CARING
FOR KIDS
WITH
SPECIAL NEEDS

Residential Treatment Programs for Children and Adolescents

Peterson's Guides
Princeton, New Jersey

Although Peterson's has made every attempt to secure timely, accurate data from reliable sources at the facilities described in this guide, it makes no claims regarding the practices of the institutions themselves. The use of this guide is intended as a first step only, and the reader is encouraged to use the contact information at the end of the profiles to obtain more information. Editorial inquiries concerning this book should be addressed to the editor at Peterson's Guides, P.O. Box 2123, Princeton, New Jersey 08543-2123.

Library of Congress Cataloging-in-Publication Data
Caring for kids with special needs: residential programs for children and adolescents.
      p.   cm.
  Includes index.
  ISBN 1-56079-168-3
    1. Children—Institutional care—United States—Directories. 2. Group homes for children—United States—Directories. 3. Teenagers—Institutional care—United States—Directories. 4. Group homes for teenagers—United States—Directories. I. Peterson's Guides, Inc.
  HV863.C35   1993
  362.7'32'0973—dc20   92-36346

Composition and design by Peterson's Guides

Printed in the United States of America

10 9 8 7 6 5 4 3 2 1

Contents

Introduction

There can be few more difficult or important decisions that a parent can face than to seek professional care for a troubled child. An estimated 12 percent of our nation's children under age 18 suffer from mental health problems, and countless others struggle with learning disabilities within our traditional school programs. For most, the professional care received while living at home is adequate. For some, however, it becomes necessary to leave the home environment—and so begins the difficult process of choosing the right facility.

For the health-care professional, social worker, student counselor, or discharge planner who has to answer the questions of a concerned parent as well as juggle the complicated needs of the patient, recommending the proper school or facility can be a daunting task.

As health-care costs continue to rise and the need to balance costs, quality, and accountability increases with the involvement of insurance companies, reliable information about mental health care providers is more crucial than ever.

This book was created to help the many thousands of professionals and parents who each year must find the best environment for a troubled child or adolescent. It is the only resource of its kind. Devoted solely to youths ages 8 to 18, the guide lists a broad range of facilities available in the United States and Canada:

- drug and alcohol rehabilitation centers
- psychiatric hospitals
- residential schools serving students with special emotional or cognitive needs
- acute-care facilities
- general hospitals with psychiatric units
- wilderness programs
- camps

The range of problems addressed by these facilities and schools is extensive:

- autism
- learning disabilities
- behavior disorders
- psychosocial disorders
- substance abuse
- eating disorders
- other compulsive/addictive disorders
- post-traumatic stress disorder
- thought, mood, and personality disorders

Severe mental retardation, although treated by some of the institutions described, is outside the scope of this book.

The information presented in this guide was obtained from facility directors or their representatives in the spring and summer of 1992 through a questionnaire that was sent to them by Peterson's. The answers they provided were entered into a computer database, from which the 817 statistical profile descriptions on pages 52-398 were generated. Some of the facilities and schools chose to describe a special feature of their program or their philosophy in announcements that appear at the end of their profile.

In addition, 35 programs elected to describe their offerings more fully. These expanded descriptions, many with photographs, begin on page 399.

Acknowledgments

We wish to thank the 800 health-care providers who generously devoted the time required to provide us with information about their facilities.

We are also very grateful to the following education and health-care professionals who lent advice and encouragement during the planning and production of this book.

Glenn Bender, Academic Dean, The Cascade School, Whitmore, CA

Thomas J. Croke, Consultant, Latrobe, PA

Lorraine Henricks, Director of the Foundry, Regents Hospital, New York, NY

Paul Henry, Managing Director, Keystone Center, Chester, PA

Karen Hollowell, Director of Admission, George School, Newtown, PA

Selden Illich, M.S.W., Princeton Psychological Associates, Princeton, NJ

Brooke Jackson, Director, U.S. Admissions, The Amity School, Arezzo, Italy

Dan Lundquist, M.S.W., Princeton, NJ

Greg MacBride, Director, Princeton House, Princeton, NJ

Nancy Manning, Psychologist, Princeton, NJ

Beth Paulin, Director of Recruitment, DeSisto School, Stockbridge, MA

Helene Reynolds, Education Consultant, Princeton, NJ

Anita Targan, Educational Consultant, Morristown, NJ

Lon Woodbury, Editor, *Woodbury Reports,* Bonners Ferry, ID

How to Use This Book

Quick-Reference Chart of Programs

The chart that appears on pages 2–50 will allow you to make a preliminary list of facilities that offer appropriate services for your client or child. Organized geographically, it presents the most important features of every facility described in the book:

- **facility name and address**
- **page number of facility's profile**
- **facility type**
  drug addiction rehabilitation center
  psychiatric hospital
  general hospital
  residential treatment center
  school
  camp
  wilderness program
  other facility type
- **security at the facility**
  unsecured, no runaway pursuit
  unsecured, runaway pursuit
  staff secured, no runaway pursuit
  staff secured, runaway pursuit
  partially locked, no runaway pursuit
  partially locked, runaway pursuit
  entirely locked, no runaway pursuit
  entirely locked, runaway pursuit
  varies with program
- **policy on admission**
  voluntary
  agreement of one parent or guardian
    necessary
  agreement of all parties
  court order necessary
  other
  variable
- **average stay**
- **ages admitted**
- **gender admitted**
- **disorders treated** (designated by the programs themselves as a main treatment focus or a secondary treatment focus)
  autism
  learning disabilities
  behavior disorders
  psychosocial disorders

substance abuse
eating disorders
other compulsive/addictive disorders
post-traumatic stress disorder
thought, mood, and personality disorders

A key to the abbreviations used in the chart appears at the bottom of each right-hand page.

You can use the chart in a number of ways. If your search is limited to one state, you can turn to that section of the chart and scan for important criteria—for example, the age range the program will accept or the facility's ability to treat a specific disorder. If your main criterion is not the location of a facility, you can scan the chart vertically for the co-occurrence of features that are important to you.

Perhaps the most useful feature of the chart is that a distinction is made between disorders accepted at a facility and disorders that form the main focus of the facility's programs. For example, a young person may be experiencing serious alcohol abuse problems as well as a learning disability. If the immediate need is treatment for substance abuse, you would scan the chart for a facility that indicates that substance abuse is a main treatment focus. You might use as a second criterion whether the facility can accommodate the educational needs of a child with a learning disability.

Once you have narrowed your search by using the Quick-Reference Chart, you are ready to turn to the Program Profiles for more information.

Program Profiles

The Program Profile section, pages 51-398, is organized alphabetically. The following data, in addition to facility name, address, and phone and fax numbers, are presented for most of the facilities in the guide. Some information may be missing for programs that could not or did not supply the information.

- **General Information**
  facility type; number of beds; year-round schedule; patient security; setting; profit/nonprofit status; affiliation; licensing; accreditation
- **Participants**
  gender and age range accepted; average stay; admission policy; main treatment focuses;

special accommodations; geographic profile of patients

- **Program**
  treatment modalities used; availability of family treatment program
- **Staff**
  total number of staff members; percentage of male and female staff members
- **Facilities**
  number of buildings; residential arrangements; dining arrangements; other physical features
- **Education**
  availability of educational program (if not a school); ages/grades served; number of teachers; curriculum accreditation; cost arrangements; availability of sports
- **Costs**
  payment plans accepted
- **Additional Services**
  brief description of any additional programs, including outpatient clinics
- **Contact**
  name, address, and phone number of person to contact for more information

A number of facilities chose to describe a special feature in an Announcement. These are found at the end of the facility's profile.

Expanded Descriptions

If a facility has chosen to write more fully about its offerings, a boldface reference to an Expanded Description will appear at the end of the Program Profile. Thirty-five such descriptions are included on pages 400–469.

These descriptions give the reader a broader picture of the programs. A representative of the school or facility provided the details in the following areas:

- **The Facility**
  A description of the location, physical setting, philosophy, and history of the institution
- **Eligibility**
  A profile of the types of treatment needs addressed by the facility and a description of the admission policy
- **Assessment**
  How a young person's diagnosis or special requirements are determined
- **Programs**
  A complete description of the programs available, a picture of student/patient schedules and activities, and a description of a typical treatment regimen
- **Staff**
  Number, duties, and credentials of staff members
- **Special Programs**
  Any additional programs offered, including summer programs and outpatient or step-down programs
- **Continuity of Treatment**
  A description of what typically happens to an alumnus of a program or school, including special transitional living or education arrangements
- **Buildings and Grounds**
  Describes the grounds, buildings, living and dining accommodations, and any additional facilities, such as libraries, gymnasiums, and recreation areas
- **Admission and Financial Information**
  Describes application procedures, costs, financial aid, and payment plans

Quick-Reference Chart

Facility Name and Address	Page Number	Type	Security	Admission	Average stay	Age range	Gender	Autism	Learning Disabilities	Behavior Disorders	Psychosocial Disorders	Substance Abuse	Eating Disorders	Other Compulsive/Addictive	Post-Traumatic Stress	Thought, Mood, and Personality
ALABAMA																
Parkside Lodge of Birmingham Warrior, AL 35180	290	RT	P/N	*		12-adult	M/F					♦	♦	◇	◇	◇
Three Springs of Courtland Courtland, AL 35618	366	RT	L/R	*	365 dy	12-17	M		◇	♦	♦	◇		♦	◇	◇
Three Springs of Paint Rock Valley Trenton, AL 35774	367	RT	U/R	*	365 dy	10-17	M/F		◇	♦	♦	◇			◇	◇
ALASKA																
Alaska Children's Services Anchorage, AK 99507	54	RT	S/N	PP	365 dy	6-18	M/F				♦					
North Star Hospital Anchorage, AK 99508	276	PH	P	*	26 dy		M/F		◇	♦	◇	♦	◇	◇	◇	◇
ARIZONA																
Anasazi Wilderness Treatment Program Payson, AZ 85547	57	W	S/R	*	51 dy	12-18	M/F		◇	◇	◇	◇	◇	◇	◇	◇
Arizona Baptist Children's Services Phoenix, AZ 85069	61	RT	S	*	9 mo		M/F	♦	◇	♦	♦	◇	◇	◇	◇	♦
Aspen Hill Hospital Flagstaff, AZ 86001	63	PH	L	*	18 dy		M/F		◇	◇	♦	◇	◇	◇	◇	◇
Desert Hills Center for Youth and Families Tucson, AZ 85745	158	PH	L	*			M/F	◇	◇	◇	◇	◇	◇	◇	◇	◇
Desert Vista Hospital Mesa, AZ 85201	158	PH	*	*	23 dy	13-adult	M/F	◇	♦	♦	♦	♦	♦	◇	♦	♦
Devereux Arizona Scottsdale, AZ 85254	160	RT	*	*	549 dy	13-17	M/F	◇		♦	♦				◇	◇
Homestead Mesa, AZ 85203	222	RT	S	*	12 mo		F	◇	♦	♦	♦	◇	◇	◇	♦	♦
Las Rosas Tucson, AZ 85749	239	DA	S	*	9 mo		F		◇	◇	◇	♦		◇	◇	◇
Parc Place Phoenix, AZ 85018	288	O	U	P	45 dy	12-20	M/F		◇	◇	◇	◇	◇		◇	◇
Pioneer Ranch Payson, AZ 85541	307	DA	S	*	9 mo		M		◇	◇	◇	♦		◇	◇	◇
St. Luke's Behavioral Health Center Phoenix, AZ 85006	336	O					M/F				♦		♦		◇	◇	◇
San Pablo Treatment Center, Inc. Phoenix, AZ 85008	344	RT	S/N	*	8 mo	12-17	M	♦	♦						♦	♦

Facility Name and Address	Page Number	Type	Security	Admission	Average stay	Age range	Gender	Autism	Learning Disabilities	Behavior Disorders	Psychosocial Disorders	Substance Abuse	Other Compulsive/Addictive	Eating Disorders	Post-Traumatic Stress	Thought, Mood, and Personality
					GENERAL INFORMATION			DISORDERS TREATED								
Scottsdale Camelback Hospital Scottsdale, AZ 85251	345	PH	L	*	1 dy	12-18	M/F	◊	♦	♦	♦	♦	♦	◊	♦	♦
Sierra Tucson Adolescent Care Tucson, AZ 85737	348	PH	S/R	PP	45 dy	13-17	M/F		◊	◊	♦	♦	◊	◊	♦	◊
Sonora Desert Hospital Tucson, AZ 85704	351	PH	L/R	*	10 dy	13-adult	M/F	◊	◊	♦	♦	♦	♦	♦	♦	♦
Touchstone Community, Inc. Phoenix, AZ 85024	368	O	S	*	4 mo	12-16	M	◊	♦	♦	◊		◊		♦	♦
Tucson Psychiatric Institute Youth Hospital Tucson, AZ 85710	370	PH	L/R	*	180 dy	13-17	M/F	◊	♦	♦	◊				◊	◊
Villa Del Sol Treatment Center Yuma, AZ 85364	377	RT	P/N	*	152 dy	12-18	M/F		◊	◊	♦	♦	◊	◊	♦	◊
Wayland Family Centers Phoenix, AZ 85029	382	RT	S	*	6 mo		M/F		◊	♦	◊			◊		♦
Wendy Paine O'Brien Treatment Center Scottsdale, AZ 85257	383	RT	S	*	3 mo		M/F	◊	◊	♦	♦	◊	◊	◊	♦	♦
Westbridge Adolescent Center Phoenix, AZ 85006	383	RT	P/N	*		12-22	M/F		◊	♦	♦	◊	◊	◊	♦	♦
Westbridge Center for Children Phoenix, AZ 85014	384	PH	P/R	*		3-14	M/F		◊	♦	♦	◊	◊	◊	♦	♦
Westcenter Rehabilitation Facility, Inc. Tucson, AZ 85719	385	DA	S/R	*	28 dy	13-adult	M/F			◊	◊	♦	◊	◊	◊	◊
West Valley Camelback Hospital Glendale, AZ 85306	386	PH	R	*	24 dy	13-adult	M/F		◊	◊	◊	◊	◊	◊	◊	◊
ARKANSAS																
Arkansas Children's Hospital Little Rock, AR 72202	61	O	P	*	9 dy		M/F	◊	◊	◊	◊	◊	◊	◊	◊	◊
Charter Hospital of Little Rock Maumelle, AR 72113	115	O	L	*			M/F		◊	◊	◊	◊		◊	◊	◊
CPC Pinnacle Pointe Hospital Little Rock, AR 72211	145	PH	L/N	*	90 dy	12-18	M/F		◊	◊	◊	◊	◊	◊	◊	◊

Type
DA = Drug addiction rehab center
PH = Psychiatric hospital
GH = General hospital
RT = Residential treatment
S = School
C = Camp
W = Wilderness program
O = Other

Security
U = Unsecured
S = Staff secured
P = Partially locked
L = Entirely locked
N = No runaway pursuit
R = Runaway pursuit
* = Varies depending on program

Admission
V = Voluntary
P = One parent
PP = All parties
C = Court order
O = Other
* = Varies

Disorders
♦ = main treatment focus
◊ = secondary treatment focus

Facility Name and Address	Page Number	Type	Security	Admission	Average stay	Age range	Gender	Autism	Learning Disabilities	Behavior Disorders	Psychosocial Disorders	Substance Abuse	Eating Disorders	Other Compulsive/Addictive	Post-Traumatic Stress	Thought, Mood, and Personality
Decision Point Springdale, AR 72764	156	DA	P	*	90 dy		M/F		◇	◇	◇	♦	◇	◇	◇	◇
Fort Smith Rehabilitation Hospital Fort Smith, AR 72901	185	O	S	*	45 dy		M/F		◇	◇	◇		◇			
Greenleaf Center, Inc. Jonesboro, AR 72401	197	PH	L	*	35 dy		M/F		◇	◇	♦	♦	♦	◇	◇	♦
Habberton House Springdale, AR 72764	201	RT	L/N	PP	180 dy	11-17	M/F		◇	◇	◇	◇	◇	◇	◇	◇
Youth Home, Inc. Little Rock, AR 72207-5245	396	RT	L/R	C	150 dy	12-18	M/F		◇	◇	◇	◇	◇	◇	◇	♦

CALIFORNIA

Facility Name and Address	Page Number	Type	Security	Admission	Average stay	Age range	Gender	Autism	Learning Disabilities	Behavior Disorders	Psychosocial Disorders	Substance Abuse	Eating Disorders	Other Compulsive/Addictive	Post-Traumatic Stress	Thought, Mood, and Personality
Adolescent Intensive Residential Service of California Pacific Medical Center San Francisco, CA 94117	53	RT	S/N	*	300 dy	11-17	M/F		◇	◇	♦				♦	♦
Alvarado Parkway Institute La Mesa, CA 91942-2352	56	O	L/R	*	12 dy	12-adult	M/F	◇	♦	♦	♦	♦	♦	◇	♦	♦
Bridges Center Malibu, CA 90265	79	RT	S/R	P	120 dy	12-17	M/F		◇	◇	◇	◇	◇			◇
Broad Horizons of Ramona, Inc. Ramona, CA 92065	81	RT	S	*	3 mo		M/F		◇	◇	◇	◇	◇	◇	◇	◇
Canyon Ridge Hospital Chino, CA 91710	94	PH	L/R	*	13 dy	12-adult	M/F		◇	◇	◇	♦	◇	◇	◇	♦
Capistrano by the Sea Hospital Dana Point, CA 92629	95	PH	L/R	PP	30 dy	10-adult	M/F	◇	◇	♦	♦	♦	♦	♦	♦	♦
Cascade School Whitmore, CA 96096	100	S	S/R	PP	730 dy	13-18	M/F		◇	♦		◇	◇		♦	
CEDU Middle School Running Springs, CA 92382	102	S	S	*	24 mo	9-13	M/F		◇	♦	◇	◇				◇
CEDU School Running Springs, CA 92382	103	S	S	*	24 mo	13-17	M/F		◇	♦	◇	◇				◇
Chamberlain's Children's Center, Inc. Hollister, CA 95024-1269	104	RT	U/R	*	2 yr	3-13	M/F		◇	◇	◇	◇				
Charter Academy Residential Treatment Center Corona, CA 91719	108	RT	S/R	*	90 dy	12-18	M/F		◇	◇	◇	◇	◇	◇	◇	◇
Charter Hospital of Bakersfield Bakersfield, CA 93309	110	PH	P	P		13-adult	M/F						♦	◇		♦
Charter Hospital of Fountain Valley Fountain Valley, CA 92708	112	PH	P/R	*	18 dy	12-adult	M/F		◇	♦	♦	♦	◇	◇	◇	♦
Charter Hospital of Long Beach Long Beach, CA 90805	115	PH	P/R	PP	17 dy	12-adult	M/F	◇	♦	♦	♦	♦	♦	♦	♦	♦

Facility Name and Address	GENERAL INFORMATION							DISORDERS TREATED								
	Page Number	Type	Security	Admission	Average stay	Age range	Gender	Autism	Learning Disabilities	Behavior Disorders	Psychosocial Disorders	Substance Abuse	Other Compulsive/Addictive	Eating Disorders	Post-Traumatic Stress	Thought, Mood, and Personality
Children's Hospital of Los Angeles Los Angeles, CA 90054	128	O	S/R	*	7 dy	11-18	M/F	◊	◊	◊	◊		◊			
Clare Foundation Youth Recovery Teen Home Santa Monica, CA 90405	131	RT	S	*	12 mo		M/F						◆			
CPC Belmont Hills Hospital Belmont, CA 94002	137	PH	P/N	*	22 dy	13-adult	M/F		◊	◆	◆	◆	◆	◆	◊	◆
CPC Fremont Hospital Fremont, CA 94538	140	PH	L	*	10 dy		M/F	◊	◆	◊	◊	◊	◊	◊	◊	◊
CPC Redwoods Hospital Santa Rosa, CA 95401	145	PH	S/N		240 dy	12-18	M/F	◊	◊	◊	◆	◊	◊	◊	◆	◆
CPC Santa Ana Hospital Santa Ana, CA 92705	146	PH	P/R	*	15 dy	12-adult	M/F		◊	◊	◊	◊	◊	◊	◊	◊
CPC Westwood Hospital Los Angeles, CA 90025	148	PH	*	*	28 dy	11-adult	M/F		◊	◆	◊	◆	◆	◊	◊	◆	◆
Devereux California Santa Barbara, CA 93102	161	RT	S/R		2 yr	11-adult	M/F	◊	◊	◊	◊				◊	◊
First Hospital Vallejo Vallejo, CA 94590	181	PH	L/R	*	14 dy	12-adult	M/F		◊	◊		◊	◊	◊	◊	◊
Fred Finch Youth Center Oakland, CA 94602	187	O	S/N	*	18 mo	11-20	M/F		◆	◆	◆	◊	◊	◊	◆	◆
Hathaway Children's Services Sylmar, CA 91392	204	RT	U	*	18 mo		M/F		◊	◊	◊		◊		◊	◊
HCA Cedar Vista Hospital Fresno, CA 93720	207	PH	P	*		13-adult	M/F		◆	◆	◊	◆	◊	◊	◆	◆
Hilltop Running Springs, CA 92382	221	RT	S	*		adult	M/F		◊	◆	◊	◊				◊
Ivy Lea Manor Rancho Palos Verdes, CA 90732	227	RT	S/N	*		7-adult	M/F	◊	◆	◆	◆	◆	◆	◆	◆	◆
Kings View Center Reedley, CA 93654	232	RT	S	*	6 mo		M/F		◊	◊	◊			◊	◊	◊
Las Encinas Hospital Pasadena, CA 91107	238	PH	L/R	P	16 dy	13-adult	M/F		◊	◊	◊	◊	◊	◊	◊	◊

Type
DA = Drug addiction rehab center
PH = Psychiatric hospital
GH = General hospital
RT = Residential treatment
S = School
C = Camp
W = Wilderness program
O = Other

Security
U = Unsecured
S = Staff secured
P = Partially locked
L = Entirely locked
N = No runaway pursuit
R = Runaway pursuit
* = Varies depending on program

Admission
V = Voluntary
P = One parent
PP = All parties
C = Court order
O = Other
* = Varies

Disorders
◆ = main treatment focus
◊ = secondary treatment focus

Facility Name and Address	GENERAL INFORMATION							DISORDERS TREATED								
	Page Number	Type	Security	Admission	Average stay	Age range	Gender	Learning Disabilities	Autism	Behavior Disorders	Psychosocial Disorders	Substance Abuse	Eating Disorders	Other Compulsive/Addictive	Post-Traumatic Stress	Thought, Mood, and Personality
Lincoln Child Center Oakland, CA 94602	244	RT	S/R	*	18 mo	12-15	M/F			◆	◆	◆		◆	◆	◆
Linden Center Los Angeles, CA 90036	245	RT	N		90 dy	5-18	M/F	◇		◆	◆	◆	◇		◆	◆
Memorial Center for Behavioral Health Bakersfield, CA 93301	253	PH	S/N	*			M/F			◆	◆			◇	◆	◆
Newport Harbor Hospital Newport Beach, CA 92663	273	PH	P/N	*	44 dy	12-18	M/F			◆	◆	◇	◆	◆	◇	◆
North American Wilderness Academy French Gulch, CA 96033	275	O	S	P		12-18	M/F			◆						
Oak Grove Institute Murrieta, CA 92562	278	RT	U/R	*	90 dy	9-18	M/F			◆	◆	◆	◇	◇	◇	◆
Pacific Lodge Boys' Home Woodland Hills, CA 91364	286	RT	U/N	*	270 dy	13-18	M			◇	◇	◆	◇		◇	◇
Palmdale Hospital Medical Center Palmdale, CA 93550	287	GH	L	P	21 dy		M/F			◇	◇	◇	◇	◇	◇	◇
Palomares Group Homes San Jose, CA 95155	287	RT	S/R	*	365 dy	11-19	M/F		◇	◆	◆	◇	◆	◇	◆	◆
Phoenix Academy Descanso, CA 91916	303	RT	S	*	15 mo		M/F							◆		
Phoenix House Venice, CA 90291	304	O	U/N	*	1 yr	12-17	M/F							◆		
Pine Grove Hospital Canoga Park, CA 91307	305	PH	P	*	14 dy		M/F				◇	◇	◇			
Pine Meadows School French Gulch, CA 96033	306	S	S	PP	18 mo	12-18	M/F		◆	◆						
Quest Boonville, CA 95415	313	O	U/R	*	2 yr		M		◆	◆						
River Oak Center for Children Sacramento, CA 95841	324	RT	S/R	*	15 mo	5-13	M/F		◇	◇	◇				◇	◇
Solono Park Hospital Fairfield, CA 94533	350	PH	P/R	*		adult			◆	◆	◆	◇	◇	◇	◆	◆
Starting Point Chemical Dependency Recovery Hospital Orangevale, CA 95662	356	DA	S/N	*	28 dy	12-adult	M/F				◇	◇	◆			
Suncrest Hospital of South Bay Torrance, CA 90505	358	O	P	*	21 dy		M/F			◇	◇	◇	◇	◇	◇	◇
Sunny Hills Children's Services San Anselmo, CA 94960	359	RT	U/R	*	545 dy	13-18	M/F	◆	◆	◆	◆	◆	◆	◆	◆	◆
Sycamores Altadena, CA 91001	360	RT	S/R	*	14 mo	6-14	M		◇	◆	◆			◆		◇

Facility Name and Address	Page Number	Type	Security	Admission	Average stay	Age range	Gender	Autism	Learning Disabilities	Behavior Disorders	Psychosocial Disorders	Substance Abuse	Other Compulsive/Addictive	Eating Disorders	Post-Traumatic Stress	Thought, Mood, and Personality
Teen Enrichment Center, Inc. Milpitas, CA 95035	364	RT	S	*	12 mo		F		◊	◊	◊	♦	◊	◊	◊	
Turnoff, Inc. Desert Hot Springs, CA 92240	371	RT	S	*	12 mo		M/F					♦				
Tustin Hospital Medical Center Tustin, CA 92680	371	GH	S	*	20 dy		M/F					♦				
Vista Del Mar Child and Family Services Los Angeles, CA 90034	379	RT	S	*	12 mo		M/F		◊	◊	◊	◊	◊	◊	◊	◊
Wide Horizons Ranch, Inc. Oak Run, CA 96069	387	RT	S/R	*	3 yr	9-17	M	◊	♦	♦					♦	♦
Woodview-Calabasas Hospital Calabasas, CA 91302	393	PH	P	*	13 dy	12-adult	M/F		◊	◊	♦	◊	◊	◊	♦	♦

COLORADO

Facility Name and Address	Page Number	Type	Security	Admission	Average stay	Age range	Gender	Autism	Learning Disabilities	Behavior Disorders	Psychosocial Disorders	Substance Abuse	Other Compulsive/Addictive	Eating Disorders	Post-Traumatic Stress	Thought, Mood, and Personality
Adolescent Program at Mapleton Center Boulder, CO 80302	53	GH	P	*	7 dy		M/F	◊	♦	♦	♦	♦	♦	♦	◊	♦
Arapahoe House Thornton, CO 80223	60	DA	S	*			M/F					♦				
Brockhurst Extended Care Programs Green Mountain Falls, CO 80819	81	RT	S/R	*	4 mo	13-18	M/F			♦	♦	♦			♦	♦
CareUnit Hospital of Colorado Aurora, CO 80012	97	PH	P/R	P	25 dy	12-adult	M/F			◊	♦	♦	◊	◊	◊	♦
Centennial Peaks Treatment Center Fort Collins, CO 80524	103	DA	S/N	PP	30 dy	12-adult	M/F		◊	◊	◊	♦	◊	◊	◊	
Cheyenne Mesa Colorado Springs, CO 80906	124	RT	S/R	V	120 dy	12-18	M/F			◊	♦	♦	◊	◊	♦	♦
Cleo Wallace Center Westminster, CO 80021	132	PH	L	*	15 dy		M/F	◊	◊	◊	◊	◊			◊	◊
Colorado Boys Ranch La Junta, CO 81050	133	RT	S/R	*	245 dy	12-18	M		◊	♦	♦	◊	◊	◊	◊	♦
Columbine Psychiatric Center Littleton, CO 80126	134	PH	S/R	*	13 dy	11-adult	M/F		◊	♦	♦	♦	♦	◊	♦	♦

Type
DA = Drug addiction rehab center
PH = Psychiatric hospital
GH = General hospital
RT = Residential treatment
S = School
C = Camp
W = Wilderness program
O = Other

Security
U = Unsecured
S = Staff secured
P = Partially locked
L = Entirely locked
N = No runaway pursuit
R = Runaway pursuit
* = Varies depending on program

Admission
V = Voluntary
P = One parent
PP = All parties
C = Court order
O = Other
* = Varies

Disorders
♦ = main treatment focus
◊ = secondary treatment focus

Facility Name and Address	Page Number	Type	Security	Admission	Average stay	Age range	Gender	Autism	Learning Disabilities	Behavior Disorders	Psychosocial Disorders	Substance Abuse	Other Compulsive/Addictive	Eating Disorders	Post-Traumatic Stress	Thought, Mood, and Personality
Denver Children's Home Denver, CO 80220	156	RT	U	PP		10-18	M/F		◊	♦	♦	◊	◊		♦	♦
El Pueblo Boys' Ranch Pueblo, CO 81006	174	RT	S/R	C	730 dy	10-18	M		◊	♦	◊	◊	◊	♦	◊	◊
Forest Heights Lodge Evergreen, CO 80439	184	RT	S/R	V	700 dy	5-14	M	◊	◊	♦	♦				◊	♦
Larico Center for Youth Addictions, Inc. Fort Collins, CO 80524	237	RT		*	9 mo		M/F					♦				
Larico Youth Homes, Inc. Fort Collins, CO 80524	237	RT	S	*	9 mo		M/F		◊	♦	◊	♦	◊	◊	◊	◊
Mountainview Place Colorado Springs, CO 80906	264	RT	S/R	*	120 dy	10-18	M/F		◊	♦	♦	◊	◊	◊	♦	♦
Mount St. Vincent Home Denver, CO 80211	266	RT	S	*	22 mo	5-16	M/F		◊	♦	◊			◊	◊	♦
North Colorado PsychCare Greeley, CO 80631	275	PH	P	*	6 dy		M/F			◊	◊		◊		◊	◊
Parker Valley Hope Parker, CO 80134	289	DA	S/R	P	30 dy	17-adult	M/F					♦				
Parkview Episcopal Medical Center—Child and Adolescent Psychiatric Service Pueblo, CO 81003	296	GH	S	*	12 dy		M/F		◊	♦	◊	◊		◊	◊	◊
St. Mary-Corwin Regional Medical Center Pueblo, CO 81004	337	GH	P/R	*	10 dy	13-adult	M/F	◊	◊	♦	◊	♦	◊	◊	◊	♦

CONNECTICUT

Facility Name and Address	Page Number	Type	Security	Admission	Average stay	Age range	Gender	Autism	Learning Disabilities	Behavior Disorders	Psychosocial Disorders	Substance Abuse	Other Compulsive/Addictive	Eating Disorders	Post-Traumatic Stress	Thought, Mood, and Personality
APT Residential Services Newtown, CT 06470	60	DA	S	*	12 mo		M/F					♦				
Children's Center Hamden, CT 06517	125	DA	S/N	*	21 dy	12-19	M/F		◊	◊	♦	♦	◊		◊	♦
Children's Home of Cromwell Cromwell, CT 06416	126	RT	S/R	*	17 mo	13-16	M/F	♦	♦	♦	◊				♦	◊
Common Ground: The Center for Adolescents at Stamford Hospital Stamford, CT 06904	135	GH	S/R	*	30 dy	13-20	M/F		◊	◊	◊	◊	◊		◊	◊
Devereux Glenholme Washington, CT 06793	163	RT	S/R	PP	545 dy	13-15	M/F		◊	♦	◊		◊		◊	◊
Founder's School East Haddam, CT 06423	185	RT	S	O	18 mo		M		◊	◊	◊	◊		◊		
Grandview Psychiatric Resource Center Waterbury, CT 06708	194	GH	L/R	*	22 dy	12-adult	M/F			♦	♦	◊	◊	◊	◊	♦

Facility Name and Address	GENERAL INFORMATION						DISORDERS TREATED								
	Page Number	Type	Security	Admission	Average stay	Age range	Gender	Autism	Learning Disabilities	Behavior Disorders	Psychosocial Disorders	Substance Abuse	Other Compulsive/Addictive	Eating Disorders	Post-Traumatic Stress	Thought, Mood, and Personality
Gray Lodge Hartford, CT 06105	195	RT	L/N	*		12-18	F		◊	♦			◊			
Grove School Madison, CT 06443	199	RT	S	*	540 dy	11-18	M/F		♦	♦	♦		◊	◊	◊	♦
Hall-Brooke Foundation Westport, CT 06880	201	PH	*	*	24 dy	10-adult	M/F		♦	♦	♦	♦	◊	♦	♦	♦
Institute of Living Hartford, CT 06106	224	PH	P/R	*	21 dy	14-adult	M/F	◊	♦	♦	♦	♦	♦	◊	◊	♦
Mohonk House, Inc. Westport, CT 06880	262	RT	S/R	*	180 dy	12-18	M		◊	♦	♦				◊	
Parkside Lodge of Connecticut Canaan, CT 06018	291	DA	S	*	30 dy	13-adult	M/F		◊	◊	◊		♦	◊		◊
Perception House Willimantic, CT 06226	301	DA	S	*	2 mo		M/F						♦			
Silver Hill Hospital New Canaan, CT 06840	349	PH	P/R	*	36 dy	13-adult	M/F		◊	♦	◊	♦	♦	◊	♦	♦
Waterford Country School Quaker Hill, CT 06375	381	RT	S/R	PP	550 dy	8-18	M/F		◊	♦	◊					♦
Wellspring Bethlehem, CT 06751-0370	383	RT	S/R	V		13-adult	M/F		◊	◊	◊	◊	◊	◊	◊	♦
Yale Psychiatric Institute New Haven, CT 06520	394	PH	P/R	*	15 dy	13-adult	M/F	♦	♦	♦	♦	◊	♦	♦	◊	♦
DELAWARE																
Greenwood Hockessin, DE 19707	198	DA	S/R	P	30 dy	12-17	M/F			♦		♦	♦	♦	♦	♦
HCA Rockford Center Newark, DE 19701	214	PH	L/R	*	14 dy	12-adult	M/F		◊	◊	◊	◊	◊		◊	◊
Meadow Wood Hospital for Children and Adolescents New Castle, DE 19720	252	PH	L/N	*	30 dy	12-18	M/F	◊	♦	♦	♦	◊	◊	◊	♦	♦
Devereux—Wrangle Hill Treatment Center Bear, DE 19701	168	RT														

Type
DA = Drug addiction rehab center
PH = Psychiatric hospital
GH = General hospital
RT = Residential treatment
S = School
C = Camp
W = Wilderness program
O = Other

Security
U = Unsecured
S = Staff secured
P = Partially locked
L = Entirely locked
N = No runaway pursuit
R = Runaway pursuit
* = Varies depending on program

Admission
V = Voluntary
P = One parent
PP = All parties
C = Court order
O = Other
* = Varies

Disorders
♦ = main treatment focus
◊ = secondary treatment focus

Facility Name and Address	Page Number	Type	Security	Admission	Average stay	Age range	Gender	Autism	Learning Disabilities	Behavior Disorders	Psychosocial Disorders	Substance Abuse	Other Compulsive/Addictive	Eating Disorders	Post-Traumatic Stress	Thought, Mood, and Personality
DISTRICT OF COLUMBIA																
Buena Vista Academy Washington, DC 20032	85	RT	S/R	*	1 yr	13-18	F			♦	♦	◊	◊	◊		◊
Episcopal Center for Children Washington, DC 20015	176	RT	U	V	3 yr	5-13	M/F		◊	◊	♦					
FLORIDA																
Agency for Community Treatment Services Seffner, FL 33584	53	DA		*	3 mo		M/F		◊	♦	♦	♦	◊	◊	◊	◊
Atlantic Shores Hospital Daytona Beach, FL 32117-4599	64	PH	L/R	*	15 dy	13-adult	M/F		◊	♦	♦	◊	◊	◊	◊	♦
Bay Harbor Residential Treatment Center Largo, FL 34648	68	RT	L	V		13-18	M/F	♦	♦	♦	♦	♦	◊	◊	♦	♦
Camp E-How-Kee Brooksville, FL 34602	87	W	S/R	*	365 dy	10-17	M		◊	♦	♦					
Camp E-Kel-Etu Silver Springs, FL 32688	88	W	S/R	*	365 dy	10-17	M		◊	♦	♦					
Camp E-Ma-Chamee Milton, FL 32570	89	W	S/R	*	365,dy	10-17	M/F		◊	♦	♦					
Camp E-Ninee-Hassee Floral City, FL 34436	90	W	S/R	*	365 dy	10-17	F		◊	♦	♦					
Camp E-Tu-Makee Clewiston, FL 33440	92	W	S/R	*	365 dy	10-17	M		◊	♦	♦					
Central Florida Human Services—Bradley Oaks Mulberry, FL 33860	103	DA	U	*	9 mo		M					♦				
Charter Glade Hospital Fort Myers, FL 33912	109	PH	P	PP	28 dy		M/F	◊	◊	◊	◊	◊	◊	◊	◊	◊
Charter Hospital of Pasco Lutz, FL 33549	118	PH	L/R	O	11 dy	11-adult	M/F	◊	◊	♦	◊	♦	◊	◊	◊	♦
Charter Hospital Orlando South Kissimmee, FL 34741	119	PH	L/N	*	22 dy	11-17	M/F		◊	◊	◊	◊	◊	◊	◊	◊
Charter Springs Hospital Ocala, FL 32674	123	PH	P	PP	15 dy		M/F		◊	◊	◊	◊		◊	◊	◊
Cloisters at Pine Island Pineland, FL 33945	132	DA	S/R	*	42 dy	16-adult	M/F				◊	♦	♦	♦	◊	
CPC Palm Bay Hospital Community Residential Center Palm Bay, FL 32905	143	O	P/R	PP	120 dy	13-18	M/F	◊	◊	♦	♦	♦	◊	◊	◊	♦
Devereux Hospital and Children's Center of Florida Melbourne, FL 32940	163	PH	P	PP	417 dy	14-17	M/F	◊	◊	◊	◊		◊		◊	◊

Facility Name and Address	Page Number	Type	Security	Admission	Average stay	Age range	Gender	Learning Disabilities	Autism	Behavior Disorders	Psychosocial Disorders	Substance Abuse	Other Compulsive/Addictive	Eating Disorders	Post-Traumatic Stress	Thought, Mood, and Personality
Devereux Orlando Center Orlando, FL 32808	167	RT	S	V	95 dy		M/F	◊	◊	♦	♦				◊	♦
Drug Abuse Treatment Association, Inc. Jupiter, FL 33477	169	DA	S	*	3 mo		M/F	◊	◊	◊		♦		◊		◊
Fairwinds Treatment Center Clearwater, FL 34616	179	RT	S/R		28 dy	12-adult	M/F		◊	♦	♦	♦	◊	♦	◊	♦
Florida Hospital Center for Psychiatry Orlando, FL 32803	183	PH	P/R	*	14 dy	12-adult	M/F	◊	◊	♦	◊	♦	◊	◊	♦	♦
Gateway Community Services, Inc.—Nancy Reagan TPC Village Jacksonville, FL 32216	189	RT	S	*	6 mo		M/F					♦				
Grove Counseling Center, Inc. Winter Springs, FL 32708	199	DA	S	*	7 mo		M/F					♦				
Growing Together, Inc. Lake Worth, FL 33460	200	O	U/N	PP	60 dy	12-21	M/F			◊	◊	♦				
HCA Grant Center Hospital Miami, FL 33187	209	PH	L/R	*	40 dy	13-adult	M/F	◊	♦	♦	♦	◊			◊	◊
La Amistad Residential Treatment Center Maitland, FL 32751	234	RT	U/R	V		14-18	M/F	◊	◊	◊					◊	◊
Leon F. Stewart Treatment Center Daytona Beach, FL 32114	242	DA	P	*	6 mo		M/F					◊	◊			
Manatee Palms Adolescent Specialty Hospital Bradenton, FL 34208	247	PH	P/R	V	75 dy	13-18	M/F	◊	◊	♦	♦	♦	♦	♦	♦	♦
Mental Health Services Incorporated of North Central Florida Gainesville, FL 32608	255	O	U	*	4 dy		M/F			◊	◊	◊			◊	◊
Montanari Residential Treatment Center Hialeah, FL 33011-1360	263	RT	P	*	18 mo		M/F	◊	◊	◊	◊	◊	◊	◊		◊
Northwest Dade Center Hialeah, FL 33012	277	PH	L	*	2 mo		M/F	◊	♦	◊		◊			◊	◊
Operation Par Largo, FL 34641	282	DA	S	*	7 mo		M/F						♦			
Palmview Hospital Lakeland, FL 33805	287	PH	L	*	21 dy		M/F	◊	◊	◊	◊	◊	◊	◊	◊	◊

Type
DA = Drug addiction rehab center
PH = Psychiatric hospital
GH = General hospital
RT = Residential treatment
S = School
C = Camp
W = Wilderness program
O = Other

Security
U = Unsecured
S = Staff secured
P = Partially locked
L = Entirely locked
N = No runaway pursuit
R = Runaway pursuit
* = Varies depending on program

Admission
V = Voluntary
P = One parent
PP = All parties
C = Court order
O = Other
* = Varies

Disorders
♦ = main treatment focus
◊ = secondary treatment focus

Facility Name and Address	Page Number	Type	Security	Admission	Average stay	Age range	Gender	Autism	Learning Disabilities	Behavior Disorders	Psychosocial Disorders	Substance Abuse	Eating Disorders	Other Compulsive/Addictive	Post-Traumatic Stress	Thought, Mood, and Personality
Pavilion/West Florida Regional Medical Center Pensacola, FL 32514	299	PH	L	*	12 dy		M/F		◊	◆	◊	◊	◊		◊	◊
Peace River Center CARE Centers Bartow, FL 33830	299	RT	*	*		6-17	M/F	◊	◊	◊	◆		◊	◊	◊	◊
Personal Enrichment through Mental Health Services Pinellas Park, FL 34666	301	RT	P/N	*	436 dy	6-17	M/F		◆	◆	◆	◊	◊	◊	◊	◆
Renfrew Center of Florida Coconut Creek, FL 33073	319	RT	S	V	7 wk	14-adult	F			◊	◊	◊	◆	◊	◊	◊
Retreat Sunrise, FL 33325	320	PH	L	*	30 dy		M/F		◊	◊	◊	◊	◊	◊	◊	◊
Sandy Pines Hospital Tequesta, FL 33469	343	PH	L/N	*	22 dy	12-18	M/F	◊	◆	◆	◆	◊	◊	◊	◊	◆
Sea Pines Rehabilitation Hospital Melbourne, FL 32901	345	RT	S	*	2 mo		M/F		◊						◊	◊
Starting Place Hollywood, FL 33020	356	DA	S	*	3 mo		M/F		◊	◆	◊	◆	◊	◊	◊	◊
Tampa Bay Academy Riverview, FL 33569	361	RT	S/R	P	150 dy	4-18	M/F		◊	◆	◆	◊	◊		◊	◆
University of South Florida Psychiatry Center Tampa, FL 33613	373	PH	L	*	14 dy		M/F		◆	◊	◊		◊	◊	◆	◊
University Pavilion Taramac, FL 33321	374	PH	L	*	17 dy		M/F			◊	◊	◊	◊	◊	◊	◊
Vanguard School Lake Wales, FL 33853	376	S	U/N	V		13-21	M/F		◆							
Venice Hospital Venice, FL 34285	376	GH	P	*			M/F	⊤	◊		◊	◊				
Water Oak Specialty Hospital Tallahassee, FL 32308	381	RT	U/R	PP	500 dy	10-16	M/F			◆	◆				◊	◊

GEORGIA

Anchor Hospital Atlanta, GA 30349	57	DA	P/R	O	30 dy	13-adult	M/F			◊	◊	◆	◊	◊	◊	◊
Bradley Center, Inc. Columbus, GA 31993	78	O	P/R	*		12-adult	M/F		◊	◆	◆	◆	◊	◊	◆	◊
Camp Barney Medintz Cleveland, GA 30528	87	C	P	V	4 wk		M/F		◊	◊						
Charter Hospital of Augusta Augusta, GA 30909	110	PH	*	O	29 dy	11-17	M/F	◊		◊	◊		◊		◊	◊
Charter Hospital of Savannah Savannah, GA 31406	118	PH	L	*	22 dy		M/F	◊	◊	◊	◊	◊	◊	◊	◊	◊

Facility Name and Address	GENERAL INFORMATION							DISORDERS TREATED								
	Page Number	Type	Security	Admission	Average stay	Age range	Gender	Autism	Learning Disabilities	Behavior Disorders	Psychosocial Disorders	Substance Abuse	Other Compulsive/Addictive	Eating Disorders	Post-Traumatic Stress	Thought, Mood, and Personality
Charter Lake Hospital Macon, GA 31209	120	PH	P	*	2 wk		M/F		◊	◊	◊	◊	◊	◊	◊	◊
CPC Parkwood Hospital Atlanta, GA 30329	144	PH	P/R	*	32 dy	12-adult	M/F			♦	◊	♦		♦	♦	♦
Davison School Atlanta, GA 30306	154	S	U	*	3 yr		M/F		◊							
Devereux Georgia Kennesaw, GA 30144	162	RT	P/R	PP	14 mo	12-18	M/F		♦	♦	♦	◊	◊	◊	♦	♦
Greenleaf Center, Inc. Fort Oglethorpe, GA 30742	197	PH	P/N	*	21 dy	12-18	M/F		◊	◊	◊	♦	◊	◊	♦	♦
HCA Coliseum Psychiatric Hospital Macon, GA 31201	207	PH	L/R	*	16 dy	12-adult	M/F			◊	◊	♦	♦	♦	◊	♦
Laurel Heights Hospital Atlanta, GA 30306	240	RT	L	*		13-17	M/F		◊	♦	♦	♦	◊	◊	♦	♦
Northridge Hospital Columbus, GA 31909	276	O	L/N	*	17 dy	13-18	M/F		◊	◊	◊	♦	◊	◊	◊	◊
Parkside Lodge of Dublin Dublin, GA 31021	292	DA	S/R	P	42 dy	13-adult	M/F					♦				
Ridgeview Institute Smyrna, GA 30080-6397	320	PH	P/R	PP	25 dy	12-adult	M/F	◊	♦	♦	♦	♦	♦	◊	♦	♦
Woodridge Adolescent Unit Clayton, GA 30525	392	PH	S/R	P	28 dy	12-adult	M/F		◊	♦	♦	♦	♦	♦	◊	♦
HAWAII																
Big Island Substance Abuse Council Hilo, HI 96721	75	DA	S	*	6 mo		M/F					♦				
Bobby Benson Center Kailua, HI 96734-4498	76	RT	U/N	*	80 dy	13-17	M/F		◊	◊	◊	♦		◊	◊	◊
Kahi Mohala, A Psychiatric Hospital Ewa Beach, HI 96706	230	PH	L	*	21 dy		M/F	◊	◊	♦	♦	♦	♦	◊	♦	♦
Salvation Army Addiction Treatment Services Honolulu, HI 96817	341	DA	S	*	9 mo		M					♦				

Type
DA = Drug addiction rehab center
PH = Psychiatric hospital
GH = General hospital
RT = Residential treatment
S = School
C = Camp
W = Wilderness program
O = Other

Security
U = Unsecured
S = Staff secured
P = Partially locked
L = Entirely locked
N = No runaway pursuit
R = Runaway pursuit
* = Varies depending on program

Admission
V = Voluntary
P = One parent
PP = All parties
C = Court order
O = Other
* = Varies

Disorders
♦ = main treatment focus
◊ = secondary treatment focus

Facility Name and Address	GENERAL INFORMATION							DISORDERS TREATED								
	Page Number	Type	Security	Admission	Average stay	Age range	Gender	Autism	Learning Disabilities	Behavior Disorders	Psychosocial Disorders	Substance Abuse	Eating Disorders	Other Compulsive/Addictive	Post-Traumatic/Addictive Stress	Thought, Mood, and Personality
Salvation Army Treatment Programs for Women and Children Honolulu, HI 96822	342	O	S	*	18 mo	1-adult	M/F			◊	◆	◆	◆	◊	◊	◊
IDAHO																
Ascent Wilderness Program Sand Point, ID 83864	62	W	U/R	PP	41 dy	13-20	M/F			◊	◆	◆	◊	◊	◊	◊
Aspen Crest Hospital Pocatello, ID 83201	62	PH	P/R	*	21 dy	12-adult	M/F			◊	◊	◊	◊	◊	◊	◊
Canyon View Hospital Twin Falls, ID 83301	95	O	L/R	*	14 dy	12-adult	M/F			◊	◆	◆	◆	◊	◊	◆	◊
CPC Intermountain Hospital Adolescent Community Residential Center Boise, ID 83704	141	RT	L/R	P		12-18	M/F		◆	◆	◆	◆	◆	◆		◆	◆
Eagle Mountain Outpost School Sagle, ID 83864	170	O	S/R	*	365 dy	10-18	M		◆	◆	◆					◊
Mercy Care Units Nampa, ID 83686	255	GH	S/R	P	18 dy	12-adult	M/F			◊	◆	◆	◆	◊		◊
New Hope Center Hospital Boise, ID 83704	272	O	S	*	4 wk		M/F			◊	◊	◆	◆	◆	◆	◆	◆
Northwest Children's Home, Inc. Lewiston, ID 83501-1288	276	RT	S	*	1 yr		M/F		◆	◊		◊		◆	◊	◊
Pine Crest Hospital Coeur d'Alene, ID 83814	304	PH	L	*			M/F	◊	◊	◆	◆	◆	◊	◆	◊	◆	◆
Rocky Mountain Academy Bonners Ferry, ID 83805	326	S	U/R	PP	30 mo	13-18	M/F		◆	◆	◆	◊	◊	◊		◊
Walker Center Gooding, ID 83330-1858	379	O	P	*	16 dy		M/F				◊	◊	◆	◊	◆	◊	◊
ILLINOIS																
Alcoholism Treatment Center of Central DuPage Hospital Winfield, IL 60190	54	DA	S/R	*		12-adult	M/F			◊	◊	◊	◊		◊	◊
Alexian Brothers Medical Center Elk Grove Village, IL 60007	55	PH	L	*	18 dy		M/F	◆	◊	◆	◆	◆	◆	◆	◆	◆
Allendale Association Lake Villa, IL 60046	55	RT	S	O	6 mo		M/F	◊	◆	◆	◆				◊	◊
Camelot Care Center, Inc. Palatine, IL 60067	86	RT	S/R	*	150 dy	13-18	M/F			◊	◆	◊	◊	◊	◊	◊	◊
Charter Barclay Hospital Chicago, IL 60640	108	PH	L/N	*	20 dy	12-adult	M/F			◊	◆	◆	◆	◊	◊	◆	◆
Chestnut Health Systems—Lighthouse Bloomington, IL 61701	123	DA	S	*	60 dy		M/F			◊	◊	◊	◆	◊		◊	◊

Facility Name and Address	Page Number	Type	Security	Admission	Average stay	Age range	Gender	Autism	Learning Disabilities	Behavior Disorders	Psychosocial Disorders	Substance Abuse	Eating Disorders	Other Compulsive/Addictive	Post-Traumatic/Stress	Thought, Mood, and Personality
Children's Memorial Hospital Chicago, IL 60614	129	O	L	*	30 dy		M/F	◊	◆	◆	◆	◊	◆	◆	◆	◆
CPC Old Orchard Hospital Skokie, IL 60076	143	PH	L	*			M/F									
CPC Streamwood Hospital Streamwood, IL 60107	147	PH	P	*			M/F									
Edgewood Program Edwardsville, IL 62025	172	DA	S	*	22 dy		M/F					◆				
Forest Hospital Des Plaines, IL 60016	184	PH	L	*	25 dy	13-18	M/F		◆	◆	◆	◆	◆	◆	◆	◆
Gateway Youth Care Foundation Lake Villa, IL 60046	190	DA	S	*	4 mo		M					◆				
Grant Hospital of Chicago Chicago, IL 60614	194	GH	S	*	6 dy		M/F	◆	◆	◆	◆		◆		◆	◆
Hill House, Inc. Carbondale, IL 62901	221	DA	S	*	9 mo		M/F					◆				
Interventions Contact Wanconda, IL 60084	225	RT	S	*	5 mo		F		◊	◊	◊	◆	◊	◊	◊	◊
Jeanine Schultz Memorial School Park Ridge, IL 60068	228	S	S		4 yr		M/F	◊	◊	◊	◊					◊
La Grange Memorial Hospital La Grange, IL 60525	235	GH	S	V			M/F					◊	◊	◊	◊	
Linden Oaks Hospital Naperville, IL 60540	245	PH	L	*			M/F	◊	◊	◆	◆	◊	◆	◆	◆	◆
Lutherbrook Children's Center Addison, IL 60101	246	RT	S	O	36 mo		M/F		◊	◆	◆	◊	◊	◊	◆	◆
Memorial Hospital Woodstock, IL 60098	254	GH	L	*	21 dy		M/F		◊	◆	◆	◊	◊	◆	◆	◆
Memorial Medical Center Springfield, IL 62781	254	GH	*	*	19 dy	12-adult	M/F		◊	◊	◊	◊	◆		◊	◆
Mercy Center for Health Care Services Aurora, IL 60506	256	PH	P/R	*	19 dy	13-adult	M/F		◊	◊	◊	◊	◊	◊	◊	◊

Type
DA = Drug addiction rehab center
PH = Psychiatric hospital
GH = General hospital
RT = Residential treatment
S = School
C = Camp
W = Wilderness program
O = Other

Security
U = Unsecured
S = Staff secured
P = Partially locked
L = Entirely locked
N = No runaway pursuit
R = Runaway pursuit
* = Varies depending on program

Admission
V = Voluntary
P = One parent
PP = All parties
C = Court order
O = Other
* = Varies

Disorders
◆ = main treatment focus
◊ = secondary treatment focus

Facility Name and Address	Page Number	Type	Security	Admission	Average stay	Age range	Gender	Autism	Learning Disabilities	Behavior Disorders	Psychosocial Disorders	Substance Abuse	Eating Disorders	Other Compulsive/Addictive	Post-Traumatic Stress	Thought, Mood, and Personality
Newman Clinic, Quincy, IL 62306	273	RT	L	*	12 dy		M/F		◊	♦	♦	♦	◊	◊		♦
Palos Community Hospital, Palos Heights, IL 60463	288	GH	L	*	3 wk		M/F		◊	◊	♦	♦	◊	◊	◊	♦
Parkside Lodge of Mundelein, Mundelein, IL 60060	293	DA	S/R	P	21 dy	13-21	M/F					♦	♦			
Parkside Youth Center, Woodridge, IL 60517	295	DA	S/R	V	90 dy	13-21	M/F				◊	◊	♦	◊		◊	◊
Parkside Youth Chemical Dependency Program, Bloomington, IL 61738	295	RT	S/N	V	24 dy	12-adult	M/F				◊	◊	♦				◊
Proctor Community Hospital, Peoria, IL 61614	311	GH	P	*	5 wk		M/F						♦			
Rehabilitation Institute of Chicago, Chicago, IL 60611	317	O	U/N	*	29 dy	12-adult	M/F		◊	◊						
Rock Creek Center, Lemont, IL 60439	326	PH	S/R	*	40 dy	12-adult	M/F		◊	◊	◊	◊	◊	◊	◊	◊
Rosecrance Center, Rockford, IL 61107	327	DA	S	*	42 dy	12-18	M/F						♦			
St. Clare's Hospital Chemical Dependency Treatment Center, Alton, IL 62002	332	O	S	*	21 dy		M/F		◊	◊	◊	♦	◊	◊	◊	◊
St. Joseph's Carondelet Child Center, Chicago, IL 60616	334	RT	S	*	2 yr		M		◊	♦	◊			◊	◊	◊
Saint Mary of Nazareth Hospital Center, Chicago, IL 60622	338	GH	P/R	P	21 dy	1-adult	M/F		♦	♦	♦	◊	◊	◊	◊	♦
Sonia Shankman Orthogenic School, Chicago, IL 60637	350	RT	S/R	*	5 yr	13-21	M/F		◊	◊	♦		◊		◊	♦
University Hospital, Chicago, IL 60651	373	O	L	*	16 dy		M/F	◊	◊	♦	♦	♦	♦	♦	♦	♦
Victory Memorial Hospital (Chemical Dependency Programs), Waukegan, IL 60085	377	GH	S/R	V	33 dy	12-adult	M/F					◊	♦		◊	◊	◊
Woodland Hospital, Hoffman Estates, IL 60194	391	PH	L/R	PP	23 dy	13-adult	M/F		♦	◊		♦		◊	♦	♦
INDIANA																
Behavioral Medicine Center at Saint Margaret Mercy Healthcare Centers, South Campus, Dyer, IN 46311	71	GH	P/R	*	25 dy	12-adult	M/F		♦	♦	♦	♦	♦	♦	♦	♦
Bloomington Meadows Hospital, Bloomington, IN 47404	75	PH	L/R	PP		12-adult	M/F			◊		◊	◊	◊	♦	♦
Challenge Program of Southlake Center for Mental Health, Schererville, IN 46375	104	RT	S/R	*	365 dy	13-17	M		◊	◊	♦				◊	◊

Facility Name and Address	GENERAL INFORMATION							DISORDERS TREATED								
	Page Number	Type	Security	Admission	Average stay	Age range	Gender	Autism	Learning Disabilities	Behavior Disorders	Psychosocial Disorders	Substance Abuse	Eating Disorders	Other Compulsive/Addictive	Post-Traumatic Stress	Thought, Mood, and Personality
Charter Beacon Hospital Fort Wayne, IN 46805	109	O	L	*	22 dy		M/F	◇	◆	◆	◆	◇	◆	◆	◆	◆
Charter Hospital of Indianapolis Indianapolis, IN 46226	114	PH	P	*			M/F	◇	◆	◆	◆	◆	◆	◆	◆	◆
Charter Hospital of Lafayette Lafayette, IN 47903	114	O	P	*			M/F	◇	◇	◇	◇	◇	◇		◇	◆
Children's Campus Mishawaka, IN 46544-1690	125	RT	S	C	18 mo		M/F	◇	◇	◆	◆	◇	◇	◇	◇	◇
CPC Valle Vista Residential Treatment Center Greenwood, IN 46143	147	RT	L/R	PP		12-20	M/F	◇	◆	◇	◇	◇	◇	◇		◆
Englishton Park Children's Center Lexington, IN 47138	175	C	U/R	O	10 dy	6-12	M/F	◇	◆	◆	◆					◇
Grant-Blackford Mental Health, Inc. Marion, IN 46952	194	O	L	*	30 dy		M/F	◇		◆	◆	◇	◇	◇	◆	◆
Hillcrest-Washington Youth Home Evansville, IN 47712	220	RT	S	*	12 mo		M/F	◇	◆	◆					◆	◆
Interventions, Inc. Youth Program Grovertown, IN 46531	226	DA	S	C	8 mo		M					◆				
Koala Hospital Columbus, IN 47201	233	PH	L	*	30 dy		M/F	◇	◇	◆	◆	◆	◇	◆	◆	◆
Koala Hospital Indianapolis, IN 46203	233	PH	L	*	18 dy		M/F	◇	◇	◆	◆	◆	◆	◆	◆	◆
Koala Hospital Plymouth Plymouth, IN 46563	233	PH	P/R	*	34 dy	12-adult	M/F	◇	◇	◆	◆	◇			◆	◆
La Porte Hospital Stress Center La Porte, IN 46350-0250	237	GH	L	*	10 dy		M/F			◆	◇	◇			◇	◇
Larue D. Carter Memorial Hospital School Indianapolis, IN 46202-2885	238	RT	S	*	6 mo		M/F	◇	◆	◆	◇	◇	◇		◆	◆
Memorial Hospital of Michigan City Michigan City, IN 46360	254	GH	P	*	3 wk		M/F							◆		
Methodist Hospital of Indiana, Inc. Indianapolis, IN 46206	258	GH	L	*	12 dy		M/F			◆	◆					◆

Type
DA = Drug addiction rehab center
PH = Psychiatric hospital
GH = General hospital
RT = Residential treatment
S = School
C = Camp
W = Wilderness program
O = Other

Security
U = Unsecured
S = Staff secured
P = Partially locked
L = Entirely locked
N = No runaway pursuit
R = Runaway pursuit
* = Varies depending on program

Admission
V = Voluntary
P = One parent
PP = All parties
C = Court order
O = Other
* = Varies

Disorders
◆ = main treatment focus
◇ = secondary treatment focus

Facility Name and Address	Page Number	Type	Security	Admission	Average stay	Age range	Gender	Autism	Learning Disabilities	Behavior Disorders	Psychosocial Disorders	Substance Abuse	Eating Disorders	Other Compulsive/Addictive	Post-Traumatic/Stress	Thought, Mood, and Personality
Methodist Hospitals, Child and Adolescent Program, Gary, IN 46402	258	GH	L	*	4 wk		M/F			◊	◊				◊	♦
Mirage Retreat, Indianapolis, IN 46208	261	DA	S	*	60 dy		M/F					♦				
Mulberry Center, Welborn Hospital, Evansville, IN 47713	267	GH	P/R	*	14 dy	13-adult	M/F		◊	♦	♦	♦	◊	♦	◊	♦
Oaklawn, Goshen, IN 46526	280	PH	P/R	*	31 dy	13-adult	M/F		◊	♦	♦	◊	◊	◊	♦	♦
Pettersen House, Hammond, IN 46320	302	RT	S	*	3 mo		M/F					♦				
Porter-Starke Service, Inc. and Vale Park Psychiatric Hospital, Valparaiso, IN 46383	308	PH	P/R	*	21 dy	10-adult	M/F	♦	♦	♦	♦	◊	◊	◊	♦	♦
Quinco Behavioral Health Systems, Columbus, IN 47201	313	PH	L	*	2 wk		M/F	◊	◊	♦	♦	♦	♦	♦	♦	♦
Renaissance Center for Addictions, Elkhart, IN 46514	317	GH	S	*	9 dy		M/F		◊	◊	♦	♦	♦	♦	◊	♦
Youth Service Bureau of Porter County—Niequist Center, Valparaiso, IN 46383	397	RT	S	*	1 yr		M/F		◊	♦	♦	◊	◊	◊	◊	◊
IOWA																
Area Substance Abuse Council, Cedar Rapids, IA 52404	60	RT	S	*	5 mo		M/F		◊	◊	◊	♦	◊	◊	◊	
Children's Square USA, Council Bluffs, IA 51502-3008	130	RT	S	*	12 mo		M/F		◊	♦	♦			◊	◊	♦
Jennie Edmundson Memorial Hospital, Council Bluffs, IA 51503	228	GH	S	*	20 dy		M/F		◊	◊	◊	◊	◊		◊	♦
Lutheran Social Service—Beloit Children's Home, Ames, IA 50010	246	RT	S	C	20 mo		M/F	◊	◊	♦	♦			◊	◊	♦	◊
Mercy Hospital, Council Bluffs, IA 51503	256	GH	P	*	14 dy		M/F	◊	◊	◊	♦		◊		◊	◊
Mercy Hospital—Chemical Dependency Services, Council Bluffs, IA 51503	257	O	S	*	19 dy		M/F					♦				
Orchard Place, Des Moines, IA 50315	284	O	S/R	*		13-18	M/F		◊	♦	♦	◊	◊	◊	♦	♦
St. Luke's Gordon Recovery Center, Sioux City, IA 51102	336	DA	S	*	65 dy		M/F					♦				
St. Luke's Hospital, Cedar Rapids, IA 52402	337	GH	L	*	3 wk		M/F		◊	♦	♦		◊		◊	♦
St. Mary's Adolescent Substance Abuse Center, Dyersville, IA 52040	338	GH	S	*	26 dy		M/F					♦				

Facility Name and Address	Page Number	Type	Security	Admission	Average stay	Age range	Gender	Autism	Learning Disabilities	Behavior Disorders	Psychosocial Disorders	Substance Abuse	Eating Disorders	Other Compulsive/Addictive	Post-Traumatic Stress	Thought, Mood, and Personality
Smith Center Residential Treatment Cedar Rapids, IA 52404	349	RT	S/R	*	14 mo	5-13	M/F		◊	◆	◆				◆	◆
Tanager Place Cedar Rapids, IA 52404	362	RT	S/N	*	280 dy	12-17	M/F		◊	◆	◊			◊	◊	◊
Youth and Shelter Services, Inc. Ames, IA 50010	396	DA	S	*	7 mo		M/F			◊	◊	◆				

KANSAS

Facility Name and Address	Page Number	Type	Security	Admission	Average stay	Age range	Gender	Autism	Learning Disabilities	Behavior Disorders	Psychosocial Disorders	Substance Abuse	Eating Disorders	Other Compulsive/Addictive	Post-Traumatic Stress	Thought, Mood, and Personality
Atchison Valley Hope Atchison, KS 66002	64	DA	U/N	P	27 dy	adult	M/F			◊	◊	◆	◊	◊	◊	◊
Cedar Ridge Hospital Shawnee, KS 66217	102	PH	P/R	*	24 dy	12-adult	M/F		◊	◆	◆	◆	◊	◊	◆	◆
Charter Hospital of Overland Park—Youth Services Program Overland Park, KS 66213	117	O	P	*	21 dy		M/F	◊	◊	◆	◆	◆	◆	◆	◆	◆
Charter Hospital of Wichita Wichita, KS 67207	119	O	L	*	25 dy		M/F	◊	◆	◆	◆	◆	◆	◊	◆	◆
CPC College Meadows Hospital Lenexa, KS 66215	138	PH	P/R	PP		13-adult	M/F	◊	◊	◊	◊	◊	◊	◊	◊	◊
CPC Great Plains Hospital Wichita, KS 67208	141	PH	L/N	*		13-adult	M/F	◊	◊	◊	◊	◊	◊	◊	◊	◊
Elm Acres Youth Home, Inc.—Boy's Facility Pittsburg, KS 66762	174	RT	U	C	18 mo		M		◊	◊	◊	◊		◊	◊	◊
Kansas Institute Overland Park, KS 66211	230	PH	L/R	*	24 dy	13-adult	M/F	◊	◆	◆	◊	◆	◆	◊	◆	◆
Meninger Clinic—Children and Adolescent Division Topeka, KS 66606	255	PH	S	*	11 mo		M/F		◊	◆		◊	◊	◊	◊	◆
Parkview Hospital of Topeka Topeka, KS 66606	296	PH	L	*	23 dy		M/F	◊	◊	◆	◆	◆	◊	◊	◆	◊
Prairie View, Inc. Newton, KS 67114	309	PH	U/R	*	30 dy	13-adult	M/F	◊	◊	◆	◆	◆	◊	◊	◆	◆
Recovery Services Council, Inc.—Recovering Adolescent Program Wichita, KS 67203	315	RT	S	*	45 dy		M/F		◊	◆	◆	◆	◊	◊	◊	◊

Type
DA = Drug addiction rehab center
PH = Psychiatric hospital
GH = General hospital
RT = Residential treatment
S = School
C = Camp
W = Wilderness program
O = Other

Security
U = Unsecured
S = Staff secured
P = Partially locked
L = Entirely locked
N = No runaway pursuit
R = Runaway pursuit
* = Varies depending on program

Admission
V = Voluntary
P = One parent
PP = All parties
C = Court order
O = Other
* = Varies

Disorders ◆ = main treatment focus
◊ = secondary treatment focus

Facility Name and Address	Page Number	Type	Security	Admission	Average stay	Age range	Gender	Autism	Learning Disabilities	Behavior Disorders	Psychosocial Disorders	Substance Abuse	Eating Disorders	Other Compulsive/Addictive	Post-Traumatic Stress	Thought, Mood, and Personality
Saint Francis Academy Incorporated Salina, KS 67401	333	PH	S/R	PP												
Saint Francis Academy, Inc. Salina, KS 67402	333	RT	S/R	*	270 dy	12-18	M		◊	♦		◊		♦	◊	◊
Stormont Vail Regional Medical Center Topeka, KS 66604	357	GH	L	*	22 dy		M/F	◊	♦	♦	♦	◊	◊		♦	♦
Sunrise, Inc. Larned, KS 67550	359	DA	S	*	180 dy		M/F						♦			
KENTUCKY																
Brooklawn Academy Louisville, KY 40232	82	RT		*	6 mo		M		◊	♦	♦	◊		◊		◊
Charter Hospital of Louisville Louisville, KY 40207	116	PH	P/R	*	25 dy	13-adult	M/F	◊	◊	◊	◊	♦	◊	◊	◊	♦
Charter Hospital of Paducah Paducah, KY 42002	117	PH	L	*	24 dy		M/F			◊	◊	◊			◊	◊
Diocesan Catholic Children's Home Fort Mitchell, KY 41017	168	RT	S/R	*	18 mo	6-13	M/F		◊	♦	◊					
Life Adventure Camp, Inc. Lexington, KY 40505	243	C	U/R	V	5 dy	10-18	M/F		◊	♦						
Our Lady of Peace Hospital Louisville, KY 40232	284	PH	P	*	27 dy		M/F	◊	◊	♦	♦	◊	◊	◊	◊	◊
Rivendell Psychiatric Center Bowling Green, KY 42103	322	PH	L	*	45 dy		M/F	♦	◊	◊	♦	♦	◊	♦	♦	♦
Ten Broeck Hospital Louisville, KY 40242	364	O	S	*	17 dy		M/F	◊	◊	◊	◊	♦	♦	◊	◊	♦
LOUISIANA																
Bayou Oaks Hospital Houma, LA 70360	69	O	L	*	16 dy		M/F	♦	◊	♦		♦	♦	♦	♦	♦
CPC East Lake Hospital New Orleans, LA 70127	139	PH	L	*	18 dy		M/F	◊	◊	♦	♦	♦	◊	◊	◊	♦
Cypress Hospital Lafayette, LA 70506	153	PH	P/R		14 dy	12-adult	M/F		◊	♦	◊	♦	◊	◊	◊	♦
DePaul Hospital New Orleans, LA 70118	157	O	P/R	PP		12-adult	M/F		◊	♦	♦	♦	◊	◊	♦	♦
Greenbriar Hospital Covington, LA 70433	195	PH	L/R	*	20 dy	13-adult	M/F	◊	◊	♦	♦	♦	◊	◊		♦
Hope Haven Center Marrero, LA 70125	222	RT	P/R	PP	300 dy	10-18	M/F		◊	♦	◊		◊	◊	◊	◊

Facility Name and Address	Page Number	Type	Security	Admission	Average stay	Age range	Gender	Autism	Learning Disabilities	Behavior Disorders	Psychosocial Disorders	Substance Abuse	Eating Disorders	Other Compulsive/Addictive	Post-Traumatic Stress	Thought, Mood, and Personality
Lake Charles Memorial Hospital, Lake Charles, LA 70601	235	GH	L/R	*	21 dy	12-18	M/F		◇	◆		◆			◇	◆
Magnolia Recovery Center, Gonzales, LA 70737	247	DA	S/R	*	6 mo	13-21	F					◆	◆		◆	
Methodist Psychiatric Pavilion, New Orleans, LA 70127	258	O	P	*	16 dy	11-adult	M/F	◇	◆	◆	◆	◆	◇	◇	◆	◆
New Beginnings of Opelousas, Opelousas, LA 70570	270	DA	S/R	*	3 mo	13-adult	M/F			◇	◇	◆	◇	◇	◇	◇
Northshore Psychiatric Hospital, Slidell, LA 70461	276	PH	P	*	25 dy		M/F			◇	◆	◇	◇	◇		◇
Opportunities, Scott, LA 70583	282	DA	*	*		13-adult	M/F			◇	◇	◆	◆	◇	◆	◇
Our Lady of the Lake Regional Medical Center—Tau Center, Baton Rouge, LA 70808	285	DA	S	*	18 dy		M/F					◆				
Parkland Hospital, Baton Rouge, LA 70808	289	PH	P/R	PP	15 dy	12-adult	M/F		◇	◆	◆	◆	◇	◇	◇	◇
Rivernorth Treatment Center, Pineville, LA 71360	323	O	L	*	18 dy		M/F	◇	◇	◆	◆	◆	◇	◇	◆	◆
River Oaks Hospital, New Orleans, LA 70123	324	O	P	*	21 dy		M/F		◇	◆	◆	◇	◆	◇	◆	◆
Tulane University Medical Center, New Orleans, LA 70112	370	GH	S	*	6 wk		M/F	◇			◇			◇		◇	◇

MAINE

Facility Name and Address	Page Number	Type	Security	Admission	Average stay	Age range	Gender	Autism	Learning Disabilities	Behavior Disorders	Psychosocial Disorders	Substance Abuse	Eating Disorders	Other Compulsive/Addictive	Post-Traumatic Stress	Thought, Mood, and Personality
Acadia Hospital, Bangor, ME 04401	52	GH	L	*			M/F	◇	◇	◇	◇			◇	◇	◇	◇
Day One, Bar Mills, ME 04004	155	DA	S	*	1 yr		M/F							◆		
Elan School, Poland Spring, ME 04274-9711	172	S	S	*	24 mo	12-20	M/F		◇	◆	◇	◇			◇	◇
Jackson Brook Institute, South Portland, ME 04106	227	PH	L	*	37 dy	13-adult	M/F	◇	◇	◇	◆	◇	◇	◇	◇	◇

Type
DA = Drug addiction rehab center
PH = Psychiatric hospital
GH = General hospital
RT = Residential treatment
S = School
C = Camp
W = Wilderness program
O = Other

Security
U = Unsecured
S = Staff secured
P = Partially locked
L = Entirely locked
N = No runaway pursuit
R = Runaway pursuit
* = Varies depending on program

Admission
V = Voluntary
P = One parent
PP = All parties
C = Court order
O = Other
* = Varies

Disorders
◆ = main treatment focus
◇ = secondary treatment focus

Facility Name and Address	Page Number	Type	Security	Admission	Average stay	Age range	Gender	Autism	Learning Disabilities	Behavior Disorders	Psychosocial Disorders	Substance Abuse	Eating Disorders	Other Compulsive/Addictive Disorders	Post-Traumatic Stress	Thought, Mood, and Personality
Project Rebound Bangor, ME 04401	312	RT	S	*	4 mo		M					♦				
Wiley House Treatment Centers of New England Ellesworth, ME 04605	388	RT	S/R	*		10-18	M/F		◊	♦	♦	◊		◊	◊	♦
MARYLAND																
Brook Lane Psychiatric Center Hagerstown, MD 21742	81	PH	S	*	40 dy		M/F	◊	◊	♦	♦	◊	◊	◊	♦	♦
Changing Point Ellicott City, MD 21041-0167	105	DA	S/R	PP	45 dy	14-adult	M/F				◊	◊	♦			◊
Changing Point South Waldorf, MD 20604	106	DA	S/R	*	47 dy	13-adult	M/F				◊	◊	◊	♦		◊
Chestnut Lodge Hospital—Rose Hill Treatment Center Rockville, MD 20850	123	PH	P	*	4 mo		M/F		◊	♦	♦	◊	♦	◊	♦	♦
Edgemeade Upper Marlboro, MD 20772	171	RT	U/N	*	547 dy	12-18	M		◊	♦	♦	◊			◊	♦
Fairbridge Residential Treatment Center Rockville, MD 20850	177	RT	R		180 dy	12-18	M/F		◊	◊	◊	◊	◊		◊	◊
Franklin Square Hospital Center Baltimore, MD 21237	187	GH	P	*	2 wk		M/F		◊	♦	♦		◊		◊	◊
Gundry Glass Hospital Baltimore, MD 21228	200	PH	L/N	*		12-adult	M/F	◊	♦	♦	♦	◊	◊	♦	♦	♦
Karma Academy at Frederick for Girls Frederick, MD 21701	231	RT	S	*	12 mo		F		◊	♦	◊	◊	◊		◊	◊
Karma Academy for Boys Rockville, MD 20850	231	DA	S	*	12 mo		M			♦		♦		♦		
Mercy Medical Center Baltimore, MD 21202	257	GH	S	*	21 dy		M/F				◊	◊	◊	♦		◊
New Beginnings at White Oak Woolford, MD 21613	270	DA	S	*	35 dy		M/F						♦			
Oakview Treatment Ellicott City, MD 21043	281	DA	P/N	*	30 dy	13-adult	M/F				◊	◊	♦			◊
Sheppard Pratt Hospital Baltimore, MD 21204	347	PH	L	O		12-adult	M/F		◊	◊	◊	◊	◊	◊	◊	◊
Taylor Manor Hospital Ellicott City, MD 21041-0396	363	PH	L/R	*	31 dy	10-adult	M/F	◊	◊	♦	♦	◊	◊	◊	♦	♦
Villa Maria Residential Treatment Center Timonium, MD 21093	378	RT	S	*	16 mo	5-13	M/F		◊	♦	♦		◊		◊	◊
Walden/Sierra, Inc. California, MD 20619	379	RT	S	*	18 mo		F				◊	◊	♦		◊	

Facility Name and Address	GENERAL INFORMATION							DISORDERS TREATED								
	Page Number	Type	Security	Admission	Average stay	Age range	Gender	Autism	Learning Disabilities	Behavior Disorders	Psychosocial Disorders	Substance Abuse	Eating Disorders	Other Compulsive/Addictive	Post-Traumatic Stress	Thought, Mood, and Personality
Woodbourne Center, Inc. Baltimore, MD 21239	390	RT	S/R	*		11-18	M/F		◆	◆	◆	◇		◇	◇	◆
MASSACHUSETTS																
Austen Riggs Center Stockbridge, MA 01262	65	PH	U/N	V		17+	M/F	◇	◇	◇	◇		◆	◇	◇	◆
Balpate Hospital, Inc. Georgetown, MA 01833	66	O	*	*	2 wk	16+	M/F	◇	◇	◇	◆	◆	◇	◆	◇	◆
Beacon Detox Center Greenfield, MA 01301	70	DA	S	*	3 dy		M/F					◆				
Bournewood Hospital Brookline, MA 02167	77	PH	L	*	19 dy		M/F	◇	◇	◆	◆	◆	◆	◆	◆	◆
Brightside, Inc. West Springfield, MA 01089	80	RT	S/R	PP	365 dy	12-18	M/F		◇	◆	◆			◆	◆	◇
Camp Half Moon Great Barrington, MA 01230	93	C	U/R	*	8 wk	6-15	M	◆								
Cardinal Cushing School and Training Center Hanover, MA 02339	96	O	S/R	V	2 yr	14-adult	M/F				◇			◇		
Charles River Hospital Wellesley, MA 02181	106	PH	P/R	P	18 dy	12-adult	M/F	◇	◇	◇	◆	◆	◆	◇	◆	◆
Charles River Hospital—West Chicopee, MA 01020	107	PH	P/R	*	21 dy	11-adult	M/F			◆	◆	◇	◇	◇	◆	◆
Children's Hospital Boston, MA 02115	128	O	S	*	20 dy		M/F	◇	◇	◇		◇				◇
DeSisto School Stockbridge, MA 01262	159	S	S	*	2 yr	13-21	M/F	◇	◇	◇	◇	◇		◇	◇	◇
Devereux Massachusetts Rutland, MA 01543-0197	166	RT	S/R	*		6-adult	M/F	◆	◆	◆	◆				◆	◆
Germaine Lawrence School Arlington, MA 02174	191	RT	S/R	PP	14 mo	12-22	F		◇	◆	◇	◆	◇	◇	◆	◇
Gosnold Treatment Center Falmouth, MA 02540	192	DA	S/R	*	40 dy	13-adult	M/F					◆				

Type
DA = Drug addiction rehab center
PH = Psychiatric hospital
GH = General hospital
RT = Residential treatment
S = School
C = Camp
W = Wilderness program
O = Other

Security
U = Unsecured
S = Staff secured
P = Partially locked
L = Entirely locked
N = No runaway pursuit
R = Runaway pursuit
* = Varies depending on program

Admission
V = Voluntary
P = One parent
PP = All parties
C = Court order
O = Other
* = Varies

Disorders
◆ = main treatment focus
◇ = secondary treatment focus

Facility Name and Address	Page Number	Type	Security	Admission	Average stay	Age range	Gender	Autism	Learning Disabilities	Behavior Disorders	Psychosocial Disorders	Substance Abuse	Other Compulsive/Addictive	Eating Disorders	Post-Traumatic Stress	Thought, Mood, and Personality
Grove Adolescent Treatment Center Northampton, MA 01060	198	RT	S/R	PP	540 dy	12-21	M/F		◊	◆	◆	◊	◊	◊	◆	◆
Italian Home For Children, Inc. Jamaica Plain, MA 02130	226	RT	S/R	PP	545 dy	4-12	M/F		◆	◆						
John Dewey Academy Great Barrington, MA 01230	228	S	U/N	*	24 mo	15-22	M/F		◆	◆	◆	◆	◆	◆	◆	
Kolburne School, Inc. New Marlborough, MA 01230	234	S	S/R	*	730 dy	8-21	M/F		◆	◆	◊	◊	◊	◊		◊
McAuley Nazareth Home For Boys Leicester, MA 01524	251	RT	S/R	*	550 dy	6-13	M		◆	◆	◆					
Orchard Home Watertown, MA 02172	283	O	S/R	*	500 dy	11-17	F		◆	◆	◆	◊	◊	◊	◆	◆
Providence Hospital First Step Holyoke, MA 01040	312	O	S	*	13 dy		M/F					◆				
Providence Hospital Honor House Holyoke, MA 01040	312	RT	S	*	3 mo		M/F					◆				
Reed Academy Framingham, MA 01701	315	S	S/R	O	720 dy	7-14	M/F		◆	◆	◊				◊	◊
Riverview School, Inc. East Sandwich, MA 02537	325	S	P/R	PP	3 yr	12-21	M/F	◊	◆				◊			
Road Back Attleboro, MA 02703	325	RT	S	*	3 mo		M/F		◊	◊	◊	◆	◊	◊	◊	◊
St. Ann's Home, Inc. Methuen, MA 01844	330	RT	S/R	*	550 dy	13-17	M/F		◆	◆	◆		◊	◊	◊	◆
Southwood Community Hospital Norfolk, MA 02056	354	GH	S	*	8 dy		M/F	◊	◊	◆	◊	◆	◊	◆	◊	◊
Valley View School North Brookfield, MA 01535	375	RT	S/N	PP		12-17	M		◊	◆	◆					◊
Waltham House Waltham, MA 02154	380	RT	S/R	*	500 dy	11-17	M/F		◆	◆	◆	◊	◊	◊	◆	◆
Westlake Academy North Grafton, MA 01536	385	RT	L/R	PP	547 dy	13-18	M/F		◊	◆	◆				◆	◆

MICHIGAN

Facility Name and Address	Page Number	Type	Security	Admission	Average stay	Age range	Gender	Autism	Learning Disabilities	Behavior Disorders	Psychosocial Disorders	Substance Abuse	Other Compulsive/Addictive	Eating Disorders	Post-Traumatic Stress	Thought, Mood, and Personality
Alpha House Ann Arbor, MI 48106	56	RT	S	*	6 mo		M/F			◊	◊		◆	◊	◊	◊
Barat Human Services Detroit, MI 48202	67	RT	U	C	10 mo		F				◊	◊		◊		◊
Bay Haven Bay City, MI 48708	68	RT	P/R	V	30 dy	12-adult	M/F			◊	◊	◆	◊	◊	◊	◊

Facility Name and Address	Page Number	Type	Security	Admission	Average stay	Age range	Gender	Autism	Learning Disabilities	Behavior Disorders	Psychosocial Disorders	Substance Abuse	Eating Disorders	Other Compulsive/Addictive	Post-Traumatic Stress	Thought, Mood, and Personality
Brighton Hospital Adolescent Center Brighton, MI 48116	80	DA	*	*	26 dy	12-18	M/F					♦				
Children's Home of Detroit Grosse Point Woods, MI 48236	127	RT	S/R	*	300 dy	13-18	M/F	♦	♦	♦				◊		♦
Havenwyck Hospital Auburn Hills, MI 48326	205	PH	L/R	*	14 dy	13-adult	M/F			♦	♦	◊	◊	◊	◊	♦
Herrick Memorial Health Care Center Tecumseh, MI 49286	218	GH	L/R	*	14 dy	12-adult	M/F				♦	◊	◊	◊	♦	♦
Judson Center Royal Oak, MI 48073	229	RT	U/N	PP		13-17	M/F	♦	◊	◊			♦	♦		♦
Maplegrove Youth Treatment Center West Bloomfield, MI 48322	249	RT		*	24 dy		M/F					♦				
Munson Medical Center—Alcohol and Drug Treatment Center Traverse City, MI 49684	267	RT	S	*	6 wk		M/F					♦				
Project Rehab—Shiloh Family Grand Rapids, MI 49503	312	DA	S	*	6 mo		M/F					♦				
Regional Mental Health Clinic Southfield, MI 48075	316	DA	U/R	*		10-adult	M/F	♦		♦		♦	◊	♦	♦	◊
St. Vincent and Sarah Fisher Center Residential Treatment Program Farmington Hills, MI 48334-4200	340	RT	U/R	*	450 dy	11-16	M/F		◊	♦	♦			◊		◊
Starr Commonwealth Albion, MI 49224	355	RT	S/R	C	365 dy	12-17	M	◊		♦	♦	◊		♦		◊
Warren Secure Residential Program Warren, MI 48092	380	RT	L/R	*	4 mo	13-18	M/F	♦		♦	♦				◊	♦

MINNESOTA

Facility Name and Address	Page Number	Type	Security	Admission	Average stay	Age range	Gender	Autism	Learning Disabilities	Behavior Disorders	Psychosocial Disorders	Substance Abuse	Eating Disorders	Other Compulsive/Addictive	Post-Traumatic Stress	Thought, Mood, and Personality
Anthony Lewis Center Blaine, MN 55434	58	DA	S/R	*	40 dy	12-adult	M/F		◊	◊	◊	♦				
Anthony Lewis Center Plymouth, MN 55441	59	DA	S	*	6 wk		M/F					♦				
Buckskin, Inc. Ely, MN 55731	84	C	S/R	*	32 dy	12-18	M/F	♦		♦	♦					

Type
DA = Drug addiction rehab center
PH = Psychiatric hospital
GH = General hospital
RT = Residential treatment
S = School
C = Camp
W = Wilderness program
O = Other

Security
U = Unsecured
S = Staff secured
P = Partially locked
L = Entirely locked
N = No runaway pursuit
R = Runaway pursuit
* = Varies depending on program

Admission
V = Voluntary
P = One parent
PP = All parties
C = Court order
O = Other
* = Varies

Disorders ♦ = main treatment focus
◊ = secondary treatment focus

Facility Name and Address	Page Number	Type	Security	Admission	Average stay	Age range	Gender	Autism	Learning Disabilities	Behavior Disorders	Psychosocial Disorders	Substance Abuse	Eating Disorders	Other Compulsive/Addictive	Post-Traumatic Stress	Thought, Mood, and Personality
Children's Residential Treatment Center Minneapolis, MN 55403		RT	P	*	328 dy	11-17	M/F		◊	♦	◊			♦	◊	♦ ♦
Fairview Deaconess Adolescent Chemical Dependency Program Minneapolis, MN 55454	178	GH	S	*	35 dy		M/F					♦				
Fairview Riverside Medical Center Minneapolis, MN 55454	179	GH	L	*	1 mo		M/F	◊	◊		♦			♦	♦	♦ ♦
Fairview Woodbury Adolescent Chemical Dependency Program Woodbury, MN 55125	179	DA	S	*	90 dy		M/F					♦				
Fountain Center/Albert Lea Albert Lea, MN 56007	185	DA	S/R	V	26 dy	13-adult	M/F					♦				◊
Hazelden Pioneer House Plymouth, MN 55441	205	RT	U	*	36 dy	14-25						♦				
St. Cloud Children's Home St. Cloud, MN 56301	332	RT	S	*	9 mo		M/F	♦	♦	♦	♦	◊			♦	♦
St. Joseph's Home For Children Minneapolis, MN 55407	335	O	S	*		13-17	M/F			♦	♦					♦
Woodbury Extended Care Woodbury, MN 55125	391	DA	S	*	60 dy		M/F					♦				

MISSISSIPPI

Facility Name and Address	Page Number	Type	Security	Admission	Average stay	Age range	Gender	Autism	Learning Disabilities	Behavior Disorders	Psychosocial Disorders	Substance Abuse	Eating Disorders	Other Compulsive/Addictive	Post-Traumatic Stress	Thought, Mood, and Personality
Laurel Wood Center Meridian, MS 39303	242	PH	*	*	15 dy	12-adult	M/F		◊	♦	♦	♦	◊			◊

MISSOURI

Facility Name and Address	Page Number	Type	Security	Admission	Average stay	Age range	Gender	Autism	Learning Disabilities	Behavior Disorders	Psychosocial Disorders	Substance Abuse	Eating Disorders	Other Compulsive/Addictive	Post-Traumatic Stress	Thought, Mood, and Personality
Arthur Center Mexico, MO 65265	62	PH	P	*	24 dy		M/F	◊	◊	◊	◊	◊	◊	◊	◊	◊
Baptist Medical Center—Adolescent Mental Health and Chemical Dependency Treatment Program Kansas City, MO 64131	67	O	L	*	20 dy	12-18	M/F		◊	♦	◊	♦		◊		♦
Boys Town of Missouri, Inc. St. James, MO 65559	77	RT	S/R	*		13-17	M/F			♦	♦	♦	◊		♦	♦ ♦
Charter Hospital of Columbia Columbia, MO 65201	111	PH	L/R	*		13-adult	M/F	◊	♦	♦	♦	♦	◊	◊	◊	◊ ♦
Child Center of Our Lady St. Louis, MO 63121	124	RT	S/R		730 dy	5-14	M/F		♦	♦	♦				◊	◊
Comprehensive Mental Health Services, Inc. Independence, MO 64052	135	DA	S/R	*	45 dy	13-adult	M/F	◊	◊	♦	♦	♦	♦	◊	◊	♦ ♦
Edgewood Children's Center St. Louis, MO 63119	171	RT	P/R	*	22 mo	5-17	M/F		♦	♦	♦			◊	◊	◊ ♦
Epworth Children's Home St. Louis, MO 63119	176	RT	P/R	PP	210 dy	11-18	M/F		♦	♦	◊	◊	◊	◊	◊	♦

Facility Name and Address	Page Number	Type	Security	Admission	Average stay	Age range	Gender	Autism	Learning Disabilities	Behavior Disorders	Psychosocial Disorders	Substance Abuse	Eating Disorders	Other Compulsive/Addictive	Post-Traumatic Stress	Thought, Mood, and Personality
GENERAL INFORMATION → / **DISORDERS TREATED** →																
Front Door Residential Program, Columbia, MO 65201	188	RT	S	*	8 mo		M		◊	◊	◊	◊				
Heartland Hospital, Nevada, MO 64772	217	PH	S	*	145 dy		M/F	◊	◊	◊	◆	◊	◊	◊	◊	◊
Lakeland Regional Hospital, Springfield, MO 65806	236	O	L	*	27 dy		M/F			◆	◊	◊	◊	◆	◆	◆
Laughlin Pavilion, Kirksville, MO 63501	239	PH	P	*	180 dy		M/F	◊	◊	◊	◆	◆	◆	◊	◆	◆
Mattie Rhodes Counseling and Art Center, Kansas City, MO 64108	250	C	U/R	P		13-adult	M/F				◆					
Menorah Medical Center, Kansas City, MO 64110	255	GH	P	*	9 dy		M/F	◊	◊	◊	◆	◊	◆	◊	◊	◆
Parkside Recovery Center at Freeman Hospital, Joplin, MO 64801	294	GH	S/N	*	12 dy	12-adult	M/F			◊	◊	◆		◊	◊	◊
Piney Ridge Center, Inc., Waynesville, MO 65583	307	RT	S/R	*	150 dy	11-18	M/F	◊	◆	◆	◆	◊	◊		◆	◆
Research Psychiatric Center, Kansas City, MO 64130	319	PH	L/R	PP	12 dy	13-adult	M/F	◊	◆	◆	◆	◊	◊	◆	◆	◆
Riverside Hospital, Jefferson City, MO 65109	324	PH	L	*	14 dy		M/F	◊	◊	◊	◊	◊	◊	◊	◊	◊
Rotary Youth Camp, Lee's Summit, MO 64063	328	C	S/R	*	6 dy	13-16	M/F	◊	◊	◊					◊	◊
St. Joseph Health Center, St. Charles, MO 63301	334	GH	L/N	PP		12-18	M/F	◊	◆	◆	◆	◊	◊		◆	◆
Trinity Lutheran Hospital, Kansas City, MO 64108	369	GH	L	*	21 dy		M/F	◊	◊	◆	◆	◊	◊	◊		◆
Two Rivers Psychiatric Hospital, Kansas City, MO 64133	371	PH	L/R	*		11-adult	M/F	◊	◆	◆	◆	◊	◊		◆	◊
MONTANA																
Expeditions, Trout Creek, MT 59874	177	W	U	P			M/F		◊	◊	◊	◊				◊

Type
DA = Drug addiction rehab center
PH = Psychiatric hospital
GH = General hospital
RT = Residential treatment
S = School
C = Camp
W = Wilderness program
O = Other

Security
U = Unsecured
S = Staff secured
P = Partially locked
L = Entirely locked
N = No runaway pursuit
R = Runaway pursuit
* = Varies depending on program

Admission
V = Voluntary
P = One parent
PP = All parties
C = Court order
O = Other
* = Varies

Disorders
◆ = main treatment focus
◊ = secondary treatment focus

Facility Name and Address	Page Number	Type	Security	Admission	Average stay	Age range	Gender	Autism	Learning Disabilities	Behavior Disorders	Psychosocial Disorders	Substance Abuse	Eating Disorders	Other Compulsive/Addictive	Post-Traumatic Stress	Thought, Mood, and Personality
Explorations, Trout Creek, MT 59874	177	RT	U	P			M/F	◊	◊	◊	◊					◊
Montana Deaconess Medical Center, Great Falls, MT 59405	262	GH	*	*	14 dy		M/F	◊	◆	◆	◆	◊	◊		◊	◊
Rimrock Foundation, Billings, MT 59107	321	O	S/R	P	35 dy	14-18	M/F	◊	◊	◊		◆	◆	◆	◊	◊
Rivendell Psychiatric Center, Butte, MT 59701	322	PH	L	*			M/F	◊	◊	◊	◊	◊	◊	◊	◆	◆
Wilderness Treatment Center, Marion, MT 59925	387	DA	U/N	P	60 dy	13-adult	M					◆				
Yellowstone Treatment Centers, Billings, MT 59106	395	RT	P	*		12-18	M/F	◆	◆	◆		◊	◊	◆	◆	◆

NEBRASKA

Facility Name and Address	Page Number	Type	Security	Admission	Average stay	Age range	Gender	Autism	Learning Disabilities	Behavior Disorders	Psychosocial Disorders	Substance Abuse	Eating Disorders	Other Compulsive/Addictive	Post-Traumatic Stress	Thought, Mood, and Personality
Father Flanagan's Boy's Home, Boys' Town, NE 68010	180	O		C	18 mo		M/F		◊	◆	◆	◊	◊			
Methodist Richard Young Residential Program, Omaha, NE 68105	259	PH	P/N	*		11-17	M/F			◆	◆	◆	◊	◊	◆	◆
NOVA Therapeutic Community, Omaha, NE 68111	277	DA	S	*	12 mo		M/F					◆				
O'Neill Valley Hope, O'Neill, NE 68763	281	DA	S/N	P		13-adult	M/F			◊	◊	◆	◊	◊	◊	◊
Rivendell Psychiatric Center, Seward, NE 68434	323	PH	L/R	*	32 dy	12-18	M/F	◆	◆	◆	◊				◆	◊
Uta Halee Girls' Village, Omaha, NE 68112	374	RT	P/R	*	15 mo	12-18	F	◊	◆	◆	◊				◆	◆

NEVADA

Facility Name and Address	Page Number	Type	Security	Admission	Average stay	Age range	Gender	Autism	Learning Disabilities	Behavior Disorders	Psychosocial Disorders	Substance Abuse	Eating Disorders	Other Compulsive/Addictive	Post-Traumatic Stress	Thought, Mood, and Personality
Adolescent Care and Treatment Center—Oikos, Inc., Reno, NV 89503	52	DA	S	*	10 mo		F					◆				
CareUnit Hospital of Nevada, Las Vegas, NV 89102	98	PH	P/R	*	20 dy	12-adult	M/F	◊	◆	◆	◆	◊		◆	◊	◆
Charter Hospital of Las Vegas, Las Vegas, NV 89117	114	PH	L/R			12-adult	M/F	◊	◆	◊	◊	◊	◊	◊	◊	◊
HCA Montevista Hospital, Las Vegas, NV 89103	212	PH	L/R	*		13-adult	M/F	◊	◆	◆	◆	◊	◊	◊		◆
HCA Willow Springs Center, Reno, NV 89502	216	RT	L	*	4 mo	13-17	M/F	◊	◆	◆	◊	◊			◆	◆
Nike House, Inc., Las Vegas, NV 89102	275	DA	S	*	9 mo		F	◊	◊	◊			◊	◊		◊

Facility Name and Address	Page Number	Type	Security	Admission	Average stay	Age range	Gender	Autism	Learning Disabilities	Behavior Disorders	Psychosocial Disorders	Substance Abuse	Eating Disorders	Other Compulsive/Addictive	Post-Traumatic/Addictive Stress	Thought, Mood, and Personality
St. Mary's Regional Medical Center, New Foundation Center for Addictions and Behavioral Health, Reno, NV 89520	339	GH	S	*	26 dy		M/F		◊	◊	◊	♦	◊	♦	♦	♦
Truckee Meadows Hospital, Reno, NV 89520	369	PH	L/R		14 dy	13-adult	M/F		◊	♦	♦	♦	◊	♦	♦	♦
NEW HAMPSHIRE																
Beech Hill Hospital, Dublin, NH 03444	71	DA	S/R	P	21 dy	14-adult	M/F					♦		◊	◊	◊
Camp E-Toh-Ahnee, Colebrook, NH 03576	91	W	S/R	*		10-17	M			◊	♦	♦				
Cragged Mountain Farm, Freedom, NH 03836	148	C	S	PP	28 dy		M/F			◊						
Crotched Mountain Preparatory School and Rehabilitation Center, Greenfield, NH 03047	150	S	S/R	*		13-adult	M/F	♦	♦	♦	♦			◊	♦	♦
Hampshire Country School, Rindge, NH 03461	202	S	U/N	*	3 yr	13-17	M/F			◊	◊	◊				
Hampstead Hospital, Hampstead, NH 03841	202	PH	P	*	20 dy		M/F	◊	♦	♦	♦	♦	◊	◊	◊	◊
Pike School, Inc., Haverhill, NH 03765	304	S	U/R	*	18 mo	11-17	M			♦	♦					◊
Seafield Pines Hospital, Keene, NH 03431	345	DA	S	*	42 dy		M/F					♦				
Spaulding Youth Center, Northfield, NH 03276	354	RT	S	*		16-21	M/F	♦	◊	♦	◊					◊
NEW JERSEY																
Bowling Green Adolescent Center, Berlin, NJ 08009	77	DA	S/R	*	42 dy	12-18	M/F			♦	◊	♦	◊	◊		
Carrier Foundation, Belle Mead, NJ 08502	99	PH	L/R	*	26 dy	12-adult	M/F	◊	♦	♦	◊	♦	◊	◊	♦	♦
Daytop, New Jersey, Mendham, NJ 07945	155	RT	S	*	8 mo		M/F					♦				

Type
DA = Drug addiction rehab center
PH = Psychiatric hospital
GH = General hospital
RT = Residential treatment
S = School
C = Camp
W = Wilderness program
O = Other

Security
U = Unsecured
S = Staff secured
P = Partially locked
L = Entirely locked
N = No runaway pursuit
R = Runaway pursuit
* = Varies depending on program

Admission
V = Voluntary
P = One parent
PP = All parties
C = Court order
O = Other
* = Varies

Disorders
♦ = main treatment focus
◊ = secondary treatment focus

Facility Name and Address	Page Number	Type	Security	Admission	Average stay	Age range	Gender	Autism	Learning Disabilities	Behavior Disorders	Psychosocial Disorders	Substance Abuse	Eating Disorders	Other Compulsive/Addictive	Post-Traumatic Stress	Thought, Mood, and Personality
Devereux Deerhaven, Chester, NJ 07930	162	O	S	O	12 mo	9+	F		◊	◊	◊				◊	◊
Devereux—New Jersey Center for Autism, Bridgeton, NJ 08302	166	RT														
Elizabeth General Medical Center, Children and Adolescent Psychiatric Inpatient Unit, Elizabeth, NJ 07201	173	GH	L	*	20 dy		M/F		◊	◊	◊	◊			◊	◊
Fair Oaks Hospital, Summit, NJ 07901	178	PH	L/R	P	27 dy	9-adult	M/F	◆	◆	◆	◆	◆	◆	◆	◆	◆
Harbor, Hoboken, NJ 07030	203	DA	S/R	P	35 dy	13-19	M/F					◆				
Newgrange School, Trenton, NJ 08610	272	S				8-18	M/F		◆							
New Hope Foundation, Marlboro, NJ 07746	272	DA	S/R	*	180 dy	13-18	M/F		◊	◊	◊	◆	◊	◊	◊	◊
Phoenix Academy, Rockleigh, NJ 07647	303	DA	S	*	1 yr		M/F					◆				
NEW MEXICO																
Aspen Meadows Hospital, Velarde, NM 87582	63	PH	P	*	30 dy		M/F		◊	◆	◆	◆	◊	◊	◆	◆
Brush Ranch School, Terrero, NM 87573	83	S	S/R	V	2 yr	10-18	M/F		◆	◊						
Charter Hospital of Albuquerque, Albuquerque, NM 87108	110	O	P	*	28 dy		M/F		◊	◆	◆	◆	◊	◊	◆	◆
HCA Heights Psychiatric Hospital, Albuquerque, NM 87109	211	PH	L/R	*	30 dy	13-adult	M/F	◊	◆	◆	◆	◆	◊	◆	◆	◆
Kaseman Presbyterian Hospital, Albuquerque, NM 87110	232	GH	L	*			M/F		◊	◆	◆	◊			◊	◊
Lea Regional Hospital, Hobbs, NM 88240	242	GH	P	*	14 dy		M/F	◊	◊	◆	◊	◊	◊	◊	◆	◆
Namaste, Los Lunas, NM 87031	268	RT	S/N	*	9 mo	6-12	M/F		◊	◊	◊	◊	◊	◊	◆	
St. Vincent's Adolescent Psychiatric Services, Santa Fe, NM 87501	341	GH	L/N	*	25 dy	12-18	M/F		◆	◆	◆	◆	◆		◆	◆
NEW YORK																
APPLE (A Program Planned for Life Enrichment), Hauppauge, NY 11788	59	RT	S	P		15-adult	M/F					◆				
Arms Acres, Carmel, NY 10512	61	DA	S/R	PP	35 dy	12-adult	M/F		◊	◊	◊	◆	◊	◊		◊

Facility Name and Address	GENERAL INFORMATION							DISORDERS TREATED								
	Page Number	Type	Security	Admission	Average stay	Age range	Gender	Autism	Learning Disabilities	Behavior Disorders	Psychosocial Disorders	Substance Abuse	Other Compulsive/Addictive	Eating Disorders	Post-Traumatic Stress	Thought, Mood, and Personality
Astor Home for Children Rhinebeck, NY 12572	63	RT	U	O	18 dy		M/F			♦	♦	◊			♦	◊
Aurora Concept, Inc. Flushing, NY 11366	65	RT	S/N	*		14-adult	M/F		◊	♦	◊	♦	◊	◊		◊
Baker Hall, Inc. Lackawanna, NY 14218	66	RT	S/R	V	15 mo	12-21	M/F		◊	♦	♦		◊		♦	♦
Benjamin Rush Center Syracuse, NY 13202	73	O	P/R	P		12-adult	M/F		◊	♦	♦	♦	♦	◊	♦	♦
Blythedale Children's Hospital Valhalla, NY 10595	76	O	S	P	140 dy		M/F	◊	♦	♦	♦		♦		◊	◊
Brunswick Hall Amityville, NY 11701	82	PH	S	P	40 dy		M/F		◊	◊	◊	◊	◊		◊	◊
Camp Cummings Brewster, NY 10509	87	C	S/R	*	26 dy	14-adult	M/F	◊	◊							
Camp Huntington High Falls, NY 12440	93	C	S/R	PP	30 dy	13-adult	M/F	◊	♦							
Children's Home of Kingston Kingston, NY 12401	127	RT	S/R	*	420 dy	13-21	M		♦	♦	♦				♦	♦
Children's Village Dobbs Ferry, NY 10522	130	RT	S/R	*	33 mo	13-15	M		♦	♦	♦				♦	♦
Conifer Park Scotia, NY 12302	136	DA	S/R	*	28 dy	12-adult	M/F		◊	◊	◊	♦	◊		◊	◊
Craig House Hospital Beacon, NY 12508	149	PH	P/R	P	45 dy	12-adult	M/F		◊	♦	♦	♦	♦	◊	◊	♦
Credo Foundation Evan Mills, NY 13637	149	O	S	*	1 yr		M/F						♦			
Daytop Village, Inc. New York, NY 10018	155	RT	S	*			M/F						♦			
DePaul Mental Health Services Rochester, NY 14611	158	RT	S	*	18 mo		M/F		◊	◊	◊		◊	◊	◊	◊
Devereux New York Red Hook, NY 12571-0040	166	O	S/R	*	3 yr	13-21	M/F	◊					◊		◊	

Type
DA = Drug addiction rehab center
PH = Psychiatric hospital
GH = General hospital
RT = Residential treatment
S = School
C = Camp
W = Wilderness program
O = Other

Security
U = Unsecured
S = Staff secured
P = Partially locked
L = Entirely locked
N = No runaway pursuit
R = Runaway pursuit
* = Varies depending on program

Admission
V = Voluntary
P = One parent
PP = All parties
C = Court order
O = Other
* = Varies

Disorders
♦ = main treatment focus
◊ = secondary treatment focus

Facility Name and Address	Page Number	Type	Security	Admission	Average stay	Age range	Gender	Autism	Learning Disabilities	Behavior Disorders	Psychosocial Disorders	Substance Abuse	Eating Disorders	Other Compulsive/Addictive Disorders	Post-Traumatic Stress	Thought, Mood, and Personality
Dynamic Youth Community, Inc. Brooklyn, NY 11230	170	RT	S	*	16 mo		M/F							♦		
Four Winds—Saratoga Saratoga Springs, NY 12866	186	PH	S/R	*		13-adult	M/F	◊	♦	◊	◊	♦	♦	♦	♦	♦
Four Winds Westchester Katonah, NY 10536	186	PH	S/R	*		13-adult	M/F		◊	♦	♦	♦	♦	♦	♦	♦
Gateway Youth and Family Services—Residential Services Williamsville, NY 14221	189	RT	S/R	C	411 dy	10-17	M/F		◊	♦	◊	◊	◊		◊	◊
Geller House Staten Island, NY 10305	190	O	U/R	*	60 dy	11-16	M/F		◊	♦	♦	◊	◊		♦	♦
Gracie Square Hospital New York, NY 10021	193	PH	P	*	30 dy		M/F								♦	
Green Chimneys School Brewster, NY 10509	196	RT	S/R	*	2 yr	12-21	M/F		◊	◊	◊				◊	◊
Henry Ittleson Center for Child Research Riverdale, NY 10471	217	RT	S/R	V	4 yr	5-12	M/F			♦	♦	♦			♦	♦
High Point Hospital Rye Brook, NY 10573	219	PH	P/R	*	90 dy	12-adult	M/F		◊	♦	♦	◊	◊	◊	♦	♦
Hill House Albany, NY 12207	220	RT	S/R	*	360 dy	12-16	M/F			◊	◊	♦	◊	◊	◊	◊
Hillside Children's Center Rochester, NY 14620	221	RT	*		540 dy	13-21	M/F		♦	♦	♦	◊	◊	◊	◊	♦
Holliswood Hospital Holliswood, NY 11423	222	PH	L	PP		12-adult	M/F		◊	♦	♦	◊	◊	◊	♦	♦
Hopevale, Inc. Hamburg, NY 14075	223	RT	S/R	*	1 yr	12-18	F			♦	♦				♦	♦
Julia Dyckman Andrus Memorial Yonkers, NY 10701	229	RT	S/R	PP	18 mo	13-15	M/F		◊	♦	♦				♦	◊
Kaplan House New York, NY 10003	231	RT	S	PP	18 mo	17-21	M			◊	◊	◊				◊
Madonna Heights Services Dix Hills, NY 11746	247	RT	P/R	*	180 dy	12-18	F		◊	♦	♦	◊				◊
Maplebrook School, Inc. Amenia, NY 12501	248	S	S/R	*	4 yr	13-adult	M/F		♦							
Mount Sinai Medical Center New York, NY 10029	266	GH	L	PP	2 mo	5-12	M/F	◊	♦	♦	◊			◊	◊	◊
New York Institute For Special Education Bronx, NY 10469	274	S	S	*	5 dy		M/F		♦	♦						

| | GENERAL INFORMATION | | | | | | | DISORDERS TREATED | | | | | | | | |
Facility Name and Address	Page Number	Type	Security	Admission	Average stay	Age range	Gender	Learning Disabilities	Autism	Behavior Disorders	Psychosocial Disorders	Substance Abuse	Eating Disorders	Other Compulsive/Addictive	Post-Traumatic Stress	Thought, Mood, and Personality
Outreach House/Brentwood, Brentwood, NY 11717	285	DA	S	*	15 mo		M/F					♦				
Outreach House/Ridgewood, Ridgewood, NY 11385	285	DA	S	*	15 mo		M/F					♦				
Pahl, Inc.—Pahl House, Troy, NY 12180	286	DA	S	*	8 mo		M/F					♦				
Park Ridge Chemical Dependency, Rochester, NY 14626	290	RT	S	*	60 dy		M/F					♦				
Parsons Child and Family Center, Albany, NY 12208	297	RT	S	*	1 yr	13-21	M/F	◊	◊	♦	♦		◊		◊	♦
Ramapo Anchorage Camp, Rhinebeck, NY 12572	314	C			27 dy		M/F			◊	◊					
Regent Hospital, New York, NY 10021	316	PH	P/N	*	30 dy	13-adult	M/F		◊	◊	◊	◊	◊	◊	◊	◊
St. Christopher's Jennie Clarkson Child Care Services—Dobbs Ferry Campus, Dobbs Ferry, NY 10522	331	RT	S/R	C		12-19	M/F	♦		◊		♦	◊		◊	◊
St. Christopher's Jennie Clarkson Child Care Services—Valhalla Campus, Valhalla, NY 10595	331	RT	S/R	C				♦		◊		♦	◊		◊	◊
St. Francis Academy—Camelot, Lake Placid, NY 12946	332	RT	S/R	*		12-18	M		◊	♦	♦	♦			◊	♦
St. Joseph's Villa, Rochester, NY 14616	335	RT	U/R	*	1 yr	11-19	M/F		♦	♦	♦	♦		◊	◊	◊
Schneider Children's Hospital of Long Island, New Hyde Park, NY 11042	344	GH	S	P	8 dy		M/F		◊	◊	◊	◊	◊	◊		◊
South Oaks, Amityville, NY 11701	353	PH	P/N	P		10-adult	M/F			♦	♦	♦	♦	♦	♦	♦
Stony Lodge Hospital, Ossining, NY 10562	356	PH	L	*	20 dy		M/F		◊	◊	◊	◊	◊	◊	◊	◊
Summit School/Children's Residence Center, Upper Nyack, NY 10960	357	RT	U/R	*	600 dy	13-adult	M/F	♦		♦	♦		◊	◊	◊	♦
Valley View/Redirection, Kenoza Lake, NY 12750	375	DA	S/R	*	42 dy	12-adult	M/F					♦				

Type
DA = Drug addiction rehab center
PH = Psychiatric hospital
GH = General hospital
RT = Residential treatment
S = School
C = Camp
W = Wilderness program
O = Other

Security
U = Unsecured
S = Staff secured
P = Partially locked
L = Entirely locked
N = No runaway pursuit
R = Runaway pursuit
* = Varies depending on program

Admission
V = Voluntary
P = One parent
PP = All parties
C = Court order
O = Other
* = Varies

Disorders
♦ = main treatment focus
◊ = secondary treatment focus

Facility Name and Address	Page Number	Type	Security	Admission	Average stay	Age range	Gender	Autism	Learning Disabilities	Behavior Disorders	Psychosocial Disorders	Substance Abuse	Eating Disorders	Other Compulsive/Addictive	Post-Traumatic Stress	Thought, Mood, and Personality
NORTH CAROLINA																
Amethyst — Charlotte, NC 28210	56	DA	S/R	*	30 dy	13-adult	M/F	◊	◊	◊	♦	◊	◊	◊	◊	◊
Appalachian Hall — Asheville, NC 28803	59	PH	P/R	*	40 dy	13-adult	M/F	♦	♦	♦	◊	◊	◊	◊	◊	◊
Brunswick Hospital Adolescent Psychiatric Unit — Supply, NC 28462	83	GH	L/R	*	30 dy	13-17	M/F			♦	♦		♦	♦	♦	♦
Brynn Marr Hospital — Jacksonville, NC 28546	83	PH	L/N	*	30 dy	13-adult	M/F			♦	♦	♦	♦	◊		♦
Camp E-Ku-Sumee — Candor, NC 27229	89	W	S/R	*	365 dy	10-17	M		◊	♦	♦					
Camp Elliott Wilderness Program — Black Mountain, NC 28711	89	RT	U/R	PP	14 mo	10-17	M		♦	♦						
Camp E-Mun-Talee — Lowgap, NC 27024	90	W	S/R	*	365 dy	10-17	M		◊	♦	♦					
Camp E-Toh-Kalu — Hendersonville, NC 28739	91	W	S/R	*	365 dy	10-17	M/F		◊	♦	♦					
Camp E-Wa-Henwu — Newport, NC 28570	92	W	S/R	*	365 dy	10-17	M/F		◊	♦	♦					
Charter Hospital of Greensboro — Greensboro, NC 27403	113	PH	P/R	O	21 dy	10-adult	M/F		♦	♦	♦	◊	◊	◊	◊	♦
Charter Northridge Hospital — Raleigh, NC 27615	121	PH	L/N	C	90 dy	12-17	M/F				◊	♦	♦		◊	◊
Cumberland Hospital — Fayetteville, NC 28304	152	PH	*	*	23 dy		M/F	◊	◊	◊	◊	◊	◊	◊	◊	◊
Duke University Hospital — Durham, NC 27710	169	GH	L	*	30 dy		M/F	◊	◊	◊	◊	♦	♦	◊	◊	◊
Durham Regional Hospital Adolescent Treatment Unit — Durham, NC 27704	169	GH	L/R	*	23 dy	12-18	M/F		◊	♦	♦	◊	◊		♦	♦
HCA Holly Hill Hospital — Raleigh, NC 27610	211	PH	L/R	PP	20 dy	13-adult	M/F	◊		♦	♦	◊	◊		♦	♦
North Carolina Baptist Hospitals, Inc. — Winston-Salem, NC 27157	275	GH	S	P	6 dy		M/F	◊	◊	◊	◊	◊	◊	◊	◊	◊
Oakhill Residential Treatment Center — Asheville, NC 28801	279	RT	S/R	PP	181 dy	12-18	M/F	◊	◊	◊	◊	◊	◊	◊	◊	◊
Talisman Summer Camp — Black Mountain, NC 28711	361	C	S/R	PP	4 wk	9-17	M/F	◊	◊							
Thompson Children's Homes — Charlotte, NC 28229	365	RT	U/R	PP	700 dy	5-18	M/F		♦	♦	♦					

Facility Name and Address	Page Number	Type	Security	Admission	Average stay	Age range	Gender	Autism	Learning Disabilities	Behavior Disorders	Psychosocial Disorders	Substance Abuse	Eating Disorders	Other Compulsive/Addictive	Post-Traumatic Stress	Thought, Mood, and Personality
Three Springs of North Carolina, Pittsboro, NC 27312	367	RT	S/R			10-17	M			◆	◆	◊				◆
NORTH DAKOTA																
Dakota Boys' Ranch, Minot, ND 58702	154	RT	S/R	*	365 dy	10-17	M		◆	◆	◆	◆	◊	◊	◆	◆
OHIO																
Bellefaire Jewish Children's Bureau, Cleveland, OH 44118	72	RT	S/R	*	420 dy	11-adult	M/F		◊	◊	◆	◊	◊	◊	◊	◆
Belmont Pine Hospital, Youngstown, OH 44505	73	PH	P/R	*	22 dy	13-adult	M/F		◊	◆	◊	◆	◊		◆	◆
Buckeye Boys Ranch, Inc., Grove City, OH 43123	84	RT	*	*		10-18	M/F		◊	◊	◊	◊			◊	◊
CareUnit Hospital of Cincinnati, Cincinnati, OH 45211	96	DA	S/R	P	20 dy	13-adult	M/F					◆				
Charter Hospital of Toledo, Inc., Maumee, OH 43537	118	PH	L/R	*	2 wk	13-18	M/F		◊	◊	◊	◊		◊	◊	◊
Children's Home of Cincinnati, Cincinnati, OH 45227	126	RT	U/N	*	12 mo	11-18	M/F			◆	◆	◆			◆	◆
Children's Hospital Medical Center, Cincinnati, OH 45229	128	PH	L/R	PP	30 dy	6-12	M/F	◊	◊	◊	◊		◊		◊	◊
Dairy Lane Group Home, Athens, OH 45701	153	RT	S	*	6 mo		M/F		◊	◆	◆			◊	◊	◆
Dettmer Hospital, Troy, OH 45373	159	PH	S/R	P	17 dy	11-adult	M/F		◆	◆	◆	◆	◊		◊	◆
Gill House, Steubenville, OH 43952	191	RT	S	*	1 yr		M		◊	◆	◊					◆
Harding Hospital, Worthington, OH 43085	203	PH	L/R	*	19 dy	1-adult	M/F	◊	◆	◆	◆	◆	◆	◊	◊	◆
Health Hill Hospital for Children, Cleveland, OH 44104-3865	217	RT	S/R	*	60 dy	18	M/F		◊	◊	◊			◊		◊	◊

Type
DA = Drug addiction rehab center
PH = Psychiatric hospital
GH = General hospital
RT = Residential treatment
S = School
C = Camp
W = Wilderness program
O = Other

Security
U = Unsecured
S = Staff secured
P = Partially locked
L = Entirely locked
N = No runaway pursuit
R = Runaway pursuit
* = Varies depending on program

Admission
V = Voluntary
P = One parent
PP = All parties
C = Court order
O = Other
* = Varies

Disorders
◆ = main treatment focus
◊ = secondary treatment focus

Facility Name and Address	Page Number	Type	Security	Admission	Average stay	Age range	Gender	Autism	Learning Disabilities	Behavior Disorders	Psychosocial Disorders	Substance Abuse	Eating Disorders	Other Compulsive/Addictive	Post-Traumatic Stress	Thought, Mood, and Personality
Interval Brotherhood Home Alcohol—Drug Rehabilitation Center Akron, OH 44319	225	DA	S/N	P	150 dy	12-17	F			◊	◊	◆	◊			
Lakeland Community Hospital, Inc. Lorain, OH 44053	236	GH	P/R	P	14 dy	13-adult	M/F					◊	◆		◊	◆
Maryhaven, Inc. Columbus, OH 43207	249	DA	S	*	35 dy		M/F					◆				
Marymount Hospital Mental Health Center Garfield Heights, OH 44125-2975	249	GH	P/R	*	22 dy	12-adult	M/F			◆	◆		◊	◊	◊	◊
McKinley Hall, Inc. Springfield, OH 45505	251	RT	S/N	*	56 dy	10-18	M/F					◊				
Meridia Recovery Center Cleveland, OH 44112	257	O	S	*	28 dy		M/F					◆				
MetroHealth Saint Luke's Adolescent Chemical Dependency Programs Cleveland, OH 44104	259	GH	P/R	P	35 dy	13-19	M/F					◆	◊			
New Directions, Inc. Pepper Pike, OH 44124	271	RT	U/R	*	120 dy	13-19	M/F		◊	◊	◊	◆	◊		◊	◊
Parmadale Parma, OH 44134	297	RT	S/R	*	9 mo	10-18	M/F	◊	◊	◆	◆	◆	◊	◊		
St. John Medical Center Steubenville, OH 43952	333	GH	S/R	*	18 dy	13-adult	M/F			◊	◊	◊			◊	◊
St. Vincent Medical Center Toledo, OH 43608-2691	340	GH	S	*	19 dy		M/F		◊	◊	◊	◊	◆	◊	◊	◊
Semi-Independent Living Steubenville, OH 43952	346	RT	S	*	1 yr		M		◊	◆	◊					◆
OKLAHOMA																
Bethany Pavilion Bethany, OK 73008	74	PH	L	*		13-adult	M/F	◊	◆	◆	◆		◆	◆	◆	◆
Christian Care Program Tulsa, OK 74128	130	PH	L	*		13-adult	M/F			◊	◆	◆	◊	◊	◊	◊
CPC Southwind Hospital Oklahoma City, OK 73159	147	PH	P	*			M/F			◊	◊	◊	◊	◊	◊	◊
High Pointe Residential Treatment Center Oklahoma City, OK 73141	219	RT	S/R	*	116 dy	11-17	M/F		◊	◆	◆	◊	◊		◆	◆
Laureate Psychiatric Clinic and Hospital Tulsa, OK 74136	239	PH	L/R	*	18 dy	1-adult	M/F		◊	◆	◊	◊	◊	◆	◊	◆
Moccasin Bend Ranch Miami, OK 74354	261	RT	U/R	*	90 dy	12-18	M/F		◊	◆	◆	◊		◊	◆	◆
Oak Crest Center Shawnee, OK 74801	277	PH	L	*	45 dy		M/F		◊	◆	◆	◊			◆	◆

Facility Name and Address	GENERAL INFORMATION							DISORDERS TREATED								
	Page Number	Type	Security	Admission	Average stay	Age range	Gender	Autism	Learning Disabilities	Behavior Disorders	Psychosocial Disorders	Substance Abuse	Eating Disorders	Other Compulsive/Addictive	Post-Traumatic Stress	Thought, Mood, and Personality
Rolling Hills Hospital Ada, OK 74820	327	PH	L/R	*	45 dy	13-adult	M/F		◊	◊	◊	◊		◊	◊	◊
Shadow Mountain Institute Tulsa, OK 74133	347	RT	P/N	*	45 dy	12-18	M/F		◊	◆	◆	◊	◊	◆	◊	◊
Wetumka General Hospital—Second Chance Wetumka, OK 74883	387	DA	S	*			M/F					◆				
OREGON																
Catherine Freer Wilderness Therapy Expeditions Albany, OR 97321	100	W	S/R	P	21 dy	12-18	M/F		◊	◆	◊	◆	◊	◊	◊	◊
Christie School Marylhurst, OR 97036	131	RT	S	*	3 yr		M/F		◊	◊	◊			◆	◆	◊
Mount Bachelor Academy Bend, OR 97708	265	S	S/N	*	730 dy	13-18	M/F		◊	◊	◊	◊	◊	◊		◊
Pacific Gateway Hospital Portland, OR 97202	285	PH	L/R	*	28 dy	11-adult	M/F		◊	◆	◆	◆	◊	◊	◆	◆
Portland Adventist Medical Center Adolescent Treatment Program Portland, OR 97216	309	GH	S	*	7 dy		M/F	◊	◊	◊	◊	◊	◊		◆	◆
Red Willow Adolescent Chemical Dependency Treatment, Inc. Beaverton, OR 97005	315	DA	S	*	45 dy		M/F					◆				
Sacred Heart General Hospital Eugene, OR 97401	329	O	L	*	22 dy		M/F		◊	◊	◆	◆	◊	◊	◆	◆
Southern Oregon Adolescent Study and Treatment Center Grants Pass, OR 97526	352	RT	S/R	*	24 mo	12-18	M		◆	◆	◊	◊		◊	◊	◆
Waverly Children's Home Portland, OR 97202	382	RT	S/R	PP	14 mo	12-adult	M/F		◆	◆	◊				◆	◊
Winnicoh Residential Treatment Center for Children Portland, OR 97225	390	PH	P/N	PP		8-14	M/F		◊	◊	◊	◊			◆	◆	◊
PENNSYLVANIA																
Aloysia Hall, Mercy Medical Center Johnstown, PA 15905	55	GH	L/R	*	18 dy	12-17	M/F	◊	◊	◆	◆	◊	◊	◊	◆	◆

Type
DA = Drug addiction rehab center
PH = Psychiatric hospital
GH = General hospital
RT = Residential treatment
S = School
C = Camp
W = Wilderness program
O = Other

Security
U = Unsecured
S = Staff secured
P = Partially locked
L = Entirely locked
N = No runaway pursuit
R = Runaway pursuit
* = Varies depending on program

Admission
V = Voluntary
P = One parent
PP = All parties
C = Court order
O = Other
* = Varies

Disorders
◆ = main treatment focus
◊ = secondary treatment focus

Facility Name and Address	Page Number	Type	Security	Admission	Average stay	Age range	Gender	Autism	Learning Disabilities	Behavior Disorders	Psychosocial Disorders	Substance Abuse	Eating Disorders	Other Compulsive/Addictive	Post-Traumatic Stress	Thought, Mood, and Personality
Bi-County Treatment Center Dubois, PA 15801	75	DA	S	*	93 dy		M/F					♦				
Camp Lee Mar Lackawaxen, PA 18435	93	C	S/R	P	7 wk	13-21	M/F	◊	◊	◊						
Chambers Hill Adolescent Care Facility Harrisburg, PA 17111	104	DA	S	*	180 dy		M/F					♦				
Charter Fairmont Institute Philadelphia, PA 19128	109	PH	L	*	2 wk		M/F	◊	◊	♦	♦	♦	◊	♦	◊	♦
Clarion Psychiatric Center Clarion, PA 16214	131	PH	L/R	*	25 dy	12-adult	M/F		◊	♦	♦	◊	◊	♦	♦	♦
Clear Brook Lodge Shickshinny, PA 18655	132	DA	S/R		42 dy	13-18	M/F					♦				
Devereux—Brandywine Treatment Center Glenmore, PA 19343-0069	161	RT	U/R	*		14-21	M		◊	♦	♦				♦	◊
Devereux—Edward L. French Center Devon, PA 19333	162	RT	S/R	*	2 yr	12-adult	M/F		◊	◊	♦				◊	◊
Devereux—Leo Kanner Center West Chester, PA 19380	165	RT	S/R	*		11-adult	M/F	♦	◊	♦	♦		◊			♦
Devereux—Mapleton Center Malvern, PA 19355-0297	165	RT	S/R	V	664 dy	13-21	M/F		◊		♦			◊	◊	♦
Elling Camp's at Rock Creek Farm Thompson, PA 18465	173	C	S/R	*	26 dy	12-adult	M/F		♦		◊					
First Hospital Wyoming Valley Wilkes-Barre, PA 18702	182	PH	P/R	*	23 dy	13-adult	M/F	♦	◊	◊	◊	◊		◊		◊
Friends Hospital Young People's Services Philadelphia, PA 19124	188	PH	P/R	P	30 dy	12-adult	M/F		◊	◊	◊			♦		◊
Gateway Meadowbrook Aliquippa, PA 15001	189	DA	S/N	PP	30 dy	13-21	M/F		◊	◊	◊		♦	◊	◊	◊
Horsham Clinic Ambler, PA 19002	223	PH	P	*	30 dy	13-adult	M/F		◊	◊	◊			◊		◊
Keystone Center Chester, PA 19013	232	DA	U/N	V		11-17	M/F		◊	◊	◊		♦		◊	◊
Ligonier Valley Treatment Center Stahlstown, PA 15687	244	DA	S/R	*	35 dy	13-adult	M/F				◊		◊	◊	◊	
Lourdesmont—Good Shepherd Youth And Family Services Clarks Summit, PA 18411-1298	245	RT	U/R	PP	365 dy	13-17	F					♦	♦	◊		◊
Meadows Psychiatric Center Centre Hall, PA 16828	251	PH	P/R	*	25 dy	13-adult	M/F	◊	◊	♦	♦	♦	◊	◊	◊	◊
Mercy Hospital Wilkes-Barre, PA 18765	257	GH	L	*	2 wk		M/F	♦	◊	♦	♦	◊	♦	♦	♦	♦

Facility Name and Address	Page Number	Type	Security	Admission	Average stay	Age range	Gender	Autism	Learning Disabilities	Behavior Disorders	Psychosocial Disorders	Substance Abuse	Eating Disorders	Other Compulsive/Addictive	Post-Traumatic Stress	Thought, Mood, and Personality
Mill Creek School Philadelphia, PA 19139	260	S	U	*	1 yr	12-18	M/F	◇	◇	◆	◇	◇	◇	◇		◆
Mirmont Treatment Center Lima, PA 19037	261	DA	S/N	*	27 dy	13-adult	M/F		◇			◆		◇		
Mountainview Rehabilitation Center, Inc. Brodheadsville, PA 18322	264	DA	S/R	*	42 dy	12-adult	M/F			◇	◇	◆				◇
Mount Sinai Hospital Philadelphia, PA 19147	266	O	P/R	V	20 dy	10-17	M/F	◆		◇	◇					◇
National Hospital for Kids in Crisis Orefield, PA 18069	268	PH	L/R	*	30 dy	13-21	M/F	◇	◆	◆	◆	◇	◇	◇		◆
Philadelphia Child Guidance Center Philadelphia, PA 19104	302	PH	*	*	25 dy	13-adult	M/F	◆	◆	◆				◆	◇	◆
Philhaven—A Continuum of Psychiatric Services Mount Gretna, PA 17064	303	O	L	*	23 dy		M/F	◆	◆	◆	◆	◇	◆	◆	◆	◆
Pressley Ridge School at Ohiopyle Ohiopyle, PA 15470	310	O	S/R	*	1 yr	10-16	M	◆	◆	◆						◆
Rehabilitation Institute of Pittsburgh Pittsburgh, PA 15217	317	O	S	*	30 dy		M/F	◆		◆	◆			◆		
Renewal Centers Quakertown, PA 19070	318	DA	S/R	*	28 dy	12-18	M/F			◇	◇	◆			◇	◇
Renfrew Center Philadelphia, PA 19128	318	O	S/R	V	45 dy	15-adult	M/F				◇	◇	◆		◇	◇
Roxbury Shippensburg, PA 17257	328	DA	S/R		42 dy	14-adult	M/F			◇	◇	◆	◇	◇	◇	◇
Summit Camp, Inc. Honesdale, PA 18431	357	C	S/R	*	53 dy	13-17	M/F		◆	◇						
Terraces Ephrata, PA 17522	365	DA	S	*	21 dy		M			◇	◇	◆				◇
Today, Inc. Newtown, PA 18940	368	DA	S/N	*	45 dy	13-adult	M/F			◇	◇	◆	◇			◇
Twin Lakes Center for Drug and Alcohol Rehabilitation Somerset, PA 15501-0909	371	DA	S/R	*	42 dy	13-adult	M/F					◆				

Type
DA = Drug addiction rehab center
PH = Psychiatric hospital
GH = General hospital
RT = Residential treatment
S = School
C = Camp
W = Wilderness program
O = Other

Security
U = Unsecured
S = Staff secured
P = Partially locked
L = Entirely locked
N = No runaway pursuit
R = Runaway pursuit
* = Varies depending on program

Admission
V = Voluntary
P = One parent
PP = All parties
C = Court order
O = Other
* = Varies

Disorders
◆ = main treatment focus
◇ = secondary treatment focus

Facility Name and Address	Page Number	Type	Security	Admission	Average stay	Age range	Gender	Autism	Learning Disabilities	Behavior Disorders	Psychosocial Disorders	Substance Abuse	Eating Disorders	Other Compulsive/Addictive	Post-Traumatic Stress	Thought, Mood, and Personality
Tyrone Hospital Detox Unit Tyrone, PA 16686	373	GH	U/N	V	5 dy	14-adult	M/F					♦				
Wiley House Treatment Centers Bethlehem, PA 18015-3998	388	RT	S/R	*		12-18	M/F		◊	♦	♦	◊	◊	◊	◊	♦
Wordsworth Residential Treatment Program Fort Washington, PA 19034	394	RT	S/R	V	18 mo	13-21	M/F		♦	♦	♦				◊	♦

RHODE ISLAND

Facility Name and Address	Page Number	Type	Security	Admission	Average stay	Age range	Gender	Autism	Learning Disabilities	Behavior Disorders	Psychosocial Disorders	Substance Abuse	Eating Disorders	Other Compulsive/Addictive	Post-Traumatic Stress	Thought, Mood, and Personality
Butler Hospital Providence, RI 02906	85	PH	S/R		10 dy	13-adult	M/F				◊	◊	◊	◊	◊	◊
Camp E-Hun-Tee Exeter, RI 02882	88	W	S/R	*		10-17	M/F		◊	♦	♦					
Emma Pendleton Bradley Hospital East Providence, RI 02915	174	PH	P/R	O	30 dy	13-18	M/F	♦	♦	♦	◊	♦	♦	◊	♦	♦
Good Hope Center Network East Greenwich, RI 02818	191	DA	S	PP	35 dy	12-adult	M		◊	◊	◊	♦	◊	◊		♦

SOUTH CAROLINA

Facility Name and Address	Page Number	Type	Security	Admission	Average stay	Age range	Gender	Autism	Learning Disabilities	Behavior Disorders	Psychosocial Disorders	Substance Abuse	Eating Disorders	Other Compulsive/Addictive	Post-Traumatic Stress	Thought, Mood, and Personality
Bruce Hall—Center for Treatment of Alcohol and Drug Dependency Florence, SC 29501	82	O	S	*	31 dy		M/F				◊	♦	♦	◊	◊	◊
Charter of Charleston Charleston, SC 29405	121	PH	P/R	*	14 dy	12-adult	M/F	◊	◊	♦	♦	◊	◊	◊	♦	♦
Charter Rivers Hospital West Columbia, SC 29169	122	PH	L/R	*	14 dy	10-adult	M/F			♦	♦	♦	◊	◊	♦	♦
Coastal Carolina Hospital—Child and Adolescent Program Conway, SC 29526	133	O	P	*	14 dy		M/F			♦	♦	♦	◊		♦	♦
Coastal Carolina Hospital—Residential Treatment Center Conway, SC 29526	133	RT	L	*	2 yr		M/F		◊	♦	♦	♦	◊	♦	♦	♦
Fenwick Hall Hospital—New Beginnings Johns Island, SC 29457	181	DA	P/R	*	19 dy	12-adult	M/F			♦	♦	♦	◊	◊	◊	♦
HCA Aurora Pavilion Aiken, SC 29802	206	PH	L/R	PP	12 dy	12-15	M/F			♦	♦	♦	◊			♦
New Hope Treatment Center Summerville, SC 29485	273	RT	L/R	*	217 dy	12-17	M/F		♦	♦	◊	◊	◊	♦	♦	♦
Spartanburg Regional Medical Center Spartanburg, SC 29303	354	GH	L	*	13 dy		M/F			♦	♦	◊	◊			♦
William S. Hall Psychiatric Institute Columbia, SC 29202	389	O	P	*	2 mo		M/F	♦	◊	♦	◊		♦		♦	♦
York Place York, SC 29745	396	RT	S/R	*	400 dy	6-12	M/F	♦	♦	♦				◊	♦	◊

Facility Name and Address	GENERAL INFORMATION							DISORDERS TREATED								
	Page Number	Type	Security	Admission	Average stay	Age range	Gender	Autism	Learning Disabilities	Behavior Disorders	Psychosocial Disorders	Substance Abuse	Eating Disorders	Other Compulsive/Addictive	Post-Traumatic Stress	Thought, Mood, and Personality
SOUTH DAKOTA																
Our Home, Inc. Huron, SD 57350	284	RT	S	*	50 dy		M/F							♦		
Rapid City Regional Hospital—Addiction Recovery Center Rapid City, SD 57702	314	RT	S	*	42 dy		M/F							♦		
Threshold Youth Services Sioux Falls, SD 57105	367	RT	S	*	1 yr		M/F			♦	◇	♦	♦	◇	♦	♦
TENNESSEE																
Blount Memorial Hospital Maryville, TN 37801	75	GH	P/R	V		13-18	M/F			◇	◇	◇	◇		◇	◇
Camelot Care Center, Inc. Kingston, TN 37763	86	O	S	*	3 mo		M/F	◇	◇	♦	♦	◇	◇	◇	♦	♦
Camp E-Sun-Alee Deerlodge, TN 37726	90	W	S/R	*	365 dy	10-17	M		◇	♦	♦					
Charter Lakeside Hospital Memphis, TN 38133	120	PH	P/R	PP	15 mo	12-adult	M/F		♦	♦	♦	♦	♦	◇	♦	♦
Cooper House Knoxville, TN 37917	136	RT	S	*	1 yr		M	◇	♦	♦	♦	◇	◇	♦	♦	♦
Cumberland Hall Hospital Nashville, TN 37207	150	PH	L/R	*	30 dy	12-18	M/F		◇	◇	◇	◇	◇	◇	◇	◇
Cumberland Hall of Chattanooga, Inc. Chattanooga, TN 37421	151	PH	L/R	*		13-18	M/F		◇	◇	◇	◇	◇	◇	◇	◇
Cumberland Heights Treatment Center Nashville, TN 37209	152	DA	S/N	PP	35 dy	13-adult	M/F					♦				
De Neuville Heights School Memphis, TN 38127	156	O	*	*	425 dy	12-17	F			◇	♦	◇				◇
Goodlark Medical Center Diagnostic Acute Care Unit Dickson, TN 37055	192	O	S	*	30 dy		M/F	◇	◇	◇	◇		◇		◇	◇
Goodlark Residential Treatment Center Dickson, TN 37055	192	RT	P	*	6 mo		M		◇	♦		◇			◇	◇

Type
DA = Drug addiction rehab center
PH = Psychiatric hospital
GH = General hospital
RT = Residential treatment
S = School
C = Camp
W = Wilderness program
O = Other

Security
U = Unsecured
S = Staff secured
P = Partially locked
L = Entirely locked
N = No runaway pursuit
R = Runaway pursuit
* = Varies depending on program

Admission
V = Voluntary
P = One parent
PP = All parties
C = Court order
O = Other
* = Varies

Disorders
♦ = main treatment focus
◇ = secondary treatment focus

Facility Name and Address	Page Number	Type	Security	Admission	Average stay	Age range	Gender	Autism	Learning Disabilities	Behavior Disorders	Psychosocial Disorders	Substance Abuse	Eating Disorders	Other Compulsive/Addictive	Post-Traumatic Stress	Thought, Mood, and Personality
Harbours at Brentwood Brentwood, TN 37024	203	DA	S/N	P	14 dy	16-adult	M/F						◆			
Haslam Center Knoxville, TN 37909	204	RT	P	*	1 yr		M/F	◊	◆	◆	◆	◊	◊	◆	◆	◆
HCA Valley Hospital Chattanooga, TN 37421	216	PH	*	*	14 dy	13-adult	M/F		◆	◆	◆	◊	◊	◊	◊	◊
Indian Path Pavilion Kingsport, TN 37660	224	O	S	*	2 wk		M/F		◆	◆	◆	◆		◊	◆	◆
Meharry-Hubbard Hospital Nashville, TN 37208	253	GH	P	*	3 wk		M/F	◊	◊	◊	◊	◊	◊	◊	◊	◊
Northwest Counseling Center—The Turning Point Program Lexington, TN 38351	277	DA	S	*	5 mo		M/F									
Parthenon Pavilion at Centennial Medical Center Nashville, TN 37203	298	PH	*	*	20 dy	12-adult	M/F		◊	◊	◊	◆	◊	◊	◊	◊
Peninsula Village Louisville, TN 37777	300	RT	P/R	*	265 dy	13-18	M/F		◊	◆	◊	◆	◊	◊	◊	◊
Ridgeview Psychiatric Hospital and Center, Inc. Oak Ridge, TN 37830	321	PH	P	*	14 dy		M/F			◆	◆		◊	◊	◊	◆
St. Mary's Medical Center Knoxville, TN 37917	339	GH	L	*	3 wk		M/F	◊	◊	◊	◊	◆	◊	◊	◊	◆
Seven Hawks Wilderness Program Waverly, TN 37185	347	W	S	*	12 mo		M/F		◊	◆		◊			◊	◊
Tennessee Christian Medical Center Madison, TN 37115	365	GH	L	*	20 dy		M/F	◊	◊	◆	◆	◆	◆	◆	◊	◆
Three Springs of Duck River Nunnelly, TN 37137	366	RT	U/R	*	365 dy	11-17	M		◊	◆	◆	◊			◊	◊
Woodridge Hospital Johnson City, TN 37604	392	O	P	*	21 dy		M/F	◊	◊	◆	◆	◆	◆	◆	◆	◆
Youth Villages—Deer Valley Campus Linden, TN 37096	397	RT	S/R	*		10-17	F		◊	◆	◆	◊	◊	◊	◊	◊
Youth Villages—Dogwood Village Campus Arlington, TN 38002	398	RT	S/R	*	12 mo	9-21	M/F		◊	◆	◆	◊	◊	◊	◊	◊
Youth Villages—Memphis Boys Town Campus Memphis, TN 38135	398	RT	S/R	*		12-21	M/F		◊	◆	◆	◊	◊	◊	◊	◊
Vanderbilt Child and Adolescent Psychiatric Hospital Nashville, TN 37212	376	PH	L	*	25 dy	4-21	M/F		◆	◆	◆	◆	◆	◆	◆	◆

TEXAS

Facility Name and Address	Page Number	Type	Security	Admission	Average stay	Age range	Gender	Autism	Learning Disabilities	Behavior Disorders	Psychosocial Disorders	Substance Abuse	Eating Disorders	Other Compulsive/Addictive	Post-Traumatic Stress	Thought, Mood, and Personality
Baylor-Parkside Lodge of Dallas/Fort Worth, Inc. Argyle, TX 76226	69	DA	S/R	*		12-adult	M/F					◊		◆	◆	◊

Facility Name and Address	Page Number	Type	Security	Admission	Average stay	Age range	Gender	Autism	Learning Disabilities	Behavior Disorders	Psychosocial Disorders	Substance Abuse	Eating Disorders	Other Compulsive/Addictive	Post-Traumatic Stress	Thought, Mood, and Personality
Baywood Hospital Webster, TX 77598	70	PH	P/N	*	21 dy	12-19	M/F	♦	♦	♦	♦	◊	◊	◊	◊	♦
Canyon Lakes Residential Treatment Center Lubbock, TX 79415	94	RT	L	*	150 dy		M/F	◊	◊	◊	◊			◊	◊	◊
CareUnit Hospital of Fort Worth Fort Worth, TX 76104	98	PH	P	PP	23 dy	12-adult	M/F			♦	♦	♦	◊	◊	◊	♦
Cedar Creek Hospital Amarillo, TX 79106	101	PH	L	PP	21 dy		M/F		◊	◊	◊	◊	◊	◊	◊	◊
Cedar Crest Residential Treatment Center Belton, TX 76513	101	RT	S/R	*	139 dy	13-17	M/F		◊	♦	♦	♦			♦	♦
Champions Psychiatric Treatment Center Houston, TX 77014	105	RT	S/R	*	6 mo	12-19	M/F		◊	♦	♦	◊	◊		◊	◊
Charter Hospital of Corpus Christi Corpus Christi, TX 78414	112	PH	L	*	26 dy		M/F		◊	◊	◊	◊	◊	◊	◊	◊
CPC Afton Oaks Hospital Community Residential Center San Antonio, TX 78232	137	O	P/R	*	120 dy	12-18	M/F		◊	♦	♦	◊	◊	◊	◊	◊
CPC Capital Hospital Austin, TX 78729	138	PH	P/R	*	22 dy	13-adult	M/F		◊	◊	♦	♦	◊			◊
CPC Cypress Point Hospital Houston, TX 77065	139	PH	P/R	*	20 dy	11-adult	M/F		◊	♦	♦	♦	◊	♦	♦	♦
CPC Oak Bend Hospital Fort Worth, TX 76132	142	PH	P/R	PP	30 dy	12-adult	M/F			♦	♦	♦	♦	♦	♦	♦
Devereux Hospital and Neurobehavioral Institute of Texas League City, TX 77573	164	PH	L/R			13-adult	M/F	♦	◊	♦	♦	◊	◊	◊		♦
Devereux Psychiatric Residential Treatment Center of Texas Victoria, TX 77902-2666	167	RT	P/R	*	180 dy	12-18	M/F	♦	♦	◊	◊				◊	◊
Faith Ranch Uvalde, TX 78802	180	O	S	PP	2 yr		M		◊	◊	◊	◊				◊
Faulkner Center, Adolescent Program Austin, TX 78705	180	DA	S/R	P	21 dy	12-adult	M/F		◊	◊	◊		♦	◊		◊
Five Oaks Residential Treatment Center Houston, TX 77005	183	RT	S/N	V	78 dy	13-adult	M/F		◊	♦	♦	♦	◊	◊	◊	♦

Type
- DA = Drug addiction rehab center
- PH = Psychiatric hospital
- GH = General hospital
- RT = Residential treatment
- S = School
- C = Camp
- W = Wilderness program
- O = Other

Security
- U = Unsecured
- S = Staff secured
- P = Partially locked
- L = Entirely locked
- N = No runaway pursuit
- R = Runaway pursuit
- * = Varies depending on program

Admission
- V = Voluntary
- P = One parent
- PP = All parties
- C = Court order
- O = Other
- * = Varies

Disorders
- ♦ = main treatment focus
- ◊ = secondary treatment focus

Facility Name and Address	Page Number	Type	Security	Admission	Average stay	Age range	Gender	Autism	Learning Disabilities	Behavior Disorders	Psychosocial Disorders	Substance Abuse	Other Compulsive/Addictive	Eating Disorders	Post-Traumatic Stress	Thought, Mood, and Personality
HCA Belle Park Hospital, Houston, TX 77072	206	PH	L/R	*	20 dy	11-adult	M/F	◊	◊	♦	◊	◊	◊	◊	◊	♦
HCA Deer Park Hospital, Deer Park, TX 77536	208	PH	L/R	*	17 dy	13-adult	M/F	◊	◊	♦	◊	♦	◊	◊	◊	◊
HCA Greenleaf Hospital, College Station, TX 77845	210	PH	L/R	PP	17 dy	12-adult	M/F			◊	◊	◊				◊
HCA Gulf Pines Hospital, Houston, TX 77090	210	PH	L/R	*	25 dy	12-adult	M/F	◊	♦	♦	♦	♦	♦	♦	♦	♦
HCA Red River Hospital, Wichita Falls, TX 76301	213	PH	P/R	P	26 dy	13-adult	M/F		◊	♦	♦	♦	♦	♦	◊	♦
HCA Richland Hospital, North Richland Hills, TX 76180	213	PH	P/R	*	20 dy	13-adult	M/F		◊	◊	◊	◊	◊	◊	◊	◊
HCA Shoal Creek Hospital, Austin, TX 78731	215	PH	P/R	*	12 dy	12-adult	M/F	◊	◊	◊	◊	♦	◊	◊	♦	◊
Intracare Hospital, Houston, TX 77054	226	DA	S	*	14 dy		M/F		◊	♦	◊	♦	◊	◊	◊	◊
Laurel Ridge Hospital, San Antonio, TX 78259	241	PH	P/R	*	180 dy	13-adult	M/F	◊	◊	♦	◊	♦	◊	◊	◊	♦
New Spirit Addictive Disorders and Mental Health Program, Houston, TX 77056	274	PH	S/R	P	10 dy	11-adult	M/F			◊	◊	◊	◊	◊		
Oak Grove Treatment Center, Burleson, TX 76028	278	RT	P/R	*	150 dy	12-18	M/F		◊	♦	♦	◊	◊	♦	♦	♦
Oaks Treatment Center, Austin, TX 78745	280	PH	P	*	6 mo		M/F	♦	♦	◊	◊	◊	◊	◊		♦
Operation Springboard, Canyon Lake, TX 78133	282	RT	S/R	*	120 dy	12-18	M/F		◊	♦	♦	♦	◊	◊	◊	♦
Parkside at Baptist Hospital of Southeast Texas, Beaumont, TX 77701	290	PH	S/R	*	21 dy	12-adult	M/F		♦	♦	♦	♦	◊			♦
Parkside Lodge of Katy, Katy, TX 77494	292	O	S/R	*	30 dy	12-adult	M/F			◊	◊	♦	♦	◊	♦	♦
Passages Residential Treatment Center, El Paso, TX 79902	298	RT	P/R	*	9 mo	13-17	M/F			◊	♦	◊			◊	♦
Pinelands Hospital, Nacogdoches, TX 75963-1004	305	PH	L/R	*	24 dy	13-adult	M/F	◊	◊	♦	◊	♦	◊	◊	◊	♦
RAPHA Adolescent Treatment Program, Grand Prairie, TX 75051	314	GH	L	*	29 dy	12-18	M/F	◊	◊	♦	◊	♦	♦	◊	♦	♦
Residential Treatment Center, Bedford, TX 76021	320	RT	L/R	*		13-18	M/F		◊	♦	♦	♦	◊	◊	♦	◊
Sandstone Center, College Station, TX 77840	342	PH	L/R	*	26 dy	13-adult	M/F	◊	◊	◊	◊	◊	◊	◊	◊	◊

Facility Name and Address	Page Number	Type	Security	Admission	Average stay	Age range	Gender	Autism	Learning Disabilities	Behavior Disorders	Psychosocial Disorders	Substance Abuse	Eating Disorders	Other Compulsive/Addictive	Post-Traumatic Stress	Thought, Mood, and Personality
San Marcos Treatment Center, A Brown Schools Neuropsychiatric Hospital, San Marcos, TX 78667-0768	343	RT	P/R	*		13-adult	M/F	♦	◊	♦	♦	◊	◊	♦	◊	♦
Settlement Home for Children, Austin, TX 78758	346	RT	U/R	PP	12 mo	9-17	F		♦	♦	♦		◊	◊	♦	♦
Southmore Medical Center, Pasadena, TX 77502	353	GH	L	*	10 dy		M/F		♦	♦	♦	◊	◊	◊	♦	♦
Spring Shadows Glen Hospital, Houston, TX 77080	355	PH	P	*		adult	M/F		◊			♦	♦	◊	◊	◊
Sundown Ranch, Inc., Canton, TX 75103	358	DA	S/R	*	120 dy	12-adult	M/F		◊	◊	◊	♦	◊	◊	◊	◊
Sun Towers Behavioral Health Center, El Paso, TX 79902	359	PH	P/R	C	19 dy	13-adult	M/F		♦	♦	◊	♦	◊		♦	♦
Willow Creek Hospital, Fort Worth, TX 76017	389	PH	L/R	PP	21 dy	11-adult	M/F			◊	◊	◊	◊	◊	◊	◊
Woods Psychiatric Institute of Central Texas, Killeen, TX 76543	393	RT	P/R	P	150 dy	6-17	M/F		◊	♦	♦	◊	◊		◊	◊

UTAH

Facility Name and Address	Page Number	Type	Security	Admission	Average stay	Age range	Gender	Autism	Learning Disabilities	Behavior Disorders	Psychosocial Disorders	Substance Abuse	Eating Disorders	Other Compulsive/Addictive	Post-Traumatic Stress	Thought, Mood, and Personality
Adolescent Center for Change, LaVerkin, UT 84745	52	RT	S/R	*	90 dy	11-17	M/F		◊	♦	♦	◊	◊	◊	◊	♦
CPC Olympus View Hospital Community Residential Center, Salt Lake City, UT 84117	143	PH	L/R	*	100 dy	12-18	M/F		◊	◊	♦	◊	◊	♦	♦	♦
Cross Creek Manor, LaVerkin, UT 84745	149	RT	S/R	P	8 mo	11-18	F		◊	♦	♦	◊	◊	◊	◊	◊
Discovery Academy, Provo, UT 84601	168	S	S/R	PP	365 dy	12-18	M/F		◊	◊	♦	◊				
Lakeview Hospital Step One Program, Bountiful, UT 84010	236	GH		*	3 wk		M/F		◊	◊	♦	♦	♦	♦	◊	♦
Mountain View Hospital, Payson, UT 84651	263	GH	R	P	15 dy	13-adult	M/F	◊	◊	♦	♦	♦	◊	◊	◊	♦
Navajo Pines Outdoor Residential Treatment Center, LaVerkin, UT 84745	269	RT	S/R	*	56 dy	13-18	M/F	♦	♦			◊	◊		◊	◊

Type
DA = Drug addiction rehab center
PH = Psychiatric hospital
GH = General hospital
RT = Residential treatment
S = School
C = Camp
W = Wilderness program
O = Other

Security
U = Unsecured
S = Staff secured
P = Partially locked
L = Entirely locked
N = No runaway pursuit
R = Runaway pursuit
* = Varies depending on program

Admission
V = Voluntary
P = One parent
PP = All parties
C = Court order
O = Other
* = Varies

Disorders
♦ = main treatment focus
◊ = secondary treatment focus

Facility Name and Address	Page Number	Type	Security	Admission	Average stay	Age range	Gender	Autism	Learning Disabilities	Behavior Disorders	Psychosocial Disorders	Substance Abuse	Eating Disorders	Other Compulsive/Addictive	Post-Traumatic Stress	Thought, Mood, and Personality
Odyssey Adolescent Program Salt Lake City, UT 84111	281	RT	U	*	9 mo		M/F		◊	◆	◆	◆	◊	◊	◆	◊
Primary Children's Residential Treatment Center Salt Lake City, UT 84010	310	RT	P/R		11 mo	6-13	M/F	◊	◊	◊	◊				◊	◊
Primary Children's Residential Treatment Program Salt Lake City, UT 84123	311	RT	S/R	*	225 dy	5-11	M		◆	◆					◊	◊
Provo Canyon School Provo, UT 84603	313	RT	P/R	*	330 dy	12-18	M/F		◊	◆	◆	◊			◊	◆
Rivendell of Utah West Jordan, UT 84088	322	RT	S/R	P	170 dy	12-18	M/F		◊	◊	◆	◊	◊	◊	◊	◆
Sorenson's Ranch School Koosharem, UT 84744	352	RT	S/R	*	365 dy	13-18	M/F		◊	◆	◊	◊	◊	◊	◊	◊
Utah Valley Regional Medical Center Provo, UT 84604	374	GH	P	*	30 dy		M/F	◊	◊	◊	◊	◊	◊	◊	◆	◆
Western Institute of Neuropsychiatry Salt Lake City, UT 84108	385	PH	L	*	14 dy		M/F	◆	◊	◆	◊	◊	◊	◊	◊	◊

VERMONT

Facility Name and Address	Page Number	Type	Security	Admission	Average stay	Age range	Gender	Autism	Learning Disabilities	Behavior Disorders	Psychosocial Disorders	Substance Abuse	Eating Disorders	Other Compulsive/Addictive	Post-Traumatic Stress	Thought, Mood, and Personality
Brattleboro Retreat Brattleboro, VT 05302	79	PH	P/R	V	36 dy	12-adult	M/F	◊	◆	◆	◆	◆	◆	◆	◆	◆
Camp E-Wen-Akee Fair Haven, VT 05743	92	W	S/R	*		10-17	M/F		◊	◆	◆					
Greenwood School Putney, VT 05346	198	S	S	P		8-15	M		◆							
Pine Ridge School Williston, VT 05461	306	S		V	3 yr	13-18	M/F		◆							

VIRGINIA

Facility Name and Address	Page Number	Type	Security	Admission	Average stay	Age range	Gender	Autism	Learning Disabilities	Behavior Disorders	Psychosocial Disorders	Substance Abuse	Eating Disorders	Other Compulsive/Addictive	Post-Traumatic Stress	Thought, Mood, and Personality
Charter Hospital of Charlottesville Charlottesville, VA 22905	111	PH	L/R	P	25 dy	13-adult	M/F		◊	◊	◊	◊	◊	◊	◊	◆
Charter Westbrook Hospital Richmond, VA 23227	123	PH	P	*	21 dy		M/F		◊	◆	◆	◆	◆	◆	◆	◆
Cumberland Hospital for Children and Adolescents New Kent, VA 23124	152	O	S/R	P	274 dy	2-22	M/F	◊	◆	◆	◊		◊			◊
Elk Hill Farm, Inc. Goochland, VA 23063	173	RT	S/R	V	1 yr	11-18	M		◆	◆	◊	◊				
Grafton School, Inc. Berryville, VA 22611	193	S	U	*	3 yr	13-adult	M/F	◆	◆	◆	◊					◆
Graydon Manor Leesburg, VA 22075	195	RT	S/R	*	270 dy	13-18	M/F		◊	◊	◆	◊	◊		◊	◆

Facility Name and Address	Page Number	Type	Security	Admission	Average stay	Age range	Gender	Autism	Learning Disabilities	Behavior Disorders	Psychosocial Disorders	Substance Abuse	Eating Disorders	Other Compulsive/Addictive	Post-Traumatic Stress	Thought, Mood, and Personality
HCA Dominion Hospital, Falls Church, VA 22044	209	PH	L/R	*	17 dy	13-18	M/F	◊	◊	◊	◊	◊	♦	◊	♦	♦
Maryview Psychiatric Hospital, Portsmouth, VA 23707	250	PH	P	*		11-adult	M/F	◊	♦	♦	♦	♦	◊	◊	♦	♦
Mountain Wood, Charlottesville, VA 22905	265	DA	U/R	PP	30 dy	13-adult	M/F					♦	♦		♦	
New Dominion School, Inc., Cumberland, VA 23040	271	O	S/R	PP	540 dy	11-18	M		♦	♦	♦	◊		◊		♦
Oakland School, Keswick, VA 22947	279	S	U/R	P	2 yr	8-17	M/F		♦							
Peninsula Psychiatric Hospital, Hampton, VA 23666	300	PH	P/R	*	12 dy	13-adult	M/F	◊	◊	◊	◊	◊	◊	◊	◊	◊
Pines Residential Treatment Center and The Phoenix at Portsmouth Psychiatric Center, Portsmouth, VA 23704	306	RT	S/R	*	548 dy	13-adult	M/F		♦	♦	♦	◊	◊	♦	♦	◊
Poplar Springs Hospital, Petersburg, VA 23805	308	PH	P/R	*	12 dy	12-adult	M/F		♦	♦	♦	♦	◊	◊	◊	◊
Saint Albans Psychiatric Hospital, Radford, VA 24143	330	PH	P	*			M/F			♦	♦	♦	♦	◊	◊	♦
Snowden at Fredericksburg, Fredericksburg, VA 22401	350	O	L	*			M/F	♦	◊	♦	♦	◊	◊	◊	♦	♦
Virginia Beach Psychiatric Center, Virginia Beach, VA 23454	378	PH	L/R	*	14 dy	12-adult	M/F	◊	◊	◊	◊	◊	◊	◊	◊	◊
Winchester Medical Center, Inc., Winchester, VA 22601	390	GH	L	*	20 dy		M/F			♦	♦	♦	◊	◊		♦

WASHINGTON

Facility Name and Address	Page Number	Type	Security	Admission	Average stay	Age range	Gender	Autism	Learning Disabilities	Behavior Disorders	Psychosocial Disorders	Substance Abuse	Eating Disorders	Other Compulsive/Addictive	Post-Traumatic Stress	Thought, Mood, and Personality
Carondelet Psychiatric Care Center, Richland, WA 99352	99	PH	L	*	1 mo		M/F		◊	◊	◊		◊		◊	◊
CPC Fairfax Hospital, Kirkland, WA 98034	140	PH	*	*	45 dy	13-adult	M/F	◊	♦	◊	◊	◊	♦	♦	◊	◊
Daybreak of Spokane, Spokane, WA 99203	154	DA	U	*	60 dy		M/F					♦				

Type
DA = Drug addiction rehab center
PH = Psychiatric hospital
GH = General hospital
RT = Residential treatment
S = School
C = Camp
W = Wilderness program
O = Other

Security
U = Unsecured
S = Staff secured
P = Partially locked
L = Entirely locked
N = No runaway pursuit
R = Runaway pursuit
* = Varies depending on program

Admission
V = Voluntary
P = One parent
PP = All parties
C = Court order
O = Other
* = Varies

Disorders
♦ = main treatment focus
◊ = secondary treatment focus

Facility Name and Address	Page Number	Type	Security	Admission	Average stay	Age range	Gender	Autism	Learning Disabilities	Behavior Disorders	Psychosocial Disorders	Substance Abuse	Other Compulsive/Addictive	Eating Disorders	Post-Traumatic Stress	Thought, Mood, and Personality
Deaconess Chemical Dependency Units, Spokane, WA 99210	155	GH	S/N	P	42 dy	12-adult	M/F					◆				
New Beginnings at Northwest, Seattle, WA 98133	269	DA	P/R	P	21 dy	12-19	M/F					◆			◆	
Sacred Heart Medical Center, Department of Psychiatry, Spokane, WA 99220-4045	329	GH	L/N	P	19 dy	12-18	M/F			◆	◆	◆		◇	◇	◆
St. Peter Chemical Dependency Center, Lacey, WA 98503	339	DA	P	*	30 dy		M/F					◆				
Seattle Indian Health Board, Seattle, WA 98114	346	RT	S	*	2 mo		M/F			◇	◇	◆	◇	◇	◇	◇
Southwest Washington Medical Center—Turnaround, Vancouver, WA 98664	353	GH	S	*	35 dy		M/F					◆				
SUWS Adolescent Program, Redmond, WA 98052	360	O	U	*	21 dy	13-18	M/F			◇	◇		◇			
Tamarack Center, Spokane, WA 99204-5202	361	RT	S	*	547 dy	12-18	M/F		◇	◇	◇	◇	◇	◇	◇	◆
Tyler Ranch, Inc., Spokane, WA 99208-3740	372	RT	S/R	PP	1 yr	12-18	M			◇	◆	◇	◇		◇	
Walla Walla General Hospital's Addiction Recovery Center, Walla Walla, WA 99362	379	GH	S	*	28 dy		M/F					◆	◆			
WEST VIRGINIA																
Barboursville School, Barboursville, WV 25504	67	RT	S/R	C	180 dy	12-17	M/F		◇	◇	◇	◇	◇	◆	◆	◆
Chestnut Ridge Hospital, Morgantown, WV 26505	124	PH	L	*	17 dy		M/F		◇	◇	◇	◇	◆	◆	◆	◆
HCA River Park Hospital, Huntington, WV 25701	214	PH	P	*	31 dy	12-adult	M/F	◇	◆	◆	◆	◆	◇	◇	◇	◆
Highland Hospital, Charleston, WV 25364	218	PH	P	*	21 dy		M/F		◇	◆	◇			◇		◆
Parkside Recovery Center at Charleston Area Medical Center, Charleston, WV 25326	293	GH	S/R	*	22 dy	13-adult	M/F				◇	◇	◆	◇	◇	◇
WISCONSIN																
Bellin Psychiatric Center, Inc., Green Bay, WI 54305-3725	73	PH	P	*	18 dy		M/F	◇	◇	◆	◆	◇	◇	◇	◇	◇
Charter Hospital of Milwaukee, West Allis, WI 53227	116	PH	L/N	*	26 dy	12-adult	M/F		◆	◆	◆	◆	◆	◆	◆	◆
CPC Greenbriar Hospital, Greenfield, WI 53228	141	O	L	*	18 dy		M/F		◇	◇	◇	◇	◇	◇	◇	◇

Facility Name and Address	GENERAL INFORMATION						DISORDERS TREATED								
	Page Number	Type	Security	Admission	Average stay	Age range	Gender	Autism	Learning Disabilities	Behavior Disorders	Psychosocial Disorders	Substance Abuse	Other Compulsive/Addictive	Eating Disorders	Post-Traumatic Stress	Thought, Mood, and Personality
DePaul Hospital Milwaukee, WI 53221	158	O	P	*	14 dy		M/F	◇	◆	◆	◆	◆	◇		◆	◆
Eau Claire Academy Eau Claire, WI 54702	170	RT	U/R	C	9 mo	11-18	M/F	◇	◇	◇	◇	◇			◇	◇
Exodus House Eau Claire, WI 54703	177	RT	S	*	6 mo		M/F	◇	◆	◆	◆	◆	◇	◇	◆	◆
Laurelbrooke Extended Care Program Brown Deer, WI 53223	240	RT	L/N	*	270 dy	5-13	M/F	◇	◆	◇			◇	◇	◇	◇
L. E. Phillips-Libertas Center, St. Joseph Hospital Chippewa Falls, WI 54729	243	GH	U	*			M/F					◆				
Libertas—St. Mary's Hospital Green Bay, WI 54303	243	O	U	*	20 dy	11-18	M/F					◆				
Lutheran Social Services—Serenity Stoughton, WI 53589	246	RT	S	*	10 mo		F	◇	◇	◇	◇	◇	◇	◇	◇	◇
Milwaukee Psychiatric Hospital Wauwatosa, WI 53213	260	PH	P	*	14 dy		M/F	◇	◆	◆	◇	◇	◇	◇	◇	◆
Parkside Lodge of Wisconsin, Inc. Edgerton, WI 53534-0111	293	DA	S/R	*	15 dy	12-adult	M/F	◇				◆				
Parkway Hospital Madison, WI 53719	296	PH	P/R	V	20 dy	13-adult	M/F	◆	◆	◆	◆	◆	◆	◇	◇	◆
Rogers Memorial Hospital Oconomowoc, WI 53066	327	PH	S	*	20 dy		M/F	◇	◇	◇	◇	◇	◇	◇	◇	◇
St. Agnes Hospital—Addiction Services Fond du Lac, WI 54935	330	GH	S	*	25 dy		M/F					◆				
St. Mary's Hill Hospital Milwaukee, WI 53211	338	PH	L	*	14 dy		M/F	◇	◆	◆	◆	◇	◆	◆	◆	◆
St. Rose Residence Milwaukee, WI 53222	339	RT	S/N	*	403 dy	13-17	F	◇	◆	◆	◇	◇	◇	◇	◆	◆
Taylor Home, Inc. Racine, WI 53405	363	RT	U/R	C	180 dy	12-17	M/F			◇				◇		
TriCenter Milwaukee, WI 53209	369	RT	S	*	1 yr		M/F	◇	◇	◇	◇					

Type
DA = Drug addiction rehab center
PH = Psychiatric hospital
GH = General hospital
RT = Residential treatment
S = School
C = Camp
W = Wilderness program
O = Other

Security
U = Unsecured
S = Staff secured
P = Partially locked
L = Entirely locked
N = No runaway pursuit
R = Runaway pursuit
* = Varies depending on program

Admission
V = Voluntary
P = One parent
PP = All parties
C = Court order
O = Other
* = Varies

Disorders
◆ = main treatment focus
◇ = secondary treatment focus

Facility Name and Address	GENERAL INFORMATION							DISORDERS TREATED								
	Page Number	Type	Security	Admission	Average stay	Age range	Gender	Autism	Learning Disabilities	Behavior Disorders	Psychosocial Disorders	Substance Abuse	Eating Disorders	Other Compulsive/Addictive	Post-Traumatic Stress	Thought, Mood, and Personality
WYOMING																
Lander Valley Medical Center Lander, WY 82520	237	GH	L	*	14 dy		M/F			♦	♦	◊	◊	◊	♦	♦
New Directions Casper, WY 82601	271	RT	S	*	45 dy		M/F					♦				
Saint Joseph's Children's Home Torrington, WY 82240	335	RT	S	*	9 mo		M/F	◊	◊	◊	◊	◊			◊	◊
Teen Challenge Christian Academy Sundance, WY 82729	364	S	S/R	PP		12-18	M/F			◊	◊	♦	◊	◊		

Type
DA = Drug addiction rehab center
PH = Psychiatric hospital
GH = General hospital
RT = Residential treatment
S = School
C = Camp
W = Wilderness program
O = Other

Security
U = Unsecured
S = Staff secured
P = Partially locked
L = Entirely locked
N = No runaway pursuit
R = Runaway pursuit
* = Varies depending on program

Admission
V = Voluntary
P = One parent
PP = All parties
C = Court order
O = Other
* = Varies

Disorders
♦ = main treatment focus
◊ = secondary treatment focus

Program Profiles

ACADIA HOSPITAL
268 Stillwater Avenue
Bangor, Maine 04401
207-945-7071

General Information General hospital for children, adolescents. Patient security: entirely locked. Not-for-profit facility affiliated with Eastern Maine Healthcare, Bangor, ME. Licensed by state of Maine. Accredited by JCAHO.

Participants Accepts: male and female children; male and female adolescents. Admission: one parent, all parties who share custody, depending on program. Treats autistic disorders; learning disabilities; behavior disorders; general psychosocial disorders; eating disorders; compulsive/addictive disorders other than substance abuse and eating disorders; post-traumatic stress disorder; thought, mood, and personality disorders.

Contact Access Department, main address above. Phone: 207-990-2300.

ADOLESCENT CARE AND TREATMENT CENTER—OIKOS, INC.
3000 Dickerson Road
Reno, Nevada 89503
702-322-4357

General Information Drug and alcohol rehabilitation center for adolescents. 8 beds for adolescents. Patient security: staff secured. Independent not-for-profit facility. Licensed by state of Nevada. Accredited by Bureau of Alcohol and Drug Abuse.

Participants Accepts: female adolescents. Average stay: 10 months. Admission: one parent, all parties who share custody, court order, voluntary, depending on program. Treats substance abuse. Accepts the vision impaired; the hearing impaired; the speech impaired; those with a history of epilepsy.

Staff Staff is all female.

Costs Average cost: $70 per day.

Additional Services Outpatient services for males and females ages 13–21. Treats substance abuse. Day treatment program for males and females ages 13–18. Treats substance abuse.

Contact Ellie Cook, Clinical Coordinator, P.O. Box 1272, Reno, NV 89503. Phone: 702-322-4357.

ADOLESCENT CENTER FOR CHANGE
215 South State
LaVerkin, Utah 84745
800-637-0701

General Information Residential treatment/subacute facility for adolescents. 24 beds for adolescents. Open year-round. Patient security: staff secured; will pursue and return runaways. Rural setting. For-profit facility affiliated with Cross Creek Manor, LaVerkin, UT. Licensed by state of Utah.

Participants Accepts: male and female adolescents ages 11–17. Average stay: 90 days. Admission: one parent, all parties who share custody, depending on program. Treats learning disabilities; behavior disorders; general psychosocial disorders; substance abuse; eating disorders; compulsive/addictive disorders other than substance abuse and eating disorders; post-traumatic stress disorder; thought, mood, and personality disorders. Accepts those with a history of harm to themselves and others; those receiving psychotropic medication.

Program Treatment modalities: reality therapy; Twelve Step Recovery; cognitive therapy; Gestalt therapy. Family treatment program available.

Staff 1 full-time direct-care staff member per adolescent. Total facility staff includes 1 physician, 1 psychologist, 1 psychiatrist, 1 registered nurse, 4 practical/vocational nurses, 2 MSW social workers, 1 social worker (non-MSW), 2 teachers, 10 counselors, 2 other direct-care staff members. Staff is 60% male, 40% female.

Facilities Single building; males and females in separate units. Central dining. Basketball courts, game room, outdoor swimming pool, ropes course, spa.

Education Academic program available at no charge. Serves ages 11–17, grades 7–12. 2 teachers on staff. Curriculum accredited or approved by Northwest Association of Schools and Colleges. Organized sports program offered.

Costs Average cost: $100 per day. Accepts private insurance, group insurance, Blue Cross/Blue Shield, public funds.

Contact Narvin Lichfield, Admissions Director, main address above. Phone: 800-637-0701.
See page 402 for full page description.

ADOLESCENT INTENSIVE RESIDENTIAL SERVICE OF CALIFORNIA PACIFIC MEDICAL CENTER
1020 Haight Street
San Francisco, California 94117
415-431-3022; Fax: 415-431-0201

General Information Residential treatment/subacute facility for adolescents. 12 beds for adolescents. Open year-round. Patient security: staff secured; no runaway pursuit. Urban setting. Not-for-profit facility affiliated with California Pacific Medical Center, San Francisco, CA. Licensed by state of California. Accredited by State of California Department of Social Services.

Participants Accepts: male and female adolescents ages 11–17. Average stay: 300 days. Admission: all parties who share custody, voluntary, depending on program. Treats learning disabilities; behavior disorders; general psychosocial disorders; post-traumatic stress disorder; thought, mood, and personality disorders. Accepts the sexually compulsive; those with a history of harm to themselves and others; those receiving psychotropic medication. Largest number of participants from California.

Program Treatment modalities: psychodynamic; family systems. Family treatment program available.

Staff 2.7 full-time direct-care staff members per adolescent. Total facility staff includes 1 psychologist, 2 psychiatrists, 1 registered nurse, 3 MSW social workers, 1 teacher, 12 counselors, 4 other direct-care staff members. Staff is 45% male, 55% female.

Facilities Single building; males and females in co-educational units. Central dining. Basketball courts.

Education Academic program available. Serves ages 11–17, ungraded. 1 teacher on staff. Curriculum accredited or approved by California State Department of Education. Organized sports program offered.

Costs Accepts public funds.

Contact Wilson Lam, Clinical Director, main address above. Phone: 415-431-3022. Fax: 415-431-0201.

THE ADOLESCENT PROGRAM AT MAPLETON CENTER
311 Mapleton Avenue
Boulder, Colorado 80302
303-449-1324; Fax: 303-441-0465

General Information General hospital for adolescents. 4 beds for adolescents. Patient security: partial-ly locked. Not-for-profit facility affiliated with Boulder Community Hospital, Boulder, CO. Licensed by state of Colorado. Accredited by JCAHO.

Participants Accepts: male and female adolescents. Average stay: 7 days. Admission: one parent, all parties who share custody, court order, voluntary, depending on program. Treats autistic disorders; learning disabilities; behavior disorders; general psychosocial disorders; substance abuse; eating disorders; compulsive/addictive disorders other than substance abuse and eating disorders; post-traumatic stress disorder; thought, mood, and personality disorders.

Costs Average cost: $900 per day.

Additional Services Day treatment for males and females ages 12–18. Treats autistic disorders; learning disabilities; behavior disorders; general psychosocial disorders; substance abuse; eating disorders; compulsive/addictive disorders other than substance abuse and eating disorders; post-traumatic stress disorder; thought, mood, and personality disorders.

Contact Barbara Hughes, Program Director, main address above. Phone: 303-449-1324. Fax: 303-441-0465.

AGENCY FOR COMMUNITY TREATMENT SERVICES
6612 Stark Road
Seffner, Florida 33584
813-621-6051; Fax: 813-272-3439

General Information Drug and alcohol rehabilitation center for children, adolescents. Independent not-for-profit facility. Licensed by state of Florida.

Participants Accepts: male and female children; male and female adolescents. Average stay: 3 months. Admission: one parent, all parties who share custody, court order, voluntary, depending on program. Treats learning disabilities; behavior disorders; general psychosocial disorders; substance abuse; eating disorders; compulsive/addictive disorders other than substance abuse and eating disorders; post-traumatic stress disorder; thought, mood, and personality disorders.

Staff Staff is 50% male, 50% female.

Additional Services Outpatient services for males and females. Treats learning disabilities; behavior disorders; general psychosocial disorders; substance abuse; eating disorders; compulsive/addictive disorders other than substance abuse and eating disorders; post-traumatic stress disorder; thought, mood, and personality disorders.

Contact Jenny Stone, Youth Program Director, main address above. Phone: 813-621-6051.

ALASKA CHILDREN'S SERVICES
4600 Abbott Road
Anchorage, Alaska 99507
907-346-2101; Fax: 907-346-2748

General Information Residential treatment/subacute facility for children, adolescents. 56 beds for children. Open year-round. Patient security: staff secured; no runaway pursuit. Suburban setting. Independent not-for-profit facility. Licensed by state of Alaska. Accredited by JCAHO.

Participants Accepts: male and female children and adolescents ages 6–18. Average stay: 365 days. Admission: all parties who share custody. Treats general psychosocial disorders. Accepts those with a history of arson; the sexually compulsive; those with a history of harm to themselves and others; those receiving psychotropic medication; those with a history of epilepsy.

Program Treatment modalities: behavior therapy; social learning models; cognitive-behavior therapy; psychiatric consultation. Family treatment program available.

Staff Total facility staff includes 1 psychologist, 1 psychiatrist, 1 registered nurse, 7 MSW social workers, 3 teachers, 1 occupational/recreational therapist, 1 dietician, 56 other direct-care staff members. Staff is 49% male, 51% female.

Facilities Multiple buildings; males and females in both coeducational and separate units depending on program. Separate dining by residential unit available. Basketball courts, game room, gymnasium, playing fields.

Education Academic program available at no charge. Serves ages 6–18, ungraded. 3 teachers on staff. Curriculum accredited or approved by Anchorage School District. Cost of educational program covered by local school district. Organized sports program offered.

Costs Average cost: $320 per day. Accepts private insurance, group insurance, public funds.

Contact Cliff Ames, Referral Coordinator, main address above. Phone: 907-346-2101. Fax: 907-346-2748.

ALCOHOLISM TREATMENT CENTER OF CENTRAL DUPAGE HOSPITAL
27 West 350 High Lake Road
Winfield, Illinois 60190
708-653-4000; Fax: 708-653-0591

General Information Drug and alcohol rehabilitation center for adolescents, adults. 20 beds for adolescents. Open year-round. Patient security: staff secured; will pursue and return runaways. Suburban setting. Not-for-profit facility affiliated with Central DuPage Health Systems, Naperville, IL. Licensed by state of Illinois. Accredited by JCAHO; Department of Alchohol and Substance Abuse.

Participants Accepts: male and female adolescents ages 12–18; male and female adults ages 18 and up. Admission: one parent, all parties who share custody, court order, voluntary, guardianship, Department of Children and Family Services, depending on program. Treats learning disabilities; behavior disorders; general psychosocial disorders; substance abuse; post-traumatic stress disorder; thought, mood, and personality disorders. Accepts the mobility impaired; the vision impaired; the hearing impaired; the speech impaired; those with a history of arson; those receiving psychotropic medication; those with a history of epilepsy. Largest number of participants from Illinois.

Program Treatment modalities: Minnesota/Illinois model. Family treatment program available.

Staff 2.5 full-time direct-care staff members per adolescent. Total facility staff includes 2 physicians, 1 psychologist, 2 psychiatrists, 11 registered nurses, 4 practical/vocational nurses, 4 MSW social workers, 1 teacher, 7 counselors, 1 occupational/recreational therapist, 1 speech pathologist, 1 dietician, 14 other direct-care staff members.

Facilities Single building; males and females in coeducational units. Separate residential quarters for adolescents. Central dining (shared with adults), in-room dining available. Basketball courts, game room, gymnasium.

Education Academic program available at no charge. Serves ages 12–18, grades 7–12. 1 teacher on staff. Cost of educational program covered by local school district. Organized sports program offered.

Costs Average cost: $13,600 per month. Accepts private insurance, group insurance, medicaid, Blue Cross/Blue Shield, public funds.

Additional Services Outpatient services for males and females ages 12–18. Treats learning disabilities; behavior disorders; general psychosocial disorders; substance abuse; post-traumatic stress disorder; thought, mood, and personality disorders.

Contact Linda F. Buckner, Community Relations, main address above. Phone: 708-653-4000. Fax: 708-653-0591.

ALEXIAN BROTHERS MEDICAL CENTER
800 Biesterfield Road
Elk Grove Village, Illinois 60007
708-437-5500; Fax: 708-945-5117

General Information Psychiatric hospital for children, adolescents. Patient security: entirely locked. Not-for-profit facility affiliated with Alexian Brothers, Elk Grove Village, IL. Licensed by state of Illinois. Accredited by JCAHO.

Participants Accepts: male and female children; male and female adolescents. Average stay: 18 days. Admission: one parent, all parties who share custody, court order, voluntary, depending on program. Treats autistic disorders; learning disabilities; behavior disorders; general psychosocial disorders; substance abuse; eating disorders; compulsive/addictive disorders other than substance abuse and eating disorders; post-traumatic stress disorder; thought, mood, and personality disorders.

Additional Services Outpatient services for males and females. Treats substance abuse.

Contact Judy Dineen, Intake Coordinator, main address above. Phone: 708-437-5500.

ALLENDALE ASSOCIATION
P.O. Box 1088
Lake Villa, Illinois 60046
708-356-2351; Fax: 708-356-0289

General Information Residential treatment/subacute facility for children, adolescents. Patient security: staff secured. Independent not-for-profit facility. Licensed by state of Illinois. Accredited by JCAHO.

Participants Accepts: male and female children; male and female adolescents. Average stay: 6 months. Admission: guardianship. Treats autistic disorders; learning disabilities; behavior disorders; general psychosocial disorders; post-traumatic stress disorder; thought, mood, and personality disorders.

Contact Laurie Frank, Intake Supervisor, main address above. Phone: 708-356-2351.

ALOYSIA HALL, MERCY MEDICAL CENTER
1020 Franklin Street
Johnstown, Pennsylvania 15905
814-533-1000; Fax: 814-533-1819

General Information General hospital for children, adolescents. Open year-round. Patient security: entirely locked; will pursue and return runaways. Small town setting. Not-for-profit facility affiliated with Mercy Health System, Cincinnati, OH. Licensed by state of Pennsylvania. Accredited by JCAHO.

Participants Accepts: male and female children ages 4–12; male and female adolescents ages 12–17. Average stay: 18 days. Admission: one parent, voluntary, depending on program. Treats autistic disorders; learning disabilities; behavior disorders; general psychosocial disorders; substance abuse; eating disorders; compulsive/addictive disorders other than substance abuse and eating disorders; post-traumatic stress disorder; thought, mood, and personality disorders. Accepts the hearing impaired; the speech impaired; those with a history of arson; the sexually compulsive; those with a history of harm to themselves and others; those receiving psychotropic medication; those with a history of epilepsy.

Program Treatment modalities: multi-disciplinary team approach. Family treatment program available.

Staff Total facility staff includes 1 physician, 2 psychologists, 1 psychiatrist, 9 registered nurses, 2 practical/vocational nurses, 1 MSW social worker, 1 teacher, 1 occupational/recreational therapist, 8 other direct-care staff members. Staff is 24% male, 76% female.

Facilities Multiple buildings; males and females in coeducational units. Separate dining by residential unit available. Game room.

Education Academic program available at no charge. Serves ages 4–17, grades K–12. 1 teacher on staff. Curriculum accredited or approved by Greater Johnstown School District. Cost of educational program covered by local school district.

Costs Average cost: $8300 per stay. Accepts private insurance, group insurance, medicaid, Blue Cross/Blue Shield.

Contact Diane Gregovich, Director, main address above. Phone: 814-533-1000. Fax: 814-533-1819.

ALPHA HOUSE
4290 Jackson Road
P.O. Box 3757
Ann Arbor, Michigan 48106
313-662-0533

General Information   Residential treatment/subacute facility for adolescents. Patient security: staff secured. Not-for-profit facility affiliated with Catherine McAuley Health System, Ann Arbor, MI. Licensed by state of Michigan. Accredited by JCAHO.

Participants   Accepts: male and female adolescents. Average stay: 6 months. Admission: one parent, all parties who share custody, court order, voluntary, depending on program. Treats learning disabilities; behavior disorders; substance abuse; compulsive/addictive disorders other than substance abuse and eating disorders; post-traumatic stress disorder; thought, mood, and personality disorders.

Staff   Staff is 60% male, 40% female.

Costs   Average cost: $131 per day.

Contact   Linda Loos, Admissions Coordinator, main address above. Phone: 313-662-0533.

ALVARADO PARKWAY INSTITUTE
7050 Parkway Drive
La Mesa, California 91942-2352
619-583-9991; Fax: 619-265-1287

General Information   Psychiatric hospital and alchohol and drug rehabilitation center for children, adolescents, adults. 11 beds for children; 26 beds for adolescents; 99 beds total. Open year-round. Patient security: entirely locked; will pursue and return runaways. Suburban setting. Not-for-profit facility affiliated with National Medical Enterprise, Santa Monica, CA. Licensed by state of California. Accredited by JCAHO.

Participants   Accepts: male and female children ages 4–11; male and female adolescents ages 12–18; male and female adults ages 18 and up. Average stay: 12 days. Admission: one parent, all parties who share custody, court order, voluntary, depending on program. Treats autistic disorders; learning disabilities; behavior disorders; general psychosocial disorders; substance abuse; eating disorders; compulsive/addictive disorders other than substance abuse and eating disorders; post-traumatic stress disorder; thought, mood, and personality disorders. Accepts the mobility impaired; the vision impaired; the hearing impaired; the speech impaired; those with a history of arson; the sexually compulsive; those with a

history of harm to themselves and others; those receiving psychotropic medication; non-English speaking individuals; those with a history of epilepsy. Special programs for the developmentally disabled.

Program   Treatment modalities: Twelve Step Recovery; psychodynamic; family systems. Family treatment program available.

Staff   Total facility staff includes 3 psychologists, 5 psychiatrists, 15 registered nurses, 1 practical/vocational nurse, 3 MSW social workers, 3 teachers, 1 counselor, 2 occupational/recreational therapists, 1 speech pathologist, 3 therapists.

Facilities   Single building; males and females in co-educational units. Separate residential quarters for children and adolescents. Central dining (not shared with adults). Basketball courts, gymnasium.

Education   Academic program available at no charge. Serves ages 4–18, grades K–12. 3 teachers on staff. Curriculum accredited or approved by State of California. Cost of educational program covered by local school district. Organized sports program offered.

Costs   Accepts private insurance, group insurance, medicare, medicaid, Blue Cross/Blue Shield.

Contact   Kathy Randall, main address above. Phone: 619-583-9991. Fax: 619-265-1287.

AMETHYST
1715 Sharon Road, West
Charlotte, North Carolina 28210
704-544-8373; Fax: 704-554-8058

General Information   Drug and alcohol rehabilitation center for adolescents, adults. Open year-round. Patient security: staff secured; will pursue and return runaways. Urban setting. Independent not-for-profit facility. Licensed by state of North Carolina. Accredited by JCAHO.

Participants   Accepts: male and female adolescents ages 13–23; male and female adults ages 19 and up. Average stay: 30 days. Admission: one parent, all parties who share custody, court order, depending on program. Treats learning disabilities; behavior disorders; general psychosocial disorders; substance abuse; eating disorders; compulsive/addictive disorders other than substance abuse and eating disorders; post-traumatic stress disorder; thought, mood, and personality disorders. Accepts the mobility impaired; the vision impaired; the speech impaired; those with a history of harm to themselves and others; those receiving psychotropic medication; those with a history of epilepsy. Special programs for the developmentally disabled; those with AIDS. Largest number of participants from Georgia, North Carolina, South Carolina.

Program Treatment modalities: Twelve Step Recovery; family of origin; cognitive-behavioral. Family treatment program available.

Staff 2.3 full-time direct-care staff members per adolescent. Total facility staff includes 2 physicians, 3 psychologists, 1 psychiatrist, 9 registered nurses, 1 MSW social worker, 3 social workers (non-MSW), 1 teacher, 12 counselors, 1 occupational/recreational therapist, 22 therapists, 1 dietician. Staff is 50% male, 50% female.

Facilities Multiple buildings; males and females in separate units. Separate residential quarters for adolescents. Separate dining by residential unit available. Basketball courts, game room, gymnasium, ropes course.

Education Academic program available at no charge. Serves ages 13–23, grades 6–12. 1 teacher on staff. Curriculum accredited or approved by Mecklenburg Schools.

Costs Average cost: $8000 per stay. Accepts private insurance, group insurance, medicare, medicaid, Blue Cross/Blue Shield.

Additional Services Residential or sub-acute services for males and females ages 13 and up. Treats learning disabilities; behavior disorders; general psychosocial disorders; substance abuse; eating disorders; compulsive/addictive disorders other than substance abuse and eating disorders; post-traumatic stress disorder; thought, mood, and personality disorders. Wilderness/survival program for males and females ages 13–23. Treats learning disabilities; behavior disorders; general psychosocial disorders; substance abuse; eating disorders; compulsive/addictive disorders other than substance abuse and eating disorders; post-traumatic stress disorder; thought, mood, and personality disorders.

Contact Kathy F. Womble, Administrative Assistant, P.O. Box 240156, Charlotte, NC 28224. Phone: 704-554-8373. Fax: 704-554-8058.

ANASAZI WILDERNESS TREATMENT PROGRAM
200 West Frontier Street
Payson, Arizona 85547
602-892-7403; Fax: 602-892-6701

General Information Wilderness/survival program for adolescents. 40 beds for adolescents. Open year-round. Patient security: staff secured; will pursue and return runaways. Small town setting. Independent

not-for-profit facility. Licensed by state of Arizona. Accredited by Arizona Department of Economic Security.

Participants Accepts: male and female adolescents ages 12–18. Average stay: 51 days. Admission: one parent, all parties who share custody, court order, depending on program. Treats learning disabilities; behavior disorders; general psychosocial disorders; substance abuse; eating disorders; compulsive/addictive disorders other than substance abuse and eating disorders; post-traumatic stress disorder; thought, mood, and personality disorders. Accepts those receiving psychotropic medication. Largest number of participants from Arizona, Utah, Texas.

Program Treatment modalities: agentative; repentance. Family treatment program available.

Staff Total facility staff includes 1 physician, 1 psychologist, 1 psychiatrist, 2 registered nurses, 1 MSW social worker, 2 social workers (non-MSW), 1 teacher, 1 therapist, 1 dietician, 25 other direct-care staff members. Staff is 80% male, 20% female.

Facilities Males and females in separate units.

Education Academic program available at no charge. Serves ages 12–18, ungraded. 1 teacher on staff.

Costs Average cost: $350 per day. Accepts private insurance, group insurance, Blue Cross/Blue Shield, public funds.

Additional Services Outpatient services for males and females ages 12–18. Treats learning disabilities; behavior disorders; general psychosocial disorders; substance abuse; eating disorders; compulsive/addictive disorders other than substance abuse and eating disorders; post-traumatic stress disorder; thought, mood, and personality disorders.

Contact Mike Merchant, Director of Marketing, 1818 E. Southern, Suite 17A, Mesa, AZ 85547. Phone: 602-892-7403. Fax: 602-892-6701.

ANCHOR HOSPITAL
5454 Yorktowne Drive
Atlanta, Georgia 30349
404-991-6044; Fax: 404-991-6044 Ext. 298

General Information Drug and alcohol rehabilitation center for adolescents, adults. 8 beds for adolescents. Open year-round. Patient security: partially locked; will pursue and return runaways. Suburban setting. Independent for-profit facility. Licensed by state of Georgia. Accredited by JCAHO.

Participants Accepts: male and female adolescents ages 13–21; male and female adults ages 18 and up.

Average stay: 30 days. Admission: legal custodial care. Treats behavior disorders; general psychosocial disorders; substance abuse; eating disorders; compulsive/addictive disorders other than substance abuse and eating disorders; post-traumatic stress disorder; thought, mood, and personality disorders. Accepts the mobility impaired; the speech impaired; those with a history of arson; the sexually compulsive; those with a history of harm to themselves and others; those receiving psychotropic medication; those with a history of epilepsy. Largest number of participants from Georgia, Florida, Tennessee.

Program Treatment modalities: Twelve Step Recovery; group therapy; family therapy; individual therapy. Family treatment program available.

Staff Total facility staff includes 22 physicians, 14 psychologists, 9 psychiatrists, 20 registered nurses, 13 practical/vocational nurses, 6 MSW social workers, 6 social workers (non-MSW), 1 teacher, 9 counselors, 3 occupational/recreational therapists, 1 dietician, 54 other direct-care staff members. Staff is 55% male, 45% female.

Facilities Single building; males and females in co-educational units. Residential arrangements vary depending on program. Central dining (shared with adults). Basketball courts, game room, outdoor swimming pool, outdoor tennis courts, playing fields.

Education Academic program available at no charge. Serves ages 13–17, ungraded. 1 teacher on staff.

Costs Accepts private insurance, group insurance, Blue Cross/Blue Shield.

Additional Services Outpatient services for males and females ages 17 and up. Treats substance abuse. Psychiatric hospital for males and females ages 13 and up. Treats behavior disorders; general psychosocial disorders; eating disorders; compulsive/addictive disorders other than substance abuse and eating disorders; post-traumatic stress disorder; thought, mood, and personality disorders.

Contact Trish Nyquist, Intake/Admissions Director, main address above. Phone: 404-991-6044. Fax: 404-991-6044 Ext. 298.

ANTHONY LEWIS CENTER
1000 Paul Parkway
Blaine, Minnesota 55434
612-757-2906; Fax: 612-757-2059

General Information Drug and alcohol rehabilitation center for adolescents, adults. 22 beds for adolescents. Open year-round. Patient security: staff secured; will pursue and return runaways. Suburban setting. For-profit facility affiliated with On-Belay of Minnesota, Inc., Minneapolis/Plymouth, MN. Licensed by state of Minnesota. Accredited by JCAHO.

Participants Accepts: male and female adolescents ages 12–17; male and female adults ages 18–19. Average stay: 40 days. Admission: one parent, all parties who share custody, court order, depending on program. Treats learning disabilities; behavior disorders; general psychosocial disorders; substance abuse. Accepts the hearing impaired; the speech impaired; those with a history of arson; those with a history of harm to themselves and others; those receiving psychotropic medication; those with a history of epilepsy. Largest number of participants from Minnesota, New Jersey.

Program Treatment modalities: Twelve Step Recovery; family systems. Family treatment program available.

Staff .1 full-time direct-care staff member per adolescent. Total facility staff includes 1 physician, 1 psychologist, 1 registered nurse, 1 social worker (non-MSW), 2 teachers, 4 counselors, 1 dietician, 7 other direct-care staff members. Staff is 45% male, 55% female.

Facilities Single building; males and females in co-educational units. Separate residential quarters for adolescents. Central dining (not shared with adults). Basketball courts, indoor swimming pool, playing fields.

Education Academic program available at no charge. Serves ages 12–18, grades 7–12. 2 teachers on staff. Curriculum accredited or approved by Anoka Henn School District. Cost of educational program covered by local school district.

Costs Average cost: $400 per day. Accepts private insurance, group insurance, Blue Cross/Blue Shield, public funds.

Additional Services Drug and alcohol rehabilitation services for males and females ages 12–19. Treats learning disabilities; behavior disorders; general psychosocial disorders; substance abuse.

Contact Melissa Brogger, Program Director, main address above. Phone: 612-757-2906. Fax: 612-757-2059.

ANTHONY LEWIS CENTER
115 Forestview Lane
Plymouth, Minnesota 55441
612-546-8008; Fax: 612-546-3349

General Information Drug and alcohol rehabilitation center for adolescents. 15 beds for adolescents. Patient security: staff secured. Not-for-profit facility affiliated with On-Belay of Minnesota, Plymouth, MN. Licensed by state of Minnesota.

Participants Accepts: male and female adolescents. Average stay: 6 weeks. Admission: one parent, all parties who share custody, court order, voluntary, depending on program. Treats substance abuse. Accepts the mobility impaired; the vision impaired; the hearing impaired; the speech impaired; those with a history of arson; the sexually compulsive; those with a history of harm to themselves and others; those receiving psychotropic medication; non-English speaking individuals; those with a history of epilepsy.

Staff Staff is 50% male, 50% female.

Costs Average cost: $300 per day.

Contact Sharlee Benson, Program Director, main address above. Phone: 612-546-8008. Fax: 612-546-3349.

APPALACHIAN HALL
60 Caledonia Road
Asheville, North Carolina 28803
704-253-3681; Fax: 704-253-8126

General Information Psychiatric hospital for children, adolescents, adults. 12 beds for children; 23 beds for adolescents; 100 beds total. Open year-round. Patient security: partially locked; will pursue and return runaways. Rural setting. For-profit facility affiliated with National Medical Enterprises, Santa Monica, CA. Licensed by state of North Carolina. Accredited by JCAHO.

Participants Accepts: male and female children ages 4–12; male and female adolescents ages 13–17; male and female adults ages 18 and up. Average stay: 40 days. Admission: all parties who share custody, court order, all children and adolescents in North Carolina must be under commitment, depending on program. Treats learning disabilities; behavior disorders; general psychosocial disorders; substance abuse; eating disorders; compulsive/addictive disorders other than substance abuse and eating disorders; post-traumatic stress disorder; thought, mood, and personality disorders. Accepts the hearing impaired; the speech impaired; those with a history of harm to themselves and

others; those receiving psychotropic medication; those with a history of epilepsy.

Program Treatment modalities: Twelve Step Recovery; biopsychosocial approach; behavior model; psychodynamic. Family treatment program available.

Staff Total facility staff includes 1 physician, 3 psychologists, 8 psychiatrists, 35 registered nurses, 7 practical/vocational nurses, 8 MSW social workers, 4 teachers, 13 counselors, 8 occupational/recreational therapists, 1 dietician, 43 other direct-care staff members.

Facilities Single building; males and females in separate units. Basketball courts, game room, outdoor tennis courts, playing fields, ropes course.

Education Academic program available at no charge. Serves ages 6–18, grades 1–12. 4 teachers on staff. Curriculum accredited or approved by State of North Carolina. Cost of educational program sometimes covered by local school district.

Costs Accepts private insurance, group insurance, medicare, medicaid, Blue Cross/Blue Shield.

Additional Services Outpatient services for males and females. Treats autistic disorders; learning disabilities; behavior disorders; general psychosocial disorders; substance abuse; eating disorders; compulsive/addictive disorders other than substance abuse and eating disorders; post-traumatic stress disorder; thought, mood, and personality disorders.

Contact Myrna Harvey, Director of Marketing, main address above. Phone: 704-253-3681. Fax: 704-253-8126.

APPLE (A PROGRAM PLANNED FOR LIFE ENRICHMENT)
1373-8 Veteran's Highway
Hauppauge, New York 11788
516-979-7300; Fax: 516-979-6890

General Information Residential treatment/subacute facility for children, adolescents, adults. 55 beds for adolescents. Open year-round. Patient security: staff secured. Suburban setting. Independent not-for-profit facility. Licensed by state of New York. Accredited by Department of Substance Abuse Services.

Participants Accepts: male and female children ages 15–18; male and female adolescents ages 18–21; male and female adults ages 21 and up. Admission: one parent. Treats substance abuse. Accepts those receiving psychotropic medication; non-English speaking individuals; those with a history of epilepsy.

Program Treatment modalities: rational emotive therapy.

Staff Total facility staff includes 3 physicians, 2 psychologists, 2 psychiatrists, 8 registered nurses, 22 MSW social workers, 20 social workers (non-MSW), 6 teachers, 40 counselors, 1 dietician, 27 other direct-care staff members.

Facilities Multiple buildings; males and females in coeducational units. Separate residential quarters for children and adolescents. Separate dining by residential unit available. Basketball courts, game room, gymnasium, weight room.

Education Academic program available at no charge. Serves ages 4–21, grades 9–12. 6 teachers on staff. Curriculum accredited or approved by New York State Education Department; Board of Cooperative Education Services. Cost of educational program covered by local school district.

Costs Accepts private insurance, group insurance, medicaid, Blue Cross/Blue Shield, public funds.

Contact Glenn Greenberg, Director of Intake, main address above. Phone: 516-366-1035.

APT RESIDENTIAL SERVICES
Fairfield Hills Hospital, Greenwich House
3rd Street
Newtown, Connecticut 06470
203-426-3344; Fax: 203-781-4792

General Information Drug and alcohol rehabilitation center for adolescents. 34 beds for adolescents. Patient security: staff secured. Not-for-profit facility affiliated with APT Foundation, New Haven, CT. Licensed by state of Connecticut. Accredited by Commission on Accreditation of Rehabilitation Facilities.

Participants Accepts: male and female adolescents. Average stay: 12 months. Admission: court order, voluntary, depending on program. Treats substance abuse. Accepts the mobility impaired; the vision impaired; the hearing impaired; the speech impaired; those with a history of harm to themselves and others; those receiving psychotropic medication; those with a history of epilepsy.

Staff Staff is 60% male, 40% female.

Contact Intake Coordinator, P.O. Box 587, Newtown, CT 06470. Phone: 203-426-3344. Fax: 203-781-4792.

ARAPAHOE HOUSE
8801 Lipan
Thornton, Colorado 80223
303-657-3700; Fax: 303-657-3727

General Information Drug and alcohol rehabilitation center for adolescents. 50 beds for adolescents. Patient security: staff secured. Independent not-for-profit facility. Licensed by state of Colorado.

Participants Accepts: male and female adolescents. Admission: one parent, all parties who share custody, court order, voluntary, depending on program. Treats substance abuse. Accepts the mobility impaired; the vision impaired; the hearing impaired; the speech impaired; those with a history of harm to themselves and others; those receiving psychotropic medication; non-English speaking individuals; those with a history of epilepsy.

Staff Staff is 50% male, 50% female.

Costs Average cost: $200 per day.

Contact Erik Stone, Assessment and Referral Coordinator, main address above. Phone: 303-657-3700. Fax: 303-657-3727.

AREA SUBSTANCE ABUSE COUNCIL
3601 16th Avenue SW
Cedar Rapids, Iowa 52404
319-390-3325

General Information Residential treatment/subacute facility for adolescents. Patient security: staff secured. Independent not-for-profit facility. Licensed by state of Iowa.

Participants Accepts: male and female adolescents. Average stay: 5 months. Admission: one parent, all parties who share custody, court order, voluntary, depending on program. Treats learning disabilities; behavior disorders; general psychosocial disorders; substance abuse; eating disorders; compulsive/addictive disorders other than substance abuse and eating disorders; post-traumatic stress disorder.

Staff Staff is 40% male, 60% female.

Costs Average cost: $100 per day.

Contact John Harbor, Youth Residential Director, main address above. Phone: 319-390-3325.

ARIZONA BAPTIST CHILDREN'S SERVICES
8920 North 23rd Avenue
Phoenix, Arizona 85069
602-943-7760; Fax: 602-943-7864

General Information Residential treatment/subacute facility for children, adolescents. Patient security: staff secured. Not-for-profit facility affiliated with Arizona Southern Baptist Convention, Phoenix, AZ. Licensed by state of Arizona. Accredited by JCAHO.

Participants Accepts: male and female children; male and female adolescents. Average stay: 9 months. Admission: one parent, all parties who share custody, court order, voluntary, depending on program. Treats autistic disorders; learning disabilities; behavior disorders; general psychosocial disorders; substance abuse; eating disorders; compulsive/addictive disorders other than substance abuse and eating disorders; post-traumatic stress disorder; thought, mood, and personality disorders.

Staff Staff is 50% male, 50% female.

Contact Margie Woodruff, Intake Coordinator, P.O. Box 39239, Phoenix, AZ 85069-9239. Phone: 602-973-8131.

ARKANSAS CHILDREN'S HOSPITAL
800 Marshall Street
Little Rock, Arkansas 72202
501-320-1100; Fax: 501-320-4777

General Information Pediatric hospital for children, adolescents. Patient security: partially locked. Independent not-for-profit facility. Licensed by state of Arkansas. Accredited by JCAHO.

Participants Accepts: male and female children; male and female adolescents. Average stay: 9 days. Admission: one parent, all parties who share custody, court order, voluntary, depending on program. Treats autistic disorders; learning disabilities; behavior disorders; general psychosocial disorders; substance abuse; eating disorders; compulsive/addictive disorders other than substance abuse and eating disorders; post-traumatic stress disorder; thought, mood, and personality disorders.

Contact Phillip Gilmore, Administrator, main address above. Phone: 501-320-1100.

ARMS ACRES
Seminary Hill Road
Carmel, New York 10512
800-989-2676; Fax: 914-225-5660

General Information Drug and alcohol rehabilitation center for adolescents, adults. 32 beds for adolescents. Open year-round. Patient security: staff secured; will pursue and return runaways. Suburban setting. For-profit facility affiliated with The Mediplex Group, Inc., Wellesley, MA. Licensed by state of New York. Accredited by JCAHO; New York State Division of Alcoholism and Alcohol Abuse, New York State Division of Substance Abuse Services.

Participants Accepts: male and female adolescents ages 12–19; male and female adults ages 18 and up. Average stay: 35 days. Admission: all parties who share custody. Treats learning disabilities; behavior disorders; general psychosocial disorders; substance abuse; eating disorders; compulsive/addictive disorders other than substance abuse and eating disorders; thought, mood, and personality disorders. Accepts the mobility impaired; the vision impaired; the hearing impaired; the speech impaired; those receiving psychotropic medication; those with a history of epilepsy.

Program Treatment modalities: Twelve Step Recovery; cognitive behavioral; psychodynamic; family. Family treatment program available.

Staff Total facility staff includes 2 physicians, 4 psychologists, 2 psychiatrists, 7 registered nurses, 7 practical/vocational nurses, 5 MSW social workers, 4 social workers (non-MSW), 2 teachers, 22 counselors, 4 occupational/recreational therapists, 8 therapists, 1 dietician. Staff is 50% male, 50% female.

Facilities Single building; males and females in both coeducational and separate units depending on program. Separate residential quarters for adolescents. Separate dining by residential unit available. Game room, gymnasium, indoor swimming pool, playing fields, sauna, jacuzzi, weight room.

Education Academic program available. Serves ages 12–19, grades 7–12. 2 teachers on staff. Curriculum accredited or approved by referring school district. Organized sports program offered.

Costs Average cost: $500 per day. Accepts private insurance, group insurance, Blue Cross/Blue Shield, public funds.

Contact Richard Dolan, Coordinator of Regional Services, main address above. Phone: 800-989-2676. Fax: 914-225-5660.

ARTHUR CENTER
704 East Monroe
Mexico, Missouri 65265
800-530-5465; Fax: 314-581-8713

General Information Psychiatric hospital for adolescents. 12 beds for adolescents. Patient security: partially locked. Not-for-profit facility affiliated with Audrain Medical Center, Mexico, MO. Licensed by state of Missouri. Accredited by JCAHO.

Participants Accepts: male and female adolescents. Average stay: 24 days. Admission: one parent, all parties who share custody, court order, voluntary, depending on program. Treats learning disabilities; behavior disorders; general psychosocial disorders; substance abuse; eating disorders; compulsive/addictive disorders other than substance abuse and eating disorders; post-traumatic stress disorder; thought, mood, and personality disorders.

Costs Average cost: $495 per day.

Additional Services Outpatient services for males and females ages 3 and up. Treats learning disabilities; behavior disorders; general psychosocial disorders; substance abuse; eating disorders; compulsive/addictive disorders other than substance abuse and eating disorders; post-traumatic stress disorder; thought, mood, and personality disorders.

Contact Sylvia Greenlee-Sawyer, Program Director, main address above. Phone: 800-530-5465. Fax: 314-581-8713.

ASCENT WILDERNESS PROGRAM
150 McGhee
Sand Point, Idaho 83864
208-265-6717; Fax: 208-265-2220

General Information Wilderness/survival program for adolescents. Open year-round. Patient security: unlocked; will pursue and return runaways. Rural setting. Independent for-profit facility.

Participants Accepts: male and female adolescents ages 13–20. Average stay: 41 days. Admission: all parties who share custody. Treats learning disabilities; behavior disorders; general psychosocial disorders; substance abuse; eating disorders; compulsive/addictive disorders other than substance abuse and eating disorders; thought, mood, and personality disorders. Largest number of participants from California, Tennessee, Georgia.

Program Treatment modalities: group psychotherapy; individualized psychotherapy. Family treatment program available.

Staff Total facility staff includes 1 psychologist, 2 teachers, 3 counselors, 3 therapists, 3 other direct-care staff members. Staff is 50% male, 50% female.

Education Academic program available at no charge. Serves ages 13–20, grades 7–12. 2 teachers on staff.

Costs Average cost: $300 per day. Accepts private insurance, group insurance.

Contact Ranel Hanson, Admissions Director, c/o Rocky Mountain Academy, Route One, Bonners Ferry, ID 83805. Phone: 208-267-7522. Fax: 208-267-3232.

Announcement Ascent's 41-day wilderness course is rigorous: physically and emotionally demanding yet with very achievable goals. Attitudes and behaviors are confronted; primary redirection and attitude adjustment are the results. Assessment is an important part of each course, and families are assisted in putting an individual plan of action into place. Parents are encouraged to participate in the family workshop at the conclusion of each course. Ascent is built upon the principles of CEDU education, utilizing a holistic approach to resolving family issues.

ASPEN CREST HOSPITAL
797 Hospital Way
Pocatello, Idaho 83201
208-234-0797; Fax: 208-234-0156

General Information Psychiatric hospital for children, adolescents, adults. 8 beds for children; 27 beds for adolescents; 62 beds total. Open year-round. Patient security: partially locked; will pursue and return runaways. Suburban setting. For-profit facility affiliated with Sterling Health Care Corporation, Bellevue, WA. Licensed by state of Idaho. Accredited by JCAHO.

Participants Accepts: male and female children ages 4–11; male and female adolescents ages 12–18; male and female adults ages 18 and up. Average stay: 21 days. Admission: one parent, court order, voluntary, depending on program. Treats learning disabilities; behavior disorders; general psychosocial disorders; substance abuse; eating disorders; compulsive/addictive disorders other than substance abuse and eating disorders; post-traumatic stress disorder; thought, mood, and personality disorders. Accepts the mobility impaired; the vision impaired; the hearing impaired; the speech impaired; those with a history of arson; the sexually compulsive; those with a history of harm to themselves and others; those receiving psychotropic medication; those with a history of epilepsy. Special programs for the chronically ill.

Program   Treatment modalities: Twelve Step Recovery; relapse prevention; recreational therapy; psychotherapy. Family treatment program available.

Staff   Total facility staff includes 2 physicians, 3 psychologists, 5 psychiatrists, 12 registered nurses, 4 practical/vocational nurses, 3 MSW social workers, 2 teachers, 5 counselors, 5 occupational/recreational therapists, 1 dietician.

Facilities   Single building; males and females in co-educational units. Separate residential quarters for children and adolescents. Central dining (shared with adults). Basketball courts, game room, gymnasium.

Education   Academic program available at no charge. Serves ages 4–18, grades K–12. 2 teachers on staff. Curriculum accredited or approved by State of Idaho Education.

Costs   Accepts private insurance, group insurance, medicare, medicaid, Blue Cross/Blue Shield, public funds.

Additional Services   Drug and alcohol rehabilitation services for males and females ages 4 and up. Treats behavior disorders; general psychosocial disorders; substance abuse; eating disorders; compulsive/addictive disorders other than substance abuse and eating disorders; post-traumatic stress disorder; thought, mood, and personality disorders. Outpatient services for males and females ages 13 and up. Treats substance abuse.

Contact   Melissa Curtis, Admissions/Intake Coordinator, main address above. Phone: 208-234-0797. Fax: 208-234-0156.

ASPEN HILL HOSPITAL
305 West Forest Avenue
Flagstaff, Arizona 86001
602-773-1060; Fax: 602-779-4388

General Information   Psychiatric hospital for adolescents. 12 beds for adolescents. Patient security: entirely locked. For-profit facility affiliated with Mental Health Management, McLean, VA. Licensed by state of Arizona. Accredited by JCAHO.

Participants   Accepts: male and female adolescents. Average stay: 18 days. Admission: one parent, all parties who share custody, court order, voluntary, depending on program. Treats learning disabilities; behavior disorders; general psychosocial disorders; substance abuse; eating disorders; compulsive/addictive disorders other than substance abuse and eating

disorders; post-traumatic stress disorder; thought, mood, and personality disorders.

Staff   Staff is 50% male, 50% female.

Costs   Average cost: $650 per day.

Contact   Cathy Bofetta, Intake Coordinator, main address above. Phone: 800-336-2773.

ASPEN MEADOWS HOSPITAL
6930 Weicker Lane
Velarde, New Mexico 87582
505-852-2704; Fax: 505-852-4612

General Information   Psychiatric hospital for adolescents. 36 beds for adolescents. Patient security: partially locked. For-profit facility affiliated with National Medical Enterprises, Santa Monica, CA. Licensed by state of New Mexico. Accredited by JCAHO.

Participants   Accepts: male and female adolescents. Average stay: 30 days. Admission: one parent, all parties who share custody, court order, voluntary, depending on program. Treats learning disabilities; behavior disorders; general psychosocial disorders; substance abuse; eating disorders; compulsive/addictive disorders other than substance abuse and eating disorders; post-traumatic stress disorder; thought, mood, and personality disorders.

Staff   Staff is 40% male, 60% female.

Costs   Average cost: $36,000 per stay.

Contact   Carole Rutten, Director of Marketing, main address above. Phone: 505-852-2704. Fax: 505-852-4612.

THE ASTOR HOME FOR CHILDREN
36 Mill Street
P.O. Box 5005
Rhinebeck, New York 12572
914-876-4081; Fax: 914-876-2020

General Information   Residential treatment/subacute facility for children. 75 beds for children. Patient security: unlocked. Independent not-for-profit facility. Licensed by state of New York. Accredited by JCAHO.

Participants   Accepts: male and female children. Average stay: 18 days. Admission: Department of Social Services or Department of Mental Health referrals. Treats learning disabilities; behavior disorders;

general psychosocial disorders; post-traumatic stress disorder; thought, mood, and personality disorders.

Contact Deborah Doolittle, Public Relations Director, main address above. Phone: 914-876-4081.

ATCHISON VALLEY HOPE
Box 312
Atchison, Kansas 66002
913-367-1618

General Information Drug and alcohol rehabilitation center for adolescents, adults. Open year-round. Patient security: unlocked; no runaway pursuit. Small town setting. Not-for-profit facility affiliated with Valley Hope Association, Norton, KS. Licensed by state of Kansas. Accredited by JCAHO.

Participants Accepts: male and female adolescents; male and female adults. Average stay: 27 days. Admission: one parent. Treats behavior disorders; general psychosocial disorders; substance abuse; eating disorders; compulsive/addictive disorders other than substance abuse and eating disorders; post-traumatic stress disorder; thought, mood, and personality disorders. Accepts the mobility impaired; the vision impaired; the speech impaired; the sexually compulsive; those with a history of harm to themselves and others; those receiving psychotropic medication; those with a history of epilepsy. Special programs for the mobility impaired; the vision impaired; the speech impaired; those with AIDS. Largest number of participants from Kansas, Missouri, Illinois.

Program Treatment modalities: individual counseling; group therapy; peer assessment; Twelve Step Recovery. Family treatment program available.

Staff 1.1 full-time direct-care staff members per adolescent. Total facility staff includes 2 physicians, 2 psychologists, 5 registered nurses, 8 practical/vocational nurses, 1 teacher, 8 counselors, 2 therapists, 4 dieticians. Staff is 34% male, 66% female.

Facilities Multiple buildings; males and females in coeducational units. Residential quarters shared with adults. Central dining (shared with adults). Basketball courts, game room.

Education 1 teacher on staff. Educational arrangements: coordinate with students' school to get assignments needed to keep current with their classes. Educational program held on-site at additional cost.

Costs Average cost: $5000 per stay. Accepts private insurance, group insurance, Blue Cross/Blue Shield.

Additional Services Outpatient services for males and females ages 16 and up. Treats substance abuse; compulsive/addictive disorders other than substance abuse and eating disorders; post-traumatic stress disorder; thought, mood, and personality disorders. Residential or sub-acute services for males and females ages 16 and up. Treats behavior disorders; general psychosocial disorders; substance abuse; compulsive/addictive disorders other than substance abuse and eating disorders; post-traumatic stress disorder; thought, mood, and personality disorders.

Contact Charles Pinkman, Business Manager, main address above. Phone: 913-367-1618.

ATLANTIC SHORES HOSPITAL
841 Jimmy Ann Drive
Daytona Beach, Florida 32117-4599
800-345-2647; Fax: 904-274-4140

General Information Psychiatric hospital for children, adolescents, adults. 35 beds for children. Open year-round. Patient security: entirely locked; will pursue and return runaways. Suburban setting. For-profit facility affiliated with Ramsay Health Care, Inc., New Orleans, LA. Licensed by state of Florida. Accredited by JCAHO.

Participants Accepts: male and female children ages up to 12; male and female adolescents ages 13–17; male and female adults ages 18 and up. Average stay: 15 days. Admission: one parent, all parties who share custody, court order, depending on program. Treats learning disabilities; behavior disorders; general psychosocial disorders; substance abuse; eating disorders; compulsive/addictive disorders other than substance abuse and eating disorders; post-traumatic stress disorder; thought, mood, and personality disorders. Accepts the mobility impaired; the vision impaired; the hearing impaired; the speech impaired; those with a history of arson; the sexually compulsive; those with a history of harm to themselves and others; those receiving psychotropic medication; non-English speaking individuals; those with a history of epilepsy. Special programs for the chronically ill; the mobility impaired; the developmentally disabled; the vision impaired; the hearing impaired; the speech impaired. Largest number of participants from Florida, Ohio.

Program Treatment modalities: psychodynamic. Family treatment program available.

Staff 1 full-time direct-care staff member per child or adolescent. Total facility staff includes 5 physicians, 1 psychologist, 7 psychiatrists, 22 registered nurses, 2 practical/vocational nurses, 5 MSW social workers, 1 social worker (non-MSW), 3 teachers, 4 counselors, 1 occupational/recreational therapist, 2 therapists, 1 dietician, 45 other direct-care staff members. Staff is 50% male, 50% female.

Facilities Single building; males and females in co-educational units. Residential quarters shared with adults. Central dining (shared with adults). Basketball courts, game room, gymnasium.

Education Academic program available at no charge. Serves ages 5–18, grades K–12. 3 teachers on staff.

Additional Services Drug and alcohol rehabilitation services for males and females ages 8 and up. Treats learning disabilities; behavior disorders; general psychosocial disorders; substance abuse; eating disorders; compulsive/addictive disorders other than substance abuse and eating disorders; post-traumatic stress disorder; thought, mood, and personality disorders.

Contact Maria Spoto, Director, Intake Services, main address above. Phone: 800-345-2647. Fax: 904-274-4140.

AURORA CONCEPT, INC.
78-31 Parsons Boulevard
Flushing, New York 11366
718-969-7000; Fax: 718-380-1775

General Information Residential treatment/subacute facility for adolescents, adults. Open year-round. Patient security: staff secured; no runaway pursuit. Urban setting. Independent not-for-profit facility. Licensed by state of New York. Accredited by New York State Division of Substance Abuse Services.

Participants Accepts: male and female adolescents ages 14–21; male and female adults ages 21 and up. Admission: one parent, significant other, depending on program. Treats learning disabilities; behavior disorders; general psychosocial disorders; substance abuse; eating disorders; compulsive/addictive disorders other than substance abuse and eating disorders; thought, mood, and personality disorders. Accepts those with a history of epilepsy. Special programs for those with AIDS.

Program Treatment modalities: therapeutic community modality (behavior modification); residential; ambulatory; medically supervised aftercare program. Family treatment program available.

Staff Total facility staff includes 2 physicians, 2 psychologists, 1 registered nurse, 1 practical/vocational nurse, 2 MSW social workers, 1 teacher, 5 counselors, 3 other direct-care staff members.

Facilities Multiple buildings; males and females in separate units. Residential quarters shared with adults. Central dining (shared with adults).

Education Academic program available at no charge. 1 teacher on staff. Curriculum accredited or approved by New York City Board of Education. Cost of educational program sometimes covered by local school district.

Costs Accepts private insurance, group insurance, medicare, medicaid, Blue Cross/Blue Shield, public funds.

Additional Services Outpatient services for males and females. Treats learning disabilities; behavior disorders; general psychosocial disorders; substance abuse; eating disorders; compulsive/addictive disorders other than substance abuse and eating disorders; thought, mood, and personality disorders.

Contact Lawrence A. Knopping, Intake Department, main address above. Phone: 718-969-7000. Fax: 718-380-1775.

AUSTEN RIGGS CENTER
25 Main Street
P.O. Box 962
Stockbridge, Massachusetts 01262
413-298-5511; Fax: 413-298-4020

General Information Psychiatric hospital for adolescents. Open year-round. Patient security: unlocked; no runaway pursuit. Small town setting. Independent not-for-profit facility. Licensed by state of Massachusetts. Accredited by JCAHO; Massachusetts Department of Mental Health, Massachusetts Hospital Association.

Participants Accepts: male and female adolescents ages 17 and up. Admission: voluntary. Treats autistic disorders; learning disabilities; behavior disorders; general psychosocial disorders; eating disorders; compulsive/addictive disorders other than substance abuse and eating disorders; post-traumatic stress disorder; thought, mood, and personality disorders. Accepts the mobility impaired; the vision impaired; those with a history of harm to themselves and others; those receiving psychotropic medication; those with a history of epilepsy. Special programs for the chronically ill. Largest number of participants from New York, New Jersey, Massachusetts.

Program Treatment modalities: psychodynamic individual therapy; psychoactive medication; milieu therapy; family therapy. Family treatment program available.

Staff Total facility staff includes 1 physician, 7 psychologists, 10 psychiatrists, 11 registered nurses, 1 MSW social worker, 1 social worker (non-MSW), 7 teachers, 1 dietician, 11 other direct-care staff members. Staff is 42% male, 58% female.

Facilities Multiple buildings; males and females in coeducational units. Residential quarters shared with adults. Central dining (shared with adults), separate dining by residential unit available. Basketball courts, game room, gymnasium, horseback riding, outdoor tennis courts, playing fields.

Education 7 teachers on staff. Educational arrangements: with local school district. Educational program held off-site at no charge. Cost of educational program covered by local school district.

Costs Accepts private insurance, group insurance, Blue Cross/Blue Shield.

Contact Janet Perachi, Admission Coordinator, main address above. Phone: 413-298-5511. Fax: 413-298-4020.

BAKER HALL, INC.
150 Martin Road
Lackawanna, New York 14218
716-828-9777; Fax: 716-828-9767

General Information Residential treatment/subacute facility for adolescents. 120 beds for adolescents. Open year-round. Patient security: staff secured; will pursue and return runaways. Suburban setting. Independent not-for-profit facility. Licensed by state of New York. Accredited by JCAHO; New York State Office of Mental Health, New York State Department of Social Services.

Participants Accepts: male and female adolescents ages 12–21. Average stay: 15 months. Admission: voluntary. Treats learning disabilities; behavior disorders; general psychosocial disorders; eating disorders; post-traumatic stress disorder; thought, mood, and personality disorders. Accepts those with a history of arson; the sexually compulsive; those with a history of harm to themselves and others; those receiving psychotropic medication; those with a history of epilepsy. Special programs for those with mental illness.

Program Treatment modalities: milieu treatment; individual, group, and family therapy; psychoeducational skill development; psychopharmacology. Family treatment program available.

Staff 2.2 full-time direct-care staff members per adolescent. Total facility staff includes 10 physicians, 2 psychologists, 1 psychiatrist, 6 registered nurses, 13 MSW social workers, 24 social workers (non-MSW), 31 teachers, 4 counselors, 4 occupational/recreational therapists, 1 speech pathologist, 1 dietician, 164 other

direct-care staff members. Staff is 40% male, 60% female.

Facilities Multiple buildings; males and females in separate units. Central dining, separate dining by residential unit available. Basketball courts, game room, gymnasium, outdoor swimming pool, playing fields, ropes course.

Education Academic program available at additional cost. Serves ages 12–18, ungraded. 31 teachers on staff. Curriculum accredited or approved by New York State Education Department. Cost of educational program covered by local school district. Organized sports program offered.

Costs Accepts private insurance, group insurance, medicaid, Blue Cross/Blue Shield, public funds.

Additional Services Outpatient services for males and females ages 5–18. Treats behavior disorders; general psychosocial disorders; compulsive/addictive disorders other than substance abuse and eating disorders; post-traumatic stress disorder; thought, mood, and personality disorders. Wilderness/survival program for males and females ages up to 21. Treats learning disabilities; behavior disorders; general psychosocial disorders; eating disorders; compulsive/addictive disorders other than substance abuse and eating disorders; post-traumatic stress disorder; thought, mood, and personality disorders. Day treatment for males and females ages 5–18. Treats learning disabilities; behavior disorders; general psychosocial disorders; compulsive/addictive disorders other than substance abuse and eating disorders; post-traumatic stress disorder; thought, mood, and personality disorders.

Contact Leslie G. Ford, PhD, Director of Quality Improvement, main address above. Phone: 716-828-9777. Fax: 716-828-9767.

BALPATE HOSPITAL, INC.
Balpate Road
Georgetown, Massachusetts 01833
508-352-2131; Fax: 508-352-6755

General Information Freestanding psychiatric/chemical dependency hospital for adolescents. 5 beds for adolescents. Patient security arrangements vary depending on program. Independent for-profit facility. Licensed by state of Massachusetts. Accredited by JCAHO.

Participants Accepts: male and female adolescents ages 16 and up. Average stay: 2 weeks. Admission: one parent, all parties who share custody, court order, voluntary, depending on program. Treats autistic disorders; learning disabilities; behavior disorders; general psychosocial disorders; substance abuse; eating disorders; compulsive/addictive disorders other than substance abuse and eating disorders; post-traumatic stress disorder; thought, mood, and personality disorders.

Costs Average cost: $500 per day.

Contact Cathy Williams, Admissions Officer, main address above. Phone: 508-352-2131.

BAPTIST MEDICAL CENTER— ADOLESCENT MENTAL HEALTH AND CHEMICAL DEPENDENCY TREATMENT PROGRAM
6601 Rockhill Road
Kansas City, Missouri 64131
816-276-7791

General Information Adolescent mental health and chemical dependency treatment program for adolescents. Patient security: entirely locked. Independent not-for-profit facility. Licensed by state of Missouri. Accredited by JCAHO.

Participants Accepts: male and female adolescents ages 12–18. Average stay: 20 days. Admission: one parent, all parties who share custody, depending on program. Treats *learning disabilities; behavior disorders; general psychosocial disorders; substance abuse; compulsive/addictive disorders other than substance abuse and eating disorders; thought, mood, and personality disorders.*

Staff Staff is 50% male, 50% female.

Costs Average cost: $573 per day.

Additional Services Drug and alcohol rehabilitation services for males and females ages 12–18. Treats *learning disabilities; behavior disorders; general psychosocial disorders; substance abuse; compulsive/addictive disorders other than substance abuse and eating disorders; thought, mood, and personality disorders.* Outpatient services for males and females ages 7 and up. Treats *learning disabilities; behavior disorders; general psychosocial disorders; substance abuse; eating disorders; compulsive/addictive disorders other than substance abuse and eating disorders; thought, mood, and personality disorders.*

Contact Robert Kelly, Provider Relations Representative, main address above. Phone: 816-276-7791.

BARAT HUMAN SERVICES
5250 John R. Street
Detroit, Michigan 48202
313-833-1525; Fax: 313-833-0902

General Information Residential treatment/subacute facility for adolescents. Patient security: unlocked. Not-for-profit facility affiliated with The League of Catholic Women, Detroit, MI. Licensed by state of Michigan. Accredited by JCAHO.

Participants Accepts: female adolescents. Average stay: 10 months. Admission: court order. Treats *behavior disorders; general psychosocial disorders; eating disorders; thought, mood, and personality disorders.*

Staff .5 full-time direct-care staff member per adolescent. Staff is 35% male, 65% female.

Contact Department of Social Services, main address above.

BARBOURSVILLE SCHOOL
1535 Martha Road
Barboursville, West Virginia 25504
304-736-0915

General Information Residential treatment/subacute facility for adolescents. 22 beds for adolescents. Open year-round. Patient security: staff secured; will pursue and return runaways. Rural setting. Not-for-profit facility affiliated with Shawnee Hills MH/MR Center, Inc., Charleston, WV. Licensed by state of West Virginia. Accredited by JCAHO.

Participants Accepts: male and female adolescents ages 12–17. Average stay: 180 days. Admission: court order. Treats *learning disabilities; behavior disorders; general psychosocial disorders; substance abuse; eating disorders; compulsive/addictive disorders other than substance abuse and eating disorders; post-traumatic stress disorder; thought, mood, and personality disorders.* Accepts *the vision impaired; the speech impaired; those with a history of arson; the sexually compulsive; those with a history of harm to themselves and others; those receiving psychotropic medication; those with a history of epilepsy.* Largest number of participants from West Virginia.

Program Treatment modalities: reality therapy; psychodynamic. Family treatment program available.

Staff Total facility staff includes 1 physician, 3 psychologists, 4 psychiatrists, 1 registered nurse, 2 social workers (non-MSW), 5 teachers, 1 occupational/recreational therapist, 1 dietician.

Facilities Multiple buildings; males and females in separate units. Separate dining by residential unit available. Basketball courts, game room, gymnasium, outdoor tennis courts, playing fields, lake for fishing.

Education Academic program available. Serves ages 12–17. 5 teachers on staff. Curriculum accredited or approved by West Virginia Board of Education.

Costs Accepts private insurance, medicaid, Blue Cross/Blue Shield.

Contact Karen Yost, Division Director, main address above. Phone: 304-736-0915.

BAY HARBOR RESIDENTIAL TREATMENT CENTER
12895 Seminole Boulevard
Largo, Florida 34648
800-683-4727; Fax: 813-584-1835

General Information Residential treatment/subacute facility for children, adolescents. 8 beds for children; 32 beds for adolescents; 40 beds total. Open year-round. Patient security: entirely locked. Suburban setting. For-profit facility affiliated with National Medical Enterprises, Santa Monica, CA. Licensed by state of California. Accredited by JCAHO; Civilian Health and Medical Program of the Uniformed Services.

Participants Accepts: male and female children ages 6–12; male and female adolescents ages 13–18. Admission: voluntary. Treats learning disabilities; behavior disorders; general psychosocial disorders; substance abuse; eating disorders; compulsive/addictive disorders other than substance abuse and eating disorders; post-traumatic stress disorder; thought, mood, and personality disorders. Accepts those with a history of arson; the sexually compulsive; those with a history of harm to themselves and others; those receiving psychotropic medication. Special programs for the developmentally disabled.

Program Treatment modalities: Twelve Step Recovery; positive peer culture model. Family treatment program available.

Contact Bill Peeke, Director, Information and Referral Services, main address above. Phone: 800-683-4727. Fax: 813-584-1835.

BAY HAVEN
713 Ninth Street
Bay City, Michigan 48708
517-894-3799; Fax: 517-893-9717

General Information Residential treatment/subacute facility for adolescents, adults. 10 beds for adolescents. Open year-round. Patient security: partially locked; will pursue and return runaways. Small town setting. Not-for-profit facility affiliated with Bay Medical Center, Bay City, MI. Licensed by state of Michigan. Accredited by JCAHO.

Participants Accepts: male and female adolescents ages 12–18; male and female adults ages 18 and up. Average stay: 30 days. Admission: voluntary. Treats behavior disorders; general psychosocial disorders; substance abuse; eating disorders; compulsive/addictive disorders other than substance abuse and eating disorders; post-traumatic stress disorder; thought, mood, and personality disorders. Accepts the mobility impaired; the vision impaired; the hearing impaired; the speech impaired; those with a history of harm to themselves and others; those receiving psychotropic medication; those with a history of epilepsy. Special programs for the mobility impaired; the vision impaired; the hearing impaired; the speech impaired. Largest number of participants from Michigan.

Program Treatment modalities: Twelve Step Recovery; disease concept. Family treatment program available.

Staff 1.1 full-time direct-care staff members per adolescent. Total facility staff includes 4 physicians, 1 psychologist, 1 psychiatrist, 4 registered nurses, 1 practical/vocational nurse, 2 MSW social workers, 1 social worker (non-MSW), 3 teachers, 5 counselors, 2 occupational/recreational therapists, 1 speech pathologist, 1 dietician, 2 other direct-care staff members. Staff is 50% male, 50% female.

Facilities Single building; males and females in co-educational units. Separate residential quarters for adolescents. Central dining (shared with adults). Basketball courts, game room, gymnasium, indoor swimming pool, outdoor swimming pool, climbing tower.

Education Academic program available at no charge. Serves ages 12–21. 3 teachers on staff. Curriculum accredited or approved by School District Homebound. Cost of educational program covered by local school district. Organized sports program offered.

Costs Accepts private insurance, group insurance, medicare, medicaid, Blue Cross/Blue Shield, public funds.

Additional Services Drug and alcohol rehabilitation services for males and females ages 12–21. Treats behavior disorders; general psychosocial disorders;

substance abuse; eating disorders; compulsive/addictive disorders other than substance abuse and eating disorders; post-traumatic stress disorder; thought, mood, and personality disorders. Outpatient services for males and females ages 3–21. Treats behavior disorders; general psychosocial disorders; substance abuse; eating disorders; compulsive/addictive disorders other than substance abuse and eating disorders; post-traumatic stress disorder; thought, mood, and personality disorders.

Contact Scott Gilman, Development Manager, main address above. Phone: 517-894-3799. Fax: 517-893-9717.

BAYLOR-PARKSIDE LODGE OF DALLAS/FORT WORTH, INC.
Route #1, Box 223AB
Orchid Hill Lane
Argyle, Texas 76226
817-455-2201; Fax: 817-455-2198

General Information Drug and alcohol rehabilitation center for children, adolescents, adults. 20 beds for children; 20 beds for adolescents; 50 beds total. Open year-round. Patient security: staff secured; will pursue and return runaways. Rural setting. Affiliated with Baylor Health Care Systems/Parkside Medical Services, Park Ridge, IL. Licensed by state of Texas. Accredited by JCAHO; Texas Commission on Alcohol and Drug Abuse.

Participants Accepts: male and female children ages 12–18; male and female adolescents ages 18–22; male and female adults ages 22–80. Admission: one parent, all parties who share custody, court order, depending on program. Treats behavior disorders; substance abuse; eating disorders; compulsive/addictive disorders other than substance abuse and eating disorders; thought, mood, and personality disorders. Accepts the vision impaired; the hearing impaired; the speech impaired. Special programs for the vision impaired; the hearing impaired; the speech impaired. Largest number of participants from Texas, Illinois, Oklahoma.

Program Treatment modalities: Twelve Step Recovery. Family treatment program available.

Staff 1 full-time direct-care staff member per child or adolescent. Total facility staff includes 1 physician, 1 psychologist, 1 psychiatrist, 6 registered nurses, 3 practical/vocational nurses, 2 MSW social workers, 2 teachers, 5 counselors, 1 occupational/recreational therapist, 1 speech pathologist, 1 dietician, 14 other

direct-care staff members. Staff is 42% male, 58% female.

Facilities Single building; males and females in co-educational units. Separate residential quarters for children and adolescents. Central dining (shared with adults). Basketball courts, game room, gymnasium, outdoor swimming pool, playing fields, ropes course, volleyball, Nautilus.

Education Academic program available at no charge. Serves ages 12–18, grades 6–12. 2 teachers on staff. Curriculum accredited or approved by Lewisville Independent School District.

Costs Accepts private insurance, group insurance, Blue Cross/Blue Shield, public funds.

Additional Services Residential or sub-acute services for males and females ages 12–18. Treats behavior disorders; substance abuse; eating disorders; compulsive/addictive disorders other than substance abuse and eating disorders; thought, mood, and personality disorders.

Contact Michelle Carpentere, Admissions Coordinator, main address above. Phone: 817-455-2201. Fax: 817-455-2198.

BAYOU OAKS HOSPITAL
934 East Main Street
Houma, Louisiana 70360
504-876-2020; Fax: 504-876-3833

General Information Psychiatric and chemical dependency hospital for children, adolescents. Patient security: entirely locked. For-profit facility affiliated with Ramsay Health Care, Inc, New Orleans, LA. Licensed by state of Louisiana. Accredited by JCAHO.

Participants Accepts: male and female children; male and female adolescents. Average stay: 16 days. Admission: one parent, all parties who share custody, court order, voluntary, depending on program. Treats autistic disorders; learning disabilities; behavior disorders; substance abuse; eating disorders; compulsive/addictive disorders other than substance abuse and eating disorders; post-traumatic stress disorder; thought, mood, and personality disorders.

Contact Timothy Speece, Program Director, main address above. Phone: 504-876-2020.

BAYWOOD HOSPITAL
709 Medical Center Boulevard
Webster, Texas 77598
713-332-9550; Fax: 713-332-1226

General Information Psychiatric hospital for children, adolescents. 34 beds for children; 38 beds for adolescents. Open year-round. Patient security: partially locked; no runaway pursuit. Suburban setting. For-profit facility affiliated with National Medical Enterprises, Santa Monica, CA. Licensed by state of Texas. Accredited by JCAHO; Civilian Health and Medical Program of the Uniformed Services.

Participants Accepts: male and female children ages 4–12; male and female adolescents ages 12–19. Average stay: 21 days. Admission: one parent, all parties who share custody, court order, voluntary, depending on program. Treats learning disabilities; behavior disorders; general psychosocial disorders; substance abuse; eating disorders; compulsive/addictive disorders other than substance abuse and eating disorders; post-traumatic stress disorder; thought, mood, and personality disorders. Accepts the mobility impaired; the vision impaired; the hearing impaired; the speech impaired; those with a history of arson; the sexually compulsive; those with a history of harm to themselves and others; those receiving psychotropic medication; non-English speaking individuals; those with a history of epilepsy. Special programs for the vision impaired; the hearing impaired; those with AIDS.

Program Treatment modalities: Twelve Step Recovery; experiential therapy; psychodrama; trauma resolution therapy. Family treatment program available.

Staff Total facility staff includes 38 physicians, 41 psychologists, 19 psychiatrists, 118 registered nurses, 3 practical/vocational nurses, 35 MSW social workers, 6 teachers, 20 counselors, 8 occupational/recreational therapists, 2 speech pathologists, 1 dietician, 26 other direct-care staff members. Staff is 40% male, 60% female.

Facilities Single building; males and females in coeducational units. Central dining (shared with adults), separate dining by residential unit available. Basketball courts, game room, gymnasium, outdoor swimming pool, outdoor tennis courts, ropes course.

Education Academic program available at no charge. Serves ages 4–19, grades K–12. 6 teachers on staff. Curriculum accredited or approved by Southern Association of Schools and Colleges. Cost of educational program sometimes covered by local school district.

Costs Accepts private insurance, group insurance, medicare, Blue Cross/Blue Shield.

Additional Services Drug and alcohol rehabilitation services for males and females ages 10 and up. Treats learning disabilities; behavior disorders; general psychosocial disorders; substance abuse; eating disorders; compulsive/addictive disorders other than substance abuse and eating disorders; post-traumatic stress disorder; thought, mood, and personality disorders. Outpatient services for males and females ages 4 and up. Treats learning disabilities; behavior disorders; general psychosocial disorders; substance abuse; compulsive/addictive disorders other than substance abuse and eating disorders; post-traumatic stress disorder; thought, mood, and personality disorders. Wilderness/survival program for males and females ages 10–19. Treats behavior disorders; general psychosocial disorders; substance abuse; post-traumatic stress disorder; thought, mood, and personality disorders.

Contact Shelly Ramono, Director of Marketing, P.O. Box 57727, Webster, TX 77598. Phone: 713-332-9550. Fax: 713-332-1226.

BEACON DETOX CENTER
164 High Street
Greenfield, Massachusetts 01301
413-774-5272

General Information Drug and alcohol rehabilitation center for children, adolescents. Patient security: staff secured. Not-for-profit facility affiliated with Bay State Health Systems, Springfield, MA. Licensed by state of Massachusetts. Accredited by JCAHO.

Participants Accepts: male and female children; male and female adolescents. Average stay: 3 days. Admission: one parent, all parties who share custody, court order, voluntary, depending on program. Treats substance abuse. Accepts the mobility impaired; the vision impaired; the hearing impaired; the speech impaired; those with a history of arson; the sexually compulsive; those with a history of harm to themselves and others; non-English speaking individuals; those with a history of epilepsy.

Staff Staff is 75% male, 25% female.

Costs Average cost: $130 per day.

Contact Linda Hoer, Program Director, main address above. Phone: 413-774-5272.

BEECH HILL HOSPITAL
New Harrisville Road
Dublin, New Hampshire 03444
603-563-8511; Fax: 603-563-8771

General Information Drug and alcohol rehabilitation center for adolescents, adults. 19 beds for adolescents. Open year-round. Patient security: staff secured; will pursue and return runaways. Rural setting. Not-for-profit facility affiliated with Las Casas Foundation New Hampshire, Inc., Atlanta, GA. Licensed by state of New Hampshire. Accredited by JCAHO; Commission on Accreditation of Rehabilitation Facilities.

Participants Accepts: male and female adolescents ages 14–19; male and female adults. Average stay: 21 days. Admission: one parent. Treats substance abuse; eating disorders; compulsive/addictive disorders other than substance abuse and eating disorders; post-traumatic stress disorder. Accepts the hearing impaired; the speech impaired. Special programs for the developmentally disabled; those with AIDS. Largest number of participants from New Hampshire, Massachusetts, Maine.

Program Treatment modalities: Twelve Step Recovery; Outward Bound experiential program for adolescents. Family treatment program available.

Staff Total facility staff includes 2 physicians, 3 psychologists, 1 psychiatrist, 24 registered nurses, 1 teacher, 15 counselors, 3 occupational/recreational therapists, 1 dietician.

Facilities Multiple buildings; males and females in separate units. Separate residential quarters for adolescents. Central dining (shared with adults). Basketball courts, game room, gymnasium, outdoor swimming pool, playing fields, ropes course.

Education Academic program available at no charge. Serves ages 14–19, grades 7–12. 1 teacher on staff. Organized sports program offered.

Costs Average cost: $10,000 per stay. Accepts private insurance, group insurance, Blue Cross/Blue Shield, public funds.

Additional Services Outpatient services for males and females ages 14 and up. Treats substance abuse; eating disorders; post-traumatic stress disorder. Wilderness/survival program for males and females ages 14–19. Treats substance abuse; eating disorders.

Contact Charles Preus, Director of Development, 950 North Main Street, Randolph, MA 02368. Phone: 617-963-7910. Fax: 617-963-7910.

THE BEHAVIORAL MEDICINE CENTER AT SAINT MARGARET MERCY HEALTHCARE CENTERS, SOUTH CAMPUS
U.S. Highway 30
Dyer, Indiana 46311
219-865-2141; Fax: 219-865-2964

General Information General hospital for children, adolescents, adults. 14 beds for children; 47 beds for adolescents; 132 beds total. Open year-round. Patient security: partially locked; will pursue and return runaways. Small town setting. Not-for-profit facility affiliated with Sisters of Saint Francis Health Services, Inc., Mishawaka, IN. Licensed by state of Indiana. Accredited by JCAHO; Indiana Department of Mental Health, Indiana Department of Addiction Services, Indiana State Board of Health.

Participants Accepts: male and female children ages 3–12; male and female adolescents ages 12–18; male and female adults ages 18 and up. Average stay: 25 days. Admission: one parent, all parties who share custody, court order, court referrals, depending on program. Treats learning disabilities; behavior disorders; general psychosocial disorders; substance abuse; eating disorders; compulsive/addictive disorders other than substance abuse and eating disorders; post-traumatic stress disorder; thought, mood, and personality disorders. Accepts the mobility impaired; the vision impaired; the hearing impaired; the speech impaired; those with a history of arson; the sexually compulsive; those with a history of harm to themselves and others; those receiving psychotropic medication; non-English speaking individuals; those with a history of epilepsy; the mentally retarded (IQ over 70). Special programs for the chronically ill; the mobility impaired; the developmentally disabled; the vision impaired; the hearing impaired; the speech impaired; those with AIDS.

Program Treatment modalities: Twelve Step Recovery; individual therapy; group therapy; family therapy. Family treatment program available.

Facilities Multiple buildings; males and females in coeducational units. Central dining (not shared with adults). Basketball courts, game room, gymnasium, horseback riding, playing fields, miniature golf, baseball diamond, par course.

Education Academic program available at no charge. Serves ages 3–18, grades K–12. Curriculum accredited or approved by client's home school district. Organized sports program offered.

Costs Accepts private insurance, group insurance, medicare, medicaid, Blue Cross/Blue Shield, public funds.

Additional Services Drug and alcohol rehabilitation services for males and females ages 12–18. Treats learning disabilities; behavior disorders; general psychosocial disorders; substance abuse; eating disorders; compulsive/addictive disorders other than substance abuse and eating disorders; post-traumatic stress disorder; thought, mood, and personality disorders. Adolescent dual diagnosis program for males and females ages 3 and up. Treats learning disabilities; behavior disorders; general psychosocial disorders; substance abuse; eating disorders; compulsive/addictive disorders other than substance abuse and eating disorders; post-traumatic stress disorder; thought, mood, and personality disorders.

Contact Linda Gadbois, Director of Community Relations, main address above. Phone: 219-865-2141. Fax: 219-865-2964.

BELLEFAIRE JEWISH CHILDREN'S BUREAU
22001 Fairmount Boulevard
Cleveland, Ohio 44118
216-932-2800; Fax: 216-932-6704

General Information Residential treatment/subacute facility for children, adolescents, adults. Open year-round. Patient security: staff secured; will pursue and return runaways. Suburban setting. Independent not-for-profit facility. Licensed by state of Ohio. Accredited by JCAHO; Ohio Department of Mental Health, Ohio Department of Human Services, Council on Accreditation of Services for Families and Children.

Participants Accepts: male and female children ages 11–12; male and female adolescents ages 13–19; male and female adults ages 20 and up. Average stay: 420 days. Admission: one parent, all parties who share custody, court order, depending on program. Treats learning disabilities; behavior disorders; general psychosocial disorders; substance abuse; eating disorders; compulsive/addictive disorders other than substance abuse and eating disorders; post-traumatic stress disorder; thought, mood, and personality disorders. Accepts the mobility impaired; the hearing impaired; the speech impaired; those with a history of arson; those with a history of harm to themselves and others; those receiving psychotropic medication; those with a history of epilepsy. Special programs for the chronically ill; the mobility impaired; the hearing impaired; the speech impaired. Largest number of participants from Ohio, Illinois, Indiana.

Program Treatment modalities: psychodynamic; Twelve Step Recovery. Family treatment program available.

Staff Total facility staff includes 2 physicians, 9 psychologists, 5 psychiatrists, 5 registered nurses, 20 MSW social workers, 20 teachers, 25 counselors, 5 occupational/recreational therapists, 1 therapist, 1 dietician, 60 other direct-care staff members.

Facilities Multiple buildings; males and females in both coeducational and separate units depending on program. Separate residential quarters for children and adolescents. Separate dining by residential unit available. Basketball courts, game room, gymnasium, indoor swimming pool, outdoor tennis courts, playing fields, ropes course, off-site camp.

Education Academic program available at additional cost. Serves ages 11–20, grades 6–12. 20 teachers on staff. Curriculum accredited or approved by Cleveland Heights/University Heights School District. Cost of educational program sometimes covered by local school district. Organized sports program offered.

Costs Average cost: $96,600 per stay. Accepts private insurance, group insurance, medicare, medicaid, Blue Cross/Blue Shield, public funds.

Additional Services Drug and alcohol rehabilitation services for males and females ages 11–20. Treats learning disabilities; behavior disorders; general psychosocial disorders; substance abuse; post-traumatic stress disorder; thought, mood, and personality disorders. Outpatient services for males and females ages 5–18. Treats behavior disorders; general psychosocial disorders; compulsive/addictive disorders other than substance abuse and eating disorders; post-traumatic stress disorder. Wilderness/survival program for males and females ages 11–20. Treats learning disabilities; behavior disorders; general psychosocial disorders; substance abuse; post-traumatic stress disorder; thought, mood, and personality disorders. Camping program for males and females ages 11–20. Treats learning disabilities; behavior disorders; general psychosocial disorders; substance abuse; post-traumatic stress disorder; thought, mood, and personality disorders.

Contact Margaret Culp, Director of Admissions, main address above. Phone: 216-932-2800. Fax: 216-932-6704.

BELLIN PSYCHIATRIC CENTER, INC.
725 South Webster Avenue
P.O. Box 23725
Green Bay, Wisconsin 54305-3725
414-433-3630; Fax: 414-433-7564

General Information Psychiatric hospital for children, adolescents. Patient security: partially locked. Not-for-profit facility. Licensed by state of Wisconsin. Accredited by JCAHO.

Participants Accepts: male and female children; male and female adolescents. Average stay: 18 days. Admission: one parent, all parties who share custody, court order, voluntary, depending on program. Treats autistic disorders; learning disabilities; behavior disorders; general psychosocial disorders; substance abuse; eating disorders; compulsive/addictive disorders other than substance abuse and eating disorders; post-traumatic stress disorder; thought, mood, and personality disorders.

Costs Average cost: $500 per day.

Contact Patrick Curren, Director of Child and Adolescent Unit, main address above. Phone: 414-433-3698.

BELMONT PINE HOSPITAL
615 Churchill-Hubbard Road
Youngstown, Ohio 44505
216-759-2700; Fax: 216-759-2776

General Information Psychiatric hospital for children, adolescents, adults. 10 beds for children; 48 beds for adolescents; 68 beds total. Open year-round. Patient security: partially locked; will pursue and return runaways. Suburban setting. Independent for-profit facility. Licensed by state of Ohio. Accredited by JCAHO.

Participants Accepts: male and female children ages 7–12; male and female adolescents ages 13–18; male and female adults ages 18–60. Average stay: 22 days. Admission: one parent, all parties who share custody, court order, depending on program. Treats learning disabilities; behavior disorders; general psychosocial disorders; substance abuse; eating disorders; post-traumatic stress disorder; thought, mood, and personality disorders. Accepts the mobility impaired; the sexually compulsive; those with a history of harm to themselves and others; those receiving psychotropic medication; those with a history of epilepsy. Special programs for the chronically ill; the mobility impaired; those with AIDS. Largest number of participants from Indiana, Pennsylvania.

Program Treatment modalities: cognitive-behavioral; psychodynamic; experiential therapy; Twelve Step Recovery. Family treatment program available.

Staff Total facility staff includes 3 physicians, 3 psychologists, 8 psychiatrists, 14 registered nurses, 2 practical/vocational nurses, 2 MSW social workers, 8 social workers (non-MSW), 3 teachers, 7 counselors, 4 occupational/recreational therapists, 1 speech pathologist, 1 therapist, 1 dietician, 32 other direct-care staff members. Staff is 55% male, 45% female.

Facilities Single building; males and females in co-educational units. Separate residential quarters for children and adolescents. Central dining (not shared with adults). Basketball courts, game room, gymnasium, indoor swimming pool, outdoor tennis courts, playing fields, ropes course.

Education Academic program available at no charge. Serves ages 7–18, grades 1–12. 3 teachers on staff. Curriculum accredited or approved by Liberty Township School System.

Costs Accepts private insurance, group insurance, Blue Cross/Blue Shield, public funds.

Additional Services Drug and alcohol rehabilitation services for males and females ages 18–60. Treats substance abuse. School for males and females ages 6–18. Treats learning disabilities; behavior disorders; general psychosocial disorders; substance abuse; eating disorders; compulsive/addictive disorders other than substance abuse and eating disorders; post-traumatic stress disorder; thought, mood, and personality disorders.

Contact John Sokol, Assessment Coordinator, main address above. Phone: 216-759-2700. Fax: 216-759-2776.

BENJAMIN RUSH CENTER
650 South Salina Street
Syracuse, New York 13202
315-476-2161

General Information Psychiatric and chemical dependency hospital for children, adolescents, adults. 9 beds for children; 30 beds for adolescents; 129 beds total. Open year-round. Patient security: partially locked; will pursue and return runaways. Urban setting. Independent for-profit facility. Licensed by state of New York. Accredited by JCAHO.

Participants Accepts: male and female children ages 5–12; male and female adolescents ages 12–18; male and female adults ages 18 and up. Admission: one parent. Treats learning disabilities; behavior disorders; general psychosocial disorders; substance abuse;

eating disorders; compulsive/addictive disorders other than substance abuse and eating disorders; post-traumatic stress disorder; thought, mood, and personality disorders. Accepts the mobility impaired; the vision impaired; the hearing impaired; the speech impaired; those with a history of harm to themselves and others; those receiving psychotropic medication; those with a history of epilepsy.

Program   Treatment modalities: eclectic (psychodynamic, behavioral); Twelve Step Recovery. Family treatment program available.

Staff   Total facility staff includes 5 physicians, 6 psychologists, 40 psychiatrists, 45 registered nurses, 8 practical/vocational nurses, 12 MSW social workers, 3 teachers, 12 counselors, 6 occupational/recreational therapists, 4 therapists, 1 dietician, 8 other direct-care staff members. Staff is 50% male, 50% female.

Facilities   Single building; males and females in co-educational units. Separate residential quarters for children and adolescents. Central dining (shared with adults). Basketball courts, game room, gymnasium, indoor swimming pool, indoor tennis courts, playing fields, pottery studio, photography studio, dance studio, arts and crafts studio.

Education   Academic program available at no charge. Serves ages 5–18, grades K–12. 3 teachers on staff. Cost of educational program covered by local school district.

Costs   Accepts private insurance, group insurance, medicare, medicaid, Blue Cross/Blue Shield.

Additional Services   Drug and alcohol rehabilitation services for males and females ages 12 and up. Treats substance abuse.

Contact   Stephanie Chin-Rinefierd, Director of Public Relations and Marketing, main address above. Phone: 315-476-2161.

THE BETHANY PAVILION
7600 Northwest 23rd Street
Bethany, Oklahoma 73008
405-495-2870; Fax: 405-495-5471

General Information   Psychiatric hospital for children, adolescents, adults. 6 beds for children; 20 beds for adolescents; 43 beds total. Open year-round. Patient security: entirely locked. Urban setting. For-profit facility affiliated with Ramsay Health Care, Inc., New Orleans, LA. Licensed by state of Oklahoma. Accredited by JCAHO.

Participants   Accepts: male and female children ages 6–12; male and female adolescents ages 13–17; male

and female adults ages 18 and up. Admission: one parent, all parties who share custody, court order, legal guardian must sign patient in, depending on program. Treats autistic disorders; learning disabilities; behavior disorders; general psychosocial disorders; eating disorders; compulsive/addictive disorders other than substance abuse and eating disorders; post-traumatic stress disorder; thought, mood, and personality disorders. Accepts the mobility impaired; the vision impaired; the hearing impaired; the speech impaired; those with a history of arson; the sexually compulsive; those with a history of harm to themselves and others; those receiving psychotropic medication; non-English speaking individuals; those with a history of epilepsy. Special programs for the chronically ill; the mobility impaired; the developmentally disabled; the vision impaired; the hearing impaired; the speech impaired; those with AIDS.

Program   Family treatment program available.

Staff   Total facility staff includes 4 psychologists, 8 psychiatrists, 46 registered nurses, 5 MSW social workers, 3 teachers, 7 occupational/recreational therapists, 1 therapist, 33 other direct-care staff members. Staff is 26% male, 74% female.

Facilities   Single building; males and females in co-educational units. Separate residential quarters for children and adolescents. Separate dining by residential unit available. Basketball courts, game room.

Education   Academic program available at no charge. Serves ages 6–18, grades K–12. 3 teachers on staff. Curriculum accredited or approved by Putnam City School District. Cost of educational program covered by local school district.

Costs   Accepts private insurance, group insurance, medicare, medicaid, Blue Cross/Blue Shield.

Additional Services   Day treatment for males and females ages 6–17. Treats autistic disorders; learning disabilities; behavior disorders; general psychosocial disorders; eating disorders; compulsive/addictive disorders other than substance abuse and eating disorders; post-traumatic stress disorder; thought, mood, and personality disorders.

Contact   Brenda Gassett, Marketing Coordinator, main address above. Phone: 405-495-2870. Fax: 405-495-5471.

BI-COUNTY TREATMENT CENTER
319 Daly Street
Dubois, Pennsylvania 15801
814-371-1522

General Information Drug and alcohol rehabilitation center for adolescents. 14 beds for adolescents. Patient security: staff secured. Independent not-for-profit facility. Licensed by state of Pennsylvania.

Participants Accepts: male and female adolescents. Average stay: 93 days. Admission: one parent, all parties who share custody, court order, voluntary, depending on program. Treats substance abuse. Accepts the mobility impaired; the vision impaired; the hearing impaired; the speech impaired; those with a history of arson; those with a history of epilepsy.

Costs Average cost: $76 per day.

Contact Jack Volpe, Director, main address above. Phone: 814-371-1522.

BIG ISLAND SUBSTANCE ABUSE
COUNCIL
1190 Waianuenue Avenue
Hilo, Hawaii 96721
808-935-4927; Fax: 808-969-1861

General Information Drug and alcohol rehabilitation center for adolescents. 30 beds for adolescents. Patient security: staff secured. Independent not-for-profit facility. Licensed by state of Hawaii.

Participants Accepts: male and female adolescents. Average stay: 6 months. Admission: one parent, all parties who share custody, court order, voluntary, depending on program. Treats substance abuse.

Staff Staff is 50% male, 50% female.

Costs Average cost: $210 per day.

Contact Majken Mechling, Chief Executive Officer, P.O. Box 38, Hilo, HI 96721. Phone: 808-935-4927. Fax: 808-969-1861.

BLOOMINGTON MEADOWS HOSPITAL
3600 North Prow Road
Bloomington, Indiana 47404

General Information Psychiatric hospital for children, adolescents, adults. Open year-round. Patient security: entirely locked; will pursue and return runaways. Suburban setting. Independent for-profit facility. Licensed by state of Indiana.

Participants Accepts: male and female children ages 3–12; male and female adolescents ages 12–18; male and female adults ages 17 and up. Admission: all parties who share custody. Treats behavior disorders; substance abuse; eating disorders; compulsive/addictive disorders other than substance abuse and eating disorders; post-traumatic stress disorder; thought, mood, and personality disorders. Accepts the mobility impaired; the vision impaired; the hearing impaired; the speech impaired; those with a history of arson; the sexually compulsive; those with a history of harm to themselves and others; those receiving psychotropic medication; those with a history of epilepsy.

Program Treatment modalities: Twelve Step Recovery; cognitive; behavioral. Family treatment program available.

Staff Total facility staff includes 6 physicians, 6 psychiatrists, 15 registered nurses, 3 MSW social workers, 6 social workers (non-MSW), 3 teachers, 6 counselors, 4 occupational/recreational therapists, 1 therapist, 1 dietician, 20 other direct-care staff members. Staff is 50% male, 50% female.

Facilities Single building; males and females in co-educational units. Basketball courts, gymnasium, ropes course.

Education Academic program available at no charge. Serves ages 6–18, grades 1–12. 3 teachers on staff. Curriculum accredited or approved by State of Indiana.

Costs Accepts private insurance, group insurance, medicare, medicaid, Blue Cross/Blue Shield, public funds.

Contact Dan Thomas, Facility Director, main address above. Phone: 812-331-8000. Fax: 812-331-8056.

BLOUNT MEMORIAL HOSPITAL
907 East Lamar Alexander Boulevard
Maryville, Tennessee 37801
615-983-7211; Fax: 615-981-2173

General Information General hospital for children, adolescents. Open year-round. Patient security: partially locked; will pursue and return runaways. Suburban setting. Independent not-for-profit facility. Accredited by JCAHO.

Participants Accepts: male and female children ages up to 12; male and female adolescents ages 13–18. Admission: voluntary. Treats behavior disorders; general psychosocial disorders; substance abuse; eating disorders; post-traumatic stress disorder; thought, mood, and personality disorders. Accepts the mobility impaired; the vision impaired; the hearing impaired; the speech impaired; those with a history of harm to themselves and others; non-English speaking individuals; those with a history of epilepsy. Special programs for the chronically ill; the mobility impaired; the developmentally disabled; the vision impaired; the hearing impaired; the speech impaired; those with AIDS.

Program   Family treatment program available.

Facilities   Multiple buildings; males and females in separate units. Separate dining by residential unit, in-room dining available. Game room, ropes course.

Costs   Accepts private insurance, group insurance, medicare, medicaid, Blue Cross/Blue Shield, public funds.

Additional Services   Drug and alcohol rehabilitation services for males and females ages 12 and up. Treats learning disabilities; eating disorders; compulsive/addictive disorders other than substance abuse and eating disorders; thought, mood, and personality disorders. Outpatient services for males and females ages 12 and up. Treats substance abuse; eating disorders.

Contact   V.C. Fuqua, Director, Marketing and Public Relations, main address above. Phone: 615-983-7211. Fax: 615-981-2173.

BLYTHEDALE CHILDREN'S HOSPITAL
Bradhurst Avenue
Valhalla, New York 10595
914-592-7555; Fax: 914-592-5844

General Information   Pediatric rehabilitation hospital for children, adolescents. Patient security: staff secured. Independent not-for-profit facility. Licensed by state of New York. Accredited by JCAHO.

Participants   Accepts: male and female children; male and female adolescents. Average stay: 140 days. Admission: one parent. Treats autistic disorders; learning disabilities; behavior disorders; general psychosocial disorders; eating disorders; post-traumatic stress disorder; thought, mood, and personality disorders.

Staff   Staff is 30% male, 70% female.

Costs   Average cost: $67,000 per stay.

Additional Services   Outpatient services for males and females ages 1–21. Treats autistic disorders; learning disabilities; behavior disorders; general psychosocial disorders; eating disorders; post-traumatic stress disorder; thought, mood, and personality disorders.

Contact   Dorothy Herbst, Director of Admissions, Bradhurst Avenue, Valhalla, NY 10595. Phone: 914-592-7555.

BOBBY BENSON CENTER
640 Ulukahiki Street
Kailua, Hawaii 96734-4498
808-263-5500; Fax: 808-263-5143

General Information   Residential treatment/subacute facility for adolescents. 32 beds for adolescents. Open year-round. Patient security: unlocked; no runaway pursuit. Small town setting. Not-for-profit facility affiliated with AHS- West, Roseville, CA. Licensed by state of Hawaii. Accredited by JCAHO.

Participants   Accepts: male and female adolescents ages 13–17. Average stay: 80 days. Admission: one parent, all parties who share custody, court order, depending on program. Treats learning disabilities; behavior disorders; general psychosocial disorders; substance abuse; compulsive/addictive disorders other than substance abuse and eating disorders; post-traumatic stress disorder; thought, mood, and personality disorders. Accepts the mobility impaired; those with a history of arson; the sexually compulsive; those with a history of harm to themselves and others; those receiving psychotropic medication; those with a history of epilepsy. Special programs for the mobility impaired; those with AIDS.

Program   Treatment modalities: Twelve Step Recovery; brief psychodynamic; cognitive. Family treatment program available.

Staff   Total facility staff includes 1 psychologist, 1 registered nurse, 2 teachers, 15 counselors, 1 occupational/recreational therapist, 1 therapist. Staff is 50% male, 50% female.

Facilities   Multiple buildings; males and females in coeducational units. Central dining. Basketball courts, game room, playing fields.

Education   Academic program available. Serves ages 13–17, ungraded. 2 teachers on staff. Cost of educational program covered by local school district.

Costs   Average cost: $30,000 per stay. Accepts private insurance, Blue Cross/Blue Shield, public funds.

Additional Services   Drug and alcohol rehabilitation services for males and females ages 12–17. Treats learning disabilities; behavior disorders; general psychosocial disorders; substance abuse; compulsive/addictive disorders other than substance abuse and eating disorders; post-traumatic stress disorder; thought, mood, and personality disorders.

Contact T. Orvin Fillman, Vice President, Behavioral Medicine Services, 640 Ulukahiki Street, Kailua, HI 96734. Phone: 808-263-5184. Fax: 808-263-5143.

BOURNEWOOD HOSPITAL
300 South Street
Brookline, Massachusetts 02167
617-469-0300; Fax: 617-469-5013

General Information Psychiatric hospital for adolescents. Patient security: entirely locked. Licensed by state of Massachusetts. Accredited by JCAHO.

Participants Accepts: male and female adolescents. Average stay: 19 days. Admission: one parent, all parties who share custody, court order, voluntary, depending on program. Treats autistic disorders; learning disabilities; behavior disorders; general psychosocial disorders; substance abuse; eating disorders; compulsive/addictive disorders other than substance abuse and eating disorders; post-traumatic stress disorder; thought, mood, and personality disorders.

Staff Staff is 50% male, 50% female.

Contact James Curran, Admissions Coordinator, 300 South Street, Brookline, MA 02167. Phone: 617-469-0300. Fax: 617-469-5013.

BOWLING GREEN ADOLESCENT CENTER
109 Jackson Road
Berlin, New Jersey 08009
609-767-3000; Fax: 609-753-9658

General Information Drug and alcohol rehabilitation center for adolescents. 24 beds for adolescents. Open year-round. Patient security: staff secured; will pursue and return runaways. Small town setting. For-profit facility affiliated with Comprehensive Addictive Programs, Vienna, VA. Licensed by state of New Jersey. Accredited by JCAHO.

Participants Accepts: male and female adolescents ages 12–18. Average stay: 42 days. Admission: one parent, all parties who share custody, court order, depending on program. Treats behavior disorders; general psychosocial disorders; substance abuse; eating disorders; compulsive/addictive disorders other than substance abuse and eating disorders. Accepts those receiving psychotropic medication. Largest

number of participants from New Jersey, Delaware, Pennsylvania.

Program Treatment modalities: Twelve Step Recovery; reality therapy; Gestalt; contextual family therapy. Family treatment program available.

Staff .3 full-time direct-care staff member per adolescent. Total facility staff includes 1 physician, 1 psychiatrist, 2 registered nurses, 4 practical/vocational nurses, 3 MSW social workers, 1 social worker (non-MSW), 4 teachers, 17 counselors, 2 occupational/recreational therapists, 1 dietician.

Facilities Multiple buildings. Central dining. Basketball courts, playing fields, ropes course.

Education Academic program available at no charge. Serves ages 12–18. 4 teachers on staff. Curriculum accredited or approved by New Jersey Department of Education. Cost of educational program sometimes covered by local school district. Organized sports program offered.

Costs Average cost: $17,000 per stay. Accepts private insurance, group insurance, Blue Cross/Blue Shield, public funds.

Additional Services Outpatient services for males and females ages 12–18. Treats learning disabilities; behavior disorders; general psychosocial disorders; substance abuse; eating disorders; compulsive/addictive disorders other than substance abuse and eating disorders; post-traumatic stress disorder; thought, mood, and personality disorders. Experiential therapy. Treats behavior disorders; general psychosocial disorders; substance abuse; eating disorders; compulsive/addictive disorders other than substance abuse and eating disorders.

Contact Steve Masapollo, Associate Executive Director, main address above. Phone: 800-232-2661. Fax: 609-753-9658.

BOYS TOWN OF MISSOURI, INC.
P.O. Box 189
St. James, Missouri 65559
314-265-3251; Fax: 314-265-5370

General Information Residential treatment/subacute facility for children, adolescents. 72 beds for children; 118 beds for adolescents; 190 beds total. Open year-round. Patient security: staff secured; will pursue and return runaways. Rural setting. Independent not-for-profit facility. Licensed by state of Missouri. Accredited by JCAHO.

Participants Accepts: male and female children ages 8–12; male and female adolescents ages 13–17. Admission: one parent, all parties who share custody, court order, depending on program. Treats learning disabilities; behavior disorders; general psychosocial disorders; substance abuse; compulsive/addictive disorders other than substance abuse and eating disorders; post-traumatic stress disorder; thought, mood, and personality disorders. Accepts the speech impaired; those with a history of arson; the sexually compulsive; those with a history of harm to themselves and others; those receiving psychotropic medication. Special programs for the speech impaired. Largest number of participants from Missouri.

Program Treatment modalities: therapeutic community; psychodynamic; sexual and substance abuse recovery program-group and psychoeducational methodologies. Family treatment program available.

Staff 1 full-time direct-care staff member per child or adolescent. Total facility staff includes 2 psychologists, 2 psychiatrists, 1 registered nurse, 4 practical/vocational nurses, 14 MSW social workers, 10 social workers (non-MSW), 21 teachers, 1 counselor, 2 occupational/recreational therapists, 1 speech pathologist, 123 other direct-care staff members. Staff is 40% male, 60% female.

Facilities Multiple buildings; males and females in separate units. Central dining. Basketball courts, game room, gymnasium, horseback riding, outdoor swimming pool, outdoor tennis courts, playing fields, ropes course, canoeing.

Education Academic program available at no charge. Serves ages 8–17, grades 2–12. 21 teachers on staff. Curriculum accredited or approved by Missouri Department of Elementary and Secondary Education. Cost of educational program covered by local school district. Organized sports program offered.

Costs Accepts private insurance, public funds.

Additional Services Drug and alcohol rehabilitation services for males and females ages 8–17. Treats learning disabilities; behavior disorders; general psychosocial disorders; substance abuse; eating disorders; compulsive/addictive disorders other than substance abuse and eating disorders; post-traumatic stress disorder; thought, mood, and personality disorders. Wilderness/survival program for males and females ages 8–17. Treats learning disabilities; behavior disorders; general psychosocial disorders; substance abuse; eating disorders; compulsive/addictive disorders other than substance abuse and eating disorders; post-traumatic stress disorder; thought, mood, and personality disorders.

Contact Judith L. Cavender, Director of Marketing, main address above. Phone: 314-265-3251. Fax: 314-265-5370.

THE BRADLEY CENTER, INC.
2000 Sixteenth Avenue
Columbus, Georgia 31993
706-649-6100; Fax: 706-649-6124

General Information Comprehensive mental health center for children, adolescents, adults. Open year-round. Patient security: partially locked; will pursue and return runaways. Suburban setting. Independent not-for-profit facility. Licensed by state of Georgia. Accredited by JCAHO.

Participants Accepts: male and female children ages 3–11; male and female adolescents ages 12–18; male and female adults ages 21 and up. Admission: one parent, all parties who share custody, voluntary, depending on program. Treats learning disabilities; behavior disorders; general psychosocial disorders; substance abuse; eating disorders; compulsive/addictive disorders other than substance abuse and eating disorders; post-traumatic stress disorder; thought, mood, and personality disorders.

Program Treatment modalities: general psychiatric diagnosis; dual diagnosis; open staff model of treatment; incorporation by request of religious or spiritual aspects in treatment. Family treatment program available.

Staff Total facility staff includes 13 psychologists, 5 psychiatrists, 39 registered nurses, 6 practical/vocational nurses, 12 MSW social workers, 6 teachers, 12 counselors, 7 occupational/recreational therapists, 2 dieticians, 26 other direct-care staff members.

Facilities Multiple buildings; males and females in coeducational units. Separate residential quarters for children and adolescents. Central dining (shared with adults). Basketball courts, game room, gymnasium, outdoor swimming pool, weight room.

Education Academic program available at no charge. Serves ages 8–17, grades 3–12. 6 teachers on staff. Curriculum accredited or approved by Georgia Board of Education.

Costs Accepts private insurance, group insurance, medicare, Blue Cross/Blue Shield.

Additional Services Drug and alcohol rehabilitation services for males and females ages 8 and up. Treats learning disabilities; behavior disorders; general psychosocial disorders; substance abuse; eating disorders; compulsive/addictive disorders other than substance abuse and eating disorders; post-traumatic stress disorder; thought, mood, and personality disorders. Outpatient services for males and females ages 3 and up. Treats learning disabilities; behavior disorders; general psychosocial disorders; substance abuse; eating disorders; compulsive/addictive disorders other than substance abuse and eating disorders; post-traumatic stress disorder; thought, mood, and personality disorders. Residential or sub-acute services for males and females ages 12–17. Treats learning disabilities; behavior disorders; general psychosocial disorders; substance abuse; eating disorders; compulsive/addictive disorders other than substance abuse and eating disorders; post-traumatic stress disorder; thought, mood, and personality disorders. Inpatient and day hospital treatment for males and females ages 8 and up. Treats learning disabilities; behavior disorders; general psychosocial disorders; substance abuse; eating disorders; compulsive/addictive disorders other than substance abuse and eating disorders; post-traumatic stress disorder; thought, mood, and personality disorders.

Contact Ruth Ann McCard, Marketing Director, main address above. Phone: 706-649-6100. Fax: 706-649-6124.

BRATTLEBORO RETREAT
75 Linden Street
Brattleboro, Vermont 05302
800-345-5550; Fax: 802-257-7785 Ext. 499

General Information Psychiatric hospital for children, adolescents, adults. 2 beds for children; 54 beds for adolescents; 130 beds total. Open year-round. Patient security: partially locked; will pursue and return runaways. Rural setting. Independent not-for-profit facility. Licensed by state of Vermont. Accredited by JCAHO; American Hospital Association.

Participants Accepts: male and female children ages 6–12; male and female adolescents ages 12–18; male and female adults ages 19–65. Average stay: 36 days. Admission: voluntary. Treats autistic disorders; learning disabilities; behavior disorders; general psychosocial disorders; substance abuse; eating disorders; compulsive/addictive disorders other than substance abuse and eating disorders; post-traumatic stress disorder; thought, mood, and personality disorders. Accepts the mobility impaired; those with a history of harm to themselves and others; those receiving psychotropic medication; those with a history of epilepsy.

Program Treatment modalities: psychodynamic; group therapy. Family treatment program available.

Staff Total facility staff includes 8 psychologists, 13 psychiatrists, 57 registered nurses, 12 MSW social workers, 8 teachers, 6 counselors, 1 dietician.

Facilities Multiple buildings; males and females in coeducational units. Separate residential quarters for children and adolescents. Separate dining by residential unit available. Basketball courts, game room, gymnasium, outdoor swimming pool, outdoor tennis courts, playing fields, ropes course.

Education Academic program available at additional cost. Serves ages 6–18, ungraded. 8 teachers on staff. Curriculum accredited or approved by State of Vermont. Cost of educational program covered by local school district.

Costs Accepts private insurance, group insurance, medicare, Blue Cross/Blue Shield.

Additional Services Residential or sub-acute services for males and females ages 12–18. Treats autistic disorders; learning disabilities; behavior disorders; general psychosocial disorders; substance abuse; eating disorders; compulsive/addictive disorders other than substance abuse and eating disorders; post-traumatic stress disorder; thought, mood, and personality disorders.

Contact Peter Albert, Director of Admissions, main address above. Phone: 800-345-5550. Fax: 802-257-7785 Ext. 499.

BRIDGES CENTER
30371 Morning View Drive
Malibu, California 90265
310-457-5802; Fax: 310-457-6093

General Information Residential treatment/subacute facility for adolescents. 6 beds for adolescents. Open year-round. Patient security: staff secured; will pursue and return runaways. Suburban setting. Independent for-profit facility. Licensed by state of California. Accredited by JCAHO.

Participants Accepts: male and female adolescents ages 12–17. Average stay: 120 days. Admission: one parent. Treats learning disabilities; behavior disorders; general psychosocial disorders; substance abuse; eating disorders; thought, mood, and personality disorders. Accepts the speech impaired; the sexually compulsive; those with a history of harm to themselves and others; those receiving psychotropic medication. Largest number of participants from California, New Mexico, Nevada.

Program Treatment modalities: eclectic psychodynamic; Twelve Step Recovery. Family treatment program available.

Staff Total facility staff includes 2 physicians, 3 psychologists, 3 psychiatrists, 2 registered nurses, 8 counselors, 1 occupational/recreational therapist, 1 speech pathologist, 1 dietician, 3 other direct-care staff members. Staff is 70% male, 30% female.

Facilities Multiple buildings; males and females in coeducational units. Central dining.

Education   Educational arrangements: local community schools. Educational program held off-site at additional cost. Cost of educational program sometimes covered by local school district. Organized sports program offered.

Costs   Average cost: $450 per day. Accepts private insurance, group insurance, Blue Cross/Blue Shield, public funds.

Contact   Martha Zimmerman, Admissions, P.O. Box 4233, Malibu, CA 90265. Phone: 310-457-5802. Fax: 310-457-6093.

BRIGHTON HOSPITAL ADOLESCENT CENTER
12851 East Grand River Avenue
Brighton, Michigan 48116
313-227-1211; Fax: 313-227-6893

General Information   Drug and alcohol rehabilitation center for adolescents. 20 beds for adolescents. Open year-round. Patient security arrangements vary depending on program; no runaway pursuit. Suburban setting. Not-for-profit facility affiliated with Brighton Hospital, Brighton, MI. Licensed by state of Michigan. Accredited by JCAHO; Michigan Departments of Social Services and of Public Health, Michigan Department of Substance Abuse Services.

Participants   Accepts: male and female adolescents ages 12–18. Average stay: 26 days. Admission: one parent, court order, depending on program. Treats substance abuse. Accepts the mobility impaired; the vision impaired; the hearing impaired; the speech impaired; those with a history of arson; the sexually compulsive; those with a history of harm to themselves and others; those receiving psychotropic medication; non-English speaking individuals; those with a history of epilepsy. Special programs for the mobility impaired; the vision impaired; the hearing impaired.

Program   Treatment modalities: Twelve Step Recovery; systemic/strategic family therapy; milieu therapy; cognitive-behavioral therapy. Family treatment program available.

Staff   Total facility staff includes 1 physician, 1 psychologist, 1 psychiatrist, 9 registered nurses, 4 MSW social workers, 1 social worker (non-MSW), 1 teacher, 3 counselors, 1 occupational/recreational therapist, 1 dietician, 7 other direct-care staff members.

Facilities   Single building; males and females in coeducational units. Central dining. Basketball courts, game room, gymnasium, outdoor tennis courts, playing fields, fishing lake, golf.

Education   Academic program available at no charge. Serves ages 12–18, ungraded. 1 teacher on staff. Organized sports program offered.

Costs   Average cost: $360 per day. Accepts private insurance, group insurance, Blue Cross/Blue Shield, public funds.

Contact   Bradley Casemore, Administrator, main address above. Phone: 313-227-1211. Fax: 313-227-6893.

BRIGHTSIDE, INC.
2112 Riverdale Street
West Springfield, Massachusetts 01089
413-788-7366; Fax: 413-747-0182

General Information   Residential treatment/subacute facility for children, adolescents. 39 beds for children; 31 beds for adolescents. Open year-round. Patient security: staff secured; will pursue and return runaways. Suburban setting. Not-for-profit facility affiliated with Sisters of Providence Health System, Springfield, MA. Licensed by state of Massachusetts. Accredited by Council on Accreditation of Services for Families and Children.

Participants   Accepts: male and female children ages 6–13; male adolescents ages 12–18. Average stay: 365 days. Admission: all parties who share custody. Treats learning disabilities; behavior disorders; general psychosocial disorders; compulsive/addictive disorders other than substance abuse and eating disorders; post-traumatic stress disorder; thought, mood, and personality disorders. Accepts those with a history of arson; the sexually compulsive; those with a history of harm to themselves and others; those receiving psychotropic medication. Largest number of participants from Massachusetts, Connecticut, New Hampshire.

Program   Treatment modalities: solution focused/outcome oriented; psychodynamic; behavioral. Family treatment program available.

Staff   1.2 full-time direct-care staff members per child or adolescent. Total facility staff includes 1 physician, 1 psychologist, 1 psychiatrist, 1 registered nurse, 20 MSW social workers, 30 social workers (non-MSW), 10 teachers, 70 counselors, 1 occupational/recreational therapist, 1 dietician. Staff is 45% male, 55% female.

Facilities   Multiple buildings; males and females in coeducational units. Central dining (shared with adults), separate dining by residential unit available. Basketball courts, game room, gymnasium, outdoor swimming pool, playing fields, ropes course.

Education Academic program available at additional cost. Serves ages 6–18, ungraded. 10 teachers on staff. Curriculum accredited or approved by Massachusetts Department of Education. Cost of educational program covered by local school district. Organized sports program offered.

Costs Average cost: $60,000 per stay. Accepts private insurance, group insurance, medicaid, Blue Cross/Blue Shield, public funds.

Additional Services Outpatient services for males and females ages 3–99. Treats learning disabilities; behavior disorders; general psychosocial disorders; substance abuse; eating disorders; compulsive/addictive disorders other than substance abuse and eating disorders; post-traumatic stress disorder; thought, mood, and personality disorders.

Contact John Ten Brook, Director of Marketing, main address above. Phone: 413-788-7366. Fax: 413-747-0182.

BROAD HORIZONS OF RAMONA, INC.
1236 H Street
Ramona, California 92065
619-789-7060; Fax: 619-789-4062

General Information Residential treatment/subacute facility for adolescents. Patient security: staff secured. For-profit facility affiliated with Pricor, Murfreesboro, TN. Licensed by state of California. Accredited by JCAHO.

Participants Accepts: male and female adolescents. Average stay: 3 months. Admission: one parent, all parties who share custody, court order, depending on program. Treats learning disabilities; behavior disorders; general psychosocial disorders; substance abuse; eating disorders; compulsive/addictive disorders other than substance abuse and eating disorders; post-traumatic stress disorder; thought, mood, and personality disorders.

Contact Admissions, P.O. Box 1920, Ramona, CA 92065. Phone: 619-789-7060.

BROCKHURST EXTENDED CARE PROGRAMS
10460 West Highway 24
Green Mountain Falls, Colorado 80819
800-223-9421; Fax: 719-636-8871

General Information Residential treatment/subacute facility for adolescents. 20 beds for adolescents.

Open year-round. Patient security: staff secured; will pursue and return runaways. Rural setting. Not-for-profit facility affiliated with Penrose—St. Francis Healthcare System, Colorado Springs, CO. Licensed by state of Colorado. Accredited by JCAHO; Civilian Health and Medical Program of the Uniformed Services.

Participants Accepts: male and female adolescents ages 13–18. Average stay: 4 months. Admission: one parent, all parties who share custody, depending on program. Treats behavior disorders; general psychosocial disorders; substance abuse; post-traumatic stress disorder; thought, mood, and personality disorders.

Program Treatment modalities: Twelve Step Recovery; behavioral cognitive. Family treatment program available.

Staff .5 full-time direct-care staff member per adolescent. Total facility staff includes 1 psychiatrist, 5 registered nurses, 1 MSW social worker, 1 teacher, 5 counselors, 1 occupational/recreational therapist, 1 therapist, 1 dietician. Staff is 40% male, 60% female.

Facilities Multiple buildings. Central dining. Basketball courts, game room, horseback riding, playing fields, ropes course, volleyball.

Education Academic program available at no charge. Serves ages 13–18, grades 7–12. 1 teacher on staff. Curriculum accredited or approved by State of Colorado. Organized sports program offered.

Costs Accepts private insurance, group insurance.

Additional Services Drug and alcohol rehabilitation services for males and females ages 13–18. Treats behavior disorders; general psychosocial disorders; substance abuse; post-traumatic stress disorder; thought, mood, and personality disorders.

Contact Barry Schultz, Manager, main address above. Phone: 719-684-9421. Fax: 719-634-6022.

BROOK LANE PSYCHIATRIC CENTER
13218 Brook Lane Drive
Hagerstown, Maryland 21742
301-733-0330; Fax: 301-733-4038

General Information Psychiatric hospital for children, adolescents. Patient security: staff secured. Independent not-for-profit facility. Licensed by state of Maryland. Accredited by JCAHO.

Participants Accepts: male and female children; male and female adolescents. Average stay: 40 days. Admission: one parent, all parties who share custody, court order, voluntary, depending on program. Treats autistic disorders; learning disabilities; behavior disorders; general psychosocial disorders; substance abuse; eating disorders; compulsive/addictive disorders other than substance abuse and eating disorders; post-traumatic stress disorder; thought, mood, and personality disorders.

Costs   Average cost: $525 per day.

Additional Services   Outpatient services for males and females ages 3–18. Treats autistic disorders; learning disabilities; behavior disorders; general psychosocial disorders; substance abuse; eating disorders; compulsive/addictive disorders other than substance abuse and eating disorders; post-traumatic stress disorder; thought, mood, and personality disorders.

Contact   Ken Toms, Evaluations and Admissions Coordinator, P.O. Box 1945, Hagerstown, MD 21742. Phone: 301-733-0330. Fax: 301-733-4038.

BROOKLAWN ACADEMY
2125 Goldsmith Lane
Louisville, Kentucky 40232
502-451-5177

General Information   Residential treatment/subacute facility for adolescents. 16 beds for adolescents. Independent not-for-profit facility. Licensed by state of Kentucky. Accredited by JCAHO.

Participants   Accepts: male adolescents. Average stay: 6 months. Admission: one parent, all parties who share custody, court order, voluntary, depending on program. Treats learning disabilities; behavior disorders; general psychosocial disorders; substance abuse; compulsive/addictive disorders other than substance abuse and eating disorders; thought, mood, and personality disorders.

Staff   1 full-time direct-care staff member per adolescent. Staff is 50% male, 50% female.

Costs   Average cost: $275 per day.

Contact   David Turner, Clinical Director, main address above. Phone: 502-451-5177.

BRUCE HALL—CENTER FOR TREATMENT OF ALCOHOL AND DRUG DEPENDENCY
601 Gregg Avenue
Florence, South Carolina 29501
803-664-3240; Fax: 803-661-4375

General Information   Inpatient alcohol and drug treatment facility for adolescents. 12 beds for adolescents. Patient security: staff secured. Independent not-for-profit facility. Licensed by state of South Carolina. Accredited by JCAHO.

Participants   Accepts: male and female adolescents. Average stay: 31 days. Admission: one parent, all parties who share custody, court order, voluntary, depending on program. Treats behavior disorders; general psychosocial disorders; substance abuse; eating disorders; compulsive/addictive disorders other than substance abuse and eating disorders; post-traumatic stress disorder.

Staff   Staff is 30% male, 70% female.

Contact   Gary Martin, Treatment Administrator, main address above. Phone: 800-221-8108.

BRUNSWICK HALL
80 Louden Avenue
Amityville, New York 11701
516-789-7000

General Information   Psychiatric hospital for adolescents. Patient security: staff secured. For-profit facility affiliated with Brunswick Hospital Center, Amityville, NY. Licensed by state of New York. Accredited by JCAHO.

Participants   Accepts: male and female adolescents. Average stay: 40 days. Admission: one parent. Treats behavior disorders; general psychosocial disorders; substance abuse; eating disorders; compulsive/addictive disorders other than substance abuse and eating disorders; post-traumatic stress disorder; thought, mood, and personality disorders.

Staff   Staff is 50% male, 50% female.

Costs   Average cost: $500 per day.

Contact   Admitting Office, main address above. Phone: 516-789-7000.

THE BRUNSWICK HOSPITAL ADOLESCENT PSYCHIATRIC UNIT
P.O. Box 139
Supply, North Carolina 28462
919-754-9809

General Information   General hospital for adolescents. 12 beds for adolescents. Open year-round. Patient security: entirely locked; will pursue and return runaways. Rural setting. Independent for-profit facility. Licensed by state of North Carolina. Accredited by JCAHO.

Participants   Accepts: male and female adolescents ages 13–17. Average stay: 30 days. Admission: one parent, all parties who share custody, depending on program. Treats behavior disorders; general psychosocial disorders; eating disorders; compulsive/addictive disorders other than substance abuse and eating disorders; post-traumatic stress disorder; thought, mood, and personality disorders. Accepts the mobility impaired; the vision impaired; the hearing impaired; the speech impaired; those with a history of arson; the sexually compulsive; those with a history of harm to themselves and others; those receiving psychotropic medication; those with a history of epilepsy.

Program   Treatment modalities: family system approach; crisis stabilization. Family treatment program available.

Staff   1.6 full-time direct-care staff members per adolescent. Total facility staff includes 1 physician, 1 psychologist, 1 psychiatrist, 2 registered nurses, 3 practical/vocational nurses, 1 MSW social worker, 8 counselors, 1 occupational/recreational therapist, 1 therapist. Staff is 40% male, 60% female.

Facilities   Multiple buildings; males and females in coeducational units.

Education   Academic program available at no charge. Serves ages 13–17, ungraded.

Costs   Accepts private insurance, group insurance, medicaid, Blue Cross/Blue Shield.

Contact   Admissions Coordinator, main address above. Phone: 919-754-9809.

BRUSH RANCH SCHOOL
Highway 63
Terrero, New Mexico 87573
505-757-6114; Fax: 505-757-6118

General Information   School for children, adolescents. Open academic year. Patient security: staff secured; will pursue and return runaways. Rural setting. Independent not-for-profit facility. Licensed by state of New Mexico.

Participants   Accepts: male and female children and adolescents ages 10–18. Average stay: 2 years. Admission: voluntary. Treats learning disabilities; behavior disorders. Accepts the vision impaired; the hearing impaired; the speech impaired; those receiving psychotropic medication; those with a history of epilepsy.

Program   Treatment modalities: multi modality; structure; behavior modification.

Staff   Total facility staff includes 2 registered nurses, 5 teachers, 15 counselors, 4 other direct-care staff members. Staff is 50% male, 50% female.

Facilities   Multiple buildings; males and females in separate units. Central dining. Basketball courts, game room, horseback riding, outdoor swimming pool, outdoor tennis courts, playing fields, ropes course.

Education   School serves ages 10–18, grades 4–12. 5 teachers on staff. Curriculum is college-preparatory; diploma granted upon completion. Curriculum accredited or approved by North Central Association of Colleges and Schools, State Board of Education. Organized sports program offered.

Costs   Average cost: $21,000 per stay. Accepts private insurance, group insurance.

Contact   David M. Floyd, Director, P.O. Box 2450, Santa Fe, NM 87504. Phone: 505-757-6114. Fax: 505-757-6118.

BRYNN MARR HOSPITAL
192 Village Drive
Jacksonville, North Carolina 28546
919-577-1400; Fax: 919-577-7365

General Information   Psychiatric hospital for children, adolescents, adults. 15 beds for children; 24 beds for adolescents; 76 beds total. Open year-round. Patient security: entirely locked; no runaway pursuit. Urban setting. For-profit facility affiliated with Ramsey Health Care, Inc., New Orleans, LA. Licensed by state of North Carolina. Accredited by JCAHO; National Association of Private Psychiatric Hospitals.

Participants   Accepts: male and female children ages 3–12; male and female adolescents ages 13–17; male and female adults ages 18 and up. Average stay: 30 days. Admission: all parties who share custody, court order, depending on program. Treats learning disabilities; behavior disorders; general psychosocial disorders; substance abuse; eating disorders; post-traumatic stress disorder; thought, mood, and personality disorders. Accepts the mobility impaired; the hearing impaired; those with a history of arson; those with a history of harm to themselves and others. Largest number of participants from North Carolina, Virginia, South Carolina.

Program Treatment modalities: Twelve Step Recovery; psychodynamic. Family treatment program available.

Staff .1 full-time direct-care staff member per child or adolescent. Total facility staff includes 3 physicians, 1 psychologist, 3 psychiatrists, 38 registered nurses, 10 practical/vocational nurses, 1 MSW social worker, 2 social workers (non-MSW), 3 teachers, 26 counselors, 3 occupational/recreational therapists, 1 dietician.

Facilities Single building; males and females in coeducational units. Separate residential quarters for children and adolescents. Separate dining by residential unit available. Basketball courts, gymnasium, horseback riding, playing fields, ropes course.

Education Academic program available at no charge. Serves ages 5–18, grades K–12. 3 teachers on staff. Curriculum accredited or approved by State of North Carolina.

Costs Average cost: $600 per day. Accepts private insurance, medicare, medicaid, Blue Cross/Blue Shield.

Additional Services Drug and alcohol rehabilitation services for males and females ages 5–17. Treats learning disabilities; behavior disorders; general psychosocial disorders; substance abuse; eating disorders; compulsive/addictive disorders other than substance abuse and eating disorders; post-traumatic stress disorder; thought, mood, and personality disorders. Outpatient services for males and females ages 12–17. Treats learning disabilities; behavior disorders; general psychosocial disorders; substance abuse; eating disorders; compulsive/addictive disorders other than substance abuse and eating disorders; post-traumatic stress disorder; thought, mood, and personality disorders. Camping program for males and females ages 5–12. Treats learning disabilities; behavior disorders.

Contact Bill Bauer, Director of Helpline, main address above. Phone: 919-577-1900.

BUCKEYE BOYS RANCH, INC.
5665 Hoover Road
Grove City, Ohio 43123
614-875-2371; Fax: 614-875-2116

General Information Residential treatment/subacute facility for children, adolescents. Open year-round. Patient security arrangements vary depending on program; no runaway pursuit. Suburban setting. Independent not-for-profit facility. Licensed by state of Ohio. Accredited by JCAHO.

Participants Accepts: male and female children ages 10–12; male and female adolescents ages 13–18. Admission: one parent, all parties who share custody, court order, custody of public agency, depending on program. Treats learning disabilities; behavior disorders; general psychosocial disorders; substance abuse; eating disorders; post-traumatic stress disorder; thought, mood, and personality disorders. Accepts the hearing impaired; those with a history of harm to themselves and others; those receiving psychotropic medication. Special programs for the hearing impaired. Largest number of participants from Ohio, Indiana, West Virginia.

Program Treatment modalities: family systems approach. Family treatment program available.

Staff Total facility staff includes 1 physician, 1 psychologist, 4 psychiatrists, 8 registered nurses, 6 MSW social workers, 15 teachers, 6 counselors, 4 occupational/recreational therapists, 1 speech pathologist, 1 dietician, 75 other direct-care staff members. Staff is 60% male, 40% female.

Facilities Multiple buildings; males and females in coeducational units. Central dining. Basketball courts, game room, gymnasium, outdoor swimming pool, outdoor tennis courts, playing fields, ropes course, creative arts center.

Education Academic program available at additional cost. Serves ages 10–17, ungraded. 15 teachers on staff. Curriculum accredited or approved by Ohio Department of Education. Organized sports program offered.

Costs Accepts private insurance, group insurance, Blue Cross/Blue Shield, public funds.

Contact Sally Pedon, Director of Admissions, main address above. Phone: 614-875-2371. Fax: 614-875-2116.

BUCKSKIN, INC.
Box 389
Ely, Minnesota 55731
218-365-2121

General Information Camp for children, adolescents. Open summer. Patient security: staff secured; will pursue and return runaways. Rural setting. Independent for-profit facility. Licensed by state of Minnesota. Accredited by American Camping Association.

Participants Accepts: male and female children ages 6–12; male and female adolescents ages 12–18. Average stay: 32 days. Admission: one parent, all parties who share custody, depending on program. Treats learning disabilities; behavior disorders; general psychosocial disorders. Accepts those receiving psychotropic medication. Special programs for the developmentally disabled. Largest number of participants from Minnesota, Illinois, Arizona.

Program Treatment modalities: behaviorally based cognitive approach.

Staff .4 full-time direct-care staff member per child or adolescent. Total facility staff includes 1 registered nurse, 1 practical/vocational nurse, 8 teachers, 44 counselors, 1 occupational/recreational therapist, 9 other direct-care staff members. Staff is 50% male, 50% female.

Facilities Multiple buildings; males and females in separate units. Central dining. Basketball courts, game room, playing fields, lake for canoeing/swimming, archery/riflery ranges, nature/hiking trails, wilderness area for camping.

Education Academic program available at no charge. Serves ages 6–18, ungraded. 8 teachers on staff. Curriculum accredited or approved by Minnesota Department of Education. Cost of educational program sometimes covered by local school district. Organized sports program offered.

Costs Average cost: $1750 per stay. Accepts public funds.

Contact Thomas R. Bauer, Assistant Director, main address above. Phone: 612-536-9749.

Announcement Buckskin serves youth with academic and/or social skill difficulties. The primary goals are to develop self-confidence, improve social skills, and enhance self-esteem. Both academic and traditional campus activities are available, in large and small group settings. The 1:3 staff to camper ratio provides ample individual attention and support.

BUENA VISTA ACADEMY
3213 Buena Vista Terrace, SE
Washington, D.C. 20032
202-889-4037; Fax: 202-682-3929

General Information Residential treatment/subacute facility for adolescents. 10 beds for adolescents. Open year-round. Patient security: staff secured; will pursue and return runaways. Urban setting. Affiliated with Metropolitan Health Associates, Inc., Washing-

ton, DC. Licensed by District of Columbia. Accredited by JCAHO.

Participants Accepts: female adolescents ages 13–18. Average stay: 1 year. Admission: all parties who share custody, court order, depending on program. Treats behavior disorders; general psychosocial disorders; substance abuse; eating disorders; compulsive/addictive disorders other than substance abuse and eating disorders; thought, mood, and personality disorders. Largest number of participants from D.C.

Program Family treatment program available.

Staff 2.6 full-time direct-care staff members per adolescent. Total facility staff includes 1 physician, 2 psychologists, 2 psychiatrists, 8 registered nurses, 2 MSW social workers, 3 teachers, 12 counselors, 1 physical therapist, 1 speech pathologist, 1 dietician. Staff is 30% male, 70% female.

Facilities Multiple buildings. Central dining. Basketball courts, game room, gymnasium.

Education Academic program available. Serves ages 13–18, ungraded. 3 teachers on staff. Curriculum accredited or approved by Washington, D.C. Public School System. Organized sports program offered.

Costs Average cost: $320 per day. Accepts private insurance, group insurance, medicare, medicaid, Blue Cross/Blue Shield, public funds.

Contact Earnest A. Green, President, main address above. Phone: 202-371-2816. Fax: 202-682-3929.

BUTLER HOSPITAL
345 Blackstone Boulevard
Providence, Rhode Island 02906
401-455-6200; Fax: 401-455-6293

General Information Psychiatric hospital for adolescents, adults. 12 beds for adolescents. Open year-round. Patient security: staff secured; will pursue and return runaways. Urban setting. Independent not-for-profit facility. Licensed by state of Rhode Island. Accredited by JCAHO.

Participants Accepts: male and female adolescents ages 13–17; male and female adults ages 18 and up. Average stay: 10 days. Treats general psychosocial disorders; substance abuse; eating disorders; compulsive/addictive disorders other than substance abuse and eating disorders; post-traumatic stress disorder; thought, mood, and personality disorders.

Program Family treatment program available.

Facilities Multiple buildings; males and females in coeducational units. Central dining (shared with adults). Gymnasium, playing fields.

Education Educational arrangements: tutoring by school district if stay is over 3 weeks.

Costs Accepts private insurance, group insurance, medicare, medicaid, Blue Cross/Blue Shield, public funds.

Additional Services Drug and alcohol rehabilitation services for males and females ages 13 and up. Treats general psychosocial disorders; substance abuse; eating disorders; compulsive/addictive disorders other than substance abuse and eating disorders; post-traumatic stress disorder; thought, mood, and personality disorders.

Contact James Hallan Jr., Director of Public Relations, main address above. Phone: 401-455-6265. Fax: 401-455-6293.

CAMELOT CARE CENTER, INC.
1502 North Northwest Highway
Palatine, Illinois 60067
708-359-5600; Fax: 708-359-2759

General Information Residential treatment/subacute facility for children, adolescents. 8 beds for children; 14 beds for adolescents; 22 beds total. Open year-round. Patient security: staff secured; will pursue and return runaways. Suburban setting. For-profit facility affiliated with Camelot Care Centers, Inc., Seminole, FL. Licensed by state of Illinois. Accredited by JCAHO; Civilian Health and Medical Program of the Uniformed Services.

Participants Accepts: male and female children ages 5–12; male and female adolescents ages 13–18. Average stay: 150 days. Admission: one parent, all parties who share custody, depending on program. Treats learning disabilities; behavior disorders; general psychosocial disorders; substance abuse; eating disorders; compulsive/addictive disorders other than substance abuse and eating disorders; post-traumatic stress disorder; thought, mood, and personality disorders. Accepts the speech impaired; those with a history of arson; the sexually compulsive; those with a history of harm to themselves and others; those receiving psychotropic medication; those with a history of epilepsy. Largest number of participants from Illinois, Indiana, Wisconsin.

Program Treatment modalities: process therapy/behavioral-developmental approach. Family treatment program available.

Staff Total facility staff includes 2 physicians, 1 psychologist, 1 psychiatrist, 6 registered nurses, 1 MSW social worker, 4 social workers (non-MSW), 6 teachers, 3 counselors, 1 occupational/recreational therapist, 1 speech pathologist, 1 dietician, 34 other direct-care staff members. Staff is 17% male, 83% female.

Facilities Multiple buildings; males and females in coeducational units. Separate dining by residential unit available. Basketball courts, game room, gymnasium, horseback riding, indoor swimming pool, outdoor swimming pool, outdoor tennis courts, playing fields.

Education Academic program available at additional cost. Serves ages 5–18, grades K–12. 6 teachers on staff. Curriculum accredited or approved by Illinois State Board of Education, North Central Association of Colleges and Schools. Cost of educational program sometimes covered by local school district. Organized sports program offered.

Costs Average cost: $66,000 per stay. Accepts private insurance, group insurance, Blue Cross/Blue Shield, public funds.

Additional Services Outpatient services for males and females ages 5–18. Treats learning disabilities; behavior disorders; general psychosocial disorders; substance abuse; eating disorders; compulsive/addictive disorders other than substance abuse and eating disorders; post-traumatic stress disorder; thought, mood, and personality disorders. Partial hospitalization and therapeutic day school for males and females ages 5–18. Treats learning disabilities; behavior disorders; general psychosocial disorders; substance abuse; eating disorders; compulsive/addictive disorders other than substance abuse and eating disorders; post-traumatic stress disorder; thought, mood, and personality disorders.

Contact Liz Doyle, Director of Social Services, main address above. Phone: 708-359-5600. Fax: 708-359-2759.

CAMELOT CARE CENTER, INC.
Route 3
Box 267-C
Kingston, Tennessee 37763
615-376-2296; Fax: 615-376-1850

General Information Residential treatment facility with partial hospitalization program and outpatient services for children, adolescents. Patient security: staff secured. Independent for-profit facility. Licensed by state of Tennessee. Accredited by JCAHO.

Participants Accepts: male and female children; male and female adolescents. Average stay: 3 months. Admission: one parent, voluntary, depending on program. Treats autistic disorders; learning disabilities; behavior disorders; general psychosocial disorders; substance abuse; eating disorders; compulsive/addictive disorders other than substance abuse and eating disorders; post-traumatic stress disorder; thought, mood, and personality disorders.

Contact Kerry Knight, Director of Admission, main address above. Phone: 615-376-2296.

CAMP BARNEY MEDINTZ
Route 3
Box 3828
Cleveland, Georgia 30528
706-865-2715; Fax: 706-865-1495

General Information Camp for children, adolescents. Patient security: partially locked. Independent not-for-profit facility affiliated with Atlanta Jewish Community Center, Atlanta, GA. Licensed by state of Georgia. Accredited by American Camping Association.

Participants Accepts: male and female children; male and female adolescents. Average stay: 4 weeks. Admission: voluntary. Treats learning disabilities; behavior disorders.

Staff Staff is 50% male, 50% female.

Costs Average cost: $1400 per stay.

Contact Mike Wolff, Assistant Director, 1745 Peachtree Road NE, Atlanta, GA 30309. Phone: 404-875-7881. Fax: 404-898-9612.

Announcement Designed for children with special needs to experience summer in a mainstreamed environment, with peers and at their own pace. Children must be independent in most self-care skills and ambulatory. Staff supervision by professionals. Children participate in all activities: waterfront, arts, music, drama, horseback riding, recreation, nature crafts.

CAMP CUMMINGS
Ballyhack Road
Brewster, New York 10509
914-279-4811

General Information Camp for children, adolescents, adults. 60 beds for children; 90 beds for adolescents; 240 beds total. Open summer. Patient security: staff secured; will pursue and return runaways. Rural setting. Not-for-profit facility affiliated with The

Educational Alliance, New York, NY. Licensed by state of New York.

Participants Accepts: male and female children ages 8–16; male and female adolescents ages 14–22; male and female adults ages 18–85. Average stay: 26 days. Admission: one parent, social worker or agency, depending on program. Treats autistic disorders; learning disabilities. Accepts the speech impaired; those with a history of epilepsy. Special programs for the developmentally disabled. Largest number of participants from New York, New Jersey, Connecticut.

Program Treatment modalities: behavior modification; therapeutic recreation; group dynamics. Family treatment program available.

Staff Total facility staff includes 1 physician, 1 psychologist, 2 registered nurses, 3 practical/vocational nurses, 2 MSW social workers, 2 teachers, 90 counselors, 1 occupational/recreational therapist, 1 speech pathologist, 10 other direct-care staff members.

Facilities Multiple buildings; males and females in coeducational units. Separate residential quarters for children and adolescents. Central dining arrangements vary. Basketball courts, game room, gymnasium, playing fields, obstacle course.

Education Academic program available at no charge. Serves ages 8–16, ungraded. 2 teachers on staff. Organized sports program offered.

Costs Average cost: $400 per week. Accepts public funds.

Contact Barbara L. Kirsh, Director, main address above. Phone: 212-475-6200 Ext. 381. Fax: 212-529-1745.

CAMP E-HOW-KEE
397 Culbreath Road
Brooksville, Florida 34602
800-554-4357

General Information Wilderness/survival program for children, adolescents. Open year-round. Patient security: staff secured; will pursue and return runaways. Rural setting. Not-for-profit facility affiliated with Eckerd Family Youth Alternatives, Inc., Clearwater, FL. Licensed by state of Florida.

Participants Accepts: male children ages 10–12; male adolescents ages 13–17. Average stay: 365 days. Admission: all parties who share custody, voluntary, depending on program. Treats learning disabilities; behavior disorders; general psychosocial disorders.

Program Treatment modalities: Twelve Step Recovery/control theory; reality therapy; Carl Rogers;

guided group interaction. Family treatment program available.

Staff Total facility staff includes 1 psychologist, 1 psychiatrist, 1 registered nurse, 4 social workers (non-MSW), 5 teachers, 17 counselors, 3 other direct-care staff members. Staff is 51% male, 49% female.

Facilities Multiple buildings. Playing fields, ropes course.

Education Academic program available at no charge. Serves ages 10–17, grades 3–12. 5 teachers on staff. Curriculum accredited or approved by State of Florida, Department of Education and the Southern Association of Colleges and Schools.

Costs Average cost: $100 per day. Accepts private insurance, group insurance, public funds.

Contact Dwight Lord, Director of Admissions, P.O. Box 7450, Clearwater, FL 34618-7450. Phone: 800-554-4357. Fax: 813-442-5911.

CAMP E-HUN-TEE
One Camp E-Hun-Tee Place
Exeter, Rhode Island 02882
800-554-4357

General Information Wilderness/survival program for children, adolescents. Open year-round. Patient security: staff secured; will pursue and return runaways. Rural setting. Not-for-profit facility affiliated with Eckerd Family Youth Alternatives, Inc., Clearwater, FL. Licensed by state of Rhode Island.

Participants Accepts: male and female children ages 10–12; male and female adolescents ages 13–17. Admission: all parties who share custody, voluntary, depending on program. Treats learning disabilities; behavior disorders; general psychosocial disorders.

Program Treatment modalities: Twelve Step Recovery/control theory; reality therapy; Carl Rogers; guided group interaction. Family treatment program available.

Staff Total facility staff includes 1 psychologist, 1 psychiatrist, 1 registered nurse, 1 MSW social worker, 4 social workers (non-MSW), 2 teachers, 15 counselors, 3 other direct-care staff members. Staff is 51% male, 49% female.

Facilities Multiple buildings; males and females in separate units. Playing fields, ropes course, canoeing, backpacking.

Education Academic program available at no charge. Serves ages 10–17, grades 3–12. 2 teachers on staff. Curriculum accredited or approved by Department of Education.

Costs Average cost: $100 per day. Accepts private insurance, group insurance, public funds.

Contact Dwight Lord, Director of Admissions, P.O. Box 7450, Clearwater, FL 34618-7450. Phone: 800-554-4357. Fax: 813-442-5911.

CAMP E-KEL-ETU
Route 3
Box 6550
Silver Springs, Florida 32688
800-554-4357

General Information Wilderness/survival program for children, adolescents. Open year-round. Patient security: staff secured; will pursue and return runaways. Rural setting. Not-for-profit facility affiliated with Eckerd Family Youth Alternatives, Inc., Clearwater, FL. Licensed by state of Florida.

Participants Accepts: male children ages 10–12; male adolescents ages 13–17. Average stay: 365 days. Admission: all parties who share custody, voluntary, depending on program. Treats learning disabilities; behavior disorders; general psychosocial disorders.

Program Treatment modalities: Twelve Step Recovery/control theory; reality therapy; Carl Rogers; guided group interaction. Family treatment program available.

Staff Total facility staff includes 1 psychologist, 1 psychiatrist, 1 registered nurse, 4 social workers (non-MSW), 5 teachers, 17 counselors, 3 other direct-care staff members. Staff is 53% male, 47% female.

Facilities Multiple buildings. Playing fields, ropes course, canoeing, backpacking.

Education Academic program available at no charge. Serves ages 10–17, grades 3–12. 5 teachers on staff. Curriculum accredited or approved by State of Florida, Department of Education and the Southern Association of Colleges and Schools.

Costs Average cost: $100 per day. Accepts private insurance, group insurance, public funds.

Contact Dwight Lord, Director of Admissions, P.O. Box 7450, Clearwater, FL 34618-7450. Phone: 800-554-4357. Fax: 813-442-5911.

CAMP E-KU-SUMEE
Route 3
Box 460
Candor, North Carolina 27229
800-554-4357

General Information Wilderness/survival program for children, adolescents. Open year-round. Patient security: staff secured; will pursue and return runaways. Rural setting. Not-for-profit facility affiliated with Eckerd Family Youth Alternatives, Inc., Clearwater, FL. Licensed by state of North Carolina.

Participants Accepts: male children ages 10–12; male adolescents ages 13–17. Average stay: 365 days. Admission: all parties who share custody, voluntary, depending on program. Treats learning disabilities; behavior disorders; general psychosocial disorders.

Program Treatment modalities: Twelve Step Recovery/control theory; reality therapy; Carl Rogers; guided group interaction. Family treatment program available.

Staff Total facility staff includes 1 psychologist, 1 psychiatrist, 1 registered nurse, 4 social workers (non-MSW), 5 teachers, 17 counselors, 3 other direct-care staff members. Staff is 53% male, 47% female.

Facilities Multiple buildings. Playing fields, ropes course, canoeing, backpacking.

Education Academic program available at no charge. Serves ages 10–17, grades 3–12. 5 teachers on staff. Curriculum accredited or approved by Southern Association of Colleges and Schools.

Costs Average cost: $100 per day. Accepts private insurance, group insurance, public funds.

Contact Dwight Lord, Director of Admissions, P.O. Box 7450, Clearwater, FL 34618-7450. Phone: 800-554-4357. Fax: 813-442-5911.

CAMP ELLIOTT WILDERNESS PROGRAM
601 Camp Elliott Road
Black Mountain, North Carolina 28711
704-669-8639; Fax: 704-669-4067

General Information Residential treatment/subacute facility for adolescents. 10 beds for adolescents. Open year-round. Patient security: unlocked; will pursue and return runaways. Rural setting. Independent not-for-profit facility affiliated with Talisman School, Inc., Black Mountain, NC. Licensed by state of North Carolina.

Participants Accepts: male adolescents ages 10–17. Average stay: 14 months. Admission: all parties who share custody. Treats learning disabilities; behavior disorders. Accepts the sexually compulsive.

Program Treatment modalities: group dynamics; positive peer culture.

Staff Total facility staff includes 1 registered nurse, 1 MSW social worker, 1 teacher, 6 counselors.

Facilities Multiple buildings. Game room, playing fields, lake.

Education Academic program available at no charge. Serves ages 10–17, grades 4–12. 1 teacher on staff. Curriculum accredited or approved by North Carolina Department of Education.

Costs Average cost: $3500 per month.

Contact Catherine Buie, Director, main address above. Phone: 704-669-8639. Fax: 704-669-4067.

CAMP E-MA-CHAMEE
Route 1
Box 178B
Milton, Florida 32570
800-554-4357

General Information Wilderness/survival program for children, adolescents. Open year-round. Patient security: staff secured; will pursue and return runaways. Rural setting. Not-for-profit facility affiliated with Eckerd Family Youth Alternatives, Inc., Clearwater, FL. Licensed by state of Florida.

Participants Accepts: male and female children ages 10–12; male and female adolescents ages 13–17. Average stay: 365 days. Admission: all parties who share custody, voluntary, depending on program. Treats learning disabilities; behavior disorders; general psychosocial disorders.

Program Treatment modalities: Twelve Step Recovery/control theory; reality therapy; Carl Rogers; guided group interaction. Family treatment program available.

Staff Total facility staff includes 1 psychologist, 1 psychiatrist, 1 registered nurse, 4 social workers (non-MSW), 5 teachers, 17 counselors, 3 other direct-care staff members. Staff is 47% male, 53% female.

Facilities Multiple buildings; males and females in separate units. Playing fields, ropes course, canoeing, backpacking.

Education Academic program available at no charge. Serves ages 10–17, grades 3–12. 5 teachers on staff. Curriculum accredited or approved by State of Florida, Department of Education and the Southern Association of Colleges and Schools.

Costs Average cost: $100 per day. Accepts private insurance, group insurance, public funds.

Contact Dwight Lord, Director of Admissions, P.O. Box 7450, Clearwater, FL 34618-7450. Phone: 800-554-4357. Fax: 813-442-5911.

CAMP E-MUN-TALEE
Route 1
Box 270
Lowgap, North Carolina 27024
800-554-4357

General Information Wilderness/survival program for children, adolescents. Open year-round. Patient security: staff secured; will pursue and return runaways. Rural setting. Not-for-profit facility affiliated with Eckerd Family Youth Alternatives, Inc., Clearwater, FL. Licensed by state of North Carolina.

Participants Accepts: male children ages 10–12; male adolescents ages 13–17. Average stay: 365 days. Admission: all parties who share custody, voluntary, depending on program. Treats learning disabilities; behavior disorders; general psychosocial disorders.

Program Treatment modalities: Twelve Step Recovery/control theory; reality therapy; Carl Rogers; guided group interaction. Family treatment program available.

Staff Total facility staff includes 1 psychologist, 1 psychiatrist, 1 registered nurse, 4 social workers (non-MSW), 5 teachers, 17 counselors, 3 other direct-care staff members. Staff is 58% male, 42% female.

Facilities Multiple buildings. Playing fields, ropes course, canoeing, backpacking.

Education Academic program available at no charge. Serves ages 10–17, grades 3–12. 5 teachers on staff. Curriculum accredited or approved by Southern Association of Colleges and Schools.

Costs Average cost: $100 per day. Accepts private insurance, group insurance, public funds.

Contact Dwight Lord, Director of Admissions, P.O. Box 7450, Clearwater, FL 34618-7450. Phone: 800-544-4357. Fax: 813-442-5911.

CAMP E-NINEE-HASSEE
7027 East Stage Coach Trail
Floral City, Florida 34436
800-554-4357

General Information Wilderness/survival program for children, adolescents. 56 beds for adolescents. Open year-round. Patient security: staff secured; will pursue and return runaways. Rural setting. Not-for-profit facility affiliated with Eckerd Family Youth Alternatives, Inc., Clearwater, FL. Licensed by state of Florida.

Participants Accepts: female children ages 10–12; female adolescents ages 13–17. Average stay: 365 days. Admission: all parties who share custody, voluntary, depending on program. Treats learning disabilities; behavior disorders; general psychosocial disorders.

Program Treatment modalities: Twelve Step Recovery/control theory; reality therapy; Carl Rogers; guided group interaction. Family treatment program available.

Staff Total facility staff includes 1 psychologist, 1 psychiatrist, 1 registered nurse, 4 social workers (non-MSW), 5 teachers, 17 counselors, 3 other direct-care staff members. Staff is 11% male, 89% female.

Facilities Multiple buildings. Playing fields, ropes course, canoeing, backpacking.

Education Academic program available at no charge. Serves ages 10–17, grades 3–12. 5 teachers on staff. Curriculum accredited or approved by State of Florida, Department of Education and the Southern Association of Colleges and Schools.

Costs Average cost: $100 per day. Accepts private insurance, group insurance, public funds.

Contact Dwight Lord, Director of Admissions, P.O. Box 7450, Clearwater, FL 34618-7450. Phone: 800-554-4357. Fax: 813-442-5911.

CAMP E-SUN-ALEE
Route 1
Box 81
Deerlodge, Tennessee 37726
800-554-4357

General Information Wilderness/survival program for children, adolescents. 56 beds for adolescents. Open year-round. Patient security: staff secured; will pursue and return runaways. Rural setting. Not-for-profit facility affiliated with Eckerd Family Youth Alternatives, Inc., Clearwater, FL. Licensed by state of Tennessee.

Participants Accepts: male children ages 10–12; male adolescents ages 13–17. Average stay: 365 days. Admission: all parties who share custody, voluntary, depending on program. Treats learning disabilities; behavior disorders; general psychosocial disorders.

Program Treatment modalities: Twelve Step Recovery/control theory; reality therapy; Carl Rogers; guided group interaction. Family treatment program available.

Staff Total facility staff includes 1 psychologist, 1 psychiatrist, 1 registered nurse, 4 social workers (non-MSW), 5 teachers, 17 counselors, 3 other direct-care staff members. Staff is 47% male, 53% female.

Facilities Multiple buildings. Playing fields, ropes course, canoeing, backpacking.

Education Academic program available at no charge. Serves ages 10–17, grades 3–12. 5 teachers on staff. Curriculum accredited or approved by Southern Association of Colleges and Schools.

Costs Average cost: $100 per day. Accepts private insurance, group insurance, public funds.

Contact Dwight Lord, Director of Admissions, P.O. Box 7450, Clearwater, FL 34618-7450. Phone: 800-554-4357. Fax: 813-442-5911.

CAMP E-TOH-AHNEE
Route 1, Box 164E
Diamond Pond Road
Colebrook, New Hampshire 03576
800-554-4357

General Information Wilderness/survival program for children, adolescents. Open year-round. Patient security: staff secured; will pursue and return runaways. Rural setting. Not-for-profit facility affiliated with Eckerd Family Youth Alternatives, Inc., Clearwater, FL. Licensed by state of New Hampshire.

Participants Accepts: male children ages 10–12; male adolescents ages 13–17. Admission: all parties who share custody, voluntary, depending on program. Treats learning disabilities; behavior disorders; general psychosocial disorders.

Program Treatment modalities: Twelve Step Recovery/control theory; reality therapy; Carl Rogers; guided group interaction. Family treatment program available.

Staff Total facility staff includes 1 psychologist, 1 psychiatrist, 1 registered nurse, 4 social workers (non-MSW), 3 teachers, 18 counselors, 3 other direct-care staff members. Staff is 57% male, 43% female.

Facilities Multiple buildings. Playing fields, ropes course, canoeing, backpacking.

Education Academic program available. Serves ages 10–17, grades 3–12. 3 teachers on staff. Curriculum accredited or approved by Department of Education.

Costs Average cost: $100 per day. Accepts private insurance, group insurance, public funds.

Contact Dwight Lord, Director of Admissions, P.O. Box 7450, Clearwater, FL 34618-7450. Phone: 800-554-4357. Fax: 813-442-5911.

CAMP E-TOH-KALU
Route 4
Box 282
Hendersonville, North Carolina 28739
800-554-4357

General Information Wilderness/survival program for children, adolescents. Open year-round. Patient security: staff secured; will pursue and return runaways. Rural setting. Not-for-profit facility affiliated with Eckerd Family Youth Alternatives, Inc., Clearwater, FL. Licensed by state of North Carolina.

Participants Accepts: male and female children ages 10–12; male and female adolescents ages 13–17. Average stay: 365 days. Admission: all parties who share custody, voluntary, depending on program. Treats learning disabilities; behavior disorders; general psychosocial disorders.

Program Treatment modalities: Twelve Step Recovery/control theory; reality therapy; Carl Rogers; guided group interaction. Family treatment program available.

Staff Total facility staff includes 1 psychologist, 1 psychiatrist, 1 registered nurse, 4 social workers (non-MSW), 5 teachers, 17 counselors, 3 other direct-care staff members. Staff is 58% male, 42% female.

Facilities Multiple buildings; males and females in separate units. Playing fields, ropes course, canoeing, backpacking.

Education Academic program available at no charge. Serves ages 10–17, grades 3–12. 5 teachers on staff. Curriculum accredited or approved by Southern Association of Colleges and Schools.

Costs Average cost: $100 per day. Accepts private insurance, group insurance, public funds.

Contact Dwight Lord, Director of Admissions, P.O. Box 7450, Clearwater, FL 34618-7450. Phone: 800-554-4357. Fax: 813-442-5911.

CAMP E-TU-MAKEE
Star Route
Box 6
Clewiston, Florida 33440
800-554-4357

General Information Wilderness/survival program for children, adolescents. Open year-round. Patient security: staff secured; will pursue and return runaways. Rural setting. Not-for-profit facility affiliated with Eckerd Family Youth Alternatives, Inc., Clearwater, FL. Licensed by state of Florida.

Participants Accepts: male children ages 10–12; male adolescents ages 13–17. Average stay: 365 days. Admission: all parties who share custody, voluntary, depending on program. Treats learning disabilities; behavior disorders; general psychosocial disorders.

Program Treatment modalities: Twelve Step Recovery/control theory; reality therapy; Carl Rogers; guided group interaction. Family treatment program available.

Staff Total facility staff includes 1 psychologist, 1 psychiatrist, 1 registered nurse, 4 social workers (non-MSW), 5 teachers, 17 counselors, 3 other direct-care staff members. Staff is 58% male, 42% female.

Facilities Multiple buildings. Playing fields, ropes course, canoeing, backpacking.

Education Academic program available at no charge. Serves ages 13–17, grades 3–12. 5 teachers on staff. Curriculum accredited or approved by State of Florida, Department of Education and the Southern Association of Colleges and Schools.

Costs Average cost: $100 per day. Accepts private insurance, group insurance, public funds.

Contact Dwight Lord, Director of Admissions, P.O. Box 7450, Clearwater, FL 34618-7450. Phone: 800-554-4357. Fax: 813-442-5911.

CAMP E-WA-HENWU
388 Nine Mile Road
Newport, North Carolina 28570
800-554-4357

General Information Wilderness/survival program for children, adolescents. Open year-round. Patient security: staff secured; will pursue and return runaways. Rural setting. Not-for-profit facility affiliated with Eckerd Family Youth Alternatives, Inc., Clearwater, FL. Licensed by state of North Carolina.

Participants Accepts: male and female children ages 10–12; male and female adolescents ages 13–17. Average stay: 365 days. Admission: all parties who share custody, voluntary, depending on program. Treats learning disabilities; behavior disorders; general psychosocial disorders.

Program Treatment modalities: Twelve Step Recovery/control theory; reality therapy; Carl Rogers; guided group interaction. Family treatment program available.

Staff Total facility staff includes 1 psychologist, 1 psychiatrist, 1 registered nurse, 4 social workers (non-MSW), 5 teachers, 17 counselors, 3 other direct-care staff members. Staff is 44% male, 56% female.

Facilities Multiple buildings; males and females in separate units. Playing fields, ropes course, canoeing, backpacking.

Education Academic program available at no charge. Serves ages 10–17, grades 3–12. 5 teachers on staff. Curriculum accredited or approved by Southern Association of Colleges and Schools.

Contact Dwight Lord, Director of Admissions, P.O. Box 7450, Clearwater, FL 34618-7450. Phone: 800-554-4357. Fax: 813-442-5911.

CAMP E-WEN-AKEE
Route 2
Box 6800
Fair Haven, Vermont 05743
800-554-4357

General Information Wilderness/survival program for children, adolescents. Open year-round. Patient security: staff secured; will pursue and return runaways. Rural setting. Not-for-profit facility affiliated with Eckerd Family Youth Alternatives, Inc., Clearwater, FL. Licensed by state of Vermont.

Participants Accepts: male and female children ages 10–12; male and female adolescents ages 13–17. Admission: all parties who share custody, voluntary, depending on program. Treats learning disabilities; behavior disorders; general psychosocial disorders. Accepts the sexually compulsive.

Program Treatment modalities: Twelve Step Recovery/control theory; reality therapy; Carl Rogers; guided group interaction. Family treatment program available.

Staff Total facility staff includes 1 psychologist, 1 psychiatrist, 1 registered nurse, 3 social workers (non-MSW), 3 teachers, 14 counselors, 3 other direct-care staff members. Staff is 57% male, 43% female.

Facilities Multiple buildings; males and females in separate units. Playing fields, ropes course, canoeing, backpacking.

Education Academic program available at no charge. Serves ages 10–17, grades 3–12. 3 teachers on staff. Curriculum accredited or approved by Department of Education.

Costs Average cost: $100 per day. Accepts private insurance, group insurance, public funds.

Contact Dwight Lord, Director of Admissions, P.O. Box 7450, Clearwater, FL 34618-7450. Phone: 800-554-4357. Fax: 813-442-5911.

CAMP HALF MOON
400 Main Street
P.O. Box 188
Great Barrington, Massachusetts 01230
413-528-0940; Fax: 413-528-0941

General Information Camp for children. 100 beds for children. Open summer. Patient security: unlocked; will pursue and return runaways. Rural setting. Independent for-profit facility. Licensed by state of Massachusetts. Accredited by American Camping Association.

Participants Accepts: male children ages 6–15. Average stay: 8 weeks. Admission: one parent, all parties who share custody, depending on program. Treats learning disabilities.

Facilities Multiple buildings; males and females in separate units. Central dining arrangements vary. Basketball courts, game room, horseback riding, outdoor tennis courts, playing fields, ropes course, lake for boating, sailing, waterskiing.

Education Academic program available at additional cost. Serves ages 6–16. Organized sports program offered.

Costs Average cost: $3600 per stay. Accepts public funds.

Contact Edward Mann, Director, main address above. Phone: 413-528-0940. Fax: 413-528-0941.

CAMP HUNTINGTON
Bruceville Road
High Falls, New York 12440
914-687-7840; Fax: 914-687-7211

General Information Camp for children, adolescents, adults. 25 beds for children; 50 beds for adolescents; 125 beds total. Open summer. Patient security: staff secured; will pursue and return runaways. Small

town setting. Independent. Licensed by state of New York. Accredited by American Camping Association.

Participants Accepts: male and female children ages 6–12; male and female adolescents ages 13–18; male and female adults ages 18–60. Average stay: 30 days. Admission: all parties who share custody. Treats autistic disorders; learning disabilities. Accepts the mobility impaired; the vision impaired; the hearing impaired; the speech impaired; those with a history of arson; those receiving psychotropic medication; non-English speaking individuals; those with a history of epilepsy; diabetics; those with hepatitis. Special programs for the developmentally disabled; the vision impaired; the hearing impaired; the speech impaired. Largest number of participants from New York, New Jersey, Connecticut.

Staff Total facility staff includes 1 psychologist, 3 registered nurses, 1 MSW social worker, 3 social workers (non-MSW), 12 teachers, 50 counselors, 2 occupational/recreational therapists, 1 speech pathologist, 10 therapists, 2 dieticians.

Facilities Multiple buildings; males and females in separate units. Separate residential quarters for children and adolescents. Separate dining by residential unit available. Basketball courts, horseback riding, outdoor swimming pool, outdoor tennis courts, playing fields, arts and crafts, music, and drama facilities.

Education Academic program available. Serves ages 6–21, grades N–6. 12 teachers on staff. Organized sports program offered.

Costs Average cost: $550 per week. Accepts private insurance, group insurance, medicare, medicaid, Blue Cross/Blue Shield, public funds.

Additional Services Outpatient services for males and females. Treats autistic disorders; learning disabilities; behavior disorders; general psychosocial disorders; substance abuse; eating disorders; compulsive/addictive disorders other than substance abuse and eating disorders; post-traumatic stress disorder; thought, mood, and personality disorders.

Contact Dr. Bruria K. Falik, Director, main address above. Phone: 914-687-7840. Fax: 914-687-7211.

See page 404 for full page description.

CAMP LEE MAR
Route 590
Lackawaxen, Pennsylvania 18435
717-685-7188

General Information Camp for children, adolescents. 100 beds for children; 80 beds for adolescents.

Open summer. Patient security: staff secured; will pursue and return runaways. Small town setting. Independent not-for-profit facility. Licensed by state of Pennsylvania. Accredited by Pennsylvania State Department of Health and Education.

Participants Accepts: male and female children ages 5–12; male and female adolescents ages 13–21. Average stay: 7 weeks. Admission: one parent. Treats autistic disorders; learning disabilities; behavior disorders. Accepts the vision impaired; the hearing impaired; the speech impaired; those with a history of epilepsy; the mentally retarded. Special programs for the speech impaired.

Program Treatment modalities: Orton.

Staff .6 full-time direct-care staff member per child or adolescent. Total facility staff includes 5 registered nurses, 12 teachers, 30 counselors, 6 occupational/recreational therapists, 10 speech pathologists. Staff is 45% male, 55% female.

Facilities Multiple buildings; males and females in separate units. Basketball courts, game room, outdoor swimming pool, outdoor tennis courts, playing fields.

Education Academic program available at no charge. Serves ages 5–21, ungraded. 12 teachers on staff. Curriculum accredited or approved by Education Department. Cost of educational program sometimes covered by local school district. Organized sports program offered.

Costs Average cost: $4200 per stay.

Contact Lee Morrone, Owner/Director, 360 East 72nd Street, Suite A711, New York, NY 10021. Phone: 212-988-7260.

CANYON LAKES RESIDENTIAL TREATMENT CENTER
2402 Canyon Lakes Drive
Lubbock, Texas 79415
806-762-5782; Fax: 806-762-0838

General Information Residential treatment/subacute facility for children, adolescents. Patient security: entirely locked. Independent for-profit facility. Licensed by state of Texas. Accredited by JCAHO.

Participants Accepts: male and female children; male and female adolescents. Average stay: 150 days. Admission: all parties who share custody, court order, depending on program. Treats learning disabilities; behavior disorders; general psychosocial disorders; eating disorders; compulsive/addictive disorders other than substance abuse and eating disorders; post-traumatic stress disorder; thought, mood, and personality disorders.

Staff Staff is 40% male, 60% female.

Costs Average cost: $10,000 per month.

Contact Lindy Fruge, Director of Social Work and Admissions, main address above. Phone: 806-762-5782. Fax: 806-762-0838.

CANYON RIDGE HOSPITAL
5353 G Street
Chino, California 91710
714-590-3700; Fax: 714-590-4019

General Information Psychiatric hospital for adolescents, adults. Open year-round. Patient security: entirely locked; will pursue and return runaways. Suburban setting. For-profit facility affiliated with Hospital Corporation of America, Nashville, TN. Licensed by state of California. Accredited by JCAHO.

Participants Accepts: male and female adolescents ages 12–17; male and female adults ages 18 and up. Average stay: 13 days. Admission: one parent, all parties who share custody, court order, involuntary hold, depending on program. Treats learning disabilities; behavior disorders; general psychosocial disorders; substance abuse; eating disorders; compulsive/addictive disorders other than substance abuse and eating disorders; post-traumatic stress disorder; thought, mood, and personality disorders. Accepts the mobility impaired; the vision impaired; the hearing impaired; the speech impaired; those with a history of arson; the sexually compulsive; those with a history of harm to themselves and others; those receiving psychotropic medication; those with a history of epilepsy.

Program Treatment modalities: cognitive therapy; Twelve Step Recovery; brief psychodynamic therapy. Family treatment program available.

Staff Total facility staff includes 1 physician, 1 psychiatrist, 5 registered nurses, 2 practical/vocational nurses, 3 MSW social workers, 1 social worker (non-MSW), 1 teacher, 1 counselor, 2 occupational/recreational therapists, 1 therapist, 1 dietician, 4 other direct-care staff members. Staff is 30% male, 70% female.

Facilities Single building; males and females in co-educational units. Separate residential quarters for adolescents. Central dining (shared with adults). Basketball courts, game room, gymnasium, outdoor swimming pool, playing fields.

Education Academic program available at no charge. Serves ages 12–17, ungraded. 1 teacher on staff. Curriculum accredited or approved by Chino

Unified School District. Cost of educational program covered by local school district.

Costs Average cost: $7500 per stay. Accepts private insurance, group insurance, medicare, Blue Cross/Blue Shield.

Additional Services Drug and alcohol rehabilitation services for males and females ages 12 and up. Treats learning disabilities; behavior disorders; general psychosocial disorders; substance abuse; eating disorders; compulsive/addictive disorders other than substance abuse and eating disorders; post-traumatic stress disorder; thought, mood, and personality disorders. Partial hospitalization for males and females ages 12 and up. Treats learning disabilities; behavior disorders; general psychosocial disorders; substance abuse; eating disorders; compulsive/addictive disorders other than substance abuse and eating disorders; post-traumatic stress disorder; thought, mood, and personality disorders.

Contact Marianne Ferretti, Director of Assessment and Referral, main address above. Phone: 714-590-3700. Fax: 714-590-4019.

CANYON VIEW HOSPITAL
228 Shoup Avenue West
Twin Falls, Idaho 83301
208-734-6760; Fax: 208-734-6764

General Information Freestanding dual diagnosis program for adolescents, adults. 10 beds for adolescents. Open year-round. Patient security: entirely locked; will pursue and return runaways. Small town setting. Independent for-profit facility. Licensed by state of Idaho. Accredited by JCAHO.

Participants Accepts: male and female adolescents ages 12–18; male and female adults ages 18 and up. Average stay: 14 days. Admission: one parent, all parties who share custody, court order, depending on program. Treats learning disabilities; behavior disorders; general psychosocial disorders; substance abuse; eating disorders; compulsive/addictive disorders other than substance abuse and eating disorders; post-traumatic stress disorder; thought, mood, and personality disorders. Accepts the mobility impaired; the vision impaired; the hearing impaired; the speech impaired; those with a history of arson; the sexually compulsive; those with a history of harm to themselves and others; those receiving psychotropic medication; non-English speaking individuals; those with a history of epilepsy.

Program Family treatment program available.

Staff 1 full-time direct-care staff member per adolescent. Total facility staff includes 1 physician, 1 psychologist, 4 psychiatrists, 8 registered nurses, 2 MSW social workers, 1 social worker (non-MSW), 1 teacher, 2 counselors, 2 occupational/recreational therapists, 4 therapists, 1 dietician, 8 other direct-care staff members. Staff is 40% male, 60% female.

Facilities Single building; males and females in co-educational units. Central dining (shared with adults). Basketball courts, game room, gymnasium, playing fields.

Education Academic program available at no charge. Academic program is ungraded. 1 teacher on staff. Organized sports program offered.

Costs Average cost: $675 per day. Accepts private insurance, group insurance, medicare, Blue Cross/Blue Shield, public funds.

Additional Services Outpatient services for males and females ages 12 and up. Treats learning disabilities; behavior disorders; general psychosocial disorders; substance abuse; eating disorders; post-traumatic stress disorder; thought, mood, and personality disorders.

Contact Kathy A. Curtiss, Program Coordinator, main address above. Phone: 208-734-6760. Fax: 208-734-6764.

CAPISTRANO BY THE SEA HOSPITAL
34000 Capistrano by the Sea Drive
Dana Point, California 92629
800-237-9506; Fax: 714-496-4464

General Information Psychiatric hospital for children, adolescents, adults. 10 beds for children; 30 beds for adolescents; 98 beds total. Open year-round. Patient security: entirely locked; will pursue and return runaways. Suburban setting. Independent for-profit facility. Licensed by state of California. Accredited by JCAHO.

Participants Accepts: male and female children ages 10–12; male and female adolescents ages 12–18; male and female adults ages 18–80. Average stay: 30 days. Admission: all parties who share custody. Treats autistic disorders; learning disabilities; behavior disorders; general psychosocial disorders; substance abuse; eating disorders; compulsive/addictive disorders other than substance abuse and eating disorders; post-traumatic stress disorder; thought, mood, and personality disorders. Accepts the mobility impaired; the vision impaired; the hearing impaired; the speech impaired; those with a history of arson; the sexually compulsive; those with a history of harm to themselves and others; those receiving psychotropic medication; those with a history of epilepsy. Largest number of participants from California, Nevada.

Program   Treatment modalities: structure/behavioral program; psychodynamic; skill building/coping skills/education. Family treatment program available.

Staff   3.7 full-time direct-care staff members per child or adolescent. Total facility staff includes 4 physicians, 40 psychologists, 30 psychiatrists, 30 registered nurses, 20 practical/vocational nurses, 3 MSW social workers, 15 social workers (non-MSW), 3 teachers, 2 counselors, 5 occupational/recreational therapists, 1 speech pathologist, 2 dieticians, 40 other direct-care staff members. Staff is 34% male, 66% female.

Facilities   Multiple buildings; males and females in coeducational units. Separate residential quarters for children and adolescents. Central dining (not shared with adults). Outdoor swimming pool, playing fields.

Education   Academic program available at no charge. Serves ages 10–18, grades 6–12. 3 teachers on staff. Curriculum accredited or approved by State Department of Education.

Costs   Accepts private insurance, group insurance, medicare, Blue Cross/Blue Shield.

Additional Services   Drug and alcohol rehabilitation services for males and females ages 10–18. Treats behavior disorders; general psychosocial disorders; substance abuse; eating disorders; compulsive/addictive disorders other than substance abuse and eating disorders; post-traumatic stress disorder; thought, mood, and personality disorders.

Contact   Larry Stednitz, PhD, Director, main address above. Phone: 800-237-9506. Fax: 714-496-4464.

CARDINAL CUSHING SCHOOL AND TRAINING CENTER
405 Washington Street
Hanover, Massachusetts 02339
617-826-6371; Fax: 617-826-6474

General Information   Day school and residential facility for children, adolescents, adults. Open eleven months. Patient security: staff secured; will pursue and return runaways. Suburban setting. Not-for-profit facility affiliated with Sisters of Saint Francis of Assissi, Milwaukee, WI. Licensed by state of Massachusetts. Accredited by Massachusetts Department of Social Services; Office for Children.

Participants   Accepts: male and female children ages 6–14; male and female adolescents ages 14–21; male and female adults ages 21–28. Average stay: 2 years. Admission: voluntary. Treats behavior disorders; eating disorders. Accepts the mobility impaired; the vision impaired; the speech impaired; those with a history of harm to themselves and others; those receiving psychotropic medication; non-English speaking individuals; those with a history of epilepsy; the mentally retarded. Special programs for the developmentally disabled; the speech impaired; those with Prader-Willi Syndrome and Williams Syndrome.

Program   Family treatment program available.

Staff   Total facility staff includes 1 physician, 1 psychologist, 1 psychiatrist, 7 registered nurses, 2 MSW social workers, 7 social workers (non-MSW), 30 teachers, 3 occupational/recreational therapists, 2 speech pathologists, 1 dietician, 90 other direct-care staff members.

Facilities   Multiple buildings; males and females in both coeducational and separate units depending on program. Separate residential quarters for children and adolescents. Central dining (not shared with adults). Basketball courts, game room, gymnasium, outdoor swimming pool, playing fields, ropes course.

Education   School serves ages 6–22, ungraded. 30 teachers on staff. Diploma granted upon completion. Tutor is available. Curriculum accredited or approved by Department of Education. Organized sports program offered.

Costs   Average cost: $175 per day. Accepts public funds.

Additional Services   Camping program for males and females ages 6–22. Treats learning disabilities; behavior disorders; general psychosocial disorders; eating disorders.

Contact   Lynne B. Goyuk, Director of Admissions, 400 Washington Street, Hanover, MA 02339. Phone: 617-826-6371. Fax: 617-826-6474.

CAREUNIT HOSPITAL OF CINCINNATI
3156 Glenmore Avenue
Cincinnati, Ohio 45211
513-481-8822; Fax: 513-481-7317

General Information   Drug and alcohol rehabilitation center for adolescents, adults. 50 beds for adolescents. Open year-round. Patient security: staff secured; will pursue and return runaways. Suburban setting. For-profit facility affiliated with Comprehensive Care Corporation, St. Louis, MO. Licensed by state of Ohio. Accredited by JCAHO.

Participants Accepts: male and female adolescents ages 13–18; male and female adults ages 18 and up. Average stay: 20 days. Admission: one parent. Treats substance abuse. Accepts the mobility impaired; the vision impaired; the hearing impaired; the speech impaired; those with a history of arson; the sexually compulsive; those with a history of harm to themselves and others; those receiving psychotropic medication; non-English speaking individuals; those with a history of epilepsy.

Program Treatment modalities: Twelve Step Recovery. Family treatment program available.

Staff Total facility staff includes 5 physicians, 2 psychologists, 1 psychiatrist, 15 registered nurses, 15 practical/vocational nurses, 2 MSW social workers, 1 teacher, 15 counselors, 1 occupational/recreational therapist, 8 therapists, 1 dietician.

Facilities Single building; males and females in co-educational units. Separate residential quarters for adolescents. Central dining (not shared with adults). Basketball courts, game room, gymnasium, playing fields.

Education Academic program available at no charge. Serves ages 13–18, grades 8–12. 1 teacher on staff. Curriculum accredited or approved by Cincinnati Public Schools. Cost of educational program sometimes covered by local school district.

Costs Average cost: $7500 per stay. Accepts private insurance, group insurance, medicare, Blue Cross/Blue Shield.

Additional Services Outpatient services for males and females ages 12 and up. Treats substance abuse.

Contact Charles Rolfsen, Director of Marketing, main address above. Phone: 513-481-8822. Fax: 513-481-7317.

CAREUNIT HOSPITAL OF COLORADO
1290 South Potomac
Aurora, Colorado 80012
303-745-2273; Fax: 303-369-9556

General Information Psychiatric hospital for adolescents, adults. 25 beds for adolescents. Open year-round. Patient security: partially locked; will pursue and return runaways. Suburban setting. For-profit facility affiliated with Comprehensive Care Corporation, Chesterfield, MO. Licensed by state of Colorado. Accredited by JCAHO.

Participants Accepts: male and female adolescents ages 12–18; male and female adults ages 18 and up. Average stay: 25 days. Admission: one parent. Treats behavior disorders; general psychosocial disorders; substance abuse; eating disorders; compulsive/addictive disorders other than substance abuse and eating disorders; post-traumatic stress disorder; thought, mood, and personality disorders. Accepts the mobility impaired; the vision impaired; the hearing impaired; the speech impaired; those with a history of harm to themselves and others; those receiving psychotropic medication; non-English speaking individuals; those with a history of epilepsy. Special programs for the mobility impaired; dual diagnosis. Largest number of participants from Colorado, Kansas, Wyoming.

Program Treatment modalities: psychodynamic; medical model; experimental groups; family focus. Family treatment program available.

Staff 4.3 full-time direct-care staff members per adolescent. Total facility staff includes 2 physicians, 8 psychologists, 6 psychiatrists, 20 registered nurses, 2 practical/vocational nurses, 4 MSW social workers, 1 social worker (non-MSW), 2 teachers, 6 counselors, 2 physical therapists, 1 occupational/recreational therapist, 2 therapists, 1 dietician, 20 other direct-care staff members. Staff is 36% male, 64% female.

Facilities Single building; males and females in co-educational units. Separate residential quarters for adolescents. Separate dining by residential unit available. Basketball courts, game room, gymnasium, playing fields, ropes course.

Education Academic program available at no charge. Serves ages 12–18, grades 6–12. 2 teachers on staff. Curriculum accredited or approved by State of Colorado Department of Education. Cost of educational program sometimes covered by local school district.

Costs Average cost: $1000 per stay. Accepts private insurance, group insurance, medicare, Blue Cross/Blue Shield.

Additional Services Drug and alcohol rehabilitation services for males and females ages 12 and up. Treats behavior disorders; general psychosocial disorders; substance abuse; eating disorders; compulsive/addictive disorders other than substance abuse and eating disorders; post-traumatic stress disorder; thought, mood, and personality disorders. Outpatient services for males and females ages 12 and up. Treats behavior disorders; general psychosocial disorders; substance abuse; eating disorders; compulsive/addictive disorders other than substance abuse and eating disorders; post-traumatic stress disorder; thought, mood, and personality disorders. Residential or sub-acute services for males and females ages 12 and up. Treats behavior disorders; general psychosocial disorders; substance abuse; eating disorders; compulsive/addictive disorders other than substance abuse and eating disorders; post-traumatic stress disorder; thought, mood, and personality disorders.

Contact Jack Gallagher, Vice President of Business Development, main address above. Phone: 303-745-2273. Fax: 303-369-9556.

CAREUNIT HOSPITAL OF FORT WORTH
1066 West Magnolia
Fort Worth, Texas 76104
817-336-2828; Fax: 817-332-3054

General Information Psychiatric hospital for adolescents, adults. 24 beds for adolescents. Open year-round. Patient security: partially locked. Urban setting. For-profit facility affiliated with Comprehensive Care Corporation, Chesterfield, MO. Licensed by state of Texas. Accredited by JCAHO; Civilian Health and Medical Program of the Uniformed Services.

Participants Accepts: male and female adolescents ages 12–18; male and female adults ages 18 and up. Average stay: 23 days. Admission: all parties who share custody. Treats behavior disorders; general psychosocial disorders; substance abuse; eating disorders; compulsive/addictive disorders other than substance abuse and eating disorders; post-traumatic stress disorder; thought, mood, and personality disorders. Accepts the mobility impaired; the vision impaired; the hearing impaired; the speech impaired; those with a history of arson; the sexually compulsive; those with a history of harm to themselves and others; those receiving psychotropic medication; non-English speaking individuals; those with a history of epilepsy.

Program Treatment modalities: Twelve Step Recovery; family systems approach; psychodynamic; rational emotive therapy. Family treatment program available.

Staff Total facility staff includes 3 physicians, 3 MSW social workers, 2 teachers, 3 occupational/recreational therapists, 1 dietician.

Facilities Single building; males and females in coeducational units. Separate residential quarters for adolescents. Central dining (shared with adults). Basketball courts, game room, ropes course.

Education Academic program available at no charge. Serves ages 12–18, grades 7–12. 2 teachers on staff. Curriculum accredited or approved by Fort Worth Independent School District. Cost of educational program covered by local school district. Organized sports program offered.

Costs Accepts private insurance, group insurance, medicare, Blue Cross/Blue Shield.

Additional Services Drug and alcohol rehabilitation services for males and females ages 12–18. Treats behavior disorders; general psychosocial disorders; substance abuse; eating disorders; compulsive/addictive disorders other than substance abuse and eating disorders; post-traumatic stress disorder; thought, mood, and personality disorders. Outpatient services for males and females ages 12–18. Treats behavior disorders; general psychosocial disorders; substance abuse; eating disorders; compulsive/addictive disorders other than substance abuse and eating disorders; post-traumatic stress disorder; thought, mood, and personality disorders.

Contact Maureen Borkowski, Assistant Administrator, main address above. Phone: 817-336-2828. Fax: 817-332-3054.

CAREUNIT HOSPITAL OF NEVADA
5100 West Sahara Avenue
Las Vegas, Nevada 89102
702-362-8404; Fax: 702-362-7846

General Information Psychiatric hospital for adolescents, adults. 5 beds for adolescents. Open year-round. Patient security: partially locked; will pursue and return runaways. Urban setting. For-profit facility affiliated with Comprehensive Care Corporation, Chesterfield, MO. Licensed by state of Nevada. Accredited by JCAHO; Bureau of Alcohol and Drug Abuse.

Participants Accepts: male and female adolescents ages 12–19; male and female adults ages 18–80. Average stay: 20 days. Admission: one parent, all parties who share custody, court order, depending on program. Treats learning disabilities; behavior disorders; general psychosocial disorders; substance abuse; eating disorders; compulsive/addictive disorders other than substance abuse and eating disorders; post-traumatic stress disorder; thought, mood, and personality disorders. Accepts the mobility impaired; the vision impaired; the hearing impaired; the speech impaired; those with a history of harm to themselves and others; those receiving psychotropic medication; those with a history of epilepsy. Largest number of participants from Nevada.

Program Treatment modalities: Twelve Step Recovery; psychodynamic; reality therapy; Gestalt therapy. Family treatment program available.

Staff Total facility staff includes 1 physician, 1 psychologist, 1 psychiatrist, 1 registered nurse, 1 MSW social worker, 4 teachers, 4 counselors, 1 occupational/recreational therapist, 1 dietician, 1 other direct-care staff member.

Facilities Multiple buildings; males and females in coeducational units. Residential quarters shared with adults. Central dining (shared with adults). Basketball courts, game room.

Education Academic program available. Serves ages 12–19, grades 7–12. 4 teachers on staff. Curriculum accredited or approved by State of Nevada. Organized sports program offered.

Costs Average cost: $5300 per stay. Accepts private insurance, group insurance, medicare, medicaid, Blue Cross/Blue Shield.

Additional Services Drug and alcohol rehabilitation services for males and females ages 12–19. Treats learning disabilities; behavior disorders; general psychosocial disorders; substance abuse; eating disorders; compulsive/addictive disorders other than substance abuse and eating disorders; post-traumatic stress disorder; thought, mood, and personality disorders. Outpatient services for males and females ages 12–19. Treats learning disabilities; behavior disorders; general psychosocial disorders; substance abuse; eating disorders; compulsive/addictive disorders other than substance abuse and eating disorders; post-traumatic stress disorder; thought, mood, and personality disorders. Residential or sub-acute services for males and females ages 12–19. Treats learning disabilities; behavior disorders; general psychosocial disorders; substance abuse; eating disorders; compulsive/addictive disorders other than substance abuse and eating disorders; post-traumatic stress disorder; thought, mood, and personality disorders.

Contact Susan Gregg, Marketing Director, main address above. Phone: 702-362-8404. Fax: 702-362-7846.

CARONDELET PSYCHIATRIC CARE CENTER
1175 Carondelet Drive
Richland, Washington 99352
509-943-9104; Fax: 509-943-7206

General Information Psychiatric hospital for children, adolescents. Patient security: entirely locked. Not-for-profit facility affiliated with Carondelet Health Systems, St. Louis, MO. Licensed by state of Washington.

Participants Accepts: male and female children; male and female adolescents. Average stay: 1 month. Admission: one parent, all parties who share custody, court order, voluntary, depending on program. Treats learning disabilities; behavior disorders; general psychosocial disorders; eating disorders; post-traumatic stress disorder; thought, mood, and personality disorders.

Contact Rusty Cooper, Administrator, main address above. Phone: 509-943-9104.

CARRIER FOUNDATION
Route 601
Belle Mead, New Jersey 08502
908-281-1000; Fax: 908-874-4818

General Information Psychiatric hospital for adolescents, adults. 36 beds for adolescents. Open year-round. Patient security: entirely locked; will pursue and return runaways. Suburban setting. Independent not-for-profit facility. Licensed by state of New Jersey. Accredited by JCAHO.

Participants Accepts: male and female adolescents ages 12–18; male and female adults ages 18 and up. Average stay: 26 days. Admission: one parent, all parties who share custody, court order, voluntary, depending on program. Treats autistic disorders; learning disabilities; behavior disorders; general psychosocial disorders; substance abuse; eating disorders; compulsive/addictive disorders other than substance abuse and eating disorders; post-traumatic stress disorder; thought, mood, and personality disorders. Accepts the mobility impaired; those with a history of harm to themselves and others; those receiving psychotropic medication; those with a history of epilepsy.

Program Treatment modalities: psychodynamic in individual and group setting; psychopharmacology; family therapy. Family treatment program available.

Staff Total facility staff includes 124 registered nurses, 11 practical/vocational nurses, 21 MSW social workers, 14 teachers, 3 physical therapists, 15 occupational/recreational therapists, 3 therapists, 1 dietician, 200 other direct-care staff members. Staff is 33% male, 67% female.

Facilities Multiple buildings; males and females in coeducational units. Separate residential quarters for adolescents. Separate dining by residential unit available. Basketball courts, game room, gymnasium, outdoor swimming pool, outdoor tennis courts, playing fields, ropes course, outdoor track.

Education Academic program available at no charge. Serves ages 13–17, grades 6–12. 14 teachers on staff. Cost of educational program covered by local school district.

Costs Average cost: $19,000 per stay. Accepts private insurance, group insurance, medicare, medicaid, Blue Cross/Blue Shield, public funds.

Additional Services Drug and alcohol rehabilitation services for males and females ages 13–17. Treats learning disabilities; behavior disorders; general psychosocial disorders; substance abuse; post-traumatic stress disorder; thought, mood, and personality disorders. Outpatient services for males and females ages 5–18. Treats autistic disorders; behavior disorders; general psychosocial disorders; substance abuse; post-traumatic stress disorder; thought, mood, and personality disorders.

Contact Sharon H. Campbell, Assistant Director of Marketing and Public Relations, main address above. Phone: 800-933-3579. Fax: 908-874-4818.

THE CASCADE SCHOOL
P.O. Box 9
Whitmore, California 96096
916-472-3031; Fax: 916-472-3414

General Information School for adolescents. 160 beds for adolescents. Open year-round. Patient security: staff secured; will pursue and return runaways. Rural setting. Independent for-profit facility.

Participants Accepts: male and female adolescents ages 13–18. Average stay: 730 days. Admission: all parties who share custody. Treats learning disabilities; behavior disorders; substance abuse; eating disorders; post-traumatic stress disorder. Accepts those receiving psychotropic medication. Special programs for those with mild speech, vision, and/or hearing impairments.

Program Treatment modalities: communication theory; self esteem development. Family treatment program available.

Staff .3 full-time direct-care staff member per adolescent. Total facility staff includes 1 registered nurse, 20 teachers, 19 counselors, 4 other direct-care staff members. Staff is 58% male, 42% female.

Facilities Multiple buildings; males and females in separate units. Central dining (shared with adults). Basketball courts, outdoor swimming pool, playing fields, fitness center, weight room, aerobics studio, climbing wall, canoeing, and fishing ponds.

Education School serves ages 13–18, grades 8–12. 20 teachers on staff. Curriculum is college-preparatory; diploma granted upon completion. Curriculum accredited or approved by Western Association of Schools and Colleges. Organized sports program offered.

Costs Accepts private insurance, group insurance. Financial aid available.

Contact Admissions Department, main address above. Phone: 916-472-3031. Fax: 916-472-3414.
See page 406 for full page description.

CATHERINE FREER WILDERNESS THERAPY EXPEDITIONS
P.O. Box 1064
Albany, Oregon 97321
503-926-7252

General Information Wilderness/survival program for adolescents. 14 beds for adolescents. Open year-round. Patient security: staff secured; will pursue and return runaways. Small town setting. For-profit facility affiliated with Cooley River Expeditions, Inc., Albany, OR. Licensed by state of Oregon. Accredited by Oregon State Alcohol and Drug Department.

Participants Accepts: male and female adolescents ages 12–18. Average stay: 21 days. Admission: one parent. Treats learning disabilities; behavior disorders; general psychosocial disorders; substance abuse; eating disorders; compulsive/addictive disorders other than substance abuse and eating disorders; post-traumatic stress disorder; thought, mood, and personality disorders. Accepts the hearing impaired; the sexually compulsive; those with a history of harm to themselves and others; those receiving psychotropic medication; those with a history of epilepsy. Largest number of participants from Oregon, California, Washington.

Program Treatment modalities: Twelve Step Recovery; structural family therapy; reality therapy; psychodynamic.

Staff .1 full-time direct-care staff member per adolescent. Total facility staff includes 1 psychologist, 3 MSW social workers, 3 counselors, 3 other direct-care staff members.

Facilities Multiple buildings; males and females in separate units.

Costs Average cost: $3800 per stay. Accepts private insurance, group insurance, Blue Cross/Blue Shield.

Additional Services Drug and alcohol rehabilitation services for males and females ages 12–18. Treats behavior disorders; general psychosocial disorders; substance abuse; eating disorders; compulsive/addictive disorders other than substance abuse and eating disorders; post-traumatic stress disorder; thought, mood, and personality disorders. Residential or subacute services for males and females ages 12–18. Treats behavior disorders; general psychosocial disorders; substance abuse; eating disorders; compulsive/addictive disorders other than substance abuse and eating disorders; post-traumatic stress disorder; thought, mood, and personality disorders.

Contact Rob Cooley, PhD, Director, main address above. Phone: 503-926-7252.

Announcement Catherine Freer Wilderness Therapy Expeditions provide quality, intensive group and individual therapy on 21-day Northwest backpacking trips. The setting is conducive to examination of behavior and values and rewards participants with emotional growth and enhanced self-esteem. Expedition staff includes MA/MSW therapists.

CEDAR CREEK HOSPITAL
7200 West Ninth Avenue
Amarillo, Texas 79106
800-926-0044

General Information Psychiatric hospital for children, adolescents. Patient security: entirely locked. For-profit facility affiliated with National Medical Enterprises, Santa Monica, CA. Licensed by state of Texas. Accredited by JCAHO.

Participants Accepts: male and female children; male and female adolescents. Average stay: 21 days. Admission: all parties who share custody. Treats learning disabilities; behavior disorders; general psychosocial disorders; substance abuse; eating disorders; compulsive/addictive disorders other than substance abuse and eating disorders; post-traumatic stress disorder; thought, mood, and personality disorders.

Costs Average cost: $17,500 per stay.

Contact Information and Referral, main address above. Phone: 800-926-0044.

CEDAR CREST RESIDENTIAL TREATMENT CENTER
3500 South Interstate Highway 35
Belton, Texas 76513
800-888-4071; Fax: 817-939-2334

General Information Residential treatment/subacute facility for children, adolescents. 30 beds for children; 40 beds for adolescents; 70 beds total. Open year-round. Patient security: staff secured; will pursue and return runaways. Rural setting. Not-for-profit facility affiliated with Hospital Corporation of America, Nashville, TN. Licensed by state of Texas. Accredited by JCAHO.

Participants Accepts: male and female children ages 4–12; male and female adolescents ages 13–17. Average stay: 139 days. Admission: one parent, court order, depending on program. Treats learning disabilities; behavior disorders; general psychosocial disorders; substance abuse; post-traumatic stress disorder; thought, mood, and personality disorders. Accepts the mobility impaired; the vision impaired; the hearing impaired; the speech impaired; those with a history of arson; the sexually compulsive; those with a history of harm to themselves and others; those receiving psychotropic medication; those with a history of epilepsy. Special programs for dual diagnosis; sexual abuse survivors; young latency. Largest number of participants from Texas, New Mexico, California.

Program Treatment modalities: psychodynamic; systems therapy; reality therapy; Twelve Step Recovery. Family treatment program available.

Staff .8 full-time direct-care staff member per child or adolescent. Total facility staff includes 1 physician, 3 psychologists, 3 psychiatrists, 12 registered nurses, 4 practical/vocational nurses, 2 MSW social workers, 2 social workers (non-MSW), 6 teachers, 4 counselors, 3 occupational/recreational therapists, 1 speech pathologist, 1 dietician, 35 other direct-care staff members. Staff is 35% male, 65% female.

Facilities Multiple buildings. Central dining. Basketball courts, gymnasium, outdoor swimming pool, playing fields, ropes course.

Education Academic program available at no charge. Serves ages 4–17, grades N–12. 6 teachers on staff. Curriculum accredited or approved by Belton Independent School District.

Costs Average cost: $415 per day. Accepts private insurance, group insurance, Blue Cross/Blue Shield.

Additional Services Drug and alcohol rehabilitation services for males and females ages 13–17. Treats behavior disorders; general psychosocial disorders; substance abuse; post-traumatic stress disorder; thought, mood, and personality disorders.

Contact Beth Porterfield, Admissions Coordinator, main address above. Phone: 800-888-4071. Fax: 817-939-2334.

See page 408 for full page description.

CEDAR RIDGE HOSPITAL
7405 Renner Road
Shawnee, Kansas 66217
913-631-1900; Fax: 913-631-7749

General Information Psychiatric hospital for adolescents, adults. 20 beds for adolescents. Open year-round. Patient security: partially locked; will pursue and return runaways. Suburban setting. For-profit facility affiliated with The Mediplex Group, Wellesley, MA. Licensed by state of Kansas. Accredited by JCAHO.

Participants Accepts: male and female adolescents ages 12–18; male and female adults ages 18–80. Average stay: 24 days. Admission: one parent, court order, depending on program. Treats learning disabilities; behavior disorders; general psychosocial disorders; substance abuse; eating disorders; compulsive/addictive disorders other than substance abuse and eating disorders; post-traumatic stress disorder; thought, mood, and personality disorders. Accepts the mobility impaired; the vision impaired; the hearing impaired; the speech impaired; those with a history of arson; the sexually compulsive; those with a history of harm to themselves and others; those receiving psychotropic medication; those with a history of epilepsy. Special programs for the mobility impaired; the developmentally disabled; the vision impaired; the hearing impaired; the speech impaired; those with AIDS. Largest number of participants from Missouri, Kansas, New York.

Program Treatment modalities: Twelve Step Recovery; cognitive behavioral; Gestalt. Family treatment program available.

Staff 1.5 full-time direct-care staff members per adolescent. Total facility staff includes 2 physicians, 4 psychologists, 10 psychiatrists, 32 registered nurses, 4 MSW social workers, 4 social workers (non-MSW), 2 teachers, 6 counselors, 3 occupational/recreational therapists, 1 therapist, 1 dietician. Staff is 40% male, 60% female.

Facilities Single building; males and females in coeducational units. Central dining (shared with adults). Basketball courts, game room, gymnasium, indoor swimming pool, playing fields.

Education Academic program available at no charge. Serves ages 12–18, grades 8–12. 2 teachers on staff. Curriculum accredited or approved by Johnson County Schools. Organized sports program offered.

Costs Average cost: $600 per stay. Accepts private insurance, group insurance, medicare, Blue Cross/Blue Shield.

Additional Services Drug and alcohol rehabilitation services for males and females ages 12–75. Treats autistic disorders; behavior disorders; general psychosocial disorders; substance abuse; eating disorders; compulsive/addictive disorders other than substance abuse and eating disorders; post-traumatic stress disorder; thought, mood, and personality disorders. Outpatient services for males and females ages 18–75. Treats behavior disorders; general psychosocial disorders; substance abuse; eating disorders; compulsive/addictive disorders other than substance abuse and eating disorders; post-traumatic stress disorder; thought, mood, and personality disorders. Day treatment for males and females ages 18–75. Treats behavior disorders; general psychosocial disorders; substance abuse; eating disorders; compulsive/addictive disorders other than substance abuse and eating disorders; post-traumatic stress disorder; thought, mood, and personality disorders.

Contact Trish Smith, Director of Intake, main address above. Phone: 913-631-1900. Fax: 913-631-7749.

CEDU MIDDLE SCHOOL
P.O. Box 1176
Running Springs, California 92382
714-867-2722; Fax: 714-867-9483

General Information School for children. Open year-round. Patient security: staff secured. Rural setting. Independent for-profit facility. Licensed by state of California.

Participants Accepts: male and female children ages 9–13. Average stay: 24 months. Admission: one parent, all parties who share custody, court order, depending on program. Treats learning disabilities; behavior disorders; general psychosocial disorders; substance abuse; thought, mood, and personality disorders.

Facilities Multiple buildings.

Education School serves ages 9–13, ungraded. Curriculum accredited or approved by Western Association of Schools and Colleges. Organized sports program offered.

Costs Average cost: $4000 per month.

Contact Saul G. Rudman, Director of Admissions, main address above. Phone: 714-867-2722. Fax: 714-867-9483.

See page 410 for full page description.

CEDU SCHOOL
P.O. Box 1176
Running Springs, California 92382
714-867-2722; Fax: 714-867-9438

General Information School for adolescents. Open year-round. Patient security: staff secured. Independent for-profit facility. Licensed by state of California.

Participants Accepts: male and female adolescents ages 13–17. Average stay: 24 months. Admission: one parent, all parties who share custody, court order, depending on program. Treats learning disabilities; behavior disorders; general psychosocial disorders; substance abuse; thought, mood, and personality disorders.

Facilities Multiple buildings.

Education School serves ages 13–17, ungraded. Curriculum is college-preparatory; diploma granted upon completion. Curriculum accredited or approved by Western Association of Schools and Colleges. Organized sports program offered.

Costs Average cost: $4000 per month.

Contact Saul G. Rudman, Director of Admissions, main address above. Phone: 714-867-2722. Fax: 714-867-9483.

See page 412 for full page description.

CENTENNIAL PEAKS TREATMENT CENTER
1225 Redwood Street
Fort Collins, Colorado 80524
303-493-3389; Fax: 303-493-1478

General Information Drug and alcohol rehabilitation center for adolescents, adults. 25 beds for adolescents. Open year-round. Patient security: staff secured; no runaway pursuit. Small town setting. For-profit facility affiliated with National Medical Enterprises, Washington, DC. Licensed by state of Colorado. Accredited by JCAHO.

Participants Accepts: male and female adolescents ages 12–18; male and female adults ages 18 and up. Average stay: 30 days. Admission: all parties who share custody. Treats learning disabilities; behavior disorders; general psychosocial disorders; substance abuse; eating disorders; compulsive/addictive disorders other than substance abuse and eating disorders; post-traumatic stress disorder. Accepts the mobility impaired; the vision impaired; the hearing impaired; the speech impaired; those with a history of arson; the sexually compulsive; those with a history of harm to themselves and others; those receiving psychotropic medication; non-English speaking individuals; those with a history of epilepsy. Special programs for the mobility impaired; the developmentally disabled; the vision impaired; the hearing impaired; the speech impaired; those with AIDS.

Program Treatment modalities: Twelve Step Recovery; behavioral therapies; experiential therapies; cognitive therapies. Family treatment program available.

Staff Total facility staff includes 1 physician, 3 psychologists, 3 psychiatrists, 10 registered nurses, 1 practical/vocational nurse, 4 MSW social workers, 1 teacher, 4 counselors, 1 dietician, 10 other direct-care staff members.

Facilities Single building; males and females in co-educational units. Separate residential quarters for adolescents. Central dining (shared with adults). Basketball courts, game room, gymnasium, outdoor swimming pool, playing fields, ropes course.

Education Academic program available at no charge. Serves ages 12–18. 1 teacher on staff. Curriculum accredited or approved by State of Colorado. Organized sports program offered.

Costs Average cost: $540 per day. Accepts private insurance, group insurance, Blue Cross/Blue Shield.

Contact Nancy McBride, Assistant Administrator, main address above. Phone: 303-493-3389. Fax: 303-493-1478.

CENTRAL FLORIDA HUMAN SERVICES—BRADLEY OAKS
6980 State Road 37 South
Mulberry, Florida 33860
800-562-5084; Fax: 813-428-2119

General Information Drug and alcohol rehabilitation center for adolescents. 26 beds for adolescents. Patient security: unlocked. Not-for-profit facility affiliated with Central Florida Human Services, Lakeland, FL. Licensed by state of Florida.

Participants Accepts: male adolescents. Average stay: 9 months. Admission: one parent, all parties who share custody, court order, voluntary, depending on program. Treats substance abuse. Accepts the mobility impaired.

Staff .5 full-time direct-care staff member per adolescent. Staff is 60% male, 40% female.

Contact John Allen, Program Director, main address above. Phone: 800-562-5084. Fax: 813-428-2119.

CHALLENGE PROGRAM OF SOUTHLAKE CENTER FOR MENTAL HEALTH
7403 Cline Avenue
Schererville, Indiana 46375
219-322-0038; Fax: 219-769-2508

General Information   Residential treatment/subacute facility for adolescents. 18 beds for adolescents. Open year-round. Patient security: staff secured; will pursue and return runaways. Suburban setting. Not-for-profit facility affiliated with Southlake Center for Mental Health, Merrillville, IN. Licensed by state of Indiana.

Participants   Accepts: male adolescents ages 13–17. Average stay: 365 days. Admission: one parent, all parties who share custody, court order, depending on program. Treats learning disabilities; behavior disorders; general psychosocial disorders; post-traumatic stress disorder; thought, mood, and personality disorders. Accepts those with a history of arson; those with a history of harm to themselves and others; those receiving psychotropic medication.

Program   Treatment modalities: reality therapy (milieu model); self psychology (psychiatric consultation); structural family therapy (intimate system intervention); narrative therapy (individual approach). Family treatment program available.

Staff   1.3 full-time direct-care staff members per adolescent. Total facility staff includes 1 psychiatrist, 1 registered nurse, 4 teachers, 1 occupational/recreational therapist, 3 therapists, 15 other direct-care staff members. Staff is 80% male, 20% female.

Facilities   Multiple buildings. Central dining (shared with adults). Basketball courts, game room, gymnasium, indoor swimming pool, playing fields.

Education   Academic program available at no charge. Serves ages 13–18, grades 7–12. 4 teachers on staff. Curriculum accredited or approved by State of Indiana. Cost of educational program covered by local school district. Organized sports program offered.

Costs   Average cost: $155 per day. Accepts private insurance, group insurance, medicaid, Blue Cross/Blue Shield, public funds.

Contact   John Ross Brown, Director, main address above. Phone: 219-322-0038. Fax: 219-769-2508.

CHAMBERLAIN'S CHILDREN'S CENTER, INC.
P.O. Box 1269
Hollister, California 95024-1269
408-637-1677; Fax: 408-636-5296

General Information   Residential treatment/subacute facility for children. 30 beds for children. Open year-round. Patient security: unlocked; will pursue and return runaways. Rural setting. Independent not-for-profit facility. Licensed by state of California.

Participants   Accepts: male and female children ages 3–13. Average stay: 2 years. Admission: all parties who share custody, court order, depending on program. Treats autistic disorders; learning disabilities; behavior disorders; general psychosocial disorders. Accepts those receiving psychotropic medication. Largest number of participants from California.

Staff   1.8 full-time direct-care staff members per child. Total facility staff includes 1 psychiatrist, 3 MSW social workers, 3 teachers, 1 therapist, 46 other direct-care staff members.

Facilities   Multiple buildings; males and females in separate units. Separate dining by residential unit available. Indoor swimming pool, playing fields.

Education   Academic program available at additional cost. Serves ages 5–12, ungraded. 3 teachers on staff. Curriculum accredited or approved by State Department of Education. Cost of educational program covered by local school district.

Costs   Average cost: $4500 per month. Accepts private insurance, group insurance, public funds.

Additional Services   Outpatient services for males and females ages 3–13. Treats behavior disorders; general psychosocial disorders; post-traumatic stress disorder; thought, mood, and personality disorders.

Contact   Beth Kirshner, Program Assistant, main address above. Phone: 408-637-1677. Fax: 408-636-5296.

THE CHAMBERS HILL ADOLESCENT CARE FACILITY
3740 Chambers Hill Road
Harrisburg, Pennsylvania 17111
717-561-0400; Fax: 717-238-9206

General Information   Drug and alcohol rehabilitation center for adolescents. 25 beds for adolescents. Patient security: staff secured. Not-for-profit facility affiliated with Gaudenzia, Inc., Philadelphia, PA. Licensed by state of Pennsylvania. Accredited by JCAHO.

Participants Accepts: male and female adolescents. Average stay: 180 days. Admission: one parent, all parties who share custody, court order, voluntary, depending on program. Treats substance abuse. Accepts the mobility impaired; the vision impaired; the hearing impaired; the speech impaired.

Staff Staff is 50% male, 50% female.

Costs Average cost: $245 per day.

Contact Jan Daddona, Program Supervisor, main address above. Phone: 717-561-0400.

CHAMPIONS PSYCHIATRIC TREATMENT CENTER
14320 Walters Road
Houston, Texas 77014
713-537-5050; Fax: 713-537-2726

General Information Residential treatment/subacute facility for children, adolescents. 16 beds for children; 32 beds for adolescents; 48 beds total. Open year-round. Patient security: staff secured; will pursue and return runaways. Suburban setting. For-profit facility affiliated with Century HealthCare Corporation, Tulsa, OK. Licensed by state of Texas. Accredited by JCAHO; Texas Department of Human Services, Texas Commission on Alcohol and Drug Abuse, Civilian Health and Medical Program of the Uniformed Services.

Participants Accepts: male and female children ages 5–12; male and female adolescents ages 12–19. Average stay: 6 months. Admission: one parent, voluntary, guardian, depending on program. Treats learning disabilities; behavior disorders; general psychosocial disorders; substance abuse; eating disorders; compulsive/addictive disorders other than substance abuse and eating disorders; post-traumatic stress disorder; thought, mood, and personality disorders. Accepts those with a history of arson; the sexually compulsive; those with a history of harm to themselves and others; those receiving psychotropic medication; non-English speaking individuals; those with a history of epilepsy; those with attachment disorders; sexual abuse victims; the adopted. Largest number of participants from Texas, Illinois.

Program Treatment modalities: milieu therapy; intensive individual and group therapy; reality therapy. Family treatment program available.

Staff Total facility staff includes 6 physicians, 6 psychologists, 29 psychiatrists, 6 registered nurses, 3 practical/vocational nurses, 8 MSW social workers, 7 teachers, 28 counselors, 1 physical therapist, 2 occupational/recreational therapists, 1 speech pathologist, 9 therapists, 1 dietician, 8 other direct-care staff members. Staff is 45% male, 55% female.

Facilities Multiple buildings; males and females in coeducational units. Central dining. Game room, outdoor swimming pool, playing fields, outdoor sports court and playscape.

Education Academic program available at no charge. Serves ages 6–19, grades N–12. 7 teachers on staff. Curriculum accredited or approved by State of Texas. Cost of educational program sometimes covered by local school district. Organized sports program offered.

Costs Average cost: $50,000 per stay. Accepts private insurance, group insurance, medicaid, Blue Cross/Blue Shield.

Additional Services Outpatient services for males and females ages 5–19. Treats learning disabilities; behavior disorders; general psychosocial disorders; substance abuse; eating disorders; compulsive/addictive disorders other than substance abuse and eating disorders; post-traumatic stress disorder; thought, mood, and personality disorders. Day hospital treatment for males and females ages 6–19. Treats learning disabilities; behavior disorders; general psychosocial disorders; substance abuse; eating disorders; compulsive/addictive disorders other than substance abuse and eating disorders; post-traumatic stress disorder; thought, mood, and personality disorders.

Contact Roger Fryou, Director of Intake and Marketing, main address above. Phone: 713-537-5050. Fax: 713-537-2726.
See page 414 for full page description.

CHANGING POINT
4100 College Avenue, P.O. Box 167
Ellicott City, Maryland 21041-0167
800-883-9500; Fax: 800-883-9500 Ext. 320

General Information Drug and alcohol rehabilitation center for adolescents, adults. 18 beds for adolescents. Open year-round. Patient security: staff secured; will pursue and return runaways. Rural setting. For-profit facility affiliated with Taylor Manor Hospital, Ellicott City, MD. Licensed by state of Maryland. Accredited by JCAHO.

Participants Accepts: male and female adolescents ages 14–18; male and female adults ages 19 and up. Average stay: 45 days. Admission: all parties who share custody. Treats behavior disorders; general psychosocial disorders; substance abuse; thought, mood, and personality disorders. Accepts the vision impaired; the speech impaired; those with a history of arson; the sexually compulsive; those with a history of epilepsy. Special programs for the vision impaired; those with AIDS. Largest number of participants from Maryland.

Program Treatment modalities: Twelve Step Recovery; Alcoholics Anonymous, Narcotics Anonymous. Family treatment program available.

Staff 1.1 full-time direct-care staff members per adolescent. Total facility staff includes 2 physicians, 6 registered nurses, 4 practical/vocational nurses, 2 MSW social workers, 1 social worker (non-MSW), 4 counselors, 1 occupational/recreational therapist. Staff is 45% male, 55% female.

Facilities Multiple buildings; males and females in coeducational units. Separate residential quarters for adolescents. Separate dining by residential unit available. Basketball courts, game room, gymnasium, outdoor swimming pool, playing fields.

Education Academic program available at no charge. Serves ages 14–18, ungraded. Curriculum accredited or approved by Howard County Board of Education. Organized sports program offered.

Costs Accepts private insurance, group insurance, medicaid, Blue Cross/Blue Shield.

Additional Services Outpatient services for males and females ages 14 and up. Treats behavior disorders; general psychosocial disorders; substance abuse; thought, mood, and personality disorders. Residential or sub-acute services for males and females ages 14 and up. Treats substance abuse.

Contact Joy Yeager, Assistant Marketing Director, main address above. Phone: 800-883-9500. Fax: 800-883-9500 Ext. 320.

CHANGING POINT SOUTH
7900 Billingsley Road
P.O. Box 2010
Waldorf, Maryland 20604
301-870-5100

General Information Drug and alcohol rehabilitation center for adolescents, adults. 23 beds for adolescents. Open year-round. Patient security: staff secured; will pursue and return runaways. Suburban setting. Independent for-profit facility. Licensed by state of Maryland. Accredited by JCAHO; Maryland Department of Mental Hygiene.

Participants Accepts: male and female adolescents ages 13–17; male and female adults ages 18 and up. Average stay: 47 days. Admission: one parent, court order, depending on program. Treats learning disabilities; behavior disorders; general psychosocial

disorders; substance abuse; eating disorders; thought, mood, and personality disorders. Accepts the mobility impaired; the vision impaired; those with a history of arson; those with a history of harm to themselves and others; those receiving psychotropic medication; those with a history of epilepsy. Largest number of participants from Maryland, D.C., Virginia.

Program Treatment modalities: therapeutic community; Twelve Step orientation; family recovery. Family treatment program available.

Staff Total facility staff includes 2 physicians, 1 psychologist, 12 registered nurses, 2 practical/vocational nurses, 1 MSW social worker, 2 social workers (non-MSW), 2 teachers, 2 counselors, 3 therapists, 1 dietician, 11 other direct-care staff members. Staff is 40% male, 60% female.

Facilities Multiple buildings; males and females in coeducational units. Separate residential quarters for adolescents. Central dining (not shared with adults), separate dining by residential unit available. Basketball courts, game room, gymnasium, outdoor swimming pool, outdoor tennis courts, playing fields, weight room.

Education Academic program available at no charge. Serves ages 13–18, grades 8–12. 2 teachers on staff. Curriculum accredited or approved by Maryland Board of Education. Cost of educational program covered by local school district. Organized sports program offered.

Costs Average cost: $21,000 per stay. Accepts private insurance, group insurance, medicaid, Blue Cross/Blue Shield, public funds.

Additional Services Outpatient services for males and females ages 13 and up. Treats learning disabilities; behavior disorders; general psychosocial disorders; substance abuse; eating disorders; thought, mood, and personality disorders.

Contact Thomas J. DeCoster, Clinical Director, main address above. Phone: 301-870-5100.

CHARLES RIVER HOSPITAL
203 Grove Street
Wellesley, Massachusetts 02181
617-235-8400; Fax: 617-237-9203

General Information Psychiatric hospital for adolescents, adults. 24 beds for adolescents. Open year-round. Patient security: partially locked; will pursue and return runaways. Suburban setting. For-profit facility affiliated with Community Care Systems, Wellesley, MA. Licensed by state of Massachusetts. Accredited by JCAHO.

Participants Accepts: male and female adolescents ages 12–18; male and female adults. Average stay: 18 days. Admission: one parent. Treats autistic disorders; learning disabilities; behavior disorders; general psychosocial disorders; substance abuse; eating disorders; compulsive/addictive disorders other than substance abuse and eating disorders; post-traumatic stress disorder; thought, mood, and personality disorders. Accepts the mobility impaired; the vision impaired; the hearing impaired; the speech impaired; those with a history of harm to themselves and others; those receiving psychotropic medication. Special programs for adolescents with diabetes. Largest number of participants from Massachusetts, New Hampshire, Connecticut.

Program Treatment modalities: family systems; psychodynamic; Twelve Step Recovery; psychoeducational. Family treatment program available.

Staff 3.9 full-time direct-care staff members per adolescent. Total facility staff includes 16 psychologists, 6 psychiatrists, 30 registered nurses, 5 MSW social workers, 2 teachers, 30 counselors, 4 occupational/recreational therapists, 1 dietician, 1 other direct-care staff member. Staff is 40% male, 60% female.

Facilities Multiple buildings; males and females in coeducational units. Separate residential quarters for adolescents. Central dining (shared with adults). Basketball courts, game room, ropes course.

Education Academic program available. Serves ages 12–18, ungraded. 2 teachers on staff. Cost of educational program covered by local school district.

Costs Average cost: $5000 per week. Accepts private insurance, group insurance, medicaid, Blue Cross/Blue Shield, public funds.

Additional Services Drug and alcohol rehabilitation services for males and females ages 12–18. Treats learning disabilities; behavior disorders; general psychosocial disorders; substance abuse; eating disorders; compulsive/addictive disorders other than substance abuse and eating disorders; post-traumatic stress disorder; thought, mood, and personality disorders.

Contact Bill Smith, Community Representative, main address above. Phone: 617-235-8400. Fax: 617-237-9203.

CHARLES RIVER HOSPITAL—WEST
350 Memorial Drive
Chicopee, Massachusetts 01020
413-594-2211; Fax: 413-594-7642

General Information Psychiatric hospital for adolescents, adults. 15 beds for adolescents. Open year-round. Patient security: partially locked; will pursue and return runaways. Urban setting. For-profit facility affiliated with Community Care Systems, Wellesley, MA. Licensed by state of Massachusetts. Accredited by JCAHO; Department of Mental Health.

Participants Accepts: male and female adolescents ages 11–18; male and female adults ages 18–75. Average stay: 21 days. Admission: one parent, all parties who share custody, court order, depending on program. Treats behavior disorders; general psychosocial disorders; substance abuse; eating disorders; compulsive/addictive disorders other than substance abuse and eating disorders; post-traumatic stress disorder; thought, mood, and personality disorders. Accepts those with a history of arson; the sexually compulsive; those with a history of harm to themselves and others; those receiving psychotropic medication; non-English speaking individuals; those with a history of epilepsy. Special programs for those with AIDS. Largest number of participants from Massachusetts.

Program Treatment modalities: Twelve Step Recovery; behavior modification; reality therapy; psychodynamic. Family treatment program available.

Staff 1 full-time direct-care staff member per adolescent. Total facility staff includes 6 physicians, 3 psychologists, 4 psychiatrists, 15 registered nurses, 8 MSW social workers, 3 teachers, 14 counselors, 8 occupational/recreational therapists, 1 dietician. Staff is 60% male, 40% female.

Facilities Single building; males and females in coeducational units. Separate residential quarters for adolescents. Central dining (shared with adults). Basketball courts, gymnasium, ropes course.

Education Academic program available at no charge. Serves ages 11–18, ungraded. 3 teachers on staff. Cost of educational program covered by local school district.

Costs Average cost: $775 per day. Accepts private insurance, group insurance, medicaid, Blue Cross/Blue Shield.

Additional Services Outpatient services for males and females ages 12 and up. Treats behavior disorders; general psychosocial disorders; substance abuse; eating disorders; compulsive/addictive disorders other than substance abuse and eating disorders; post-traumatic stress disorder; thought, mood, and personality disorders.

Contact   Kathryn Adams, Marketing Executive, main address above. Phone: 413-594-2211. Fax: 413-594-7642.

CHARTER ACADEMY RESIDENTIAL TREATMENT CENTER
2055 Kellogg Avenue
Corona, California 91719
714-735-2910; Fax: 714-735-2092

General Information   Residential treatment/subacute facility for adolescents. 30 beds for adolescents. Open year-round. Patient security: staff secured; will pursue and return runaways. Suburban setting. For-profit facility affiliated with Charter Medical Corporation, Macon, GA. Licensed by state of California. Accredited by JCAHO.

Participants   Accepts: male and female adolescents ages 12–18. Average stay: 90 days. Admission: one parent, all parties who share custody, court order, depending on program. Treats learning disabilities; behavior disorders; general psychosocial disorders; substance abuse; eating disorders; compulsive/addictive disorders other than substance abuse and eating disorders; post-traumatic stress disorder; thought, mood, and personality disorders. Accepts the mobility impaired; the vision impaired; the hearing impaired; the speech impaired; those with a history of arson; the sexually compulsive; those with a history of harm to themselves and others; those receiving psychotropic medication; non-English speaking individuals; those with a history of epilepsy. Special programs for the chronically ill; the mobility impaired; the developmentally disabled; the vision impaired; the hearing impaired; the speech impaired; those with AIDS. Largest number of participants from California, Maryland, Florida.

Program   Treatment modalities: psychodynamic; Twelve Step Recovery; biopsychosocial model; situational decision making process. Family treatment program available.

Staff   1.1 full-time direct-care staff members per adolescent. Total facility staff includes 2 physicians, 2 psychologists, 4 psychiatrists, 8 registered nurses, 3 practical/vocational nurses, 2 MSW social workers, 1 teacher, 8 counselors, 1 occupational/recreational therapist, 1 speech pathologist, 1 dietician.

Facilities   Multiple buildings; males and females in coeducational units. Central dining (shared with adults). Game room, gymnasium, outdoor swimming pool, outdoor tennis courts, playing fields, outdoor track.

Education   Academic program available at no charge. Serves ages 12–18, ungraded. 1 teacher on staff. Curriculum accredited or approved by California Department of Education, Riverside County Education Department. Cost of educational program sometimes covered by local school district.

Costs   Average cost: $495 per day. Accepts private insurance, group insurance, medicare, medicaid, Blue Cross/Blue Shield, public funds.

Additional Services   Drug and alcohol rehabilitation services for males and females ages 12–18. Treats learning disabilities; behavior disorders; general psychosocial disorders; substance abuse; eating disorders; compulsive/addictive disorders other than substance abuse and eating disorders; post-traumatic stress disorder; thought, mood, and personality disorders.

Contact   Deborah Glynn, Program Manager, main address above. Phone: 714-735-2910. Fax: 714-734-2092.

CHARTER BARCLAY HOSPITAL
4700 North Clarendon Avenue
Chicago, Illinois 60640
312-728-7100; Fax: 312-728-7383

General Information   Psychiatric hospital for adolescents, adults. 23 beds for adolescents. Open year-round. Patient security: entirely locked; no runaway pursuit. Urban setting. For-profit facility affiliated with Charter Medical Corporation, Macon, GA. Licensed by state of Illinois. Accredited by JCAHO; Health Care Financing Administration.

Participants   Accepts: male and female adolescents ages 12–18; male and female adults ages 18 and up. Average stay: 20 days. Admission: one parent, all parties who share custody, court order, voluntary, depending on program. Treats learning disabilities; behavior disorders; general psychosocial disorders; substance abuse; eating disorders; compulsive/addictive disorders other than substance abuse and eating disorders; post-traumatic stress disorder; thought, mood, and personality disorders. Accepts the mobility impaired; the sexually compulsive; those with a history of harm to themselves and others; those receiving psychotropic medication; non-English speaking individuals. Special programs for those with AIDS.

Program Treatment modalities: Twelve Step Recovery; psychodynamic; psychoanalytic. Family treatment program available.

Staff Total facility staff includes 20 physicians, 200 psychologists, 100 psychiatrists, 50 registered nurses, 50 MSW social workers, 3 teachers, 25 counselors, 7 occupational/recreational therapists, 7 dieticians. Staff is 50% male, 50% female.

Facilities Multiple buildings; males and females in coeducational units. Central dining (shared with adults), in-room dining available. Game room, gymnasium, playing fields, outdoor play area.

Education Academic program available. Serves ages 12–18, grades 6–12. 3 teachers on staff.

Costs Accepts private insurance, group insurance, medicare, medicaid, Blue Cross/Blue Shield, public funds.

Additional Services Outpatient services for males and females. Treats autistic disorders; learning disabilities; behavior disorders; general psychosocial disorders; substance abuse; eating disorders; compulsive/addictive disorders other than substance abuse and eating disorders; post-traumatic stress disorder; thought, mood, and personality disorders.

Contact Kathy Maloney, Assistant Director of Marketing, main address above. Phone: 312-728-7100. Fax: 312-728-7383.

CHARTER BEACON HOSPITAL
1720 Beacon Street
Fort Wayne, Indiana 46805
219-423-3651

General Information Freestanding psychiatric and chemical dependency treatment facility for children, adolescents. Patient security: entirely locked. For-profit facility affiliated with Charter Medical Corporation, Macon, GA. Licensed by state of Indiana. Accredited by JCAHO.

Participants Accepts: male and female children; male and female adolescents. Average stay: 22 days. Admission: one parent, all parties who share custody, court order, voluntary, depending on program. Treats learning disabilities; behavior disorders; general psychosocial disorders; substance abuse; eating disorders; compulsive/addictive disorders other than substance abuse and eating disorders; post-traumatic stress disorder; thought, mood, and personality disorders.

Contact Ron Shivley, Needs Assessment Manager, main address above. Phone: 219-423-3651.

CHARTER FAIRMONT INSTITUTE
561 Fairthorne Avenue
Philadelphia, Pennsylvania 19128
215-487-4000; Fax: 215-483-8187

General Information Psychiatric hospital for adolescents. 44 beds for adolescents. Patient security: entirely locked. For-profit facility affiliated with Charter Medical Corporation, Macon, GA. Licensed by state of Pennsylvania. Accredited by JCAHO.

Participants Accepts: male and female adolescents. Average stay: 2 weeks. Admission: one parent, all parties who share custody, court order, voluntary, depending on program. Treats autistic disorders; learning disabilities; behavior disorders; general psychosocial disorders; substance abuse; eating disorders; compulsive/addictive disorders other than substance abuse and eating disorders; post-traumatic stress disorder; thought, mood, and personality disorders.

Contact Jean Griffea, Director of Admissions, main address above. Phone: 215-487-4000.

CHARTER GLADE HOSPITAL
3550 Colonial Boulevard
Fort Myers, Florida 33912
813-939-0403; Fax: 813-939-4695

General Information Psychiatric hospital for children, adolescents. Patient security: partially locked. For-profit facility affiliated with Charter Medical Corporation, Macon, GA. Licensed by state of Florida. Accredited by JCAHO.

Participants Accepts: male and female children; male and female adolescents. Average stay: 28 days. Admission: all parties who share custody. Treats autistic disorders; learning disabilities; behavior disorders; general psychosocial disorders; substance abuse; eating disorders; compulsive/addictive disorders other than substance abuse and eating disorders; post-traumatic stress disorder; thought, mood, and personality disorders.

Staff Staff is 30% male, 70% female.

Contact Jeanie Mapes, Marketing, P.O. Box 06120, Fort Myers, FL 33906. Phone: 813-939-0403.

CHARTER HOSPITAL OF ALBUQUERQUE
5901 Zuni Road Southwest
Albuquerque, New Mexico 87108
505-265-8800; Fax: 505-260-5401

General Information Freestanding psychiatric and chemical dependency hospital for children, adolescents. Patient security: partially locked. For-profit facility affiliated with Charter Medical Corporation, Macon, GA. Licensed by state of New Mexico. Accredited by JCAHO.

Participants Accepts: male and female children; male and female adolescents. Average stay: 28 days. Admission: one parent, all parties who share custody, court order, depending on program. Treats learning disabilities; behavior disorders; general psychosocial disorders; substance abuse; eating disorders; compulsive/addictive disorders other than substance abuse and eating disorders; post-traumatic stress disorder; thought, mood, and personality disorders.

Contact Beth Larsen, Director of Marketing, main address above. Phone: 505-265-8800.

CHARTER HOSPITAL OF AUGUSTA
3100 Perimeter Parkway
Augusta, Georgia 30909
706-868-6625; Fax: 706-860-6238

General Information Psychiatric hospital for children, adolescents. 27 beds for children; 36 beds for adolescents. Open year-round. Patient security arrangements vary depending on program; will pursue and return runaways. For-profit facility affiliated with Charter Medical Corporation, Macon, GA. Licensed by state of Georgia. Accredited by JCAHO.

Participants Accepts: male and female children ages 3–11; male and female adolescents ages 11–17. Average stay: 29 days. Admission: legal guardian. Treats autistic disorders; behavior disorders; general psychosocial disorders; eating disorders; post-traumatic stress disorder; thought, mood, and personality disorders. Accepts the vision impaired; the hearing impaired; the speech impaired; those with a history of arson; those with a history of harm to themselves and others; those receiving psychotropic medication. Special programs for the developmentally disabled; the hearing impaired; the speech impaired; those with AIDS.

Program Family treatment program available.

Staff Total facility staff includes 4 physicians, 4 psychologists, 4 psychiatrists, 4 MSW social workers, 4 teachers, 2 occupational/recreational therapists, 1 speech pathologist, 1 dietician.

Facilities Single building; males and females in co-educational units. Central dining, separate dining by residential unit available. Basketball courts, gymnasium, outdoor swimming pool, outdoor tennis courts, playing fields, ropes course.

Education Academic program available. Serves ages 3–18, grades N–12. 4 teachers on staff.

Costs Accepts private insurance, group insurance, medicaid, Blue Cross/Blue Shield, public funds.

Additional Services Drug and alcohol rehabilitation services for males and females ages 3–17. Treats autistic disorders; learning disabilities; behavior disorders; general psychosocial disorders; eating disorders; compulsive/addictive disorders other than substance abuse and eating disorders; post-traumatic stress disorder; thought, mood, and personality disorders. Outpatient services for males and females ages 3–17. Treats learning disabilities; behavior disorders; general psychosocial disorders; compulsive/addictive disorders other than substance abuse and eating disorders. Residential or sub-acute services for males and females ages 4–14. Treats autistic disorders; behavior disorders; eating disorders; compulsive/addictive disorders other than substance abuse and eating disorders; post-traumatic stress disorder; thought, mood, and personality disorders.

Contact Sheri Luthi, Needs Assessment Director, main address above. Phone: 706-868-6625. Fax: 706-860-6238.

CHARTER HOSPITAL OF BAKERSFIELD
5201 White Lane
Bakersfield, California 93309
805-398-1800; Fax: 805-837-0755

General Information Psychiatric hospital for children, adolescents, adults. 12 beds for children; 12 beds for adolescents; 60 beds total. Open year-round. Patient security: partially locked. Suburban setting. For-profit facility affiliated with Charter Medical Corporation, Macon, GA. Licensed by state of California. Accredited by JCAHO.

Participants Accepts: male and female children ages 5–12; male and female adolescents ages 13–17; male and female adults ages 18 and up. Admission: one parent. Treats substance abuse; eating disorders; thought, mood, and personality disorders. Accepts the mobility impaired; the vision impaired; the hearing impaired; the speech impaired; those with a history of arson; the sexually compulsive; those with a history of harm to themselves and others; those receiving psychotropic medication; those with a history of epilepsy.

Program Treatment modalities: psychodynamic: individual and group; cognitive therapy; Twelve Step Recovery (addictive disease).

Staff Total facility staff includes 14 physicians, 13 psychologists, 11 psychiatrists, 16 registered nurses, 2 practical/vocational nurses, 6 MSW social workers, 1 teacher, 6 counselors, 2 occupational/recreational therapists, 1 speech pathologist, 1 therapist, 1 dietician.

Facilities Single building; males and females in coeducational units. Separate residential quarters for children and adolescents. Central dining (shared with adults). Basketball courts, game room, gymnasium, outdoor swimming pool, outdoor tennis courts, ropes course, playground.

Education Academic program available at no charge. Serves ages 5–17, grades K–12. 1 teacher on staff. Curriculum accredited or approved by Kern County Superintendent of Schools.

Costs Accepts private insurance, group insurance, medicare, Blue Cross/Blue Shield.

Additional Services Outpatient services for males and females ages 5 and up. Treats behavior disorders; general psychosocial disorders; substance abuse; compulsive/addictive disorders other than substance abuse and eating disorders; thought, mood, and personality disorders.

Contact Tim Ross, Director of Marketing, main address above. Phone: 805-398-1800. Fax: 805-837-0755.

chosocial disorders; substance abuse; eating disorders; compulsive/addictive disorders other than substance abuse and eating disorders; post-traumatic stress disorder; thought, mood, and personality disorders. Accepts the mobility impaired; the vision impaired; the hearing impaired; the speech impaired; those with a history of arson; the sexually compulsive; those with a history of harm to themselves and others; those receiving psychotropic medication; those with a history of epilepsy. Special programs for the chronically ill; the developmentally disabled; the vision impaired; the hearing impaired; the speech impaired; those with AIDS.

Program Treatment modalities: psychodynamic; Twelve Step Recovery. Family treatment program available.

Staff Total facility staff includes 6 physicians, 2 MSW social workers, 1 teacher, 1 occupational/recreational therapist, 1 dietician, 3 other direct-care staff members.

Facilities Single building; males and females in coeducational units. Central dining (shared with adults). Basketball courts, gymnasium, ropes course.

Education Academic program available at additional cost. Serves ages 13–18, grades 6–12. 1 teacher on staff. Curriculum accredited or approved by County of Albemarle, City of Charlottesville. Cost of educational program sometimes covered by local school district.

Costs Average cost: $700 per day. Accepts private insurance, group insurance, medicare, Blue Cross/Blue Shield, public funds.

Contact Bonnie Cady, Community Services, main address above. Phone: 804-977-1120. Fax: 804-295-0984.

CHARTER HOSPITAL OF CHARLOTTESVILLE
2101 Arlington Boulevard
Charlottesville, Virginia 22905
804-977-1120; Fax: 804-295-0984

General Information Psychiatric hospital for adolescents, adults. 15 beds for adolescents. Open year-round. Patient security: entirely locked; will pursue and return runaways. Urban setting. For-profit facility affiliated with Charter Medical Corporation, Macon, GA. Licensed by state of Virginia. Accredited by JCAHO.

Participants Accepts: male and female adolescents ages 13–18; male and female adults ages 18 and up. Average stay: 25 days. Admission: one parent. Treats learning disabilities; behavior disorders; general psy-

CHARTER HOSPITAL OF COLUMBIA
200 Portland Street
Columbia, Missouri 65201
314-876-8000; Fax: 314-449-4811

General Information Psychiatric hospital for children, adolescents, adults. 16 beds for children; 24 beds for adolescents; 64 beds total. Open year-round. Patient security: entirely locked; will pursue and return runaways. Urban setting. For-profit facility affiliated with Charter Medical Corporation, Macon, GA. Licensed by state of Missouri. Accredited by JCAHO; Health Care Financing Administration.

Participants Accepts: male and female children ages 4–12; male and female adolescents ages 13–17; male and female adults ages 18 and up. Admission: one parent, all parties who share custody, court order, voluntary, committed, depending on program. Treats autistic disorders; learning disabilities; behavior disorders; general psychosocial disorders; substance abuse; eating disorders; compulsive/addictive disorders other than substance abuse and eating disorders; post-traumatic stress disorder; thought, mood, and personality disorders. Accepts the mobility impaired; the hearing impaired; those with a history of arson; the sexually compulsive; those with a history of harm to themselves and others; those receiving psychotropic medication; those with a history of epilepsy.

Program Treatment modalities: reality therapy, group therapy; play therapy, individual therapy, family therapy; Twelve Step Recovery; behavioral contracting. Family treatment program available.

Staff .4 full-time direct-care staff member per child or adolescent. Total facility staff includes 41 registered nurses, 6 practical/vocational nurses, 6 MSW social workers, 2 social workers (non-MSW), 2 teachers, 2 occupational/recreational therapists, 1 speech pathologist, 65 other direct-care staff members. Staff is 41% male, 59% female.

Facilities Single building; males and females in co-educational units. Separate residential quarters for children and adolescents. Central dining (shared with adults). Basketball courts, game room, gymnasium, outdoor tennis courts, playing fields, ropes course, wooden playground.

Education 2 teachers on staff. Educational arrangements: assignments made through the patient's home school district. Cost of educational program covered by local school district.

Costs Accepts private insurance, group insurance, medicare, medicaid, Blue Cross/Blue Shield.

Additional Services Drug and alcohol rehabilitation services for males and females ages 13 and up. Treats learning disabilities; behavior disorders; general psychosocial disorders; substance abuse; eating disorders; compulsive/addictive disorders other than substance abuse and eating disorders; post-traumatic stress disorder; thought, mood, and personality disorders. Outpatient services for males and females ages 18 and up. Treats substance abuse; compulsive/addictive disorders other than substance abuse and eating disorders. Residential or sub-acute services for males and females ages 4–17. Treats learning disabilities; behavior disorders; general psychosocial disorders; substance abuse; eating disorders; compulsive/addictive disorders other than substance abuse and eating disorders; post-traumatic stress disorder; thought, mood, and personality disorders.

Contact Susan Harris, Director of Marketing, main address above. Phone: 314-876-8207. Fax: 314-449-4811.

CHARTER HOSPITAL OF CORPUS CHRISTI
3126 Rodd Field Road
Corpus Christi, Texas 78414
512-993-8893; Fax: 512-993-5360

General Information Psychiatric hospital for children, adolescents. Patient security: entirely locked. For-profit facility affiliated with Charter Medical Corporation, Macon, GA. Licensed by state of Texas. Accredited by JCAHO.

Participants Accepts: male and female children; male and female adolescents. Average stay: 26 days. Admission: one parent, all parties who share custody, court order, voluntary, depending on program. Treats learning disabilities; behavior disorders; general psychosocial disorders; substance abuse; eating disorders; compulsive/addictive disorders other than substance abuse and eating disorders; post-traumatic stress disorder; thought, mood, and personality disorders.

Staff Staff is 50% male, 50% female.

Additional Services Drug and alcohol rehabilitation services for males and females ages 4 and up. Treats learning disabilities; behavior disorders; general psychosocial disorders; substance abuse; eating disorders; compulsive/addictive disorders other than substance abuse and eating disorders; post-traumatic stress disorder; thought, mood, and personality disorders.

Contact Intake Office, main address above. Phone: 512-993-8893 Ext. 134.

CHARTER HOSPITAL OF FOUNTAIN VALLEY
11250 Warner Avenue
Fountain Valley, California 92708
714-668-9000; Fax: 714-540-0938

General Information Psychiatric hospital for adolescents, adults. 20 beds for adolescents. Open year-round. Patient security: partially locked; will pursue and return runaways. Suburban setting. For-profit facility affiliated with Charter Hospital, Macon, GA. Licensed by state of California. Accredited by JCAHO.

Participants Accepts: male and female adolescents ages 12–18; male and female adults ages 18 and up. Average stay: 18 days. Admission: one parent, all parties who share custody, court order, voluntary, depending on program. Treats learning disabilities; behavior disorders; general psychosocial disorders;

substance abuse; eating disorders; compulsive/addictive disorders other than substance abuse and eating disorders; post-traumatic stress disorder; thought, mood, and personality disorders. Accepts the mobility impaired; the vision impaired; the hearing impaired; the speech impaired; those with a history of arson; the sexually compulsive; those with a history of harm to themselves and others; those receiving psychotropic medication; those with a history of epilepsy. Largest number of participants from California.

Program Treatment modalities: cognitive therapy; Twelve Step Recovery; behavior modification and reality; psychodynamic. Family treatment program available.

Staff Total facility staff includes 8 physicians, 27 psychologists, 18 psychiatrists, 16 registered nurses, 4 practical/vocational nurses, 2 MSW social workers, 6 social workers (non-MSW), 2 teachers, 15 counselors, 2 physical therapists, 2 occupational/recreational therapists, 1 speech pathologist, 25 therapists, 1 dietician. Staff is 50% male, 50% female.

Facilities Single building; males and females in coeducational units. Separate residential quarters for adolescents. Central dining (shared with adults), in-room dining available. Basketball courts, game room, indoor swimming pool, indoor weight room.

Education Academic program available at no charge. Serves ages 12–18, grades 5–12. 2 teachers on staff. Curriculum accredited or approved by State of California Department of Education.

Costs Average cost: $650 per day. Accepts private insurance, group insurance, Blue Cross/Blue Shield, public funds.

Additional Services Outpatient services for males and females ages 12 and up. Treats learning disabilities; behavior disorders; general psychosocial disorders; substance abuse; eating disorders; compulsive/addictive disorders other than substance abuse and eating disorders; post-traumatic stress disorder; thought, mood, and personality disorders.

Contact Jan Pfeffer, Program Manager, main address above. Phone: 714-668-9000. Fax: 714-540-0938.

CHARTER HOSPITAL OF GREENSBORO
700 Walter Reed Drive
Greensboro, North Carolina 27403
919-852-4821; Fax: 919-852-7224

General Information Psychiatric hospital for adolescents, adults. 32 beds for adolescents. Open year-round. Patient security: partially locked; will pursue and return runaways. Urban setting. For-profit facility affiliated with Charter Medical Corporation, Macon, GA. Licensed by state of North Carolina. Accredited by JCAHO.

Participants Accepts: male and female adolescents ages 10–18; male and female adults ages 18 and up. Average stay: 21 days. Admission: parent or legal guardian. Treats learning disabilities; behavior disorders; general psychosocial disorders; substance abuse; eating disorders; compulsive/addictive disorders other than substance abuse and eating disorders; post-traumatic stress disorder; thought, mood, and personality disorders. Accepts the mobility impaired; the speech impaired; those with a history of harm to themselves and others; those receiving psychotropic medication; those with a history of epilepsy. Special programs for the developmentally disabled; the sexually abused.

Program Treatment modalities: Twelve Step Recovery; psychodynamic; psycho-educational; reality therapy. Family treatment program available.

Staff Total facility staff includes 1 psychologist, 18 psychiatrists, 71 registered nurses, 4 practical/vocational nurses, 8 MSW social workers, 3 teachers, 4 counselors, 2 occupational/recreational therapists, 5 therapists, 1 dietician, 53 other direct-care staff members. Staff is 25% male, 75% female.

Facilities Single building; males and females in coeducational units. Separate residential quarters for adolescents. Central dining (shared with adults). Basketball courts, game room, gymnasium, outdoor swimming pool.

Education Academic program available at no charge. Serves ages 10–18, grades 5–12. 3 teachers on staff. Curriculum accredited or approved by North Carolina Department of Non-Public Institutions. Organized sports program offered.

Costs Average cost: $800 per day. Accepts private insurance, group insurance, medicare, medicaid, Blue Cross/Blue Shield, public funds.

Additional Services Drug and alcohol rehabilitation services for males and females ages 10 and up. Treats learning disabilities; behavior disorders; general psychosocial disorders; substance abuse; eating disorders; compulsive/addictive disorders other than substance abuse and eating disorders; post-traumatic stress disorder; thought, mood, and personality disorders. Outpatient services for males and females ages 5 and up. Treats learning disabilities; behavior disorders; general psychosocial disorders; substance abuse; eating disorders; compulsive/addictive disorders other than substance abuse and eating disorders; post-traumatic stress disorder; thought, mood, and personality disorders. Camping program for males and females ages 8–12. Treats learning disabilities; behavior disorders; general psychosocial disorders; post-traumatic stress disorder; thought, mood, and personality disorders. Partial hospitalization for males and females ages 10 and up. Treats learning disabilities; behavior disorders; general psychosocial disorders; substance abuse; eating disorders; compulsive/addictive disorders other than substance abuse and eating disorders; post-traumatic stress disorder; thought, mood, and personality disorders.

Contact Robin Bartlett, Program Administrator, main address above. Phone: 919-852-4821. Fax: 919-852-7224.

CHARTER HOSPITAL OF INDIANAPOLIS
5602 Caito
Indianapolis, Indiana 46226
317-545-2111

General Information Psychiatric hospital for children, adolescents. Patient security: partially locked. Not-for-profit facility affiliated with Charter Medical Corporation, Macon, GA. Licensed by state of Indiana. Accredited by JCAHO.

Participants Accepts: male and female children; male and female adolescents. Admission: one parent, all parties who share custody, court order, depending on program. Treats learning disabilities; behavior disorders; general psychosocial disorders; substance abuse; eating disorders; compulsive/addictive disorders other than substance abuse and eating disorders; post-traumatic stress disorder; thought, mood, and personality disorders.

Contact Needs Assessment, main address above. Phone: 317-545-2111.

CHARTER HOSPITAL OF LAFAYETTE
3700 Rome Drive
Lafayette, Indiana 47903
317-448-6999

General Information Mental health hospital for children, adolescents. Patient security: partially locked. For-profit facility affiliated with Charter Medical Corporation, Macon, GA. Licensed by state of Indiana. Accredited by JCAHO.

Participants Accepts: male and female children; male and female adolescents. Admission: one parent, all parties who share custody, court order, voluntary,

depending on program. Treats autistic disorders; learning disabilities; behavior disorders; general psychosocial disorders; substance abuse; eating disorders; post-traumatic stress disorder; thought, mood, and personality disorders.

Staff Staff is 35% male, 65% female.

Contact Needs Assessment and Referral Center, P.O. Box 5969, Lafayette, IN 47903. Phone: 800-544-1564.

CHARTER HOSPITAL OF LAS VEGAS
7000 West Spring Mountain Road
Las Vegas, Nevada 89117
702-876-4357; Fax: 702-876-1897

General Information Psychiatric hospital for children, adolescents, adults. Open year-round. Patient security: entirely locked; will pursue and return runaways. Urban setting. For-profit facility affiliated with Charter Medical Corporation, Macon, GA. Licensed by state of Nevada. Accredited by JCAHO; American Hospital Association.

Participants Accepts: male and female children ages 5–11; male and female adolescents ages 12–17; male and female adults ages 18 and up. Treats learning disabilities; behavior disorders; general psychosocial disorders; substance abuse; eating disorders; compulsive/addictive disorders other than substance abuse and eating disorders; post-traumatic stress disorder; thought, mood, and personality disorders. Accepts those with a history of arson; the sexually compulsive; those with a history of harm to themselves and others; those receiving psychotropic medication; non-English speaking individuals; those with a history of epilepsy.

Program Treatment modalities: Twelve Step Recovery; psychodynamic; behavioral. Family treatment program available.

Staff Total facility staff includes 8 physicians, 20 psychologists, 6 psychiatrists, 45 registered nurses, 5 practical/vocational nurses, 3 MSW social workers, 1 social worker (non-MSW), 2 teachers, 4 occupational/recreational therapists, 10 therapists, 1 dietician.

Facilities Single building; males and females in co-educational units. Separate residential quarters for children and adolescents. Central dining (shared with adults). Gymnasium, outdoor swimming pool, play area for 5-11 year olds.

Education Academic program available at no charge. Serves ages 5–17, grades K–12. 2 teachers on staff. Curriculum accredited or approved by Clark County School District—Homebound.

Costs   Average cost: $480 per day. Accepts private insurance, group insurance, medicare, medicaid, Blue Cross/Blue Shield.

Additional Services   Drug and alcohol rehabilitation services for males and females ages 11–18. Treats behavior disorders; general psychosocial disorders; substance abuse; thought, mood, and personality disorders.

Contact   Bobbie Stenger, Adolescent/Child Program Manager, main address above. Phone: 702-876-4357. Fax: 702-876-1897.

CHARTER HOSPITAL OF LITTLE ROCK
1601 Murphy Drive
Maumelle, Arkansas 72113
501-851-8700; Fax: 501-851-8659

General Information   Freestanding psychiatric, drug, and alcohol rehabilitation center for children, adolescents. Patient security: entirely locked. For-profit facility affiliated with Charter Medical Corporation, Macon, GA. Licensed by state of Arkansas. Accredited by JCAHO.

Participants   Accepts: male and female children; male and female adolescents. Admission: one parent, all parties who share custody, court order, voluntary, depending on program. Treats learning disabilities; behavior disorders; general psychosocial disorders; substance abuse; compulsive/addictive disorders other than substance abuse and eating disorders; post-traumatic stress disorder; thought, mood, and personality disorders.

Contact   Needs Assessment Department, main address above. Phone: 800-842-4282.

CHARTER HOSPITAL OF LONG BEACH
6060 Paramount Boulevard
Long Beach, California 90805
310-220-1000

General Information   Psychiatric hospital for children, adolescents, adults. 17 beds for children; 26 beds for adolescents; 93 beds total. Open year-round. Patient security: partially locked; will pursue and return runaways. Urban setting. Not-for-profit facility affiliated with Charter Medical Corporation, Macon, GA. Operated by Charter Medical Corporation, Macon, GA. Licensed by state of California. Accredited by JCAHO.

Participants   Accepts: male and female children ages 5–12; male and female adolescents ages 12–17; male and female adults ages 18 and up. Average stay: 17 days. Admission: all parties who share custody. Treats autistic disorders; learning disabilities; behavior disorders; general psychosocial disorders; substance abuse; eating disorders; compulsive/addictive disorders other than substance abuse and eating disorders; post-traumatic stress disorder; thought, mood, and personality disorders. Accepts the mobility impaired; the vision impaired; the hearing impaired; the speech impaired; those with a history of arson; the sexually compulsive; those with a history of harm to themselves and others; those receiving psychotropic medication; non-English speaking individuals; those with a history of epilepsy. Special programs for the mobility impaired.

Program   Treatment modalities: Twelve Step Recovery; psychodynamic. Family treatment program available.

Facilities   Multiple buildings; males and females in coeducational units. Separate residential quarters for children and adolescents. Central dining (shared with adults). Basketball courts, game room, gymnasium, outdoor swimming pool, playing fields, ropes course, outdoor volleyball court.

Education   Academic program available at no charge. Serves ages 5–18, grades K–12. Curriculum accredited or approved by Long Beach Unified.

Additional Services   Drug and alcohol rehabilitation services for males and females ages 5 and up. Treats autistic disorders; learning disabilities; behavior disorders; general psychosocial disorders; substance abuse; eating disorders; compulsive/addictive disorders other than substance abuse and eating disorders; post-traumatic stress disorder; thought, mood, and personality disorders. Outpatient services for males and females ages 5 and up. Treats autistic disorders; learning disabilities; behavior disorders; general psychosocial disorders; substance abuse; eating disorders; compulsive/addictive disorders other than substance abuse and eating disorders; post-traumatic stress disorder; thought, mood, and personality disorders.

Contact   Debe G. Peterson, Youth Services Program Manager, main address above. Phone: 310-220-1000.

CHARTER HOSPITAL OF LOUISVILLE
1405 Browns Lane
Louisville, Kentucky 40207
502-896-0495

General Information   Psychiatric hospital for adolescents, adults. 20 beds for adolescents. Open year-round. Patient security: partially locked; will pursue and return runaways. Suburban setting. For-profit facility affiliated with Charter Medical Corporation, Macon, GA. Licensed by state of Kentucky. Accredited by JCAHO.

Participants   Accepts: male and female adolescents ages 13–18; male and female adults ages 18 and up. Average stay: 25 days. Admission: one parent, all parties who share custody, court order, voluntary, state custody, depending on program. Treats autistic disorders; learning disabilities; behavior disorders; general psychosocial disorders; substance abuse; eating disorders; compulsive/addictive disorders other than substance abuse and eating disorders; post-traumatic stress disorder; thought, mood, and personality disorders. Accepts the mobility impaired; the vision impaired; the hearing impaired; the speech impaired; those with a history of arson; the sexually compulsive; those with a history of harm to themselves and others; those receiving psychotropic medication; non-English speaking individuals; those with a history of epilepsy; those with Tourette's Syndrome.

Program   Treatment modalities: Twelve Step Recovery; behavior modification for adolescents; psychodynamic/cognitive. Family treatment program available.

Staff   Total facility staff includes 3 physicians, 6 psychiatrists, 37 registered nurses, 4 practical/vocational nurses, 3 MSW social workers, 3 social workers (non-MSW), 1 teacher, 3 occupational/recreational therapists, 25 other direct-care staff members. Staff is 43% male, 57% female.

Facilities   Single building; males and females in co-educational units. Separate residential quarters for adolescents. Central dining (shared with adults), in-room dining available. Basketball courts, gymnasium, outdoor tennis courts, playing fields, fitness trail.

Education   Academic program available at no charge. Serves ages 13–18, grades 8–12. 1 teacher on staff. Curriculum accredited or approved by Jefferson County Board of Education.

Costs   Accepts private insurance, group insurance, medicare, medicaid, Blue Cross/Blue Shield.

Additional Services   Drug and alcohol rehabilitation services for males and females ages 13 and up. Treats autistic disorders; learning disabilities; behavior disorders; general psychosocial disorders; substance abuse; eating disorders; compulsive/addictive disord-ers other than substance abuse and eating disorders; post-traumatic stress disorder; thought, mood, and personality disorders. Outpatient services for males and females ages 8 and up. Treats autistic disorders; learning disabilities; behavior disorders; general psychosocial disorders; substance abuse; eating disorders; compulsive/addictive disorders other than substance abuse and eating disorders; post-traumatic stress disorder; thought, mood, and personality disorders.

Contact   Toni Bryan, Director of Marketing, main address above. Phone: 502-896-0495.

CHARTER HOSPITAL OF MILWAUKEE
11101 West Lincoln Avenue
West Allis, Wisconsin 53227
414-327-3000; Fax: 414-327-6045

General Information   Psychiatric hospital for children, adolescents, adults. 8 beds for children; 16 beds for adolescents; 80 beds total. Open year-round. Patient security: entirely locked; no runaway pursuit. Suburban setting. For-profit facility affiliated with Charter Medical Corporation, Macon, GA. Licensed by state of Wisconsin. Accredited by JCAHO; Health Care Financing Administration.

Participants   Accepts: male and female children ages 4–11; male and female adolescents ages 12–18; male and female adults ages 18 and up. Average stay: 26 days. Admission: one parent, all parties who share custody, court order, voluntary, depending on program. Treats learning disabilities; behavior disorders; general psychosocial disorders; substance abuse; eating disorders; compulsive/addictive disorders other than substance abuse and eating disorders; post-traumatic stress disorder; thought, mood, and personality disorders. Accepts the mobility impaired; the vision impaired; the hearing impaired; the speech impaired; those with a history of arson; the sexually compulsive; those with a history of harm to themselves and others; those receiving psychotropic medication; those with a history of epilepsy. Special programs for the chronically ill; the mobility impaired; the developmentally disabled; the vision impaired; the hearing impaired; the speech impaired; those with AIDS. Largest number of participants from Wisconsin.

Program   Treatment modalities: milieu/psychoeducational; Twelve Step Recovery; psychodynamic. Family treatment program available.

Staff   Total facility staff includes 12 physicians, 19 psychologists, 9 psychiatrists, 46 registered nurses, 3 practical/vocational nurses, 3 MSW social workers,

13 social workers (non-MSW), 3 teachers, 4 counselors, 4 occupational/recreational therapists, 1 speech pathologist, 1 dietician, 28 other direct-care staff members. Staff is 26% male, 74% female.

Facilities Single building; males and females in co-educational units. Separate residential quarters for children and adolescents. Central dining (not shared with adults). Basketball courts, gymnasium, outdoor tennis courts, ropes course.

Education Academic program available at no charge. Serves ages 4–17, grades K–12. 3 teachers on staff. Curriculum accredited or approved by North Central Association of Colleges and Schools. Organized sports program offered.

Costs Accepts private insurance, group insurance, medicare, medicaid, Blue Cross/Blue Shield.

Additional Services Drug and alcohol rehabilitation services for males and females ages 12 and up. Treats learning disabilities; behavior disorders; general psychosocial disorders; substance abuse; eating disorders; compulsive/addictive disorders other than substance abuse and eating disorders; post-traumatic stress disorder; thought, mood, and personality disorders. Outpatient services for males and females ages 4 and up. Treats autistic disorders; learning disabilities; behavior disorders; general psychosocial disorders; substance abuse; eating disorders; compulsive/addictive disorders other than substance abuse and eating disorders; post-traumatic stress disorder; thought, mood, and personality disorders. Women's program for females ages 18 and up. Treats general psychosocial disorders; substance abuse; eating disorders; compulsive/addictive disorders other than substance abuse and eating disorders; post-traumatic stress disorder; thought, mood, and personality disorders.

Contact Laurie K. Maes, Marketing Director, main address above. Phone: 414-327-3000. Fax: 414-327-6045.

CHARTER HOSPITAL OF OVERLAND PARK—YOUTH SERVICES PROGRAM
8000 West 127th Street
Overland Park, Kansas 66213
800-842-9355; Fax: 913-897-2046

General Information Freestanding psychiatric/drug and alcohol rehabilitation hospital for adolescents. 12 beds for adolescents. Patient security: partially locked. For-profit facility affiliated with Charter Medical Corporation, Macon, GA. Licensed by state of Kansas. Accredited by JCAHO.

Participants Accepts: male and female adolescents. Average stay: 21 days. Admission: one parent, all parties who share custody, court order, voluntary, depending on program. Treats autistic disorders; learning disabilities; behavior disorders; general psychosocial disorders; substance abuse; eating disorders; compulsive/addictive disorders other than substance abuse and eating disorders; post-traumatic stress disorder; thought, mood, and personality disorders.

Staff Staff is 30% male, 70% female.

Costs Average cost: $975 per day.

Additional Services Outpatient services for males and females ages 12–18. Treats autistic disorders; learning disabilities; behavior disorders; general psychosocial disorders; substance abuse; eating disorders; compulsive/addictive disorders other than substance abuse and eating disorders; post-traumatic stress disorder; thought, mood, and personality disorders.

Contact Mike Truman, Intake Coordinator, main address above. Phone: 800-842-9355. Fax: 913-897-2046.

CHARTER HOSPITAL OF PADUCAH
435 Berger Road
Paducah, Kentucky 42002
502-444-0444; Fax: 502-443-3768

General Information Psychiatric hospital for children, adolescents. Patient security: entirely locked. For-profit facility affiliated with Charter Medical Corporation, Macon, GA. Licensed by state of Kentucky. Accredited by JCAHO.

Participants Accepts: male and female children; male and female adolescents. Average stay: 24 days. Admission: one parent, voluntary, depending on program. Treats behavior disorders; general psychosocial disorders; substance abuse; post-traumatic stress disorder; thought, mood, and personality disorders.

Contact Sherri Fouty, Human Resource Director, P.O. Box 7609, Paducah, KY 42002. Phone: 502-444-0444. Fax: 502-443-3768.

CHARTER HOSPITAL OF PASCO
21808 S.R. 54
Lutz, Florida 33549
800-322-2673; Fax: 813-948-2805

General Information Psychiatric hospital for children, adolescents, adults. 15 beds for children; 15 beds for adolescents; 72 beds total. Open year-round. Patient security: entirely locked; will pursue and return runaways. Suburban setting. For-profit facility affiliated with Charter Medical Corporation, Macon, GA. Licensed by state of Florida. Accredited by JCAHO; National Association of Private Psychiatric Hospitals.

Participants Accepts: male and female children ages 3–13; male and female adolescents ages 11–19; male and female adults ages 18 and up. Average stay: 11 days. Admission: voluntary and involuntary per Baker Act Guidelines. Treats autistic disorders; learning disabilities; behavior disorders; general psychosocial disorders; substance abuse; eating disorders; compulsive/addictive disorders other than substance abuse and eating disorders; post-traumatic stress disorder; thought, mood, and personality disorders. Accepts the mobility impaired; the vision impaired; the hearing impaired; the speech impaired; those with a history of arson; the sexually compulsive; those with a history of harm to themselves and others; those receiving psychotropic medication; non-English speaking individuals; those with a history of epilepsy. Special programs for the chronically ill; the mobility impaired; the speech impaired.

Program Treatment modalities: Twelve Step Recovery; expressive therapy; pyschodynamic; family therapy. Family treatment program available.

Staff .1 full-time direct-care staff member per child or adolescent. Total facility staff includes 17 physicians, 37 psychologists, 14 psychiatrists, 6 registered nurses, 1 MSW social worker, 1 teacher, 7 counselors, 2 occupational/recreational therapists, 1 dietician, 1 other direct-care staff member. Staff is 30% male, 70% female.

Facilities Single building; males and females in co-educational units. Separate residential quarters for children and adolescents. Central dining (shared with adults). Basketball courts, game room, outdoor swimming pool, outdoor tennis courts, playing fields, ropes course.

Education Academic program available at no charge. Serves ages 3–19, grades K–12. 1 teacher on staff. Curriculum accredited or approved by Alternative Education of Pasco County.

Costs Average cost: $985 per stay. Accepts private insurance, group insurance, medicare, Blue Cross/Blue Shield.

Additional Services Drug and alcohol rehabilitation services for males and females ages 3–90. Treats autistic disorders; learning disabilities; behavior disorders; general psychosocial disorders; substance abuse; eating disorders; compulsive/addictive disorders other than substance abuse and eating disorders; post-traumatic stress disorder; thought, mood, and personality disorders. Outpatient services for males and females ages 3–90. Treats autistic disorders; learning disabilities; behavior disorders; general psychosocial disorders; substance abuse; eating disorders; compulsive/addictive disorders other than substance abuse and eating disorders; post-traumatic stress disorder; thought, mood, and personality disorders.

Contact Phyllis Gilker Lancaster, Marketing Director, main address above. Phone: 813-948-2441 Ext. 304. Fax: 813-948-2805.

CHARTER HOSPITAL OF SAVANNAH
1150 Cornall Avenue
Savannah, Georgia 31406
912-354-3911; Fax: 912-354-0352

General Information Psychiatric hospital for children, adolescents. Patient security: entirely locked. For-profit facility affiliated with Charter Medical Corporation, Macon, GA. Licensed by state of Georgia. Accredited by JCAHO.

Participants Accepts: male and female children; male and female adolescents. Average stay: 22 days. Admission: one parent, all parties who share custody, court order, voluntary, depending on program. Treats autistic disorders; learning disabilities; behavior disorders; general psychosocial disorders; substance abuse; eating disorders; compulsive/addictive disorders other than substance abuse and eating disorders; post-traumatic stress disorder; thought, mood, and personality disorders.

Costs Average cost: $700 per day.

Contact Needs Assessment Department, main address above. Phone: 912-354-3911.

CHARTER HOSPITAL OF TOLEDO, INC.
1725 Timber Line Road
Maumee, Ohio 43537
419-891-9333; Fax: 419-891-9330

General Information Psychiatric hospital for children, adolescents. 18 beds for children; 20 beds for adolescents; 38 beds total. Open year-round. Patient security: entirely locked; will pursue and return runaways. Urban setting. For-profit facility affiliated with Charter Medical Corporation, Macon, GA. Accredited by JCAHO.

Participants Accepts: male and female children ages 4–12; male and female adolescents ages 13–18. Average stay: 2 weeks. Admission: one parent, court order, depending on program. Treats learning disabilities; behavior disorders; general psychosocial disorders; substance abuse; eating disorders; compulsive/addictive disorders other than substance abuse and eating disorders; post-traumatic stress disorder; thought, mood, and personality disorders. Accepts the mobility impaired; the speech impaired; those with a history of arson; those with a history of harm to themselves and others; those receiving psychotropic medication. Special programs for the developmentally disabled.

Program Treatment modalities: family systems; behavior modification. Family treatment program available.

Facilities Single building; males and females in co-educational units. Central dining, in-room dining available. Basketball courts, game room, gymnasium, outdoor tennis courts.

Education Academic program available at no charge. Serves ages 4–18. Curriculum accredited or approved by Lucas County Board of Education.

Costs Accepts private insurance, medicaid, Blue Cross/Blue Shield.

Additional Services Drug and alcohol rehabilitation services for males and females ages 13–18. Treats substance abuse. Outpatient services for males and females. Treats learning disabilities; behavior disorders; general psychosocial disorders; substance abuse; eating disorders; compulsive/addictive disorders other than substance abuse and eating disorders; post-traumatic stress disorder; thought, mood, and personality disorders.

Contact Needs Assessment Department, main address above. Phone: 800-766-9355.

CHARTER HOSPITAL OF WICHITA
8901 East Orme
Wichita, Kansas 67207
316-686-5000

General Information Freestanding psychiatric and chemical dependency hospital for children, adolescents. Patient security: entirely locked. For-profit facility affiliated with Charter Medical Corporation, Macon, GA. Licensed by state of Kansas. Accredited by JCAHO.

Participants Accepts: male and female children; male and female adolescents. Average stay: 25 days. Admission: one parent, all parties who share custody, court order, voluntary, depending on program. Treats autistic disorders; learning disabilities; behavior disorders; general psychosocial disorders; substance abuse; eating disorders; compulsive/addictive disorders other than substance abuse and eating disorders; post-traumatic stress disorder; thought, mood, and personality disorders.

Staff Staff is 30% male, 70% female.

Contact Linda Long, Needs Assessment Manager, main address above. Phone: 316-686-5000.

CHARTER HOSPITAL ORLANDO SOUTH
206 Park Place Drive
Kissimmee, Florida 34741
407-846-0444; Fax: 407-846-4216

General Information Psychiatric hospital for adolescents. 20 beds for adolescents. Open year-round. Patient security: entirely locked; no runaway pursuit. Suburban setting. For-profit facility affiliated with Charter Medical Corporation, Macon, GA. Licensed by state of Florida. Accredited by JCAHO.

Participants Accepts: male and female adolescents ages 11–17. Average stay: 22 days. Admission: one parent, all parties who share custody, court order, depending on program. Treats learning disabilities; behavior disorders; general psychosocial disorders; substance abuse; eating disorders; compulsive/addictive disorders other than substance abuse and eating disorders; post-traumatic stress disorder; thought, mood, and personality disorders. Accepts the mobility impaired; those with a history of arson; the sexually compulsive; those with a history of harm to themselves and others; those receiving psychotropic medication; those with a history of epilepsy. Largest number of participants from Florida.

Program Treatment modalities: systems therapy; cognitive behavioral. Family treatment program available.

Staff Total facility staff includes 15 psychologists, 10 psychiatrists, 10 registered nurses, 3 MSW social workers, 1 teacher, 1 counselor, 1 occupational/recreational therapist, 1 dietician, 25 other direct-care staff members. Staff is 25% male, 75% female.

Facilities Single building; males and females in co-educational units. Central dining (shared with adults). Basketball courts, gymnasium.

Education Academic program available at no charge. Serves ages 11–17, grades 5–12. 1 teacher on staff. Curriculum accredited or approved by State of Florida. Organized sports program offered.

Costs Accepts private insurance, group insurance, medicare, Blue Cross/Blue Shield.

Additional Services Outpatient services for males and females ages 6–85. Treats autistic disorders; learning disabilities; behavior disorders; general psychosocial disorders; substance abuse; eating disorders; compulsive/addictive disorders other than substance abuse and eating disorders; post-traumatic stress disorder; thought, mood, and personality disorders.

Contact Bill Jennings, Needs Assessment Manager, main address above. Phone: 800-877-5863. Fax: 407-846-4216.

CHARTER LAKE HOSPITAL
3500 Riverside Drive
Macon, Georgia 31209
912-474-6200; Fax: 912-474-6709

General Information Psychiatric hospital for children, adolescents. Patient security: partially locked. For-profit facility affiliated with Charter Medical Corporation, Macon, GA. Licensed by state of Georgia. Accredited by JCAHO.

Participants Accepts: male and female children; male and female adolescents. Average stay: 2 weeks. Admission: one parent, all parties who share custody, court order, voluntary, depending on program. Treats learning disabilities; behavior disorders; general psychosocial disorders; substance abuse; eating disorders; compulsive/addictive disorders other than substance abuse and eating disorders; post-traumatic stress disorder; thought, mood, and personality disorders.

Costs Average cost: $600 per day.

Contact Needs Assessment Referral Department, P.O. Box 7067, Macon, GA 31209. Phone: 912-474-6200.

CHARTER LAKESIDE HOSPITAL
2911 Brunswick Road
Memphis, Tennessee 38133
901-377-4700; Fax: 901-373-0912

General Information Psychiatric hospital for children, adolescents, adults. Open year-round. Patient security: partially locked; will pursue and return runaways. Suburban setting. For-profit facility affiliated with Charter Medical Corporation, Macon, GA. Licensed by state of Tennessee. Accredited by JCAHO; State of Tennessee Mental Health and Mental Retardation, Civilian Health and Medical Program of the Uniformed Services.

Participants Accepts: male and female children ages 5–12; male and female adolescents ages 12–17; male and female adults ages 18 and up. Average stay: 15 months. Admission: all parties who share custody. Treats learning disabilities; behavior disorders; general psychosocial disorders; substance abuse; eating disorders; compulsive/addictive disorders other than substance abuse and eating disorders; post-traumatic stress disorder; thought, mood, and personality disorders. Accepts the mobility impaired; the vision impaired; the hearing impaired; the speech impaired; those with a history of arson; the sexually compulsive; those with a history of harm to themselves and others; those receiving psychotropic medication. Special programs for the chronically ill; the mobility impaired; the developmentally disabled; the vision impaired; the hearing impaired; the speech impaired; those with AIDS.

Program Treatment modalities: multi-disciplinary; Twelve Step Recovery. Family treatment program available.

Facilities Multiple buildings; males and females in coeducational units. Separate residential quarters for children and adolescents. Central dining (not shared with adults), separate dining by residential unit available. Basketball courts, gymnasium, outdoor swimming pool, outdoor tennis courts, ropes course.

Education Academic program available at no charge. Serves ages 5–17, grades K–12. Curriculum accredited or approved by Tennessee State Department of Education. Cost of educational program sometimes covered by local school district.

Costs Accepts private insurance, group insurance, medicare, medicaid, Blue Cross/Blue Shield.

Additional Services Drug and alcohol rehabilitation services for males and females ages 5 and up. Treats learning disabilities; behavior disorders; general psychosocial disorders; substance abuse; eating disorders; compulsive/addictive disorders other than substance abuse and eating disorders; post-traumatic stress disorder; thought, mood, and personality disorders. Outpatient services for males and females ages 5 and up. Treats learning disabilities; behavior disorders; general psychosocial disorders; substance abuse; eating disorders; compulsive/addictive disorders other than substance abuse and eating disorders; post-traumatic stress disorder; thought, mood, and personality disorders. Camping program for males and females ages 6–17. Treats learning disabilities; behavior disorders.

Contact Beth Quinn, Program Administrator, Child and Adolescent Services, main address above. Phone: 901-377-4700. Fax: 901-373-0912.

CHARTER NORTHRIDGE HOSPITAL
400 Newton Road
Raleigh, North Carolina 27615
919-847-0008; Fax: 919-870-6739

General Information Psychiatric hospital for adolescents. 37 beds for adolescents. Open year-round. Patient security: entirely locked; no runaway pursuit. Suburban setting. For-profit facility affiliated with Charter Medical Corporation, Macon, GA. Licensed by state of North Carolina. Accredited by JCAHO.

Participants Accepts: male and female adolescents ages 12–17. Average stay: 90 days. Admission: court order. Treats behavior disorders; general psychosocial disorders; substance abuse; post-traumatic stress disorder; thought, mood, and personality disorders. Accepts those with a history of harm to themselves and others; those receiving psychotropic medication. Largest number of participants from North Carolina.

Program Treatment modalities: Twelve Step Recovery; cognitive behavioral; rational emotive therapy; reality therapy. Family treatment program available.

Staff Total facility staff includes 1 physician, 1 psychologist, 1 psychiatrist, 5 registered nurses, 2 MSW social workers, 2 teachers, 3 counselors, 1 occupational/recreational therapist, 1 therapist. Staff is 40% male, 60% female.

Facilities Single building; males and females in separate units. Central dining (shared with adults). Basketball courts, game room, gymnasium, outdoor swimming pool, outdoor tennis courts, ropes course.

Education Academic program available at no charge. Serves ages 12–17, grades 6–12. 2 teachers on staff. Curriculum accredited or approved by State of North Carolina Department of Public Instruction.

Costs Average cost: $325 per day. Accepts private insurance, group insurance, Blue Cross/Blue Shield, public funds.

Additional Services Drug and alcohol rehabilitation services for males and females ages 12–17. Treats general psychosocial disorders; substance abuse; post-traumatic stress disorder; thought, mood, and personality disorders. Residential or sub-acute services for males and females ages 12–17. Treats behavior disorders; general psychosocial disorders; substance abuse; compulsive/addictive disorders other than substance abuse and eating disorders; post-traumatic stress disorder; thought, mood, and personality disorders.

Contact Andy Delbridge, Marketing Director, main address above. Phone: 919-847-0008. Fax: 919-870-6739.

CHARTER OF CHARLESTON
2777 Speissegger Drive
Charleston, South Carolina 29405
803-747-5830

General Information Psychiatric hospital for children, adolescents, adults. 18 beds for children; 18 beds for adolescents. Open year-round. Patient security: partially locked; will pursue and return runaways. Urban setting. For-profit facility affiliated with Charter Medical Corporation, Macon, GA. Licensed by state of South Carolina. Accredited by JCAHO.

Participants Accepts: male and female children ages 3–14; male and female adolescents ages 12–19; male and female adults ages 17 and up. Average stay: 14 days. Admission: one parent, court order, depending on program. Treats autistic disorders; learning disabilities; behavior disorders; general psychosocial disorders; substance abuse; eating disorders; compulsive/addictive disorders other than substance abuse and eating disorders; post-traumatic stress disorder; thought, mood, and personality disorders. Accepts the mobility impaired; the vision impaired; the hearing impaired; the speech impaired; those with a history of arson; the sexually compulsive; those with a history of harm to themselves and others; those receiving psychotropic medication; non-English speaking individuals; those with a history of epilepsy. Special programs for the mobility impaired; the developmentally disabled; the vision impaired; the hearing impaired; the speech impaired.

Program Treatment modalities: family therapy (structural, system); behavior modification; psychodynamic; Twelve Step Recovery. Family treatment program available.

Staff .7 full-time direct-care staff member per child or adolescent. Total facility staff includes 10 physicians, 4 psychologists, 10 psychiatrists, 10 registered nurses, 3 practical/vocational nurses, 6 MSW social workers, 1 social worker (non-MSW), 4 teachers, 20 counselors, 5 occupational/recreational therapists, 1 speech pathologist, 1 therapist, 1 dietician, 5 other direct-care staff members. Staff is 25% male, 75% female.

Facilities Multiple buildings; males and females in coeducational units. Separate residential quarters for children and adolescents. Central dining (shared with adults). Basketball courts, game room, gymnasium, playing fields, ropes course.

Education Academic program available at no charge. Serves ages 4–18, grades N–12. 4 teachers on staff. Curriculum accredited or approved by State of South Carolina. Cost of educational program covered by local school district.

Costs Average cost: $780 per day. Accepts private insurance, group insurance, medicare, medicaid, Blue Cross/Blue Shield, public funds.

Additional Services Residential or sub-acute services for males and females ages 12–18. Treats learning disabilities; behavior disorders; general psychosocial disorders; substance abuse; eating disorders; compulsive/addictive disorders other than substance abuse and eating disorders; post-traumatic stress disorder; thought, mood, and personality disorders. Dual diagnosis program for males and females ages 12–18. Treats learning disabilities; behavior disorders; general psychosocial disorders; substance abuse; compulsive/addictive disorders other than substance abuse and eating disorders; post-traumatic stress disorder; thought, mood, and personality disorders.Day treatment program for males and females ages 12–17. Treats learning disabilities; behavior disorders; general psychosocial disorders; substance abuse; eating disorders; compulsive/addictive disorders other than substance abuse and eating disorders; post-traumatic stress disorder; thought, mood, and personality disorders.

Contact Don Elsey, Program Administrator, main address above. Phone: 803-745-5128.

CHARTER RIVERS HOSPITAL
2900 Sunset Boulevard
West Columbia, South Carolina 29169
803-796-9911; Fax: 803-791-7622

General Information Psychiatric hospital for adolescents, adults. 16 beds for adolescents. Open year-round. Patient security: entirely locked; will pursue and return runaways. Urban setting. For-profit facility affiliated with Charter Medical Corporation,

Macon, GA. Licensed by state of South Carolina. Accredited by JCAHO.

Participants Accepts: male and female adolescents ages 10–17; male and female adults ages 18 and up. Average stay: 14 days. Admission: one parent, court order, depending on program. Treats behavior disorders; general psychosocial disorders; substance abuse; eating disorders; compulsive/addictive disorders other than substance abuse and eating disorders; post-traumatic stress disorder; thought, mood, and personality disorders. Accepts the mobility impaired; the vision impaired; the hearing impaired; the speech impaired; those with a history of arson; the sexually compulsive; those with a history of harm to themselves and others; those receiving psychotropic medication; non-English speaking individuals; those with a history of epilepsy. Largest number of participants from South Carolina.

Program Treatment modalities: Twelve Step Recovery; psychotherapy. Family treatment program available.

Staff Total facility staff includes 42 registered nurses, 8 practical/vocational nurses, 4 MSW social workers, 2 social workers (non-MSW), 2 teachers, 7 counselors, 4 occupational/recreational therapists, 22 therapists, 1 dietician, 11 other direct-care staff members. Staff is 33% male, 67% female.

Facilities Single building; males and females in coeducational units. Separate residential quarters for adolescents. Central dining (shared with adults). Basketball courts, game room, gymnasium, horseback riding, outdoor swimming pool, outdoor tennis courts, playing fields, ropes course, fitness trail.

Education Academic program available at no charge. Serves ages 10–18, ungraded. 2 teachers on staff. Curriculum accredited or approved by South Carolina Board of Education.

Costs Accepts private insurance, group insurance, medicare, medicaid, Blue Cross/Blue Shield.

Additional Services Drug and alcohol rehabilitation services for males and females ages 10 and up. Treats behavior disorders; substance abuse. Outpatient services for males and females ages 10 and up. Treats substance abuse; compulsive/addictive disorders other than substance abuse and eating disorders. Partial hospitalization for males and females ages 10–18. Treats behavior disorders; general psychosocial disorders; substance abuse; eating disorders; compulsive/addictive disorders other than substance abuse and eating disorders; post-traumatic stress disorder; thought, mood, and personality disorders.

Contact Needs Assessment/Referral Center, main address above. Phone: 803-796-9911. Fax: 803-791-7622.

CHARTER SPRINGS HOSPITAL
3130 Southwest 27th Avenue
Ocala, Florida 32674
904-237-7293; Fax: 904-854-4295

General Information Psychiatric hospital for children, adolescents. Patient security: partially locked. For-profit facility affiliated with Charter Medical Corporation, Macon, GA. Licensed by state of Florida. Accredited by JCAHO.

Participants Accepts: male and female children; male and female adolescents. Average stay: 15 days. Admission: all parties who share custody. Treats learning disabilities; behavior disorders; general psychosocial disorders; substance abuse; compulsive/addictive disorders other than substance abuse and eating disorders; post-traumatic stress disorder; thought, mood, and personality disorders.

Costs Average cost: $13,500 per stay.

Contact Rich Schleicher, Marketing Director, P.O. Box 3338, Ocala, FL 32674. Phone: 904-237-7293.

CHARTER WESTBROOK HOSPITAL
1500 Westbrook Avenue
Richmond, Virginia 23227
804-266-9671; Fax: 804-262-1201

General Information Psychiatric hospital for children, adolescents. Patient security: partially locked. For-profit facility affiliated with Charter Medical Corporation, Macon, GA. Licensed by state of Virginia. Accredited by JCAHO.

Participants Accepts: male and female children; male and female adolescents. Average stay: 21 days. Admission: one parent, all parties who share custody, court order, voluntary, depending on program. Treats learning disabilities; behavior disorders; general psychosocial disorders; substance abuse; eating disorders; compulsive/addictive disorders other than substance abuse and eating disorders; post-traumatic stress disorder; thought, mood, and personality disorders.

Contact Terry Tysinger, Director of Marketing, main address above. Phone: 804-266-9671.

CHESTNUT HEALTH SYSTEMS— LIGHTHOUSE
1003 Martin Luther King Drive
Bloomington, Illinois 61701
309-827-6026; Fax: 309-827-6496

General Information Drug and alcohol rehabilitation center for adolescents. Patient security: staff secured. Independent not-for-profit facility. Licensed by state of Illinois. Accredited by JCAHO.

Participants Accepts: male and female adolescents. Average stay: 60 days. Admission: one parent, court order, guardianship, depending on program. Treats learning disabilities; behavior disorders; general psychosocial disorders; substance abuse; eating disorders; post-traumatic stress disorder; thought, mood, and personality disorders.

Staff Staff is 40% male, 60% female.

Contact Gary Roberts, Intake Coordinator, main address above. Phone: 309-827-6026.

CHESTNUT LODGE HOSPITAL—ROSE HILL TREATMENT CENTER
500 West Montgomery Avenue
Rockville, Maryland 20850
301-424-8300; Fax: 301-762-2050

General Information Psychiatric hospital for children, adolescents. Patient security: partially locked. For-profit facility. Licensed by state of Maryland. Accredited by JCAHO.

Participants Accepts: male and female children; male and female adolescents. Average stay: 4 months. Admission: one parent, all parties who share custody, court order, voluntary, depending on program. Treats learning disabilities; behavior disorders; general psychosocial disorders; substance abuse; eating disorders; compulsive/addictive disorders other than substance abuse and eating disorders; post-traumatic stress disorder; thought, mood, and personality disorders.

Staff Staff is 50% male, 50% female.

Costs Average cost: $550 per day.

Contact Marika Cutler, Director of Clinical Resources, main address above. Phone: 301-424-8300. Fax: 301-762-2050.

CHESTNUT RIDGE HOSPITAL
930 Chestnut Ridge Road
Morgantown, West Virginia 26505
304-293-4000; Fax: 304-293-5555

General Information Psychiatric hospital for adolescents. 14 beds for adolescents. Patient security: entirely locked. For-profit facility affiliated with Ramsey Health Care, Inc., New Orleans, LA. Licensed by state of West Virginia. Accredited by JCAHO.

Participants Accepts: male and female adolescents. Average stay: 17 days. Admission: one parent, all parties who share custody, court order, voluntary, depending on program. Treats learning disabilities; behavior disorders; general psychosocial disorders; substance abuse; eating disorders; compulsive/addictive disorders other than substance abuse and eating disorders; post-traumatic stress disorder; thought, mood, and personality disorders.

Contact Lisa Simmons, Referral Coordinator, main address above. Phone: 304-293-4000. Fax: 304-293-5555.

CHEYENNE MESA
1353 South Eighth Street
Colorado Springs, Colorado 80906
719-520-1400; Fax: 719-475-1527

General Information Residential treatment/subacute facility for adolescents. 22 beds for adolescents. Open year-round. Patient security: staff secured; will pursue and return runaways. Urban setting. For-profit facility affiliated with Century HealthCare Corporation, Tulsa, OK. Licensed by state of Colorado. Accredited by JCAHO.

Participants Accepts: male and female adolescents ages 12–18. Average stay: 120 days. Admission: voluntary. Treats learning disabilities; behavior disorders; general psychosocial disorders; substance abuse; eating disorders; post-traumatic stress disorder; thought, mood, and personality disorders. Accepts the sexually compulsive; those with a history of harm to themselves and others; those receiving psychotropic medication; those with a history of epilepsy. Largest number of participants from Colorado, New Mexico, Illinois.

Program Treatment modalities: psychodynamic; Twelve Step Recovery.

Staff 1.8 full-time direct-care staff members per adolescent. Total facility staff includes 2 psychiatrists, 2 registered nurses, 2 practical/vocational nurses, 7

MSW social workers, 1 social worker (non-MSW), 7 teachers, 1 occupational/recreational therapist, 2 therapists, 15 other direct-care staff members. Staff is 33% male, 67% female.

Facilities Multiple buildings; males and females in coeducational units. Central dining. Basketball courts, game room, gymnasium, playing fields.

Education Academic program available at no charge. Serves ages 11–18, grades 5–12. 7 teachers on staff. Curriculum accredited or approved by Colorado State Department of Education. Cost of educational program covered by local school district. Organized sports program offered.

Costs Average cost: $375 per day. Accepts private insurance, group insurance, public funds.

Additional Services Drug and alcohol rehabilitation services for males and females ages 12–18. Treats learning disabilities; behavior disorders; general psychosocial disorders; substance abuse; eating disorders; post-traumatic stress disorder; thought, mood, and personality disorders. Residential or sub-acute services for males and females ages 12–18. Treats learning disabilities; behavior disorders; general psychosocial disorders; substance abuse; eating disorders; post-traumatic stress disorder; thought, mood, and personality disorders. Day treatment ages 11–18. Treats learning disabilities; behavior disorders; general psychosocial disorders; substance abuse; eating disorders; post-traumatic stress disorder; thought, mood, and personality disorders.

Contact Betteanne Barash, Marketing Director, main address above. Phone: 719-520-1400. Fax: 719-475-1527.

See page 414 for full page description.

CHILD CENTER OF OUR LADY
7900 Natural Bridge
St. Louis, Missouri 63121
314-383-0200; Fax: 314-383-6334

General Information Residential treatment/subacute facility for children. 18 beds for children. Open year-round. Patient security: staff secured; will pursue and return runaways. Suburban setting. Independent not-for-profit facility. Licensed by state of Missouri. Accredited by JCAHO.

Participants Accepts: male and female children ages 5–14. Average stay: 730 days. Treats learning disabilities; behavior disorders; general psychosocial disorders; post-traumatic stress disorder; thought, mood, and personality disorders. Accepts those with a history of harm to themselves and others; those receiving psychotropic medication. Largest number of participants from Missouri, Illinois.

Program Treatment modalities: psychodynamic; cognitive-behavioral; systems theory; behavior modification.

Staff 1.7 full-time direct-care staff members per child. Total facility staff includes 1 psychologist, 1 psychiatrist, 2 MSW social workers, 3 teachers, 1 counselor, 1 physical therapist, 1 occupational/recreational therapist, 1 speech pathologist, 3 therapists, 17 other direct-care staff members. Staff is 65% male, 35% female.

Facilities Multiple buildings; males and females in coeducational units. Separate dining by residential unit available. Basketball courts, gymnasium, outdoor swimming pool, playing fields.

Education Academic program available at additional cost. Serves ages 5–14, ungraded. 3 teachers on staff. Curriculum accredited or approved by Missouri Department of Elementary and Secondary Education. Cost of educational program sometimes covered by local school district.

Costs Average cost: $205 per day. Accepts private insurance, group insurance, Blue Cross/Blue Shield, public funds.

Contact Ashley Parriott, Director of Development, main address above. Phone: 314-383-0200. Fax: 314-383-6334.

THE CHILDREN'S CAMPUS
1411 Lincoln Way, West
Mishawaka, Indiana 46544-1690
219-259-5666; Fax: 219-232-7756

General Information Residential treatment/subacute facility for children, adolescents. Patient security: staff secured. Independent not-for-profit facility. Licensed by state of Indiana. Accredited by JCAHO.

Participants Accepts: male and female children; male and female adolescents. Average stay: 18 months. Admission: court order. Treats autistic disorders; learning disabilities; behavior disorders; general psychosocial disorders; substance abuse; eating disorders; compulsive/addictive disorders other than substance abuse and eating disorders; post-traumatic stress disorder; thought, mood, and personality disorders.

Contact Barbara Merritt, Director of Admissions, main address above. Phone: 219-259-5666.

THE CHILDREN'S CENTER
1400 Whitney Avenue
Hamden, Connecticut 06517
203-248-2115; Fax: 203-248-2572

General Information Drug and alcohol rehabilitation center for adolescents. 20 beds for adolescents. Open year-round. Patient security: staff secured; no runaway pursuit. Suburban setting. Independent not-for-profit facility. Licensed by state of Connecticut. Accredited by JCAHO.

Participants Accepts: male and female adolescents ages 12–19. Average stay: 21 days. Admission: one parent, all parties who share custody, court order, voluntary, self-admit, depending on program. Treats learning disabilities; behavior disorders; general psychosocial disorders; substance abuse; eating disorders; post-traumatic stress disorder; thought, mood, and personality disorders. Accepts those with a history of arson; those with a history of harm to themselves and others; those receiving psychotropic medication; those with a history of epilepsy. Largest number of participants from Connecticut.

Program Treatment modalities: psychodynamics; family systems treatment; reality therapy; Twelve Step Recovery. Family treatment program available.

Staff 2.5 full-time direct-care staff members per adolescent. Total facility staff includes 1 psychiatrist, 1 registered nurse, 3 MSW social workers, 3 social workers (non-MSW), 5 teachers, 10 counselors, 2 other direct-care staff members. Staff is 52% male, 48% female.

Facilities Multiple buildings; males and females in coeducational units. Central dining. Basketball courts, game room, gymnasium, outdoor swimming pool, playing fields.

Education Academic program available at additional cost. Serves ages 12–19, grades 7–12. 5 teachers on staff. Curriculum accredited or approved by Connecticut State Department of Education. Cost of educational program sometimes covered by local school district.

Costs Average cost: $323 per day. Accepts private insurance, group insurance, medicaid, Blue Cross/Blue Shield, public funds.

Additional Services Residential or sub-acute services for males and females ages 7–18. Treats learning disabilities; behavior disorders; general psychosocial disorders; post-traumatic stress disorder; thought, mood, and personality disorders. Specialized foster care for males and females ages 4–18. Treats learning disabilities; behavior disorders; general psychosocial disorders; substance abuse; eating disorders; post-traumatic stress disorder; thought, mood, and personality disorders.

Contact Daniel Lyga, Administrator for Programs, main address above. Phone: 203-248-2115. Fax: 203-248-2572.

THE CHILDREN'S HOME OF CINCINNATI
5050 Madison Road
Cincinnati, Ohio 45227
513-272-2800; Fax: 513-272-2807

General Information Residential treatment/subacute facility for adolescents. 36 beds for adolescents. Open year-round. Patient security: unlocked; no runaway pursuit. Urban setting. Independent not-for-profit facility. Licensed by state of Ohio. Accredited by Council on Accreditation of Services for Families and Children.

Participants Accepts: male and female adolescents ages 11–18. Average stay: 12 months. Admission: one parent, all parties who share custody, court order, voluntary, depending on program. Treats learning disabilities; behavior disorders; general psychosocial disorders; post-traumatic stress disorder; thought, mood, and personality disorders. Accepts those with a history of arson; those with a history of harm to themselves and others; those receiving psychotropic medication; those with a history of epilepsy. Largest number of participants from Ohio, Kentucky, Indiana.

Program Treatment modalities: psychodynamic; structural/strategic. Family treatment program available.

Staff 1 full-time direct-care staff member per adolescent. Total facility staff includes 1 psychologist, 1 psychiatrist, 1 registered nurse, 5 MSW social workers, 2 occupational/recreational therapists, 23 other direct-care staff members.

Facilities Multiple buildings; males and females in separate units. Basketball courts, game room, gymnasium, outdoor swimming pool, outdoor tennis courts, playing fields, recreation building.

Education Academic program available. Serves ages 11–18, grades 4–12. Curriculum accredited or approved by Ohio State Department of Education. Cost of educational program sometimes covered by local school district. Organized sports program offered.

Costs Average cost: $183 per day. Accepts private insurance, group insurance, Blue Cross/Blue Shield, public funds.

Additional Services Outpatient services for males and females. Treats learning disabilities; behavior disorders; general psychosocial disorders; eating disorders; compulsive/addictive disorders other than substance abuse and eating disorders; post-traumatic stress disorder; thought, mood, and personality disorders.

Contact Kathy McLaughlin LISW, Intake Social Worker, main address above. Phone: 513-272-2800. Fax: 513-272-2807.

Announcement The Children's Home of Cincinnati, Ohio, provides an individualized, comprehensive treatment milieu for emotionally disturbed adolescent boys and girls. Within the Children's Home's structured, caring environment, children are able to safely work through problems involving peer, school, and family relationships and the difficult emotions often involved with both.

THE CHILDREN'S HOME OF CROMWELL
60 Hicksville Road
Cromwell, Connecticut 06416
203-635-6010; Fax: 203-635-3425

General Information Residential treatment/subacute facility for children, adolescents. 30 beds for children; 41 beds for adolescents; 71 beds total. Open year-round. Patient security: staff secured; will pursue and return runaways. Suburban setting. Not-for-profit facility affiliated with The Evangelical Covenant Church, East Coast Conference. Licensed by state of Connecticut.

Participants Accepts: male and female children ages 9–12; male and female adolescents ages 13–16. Average stay: 17 months. Admission: one parent, all parties who share custody, court order, depending on program. Treats learning disabilities; behavior disorders; general psychosocial disorders; substance abuse; post-traumatic stress disorder; thought, mood, and personality disorders. Accepts the vision impaired; the speech impaired; those with a history of harm to themselves and others; those receiving psychotropic medication. Largest number of participants from Connecticut, Vermont, Rhode Island.

Program Treatment modalities: systematic family therapy; group therapy; milieu therapy; individual psychodynamic therapy. Family treatment program available.

Staff .5 full-time direct-care staff member per child or adolescent. Total facility staff includes 1 physician, 1 psychologist, 1 psychiatrist, 1 registered nurse, 2 practical/vocational nurses, 2 MSW social workers, 3 social workers (non-MSW), 10 teachers, 1 occupational/recreational therapist, 1 speech pathologist, 2 therapists, 1 dietician, 37 other direct-care staff members. Staff is 20% male, 80% female.

Facilities Multiple buildings; males and females in separate units. Central dining. Basketball courts, game room, gymnasium, outdoor swimming pool, outdoor tennis courts, playing fields, ropes course.

Education Academic program available at additional cost. Serves ages 9–18, grades K–12. 10 teachers on staff. Curriculum accredited or approved by State Department of Education. Cost of educational program covered by local school district. Organized sports program offered.

Costs Average cost: $94 per day. Accepts private insurance, medicaid, public funds.

Contact David J. Carlson, Executive Director, main address above. Phone: 203-635-6010. Fax: 203-635-3425.

CHILDREN'S HOME OF DETROIT
900 Cook Road
Grosse Point Woods, Michigan 48236
313-886-0800; Fax: 313-886-9446

General Information Residential treatment/subacute facility for children, adolescents. 50 beds for children; 22 beds for adolescents; 72 beds total. Open year-round. Patient security: staff secured; will pursue and return runaways. Suburban setting. Independent not-for-profit facility. Licensed by state of Michigan. Accredited by JCAHO.

Participants Accepts: male and female children ages 6–13; male and female adolescents ages 13–18. Average stay: 300 days. Admission: voluntary, voluntary placements funded by mental health, social service, and juvenile courts, depending on program. Treats learning disabilities; behavior disorders; general psychosocial disorders; compulsive/addictive disorders other than substance abuse and eating disorders; thought, mood, and personality disorders. Accepts those with a history of harm to themselves and others; those receiving psychotropic medication; those with a history of epilepsy. Largest number of participants from Michigan.

Program Treatment modalities: psychodynamic; behavioral; cognitive. Family treatment program available.

Facilities Multiple buildings; males and females in separate units. Separate dining by residential unit available. Basketball courts, game room, gymnasium, outdoor swimming pool, outdoor tennis courts, playing fields, picinic areas, obstacle courses.

Education Academic program available at no charge. Serves ages 6–18, grades 1–12. Curriculum accredited or approved by North Central Association of Colleges and Schools. Cost of educational program covered by local school district.

Costs Average cost: $132 per day. Accepts private insurance, group insurance, public funds.

Additional Services Camping program for males and females ages 6–18. Treats learning disabilities; behavior disorders; general psychosocial disorders; compulsive/addictive disorders other than substance abuse and eating disorders; thought, mood, and personality disorders.

Contact Patricia Shomaker, Director of Social Services, main address above. Phone: 313-886-0800.

THE CHILDREN'S HOME OF KINGSTON
26 Grove Street
Kingston, New York 12401
914-331-1448; Fax: 914-331-1448

General Information Residential treatment/subacute facility for children, adolescents. Open year-round. Patient security: staff secured; will pursue and return runaways. Small town setting. Independent not-for-profit facility. Licensed by state of New York. Accredited by Council on Accreditation of Services for Families and Children.

Participants Accepts: male children ages 9–13; male adolescents ages 13–21. Average stay: 420 days. Admission: court order, referrals from school districts and social service departments, depending on program. Treats learning disabilities; behavior disorders; general psychosocial disorders; post-traumatic stress disorder; thought, mood, and personality disorders. Accepts the speech impaired; those with a history of harm to themselves and others; those receiving psychotropic medication. Largest number of participants from New York.

Program Treatment modalities: psychodynamic. Family treatment program available.

Staff Total facility staff includes 1 psychologist, 1 psychiatrist, 1 registered nurse, 1 practical/vocational nurse, 6 MSW social workers, 12 teachers, 40 counselors, 1 occupational/recreational therapist, 10 other direct-care staff members. Staff is 50% male, 50% female.

Facilities Multiple buildings. Separate dining by residential unit available. Basketball courts, game room, gymnasium, outdoor swimming pool, playing fields.

Education Academic program available at no charge. Serves ages 9–15, grades 3–10. 12 teachers on staff. Curriculum accredited or approved by New York State Education Department; Council on Accreditation. Cost of educational program sometimes covered by local school district. Organized sports program offered.

Costs Average cost: $200 per day. Accepts medicaid, public funds.

Contact William House, Director of Health and Intake, main address above. Phone: 914-331-1448. Fax: 914-331-1448 Ext. 119.

THE CHILDREN'S HOSPITAL
300 Longwood Avenue
Boston, Massachusetts 02115
617-735-6000; Fax: 617-735-6434

General Information Children's hospital for children, adolescents. Patient security: staff secured. Independent not-for-profit facility. Licensed by state of Massachusetts. Accredited by JCAHO.

Participants Accepts: male and female children; male and female adolescents. Average stay: 20 days. Admission: one parent, court order, depending on program. Treats learning disabilities; behavior disorders; general psychosocial disorders; eating disorders; thought, mood, and personality disorders.

Contact Dr. William Beardsell, Director of Psychiatric Unit, 300 Longwood Avenue, Boston, MA 02115. Phone: 617-735-6000. Fax: 617-735-6434.

CHILDREN'S HOSPITAL MEDICAL CENTER
Elland and Bethesda Avenues
Pavilion Building
Cincinnati, Ohio 45229
513-559-4200; Fax: 513-559-7431

General Information Psychiatric hospital for children. 14 beds for children. Open year-round. Patient security: entirely locked; will pursue and return runaways. Urban setting. Independent. Operated by Children's Hospital Medical Center, Cincinnati, OH. Licensed by state of Ohio. Accredited by JCAHO.

Participants Accepts: male and female children ages 6–12. Average stay: 30 days. Admission: all parties who share custody. Treats autistic disorders; learning disabilities; behavior disorders; general psychosocial disorders; eating disorders; compulsive/addictive dis-

orders other than substance abuse and eating disorders; post-traumatic stress disorder; thought, mood, and personality disorders. Accepts the mobility impaired; the vision impaired; the hearing impaired; the speech impaired; those with a history of arson; the sexually compulsive; those with a history of harm to themselves and others; those receiving psychotropic medication; non-English speaking individuals; those with a history of epilepsy. Special programs for the developmentally disabled; the hearing impaired.

Program Family treatment program available.

Staff Total facility staff includes 2 physicians, 1 psychologist, 2 psychiatrists, 1 MSW social worker, 2 teachers.

Facilities Single building; males and females in separate units. Central dining. Game room, playground.

Education Academic program available at no charge. Serves ages 6–12, grades K–12. 2 teachers on staff. Curriculum accredited or approved by Cincinnati Public Schools. Cost of educational program sometimes covered by local school district.

Costs Average cost: $300 per day. Accepts private insurance, medicaid, Blue Cross/Blue Shield.

Contact Dr. Leonard Harris, Director, main address above. Phone: 513-559-4606. Fax: 513-559-7882.

CHILDREN'S HOSPITAL OF LOS ANGELES
4650 Sunset Boulevard
Los Angeles, California 90054
213-660-2450; Fax: 213-664-6917

General Information Pediatric academic medical center for children, adolescents. Open year-round. Patient security: staff secured; will pursue and return runaways. Urban setting. Independent not-for-profit facility. Licensed by state of California. Accredited by JCAHO.

Participants Accepts: male and female children ages up to 10; male and female adolescents ages 11–18. Average stay: 7 days. Admission: one parent, all parties who share custody, court order, voluntary, depending on program. Treats autistic disorders; learning disabilities; behavior disorders; general psychosocial disorders; eating disorders. Accepts the mobility impaired; the vision impaired; the hearing impaired; the speech impaired; those with a history of arson; the sexually compulsive; those with a history of harm to themselves and others; those receiving psychotropic medication; non-English speaking individuals; those with a history of epilepsy. Special programs for the chronically ill; the mobility impaired; the developmentally disabled; the vision impaired; the hearing impaired; the speech impaired; those with AIDS. Largest number of participants from Arizona, Nevada.

Staff Total facility staff includes 620 physicians, 3 psychologists, 1 psychiatrist, 2300 registered nurses, 53 practical/vocational nurses, 24 MSW social workers, 3 teachers, 7 counselors, 9 physical therapists, 3 occupational/recreational therapists, 4 speech pathologists, 9 dieticians, 330 other direct-care staff members.

Facilities Multiple buildings; males and females in coeducational units. In-room dining available Game room.

Education Academic program available at no charge. Serves ages 4–18, grades K–12. 3 teachers on staff. Curriculum accredited or approved by State of California. Cost of educational program covered by local school district.

Costs Accepts private insurance, group insurance, medicare, Blue Cross/Blue Shield, public funds.

Additional Services Outpatient services for males and females. Treats autistic disorders; learning disabilities; behavior disorders; eating disorders; compulsive/addictive disorders other than substance abuse and eating disorders; post-traumatic stress disorder.

Contact Ted S. Burnett, Director of Business Development, main address above. Phone: 213-669-2502. Fax: 213-660-1116.

THE CHILDREN'S MEMORIAL HOSPITAL
2300 Children's Plaza
Chicago, Illinois 60614
312-880-4000; Fax: 312-880-3068

General Information Freestanding children's specialty hospital for children, adolescents. Patient security: entirely locked. Independent not-for-profit facility. Licensed by state of Illinois. Accredited by JCAHO.

Participants Accepts: male and female children; male and female adolescents. Average stay: 30 days. Admission: one parent, all parties who share custody, voluntary, depending on program. Treats autistic disorders; learning disabilities; behavior disorders; general psychosocial disorders; substance abuse; eating disorders; compulsive/addictive disorders other than substance abuse and eating disorders; post-traumatic

stress disorder; thought, mood, and personality disorders.

Contact Dennis Kepchar, Vice President of Planning and Marketing, main address above. Phone: 312-880-4743.

CHILDREN'S RESIDENTIAL TREATMENT CENTER
143 East 19th Street
Minneapolis, Minnesota 55403
612-863-5140

General Information Residential treatment/subacute facility for children, adolescents. 24 beds for adolescents. Open year-round. Patient security: partially locked. Urban setting. Not-for-profit facility affiliated with Behavioralcare Network, Minneapolis, MN. Licensed by state of Minnesota. Accredited by JCAHO.

Participants Accepts: male and female children and adolescents ages 11–17. Average stay: 328 days. Admission: one parent, all parties who share custody, court order, depending on program. Treats learning disabilities; behavior disorders; general psychosocial disorders; eating disorders; compulsive/addictive disorders other than substance abuse and eating disorders; post-traumatic stress disorder; thought, mood, and personality disorders. Accepts those with a history of harm to themselves and others; those receiving psychotropic medication; those with a history of epilepsy. Largest number of participants from Minnesota, Iowa.

Program Treatment modalities: psychodynamic; family systems; cognitive-behavioral. Family treatment program available.

Staff Total facility staff includes 1 psychologist, 1 psychiatrist, 1 registered nurse, 2 MSW social workers, 2 social workers (non-MSW), 3 teachers, 21 counselors. Staff is 39% male, 61% female.

Facilities Single building; males and females in coeducational units. Central dining. Game room, gymnasium, indoor swimming pool.

Education Academic program available. Serves ages 11–17, ungraded. 3 teachers on staff. Curriculum accredited or approved by Minneapolis Public Schools. Cost of educational program sometimes covered by local school district. Organized sports program offered.

Costs Accepts private insurance, group insurance, public funds.

Contact Mary Regan, main address above. Phone: 612-863-5141.

CHILDREN'S SQUARE USA
North Sixth Street and Avenue E
Council Bluffs, Iowa 51502-3008
712-322-3700; Fax: 712-325-0913

General Information Residential treatment/subacute facility for children, adolescents. Patient security: staff secured. Not-for-profit facility affiliated with Children's Square USA, Council Bluffs, IA. Licensed by state of Iowa. Accredited by JCAHO; National Association of Home Services for Children, Council on Accreditation.

Participants Accepts: male and female children; male and female adolescents. Average stay: 12 months. Admission: court order, voluntary, depending on program. Treats learning disabilities; behavior disorders; general psychosocial disorders; eating disorders; compulsive/addictive disorders other than substance abuse and eating disorders; thought, mood, and personality disorders.

Costs Average cost: $200 per day.

Contact Bob DiBlasi, Director of Residential Services, P.O. Box 8-C, Council Bluffs, IA 51502-3008. Phone: 712-322-3700. Fax: 712-325-0913.

CHILDREN'S VILLAGE
Dobbs Ferry, New York 10522
914-693-0600; Fax: 914-693-7708

General Information Residential treatment/subacute facility for children, adolescents. 250 beds for children; 50 beds for adolescents; 300 beds total. Open year-round. Patient security: staff secured; will pursue and return runaways. Suburban setting. Independent not-for-profit facility. Licensed by state of New York. Accredited by JCAHO; Council on Accreditation of Services for Families and Children, Child Welfare League of America.

Participants Accepts: male children ages 5–12; male adolescents ages 13–15. Average stay: 33 months. Admission: one parent, court order, Department of Social Services, depending on program. Treats learning disabilities; behavior disorders; general psychosocial disorders; post-traumatic stress disorder; thought, mood, and personality disorders. Accepts the speech impaired; those with a history of arson; those with a history of harm to themselves and others; those receiving psychotropic medication; non-English speaking individuals; those with a history of epilepsy. Largest number of participants from New York.

Program Treatment modalities: systemic family therapy; milieu therapy; psychodynamic therapy;

behavioral therapy. Family treatment program available.

Staff 1 full-time direct-care staff member per child or adolescent. Total facility staff includes 2 physicians, 9 psychologists, 4 psychiatrists, 7 registered nurses, 2 practical/vocational nurses, 45 MSW social workers, 8 social workers (non-MSW), 200 counselors, 4 occupational/recreational therapists, 1 dietician. Staff is 60% male, 40% female.

Facilities Multiple buildings. Separate dining by residential unit available. Basketball courts, game room, gymnasium, indoor swimming pool, playing fields.

Education Academic program available at no charge. Serves ages 5–15, ungraded. Curriculum accredited or approved by New York State Education Department. Cost of educational program covered by local school district. Organized sports program offered.

Costs Average cost: $140 per day. Accepts public funds.

Contact Mona Swanson, Associate Executive Director for QA, main address above. Phone: 914-693-0600. Fax: 914-693-7708.

CHRISTIAN CARE PROGRAM
201 South Garnett Road
Tulsa, Oklahoma 74128
918-438-4257; Fax: 918-438-8016

General Information Psychiatric hospital for adolescents, adults. 6 beds for adolescents. Open year-round. Patient security: entirely locked. Suburban setting. For-profit facility affiliated with Rehabilitation Institute of America, Emoryville, CA. Licensed by state of Oklahoma. Accredited by JCAHO.

Participants Accepts: male and female adolescents ages 13–18; male and female adults ages 18 and up. Admission: one parent, all parties who share custody, court order, depending on program. Treats behavior disorders; general psychosocial disorders; substance abuse; eating disorders; compulsive/addictive disorders other than substance abuse and eating disorders; post-traumatic stress disorder; thought, mood, and personality disorders. Accepts the mobility impaired; the vision impaired; the hearing impaired; the speech impaired; those with a history of harm to themselves and others; those receiving psychotropic medication. Special programs for the speech impaired.

Program Treatment modalities: family systems; dual diagnosis (Twelve Step Recovery); cognitive-behavioral; Christ-centered. Family treatment program available.

Staff Total facility staff includes 3 physicians, 8 psychologists, 4 psychiatrists, 10 registered nurses, 2 practical/vocational nurses, 1 MSW social worker, 1 teacher, 2 occupational/recreational therapists, 1 therapist, 15 other direct-care staff members.

Facilities Single building; males and females in co-educational units. Separate residential quarters for adolescents. Central dining (shared with adults). Basketball courts, game room, volleyball court, open area.

Education Academic program available at no charge. Serves ages 13–18, grades 8–12. 1 teacher on staff. Curriculum accredited or approved by Tulsa Public Schools. Cost of educational program covered by local school district.

Costs Average cost: $620 per day. Accepts private insurance, group insurance, medicare, Blue Cross/Blue Shield, public funds.

Contact Joseph Wilkerson, Community Relations Director, main address above. Phone: 918-438-4257. Fax: 918-438-8016.

THE CHRISTIE SCHOOL
P.O. Box 368
Marylhurst, Oregon 97036
503-635-3416; Fax: 503-697-6932

General Information Residential treatment/subacute facility for children, adolescents. Patient security: staff secured. Independent not-for-profit facility. Licensed by state of Oregon. Accredited by JCAHO.

Participants Accepts: male and female children; male and female adolescents. Average stay: 3 years. Admission: court order, Children Services Division, depending on program. Treats learning disabilities; behavior disorders; general psychosocial disorders; compulsive/addictive disorders other than substance abuse and eating disorders; post-traumatic stress disorder; thought, mood, and personality disorders.

Staff Staff is 50% male, 50% female.

Contact Daniel A. Mahler, Executive Director, main address above. Phone: 503-635-3416. Fax: 503-697-6932.

CLARE FOUNDATION YOUTH RECOVERY TEEN HOME
844 Pico Boulevard
Santa Monica, California 90405
310-314-6247; Fax: 310-396-6974

General Information Residential treatment/subacute facility for adolescents. Patient security: staff secured. Not-for-profit facility affiliated with Clare Foundation, Santa Monica, CA. Licensed by state of California.

Participants Accepts: male and female adolescents. Average stay: 12 months. Admission: one parent, court order, voluntary, depending on program. Treats substance abuse.

Staff Staff is 50% male, 50% female.

Contact Debbie Gibbs, Director, main address above. Phone: 310-314-6247. Fax: 310-396-6974.

CLARION PSYCHIATRIC CENTER
Two Hospital Drive
RD 3, P.O. Box 188
Clarion, Pennsylvania 16214
814-226-9545; Fax: 814-226-9622

General Information Psychiatric hospital for children, adolescents, adults. 13 beds for children; 13 beds for adolescents; 52 beds total. Open year-round. Patient security: entirely locked; will pursue and return runaways. Small town setting. For-profit facility affiliated with First Hospital Corporation, Norfolk, VA. Licensed by state of Pennsylvania. Accredited by JCAHO.

Participants Accepts: male and female children ages 5–12; male and female adolescents ages 12–18; male and female adults ages 18 and up. Average stay: 25 days. Admission: all parties who share custody, voluntary, involuntary, depending on program. Treats learning disabilities; behavior disorders; general psychosocial disorders; substance abuse; eating disorders; compulsive/addictive disorders other than substance abuse and eating disorders; post-traumatic stress disorder; thought, mood, and personality disorders. Accepts the mobility impaired; the vision impaired; the hearing impaired; the speech impaired; those with a history of arson; the sexually compulsive; those with a history of harm to themselves and others; those receiving psychotropic medication; those with a history of epilepsy. Largest number of participants from Pennsylvania.

Program Treatment modalities: behavior modification; psychotherapy; group therapy; abuse therapy.

Staff Total facility staff includes 2 psychologists, 4 psychiatrists, 22 registered nurses, 7 practical/vocational nurses, 3 MSW social workers, 1 social worker (non-MSW), 2 teachers, 4 occupational/recreational therapists, 1 dietician, 17 other direct-care staff members. Staff is 29% male, 71% female.

Facilities Single building; males and females in coeducational units. Separate residential quarters for children and adolescents. Central dining (not shared with adults). Gymnasium, playing fields.

Education Academic program available at no charge. Serves ages 5–18, grades 1–12. 2 teachers on staff. Curriculum accredited or approved by Pennsylvania Department of Education.

Costs Average cost: $18,791 per stay. Accepts private insurance, group insurance, medicare, medicaid, Blue Cross/Blue Shield, public funds.

Additional Services Drug and alcohol rehabilitation services for males and females ages 18 and up. Treats behavior disorders; general psychosocial disorders; substance abuse; eating disorders; compulsive/addictive disorders other than substance abuse and eating disorders; post-traumatic stress disorder; thought, mood, and personality disorders.

Contact David Venanzi, Director of Call Management, main address above. Phone: 814-226-9545. Fax: 814-226-9622.

CLEAR BROOK LODGE
Road #2
P.O. Box 2166
Shickshinny, Pennsylvania 18655
717-864-3116; Fax: 717-864-2812

General Information Drug and alcohol rehabilitation center for adolescents. 50 beds for adolescents. Open year-round. Patient security: staff secured; will pursue and return runaways. Rural setting. Independent not-for-profit facility. Licensed by state of Pennsylvania. Accredited by JCAHO.

Participants Accepts: male and female adolescents ages 13–18. Average stay: 42 days. Treats substance abuse.

Program Treatment modalities: Twelve Step Recovery. Family treatment program available.

Facilities Multiple buildings; males and females in separate units. Central dining. Basketball courts, game room, gymnasium, playing fields.

Education

Costs Average cost: $8000 per stay. Accepts private insurance, group insurance, Blue Cross/Blue Shield, public funds.

Contact Sandy Milazzo, Admissions Coordinator, 1100 East Northampton Street, Wilkes Barre, PA 18702. Phone: 717-823-1171. Fax: 717-823-1582.

CLEO WALLACE CENTER
8405 West 100 Avenue
Westminster, Colorado 80021
303-466-7391; Fax: 303-466-0904

General Information Psychiatric hospital for children, adolescents. Patient security: entirely locked. Not-for-profit facility. Licensed by state of Colorado. Accredited by JCAHO.

Participants Accepts: male and female children; male and female adolescents. Average stay: 15 days. Admission: one parent, all parties who share custody, court order, voluntary, depending on program. Treats autistic disorders; learning disabilities; behavior disorders; general psychosocial disorders; substance abuse; compulsive/addictive disorders other than substance abuse and eating disorders; post-traumatic stress disorder; thought, mood, and personality disorders.

Contact Jane Harris, Supervisor of Intake Department, main address above. Phone: 303-466-7391.

THE CLOISTERS AT PINE ISLAND
13771 Waterfront Drive
Pineland, Florida 33945
813-283-1019; Fax: 813-283-3079

General Information Drug and alcohol rehabilitation center for adolescents, adults. 4 beds for adolescents. Open year-round. Patient security: staff secured; will pursue and return runaways. Rural setting. For-profit facility affiliated with First Hospital Corporation, Norfolk, VA. Licensed by state of Florida. Accredited by JCAHO.

Participants Accepts: male and female adolescents ages 16–18; male and female adults ages 18 and up. Average stay: 42 days. Admission: one parent, court order, voluntary, depending on program. Treats general psychosocial disorders; substance abuse; eating disorders; compulsive/addictive disorders other than substance abuse and eating disorders; post-traumatic stress disorder. Accepts the mobility impaired; the vision impaired; the hearing impaired; the speech impaired; those with a history of harm to themselves and others; those receiving psychotropic medication; those with a history of epilepsy. Special programs for the chronically ill; the mobility impaired; the developmentally disabled; the vision impaired; the hearing impaired; the speech impaired; those with AIDS. Largest number of participants from Florida, Ohio.

Program   Treatment modalities: Twelve Step Recovery; individual and group psychotherapy; family therapy. Family treatment program available.

Staff   Total facility staff includes 2 physicians, 1 psychiatrist, 4 registered nurses, 4 practical/vocational nurses, 1 social worker (non-MSW), 9 counselors, 1 occupational/recreational therapist, 1 dietician. Staff is 40% male, 60% female.

Facilities   Multiple buildings; males and females in coeducational units. Separate residential quarters for adolescents. Central dining (shared with adults). Basketball courts, outdoor swimming pool, weight room, stationary bikes, Ping Pong.

Education   Academic program available at no charge. Serves ages 16–18, grades K–12. Curriculum accredited or approved by Lee County School District.

Costs   Average cost: $405 per day. Accepts private insurance, group insurance, Blue Cross/Blue Shield.

Contact   Tom F. Zercher, Clinical Director, main address above. Phone: 813-283-1019. Fax: 813-283-3079.

COASTAL CAROLINA HOSPITAL— CHILD AND ADOLESCENT PROGRAM
152 Waccamaw Medical Park Drive
Conway, South Carolina 29526
800-922-0742; Fax: 803-347-7176

General Information   Freestanding psychiatric/drug and alcohol rehabilitation hospital for adolescents. 15 beds for adolescents. Patient security: partially locked. Independent for-profit facility. Licensed by state of South Carolina. Accredited by JCAHO.

Participants   Accepts: male and female adolescents. Average stay: 14 days. Admission: one parent, court order, voluntary, depending on program. Treats behavior disorders; general psychosocial disorders; substance abuse; eating disorders; compulsive/addictive disorders other than substance abuse and eating disorders; post-traumatic stress disorder; thought, mood, and personality disorders.

Staff   Staff is 50% male, 50% female.

Contact   Lance Kennedy, Admissions Director, main address above. Phone: 800-922-0742. Fax: 803-347-7176.

COASTAL CAROLINA HOSPITAL— RESIDENTIAL TREATMENT CENTER
152 Waccamaw Medical Park Drive
Conway, South Carolina 29526
800-922-0742; Fax: 803-347-7176

General Information   Residential treatment/subacute facility for adolescents. 20 beds for adolescents. Patient security: entirely locked. Independent for-profit facility. Licensed by state of South Carolina. Accredited by JCAHO.

Participants   Accepts: male and female adolescents. Average stay: 2 years. Admission: voluntary, custody of state, depending on program. Treats learning disabilities; behavior disorders; general psychosocial disorders; substance abuse; eating disorders; compulsive/addictive disorders other than substance abuse and eating disorders; post-traumatic stress disorder; thought, mood, and personality disorders.

Staff   Staff is 40% male, 60% female.

Additional Services   Outpatient services for males and females ages 13 and up. Treats behavior disorders; general psychosocial disorders; substance abuse; eating disorders; compulsive/addictive disorders other than substance abuse and eating disorders; post-traumatic stress disorder; thought, mood, and personality disorders.

Contact   Lance Kennedy, Admissions Director, main address above. Phone: 800-922-0742. Fax: 803-347-7176.

COLORADO BOYS RANCH
28071 Highway 109
La Junta, Colorado 81050
719-384-5981; Fax: 719-384-8119

General Information   Residential treatment/subacute facility for adolescents. 93 beds for adolescents. Open year-round. Patient security: staff secured; will pursue and return runaways. Rural setting. Independent not-for-profit facility. Licensed by state of Colorado. Accredited by JCAHO; Colorado Department of Mental Health.

Participants   Accepts: male adolescents ages 12–18. Average stay: 245 days. Admission: one parent, all parties who share custody, court order, depending on program. Treats learning disabilities; behavior disorders; general psychosocial disorders; substance abuse; eating disorders; compulsive/addictive disorders other than substance abuse and eating disorders; posttraumatic stress disorder; thought, mood, and personality disorders. Accepts the sexually compulsive; those with a history of harm to themselves and others; those receiving psychotropic medication; those with a history of epilepsy. Special programs for the chronically ill.

Program Family treatment program available.

Staff Total facility staff includes 2 physicians, 2 psychologists, 1 psychiatrist, 4 registered nurses, 3 practical/vocational nurses, 2 MSW social workers, 6 social workers (non-MSW), 8 teachers, 87 counselors, 2 occupational/recreational therapists, 5 other direct-care staff members. Staff is 83% male, 17% female.

Facilities Multiple buildings. Central dining. Basketball courts, game room, gymnasium, horseback riding, outdoor swimming pool, outdoor tennis courts, playing fields, baseball field, volleyball court.

Education Academic program available at no charge. Serves ages 12–18, grades K–12. 8 teachers on staff. Curriculum accredited or approved by Colorado Department of Education. Cost of educational program sometimes covered by local school district. Organized sports program offered.

Costs Accepts private insurance, group insurance, medicare, medicaid, Blue Cross/Blue Shield, public funds.

Contact David Wright, Admissions Director, 1355 South Colorado Boulevard, Suite 601, Denver, CO 80222. Phone: 303-691-6095. Fax: 303-691-0890.

Announcement Colorado Boys Ranch is a residential psychiatric treatment facility for adolescent youth with severe emotional/behavioral problems. Individualized, focused treatment is offered in a rural, noninstitutional setting. Unique programs include horsemanship, chaplaincy, therapeutic recreation, wilderness camping, and paid work and money management as well as special education and pre-vocational training opportunities.

COLUMBINE PSYCHIATRIC CENTER
8565 South Poplar Way
Littleton, Colorado 80126
303-470-1440; Fax: 303-470-0607

General Information Psychiatric hospital for adolescents, adults. 20 beds for adolescents. Open year-round. Patient security: staff secured; will pursue and return runaways. Suburban setting. For-profit facility affiliated with Hospital Corporation of America, Nashville, TN. Licensed by state of Colorado. Accredited by JCAHO.

Participants Accepts: male and female adolescents ages 11–18; male and female adults ages 18–75. Average stay: 13 days. Admission: one parent, court order, depending on program. Treats learning disabilities; behavior disorders; general psychosocial disorders; substance abuse; eating disorders; compulsive/addictive disorders other than substance abuse and eating disorders; post-traumatic stress disorder; thought, mood, and personality disorders. Accepts the mobility impaired; the vision impaired; the hearing impaired; the speech impaired; those with a history of arson; the sexually compulsive; those with a history of harm to themselves and others; those receiving psychotropic medication; non-English speaking individuals; those with a history of epilepsy.

Program Treatment modalities: cognitive/behavioral; milieu and individual therapy; psychodynamic. Family treatment program available.

Staff Total facility staff includes 10 physicians, 20 psychologists, 20 psychiatrists, 40 registered nurses, 6 MSW social workers, 2 social workers (non-MSW), 2 teachers, 40 counselors, 5 occupational/recreational therapists, 1 speech pathologist, 2 therapists, 1 dietician, 20 other direct-care staff members. Staff is 30% male, 70% female.

Facilities Single building; males and females in co-educational units. Separate residential quarters for adolescents. Central dining arrangements vary. Basketball courts, game room, gymnasium, ropes course, exercise equipment.

Education Academic program available at no charge. Serves ages 11–19, grades 6–12. 2 teachers on staff. Curriculum accredited or approved by State of Colorado. Cost of educational program covered by local school district. Organized sports program offered.

Costs Average cost: $500 per day. Accepts private insurance, group insurance, Blue Cross/Blue Shield, public funds.

Additional Services Drug and alcohol rehabilitation services for males and females ages 11 and up. Treats learning disabilities; behavior disorders; general psychosocial disorders; substance abuse; eating disorders; compulsive/addictive disorders other than substance abuse and eating disorders; post-traumatic stress disorder; thought, mood, and personality disorders. Outpatient services for males and females ages 11 and up. Treats learning disabilities; behavior disorders; general psychosocial disorders; substance abuse; eating disorders; compulsive/addictive disorders other than substance abuse and eating disorders; post-traumatic stress disorder; thought, mood, and personality disorders.

Contact Dr. Michael Weinberg, Director of Front End Systems, main address above. Phone: 303-470-1440. Fax: 303-470-0607.

COMMON GROUND: THE CENTER FOR ADOLESCENTS AT STAMFORD HOSPITAL
Shelburne Road at One West Broad Street
P.O. Box 9317
Stamford, Connecticut 06904
203-325-7111; Fax: 203-325-7699

General Information General hospital for adolescents. 10 beds for adolescents. Open year-round. Patient security: staff secured; will pursue and return runaways. Suburban setting. Independent not-for-profit facility. Licensed by state of Connecticut. Accredited by JCAHO; Health Care Financing Administration.

Participants Accepts: male and female adolescents ages 13–20. Average stay: 30 days. Admission: one parent, voluntary, depending on program. Treats learning disabilities; behavior disorders; general psychosocial disorders; substance abuse; eating disorders; post-traumatic stress disorder; thought, mood, and personality disorders. Accepts those with a history of harm to themselves and others; those receiving psychotropic medication; those with a history of epilepsy. Largest number of participants from Connecticut.

Program Treatment modalities: cognitive; psychodynamic; behavior modification; psychopharmacology. Family treatment program available.

Staff Total facility staff includes 2 psychologists, 5 psychiatrists, 3 MSW social workers, 1 teacher, 1 occupational/recreational therapist, 1 dietician.

Facilities Single building; males and females in coeducational units. Residential quarters shared with adults. Central dining (shared with adults).

Education Academic program available. Serves ages 13–20, grades 7–12. 1 teacher on staff. Curriculum accredited or approved by Stamford School District. Cost of educational program sometimes covered by local school district.

Costs Accepts private insurance, group insurance, medicare, medicaid, Blue Cross/Blue Shield.

Additional Services Outpatient services for males and females ages 13–20. Treats learning disabilities; behavior disorders; general psychosocial disorders; substance abuse; eating disorders; post-traumatic stress disorder; thought, mood, and personality disorders. Partial hospital program for males and females ages 13–20. Treats learning disabilities; behavior disorders; general psychosocial disorders; substance abuse; eating disorders; post-traumatic stress disorder; thought, mood, and personality disorders.

Contact Dr. Edward Hall, Medical Director, Adolescent Psychiatric Services, main address above. Phone: 203-325-7469. Fax: 203-325-7699.

COMPREHENSIVE MENTAL HEALTH SERVICES, INC.
10901 Winner Road
Independence, Missouri 64052
816-254-3652; Fax: 816-254-9243

General Information Drug and alcohol rehabilitation center for children, adolescents, adults. 12 beds for adolescents. Open year-round. Patient security: staff secured; will pursue and return runaways. Urban setting. Independent not-for-profit facility. Licensed by state of Missouri. Accredited by JCAHO; Missouri Department of Mental Health.

Participants Accepts: male and female children ages 2–12; male and female adolescents ages 13–18; male and female adults ages 19 and up. Average stay: 45 days. Admission: one parent, all parties who share custody, court order, depending on program. Treats autistic disorders; learning disabilities; behavior disorders; general psychosocial disorders; substance abuse; eating disorders; compulsive/addictive disorders other than substance abuse and eating disorders; post-traumatic stress disorder; thought, mood, and personality disorders. Accepts those with a history of arson; the sexually compulsive; those with a history of harm to themselves and others; those receiving psychotropic medication; those with a history of epilepsy; those with behavior disorders.

Program Treatment modalities: psychoeducational; cognitive/behavioral; Twelve Step Recovery; family systems. Family treatment program available.

Staff Total facility staff includes 1 physician, 1 psychologist, 1 psychiatrist, 3 MSW social workers, 4 social workers (non-MSW), 1 teacher, 12 counselors, 1 occupational/recreational therapist, 3 therapists, 1 dietician, 12 other direct-care staff members. Staff is 70% male, 30% female.

Facilities Multiple buildings; males and females in coeducational units. Residential arrangements vary depending on program. Central dining arrangements vary. Outdoor swimming pool.

Education Academic program available at no charge. Serves ages 13–18, ungraded. 1 teacher on staff. Cost of educational program sometimes covered by local school district.

Costs Average cost: $200 per day. Accepts private insurance, group insurance, medicare, medicaid, Blue Cross/Blue Shield, public funds.

Additional Services Outpatient services for males and females ages 2 and up. Treats autistic disorders; learning disabilities; behavior disorders; general psychosocial disorders; substance abuse; eating disorders; compulsive/addictive disorders other than substance abuse and eating disorders; post-traumatic stress disorder; thought, mood, and personality disorders. Residential or sub-acute services for males and females ages 12 and up. Treats learning disabilities; behavior disorders; general psychosocial disorders; substance abuse; eating disorders; compulsive/addictive disorders other than substance abuse and eating disorders; post-traumatic stress disorder; thought, mood, and personality disorders. Therapeutic foster care program for males and females ages 6–18. Treats learning disabilities; behavior disorders; general psychosocial disorders; substance abuse; eating disorders; compulsive/addictive disorders other than substance abuse and eating disorders; post-traumatic stress disorder; thought, mood, and personality disorders.

Contact Kay Murphy-Collins, Director of Family and Youth Services, main address above. Phone: 816-254-3652. Fax: 816-254-9243.

CONIFER PARK
150 Glenridge Road
Scotia, New York 12302
518-399-6446; Fax: 518-399-1361

General Information Drug and alcohol rehabilitation center for adolescents, adults. 35 beds for adolescents. Open year-round. Patient security: staff secured; will pursue and return runaways. Suburban setting. Independent for-profit facility. Operated by Mediplex Group, Inc., Wellesley, MA. Licensed by state of New York. Accredited by JCAHO; New York State Division of Alcoholism and Alcohol Abuse, New York State Division of Substance Abuse Services.

Participants Accepts: male and female adolescents ages 12–18; male and female adults ages 18 and up. Average stay: 28 days. Admission: one parent, court order, voluntary, medical admission, depending on program. Treats learning disabilities; behavior disorders; general psychosocial disorders; substance abuse; eating disorders; post-traumatic stress disorder; thought, mood, and personality disorders. Accepts the mobility impaired; the vision impaired; those with a history of harm to themselves and others; those receiving psychotropic medication; non-English speaking individuals. Special programs for those with AIDS.

Program Treatment modalities: Twelve Step Recovery; psycosocial model; individual, group, family counseling; disease model of chemical dependency. Family treatment program available.

Staff Total facility staff includes 2 physicians, 5 psychologists, 3 psychiatrists, 15 registered nurses, 8 practical/vocational nurses, 9 MSW social workers, 1 teacher, 41 counselors, 4 occupational/recreational therapists, 1 dietician, 25 other direct-care staff members. Staff is 40% male, 60% female.

Facilities Single building; males and females in both coeducational and separate units depending on program. Separate residential quarters for adolescents. Central dining (shared with adults). Basketball courts, gymnasium, indoor swimming pool, playing fields, ropes course, volleyball court.

Education Academic program available at no charge. Serves ages 12–18, grades 7–12. 1 teacher on staff.

Costs Average cost: $525 per day. Accepts private insurance, group insurance, Blue Cross/Blue Shield.

Additional Services Outpatient services for males and females ages 12 and up. Treats substance abuse.

Contact Tim Ruhle, Coordinator of Regional Services, main address above. Phone: 518-399-6446. Fax: 518-399-1361.

COOPER HOUSE
1206 Lutrell Street
Knoxville, Tennessee 37917
615-546-7447; Fax: 615-558-8342

General Information Residential treatment/subacute facility for children, adolescents. Patient security: staff secured. Not-for-profit facility affiliated with Child and Family Services, Knoxville, TN. Licensed by state of Tennessee. Accredited by JCAHO; Family Service America, Child Welfare League of America.

Participants Accepts: male children; male adolescents. Average stay: 1 year. Admission: one parent, all parties who share custody, court order, voluntary, depending on program. Treats autistic disorders;

learning disabilities; behavior disorders; general psychosocial disorders; substance abuse; eating disorders; compulsive/addictive disorders other than substance abuse and eating disorders; post-traumatic stress disorder; thought, mood, and personality disorders.

Staff   Staff is 50% male, 50% female.

Costs   Average cost: $190 per day.

Contact   Randy Dillon, Coordinator of Psychiatric Residential Treatment, 3006 Lake Brook Boulevard, Knoxville, TN 37909. Phone: 615-558-6361. Fax: 615-558-8342.

CPC AFTON OAKS HOSPITAL
COMMUNITY RESIDENTIAL CENTER
620 East Afton Oaks Boulevard
San Antonio, Texas 78232
512-494-1060; Fax: 512-496-7499

General Information   Hospital-based residential treatment center for children, adolescents. 10 beds for children; 20 beds for adolescents; 30 beds total. Open year-round. Patient security: partially locked; will pursue and return runaways. Suburban setting. For-profit facility affiliated with Community Psychiatric Centers, Laguna Hills, CA. Licensed by state of Texas. Accredited by JCAHO; Texas Department of Human Services, Texas Department of Mental Health and Mental Retardation.

Participants   Accepts: male and female children ages 6–11; male and female adolescents ages 12–18. Average stay: 120 days. Admission: all parties who share custody, voluntary, depending on program. Treats learning disabilities; behavior disorders; general psychosocial disorders; substance abuse; eating disorders; compulsive/addictive disorders other than substance abuse and eating disorders; post-traumatic stress disorder; thought, mood, and personality disorders. Accepts the mobility impaired; the vision impaired; the speech impaired; those with a history of arson; the sexually compulsive; those with a history of harm to themselves and others; those receiving psychotropic medication; non-English speaking individuals; those with a history of epilepsy. Special programs for the chronically ill; the mobility impaired; those with AIDS. Largest number of participants from Texas.

Program   Treatment modalities: Twelve Step Recovery; psychodynamic; behavioral. Family treatment program available.

Staff   .8 full-time direct-care staff member per child or adolescent. Total facility staff includes 2 physicians, 2 psychologists, 5 psychiatrists, 6 registered nurses, 2 practical/vocational nurses, 1 MSW social worker, 1 social worker (non-MSW), 3 teachers, 2 occupational/recreational therapists, 1 speech pathologist, 1 therapist, 1 dietician, 6 other direct-care staff members. Staff is 50% male, 50% female.

Facilities   Single building; males and females in co-educational units. Basketball courts, game room, gymnasium, outdoor swimming pool.

Education   Academic program available at no charge. Serves ages 6–18, grades 1–12. 3 teachers on staff. Curriculum accredited or approved by Texas Education Agency. Cost of educational program covered by local school district.

Costs   Average cost: $320 per day. Accepts private insurance, group insurance, Blue Cross/Blue Shield, public funds.

Contact   Pat McLemore, Program Director, main address above. Phone: 512-494-1060. Fax: 512-496-7499.

CPC BELMONT HILLS HOSPITAL
1301 Ralston Avenue
Belmont, California 94002
415-593-2143; Fax: 415-595-8922

General Information   Psychiatric hospital for children, adolescents, adults. 11 beds for children; 19 beds for adolescents; 84 beds total. Open year-round. Patient security: partially locked; no runaway pursuit. Suburban setting. For-profit facility affiliated with Community Psychiatric Centers, Laguna Hills, CA. Licensed by state of California. Accredited by JCAHO.

Participants   Accepts: male and female children ages 4–12; male and female adolescents ages 13–17; male and female adults ages 19 and up. Average stay: 22 days. Admission: one parent, all parties who share custody, court order, voluntary, involuntary hold, depending on program. Treats learning disabilities; behavior disorders; general psychosocial disorders; substance abuse; eating disorders; compulsive/addictive disorders other than substance abuse and eating disorders; post-traumatic stress disorder; thought, mood, and personality disorders. Accepts the mobility impaired; the vision impaired; the speech impaired; those with a history of arson; the sexually compulsive; those with a history of harm to themselves and others; those receiving psychotropic medication; those with a history of epilepsy. Special programs for those with AIDS; lesbian/gay/bisexual with psychiatric diagnosis; multiple personality disorder.

Program Treatment modalities: psychodynamic; milieu therapy; Twelve Step Recovery; behavioral therapy. Family treatment program available.

Facilities Multiple buildings; males and females in coeducational units. Separate residential quarters for children and adolescents. Central dining (not shared with adults). Basketball courts, game room, playing fields, volleyball court, weight machine, picnic area.

Education Academic program available at no charge. Serves ages 5–18, ungraded. Cost of educational program sometimes covered by local school district.

Costs Average cost: $1200 per day. Accepts private insurance, group insurance, medicare, medicaid, Blue Cross/Blue Shield, public funds.

Additional Services Outpatient services for males and females ages 4 and up. Treats behavior disorders; general psychosocial disorders; substance abuse; eating disorders; compulsive/addictive disorders other than substance abuse and eating disorders.

Contact Wendy Lane, Director of Marketing, main address above. Phone: 415-593-2143. Fax: 415-595-8922.

CPC CAPITAL HOSPITAL
12151 Hunters Chase Drive
Austin, Texas 78729
512-250-8667; Fax: 512-331-5140

General Information Psychiatric hospital for children, adolescents, adults. 16 beds for children; 38 beds for adolescents; 98 beds total. Open year-round. Patient security: partially locked; will pursue and return runaways. Suburban setting. For-profit facility affiliated with Community Psychiatric Centers, Laguna Hills, CA. Licensed by state of Texas. Accredited by JCAHO; Texas Department of Mental Health and Mental Retardation, Texas Commission on Alcohol and Drug Abuse, Texas Association of Alcohol and Drug Abuse Commissions.

Participants Accepts: male and female children ages 6–12; male and female adolescents ages 13–18; male and female adults ages 18–80. Average stay: 22 days. Admission: one parent, all parties who share custody, court order, voluntary, depending on program. Treats learning disabilities; behavior disorders; general psychosocial disorders; substance abuse; eating disorders; compulsive/addictive disorders other than substance abuse and eating disorders; post-traumatic stress disorder; thought, mood, and personality disorders. Accepts the vision impaired; the hearing impaired; the speech impaired; those with a history of

arson; the sexually compulsive; those with a history of harm to themselves and others; those receiving psychotropic medication; non-English speaking individuals; those with a history of epilepsy. Special programs for the vision impaired; the hearing impaired.

Program Treatment modalities: Twelve Step Recovery; psychodynamic; cognitive. Family treatment program available.

Staff 6.7 full-time direct-care staff members per child or adolescent. Total facility staff includes 25 physicians, 15 psychologists, 15 psychiatrists, 20 registered nurses, 25 practical/vocational nurses, 10 MSW social workers, 4 teachers, 5 counselors, 1 physical therapist, 2 occupational/recreational therapists, 3 therapists, 1 dietician, 35 other direct-care staff members.

Facilities Single building; males and females in coeducational units. Separate residential quarters for children and adolescents. Central dining (shared with adults). Basketball courts, game room, gymnasium, outdoor swimming pool, ropes course.

Education Academic program available at no charge. Serves ages 6–18, grades K–12. 4 teachers on staff. Curriculum accredited or approved by Texas Education Agency, Round Rock Independent School District.

Costs Average cost: $650 per day. Accepts private insurance, group insurance, medicare, medicaid, Blue Cross/Blue Shield, public funds.

Additional Services Drug and alcohol rehabilitation services for males and females ages 13–18. Treats behavior disorders; general psychosocial disorders; substance abuse; compulsive/addictive disorders other than substance abuse and eating disorders; post-traumatic stress disorder; thought, mood, and personality disorders. Outpatient services for males and females ages 18 and up. Treats learning disabilities; substance abuse.

Contact Barb Williams, Marketing Director, main address above. Phone: 512-250-8667. Fax: 512-331-5140.

CPC COLLEGE MEADOWS HOSPITAL
14425 College Boulevard
Lenexa, Kansas 66215
913-469-1100; Fax: 913-469-4261

General Information Psychiatric hospital for children, adolescents, adults. 20 beds for children; 40 beds for adolescents; 120 beds total. Open year-round. Patient security: partially locked; will pursue and return runaways. Suburban setting. For-profit facility affiliated with Community Psychiatric Centers, Laguna Hills, CA. Licensed by state of Kansas. Accredited by JCAHO.

Participants Accepts: male and female children ages 5–12; male and female adolescents ages 13–17; male and female adults ages 18 and up. Admission: all parties who share custody. Treats autistic disorders; learning disabilities; behavior disorders; general psychosocial disorders; substance abuse; eating disorders; compulsive/addictive disorders other than substance abuse and eating disorders; post-traumatic stress disorder; thought, mood, and personality disorders. Accepts the mobility impaired; the vision impaired; the hearing impaired; the speech impaired; those with a history of arson; the sexually compulsive; those with a history of harm to themselves and others; those receiving psychotropic medication; non-English speaking individuals; those with a history of epilepsy.

Program Treatment modalities: Twelve Step Recovery; psychotherapy; dual diagnosis; eclectic. Family treatment program available.

Facilities Single building; males and females in co-educational units. Separate residential quarters for children and adolescents. Central dining (not shared with adults), separate dining by residential unit available. Basketball courts, game room, gymnasium, outdoor swimming pool, playing fields.

Education Academic program available at no charge. Serves ages 5–18, grades 1–12. Curriculum accredited or approved by Olathe District Schools.

Costs Accepts private insurance, group insurance, medicare, Blue Cross/Blue Shield.

Additional Services Drug and alcohol rehabilitation services for males and females ages 13 and up. Treats autistic disorders; learning disabilities; behavior disorders; general psychosocial disorders; substance abuse; eating disorders; compulsive/addictive disorders other than substance abuse and eating disorders; post-traumatic stress disorder; thought, mood, and personality disorders.

Contact Lisa Coleman, Marketing Director, main address above. Phone: 913-469-1100. Fax: 913-469-4261.

CPC CYPRESS POINT HOSPITAL
11297 Fallbrook Drive
Houston, Texas 77065
713-955-6550; Fax: 713-894-6587

General Information Psychiatric hospital for children, adolescents, adults. Open year-round. Patient security: partially locked; will pursue and return runaways. Suburban setting. For-profit facility affiliated with Community Psychiatric Centers, Laguna Hills, CA. Licensed by state of Texas. Accredited by JCAHO.

Participants Accepts: male and female children ages 2–10; male and female adolescents ages 11–18; male and female adults ages 19 and up. Average stay: 20 days. Admission: one parent, all parties who share custody, court order, voluntary, depending on program. Treats learning disabilities; behavior disorders; general psychosocial disorders; substance abuse; eating disorders; compulsive/addictive disorders other than substance abuse and eating disorders; post-traumatic stress disorder; thought, mood, and personality disorders. Accepts the speech impaired; the sexually compulsive; those with a history of harm to themselves and others; non-English speaking individuals.

Program Treatment modalities: Twelve Step Recovery; psychodynamic. Family treatment program available.

Facilities Single building; males and females in co-educational units. Separate residential quarters for children and adolescents. Central dining (shared with adults). Gymnasium, outdoor swimming pool, ropes course.

Education Academic program available. Serves ages 5–18, grades K–12. Curriculum accredited or approved by Texas Education Agency.

Costs Accepts private insurance, group insurance, medicare, medicaid, Blue Cross/Blue Shield.

Additional Services Drug and alcohol rehabilitation services for males and females ages 11 and up. Treats substance abuse; compulsive/addictive disorders other than substance abuse and eating disorders.

Contact Linda Meyer, Student Assistance and Intervention Program Coordinator, main address above. Phone: 713-955-6550. Fax: 713-894-6587.

CPC EAST LAKE HOSPITAL
5650 Read Boulevard
New Orleans, Louisiana 70127
504-241-0888; Fax: 504-245-0468

General Information Psychiatric hospital for children, adolescents. Patient security: entirely locked. For-profit facility affiliated with Community Psychiatric Centers, Laguna Hills, CA. Licensed by state of California. Accredited by JCAHO.

Participants Accepts: male and female children; male and female adolescents. Average stay: 18 days.

Admission: one parent, all parties who share custody, court order, voluntary, depending on program. Treats autistic disorders; learning disabilities; behavior disorders; general psychosocial disorders; substance abuse; eating disorders; compulsive/addictive disorders other than substance abuse and eating disorders; post-traumatic stress disorder; thought, mood, and personality disorders.

Contact Jeana Blailock, Intake Coordinator, main address above. Phone: 504-241-0888.

CPC FAIRFAX HOSPITAL
10200 Northeast 132nd Avenue
Kirkland, Washington 98034
206-821-2000; Fax: 206-821-9010

General Information Psychiatric hospital for children, adolescents, adults. 30 beds for children; 60 beds for adolescents; 120 beds total. Open year-round. Patient security arrangements vary depending on program; will pursue and return runaways. Suburban setting. For-profit facility affiliated with Community Psychiatric Centers, Laguna Hills, CA. Licensed by state of Washington. Accredited by JCAHO.

Participants Accepts: male and female children ages 4–13; male and female adolescents ages 13–18; male and female adults ages 18 and up. Average stay: 45 days. Admission: one parent, all parties who share custody, court order, voluntary, depending on program. Treats autistic disorders; learning disabilities; behavior disorders; general psychosocial disorders; substance abuse; eating disorders; compulsive/addictive disorders other than substance abuse and eating disorders; post-traumatic stress disorder; thought, mood, and personality disorders. Accepts the mobility impaired; the vision impaired; the hearing impaired; the speech impaired; those with a history of arson; the sexually compulsive; those with a history of harm to themselves and others; those receiving psychotropic medication; non-English speaking individuals; those with a history of epilepsy; those receiving acute psychiatric diagnosis with limited cognitive disability. Special programs for those with AIDS.

Program Treatment modalities: cognitive/behavioral; psychodynamic; Twelve Step Recovery. Family treatment program available.

Staff 2.2 full-time direct-care staff members per child or adolescent. Total facility staff includes 20 physicians, 15 psychologists, 100 registered nurses, 10 MSW social workers, 6 teachers, 50 counselors, 10 occupational/recreational therapists, 2 dieticians.

Facilities Single building; males and females in co-educational units. Separate residential quarters for children and adolescents. Central dining (not shared with adults), in-room dining available. Basketball courts, gymnasium, outdoor tennis courts, playing fields.

Education Academic program available at no charge. Serves ages 4–18, ungraded. 6 teachers on staff. Curriculum accredited or approved by Lake Washington School District.

Costs Average cost: $800 per stay. Accepts private insurance, group insurance, Blue Cross/Blue Shield.

Additional Services Acute partial-hospitalization program for males and females ages 13 and up. Treats behavior disorders; general psychosocial disorders; eating disorders; compulsive/addictive disorders other than substance abuse and eating disorders; post-traumatic stress disorder; thought, mood, and personality disorders.

Contact Linda Crome, Director of Intake, main address above. Phone: 206-821-2000. Fax: 206-821-9010.

CPC FREMONT HOSPITAL
39001 Sundale Drive
Fremont, California 94538
510-796-1100; Fax: 510-796-5814

General Information Psychiatric hospital for adolescents. 20 beds for adolescents. Patient security: entirely locked. Not-for-profit facility affiliated with Community Psychiatric Centers, Laguna Hills, CA. Licensed by state of California. Accredited by JCAHO.

Participants Accepts: male and female adolescents. Average stay: 10 days. Admission: one parent, all parties who share custody, court order, voluntary, depending on program. Treats autistic disorders; learning disabilities; behavior disorders; general psychosocial disorders; substance abuse; eating disorders; compulsive/addictive disorders other than substance abuse and eating disorders; post-traumatic stress disorder; thought, mood, and personality disorders.

Contact Adolescent Services, main address above. Phone: 510-796-1100.

CPC GREAT PLAINS HOSPITAL
5111 East 21st Street
Wichita, Kansas 67208
316-681-1800; Fax: 316-681-1805

General Information   Psychiatric hospital for children, adolescents, adults. 20 beds for children; 20 beds for adolescents; 79 beds total. Open year-round. Patient security: entirely locked; no runaway pursuit. Urban setting. For-profit facility affiliated with Community Psychiatric Centers, Laguna Hills, CA. Licensed by state of Kansas. Accredited by JCAHO; National Association of Private Psychiatric Hospitals.

Participants   Accepts: male and female children ages 2–11; male and female adolescents ages 13–18; male and female adults ages 18 and up. Admission: all parties who share custody, court order, depending on program. Treats autistic disorders; learning disabilities; behavior disorders; general psychosocial disorders; substance abuse; eating disorders; compulsive/addictive disorders other than substance abuse and eating disorders; post-traumatic stress disorder; thought, mood, and personality disorders. Accepts the mobility impaired; the vision impaired; the hearing impaired; the speech impaired; those with a history of arson; the sexually compulsive; those with a history of harm to themselves and others; those receiving psychotropic medication; non-English speaking individuals; those with a history of epilepsy.

Program   Treatment modalities: Twelve Step Recovery; psychodynamic; behavioral; cognitive. Family treatment program available.

Facilities   Single building; males and females in coeducational units. Separate residential quarters for children and adolescents. Central dining (shared with adults), in-room dining available. Gymnasium, outdoor swimming pool.

Education   Academic program available at no charge. Serves ages 5–18, grades K–12. Curriculum accredited or approved by local school district.

Costs   Accepts private insurance, group insurance, medicare, Blue Cross/Blue Shield, public funds.

Additional Services   Drug and alcohol rehabilitation services for males and females ages 5 and up. Treats autistic disorders; learning disabilities; behavior disorders; general psychosocial disorders; substance abuse; eating disorders; compulsive/addictive disorders other than substance abuse and eating disorders; post-traumatic stress disorder; thought, mood, and personality disorders. Outpatient services for males and females ages 5 and up. Treats autistic disorders; learning disabilities; behavior disorders; general psychosocial disorders; substance abuse; eating disorders; compulsive/addictive disorders other than

substance abuse and eating disorders; post-traumatic stress disorder; thought, mood, and personality disorders.

Contact   Cynthia Mullin, Administrator, main address above. Phone: 316-681-1800. Fax: 316-681-1805.

CPC GREENBRIAR HOSPITAL
5015 South 110th Street
Greenfield, Wisconsin 53228
414-425-8000

General Information   Psychiatric/substance abuse facility for children, adolescents. Patient security: entirely locked. For-profit facility affiliated with Community Psychiatric Centers, Laguna Hills, CA. Licensed by state of Wisconsin. Accredited by JCAHO.

Participants   Accepts: male and female children; male and female adolescents. Average stay: 18 days. Admission: one parent, voluntary, depending on program. Treats learning disabilities; behavior disorders; general psychosocial disorders; substance abuse; eating disorders; compulsive/addictive disorders other than substance abuse and eating disorders; post-traumatic stress disorder; thought, mood, and personality disorders.

Staff   Staff is 50% male, 50% female.

Costs   Average cost: $650 per day.

Contact   Pete Carlson, Director of Intake Department, main address above. Phone: 414-425-8000.

CPC INTERMOUNTAIN HOSPITAL ADOLESCENT COMMUNITY RESIDENTIAL CENTER
303 North Allumbaugh
Boise, Idaho 83704
208-377-8400; Fax: 208-377-8523

General Information   Residential treatment/subacute facility for children, adolescents. 20 beds for children; 40 beds for adolescents. Patient security: entirely locked; will pursue and return runaways. Rural setting. For-profit facility affiliated with Community Psychiatric Centers, Laguna Hills, CA. Licensed by state of Idaho. Accredited by JCAHO; Civilian Health and Medical Program of the Uniformed Services.

Participants Accepts: male and female children ages 4–13; male and female adolescents ages 12–18. Admission: one parent. Treats learning disabilities; behavior disorders; general psychosocial disorders; substance abuse; eating disorders; post-traumatic stress disorder; thought, mood, and personality disorders. Accepts the mobility impaired; those with a history of harm to themselves and others; those receiving psychotropic medication; those with a history of epilepsy. Special programs for those with AIDS.

Program Treatment modalities: Twelve Step Plus-cognitive therapy; group psychotherapy-reality therapy; individual therapy; family therapy. Family treatment program available.

Staff 1.1 full-time direct-care staff members per child or adolescent. Total facility staff includes 19 registered nurses, 4 practical/vocational nurses, 8 MSW social workers, 4 teachers, 4 counselors, 1 occupational/recreational therapist, 1 dietician, 35 other direct-care staff members. Staff is 32% male, 68% female.

Facilities Multiple buildings; males and females in coeducational units. Central dining (shared with adults). Basketball courts, gymnasium, ropes course, volleyball.

Education Academic program available at no charge. Serves ages 4–18, grades K–12. 4 teachers on staff. Curriculum accredited or approved by Northwest Association of Schools and Colleges. Organized sports program offered.

Costs Average cost: $1000 per stay. Accepts private insurance, group insurance, medicare, Blue Cross/ Blue Shield, public funds.

Contact Cindy Clark, CRC Program Director, main address above. Phone: 208-377-8400. Fax: 208-377-8523.

CPC OAK BEND HOSPITAL
7800 Oakmont Boulevard
Fort Worth, Texas 76132
817-346-6043; Fax: 817-346-1641

General Information Psychiatric hospital for children, adolescents, adults. 16 beds for children; 22 beds for adolescents; 74 beds total. Open year-round. Patient security: partially locked; will pursue and return runaways. Suburban setting. For-profit facility affiliated with Community Psychiatric Centers, Laguna Hills, CA. Licensed by state of Texas. Accredited by JCAHO.

Participants Accepts: male and female children ages 4–12; male and female adolescents ages 12–17; male and female adults ages 18 and up. Average stay: 30 days. Admission: all parties who share custody. Treats behavior disorders; general psychosocial disorders; substance abuse; eating disorders; compulsive/addictive disorders other than substance abuse and eating disorders; post-traumatic stress disorder; thought, mood, and personality disorders. Accepts the mobility impaired; the vision impaired; the speech impaired; those with a history of arson; those with a history of harm to themselves and others; those receiving psychotropic medication. Special programs for the chronically ill; the mobility impaired; the developmentally disabled; the vision impaired. Largest number of participants from Texas.

Program Treatment modalities: psychodynamic; Twelve Step Recovery; rational emotive therapy. Family treatment program available.

Staff Total facility staff includes 12 physicians, 20 psychologists, 28 psychiatrists, 20 registered nurses, 12 practical/vocational nurses, 4 MSW social workers, 1 social worker (non-MSW), 3 teachers, 4 counselors, 4 occupational/recreational therapists, 1 therapist, 1 dietician, 24 other direct-care staff members. Staff is 35% male, 65% female.

Facilities Single building; males and females in coeducational units. Separate residential quarters for children and adolescents. Central dining (shared with adults). Basketball courts, game room, gymnasium, outdoor swimming pool, ropes course.

Education Academic program available at no charge. Serves ages 3–21, grades K–12. 3 teachers on staff. Curriculum accredited or approved by Crowley Independent School District. Cost of educational program sometimes covered by local school district.

Costs Average cost: $1100 per day. Accepts private insurance, group insurance, medicare, medicaid, Blue Cross/Blue Shield.

Additional Services Drug and alcohol rehabilitation services for males and females ages 13 and up. Treats learning disabilities; behavior disorders; general psychosocial disorders; substance abuse; thought, mood, and personality disorders. Outpatient services for males and females ages 3 and up. Treats learning disabilities; behavior disorders; general psychosocial disorders; substance abuse; thought, mood, and personality disorders. Residential or sub-acute services for males and females ages 3–12. Treats behavior disorders; general psychosocial disorders. Camping program for males and females ages 6–12. Treats learning disabilities; behavior disorders; general psychosocial disorders; thought, mood, and personality disorders. Emotional trauma program for males and females ages 18 and up. Treats post-traumatic stress disorder.

Contact Dean Paret, Director of Clinical Services, main address above. Phone: 817-346-6043. Fax: 817-346-1641.

CPC OLD ORCHARD HOSPITAL
9700 Kenton Avenue
Skokie, Illinois 60076
708-679-0760; Fax: 708-679-5061

General Information Psychiatric hospital for children, adolescents. Patient security: entirely locked. For-profit facility affiliated with Community Psychiatric Centers, Laguna Hills, CA. Licensed by state of Illinois. Accredited by JCAHO.

Participants Accepts: male and female children; male and female adolescents. Admission: voluntary, family members, depending on program.

Contact Client Service Administration, main address above. Phone: 708-679-0760.

CPC OLYMPUS VIEW HOSPITAL
COMMUNITY RESIDENTIAL CENTER
1430 East 4500 South
Salt Lake City, Utah 84117
801-272-8000; Fax: 801-272-4952

General Information Psychiatric hospital for adolescents. 20 beds for adolescents. Open year-round. Patient security: entirely locked; will pursue and return runaways. Suburban setting. For-profit facility affiliated with Community Psychiatric Centers, Laguna Hills, CA. Licensed by state of Utah. Accredited by JCAHO.

Participants Accepts: male and female adolescents ages 12–18. Average stay: 100 days. Admission: one parent, all parties who share custody, court order, voluntary, depending on program. Treats learning disabilities; behavior disorders; general psychosocial disorders; substance abuse; eating disorders; post-traumatic stress disorder; thought, mood, and personality disorders. Accepts those with a history of harm to themselves and others; those receiving psychotropic medication; those with a history of epilepsy. Special programs for the chronically ill; those with AIDS; survivors of abuse/substance abuse. Largest number of participants from Utah, Nevada, California.

Program Treatment modalities: biopsychosocial model; Twelve Step Recovery. Family treatment program available.

Staff 3.6 full-time direct-care staff members per adolescent. Total facility staff includes 1 physician, 2 psychologists, 3 psychiatrists, 5 registered nurses, 1 practical/vocational nurse, 4 MSW social workers, 2 teachers, 1 counselor, 5 occupational/recreational therapists, 2 therapists, 1 dietician, 10 other direct-care staff members. Staff is 50% male, 50% female.

Facilities Single building; males and females in co-educational units. Central dining. Basketball courts, game room, gymnasium, outdoor swimming pool, playing fields, ropes course.

Education Academic program available at no charge. Serves ages 12–18, grades 7–12. 2 teachers on staff. Curriculum accredited or approved by Northwest Association of Schools and Colleges for California and Utah. Organized sports program offered.

Costs Average cost: $44,000 per stay. Accepts private insurance, group insurance, Blue Cross/Blue Shield, public funds.

Additional Services Drug and alcohol rehabilitation services for males and females ages 18 and up. Treats general psychosocial disorders; substance abuse; thought, mood, and personality disorders. Residential or sub-acute services for males and females ages 12–18. Treats general psychosocial disorders; substance abuse; eating disorders; post-traumatic stress disorder; thought, mood, and personality disorders. Adolescent acute program ages 12–18. Treats behavior disorders; general psychosocial disorders; substance abuse; post-traumatic stress disorder; thought, mood, and personality disorders.

Contact Robyn Theuer, Program Director, main address above. Phone: 801-272-8000. Fax: 801-272-4952.

CPC PALM BAY HOSPITAL
COMMUNITY RESIDENTIAL CENTER
4400 Dixie Highway, NE
Palm Bay, Florida 32905
407-729-0500; Fax: 407-728-7164

General Information Freestanding psychiatric and substance abuse hospital for children, adolescents. 15 beds for children; 25 beds for adolescents; 40 beds total. Open year-round. Patient security: partially locked; will pursue and return runaways. Suburban setting. For-profit facility affiliated with Community Psychiatric Centers, Laguna Hills, CA. Licensed by state of Florida. Accredited by JCAHO.

Participants Accepts: male and female children ages 5–12; male and female adolescents ages 13–18. Average stay: 120 days. Admission: all parties who share custody. Treats autistic disorders; learning disabilities; behavior disorders; general psychosocial disorders; substance abuse; eating disorders; compulsive/ addictive disorders other than substance abuse and eating disorders; post-traumatic stress disorder; thought, mood, and personality disorders. Accepts the speech impaired; those with a history of harm to themselves and others; those receiving psychotropic medication; non-English speaking individuals. Special programs for the developmentally disabled; the speech impaired. Largest number of participants from Florida, D.C., Kentucky.

Program   Treatment modalities: Twelve Step Recovery; psychodynamic; milieu management; group therapy. Family treatment program available.

Staff   .5 full-time direct-care staff member per child or adolescent. Total facility staff includes 1 psychologist, 2 psychiatrists, 4 registered nurses, 2 MSW social workers, 2 teachers, 3 counselors, 1 occupational/ recreational therapist, 1 therapist, 1 dietician, 3 other direct-care staff members. Staff is 40% male, 60% female.

Facilities   Single building; males and females in co-educational units. Central dining. Basketball courts, game room, gymnasium, outdoor swimming pool, playing fields, ropes course.

Education   Academic program available at no charge. Serves ages 5–18, grades K–12. 2 teachers on staff. Curriculum accredited or approved by State of Florida Accreditation. Cost of educational program covered by local school district. Organized sports program offered.

Costs   Average cost: $500 per day. Accepts private insurance, group insurance, Blue Cross/Blue Shield.

Additional Services   Drug and alcohol rehabilitation services for males and females ages 5–18. Treats autistic disorders; learning disabilities; behavior disorders; general psychosocial disorders; substance abuse; eating disorders; compulsive/addictive disorders other than substance abuse and eating disorders; post-traumatic stress disorder; thought, mood, and personality disorders. Outpatient services for males and females ages 5–18. Treats behavior disorders; general psychosocial disorders; substance abuse; thought, mood, and personality disorders.

Contact   Mai Lee Fleury, Marketing Director, main address above. Phone: 407-729-0500. Fax: 407-728-7164.

CPC PARKWOOD HOSPITAL
1999 Cliff Valley Way, NE
Atlanta, Georgia 30329
404-633-8431; Fax: 404-633-9300

General Information   Psychiatric hospital for children, adolescents, adults. 15 beds for children; 35 beds for adolescents; 152 beds total. Open year-round. Patient security: partially locked; will pursue and return runaways. Urban setting. For-profit facility affiliated with Community Psychiatric Centers, Laguna Hills, CA. Licensed by state of Georgia. Accredited by JCAHO.

Participants   Accepts: male and female children ages 4–11; male and female adolescents ages 12–17; male and female adults ages 18 and up. Average stay: 32 days. Admission: one parent, all parties who share custody, court order, depending on program. Treats behavior disorders; general psychosocial disorders; substance abuse; compulsive/addictive disorders other than substance abuse and eating disorders; post-traumatic stress disorder; thought, mood, and personality disorders. Accepts those with a history of arson; the sexually compulsive; those with a history of harm to themselves and others; those receiving psychotropic medication. Special programs for those with AIDS.

Program   Treatment modalities: Twelve Step Recovery; cognitive behavior therapy. Family treatment program available.

Staff   Total facility staff includes 6 physicians, 80 psychologists, 150 psychiatrists, 20 registered nurses, 30 practical/vocational nurses, 30 MSW social workers, 6 teachers, 10 counselors, 3 occupational/recreational therapists, 2 dieticians.

Facilities   Single building; males and females in co-educational units. Separate residential quarters for children and adolescents. Separate dining by residential unit available. Basketball courts, game room, gymnasium, outdoor swimming pool, playing fields.

Education   Academic program available at no charge. Serves ages 5–18, grades K–12. 6 teachers on staff. Curriculum accredited or approved by State of Georgia.

Costs   Average cost: $475 per day. Accepts private insurance, group insurance, medicare, Blue Cross/ Blue Shield, public funds.

Additional Services   Drug and alcohol rehabilitation services for males and females ages 4 and up. Treats behavior disorders; general psychosocial disorders; substance abuse; compulsive/addictive disorders other than substance abuse and eating disorders; post-traumatic stress disorder; thought, mood, and personality disorders. Residential or sub-acute services for males and females ages 13–17. Treats general psychosocial disorders; substance abuse; compulsive/addictive disorders other than substance abuse and eating disorders; post-traumatic stress disorder; thought, mood, and personality disorders.

Contact Barbara Nut, Program Manager for Wings, main address above. Phone: 404-633-8431. Fax: 404-633-9300.

CPC PINNACLE POINTE HOSPITAL
11501 Financial Center Parkway
Little Rock, Arkansas 72211
501-223-3322; Fax: 501-224-7528

General Information Psychiatric hospital for children, adolescents. 18 beds for children; 68 beds for adolescents; 86 beds total. Open year-round. Patient security: entirely locked; no runaway pursuit. Suburban setting. For-profit facility affiliated with Community Psychiatric Centers, Laguna Hills, CA. Licensed by state of Arkansas. Accredited by JCAHO.

Participants Accepts: male and female children ages 6–12; male and female adolescents ages 12–18. Average stay: 90 days. Admission: one parent, all parties who share custody, court order, depending on program. Treats learning disabilities; behavior disorders; general psychosocial disorders; substance abuse; eating disorders; compulsive/addictive disorders other than substance abuse and eating disorders; post-traumatic stress disorder; thought, mood, and personality disorders. Accepts the mobility impaired; the vision impaired; the hearing impaired; the speech impaired; those with a history of arson; the sexually compulsive; those with a history of harm to themselves and others; those receiving psychotropic medication; non-English speaking individuals; those with a history of epilepsy. Special programs for the mobility impaired; the developmentally disabled; the vision impaired; the hearing impaired; the speech impaired; those with AIDS.

Program Treatment modalities: Twelve Step Recovery; psychodynamic. Family treatment program available.

Staff Total facility staff includes 2 physicians, 1 psychologist, 10 psychiatrists, 23 registered nurses, 5 practical/vocational nurses, 6 MSW social workers, 5 teachers, 2 counselors, 3 occupational/recreational therapists, 8 therapists, 1 dietician, 17 other direct-care staff members. Staff is 47% male, 53% female.

Facilities Single building. Central dining (shared with adults). Basketball courts, gymnasium, outdoor swimming pool.

Education Academic program available at no charge. Serves ages 6–21, grades K–12. 5 teachers on staff. Curriculum accredited or approved by Arkansas Department of Education; Division of Special Education. Cost of educational program sometimes covered by local school district.

Costs Accepts private insurance, group insurance, medicare, medicaid, Blue Cross/Blue Shield, public funds.

Additional Services Drug and alcohol rehabilitation services for males and females ages 13 and up. Treats learning disabilities; behavior disorders; general psychosocial disorders; substance abuse; eating disorders; compulsive/addictive disorders other than substance abuse and eating disorders; post-traumatic stress disorder; thought, mood, and personality disorders. Residential or sub-acute services for males and females ages 6–18. Treats learning disabilities; behavior disorders; general psychosocial disorders; substance abuse; eating disorders; compulsive/addictive disorders other than substance abuse and eating disorders; post-traumatic stress disorder; thought, mood, and personality disorders. Partial hospitalization for males and females ages 6 and up. Treats learning disabilities; behavior disorders; general psychosocial disorders; substance abuse; eating disorders; compulsive/addictive disorders other than substance abuse and eating disorders; post-traumatic stress disorder; thought, mood, and personality disorders.

Contact Susan Johns, Director of Intake, main address above. Phone: 501-223-3322. Fax: 501-224-7528.

CPC REDWOODS HOSPITAL
1287 Fulton Road
Santa Rosa, California 95401
707-578-4500; Fax: 707-578-4969

General Information Psychiatric hospital for adolescents. 14 beds for adolescents. Open year-round. Patient security: staff secured; no runaway pursuit. Small town setting. For-profit facility affiliated with Community Psychiatric Centers, Laguna Hills, CA. Licensed by state of California. Accredited by JCAHO.

Participants Accepts: male and female adolescents ages 12–18. Average stay: 240 days. Treats autistic disorders; learning disabilities; behavior disorders; general psychosocial disorders; substance abuse; eating disorders; compulsive/addictive disorders other than substance abuse and eating disorders; post-traumatic stress disorder; thought, mood, and personality disorders. Accepts the mobility impaired; the vision impaired; the hearing impaired; the speech impaired; those with a history of arson; the sexually compulsive; those with a history of harm to themselves and others; those receiving psychotropic medication; those with a history of epilepsy. Special programs for the mobility impaired; the developmentally disabled; the vision impaired; the hearing impaired; the speech impaired; those with AIDS.

Program Treatment modalities: Twelve Step Recovery; psychodynamic; psychotherapy. Family treatment program available.

Staff Total facility staff includes 4 physicians, 2 psychologists, 2 psychiatrists, 2 registered nurses, 3 practical/vocational nurses, 1 MSW social worker, 1 social worker (non-MSW), 2 teachers, 2 counselors, 1 physical therapist, 1 occupational/recreational therapist, 1 speech pathologist, 1 therapist, 1 dietician, 6 other direct-care staff members. Staff is 50% male, 50% female.

Facilities Multiple buildings; males and females in coeducational units. Basketball courts, game room, gymnasium, outdoor swimming pool, playing fields.

Education Academic program available at no charge. Serves ages 12–18, grades 6–12. 2 teachers on staff. Curriculum accredited or approved by Sonoma County Office of Education.

Costs Average cost: $465 per day. Accepts private insurance, group insurance, Blue Cross/Blue Shield, public funds.

Additional Services Drug and alcohol rehabilitation services for males and females ages 12–18. Treats learning disabilities; behavior disorders; substance abuse; eating disorders; compulsive/addictive disorders other than substance abuse and eating disorders; post-traumatic stress disorder; thought, mood, and personality disorders. Residential or sub-acute services for males and females ages 12–18. Treats learning disabilities; behavior disorders; general psychosocial disorders; substance abuse; eating disorders; compulsive/addictive disorders other than substance abuse and eating disorders; post-traumatic stress disorder; thought, mood, and personality disorders.

Contact Ken Barnes, Program Director, main address above. Phone: 707-578-4500 Ext. 231. Fax: 707-578-4969.

CPC SANTA ANA HOSPITAL
2212 East Fourth Street
Santa Ana, California 92705
714-543-8481; Fax: 714-836-0144

General Information Psychiatric hospital for adolescents, adults. 61 beds for adolescents. Open year-round. Patient security: partially locked; will pursue and return runaways. Suburban setting. Independent for-profit facility. Licensed by state of California. Accredited by JCAHO.

Participants Accepts: male and female adolescents ages 12–17; male and female adults ages 18 and up. Average stay: 15 days. Admission: one parent, all parties who share custody, court order, depending on program. Treats learning disabilities; behavior disorders; general psychosocial disorders; substance abuse; eating disorders; compulsive/addictive disorders other than substance abuse and eating disorders; post-traumatic stress disorder; thought, mood, and personality disorders. Accepts the mobility impaired; the vision impaired; the hearing impaired; the speech impaired; those with a history of arson; those with a history of harm to themselves and others; those receiving psychotropic medication; non-English speaking individuals; those with a history of epilepsy. Special programs for the chronically ill; the mobility impaired; the developmentally disabled; the vision impaired; the hearing impaired; the speech impaired; those with AIDS. Largest number of participants from California.

Program Treatment modalities: cognitive therapy; dual diagnosis; Twelve Step Recovery; psychodynamic. Family treatment program available.

Staff Total facility staff includes 3 physicians, 10 psychologists, 26 psychiatrists, 16 registered nurses, 9 practical/vocational nurses, 3 MSW social workers, 1 social worker (non-MSW), 3 teachers, 4 occupational/recreational therapists, 1 speech pathologist, 15 therapists, 2 dieticians, 33 other direct-care staff members.

Facilities Single building; males and females in coeducational units. Central dining (shared with adults). Basketball courts, game room, gymnasium, outdoor swimming pool, playing fields, ropes course.

Education Academic program available at no charge. Serves ages 12–17, grades 5–12. 3 teachers on staff. Curriculum accredited or approved by Tustin Unified School District. Cost of educational program sometimes covered by local school district.

Costs Average cost: $1250 per stay. Accepts private insurance, group insurance, medicare, Blue Cross/Blue Shield, public funds.

Contact Debra Sterns, Marketing Director, main address above. Phone: 714-543-8481. Fax: 714-836-0144.

CPC SOUTHWIND HOSPITAL
3100 Southwest 89th Street
Oklahoma City, Oklahoma 73159
405-691-5100; Fax: 405-692-2394

General Information Psychiatric hospital for children, adolescents. Patient security: partially locked. For-profit facility affiliated with Community Psychiatric Centers, Laguna Hills, CA. Licensed by state of Oklahoma. Accredited by JCAHO.

Participants Accepts: male and female children; male and female adolescents. Admission: one parent, all parties who share custody, court order, voluntary, depending on program. Treats learning disabilities; behavior disorders; general psychosocial disorders; substance abuse; eating disorders; compulsive/addictive disorders other than substance abuse and eating disorders; post-traumatic stress disorder; thought, mood, and personality disorders.

Costs Average cost: $850 per day.

Contact Ray Walker, Client Services Administrator, main address above. Phone: 405-691-5100. Fax: 405-692-2394.

CPC STREAMWOOD HOSPITAL
1400 East Irving Park Road
Streamwood, Illinois 60107
708-837-9000; Fax: 708-837-2710

General Information Psychiatric hospital for children, adolescents. Patient security: partially locked. For-profit facility affiliated with Community Psychiatric Centers, Laguna Hills, CA. Licensed by state of Illinois. Accredited by JCAHO.

Participants Accepts: male and female children; male and female adolescents. Admission: one parent, all parties who share custody, court order, voluntary, depending on program.

Contact Karen diRenzo, Director of Intake, main address above. Phone: 708-837-9000. Fax: 708-837-2710.

CPC VALLE VISTA RESIDENTIAL TREATMENT CENTER
898 East Main Street
Greenwood, Indiana 46143
317-887-1348; Fax: 317-888-1104

General Information Residential treatment/subacute facility for adolescents. 24 beds for adolescents. Open year-round. Patient security: entirely locked; will pursue and return runaways. Suburban setting. For-profit facility affiliated with Community Psychiatric Centers, Laguna Hills, CA. Licensed by state of Indiana. Accredited by JCAHO.

Participants Accepts: male and female adolescents ages 12–20. Admission: all parties who share custody. Treats learning disabilities; behavior disorders; general psychosocial disorders; substance abuse; eating disorders; compulsive/addictive disorders other than substance abuse and eating disorders; post-traumatic stress disorder; thought, mood, and personality disorders. Accepts the speech impaired; those with a history of arson; the sexually compulsive; those with a history of harm to themselves and others; those receiving psychotropic medication; those with a history of epilepsy. Special programs for the developmentally disabled. Largest number of participants from Indiana, Kentucky, Illinois.

Program Treatment modalities: psychodynamic; Twelve Step Recovery; milieu therapy; behavior contingency. Family treatment program available.

Staff 1.5 full-time direct-care staff members per adolescent. Total facility staff includes 3 psychiatrists, 5 registered nurses, 2 MSW social workers, 2 teachers, 1 counselor, 2 occupational/recreational therapists, 7 other direct-care staff members. Staff is 50% male, 50% female.

Facilities Single building; males and females in co-educational units. Central dining (shared with adults). Game room, gymnasium, outdoor swimming pool, playing fields.

Education Academic program available at no charge. Serves ages 12–20, grades 1–12. 2 teachers on staff. Cost of educational program sometimes covered by local school district.

Costs Average cost: $440 per day. Accepts private insurance, group insurance, Blue Cross/Blue Shield, public funds.

Contact Mary Meyers, main address above. Phone: 317-887-1348. Fax: 317-888-1104.

CPC WESTWOOD HOSPITAL
2112 South Barrington Avenue
Los Angeles, California 90025
310-479-4281; Fax: 310-479-5918

General Information Psychiatric hospital for adolescents, adults. 53 beds for adolescents. Open year-round. Patient security arrangements vary depending on program; will pursue and return runaways. Suburban setting. For-profit facility affiliated with Community Psychiatric Centers, Laguna Hills, CA. Licensed by state of California. Accredited by JCAHO.

Participants Accepts: male and female adolescents ages 11–18; male and female adults ages 18 and up. Average stay: 28 days. Admission: one parent, all parties who share custody, court order, voluntary, depending on program. Treats learning disabilities; behavior disorders; general psychosocial disorders; substance abuse; eating disorders; compulsive/addictive disorders other than substance abuse and eating disorders; post-traumatic stress disorder; thought, mood, and personality disorders. Accepts the mobility impaired; the vision impaired; the hearing impaired; the speech impaired; those with a history of arson; the sexually compulsive; those with a history of harm to themselves and others; those receiving psychotropic medication; non-English speaking individuals. Special programs for the chronically ill; the mobility impaired; the developmentally disabled; the hearing impaired; the speech impaired; those with AIDS.

Program Treatment modalities: Twelve Step Recovery; psychodynamic; life skills; art therapy, movement therapy, psychodrama. Family treatment program available.

Staff .4 full-time direct-care staff member per adolescent. Total facility staff includes 10 physicians, 80 psychologists, 120 psychiatrists, 35 registered nurses, 15 practical/vocational nurses, 10 MSW social workers, 2 social workers (non-MSW), 5 teachers, 6 counselors, 5 occupational/recreational therapists, 1 speech pathologist, 10 therapists, 1 dietician, 15 other direct-care staff members. Staff is 50% male, 50% female.

Facilities Multiple buildings; males and females in coeducational units. Separate residential quarters for adolescents. Central dining (shared with adults), in-room dining available. Basketball courts, game room, gymnasium, outdoor swimming pool, outdoor tennis courts.

Education Academic program available at no charge. Serves ages 11–18, grades 5–12. 5 teachers on staff. Curriculum accredited or approved by California State Department of Education. Cost of educational program sometimes covered by local school district.

Costs Average cost: $28,000 per stay. Accepts private insurance, group insurance, medicare, Blue Cross/Blue Shield, public funds.

Additional Services Drug and alcohol rehabilitation services for males and females ages 11 and up. Treats learning disabilities; behavior disorders; general psychosocial disorders; substance abuse; eating disorders; compulsive/addictive disorders other than substance abuse and eating disorders; post-traumatic stress disorder; thought, mood, and personality disorders. Outpatient services for males and females ages 18 and up. Treats general psychosocial disorders; substance abuse; eating disorders; compulsive/addictive disorders other than substance abuse and eating disorders; post-traumatic stress disorder; thought, mood, and personality disorders. Residential or sub-acute services for males and females ages 11–18. Treats learning disabilities; behavior disorders; general psychosocial disorders; substance abuse; eating disorders; compulsive/addictive disorders other than substance abuse and eating disorders; post-traumatic stress disorder; thought, mood, and personality disorders. Dual diagnosis for males and females ages 11 and up. Treats learning disabilities; behavior disorders; general psychosocial disorders; substance abuse; eating disorders; compulsive/addictive disorders other than substance abuse and eating disorders; post-traumatic stress disorder; thought, mood, and personality disorders.

Contact Pamela Goldman, Director of Marketing, main address above. Phone: 310-479-4281 Ext. 112. Fax: 310-479-5918.

CRAGGED MOUNTAIN FARM
Freedom, New Hampshire 03836
603-539-4070

General Information Camp for children, adolescents. Patient security: staff secured. Independent for-profit facility. Licensed by state of New Hampshire. Accredited by American Camping Association.

Participants Accepts: male and female children; male and female adolescents. Average stay: 28 days. Admission: all parties who share custody. Treats learning disabilities.

Costs Average cost: $1075 per month.

Contact Tim Reed, Director, main address above. Phone: 603-539-4070.

CRAIG HOUSE HOSPITAL
Howland Avenue
Beacon, New York 12508
914-831-1200; Fax: 914-831-1241

General Information   Psychiatric hospital for adolescents, adults. 24 beds for adolescents. Open year-round. Patient security: partially locked; will pursue and return runaways. Small town setting. Independent for-profit facility. Licensed by state of New York. Accredited by JCAHO.

Participants   Accepts: male and female adolescents ages 12–18; male and female adults ages 18 and up. Average stay: 45 days. Admission: one parent. Treats learning disabilities; behavior disorders; general psychosocial disorders; substance abuse; eating disorders; compulsive/addictive disorders other than substance abuse and eating disorders; post-traumatic stress disorder; thought, mood, and personality disorders. Accepts those with a history of harm to themselves and others; those receiving psychotropic medication; non-English speaking individuals; those with a history of epilepsy.

Program   Treatment modalities: multi-model; Twelve Step Recovery. Family treatment program available.

Staff   Total facility staff includes 5 psychologists, 9 psychiatrists, 5 MSW social workers, 4 teachers, 1 dietician.

Facilities   Multiple buildings; males and females in coeducational units. Separate residential quarters for adolescents. Central dining (not shared with adults), in-room dining available. Basketball courts, game room, gymnasium, indoor swimming pool, outdoor swimming pool, outdoor tennis courts, playing fields, ropes course.

Education   Academic program available at no charge. Serves ages 12–21, grades 7–12. 4 teachers on staff. Cost of educational program covered by local school district.

Costs   Accepts private insurance, group insurance.

Additional Services   Drug and alcohol rehabilitation services for males and females ages 12 and up. Treats learning disabilities; behavior disorders; general psychosocial disorders; substance abuse; eating disorders; compulsive/addictive disorders other than substance abuse and eating disorders; post-traumatic stress disorder; thought, mood, and personality disorders. Dual diagnosis for males and females ages 12 and up. Treats eating disorders.

Contact   Catherine Cherico, Director of Community Relations, main address above. Phone: 914-831-1200. Fax: 914-831-1241.

CREDO FOUNDATION
Route 1
Box 413
Evan Mills, New York 13637
315-629-4441; Fax: 315-629-5473

General Information   Freestanding drug rehabilitation center for adolescents. 30 beds for adolescents. Patient security: staff secured. Independent not-for-profit facility. Licensed by state of New York.

Participants   Accepts: male and female adolescents. Average stay: 1 year. Admission: one parent, all parties who share custody, court order, voluntary, depending on program. Treats substance abuse. Accepts the mobility impaired; the vision impaired; those with a history of arson; those receiving psychotropic medication; those with a history of epilepsy.

Contact   Leslie Bonney, Clinical Director, main address above. Phone: 315-629-4441. Fax: 315-629-5473.

CROSS CREEK MANOR
591 North State
LaVerkin, Utah 84745
801-635-2300

General Information   Residential treatment/subacute facility for adolescents. 54 beds for adolescents. Open year-round. Patient security: staff secured; will pursue and return runaways. Rural setting. Independent for-profit facility. Licensed by state of Utah.

Participants   Accepts: female adolescents ages 11–18. Average stay: 8 months. Admission: one parent. Treats learning disabilities; behavior disorders; general psychosocial disorders; substance abuse; eating disorders; compulsive/addictive disorders other than substance abuse and eating disorders; post-traumatic stress disorder; thought, mood, and personality disorders. Accepts those with a history of harm to themselves and others; those receiving psychotropic medication.

Program   Treatment modalities: reality therapy; Twelve Step Recovery. Family treatment program available.

Staff   .6 full-time direct-care staff member per adolescent. Total facility staff includes 1 physician, 1 psychologist, 1 psychiatrist, 4 MSW social workers, 3 teachers, 22 counselors. Staff is 30% male, 70% female.

Facilities   Single building. Separate dining by residential unit available. Outdoor swimming pool, playing fields, spa, volleyball court.

Education   Academic program available at no charge. Serves ages 11–17, grades 7–12. 3 teachers on staff. Curriculum accredited or approved by Northwest Association of Schools and Colleges.

Costs   Average cost: $90 per day. Accepts private insurance, group insurance.

Contact   Brent Facer, Administrator, main address above. Phone: 801-635-2300.

CROTCHED MOUNTAIN PREPARATORY SCHOOL AND REHABILITATION CENTER
1 Verney Drive
Greenfield, New Hampshire 03047
603-547-3311; Fax: 603-547-3232

General Information   School for children, adolescents, adults. Open year-round. Patient security: staff secured; will pursue and return runaways. Rural setting. Not-for-profit facility affiliated with Crotched Mountain Foundation, Greenfield, NH. Licensed by state of New Hampshire.

Participants   Accepts: male and female children ages 6–12; male and female adolescents ages 13–22; male and female adults ages 18–44. Admission: one parent, all parties who share custody, court order, voluntary, local education agencies, depending on program. Treats autistic disorders; learning disabilities; behavior disorders; general psychosocial disorders; eating disorders; post-traumatic stress disorder; thought, mood, and personality disorders. Accepts the mobility impaired; the vision impaired; the hearing impaired; the speech impaired; those receiving psychotropic medication; those with a history of epilepsy; the nonverbal. Special programs for the chronically ill; the mobility impaired; the developmentally disabled; the vision impaired; the hearing impaired; the speech impaired; those with traumatic head injury, spinal cord injury, spina bifida, cerebral palsy. Largest number of participants from Massachusetts, New York, New Hampshire.

Program   Treatment modalities: multi-disciplinary team approach; behavior management; holistic educational/clinical service. Family treatment program available.

Staff   2.1 full-time direct-care staff members per child or adolescent. Total facility staff includes 3 physicians, 6 psychologists, 1 psychiatrist, 8 registered nurses, 3 practical/vocational nurses, 3 MSW social workers, 2 social workers (non-MSW), 27 teachers, 98 counselors, 7 physical therapists, 11 occupational/recreational therapists, 7 speech pathologists, 1 dietician, 40 other direct-care staff members. Staff is 24% male, 76% female.

Facilities   Multiple buildings; males and females in coeducational units. Separate residential quarters for children and adolescents. Central dining (not shared with adults), separate dining by residential unit available. Basketball courts, game room, gymnasium, horseback riding, indoor swimming pool, outdoor tennis courts, playing fields, ropes course.

Education   School serves ages 6–22. 27 teachers on staff. Curriculum is college-preparatory; diploma granted upon completion. Curriculum accredited or approved by Ind. Schools Assoc. of Northern New England, Nat. Assoc. of Private Schools for Exceptional Children. Organized sports program offered.

Costs   Accepts private insurance, group insurance, medicare, medicaid, Blue Cross/Blue Shield, public funds. Financial aid available.

Additional Services   School with residential component for males and females ages 6–22. Treats autistic disorders; learning disabilities; behavior disorders; general psychosocial disorders; eating disorders; compulsive/addictive disorders other than substance abuse and eating disorders; post-traumatic stress disorder; thought, mood, and personality disorders.

Contact   Debra Flanders, Registrar, main address above. Phone: 603-547-3311. Fax: 603-547-3232.
See page 416 for full page description.

CUMBERLAND HALL HOSPITAL
804 Youngs Lane
Nashville, Tennessee 37207
615-228-4848; Fax: 615-262-8130

General Information   Psychiatric hospital for children, adolescents. 14 beds for children; 86 beds for adolescents; 100 beds total. Open year-round. Patient security: entirely locked; will pursue and return runaways. Urban setting. For-profit facility affiliated with Cumberland Health Systems, Inc., Nashville, TN. Licensed by state of Tennessee. Accredited by JCAHO.

Participants   Accepts: male and female children ages 4–11; male and female adolescents ages 12–18. Average stay: 30 days. Admission: one parent, all parties who share custody, court order, voluntary, depending on program. Treats learning disabilities; behavior disorders; general psychosocial disorders; substance abuse; eating disorders; compulsive/addictive disorders other than substance abuse and eating disorders; post-traumatic stress disorder; thought, mood, and personality disorders. Accepts those with a history of arson; the sexually compulsive; those with a history of harm to themselves and others; those receiving psychotropic medication. Special programs for sexual perpetrators (male 10-14).

Program Treatment modalities: thought-stopping (cognitive-behavioral); Ann Burgess Trauma Model; Twelve Step Recovery; psychodynamic. Family treatment program available.

Staff Total facility staff includes 7 physicians, 4 psychologists, 7 psychiatrists, 79 registered nurses, 7 MSW social workers, 3 social workers (non-MSW), 8 teachers, 12 occupational/recreational therapists, 1 dietician.

Facilities Multiple buildings; males and females in coeducational units. Central dining. Basketball courts, game room, gymnasium, outdoor tennis courts, playing fields, ropes course.

Education Academic program available at no charge. Serves ages 4–18, grades K–12. 8 teachers on staff. Organized sports program offered.

Costs Accepts private insurance, group insurance, medicare, medicaid, Blue Cross/Blue Shield.

Additional Services Outpatient services for males and females. Treats learning disabilities; behavior disorders; general psychosocial disorders; substance abuse; eating disorders; compulsive/addictive disorders other than substance abuse and eating disorders; post-traumatic stress disorder; thought, mood, and personality disorders. Residential or sub-acute services for males and females ages 12–18. Treats behavior disorders; general psychosocial disorders; post-traumatic stress disorder; thought, mood, and personality disorders.

Contact Lydia Armistead, Director of Marketing, main address above. Phone: 800-467-4848. Fax: 615-262-8130.

CUMBERLAND HALL OF CHATTANOOGA, INC.
7351 Standifer Gap Road
Chattanooga, Tennessee 37421
615-499-9007; Fax: 615-499-9757

General Information Psychiatric hospital for children, adolescents. 32 beds for children; 32 beds for adolescents; 64 beds total. Open year-round. Patient security: entirely locked; will pursue and return runaways. Suburban setting. For-profit facility affiliated with Cumberland Health Systems, Inc., Nashville, TN. Licensed by state of Tennessee. Accredited by JCAHO.

Participants Accepts: male and female children ages 4–12; male and female adolescents ages 13–18. Admission: one parent, court order, depending on program. Treats learning disabilities; behavior disorders; general psychosocial disorders; substance abuse; eating disorders; compulsive/addictive disorders other than substance abuse and eating disorders; post-traumatic stress disorder; thought, mood, and personality disorders. Accepts the mobility impaired; the vision impaired; the hearing impaired; the speech impaired; those with a history of arson; those with a history of harm to themselves and others; those receiving psychotropic medication.

Program Treatment modalities: positive-based behavioral modification; experimental therapy; Twelve Step Recovery; family therapy. Family treatment program available.

Staff Total facility staff includes 6 physicians, 16 psychologists, 12 psychiatrists, 13 registered nurses, 2 practical/vocational nurses, 4 MSW social workers, 5 social workers (non-MSW), 6 teachers, 27 counselors, 1 speech pathologist, 5 therapists, 1 dietician, 5 other direct-care staff members.

Facilities Single building; males and females in separate units. Central dining. Basketball courts, gymnasium, outdoor swimming pool, playing fields, ropes course, outdoor playground.

Education Academic program available at no charge. Serves ages 6–18, grades 1–12. 6 teachers on staff. Curriculum accredited or approved by Tennessee State Department of Education. Cost of educational program sometimes covered by local school district. Organized sports program offered.

Costs Average cost: $632 per day. Accepts private insurance, group insurance, medicare, medicaid, Blue Cross/Blue Shield, public funds.

Additional Services Residential or sub-acute services for males and females ages 13–18. Treats autistic disorders; learning disabilities; behavior disorders; general psychosocial disorders; substance abuse; eating disorders; compulsive/addictive disorders other than substance abuse and eating disorders; post-traumatic stress disorder; thought, mood, and personality disorders.

Contact Rick Daugherty, Assistant Administrator, main address above. Phone: 615-499-9007. Fax: 615-499-9757.

CUMBERLAND HEIGHTS TREATMENT CENTER
River Road
P.O. Box 90727
Nashville, Tennessee 37209
615-352-1757; Fax: 615-353-4300

General Information Drug and alcohol rehabilitation center for adolescents, adults. 16 beds for adolescents. Open year-round. Patient security: staff secured; no runaway pursuit. Rural setting. Independent not-for-profit facility. Licensed by state of Tennessee. Accredited by JCAHO.

Participants Accepts: male and female adolescents ages 13–21; male and female adults ages 21 and up. Average stay: 35 days. Admission: all parties who share custody. Treats substance abuse. Accepts the vision impaired; those receiving psychotropic medication. Special programs for relapsed substance abusers; cocaine users.

Program Treatment modalities: Twelve Step Recovery; Gestalt/psychodrama; cognitive; therapeutic recreation. Family treatment program available.

Staff Total facility staff includes 1 physician, 1 psychologist, 1 registered nurse, 2 practical/vocational nurses, 1 MSW social worker, 2 social workers (non-MSW), 1 teacher, 14 counselors, 2 occupational/recreational therapists, 1 dietician, 10 other direct-care staff members. Staff is 50% male, 50% female.

Facilities Multiple buildings; males and females in coeducational units. Separate residential quarters for adolescents. Central dining (shared with adults). Game room, playing fields.

Education Academic program available at no charge. Serves ages 13–18, ungraded. 1 teacher on staff.

Costs Average cost: $205 per day. Accepts private insurance, group insurance, Blue Cross/Blue Shield.

Contact Byron Metcalf, Adolescent Therapy Supervisor, main address above. Phone: 615-352-1757. Fax: 615-353-4300.

CUMBERLAND HOSPITAL
3425 Melrose Road
Fayetteville, North Carolina 28304
919-485-7181; Fax: 919-485-8465

General Information Psychiatric hospital for children, adolescents. Patient security arrangements vary depending on program. For-profit facility affiliated with Ramsay Health Care, Inc., New Orleans, LA.

Licensed by state of North Carolina. Accredited by JCAHO.

Participants Accepts: male and female children; male and female adolescents. Average stay: 23 days. Admission: one parent, all parties who share custody, court order, voluntary, depending on program. Treats autistic disorders; learning disabilities; behavior disorders; general psychosocial disorders; substance abuse; eating disorders; compulsive/addictive disorders other than substance abuse and eating disorders; post-traumatic stress disorder; thought, mood, and personality disorders.

Staff Staff is 35% male, 65% female.

Contact Kathy Wood, Director of Admissions, main address above. Phone: 919-485-7181 Ext. 8554.

CUMBERLAND HOSPITAL FOR CHILDREN AND ADOLESCENTS
9407 Cumberland Road
New Kent, Virginia 23124
800-368-3472; Fax: 804-966-5639

General Information Specialty rehabilitation hospital for children, adolescents. Open year-round. Patient security: staff secured; will pursue and return runaways. Rural setting. For-profit facility affiliated with Healthcare International, Inc., Austin, TX. Licensed by state of Virginia. Accredited by JCAHO.

Participants Accepts: male and female children and adolescents ages 2–22. Average stay: 274 days. Admission: one parent. Treats autistic disorders; learning disabilities; behavior disorders; general psychosocial disorders; eating disorders; thought, mood, and personality disorders. Accepts the mobility impaired; the vision impaired; the hearing impaired; the speech impaired; those with a history of harm to themselves and others; those receiving psychotropic medication; non-English speaking individuals; those with a history of epilepsy. Special programs for the chronically ill; the mobility impaired; the developmentally disabled; the vision impaired; the hearing impaired; the speech impaired. Largest number of participants from Virginia, North Carolina, New York.

Program Treatment modalities: medical/rehabilitation; cognitive behavioral; psychoeducational; behavior modification. Family treatment program available.

Staff Total facility staff includes 4 physicians, 2 psychologists, 1 psychiatrist, 28 registered nurses, 25 practical/vocational nurses, 4 MSW social workers, 4 social workers (non-MSW), 6 teachers, 35 counselors, 2 physical therapists, 10 occupational/recreational therapists, 4 speech pathologists, 4 therapists, 2 dieticians, 6 other direct-care staff members. Staff is 26% male, 74% female.

Facilities Multiple buildings; males and females in coeducational units. Central dining. Basketball courts, game room, gymnasium, outdoor swimming pool, playing fields, ropes course.

Education Academic program available. Serves ages 2–22, ungraded. 6 teachers on staff. Curriculum accredited or approved by Commonwealth of Virginia Board of Education. Organized sports program offered.

Costs Accepts private insurance, group insurance, medicaid, Blue Cross/Blue Shield.

Contact Gay Brooks, Admission Coordinator, P.O. Box 150, New Kent, VA 23124-0150. Phone: 800-368-3472.

CYPRESS HOSPITAL
302 Dulles Drive
Lafayette, Louisiana 70506
318-233-9024

General Information Psychiatric hospital for children, adolescents, adults. 6 beds for children; 10 beds for adolescents; 94 beds total. Open year-round. Patient security: partially locked; will pursue and return runaways. Urban setting. For-profit facility affiliated with Hospital Corporation of America, Nashville, TN. Licensed by state of Louisiana. Accredited by JCAHO.

Participants Accepts: male and female children ages 6–12; male and female adolescents ages 12–18; male and female adults ages 18 and up. Average stay: 14 days. Treats learning disabilities; behavior disorders; general psychosocial disorders; substance abuse; eating disorders; compulsive/addictive disorders other than substance abuse and eating disorders; post-traumatic stress disorder; thought, mood, and personality disorders. Accepts the mobility impaired; the vision impaired; the hearing impaired; the speech impaired; those with a history of arson; the sexually compulsive; those with a history of harm to themselves and others; those receiving psychotropic medication; non-English speaking individuals; those with a history of epilepsy. Largest number of participants from Mississippi, Texas.

Program Treatment modalities: Twelve Step Recovery; individual and group therapy; family therapy; adjunctive therapy. Family treatment program available.

Staff Total facility staff includes 1 physician, 3 psychologists, 3 psychiatrists, 5 registered nurses, 5 practical/vocational nurses, 1 MSW social worker, 2 teachers, 2 counselors, 3 occupational/recreational therapists, 1 dietician, 4 other direct-care staff members. Staff is 30% male, 70% female.

Facilities Single building; males and females in coeducational units. Separate residential quarters for children and adolescents. Central dining (not shared with adults). Basketball courts, game room, gymnasium, outdoor swimming pool, ropes course.

Education Academic program available at no charge. Serves ages 6–18, grades 1–12. 2 teachers on staff. Curriculum accredited or approved by State Department of Education.

Costs Accepts private insurance, group insurance, medicare.

Additional Services Drug and alcohol rehabilitation services for males and females ages 18 and up. Treats behavior disorders; general psychosocial disorders; substance abuse; eating disorders; compulsive/addictive disorders other than substance abuse and eating disorders; thought, mood, and personality disorders.

Contact Noemi Perillo, CAP Director, main address above. Phone: 318-233-9024.

DAIRY LANE GROUP HOME
8044 Dairy Lane
Athens, Ohio 45701
614-594-3531; Fax: 614-594-5642

General Information Residential treatment/subacute facility for adolescents. 10 beds for adolescents. Patient security: staff secured. Not-for-profit facility affiliated with Tri-County Mental Health and Couseling, Inc., Athens, OH. Licensed by state of Ohio.

Participants Accepts: male and female adolescents. Average stay: 6 months. Admission: one parent, all parties who share custody, court order, voluntary, depending on program. Treats learning disabilities; behavior disorders; general psychosocial disorders; eating disorders; compulsive/addictive disorders other than substance abuse and eating disorders; post-traumatic stress disorder; thought, mood, and personality disorders.

Staff Staff is 50% male, 50% female.

Costs Average cost: $117 per day.

Contact Michele Cain, Director, main address above. Phone: 614-594-3531.

DAKOTA BOYS' RANCH
P.O. Box 5007
Minot, North Dakota 58702
701-852-3628; Fax: 701-839-5541

General Information Residential treatment/subacute facility for adolescents. 58 beds for adolescents. Open year-round. Patient security: staff secured; will pursue and return runaways. Rural setting. Independent not-for-profit facility. Licensed by state of North Dakota. Accredited by Council on Accreditation of Services for Families and Children.

Participants Accepts: male adolescents ages 10–17. Average stay: 365 days. Admission: one parent, all parties who share custody, court order, depending on program. Treats learning disabilities; behavior disorders; general psychosocial disorders; substance abuse; eating disorders; compulsive/addictive disorders other than substance abuse and eating disorders; post-traumatic stress disorder; thought, mood, and personality disorders. Accepts those with a history of arson; those with a history of harm to themselves and others; those receiving psychotropic medication; those with a history of epilepsy. Largest number of participants from North Dakota, Minnesota, Illinois.

Program Treatment modalities: reality therapy; Twelve Step Recovery; cognitive-behavioral; developmental. Family treatment program available.

Staff 1.1 full-time direct-care staff members per adolescent. Total facility staff includes 1 physician, 1 psychologist, 1 psychiatrist, 2 registered nurses, 3 MSW social workers, 3 social workers (non-MSW), 9 teachers, 2 counselors, 1 occupational/recreational therapist, 1 therapist, 1 dietician, 45 other direct-care staff members. Staff is 52% male, 48% female.

Facilities Multiple buildings. Central dining (shared with adults). Basketball courts, game room, gymnasium, horseback riding, outdoor tennis courts, playing fields.

Education Academic program available at additional cost. Serves ages 10–17, grades 6–12. 9 teachers on staff. Curriculum accredited or approved by Department of Public Institutions. Cost of educational program covered by local school district. Organized sports program offered.

Costs Accepts private insurance, group insurance, medicaid, Blue Cross/Blue Shield, public funds.

Additional Services Drug and alcohol rehabilitation services for males ages 10–17. Treats learning disabilities; behavior disorders; general psychosocial disorders; substance abuse; eating disorders; compulsive/addictive disorders other than substance abuse and eating disorders; post-traumatic stress disorder; thought, mood, and personality disorders.

Contact Gene Kozeman, Executive Director, main address above. Phone: 701-852-3628. Fax: 701-839-5541.

THE DAVISON SCHOOL
1500 North Decatur Road, NE
Atlanta, Georgia 30306
404-373-7288

General Information School for children, adolescents. Patient security: unlocked. Independent not-for-profit facility. Licensed by state of Georgia. Accredited by American Speech-Language-Hearing Association.

Participants Accepts: male and female children; male and female adolescents. Average stay: 3 years. Admission: one parent, recommendations by professionals, depending on program. Treats learning disabilities.

Education School serves ages 3–18, grades N–12.

Costs Average cost: $20,000 per year.

Contact Sandra Mullins, Director of Enrollment, main address above. Phone: 404-373-7288.

DAYBREAK OF SPOKANE
South 3220 Grand Boulevard
Spokane, Washington 99203
509-747-3088

General Information Drug and alcohol rehabilitation center for adolescents. 20 beds for adolescents. Patient security: unlocked. Independent not-for-profit facility. Licensed by state of Washington.

Participants Accepts: male and female adolescents. Average stay: 60 days. Admission: one parent, all parties who share custody, depending on program. Treats substance abuse. Accepts the mobility impaired; the vision impaired; the hearing impaired; the speech impaired; those with a history of arson; those with a history of harm to themselves and others; those receiving psychotropic medication; non-English speaking individuals; those with a history of epilepsy.

Staff Staff is 50% male, 50% female.

Costs Average cost: $103 per day.

Contact Tim Smith, Executive Director, P.O. Box 8616, Spokane, WA 99203. Phone: 509-747-3088.

DAY ONE
Route 4A
Bar Mills, Maine 04004
207-929-5166

General Information Drug and alcohol rehabilitation center for adolescents. 11 beds for adolescents. Patient security: staff secured. Independent not-for-profit facility. Licensed by state of Maine.

Participants Accepts: male and female adolescents. Average stay: 1 year. Admission: one parent, all parties who share custody, voluntary, depending on program. Treats substance abuse. Accepts the mobility impaired; the hearing impaired; the speech impaired; those with a history of harm to themselves and others; those with a history of epilepsy.

Staff Staff is 60% male, 40% female.

Contact Ray Girous, House Manager, P.O. Box 41, Bar Mills, ME 04004. Phone: 207-929-5166.

DAYTOP, NEW JERSEY
80 West Main Street
Mendham, New Jersey 07945
201-543-5656; Fax: 201-543-7502

General Information Residential treatment/subacute facility for adolescents. Patient security: staff secured. Independent not-for-profit facility. Licensed by state of New Jersey.

Participants Accepts: male and female adolescents. Average stay: 8 months. Admission: one parent, all parties who share custody, court order, voluntary, depending on program. Treats substance abuse. Accepts the mobility impaired; those with a history of epilepsy.

Staff Staff is 65% male, 35% female.

Costs Average cost: $54 per day.

Contact Joseph Hennen, Executive Director, main address above. Phone: 201-543-5656. Fax: 201-543-7502.

DAYTOP VILLAGE, INC.
54 West 40th Street
New York, New York 10018
212-345-6000

General Information Residential treatment/subacute facility for adolescents. 200 beds for adolescents.

Patient security: staff secured. Independent not-for-profit facility. Licensed by state of New York.

Participants Accepts: male and female adolescents. Admission: one parent, all parties who share custody, court order, voluntary, depending on program. Treats substance abuse. Accepts the mobility impaired; the vision impaired; the hearing impaired; the speech impaired; those receiving psychotropic medication.

Staff Staff is 50% male, 50% female.

Education Academic program available at no charge. Serves ages 12–21. Curriculum accredited or approved by New York State Education Department. Cost of educational program covered by local school district. Organized sports program offered.

Additional Services Outpatient services for males and females ages 12–21. Treats learning disabilities; behavior disorders; general psychosocial disorders; substance abuse; eating disorders; compulsive/addictive disorders other than substance abuse and eating disorders; post-traumatic stress disorder.

Contact Steven Conforte, Intake, 316 Beach 65th Street, Auburn, NY 11692. Phone: 718-474-3800.

DEACONESS CHEMICAL DEPENDENCY UNITS
800 West Fifth Avenue
Spokane, Washington 99210
509-958-7000

General Information General hospital for adolescents, adults. 10 beds for adolescents. Open year-round. Patient security: staff secured; no runaway pursuit. Urban setting. Independent not-for-profit facility. Licensed by state of Washington. Accredited by JCAHO; Department of Alcohol and Substance Abuse.

Participants Accepts: male and female adolescents ages 12–17; male and female adults ages 18 and up. Average stay: 42 days. Admission: one parent. Treats substance abuse. Accepts the mobility impaired; the vision impaired; the hearing impaired; the speech impaired; those with a history of harm to themselves and others; those receiving psychotropic medication; non-English speaking individuals; those with a history of epilepsy; the pregnant and addicted. Special programs for the mobility impaired; the developmentally disabled; the vision impaired; the hearing impaired; the speech impaired; diabetics; pregnant patients. Largest number of participants from Washington, Idaho.

Program Treatment modalities: Twelve Step Recovery; psychodynamic; group process; abstinence based. Family treatment program available.

Staff .2 full-time direct-care staff member per adolescent. Total facility staff includes 22 registered nurses, 13 practical/vocational nurses, 1 teacher, 11 counselors, 1 occupational/recreational therapist, 24 other direct-care staff members. Staff is 30% male, 70% female.

Facilities Single building; males and females in co-educational units. Separate residential quarters for adolescents. Central dining (not shared with adults). Game room, weight and exercise room.

Education Academic program available at no charge. Serves ages 12–18, ungraded. 1 teacher on staff. Cost of educational program covered by local school district.

Costs Average cost: $14,000 per stay. Accepts private insurance, group insurance, medicare, medicaid, Blue Cross/Blue Shield, public funds.

Additional Services Drug and alcohol rehabilitation services for males and females ages 12 and up. Treats substance abuse. Outpatient services for males and females ages 12 and up. Treats substance abuse.

Contact Susan Kent, Registered Nurse, main address above. Phone: 509-958-7000.

DECISION POINT
301 Holcomb
Springdale, Arkansas 72764
501-756-1060

General Information Drug and alcohol rehabilitation center for adolescents. 20 beds for adolescents. Patient security: partially locked. Independent not-for-profit facility. Licensed by state of Arkansas.

Participants Accepts: male and female adolescents. Average stay: 90 days. Admission: one parent, all parties who share custody, court order, voluntary, depending on program. Treats learning disabilities; behavior disorders; general psychosocial disorders; substance abuse; eating disorders; compulsive/addictive disorders other than substance abuse and eating disorders; post-traumatic stress disorder; thought, mood, and personality disorders.

Staff Staff is 75% male, 25% female.

Costs Average cost: $34 per day.

Contact Steve Sargent, Executive Director, P.O. Box 1174, Springdale, AR 72764. Phone: 501-756-1060.

DE NEUVILLE HEIGHTS SCHOOL
3060 Baskin Street
Memphis, Tennessee 38127
901-357-7316; Fax: 901-357-0554

General Information Child care facility and campus school for adolescents. 52 beds for adolescents. Open year-round. Patient security arrangements vary depending on program; no runaway pursuit. Urban setting. Not-for-profit facility affiliated with Sisters of the Good Shepherd, St. Louis, MO. Licensed by state of Tennessee.

Participants Accepts: female adolescents ages 12–17. Average stay: 425 days. Admission: one parent, all parties who share custody, state custody, depending on program. Treats learning disabilities; behavior disorders; general psychosocial disorders; post-traumatic stress disorder. Largest number of participants from Tennessee, Alabama, Mississippi.

Staff .7 full-time direct-care staff member per adolescent. Total facility staff includes 6 psychologists, 3 MSW social workers, 1 social worker (non-MSW), 10 teachers, 13 other direct-care staff members. Staff is 20% male, 80% female.

Facilities Multiple buildings. Separate dining by residential unit available. Basketball courts, gymnasium, outdoor swimming pool.

Education Academic program available. Serves ages 12–17, grades 7–12. 10 teachers on staff. Curriculum accredited or approved by Tennessee State Department of Education. Organized sports program offered.

Costs Average cost: $950 per month. Accepts private insurance, public funds.

Contact Marilyn Walker, Social Worker, main address above. Phone: 901-357-7316. Fax: 901-357-0554.

DENVER CHILDREN'S HOME
1501 Albion Steeet
Denver, Colorado 80220
303-399-4890; Fax: 303-399-9846

General Information Residential treatment/subacute facility for adolescents. 68 beds for adolescents. Open year-round. Patient security: unlocked. Urban setting. Independent not-for-profit facility. Licensed by state of Colorado.

Participants Accepts: male and female adolescents ages 10–18. Admission: all parties who share custody. Treats learning disabilities; behavior disorders; general psychosocial disorders; substance abuse; eating disorders; post-traumatic stress disorder; thought, mood, and personality disorders. Accepts those with a history of harm to themselves and others; those receiving psychotropic medication; those with a history of epilepsy.

Program Treatment modalities: psychodymanic; family systems approach. Family treatment program available.

Staff 1.3 full-time direct-care staff members per adolescent. Total facility staff includes 6 psychologists, 5 psychiatrists, 1 registered nurse, 4 MSW social workers, 1 social worker (non-MSW), 21 teachers, 54 counselors, 1 speech pathologist, 1 dietician, 6 other direct-care staff members. Staff is 50% male, 50% female.

Facilities Single building; males and females in separate units. Central dining. Basketball courts, game room, playing fields.

Education Academic program available at additional cost. Serves ages 10–18, ungraded. 21 teachers on staff. Curriculum accredited or approved by Colorado State Department of Education. Cost of educational program sometimes covered by local school district. Organized sports program offered.

Costs Average cost: $175 per day. Accepts private insurance, group insurance, public funds.

Additional Services Drug and alcohol rehabilitation services for males and females ages 10–18. Treats learning disabilities; behavior disorders; general psychosocial disorders; substance abuse; eating disorders; compulsive/addictive disorders other than substance abuse and eating disorders; post-traumatic stress disorder; thought, mood, and personality disorders. Outpatient services for males and females ages 6–18. Treats learning disabilities; behavior disorders; general psychosocial disorders; substance abuse; eating disorders; compulsive/addictive disorders other than substance abuse and eating disorders; post-traumatic stress disorder; thought, mood, and personality disorders.

Contact Babe McLagan, Intake Director, main address above. Phone: 303-399-4890. Fax: 303-399-9846.

DEPAUL HOSPITAL
1040 Calhoun Street
New Orleans, Louisiana 70118
800-548-4183; Fax: 504-897-5755

General Information Psychiatric hospital and residential treatment center for children, adolescents, adults. Open year-round. Patient security: partially locked; will pursue and return runaways. Urban setting. For-profit facility affiliated with Hospital Corporation of America, Nashville, TN. Licensed by state of Louisiana. Accredited by JCAHO; Civilian Health and Medical Program of the Uniformed Services.

Participants Accepts: male and female children ages 4–12; male and female adolescents ages 12–18; male and female adults ages 19 and up. Admission: all parties who share custody. Treats learning disabilities; behavior disorders; general psychosocial disorders; substance abuse; eating disorders; compulsive/addictive disorders other than substance abuse and eating disorders; post-traumatic stress disorder; thought, mood, and personality disorders. Accepts the mobility impaired; the vision impaired; those with a history of harm to themselves and others; those receiving psychotropic medication; those with a history of epilepsy. Special programs for the developmentally disabled; the hearing impaired; the speech impaired. Largest number of participants from Louisiana, Mississippi.

Program Treatment modalities: behavior modification; Twelve Step Recovery; biopsychosocial model; cognitive restructuring. Family treatment program available.

Staff Total facility staff includes 1 physician, 2 psychologists, 6 psychiatrists, 12 registered nurses, 2 practical/vocational nurses, 7 social workers (non-MSW), 8 teachers, 2 counselors, 1 physical therapist, 3 occupational/recreational therapists, 1 speech pathologist, 1 therapist, 1 dietician, 25 other direct-care staff members. Staff is 56% male, 44% female.

Facilities Multiple buildings; males and females in coeducational units. Separate residential quarters for children and adolescents. Central dining (shared with adults). Basketball courts, gymnasium, outdoor swimming pool, outdoor tennis courts, playing fields, gardening plots, play equipment.

Education Academic program available at no charge. Serves ages 4–18, grades K–12. 8 teachers on staff. Curriculum accredited or approved by Louisiana State Board of Education, Mississippi State Board of Education.

Contact Nancy Cranton, Director of RESPOND, main address above. Phone: 800-548-4183. Fax: 504-897-5755.

See page 418 for full page description.

DEPAUL HOSPITAL
4143 South 13th Street
Milwaukee, Wisconsin 53221
414-281-3572; Fax: 414-281-7294

General Information Chemical dependency treatment facility and psychiatric hospital with in-patient and out-patient programs for adolescents. Patient security: partially locked. Independent not-for-profit facility. Licensed by state of Wisconsin. Accredited by JCAHO.

Participants Accepts: male and female adolescents. Average stay: 14 days. Admission: one parent, all parties who share custody, voluntary, depending on program. Treats learning disabilities; behavior disorders; general psychosocial disorders; substance abuse; eating disorders; compulsive/addictive disorders other than substance abuse and eating disorders; post-traumatic stress disorder; thought, mood, and personality disorders.

Staff Staff is 40% male, 60% female.

Additional Services Outpatient services for males and females ages 3–18. Treats learning disabilities; behavior disorders; general psychosocial disorders; substance abuse; eating disorders; compulsive/addictive disorders other than substance abuse and eating disorders; post-traumatic stress disorder; thought, mood, and personality disorders.

Contact Debbie Dolata-Drent, Director of Child and Adolescent Services, main address above. Phone: 414-281-3572. Fax: 414-281-7294.

DEPAUL MENTAL HEALTH SERVICES
855 West Main Street
Rochester, New York 14611
716-436-8020; Fax: 716-436-4836

General Information Residential treatment/subacute facility for adolescents. 30 beds for adolescents. Patient security: staff secured. Independent not-for-profit facility. Licensed by state of New York. Accredited by JCAHO.

Participants Accepts: male and female adolescents. Average stay: 18 months. Admission: all parties who share custody, court order, voluntary, depending on program. Treats learning disabilities; behavior disorders; general psychosocial disorders; eating disorders; compulsive/addictive disorders other than substance abuse and eating disorders; post-traumatic stress disorder; thought, mood, and personality disorders.

Contact Tanya MacNaughton, Assistant Director, Adolescent Program/Intake Coordinator, main address above. Phone: 716-436-8020.

DESERT HILLS CENTER FOR YOUTH AND FAMILIES
2797 North Introspect
Tucson, Arizona 85745
602-622-5437; Fax: 602-792-6249

General Information Psychiatric hospital for children, adolescents. Patient security: entirely locked. Independent for-profit facility. Licensed by state of Arizona. Accredited by JCAHO; Civilian Health and Medical Program of the Uniformed Services.

Participants Accepts: male and female children; male and female adolescents. Admission: one parent, all parties who share custody, court order, voluntary, depending on program. Treats autistic disorders; learning disabilities; behavior disorders; general psychosocial disorders; substance abuse; eating disorders; compulsive/addictive disorders other than substance abuse and eating disorders; post-traumatic stress disorder; thought, mood, and personality disorders.

Contact Lisa Logan, Clinical Liaison, main address above. Phone: 602-622-5437. Fax: 602-792-6249.

DESERT VISTA HOSPITAL
570 West Brown Road
Mesa, Arizona 85201
602-962-3900; Fax: 602-827-0412

General Information Psychiatric hospital for children, adolescents, adults. 16 beds for children; 24 beds for adolescents. Open year-round. Patient security arrangements vary depending on program; will pursue and return runaways. Suburban setting. For-profit facility affiliated with Ramsay Health Care, Inc., New Orleans, LA. Licensed by state of Arizona. Accredited by JCAHO; Health Care Financing Administration, National Association of Private Psychiatric Hospitals.

Participants Accepts: male and female children ages 5–12; male and female adolescents ages 13–18; male and female adults ages 19 and up. Average stay: 23 days. Admission: one parent, all parties who share custody, court order, depending on program. Treats autistic disorders; learning disabilities; behavior disorders; general psychosocial disorders; substance abuse; eating disorders; compulsive/addictive disorders other than substance abuse and eating disorders; post-traumatic stress disorder; thought, mood, and personality disorders. Accepts those with a history of arson; those with a history of harm to themselves and others; those receiving psychotropic medication; those with a history of epilepsy.

Program   Treatment modalities: psychodynamic; behavior modification; Twelve Step Recovery. Family treatment program available.

Staff   Total facility staff includes 45 physicians, 32 psychologists, 17 psychiatrists, 51 registered nurses, 6 practical/vocational nurses, 5 MSW social workers, 4 teachers, 4 counselors, 2 occupational/recreational therapists, 15 therapists, 1 dietician, 62 other direct-care staff members. Staff is 35% male, 65% female.

Facilities   Single building; males and females in co-educational units. Separate residential quarters for children and adolescents. Central dining (shared with adults), in-room dining available. Basketball courts, game room, gymnasium, horseback riding, outdoor swimming pool, outdoor tennis courts, playing fields.

Education   Academic program available at no charge. Serves ages 5–18, grades 1–12. 4 teachers on staff. Curriculum accredited or approved by Maricopa County Accommodations School District through Arizona Department of Education. Cost of educational program sometimes covered by local school district. Organized sports program offered.

Costs   Accepts private insurance, group insurance, medicare, Blue Cross/Blue Shield, public funds.

Additional Services   Drug and alcohol rehabilitation services for males and females ages 13 and up. Treats behavior disorders; general psychosocial disorders; substance abuse; eating disorders; compulsive/addictive disorders other than substance abuse and eating disorders; post-traumatic stress disorder; thought, mood, and personality disorders. Outpatient services for males and females ages 5 and up. Treats behavior disorders; general psychosocial disorders; substance abuse; eating disorders; compulsive/addictive disorders other than substance abuse and eating disorders; post-traumatic stress disorder; thought, mood, and personality disorders. Camping program ages 5–18. Treats autistic disorders; learning disabilities; behavior disorders; general psychosocial disorders; substance abuse; eating disorders; compulsive/addictive disorders other than substance abuse and eating disorders; post-traumatic stress disorder; thought, mood, and personality disorders.

Contact   Rea A. Oliver, Senior Administrator, main address above. Phone: 602-962-3900. Fax: 602-827-0412.

THE DESISTO SCHOOL
Route 183
Stockbridge, Massachusetts 01262
413-298-3776; Fax: 413-298-5175

General Information   School for adolescents. Open year-round. Patient security: staff secured. Rural setting. Independent not-for-profit facility. Licensed by state of Massachusetts.

Participants   Accepts: male and female adolescents ages 13–21. Average stay: 2 years. Admission: one parent, all parties who share custody, court order, depending on program. Treats learning disabilities; behavior disorders; general psychosocial disorders; substance abuse; eating disorders; compulsive/addictive disorders other than substance abuse and eating disorders; post-traumatic stress disorder; thought, mood, and personality disorders.

Program   Treatment modalities: behavior modification; individual psychotherapy; group psychotherapy; Twelve Step Recovery. Family treatment program available.

Staff   Staff is 60% male, 40% female.

Facilities   Multiple buildings.

Education   School serves ages 13–21, ungraded. Curriculum is college-preparatory; diploma granted upon completion. Curriculum accredited or approved by Berkshire Hills Regional School District. Organized sports program offered.

Costs   Average cost: $40,000 per year. Financial aid available.

Contact   Constance Real, Admissions Director, main address above. Phone: 413-298-3776. Fax: 413-298-5175.

See page 420 for full page description.

DETTMER HOSPITAL
3130 North Dixie Highway
Troy, Ohio 45373
800-772-5538

General Information   Psychiatric hospital for children, adolescents, adults. 12 beds for children; 22 beds for adolescents; 53 beds total. Open year-round. Patient security: staff secured; will pursue and return runaways. Rural setting. Independent not-for-profit facility. Licensed by state of Ohio. Accredited by JCAHO.

Participants   Accepts: male and female children ages 5–11; male and female adolescents ages 11–18; male and female adults ages 18 and up. Average stay: 17 days. Admission: one parent. Treats learning disabilities; behavior disorders; general psychosocial disorders; substance abuse; eating disorders; post-traumatic stress disorder; thought, mood, and personality disorders. Accepts the speech impaired; those with a history of arson; those with a history of harm to themselves and others; those receiving psychotropic medication. Special programs for the chronically ill; the developmentally disabled; those with AIDS.

Program Treatment modalities: Twelve Step Recovery; family therapy; reality therapy; play therapy. Family treatment program available.

Staff Total facility staff includes 3 physicians, 1 psychologist, 3 psychiatrists, 25 registered nurses, 5 MSW social workers, 2 teachers, 4 counselors, 2 occupational/recreational therapists, 1 therapist, 1 dietician.

Facilities Single building; males and females in coeducational units. Separate residential quarters for children and adolescents. Central dining (not shared with adults). Game room, gymnasium, playing fields, ropes course, playground.

Education Academic program available at no charge. Serves ages 5–18, grades 1–12. 2 teachers on staff. Curriculum accredited or approved by state-approved tutorial services. Cost of educational program sometimes covered by local school district.

Costs Average cost: $668 per stay. Accepts private insurance, group insurance, medicare, medicaid, Blue Cross/Blue Shield, public funds.

Additional Services Outpatient services for males and females ages 5 and up. Treats behavior disorders; general psychosocial disorders; substance abuse; eating disorders; compulsive/addictive disorders other than substance abuse and eating disorders; post-traumatic stress disorder; thought, mood, and personality disorders. Residential or sub-acute services for males and females ages 12–18. Treats behavior disorders; general psychosocial disorders; substance abuse; compulsive/addictive disorders other than substance abuse and eating disorders; post-traumatic stress disorder; thought, mood, and personality disorders.

Contact Kris Curry, Director of Admissions, main address above. Phone: 800-772-5538. Fax: 513-332-7739.

DEVEREUX ARIZONA
6436 East Sweetwater Avenue
Scottsdale, Arizona 85254
602-998-2920; Fax: 602-443-5589

General Information Residential treatment/subacute facility for children, adolescents. 35 beds for chil-

dren; 33 beds for adolescents; 68 beds total. Open year-round. Patient security arrangements vary depending on program; will pursue and return runaways. Suburban setting. Not-for-profit facility affiliated with Devereux Foundation, Devon, PA. Licensed by state of Arizona. Accredited by JCAHO; Civilian Health and Medical Program of the Uniformed Services, Arizona Department of Health Services, Arizona Department of Economic Security.

Participants Accepts: male and female children ages 3–12; male and female adolescents ages 13–17. Average stay: 549 days. Admission: all parties who share custody, court order, depending on program. Treats autistic disorders; behavior disorders; general psychosocial disorders; post-traumatic stress disorder; thought, mood, and personality disorders. Accepts the mobility impaired; the vision impaired; the hearing impaired; the speech impaired; those with a history of harm to themselves and others; those receiving psychotropic medication; those with a history of epilepsy; the seriously emotionally disturbed. Special programs for the developmentally disabled.

Program Treatment modalities: psychodynamic; behavior modification; cognitive behavioral. Family treatment program available.

Staff 1.4 full-time direct-care staff members per child or adolescent. Total facility staff includes 3 psychologists, 1 psychiatrist, 5 registered nurses, 6 MSW social workers, 11 teachers, 5 counselors, 3 occupational/recreational therapists, 2 speech pathologists, 1 dietician, 58 other direct-care staff members. Staff is 30% male, 70% female.

Facilities Multiple buildings; males and females in coeducational units. Central dining, separate dining by residential unit available. Basketball courts, outdoor swimming pool, outdoor tennis courts, playing fields.

Education Academic program available at additional cost. Serves ages 3–17, ungraded. 11 teachers on staff. Curriculum accredited or approved by Arizona Department of Education, California Department of Education. Cost of educational program sometimes covered by local school district.

Costs Average cost: $185 per day. Accepts private insurance, group insurance, medicaid, Blue Cross/Blue Shield, public funds.

Contact Judith Sindlinger, Admission Coordinator, main address above. Phone: 602-998-2920. Fax: 602-443-5589.

See page 422 for full page description.

DEVEREUX—BRANDYWINE TREATMENT CENTER
P.O. Box 69
Glenmore, Pennsylvania 19343-0069
215-942-5967; Fax: 215-942-5959

General Information Residential treatment/subacute facility for children, adolescents. Open year-round. Patient security: unlocked; will pursue and return runaways. Rural setting. Not-for-profit facility affiliated with Devereux Foundation, Devon, PA. Licensed by state of Pennsylvania. Accredited by JCAHO.

Participants Accepts: male children ages 8–14; male adolescents ages 14–21. Admission: one parent, all parties who share custody, voluntary, depending on program. Treats learning disabilities; behavior disorders; general psychosocial disorders; post-traumatic stress disorder; thought, mood, and personality disorders. Accepts the hearing impaired; the speech impaired; those with a history of harm to themselves and others; those receiving psychotropic medication. Special programs for the developmentally disabled; the hearing impaired; the speech impaired. Largest number of participants from Pennsylvania, New Jersey, New York.

Program Treatment modalities: behavioral-structured approach; cognitive-reality based; psychoeducational; family therapy. Family treatment program available.

Staff Total facility staff includes 1 physician, 8 psychologists, 3 psychiatrists, 6 registered nurses, 5 MSW social workers, 23 teachers, 70 counselors, 1 speech pathologist, 1 dietician. Staff is 75% male, 25% female.

Facilities Multiple buildings. Central dining. Basketball courts, game room, gymnasium, outdoor swimming pool, outdoor tennis courts, playing fields, ropes course, stocked lake, nature trails.

Education Academic program available at no charge. Serves ages 8–21, ungraded. 23 teachers on staff. Curriculum accredited or approved by Pennsylvania Department of Education. Cost of educational program sometimes covered by local school district. Organized sports program offered.

Costs Accepts private insurance, group insurance, public funds.

Contact John Ezell, Director of Community Relations, main address above. Phone: 215-942-5967. Fax: 215-942-5959.
See page 422 for full page description.

DEVEREUX CALIFORNIA
P.O. Box 1079
Santa Barbara, California 93102
805-968-2525; Fax: 805-968-3247

General Information Residential treatment/subacute facility for children, adolescents, adults. 100 beds for adolescents. Open year-round. Patient security: staff secured; will pursue and return runaways. Suburban setting. Not-for-profit facility affiliated with Devereux Foundation, Devon, PA. Licensed by state of California. Accredited by Commission on Accreditation of Rehabilitation Facilities.

Participants Accepts: male and female children and adolescents ages 11–18; male and female adults ages 18 and up. Average stay: 2 years. Treats autistic disorders; learning disabilities; behavior disorders; general psychosocial disorders; post-traumatic stress disorder; thought, mood, and personality disorders. Accepts the mobility impaired; the vision impaired; the hearing impaired; the speech impaired; those with a history of harm to themselves and others; those receiving psychotropic medication; those with a history of epilepsy. Special programs for the developmentally disabled.

Staff Total facility staff includes 1 physician, 3 psychologists, 1 psychiatrist, 4 registered nurses, 6 MSW social workers, 12 teachers, 156 counselors, 3 speech pathologists, 1 therapist, 1 dietician.

Facilities Multiple buildings; males and females in both coeducational and separate units depending on program. Separate residential quarters for children and adolescents. Basketball courts, game room, outdoor swimming pool, outdoor tennis courts, playing fields.

Education Academic program available at additional cost. Serves ages 10–22, ungraded. 12 teachers on staff. Curriculum accredited or approved by California Department of Education. Cost of educational program sometimes covered by local school district. Organized sports program offered.

Costs Average cost: $6555 per month. Accepts private insurance, group insurance, medicare, medicaid, public funds.

Contact Anne McNiff, Marketing and Referral Coordinator, main address above. Phone: 805-968-2525. Fax: 805-968-3247.
See page 422 for full page description.

DEVEREUX DEERHAVEN
Pottersville Road
P.O. Box 520
Chester, New Jersey 07930
908-879-4500; Fax: 908-879-6370

General Information Residential treatment facility and school for children, adolescents. Patient security: staff secured. Not-for-profit facility affiliated with Devereux Foundation, Devon, PA. Licensed by state of New Jersey. Accredited by New Jersey Division of Youth and Family Services.

Participants Accepts: female children ages 9 and up; female adolescents. Average stay: 12 months. Admission: referrals. Treats learning disabilities; behavior disorders; general psychosocial disorders; post-traumatic stress disorder; thought, mood, and personality disorders.

Education Academic program available. Academic program is ungraded. Curriculum accredited or approved by New Jersey Department of Education.

Contact Kristy Hartman, Admissions Director, main address above. Phone: 908-879-4166. Fax: 908-879-6370.
See page 422 for full page description.

DEVEREUX—EDWARD L. FRENCH CENTER
119 Old Lancaster Road
Devon, Pennsylvania 19333
215-964-3212; Fax: 215-971-4603

General Information Residential treatment/subacute facility for adolescents, adults. 68 beds for adolescents. Open year-round. Patient security: staff secured; will pursue and return runaways. Suburban setting. Not-for-profit facility affiliated with Devereux Foundation, Devon, PA. Licensed by state of Pennsylvania. Accredited by JCAHO; Commission on Accreditation of Rehabilitation Facilities.

Participants Accepts: male and female adolescents ages 12–18; male and female adults ages 18 and up. Average stay: 2 years. Admission: one parent, all parties who share custody, voluntary, depending on program. Treats learning disabilities; behavior disorders; general psychosocial disorders; post-traumatic stress disorder; thought, mood, and personality disorders. Accepts the speech impaired; those with a history of harm to themselves and others; those receiving psychotropic medication; those with a history of epilepsy; those with mild visual impairments. Special programs for the developmentally disabled; the speech impaired; those with traumatic brain injury.

Program Treatment modalities: cognitive-behavioral; social milieu treatment planning; psycho-educational. Family treatment program available.

Staff Total facility staff includes 1 physician, 5 psychologists, 2 psychiatrists, 4 registered nurses, 1 MSW social worker, 1 social worker (non-MSW), 7 teachers, 1 speech pathologist, 1 dietician, 20 other direct-care staff members.

Facilities Multiple buildings; males and females in separate units. Separate residential quarters for adolescents. Separate dining by residential unit available. Gymnasium, outdoor swimming pool, playing fields.

Education Academic program available at no charge. Serves ages 12–22, ungraded. 7 teachers on staff. Curriculum accredited or approved by Pennsylvania Department of Education.

Costs Average cost: $5700 per month. Accepts private insurance, group insurance, public funds.

Additional Services Traumatic head injury ages 16 and up. Treats behavior disorders; general psychosocial disorders; post-traumatic stress disorder; thought, mood, and personality disorders.

Contact Bonnie Elliott, main address above. Phone: 215-964-3269. Fax: 215-964-3293.
See page 422 for full page description.

DEVEREUX GEORGIA
1291 Stanley Road
Kennesaw, Georgia 30144
404-427-0147; Fax: 404-425-1413

General Information Residential treatment/subacute facility for adolescents. 105 beds for adolescents. Open year-round. Patient security: partially locked; will pursue and return runaways. Suburban setting. Not-for-profit facility affiliated with Devereux Foundation, Devon, PA. Licensed by state of Georgia. Accredited by JCAHO.

Participants Accepts: male and female adolescents ages 12–18. Average stay: 14 months. Admission: all parties who share custody. Treats learning disabilities; behavior disorders; general psychosocial disorders; substance abuse; eating disorders; compulsive/addictive disorders other than substance abuse and eating disorders; post-traumatic stress disorder; thought, mood, and personality disorders. Accepts the speech impaired; those with a history of harm to themselves and others; those receiving psychotropic medication; those with a history of epilepsy. Special programs for the developmentally disabled; the speech impaired. Largest number of participants from Georgia, Maryland, D.C.

Program Treatment modalities: cognitive-behavior therapy; psychodynamic; learning disorders; vocational rehabilitation. Family treatment program available.

Staff 1.5 full-time direct-care staff members per adolescent. Total facility staff includes 1 physician, 2 psychologists, 2 psychiatrists, 15 registered nurses, 11 practical/vocational nurses, 7 MSW social workers, 7 social workers (non-MSW), 12 teachers, 5 occupational/recreational therapists, 1 speech pathologist, 1 dietician, 115 other direct-care staff members. Staff is 52% male, 48% female.

Facilities Multiple buildings; males and females in coeducational units. Central dining. Basketball courts, game room, gymnasium, outdoor swimming pool, playing fields, ropes course.

Education Academic program available at no charge. Serves ages 12–18, ungraded. 12 teachers on staff. Curriculum accredited or approved by Georgia Department of Education. Cost of educational program sometimes covered by local school district. Organized sports program offered.

Costs Average cost: $267 per day. Accepts private insurance, group insurance, Blue Cross/Blue Shield, public funds.

Contact Carolyn Moffitt, Admission Officer, main address above. Phone: 404-427-0147. Fax: 404-425-1413.

See page 422 for full page description.

DEVEREUX GLENHOLME
81 Sabbaday Lane
Washington, Connecticut 06793
203-868-7377; Fax: 203-868-7894

General Information Residential treatment/subacute facility for children, adolescents. 50 beds for children; 65 beds for adolescents. Open year-round. Patient security: staff secured; will pursue and return runaways. Small town setting. Not-for-profit facility affiliated with Devereux Foundation, Devon, PA. Licensed by state of Connecticut. Accredited by Connecticut Department of Children and Youth Services.

Participants Accepts: male and female children ages 5–12; male and female adolescents ages 13–15. Average stay: 545 days. Admission: all parties who share custody. Treats learning disabilities; behavior disorders; general psychosocial disorders; eating disorders; post-traumatic stress disorder; thought, mood, and personality disorders. Accepts the hearing impaired;

the speech impaired; those with a history of harm to themselves and others; those receiving psychotropic medication; those with a history of epilepsy. Special programs for the hearing impaired; the speech impaired.

Program Treatment modalities: behavioral/milieu treatment; psychodynamic. Family treatment program available.

Staff Total facility staff includes 1 physician, 2 psychologists, 1 psychiatrist, 5 registered nurses, 5 MSW social workers, 20 teachers, 15 counselors, 15 occupational/recreational therapists, 1 speech pathologist, 8 other direct-care staff members.

Facilities Multiple buildings; males and females in separate units. Central dining. Basketball courts, game room, gymnasium, indoor swimming pool, outdoor swimming pool, outdoor tennis courts, playing fields, hiking trail, volleyball area, Honda pilot track, baseball field.

Education Academic program available at no charge. Serves ages 5–15, grades K–10. 20 teachers on staff. Curriculum accredited or approved by Connecticut State Department of Education. Organized sports program offered.

Costs Average cost: $4472 per month. Accepts private insurance, public funds.

Additional Services Residential or sub-acute services for males and females ages 5–15. Treats learning disabilities; behavior disorders; general psychosocial disorders; eating disorders; post-traumatic stress disorder; thought, mood, and personality disorders. Camping program for males and females ages 5–15. Treats learning disabilities; behavior disorders.

Contact Kathi Fitzherbert, Director of Admissions, main address above. Phone: 203-868-7377. Fax: 203-868-7894.

See page 422 for full page description.

DEVEREUX HOSPITAL AND CHILDREN'S CENTER OF FLORIDA
8000 Devereux Drive
Melbourne, Florida 32940
407-242-9100; Fax: 407-259-0786

General Information Psychiatric hospital for children, adolescents. 25 beds for children; 75 beds for adolescents; 100 beds total. Open year-round. Patient security: partially locked. Small town setting. Not-for-profit facility affiliated with Devereux Foundation, Devon, PA. Licensed by state of Florida. Accredited by JCAHO.

Participants Accepts: male and female children ages 3–13; male and female adolescents ages 14–17. Average stay: 417 days. Admission: all parties who share custody. Treats autistic disorders; learning disabilities; behavior disorders; general psychosocial disorders; eating disorders; post-traumatic stress disorder; thought, mood, and personality disorders. Accepts the mobility impaired; the vision impaired; the hearing impaired; the speech impaired; those with a history of arson; those with a history of harm to themselves and others; those receiving psychotropic medication; those with a history of epilepsy. Special programs for the chronically ill; the mobility impaired; the developmentally disabled; the vision impaired; the hearing impaired; the speech impaired. Largest number of participants from Florida, D.C., Maryland.

Program Treatment modalities: behavioral therapy/modification; psychodynamic; group psychodynamic; family therapy. Family treatment program available.

Staff 2.2 full-time direct-care staff members per child or adolescent. Total facility staff includes 3 physicians, 4 psychologists, 3 psychiatrists, 61 registered nurses, 1 practical/vocational nurse, 14 MSW social workers, 3 social workers (non-MSW), 26 teachers, 8 occupational/recreational therapists, 5 speech pathologists, 3 therapists, 1 dietician, 242 other direct-care staff members. Staff is 35% male, 65% female.

Facilities Multiple buildings; males and females in coeducational units. Central dining. Basketball courts, game room, gymnasium, outdoor swimming pool, playing fields, ropes course.

Education Academic program available at no charge. Serves ages 5–17, grades K–12. 26 teachers on staff. Curriculum accredited or approved by Florida Council of Independent Schools, Brevard District Schools. Cost of educational program sometimes covered by local school district.

Costs Average cost: $154,707 per stay. Accepts private insurance, group insurance, medicaid, public funds.

Additional Services Outpatient services for males and females ages 3 and up. Treats autistic disorders; learning disabilities; behavior disorders; general psychosocial disorders; compulsive/addictive disorders other than substance abuse and eating disorders; post-traumatic stress disorder; thought, mood, and personality disorders. Residential or sub-acute services for males and females ages 5–17. Treats autistic disorders; learning disabilities; behavior disorders; general psychosocial disorders; compulsive/addictive disorders other than substance abuse and eating disorders; post-traumatic stress disorder; thought, mood, and personality disorders.

Contact Tonie Vogt, Director of Marketing, main address above. Phone: 407-242-9100. Fax: 407-259-0786.

See page 422 for full page description.

DEVEREUX HOSPITAL AND NEUROBEHAVIORAL INSTITUTE OF TEXAS
1150 Devereux Drive
League City, Texas 77573
713-335-1000; Fax: 713-332-2301

General Information Psychiatric hospital for children, adolescents, adults. 66 beds for children; 44 beds for adolescents; 132 beds total. Open year-round. Patient security: entirely locked; will pursue and return runaways. Small town setting. Not-for-profit facility affiliated with Devereux Foundation, Devon, PA. Licensed by state of Texas.

Participants Accepts: male and female children ages 5–13; male and female adolescents ages 13–18; male and female adults ages 18 and up. Treats autistic disorders; learning disabilities; behavior disorders; general psychosocial disorders; substance abuse; eating disorders; compulsive/addictive disorders other than substance abuse and eating disorders; thought, mood, and personality disorders. Accepts the mobility impaired; the vision impaired; the hearing impaired; the speech impaired; those with a history of arson; the sexually compulsive; those with a history of harm to themselves and others; those receiving psychotropic medication. Special programs for the mobility impaired; the developmentally disabled; the vision impaired; the speech impaired.

Program Treatment modalities: behavior modification; client-centered therapy. Family treatment program available.

Staff Total facility staff includes 1 physician, 6 psychologists, 3 psychiatrists, 15 registered nurses, 15 practical/vocational nurses, 6 MSW social workers, 12 teachers, 1 counselor, 1 physical therapist, 4 occupational/recreational therapists, 5 speech pathologists, 8 therapists, 1 dietician, 228 other direct-care staff members. Staff is 40% male, 60% female.

Facilities Multiple buildings; males and females in coeducational units. Separate residential quarters for children and adolescents. Central dining (not shared with adults), separate dining by residential unit available. Basketball courts, game room, gymnasium, outdoor swimming pool, playing fields.

Education Academic program available. Serves ages 6–18, grades 1–12. 12 teachers on staff.

Costs Average cost: $395 per day. Accepts private insurance, group insurance, medicaid, Blue Cross/ Blue Shield, public funds.

Additional Services Outpatient services for males and females ages 6–21. Treats autistic disorders; learning disabilities; behavior disorders; general psychosocial disorders; substance abuse; eating disorders; compulsive/addictive disorders other than substance abuse and eating disorders; post-traumatic stress disorder; thought, mood, and personality disorders. Camping program for males and females ages 6–18. Treats autistic disorders; behavior disorders; compulsive/addictive disorders other than substance abuse and eating disorders.

Contact Office of Admissions, main address above. Phone: 713-335-1000. Fax: 713-332-2301.
See page 422 for full page description.

DEVEREUX—LEO KANNER CENTER
390 East Boot Road
West Chester, Pennsylvania 19380
215-431-8174; Fax: 215-431-3155

General Information Residential treatment/subacute facility for children, adolescents, adults. 85 beds for children; 85 beds for adolescents; 220 beds total. Open year-round. Patient security: staff secured; will pursue and return runaways. Suburban setting. Not-for-profit facility affiliated with Devereux Foundation, Devon, PA. Licensed by state of Pennsylvania.

Participants Accepts: male and female children ages 6–13; male and female adolescents ages 11–21; male adults ages 21–49. Admission: one parent, all parties who share custody, court order, depending on program. Treats autistic disorders; learning disabilities; behavior disorders; general psychosocial disorders; eating disorders; thought, mood, and personality disorders. Accepts the speech impaired; those with a history of harm to themselves and others; those receiving psychotropic medication; those with a history of epilepsy. Special programs for the developmentally disabled; the speech impaired. Largest number of participants from New Jersey, New York, Pennsylvania.

Program Treatment modalities: behavioral anaylysis; individual and group psychotherapy; speech and language.

Staff 1.6 full-time direct-care staff members per child or adolescent. Total facility staff includes 3 physicians, 6 psychologists, 3 psychiatrists, 5 registered nurses, 5 social workers (non-MSW), 40 teachers, 70 counselors, 3 physical therapists, 15 occupational/recreational therapists, 2 speech pathologists, 1 therapist, 1 dietician, 125 other direct-care staff members. Staff is 40% male, 60% female.

Facilities Multiple buildings; males and females in both coeducational and separate units depending on program. Separate residential quarters for children and adolescents. Central dining (not shared with adults). Basketball courts, game room, gymnasium, horseback riding, indoor swimming pool, outdoor swimming pool, outdoor tennis courts, playing fields.

Education Academic program available at no charge. Serves ages 5–21, ungraded. 40 teachers on staff. Curriculum accredited or approved by Pennsylvania Department of Education. Cost of educational program covered by local school district. Organized sports program offered.

Costs Average cost: $57,000 per stay. Accepts private insurance, group insurance, public funds.

Contact Carl D. Villarini, Admissions Director, main address above. Phone: 215-431-8174. Fax: 215-431-3155.
See page 422 for full page description.

DEVEREUX—MAPLETON CENTER
655 Sugartown Road
Box 297
Malvern, Pennsylvania 19355-0297
215-296-6923; Fax: 215-296-6949

General Information Residential treatment/subacute facility for adolescents. 90 beds for adolescents. Open year-round. Patient security: staff secured; will pursue and return runaways. Suburban setting. Not-for-profit facility affiliated with Devereux Foundation, Devon, PA. Licensed by state of Pennsylvania. Accredited by JCAHO.

Participants Accepts: male and female adolescents ages 13–21. Average stay: 664 days. Admission: voluntary. Treats learning disabilities; general psychosocial disorders; eating disorders; post-traumatic stress disorder; thought, mood, and personality disorders. Accepts the speech impaired; those with a history of harm to themselves and others; those receiving psychotropic medication; those with a history of epilepsy; those with severe psychiatric disorders. Largest number of participants from Pennsylvania, New York, Maryland.

Program Treatment modalities: developmental; psychodynamic; cognitive; interpersonal/systems. Family treatment program available.

Staff .9 full-time direct-care staff member per adolescent. Total facility staff includes 2 physicians, 7 psychologists, 2 psychiatrists, 5 registered nurses,

2 practical/vocational nurses, 2 MSW social workers, 15 teachers, 1 occupational/recreational therapist, 1 speech pathologist, 1 dietician, 40 other direct-care staff members. Staff is 46% male, 54% female.

Facilities Multiple buildings; males and females in separate units. Central dining. Basketball courts, game room, gymnasium, outdoor swimming pool, outdoor tennis courts, playing fields.

Education Academic program available at additional cost. Serves ages 13–21, grades 7–12. 15 teachers on staff. Curriculum accredited or approved by Pennsylvania Department of Education. Cost of educational program sometimes covered by local school district. Organized sports program offered.

Costs Average cost: $278 per day. Accepts private insurance, public funds.

Contact Laura Kearns, Director, Admissions/Marketing, main address above. Phone: 215-296-6975. Fax: 215-296-5866.
See page 422 for full page description.

DEVEREUX MASSACHUSETTS
60 Miles Road
P.O. Box 197
Rutland, Massachusetts 01543-0197
508-886-4746; Fax: 508-886-2274

General Information Residential treatment/subacute facility for children, adolescents, adults. Open year-round. Patient security: staff secured; will pursue and return runaways. Small town setting. Not-for-profit facility affiliated with Devereux Foundation, Devon, PA. Licensed by state of Massachusetts.

Participants Accepts: male and female children and adolescents ages 6–22; male and female adults. Admission: one parent, all parties who share custody, court order, public agencies, depending on program. Treats autistic disorders; learning disabilities; behavior disorders; general psychosocial disorders; post-traumatic stress disorder; thought, mood, and personality disorders. Accepts the speech impaired; those with a history of arson; those with a history of harm to themselves and others; those receiving psychotropic medication; sexual abuse survivors; low-risk offenders. Special programs for the developmentally disabled; sexual abuse survivors; low-risk offenders.

Program Treatment modalities: psychodynamic; systems approach; eclectics. Family treatment program available.

Staff Total facility staff includes 1 physician, 1 psychologist, 2 psychiatrists, 13 registered nurses, 1 practical/vocational nurse, 2 MSW social workers, 8 social workers (non-MSW), 20 teachers, 18 counselors, 1 occupational/recreational therapist, 2 speech pathologists, 2 therapists, 71 other direct-care staff members.

Facilities Multiple buildings; males and females in both coeducational and separate units depending on program. Separate residential quarters for children and adolescents. Central dining (shared with adults), separate dining by residential unit available. Basketball courts, game room, gymnasium, playing fields, ropes course.

Education Academic program available. Serves ages 6–22, grades N–10. 20 teachers on staff. Curriculum accredited or approved by Massachusetts Department of Education. Cost of educational program sometimes covered by local school district. Organized sports program offered.

Costs Accepts private insurance, group insurance, public funds.

Contact Kenneth M. Ayers, Director of Admissions, main address above. Phone: 508-886-4746. Fax: 508-886-2274.
See page 422 for full page description.

DEVEREUX—NEW JERSEY CENTER FOR AUTISM
186 Roadstown Road
Bridgeton, New Jersey 08302
609-455-7200; Fax: 609-455-2765

Contact Vincent Winterling, main address above. Phone: 609-455-7200. Fax: 609-455-2765.
See page 422 for full page description.

DEVEREUX NEW YORK
Route 9, North
P.O. Box 40
Red Hook, New York 12571-0040
914-758-1899; Fax: 914-758-1817

General Information Residential school and treatment program for developmentally disabled children and adolescents for children, adolescents. Open year-round. Patient security: staff secured; will pursue and return runaways. Rural setting. Not-for-profit facility affiliated with Devereux Foundation, Devon, PA. Licensed by state of New York. Accredited by New York State Office for Mental Retardation and Developmental Disabilities.

Participants Accepts: male and female children ages 7–12; male and female adolescents ages 13–21. Average stay: 3 years. Admission: all parties who share custody, Department of Social Services, depending on program. Treats autistic disorders; eating disorders; post-traumatic stress disorder. Accepts the mobility impaired; the vision impaired; the hearing impaired; the speech impaired; those with a history of harm to themselves and others; those receiving psychotropic medication; non-English speaking individuals; those with a history of epilepsy. Special programs for the mobility impaired; the developmentally disabled; the speech impaired; students with Prader-Willi Syndrome needing special dietary and behavioral training.

Program Treatment modalities: milieu therapy; behavior modification; individual and group counseling.

Staff Total facility staff includes 1 psychologist, 1 psychiatrist, 4 registered nurses, 2 practical/vocational nurses, 5 MSW social workers, 11 social workers (non-MSW), 24 teachers, 93 counselors, 2 physical therapists, 3 speech pathologists, 1 dietician, 28 other direct-care staff members. Staff is 30% male, 70% female.

Facilities Multiple buildings; males and females in both coeducational and separate units depending on program. Central dining, separate dining by residential unit available. Basketball courts, game room, gymnasium, outdoor swimming pool, playing fields, ropes course.

Education Academic program available. Serves ages 7–21, ungraded. 24 teachers on staff. Curriculum accredited or approved by New York State Education Department; Office for Children with Handicapped Conditions. Organized sports program offered.

Costs Average cost: $84,000 per year. Accepts medicaid, public funds.

Contact Mary L. Carey, Intake Coordinator, main address above. Phone: 914-758-1899. Fax: 914-758-1817.

See page 422 for full page description.

DEVEREUX ORLANDO CENTER
6147 Christian Way
Orlando, Florida 32808
407-296-5300; Fax: 407-296-5331

General Information Residential treatment/subacute facility for children, adolescents. Patient security: staff secured. Not-for-profit facility affiliated with Devereux Foundation, Devon, PA. Licensed by state of Florida. Accredited by JCAHO.

Participants Accepts: male and female children; male and female adolescents. Average stay: 95 days. Admission: voluntary. Treats autistic disorders; learning disabilities; behavior disorders; general psychosocial disorders; post-traumatic stress disorder; thought, mood, and personality disorders.

Staff Staff is 42% male, 58% female.

Costs Average cost: $260 per day.

Contact Bev Aleo, Director of Admissions, main address above. Phone: 407-296-5300. Fax: 407-296-5331.

See page 422 for full page description.

DEVEREUX PSYCHIATRIC RESIDENTIAL TREATMENT CENTER OF TEXAS
120 David Wade Drive
Victoria, Texas 77902-2666
512-575-8271; Fax: 512-515-6520

General Information Residential treatment/subacute facility for children, adolescents. 24 beds for children; 110 beds for adolescents; 134 beds total. Open year-round. Patient security: partially locked; will pursue and return runaways. Rural setting. Not-for-profit facility affiliated with Devereux Foundation, Devon, PA. Licensed by state of Texas. Accredited by JCAHO; Texas Mental Health and Mental Retardation, Texas Department of Human Services.

Participants Accepts: male children ages 6–13; male and female adolescents ages 12–18. Average stay: 180 days. Admission: one parent, all parties who share custody, court order, depending on program. Treats learning disabilities; behavior disorders; general psychosocial disorders; substance abuse; post-traumatic stress disorder; thought, mood, and personality disorders. Accepts those with a history of harm to themselves and others; those receiving psychotropic medication; non-English speaking individuals; those with a history of epilepsy.

Program Treatment modalities: Twelve Step Recovery; insight-oriented; reality therapy; cognitive-behavioral. Family treatment program available.

Staff 1.4 full-time direct-care staff members per child or adolescent. Total facility staff includes 1 physician, 3 psychologists, 3 psychiatrists, 8 registered nurses, 15 practical/vocational nurses, 1 MSW social worker, 6 social workers (non-MSW), 15 teachers, 7 counselors, 1 occupational/recreational therapist, 1 speech pathologist, 8 therapists, 1 dietician, 76 other direct-care staff members. Staff is 52% male, 48% female.

Facilities Multiple buildings; males and females in coeducational units. Central dining. Basketball courts, game room, gymnasium, outdoor swimming pool, outdoor tennis courts, playing fields, fishing.

Education Academic program available at no charge. Serves ages 6–18, grades K–12. 15 teachers on staff. Curriculum accredited or approved by Texas Education Agency, Southern Association of Colleges and Schools.

Costs Average cost: $340 per day. Accepts private insurance, group insurance, Blue Cross/Blue Shield, public funds.

Contact Par Franke, Admissions Director, main address above. Phone: 512-575-8721. Fax: 512-515-6520.
    See page 422 for full page description.

DEVEREUX—WRANGLE HILL TREATMENT CENTER
3560 Wrangle Hill Road
Bear, Delaware 19701
302-834-8416

Contact Jeff Peck, Administrator, main address above. Phone: 302-834-8416.
    See page 422 for full page description.

DIOCESAN CATHOLIC CHILDREN'S HOME
75 Orphanage Road
Fort Mitchell, Kentucky 41017
606-331-2040

General Information Residential treatment/subacute facility for children. 28 beds for children. Open year-round. Patient security: staff secured; will pursue and return runaways. Suburban setting. Not-for-profit facility. Licensed by state of Kentucky. Accredited by Commission on Accreditation of Services for Families and Children.

Participants Accepts: male and female children ages 6–13. Average stay: 18 months. Admission: all parties who share custody, court order, depending on program. Treats learning disabilities; behavior disorders; general psychosocial disorders. Accepts the vision impaired; the speech impaired; those with a history of harm to themselves and others; those receiving

psychotropic medication. Special programs for the developmentally disabled; the speech impaired.

Program Treatment modalities: behavioral; milieu; psychodynamic; eclectic. Family treatment program available.

Staff 1.8 full-time direct-care staff members per child. Total facility staff includes 1 psychologist, 1 psychiatrist, 4 MSW social workers, 4 teachers, 4 occupational/recreational therapists, 1 speech pathologist, 1 therapist, 30 other direct-care staff members.

Facilities Multiple buildings; males and females in separate units. Separate dining by residential unit available. Basketball courts, game room, gymnasium, outdoor swimming pool, playing fields.

Education Academic program available at no charge. Serves ages 6–12, grades 1–6. 4 teachers on staff. Curriculum accredited or approved by Kentucky Education Department.

Costs Average cost: $75 per day. Accepts private insurance, group insurance, medicare, medicaid.

Contact John Ross, main address above. Phone: 606-331-2040.

DISCOVERY ACADEMY
1460 South University Avenue
Provo, Utah 84601
801-374-2121; Fax: 801-373-4451

General Information School for adolescents. 60 beds for adolescents. Open year-round. Patient security: staff secured; will pursue and return runaways. Urban setting. For-profit facility affiliated with Discovery Foundation, Provo, UT. Licensed by state of Utah. Accredited by Utah Division of Social Services.

Participants Accepts: male and female adolescents ages 12–18. Average stay: 365 days. Admission: all parties who share custody. Treats learning disabilities; behavior disorders; general psychosocial disorders; substance abuse. Accepts those receiving psychotropic medication; those with a history of epilepsy. Special programs for those needing academic remediation. Largest number of participants from California, Florida, Washington.

Program Treatment modalities: cognitive-behavioral; competency-based education; milieu therapy. Family treatment program available.

Staff .9 full-time direct-care staff member per adolescent. Total facility staff includes 2 physicians, 3 psychologists, 1 psychiatrist, 1 registered nurse, 1 MSW social worker, 10 teachers, 30 counselors, 1 occupational/recreational therapist. Staff is 60% male, 40% female.

Facilities Multiple buildings; males and females in separate units. Central dining. Basketball courts, game room, gymnasium, outdoor swimming pool, outdoor tennis courts, playing fields.

Education School serves ages 12–18, grades 6–12. 10 teachers on staff. Curriculum is college-preparatory; diploma granted upon completion. Curriculum accredited or approved by Northwest Association of Schools and Colleges. Organized sports program offered.

Costs Average cost: $33,600 per stay. Accepts private insurance, group insurance, public funds. Financial aid available.

Contact Kathryn Moody, Admissions Officer, main address above. Phone: 801-374-2121. Fax: 801-373-4451.

DRUG ABUSE TREATMENT ASSOCIATION, INC.
1016 North Clemons Street
Suite 406
Jupiter, Florida 33477
407-743-1034; Fax: 407-743-1037

General Information Drug and alcohol rehabilitation center for adolescents. Patient security: staff secured. Independent not-for-profit facility. Licensed by state of Florida.

Participants Accepts: male and female adolescents. Average stay: 3 months. Admission: one parent, all parties who share custody, court order, voluntary, depending on program. Treats learning disabilities; behavior disorders; general psychosocial disorders; substance abuse; compulsive/addictive disorders other than substance abuse and eating disorders; thought, mood, and personality disorders.

Staff Staff is 50% male, 50% female.

Costs Average cost: $800 per stay.

Contact Pam Middleton, Deputy Director, main address above. Phone: 407-743-1034.

DUKE UNIVERSITY HOSPITAL
Erwin Road
Durham, North Carolina 27710
919-684-8111; Fax: 919-684-8663

General Information General hospital for children, adolescents. Patient security: entirely locked. Not-for-profit facility affiliated with Duke University,

Durham, NC. Licensed by state of North Carolina. Accredited by JCAHO.

Participants Accepts: male and female children; male and female adolescents. Average stay: 30 days. Admission: one parent, all parties who share custody, court order, depending on program. Treats learning disabilities; behavior disorders; general psychosocial disorders; substance abuse; eating disorders; compulsive/addictive disorders other than substance abuse and eating disorders; post-traumatic stress disorder; thought, mood, and personality disorders.

Costs Average cost: $24,000 per stay.

Contact Referral Coordinator, P.O. Box 3313, Durham, NC 27710. Phone: 919-684-5484.

DURHAM REGIONAL HOSPITAL ADOLESCENT TREATMENT UNIT
3643 North Roxboro Road
Durham, North Carolina 27704
919-470-4000; Fax: 919-470-7390

General Information General hospital for adolescents. 12 beds for adolescents. Open year-round. Patient security: entirely locked; will pursue and return runaways. Urban setting. Independent not-for-profit facility. Licensed by state of North Carolina. Accredited by JCAHO.

Participants Accepts: male and female adolescents ages 12–18. Average stay: 23 days. Admission: one parent, all parties who share custody, court order, depending on program. Treats learning disabilities; behavior disorders; general psychosocial disorders; substance abuse; eating disorders; post-traumatic stress disorder; thought, mood, and personality disorders. Accepts the mobility impaired; the vision impaired; the hearing impaired; the speech impaired; those with a history of arson; the sexually compulsive; those with a history of harm to themselves and others; those receiving psychotropic medication; non-English speaking individuals; those with a history of epilepsy. Largest number of participants from North Carolina.

Program Treatment modalities: Psychodynamic Biopsychosocial Development Assessment Model; eclectic treatment; individualized Twelve Step Recovery program. Family treatment program available.

Staff 1.5 full-time direct-care staff members per adolescent. Total facility staff includes 15 physicians, 3 psychologists, 2 psychiatrists, 6 registered nurses, 1 teacher, 1 occupational/recreational therapist, 12 other direct-care staff members.

Facilities Single building; males and females in co-educational units. Central dining. Game room, weight room.

Education Academic program available at no charge. Serves ages 12–18, grades 5–12. 1 teacher on staff. Curriculum accredited or approved by Durham County Public Schools. Cost of educational program covered by local school district.

Costs Average cost: $410 per day. Accepts private insurance, group insurance, medicaid, Blue Cross/Blue Shield, public funds.

Contact Elizabeth Rogsdale, Administrative Assistant, main address above. Phone: 919-470-6226. Fax: 919-470-7390.

DYNAMIC YOUTH COMMUNITY, INC.
1830 Coney Island Avenue
Brooklyn, New York 11230
718-376-7923; Fax: 718-998-9878

General Information Residential treatment/subacute facility for adolescents. 56 beds for adolescents. Patient security: staff secured. Independent not-for-profit facility. Licensed by state of New York.

Participants Accepts: male and female adolescents. Average stay: 16 months. Admission: one parent, all parties who share custody, court order, voluntary, depending on program. Treats substance abuse. Accepts those with a history of epilepsy.

Contact Barbara Green, Intake Coordinator, main address above. Phone: 718-376-7923. Fax: 718-998-9878.

EAGLE MOUNTAIN OUTPOST SCHOOL
2835 Lakeshore Drive
Sagle, Idaho 83864
208-263-3447; Fax: 208-263-7353

General Information Special purpose school for children, adolescents. Open year-round. Patient security: staff secured; will pursue and return runaways. Rural setting. Not-for-profit facility affiliated with Eagle Canyon Outpost, Inc., Albuquerque, NM. Licensed by state of Idaho.

Participants Accepts: male children and adolescents ages 10–18. Average stay: 365 days. Admission: one parent, all parties who share custody, court order, depending on program. Treats learning disabilities; behavior disorders; general psychosocial disorders;

thought, mood, and personality disorders. Accepts those receiving psychotropic medication; those with a history of epilepsy. Largest number of participants from Washington, California, Oregon.

Program Treatment modalities: milieu therapeutic approach; behavior modification; individualized; Twelve Step Recovery.

Staff .3 full-time direct-care staff member per child or adolescent. Total facility staff includes 1 psychologist, 1 MSW social worker, 5 teachers, 2 counselors, 1 occupational/recreational therapist, 2 therapists, 5 other direct-care staff members. Staff is 70% male, 30% female.

Facilities Multiple buildings. Gymnasium, horseback riding, outdoor swimming pool, playing fields.

Education School serves ages 10–18, grades 4–12. 5 teachers on staff. Curriculum is college-preparatory; diploma granted upon completion. Curriculum accredited or approved by Northwest Association of Schools and Colleges, State of Idaho. Organized sports program offered.

Costs Average cost: $2200 per month. Accepts private insurance, group insurance, Blue Cross/Blue Shield, public funds.

Contact Michael Bishop, Co-Director, P.O. Box 1506, Sandpoint, ID 83864. Phone: 800-654-0307. Fax: 208-263-7353.

Announcement Eagle Mountain boys overcome negative behavior patterns and academic failure in therapeutic milieu that provides personalized, experiential learning. Group and individual counseling, point and level system help boys develop honesty, respect, responsibility. Beautiful wooded area on lake near ski basin is setting for year-round sports program.

EAU CLAIRE ACADEMY
550 North Dewey Street
P.O. Box 1168
Eau Claire, Wisconsin 54702
715-834-6681; Fax: 715-834-9954

General Information Residential treatment/subacute facility for children, adolescents. 12 beds for children; 123 beds for adolescents; 135 beds total. Open year-round. Patient security: unlocked; will pursue and return runaways. Small town setting. For-profit facility affiliated with Clinicare Corporation, Waukisha, WI. Licensed by state of Wisconsin. Accredited by JCAHO.

Participants Accepts: male and female children ages 11–13; male and female adolescents ages 13–18. Average stay: 9 months. Admission: court order. Treats learning disabilities; behavior disorders; general psychosocial disorders; substance abuse; eating disorders; post-traumatic stress disorder; thought, mood, and personality disorders. Accepts the speech impaired; those with a history of harm to themselves and others; those receiving psychotropic medication; those with a history of epilepsy. Special programs for the speech impaired.

Program Treatment modalities: Twelve Step Recovery; reality therapy; psychodynamic; multi-disciplinary approach with team. Family treatment program available.

Staff Total facility staff includes 1 psychologist, 3 psychiatrists, 3 registered nurses, 2 practical/vocational nurses, 4 MSW social workers, 9 social workers (non-MSW), 15 teachers, 1 counselor, 1 speech pathologist, 1 dietician, 190 other direct-care staff members.

Facilities Single building; males and females in both coeducational and separate units depending on program. Central dining. Basketball courts, game room, gymnasium.

Education Academic program available. Serves ages 11–18. 15 teachers on staff. Organized sports program offered.

Costs Average cost: $151 per day. Accepts private insurance, group insurance, medicare, medicaid, public funds.

Additional Services Drug and alcohol rehabilitation services for males and females ages 11–18. Treats learning disabilities; behavior disorders; general psychosocial disorders; substance abuse; eating disorders; compulsive/addictive disorders other than substance abuse and eating disorders; post-traumatic stress disorder; thought, mood, and personality disorders.

Contact Judith A. Kistner, Director of Admissions, main address above. Phone: 715-834-6681. Fax: 715-834-9954.

EDGEMEADE
13400 Edgemeade Road
Upper Marlboro, Maryland 20772
301-888-1330; Fax: 301-888-2693

General Information Residential treatment/subacute facility for adolescents. 65 beds for adolescents. Open year-round. Patient security: unlocked; no runaway pursuit. Rural setting. Independent not-for-profit facility. Licensed by state of Maryland. Accredited by JCAHO; Department of Health and Mental Hygiene.

Participants Accepts: male adolescents ages 12–18. Average stay: 547 days. Admission: voluntary, legal guardian must agree, depending on program. Treats learning disabilities; behavior disorders; general psychosocial disorders; substance abuse; post-traumatic stress disorder; thought, mood, and personality disorders. Accepts the speech impaired; those receiving psychotropic medication. Special programs for the speech impaired. Largest number of participants from Maryland, D.C.

Program Treatment modalities: psychotherapy; Twelve Step Recovery; behavior modification. Family treatment program available.

Facilities Single building. Central dining. Basketball courts, game room, gymnasium, outdoor swimming pool, playing fields.

Education Academic program available. Serves ages 12–18, grades 7–12. Curriculum accredited or approved by Maryland State Department of Education. Organized sports program offered.

Costs Average cost: $327 per day. Accepts medicaid, public funds.

Additional Services Drug and alcohol rehabilitation services for males ages 12–18. Treats learning disabilities; behavior disorders; general psychosocial disorders; substance abuse; post-traumatic stress disorder; thought, mood, and personality disorders.

Contact Cindy J. Spiller, Director of Admissions, main address above. Phone: 301-888-1330. Fax: 301-888-2693.

EDGEWOOD CHILDREN'S CENTER
330 North Gore Avenue
St. Louis, Missouri 63119
314-968-2060; Fax: 314-968-8308

General Information Residential treatment/subacute facility for children. 52 beds for children. Open year-round. Patient security: partially locked; will pursue and return runaways. Suburban setting. Independent not-for-profit facility. Licensed by state of Missouri. Accredited by Council on Accreditation of Services for Families and Children.

Participants Accepts: male and female children ages 5–17. Average stay: 22 months. Admission: all parties who share custody, court order, depending on program. Treats learning disabilities; behavior disorders; general psychosocial disorders; eating disorders; compulsive/addictive disorders other than substance abuse and eating disorders; post-traumatic stress disorder; thought, mood, and personality disorders. Accepts the speech impaired; those with a history of arson; the sexually compulsive; those with a history of harm to themselves and others; those receiving psychotropic medication; those with a history of epilepsy. Special programs for the developmentally disabled; the speech impaired.

Program Treatment modalities: milieu therapy; psychosocial; behavioral. Family treatment program available.

Staff 1.1 full-time direct-care staff members per child. Total facility staff includes 1 physician, 2 psychologists, 1 psychiatrist, 1 registered nurse, 8 MSW social workers, 6 teachers, 3 occupational/recreational therapists, 1 speech pathologist, 2 therapists, 35 other direct-care staff members. Staff is 35% male, 65% female.

Facilities Multiple buildings; males and females in both coeducational and separate units depending on program. Central dining. Basketball courts, game room, gymnasium, playing fields.

Education Academic program available. Serves ages 5–17, ungraded. 6 teachers on staff. Curriculum accredited or approved by Missouri and Illinois Departments of Education. Organized sports program offered.

Costs Accepts private insurance, group insurance, public funds.

Additional Services Outpatient services for males and females ages 5–17. Treats learning disabilities; behavior disorders; general psychosocial disorders; post-traumatic stress disorder; thought, mood, and personality disorders.

Contact Katie Burckhalter, Public Relations Manager, main address above. Phone: 314-968-2060. Fax: 314-968-8308.

THE EDGEWOOD PROGRAM
1121 University Drive
Edwardsville, Illinois 62025
618-656-6730; Fax: 618-692-9842

General Information Drug and alcohol rehabilitation center for adolescents. Patient security: staff secured. Not-for-profit facility affiliated with Saint Elizabeth Medical Center, Granite City, IL. Operated by Edgewood Program-Saint John's Mercy Medical Center, St. Louis, MO. Licensed by state of Illinois. Accredited by JCAHO.

Participants Accepts: male and female adolescents. Average stay: 22 days. Admission: one parent, all

parties who share custody, court order, voluntary, depending on program. Treats substance abuse. Accepts the mobility impaired; the vision impaired; the hearing impaired; the speech impaired; those with a history of arson; those receiving psychotropic medication; those with a history of epilepsy.

Staff Staff is 70% male, 30% female.

Costs Average cost: $420 per day.

Contact Dan Duncan, Department Supervisor, main address above. Phone: 618-656-6730. Fax: 618-692-9842.

ELAN SCHOOL
RR 1, Box 370
Poland Spring, Maine 04274-9711
207-998-4666; Fax: 207-998-4660

General Information School for adolescents. Open year-round. Patient security: staff secured. Rural setting. For-profit facility. Licensed by state of Maine.

Participants Accepts: male and female adolescents ages 12–20. Average stay: 24 months. Admission: all parties who share custody, court order, depending on program. Treats learning disabilities; behavior disorders; general psychosocial disorders; substance abuse; post-traumatic stress disorder; thought, mood, and personality disorders.

Staff Total facility staff includes 22 teachers.

Facilities Multiple buildings.

Education School serves ages 12–20, grades 7–12. 22 teachers on staff. Curriculum is college-preparatory; diploma granted upon completion. Curriculum accredited or approved by Maine Department of Education. Organized sports program offered.

Costs Average cost: $40,000 per year.

Contact Deanna Atkinson, Admissions Director, main address above. Phone: 207-998-4666. Fax: 207-998-4660.

See page 424 for full page description.

ELIZABETH GENERAL MEDICAL CENTER, CHILDREN AND ADOLESCENT PSYCHIATRIC INPATIENT UNIT
925 East Jersey Street
Elizabeth, New Jersey 07201
908-289-8600; Fax: 908-558-8103

General Information General hospital for children, adolescents. Patient security: entirely locked. Independent not-for-profit facility. Licensed by state of New Jersey. Accredited by JCAHO.

Participants Accepts: male and female children; male and female adolescents. Average stay: 20 days. Admission: one parent, all parties who share custody, court order, voluntary, depending on program. Treats learning disabilities; behavior disorders; general psychosocial disorders; substance abuse; post-traumatic stress disorder; thought, mood, and personality disorders.

Contact Beth Dorogusker, Program Director, Children and Adolescent Psychiatric Inpatient Unit, main address above. Phone: 908-965-7450.

ELK HILL FARM, INC.
Route 608, South
P.O. Box 99
Goochland, Virginia 23063
804-784-4392; Fax: 804-784-4437

General Information Residential treatment/subacute facility for adolescents. 40 beds for adolescents. Open year-round. Patient security: staff secured; will pursue and return runaways. Rural setting. Independent not-for-profit facility. Licensed by state of Virginia.

Participants Accepts: male adolescents ages 11–18. Average stay: 1 year. Admission: voluntary. Treats learning disabilities; behavior disorders; general psychosocial disorders; substance abuse. Accepts the hearing impaired; the speech impaired; those with a history of harm to themselves and others; those receiving psychotropic medication.

Program Treatment modalities: positive peer culture; behavior modification; family systems. Family treatment program available.

Staff .6 full-time direct-care staff member per adolescent. Total facility staff includes 1 psychologist, 2 MSW social workers, 7 teachers, 14 counselors, 2 occupational/recreational therapists. Staff is 70% male, 30% female.

Facilities Multiple buildings. Central dining. Basketball courts, game room, gymnasium, outdoor swimming pool, playing fields, ropes course.

Education Academic program available. Serves ages 11–18, grades 6–12. 7 teachers on staff. Curriculum accredited or approved by Virginia Association for Independent Special Education Facilities. Organized sports program offered.

Costs Average cost: $36,000 per year. Accepts public funds.

Additional Services Drug and alcohol rehabilitation services for males ages 11–18. Treats learning disabilities; behavior disorders; general psychosocial disorders; substance abuse. Wilderness/survival program for males ages 11–18. Treats learning disabilities; behavior disorders; general psychosocial disorders; substance abuse.

Contact Michael C. Farley, Resident Director, main address above. Phone: 804-784-4392. Fax: 804-784-4437.

ELLING CAMP'S AT ROCK CREEK FARM
RR #1
Box 54
Thompson, Pennsylvania 18465
717-756-2706

General Information Camp for children, adolescents, adults. 38 beds for children; 40 beds for adolescents; 96 beds total. Open summer. Patient security: staff secured; will pursue and return runaways. Rural setting. Independent for-profit facility. Licensed by state of Pennsylvania. Accredited by American Camping Association.

Participants Accepts: male and female children ages 6–12; male and female adolescents ages 12–17; male and female adults ages 17–20. Average stay: 26 days. Admission: all parties who share custody, social agency, depending on program. Treats learning disabilities; general psychosocial disorders. Accepts the vision impaired; the hearing impaired; the speech impaired; non-English speaking individuals; those with a history of epilepsy. Largest number of participants from New York, Virginia, New Jersey.

Program Treatment modalities: reality therapy; positive enhancement; differential reinforcement; structured programming.

Staff .7 full-time direct-care staff member per child or adolescent. Total facility staff includes 1 physician, 2 psychologists, 2 registered nurses, 1 MSW social worker, 1 social worker (non-MSW), 3 teachers, 20 counselors, 2 occupational/recreational therapists, 1 dietician, 45 other direct-care staff members. Staff is 60% male, 40% female.

Facilities Multiple buildings; males and females in coeducational units. Separate residential quarters for children and adolescents. Central dining (not shared with adults). Basketball courts, game room, gymnasium, playing fields, ropes course, pond, boating.

Education Academic program available at additional cost. Serves ages 6–17, ungraded. 3 teachers on staff. Organized sports program offered.

Costs Average cost: $2675 per stay. Accepts private insurance, group insurance, public funds.

Contact Lloyd E. Elling, Director, main address above. Phone: 717-756-2706.

**ELM ACRES YOUTH HOME, INC.—
BOY'S FACILITY**
1001 East Jackson Street
Pittsburg, Kansas 66762
316-231-6129; Fax: 316-231-8103

General Information Residential treatment/subacute facility for adolescents. 31 beds for adolescents. Patient security: unlocked. Independent not-for-profit facility. Licensed by state of Kansas.

Participants Accepts: male adolescents. Average stay: 18 months. Admission: court order. Treats learning disabilities; behavior disorders; general psychosocial disorders; substance abuse; compulsive/addictive disorders other than substance abuse and eating disorders; post-traumatic stress disorder; thought, mood, and personality disorders.

Staff .8 full-time direct-care staff member per adolescent. Staff is 50% male, 50% female.

Contact Keith Yoakam, Program Coordinator, P.O. Box 1135, Pittsburg, KS 66762. Phone: 316-231-6129. Fax: 316-231-8103.

EL PUEBLO BOYS' RANCH
1591 Taos Avenue
Pueblo, Colorado 81006
719-544-7496; Fax: 719-544-7705

General Information Residential treatment/subacute facility for adolescents. 40 beds for adolescents. Open year-round. Patient security: staff secured; will pursue and return runaways. Rural setting. Independent not-for-profit facility. Licensed by state of

Colorado. Accredited by Colorado Department of Social Services.

Participants Accepts: male adolescents ages 10–18. Average stay: 730 days. Admission: court order. Treats learning disabilities; behavior disorders; general psychosocial disorders; substance abuse; eating disorders; compulsive/addictive disorders other than substance abuse and eating disorders; post-traumatic stress disorder; thought, mood, and personality disorders. Accepts the sexually compulsive; those with a history of epilepsy. Largest number of participants from Colorado, Kansas, Nebraska.

Program Treatment modalities: Twelve Step Recovery: sexual-specific treatment; behavior management; psychodrama; reality therapy. Family treatment program available.

Staff .4 full-time direct-care staff member per adolescent. Total facility staff includes 2 psychologists, 1 psychiatrist, 1 MSW social worker, 2 social workers (non-MSW), 6 teachers, 14 counselors, 1 occupational/recreational therapist, 2 therapists, 3 other direct-care staff members. Staff is 75% male, 25% female.

Facilities Multiple buildings. Central dining. Basketball courts, game room, gymnasium, outdoor tennis courts, playing fields.

Education School serves ages 10–18, grades K–12. 6 teachers on staff. Curriculum is college-preparatory; diploma granted upon completion. Curriculum accredited or approved by Colorado Division of Education. Organized sports program offered.

Costs Average cost: $4200 per month. Accepts public funds.

Additional Services Adolescent sexual offenders program for males ages 10–18. Treats learning disabilities; behavior disorders; general psychosocial disorders; substance abuse; eating disorders; compulsive/addictive disorders other than substance abuse and eating disorders; post-traumatic stress disorder; thought, mood, and personality disorders.

Contact Edward H. Behling, Program Director, main address above. Phone: 719-544-7496. Fax: 719-544-7705.

**EMMA PENDLETON BRADLEY
HOSPITAL**
1011 Veterans Memorial Hospital
East Providence, Rhode Island 02915
401-434-3400; Fax: 401-438-5149

General Information Psychiatric hospital for children, adolescents. 20 beds for children; 40 beds for adolescents. Open year-round. Patient security: partially locked; will pursue and return runaways. Suburban setting. Independent not-for-profit facility. Licensed by state of Rhode Island. Accredited by JCAHO.

Participants   Accepts: male and female children ages 2–12; male and female adolescents ages 13–18. Average stay: 30 days. Admission: voluntary, emergency certification. Treats autistic disorders; learning disabilities; behavior disorders; general psychosocial disorders; substance abuse; eating disorders; compulsive/addictive disorders other than substance abuse and eating disorders; post-traumatic stress disorder; thought, mood, and personality disorders. Accepts the mobility impaired; the vision impaired; the hearing impaired; the speech impaired; those with a history of arson; the sexually compulsive; those with a history of harm to themselves and others; those receiving psychotropic medication; non-English speaking individuals; those with a history of epilepsy. Special programs for the developmentally disabled; the speech impaired.

Program   Treatment modalities: family systems; psychodynamic; behavioral; therapeutic community. Family treatment program available.

Staff   2.8 full-time direct-care staff members per child or adolescent. Total facility staff includes 3 physicians, 5 psychologists, 9 psychiatrists, 35 registered nurses, 18 MSW social workers, 17 teachers, 2 occupational/recreational therapists, 3 speech pathologists, 1 dietician, 80 other direct-care staff members. Staff is 44% male, 56% female.

Facilities   Multiple buildings; males and females in coeducational units. Central dining. Basketball courts, gymnasium, outdoor swimming pool, outdoor tennis courts, playing fields.

Education   Academic program available at no charge. Serves ages 2–18, grades K–12. 17 teachers on staff. Curriculum accredited or approved by Rhode Island and Massachusetts Departments of Education. Cost of educational program sometimes covered by local school district. Organized sports program offered.

Costs   Average cost: $625 per day. Accepts private insurance, group insurance, medicaid, Blue Cross/Blue Shield, public funds.

Additional Services   Drug and alcohol rehabilitation services for males and females ages 13–18. Treats substance abuse. Outpatient services for males and females ages 2–18. Treats autistic disorders; learning disabilities; behavior disorders; general psychosocial disorders; substance abuse; eating disorders; compulsive/addictive disorders other than substance abuse and eating disorders; post-traumatic stress disorder; thought, mood, and personality disorders. Residential

or sub-acute services for males and females ages 6–17. Treats autistic disorders; behavior disorders; general psychosocial disorders; post-traumatic stress disorder; thought, mood, and personality disorders. Day treatment (partial hospitalization) for males and females ages 2–18. Treats autistic disorders; learning disabilities; behavior disorders; general psychosocial disorders; substance abuse; eating disorders; compulsive/addictive disorders other than substance abuse and eating disorders; post-traumatic stress disorder; thought, mood, and personality disorders.

Contact   Paul Kline, Director of Outpatient Services, main address above. Phone: 401-434-3400. Fax: 401-438-5149.

ENGLISHTON PARK CHILDREN'S CENTER
Route 203, North
Lexington, Indiana 47138
812-889-2046

General Information   Camp for children. 36 beds for children. Open summer. Patient security: unlocked; will pursue and return runaways. Rural setting. Not-for-profit facility affiliated with Englishton Park United Presbyterian Ministries, Inc., Lexington, IN. Licensed by state of Indiana. Accredited by American Camping Association.

Participants   Accepts: male and female children ages 6–12. Average stay: 10 days. Admission: referral agency only. Treats autistic disorders; learning disabilities; behavior disorders; general psychosocial disorders; thought, mood, and personality disorders. Accepts the vision impaired; the hearing impaired; the speech impaired; those with a history of arson; the sexually compulsive; those with a history of harm to themselves and others; those receiving psychotropic medication; non-English speaking individuals; those with a history of epilepsy. Largest number of participants from Indiana, Kentucky, Ohio.

Program   Treatment modalities: cognitive behavior modification.

Staff   .1 full-time direct-care staff member per child. Total facility staff includes 3 psychologists, 1 practical/vocational nurse, 1 MSW social worker, 8 teachers, 2 counselors, 1 therapist, 1 dietician. Staff is 50% male, 50% female.

Facilities   Multiple buildings; males and females in separate units. Central dining. Basketball courts, game room, outdoor swimming pool.

Education   Academic program available at no charge. Serves ages 6–12, grades 1–6. 8 teachers on staff.

Costs   Average cost: $150 per stay. Accepts public funds.

Contact   Dr. Harve E. Rawson, Director, main address above. Phone: 812-866-7307.

THE EPISCOPAL CENTER FOR CHILDREN
5901 Utah Avenue, NW
Washington, D.C. 20015
202-363-1333

General Information   Residential treatment/subacute facility for children. 21 beds for children. Open September to July. Patient security: unlocked. Urban setting. Independent not-for-profit facility. Licensed by District of Columbia. Accredited by American Association of Psychiatric Services for Children.

Participants   Accepts: male and female children ages 5–13. Average stay: 3 years. Admission: voluntary. Treats learning disabilities; behavior disorders; general psychosocial disorders. Accepts those receiving psychotropic medication. Largest number of participants from Maryland, D.C., Virginia.

Program   Treatment modalities: psychodynamic. Family treatment program available.

Staff   1.7 full-time direct-care staff members per child. Total facility staff includes 1 psychologist, 2 psychiatrists, 1 registered nurse, 6 MSW social workers, 7 teachers, 14 counselors, 1 speech pathologist, 4 therapists, 1 dietician. Staff is 34% male, 66% female.

Facilities   Multiple buildings; males and females in coeducational units. Central dining. Basketball courts, game room, gymnasium, outdoor swimming pool, playing fields.

Education   7 teachers on staff.

Costs   Average cost: $36,000 per year. Accepts public funds.

Contact   Alan C. Korz, Director, main address above. Phone: 202-363-1333.

EPWORTH CHILDREN'S HOME
110 North Elm Avenue
St. Louis, Missouri 63119
314-961-5718; Fax: 314-961-3503

General Information   Residential treatment/subacute facility for adolescents. 71 beds for adolescents. Open year-round. Patient security: partially locked; will pursue and return runaways. Suburban setting. Independent not-for-profit facility. Licensed by state of Missouri. Accredited by JCAHO; Council on Accreditation of Services for Families and Children.

Participants   Accepts: male and female adolescents ages 11–18. Average stay: 210 days. Admission: all parties who share custody. Treats learning disabilities; behavior disorders; general psychosocial disorders; substance abuse; eating disorders; compulsive/addictive disorders other than substance abuse and eating disorders; post-traumatic stress disorder; thought, mood, and personality disorders. Accepts those with a history of harm to themselves and others; those receiving psychotropic medication. Special programs for the developmentally disabled. Largest number of participants from Missouri, Illinois, Indiana.

Program   Treatment modalities: psychodynamic-individual therapy; group therapy; reality therapy; milieu therapy. Family treatment program available.

Staff   .7 full-time direct-care staff member per adolescent. Total facility staff includes 1 psychiatrist, 7 registered nurses, 12 MSW social workers, 2 social workers (non-MSW), 10 teachers, 8 occupational/recreational therapists, 1 speech pathologist, 2 therapists, 1 dietician, 16 other direct-care staff members. Staff is 33% male, 67% female.

Facilities   Multiple buildings; males and females in separate units. Central dining, separate dining by residential unit available. Basketball courts, game room, gymnasium, outdoor swimming pool, outdoor tennis courts, playing fields, music and art therapy rooms, kitchen.

Education   Academic program available. Serves ages 11–18, grades 5–12. 10 teachers on staff. Curriculum accredited or approved by Special School District of St. Louis; State of Missouri. Organized sports program offered.

Costs   Average cost: $279 per day. Accepts private insurance, group insurance, Blue Cross/Blue Shield, public funds.

Additional Services   Independent Living Program for males and females. Treats learning disabilities; behavior disorders.

Contact   Roger Drake, Director of Utilization Review, main address above. Phone: 314-961-5718. Fax: 314-961-3503.

EXODUS HOUSE
3042 Kilbourne Avenue
Eau Claire, Wisconsin 54703
715-835-7582; Fax: 715-835-7582

General Information Residential treatment/subacute facility for adolescents. 20 beds for adolescents. Patient security: staff secured. Not-for-profit facility affiliated with Lutheran Social Services of Wisconsin and Upper Michigan, Milwaukee, WI. Licensed by state of Wisconsin. Accredited by Council on Accreditation of Services for Families and Children.

Participants Accepts: male and female adolescents. Average stay: 6 months. Admission: one parent, all parties who share custody, court order, voluntary, depending on program. Treats autistic disorders; learning disabilities; behavior disorders; general psychosocial disorders; substance abuse; eating disorders; compulsive/addictive disorders other than substance abuse and eating disorders; post-traumatic stress disorder; thought, mood, and personality disorders.

Staff Staff is 40% male, 60% female.

Education Academic program available at no charge. Serves ages 12–17, grades 7–12. Curriculum accredited or approved by Wisconsin Department of Public Instruction. Cost of educational program sometimes covered by local school district.

Costs Average cost: $125 per day.

Contact Myrthe McCarthy, Program Director, main address above. Phone: 715-835-7582. Fax: 715-835-7582.

EXPEDITIONS
P.O. Box 1303
Trout Creek, Montana 59874
406-827-3863; Fax: 406-827-4210

General Information Wilderness/survival program for children, adolescents. Patient security: unlocked. Independent for-profit facility. Licensed by state of Montana.

Participants Accepts: male and female children; male and female adolescents. Admission: one parent. Treats learning disabilities; behavior disorders; general psychosocial disorders; substance abuse; thought, mood, and personality disorders.

Staff Staff is 50% male, 50% female.

Costs Average cost: $3400 per stay.

Contact Lorne Riddell, Program Head, main address above. Phone: 406-827-3863. Fax: 406-827-4210.

EXPLORATIONS
P.O. Box 1303
Trout Creek, Montana 59874
406-827-3863; Fax: 406-827-4210

General Information Residential treatment/subacute facility for children, adolescents. Patient security: unlocked. Independent for-profit facility. Licensed by state of Montana.

Participants Accepts: male and female children; male and female adolescents. Admission: one parent. Treats learning disabilities; behavior disorders; general psychosocial disorders; substance abuse; thought, mood, and personality disorders.

Staff Staff is 40% male, 60% female.

Costs Average cost: $1800 per month.

Contact Lorne Riddell, Program Head, main address above. Phone: 406-827-3863. Fax: 406-827-4210.

Announcement Explorations programs offer emotionally stimulating and experience-rich living, travel, and wilderness experiences for adolescents and young adults. Offerings include intimate family-based residential living, the challenging Wilderness Assessment Course, a 10-week summer adventure program, parent/child excursions, and custom-designed experiences. Each program ensures personalized attention by maintaining small group numbers. Reasonable fees.

FAIRBRIDGE RESIDENTIAL TREATMENT CENTER
14907 Broschart Road
Rockville, Maryland 20850
301-217-9010; Fax: 301-424-3841

General Information Residential treatment/subacute facility for children, adolescents. 24 beds for children; 36 beds for adolescents; 60 beds total. Open year-round. will pursue and return runaways. Suburban setting. For-profit facility affiliated with National Medical Enterprises, Santa Monica, CA. Licensed by state of Maryland. Accredited by JCAHO.

Participants Accepts: male and female children ages 5–12; male and female adolescents ages 12–18. Average stay: 180 days. Treats learning disabilities; behavior disorders; general psychosocial disorders; substance abuse; eating disorders; post-traumatic stress disorder; thought, mood, and personality disorders. Accepts those with a history of harm to themselves and others; those receiving psychotropic medication; those with a history of epilepsy. Largest number of participants from Maryland, Virginia, Pennsylvania.

Program Treatment modalities: Twelve Step Recovery; psychodynamic; family therapy; expressive therapy. Family treatment program available.

Staff 1.5 full-time direct-care staff members per child or adolescent. Total facility staff includes 2 physicians, 5 psychologists, 4 psychiatrists, 12 registered nurses, 6 MSW social workers, 10 teachers, 2 counselors, 2 occupational/recreational therapists, 4 dieticians, 30 other direct-care staff members. Staff is 33% male, 67% female.

Facilities Single building; males and females in coeducational units. Central dining. Basketball courts, game room, gymnasium, playing fields.

Education Academic program available at additional cost. Serves ages 5–18. 10 teachers on staff. Curriculum accredited or approved by State of Maryland. Cost of educational program sometimes covered by local school district. Organized sports program offered.

Costs Accepts private insurance, group insurance, medicaid, public funds.

Contact Warren Hurlbut, Clinical Director, main address above. Phone: 800-344-3057. Fax: 301-424-3841.

FAIR OAKS HOSPITAL
19 Prospect Street
Summit, New Jersey 07901
908-522-7000; Fax: 908-522-7001

General Information Psychiatric hospital for adolescents, adults. Open year-round. Patient security: entirely locked; will pursue and return runaways. Suburban setting. For-profit facility affiliated with National Medical Enterprises, Santa Monica, CA. Licensed by state of New Jersey. Accredited by JCAHO.

Participants Accepts: male and female adolescents ages 9–17; male and female adults ages 18 and up. Average stay: 27 days. Admission: one parent. Treats autistic disorders; learning disabilities; behavior disorders; general psychosocial disorders; substance abuse; eating disorders; compulsive/addictive disorders other than substance abuse and eating disorders; post-traumatic stress disorder; thought, mood, and personality disorders. Accepts the mobility impaired; the vision impaired; the hearing impaired; the speech impaired; those with a history of arson; the sexually compulsive; those with a history of harm to them-

selves and others; those receiving psychotropic medication; those with a history of epilepsy. Special programs for those with AIDS. Largest number of participants from New Jersey.

Program Treatment modalities: Twelve Step Recovery; family systems approaches; group therapy; biopsychiatry. Family treatment program available.

Staff Total facility staff includes 12 physicians, 4 psychologists, 12 psychiatrists, 40 registered nurses, 10 MSW social workers, 8 counselors, 6 occupational/recreational therapists, 2 dieticians, 60 other direct-care staff members.

Facilities Multiple buildings; males and females in coeducational units. Separate residential quarters for adolescents. Central dining (shared with adults), in-room dining available. Basketball courts, indoor swimming pool, weight room, volleyball courts, arts and crafts building.

Education Academic program available at additional cost. Serves ages 9–21, grades 3–12. Curriculum accredited or approved by New Jersey Department of Education. Cost of educational program covered by local school district.

Costs Average cost: $1500 per day. Accepts private insurance, group insurance, medicare, medicaid, Blue Cross/Blue Shield.

Additional Services Drug and alcohol rehabilitation services for males and females ages 12 and up. Treats substance abuse; compulsive/addictive disorders other than substance abuse and eating disorders. Outpatient services for males and females ages 18 and up. Treats learning disabilities; behavior disorders; general psychosocial disorders; substance abuse; eating disorders; post-traumatic stress disorder; thought, mood, and personality disorders.

Contact Admissions Counselor, main address above. Phone: 908-522-7000. Fax: 908-522-7001.

FAIRVIEW DEACONESS ADOLESCENT CHEMICAL DEPENDENCY PROGRAM
2450 Riverside Avenue South
Minneapolis, Minnesota 55454
800-233-7503; Fax: 612-337-4113

General Information General hospital for adolescents. Patient security: staff secured. Not-for-profit facility affiliated with Fairview Corporation, Minneapolis, MN. Licensed by state of Minnesota. Accredited by JCAHO.

Participants Accepts: male and female adolescents. Average stay: 35 days. Admission: one parent, all parties who share custody, court order, voluntary, depending on program. Treats substance abuse. Accepts the mobility impaired; the vision impaired; the hearing impaired; the speech impaired; those with a history of arson; the sexually compulsive; those with a history of harm to themselves and others; those receiving psychotropic medication; those with a history of epilepsy.

Staff   Staff is 45% male, 55% female.

Costs   Average cost: $450 per day.

Contact   Steve Oman, Intake Coordinator for Chemical Dependency Program, main address above.

FAIRVIEW RIVERSIDE MEDICAL CENTER
2450 Riverside Avenue South
Minneapolis, Minnesota 55454
612-371-6600; Fax: 612-371-6159

General Information   General hospital for children, adolescents. Patient security: entirely locked. Not-for-profit facility affiliated with Fairview Corporation, Minneapolis, MN. Licensed by state of Minnesota. Accredited by JCAHO.

Participants   Accepts: male and female children; male and female adolescents. Average stay: 1 month. Admission: one parent, all parties who share custody, court order, voluntary, depending on program. Treats autistic disorders; learning disabilities; behavior disorders; eating disorders; compulsive/addictive disorders other than substance abuse and eating disorders; post-traumatic stress disorder; thought, mood, and personality disorders.

Costs   Average cost: $550 per day.

Contact   Keith Schendel, Supervisor, main address above. Phone: 612-371-6600. Fax: 612-371-6159.

FAIRVIEW WOODBURY ADOLESCENT CHEMICAL DEPENDENCY PROGRAM
1665 Woodbury Drive
Woodbury, Minnesota 55125
800-233-7503

General Information   Drug and alcohol rehabilitation center for adolescents. 40 beds for adolescents. Patient security: staff secured. Not-for-profit facility affiliated with Fairview Corporation, Minneapolis, MN. Licensed by state of Minnesota. Accredited by JCAHO.

Participants   Accepts: male and female adolescents. Average stay: 90 days. Admission: one parent, all parties who share custody, court order, voluntary, depending on program. Treats substance abuse. Accepts the mobility impaired; the vision impaired; the hearing impaired; the speech impaired; those with a history of arson; those receiving psychotropic medication; those with a history of epilepsy.

Staff   Staff is 50% male, 50% female.

Costs   Average cost: $175 per day.

Contact   Steve Oman, Intake Coordinator for Chemical Dependency Program, 2450 Riverside Avenue South, Minneapolis, MN 55454. Phone: 800-233-7503.

FAIRWINDS TREATMENT CENTER
1569 South Fort Harrison
Clearwater, Florida 34616
800-226-0301; Fax: 813-446-1022

General Information   Residential treatment/subacute facility for adolescents, adults. 12 beds for adolescents. Open year-round. Patient security: staff secured; will pursue and return runaways. Suburban setting. Independent for-profit facility. Licensed by state of Florida. Accredited by JCAHO.

Participants   Accepts: male and female adolescents ages 12–17; male and female adults ages 18 and up. Average stay: 28 days. Treats learning disabilities; behavior disorders; general psychosocial disorders; substance abuse; eating disorders; compulsive/addictive disorders other than substance abuse and eating disorders; post-traumatic stress disorder; thought, mood, and personality disorders. Accepts the mobility impaired; those with a history of arson; those with a history of harm to themselves and others; those receiving psychotropic medication.

Program   Treatment modalities: psychodynamic; Twelve Step Recovery; recreation therapy; life skills group. Family treatment program available.

Staff   1.3 full-time direct-care staff members per adolescent. Total facility staff includes 13 physicians, 13 psychologists, 12 psychiatrists, 2 registered nurses, 3 practical/vocational nurses, 2 MSW social workers, 1 teacher, 2 counselors, 1 occupational/recreational therapist, 1 therapist, 1 dietician, 7 other direct-care staff members. Staff is 40% male, 60% female.

Facilities   Single building; males and females in coeducational units. Residential quarters shared with adults. Central dining (shared with adults). Basketball courts, game room, outdoor swimming pool, playing fields.

Education   Academic program available at no charge. Serves ages 12–18, grades 6–12. 1 teacher on staff. Curriculum accredited or approved by Pinellas County School System. Cost of educational program covered by local school district.

Costs   Average cost: $450 per day. Accepts private insurance, group insurance, Blue Cross/Blue Shield.

Additional Services   Drug and alcohol rehabilitation services for males and females ages 12 and up. Treats learning disabilities; behavior disorders; general psychosocial disorders; eating disorders; compulsive/addictive disorders other than substance abuse and eating disorders; post-traumatic stress disorder; thought, mood, and personality disorders. Outpatient services for males and females ages 12 and up. Treats learning disabilities; behavior disorders; general psychosocial disorders; eating disorders; compulsive/addictive disorders other than substance abuse and eating disorders; post-traumatic stress disorder; thought, mood, and personality disorders. Day treatment for males and females ages 12 and up. Treats learning disabilities; behavior disorders; general psychosocial disorders; substance abuse; eating disorders; compulsive/addictive disorders other than substance abuse and eating disorders; post-traumatic stress disorder; thought, mood, and personality disorders.

Contact   Sam Teresi, Director of Marketing, main address above. Phone: 800-226-0301. Fax: 813-446-1022.

FAITH RANCH
Box 1015
Uvalde, Texas 78802
512-232-6611

General Information   Treatment type facility and school for adolescents. Patient security: staff secured. Independent not-for-profit facility. Licensed by state of Texas.

Participants   Accepts: male adolescents. Average stay: 2 years. Admission: all parties who share custody. Treats learning disabilities; behavior disorders; general psychosocial disorders; substance abuse; thought, mood, and personality disorders.

Staff   Staff is 55% male, 45% female.

Costs   Average cost: $650 per month.

Additional Services   School for males ages 11–18. Treats learning disabilities; behavior disorders; general psychosocial disorders; thought, mood, and personality disorders.

Contact   Mary Ann Glascock, Counselor, main address above. Phone: 512-232-6611.

FATHER FLANAGAN'S BOY'S HOME
Boys' Town, Nebraska 68010
402-498-1111; Fax: 402-498-1125

General Information   Long term residential care facility for children, adolescents. Independent not-for-profit facility. Licensed by state of Nebraska. Accredited by Council on Accreditation of Services for Families and Children.

Participants   Accepts: male and female children; male and female adolescents. Average stay: 18 months. Admission: court order. Treats learning disabilities; behavior disorders; general psychosocial disorders; substance abuse; eating disorders.

Contact   Main address above. Phone: 800-448-3000.

THE FAULKNER CENTER, ADOLESCENT PROGRAM
1900 Rio Grande
Austin, Texas 78705
800-486-0075; Fax: 512-469-9453

General Information   Drug and alcohol rehabilitation center for adolescents, adults. 29 beds for adolescents. Open year-round. Patient security: staff secured; will pursue and return runaways. Urban setting. Not-for-profit facility affiliated with Parkside Medical Services Corporation, Park Ridge, IL. Licensed by state of Texas. Accredited by JCAHO; Texas Commission on Alcohol and Drug Abuse.

Participants   Accepts: male and female adolescents ages 12–18; male and female adults ages 19 and up. Average stay: 21 days. Admission: one parent. Treats learning disabilities; behavior disorders; general psychosocial disorders; substance abuse; eating disorders; post-traumatic stress disorder. Accepts the mobility impaired; the vision impaired; the speech impaired; those with a history of harm to themselves and others; those receiving psychotropic medication; those with a history of epilepsy. Largest number of participants from Texas.

Program   Treatment modalities: Twelve Step Recovery; group/family therapy; education therapy. Family treatment program available.

Staff   .6 full-time direct-care staff member per adolescent. Total facility staff includes 1 physician, 1 psychologist, 1 psychiatrist, 1 registered nurse, 2 practical/vocational nurses, 2 MSW social workers, 1 teacher, 1 occupational/recreational therapist, 1 therapist, 1 dietician, 5 other direct-care staff members. Staff is 33% male, 67% female.

Facilities Single building; males and females in co-educational units. Separate residential quarters for adolescents. Separate dining by residential unit available. Game room, gymnasium, ropes course, weight room.

Education Academic program available at no charge. Serves ages 12–18, grades 6–12. 1 teacher on staff. Curriculum accredited or approved by Austin Independent School District.

Costs Accepts private insurance, group insurance, Blue Cross/Blue Shield, public funds.

Additional Services Outpatient services for males and females ages 12–18. Treats learning disabilities; behavior disorders; general psychosocial disorders; substance abuse; compulsive/addictive disorders other than substance abuse and eating disorders; post-traumatic stress disorder; thought, mood, and personality disorders.

Contact Alicia Locke, Program Manager of Adolescent Services, main address above. Phone: 800-486-0075. Fax: 512-469-9453.

pregnant addicted patients. Largest number of participants from South Carolina, North Carolina.

Program Treatment modalities: Twelve Step Recovery; cognitive. Family treatment program available.

Staff Total facility staff includes 1 physician, 1 psychologist, 3 psychiatrists, 9 registered nurses, 5 practical/vocational nurses, 1 MSW social worker, 3 social workers (non-MSW), 1 teacher, 6 counselors, 2 occupational/recreational therapists, 1 dietician, 4 other direct-care staff members.

Facilities Multiple buildings; males and females in separate units. Separate residential quarters for adolescents. Central dining (shared with adults). Basketball courts, game room, gymnasium, indoor swimming pool, outdoor tennis courts, playing fields.

Education Academic program available at no charge. Serves ages 12–18, ungraded. 1 teacher on staff. Curriculum accredited or approved by Charleston County School District or client's home school district. Cost of educational program covered by local school district. Organized sports program offered.

Costs Accepts private insurance, group insurance, public funds.

Contact Sherry Edwards, Coordinator of Adolescent and Psychiatric Services, main address above. Phone: 803-559-2461. Fax: 803-559-6202.

FENWICK HALL HOSPITAL—NEW BEGINNINGS
1709 River Road
P.O. Box 688
Johns Island, South Carolina 29457
803-559-2461; Fax: 803-559-6202

General Information Drug and alcohol rehabilitation center for adolescents, adults. Open year-round. Patient security: partially locked; will pursue and return runaways. Rural setting. For-profit facility affiliated with National Medical Enterprises, Santa Monica, CA. Licensed by state of South Carolina. Accredited by JCAHO.

Participants Accepts: male and female adolescents ages 12–18; male and female adults ages 18 and up. Average stay: 19 days. Treats behavior disorders; general psychosocial disorders; substance abuse; eating disorders; compulsive/addictive disorders other than substance abuse and eating disorders; post-traumatic stress disorder; thought, mood, and personality disorders. Accepts those with a history of arson; those with a history of harm to themselves and others; those receiving psychotropic medication; those with a history of epilepsy. Special programs for those with AIDS;

FIRST HOSPITAL VALLEJO
525 Oregon Street
Vallejo, California 94590
707-648-2200; Fax: 707-642-3640

General Information Psychiatric hospital for children, adolescents, adults. 9 beds for children; 13 beds for adolescents; 44 beds total. Open year-round. Patient security: entirely locked; will pursue and return runaways. Suburban setting. For-profit facility affiliated with First Hospital Corporation, Norfolk, VA. Licensed by state of California. Accredited by JCAHO.

Participants Accepts: male and female children ages 3–13; male and female adolescents ages 12–18; male and female adults ages 18 and up. Average stay: 14 days. Admission: one parent, all parties who share custody, court order, voluntary, emancipated minors, depending on program. Treats learning disabilities; behavior disorders; substance abuse; eating disorders; compulsive/addictive disorders other than substance abuse and eating disorders; post-traumatic stress disorder; thought, mood, and personality disorders. Accepts the mobility impaired; the vision impaired; the hearing impaired; the speech impaired; those with a history of arson; the sexually compulsive; those with a history of harm to themselves and others; those receiving psychotropic medication; non-English speaking individuals; those with a history of epilepsy. Special programs for the chronically ill; the mobility impaired; the developmentally disabled; the vision impaired; the hearing impaired; the speech impaired; those with AIDS.

Program Treatment modalities: milieu therapy; individual and group psychotherapy; psychopharmacology; Twelve Step Recovery. Family treatment program available.

Staff Total facility staff includes 10 physicians, 5 psychiatrists, 28 registered nurses, 10 practical/vocational nurses, 3 MSW social workers, 1 teacher, 50 counselors, 1 occupational/recreational therapist, 1 therapist, 1 dietician, 3 other direct-care staff members. Staff is 40% male, 60% female.

Facilities Single building; males and females in co-educational units. Separate residential quarters for children and adolescents. Central dining (not shared with adults), in-room dining available. Basketball courts, game room, gymnasium, playing fields.

Education Academic program available at no charge. Serves ages 5–18, grades K–12. 1 teacher on staff. Curriculum accredited or approved by Vallejo Unified School District. Cost of educational program covered by local school district.

Costs Average cost: $8400 per stay. Accepts private insurance, group insurance, medicare, medicaid, Blue Cross/Blue Shield.

Additional Services Partial hospitalization for males and females ages 3 and up. Treats learning disabilities; behavior disorders; substance abuse; eating disorders; compulsive/addictive disorders other than substance abuse and eating disorders; post-traumatic stress disorder; thought, mood, and personality disorders. Dual diagnosis for males and females ages 12 and up. Treats substance abuse.

Contact Barbara Darrow, Marketing Director, main address above. Phone: 707-648-2200 Ext. 247. Fax: 707-642-3640.

FIRST HOSPITAL WYOMING VALLEY
149 Dana Street
Wilkes-Barre, Pennsylvania 18702
717-829-7900; Fax: 717-829-7943

General Information Psychiatric hospital for children, adolescents, adults. 15 beds for children; 33 beds for adolescents; 96 beds total. Open year-round. Patient security: partially locked; will pursue and return runaways. Small town setting. For-profit facility affiliated with First Hospital Corporation, Norfolk, VA. Licensed by state of Pennsylvania. Accredited by JCAHO.

Participants Accepts: male and female children ages 4–12; male and female adolescents ages 13–18; male and female adults ages 18 and up. Average stay: 23 days. Admission: one parent, all parties who share custody, court order, mental health commitment, depending on program. Treats autistic disorders; learning disabilities; behavior disorders; general psychosocial disorders; substance abuse; compulsive/addictive disorders other than substance abuse and eating disorders; post-traumatic stress disorder; thought, mood, and personality disorders. Accepts the mobility impaired; the vision impaired; the hearing impaired; the speech impaired; those with a history of arson; the sexually compulsive; those with a history of harm to themselves and others; those receiving psychotropic medication; those with a history of epilepsy. Largest number of participants from Pennsylvania, New York, New Jersey.

Program Treatment modalities: Twelve Step Recovery; psychodynamic. Family treatment program available.

Staff Total facility staff includes 1 physician, 4 psychologists, 6 psychiatrists, 47 registered nurses, 6 MSW social workers, 7 social workers (non-MSW), 6 teachers, 1 occupational/recreational therapist, 7 therapists, 1 dietician, 160 other direct-care staff members. Staff is 32% male, 68% female.

Facilities Single building; males and females in co-educational units. Separate residential quarters for children and adolescents. Central dining (shared with adults). Basketball courts, game room.

Education Academic program available at no charge. Serves ages 4–18, grades K–12. 6 teachers on staff. Curriculum accredited or approved by Pennsylvania Department of Education.

Costs Accepts private insurance, group insurance, medicare, medicaid, Blue Cross/Blue Shield, public funds.

Additional Services Outpatient services for males and females ages 4–18. Treats autistic disorders; learning disabilities; behavior disorders; general psychosocial disorders; substance abuse; eating disorders; compulsive/addictive disorders other than substance abuse and eating disorders; post-traumatic stress disorder; thought, mood, and personality disorders.

Contact Frank Mariano, Director Education/Marketing, main address above. Phone: 717-829-7900. Fax: 717-829-7943.

FIVE OAKS RESIDENTIAL TREATMENT CENTER
1122 Bissonnet
Houston, Texas 77005
713-524-4611; Fax: 713-942-8322

General Information Residential treatment/subacute facility for children, adolescents, adults. 11 beds for children; 33 beds for adolescents; 56 beds total. Open year-round. Patient security: staff secured; no runaway pursuit. Urban setting. Independent for-profit facility. Licensed by state of Texas. Accredited by JCAHO; Texas Department of Human Services, Texas Commission on Alcohol and Drug Abuse.

Participants Accepts: male and female children ages 5–12; male and female adolescents ages 13–17; male and female adults ages 18–24. Average stay: 78 days. Admission: voluntary. Treats learning disabilities; behavior disorders; general psychosocial disorders; substance abuse; eating disorders; compulsive/addictive disorders other than substance abuse and eating disorders; post-traumatic stress disorder; thought, mood, and personality disorders. Accepts the mobility impaired; the speech impaired; those with a history of arson; those with a history of harm to themselves and others; those receiving psychotropic medication; those with a history of epilepsy. Largest number of participants from Texas.

Program Treatment modalities: psychodynamic; Twelve Step Recovery; family systems. Family treatment program available.

Staff 1.3 full-time direct-care staff members per child or adolescent. Total facility staff includes 1 physician, 3 psychiatrists, 1 registered nurse, 1 MSW social worker, 1 social worker (non-MSW), 4 teachers, 20 counselors, 3 therapists. Staff is 35% male, 65% female.

Facilities Multiple buildings; males and females in coeducational units. Separate residential quarters for children and adolescents. Central dining (not shared with adults). Basketball courts, game room, gymnasium, playing fields.

Education Academic program available at no charge. Serves ages 5–18, grades K–12. 4 teachers on staff. Curriculum accredited or approved by Houston Independent School District. Cost of educational program covered by local school district. Organized sports program offered.

Costs Accepts private insurance, group insurance.

Additional Services Drug and alcohol rehabilitation services for males and females ages 5–24. Treats learning disabilities; behavior disorders; general psychosocial disorders; substance abuse; eating disorders; compulsive/addictive disorders other than substance abuse and eating disorders; post-traumatic

stress disorder; thought, mood, and personality disorders.

Contact Dan R. Riley, Chairman/Chief Executive Officer, main address above. Phone: 713-524-4611. Fax: 713-942-8322.

FLORIDA HOSPITAL CENTER FOR PSYCHIATRY
601 East Rollins Street
Orlando, Florida 32803
407-895-7880; Fax: 407-891-5778

General Information Psychiatric hospital for adolescents, adults. 16 beds for adolescents. Open year-round. Patient security: partially locked; will pursue and return runaways. Suburban setting. Not-for-profit facility affiliated with Florida Hospital, Orlando, FL. Operated by Parkside Medical Services Corporation, Park Ridge, IL. Licensed by state of Florida. Accredited by JCAHO; Health and Rehabilitative Services.

Participants Accepts: male and female adolescents ages 12–17; male and female adults ages 18 and up. Average stay: 14 days. Admission: one parent, all parties who share custody, court order, involuntary admission, depending on program. Treats autistic disorders; learning disabilities; behavior disorders; general psychosocial disorders; substance abuse; eating disorders; compulsive/addictive disorders other than substance abuse and eating disorders; post-traumatic stress disorder; thought, mood, and personality disorders. Accepts the mobility impaired; the vision impaired; the hearing impaired; the speech impaired; those with a history of arson; the sexually compulsive; those with a history of harm to themselves and others; those receiving psychotropic medication; non-English speaking individuals; those with a history of epilepsy. Largest number of participants from Florida, New York.

Program Treatment modalities: behavior modification; group therapy; family therapy; Twelve Step Recovery/dual diagnosis. Family treatment program available.

Staff 3.3 full-time direct-care staff members per adolescent. Total facility staff includes 1 psychologist, 8 psychiatrists, 9 registered nurses, 1 practical/vocational nurse, 2 MSW social workers, 2 teachers, 3 counselors, 1 occupational/recreational therapist, 2 dieticians, 1 other direct-care staff member. Staff is 30% male, 70% female.

Facilities Multiple buildings; males and females in coeducational units. Separate residential quarters for adolescents. Separate dining by residential unit available. Game room, outdoor swimming pool, playing fields, volleyball court, weight room.

Education Academic program available at no charge. Serves ages 12–17, grades 6–12. 2 teachers on staff. Curriculum accredited or approved by Orange County Public Schools. Cost of educational program covered by local school district. Organized sports program offered.

Costs Accepts private insurance, group insurance, medicare, medicaid, Blue Cross/Blue Shield, public funds.

Additional Services Drug and alcohol rehabilitation services for males and females ages 18 and up. Treats behavior disorders; substance abuse; compulsive/addictive disorders other than substance abuse and eating disorders; thought, mood, and personality disorders. Outpatient services for males and females. Treats behavior disorders; general psychosocial disorders; substance abuse; eating disorders; compulsive/addictive disorders other than substance abuse and eating disorders; post-traumatic stress disorder; thought, mood, and personality disorders.

Contact Dana Hollifield, Community Relations Representative, main address above. Phone: 407-895-7880. Fax: 407-891-5778.

FOREST HEIGHTS LODGE
4801 Forest Hill Road
P.O. Box 789
Evergreen, Colorado 80439
303-674-6691; Fax: 303-674-6805

General Information Residential treatment/subacute facility for children. 24 beds for children. Open year-round. Patient security: staff secured; will pursue and return runaways. Small town setting. Independent not-for-profit facility. Licensed by state of Colorado. Accredited by JCAHO.

Participants Accepts: male children ages 5–14. Average stay: 700 days. Admission: voluntary. Treats autistic disorders; learning disabilities; behavior disorders; general psychosocial disorders; post-traumatic stress disorder; thought, mood, and personality disorders. Accepts the hearing impaired; the speech impaired; those with a history of harm to themselves and others; those receiving psychotropic medication; those with a history of epilepsy. Special programs for the speech impaired. Largest number of participants from California, Florida, Wyoming.

Program Treatment modalities: attachment model; psychodynamic; experiential-milieu. Family treatment program available.

Staff 1 full-time direct-care staff member per child. Total facility staff includes 1 physician, 1 psychologist, 2 psychiatrists, 1 registered nurse, 7 MSW social workers, 4 teachers, 1 therapist, 1 dietician, 5 other direct-care staff members. Staff is 79% male, 21% female.

Facilities Multiple buildings. Central dining (shared with adults). Basketball courts, game room, gymnasium, indoor swimming pool, outdoor swimming pool, outdoor tennis courts, playing fields.

Education Academic program available at no charge. Serves ages 6–18. 4 teachers on staff. Curriculum accredited or approved by Colorado Department of Education.

Costs Accepts private insurance, group insurance, public funds.

Additional Services Outpatient services for males and females ages 1–18. Treats learning disabilities; general psychosocial disorders; post-traumatic stress disorder; thought, mood, and personality disorders.

Contact Russ Colburn, Executive Director, main address above. Phone: 303-674-6691. Fax: 303-674-6805.

FOREST HOSPITAL
555 Wilson Lane
Des Plaines, Illinois 60016
708-635-4100; Fax: 708-827-0368

General Information Psychiatric hospital for children, adolescents. 19 beds for children; 67 beds for adolescents; 86 beds total. Open year-round. Patient security: entirely locked. Suburban setting. Independent for-profit facility. Licensed by state of Illinois. Accredited by JCAHO.

Participants Accepts: male and female children ages 3–12; male and female adolescents ages 13–18. Average stay: 25 days. Admission: one parent, all parties who share custody, court order, voluntary, depending on program. Treats learning disabilities; behavior disorders; general psychosocial disorders; substance abuse; eating disorders; compulsive/addictive disorders other than substance abuse and eating disorders; post-traumatic stress disorder; thought, mood, and personality disorders. Accepts those with a history of arson; the sexually compulsive; those with a history of harm to themselves and others; those receiving psychotropic medication.

Program Treatment modalities: multiple family programming; family counseling/systems approach; Twelve Step Recovery. Family treatment program available.

Facilities Single building; males and females in co-educational units. Central dining (shared with adults). Basketball courts, gymnasium, indoor swimming pool, ropes course, weight and exercise room.

Education Academic program available at additional cost. Serves ages 5–17, grades K–12. Curriculum accredited or approved by North Central Association of Colleges and Schools. Cost of educational program covered by local school district.

Costs Accepts private insurance, group insurance, Blue Cross/Blue Shield.

Additional Services Drug and alcohol rehabilitation services for males and females ages 5 and up. Treats learning disabilities; behavior disorders; general psychosocial disorders; substance abuse; eating disorders; compulsive/addictive disorders other than substance abuse and eating disorders; post-traumatic stress disorder; thought, mood, and personality disorders. Outpatient services for males and females ages 5 and up. Treats learning disabilities; behavior disorders; general psychosocial disorders; substance abuse; eating disorders; compulsive/addictive disorders other than substance abuse and eating disorders; post-traumatic stress disorder; thought, mood, and personality disorders.

Contact Susan Sardo, Public Relations Director, main address above. Phone: 708-635-4100 Ext. 363. Fax: 708-827-0368.

FORT SMITH REHABILITATION HOSPITAL
1401 South J Street
Fort Smith, Arkansas 72901
501-785-3300; Fax: 501-785-8599

General Information Freestanding cognitive and physical rehabilitation center for children, adolescents. Patient security: staff secured. For-profit facility affiliated with National Medical Enterprises, Los Angeles, CA. Licensed by state of Arkansas. Accredited by JCAHO; Commission on Accreditation of Rehabilitation Facilities.

Participants Accepts: male and female children; male and female adolescents. Average stay: 45 days. Admission: one parent, all parties who share custody, court order, depending on program. Treats autistic disorders; learning disabilities; behavior disorders; eating disorders.

Staff Staff is 20% male, 80% female.

Contact Jean Kolljeski, Pediatric Program Director, main address above. Phone: 501-785-3300.

FOUNDER'S SCHOOL
106 River Road
East Haddam, Connecticut 06423
203-873-1489; Fax: 203-873-9011

General Information Residential treatment/subacute facility for adolescents. 36 beds for adolescents. Patient security: staff secured. Independent not-for-profit facility. Licensed by state of Connecticut. Accredited by Department of Children and Youth Services.

Participants Accepts: male adolescents. Average stay: 18 months. Admission: Department of Children and Youth Services. Treats learning disabilities; behavior disorders; general psychosocial disorders; substance abuse; compulsive/addictive disorders other than substance abuse and eating disorders.

Contact Roy Pietro, Associate Director, main address above. Phone: 203-873-1489.

FOUNTAIN CENTER/ALBERT LEA
408 Fountain Street
Albert Lea, Minnesota 56007
507-377-6411; Fax: 507-377-6453

General Information Drug and alcohol rehabilitation center for adolescents, adults. 11 beds for adolescents. Open year-round. Patient security: staff secured; will pursue and return runaways. Small town setting. Not-for-profit facility affiliated with Naeve Health Care Association, Albert Lea, MN. Licensed by state of Minnesota. Accredited by JCAHO.

Participants Accepts: male and female adolescents ages 13–18; male and female adults ages 18 and up. Average stay: 26 days. Admission: voluntary. Treats substance abuse; thought, mood, and personality disorders. Accepts the mobility impaired; the vision impaired; those with a history of harm to themselves and others; those receiving psychotropic medication; non-English speaking individuals. Largest number of participants from Minnesota, Iowa, Wisconsin.

Program Treatment modalities: Twelve Step Recovery; reality therapy; multimodal; whole person. Family treatment program available.

Staff 2.3 full-time direct-care staff members per adolescent. Total facility staff includes 2 physicians, 1 psychologist, 1 psychiatrist, 4 registered nurses, 4 practical/vocational nurses, 1 social worker (non-MSW), 2 teachers, 4 counselors, 1 occupational/recreational therapist, 1 dietician, 4 other direct-care staff members. Staff is 30% male, 70% female.

Facilities Single building; males and females in co-educational units. Separate residential quarters for adolescents. Central dining (shared with adults). Basketball courts, game room, gymnasium, playing fields.

Education Academic program available at no charge. Serves ages 13–18, ungraded. 2 teachers on staff. Curriculum accredited or approved by Minnesota Department of Education. Cost of educational program covered by local school district.

Costs Average cost: $11,000 per stay. Accepts private insurance, group insurance, medicare, medicaid, Blue Cross/Blue Shield, public funds.

Additional Services Outpatient services for males and females ages 13 and up. Treats substance abuse.

Contact Linda Pederson, Admissions Coordinator, main address above. Phone: 800-533-1616. Fax: 507-377-6453.

FOUR WINDS—SARATOGA
30 Crescent Avenue
Saratoga Springs, New York 12866
800-888-5448; Fax: 518-584-3127

General Information Psychiatric hospital for adolescents, adults. 38 beds for adolescents. Open year-round. Patient security: staff secured; will pursue and return runaways. Small town setting. For-profit facility affiliated with Four Winds Hospital, Katonah, NY. Licensed by state of New York. Accredited by JCAHO.

Participants Accepts: male and female adolescents ages 13–17; male and female adults ages 17–24. Admission: one parent, all parties who share custody, voluntary, depending on program. Treats autistic disorders; learning disabilities; behavior disorders; general psychosocial disorders; substance abuse; eating disorders; compulsive/addictive disorders other than substance abuse and eating disorders; post-traumatic stress disorder; thought, mood, and personality disorders. Accepts the mobility impaired; the vision impaired; the speech impaired; those with a history of harm to themselves and others; those receiving psychotropic medication; those with a history of epilepsy;

those with a mild mental handicap. Special programs for the vision impaired; diabetics.

Program Treatment modalities: psychiatric treatment/pharmacological intervention; individual/group/family therapies; expressive arts therapy; art, music, psychodrama; chemical dependency counseling, Twelve Step Recovery. Family treatment program available.

Staff Total facility staff includes 12 psychologists, 9 psychiatrists, 35 registered nurses, 15 MSW social workers, 5 social workers (non-MSW), 6 teachers, 4 counselors, 4 occupational/recreational therapists, 3 dieticians, 40 other direct-care staff members. Staff is 50% male, 50% female.

Facilities Multiple buildings; males and females in coeducational units. Separate residential quarters for adolescents. Central dining (shared with adults). Game room, playing fields.

Education Academic program available at additional cost. Serves ages 13–18, ungraded. 6 teachers on staff. Cost of educational program sometimes covered by local school district.

Costs Accepts private insurance, medicare, medicaid, Blue Cross/Blue Shield.

Contact Frank Arcangelo, PhD, Director of Admissions and Community Relations, main address above. Phone: 800-888-5448. Fax: 518-584-3127.

Announcement Four Winds-Saratoga, a private psychiatric hospital in Saratoga Springs, New York, provides inpatient care for adolescents, including programs for eating disorders, chemical dependency associated with psychiatric illness, and trauma-related disorders. Schooling is coordinated with home districts. Outpatient assessments are available. Education for college-age patients is in affiliation with Skidmore College.

FOUR WINDS WESTCHESTER
800 Cross River Road
Katonah, New York 10536
914-763-8151; Fax: 914-763-9597

General Information Psychiatric hospital for adolescents, adults. 60 beds for adolescents. Open year-round. Patient security: staff secured; will pursue and return runaways. Suburban setting. Independent for-profit facility. Licensed by state of New York. Accredited by JCAHO.

Participants Accepts: male and female adolescents ages 13–17; male and female adults ages 18 and up. Admission: one parent, all parties who share custody, depending on program. Treats learning disabilities; behavior disorders; general psychosocial disorders; substance abuse; eating disorders; compulsive/addictive disorders other than substance abuse and eating disorders; post-traumatic stress disorder; thought, mood, and personality disorders. Accepts the mobility impaired; the vision impaired; the speech impaired; those with a history of arson; the sexually compulsive; those with a history of harm to themselves and others; those receiving psychotropic medication; non-English speaking individuals; those with a history of epilepsy. Special programs for the chronically ill.

Program Treatment modalities: psychotherapy, individual and group; family therapy and multiple family therapy; ancillary therapies including psychodrama and therapeutic activities; Twelve Step Recovery. Family treatment program available.

Staff 1.9 full-time direct-care staff members per adolescent. Total facility staff includes 2 physicians, 5 psychologists, 6 psychiatrists, 29 registered nurses, 39 practical/vocational nurses, 5 MSW social workers, 11 teachers, 4 counselors, 11 occupational/recreational therapists, 1 dietician, 3 other direct-care staff members. Staff is 40% male, 60% female.

Facilities Multiple buildings; males and females in coeducational units. Separate residential quarters for adolescents. Central dining (shared with adults). Basketball courts, game room, gymnasium, outdoor swimming pool, outdoor tennis courts, playing fields, ropes course.

Education Academic program available at no charge. Serves ages 12–18, grades 6–12. 11 teachers on staff. Curriculum accredited or approved by State of New York. Cost of educational program covered by local school district.

Costs Accepts private insurance, group insurance, medicare, medicaid, Blue Cross/Blue Shield.

Additional Services Drug and alcohol rehabilitation services for males and females ages 13 and up. Treats substance abuse. Outpatient services for males and females ages 2–12. Treats learning disabilities; behavior disorders; general psychosocial disorders.

Contact Monica Broderick, Director of Marketing and Managed Care, main address above. Phone: 914-763-8151. Fax: 914-763-9597.

See page 426 for full page description.

FRANKLIN SQUARE HOSPITAL CENTER
9000 Franklin Square Drive
Baltimore, Maryland 21237
410-682-7260

General Information General hospital for children, adolescents. Patient security: partially locked. Independent not-for-profit facility. Licensed by state of Maryland. Accredited by JCAHO.

Participants Accepts: male and female children; male and female adolescents. Average stay: 2 weeks. Admission: one parent, all parties who share custody, court order, voluntary, depending on program. Treats learning disabilities; behavior disorders; general psychosocial disorders; eating disorders; post-traumatic stress disorder; thought, mood, and personality disorders.

Staff Staff is 20% male, 80% female.

Contact Dr. George Strutt, Director of Child and Adolescent Services, main address above. Phone: 410-682-7785.

FRED FINCH YOUTH CENTER
3800 Coolidge Avenue
Oakland, California 94602
510-482-2244; Fax: 510-530-2047

General Information Residential treatment/subacute facility and special education center for adolescents. 50 beds for adolescents. Open year-round. Patient security: staff secured; no runaway pursuit. Urban setting. Independent not-for-profit facility. Licensed by state of California. Accredited by Child Welfare League of America, California Services for Children.

Participants Accepts: male and female adolescents ages 11–20. Average stay: 18 months. Admission: all parties who share custody, court order, voluntary, depending on program. Treats learning disabilities; behavior disorders; general psychosocial disorders; substance abuse; eating disorders; compulsive/addictive disorders other than substance abuse and eating disorders; post-traumatic stress disorder; thought, mood, and personality disorders. Accepts those with a history of arson; the sexually compulsive; those with a history of harm to themselves and others; those receiving psychotropic medication; those with a history of epilepsy. Largest number of participants from California.

Program Treatment modalities: psychodynamic; family systems; behavior modification. Family treatment program available.

Staff 1.5 full-time direct-care staff members per adolescent. Total facility staff includes 1 psychiatrist, 1 registered nurse, 1 practical/vocational nurse, 10 MSW social workers, 7 teachers, 40 counselors, 5 occupational/recreational therapists, 1 speech pathologist, 1 dietician, 7 other direct-care staff members. Staff is 40% male, 60% female.

Facilities Multiple buildings; males and females in coeducational units. Central dining (shared with adults), separate dining by residential unit available. Basketball courts, game room, gymnasium, horseback riding, playing fields, weight room.

Education Academic program available. Serves ages 11–20, grades 2–12. 7 teachers on staff. Curriculum accredited or approved by State of California. Organized sports program offered.

Costs Average cost: $6863 per month. Accepts private insurance, group insurance, medicare, medicaid, Blue Cross/Blue Shield, public funds.

Contact Roger Spence, PhD, Director of Treatment Services, main address above. Phone: 510-482-2244. Fax: 510-530-2047.

Staff .2 full-time direct-care staff member per adolescent. Total facility staff includes 1 psychologist, 3 psychiatrists, 11 registered nurses, 2 MSW social workers, 2 teachers, 1 occupational/recreational therapist, 1 therapist, 15 other direct-care staff members. Staff is 55% male, 45% female.

Facilities Multiple buildings; males and females in coeducational units. Separate residential quarters for adolescents. Central dining (not shared with adults). Basketball courts, game room, gymnasium, outdoor tennis courts, playing fields.

Education Academic program available at no charge. Serves ages 12–21, grades 7–12. 2 teachers on staff. Cost of educational program covered by local school district. Organized sports program offered.

Costs Average cost: $23,700 per stay. Accepts private insurance, group insurance, medicaid, Blue Cross/Blue Shield.

Additional Services Drug and alcohol rehabilitation services for males and females ages 12–21. Treats learning disabilities; behavior disorders; general psychosocial disorders; substance abuse; eating disorders; post-traumatic stress disorder.

Contact Marianne Mallon, Intake and Referral Coordinator, main address above. Phone: 215-831-4870.

FRIENDS HOSPITAL YOUNG PEOPLE'S SERVICES
4641 Roosevelt Boulevard
Philadelphia, Pennsylvania 19124
215-831-4600; Fax: 215-289-9260

General Information Psychiatric hospital for adolescents, adults. 24 beds for adolescents. Open year-round. Patient security: partially locked; will pursue and return runaways. Suburban setting. Independent not-for-profit facility. Licensed by state of Pennsylvania. Accredited by JCAHO.

Participants Accepts: male and female adolescents ages 12–21; male and female adults ages 21 and up. Average stay: 30 days. Admission: one parent. Treats learning disabilities; behavior disorders; general psychosocial disorders; substance abuse; eating disorders; compulsive/addictive disorders other than substance abuse and eating disorders; post-traumatic stress disorder; thought, mood, and personality disorders. Accepts the mobility impaired; the vision impaired; those with a history of harm to themselves and others; those receiving psychotropic medication.

Program Treatment modalities: Twelve Step Recovery for dual diagnosis; milieu therapy. Family treatment program available.

THE FRONT DOOR RESIDENTIAL PROGRAM
800 North 8th Street
Columbia, Missouri 65201
314-875-1366

General Information Residential treatment/subacute facility for children, adolescents. Patient security: staff secured. Not-for-profit facility affiliated with Comprehensive Human Services, Columbia, MO. Licensed by state of Missouri.

Participants Accepts: male children; male adolescents. Average stay: 8 months. Admission: one parent, all parties who share custody, court order, voluntary, depending on program. Treats learning disabilities; behavior disorders; general psychosocial disorders; substance abuse.

Staff Staff is all male.

Contact Rick Blakemore, Program Director, main address above. Phone: 314-875-1366.

GATEWAY COMMUNITY SERVICES, INC.—NANCY REAGAN TPC VILLAGE
2761 Huffman Boulevard
Jacksonville, Florida 32216
904-646-4889; Fax: 904-646-0791

General Information Residential treatment/subacute facility for adolescents. 46 beds for adolescents. Patient security: staff secured. Not-for-profit facility affiliated with Gateway Community Services, Inc., Jacksonville, FL. Licensed by state of Florida.

Participants Accepts: male and female adolescents. Average stay: 6 months. Admission: one parent, all parties who share custody, court order, voluntary, depending on program. Treats substance abuse. Accepts the mobility impaired; the vision impaired; the hearing impaired; the speech impaired; those with a history of arson; the sexually compulsive; those with a history of harm to themselves and others; those receiving psychotropic medication; non-English speaking individuals; those with a history of epilepsy.

Staff Staff is 40% male, 60% female.

Additional Services Outpatient services for males and females ages 13–17. Treats substance abuse.

Contact Linda Wierzba, Intake-Assessment Counselor, main address above. Phone: 904-646-4889. Fax: 904-646-0791.

GATEWAY MEADOWBROOK
Moffett Run Road
Aliquippa, Pennsylvania 15001
412-766-8700; Fax: 412-375-8815

General Information Drug and alcohol rehabilitation center for adolescents. Open year-round. Patient security: staff secured; no runaway pursuit. Suburban setting. Not-for-profit facility affiliated with Gateway Rehabilitation Center, Aliquippa, PA. Licensed by state of Pennsylvania. Accredited by JCAHO.

Participants Accepts: male and female adolescents ages 13–21. Average stay: 30 days. Admission: all parties who share custody. Treats learning disabilities; behavior disorders; general psychosocial disorders; substance abuse; eating disorders; compulsive/addictive disorders other than substance abuse and eating disorders; post-traumatic stress disorder; thought, mood, and personality disorders. Accepts the mobility impaired; the vision impaired; the hearing impaired; the speech impaired; those with a history of harm to themselves and others; those receiving psychotropic medication; non-English speaking individuals; those with a history of epilepsy. Special

programs for the developmentally disabled; the vision impaired; the hearing impaired.

Program Treatment modalities: Twelve Step Recovery; Gestalt; psychodrama; adventure-based counseling. Family treatment program available.

Staff 1.5 full-time direct-care staff members per adolescent. Total facility staff includes 1 physician, 1 psychologist, 1 psychiatrist, 8 registered nurses, 1 social worker (non-MSW), 1 teacher, 4 counselors, 1 occupational/recreational therapist, 1 dietician, 7 other direct-care staff members. Staff is 50% male, 50% female.

Facilities Single building; males and females in co-educational units. Separate dining by residential unit available. Basketball courts, game room, gymnasium, playing fields, ropes course.

Education Academic program available at no charge. Serves ages 13–18, ungraded. 1 teacher on staff.

Costs Average cost: $395 per stay. Accepts private insurance, group insurance, Blue Cross/Blue Shield, public funds.

Contact Sam Anderson, Community Relations Representative, main address above. Phone: 412-766-8700. Fax: 412-375-8815.

GATEWAY YOUTH AND FAMILY SERVICES—RESIDENTIAL SERVICES
6350 Main Street
Williamsville, New York 14221
716-633-7266; Fax: 716-633-7395

General Information Residential treatment/subacute facility for children, adolescents. Open year-round. Patient security: staff secured; will pursue and return runaways. Suburban setting. Independent not-for-profit facility. Licensed by state of New York. Accredited by New York State Department of Social Services, Council on Accreditation of Services for Families and Children, Eagle Program, United Methodist Association of Health and Welfare Ministries.

Participants Accepts: male and female children ages 10–12; male and female adolescents ages 13–17. Average stay: 411 days. Admission: court order. Treats learning disabilities; behavior disorders; general psychosocial disorders; substance abuse; eating disorders; post-traumatic stress disorder; thought, mood, and personality disorders. Accepts the speech impaired; those with a history of harm to themselves and others; those receiving psychotropic medication. Special programs for the speech impaired. Largest number of participants from New York.

Program Treatment modalities: behavior modification; reality therapy; family systems. Family treatment program available.

Staff Total facility staff includes 1 physician, 1 psychologist, 1 psychiatrist, 1 registered nurse, 13 MSW social workers, 11 teachers, 4 occupational/recreational therapists, 1 speech pathologist, 1 therapist, 48 other direct-care staff members. Staff is 32% male, 68% female.

Facilities Multiple buildings; males and females in separate units. Central dining. Basketball courts, gymnasium, outdoor swimming pool, playing fields, nature trail.

Education Academic program available. Serves ages 10–17, grades K–12. 11 teachers on staff. Curriculum accredited or approved by New York State Education Department. Cost of educational program covered by local school district. Organized sports program offered.

Costs Average cost: $60,000 per year. Accepts public funds.

Additional Services Supervised Independent Living Program for males and females ages 16–21. Treats behavior disorders; general psychosocial disorders.- Therapeutic preschool for males and females ages 2–5. Treats learning disabilities; behavior disorders; general psychosocial disorders.Day school/day treatment for males and females ages 6–17. Treats learning disabilities; behavior disorders; general psychosocial disorders; thought, mood, and personality disorders.

Contact Bruce Nisbet, Executive Vice President, main address above. Phone: 716-633-7266. Fax: 716-633-7395.

GATEWAY YOUTH CARE FOUNDATION
25480 West Cedarcrest Lane
Lake Villa, Illinois 60046
708-356-8292

General Information Drug and alcohol rehabilitation center for adolescents. 39 beds for adolescents. Patient security: staff secured. Not-for-profit facility affiliated with Gateway Foundation, Chicago, IL. Licensed by state of Illinois. Accredited by Commission on Accreditation of Rehabilitation Facilities.

Participants Accepts: male adolescents. Average stay: 4 months. Admission: one parent, all parties who share custody, court order, voluntary, depending on program. Treats substance abuse. Accepts the mobility impaired; the vision impaired; the hearing impaired; the speech impaired; those receiving psychotropic medication.

Staff Staff is 50% male, 50% female.

Costs Average cost: $120 per day.

Contact Peggy Decker, Intake Coordinator, main address above. Phone: 708-356-8292.

GELLER HOUSE
77 Chicago Avenue
Staten Island, New York 10305
718-442-7828; Fax: 718-720-0762

General Information Diagnostic/emergency care for adolescents. 24 beds for adolescents. Open year-round. Patient security: unlocked; will pursue and return runaways. Suburban setting. Not-for-profit facility affiliated with Jewish Board of Family and Children's Services, New York, NY. Licensed by state of New York. Accredited by JCAHO.

Participants Accepts: male and female adolescents ages 11–16. Average stay: 60 days. Admission: court order, Child Welfare Administration referral, depending on program. Treats learning disabilities; behavior disorders; general psychosocial disorders; substance abuse; eating disorders; post-traumatic stress disorder; thought, mood, and personality disorders. Accepts those with a history of harm to themselves and others; those receiving psychotropic medication; non-English speaking individuals.

Program Treatment modalities: psychodynamic; milieu therapy. Family treatment program available.

Staff Total facility staff includes 2 physicians, 1 psychologist, 1 psychiatrist, 3 registered nurses, 2 practical/vocational nurses, 2 MSW social workers, 6 social workers (non-MSW), 1 teacher, 15 other direct-care staff members.

Facilities Single building; males and females in separate units. Basketball courts, game room.

Education Academic program available at no charge. Serves ages 11–16, ungraded. 1 teacher on staff. Curriculum accredited or approved by New York State Education Department. Cost of educational program covered by local school district.

Costs Accepts public funds.

Contact Beryl Kende, Director, main address above. Phone: 718-442-7828. Fax: 718-720-0762.

THE GERMAINE LAWRENCE SCHOOL
18 Claremont Avenue
Arlington, Massachusetts 02174
617-648-6200; Fax: 617-646-9106

General Information   Residential treatment/subacute facility for adolescents. 58 beds for adolescents. Open year-round. Patient security: staff secured; will pursue and return runaways. Suburban setting. Independent not-for-profit facility. Licensed by state of Massachusetts.

Participants   Accepts: female adolescents ages 12–22. Average stay: 14 months. Admission: all parties who share custody. Treats learning disabilities; behavior disorders; general psychosocial disorders; substance abuse; eating disorders; compulsive/addictive disorders other than substance abuse and eating disorders; post-traumatic stress disorder; thought, mood, and personality disorders. Accepts the vision impaired; those with a history of arson; the sexually compulsive; those with a history of harm to themselves and others; those receiving psychotropic medication; those with a history of epilepsy; sexual abuse survivors. Largest number of participants from Massachusetts, New Hampshire, Rhode Island.

Program   Treatment modalities: cognitive-behavioral; Twelve Step Recovery; psychoeducational; psychodynamic. Family treatment program available.

Staff   2.3 full-time direct-care staff members per adolescent. Total facility staff includes 3 psychologists, 1 psychiatrist, 1 practical/vocational nurse, 13 MSW social workers, 12 teachers, 1 occupational/ recreational therapist, 93 therapists, 5 other direct-care staff members. Staff is 10% male, 90% female.

Facilities   Multiple buildings. Separate dining by residential unit available. Basketball courts, gymnasium, playing fields, fitness center equipped with cardiovascular fitness equipment and aerobic dance floor.

Education   Academic program available at no charge. Serves ages 12–22, grades 7–12. 12 teachers on staff. Curriculum accredited or approved by Department of Education. Cost of educational program sometimes covered by local school district.

Costs   Average cost: $178 per day. Accepts private insurance, public funds.

Additional Services   School for females ages 12–22. Treats learning disabilities; behavior disorders; general psychosocial disorders; substance abuse; eating disorders; compulsive/addictive disorders other than substance abuse and eating disorders; post-traumatic stress disorder; thought, mood, and personality disorders.

Contact   Nora Frank, Director of Admissions, main address above. Phone: 617-648-6200. Fax: 617-646-9106.

GILL HOUSE
740 North 6th Street
Steubenville, Ohio 43952
614-282-5338

General Information   Residential treatment/subacute facility for adolescents. 11 beds for adolescents. Patient security: staff secured. Not-for-profit facility affiliated with Jefferson County Mental Health Services Board, Inc., Steubenville, OH. Licensed by state of Ohio.

Participants   Accepts: male adolescents. Average stay: 1 year. Admission: one parent, all parties who share custody, court order, voluntary, depending on program. Treats learning disabilities; behavior disorders; general psychosocial disorders; thought, mood, and personality disorders.

Staff   .7 full-time direct-care staff member per adolescent. Staff is 10% male, 90% female.

Costs   Average cost: $4500 per month.

Contact   Deborah McGee, Administrative Director, main address above. Phone: 614-282-5338.

GOOD HOPE CENTER NETWORK
P.O. Box 470
East Greenwich, Rhode Island 02818
401-826-2750

General Information   Drug and alcohol rehabilitation center for children, adolescents, adults. Open year-round. Patient security: staff secured. Rural setting. Independent for-profit facility. Licensed by state of Rhode Island. Accredited by JCAHO.

Participants   Accepts: male children; male adolescents ages 12–18; male and female adults ages 18–80. Average stay: 35 days. Admission: all parties who share custody. Treats learning disabilities; behavior disorders; general psychosocial disorders; substance abuse; eating disorders; compulsive/addictive disorders other than substance abuse and eating disorders; thought, mood, and personality disorders. Accepts the mobility impaired; the vision impaired; the hearing impaired; the speech impaired; the sexually compulsive; those with a history of harm to themselves and others; those receiving psychotropic medication; non-English speaking individuals; those with a history of epilepsy. Special programs for those with AIDS.

Program   Treatment modalities: Twelve Step Recovery; behavior modification. Family treatment program available.

Staff   Total facility staff includes 2 physicians, 2 psychologists, 1 psychiatrist, 2 registered nurses, 2

MSW social workers, 1 social worker (non-MSW), 11 counselors, 1 therapist, 1 dietician. Staff is 35% male, 65% female.

Facilities   Multiple buildings; males and females in coeducational units. Residential quarters shared with adults. Central dining (shared with adults). Basketball courts, game room, playing fields, volleyball.

Education   Educational arrangements: in-house consultants or off-site. Educational program held on-site at no charge. Educational program held off-site at no charge. Cost of educational program sometimes covered by local school district. Organized sports program offered.

Costs   Average cost: $350 per day. Accepts private insurance, group insurance, Blue Cross/Blue Shield, public funds.

Additional Services   Outpatient services for males and females ages 11–18. Treats learning disabilities; behavior disorders; general psychosocial disorders; substance abuse; eating disorders; compulsive/addictive disorders other than substance abuse and eating disorders; thought, mood, and personality disorders.

Contact   Peter Fratantuono, Clinic Director, main address above. Phone: 401-826-2750.

GOODLARK MEDICAL CENTER DIAGNOSTIC ACUTE CARE UNIT
111 Highway 70 East
Dickson, Tennessee 37055
615-441-2512; Fax: 615-441-2519

General Information   Acute care psychiatric unit for children, adolescents. Patient security: staff secured. Not-for-profit facility affiliated with Residential Management Services, Dickson, TN. Licensed by state of Tennessee. Accredited by JCAHO.

Participants   Accepts: male and female children; male and female adolescents. Average stay: 30 days. Admission: one parent, all parties who share custody, court order, voluntary, depending on program. Treats autistic disorders; learning disabilities; behavior disorders; general psychosocial disorders; eating disorders; post-traumatic stress disorder; thought, mood, and personality disorders.

Staff   Staff is 50% male, 50% female.

Costs   Average cost: $550 per day.

Contact   Kim Webb, Business Manager, main address above. Phone: 615-441-2512. Fax: 615-441-2519.

GOODLARK RESIDENTIAL TREATMENT CENTER
222 Church Street
Dickson, Tennessee 37055
615-446-3900; Fax: 615-446-3985

General Information   Residential treatment/subacute facility for children, adolescents. Patient security: partially locked. For-profit facility affiliated with Residential Management Services, Dickson, TN. Licensed by state of Tennessee. Accredited by JCAHO.

Participants   Accepts: male children; male adolescents. Average stay: 6 months. Admission: one parent, all parties who share custody, court order, voluntary, depending on program. Treats learning disabilities; behavior disorders; substance abuse; post-traumatic stress disorder; thought, mood, and personality disorders.

Staff   Staff is 70% male, 30% female.

Education   Academic program available at no charge. Serves ages 10–18, grades K–12. Curriculum accredited or approved by State of Tennessee. Organized sports program offered.

Costs   Average cost: $400 per day.

Contact   Kim Moore, Admissions Director, main address above. Phone: 800-467-2206. Fax: 615-446-3985.

GOSNOLD TREATMENT CENTER
200 Ter Heun Drive
Falmouth, Massachusetts 02540
508-540-6550; Fax: 508-540-6550

General Information   Drug and alcohol rehabilitation center for adolescents, adults. 32 beds for adolescents. Open year-round. Patient security: staff secured; will pursue and return runaways. Small town setting. Independent not-for-profit facility. Licensed by state of Massachusetts. Accredited by JCAHO.

Participants   Accepts: male and female adolescents ages 13–18; male and female adults ages 18 and up. Average stay: 40 days. Admission: one parent, voluntary, depending on program. Treats substance abuse. Accepts the hearing impaired; the speech impaired; those receiving psychotropic medication; those with a history of epilepsy. Special programs for the hearing impaired.

Program   Treatment modalities: Twelve Step Recovery; adventure-based counseling; group and individual psychotherapy. Family treatment program available.

Staff 1.1 full-time direct-care staff members per adolescent. Total facility staff includes 1 physician, 2 psychologists, 13 registered nurses, 1 practical/vocational nurse, 3 MSW social workers, 1 teacher, 12 counselors, 1 occupational/recreational therapist, 1 dietician. Staff is 35% male, 65% female.

Facilities Multiple buildings; males and females in separate units. Residential arrangements vary depending on program. Central dining (shared with adults). Game room, gymnasium, playing fields, ropes course.

Education Academic program available at no charge. Serves ages 13–17, grades 8–12. 1 teacher on staff. Curriculum accredited or approved by Massachusetts Department of Education. Cost of educational program covered by local school district.

Costs Average cost: $135 per day. Accepts private insurance, group insurance, Blue Cross/Blue Shield.

Contact Raymond Tamasi, Vice President, main address above. Phone: 508-540-6550. Fax: 508-540-6550.

GRACIE SQUARE HOSPITAL
420 East 76th Street
New York, New York 10021
212-988-4400; Fax: 212-472-1431

General Information Psychiatric hospital for adolescents. 20 beds for adolescents. Patient security: partially locked. Independent for-profit facility. Licensed by state of New York. Accredited by JCAHO.

Participants Accepts: male and female adolescents. Average stay: 30 days. Admission: one parent, voluntary, involuntary with physician's consent, depending on program. Treats eating disorders.

Contact Dr. Charles Murkofsky, Medical Director, Eating Disorders Program, main address above. Phone: 800-382-2832.

GRAFTON SCHOOL, INC.
P.O. Box 112
Route 7 East
Berryville, Virginia 22611
703-955-2400; Fax: 703-955-3496

General Information School for children, adolescents, adults. 48 beds for children; 91 beds for adolescents; 169 beds total. Open year-round. Patient security: unlocked. Rural setting. Independent not-for-profit facility. Licensed by state of Virginia. Accredited by Department of Mental Health and Mental Retardation, Department of Social Services and Corrections.

Participants Accepts: male and female children ages 3–12; male and female adolescents ages 13–17; male and female adults ages 18–24. Average stay: 3 years. Admission: one parent, all parties who share custody, court order, voluntary, depending on program. Treats autistic disorders; learning disabilities; behavior disorders; general psychosocial disorders; thought, mood, and personality disorders. Accepts the mobility impaired; the vision impaired; the hearing impaired; the speech impaired; those with a history of harm to themselves and others; those receiving psychotropic medication; those with a history of epilepsy. Special programs for the developmentally disabled; the hearing impaired; the speech impaired. Largest number of participants from Virginia, Maryland, D.C.

Program Treatment modalities: behavior modification; whole-language approach; facilitative communication.

Staff 2.1 full-time direct-care staff members per child or adolescent. Total facility staff includes 2 registered nurses, 1 practical/vocational nurse, 33 teachers, 8 counselors, 6 occupational/recreational therapists, 13 speech pathologists, 1 dietician, 234 other direct-care staff members. Staff is 32% male, 68% female.

Facilities Multiple buildings; males and females in separate units. Residential quarters shared with adults. Central dining (shared with adults). Basketball courts, gymnasium, playing fields.

Education School serves ages 3–21, ungraded. 33 teachers on staff. Curriculum accredited or approved by Virginia Department of Education. Organized sports program offered.

Costs Average cost: $70,000 per year. Accepts medicaid, public funds.

Additional Services Residential or sub-acute services for males and females ages 3–21. Treats autistic disorders; learning disabilities; behavior disorders; general psychosocial disorders; post-traumatic stress disorder; thought, mood, and personality disorders. Day program for males and females ages 3–21. Treats autistic disorders; learning disabilities; behavior disorders; general psychosocial disorders; post-traumatic stress disorder; thought, mood, and personality disorders.

Contact Admissions Office, main address above. Phone: 703-955-2400. Fax: 703-955-3496.

GRANDVIEW PSYCHIATRIC RESOURCE CENTER
88 Grandview Avenue
Waterbury, Connecticut 06708
203-573-7295; Fax: 203-573-6284

General Information General hospital for adolescents, adults. 14 beds for adolescents. Open year-round. Patient security: entirely locked; will pursue and return runaways. Urban setting. Independent not-for-profit facility. Licensed by state of Connecticut. Accredited by JCAHO.

Participants Accepts: male and female adolescents ages 12–18; male and female adults ages 18 and up. Average stay: 22 days. Admission: one parent, voluntary, depending on program. Treats behavior disorders; general psychosocial disorders; substance abuse; eating disorders; compulsive/addictive disorders other than substance abuse and eating disorders; post-traumatic stress disorder; thought, mood, and personality disorders. Accepts the vision impaired; the hearing impaired; the speech impaired; those receiving psychotropic medication; non-English speaking individuals; those with a history of epilepsy. Special programs for the chronically ill.

Program Family treatment program available.

Staff Total facility staff includes 3 psychologists, 10 psychiatrists, 34 registered nurses, 6 MSW social workers, 17 social workers (non-MSW), 4 occupational/recreational therapists.

Facilities Multiple buildings; males and females in coeducational units. Separate residential quarters for adolescents. In-room dining available Basketball courts, game room, gymnasium, outdoor tennis courts, playing fields.

Education Academic program available at no charge. Serves ages 12–18, ungraded. Curriculum accredited or approved by school district tutor.

Costs Average cost: $900 per stay. Accepts private insurance, group insurance, medicare, medicaid, Blue Cross/Blue Shield, public funds.

Additional Services Outpatient services for males and females ages 12 and up. Treats behavior disorders; general psychosocial disorders; substance abuse; eating disorders; compulsive/addictive disorders other than substance abuse and eating disorders; post-traumatic stress disorder; thought, mood, and personality disorders.

Contact Anthony Teta, Director of Administration, main address above. Phone: 203-573-6288. Fax: 203-573-6284.

GRANT-BLACKFORD MENTAL HEALTH, INC.
505 Wabash Avenue
Marion, Indiana 46952
317-662-3971; Fax: 317-662-7480

General Information Community mental health center with inpatient unit for children, adolescents. Patient security: entirely locked. Independent not-for-profit facility. Licensed by state of Indiana. Accredited by JCAHO.

Participants Accepts: male and female children; male and female adolescents. Average stay: 30 days. Admission: all parties who share custody, voluntary, depending on program. Treats autistic disorders; behavior disorders; general psychosocial disorders; substance abuse; eating disorders; compulsive/addictive disorders other than substance abuse and eating disorders; post-traumatic stress disorder; thought, mood, and personality disorders.

Staff Staff is 30% male, 70% female.

Contact Sharon Lane, Executive Assistant, main address above. Phone: 317-662-3971.

GRANT HOSPITAL OF CHICAGO
550 West Webster Avenue
Chicago, Illinois 60614
312-883-2000; Fax: 312-883-5168

General Information General hospital for children, adolescents. Patient security: staff secured. Independent not-for-profit facility. Licensed by state of Illinois. Accredited by JCAHO.

Participants Accepts: male and female children; male and female adolescents. Average stay: 6 days. Admission: court order, Department of Children and Family Services, private agency referrals, depending on program. Treats autistic disorders; learning disabilities; behavior disorders; general psychosocial disorders; eating disorders; post-traumatic stress disorder; thought, mood, and personality disorders.

Contact Dr. Howard Levy, Medical Director, Pediatric Ecology Program, main address above. Phone: 312-883-3555.

GRAYDON MANOR
301 Children's Center Road
Leesburg, Virginia 22075
703-777-3485; Fax: 703-777-4887

General Information   Residential treatment/subacute facility for children, adolescents. 17 beds for children; 44 beds for adolescents; 61 beds total. Open year-round. Patient security: staff secured; will pursue and return runaways. Small town setting. Not-for-profit facility affiliated with National Children's Rehabilitation Center, Leesburg, VA. Licensed by state of Virginia. Accredited by JCAHO.

Participants   Accepts: male children ages 7–12; male and female adolescents ages 13–18. Average stay: 270 days. Admission: all parties who share custody, voluntary, depending on program. Treats learning disabilities; behavior disorders; general psychosocial disorders; substance abuse; eating disorders; post-traumatic stress disorder; thought, mood, and personality disorders. Accepts those with a history of harm to themselves and others; those receiving psychotropic medication; those with a history of epilepsy. Largest number of participants from Virginia, Maryland, D.C.

Program   Treatment modalities: individual and group psychotherapy; family therapy; psychopharmocology; social learning models. Family treatment program available.

Staff   1.1 full-time direct-care staff members per child or adolescent. Total facility staff includes 2 physicians, 2 psychologists, 3 psychiatrists, 8 registered nurses, 2 practical/vocational nurses, 7 MSW social workers, 9 teachers, 30 counselors, 1 occupational/recreational therapist, 2 therapists, 1 dietician.

Facilities   Multiple buildings; males and females in separate units. Central dining. Basketball courts, game room, gymnasium, outdoor swimming pool, outdoor tennis courts, playing fields, ropes course.

Education   Academic program available at no charge. Serves ages 7–18. 9 teachers on staff. Curriculum accredited or approved by States of Virginia and Maryland and the District of Columbia. Cost of educational program sometimes covered by local school district.

Costs   Average cost: $350 per day. Accepts private insurance, group insurance, medicaid, Blue Cross/Blue Shield, public funds.

Additional Services   Outpatient services for males and females ages 2 and up. Treats learning disabilities; behavior disorders; general psychosocial disorders; substance abuse; eating disorders; compulsive/addictive disorders other than substance abuse and eating disorders; post-traumatic stress disorder; thought, mood, and personality disorders.

Contact   William J. Kropp, Director of Marketing and Admissions, main address above. Phone: 703-777-3485. Fax: 703-777-4887.

GRAY LODGE
105 Spring Street
Hartford, Connecticut 06105
203-522-9363

General Information   Residential treatment/subacute facility for children, adolescents. Open year-round. Patient security: entirely locked; no runaway pursuit. Urban setting. Independent not-for-profit facility. Licensed by state of Connecticut. Accredited by Department of Children and Youth Services.

Participants   Accepts: female children and adolescents ages 12–18. Admission: all parties who share custody, court order, depending on program. Treats learning disabilities; behavior disorders; substance abuse. Accepts those receiving psychotropic medication.

Program   Family treatment program available.

Staff   Total facility staff includes 1 registered nurse, 4 teachers, 3 counselors. Staff is 34% male, 66% female.

Facilities   Single building. Central dining (shared with adults).

Education   Academic program available at additional cost. Serves ages 12–18, grades 7–12. 4 teachers on staff. Cost of educational program covered by local school district.

Costs   Average cost: $20,000 per stay. Accepts public funds.

Additional Services   Drug and alcohol rehabilitation services for females ages 12–18. Treats learning disabilities; behavior disorders; general psychosocial disorders.

Contact   David Luce, Administrative Director, main address above. Phone: 203-522-9363.

GREENBRIAR HOSPITAL
201 Greenbriar Boulevard
Covington, Louisiana 70433
504-893-2970; Fax: 504-893-6801

General Information   Psychiatric hospital for children, adolescents, adults. Open year-round. Patient security: entirely locked; will pursue and return runaways. Small town setting. For-profit facility affiliated with Ramsey Health Care, Inc., New Orleans, LA. Licensed by state of Louisiana. Accredited by JCAHO; National Association of Private Psychiatric Hospitals.

Participants Accepts: male and female children ages 9–12; male and female adolescents ages 13–17; male and female adults ages 18 and up. Average stay: 20 days. Admission: one parent, all parties who share custody, voluntary, depending on program. Treats autistic disorders; learning disabilities; behavior disorders; general psychosocial disorders; substance abuse; eating disorders; compulsive/addictive disorders other than substance abuse and eating disorders; post-traumatic stress disorder; thought, mood, and personality disorders. Accepts the mobility impaired; the vision impaired; the hearing impaired; the speech impaired; those with a history of arson; the sexually compulsive; those with a history of harm to themselves and others; those receiving psychotropic medication; those with a history of epilepsy. Special programs for the chronically ill; the mobility impaired; the developmentally disabled; the vision impaired; the hearing impaired; the speech impaired.

Program Treatment modalities: psychodynamic; Twelve Step Recovery; behavioral program component; pharmacological. Family treatment program available.

Staff Total facility staff includes 3 psychologists, 11 psychiatrists, 50 registered nurses, 2 practical/vocational nurses, 4 social workers (non-MSW), 4 teachers, 2 occupational/recreational therapists, 1 dietician, 32 other direct-care staff members.

Facilities Single building; males and females in co-educational units. Central dining (shared with adults). Basketball courts, gymnasium, outdoor swimming pool, outdoor tennis courts, ropes course.

Education Academic program available at no charge. Serves grades 1–12. 4 teachers on staff. Curriculum accredited or approved by Saint Lammany Parish School Board. Cost of educational program covered by local school district.

Costs Accepts private insurance, group insurance, medicare, Blue Cross/Blue Shield.

Contact Harriet Pickett, Marketing Director, main address above. Phone: 504-893-2970. Fax: 504-893-6801.

GREEN CHIMNEYS SCHOOL
Putnam Lake Road
P.O. Box 719
Brewster, New York 10509
914-279-2995; Fax: 914-279-2714

General Information Residential treatment/subacute facility for children, adolescents. 88 beds for children; 14 beds for adolescents; 102 beds total. Open year-round. Patient security: staff secured; will pursue and return runaways. Suburban setting. Independent not-for-profit facility. Licensed by state of New York. Accredited by JCAHO.

Participants Accepts: male and female children ages 6–12; male and female adolescents ages 12–21. Average stay: 2 years. Admission: all parties who share custody, court order, referral by local social service/public education authority, depending on program. Treats learning disabilities; behavior disorders; general psychosocial disorders; post-traumatic stress disorder; thought, mood, and personality disorders. Accepts the mobility impaired; the vision impaired; the hearing impaired; the speech impaired; those with a history of harm to themselves and others; those receiving psychotropic medication; those with a history of epilepsy. Special programs for the mobility impaired; the vision impaired; the hearing impaired; the speech impaired.

Program Treatment modalities: milieu therapy; animal-assisted therapy; psychotherapy; re-education. Family treatment program available.

Staff 1.6 full-time direct-care staff members per child or adolescent. Total facility staff includes 1 physician, 3 psychologists, 6 psychiatrists, 5 registered nurses, 6 practical/vocational nurses, 11 MSW social workers, 1 social worker (non-MSW), 29 teachers, 60 counselors, 4 occupational/recreational therapists, 1 speech pathologist, 38 therapists, 1 dietician. Staff is 41% male, 59% female.

Facilities Multiple buildings; males and females in separate units. Central dining (shared with adults). Basketball courts, game room, gymnasium, horseback riding, indoor swimming pool, playing fields, ropes course, farm and wildlife program.

Education Academic program available. Serves ages 6–21, ungraded. 29 teachers on staff. Curriculum accredited or approved by New York State Education Department. Cost of educational program covered by local school district. Organized sports program offered.

Costs Accepts private insurance, group insurance, medicaid, Blue Cross/Blue Shield, public funds.

Contact Myra M. Ross, main address above. Phone: 914-279-2995 Ext. 218. Fax: 914-279-2714.

GREENLEAF CENTER, INC.
2712 East Johnson Avenue
Jonesboro, Arkansas 72401
501-932-2800; Fax: 501-932-2800 Ext. 103

General Information Psychiatric hospital for adolescents. Patient security: entirely locked. For-profit facility affiliated with Greenleaf Health Systems, Chattanooga, TN. Accredited by JCAHO.

Participants Accepts: male and female adolescents. Average stay: 35 days. Admission: one parent, all parties who share custody, court order, voluntary, depending on program. Treats autistic disorders; learning disabilities; behavior disorders; general psychosocial disorders; substance abuse; eating disorders; compulsive/addictive disorders other than substance abuse and eating disorders; post-traumatic stress disorder; thought, mood, and personality disorders.

Contact SueAnn Pace, Marketing Director, main address above.

GREENLEAF CENTER, INC.
500 Greenleaf Circle
Fort Oglethorpe, Georgia 30742
706-861-4357; Fax: 706-866-3376

General Information Psychiatric hospital for children, adolescents. 10 beds for children; 24 beds for adolescents; 34 beds total. Open year-round. Patient security: partially locked; no runaway pursuit. Small town setting. For-profit facility affiliated with Greenleaf Health Systems, Chattanooga, TN. Licensed by state of Georgia. Accredited by JCAHO.

Participants Accepts: male and female children ages 3–12; male and female adolescents ages 12–18. Average stay: 21 days. Admission: one parent, all parties who share custody, depending on program. Treats learning disabilities; behavior disorders; general psychosocial disorders; substance abuse; eating disorders; compulsive/addictive disorders other than substance abuse and eating disorders; post-traumatic stress disorder; thought, mood, and personality disorders. Accepts the mobility impaired; the vision impaired; the hearing impaired; the speech impaired; those with a history of arson; the sexually compulsive; those with a history of harm to themselves and others; those receiving psychotropic medication; non-English speaking individuals; those with a history of epilepsy. Special programs for the developmentally disabled; the vision impaired; the hearing impaired; the speech impaired; those with AIDS.

Program Treatment modalities: Twelve Step Recovery. Family treatment program available.

Staff Total facility staff includes 21 physicians, 9 psychologists, 10 psychiatrists, 12 registered nurses, 3 practical/vocational nurses, 6 MSW social workers, 3 teachers, 6 counselors, 2 occupational/recreational therapists, 2 dieticians, 5 other direct-care staff members.

Facilities Males and females in coeducational units. Central dining (shared with adults), separate dining by residential unit, in-room dining available. Basketball courts, game room, gymnasium, indoor swimming pool, outdoor swimming pool, outdoor tennis courts, ropes course, nature walk, greenhouse, ceramics shop.

Education Academic program available at no charge. Serves ages 4–18, grades K–12. 3 teachers on staff. Organized sports program offered.

Costs Accepts private insurance, group insurance, medicare, Blue Cross/Blue Shield.

Additional Services Drug and alcohol rehabilitation services for males and females ages 12–18. Treats learning disabilities; behavior disorders; general psychosocial disorders; substance abuse; eating disorders; compulsive/addictive disorders other than substance abuse and eating disorders; post-traumatic stress disorder; thought, mood, and personality disorders. Outpatient services for males and females ages 3–18. Treats behavior disorders; substance abuse; eating disorders; compulsive/addictive disorders other than substance abuse and eating disorders; post-traumatic stress disorder; thought, mood, and personality disorders. Residential or sub-acute services for males and females ages 4–18. Treats learning disabilities; behavior disorders; general psychosocial disorders; substance abuse; eating disorders; compulsive/addictive disorders other than substance abuse and eating disorders; post-traumatic stress disorder; thought, mood, and personality disorders. Camping program for males and females ages 8–13. Treats learning disabilities; behavior disorders; general psychosocial disorders.

Contact Robin Howard, Coordinator, Children's Programs, main address above. Phone: 706-861-4357. Fax: 706-866-3376.

GREENWOOD
1000 Old Lancaster Pike
Hockessin, Delaware 19707
302-239-3410; Fax: 302-239-3418

General Information Drug and alcohol rehabilitation center for adolescents. 12 beds for adolescents. Open year-round. Patient security: staff secured; will pursue and return runaways. Suburban setting. For-profit facility affiliated with Forrestvilla, Hockessin, DE. Licensed by state of Delaware. Accredited by JCAHO.

Participants Accepts: male and female adolescents ages 12–17. Average stay: 30 days. Admission: one parent. Treats behavior disorders; substance abuse; eating disorders; compulsive/addictive disorders other than substance abuse and eating disorders; post-traumatic stress disorder; thought, mood, and personality disorders. Accepts the mobility impaired; the hearing impaired; the speech impaired. Largest number of participants from Delaware, Pennsylvania, New Jersey.

Program Treatment modalities: Twelve Step Recovery; psychodynamic group. Family treatment program available.

Staff 1.8 full-time direct-care staff members per adolescent. Total facility staff includes 1 physician, 2 psychologists, 1 psychiatrist, 3 registered nurses, 8 practical/vocational nurses, 1 teacher, 5 counselors, 1 dietician. Staff is 50% male, 50% female.

Facilities Single building; males and females in co-educational units. Residential quarters shared with adults. Central dining (shared with adults). Basketball courts, game room.

Education Academic program available at no charge. Serves ages 12–17, grades 8–12. 1 teacher on staff. Curriculum accredited or approved by Board of Education.

Costs Average cost: $300 per day. Accepts private insurance, group insurance, Blue Cross/Blue Shield, public funds.

Contact A. L. Gibson, Director, Marketing, main address above. Phone: 302-239-3410. Fax: 302-239-3418.

THE GREENWOOD SCHOOL
Watt Pond Road
RR 2, Box 270
Putney, Vermont 05346
802-387-4545; Fax: 802-387-5396

General Information School for children, adolescents. Patient security: staff secured. Independent not-for-profit facility. Licensed by state of Vermont.

Participants Accepts: male children and adolescents ages 8–15. Admission: one parent. Treats learning disabilities.

Staff Staff is 50% male, 50% female.

Facilities Multiple buildings.

Education School serves ages 8–15, ungraded. Curriculum accredited or approved by State of Vermont, New England Association of Schools and Colleges. Organized sports program offered.

Costs Average cost: $27,000 per year. Financial aid available.

Contact John Alexander, Admissions Coordinator, main address above. Phone: 802-387-4545. Fax: 802-387-5396.

See page 428 for full page description.

THE GROVE ADOLESCENT TREATMENT CENTER
320 Riverside Drive
Northampton, Massachusetts 01060
413-586-6210; Fax: 413-586-7852

General Information Residential treatment/subacute facility for adolescents. 19 beds for adolescents. Open year-round. Patient security: staff secured; will pursue and return runaways. Small town setting. Not-for-profit facility affiliated with Tri-County Youth Programs, Inc., Northampton, MA. Licensed by state of Massachusetts. Accredited by JCAHO; Massachusetts Department of Mental Health; Office for Children.

Participants Accepts: male and female adolescents ages 12–21. Average stay: 540 days. Admission: all parties who share custody. Treats learning disabilities; behavior disorders; general psychosocial disorders; substance abuse; eating disorders; compulsive/addictive disorders other than substance abuse and eating disorders; post-traumatic stress disorder; thought, mood, and personality disorders. Accepts the hearing impaired; the speech impaired; those with a history of harm to themselves and others; those receiving psychotropic medication; those with a history of epilepsy. Largest number of participants from Massachusetts.

Program Treatment modalities: psychoeducational; psychodynamic. Family treatment program available.

Staff 2.5 full-time direct-care staff members per adolescent. Total facility staff includes 2 psychologists, 2 registered nurses, 1 MSW social worker, 6 teachers, 1 occupational/recreational therapist, 2 therapists, 33 other direct-care staff members. Staff is 50% male, 50% female.

Facilities Multiple buildings; males and females in both coeducational and separate units depending on program. Separate dining by residential unit available. Basketball courts, playing fields.

Education Academic program available at additional cost. Serves ages 12–21, ungraded. 6 teachers on staff. Cost of educational program covered by local school district. Organized sports program offered.

Costs Average cost: $299 per day. Accepts medicaid, public funds.

Additional Services Outpatient services for males and females ages 12–22. Treats learning disabilities; behavior disorders; general psychosocial disorders; substance abuse; eating disorders; compulsive/addictive disorders other than substance abuse and eating disorders; post-traumatic stress disorder; thought, mood, and personality disorders.

Contact Jennifer Smith, Treatment Coordinator, main address above. Phone: 413-586-6210. Fax: 413-586-7852.

THE GROVE COUNSELING CENTER, INC.
580 Old Sanford-Oviedo Road
Winter Springs, Florida 32708
407-327-1765

General Information Drug and alcohol rehabilitation center for adolescents. Patient security: staff secured. Independent not-for-profit facility. Licensed by state of Florida.

Participants Accepts: male and female adolescents. Average stay: 7 months. Admission: one parent, all parties who share custody, court order, voluntary, depending on program. Treats substance abuse.

Contact Paulette Rhodes, Evaluator, main address above. Phone: 407-327-1765.

GROVE SCHOOL
175 Copse Road
P.O. Box 646
Madison, Connecticut 06443
203-245-2778; Fax: 203-245-6098

General Information Residential treatment/subacute facility for adolescents. 84 beds for adolescents. Open year-round. Patient security: staff secured. Small town setting. Independent for-profit facility. Licensed by state of Connecticut. Accredited by Connecticut Department of Children and Youth Services, American Association of Psychiatric Services for Children, American Association of Childrens' Residential Centers.

Participants Accepts: male and female adolescents ages 11–18. Average stay: 540 days. Admission: one parent, all parties who share custody, voluntary, depending on program. Treats learning disabilities; behavior disorders; general psychosocial disorders; eating disorders; compulsive/addictive disorders other than substance abuse and eating disorders; post-traumatic stress disorder; thought, mood, and personality disorders. Accepts the mobility impaired; the vision impaired; the hearing impaired; the speech impaired; those receiving psychotropic medication. Special programs for the developmentally disabled. Largest number of participants from Connecticut, New Jersey, Rhode Island.

Program Treatment modalities: interpersonal relationships; psychotherapy; group work; activities therapy. Family treatment program available.

Staff Total facility staff includes 2 physicians, 3 psychologists, 4 psychiatrists, 1 registered nurse, 2 MSW social workers, 20 teachers, 3 occupational/recreational therapists, 1 speech pathologist, 1 dietician, 1 other direct-care staff member. Staff is 60% male, 40% female.

Facilities Multiple buildings; males and females in separate units. Residential quarters shared with adults. Central dining (shared with adults). Game room, gymnasium, horseback riding, outdoor swimming pool, playing fields.

Education School serves ages 11–21, grades 5–12. 20 teachers on staff. Curriculum is college-preparatory; diploma granted upon completion. Curriculum accredited or approved by Connecticut State Department of Education. Organized sports program offered.

Costs Accepts private insurance, group insurance, Blue Cross/Blue Shield, public funds.

Contact Ethel A. Chorney, Associate Director/Admissions, main address above. Phone: 203-245-2778. Fax: 203-245-6098.

GROWING TOGETHER, INC.
1013 Lucerne Avenue
Lake Worth, Florida 33460
407-585-0892; Fax: 407-588-9971

General Information Drug and alcohol rehabilitation center and residential treatment facility for adolescents. 40 beds for adolescents. Open year-round. Patient security: unlocked; no runaway pursuit. Small town setting. Independent not-for-profit facility. Licensed by state of Florida. Accredited by JCAHO.

Participants Accepts: male and female adolescents ages 12–21. Average stay: 60 days. Admission: all parties who share custody. Treats behavior disorders; general psychosocial disorders; substance abuse. Accepts those with a history of harm to themselves and others; those receiving psychotropic medication. Largest number of participants from Florida.

Program Treatment modalities: Twelve Step Recovery; cognitive/rational emotive therapy; behavioral; reality therapy. Family treatment program available.

Staff .5 full-time direct-care staff member per adolescent. Total facility staff includes 1 physician, 2 psychologists, 1 psychiatrist, 1 registered nurse, 1 teacher, 10 counselors, 4 therapists, 1 dietician. Staff is 50% male, 50% female.

Facilities Single building; males and females in separate units. Central dining. Game room.

Education Academic program available at no charge. Serves ages 12–21, grades 7–12. 1 teacher on staff. Curriculum accredited or approved by Palm Beach County School Board. Cost of educational program covered by local school district.

Costs Average cost: $8000 per stay. Accepts private insurance, group insurance, Blue Cross/Blue Shield, public funds.

Additional Services Outpatient services for males and females ages 12–21. Treats behavior disorders; general psychosocial disorders; substance abuse.

Contact Mickey Blanchard, Program Director, main address above. Phone: 407-585-0892. Fax: 407-588-9971.

GUNDRY GLASS HOSPITAL
2 North Wickham Road
Baltimore, Maryland 21228
410-644-9917; Fax: 410-368-6082

General Information Psychiatric hospital for children, adolescents, adults. 29 beds for children; 22 beds for adolescents; 85 beds total. Open year-round.

Patient security: entirely locked; no runaway pursuit. Suburban setting. For-profit facility affiliated with Glass Health Systems, Baltimore, MD. Licensed by state of Maryland. Accredited by JCAHO; Health Care Financing Administration.

Participants Accepts: male and female children ages 4–12; male and female adolescents ages 12–17; male and female adults ages 18 and up. Admission: one parent, agency with guardianship, depending on program. Treats autistic disorders; learning disabilities; behavior disorders; general psychosocial disorders; substance abuse; eating disorders; compulsive/addictive disorders other than substance abuse and eating disorders; post-traumatic stress disorder; thought, mood, and personality disorders. Accepts the mobility impaired; the vision impaired; the hearing impaired; the speech impaired; those with a history of arson; the sexually compulsive; those with a history of harm to themselves and others; those receiving psychotropic medication; non-English speaking individuals; those with a history of epilepsy. Special programs for the chronically ill; the mobility impaired; the developmentally disabled; fire setters.

Program Treatment modalities: behavioral; biological; cognitive; educational. Family treatment program available.

Staff Total facility staff includes 3 psychologists, 69 registered nurses, 15 practical/vocational nurses, 9 MSW social workers, 2 teachers, 5 occupational/recreational therapists, 7 therapists, 62 other direct-care staff members.

Facilities Multiple buildings; males and females in coeducational units. Separate residential quarters for children and adolescents. Central dining (not shared with adults). Basketball courts, game room, playing fields.

Education Academic program available at no charge. Serves ages 4–17, ungraded. 2 teachers on staff. Cost of educational program sometimes covered by local school district.

Costs Accepts private insurance, group insurance, medicare, medicaid, Blue Cross/Blue Shield, public funds.

Additional Services Outpatient services for males and females. Treats learning disabilities; behavior disorders; general psychosocial disorders; substance abuse; compulsive/addictive disorders other than substance abuse and eating disorders; post-traumatic stress disorder; thought, mood, and personality disorders. Day treatment for males and females. Treats learning disabilities; behavior disorders; general psychosocial disorders; substance abuse; compulsive/addictive disorders other than substance abuse and eating disorders; post-traumatic stress disorder; thought, mood, and personality disorders.

Contact Elliott Neal White, Chief Operating Officer, Commercenter East, Suite 345, 1777 Reisterstown Road, Pikesville, MD 21208. Phone: 410-484-2700. Fax: 410-484-1949.

HABBERTON HOUSE
P.O. Box 1340
Springdale, Arkansas 72764
501-750-2020; Fax: 501-751-4346

General Information Residential treatment/subacute facility for adolescents. 25 beds for adolescents. Open year-round. Patient security: entirely locked; no runaway pursuit. Small town setting. Not-for-profit facility affiliated with Ozark Guidance Center, Springdale, AR. Licensed by state of Arkansas. Accredited by JCAHO.

Participants Accepts: male and female adolescents ages 11–17. Average stay: 180 days. Admission: all parties who share custody. Treats learning disabilities; behavior disorders; general psychosocial disorders; substance abuse; eating disorders; compulsive/addictive disorders other than substance abuse and eating disorders; post-traumatic stress disorder; thought, mood, and personality disorders. Accepts the mobility impaired; the vision impaired; the hearing impaired; the speech impaired; those with a history of arson; the sexually compulsive; those with a history of harm to themselves and others; those receiving psychotropic medication; those with a history of epilepsy. Special programs for the speech impaired.

Program Treatment modalities: cognitive-behavioral; insight-oriented. Family treatment program available.

Staff 2.4 full-time direct-care staff members per adolescent. Total facility staff includes 1 psychologist, 1 psychiatrist, 5 registered nurses, 3 practical/vocational nurses, 1 MSW social worker, 3 teachers, 1 counselor, 1 occupational/recreational therapist, 1 speech pathologist, 3 therapists, 1 dietician, 40 other direct-care staff members. Staff is 40% male, 60% female.

Facilities Single building; males and females in separate units. Central dining. Basketball courts, game room, gymnasium, playing fields.

Education Academic program available at no charge. Serves ages 11–17, grades 6–12. 3 teachers on staff. Curriculum accredited or approved by Arkansas State Board of Special Education.

Costs Average cost: $350 per day. Accepts private insurance, group insurance, medicaid, Blue Cross/Blue Shield, public funds.

Additional Services Outpatient services for males and females ages 3 and up. Treats learning disabilities; behavior disorders; general psychosocial disorders; substance abuse; eating disorders; compulsive/addictive disorders other than substance abuse and eating disorders; post-traumatic stress disorder; thought, mood, and personality disorders.

Contact Daphne Morris, Admissions Coordinator, main address above. Phone: 501-750-2020. Fax: 501-751-4346.

HALL-BROOKE FOUNDATION
47 Long Lots Road
Westport, Connecticut 06880
203-227-1251; Fax: 203-227-0547

General Information Psychiatric hospital for adolescents, adults. 26 beds for adolescents. Open year-round. Patient security arrangements vary depending on program; will pursue and return runaways. Small town setting. Independent not-for-profit facility. Licensed by state of Connecticut. Accredited by JCAHO.

Participants Accepts: male and female adolescents ages 10–21; male and female adults ages 18 and up. Average stay: 24 days. Admission: one parent, all parties who share custody, court order, voluntary, depending on program. Treats learning disabilities; behavior disorders; general psychosocial disorders; substance abuse; eating disorders; compulsive/addictive disorders other than substance abuse and eating disorders; post-traumatic stress disorder; thought, mood, and personality disorders. Accepts the mobility impaired; the vision impaired; the hearing impaired; the speech impaired; those with a history of arson; the sexually compulsive; those with a history of harm to themselves and others; those receiving psychotropic medication; non-English speaking individuals; those with a history of epilepsy. Special programs for the chronically ill; the mobility impaired; the developmentally disabled; the vision impaired; the hearing impaired; the speech impaired; those with AIDS.

Program Treatment modalities: cognitive and psychodynamic therapy; psychiatric education; stabilization; Twelve Step Recovery. Family treatment program available.

Staff Total facility staff includes 1 physician, 3 psychologists, 8 psychiatrists, 27 registered nurses, 3 practical/vocational nurses, 8 MSW social workers, 6 teachers, 2 counselors, 3 occupational/recreational therapists, 1 dietician, 37 other direct-care staff members.

Facilities Multiple buildings; males and females in coeducational units. Residential arrangements vary depending on program. Central dining (shared with adults), in-room dining available. Basketball courts, game room, playing fields.

Education Academic program available at no charge. Serves ages 10–21, ungraded. 6 teachers on staff. Curriculum accredited or approved by State of Connecticut Department of Education. Cost of educational program covered by local school district. Organized sports program offered.

Costs Average cost: $5500 per week. Accepts private insurance, group insurance, medicare, medicaid, Blue Cross/Blue Shield.

Additional Services Drug and alcohol rehabilitation services for males and females ages 10 and up. Treats learning disabilities; behavior disorders; general psychosocial disorders; substance abuse; eating disorders; compulsive/addictive disorders other than substance abuse and eating disorders; post-traumatic stress disorder; thought, mood, and personality disorders. Outpatient services for males and females ages 10 and up. Treats learning disabilities; behavior disorders; general psychosocial disorders; substance abuse; eating disorders; compulsive/addictive disorders other than substance abuse and eating disorders; post-traumatic stress disorder; thought, mood, and personality disorders. Residential or sub-acute services for males and females ages 10 and up. Treats learning disabilities; behavior disorders; general psychosocial disorders; substance abuse; eating disorders; compulsive/addictive disorders other than substance abuse and eating disorders; post-traumatic stress disorder; thought, mood, and personality disorders. Special education school for males and females ages 10–21. Treats learning disabilities; behavior disorders; general psychosocial disorders; substance abuse; eating disorders; compulsive/addictive disorders other than substance abuse and eating disorders; post-traumatic stress disorder; thought, mood, and personality disorders.

Contact Janet Nevas, Director, Community Relations, main address above. Phone: 203-227-1251 Ext. 231. Fax: 203-227-0547.

HAMPSHIRE COUNTRY SCHOOL
Rindge, New Hampshire 03461
603-899-3325

General Information School for children, adolescents. 15 beds for children; 10 beds for adolescents; 25 beds total. Open year-round. Patient security: un-locked; no runaway pursuit. Rural setting. Independent not-for-profit facility. Licensed by state of New Hampshire.

Participants Accepts: male and female children ages 8–12; male and female adolescents ages 13–17. Average stay: 3 years. Admission: all parties who share custody, voluntary, depending on program. Treats learning disabilities; behavior disorders; general psychosocial disorders. Largest number of participants from New York, Florida, Washington.

Contact William Dickerman, Admissions Director, main address above. Phone: 603-899-3325.

Announcement Hampshire Country School is a personal, highly structured, camplike school for about 30 high-ability boys and girls needing an unusual amount of adult time, attention, and direction. It is not a treatment program. The ideal entering age is from 8 to 12. Students may stay through high school.

HAMPSTEAD HOSPITAL
East Road
Hampstead, New Hampshire 03841
603-329-5311; Fax: 603-329-4746

General Information Psychiatric hospital for children, adolescents. Patient security: partially locked. Independent for-profit facility. Licensed by state of New Hampshire. Accredited by JCAHO.

Participants Accepts: male and female children; male and female adolescents. Average stay: 20 days. Admission: one parent, all parties who share custody, depending on program. Treats autistic disorders; learning disabilities; behavior disorders; general psychosocial disorders; substance abuse; eating disorders; compulsive/addictive disorders other than substance abuse and eating disorders; post-traumatic stress disorder; thought, mood, and personality disorders.

Staff Staff is 33% male, 67% female.

Costs Average cost: $12,000 per stay.

Contact David Haseltine, Director of Admissions, main address above. Phone: 603-329-5311.

THE HARBOR
1405 Clinton Street
Hoboken, New Jersey 07030
201-656-4040; Fax: 201-656-5308

General Information Drug and alcohol rehabilitation center for adolescents. 50 beds for adolescents. Open year-round. Patient security: staff secured; will pursue and return runaways. Urban setting. Independent for-profit facility. Licensed by state of New Jersey. Accredited by JCAHO.

Participants Accepts: male and female adolescents ages 13–19. Average stay: 35 days. Admission: one parent. Treats substance abuse. Accepts the mobility impaired; those receiving psychotropic medication.

Program Treatment modalities: Twelve Step Recovery; group therapy and individual therapy; skills training groups and activity groups; schooling. Family treatment program available.

Staff Total facility staff includes 2 physicians, 1 psychologist, 1 psychiatrist, 4 registered nurses, 3 practical/vocational nurses, 1 MSW social worker, 1 teacher, 7 counselors, 1 occupational/recreational therapist, 2 dieticians, 15 other direct-care staff members. Staff is 73% male, 27% female.

Facilities Single building; males and females in coeducational units. Residential quarters shared with adults. Central dining (shared with adults). Basketball courts, ropes course, weight room.

Education Academic program available at no charge. Serves ages 13–19, grades 8–12. 1 teacher on staff.

Costs Accepts private insurance, group insurance, Blue Cross/Blue Shield.

Additional Services Drug and alcohol rehabilitation services for males and females ages 13–19. Treats substance abuse. Wilderness/survival program for males and females ages 13–19. Treats substance abuse.

Contact Lori Yarusi, Director of Community Relations, main address above. Phone: 201-656-4040. Fax: 201-656-5308.

HARBOURS AT BRENTWOOD
209 Ward Circle
Box 1644
Brentwood, Tennessee 37024
615-373-8700; Fax: 615-373-1899

General Information Drug and alcohol rehabilitation center for adolescents, adults. Open year-round. Patient security: staff secured; no runaway pursuit. Suburban setting. For-profit facility affiliated with First Hospital Corporation, Norfolk, VA. Licensed by state of Tennessee. Accredited by JCAHO.

Participants Accepts: male and female adolescents ages 16–18; male and female adults ages 18–65. Average stay: 14 days. Admission: one parent. Treats substance abuse.

Program Treatment modalities: Twelve Step Recovery; reality therapy; rational emotive therapy. Family treatment program available.

Staff Total facility staff includes 1 physician, 1 psychologist, 1 psychiatrist, 1 registered nurse, 5 practical/vocational nurses, 1 MSW social worker, 4 counselors, 1 dietician, 5 other direct-care staff members.

Facilities Multiple buildings; males and females in coeducational units. Residential quarters shared with adults. Central dining (shared with adults). Basketball courts, game room, indoor swimming pool.

Costs Average cost: $5000 per stay. Accepts private insurance, group insurance, Blue Cross/Blue Shield.

Additional Services Outpatient services for males and females. Treats substance abuse.

Contact Mike Gibbs, Director, Community Relations, main address above. Phone: 615-373-8700. Fax: 615-373-1899.

HARDING HOSPITAL
445 East Granville Road
Worthington, Ohio 43085
614-885-5381; Fax: 614-885-9813

General Information Psychiatric hospital for children, adolescents, adults. 10 beds for children; 50 beds for adolescents; 120 beds total. Open year-round. Patient security: entirely locked; will pursue and return runaways. Suburban setting. Independent not-for-profit facility. Licensed by state of Ohio. Accredited by JCAHO.

Participants Accepts: male and female children ages 1–11; male and female adolescents ages 12–17; male and female adults ages 18 and up. Average stay: 19 days. Admission: one parent, all parties who share custody, court order, depending on program. Treats autistic disorders; learning disabilities; behavior disorders; general psychosocial disorders; substance abuse; eating disorders; compulsive/addictive disorders other than substance abuse and eating disorders; post-traumatic stress disorder; thought, mood, and personality disorders. Accepts the mobility impaired; the vision impaired; the hearing impaired; the speech impaired; those with a history of arson; those with a history of harm to themselves and others; those receiving psychotropic medication; non-English speaking individuals; those with a history of epilepsy. Largest number of participants from Ohio, Michigan, West Virginia.

Program Treatment modalities: psychoeducational; Twelve Step Recovery; biopsychosocial; psychodynamic. Family treatment program available.

Staff 2.7 full-time direct-care staff members per child or adolescent. Total facility staff includes 1 physician, 5 psychologists, 6 psychiatrists, 24 registered nurses, 7 MSW social workers, 8 teachers, 6 occupational/recreational therapists, 1 speech pathologist, 2 dieticians, 12 other direct-care staff members. Staff is 35% male, 65% female.

Facilities Multiple buildings; males and females in coeducational units. Separate residential quarters for children and adolescents. Central dining (shared with adults), separate dining by residential unit available. Basketball courts, game room, gymnasium, outdoor tennis courts, playing fields, ropes course.

Education Academic program available at additional cost. Serves ages 6–21, grades 1–12. 8 teachers on staff. Curriculum accredited or approved by Ohio Education Association. Cost of educational program covered by local school district.

Costs Average cost: $14,500 per stay. Accepts private insurance, group insurance, medicare, Blue Cross/Blue Shield.

Additional Services Drug and alcohol rehabilitation services for males and females ages 11 and up. Treats autistic disorders; learning disabilities; behavior disorders; general psychosocial disorders; substance abuse; eating disorders; compulsive/addictive disorders other than substance abuse and eating disorders; post-traumatic stress disorder; thought, mood, and personality disorders. Outpatient services for males and females ages 2 and up. Treats autistic disorders; learning disabilities; behavior disorders; general psychosocial disorders; substance abuse; eating disorders; compulsive/addictive disorders other than substance abuse and eating disorders; post-traumatic stress disorder; thought, mood, and personality disorders. Residential or sub-acute services for males and females ages 12–18. Treats autistic disorders; learning disabilities; behavior disorders; general psychosocial disorders; substance abuse; eating disorders; compulsive/addictive disorders other than substance abuse and eating disorders; post-traumatic stress disorder; thought, mood, and personality disorders. Full-continuum eating disorders program for males and females ages 12 and up. Treats behavior disorders; general psychosocial disorders; eating disorders; compulsive/addictive disorders other than substance abuse and eating disorders; post-traumatic stress disorder; thought, mood, and personality disorders.

Contact Ray Dutton, Director of Admissions, main address above. Phone: 614-785-7400. Fax: 614-885-9813.

HASLAM CENTER
3006 Lake Brook Boulevard
Knoxville, Tennessee 37909
615-558-6361; Fax: 615-558-8342

General Information Residential treatment/subacute facility for children, adolescents. Patient security: partially locked. Not-for-profit facility affiliated with Child and Family Services, Knoxville, TN. Licensed by state of Tennessee. Accredited by JCAHO; Family Service America, Child Welfare League of America.

Participants Accepts: male and female children; male and female adolescents. Average stay: 1 year. Admission: one parent, all parties who share custody, court order, voluntary, depending on program. Treats autistic disorders; learning disabilities; behavior disorders; general psychosocial disorders; substance abuse; eating disorders; compulsive/addictive disorders other than substance abuse and eating disorders; post-traumatic stress disorder; thought, mood, and personality disorders.

Staff Staff is 55% male, 45% female.

Contact Randy Dillon, Coordinator of Psychiatric Residential Treatment, main address above. Phone: 615-558-6361. Fax: 615-558-8342.

HATHAWAY CHILDREN'S SERVICES
8955 West Gold Creek Road
Sylmar, California 91392
818-896-2474

General Information Residential treatment/subacute facility for children, adolescents. Patient security: unlocked. Independent not-for-profit facility. Licensed by state of California.

Participants Accepts: male and female children; male and female adolescents. Average stay: 18 months. Admission: one parent, all parties who share custody, court order, voluntary, depending on program. Treats learning disabilities; behavior disorders; general psychosocial disorders; eating disorders; post-traumatic stress disorder; thought, mood, and personality disorders.

Costs   Average cost: $3992 per month.

Contact   Kita Curry, Intake Coordinator, P.O. Box 923670, Sylmar, CA 91392-3670. Phone: 818-896-2474 Ext. 235.

HAVENWYCK HOSPITAL
1525 University Drive
Auburn Hills, Michigan 48326
313-373-9200; Fax: 313-373-0528

General Information   Psychiatric hospital for children, adolescents, adults. Open year-round. Patient security: entirely locked; will pursue and return runaways. Suburban setting. For-profit facility affiliated with Ramsey Health Care, Inc., New Orleans, LA. Licensed by state of Michigan. Accredited by JCAHO.

Participants   Accepts: male and female children ages 4–12; male and female adolescents ages 13–17; male and female adults ages 18 and up. Average stay: 14 days. Admission: one parent, all parties who share custody, depending on program. Treats behavior disorders; general psychosocial disorders; substance abuse; eating disorders; compulsive/addictive disorders other than substance abuse and eating disorders; post-traumatic stress disorder; thought, mood, and personality disorders. Accepts the mobility impaired; the vision impaired; those with a history of arson; the sexually compulsive; those with a history of harm to themselves and others; those receiving psychotropic medication; non-English speaking individuals; those with a history of epilepsy.

Program   Treatment modalities: parent support group; psychodynamic; family systems. Family treatment program available.

Facilities   Multiple buildings; males and females in separate units. Separate residential quarters for children and adolescents. Central dining (shared with adults). Basketball courts, game room, gymnasium, playing fields.

Education   Academic program available at no charge. Serves ages 4–18, ungraded.

Costs   Accepts private insurance, group insurance, medicare, medicaid, Blue Cross/Blue Shield.

Contact   Wayne Isbell, Director, Community Relations/Marketing, main address above. Phone: 313-373-9200. Fax: 313-373-0528.

HAZELDEN PIONEER HOUSE
11505 36th Avenue, North
Plymouth, Minnesota 55441
612-559-2022; Fax: 612-559-0149

General Information   Residential treatment/subacute facility for adolescents. Open year-round. Patient security: unlocked. Suburban setting. Not-for-profit facility affiliated with Hazeldon Foundation, Center City, MN. Licensed by state of Minnesota. Accredited by JCAHO.

Participants   ages 14–25. Average stay: 36 days. Admission: one parent, all parties who share custody, court order, voluntary, depending on program. Treats substance abuse. Accepts the mobility impaired; the vision impaired; those receiving psychotropic medication; those with a history of epilepsy.

Program   Treatment modalities: Twelve Step Recovery; reality therapy; parenting skills for parents. Family treatment program available.

Staff   Staff is 50% male, 50% female.

Facilities   Single building. Residential arrangements vary depending on program. Central dining arrangements vary. Separate dining by residential unit, in-room dining available. Game room, gymnasium, indoor swimming pool, playing fields.

Education   Academic program available. Serves ages 14–25, grades 7–12. Curriculum accredited or approved by school district.

Costs   Average cost: $9000 per stay. Accepts private insurance, group insurance, Blue Cross/Blue Shield, public funds.

Contact   Miles Thompson, Community Relations, main address above. Phone: 612-559-2022. Fax: 612-559-0149.

Announcement   A service of Hazelden Foundation, Hazelden Pioneer House provides chemical dependency treatment for adolescents and young adults, ages 14 to 25. Program highlights include a separate 7- to 10-day evaluation unit and residential assessment process to determine whether or not chemical dependency treatment is required and a 3-day Parenting Program for parents with chemically dependent children.

HCA AURORA PAVILION
655 Medical Park Drive
Box 1073
Aiken, South Carolina 29802
803-641-5900; Fax: 803-641-5923

General Information Psychiatric hospital for children, adolescents. Open year-round. Patient security: entirely locked; will pursue and return runaways. Small town setting. For-profit facility affiliated with Hospital Corporation of America, Nashville, TN. Licensed by state of South Carolina. Accredited by JCAHO.

Participants Accepts: male and female children ages 6–11; male and female adolescents ages 12–15. Average stay: 12 days. Admission: all parties who share custody. Treats learning disabilities; behavior disorders; general psychosocial disorders; substance abuse; thought, mood, and personality disorders. Accepts the vision impaired; the hearing impaired; the speech impaired; those receiving psychotropic medication.

Program Treatment modalities: Twelve Step Recovery; psychodynamic. Family treatment program available.

Staff Total facility staff includes 2 physicians, 1 psychologist, 2 psychiatrists, 10 registered nurses, 5 practical/vocational nurses, 2 MSW social workers, 1 teacher, 5 counselors, 4 occupational/recreational therapists. Staff is 60% male, 40% female.

Facilities Single building; males and females in coeducational units. Central dining (shared with adults). Basketball courts, game room, gymnasium, indoor swimming pool.

Education Academic program available at no charge. Serves ages 6–15, grades 1–12. 1 teacher on staff. Curriculum accredited or approved by local school district.

Costs Average cost: $700 per day. Accepts private insurance, group insurance, Blue Cross/Blue Shield.

Additional Services Drug and alcohol rehabilitation services for males and females ages 6–15. Treats learning disabilities; behavior disorders; general psychosocial disorders; substance abuse; eating disorders; compulsive/addictive disorders other than substance abuse and eating disorders; post-traumatic stress disorder; thought, mood, and personality disorders. Outpatient services for males and females ages 6–15. Treats learning disabilities; behavior disorders; general psychosocial disorders; substance abuse; eating disorders; compulsive/addictive disorders other than substance abuse and eating disorders; post-traumatic stress disorder; thought, mood, and personality disorders. Residential or sub-acute services for males and females ages 6–15. Treats learning disabilities; behavior disorders; general psychosocial disorders; substance abuse; eating disorders; compulsive/addictive disorders other than substance abuse and eating disorders; post-traumatic stress disorder; thought, mood, and personality disorders.

Contact Robert Carlton, Program Director, main address above. Phone: 803-641-5900.

HCA BELLE PARK HOSPITAL
4427 Belle Park Drive
Houston, Texas 77072
713-933-6000; Fax: 713-983-3423

General Information Psychiatric hospital for children, adolescents, adults. 12 beds for children; 28 beds for adolescents; 40 beds total. Open year-round. Patient security: entirely locked; will pursue and return runaways. Suburban setting. For-profit facility affiliated with Hospital Corporation of America, Nashville, TN. Licensed by state of Texas. Accredited by JCAHO; Mental Health and Mental Retardation.

Participants Accepts: male and female children ages 4–12; male and female adolescents ages 11–18; male and female adults ages 17 and up. Average stay: 20 days. Admission: court order, voluntary, depending on program. Treats autistic disorders; learning disabilities; behavior disorders; general psychosocial disorders; substance abuse; eating disorders; compulsive/addictive disorders other than substance abuse and eating disorders; post-traumatic stress disorder; thought, mood, and personality disorders. Accepts the mobility impaired; the vision impaired; the hearing impaired; the speech impaired; those with a history of arson; the sexually compulsive; those with a history of harm to themselves and others; those receiving psychotropic medication; non-English speaking individuals; those with a history of epilepsy. Special programs for the chronically ill.

Program Treatment modalities: psychodynamic/behavioral short term therapy; Twelve Step Recovery for children; behavior management-positive: adolescent and child. Family treatment program available.

Staff Total facility staff includes 83 physicians, 126 psychologists, 95 psychiatrists, 88 registered nurses, 4 practical/vocational nurses, 87 MSW social workers, 1 social worker (non-MSW), 3 teachers, 5 counselors, 6 occupational/recreational therapists, 16 therapists, 1 dietician, 66 other direct-care staff members. Staff is 64% male, 36% female.

Facilities Multiple buildings; males and females in coeducational units. Separate residential quarters for children and adolescents. Central dining (shared with adults), in-room dining available. Basketball courts, game room, gymnasium, outdoor swimming pool, playing fields, ropes course.

Education Academic program available at no charge. Serves ages 6–19, grades 1–12. 3 teachers on staff. Cost of educational program sometimes covered by local school district. Organized sports program offered.

Costs Accepts private insurance, group insurance, Blue Cross/Blue Shield.

Additional Services Drug and alcohol rehabilitation services for males and females ages 11 and up. Treats substance abuse; eating disorders; compulsive/addictive disorders other than substance abuse and eating disorders. Outpatient services for males and females ages 5 and up. Treats behavior disorders; general psychosocial disorders; substance abuse; eating disorders; compulsive/addictive disorders other than substance abuse and eating disorders; post-traumatic stress disorder; thought, mood, and personality disorders.

Contact Beth Kastner, Director of Admissions, main address above. Phone: 713-933-6000.

HCA CEDAR VISTA HOSPITAL
7171 North Cedar Avenue
Fresno, California 93720
209-449-8000; Fax: 209-431-5947

General Information Psychiatric hospital for children, adolescents, adults. 8 beds for children; 16 beds for adolescents; 60 beds total. Open year-round. Patient security: partially locked. Urban setting. For-profit facility affiliated with Hospital Corporation of America, Nashville, TN. Licensed by state of California. Accredited by JCAHO.

Participants Accepts: male and female children ages 3–12; male and female adolescents ages 13–17; male and female adults ages 18 and up. Admission: one parent, court order, depending on program. Treats learning disabilities; behavior disorders; general psychosocial disorders; substance abuse; eating disorders; compulsive/addictive disorders other than substance abuse and eating disorders; post-traumatic stress disorder; thought, mood, and personality disorders. Accepts those with a history of arson; those with a history of harm to themselves and others; those receiving psychotropic medication; those with a history of epilepsy. Largest number of participants from California.

Program Family treatment program available.

Staff Total facility staff includes 9 registered nurses, 1 MSW social worker, 1 social worker (non-MSW),

3 teachers, 2 occupational/recreational therapists, 1 dietician, 4 other direct-care staff members. Staff is 20% male, 80% female.

Facilities Single building; males and females in co-educational units. Separate residential quarters for children and adolescents. Gymnasium, outdoor swimming pool, ropes course.

Education Academic program available at no charge. Serves ages 5–17, grades K–12. 3 teachers on staff. Curriculum accredited or approved by Clovis Unified School District.

Costs Accepts private insurance, group insurance, medicare, Blue Cross/Blue Shield.

Additional Services Partial hospitalization services for males and females ages 3 and up. Treats learning disabilities; behavior disorders; general psychosocial disorders; substance abuse; eating disorders; compulsive/addictive disorders other than substance abuse and eating disorders; post-traumatic stress disorder; thought, mood, and personality disorders.

Contact Sylvie Coutant, Director of Front End Systems, main address above. Phone: 209-449-8000. Fax: 209-431-5947.

HCA COLISEUM PSYCHIATRIC HOSPITAL
340 Hospital Drive
Macon, Georgia 31201
912-741-1355; Fax: 912-743-0459

General Information Psychiatric hospital for children, adolescents, adults. 8 beds for children; 30 beds for adolescents; 92 beds total. Open year-round. Patient security: entirely locked; will pursue and return runaways. Urban setting. For-profit facility affiliated with Hospital Corporation of America, Nashville, TN. Licensed by state of Georgia. Accredited by JCAHO.

Participants Accepts: male and female children ages 3–13; male and female adolescents ages 12–18; male and female adults ages 17 and up. Average stay: 16 days. Admission: one parent, all parties who share custody, court order, voluntary, depending on program. Treats learning disabilities; behavior disorders; general psychosocial disorders; substance abuse; eating disorders; compulsive/addictive disorders other than substance abuse and eating disorders; post-traumatic stress disorder; thought, mood, and personality disorders. Accepts the mobility impaired; the vision impaired; the hearing impaired; the speech impaired; those with a history of arson; the sexually compulsive; those with a history of harm to themselves and others; those receiving psychotropic medication; those with a history of epilepsy; those with emerging conduct disorder. Special programs for the hearing impaired; the speech impaired. Largest number of participants from Georgia, South Carolina.

Program Treatment modalities: psychodynamic; family therapy/family systems; Twelve Step Recovery; psychotherapeutic. Family treatment program available.

Staff .1 full-time direct-care staff member per child or adolescent. Total facility staff includes 3 physicians, 8 psychologists, 11 psychiatrists, 25 registered nurses, 5 practical/vocational nurses, 5 MSW social workers, 3 teachers, 2 counselors, 6 occupational/recreational therapists, 5 therapists, 15 other direct-care staff members. Staff is 25% male, 75% female.

Facilities Single building; males and females in co-educational units. Separate residential quarters for children and adolescents. Basketball courts, game room, gymnasium, outdoor swimming pool, courtyard with play equipment.

Education Academic program available at no charge. Serves ages 5–18. 3 teachers on staff. Curriculum accredited or approved by Georgia Accrediting Commission, Inc.

Costs Accepts private insurance, group insurance, medicare, Blue Cross/Blue Shield.

Additional Services Drug and alcohol rehabilitation services for males and females ages 13 and up. Treats learning disabilities; behavior disorders; general psychosocial disorders; substance abuse; eating disorders; compulsive/addictive disorders other than substance abuse and eating disorders; post-traumatic stress disorder; thought, mood, and personality disorders. Outpatient services for males and females. Treats learning disabilities; behavior disorders; general psychosocial disorders; substance abuse; eating disorders; compulsive/addictive disorders other than substance abuse and eating disorders; post-traumatic stress disorder; thought, mood, and personality disorders.

Contact Lynn Hamilton, Director of Lifeline, main address above. Phone: 912-741-1355. Fax: 912-743-0459.

HCA DEER PARK HOSPITAL
4525 Glenwood Avenue
Deer Park, Texas 77536
713-479-0955; Fax: 713-476-1923

General Information Psychiatric hospital for children, adolescents, adults. 12 beds for children; 44 beds for adolescents; 154 beds total. Open year-round. Patient security: entirely locked; will pursue and return runaways. Small town setting. For-profit facility affiliated with Hospital Corporation of America, Nashville, TN. Licensed by state of Texas. Accredited by JCAHO.

Participants Accepts: male and female children ages 4–12; male and female adolescents ages 13–17; male and female adults ages 18 and up. Average stay: 17 days. Admission: one parent, all parties who share custody, court order, voluntary, depending on program. Treats autistic disorders; learning disabilities; behavior disorders; general psychosocial disorders; substance abuse; eating disorders; compulsive/addictive disorders other than substance abuse and eating disorders; post-traumatic stress disorder; thought, mood, and personality disorders. Accepts the mobility impaired; the vision impaired; the sexually compulsive; those with a history of harm to themselves and others; those receiving psychotropic medication; non-English speaking individuals; those with a history of epilepsy.

Program Treatment modalities: psychodynamic; Twelve Step Recovery; psychodrama/cognitive. Family treatment program available.

Staff Total facility staff includes 2 physicians, 5 psychologists, 15 psychiatrists, 16 registered nurses, 3 MSW social workers, 2 social workers (non-MSW), 5 teachers, 3 counselors, 1 dietician. Staff is 50% male, 50% female.

Facilities Single building; males and females in co-educational units. Separate residential quarters for children and adolescents. Central dining (shared with adults). Basketball courts, game room, gymnasium, outdoor swimming pool, playing fields.

Education Academic program available at no charge. Serves ages 5–17, grades 1–12. 5 teachers on staff. Curriculum accredited or approved by Deer Park Independent School District. Cost of educational program covered by local school district. Organized sports program offered.

Costs Accepts private insurance, group insurance, Blue Cross/Blue Shield, public funds.

Contact Collette Sink, Director of Intake and Referral, main address above. Phone: 713-479-0955. Fax: 713-476-1923.

HCA DOMINION HOSPITAL
2960 Sleepy Hollow Road
Falls Church, Virginia 22044
703-538-2872; Fax: 703-237-3537

General Information Psychiatric hospital for children, adolescents. 12 beds for children; 30 beds for adolescents; 42 beds total. Open year-round. Patient security: entirely locked; will pursue and return runaways. Urban setting. For-profit facility affiliated with Hospital Corporation of America, Nashville, TN. Licensed by state of Virginia. Accredited by JCAHO.

Participants Accepts: male and female children ages 3–12; male and female adolescents ages 13–18. Average stay: 17 days. Admission: one parent, all parties who share custody, court order, temporary detention order, depending on program. Treats autistic disorders; learning disabilities; behavior disorders; general psychosocial disorders; substance abuse; eating disorders; compulsive/addictive disorders other than substance abuse and eating disorders; post-traumatic stress disorder; thought, mood, and personality disorders. Accepts the mobility impaired; the vision impaired; the hearing impaired; the speech impaired; those with a history of arson; those with a history of harm to themselves and others; those receiving psychotropic medication; non-English speaking individuals; those with a history of epilepsy. Special programs for the chronically ill.

Program Treatment modalities: crisis intervention and stabilization; family systems approach; biopsychological approach. Family treatment program available.

Staff Total facility staff includes 1 physician, 1 psychologist, 26 psychiatrists, 23 registered nurses, 2 MSW social workers, 2 social workers (non-MSW), 2 teachers, 2 counselors, 2 occupational/recreational therapists, 1 speech pathologist, 1 dietician. Staff is 20% male, 80% female.

Facilities Single building; males and females in coeducational units. Central dining (shared with adults). Basketball courts, game room, gymnasium, volleyball.

Education Academic program available at no charge. Serves ages 6–18, grades 1–12. 2 teachers on staff. Organized sports program offered.

Costs Average cost: $1000 per day. Accepts private insurance, group insurance, medicare, Blue Cross/Blue Shield.

Additional Services Drug and alcohol rehabilitation services for males and females ages 6 and up. Treats learning disabilities; behavior disorders; general psychosocial disorders; substance abuse; eating disorders; compulsive/addictive disorders other than substance abuse and eating disorders; post-traumatic

stress disorder; thought, mood, and personality disorders.

Contact Linda Pittman, Director of First Step, main address above. Phone: 703-538-2872.

HCA GRANT CENTER HOSPITAL
20601 Southwest 157th Avenue
Miami, Florida 33187
305-251-0710; Fax: 305-253-1005

General Information Psychiatric hospital for children, adolescents, adults. 28 beds for children; 90 beds for adolescents; 140 beds total. Open year-round. Patient security: entirely locked; will pursue and return runaways. Rural setting. For-profit facility affiliated with Hospital Corporation of America, Nashville, TN. Licensed by state of Florida. Accredited by JCAHO; National Association of Private Psychiatric Hospitals.

Participants Accepts: male and female children ages 4–12; male and female adolescents ages 13–18; male and female adults ages 19 and up. Average stay: 40 days. Admission: all parties who share custody, court order, depending on program. Treats autistic disorders; learning disabilities; behavior disorders; general psychosocial disorders; substance abuse; post-traumatic stress disorder; thought, mood, and personality disorders. Accepts the mobility impaired; the vision impaired; the hearing impaired; the speech impaired; those with a history of harm to themselves and others; those receiving psychotropic medication; non-English speaking individuals; those with a history of epilepsy. Largest number of participants from Florida, Indiana, New York.

Program Treatment modalities: eclectic; therapeutic community. Family treatment program available.

Staff .3 full-time direct-care staff member per child or adolescent. Total facility staff includes 20 physicians, 2 psychologists, 25 psychiatrists, 35 registered nurses, 4 MSW social workers, 7 social workers (non-MSW), 10 teachers, 65 counselors, 12 occupational/recreational therapists, 1 speech pathologist, 1 dietician, 10 other direct-care staff members. Staff is 30% male, 70% female.

Facilities Multiple buildings; males and females in coeducational units. Separate residential quarters for children and adolescents. Central dining (shared with adults). Basketball courts, game room, horseback riding, outdoor swimming pool, outdoor tennis courts, playing fields.

Education Academic program available at no charge. Serves ages 5–18, grades K–12. 10 teachers on staff. Curriculum accredited or approved by Florida Council of Independent Schools, Southern Association of Colleges and Schools. Organized sports program offered.

Costs   Accepts private insurance, group insurance, medicare, Blue Cross/Blue Shield, public funds.

Additional Services   Outpatient services for males and females ages 3 and up. Treats learning disabilities; behavior disorders; general psychosocial disorders; eating disorders; compulsive/addictive disorders other than substance abuse and eating disorders; post-traumatic stress disorder; thought, mood, and personality disorders. Residential or sub-acute services for males and females ages 6–18. Treats learning disabilities; behavior disorders; general psychosocial disorders; substance abuse; compulsive/addictive disorders other than substance abuse and eating disorders; post-traumatic stress disorder; thought, mood, and personality disorders. Specialized outpatient ADD/ADHD program for males and females ages 4 and up. Treats learning disabilities; behavior disorders.

Contact   John Guglietta, Director of Respond, main address above. Phone: 305-251-0710 Ext. 1800. Fax: 305-253-1005.

See page 430 for full page description.

HCA GREENLEAF HOSPITAL
200 Greens Prairie Road
College Station, Texas 77845
409-690-0039; Fax: 409-690-0202

General Information   Psychiatric hospital for children, adolescents, adults. 6 beds for children; 16 beds for adolescents. Open year-round. Patient security: entirely locked; will pursue and return runaways. Suburban setting. For-profit facility affiliated with Hospital Corporation of America-Texas Psychiatric Co., Nashville, TN. Licensed by state of Texas. Accredited by JCAHO.

Participants   Accepts: male and female children ages 5–11; male and female adolescents ages 12–17; male and female adults ages 18 and up. Average stay: 17 days. Admission: all parties who share custody. Treats learning disabilities; behavior disorders; general psychosocial disorders; thought, mood, and personality disorders. Accepts the mobility impaired; the hearing impaired; the speech impaired; those receiving psychotropic medication.

Program   Treatment modalities: Twelve Step Recovery. Family treatment program available.

Staff   Total facility staff includes 7 psychiatrists, 23 registered nurses, 5 practical/vocational nurses, 1 MSW social worker, 3 social workers (non-MSW), 1 teacher, 4 counselors, 3 occupational/recreational therapists, 2 dieticians, 5 other direct-care staff members. Staff is 10% male, 90% female.

Facilities   Single building; males and females in co-educational units. Separate residential quarters for children and adolescents. Central dining (shared with adults). Basketball courts, game room, gymnasium, outdoor swimming pool, playing fields, ropes course.

Education   1 teacher on staff.

Costs   Accepts private insurance, group insurance, medicare, Blue Cross/Blue Shield.

Contact   Wesley Luker, Director of Admissions, main address above. Phone: 409-690-0039. Fax: 409-690-0202.

HCA GULF PINES HOSPITAL
205 Hollow Tree Lane
Houston, Texas 77090
713-537-0700; Fax: 713-537-7230

General Information   Psychiatric hospital for children, adolescents, adults. 22 beds for children; 50 beds for adolescents; 140 beds total. Open year-round. Patient security: entirely locked; will pursue and return runaways. Suburban setting. For-profit facility affiliated with Hospital Corporation of America, Nashville, TN. Licensed by state of Texas. Accredited by JCAHO; Texas Department of Mental Health and Mental Retardation.

Participants   Accepts: male and female children ages 3–12; male and female adolescents ages 12–18; male and female adults ages 18 and up. Average stay: 25 days. Admission: one parent, all parties who share custody, court order, voluntary, depending on program. Treats autistic disorders; learning disabilities; behavior disorders; general psychosocial disorders; substance abuse; eating disorders; compulsive/addictive disorders other than substance abuse and eating disorders; post-traumatic stress disorder; thought, mood, and personality disorders. Accepts the mobility impaired; the vision impaired; the hearing impaired; the speech impaired; those with a history of arson; the sexually compulsive; those with a history of harm to themselves and others; those receiving psychotropic medication; non-English speaking individuals; those with a history of epilepsy. Special programs for the mobility impaired; the developmentally disabled; the vision impaired; the hearing impaired; the speech impaired; those with AIDS.

Program Treatment modalities: Twelve Step Recovery; disease concept; cognitive-behavioral; psychotherapeutic. Family treatment program available.

Facilities Single building; males and females in co-educational units. Separate residential quarters for children and adolescents. Central dining (shared with adults). Basketball courts, game room, gymnasium, outdoor swimming pool, playing fields, ropes course, weight/exercise room.

Education Academic program available at no charge. Serves ages 3–18, grades N–12. Curriculum accredited or approved by Spring Independent School District. Cost of educational program covered by local school district.

Costs Accepts private insurance, group insurance, medicare, Blue Cross/Blue Shield.

Additional Services Drug and alcohol rehabilitation services for males and females ages 12 and up. Treats autistic disorders; learning disabilities; behavior disorders; general psychosocial disorders; substance abuse; eating disorders; compulsive/addictive disorders other than substance abuse and eating disorders; post-traumatic stress disorder; thought, mood, and personality disorders. Outpatient services for males and females ages 18 and up. Treats substance abuse.

Contact Jayne Crabtree, Director of Admissions, main address above. Phone: 713-537-0700. Fax: 713-537-7230.

HCA HEIGHTS PSYCHIATRIC HOSPITAL
103 Hospital Loop, NE
Albuquerque, New Mexico 87109
505-883-8777; Fax: 505-888-3128

General Information Psychiatric hospital for children, adolescents, adults. 24 beds for children; 24 beds for adolescents; 92 beds total. Open year-round. Patient security: entirely locked; will pursue and return runaways. Urban setting. For-profit facility affiliated with Hospital Corporation of America, Nashville, TN. Licensed by state of New Mexico. Accredited by JCAHO.

Participants Accepts: male and female children ages 3–13; male and female adolescents ages 13–18; male and female adults ages 18–90. Average stay: 30 days. Admission: all parties who share custody, court order, depending on program. Treats autistic disorders; learning disabilities; behavior disorders; general psychosocial disorders; substance abuse; eating disorders; compulsive/addictive disorders other than substance abuse and eating disorders; post-traumatic

stress disorder; thought, mood, and personality disorders. Accepts the mobility impaired; the vision impaired; the hearing impaired; the speech impaired; those with a history of arson; the sexually compulsive; those with a history of harm to themselves and others; those receiving psychotropic medication; non-English speaking individuals; those with a history of epilepsy.

Program Treatment modalities: Twelve Step Recovery; behavioral; psychodynamic; cognitive. Family treatment program available.

Staff .6 full-time direct-care staff member per child or adolescent. Total facility staff includes 39 physicians, 47 psychologists, 28 psychiatrists, 33 registered nurses, 2 practical/vocational nurses, 3 MSW social workers, 1 social worker (non-MSW), 5 teachers, 3 counselors, 4 occupational/recreational therapists, 11 therapists, 18 other direct-care staff members. Staff is 36% male, 64% female.

Facilities Single building; males and females in co-educational units. Separate residential quarters for children and adolescents. Central dining (shared with adults). Basketball courts, game room, gymnasium, indoor swimming pool, outdoor swimming pool, playing fields, ropes course.

Education Academic program available at no charge. Serves ages 5–18, grades K–12. 5 teachers on staff. Curriculum accredited or approved by North Central Association of Colleges and Schools, State of New Mexico.

Costs Average cost: $650 per day. Accepts private insurance, group insurance, medicare, medicaid, Blue Cross/Blue Shield, public funds.

Contact Jane Tulloch, Director of Community Relations, main address above. Phone: 505-883-8777. Fax: 505-888-3128.

HCA HOLLY HILL HOSPITAL
3019 Falstaff Road
Raleigh, North Carolina 27610
919-250-7000; Fax: 919-231-3231

General Information Psychiatric hospital for children, adolescents, adults. 12 beds for children; 25 beds for adolescents; 87 beds total. Open year-round. Patient security: entirely locked; will pursue and return runaways. Urban setting. For-profit facility affiliated with Hospital Corporation of America, Nashville, TN. Licensed by state of North Carolina. Accredited by JCAHO; North Carolina Division of Facility Services.

Participants Accepts: male and female children ages 8–12; male and female adolescents ages 13–18; male and female adults ages 19 and up. Average stay: 20 days. Admission: all parties who share custody. Treats autistic disorders; behavior disorders; general psychosocial disorders; substance abuse; eating disorders; compulsive/addictive disorders other than substance abuse and eating disorders; post-traumatic stress disorder; thought, mood, and personality disorders. Accepts the mobility impaired; the vision impaired; the hearing impaired; the speech impaired; those with a history of arson; the sexually compulsive; those with a history of harm to themselves and others; those receiving psychotropic medication; non-English speaking individuals; those with a history of epilepsy. Special programs for the mobility impaired; the developmentally disabled; the vision impaired; the hearing impaired; the speech impaired; those with AIDS. Largest number of participants from North Carolina, Virginia.

Program Treatment modalities: crisis intervention and stabilization—O'Hanlon model; Twelve Step Recovery; cognitive therapy; group therapy. Family treatment program available.

Staff Total facility staff includes 25 physicians, 2 psychologists, 40 registered nurses, 8 MSW social workers, 5 teachers, 4 occupational/recreational therapists.

Facilities Single building; males and females in coeducational units. Separate residential quarters for children and adolescents. Central dining (not shared with adults), in-room dining available. Basketball courts, gymnasium, playing fields, ropes course.

Education Academic program available at no charge. Serves ages 8–18, ungraded. 5 teachers on staff. Curriculum accredited or approved by patient's home school. Organized sports program offered.

Costs Accepts private insurance, group insurance, medicare, medicaid, Blue Cross/Blue Shield, public funds.

Additional Services Drug and alcohol rehabilitation services for males and females ages 18 and up. Treats substance abuse. Outpatient services for males and females ages 8–18. Treats autistic disorders; learning disabilities; behavior disorders; general psychosocial disorders; substance abuse; eating disorders; compulsive/addictive disorders other than substance abuse and eating disorders; post-traumatic stress disorder; thought, mood, and personality disorders. Camping program for males and females ages 8–12. Treats learning disabilities; behavior disorders; general psychosocial disorders. Dual diagnosis inpatient and structured day program for males and females ages 13–18. Treats behavior disorders; general psychosocial disorders; substance abuse; compulsive/addictive disorders other than substance abuse and eating disorders; thought, mood, and personality disorders.

Contact Charlotte Craver, Director of Respond, main address above. Phone: 919-250-7000. Fax: 919-231-3231.

HCA MONTEVISTA HOSPITAL
5900 West Rochelle Avenue
Las Vegas, Nevada 89103
702-364-1111; Fax: 702-364-8183

General Information Psychiatric hospital for adolescents, adults. 32 beds for adolescents. Open year-round. Patient security: entirely locked; will pursue and return runaways. Suburban setting. For-profit facility affiliated with Hospital Corporation of America Psychiatric Company, Nashville, TN. Licensed by state of Nevada. Accredited by JCAHO; National Association of Private Psychiatric Hospitals.

Participants Accepts: male and female adolescents ages 13–17; male and female adults ages 18 and up. Admission: one parent, all parties who share custody, court order, depending on program. Treats learning disabilities; behavior disorders; general psychosocial disorders; substance abuse; eating disorders; compulsive/addictive disorders other than substance abuse and eating disorders; post-traumatic stress disorder; thought, mood, and personality disorders. Accepts the mobility impaired; the vision impaired; the hearing impaired; the speech impaired; those with a history of arson; the sexually compulsive; those with a history of harm to themselves and others; those receiving psychotropic medication; non-English speaking individuals; those with a history of epilepsy. Special programs for the chronically ill; the mobility impaired; the developmentally disabled; the vision impaired; the hearing impaired; the speech impaired; those with AIDS. Largest number of participants from Nevada, Arizona, California.

Program Treatment modalities: Twelve Step Recovery; cognitive/behavioral; Miniuchin's structured family therapy; group psychotherapy-Yalom. Family treatment program available.

Staff 1.2 full-time direct-care staff members per adolescent. Total facility staff includes 20 physicians, 15 psychologists, 17 psychiatrists, 60 registered nurses, 8 practical/vocational nurses, 35 MSW social workers, 2 teachers, 2 counselors, 1 physical therapist, 5 occupational/recreational therapists, 1 speech pathologist, 45 therapists, 1 dietician, 30 other direct-care staff members. Staff is 45% male, 55% female.

Facilities Multiple buildings; males and females in coeducational units. Separate residential quarters for adolescents. Central dining (not shared with adults).

Basketball courts, game room, gymnasium, outdoor swimming pool, playing fields, ropes course, exercise track, playground.

Education   Academic program available at no charge. Serves ages 13–17, grades 7–12. 2 teachers on staff. Curriculum accredited or approved by Clark County School District.

Costs   Accepts private insurance, group insurance, medicare, medicaid, Blue Cross/Blue Shield, public funds.

Additional Services   Drug and alcohol rehabilitation services for males and females ages 18 and up. Treats substance abuse; compulsive/addictive disorders other than substance abuse and eating disorders.

Contact   Judy Povilaitis, Education Director, main address above. Phone: 702-364-1111. Fax: 702-364-8183.

HCA RED RIVER HOSPITAL
1505 Eighth Street
Wichita Falls, Texas 76301
817-322-3171; Fax: 817-720-3990

General Information   Psychiatric hospital for adolescents, adults. 14 beds for adolescents. Open year-round. Patient security: partially locked; will pursue and return runaways. Urban setting. For-profit facility affiliated with Hospital Corporation of America, Wichita Falls, TX. Licensed by state of Texas. Accredited by JCAHO.

Participants   Accepts: male and female adolescents ages 13–17; male and female adults ages 18 and up. Average stay: 26 days. Admission: one parent. Treats learning disabilities; behavior disorders; general psychosocial disorders; substance abuse; eating disorders; compulsive/addictive disorders other than substance abuse and eating disorders; post-traumatic stress disorder; thought, mood, and personality disorders. Accepts the speech impaired; those with a history of arson; the sexually compulsive; those with a history of harm to themselves and others; those receiving psychotropic medication; those with a history of epilepsy.

Program   Treatment modalities: Twelve Step Recovery; behavioral therapy; individual/group/family therapy. Family treatment program available.

Staff   1.4 full-time direct-care staff members per adolescent. Total facility staff includes 1 physician, 1 psychologist, 4 psychiatrists, 3 registered nurses, 1 practical/vocational nurse, 1 MSW social worker, 2 teachers, 1 counselor, 2 occupational/recreational

therapists, 1 dietician, 3 other direct-care staff members. Staff is 50% male, 50% female.

Facilities   Single building; males and females in co-educational units. Separate residential quarters for adolescents. Central dining (shared with adults). Basketball courts, game room.

Education   Academic program available at no charge. Serves ages 13–17, grades 7–12. 2 teachers on staff. Curriculum accredited or approved by Wichita Falls Independent School District.

Costs   Accepts private insurance, group insurance, medicare, Blue Cross/Blue Shield, public funds.

Additional Services   Drug and alcohol rehabilitation services for males and females ages 13–17. Treats behavior disorders; general psychosocial disorders; substance abuse; eating disorders; compulsive/addictive disorders other than substance abuse and eating disorders; post-traumatic stress disorder; thought, mood, and personality disorders.

Contact   Tammy Kimrey, Director of Respond, main address above. Phone: 817-322-3171. Fax: 817-720-3990.

HCA RICHLAND HOSPITAL
7501 Glenview Drive
North Richland Hills, Texas 76180
817-595-5000; Fax: 817-595-5041

General Information   Psychiatric hospital for children, adolescents, adults. Open year-round. Patient security: partially locked; will pursue and return runaways. Suburban setting. For-profit facility affiliated with Hospital Corporation of America, Nashville, TN. Licensed by state of Texas. Accredited by JCAHO.

Participants   Accepts: male and female children ages 6–12; male and female adolescents ages 13–18; male and female adults ages 19 and up. Average stay: 20 days. Admission: one parent, all parties who share custody, court order, voluntary, depending on program. Treats learning disabilities; behavior disorders; general psychosocial disorders; substance abuse; eating disorders; compulsive/addictive disorders other than substance abuse and eating disorders; post-traumatic stress disorder; thought, mood, and personality disorders. Accepts the mobility impaired; those with a history of arson; the sexually compulsive; those with a history of harm to themselves and others; those receiving psychotropic medication; non-English speaking individuals; those with a history of epilepsy. Special programs for the developmentally disabled.

Program Treatment modalities: Twelve Step Recovery; psychodynamic group process; psychodrama; family therapy. Family treatment program available.

Staff Total facility staff includes 1 psychologist, 7 psychiatrists, 5 registered nurses, 1 practical/vocational nurse, 2 MSW social workers, 5 teachers, 1 speech pathologist, 2 other direct-care staff members. Staff is 25% male, 75% female.

Facilities Multiple buildings; males and females in coeducational units. Separate residential quarters for children and adolescents. Central dining (shared with adults). Basketball courts, game room, gymnasium, indoor swimming pool, ropes course.

Education Academic program available at no charge. Serves ages 5–19, grades K–12. 5 teachers on staff. Curriculum accredited or approved by Birdville Independent School District. Cost of educational program covered by local school district.

Costs Accepts private insurance, group insurance, medicare, Blue Cross/Blue Shield.

Additional Services Drug and alcohol rehabilitation services for males and females ages 6–19. Treats learning disabilities; behavior disorders; general psychosocial disorders; substance abuse; eating disorders; compulsive/addictive disorders other than substance abuse and eating disorders; post-traumatic stress disorder; thought, mood, and personality disorders. Partial hospitalization (day treatment) for males and females ages 6–19. Treats learning disabilities; behavior disorders; general psychosocial disorders; substance abuse; eating disorders; compulsive/addictive disorders other than substance abuse and eating disorders; post-traumatic stress disorder; thought, mood, and personality disorders.

Contact Toni Amfahr, Director of Assessment and Referrals, main address above. Phone: 817-595-5000. Fax: 817-595-5041.

HCA RIVER PARK HOSPITAL
1230 Sixth Avenue
Huntington, West Virginia 25701
304-526-9111; Fax: 304-526-9361

General Information Psychiatric hospital for children, adolescents, adults. 14 beds for children; 28 beds for adolescents; 115 beds total. Open year-round. Patient security: partially locked. Small town setting. For-profit facility affiliated with Hospital Corporation of America, Nashville, TN. Licensed by state of West Virginia. Accredited by JCAHO.

Participants Accepts: male and female children ages 6–12; male and female adolescents ages 12–18; male

and female adults ages 18 and up. Average stay: 31 days. Admission: one parent, all parties who share custody, court order, depending on program. Treats autistic disorders; learning disabilities; behavior disorders; general psychosocial disorders; substance abuse; eating disorders; compulsive/addictive disorders other than substance abuse and eating disorders; post-traumatic stress disorder; thought, mood, and personality disorders. Accepts those with a history of arson; the sexually compulsive; those with a history of harm to themselves and others; those receiving psychotropic medication; those with a history of epilepsy.

Program Treatment modalities: cognitive-behavioral; psychodynamic; family system; Twelve Step Recovery. Family treatment program available.

Staff Total facility staff includes 1 physician, 2 psychologists, 8 psychiatrists, 14 registered nurses, 3 practical/vocational nurses, 1 social worker (non-MSW), 2 teachers, 2 counselors, 1 physical therapist, 1 occupational/recreational therapist, 1 speech pathologist, 8 therapists, 1 dietician, 12 other direct-care staff members. Staff is 30% male, 70% female.

Facilities Single building; males and females in coeducational units. Separate residential quarters for children and adolescents. Central dining (shared with adults), in-room dining available. Basketball courts, game room, gymnasium, playing fields.

Education Academic program available at no charge. Serves ages 6–18, grades K–12. 2 teachers on staff. Curriculum accredited or approved by local school board.

Costs Accepts private insurance, group insurance, medicare, medicaid, Blue Cross/Blue Shield, public funds.

Contact Cathy Bellew, Director of Copes, main address above. Phone: 304-526-9111.

HCA ROCKFORD CENTER
100 Rockford Drive
Newark, Delaware 19701
302-996-5480; Fax: 302-996-0269

General Information Psychiatric hospital for children, adolescents, adults. 10 beds for children; 32 beds for adolescents. Open year-round. Patient security: entirely locked; will pursue and return runaways. Suburban setting. For-profit facility affiliated with Hospital Corporation of America, Nashville, TN. Licensed by state of Delaware. Accredited by JCAHO.

Participants Accepts: male and female children ages 5–12; male and female adolescents ages 12–17; male and female adults ages 18 and up. Average stay: 14 days. Admission: one parent, all parties who share custody, court order, voluntary, depending on program. Treats learning disabilities; behavior disorders; general psychosocial disorders; substance abuse; eating disorders; post-traumatic stress disorder; thought, mood, and personality disorders. Accepts those with a history of arson; those with a history of harm to themselves and others; those receiving psychotropic medication; those with a history of epilepsy. Largest number of participants from Delaware, Pennsylvania, Maryland.

Program Treatment modalities: multidisciplinary/milieu treatment; family systems therapy. Family treatment program available.

Staff Total facility staff includes 1 physician, 6 psychologists, 32 psychiatrists, 40 registered nurses, 2 practical/vocational nurses, 11 MSW social workers, 2 social workers (non-MSW), 7 teachers, 8 counselors, 6 occupational/recreational therapists, 1 therapist, 1 dietician, 31 other direct-care staff members. Staff is 34% male, 66% female.

Facilities Single building; males and females in separate units. Separate residential quarters for children and adolescents. Central dining (not shared with adults). Basketball courts, game room, gymnasium, outdoor swimming pool, outdoor play area.

Education Academic program available at no charge. Academic program is ungraded. 7 teachers on staff. Curriculum accredited or approved by State of Delaware. Cost of educational program covered by local school district.

Costs Average cost: $850 per day. Accepts private insurance, group insurance, medicare, Blue Cross/Blue Shield, public funds.

Additional Services Outpatient services for males and females ages 4 and up. Treats learning disabilities; behavior disorders; general psychosocial disorders; post-traumatic stress disorder; thought, mood, and personality disorders. Sexual abuse treatment track; dual diagnosis treatment track for males and females ages 5 and up. Treats learning disabilities; behavior disorders; general psychosocial disorders; post-traumatic stress disorder; thought, mood, and personality disorders.

Contact Irene B. Miller, Respond Director, main address above. Phone: 302-996-5480. Fax: 302-996-0269.

HCA SHOAL CREEK HOSPITAL
3501 Mills Avenue
Austin, Texas 78731
800-452-0361; Fax: 512-371-6566

General Information Psychiatric hospital for children, adolescents, adults. 10 beds for children; 26 beds for adolescents; 160 beds total. Open year-round. Patient security: partially locked; will pursue and return runaways. Urban setting. For-profit facility affiliated with Hospital Corporation of America, Nashville, TN. Licensed by state of Texas. Accredited by JCAHO; Texas Department of Mental Health and Mental Retardation.

Participants Accepts: male and female children ages 5–12; male and female adolescents ages 12–18; male and female adults ages 18 and up. Average stay: 12 days. Admission: one parent, court order, depending on program. Treats autistic disorders; learning disabilities; behavior disorders; general psychosocial disorders; substance abuse; eating disorders; compulsive/addictive disorders other than substance abuse and eating disorders; post-traumatic stress disorder; thought, mood, and personality disorders. Accepts the mobility impaired; the vision impaired; the hearing impaired; the speech impaired; those with a history of arson; the sexually compulsive; those with a history of harm to themselves and others; those receiving psychotropic medication; non-English speaking individuals; those with a history of epilepsy. Largest number of participants from Texas.

Program Treatment modalities: Twelve Step Recovery; brief therapy/crisis intervention model.

Staff 1.3 full-time direct-care staff members per child or adolescent. Total facility staff includes 227 physicians, 89 psychologists, 74 psychiatrists, 50 registered nurses, 2 practical/vocational nurses, 7 MSW social workers, 1 social worker (non-MSW), 3 teachers, 1 counselor, 1 physical therapist, 4 occupational/recreational therapists, 1 speech pathologist, 3 therapists, 2 dieticians, 15 other direct-care staff members.

Facilities Single building; males and females in co-educational units. Separate residential quarters for children and adolescents. Central dining (shared with adults). Basketball courts, game room, gymnasium, playscape.

Education Academic program available at no charge. Serves ages 5–18, grades K–12. 3 teachers on staff. Curriculum accredited or approved by Austin Independent School District.

Costs Accepts private insurance, group insurance, medicare, Blue Cross/Blue Shield.

Additional Services Drug and alcohol rehabilitation services for males and females ages 18 and up. Treats general psychosocial disorders; eating disorders; compulsive/addictive disorders other than substance abuse and eating disorders; post-traumatic stress disorder; thought, mood, and personality disorders. Camping program for males and females ages 5–12. Treats learning disabilities; behavior disorders.

Contact John Moore, Director of Information and Referral, main address above. Phone: 800-452-0361. Fax: 512-371-6566.

HCA VALLEY HOSPITAL
2200 Morris Hill Road
Chattanooga, Tennessee 37421
615-894-4220; Fax: 615-499-1201

General Information Psychiatric hospital for children, adolescents, adults. 10 beds for children; 40 beds for adolescents; 100 beds total. Open year-round. Patient security arrangements vary depending on program; will pursue and return runaways. Suburban setting. For-profit facility affiliated with Hospital Corporation of America, Nashville, TN. Licensed by state of Tennessee. Accredited by JCAHO; National Association of Private Psychiatric Hospitals.

Participants Accepts: male and female children ages 6–12; male and female adolescents ages 13–18; male and female adults ages 18 and up. Average stay: 14 days. Admission: one parent, all parties who share custody, court order, depending on program. Treats learning disabilities; behavior disorders; general psychosocial disorders; substance abuse; eating disorders; compulsive/addictive disorders other than substance abuse and eating disorders; post-traumatic stress disorder; thought, mood, and personality disorders. Accepts the mobility impaired; the vision impaired; the hearing impaired; the sexually compulsive; those with a history of harm to themselves and others; those receiving psychotropic medication.

Program Treatment modalities: Twelve Step Recovery; psychodynamic. Family treatment program available.

Staff Total facility staff includes 26 psychologists, 20 psychiatrists, 29 registered nurses, 4 MSW social workers, 8 teachers, 6 occupational/recreational therapists, 1 dietician.

Facilities Multiple buildings; males and females in coeducational units. Separate residential quarters for children and adolescents. Central dining (shared with adults). Basketball courts, gymnasium, outdoor swimming pool, outdoor tennis courts, playing fields, ropes course.

Education Academic program available at no charge. Serves ages 6–18, grades K–12. 8 teachers on

staff. Curriculum accredited or approved by Tennessee State Department of Education.

Costs Accepts private insurance, group insurance, medicare, medicaid, Blue Cross/Blue Shield.

Additional Services Drug and alcohol rehabilitation services for males and females ages 6–90. Treats substance abuse; compulsive/addictive disorders other than substance abuse and eating disorders; post-traumatic stress disorder. Outpatient services for males and females ages 6–90. Treats learning disabilities; behavior disorders; general psychosocial disorders; substance abuse; compulsive/addictive disorders other than substance abuse and eating disorders; post-traumatic stress disorder; thought, mood, and personality disorders. Residential or sub-acute services for males and females ages 12–18. Treats learning disabilities; behavior disorders; general psychosocial disorders; substance abuse; eating disorders; compulsive/addictive disorders other than substance abuse and eating disorders; post-traumatic stress disorder; thought, mood, and personality disorders.

Contact Robert Hagemann, Director of Admissions, main address above. Phone: 615-499-1206. Fax: 615-499-1201.

HCA WILLOW SPRINGS CENTER
690 Edison Way
Reno, Nevada 89502
702-858-3303; Fax: 702-858-4585

General Information Residential treatment/subacute facility for children, adolescents. 10 beds for children; 64 beds for adolescents; 74 beds total. Patient security: entirely locked. For-profit facility affiliated with Hospital Corporation of America, Nashville, TN. Licensed by state of Nevada. Accredited by JCAHO; Civilian Health and Medical Program of the Uniformed Services.

Participants Accepts: male and female children ages 5–12; male and female adolescents ages 13–17. Average stay: 4 months. Admission: one parent, all parties who share custody, court order, voluntary, those in state custody, depending on program. Treats learning disabilities; behavior disorders; general psychosocial disorders; substance abuse; eating disorders; post-traumatic stress disorder; thought, mood, and personality disorders.

Staff Staff is 50% male, 50% female.

Education Educational arrangements: fully accredited elementary and secondary education provided at Truckee Meadows School. Educational program held off-site.

Contact Wayne Hoff, main address above. Phone: 702-858-3303. Fax: 702-858-4585.

See page 432 for full page description.

HEALTH HILL HOSPITAL FOR CHILDREN
2801 Martin Luther King Jr. Drive
Cleveland, Ohio 44104-3865
216-721-5400; Fax: 216-231-2010

General Information Residential treatment/subacute facility for children. 52 beds for children. Open year-round. Patient security: staff secured; will pursue and return runaways. Suburban setting. Independent not-for-profit facility. Licensed by state of Ohio. Accredited by JCAHO.

Participants Accepts: male and female children ages up to 18. Average stay: 60 days. Admission: one parent, all parties who share custody, depending on program. Treats learning disabilities; behavior disorders; general psychosocial disorders; eating disorders; post-traumatic stress disorder; thought, mood, and personality disorders. Accepts the mobility impaired; the vision impaired; the hearing impaired; the speech impaired; non-English speaking individuals; those with a history of epilepsy; the head injured; the chronically ill. Special programs for the chronically ill; the mobility impaired; the developmentally disabled; the vision impaired; the hearing impaired; the speech impaired; those with AIDS; the physically disabled. Largest number of participants from Ohio.

Staff 2.1 full-time direct-care staff members per child. Total facility staff includes 4 physicians, 1 psychologist, 38 registered nurses, 16 practical/vocational nurses, 5 MSW social workers, 1 teacher, 5 physical therapists, 11 occupational/recreational therapists, 5 speech pathologists, 5 therapists, 2 dieticians, 17 other direct-care staff members. Staff is 5% male, 95% female.

Facilities Single building; males and females in co-educational units. Separate dining by residential unit available. Basketball courts, game room, gymnasium, indoor swimming pool, playing fields.

Education Academic program available at no charge. Serves ages 6–18, grades 1–12. 1 teacher on staff. Curriculum accredited or approved by Cleveland Board of Education. Cost of educational program covered by local school district.

Costs Average cost: $40,000 per stay. Accepts private insurance, group insurance, medicare, medicaid, Blue Cross/Blue Shield, public funds.

Contact Beverly Sload, Director of Development and Public Relations, main address above. Phone: 216-721-5400. Fax: 216-231-2010.

HEARTLAND HOSPITAL
1500 West Ashland
Nevada, Missouri 64772
417-667-2666; Fax: 417-667-9563

General Information Psychiatric hospital for children, adolescents. Patient security: staff secured. For-profit facility affiliated with Ramsay Health Care, Inc., New Orleans, LA. Licensed by state of Missouri. Accredited by JCAHO.

Participants Accepts: male and female children; male and female adolescents. Average stay: 145 days. Admission: one parent, all parties who share custody, voluntary, depending on program. Treats autistic disorders; learning disabilities; behavior disorders; general psychosocial disorders; substance abuse; eating disorders; compulsive/addictive disorders other than substance abuse and eating disorders; post-traumatic stress disorder; thought, mood, and personality disorders.

Contact David Johnston, Program Coordinator, main address above. Phone: 417-667-2666. Fax: 417-667-9563.

THE HENRY ITTLESON CENTER FOR CHILD RESEARCH
5050 Iselin Avenue
Riverdale, New York 10471
212-549-6700; Fax: 212-796-4614

General Information Residential treatment/subacute facility for children. 30 beds for children. Open year-round. Patient security: staff secured; will pursue and return runaways. Suburban setting. Not-for-profit facility affiliated with Jewish Board of Family Services, New York, NY. Licensed by state of New York. Accredited by JCAHO.

Participants Accepts: male and female children ages 5–12. Average stay: 4 years. Admission: voluntary. Treats behavior disorders; general psychosocial disorders; substance abuse; post-traumatic stress disorder; thought, mood, and personality disorders. Accepts those with a history of harm to themselves and others; those receiving psychotropic medication; those with a history of epilepsy. Largest number of participants from New York.

Program Treatment modalities: psychodynamic. Family treatment program available.

Staff 1.9 full-time direct-care staff members per child. Total facility staff includes 1 physician, 3 psychologists, 2 psychiatrists, 4 registered nurses, 6 practical/vocational nurses, 20 teachers, 33 counselors, 1 occupational/recreational therapist, 1 speech pathologist, 1 dietician, 1 other direct-care staff member.

Facilities Multiple buildings; males and females in separate units. Separate dining by residential unit available. Basketball courts, gymnasium, playing fields, playground.

Education Academic program available at no charge. Serves ages 5–13. 20 teachers on staff. Curriculum accredited or approved by Board of Education. Cost of educational program covered by local school district.

Costs Accepts private insurance, medicaid, Blue Cross/Blue Shield.

Additional Services Day treatment services for males and females ages 5–12. Treats learning disabilities; behavior disorders; general psychosocial disorders; post-traumatic stress disorder; thought, mood, and personality disorders.

Contact Sherry Waldman, Assistant Director, main address above. Phone: 212-549-6700.

HERRICK MEMORIAL HEALTH CARE CENTER
500 East Pottawatamie Street
Tecumseh, Michigan 49286
517-423-2141; Fax: 517-423-7450

General Information General hospital for adolescents, adults. 5 beds for adolescents. Open year-round. Patient security: entirely locked; will pursue and return runaways. Small town setting. Independent not-for-profit facility. Licensed by state of Michigan. Accredited by JCAHO; American Orthopsychiatric Association.

Participants Accepts: male and female adolescents ages 12–17; male and female adults ages 18 and up. Average stay: 14 days. Admission: all parties who share custody, court order, depending on program. Treats general psychosocial disorders; substance abuse; eating disorders; compulsive/addictive disorders other than substance abuse and eating disorders; post-traumatic stress disorder; thought, mood, and personality disorders. Accepts the vision impaired; the sexually compulsive; those with a history of harm to themselves and others; those receiving psychotropic medication; those with a history of epilepsy. Special programs for the developmentally disabled; those with AIDS. Largest number of participants from Michigan.

Program Treatment modalities: psychodynamic. Family treatment program available.

Staff Total facility staff includes 2 psychologists, 4 psychiatrists, 15 registered nurses, 3 MSW social workers, 1 teacher, 3 occupational/recreational therapists, 1 dietician, 14 other direct-care staff members.

Facilities Multiple buildings; males and females in coeducational units. Separate residential quarters for adolescents. Central dining (not shared with adults). Gymnasium.

Education Academic program available at no charge. Serves ages 12–18, ungraded. 1 teacher on staff. Curriculum accredited or approved by Lenawee County Intermediate School District, Michigan State Department of Education.

Costs Accepts private insurance, group insurance, medicare, medicaid, Blue Cross/Blue Shield.

Additional Services Outpatient services for males and females ages 12 and up. Treats learning disabilities; general psychosocial disorders; eating disorders; compulsive/addictive disorders other than substance abuse and eating disorders; post-traumatic stress disorder; thought, mood, and personality disorders. Day treatment (partial hospitalization) for males and females ages 12–17. Treats general psychosocial disorders; compulsive/addictive disorders other than substance abuse and eating disorders; post-traumatic stress disorder; thought, mood, and personality disorders.

Contact Ricardo Rodriguez, Outpatient Program Manager, main address above. Phone: 517-423-2141 Ext. 3392. Fax: 517-423-7450.

HIGHLAND HOSPITAL
300 56th Street
Charleston, West Virginia 25364
304-925-4756; Fax: 304-925-4758

General Information Psychiatric hospital for children. Patient security: partially locked. Independent not-for-profit facility. Licensed by state of West Virginia. Accredited by JCAHO.

Participants Accepts: male and female children. Average stay: 21 days. Admission: one parent, all parties who share custody, court order, voluntary, depending on program. Treats learning disabilities; behavior disorders; general psychosocial disorders;

eating disorders; thought, mood, and personality disorders.

Staff Staff is 40% male, 60% female.

Contact Carla Hall, Children's Unit Supervisor, main address above. Phone: 304-925-4756.

HIGH POINTE RESIDENTIAL TREATMENT CENTER
6501 Northeast Fiftieth Street
Oklahoma City, Oklahoma 73141
800-342-4642; Fax: 405-424-0729

General Information Residential treatment/subacute facility for children, adolescents. 8 beds for children; 24 beds for adolescents; 32 beds total. Open year-round. Patient security: staff secured; will pursue and return runaways. Suburban setting. For-profit facility affiliated with Century Healthcare Corporation, Tulsa, OK. Licensed by state of Oklahoma. Accredited by JCAHO; Oklahoma Department of Health, Oklahoma Department of Human Resources.

Participants Accepts: male and female children ages 11–12; male and female adolescents ages 13–17. Average stay: 116 days. Admission: one parent, all parties who share custody, court order, state custody, depending on program. Treats learning disabilities; behavior disorders; general psychosocial disorders; substance abuse; eating disorders; compulsive/addictive disorders other than substance abuse and eating disorders; post-traumatic stress disorder; thought, mood, and personality disorders. Accepts the mobility impaired; the vision impaired; the hearing impaired; the speech impaired; those with a history of arson; the sexually compulsive; those with a history of harm to themselves and others; those receiving psychotropic medication; those with a history of epilepsy; those with AIDS. Special programs for the chronically ill; the mobility impaired; the developmentally disabled; the vision impaired; the hearing impaired; the speech impaired. Largest number of participants from Oklahoma.

Program Treatment modalities: psychodynamic; medical model; behavior modification; cognitive therapy. Family treatment program available.

Staff 1 full-time direct-care staff member per child or adolescent. Total facility staff includes 12 registered nurses, 11 practical/vocational nurses, 4 occupational/recreational therapists, 7 therapists, 29 other direct-care staff members. Staff is 45% male, 55% female.

Facilities Multiple buildings; males and females in coeducational units. Central dining. Basketball courts, horseback riding, outdoor swimming pool, playing fields, ropes course.

Education Academic program available at no charge. Serves ages 11–17, ungraded. Curriculum accredited or approved by Oklahoma State Department of Education. Cost of educational program covered by local school district. Organized sports program offered.

Costs Average cost: $389 per day. Accepts private insurance, group insurance, medicare, medicaid, Blue Cross/Blue Shield, public funds.

Additional Services Psychiatric inpatient/acute hospitalization for males and females ages 6–17. Treats learning disabilities; behavior disorders; general psychosocial disorders; eating disorders; compulsive/addictive disorders other than substance abuse and eating disorders; post-traumatic stress disorder; thought, mood, and personality disorders.

Contact Susie Meyerson, Intake Coordinator, main address above. Phone: 800-342-4642. Fax: 405-424-0729.
See page 414 for full page description.

HIGH POINT HOSPITAL
Upper King Street
Rye Brook, New York 10573
914-939-4420; Fax: 914-939-6847

General Information Psychiatric hospital for adolescents, adults. 35 beds for adolescents. Open year-round. Patient security: partially locked; will pursue and return runaways. Suburban setting. Independent for-profit facility. Licensed by state of New York. Accredited by JCAHO.

Participants Accepts: male and female adolescents ages 12–22; male and female adults ages 22 and up. Average stay: 90 days. Admission: one parent, court order, two-psychiatrist certification, depending on program. Treats learning disabilities; behavior disorders; general psychosocial disorders; substance abuse; eating disorders; compulsive/addictive disorders other than substance abuse and eating disorders; post-traumatic stress disorder; thought, mood, and personality disorders. Accepts those with a history of harm to themselves and others; those receiving psychotropic medication. Special programs for the chronically ill.

Program Treatment modalities: insight-oriented (individual/group); expressive therapies; milieu therapy; behavior modification and psychosocial rehabilitation. Family treatment program available.

Staff .9 full-time direct-care staff member per adolescent. Total facility staff includes 1 psychologist, 6 psychiatrists, 5 registered nurses, 2 MSW social workers, 2 teachers, 12 counselors, 1 occupational/recreational therapist, 1 dietician. Staff is 50% male, 50% female.

Facilities Multiple buildings; males and females in coeducational units. Residential quarters shared with adults. Central dining (shared with adults). Basketball courts, gymnasium, outdoor swimming pool, playing fields.

Education Academic program available at additional cost. Serves ages 12–18, ungraded. 2 teachers on staff. Organized sports program offered.

Costs Average cost: $800 per day. Accepts private insurance, group insurance, medicaid.

Contact Jonathan Morgenstern, Director of Community Programs, main address above. Phone: 914-939-4420. Fax: 914-939-6847.

HILLCREST-WASHINGTON YOUTH HOME
2700 West Indiana Street
Evansville, Indiana 47712
812-428-0698

General Information Residential treatment/subacute facility for children, adolescents. Patient security: staff secured. Independent not-for-profit facility. Licensed by state of Indiana. Accredited by Indiana Association for Residential Child Care Agencies.

Participants Accepts: male and female children; male and female adolescents. Average stay: 12 months. Admission: one parent, all parties who share custody, court order, depending on program. Treats learning disabilities; behavior disorders; general psychosocial disorders; post-traumatic stress disorder; thought, mood, and personality disorders.

Staff Staff is 50% male, 50% female.

Costs Average cost: $82 per day.

Contact Gary Barnett, Program Director, P.O. Box 6347, Evansville, IN 47712. Phone: 812-428-0698.

HILL HOUSE
44 Tivoli Street
Albany, New York 12207
518-465-7879; Fax: 518-432-4699

General Information Residential treatment/subacute facility for adolescents. 14 beds for adolescents. Open year-round. Patient security: staff secured; will pursue and return runaways. Suburban setting. Independent not-for-profit facility. Licensed by state of New York. Accredited by JCAHO.

Participants Accepts: male and female adolescents ages 12–16. Average stay: 360 days. Admission: one parent, all parties who share custody, court order, voluntary, depending on program. Treats behavior disorders; general psychosocial disorders; substance abuse; eating disorders; compulsive/addictive disorders other than substance abuse and eating disorders; post-traumatic stress disorder; thought, mood, and personality disorders. Largest number of participants from New York.

Program Treatment modalities: Twelve Step Recovery; psychotherapy. Family treatment program available.

Staff Total facility staff includes 1 physician, 1 psychologist, 1 psychiatrist, 1 registered nurse, 1 MSW social worker, 1 social worker (non-MSW), 1 teacher, 3 counselors, 1 occupational/recreational therapist, 10 other direct-care staff members. Staff is 30% male, 70% female.

Facilities Single building; males and females in separate units. Central dining. Basketball courts, game room.

Education Academic program available at no charge. Serves ages 12–16, grades 6–12. 1 teacher on staff.

Costs Accepts private insurance, group insurance, medicare, medicaid, Blue Cross/Blue Shield, public funds.

Additional Services Drug and alcohol rehabilitation services for males and females ages 12–16. Treats learning disabilities; behavior disorders; general psychosocial disorders; substance abuse; eating disorders; compulsive/addictive disorders other than substance abuse and eating disorders; post-traumatic stress disorder; thought, mood, and personality disorders.

Contact Daniel DiNola, Clinical Assessment Coordinator, main address above. Phone: 518-465-7879. Fax: 518-432-4699.

HILL HOUSE, INC.
1080 Park Street
Carbondale, Illinois 62901
618-529-1151

General Information Drug and alcohol rehabilitation center for adolescents. 60 beds for adolescents. Patient security: staff secured. Independent not-for-profit facility. Licensed by state of Illinois. Accredited by Commission on Accreditation of Rehabilitation Facilities.

Participants Accepts: male and female adolescents. Average stay: 9 months. Admission: one parent, all parties who share custody, court order, voluntary, depending on program. Treats substance abuse. Accepts the mobility impaired; non-English speaking individuals.

Staff Staff is 50% male, 50% female.

Costs Average cost: $100 per day.

Contact Intake Coordinator, main address above. Phone: 618-529-1151.

HILLSIDE CHILDREN'S CENTER
1183 Monroe Avenue
Rochester, New York 14620
716-256-7500; Fax: 716-256-7510

General Information Residential treatment/subacute facility for children, adolescents. Open year-round. Patient security: staff secured; pursuit policy depends on program. Urban setting. Independent not-for-profit facility. Licensed by state of New York. Accredited by JCAHO; Council on Accreditation of Services for Families and Children.

Participants Accepts: male and female children ages 6–12; male and female adolescents ages 13–21. Average stay: 540 days. Treats learning disabilities; behavior disorders; general psychosocial disorders; substance abuse; eating disorders; compulsive/addictive disorders other than substance abuse and eating disorders; post-traumatic stress disorder; thought, mood, and personality disorders. Accepts the vision impaired; the hearing impaired; the speech impaired; those with a history of arson; the sexually compulsive; those with a history of harm to themselves and others; those receiving psychotropic medication; non-English speaking individuals; those with a history of epilepsy. Special programs for the vision impaired; the hearing impaired; the speech impaired. Largest number of participants from New York.

Program Treatment modalities: family systems; milieu therapy; eclectic. Family treatment program available.

Staff Total facility staff includes 1 physician, 3 psychologists, 1 psychiatrist, 13 registered nurses, 12 MSW social workers, 1 social worker (non-MSW), 15 teachers, 100 counselors, 9 occupational/recreational therapists, 2 speech pathologists, 3 therapists, 1 dietician, 10 other direct-care staff members. Staff is 57% male, 43% female.

Facilities Multiple buildings; males and females in both coeducational and separate units depending on program. Separate dining by residential unit available. Basketball courts, game room, gymnasium, indoor swimming pool, playing fields, ropes course.

Education Academic program available at additional cost. Serves ages 6–21, ungraded. 15 teachers on staff. Curriculum accredited or approved by New York State Education Department. Cost of educational program sometimes covered by local school district. Organized sports program offered.

Costs Average cost: $172 per day. Accepts medicaid, public funds.

Additional Services Child Welfare Services for males and females. Treats learning disabilities; behavior disorders; general psychosocial disorders; substance abuse; eating disorders; compulsive/addictive disorders other than substance abuse and eating disorders; post-traumatic stress disorder; thought, mood, and personality disorders.

Contact Jane M. Cumbie, Director of Public Relations, main address above. Phone: 716-256-7540. Fax: 716-256-7510.

HILLTOP
P.O. Box 595
Running Springs, California 92382
714-867-7054; Fax: 714-867-4952

General Information Residential treatment/subacute facility for adolescents, adults. Patient security: staff secured. For-profit facility. Licensed by state of California.

Participants Accepts: male and female adolescents; male and female adults. Admission: all parties who share custody, court order, voluntary, depending on program. Treats learning disabilities; behavior disorders; general psychosocial disorders; substance abuse; thought, mood, and personality disorders.

Staff Staff is 50% male, 50% female.

Education Academic program available. Serves ages 15–26.

Costs Average cost: $3600 per month.

Contact Saul Rudman, Director of Admissions, main address above. Phone: 714-867-9545. Fax: 714-867-4952.

See page 434 for full page description.

HOLLISWOOD HOSPITAL
87-37 Palermo Street
Holliswood, New York 11423
718-776-8181; Fax: 718-776-8551

General Information Psychiatric hospital for adolescents, adults. 25 beds for adolescents. Open year-round. Patient security: entirely locked. Urban setting. For-profit facility affiliated with Mediplex, Inc., Wellesley, MA. Licensed by state of New York. Accredited by JCAHO; Office of Mental Health, American Hospital Association, National Association of Psychiatric Hospitals.

Participants Accepts: male and female adolescents ages 12–19; male and female adults ages 18 and up. Admission: all parties who share custody. Treats learning disabilities; behavior disorders; general psychosocial disorders; substance abuse; eating disorders; compulsive/addictive disorders other than substance abuse and eating disorders; post-traumatic stress disorder; thought, mood, and personality disorders. Accepts the speech impaired; those with a history of harm to themselves and others; those receiving psychotropic medication. Special programs for the speech impaired; those with AIDS.

Program Treatment modalities: cognitive therapy; reality therapy; Twelve Step Recovery. Family treatment program available.

Staff Total facility staff includes 9 physicians, 5 psychologists, 40 registered nurses, 2 practical/vocational nurses, 12 MSW social workers, 2 social workers (non-MSW), 5 teachers, 39 counselors, 3 occupational/recreational therapists, 7 therapists, 1 dietician, 4 other direct-care staff members. Staff is 36% male, 64% female.

Facilities Single building; males and females in co-educational units. Separate residential quarters for adolescents. Separate dining by residential unit available. Basketball courts, gymnasium, playing fields.

Education Academic program available. 5 teachers on staff. Curriculum accredited or approved by New York School Board.

Costs Accepts private insurance, group insurance, Blue Cross/Blue Shield.

Additional Services Outpatient services for males and females ages 12–18. Treats behavior disorders; general psychosocial disorders; substance abuse; eating disorders; compulsive/addictive disorders other than substance abuse and eating disorders; post-traumatic stress disorder; thought, mood, and personality disorders.

Contact Janet Reiss, Director, Referral Office, main address above. Phone: 718-776-8181. Fax: 718-776-8551.

HOMESTEAD
1131 East University
Mesa, Arizona 85203
602-969-8961; Fax: 602-969-0039

General Information Residential treatment/subacute facility for adolescents. 13 beds for adolescents. Patient security: staff secured. Not-for-profit facility affiliated with Prehab of Arizona, Mesa, AZ. Licensed by state of Arizona.

Participants Accepts: female adolescents. Average stay: 12 months. Admission: one parent, all parties who share custody, court order, voluntary, depending on program. Treats autistic disorders; learning disabilities; behavior disorders; general psychosocial disorders; substance abuse; eating disorders; compulsive/addictive disorders other than substance abuse and eating disorders; post-traumatic stress disorder; thought, mood, and personality disorders.

Staff .8 full-time direct-care staff member per adolescent. Staff is 40% male, 60% female.

Contact Rebecca Martin, Program Director, main address above. Phone: 602-969-8961. Fax: 602-969-0039.

HOPE HAVEN CENTER
1101 Barataria Boulevard
Marrero, Louisiana 70125
504-347-5581; Fax: 504-340-2075

General Information Residential treatment/subacute facility for children, adolescents. 30 beds for children; 95 beds for adolescents; 125 beds total. Open year-round. Patient security: partially locked; will pursue and return runaways. Suburban setting. Not-for-profit facility affiliated with Associated Catholic Charities, New Orleans, LA. Licensed by state of Louisiana. Accredited by JCAHO.

Participants Accepts: male and female children ages 10–18; male and female adolescents ages 10–18. Average stay: 300 days. Admission: all parties who share custody. Treats learning disabilities; behavior disorders; general psychosocial disorders; eating disorders; compulsive/addictive disorders other than substance abuse and eating disorders; post-traumatic stress disorder; thought, mood, and personality disorders. Accepts the hearing impaired; the speech impaired; those with a history of arson; the sexually compulsive; those with a history of harm to themselves and others; those receiving psychotropic medication; non-English speaking individuals; those with a history of epilepsy.

Program Treatment modalities: social-learning; cognitive-behavioral. Family treatment program available.

Staff 1.4 full-time direct-care staff members per child or adolescent. Total facility staff includes 1 physician, 2 psychologists, 2 psychiatrists, 1 registered nurse, 6 practical/vocational nurses, 10 MSW social workers, 17 teachers, 4 counselors, 1 occupational/recreational therapist, 2 dieticians, 130 other direct-care staff members. Staff is 40% male, 60% female.

Facilities Multiple buildings; males and females in separate units. Central dining, separate dining by residential unit, in-room dining available. Basketball courts, game room, gymnasium, outdoor swimming pool, playing fields, activity center.

Education Academic program available at no charge. Serves ages 10–18, ungraded. 17 teachers on staff. Curriculum accredited or approved by Louisiana State Board of Education. Cost of educational program covered by local school district.

Costs Accepts private insurance, group insurance, public funds.

Contact Laurie Buckley, Admissions Coordinator, main address above. Phone: 504-347-5581. Fax: 504-340-2075.

HOPEVALE, INC.
3780 Howard Road
Hamburg, New York 14075
716-648-1964; Fax: 716-648-5266

General Information Residential treatment/subacute facility for adolescents. 100 beds for adolescents. Open year-round. Patient security: staff secured; will pursue and return runaways. Suburban setting. Independent not-for-profit facility. Licensed by state of New York. Accredited by JCAHO.

Participants Accepts: female adolescents ages 12–18. Average stay: 1 year. Admission: court order, voluntary, neglect, depending on program. Treats behavior disorders; general psychosocial disorders;

post-traumatic stress disorder; thought, mood, and personality disorders. Accepts those with a history of harm to themselves and others; those receiving psychotropic medication. Special programs for victims of sexual, physical, and/or emotional abuse.

Program Treatment modalities: psychodynamic; behavior modification; parenting training; community linkages. Family treatment program available.

Staff 1 full-time direct-care staff member per adolescent. Total facility staff includes 2 physicians, 1 psychologist, 3 psychiatrists, 7 registered nurses, 11 MSW social workers, 5 social workers (non-MSW), 7 therapists, 1 dietician, 11 other direct-care staff members. Staff is 20% male, 80% female.

Facilities Multiple buildings. Central dining, separate dining by residential unit available. Basketball courts, gymnasium, horseback riding, indoor swimming pool, playing fields.

Education Academic program available at additional cost. Serves ages 12–18, grades 7–12. Curriculum accredited or approved by New York State Education Department.

Costs Average cost: $219 per day. Accepts public funds.

Contact Donna LaPatra, Director of Intake, main address above. Phone: 716-648-1586. Fax: 716-648-5266.

THE HORSHAM CLINIC
772 East Butler Pike
Ambler, Pennsylvania 19002
215-540-1628; Fax: 215-643-5384

General Information Psychiatric hospital for children, adolescents, adults. 16 beds for children; 56 beds for adolescents. Open year-round. Patient security: partially locked. Suburban setting. For-profit facility affiliated with First Hospital Corporation, Norfolk, VA. Licensed by state of Pennsylvania. Accredited by JCAHO; Commonwealth of Pennsylvania Department of Public Welfare.

Participants Accepts: male and female children ages 7–12; male and female adolescents ages 13–18; male and female adults ages 18 and up. Average stay: 30 days. Admission: one parent, all parties who share custody, court order, depending on program. Treats autistic disorders; learning disabilities; behavior disorders; general psychosocial disorders; substance abuse; eating disorders; compulsive/addictive disorders other than substance abuse and eating disorders; post-traumatic stress disorder; thought, mood, and personality disorders. Accepts the vision impaired;

the hearing impaired; the speech impaired; those with a history of arson; those with a history of harm to themselves and others; those receiving psychotropic medication; those with a history of epilepsy. Largest number of participants from Pennsylvania, New Jersey.

Program Treatment modalities: Twelve Step Recovery; psychopharmocological; milieu therapy. Family treatment program available.

Staff Total facility staff includes 2 psychologists, 4 psychiatrists, 63 registered nurses, 3 practical/vocational nurses, 15 MSW social workers, 7 teachers, 4 counselors, 13 occupational/recreational therapists, 1 dietician, 36 other direct-care staff members.

Facilities Multiple buildings; males and females in coeducational units. Separate residential quarters for children and adolescents. Central dining (shared with adults). Basketball courts, gymnasium, playing fields, ropes course.

Education Academic program available at no charge. Serves ages 7–18, ungraded. 7 teachers on staff. Curriculum accredited or approved by homebound instruction.

Costs Average cost: $1000 per day. Accepts private insurance, group insurance, medicare, medicaid, Blue Cross/Blue Shield, public funds.

Additional Services Drug and alcohol rehabilitation services for males and females ages 13 and up. Treats learning disabilities; behavior disorders; general psychosocial disorders; substance abuse; compulsive/addictive disorders other than substance abuse and eating disorders; post-traumatic stress disorder; thought, mood, and personality disorders. Partial hospitalization program for pre-teens and adolescents for males and females ages 7–18. Treats learning disabilities; behavior disorders; general psychosocial disorders; substance abuse; eating disorders; compulsive/addictive disorders other than substance abuse and eating disorders; post-traumatic stress disorder; thought, mood, and personality disorders.

Contact Catherine Kann, Director of Marketing, main address above. Phone: 215-540-1628. Fax: 215-643-5384.

INDIAN PATH PAVILION
2300 Pavilion Drive
Kingsport, Tennessee 37660
615-378-7500; Fax: 615-378-5616

General Information Freestanding psychiatric drug and alcohol hospital for adolescents. 20 beds for adolescents. Patient security: staff secured. For-profit facility affiliated with Hospital Corporation of America, Nashville, TN. Licensed by state of Tennessee. Accredited by JCAHO.

Participants Accepts: male and female adolescents. Average stay: 2 weeks. Admission: one parent, all parties who share custody, court order, voluntary, depending on program. Treats learning disabilities; behavior disorders; general psychosocial disorders; substance abuse; compulsive/addictive disorders other than substance abuse and eating disorders; post-traumatic stress disorder; thought, mood, and personality disorders.

Contact Respond Program, main address above. Phone: 615-378-7500.

INSTITUTE OF LIVING
400 Washington Street
Hartford, Connecticut 06106
203-241-8000

General Information Psychiatric hospital for children, adolescents, adults. 15 beds for adolescents. Open year-round. Patient security: partially locked; will pursue and return runaways. Urban setting. Independent not-for-profit facility. Licensed by state of Connecticut. Accredited by JCAHO; Connecticut State Department of Children and Youth Services.

Participants Accepts: male and female children ages 3–13; male and female adolescents ages 14–18; male and female adults ages 19 and up. Average stay: 21 days. Admission: one parent, all parties who share custody, court order, ward of the state, depending on program. Treats autistic disorders; learning disabilities; behavior disorders; general psychosocial disorders; substance abuse; eating disorders; compulsive/addictive disorders other than substance abuse and eating disorders; post-traumatic stress disorder; thought, mood, and personality disorders. Accepts the mobility impaired; the vision impaired; the hearing impaired; the speech impaired; the sexually compulsive; those with a history of harm to themselves and others; those receiving psychotropic medication; non-English speaking individuals; those with a history of epilepsy. Special programs for the chronically ill; the developmentally disabled.

Program Treatment modalities: psychodynamic; milieu therapy. Family treatment program available.

Staff Total facility staff includes 4 physicians, 16 psychologists, 30 psychiatrists, 110 registered nurses, 22 MSW social workers, 4 social workers (non-MSW), 25 teachers, 20 counselors, 17 occupational/

recreational therapists, 1 speech pathologist, 3 dieticians, 103 other direct-care staff members.

Facilities Multiple buildings; males and females in coeducational units. Residential quarters shared with adults. Separate dining by residential unit available. Basketball courts, game room, gymnasium, indoor swimming pool, outdoor swimming pool, outdoor tennis courts, playing fields, ropes course.

Education Academic program available at additional cost. Serves ages 4–18, grades K–12. 25 teachers on staff. Curriculum accredited or approved by Connecticut State Department of Education. Cost of educational program covered by local school district.

Costs Average cost: $750 per day. Accepts private insurance, group insurance, medicare, medicaid, Blue Cross/Blue Shield, public funds.

Additional Services Drug and alcohol rehabilitation services for males and females ages 12 and up. Treats learning disabilities; behavior disorders; general psychosocial disorders; substance abuse; eating disorders; compulsive/addictive disorders other than substance abuse and eating disorders; post-traumatic stress disorder; thought, mood, and personality disorders. Outpatient services for males and females ages 3 and up. Treats autistic disorders; learning disabilities; behavior disorders; general psychosocial disorders; substance abuse; eating disorders; compulsive/addictive disorders other than substance abuse and eating disorders; post-traumatic stress disorder; thought, mood, and personality disorders. Residential or sub-acute services for males and females ages 17 and up. Treats learning disabilities; behavior disorders; general psychosocial disorders; substance abuse; eating disorders; compulsive/addictive disorders other than substance abuse and eating disorders; post-traumatic stress disorder; thought, mood, and personality disorders. Camping program for males and females ages 7–12. Treats learning disabilities; behavior disorders; general psychosocial disorders; thought, mood, and personality disorders. Partial hospital programs for males and females ages 5 and up. Treats learning disabilities; behavior disorders; general psychosocial disorders; substance abuse; eating disorders; compulsive/addictive disorders other than substance abuse and eating disorders; post-traumatic stress disorder; thought, mood, and personality disorders.

Contact Dr. Robert A. Lobis, Senior Service Director, main address above. Phone: 203-241-8020.

INTERVAL BROTHERHOOD HOME ALCOHOL—DRUG REHABILITATION CENTER
3445 South Main Street
Akron, Ohio 44319
216-644-4095; Fax: 216-645-2031

General Information Drug and alcohol rehabilitation center for adolescents. 15 beds for adolescents. Open year-round. Patient security: staff secured; no runaway pursuit. Suburban setting. Independent not-for-profit facility. Licensed by state of Ohio. Accredited by JCAHO.

Participants Accepts: female adolescents ages 12–17. Average stay: 150 days. Admission: one parent. Treats behavior disorders; general psychosocial disorders; substance abuse; eating disorders. Accepts the mobility impaired; the vision impaired; the hearing impaired; the speech impaired.

Program Treatment modalities: Twelve Step. Family treatment program available.

Staff 2.7 full-time direct-care staff members per adolescent. Total facility staff includes 1 physician, 1 psychologist, 1 psychiatrist, 2 registered nurses, 2 practical/vocational nurses, 1 MSW social worker, 3 teachers, 11 counselors, 1 dietician, 18 other direct-care staff members. Staff is 49% male, 51% female.

Facilities Multiple buildings; males and females in separate units. Separate dining by residential unit available. Basketball courts, game room, playing fields.

Education Academic program available at no charge. Serves ages 12–17, grades 7–12. 3 teachers on staff. Curriculum accredited or approved by County Township School Board. Cost of educational program covered by local school district. Organized sports program offered.

Costs Accepts private insurance, group insurance, medicare, medicaid, Blue Cross/Blue Shield, public funds.

Contact Fr. Sam R. Ciccolini, Executive Director, main address above. Phone: 216-644-4095. Fax: 216-645-2031.

INTERVENTIONS CONTACT
26991 Anderson Road
Wanconda, Illinois 60084
708-526-0404; Fax: 708-526-0472

General Information Residential treatment/subacute facility for adolescents. 20 beds for adolescents. Patient security: staff secured. Not-for-profit facility affiliated with Interventions, Inc., Chicago, IL. Licensed by state of Illinois.

Participants Accepts: female adolescents. Average stay: 5 months. Admission: one parent, all parties who share custody, court order, voluntary, depending on program. Treats learning disabilities; behavior disorders; general psychosocial disorders; substance abuse; eating disorders; compulsive/addictive disorders other than substance abuse and eating disorders; post-traumatic stress disorder; thought, mood, and personality disorders.

Staff .5 full-time direct-care staff member per adolescent. Staff is 30% male, 70% female.

Costs Average cost: $30,000 per stay.

Contact Tim McElroy, Program Director, main address above. Phone: 708-526-0404. Fax: 708-526-0472.

INTERVENTIONS, INC. YOUTH PROGRAM
5240 North Highway 23
Grovertown, Indiana 46531
219-867-4571; Fax: 219-867-1872

General Information Drug and alcohol rehabilitation center for adolescents. 37 beds for adolescents. Patient security: staff secured. Not-for-profit facility affiliated with Interventions, Inc., Chicago, IL. Licensed by state of Indiana.

Participants Accepts: male adolescents. Average stay: 8 months. Admission: court order. Treats substance abuse.

Staff .5 full-time direct-care staff member per adolescent. Staff is 80% male, 20% female.

Costs Average cost: $90 per day.

Contact Kathy Scott, Intake Coordinator, main address above. Phone: 218-867-4571.

INTRACARE HOSPITAL
7601 Fannin
Houston, Texas 77054
713-790-0949; Fax: 713-790-0456

General Information Drug and alcohol rehabilitation center for children, adolescents. Patient security: staff secured. For-profit facility affiliated with Cambridge International, Houston, TX. Licensed by state of Texas. Accredited by JCAHO.

Participants Accepts: male and female children; male and female adolescents. Average stay: 14 days. Admission: one parent, all parties who share custody, voluntary, depending on program. Treats learning disabilities; behavior disorders; general psychosocial disorders; substance abuse; eating disorders; compulsive/addictive disorders other than substance abuse and eating disorders; post-traumatic stress disorder; thought, mood, and personality disorders.

Contact The Care Line, main address above. Phone: 713-790-0949.

ITALIAN HOME FOR CHILDREN, INC.
1125 Centre Street
Jamaica Plain, Massachusetts 02130
617-524-3116; Fax: 617-983-5372

General Information Residential treatment/subacute facility for children. 56 beds for children. Open year-round. Patient security: staff secured; will pursue and return runaways. Urban setting. Independent not-for-profit facility. Licensed by state of Massachusetts. Accredited by Massachusetts Department of Social Services; Office for Children.

Participants Accepts: male and female children ages 4–12. Average stay: 545 days. Admission: all parties who share custody. Treats learning disabilities; behavior disorders. Accepts the speech impaired; those with a history of arson; the sexually compulsive; those with a history of harm to themselves and others; those receiving psychotropic medication. Largest number of participants from Massachusetts.

Program Treatment modalities: family preservation. Family treatment program available.

Staff 1.1 full-time direct-care staff members per child. Total facility staff includes 1 registered nurse, 6 MSW social workers, 1 social worker (non-MSW), 5 teachers, 50 other direct-care staff members. Staff is 44% male, 56% female.

Facilities Multiple buildings; males and females in coeducational units. Central dining. Basketball courts, gymnasium, outdoor swimming pool, playing fields.

Education Academic program available. Serves ages 4–12, ungraded. 5 teachers on staff. Curriculum accredited or approved by Massachusetts Department of Education. Cost of educational program covered by local school district. Organized sports program offered.

Costs Average cost: $140 per day. Accepts private insurance, medicaid.

Contact   Carole Center, Intake Coordinator, main address above. Phone: 617-524-3116. Fax: 617-983-5372.

IVY LEA MANOR
28901 South Western Avenue, #806
Rancho Palos Verdes, California 90732
310-547-4535

General Information   Residential treatment/subacute facility for children, adolescents, adults. Open year-round. Patient security: staff secured; no runaway pursuit. Urban setting. Independent for-profit facility. Licensed by state of California. Accredited by JCAHO.

Participants   Accepts: male and female children and adolescents ages 7–17; male and female adults ages 18–69. Admission: one parent, all parties who share custody, court order, depending on program. Treats autistic disorders; learning disabilities; behavior disorders; general psychosocial disorders; substance abuse; eating disorders; compulsive/addictive disorders other than substance abuse and eating disorders; post-traumatic stress disorder; thought, mood, and personality disorders. Accepts the vision impaired; the hearing impaired; the speech impaired; those with a history of arson; the sexually compulsive; those with a history of harm to themselves and others; those receiving psychotropic medication; non-English speaking individuals; those with a history of epilepsy. Special programs for the chronically ill; the developmentally disabled; the vision impaired; the hearing impaired; the speech impaired. Largest number of participants from California, Florida, Pennsylvania.

Program   Treatment modalities: cognitive behavioral therapy; Twelve Step Recovery; social learning rehabilitation model; neuro-diagnostic model. Family treatment program available.

Facilities   Multiple buildings; males and females in coeducational units. Separate residential quarters for children and adolescents. Separate dining by residential unit available.

Education   Educational arrangements: contracted with local accredited facilities. Educational program held off-site. Cost of educational program sometimes covered by local school district.

Costs   Accepts private insurance, group insurance, Blue Cross/Blue Shield, public funds.

Additional Services   Day treatment for males and females ages 7–69. Treats autistic disorders; learning disabilities; behavior disorders; general psychosocial disorders; substance abuse; eating disorders; compul-

sive/addictive disorders other than substance abuse and eating disorders; post-traumatic stress disorder; thought, mood, and personality disorders.

Contact   Casey Smart, Clinical Director, main address above. Phone: 310-547-4535.

JACKSON BROOK INSTITUTE
175 Running Hill Road
South Portland, Maine 04106
207-761-2200; Fax: 207-761-2108

General Information   Psychiatric hospital for children, adolescents, adults. 30 beds for children; 30 beds for adolescents; 106 beds total. Open year-round. Patient security: entirely locked. Suburban setting. For-profit facility affiliated with Community Care Systems, Inc., Wellesley, MA. Licensed by state of Maine. Accredited by JCAHO.

Participants   Accepts: male and female children ages 4–12; male and female adolescents ages 13–19; male and female adults ages 20 and up. Average stay: 37 days. Admission: one parent, all parties who share custody, court order, depending on program. Treats autistic disorders; learning disabilities; behavior disorders; general psychosocial disorders; substance abuse; eating disorders; compulsive/addictive disorders other than substance abuse and eating disorders; post-traumatic stress disorder; thought, mood, and personality disorders. Accepts the mobility impaired; the vision impaired; the hearing impaired; the speech impaired; those with a history of arson; the sexually compulsive; those with a history of harm to themselves and others; those receiving psychotropic medication; non-English speaking individuals; those with a history of epilepsy. Special programs for the mobility impaired; the developmentally disabled; the vision impaired; the hearing impaired; the speech impaired; those with AIDS.

Program   Treatment modalities: Twelve Step Recovery; psychodynamic; biopsychosocial; behavior modification. Family treatment program available.

Staff   Total facility staff includes 2 physicians, 5 psychologists, 11 psychiatrists, 78 registered nurses, 1 practical/vocational nurse, 40 MSW social workers, 5 social workers (non-MSW), 5 teachers, 9 occupational/recreational therapists, 1 dietician, 100 other direct-care staff members. Staff is 40% male, 60% female.

Facilities   Multiple buildings; males and females in coeducational units. Separate residential quarters for children and adolescents. Central dining (shared with adults), separate dining by residential unit, in-room dining available. Gymnasium, ropes course, softball diamond.

Education Academic program available at no charge. Serves ages 6–16, ungraded. 5 teachers on staff. Curriculum accredited or approved by Spurwich School. Cost of educational program sometimes covered by local school district. Organized sports program offered.

Costs Average cost: $26,750 per stay. Accepts private insurance, group insurance, medicare, medicaid, Blue Cross/Blue Shield, public funds.

Additional Services Outpatient services for males and females ages 6 and up. Treats behavior disorders; general psychosocial disorders; substance abuse; eating disorders; compulsive/addictive disorders other than substance abuse and eating disorders; post-traumatic stress disorder; thought, mood, and personality disorders. Partial hospitalization for males and females ages 16 and up. Treats behavior disorders; general psychosocial disorders; substance abuse; eating disorders; compulsive/addictive disorders other than substance abuse and eating disorders; post-traumatic stress disorder; thought, mood, and personality disorders.

Contact Admissions Office, main address above. Phone: 207-761-2200.

JEANINE SCHULTZ MEMORIAL SCHOOL
2101 West Oakton Street
Park Ridge, Illinois 60068
708-696-3315

General Information School for children, adolescents. Patient security: staff secured. Independent not-for-profit facility.

Participants Accepts: male and female children; male and female adolescents. Average stay: 4 years. Treats autistic disorders; learning disabilities; behavior disorders; general psychosocial disorders; eating disorders; compulsive/addictive disorders other than substance abuse and eating disorders; thought, mood, and personality disorders.

Staff Staff is 20% male, 80% female.

Education School serves ages 5–21, grades K–12.

Contact Harriet Shadoan, Principal and Associate Director, main address above. Phone: 708-696-3315.

JENNIE EDMUNDSON MEMORIAL HOSPITAL
933 East Pierce Street
Council Bluffs, Iowa 51503
712-328-6044; Fax: 712-328-7708

General Information General hospital for children, adolescents. Patient security: staff secured. Independent not-for-profit facility. Licensed by state of Iowa. Accredited by JCAHO.

Participants Accepts: male and female children; male and female adolescents. Average stay: 20 days. Admission: one parent, all parties who share custody, court order, voluntary, depending on program. Treats learning disabilities; behavior disorders; general psychosocial disorders; substance abuse; eating disorders; post-traumatic stress disorder; thought, mood, and personality disorders.

Education Academic program available at no charge. Serves ages 3–18, grades N–12. Curriculum accredited or approved by Iowa Department of Public Education. Cost of educational program sometimes covered by local school district. Organized sports program offered.

Costs Average cost: $460 per day.

Contact Judy Kelly, Director of Psychiatric Services, main address above. Phone: 712-328-6044. Fax: 712-328-7708.

THE JOHN DEWEY ACADEMY
Searles Castle
389 Main Street
Great Barrington, Massachusetts 01230
413-528-9800; Fax: 413-528-5662

General Information School for adolescents. 48 beds for adolescents. Open year-round. Patient security: unlocked; no runaway pursuit. Small town setting. Independent for-profit facility.

Participants Accepts: male and female adolescents ages 15–22. Average stay: 24 months. Admission: all parties who share custody, voluntary, depending on program. Treats learning disabilities; behavior disorders; general psychosocial disorders; substance abuse; eating disorders; compulsive/addictive disorders other than substance abuse and eating disorders; post-traumatic stress disorder. Largest number of participants from New York, Illinois, California.

Program Treatment modalities: reality therapy; confrontational-cognitive. Family treatment program available.

Staff .1 full-time direct-care staff member per adolescent. Total facility staff includes 2 psychologists, 1 MSW social worker, 2 counselors. Staff is 60% male, 40% female.

Facilities Multiple buildings; males and females in coeducational units. Central dining. Playing fields.

Education School serves ages 15–22, grades 10–PG. Curriculum is college-preparatory; diploma granted upon completion. Curriculum accredited or approved by National Independent Private Schools Association, New England Association of Schools and Colleges.

Costs Average cost: $38,000 per year. Accepts private insurance. Financial aid available.

Additional Services Residential or sub-acute services for males and females ages 15–22. Treats learning disabilities; behavior disorders; general psychosocial disorders; substance abuse; eating disorders; compulsive/addictive disorders other than substance abuse and eating disorders; post-traumatic stress disorder.

Contact Thomas Edward Bratter, President, main address above. Phone: 413-528-9800. Fax: 413-528-5662.

See page 436 for full page description.

tive therapy; reality therapy. Family treatment program available.

Staff 1.3 full-time direct-care staff members per child or adolescent. Total facility staff includes 1 psychiatrist, 3 MSW social workers, 3 social workers (non-MSW), 2 teachers, 1 counselor, 1 therapist, 32 other direct-care staff members. Staff is 40% male, 60% female.

Facilities Multiple buildings; males and females in both coeducational and separate units depending on program. Separate dining by residential unit available. Basketball courts, game room, indoor tennis courts, playing fields.

Education Academic program available at no charge. Serves ages 9–17, grades 4–12. 2 teachers on staff. Curriculum accredited or approved by Michigan North Central Accreditation through Royal Oak Public Schools. Cost of educational program covered by local school district.

Costs Accepts medicaid, public funds.

Additional Services Outpatient services for males and females. Treats substance abuse.

Contact Herbert Johnson, Program Director, main address above. Phone: 313-549-4339. Fax: 313-549-8955.

JUDSON CENTER
4410 West Thirteen Mile Road
Royal Oak, Michigan 48073
313-549-4339; Fax: 313-549-8955

General Information Residential treatment/subacute facility for children, adolescents. 12 beds for children; 24 beds for adolescents; 36 beds total. Open year-round. Patient security: unlocked; no runaway pursuit. Suburban setting. Independent not-for-profit facility. Licensed by state of Michigan. Accredited by Council on Accreditation of Services for Families and Children.

Participants Accepts: male and female children ages 9–12; male and female adolescents ages 13–17. Admission: all parties who share custody. Treats learning disabilities; behavior disorders; general psychosocial disorders; substance abuse; eating disorders; thought, mood, and personality disorders. Accepts the mobility impaired; those with a history of harm to themselves and others; those receiving psychotropic medication; those with a history of epilepsy. Largest number of participants from Michigan.

Program Treatment modalities: behavior therapy; structural and strategic family therapy; rational emo-

JULIA DYCKMAN ANDRUS MEMORIAL
1156 North Broadway
Yonkers, New York 10701
914-965-3700; Fax: 914-965-3883

General Information Residential treatment/subacute facility for children, adolescents. Open year-round. Patient security: staff secured; will pursue and return runaways. Suburban setting. Independent not-for-profit facility. Licensed by state of New York. Accredited by Council on Accreditation of Services for Families and Children.

Participants Accepts: male and female children ages 5–12; male and female adolescents ages 13–15. Average stay: 18 months. Admission: all parties who share custody. Treats learning disabilities; behavior disorders; general psychosocial disorders; post-traumatic stress disorder; thought, mood, and personality disorders. Accepts the vision impaired; the hearing impaired; the speech impaired; those with a history of harm to themselves and others; those receiving psychotropic medication; those with a history of epilepsy. Largest number of participants from New York, New Jersey, Connecticut.

Program Treatment modalities: multimodal treatment including individual, group, and family; adventure-based counseling; milieu therapy. Family treatment program available.

Staff 1.6 full-time direct-care staff members per child or adolescent. Total facility staff includes 1 registered nurse, 3 practical/vocational nurses, 5 MSW social workers, 11 teachers, 46 counselors, 4 occupational/recreational therapists, 1 dietician, 32 other direct-care staff members. Staff is 60% male, 40% female.

Facilities Multiple buildings; males and females in separate units. Separate dining by residential unit available. Basketball courts, game room, gymnasium, indoor swimming pool, outdoor tennis courts, playing fields, ropes course.

Education Academic program available at additional cost. Serves ages 5–14, grades K–9. 11 teachers on staff. Curriculum accredited or approved by New York State Education Department. Cost of educational program sometimes covered by local school district. Organized sports program offered.

Costs Average cost: $134 per day. Accepts medicaid, public funds.

Additional Services Outpatient services for males and females ages 5–13. Treats learning disabilities; behavior disorders; general psychosocial disorders; thought, mood, and personality disorders. Diagnostic center for males and females ages 5–10. Treats behavior disorders; general psychosocial disorders; post-traumatic stress disorder; thought, mood, and personality disorders.

Contact Sheri Bloom, Director of Admissions, main address above. Phone: 914-965-3700. Fax: 914-965-3883.

See page 438 for full page description.

KAHI MOHALA, A PSYCHIATRIC HOSPITAL
91-2301 Fort Weaver Road
Ewa Beach, Hawaii 96706
808-671-8511; Fax: 808-677-2570

General Information Psychiatric hospital for children, adolescents. Patient security: entirely locked. For-profit facility affiliated with Healthcare International, Inc., Austin, TX. Licensed by state of Hawaii. Accredited by JCAHO.

Participants Accepts: male and female children; male and female adolescents. Average stay: 21 days. Admission: one parent, all parties who share custody, court order, voluntary, depending on program. Treats autistic disorders; learning disabilities; behavior disorders; general psychosocial disorders; substance abuse; eating disorders; compulsive/addictive disorders other than substance abuse and eating disorders; post-traumatic stress disorder; thought, mood, and personality disorders.

Contact Lynn Oamda, Community Relations Coordinator, main address above. Phone: 808-671-8511.

THE KANSAS INSTITUTE
5808 West 110th Street
Overland Park, Kansas 66211
913-451-1700; Fax: 913-451-4419

General Information Psychiatric hospital for children, adolescents, adults. 20 beds for children; 30 beds for adolescents; 106 beds total. Open year-round. Patient security: entirely locked; will pursue and return runaways. Suburban setting. For-profit facility affiliated with United Psychiatric Group, Washington, DC. Licensed by state of Kansas. Accredited by JCAHO; State of Kansas Department of Social and Rehabilitative Services.

Participants Accepts: male and female children ages 2–12; male and female adolescents ages 13–18; male and female adults ages 18 and up. Average stay: 24 days. Admission: all parties who share custody, court order, depending on program. Treats autistic disorders; learning disabilities; behavior disorders; general psychosocial disorders; substance abuse; eating disorders; compulsive/addictive disorders other than substance abuse and eating disorders; post-traumatic stress disorder; thought, mood, and personality disorders. Accepts the mobility impaired; the vision impaired; the hearing impaired; the speech impaired; those with a history of arson; those with a history of harm to themselves and others; those receiving psychotropic medication; non-English speaking individuals; those with a history of epilepsy; diabetics; post head-injury patients. Special programs for the mobility impaired; the hearing impaired; the speech impaired; those with AIDS; Native American adolescents.

Program Treatment modalities: cognitive/behavioral; competency-based; Twelve Step Recovery.

Staff Total facility staff includes 32 physicians, 37 psychologists, 16 psychiatrists, 45 registered nurses, 5 MSW social workers, 1 social worker (non-MSW), 4 teachers, 4 counselors, 2 physical therapists, 4 occupational/recreational therapists, 2 speech pathologists, 2 therapists, 2 dieticians, 45 other direct-care staff members. Staff is 40% male, 60% female.

Facilities Single building; males and females in co-educational units. Separate residential quarters for children and adolescents. Central dining (shared with adults). Game room, gymnasium, outdoor swimming pool, playing fields, ropes course.

Education Academic program available at additional cost. Serves ages 5–18, ungraded. 4 teachers on staff. Curriculum accredited or approved by patient's home school district. Cost of educational program sometimes covered by local school district.

Costs Average cost: $1000 per stay. Accepts private insurance, group insurance, medicare, Blue Cross/Blue Shield, public funds.

Additional Services Drug and alcohol rehabilitation services for males and females ages 12–18. Treats substance abuse. Acute psychiatric care for males and females ages 2–18. Treats autistic disorders; learning disabilities; behavior disorders; general psychosocial disorders; substance abuse; eating disorders; compulsive/addictive disorders other than substance abuse and eating disorders; post-traumatic stress disorder; thought, mood, and personality disorders.

Contact Wayne Richards, Regional Marketing Director, main address above. Phone: 913-451-1700. Fax: 913-451-4419.

KAPLAN HOUSE
74 Saint Mark's Place
New York, New York 10003
212-477-1565

General Information Residential treatment/subacute facility for adolescents. Patient security: staff secured. Not-for-profit facility affiliated with Jewish Board of Family and Children's Services, New York, NY. Licensed by state of New York. Accredited by JCAHO.

Participants Accepts: male adolescents ages 17–21. Average stay: 18 months. Admission: all parties who share custody. Treats behavior disorders; general psychosocial disorders; substance abuse; thought, mood, and personality disorders.

Staff .7 full-time direct-care staff member per adolescent.

Costs Average cost: $180 per day.

Contact Child Welfare Administration, 80 Lafayette Street, New York, NY 10013. Phone: 212-266-2000.

KARMA ACADEMY AT FREDERICK FOR GIRLS
13 West 3rd Street
Frederick, Maryland 21701
301-831-4007

General Information Residential treatment/subacute facility for adolescents. 12 beds for adolescents. Patient security: staff secured. Not-for-profit facility affiliated with Karma House, Inc., Rockville, MD. Licensed by state of Maryland.

Participants Accepts: female adolescents. Average stay: 12 months. Admission: one parent, all parties who share custody, court order, voluntary, depending on program. Treats learning disabilities; behavior disorders; general psychosocial disorders; substance abuse; eating disorders; post-traumatic stress disorder; thought, mood, and personality disorders.

Staff .6 full-time direct-care staff member per adolescent. Staff is all female.

Contact Edward Kilcullen, Program Director, main address above. Phone: 301-831-4007.

KARMA ACADEMY FOR BOYS
175 Watts Branch Parkway
Rockville, Maryland 20850
301-340-8880; Fax: 301-984-1150

General Information Drug and alcohol rehabilitation center for adolescents. 13 beds for adolescents. Patient security: staff secured. Not-for-profit facility affiliated with Karma House, Inc., Rockville, MD. Licensed by state of Maryland.

Participants Accepts: male adolescents. Average stay: 12 months. Admission: one parent, all parties who share custody, court order, voluntary, depending on program. Treats behavior disorders; substance abuse; compulsive/addictive disorders other than substance abuse and eating disorders.

Staff 1.3 full-time direct-care staff members per adolescent. Staff is 60% male, 40% female.

Contact Renee Jones, Program Director, main address above. Phone: 301-341-8880.

KASEMAN PRESBYTERIAN HOSPITAL
8300 Constitution, NE
Albuquerque, New Mexico 87110
505-291-2542

General Information General hospital for children, adolescents. Patient security: entirely locked. Not-for-profit facility affiliated with Presbyterian Healthcare Services, Albuquerque, NM. Licensed by state of New Mexico. Accredited by JCAHO.

Participants Accepts: male and female children; male and female adolescents. Admission: one parent, all parties who share custody, voluntary, under custody of Department of Social Services, depending on program. Treats learning disabilities; behavior disorders; general psychosocial disorders; substance abuse; post-traumatic stress disorder; thought, mood, and personality disorders.

Staff Staff is 50% male, 50% female.

Additional Services Partial hospitalization for males and females ages 4–18. Treats learning disabilities; behavior disorders; general psychosocial disorders; substance abuse; post-traumatic stress disorder; thought, mood, and personality disorders.

Contact Pam Garrett, Clinical Coordinator, main address above. Phone: 505-291-2542.

KEYSTONE CENTER
2001 Providence Avenue
Chester, Pennsylvania 19013
215-876-9000; Fax: 215-876-5441

General Information Drug and alcohol rehabilitation center for adolescents. 12 beds for adolescents. Open year-round. Patient security: unlocked; no runaway pursuit. Suburban setting. For-profit facility affiliated with Universal Health Services, King of Prussia, PA. Licensed by state of Pennsylvania. Accredited by JCAHO.

Participants Accepts: male and female adolescents ages 11–17. Admission: voluntary. Treats learning disabilities; behavior disorders; general psychosocial disorders; substance abuse; eating disorders; post-traumatic stress disorder; thought, mood, and personality disorders. Accepts the mobility impaired; those with a history of harm to themselves and others; those receiving psychotropic medication; those with a history of epilepsy. Special programs for the chronically ill; the mobility impaired; the developmentally disabled; those with AIDS. Largest number of participants from Pennsylvania, New Jersey, New York.

Program Treatment modalities: Twelve Step Recovery. Family treatment program available.

Staff 2.3 full-time direct-care staff members per adolescent. Total facility staff includes 2 physicians, 2 psychologists, 1 psychiatrist, 7 registered nurses, 7 practical/vocational nurses, 1 social worker (non-MSW), 1 teacher, 1 counselor, 2 occupational/recreational therapists, 1 dietician, 2 other direct-care staff members. Staff is 25% male, 75% female.

Facilities Single building; males and females in separate units. Central dining (shared with adults). Basketball courts, game room.

Education Academic program available at additional cost. Serves ages 12–17, grades 7–12. 1 teacher on staff. Curriculum accredited or approved by Chester Upland School District. Cost of educational program covered by local school district.

Costs Average cost: $14,000 per stay. Accepts private insurance, group insurance, Blue Cross/Blue Shield.

Additional Services Outpatient services for males and females ages 12–17. Treats learning disabilities; behavior disorders; general psychosocial disorders; substance abuse; eating disorders; compulsive/addictive disorders other than substance abuse and eating disorders; post-traumatic stress disorder; thought, mood, and personality disorders.

Contact Mark Snow, Director of Admissions, main address above. Phone: 215-876-9000. Fax: 215-876-5441.

KINGS VIEW CENTER
42675 Road 44
Reedley, California 93654
209-638-2505; Fax: 209-244-6767

General Information Residential treatment/subacute facility for children, adolescents. Patient security: staff secured. Independent not-for-profit facility. Licensed by state of California. Accredited by JCAHO.

Participants Accepts: male and female children; male and female adolescents. Average stay: 6 months. Admission: one parent, all parties who share custody, court order, voluntary, depending on program. Treats learning disabilities; behavior disorders; general psychosocial disorders; compulsive/addictive disorders other than substance abuse and eating disorders; post-traumatic stress disorder; thought, mood, and personality disorders.

Costs Average cost: $375 per day.

Contact Assessment Referral Department, main address above. Phone: 800-348-5577.

KOALA HOSPITAL
2223 Poshard Drive
Columbus, Indiana 47201
800-562-5213; Fax: 812-376-0801

General Information Psychiatric hospital for adolescents. 20 beds for adolescents. Patient security: entirely locked. For-profit facility affiliated with Sterling Health Care Corporation, Bellevue, WA. Licensed by state of Indiana. Accredited by JCAHO.

Participants Accepts: male and female adolescents. Average stay: 30 days. Admission: one parent, all parties who share custody, court order, voluntary, depending on program. Treats autistic disorders; learning disabilities; behavior disorders; general psychosocial disorders; substance abuse; eating disorders; compulsive/addictive disorders other than substance abuse and eating disorders; post-traumatic stress disorder; thought, mood, and personality disorders.

Costs Average cost: $595 per day.

Contact Kim Moore, Program Director, main address above. Phone: 800-562-5213. Fax: 812-376-0801.

KOALA HOSPITAL
1404 South State Avenue
Indianapolis, Indiana 46203
317-783-4084; Fax: 317-782-3801

General Information Psychiatric hospital for adolescents. 76 beds for adolescents. Patient security: entirely locked. For-profit facility affiliated with Sterling Health Care Corporation, Bellevue, WA. Licensed by state of Indiana. Accredited by JCAHO.

Participants Accepts: male and female adolescents. Average stay: 18 days. Admission: one parent, all parties who share custody, court order, voluntary, depending on program. Treats autistic disorders; learning disabilities; behavior disorders; general psychosocial disorders; substance abuse; eating disorders; compulsive/addictive disorders other than substance abuse and eating disorders; post-traumatic stress disorder; thought, mood, and personality disorders.

Staff Staff is 25% male, 75% female.

Costs Average cost: $600 per day.

Additional Services Outpatient services for males and females ages 12–18. Treats autistic disorders; learning disabilities; behavior disorders; general psychosocial disorders; substance abuse; eating disorders; compulsive/addictive disorders other than substance abuse and eating disorders; post-traumatic stress disorder; thought, mood, and personality disorders.

Contact Steve Gambel, Director of Admissions, main address above. Phone: 317-783-4084. Fax: 317-782-3801.

KOALA HOSPITAL PLYMOUTH
1800 North Oak Road
Plymouth, Indiana 46563
219-936-3784; Fax: 219-936-2887

General Information Psychiatric hospital for adolescents, adults. 40 beds for adolescents. Open year-round. Patient security: partially locked; will pursue and return runaways. Rural setting. For-profit facility affiliated with K. Hospitals Indiana, Inc., Lebanon, IN. Licensed by state of Indiana. Accredited by JCAHO.

Participants Accepts: male and female adolescents ages 12–18; male and female adults ages 18–65. Average stay: 34 days. Admission: one parent, all parties who share custody, court order, depending on program. Treats learning disabilities; behavior disorders; general psychosocial disorders; substance abuse; eating disorders; post-traumatic stress disorder; thought, mood, and personality disorders. Accepts those with a history of harm to themselves and others; those receiving psychotropic medication. Largest number of participants from Indiana, Michigan, Illinois.

Program Treatment modalities: psychodynamic; psychopharmacology; Twelve Step Recovery. Family treatment program available.

Staff .8 full-time direct-care staff member per adolescent. Total facility staff includes 3 physicians, 4 psychologists, 1 psychiatrist, 15 registered nurses, 5 practical/vocational nurses, 2 MSW social workers, 4 social workers (non-MSW), 2 teachers, 9 counselors, 12 therapists, 1 dietician, 10 other direct-care staff members. Staff is 50% male, 50% female.

Facilities Single building; males and females in coeducational units. Separate residential quarters for adolescents. Central dining (shared with adults). Basketball courts, gymnasium, playing fields.

Education   Academic program available at no charge. Serves ages 12–18, ungraded. 2 teachers on staff.

Costs   Accepts private insurance, group insurance, medicaid, Blue Cross/Blue Shield.

Additional Services   Drug and alcohol rehabilitation services for males and females ages 12–18. Treats learning disabilities; behavior disorders; general psychosocial disorders; substance abuse; compulsive/addictive disorders other than substance abuse and eating disorders; post-traumatic stress disorder; thought, mood, and personality disorders. Outpatient services for males and females ages 12–18. Treats learning disabilities; behavior disorders; general psychosocial disorders; substance abuse; compulsive/addictive disorders other than substance abuse and eating disorders; post-traumatic stress disorder; thought, mood, and personality disorders.

Contact   Charlotte Pontius, Administrator, main address above. Phone: 219-936-3784. Fax: 219-936-2887.

THE KOLBURNE SCHOOL, INC.
Southfield Road
New Marlborough, Massachusetts 01230
413-229-8787; Fax: 413-229-7708

General Information   School for children, adolescents. Open year-round. Patient security: staff secured; will pursue and return runaways. Rural setting. Independent for-profit facility. Licensed by state of Massachusetts. Accredited by JCAHO; Massachusetts Department of Social Services; Office for Children.

Participants   Accepts: male and female children and adolescents ages 8–21. Average stay: 730 days. Admission: all parties who share custody, court order, depending on program. Treats learning disabilities; behavior disorders; general psychosocial disorders; substance abuse; eating disorders; compulsive/addictive disorders other than substance abuse and eating disorders; thought, mood, and personality disorders. Accepts the speech impaired; those with a history of arson; the sexually compulsive; those with a history of harm to themselves and others; those receiving psychotropic medication; those with a history of epilepsy. Special programs for the developmentally disabled. Largest number of participants from New York, Maryland, Massachusetts.

Program   Treatment modalities: behavioral treatment—achievement place model; Alcoholics Anony-

mous; Orton; vocational program. Family treatment program available.

Staff   Total facility staff includes 1 physician, 6 psychologists, 1 psychiatrist, 1 registered nurse, 4 practical/vocational nurses, 3 MSW social workers, 30 teachers, 2 occupational/recreational therapists, 4 speech pathologists, 1 dietician, 140 other direct-care staff members.

Facilities   Multiple buildings; males and females in both coeducational and separate units depending on program. Central dining. Basketball courts, game room, gymnasium, indoor swimming pool, outdoor tennis courts, playing fields.

Education   School serves ages 8–21, grades K–12. 30 teachers on staff. Curriculum is college-preparatory; diploma granted upon completion. Curriculum accredited or approved by Massachusetts Department of Education. Organized sports program offered.

Costs   Accepts private insurance, group insurance, Blue Cross/Blue Shield, public funds.

Additional Services   Wilderness/survival program for males and females ages 8–21. Treats learning disabilities; behavior disorders; general psychosocial disorders; substance abuse; eating disorders; compulsive/addictive disorders other than substance abuse and eating disorders; post-traumatic stress disorder; thought, mood, and personality disorders.

Contact   Kathy Grecco, Director of Intake, main address above. Phone: 413-229-8787. Fax: 413-229-7708.

LA AMISTAD RESIDENTIAL
TREATMENT CENTER
201 Alpine Drive
Maitland, Florida 32751
407-647-0660; Fax: 407-647-3060

General Information   Residential treatment/subacute facility for children, adolescents. 8 beds for children; 32 beds for adolescents; 40 beds total. Open year-round. Patient security: unlocked; will pursue and return runaways. Urban setting. For-profit facility affiliated with Universal Health Services, Inc., King of Prussia, PA. Licensed by state of Florida. Accredited by JCAHO; Civilian Health and Medical Program of the Uniformed Services.

Participants   Accepts: male and female children ages 6–13; male and female adolescents ages 14–18. Admission: voluntary. Treats learning disabilities; behavior disorders; general psychosocial disorders; post-traumatic stress disorder; thought, mood, and personality disorders. Accepts those with a history of harm to themselves and others; those receiving psychotropic medication; those with a history of epilepsy. Special programs for those with psychiatric disorders; dual diagnosis; sexual abuse victims.

Program Treatment modalities: psychodynamic; Twelve Step Recovery; behavior modification; family therapy. Family treatment program available.

Staff Total facility staff includes 1 psychologist, 7 psychiatrists, 6 registered nurses, 5 practical/vocational nurses, 8 MSW social workers, 8 therapists, 30 other direct-care staff members. Staff is 35% male, 65% female.

Facilities Multiple buildings; males and females in separate units. Separate dining by residential unit available. Game room, gymnasium, playing fields.

Education Academic program available at no charge. Serves ages 6–19, grades 1–12. Curriculum accredited or approved by State of Florida. Cost of educational program covered by local school district.

Costs Accepts private insurance, group insurance, Blue Cross/Blue Shield.

Contact Steve Dolliver, Director of Admissions, main address above. Phone: 407-647-0660. Fax: 407-647-3060.

LA GRANGE MEMORIAL HOSPITAL
5101 South Willow Springs Road
La Grange, Illinois 60525
708-352-1200; Fax: 708-579-4930

General Information General hospital for children, adolescents. Patient security: staff secured. Not-for-profit facility affiliated with La Grange Memorial Health System, La Grange, IL. Licensed by state of Illinois. Accredited by JCAHO.

Participants Accepts: male and female children; male and female adolescents. Admission: voluntary. Treats general psychosocial disorders; substance abuse; eating disorders; compulsive/addictive disorders other than substance abuse and eating disorders.

Contact Health Bank, main address above. Phone: 708-354-7070.

LAKE CHARLES MEMORIAL HOSPITAL
1701 Oak Park Boulevard
Lake Charles, Louisiana 70601
318-494-3000

General Information General hospital for adolescents. 20 beds for adolescents. Open year-round. Patient security: entirely locked; will pursue and return runaways. Suburban setting. Independent not-for-profit facility. Licensed by state of Louisiana. Accredited by JCAHO.

Participants Accepts: male and female adolescents ages 12–18. Average stay: 21 days. Admission: all parties who share custody, commitment by coroner, depending on program. Treats learning disabilities; behavior disorders; substance abuse; post-traumatic stress disorder; thought, mood, and personality disorders. Accepts those with a history of harm to themselves and others; those receiving psychotropic medication; those with a history of epilepsy.

Program Treatment modalities: Twelve Step Recovery; psychodynamic; behavior modification. Family treatment program available.

Staff Total facility staff includes 1 physician, 2 psychologists, 3 psychiatrists, 7 registered nurses, 3 MSW social workers, 2 teachers, 2 counselors, 2 occupational/recreational therapists, 1 speech pathologist, 1 dietician.

Facilities Single building; males and females in co-educational units. Central dining. Basketball courts, game room, playing fields, recreation and physical activity floor.

Education Academic program available. Serves ages 12–18, grades 6–12. 2 teachers on staff. Curriculum accredited or approved by Louisiana State Board of Education. Organized sports program offered.

Costs Average cost: $18,000 per stay. Accepts private insurance, group insurance, Blue Cross/Blue Shield.

Additional Services Drug and alcohol rehabilitation services for males and females ages 12–18. Treats learning disabilities; behavior disorders; general psychosocial disorders; substance abuse; post-traumatic stress disorder; thought, mood, and personality disorders. Outpatient services for males and females ages 12–18. Treats learning disabilities; behavior disorders; general psychosocial disorders; substance abuse; post-traumatic stress disorder; thought, mood, and personality disorders.

Contact Mark Severns, Program Director of Recovery Center, main address above. Phone: 318-494-3000.

LAKELAND COMMUNITY HOSPITAL, INC.
3700 Kolbe Road
Lorain, Ohio 44053
216-960-4730; Fax: 216-960-4637

General Information   General hospital for adolescents, adults. 22 beds for adolescents. Open year-round. Patient security: partially locked; will pursue and return runaways. Suburban setting. Independent not-for-profit facility. Licensed by state of Ohio. Accredited by JCAHO; Ohio Department of Mental Health, Ohio Department of Alcohol and Drug Addiction Services.

Participants   Accepts: male and female adolescents ages 13–19; male and female adults ages 18 and up. Average stay: 14 days. Admission: one parent. Treats general psychosocial disorders; substance abuse; post-traumatic stress disorder; thought, mood, and personality disorders. Accepts the mobility impaired; the vision impaired; those receiving psychotropic medication; those with a history of epilepsy. Special programs for the mobility impaired. Largest number of participants from Ohio.

Program   Treatment modalities: individual, couples, family, and group psychotherapy; psychotropic medication management; Twelve Step Recovery; psycheducation. Family treatment program available.

Staff   1.1 full-time direct-care staff members per adolescent. Total facility staff includes 3 physicians, 3 psychologists, 7 psychiatrists, 30 registered nurses, 2 practical/vocational nurses, 5 MSW social workers, 2 teachers, 22 counselors, 1 physical therapist, 2 occupational/recreational therapists, 1 speech pathologist, 1 dietician. Staff is 20% male, 80% female.

Facilities   Multiple buildings; males and females in coeducational units. Separate residential quarters for adolescents. Central dining (not shared with adults). Basketball courts, game room, gymnasium, par course, volleyball courts.

Education   Academic program available at no charge. Serves ages 13–19, grades 7–12. 2 teachers on staff. Curriculum accredited or approved by Amherst School District, State of Ohio. Cost of educational program sometimes covered by local school district.

Costs   Average cost: $500 per day. Accepts private insurance, group insurance, medicare, Blue Cross/Blue Shield.

Additional Services   Drug and alcohol rehabilitation services for males and females ages 13 and up. Treats general psychosocial disorders; substance abuse; thought, mood, and personality disorders. Outpatient services for males and females ages 13 and up. Treats general psychosocial disorders; substance abuse; post-traumatic stress disorder; thought, mood, and personality disorders. Residential or sub-acute services for males and females ages 13 and up. Treats general psychosocial disorders; substance abuse; post-traumatic stress disorder; thought, mood, and personality disorders.

Contact   Marilyn Higgins, Intake Specialist, main address above. Phone: 216-960-3500. Fax: 216-960-4637.

LAKELAND REGIONAL HOSPITAL
440 South Market
Springfield, Missouri 65806
417-865-5581; Fax: 417-865-5964

General Information   Psychiatric hospital with dual diagnosis program for children, adolescents. 18 beds for children; 42 beds for adolescents; 60 beds total. Patient security: entirely locked. For-profit facility affiliated with Psychiatric Hospital Corporation, Birmingham, AL. Licensed by state of Missouri. Accredited by JCAHO.

Participants   Accepts: male and female children; male and female adolescents. Average stay: 27 days. Admission: one parent, all parties who share custody, court order, voluntary, depending on program. Treats behavior disorders; general psychosocial disorders; substance abuse; eating disorders; compulsive/addictive disorders other than substance abuse and eating disorders; post-traumatic stress disorder; thought, mood, and personality disorders.

Staff   Staff is 35% male, 65% female.

Contact   Helen Bradley, Director of Social Work, main address above. Phone: 417-865-5581 Ext. 442. Fax: 417-865-5964.

LAKEVIEW HOSPITAL STEP ONE PROGRAM
630 East Medical Drive
Bountiful, Utah 84010
801-299-2186; Fax: 801-299-2511

General Information   General hospital for adolescents. 42 beds for adolescents. For-profit facility affiliated with Health Trust, Inc., Nashville, TN. Licensed by state of Utah. Accredited by JCAHO.

Participants   Accepts: male and female adolescents. Average stay: 3 weeks. Admission: one parent, all parties who share custody, court order, voluntary, depending on program. Treats learning disabilities; behavior disorders; general psychosocial disorders;

substance abuse; eating disorders; compulsive/addictive disorders other than substance abuse and eating disorders; post-traumatic stress disorder; thought, mood, and personality disorders.

Staff Staff is 50% male, 50% female.

Additional Services Day treatment program for males and females ages 13–18. Treats learning disabilities; behavior disorders; general psychosocial disorders; substance abuse; eating disorders; compulsive/addictive disorders other than substance abuse and eating disorders; post-traumatic stress disorder; thought, mood, and personality disorders.

Contact Randy Moss, Coordinator of Adolescent Services, main address above. Phone: 801-299-2186. Fax: 801-299-2511.

LANDER VALLEY MEDICAL CENTER
1320 Bishop Randall Drive
Lander, Wyoming 82520
307-332-5700

General Information General hospital for adolescents. Patient security: entirely locked. For-profit facility affiliated with OrNda Corporation, Nashville, TN. Licensed by state of Wyoming. Accredited by JCAHO.

Participants Accepts: male and female adolescents. Average stay: 14 days. Admission: one parent, voluntary, depending on program. Treats behavior disorders; general psychosocial disorders; substance abuse; eating disorders; compulsive/addictive disorders other than substance abuse and eating disorders; post-traumatic stress disorder; thought, mood, and personality disorders.

Staff Staff is 30% male, 70% female.

Costs Average cost: $600 per day.

Contact Theresa Alfertig, Intake Coordinator, main address above. Phone: 307-332-5700.

LA PORTE HOSPITAL STRESS CENTER
State and Madison
La Porte, Indiana 46350-0250
219-326-2420; Fax: 219-326-2509

General Information General hospital for adolescents. 10 beds for adolescents. Patient security: entirely locked. Independent not-for-profit facility. Operated by Mental Health Management, Inc.,

McLean, VA. Licensed by state of Indiana. Accredited by JCAHO.

Participants Accepts: male and female adolescents. Average stay: 10 days. Admission: one parent, all parties who share custody, court order, voluntary, depending on program. Treats behavior disorders; general psychosocial disorders; substance abuse; post-traumatic stress disorder; thought, mood, and personality disorders.

Staff Staff is all female.

Costs Average cost: $455 per day.

Contact Paula Athens, Director of Social Services, P.O. Box 250, La Porte, IN 46350-0250. Phone: 219-326-2420. Fax: 219-326-2509.

LARICO CENTER FOR YOUTH ADDICTIONS, INC.
640 West Prospect Street
Fort Collins, Colorado 80524
303-482-1037

General Information Residential treatment/subacute facility for adolescents. 11 beds for adolescents. Independent not-for-profit facility. Licensed by state of Colorado. Accredited by Colorado Alcohol and Drug Division.

Participants Accepts: male and female adolescents. Average stay: 9 months. Admission: court order, voluntary, Department of Social Services, depending on program. Treats substance abuse. Accepts the vision impaired; the speech impaired; those receiving psychotropic medication; those with a history of epilepsy.

Staff Staff is 40% male, 60% female.

Costs Average cost: $80 per day.

Contact Julia Landis, Program Director, 614 South Matthews Street, Fort Collins, CO 80524. Phone: 303-221-4040.

LARICO YOUTH HOMES, INC.
614 South Matthews Street
Fort Collins, Colorado 80524
303-221-4040

General Information Residential treatment/subacute facility for adolescents. 12 beds for adolescents. Patient security: staff secured. Independent not-for-profit facility. Licensed by state of Colorado. Accredited by Colorado Alcohol and Drug Division.

Participants Accepts: male and female adolescents. Average stay: 9 months. Admission: court order, voluntary, Department of Social Services, depending on program. Treats learning disabilities; behavior disorders; general psychosocial disorders; substance abuse; eating disorders; compulsive/addictive disorders other than substance abuse and eating disorders; post-traumatic stress disorder; thought, mood, and personality disorders.

Staff Staff is 40% male, 60% female.

Costs Average cost: $80 per day.

Contact Julia Landis, Program Director, main address above. Phone: 303-221-4040.

LARUE D. CARTER MEMORIAL HOSPITAL SCHOOL
1315 West 10th Street
Indianapolis, Indiana 46202-2885
317-634-8401 Ext. 451; Fax: 317-634-1103

General Information Residential treatment/subacute facility for children, adolescents. 16 beds for children; 18 beds for adolescents. Patient security: staff secured. Independent not-for-profit facility. Licensed by state of Indiana. Accredited by JCAHO.

Participants Accepts: male and female children; male and female adolescents. Average stay: 6 months. Admission: one parent, all parties who share custody, court order, voluntary, depending on program. Treats learning disabilities; behavior disorders; general psychosocial disorders; substance abuse; eating disorders; compulsive/addictive disorders other than substance abuse and eating disorders; post-traumatic stress disorder; thought, mood, and personality disorders.

Education Academic program available. Serves ages 6–18, grades K–12. Curriculum accredited or approved by Department of Education.

Costs Average cost: $325 per day. Accepts medicaid.

Contact John Somers, Principal, main address above. Phone: 317-634-8401 Ext. 451. Fax: 317-634-1103.

LAS ENCINAS HOSPITAL
2900 East Del Mar Boulevard
Pasadena, California 91107
818-795-9901; Fax: 818-792-2919

General Information Psychiatric hospital for children, adolescents, adults. 7 beds for children; 13 beds for adolescents; 153 beds total. Open year-round. Patient security: entirely locked; will pursue and return runaways. Suburban setting. For-profit facility affiliated with Hospital Corporation of America, Nashville, TN. Licensed by state of California. Accredited by JCAHO; California Department of Health Services.

Participants Accepts: male and female children ages 5–12; male and female adolescents ages 13–17; male and female adults ages 18 and up. Average stay: 16 days. Admission: one parent. Treats learning disabilities; behavior disorders; general psychosocial disorders; substance abuse; eating disorders; compulsive/addictive disorders other than substance abuse and eating disorders; post-traumatic stress disorder; thought, mood, and personality disorders. Accepts those with a history of harm to themselves and others; those receiving psychotropic medication; non-English speaking individuals; those with a history of epilepsy. Largest number of participants from California.

Program Treatment modalities: social skills model. Family treatment program available.

Staff Total facility staff includes 1 physician, 1 psychologist, 1 psychiatrist, 3 registered nurses, 8 practical/vocational nurses, 1 MSW social worker, 1 teacher, 1 counselor, 1 occupational/recreational therapist, 1 dietician, 3 other direct-care staff members. Staff is 50% male, 50% female.

Facilities Multiple buildings; males and females in coeducational units. Separate residential quarters for children and adolescents. Central dining (shared with adults). Basketball courts, outdoor swimming pool, outdoor tennis courts, playing fields.

Education Academic program available at no charge. Serves ages 5–17, grades 1–12. 1 teacher on staff. Curriculum accredited or approved by California State Department of Education.

Costs Accepts private insurance, group insurance, Blue Cross/Blue Shield.

Additional Services Drug and alcohol rehabilitation services for males and females ages 5–17. Treats learning disabilities; behavior disorders; general psychosocial disorders; substance abuse; eating disorders; compulsive/addictive disorders other than substance abuse and eating disorders; post-traumatic stress disorder; thought, mood, and personality disorders. Outpatient services for males and females ages 5–17. Treats learning disabilities; behavior disorders;

general psychosocial disorders; substance abuse; eating disorders; compulsive/addictive disorders other than substance abuse and eating disorders; post-traumatic stress disorder; thought, mood, and personality disorders.

Contact Vicki Miller, Director of Specialized Services, main address above. Phone: 818-795-9901. Fax: 818-792-2919.

LAS ROSAS
10755 East Tanque Verde
Tucson, Arizona 85749
602-749-5980; Fax: 602-749-7192

General Information Drug and alcohol rehabilitation center for adolescents. 30 beds for adolescents. Patient security: staff secured. Not-for-profit facility affiliated with Amity, Inc., Tucson, AZ. Licensed by state of Arizona.

Participants Accepts: female adolescents. Average stay: 9 months. Admission: one parent, all parties who share custody, court order, voluntary, depending on program. Treats learning disabilities; behavior disorders; general psychosocial disorders; substance abuse; compulsive/addictive disorders other than substance abuse and eating disorders; post-traumatic stress disorder; thought, mood, and personality disorders.

Staff Staff is 40% male, 60% female.

Costs Average cost: $122 per day.

Contact Liz Bonorand, Program Manager, P.O. Box 32200, Tucson, AZ 85751-2200. Phone: 602-749-5980. Fax: 602-749-7192.

LAUGHLIN PAVILION
900 East Laharpe
Kirksville, Missouri 63501
816-665-5171; Fax: 816-665-2102

General Information Psychiatric hospital for children, adolescents. Patient security: partially locked. For-profit facility affiliated with National Medical Enterprises, Santa Monica, CA. Licensed by state of Missouri. Accredited by American Osteopathic Association.

Participants Accepts: male and female children; male and female adolescents. Average stay: 180 days. Admission: one parent, all parties who share custody, court order, voluntary, depending on program. Treats

autistic disorders; learning disabilities; behavior disorders; general psychosocial disorders; substance abuse; eating disorders; compulsive/addictive disorders other than substance abuse and eating disorders; post-traumatic stress disorder; thought, mood, and personality disorders.

Staff Staff is 40% male, 60% female.

Contact Tom Holman, Director of Inpatient Services, main address above. Phone: 816-665-5171. Fax: 816-665-2102.

LAUREATE PSYCHIATRIC CLINIC AND HOSPITAL
6655 South Yale
Tulsa, Oklahoma 74136
918-481-4000

General Information Psychiatric hospital for children, adolescents, adults. Open year-round. Patient security: entirely locked; will pursue and return runaways. Suburban setting. Independent not-for-profit facility. Licensed by state of Oklahoma. Accredited by JCAHO; National Association of Private Psychiatric Hospitals, Health Care Financing Administration.

Participants Accepts: male and female children ages 1–13; male and female adolescents ages 13–18; male and female adults ages 18 and up. Average stay: 18 days. Admission: one parent, all parties who share custody, depending on program. Treats autistic disorders; learning disabilities; behavior disorders; general psychosocial disorders; substance abuse; eating disorders; compulsive/addictive disorders other than substance abuse and eating disorders; post-traumatic stress disorder; thought, mood, and personality disorders. Accepts the mobility impaired; the vision impaired; the hearing impaired; the speech impaired; those with a history of arson; the sexually compulsive; those with a history of harm to themselves and others; those receiving psychotropic medication; those with a history of epilepsy. Special programs for the chronically ill; the developmentally disabled.

Program Treatment modalities: psychodynamic; supportive; Twelve Step Recovery; behavioral. Family treatment program available.

Staff Total facility staff includes 9 physicians, 10 psychologists, 12 psychiatrists, 45 registered nurses, 1 practical/vocational nurse, 15 MSW social workers, 1 social worker (non-MSW), 3 teachers, 7 counselors, 2 occupational/recreational therapists, 1 dietician, 60 other direct-care staff members.

Facilities Multiple buildings; males and females in coeducational units. Separate residential quarters for children and adolescents. Central dining (shared with adults). Basketball courts, game room, gymnasium, indoor swimming pool, outdoor swimming pool, racquetball courts.

Education Academic program available at no charge. Serves ages 13–18, ungraded. 3 teachers on staff. Curriculum accredited or approved by Tulsa Public Schools. Organized sports program offered.

Costs Average cost: $650 per day. Accepts private insurance, group insurance, medicare, Blue Cross/Blue Shield.

Additional Services Drug and alcohol rehabilitation services for males and females ages 13 and up. Treats learning disabilities; behavior disorders; general psychosocial disorders; substance abuse; eating disorders; compulsive/addictive disorders other than substance abuse and eating disorders; post-traumatic stress disorder; thought, mood, and personality disorders. Outpatient services for males and females ages 1 and up. Treats autistic disorders; learning disabilities; behavior disorders; general psychosocial disorders; substance abuse; eating disorders; compulsive/addictive disorders other than substance abuse and eating disorders; post-traumatic stress disorder; thought, mood, and personality disorders. Residential or sub-acute services for males and females ages 13 and up. Treats autistic disorders; learning disabilities; behavior disorders; general psychosocial disorders; substance abuse; eating disorders; compulsive/addictive disorders other than substance abuse and eating disorders; post-traumatic stress disorder; thought, mood, and personality disorders.

Contact Dona Ghazal, Manager of Referrals, main address above. Phone: 918-481-4000.

LAURELBROOKE EXTENDED CARE PROGRAM
4600 West Shroeder Drive
Brown Deer, Wisconsin 53223
414-355-2273

General Information Residential treatment/subacute facility for children. 25 beds for children. Open year-round. Patient security: entirely locked; no runaway pursuit. Suburban setting. For-profit facility affiliated with National Medical Enterprises, Washington, DC. Licensed by state of Wisconsin. Accredited by JCAHO; Occupational Safety and Health Administration.

Participants Accepts: male and female children ages 5–13. Average stay: 270 days. Admission: all parties who share custody, court order, depending on program. Treats learning disabilities; behavior disorders; general psychosocial disorders; eating disorders; compulsive/addictive disorders other than substance abuse and eating disorders; post-traumatic stress disorder; thought, mood, and personality disorders. Accepts the mobility impaired; the vision impaired; the hearing impaired; the speech impaired; those with a history of arson; the sexually compulsive; those with a history of harm to themselves and others; those receiving psychotropic medication; those with a history of epilepsy. Largest number of participants from Indiana, Wisconsin, Illinois.

Program Treatment modalities: psychodynamic. Family treatment program available.

Staff 1.2 full-time direct-care staff members per child. Total facility staff includes 1 psychiatrist, 5 registered nurses, 2 MSW social workers, 3 teachers, 10 counselors, 5 occupational/recreational therapists, 4 other direct-care staff members.

Facilities Single building; males and females in coeducational units. Central dining (shared with adults). Basketball courts, gymnasium, outdoor swimming pool, playing fields, ropes course.

Education Academic program available at no charge. Serves ages 5–13, grades K–8. 3 teachers on staff.

Costs Average cost: $400 per day. Accepts private insurance, Blue Cross/Blue Shield.

Contact Jeff Kazmierczak, Program Director, main address above. Phone: 414-355-2273.

LAUREL HEIGHTS HOSPITAL
934 Briarcliff Road, NE
Atlanta, Georgia 30306
404-888-7860; Fax: 404-872-5088

General Information Residential treatment/subacute facility for children, adolescents. 28 beds for children; 74 beds for adolescents; 102 beds total. Open year-round. Patient security: entirely locked. Urban setting. For-profit facility affiliated with National Medical Enterprises, Santa Monica, CA. Licensed by state of Georgia. Accredited by JCAHO.

Participants Accepts: male and female children ages 5–11; male and female adolescents ages 13–17. Admission: one parent, court order, depending on program. Treats learning disabilities; behavior disorders; general psychosocial disorders; substance abuse; eating disorders; compulsive/addictive disorders other than substance abuse and eating disorders; post-traumatic stress disorder; thought, mood, and personality disorders. Accepts those with a history of arson; those with a history of harm to themselves and others; those receiving psychotropic medication. Largest number of participants from Georgia, South Carolina, Indiana.

Program Treatment modalities: psychodynamic; behavioral; cognitive/behavioral; Twelve Step Recovery. Family treatment program available.

Staff 2 full-time direct-care staff members per child or adolescent. Total facility staff includes 2 physicians, 13 psychologists, 22 psychiatrists, 34 registered nurses, 4 practical/vocational nurses, 9 MSW social workers, 12 teachers, 98 counselors, 6 occupational/recreational therapists, 1 dietician. Staff is 41% male, 59% female.

Facilities Multiple buildings; males and females in coeducational units. Central dining. Basketball courts, gymnasium, outdoor swimming pool, playing fields, ropes course, playscape for children.

Education Academic program available at no charge. Serves ages 5–17, grades 1–12. 12 teachers on staff. Curriculum accredited or approved by State of Georgia.

Costs Accepts private insurance, group insurance, public funds.

Contact Kevin Rohrer, Intake Director, main address above. Phone: 404-888-7868. Fax: 404-872-5088.

LAUREL RIDGE HOSPITAL
17720 Corporate Woods Drive
San Antonio, Texas 78259
512-491-9400; Fax: 512-491-3550

General Information Psychiatric hospital for children, adolescents, adults. 26 beds for children; 118 beds for adolescents; 180 beds total. Open year-round. Patient security: partially locked; will pursue and return runaways. Suburban setting. For-profit facility affiliated with Healthcare International, Inc., Austin, TX. Licensed by state of Texas. Accredited by JCAHO; Texas Mental Health and Mental Retardation, Texas Department of Human Services, Texas Commission on Alcohol and Drug Abuse.

Participants Accepts: male and female children ages 3–12; male and female adolescents ages 13–18; male and female adults ages 19 and up. Average stay: 180 days. Admission: one parent, court order, depending on program. Treats autistic disorders; learning disabilities; behavior disorders; general psychosocial

disorders; substance abuse; eating disorders; compulsive/addictive disorders other than substance abuse and eating disorders; post-traumatic stress disorder; thought, mood, and personality disorders. Accepts the mobility impaired; the vision impaired; the hearing impaired; the speech impaired; those with a history of arson; the sexually compulsive; those with a history of harm to themselves and others; those receiving psychotropic medication; non-English speaking individuals; those with a history of epilepsy.

Program Treatment modalities: psychodynamic; behavior management; milieu; Twelve Step Recovery. Family treatment program available.

Staff Total facility staff includes 4 physicians, 1 psychologist, 23 psychiatrists, 56 registered nurses, 18 practical/vocational nurses, 9 MSW social workers, 4 social workers (non-MSW), 7 teachers, 3 counselors, 1 occupational/recreational therapist, 1 speech pathologist, 3 therapists, 1 dietician, 22 other direct-care staff members.

Facilities Multiple buildings; males and females in coeducational units. Separate residential quarters for children and adolescents. Central dining (shared with adults). Basketball courts, game room, gymnasium, outdoor swimming pool, ropes course.

Education Academic program available at no charge. Serves ages 4–20, grades K–12. 7 teachers on staff. Curriculum accredited or approved by Southern Association of Colleges and Schools, Northeast Independent School District. Cost of educational program covered by local school district.

Costs Accepts private insurance, group insurance, medicare, Blue Cross/Blue Shield, public funds.

Additional Services Drug and alcohol rehabilitation services for males and females ages 13 and up. Treats behavior disorders; general psychosocial disorders; substance abuse; eating disorders; compulsive/addictive disorders other than substance abuse and eating disorders; post-traumatic stress disorder; thought, mood, and personality disorders. Day treatment for males and females ages 3 and up. Treats autistic disorders; learning disabilities; behavior disorders; general psychosocial disorders; substance abuse; eating disorders; compulsive/addictive disorders other than substance abuse and eating disorders; post-traumatic stress disorder; thought, mood, and personality disorders.

Contact Pita Kresh, Admissions Director, main address above. Phone: 512-491-9400. Fax: 512-491-3550.

LAUREL WOOD CENTER
Highway 39, North
Meridian, Mississippi 39303
601-483-6211; Fax: 601-482-3207

General Information Psychiatric hospital for adolescents, adults. 22 beds for adolescents. Open year-round. Patient security arrangements vary depending on program; will pursue and return runaways. Suburban setting. Independent for-profit facility. Licensed by state of Mississippi. Accredited by JCAHO; Health Care Financing Administration.

Participants Accepts: male and female adolescents ages 12–18; male and female adults ages 19 and up. Average stay: 15 days. Admission: one parent, all parties who share custody, court order, depending on program. Treats learning disabilities; behavior disorders; general psychosocial disorders; substance abuse; eating disorders; thought, mood, and personality disorders. Accepts the mobility impaired; the vision impaired; the speech impaired; those receiving psychotropic medication. Special programs for the chronically ill; the mobility impaired.

Program Treatment modalities: Twelve Step Recovery; psycho-educational groups; behavioral management. Family treatment program available.

Staff Total facility staff includes 1 physician, 2 psychologists, 2 psychiatrists, 9 registered nurses, 1 MSW social worker, 1 teacher, 3 counselors, 2 physical therapists, 1 therapist. Staff is 50% male, 50% female.

Facilities Multiple buildings; males and females in coeducational units. Separate residential quarters for adolescents. Central dining (shared with adults). Basketball courts, game room, playing fields.

Education Academic program available at no charge. Serves ages 12–18, ungraded. 1 teacher on staff.

Costs Average cost: $150 per day. Accepts private insurance, group insurance, medicare, medicaid, Blue Cross/Blue Shield.

Additional Services Drug and alcohol rehabilitation services for males and females ages 19 and up. Treats general psychosocial disorders; substance abuse; eating disorders; compulsive/addictive disorders other than substance abuse and eating disorders; post-traumatic stress disorder; thought, mood, and personality disorders. Outpatient services for males and females ages 17 and up. Treats substance abuse; eating disorders; compulsive/addictive disorders other than substance abuse and eating disorders; post-traumatic stress disorder; thought, mood, and personality disorders.

Contact Ricardo Gillispie, Executive Director of Children's Programming, main address above. Phone: 601-483-6211. Fax: 601-482-3207.

LEA REGIONAL HOSPITAL
5419 North Lovington Highway
Hobbs, New Mexico 88240
505-392-6581; Fax: 505-392-2489

General Information General hospital for adolescents. 20 beds for adolescents. Patient security: partially locked. For-profit facility affiliated with Hospital Corporation of America, Nashville, TN. Licensed by state of New Mexico. Accredited by JCAHO.

Participants Accepts: male and female adolescents. Average stay: 14 days. Admission: one parent, all parties who share custody, court order, voluntary, depending on program. Treats autistic disorders; learning disabilities; behavior disorders; general psychosocial disorders; substance abuse; eating disorders; compulsive/addictive disorders other than substance abuse and eating disorders; post-traumatic stress disorder; thought, mood, and personality disorders.

Staff Staff is 20% male, 80% female.

Contact Judy Lund-Green, Director of Pavilion Services, P.O. Box 3000, Hobbs, NM 88240. Phone: 505-392-6581.

LEON F. STEWART TREATMENT CENTER
120 Michigan Avenue
Daytona Beach, Florida 32114
904-255-0447; Fax: 904-255-0447

General Information Drug and alcohol rehabilitation center for children, adolescents. Patient security: partially locked. Independent not-for-profit facility. Licensed by state of Florida. Accredited by JCAHO.

Participants Accepts: male and female children; male and female adolescents. Average stay: 6 months. Admission: all parties who share custody, court order, voluntary, depending on program. Treats general psychosocial disorders; substance abuse.

Staff Staff is 50% male, 50% female.

Contact Holly Morehouse, Finance Director, main address above. Phone: 904-255-0447.

L. E. PHILLIPS-LIBERTAS CENTER, ST. JOSEPH HOSPITAL
2661 County Road I
Chippewa Falls, Wisconsin 54729
715-723-5585; Fax: 715-723-9561

General Information General hospital for adolescents. Patient security: unlocked. Not-for-profit facility affiliated with Hospital Sisters of the Third Order of St. Francis, Springfield, IL. Licensed by state of Wisconsin. Accredited by JCAHO.

Participants Accepts: male and female adolescents. Admission: one parent, all parties who share custody, court order, voluntary, depending on program. Treats substance abuse. Accepts the mobility impaired; the vision impaired; the hearing impaired; the speech impaired; those with a history of arson; the sexually compulsive; those with a history of harm to themselves and others; those receiving psychotropic medication; those with a history of epilepsy.

Costs Average cost: $209 per day.

Contact Carolyn Coffman, Acting Director, main address above. Phone: 715-723-5585. Fax: 715-723-9561.

LIBERTAS—ST. MARY'S HOSPITAL
1701 Dousman Street
Green Bay, Wisconsin 54303
414-498-8600; Fax: 414-496-2027

General Information Adolescent in-patient unit for adolescents. 24 beds for adolescents. Open year-round. Patient security: unlocked. Urban setting. Not-for-profit facility affiliated with St. Joseph's Hospital, Chippewa Falls, WI. Licensed by state of Wisconsin. Accredited by JCAHO.

Participants Accepts: male and female adolescents ages 11–18. Average stay: 20 days. Admission: one parent, all parties who share custody, court order, self-admit, depending on program. Treats substance abuse. Accepts the mobility impaired; those with a history of epilepsy. Largest number of participants from Michigan.

Program Treatment modalities: medical model; Twelve Step Recovery. Family treatment program available.

Staff .9 full-time direct-care staff member per adolescent. Total facility staff includes 10 physicians, 1 psychologist, 1 psychiatrist, 7 registered nurses, 4 counselors.

Facilities Single building; males and females in co-educational units. Central dining. Basketball courts, game room, gymnasium, volleyball.

Education Educational arrangements: monitoring and assistance with school assignments.

Costs Average cost: $5600 per stay. Accepts private insurance, group insurance, medicaid, Blue Cross/Blue Shield, public funds.

Contact Patrick Ryan, Program Director, main address above. Phone: 414-498-8600. Fax: 414-496-2027.

LIFE ADVENTURE CAMP, INC.
1122 Oak Hill Drive
Lexington, Kentucky 40505
606-252-4733

General Information Camp for children, adolescents. 90 beds for children; 102 beds for adolescents; 192 beds total. Open year-round. Patient security: unlocked; will pursue and return runaways. Rural setting. Independent not-for-profit facility. Licensed by state of Kentucky. Accredited by American Camping Association.

Participants Accepts: male and female children ages 10–12; male and female adolescents ages 13–18. Average stay: 5 days. Admission: voluntary. Treats learning disabilities; behavior disorders. Accepts the vision impaired; the hearing impaired; the speech impaired. Largest number of participants from Kentucky.

Staff Total facility staff includes 12 counselors, 1 dietician, 4 other direct-care staff members. Staff is 50% male, 50% female.

Facilities Males and females in separate units. Playing fields, ropes course.

Costs Average cost: $330 per stay. Accepts public funds.

Additional Services Wilderness/survival program for males and females ages 10–18. Treats learning disabilities; behavior disorders.

Contact Michael Knight, Program Director, main address above. Phone: 606-252-4733.

LIGONIER VALLEY TREATMENT CENTER
RR 1
P.O. Box 190
Stahlstown, Pennsylvania 15687
412-593-6311; Fax: 412-593-6375

General Information Drug and alcohol rehabilitation center for adolescents, adults. 18 beds for adolescents. Open year-round. Patient security: staff secured; will pursue and return runaways. Rural setting. Independent for-profit facility. Licensed by state of Pennsylvania. Accredited by JCAHO.

Participants Accepts: male and female adolescents ages 13–18; male and female adults ages 19 and up. Average stay: 35 days. Admission: all parties who share custody, court order, depending on program. Treats behavior disorders; substance abuse; eating disorders; compulsive/addictive disorders other than substance abuse and eating disorders; post-traumatic stress disorder. Largest number of participants from Pennsylvania, New York.

Program Treatment modalities: Twelve Step Recovery; reality therapy; rational emotive therapy. Family treatment program available.

Staff 1.1 full-time direct-care staff members per adolescent. Total facility staff includes 2 physicians, 1 psychologist, 1 psychiatrist, 6 registered nurses, 3 practical/vocational nurses, 1 teacher, 4 counselors, 1 occupational/recreational therapist, 1 dietician, 3 other direct-care staff members. Staff is 50% male, 50% female.

Facilities Multiple buildings; males and females in coeducational units. Residential quarters shared with adults. Central dining (shared with adults). Game room, gymnasium, playing fields, ropes course.

Education Academic program available at no charge. Serves ages 12–19, grades 6–12. 1 teacher on staff. Cost of educational program sometimes covered by local school district.

Costs Average cost: $300 per day. Accepts private insurance, group insurance, Blue Cross/Blue Shield, public funds.

Additional Services Outpatient services for males and females ages 12–18. Treats learning disabilities; behavior disorders; general psychosocial disorders; substance abuse; eating disorders; compulsive/addictive disorders other than substance abuse and eating disorders; post-traumatic stress disorder; thought, mood, and personality disorders.

Contact Patrick Shields, Patient Accounts Manager, main address above. Phone: 412-593-6311. Fax: 412-593-6375.

LINCOLN CHILD CENTER
4368 Lincoln Avenue
Oakland, California 94602
510-531-3111; Fax: 510-531-8968

General Information Residential treatment/subacute facility for children, adolescents. 38 beds for children; 7 beds for adolescents; 45 beds total. Open year-round. Patient security: staff secured; will pursue and return runaways. Urban setting. Independent not-for-profit facility. Licensed by state of California. Accredited by Council on Accreditation of Services for Families and Children.

Participants Accepts: male and female children ages 6–11; male and female adolescents ages 12–15. Average stay: 18 months. Admission: court order, voluntary, depending on program. Treats learning disabilities; behavior disorders; general psychosocial disorders; eating disorders; post-traumatic stress disorder; thought, mood, and personality disorders. Accepts the speech impaired; those with a history of harm to themselves and others; those receiving psychotropic medication; those with a history of epilepsy. Largest number of participants from California.

Program Treatment modalities: psychodynamic. Family treatment program available.

Staff Total facility staff includes 3 psychiatrists, 1 registered nurse, 10 MSW social workers, 8 teachers, 55 counselors, 1 speech pathologist, 1 dietician.

Facilities Multiple buildings; males and females in coeducational units. Central dining. Basketball courts, game room, playing fields.

Education Academic program available at no charge. Serves ages 6–16, grades 1–8. 8 teachers on staff. Curriculum accredited or approved by California Department of Education. Cost of educational program covered by local school district. Organized sports program offered.

Costs Average cost: $4600 per month. Accepts public funds.

Additional Services Day treatment for males and females ages 6–12. Treats learning disabilities; behavior disorders; general psychosocial disorders; post-traumatic stress disorder; thought, mood, and personality disorders.

Contact Baba Shabbas, Program Director, main address above. Phone: 510-531-3111. Fax: 510-531-8968.

THE LINDEN CENTER
5750 Wilshire Boulevard
Suite 535
Los Angeles, California 90036
213-937-3999; Fax: 213-937-4406

General Information   Residential treatment/subacute facility for children, adolescents. Open year-round. no runaway pursuit. Urban setting. Independent not-for-profit facility. Licensed by state of California. Accredited by JCAHO.

Participants   Accepts: male and female children ages 5–18; male and female adolescents ages 5–18. Average stay: 90 days. Treats autistic disorders; learning disabilities; behavior disorders; general psychosocial disorders; substance abuse; post-traumatic stress disorder; thought, mood, and personality disorders. Accepts the speech impaired; the sexually compulsive; those with a history of harm to themselves and others; those receiving psychotropic medication. Special programs for the speech impaired. Largest number of participants from California, Texas, Nevada.

Program   Family treatment program available.

Staff   Total facility staff includes 1 physician, 3 psychologists, 1 psychiatrist, 5 MSW social workers, 8 teachers, 25 counselors, 1 speech pathologist, 1 dietician, 8 other direct-care staff members. Staff is 50% male, 50% female.

Facilities   Multiple buildings; males and females in coeducational units. Separate dining by residential unit available. Game room.

Education   Academic program available. Serves ages 5–18, grades K–12. 8 teachers on staff.

Costs   Average cost: $400 per day. Accepts private insurance.

Contact   Dr. Ronald E. Ricker, Executive Director, main address above. Phone: 213-937-3999. Fax: 213-937-4406.

LINDEN OAKS HOSPITAL
852 West Street
Naperville, Illinois 60540
708-305-5500; Fax: 708-305-5083

General Information   Psychiatric hospital for children, adolescents. Patient security: entirely locked. For-profit facility affiliated with Naperville Health Ventures, Santa Monica, CA. Licensed by state of Illinois. Accredited by JCAHO.

Participants   Accepts: male and female children; male and female adolescents. Admission: one parent, all parties who share custody, court order, voluntary, depending on program. Treats autistic disorders; learning disabilities; behavior disorders; general psychosocial disorders; substance abuse; eating disorders; compulsive/addictive disorders other than substance abuse and eating disorders; post-traumatic stress disorder; thought, mood, and personality disorders.

Staff   Staff is 50% male, 50% female.

Contact   Admissions, main address above. Phone: 708-305-5500. Fax: 708-305-5083.

LOURDESMONT—GOOD SHEPHERD YOUTH AND FAMILY SERVICES
537 Venard Road
Clarks Summit, Pennsylvania 18411-1298
717-587-4741; Fax: 717-586-0030

General Information   Residential treatment/subacute facility for adolescents. Open year-round. Patient security: unlocked; will pursue and return runaways. Suburban setting. Not-for-profit facility affiliated with Good Shepherd Corporation, Silver Spring, MD. Licensed by state of Pennsylvania. Accredited by Council on Accreditation of Services for Families and Children.

Participants   Accepts: female adolescents ages 13–17. Average stay: 365 days. Admission: all parties who share custody. Treats general psychosocial disorders; substance abuse; eating disorders; thought, mood, and personality disorders. Accepts those with a history of harm to themselves and others; those receiving psychotropic medication. Largest number of participants from Pennsylvania.

Program   Treatment modalities: Twelve Step Recovery; psychodynamic. Family treatment program available.

Staff   2 full-time direct-care staff members per adolescent. Total facility staff includes 1 physician, 1 psychologist, 2 psychiatrists, 2 registered nurses, 4 MSW social workers, 3 social workers (non-MSW), 13 teachers, 2 therapists, 2 dieticians, 40 other direct-care staff members. Staff is 7% male, 93% female.

Facilities   Multiple buildings. Central dining. Basketball courts, game room, gymnasium, outdoor swimming pool, playing fields.

Education   Academic program available at no charge. Serves ages 13–17, grades 7–12. 13 teachers on staff. Curriculum accredited or approved by private academic license. Cost of educational program sometimes covered by local school district. Organized sports program offered.

Costs   Average cost: $102 per day. Accepts medicare, public funds.

Additional Services   Drug and alcohol rehabilitation services for males and females ages 13–17. Treats general psychosocial disorders; substance abuse; thought, mood, and personality disorders. Outpatient services for males and females ages 13–17. Treats general psychosocial disorders; substance abuse; thought, mood, and personality disorders.

Contact   Alice Caulson, Admissions Director, main address above. Phone: 717-587-4741. Fax: 717-586-0030.

LUTHERAN SOCIAL SERVICE—BELOIT CHILDREN'S HOME
1323 Northwestern
Ames, Iowa 50010
515-232-7262; Fax: 515-233-5288

General Information   Residential treatment/subacute facility for children, adolescents. Patient security: staff secured. Not-for-profit facility affiliated with Evangelical Lutheran Church of America, Minneapolis, MN. Licensed by state of Iowa. Accredited by JCAHO; Council on Accreditation of Services for Families and Children.

Participants   Accepts: male and female children; male and female adolescents. Average stay: 20 months. Admission: court order. Treats autistic disorders; learning disabilities; behavior disorders; general psychosocial disorders; eating disorders; compulsive/addictive disorders other than substance abuse and eating disorders; post-traumatic stress disorder; thought, mood, and personality disorders.

Staff   Staff is 34% male, 66% female.

Costs   Average cost: $125 per day.

Additional Services   Outpatient services for males and females ages 3–18. Treats autistic disorders; learning disabilities; behavior disorders; general psychosocial disorders; eating disorders; compulsive/addictive disorders other than substance abuse and eating disorders; post-traumatic stress disorder; thought, mood, and personality disorders.

Contact   Julie Baldus, Admissions Coordinator, main address above. Phone: 515-232-7262. Fax: 515-233-5288.

LUTHERAN SOCIAL SERVICES—SERENITY
P.O. Box 576
Stoughton, Wisconsin 53589
608-873-3103; Fax: 608-873-1999

General Information   Residential treatment/subacute facility for adolescents. 12 beds for adolescents. Patient security: staff secured. Not-for-profit facility affiliated with Lutheran Social Services, Milwaukee, WI. Licensed by state of Wisconsin. Accredited by Council on Accreditation of Services for Families and Children.

Participants   Accepts: female adolescents. Average stay: 10 months. Admission: court order, voluntary, state, depending on program. Treats learning disabilities; behavior disorders; general psychosocial disorders; substance abuse; eating disorders; compulsive/addictive disorders other than substance abuse and eating disorders; post-traumatic stress disorder; thought, mood, and personality disorders.

Staff   Staff is all female.

Costs   Average cost: $137 per day.

Contact   Jennifer Tivang, Program Director, main address above. Phone: 608-873-3103. Fax: 608-873-1999.

LUTHERBROOK CHILDREN'S CENTER
343 West Lake Street
Addison, Illinois 60101
708-543-6900; Fax: 708-543-7910

General Information   Residential treatment/subacute facility for children. Patient security: staff secured. Not-for-profit facility affiliated with Lutheran Child and Family Services, River Forest, IL. Licensed by state of Illinois. Accredited by Council on Accreditation of Services for Families and Children.

Participants   Accepts: male and female children. Average stay: 36 months. Admission: guardianship. Treats learning disabilities; behavior disorders; general psychosocial disorders; substance abuse; eating disorders; compulsive/addictive disorders other than substance abuse and eating disorders; post-traumatic stress disorder; thought, mood, and personality disorders.

Contact   Brent Diers, Social Work Specialist, main address above. Phone: 708-543-6900. Fax: 708-543-7910.

MADONNA HEIGHTS SERVICES
151 Burns Lane
Dix Hills, New York 11746
516-643-8800; Fax: 516-491-4440

General Information Residential treatment/subacute facility for adolescents. 70 beds for adolescents. Open year-round. Patient security: partially locked; will pursue and return runaways. Suburban setting. Independent not-for-profit facility. Licensed by state of New York. Accredited by JCAHO.

Participants Accepts: female adolescents ages 12–18. Average stay: 180 days. Admission: court order, Department of Social Services referrals, school referrals, depending on program. Treats learning disabilities; behavior disorders; general psychosocial disorders; substance abuse; thought, mood, and personality disorders. Accepts those receiving psychotropic medication.

Program Family treatment program available.

Staff 1.1 full-time direct-care staff members per adolescent. Total facility staff includes 1 physician, 2 psychologists, 2 psychiatrists, 2 registered nurses, 3 practical/vocational nurses, 6 MSW social workers, 4 social workers (non-MSW), 17 teachers, 1 dietician, 25 other direct-care staff members. Staff is all female.

Facilities Single building. Central dining. Basketball courts, gymnasium, outdoor swimming pool, outdoor tennis courts, playing fields.

Education Academic program available at no charge. Serves ages 12–18, grades 7–12. 17 teachers on staff. Curriculum accredited or approved by New York State Education Department. Organized sports program offered.

Costs Average cost: $108 per day. Accepts public funds.

Additional Services Outpatient services for males and females ages 5–65. Treats general psychosocial disorders.

Contact Mary Alice O'Brien, Director of Development, main address above. Phone: 516-643-8800. Fax: 516-491-4440.

MAGNOLIA RECOVERY CENTER
410 East Cornerview
Gonzales, Louisiana 70737
504-647-1777; Fax: 504-647-0611

General Information Drug and alcohol rehabilitation center for adolescents. Open year-round. Patient security: staff secured; will pursue and return runaways. Small town setting. Not-for-profit facility affiliated with Reality Counseling and Recovery Center, Gonzales, LA. Licensed by state of Louisiana.

Participants Accepts: female adolescents ages 13–21. Average stay: 6 months. Admission: all parties who share custody, court order, depending on program. Treats substance abuse; eating disorders; post-traumatic stress disorder.

Program Treatment modalities: Twelve Step Recovery; reality therapy. Family treatment program available.

Staff Total facility staff includes 1 physician, 1 psychiatrist, 1 registered nurse, 1 practical/vocational nurse, 1 social worker (non-MSW), 2 counselors, 1 dietician. Staff is all female.

Facilities Multiple buildings. Residential quarters shared with adults. Central dining (shared with adults). Outdoor swimming pool, outdoor tennis courts, track.

Education Academic program available at no charge. Serves ages 13–18, grades 8–12. Curriculum accredited or approved by Ascension Parish School Board. Cost of educational program covered by local school district. Organized sports program offered.

Costs Accepts private insurance.

Additional Services Outpatient services for females ages 13–21. Treats substance abuse; eating disorders; compulsive/addictive disorders other than substance abuse and eating disorders; post-traumatic stress disorder. Residential or sub-acute services for females ages 13–21. Treats substance abuse; eating disorders; compulsive/addictive disorders other than substance abuse and eating disorders; post-traumatic stress disorder.

Contact Sheila Howard, Admissions Counselor, main address above. Phone: 504-647-1777. Fax: 504-647-0611.

MANATEE PALMS ADOLESCENT SPECIALTY HOSPITAL
1324 37th Avenue, East
Bradenton, Florida 34208
813-746-1388; Fax: 813-746-2690

General Information Psychiatric hospital for children, adolescents. 15 beds for children; 45 beds for adolescents; 60 beds total. Open year-round. Patient security: partially locked; will pursue and return runaways. Small town setting. For-profit facility affiliated with National Medical Enterprises, Washington, DC. Licensed by state of Florida. Accredited by JCAHO; American Hospital Association, Health and Rehabilitative Services.

Participants Accepts: male and female children ages 3–12; male and female adolescents ages 13–18. Average stay: 75 days. Admission: voluntary. Treats autistic disorders; learning disabilities; behavior disorders; general psychosocial disorders; substance abuse; eating disorders; compulsive/addictive disorders other than substance abuse and eating disorders; post-traumatic stress disorder; thought, mood, and personality disorders. Accepts the mobility impaired; the vision impaired; the hearing impaired; the speech impaired; those with a history of arson; the sexually compulsive; those with a history of harm to themselves and others; those receiving psychotropic medication.

Program Treatment modalities: Twelve Step Recovery; behavior modification. Family treatment program available.

Staff Total facility staff includes 1 physician, 5 psychologists, 4 psychiatrists, 2 MSW social workers, 2 social workers (non-MSW), 5 teachers, 4 occupational/recreational therapists, 1 dietician.

Facilities Multiple buildings; males and females in coeducational units. Central dining. Basketball courts, gymnasium, outdoor swimming pool, playing fields, ropes course.

Education Academic program available at no charge. Serves ages 6–18, grades K–12. 5 teachers on staff. Curriculum accredited or approved by Manatee County School Board. Cost of educational program covered by local school district. Organized sports program offered.

Costs Accepts private insurance, group insurance, Blue Cross/Blue Shield.

Additional Services Drug and alcohol rehabilitation services for males and females ages 6–18. Treats behavior disorders; general psychosocial disorders; substance abuse; eating disorders; compulsive/addictive disorders other than substance abuse and eating disorders; post-traumatic stress disorder; thought, mood, and personality disorders. Residential or subacute services for males and females ages 13–18. Treats behavior disorders; general psychosocial disorders; substance abuse; eating disorders; compulsive/addictive disorders other than substance abuse and eating disorders; post-traumatic stress disorder; thought, mood, and personality disorders.

Contact Susan Hennessey, Director of Marketing, main address above. Phone: 813-746-1388. Fax: 813-746-2690.

MAPLEBROOK SCHOOL, INC.
Route 22
Amenia, New York 12501
914-373-8191; Fax: 914-373-7029

General Information School for children, adolescents, adults. 6 beds for children; 40 beds for adolescents; 75 beds total. Open year-round. Patient security: staff secured; will pursue and return runaways. Small town setting. Independent not-for-profit facility. Licensed by state of New York.

Participants Accepts: male and female children ages 8–12; male and female adolescents ages 13–18; male and female adults ages 18–22. Average stay: 4 years. Admission: one parent, all parties who share custody, depending on program. Treats learning disabilities. Accepts the vision impaired; the hearing impaired; the speech impaired. Largest number of participants from New York, New Jersey, Florida.

Program Treatment modalities: Orton-Gillingham; multisensory feedback and teaching strategies; learning styles.

Staff .1 full-time direct-care staff member per child or adolescent. Total facility staff includes 1 psychologist, 1 registered nurse, 10 teachers, 3 counselors, 1 speech pathologist, 3 other direct-care staff members. Staff is 30% male, 70% female.

Facilities Multiple buildings; males and females in separate units. Separate residential quarters for children and adolescents. Central dining (shared with adults). Game room, gymnasium, horseback riding, indoor swimming pool, outdoor tennis courts, playing fields, fitness center.

Education School serves ages 8–22, ungraded. 10 teachers on staff. Diploma granted upon completion. Tutor is available. Curriculum accredited or approved by New York State Association of Independent Schools, Middle States Association of Colleges and Schools. Organized sports program offered.

Costs Average cost: $27,000 per year. Accepts private insurance. Financial aid available.

Additional Services Camping program for males and females ages 8–18. Treats learning disabilities.

Contact Lori S. Hale, Director of Enrollment Services, main address above. Phone: 914-373-8191. Fax: 914-373-7029.

MAPLEGROVE YOUTH TREATMENT CENTER
6773 West Maple Road
West Bloomfield, Michigan 48322
313-661-6500; Fax: 313-661-6184

General Information Residential treatment/subacute facility for adolescents. Not-for-profit facility affiliated with Henry Ford Health System, Detroit, MI. Licensed by state of Michigan. Accredited by JCAHO.

Participants Accepts: male and female adolescents. Average stay: 24 days. Admission: one parent, all parties who share custody, court order, voluntary, depending on program. Treats substance abuse. Accepts the mobility impaired; the vision impaired; the speech impaired.

Costs Average cost: $350 per day.

Additional Services Day treatment program for males and females ages 13–18. Treats substance abuse.

Contact Maureen Harte, Intake Receptionist, main address above. Phone: 313-661-6500. Fax: 313-661-6184.

MARYHAVEN, INC.
1755 Alum Creek Drive
Columbus, Ohio 43207
614-445-8131; Fax: 614-445-7808

General Information Drug and alcohol rehabilitation center for adolescents. Patient security: staff secured. Independent not-for-profit facility. Licensed by state of Ohio. Accredited by JCAHO; Ohio Department of Alcohol and Drug Addiction Services.

Participants Accepts: male and female adolescents. Average stay: 35 days. Admission: one parent, all parties who share custody, court order, voluntary, depending on program. Treats substance abuse. Accepts the mobility impaired; the vision impaired; the hearing impaired; the speech impaired; those with a history of arson; the sexually compulsive; those with a history of harm to themselves and others; those receiving psychotropic medication; non-English speaking individuals; those with a history of epilepsy.

Staff Staff is 50% male, 50% female.

Contact Holly Bostian, Clinical Supervisor, main address above. Phone: 614-445-8131. Fax: 614-445-7808.

MARYMOUNT HOSPITAL MENTAL HEALTH CENTER
12300 McCracken Road
Garfield Heights, Ohio 44125-2975
216-581-0500; Fax: 216-587-8298

General Information General hospital for adolescents, adults. Open year-round. Patient security: partially locked; will pursue and return runaways. Suburban setting. Not-for-profit facility affiliated with Marymount Health Care System, Garfield Heights, OH. Licensed by state of Ohio. Accredited by JCAHO; Cuyahoga County Community Mental Health Board, Ohio Department of Mental Health, National Institute of Mental Health.

Participants Accepts: male and female adolescents ages 12–17; male and female adults ages 18 and up. Average stay: 22 days. Admission: one parent, all parties who share custody, court order, depending on program. Treats behavior disorders; general psychosocial disorders; eating disorders; compulsive/addictive disorders other than substance abuse and eating disorders; post-traumatic stress disorder; thought, mood, and personality disorders. Accepts the mobility impaired; the vision impaired; the hearing impaired; the speech impaired; the sexually compulsive; those with a history of harm to themselves and others; those receiving psychotropic medication; non-English speaking individuals; those with a history of epilepsy. Largest number of participants from Ohio.

Program Treatment modalities: psychodynamic; individual; group; family therapy. Family treatment program available.

Staff Total facility staff includes 3 psychologists, 14 psychiatrists, 15 registered nurses, 36 practical/vocational nurses, 2 MSW social workers, 1 teacher, 6 occupational/recreational therapists.

Facilities Single building; males and females in co-educational units. Separate residential quarters for adolescents. Central dining (shared with adults). Basketball courts, game room, gymnasium, exercise equipment and par course.

Education Academic program available at no charge. Serves ages 12–19, grades 6–12. 1 teacher on staff. Curriculum accredited or approved by State of Ohio.

Costs Average cost: $17,670 per stay. Accepts private insurance, group insurance, medicare, medicaid, Blue Cross/Blue Shield.

Additional Services Drug and alcohol rehabilitation services for males and females ages 12 and up. Treats substance abuse. Outpatient services for males and females ages 2 and up. Treats behavior disorders; general psychosocial disorders; substance abuse; eating disorders; compulsive/addictive disorders other than substance abuse and eating disorders; post-traumatic stress disorder; thought, mood, and personality disorders. Partial hospitalization for males and females ages 12 and up. Treats behavior disorders; general psychosocial disorders; substance abuse; eating disorders; compulsive/addictive disorders other than substance abuse and eating disorders; post-traumatic stress disorder; thought, mood, and personality disorders.

Contact   Tom Supan, Intake Worker, main address above. Phone: 216-581-8350. Fax: 216-587-8298.

MARYVIEW PSYCHIATRIC HOSPITAL
3636 High Street
Portsmouth, Virginia 23707
804-398-2367; Fax: 804-398-2163

General Information   Psychiatric hospital for adolescents, adults. Open year-round. Patient security: partially locked. Suburban setting. Not-for-profit facility affiliated with Bon Secours Health Systems, Marriottsville, MD. Licensed by state of Virginia. Accredited by JCAHO.

Participants   Accepts: male and female adolescents ages 11–18; male and female adults ages 18–70. Admission: one parent, all parties who share custody, court order, depending on program. Treats autistic disorders; learning disabilities; behavior disorders; general psychosocial disorders; substance abuse; eating disorders; compulsive/addictive disorders other than substance abuse and eating disorders; post-traumatic stress disorder; thought, mood, and personality disorders. Accepts the mobility impaired; those with a history of arson; the sexually compulsive; those with a history of harm to themselves and others; those receiving psychotropic medication; those with a history of epilepsy. Special programs for the mobility impaired; the developmentally disabled; those with AIDS.

Program   Treatment modalities: Twelve Step Recovery; psychodynamic. Family treatment program available.

Staff   Total facility staff includes 1 psychologist, 2 psychiatrists, 2 registered nurses, 1 practical/vocational nurse, 2 MSW social workers, 1 teacher, 2 counselors, 1 occupational/recreational therapist, 1 therapist, 4 other direct-care staff members.

Facilities   Single building; males and females in coeducational units. Separate residential quarters for adolescents. Central dining (not shared with adults). Basketball courts, game room, exercise room.

Education   Academic program available at no charge. Serves ages 11–18, grades 5–12. 1 teacher on staff.

Costs   Average cost: $600 per day. Accepts private insurance, group insurance, medicaid, Blue Cross/Blue Shield, public funds.

Additional Services   Drug and alcohol rehabilitation services for males and females ages 11–75. Treats learning disabilities; behavior disorders; general psychosocial disorders; substance abuse; eating disorders; compulsive/addictive disorders other than substance abuse and eating disorders; post-traumatic stress disorder; thought, mood, and personality disorders. Partial hospitalization for males and females ages 11–75. Treats learning disabilities; behavior disorders; general psychosocial disorders; substance abuse; eating disorders; compulsive/addictive disorders other than substance abuse and eating disorders; post-traumatic stress disorder; thought, mood, and personality disorders.

Contact   Richard Jaglowski, Adolescent Program Coordinator, main address above. Phone: 804-398-2564.

MATTIE RHODES COUNSELING AND ART CENTER
1740 Jefferson
Kansas City, Missouri 64108
816-471-2536

General Information   Camp for children, adolescents, adults. Open year-round. Patient security: unlocked; will pursue and return runaways. Urban setting. Independent not-for-profit facility. Licensed by state of Missouri.

Participants   Accepts: male and female children ages 5–12; male and female adolescents ages 13–18; male and female adults ages 18 and up. Admission: one parent. Treats behavior disorders. Accepts those with a history of harm to themselves and others; those receiving psychotropic medication; non-English speaking individuals.

Program   Treatment modalities: family systems; psychodynamics. Family treatment program available.

Staff   Total facility staff includes 2 psychologists, 5 MSW social workers. Staff is 20% male, 80% female.

Facilities   Multiple buildings; males and females in separate units. Game room.

Costs   Accepts public funds.

Additional Services   Outpatient services for males and females ages 5 and up. Treats behavior disorders;

general psychosocial disorders; thought, mood, and personality disorders. Group therapy/socialization program for males and females ages 6–16. Treats learning disabilities; behavior disorders; general psychosocial disorders.

Contact Jim Ranch, Clinical Director, main address above. Phone: 816-471-2536.

MCAULEY NAZARETH HOME FOR BOYS
77 Mulberry Street
Leicester, Massachusetts 01524
508-892-4886

General Information Residential treatment/subacute facility for children. 18 beds for children. Open year-round. Patient security: staff secured; will pursue and return runaways. Small town setting. Independent not-for-profit facility. Licensed by state of Massachusetts.

Participants Accepts: male children ages 6–13. Average stay: 550 days. Admission: all parties who share custody, voluntary, depending on program. Treats learning disabilities; behavior disorders; general psychosocial disorders. Accepts those with a history of harm to themselves and others; those receiving psychotropic medication.

Program Family treatment program available.

Staff 1 full-time direct-care staff member per child. Total facility staff includes 1 psychologist, 1 practical/vocational nurse, 1 MSW social worker, 4 teachers, 11 counselors. Staff is 39% male, 61% female.

Facilities Multiple buildings. Separate dining by residential unit available. Basketball courts, game room, outdoor swimming pool, playing fields.

Education Academic program available at no charge. Serves ages 6–14, grades K–8. 4 teachers on staff. Curriculum accredited or approved by Department of Education. Cost of educational program sometimes covered by local school district. Organized sports program offered.

Costs Average cost: $43,208 per year. Accepts public funds.

Contact Sr. Mary Barry, Administrator, main address above. Phone: 508-892-4886.

MCKINLEY HALL, INC.
1101 East High Street
Springfield, Ohio 45505
513-328-5300

General Information Residential treatment/subacute facility for adolescents. 15 beds for adolescents. Open year-round. Patient security: staff secured; no runaway pursuit. Urban setting. Independent not-for-profit facility. Licensed by state of Ohio. Accredited by JCAHO; Ohio Department of Alcohol and Drug Addiction Services.

Participants Accepts: male and female adolescents ages 10–18. Average stay: 56 days. Admission: one parent, all parties who share custody, court order, depending on program. Treats substance abuse. Largest number of participants from Ohio.

Program Treatment modalities: Twelve Step Recovery; experiential. Family treatment program available.

Staff 2.5 full-time direct-care staff members per adolescent. Total facility staff includes 1 physician, 1 psychologist, 1 registered nurse, 1 teacher, 5 counselors, 1 occupational/recreational therapist, 27 other direct-care staff members. Staff is 34% male, 66% female.

Facilities Multiple buildings; males and females in coeducational units. Separate dining by residential unit available. Gymnasium.

Education Academic program available at no charge. Serves ages 10–18, ungraded. 1 teacher on staff. Curriculum accredited or approved by Springfield City Schools. Cost of educational program covered by local school district.

Costs Average cost: $260 per day. Accepts private insurance, group insurance, medicaid, Blue Cross/Blue Shield, public funds.

Additional Services Day treatment program for males and females ages 10–18. Treats substance abuse.

Contact Glenda R. Emery, Adolescent Program Director, main address above. Phone: 513-328-5314.

THE MEADOWS PSYCHIATRIC CENTER
RD 1
Box 259
Centre Hall, Pennsylvania 16828
800-641-7529; Fax: 814-364-9742

General Information Psychiatric hospital for children, adolescents, adults. 12 beds for children; 30 beds for adolescents; 100 beds total. Open year-round.

Patient security: partially locked; will pursue and return runaways. Rural setting. For-profit facility affiliated with First Hospital Corporation, Norfolk, VA. Licensed by state of Pennsylvania. Accredited by JCAHO.

Participants Accepts: male and female children ages 4–12; male and female adolescents ages 13–18; male and female adults ages 19 and up. Average stay: 25 days. Admission: one parent, all parties who share custody, court order, voluntary, depending on program. Treats autistic disorders; learning disabilities; behavior disorders; general psychosocial disorders; substance abuse; eating disorders; compulsive/addictive disorders other than substance abuse and eating disorders; post-traumatic stress disorder; thought, mood, and personality disorders. Accepts the mobility impaired; the vision impaired; the speech impaired; those with a history of arson; the sexually compulsive; those with a history of harm to themselves and others; those receiving psychotropic medication; those with a history of epilepsy. Special programs for the mobility impaired; the developmentally disabled; the vision impaired; the speech impaired; those with AIDS.

Program Treatment modalities: dual diagnosis; Twelve Step Recovery; psychodynamic. Family treatment program available.

Staff Total facility staff includes 5 physicians, 8 psychologists, 5 psychiatrists, 46 registered nurses, 15 practical/vocational nurses, 7 MSW social workers, 3 social workers (non-MSW), 7 teachers, 4 counselors, 5 occupational/recreational therapists, 1 dietician.

Facilities Multiple buildings; males and females in coeducational units. Separate residential quarters for children and adolescents. Central dining (shared with adults). Basketball courts, gymnasium, playing fields.

Education Academic program available at no charge. Serves ages 4–18, grades K–12. 7 teachers on staff. Cost of educational program sometimes covered by local school district.

Costs Accepts private insurance, group insurance, medicare, medicaid, Blue Cross/Blue Shield, public funds.

Additional Services Drug and alcohol rehabilitation services for males and females ages 13 and up. Treats learning disabilities; behavior disorders; general psychosocial disorders; substance abuse; eating disorders; compulsive/addictive disorders other than substance abuse and eating disorders; post-traumatic stress disorder; thought, mood, and personality disorders.

Contact Ronald Fry, Director of Marketing, main address above. Phone: 814-364-2161. Fax: 814-364-9742.

MEADOW WOOD HOSPITAL FOR CHILDREN AND ADOLESCENTS
575 South DuPont Highway
New Castle, Delaware 19720
302-328-3330; Fax: 302-328-9336

General Information Psychiatric hospital for children, adolescents. 10 beds for children; 40 beds for adolescents; 50 beds total. Open year-round. Patient security: entirely locked; no runaway pursuit. Suburban setting. For-profit facility affiliated with Psych Group, Inc., Wayne, PA. Licensed by state of Delaware. Accredited by JCAHO.

Participants Accepts: male and female children ages 7–12; male and female adolescents ages 12–18. Average stay: 30 days. Admission: one parent, all parties who share custody, depending on program. Treats autistic disorders; learning disabilities; behavior disorders; general psychosocial disorders; substance abuse; eating disorders; compulsive/addictive disorders other than substance abuse and eating disorders; post-traumatic stress disorder; thought, mood, and personality disorders. Accepts those with a history of arson; those with a history of harm to themselves and others; those receiving psychotropic medication. Special programs for the developmentally disabled.

Program Family treatment program available.

Staff Total facility staff includes 3 physicians, 2 psychologists, 6 psychiatrists, 50 registered nurses, 7 MSW social workers, 1 social worker (non-MSW), 7 teachers, 1 counselor, 6 occupational/recreational therapists, 2 therapists, 1 dietician, 20 other direct-care staff members.

Facilities Single building; males and females in coeducational units. Central dining. Basketball courts, game room, gymnasium, outdoor swimming pool, outdoor tennis courts, playing fields.

Education Academic program available at no charge. Serves ages 7–18, grades 2–12. 7 teachers on staff. Curriculum accredited or approved by by the child's home school district. Cost of educational program covered by local school district.

Costs Accepts private insurance, group insurance, Blue Cross/Blue Shield, public funds.

Additional Services Drug and alcohol rehabilitation services for males and females ages 8–19. Treats autistic disorders; learning disabilities; behavior disorders; general psychosocial disorders; substance abuse; eating disorders; compulsive/addictive disorders other than substance abuse and eating disorders; post-traumatic stress disorder; thought, mood, and personality disorders. Outpatient services for males and females. Treats autistic disorders; learning disabilities; behavior disorders; general psychosocial disorders; substance abuse; eating disorders; compulsive/addictive disorders other than substance abuse and eating disorders; post-traumatic stress disorder; thought, mood, and personality disorders.

Contact Kristie Augenblick, Director of Public Relations, main address above. Phone: 302-328-3330. Fax: 302-328-9336.

MEHARRY-HUBBARD HOSPITAL
1005 D.B. Todd Boulevard
Nashville, Tennessee 37208
615-327-5500; Fax: 615-327-5889

General Information General hospital for children, adolescents. Patient security: partially locked. Independent not-for-profit facility. Licensed by state of Tennessee. Accredited by JCAHO.

Participants Accepts: male and female children; male and female adolescents. Average stay: 3 weeks. Admission: one parent, all parties who share custody, court order, voluntary, depending on program. Treats learning disabilities; behavior disorders; general psychosocial disorders; substance abuse; eating disorders; compulsive/addictive disorders other than substance abuse and eating disorders; post-traumatic stress disorder; thought, mood, and personality disorders.

Staff Staff is 50% male, 50% female.

Costs Average cost: $400 per day.

Contact Carol Campbell, Clinical Specialist and Program Director, main address above. Phone: 615-327-6910. Fax: 615-327-5889.

MEMORIAL CENTER FOR BEHAVIORAL HEALTH
3600 San Dimas Street
Bakersfield, California 93301
805-327-7621; Fax: 805-325-8726

General Information Psychiatric hospital for adolescents. 9 beds for adolescents. Open year-round. Patient security: staff secured; no runaway pursuit. Rural setting. Independent not-for-profit facility. Licensed by state of California. Accredited by JCAHO; California Department of Social Services.

Participants Accepts: male and female adolescents. Admission: one parent, all parties who share custody, court order, voluntary, depending on program. Treats behavior disorders; general psychosocial disorders; eating disorders; post-traumatic stress disorder;

thought, mood, and personality disorders. Accepts the mobility impaired; the vision impaired; the hearing impaired; the speech impaired; those with a history of harm to themselves and others; those receiving psychotropic medication; those with a history of epilepsy.

Program Treatment modalities: psychodynamic; cognitive; behavior modification. Family treatment program available.

Staff Total facility staff includes 1 physician, 1 psychiatrist, 1 MSW social worker, 1 teacher, 1 counselor, 1 dietician, 6 other direct-care staff members. Staff is 50% male, 50% female.

Facilities Single building; males and females in coeducational units. Separate dining by residential unit available. Basketball courts, game room, outdoor swimming pool, outdoor tennis courts, playing fields.

Education Academic program available at no charge. Serves ages 12–18, grades 8–12. 1 teacher on staff. Curriculum accredited or approved by California Department of Education.

Costs Average cost: $300 per day. Accepts private insurance, group insurance, medicare, Blue Cross/Blue Shield, public funds.

Additional Services Outpatient services for males and females. Treats autistic disorders; learning disabilities; behavior disorders; general psychosocial disorders; substance abuse; eating disorders; compulsive/addictive disorders other than substance abuse and eating disorders; post-traumatic stress disorder; thought, mood, and personality disorders. Residential or sub-acute services for males and females ages 12–18. Treats behavior disorders; general psychosocial disorders; eating disorders; post-traumatic stress disorder; thought, mood, and personality disorders. Day hospital and adolescent day treatment for males and females ages 12–18. Treats autistic disorders; learning disabilities; behavior disorders; general psychosocial disorders; substance abuse; eating disorders; compulsive/addictive disorders other than substance abuse and eating disorders; post-traumatic stress disorder; thought, mood, and personality disorders.

Contact Gene Wood, Admissions Director, main address above. Phone: 805-327-7621. Fax: 805-325-8726.

MEMORIAL HOSPITAL
527 West South Street
Woodstock, Illinois 60098
815-338-2500; Fax: 815-338-5139

General Information General hospital for adolescents. 10 beds for adolescents. Patient security: entirely locked. Independent not-for-profit facility. Licensed by state of Illinois. Accredited by JCAHO.

Participants Accepts: male and female adolescents. Average stay: 21 days. Admission: one parent, all parties who share custody, court order, voluntary, depending on program. Treats learning disabilities; behavior disorders; general psychosocial disorders; substance abuse; eating disorders; compulsive/addictive disorders other than substance abuse and eating disorders; post-traumatic stress disorder; thought, mood, and personality disorders.

Staff Staff is 25% male, 75% female.

Costs Average cost: $700 per day.

Contact Shira Greenfield, Clinical Director, main address above. Phone: 815-338-2500 Ext. 3554. Fax: 815-338-5139.

MEMORIAL HOSPITAL OF MICHIGAN CITY
5th and Pine Street
Michigan City, Indiana 46360
219-872-9134; Fax: 219-873-2495

General Information General hospital for adolescents. 6 beds for adolescents. Patient security: partially locked. Independent not-for-profit facility. Licensed by state of Indiana. Accredited by JCAHO.

Participants Accepts: male and female adolescents. Average stay: 3 weeks. Admission: one parent, all parties who share custody, court order, voluntary, depending on program. Treats substance abuse. Accepts the mobility impaired; the vision impaired; the hearing impaired; the speech impaired; those with a history of harm to themselves and others; those with a history of epilepsy.

Costs Average cost: $375 per day.

Contact Colleen Jackson, Intake Therapist, main address above. Phone: 219-872-9134. Fax: 219-873-2495.

MEMORIAL MEDICAL CENTER
800 North Rutledge
Springfield, Illinois 62781
217-788-3000; Fax: 217-788-5544

General Information General hospital for adolescents, adults. 23 beds for adolescents. Open year-round. Patient security arrangements vary depending on program; no runaway pursuit. Suburban setting. Independent not-for-profit facility. Licensed by state of Illinois. Accredited by JCAHO; Public Health of Illinois.

Participants Accepts: male and female adolescents ages 12–17; male and female adults ages 18 and up. Average stay: 19 days. Admission: one parent, court order, depending on program. Treats learning disabilities; behavior disorders; general psychosocial disorders; substance abuse; eating disorders; post-traumatic stress disorder; thought, mood, and personality disorders. Accepts the mobility impaired; the vision impaired; the hearing impaired; those with a history of harm to themselves and others; those receiving psychotropic medication; those with a history of epilepsy.

Program Treatment modalities: family-based; reality-based. Family treatment program available.

Staff Total facility staff includes 2 psychologists, 4 psychiatrists, 15 registered nurses, 6 practical/vocational nurses, 1 MSW social worker, 2 teachers, 3 counselors, 1 physical therapist, 1 occupational/recreational therapist, 1 speech pathologist, 1 dietician, 10 other direct-care staff members.

Facilities Multiple buildings; males and females in coeducational units. Separate residential quarters for adolescents. Central dining (not shared with adults). Game room, contracts with gym/fitness center and swimming facility.

Education Academic program available at no charge. Serves ages 12–17. 2 teachers on staff. Curriculum accredited or approved by Springfield School District 186. Cost of educational program covered by local school district.

Costs Accepts private insurance, group insurance, medicare, medicaid, Blue Cross/Blue Shield, public funds.

Additional Services Drug and alcohol rehabilitation services for males and females ages 12–17. Treats learning disabilities; behavior disorders; general psychosocial disorders; substance abuse; eating disorders; compulsive/addictive disorders other than substance abuse and eating disorders; post-traumatic stress disorder; thought, mood, and personality disorders.

Contact Kirk W. Boyenga, PhD, main address above. Phone: 217-788-3000. Fax: 217-788-5544.

MENINGER CLINIC—CHILDREN AND ADOLESCENT DIVISION
325 Frazier
Topeka, Kansas 66606
800-351-9058; Fax: 913-232-6524

General Information Psychiatric hospital for children, adolescents. Patient security: staff secured. Independent not-for-profit facility. Licensed by state of Kansas. Accredited by JCAHO.

Participants Accepts: male and female children; male and female adolescents. Average stay: 11 months. Admission: one parent, all parties who share custody, voluntary, depending on program. Treats learning disabilities; behavior disorders; substance abuse; eating disorders; compulsive/addictive disorders other than substance abuse and eating disorders; post-traumatic stress disorder; thought, mood, and personality disorders.

Staff Staff is 50% male, 50% female.

Additional Services Outpatient services for males and females ages 1–18. Treats autistic disorders; learning disabilities; behavior disorders; substance abuse; eating disorders; compulsive/addictive disorders other than substance abuse and eating disorders; post-traumatic stress disorder; thought, mood, and personality disorders.

Contact Les Little, Director of Admissions for Children and Adolescent Services, P.O. Box 827, Topeka, KS 66601. Phone: 800-351-9058. Fax: 913-232-6524.

MENORAH MEDICAL CENTER
4949 Rockhill Road
Kansas City, Missouri 64110
816-276-8000; Fax: 816-276-8943

General Information General hospital for adolescents. 8 beds for adolescents. Patient security: partially locked. Independent not-for-profit facility. Licensed by state of Missouri. Accredited by JCAHO.

Participants Accepts: male and female adolescents. Average stay: 9 days. Admission: one parent, all parties who share custody, court order, voluntary, depending on program. Treats autistic disorders; learning disabilities; behavior disorders; general psychosocial disorders; substance abuse; eating disorders; compulsive/addictive disorders other than substance abuse and eating disorders; post-traumatic stress disorder; thought, mood, and personality disorders.

Staff Staff is 40% male, 60% female.

Costs Average cost: $650 per day.

Additional Services Partial hospitalization program for males and females ages 12–18. Treats autistic disorders; learning disabilities; behavior disorders; general psychosocial disorders; substance abuse; eating disorders; compulsive/addictive disorders other than substance abuse and eating disorders; post-traumatic stress disorder; thought, mood, and personality disorders.

Contact Bud Elliot, Manager, Attn: 1 East, 4949 Rockhill Road, Kansas City, MO 64110. Phone: 816-276-8591. Fax: 816-276-8943.

MENTAL HEALTH SERVICES INCORPORATED OF NORTH CENTRAL FLORIDA
4300 Southwest 13th Street
Gainesville, Florida 32608
904-374-5600; Fax: 904-371-9841

General Information Crisis stabilization unit-acute care services for children, adolescents. Patient security: unlocked. Independent not-for-profit facility. Licensed by state of Florida. Accredited by JCAHO.

Participants Accepts: male and female children; male and female adolescents. Average stay: 4 days. Admission: all parties who share custody, court order, depending on program. Treats behavior disorders; general psychosocial disorders; substance abuse; compulsive/addictive disorders other than substance abuse and eating disorders; post-traumatic stress disorder; thought, mood, and personality disorders.

Contact Casey Smith, Resource Development Coordinator, main address above. Phone: 904-374-5600.

MERCY CARE UNITS
1512 12th Ave Road
Nampa, Idaho 83686
208-466-4531; Fax: 208-463-5775

General Information General hospital for adolescents, adults. 16 beds for adolescents. Open year-round. Patient security: staff secured; will pursue and return runaways. Small town setting. Not-for-profit facility affiliated with Sisters of Mercy, Omaha, NE. Operated by CareUnit, Inc., Chesterfield, MO. Licensed by state of Idaho. Accredited by JCAHO.

Participants Accepts: male and female adolescents ages 12–17; male and female adults ages 18 and up. Average stay: 18 days. Admission: one parent. Treats learning disabilities; behavior disorders; general psychosocial disorders; substance abuse; eating disorders; thought, mood, and personality disorders. Accepts the mobility impaired; the vision impaired; the hearing impaired; the speech impaired; those with a history of harm to themselves and others; those receiving psychotropic medication; non-English speaking individuals; those with a history of epilepsy. Special programs for the developmentally disabled; the hearing impaired; the speech impaired; those with AIDS.

Program Treatment modalities: developmental model of recovery; family system; cognitive behavioral methods; didactive lectures. Family treatment program available.

Staff 3.9 full-time direct-care staff members per adolescent. Total facility staff includes 1 physician, 1 psychologist, 1 psychiatrist, 6 registered nurses, 11 practical/vocational nurses, 1 MSW social worker, 4 social workers (non-MSW), 1 teacher, 4 counselors, 1 occupational/recreational therapist, 1 speech pathologist, 1 dietician. Staff is 20% male, 80% female.

Facilities Single building; males and females in coeducational units. Separate residential quarters for adolescents. Central dining (not shared with adults). Basketball courts, game room, gymnasium, indoor swimming pool, outdoor swimming pool, outdoor tennis courts, playing fields, bowling alley.

Education Academic program available. Serves ages 12–17, ungraded. 1 teacher on staff.

Costs Average cost: $500 per day. Accepts private insurance, group insurance, medicare, medicaid, Blue Cross/Blue Shield, public funds.

Additional Services Outpatient services for males and females ages 12 and up. Treats substance abuse; compulsive/addictive disorders other than substance abuse and eating disorders.

Contact Keri Christian, Program Manager, main address above. Phone: 208-466-4531. Fax: 208-463-5775.

MERCY CENTER FOR HEALTH CARE SERVICES
1325 North Highland Avenue
Aurora, Illinois 60506
708-859-2222; Fax: 708-801-2559

General Information Psychiatric hospital for children, adolescents, adults. 14 beds for children; 24 beds for adolescents. Open year-round. Patient security: partially locked; will pursue and return runaways. Suburban setting. Not-for-profit facility. Licensed by state of Illinois. Accredited by JCAHO.

Participants Accepts: male and female children ages 2–13; male and female adolescents ages 13–18; male and female adults ages 18 and up. Average stay: 19 days. Admission: all parties who share custody, court order, depending on program. Treats autistic disorders; learning disabilities; behavior disorders; general psychosocial disorders; substance abuse; eating disorders; compulsive/addictive disorders other than substance abuse and eating disorders; post-traumatic stress disorder; thought, mood, and personality disorders. Accepts the hearing impaired; the speech impaired; those with a history of arson; the sexually compulsive; those with a history of harm to themselves and others; those receiving psychotropic medication; those with a history of epilepsy. Special programs for the developmentally disabled.

Program Treatment modalities: psychodynamic; behavior management; psychopharmacology; patient education/family therapy. Family treatment program available.

Staff Total facility staff includes 250 physicians, 3 psychologists, 15 psychiatrists, 400 registered nurses, 2 MSW social workers, 10 social workers (non-MSW), 4 teachers, 10 counselors, 2 physical therapists, 2 occupational/recreational therapists, 1 speech pathologist, 1 dietician. Staff is 40% male, 60% female.

Facilities Multiple buildings; males and females in coeducational units. Separate residential quarters for children and adolescents. Central dining (shared with adults). Basketball courts, game room, gymnasium, playing fields.

Education Academic program available at no charge. Serves ages 2–8, grades K–12. 4 teachers on staff. Cost of educational program covered by local school district.

Costs Average cost: $800 per day. Accepts private insurance, group insurance, medicare, medicaid, Blue Cross/Blue Shield.

Additional Services Outpatient services for males and females ages 12–18. Treats substance abuse.

Contact Louise Warren, Psychiatric Services Communication Liaison, main address above. Phone: 708-859-2222 Ext. 3454.

MERCY HOSPITAL
800 Mercy Drive
Council Bluffs, Iowa 51503
712-328-5000

General Information General hospital for children, adolescents. Patient security: partially locked. Not-for-profit facility affiliated with Mercy Midlands, Omaha, NE. Licensed by state of Iowa. Accredited by JCAHO.

Participants   Accepts: male and female children; male and female adolescents. Average stay: 14 days. Admission: one parent, all parties who share custody, court order, voluntary, depending on program. Treats autistic disorders; learning disabilities; behavior disorders; general psychosocial disorders; eating disorders; post-traumatic stress disorder; thought, mood, and personality disorders.

Contact   Ann Shumacher, Unit Coordinator, main address above. Phone: 712-328-5311.

MERCY HOSPITAL
25 Church Street
Wilkes-Barre, Pennsylvania 18765
717-826-3100; Fax: 717-823-0997

General Information   General hospital for children, adolescents. Patient security: entirely locked. Not-for-profit facility affiliated with Mercy Health System, Cincinnati, OH. Licensed by state of Pennsylvania. Accredited by JCAHO.

Participants   Accepts: male and female children; male and female adolescents. Average stay: 2 weeks. Admission: one parent, all parties who share custody, court order, voluntary, depending on program. Treats autistic disorders; learning disabilities; behavior disorders; general psychosocial disorders; substance abuse; eating disorders; compulsive/addictive disorders other than substance abuse and eating disorders; post-traumatic stress disorder; thought, mood, and personality disorders.

Contact   Mary Jarrett, Director, Adolescent Program, main address above. Phone: 717-826-3207.

MERCY HOSPITAL—CHEMICAL
DEPENDENCY SERVICES
800 Mercy Drive
Council Bluffs, Iowa 51503
712-328-5113; Fax: 712-328-5091

General Information   Chemical dependency service for adolescents. 10 beds for adolescents. Patient security: staff secured. Not-for-profit facility affiliated with Mercy Midlands, Omaha, NE. Licensed by state of Iowa. Accredited by JCAHO.

Participants   Accepts: male and female adolescents. Average stay: 19 days. Admission: one parent, all

parties who share custody, court order, voluntary, depending on program. Treats substance abuse. Accepts the mobility impaired; the vision impaired; the speech impaired; those with a history of arson; the sexually compulsive; those with a history of harm to themselves and others; those receiving psychotropic medication; those with a history of epilepsy.

Staff   Staff is 25% male, 75% female.

Costs   Average cost: $310 per day.

Contact   Melra Denholm, Intake and Assessment Coordinator, main address above. Phone: 712-328-5992. Fax: 712-328-5091.

MERCY MEDICAL CENTER
301 Saint Paul Place
Baltimore, Maryland 21202
410-332-9000

General Information   General hospital for children, adolescents. Patient security: staff secured. Independent not-for-profit facility. Licensed by state of Maryland. Accredited by JCAHO.

Participants   Accepts: male and female children; male and female adolescents. Average stay: 21 days. Admission: one parent, all parties who share custody, voluntary, depending on program. Treats behavior disorders; general psychosocial disorders; substance abuse; eating disorders; post-traumatic stress disorder.

Staff   Staff is 20% male, 80% female.

Contact   Dr. Harry Brandt, main address above. Phone: 410-332-9000.

MERIDIA RECOVERY CENTER
13951 Terrace Road
Cleveland, Ohio 44112
216-761-2851; Fax: 216-761-3570

General Information   General hospital with drug and alcohol rehabilitation program for adolescents. 10 beds for adolescents. Patient security: staff secured. Not-for-profit facility affiliated with Meridia Hospital Corporation, Cleveland, OH. Licensed by state of Ohio. Accredited by JCAHO.

Participants   Accepts: male and female adolescents. Average stay: 28 days. Admission: one parent, all parties who share custody, court order, voluntary, depending on program. Treats substance abuse. Accepts the mobility impaired; the vision impaired; the hearing impaired; the speech impaired; those with a history of arson; the sexually compulsive; those with a history of harm to themselves and others; those receiving psychotropic medication; those with a history of epilepsy.

Costs Average cost: $500 per day.

Contact Donna Zunt, Admissions Coordinator, main address above. Phone: 216-761-2851. Fax: 216-761-3570.

METHODIST HOSPITAL OF INDIANA, INC.
1701 North Senate Boulevard
Indianapolis, Indiana 46206
317-929-2000; Fax: 317-929-2787

General Information General hospital for adolescents. 16 beds for adolescents. Patient security: entirely locked. Independent not-for-profit facility. Licensed by state of Indiana. Accredited by JCAHO.

Participants Accepts: male and female adolescents. Average stay: 12 days. Admission: one parent, all parties who share custody, court order, voluntary, depending on program. Treats behavior disorders; general psychosocial disorders; thought, mood, and personality disorders.

Staff Staff is 20% male, 80% female.

Costs Average cost: $4500 per stay.

Contact Health Information, main address above. Phone: 317-929-2622.

THE METHODIST HOSPITALS, CHILD AND ADOLESCENT PROGRAM
600 Grant Street
Gary, Indiana 46402
219-886-4723

General Information General hospital for children, adolescents. Patient security: entirely locked. Independent not-for-profit facility. Licensed by state of Indiana. Accredited by JCAHO.

Participants Accepts: male and female children; male and female adolescents. Average stay: 4 weeks. Admission: one parent, all parties who share custody, court order, voluntary, depending on program. Treats behavior disorders; general psychosocial disorders; post-traumatic stress disorder; thought, mood, and personality disorders.

Staff Staff is 30% male, 70% female.

Costs Average cost: $500 per day.

Contact Betty May Reshkin, Admissions Coordinator, main address above. Phone: 219-886-4723.

METHODIST PSYCHIATRIC PAVILION
5610 Read Boulevard
New Orleans, Louisiana 70127
504-244-5661; Fax: 504-246-9150

General Information Freestanding psychiatric and substance abuse hospital for adolescents, adults. 10 beds for adolescents. Open year-round. Patient security: partially locked. Suburban setting. For-profit facility affiliated with Pendeton Memorial Methodist Hospital, New Orleans, LA. Licensed by state of Louisiana. Accredited by JCAHO.

Participants Accepts: male and female adolescents ages 11–18; male and female adults ages 18 and up. Average stay: 16 days. Admission: one parent, all parties who share custody, court order, voluntary, Physician Emergency Certificate, depending on program. Treats autistic disorders; learning disabilities; behavior disorders; general psychosocial disorders; substance abuse; eating disorders; compulsive/addictive disorders other than substance abuse and eating disorders; post-traumatic stress disorder; thought, mood, and personality disorders. Accepts the mobility impaired; the vision impaired; the hearing impaired; the speech impaired; those with a history of arson; the sexually compulsive; those with a history of harm to themselves and others; those receiving psychotropic medication; those with a history of epilepsy. Special programs for the chronically ill; the developmentally disabled; those with psychiatric disorders; those who are chemically dependent; those with school-related difficulties. Largest number of participants from Louisiana, Mississippi, Alabama.

Program Treatment modalities: family and individual psychotherapy; behavior modification; school intervention; medication management. Family treatment program available.

Staff Total facility staff includes 2 physicians, 3 psychologists, 2 psychiatrists, 5 registered nurses, 1 practical/vocational nurse, 2 MSW social workers, 8 social workers (non-MSW), 2 teachers, 4 counselors, 2 occupational/recreational therapists, 1 dietician, 6 other direct-care staff members. Staff is 50% male, 50% female.

Facilities Single building; males and females in coeducational units. Separate residential quarters for adolescents. Central dining (not shared with adults). Basketball courts, ropes course, volleyball.

Education Academic program available. Serves ages 11–18, grades 5–12. 2 teachers on staff. Curriculum accredited or approved by Orleans Parish School Board. Cost of educational program sometimes covered by local school district.

Costs Accepts private insurance, group insurance, medicare, Blue Cross/Blue Shield, public funds.

Additional Services Outpatient services for males and females ages 4–18. Treats autistic disorders; learning disabilities; behavior disorders; general psychosocial disorders; substance abuse; eating disorders; compulsive/addictive disorders other than substance abuse and eating disorders; post-traumatic stress disorder; thought, mood, and personality disorders. Day patient program ages 11–18. Treats autistic disorders; learning disabilities; behavior disorders; general psychosocial disorders; substance abuse; eating disorders; compulsive/addictive disorders other than substance abuse and eating disorders; post-traumatic stress disorder; thought, mood, and personality disorders.

Contact Joni Perelle, Assessment Specialist, main address above. Phone: 504-244-5661.

METHODIST RICHARD YOUNG RESIDENTIAL PROGRAM
515 South 26th Street
Omaha, Nebraska 68105
402-536-6939; Fax: 402-536-6648

General Information Psychiatric hospital for adolescents. Open year-round. Patient security: partially locked; no runaway pursuit. Urban setting. Not-for-profit facility affiliated with Nebraska Methodist Health System, Inc., Omaha, NE. Licensed by state of Nebraska. Accredited by JCAHO.

Participants Accepts: male and female adolescents ages 11–17. Admission: all parties who share custody, court order, voluntary, depending on program. Treats behavior disorders; general psychosocial disorders; substance abuse; eating disorders; compulsive/addictive disorders other than substance abuse and eating disorders; post-traumatic stress disorder; thought, mood, and personality disorders. Accepts the mobility impaired; the vision impaired; those with a history of harm to themselves and others; those receiving psychotropic medication. Largest number of participants from Nebraska, Iowa.

Program Treatment modalities: family systems model; Twelve Step Recovery. Family treatment program available.

Staff Total facility staff includes 10 physicians, 1 psychologist, 10 psychiatrists, 2 registered nurses, 2 practical/vocational nurses, 1 social worker (non-MSW), 1 occupational/recreational therapist, 1 dietician, 10 other direct-care staff members.

Facilities Multiple buildings; males and females in coeducational units. Separate dining by residential unit available. Basketball courts, game room, gymnasium, playing fields, whirlpool.

Education Academic program available. Serves ages 11–17, grades 5–12. Curriculum accredited or approved by State of Nebraska. Cost of educational program sometimes covered by local school district.

Costs Average cost: $295 per day. Accepts private insurance, group insurance, medicaid, public funds.

Additional Services Drug and alcohol rehabilitation services for males and females ages 11 and up. Treats learning disabilities; behavior disorders; general psychosocial disorders; substance abuse; eating disorders; compulsive/addictive disorders other than substance abuse and eating disorders; post-traumatic stress disorder; thought, mood, and personality disorders. Outpatient services for males and females ages 5 and up. Treats learning disabilities; behavior disorders; general psychosocial disorders; substance abuse; eating disorders; compulsive/addictive disorders other than substance abuse and eating disorders; post-traumatic stress disorder; thought, mood, and personality disorders. Residential or sub-acute services for males and females ages 11–17. Treats learning disabilities; behavior disorders; general psychosocial disorders; substance abuse; eating disorders; compulsive/addictive disorders other than substance abuse and eating disorders; post-traumatic stress disorder; thought, mood, and personality disorders.

Contact Jean Sassatelli, Program Manager, main address above. Phone: 402-536-6307. Fax: 402-536-6471.

METROHEALTH SAINT LUKE'S ADOLESCENT CHEMICAL DEPENDENCY PROGRAMS
11311 Shaker Boulevard
Cleveland, Ohio 44104
216-368-7970; Fax: 216-368-7944

General Information General hospital for adolescents. 16 beds for adolescents. Open year-round. Patient security: partially locked; will pursue and return runaways. Urban setting. Not-for-profit facility affiliated with The MetroHealth System, Cleveland,

OH. Licensed by state of Ohio. Accredited by JCAHO.

Participants Accepts: male and female adolescents ages 13–19. Average stay: 35 days. Admission: one parent. Treats general psychosocial disorders; substance abuse. Accepts the mobility impaired; the vision impaired; the hearing impaired; the speech impaired; those with a history of arson; those with a history of harm to themselves and others; those receiving psychotropic medication; those with a history of epilepsy. Special programs for the chronically ill; the mobility impaired; the vision impaired; the hearing impaired; the speech impaired; those with AIDS. Largest number of participants from Ohio, Michigan, New York.

Program Treatment modalities: Gestalt; reality therapy; Twelve Step Recovery; individual and group counseling/family groups. Family treatment program available.

Staff Total facility staff includes 2 physicians, 2 psychiatrists, 4 registered nurses, 3 practical/vocational nurses, 1 teacher, 8 counselors, 1 occupational/recreational therapist, 11 other direct-care staff members. Staff is 30% male, 70% female.

Facilities Multiple buildings; males and females in coeducational units. Separate dining by residential unit available. Basketball courts, game room.

Education Academic program available at no charge. Serves ages 13–19, grades 7–12. 1 teacher on staff.

Costs Average cost: $411 per day. Accepts private insurance, group insurance, medicaid, Blue Cross/Blue Shield.

Additional Services Outpatient services for males and females ages 8–19. Treats general psychosocial disorders; substance abuse; eating disorders; compulsive/addictive disorders other than substance abuse and eating disorders; post-traumatic stress disorder. Wilderness/survival program for males and females ages 13–19. Treats general psychosocial disorders; substance abuse.

Contact Luanne Brown-Johnson, Community Relations Coordinator, main address above. Phone: 216-368-7989. Fax: 216-368-7944.

MILL CREEK SCHOOL
111 North 49th Street
Philadelphia, Pennsylvania 19139
215-471-2169; Fax: 215-471-2833

General Information School for adolescents. Patient security: unlocked. Not-for-profit facility affiliated with Pennsylvania Hospital, Philadelphia, PA.

Participants Accepts: male and female adolescents ages 12–18. Average stay: 1 year. Admission: all parties who share custody, voluntary, depending on program. Treats learning disabilities; behavior disorders; general psychosocial disorders; substance abuse; eating disorders; compulsive/addictive disorders other than substance abuse and eating disorders; post-traumatic stress disorder; thought, mood, and personality disorders.

Education School serves ages 12–18, grades 7–12.

Contact Stanley C. Diamond, Director, main address above. Phone: 215-471-2169. Fax: 215-471-2833.

Announcement The Mill Creek School, opened in 1971, offers a supportive environment for students ages 12 to 18 with emotional and/or psychological problems. This small, fully licensed high school provides a college-prep and vocational curriculum as well as programs for the learning disabled. The program accepts day students and patients in treatment at the Institute of Pennsylvania Hospital.

MILWAUKEE PSYCHIATRIC HOSPITAL
1220 Dewey Avenue
Wauwatosa, Wisconsin 53213
414-258-2600; Fax: 414-258-0520

General Information Psychiatric hospital for children, adolescents. Patient security: partially locked. Independent not-for-profit facility. Licensed by state of Wisconsin. Accredited by JCAHO.

Participants Accepts: male and female children; male and female adolescents. Average stay: 14 days. Admission: one parent, all parties who share custody, court order, voluntary, depending on program. Treats autistic disorders; learning disabilities; behavior disorders; general psychosocial disorders; substance abuse; eating disorders; compulsive/addictive disorders other than substance abuse and eating disorders; post-traumatic stress disorder; thought, mood, and personality disorders.

Costs Average cost: $8696 per stay.

Contact Joel Rynders, Triage Coordinator, main address above. Phone: 414-258-2600. Fax: 414-258-0520.

MIRAGE RETREAT
4615 North Michigan Road
Indianapolis, Indiana 46208
317-925-5378; Fax: 317-923-9271

General Information Drug and alcohol rehabilitation center for adolescents. Patient security: staff secured. Not-for-profit facility affiliated with Community Centers of Indianapolis, Indianapolis, IN. Licensed by state of Indiana.

Participants Accepts: male and female adolescents. Average stay: 60 days. Admission: one parent, all parties who share custody, court order, voluntary, depending on program. Treats substance abuse. Accepts the vision impaired; the hearing impaired; the speech impaired; those with a history of harm to themselves and others; those receiving psychotropic medication; those with a history of epilepsy.

Staff Staff is 40% male, 60% female.

Costs Average cost: $152 per day.

Contact Judith Smith, Residential Director, main address above. Phone: 317-925-5378.

MIRMONT TREATMENT CENTER
100 Yearsley Mill Road
Lima, Pennsylvania 19037
215-565-9232; Fax: 215-565-7497

General Information Drug and alcohol rehabilitation center for adolescents, adults. 30 beds for adolescents. Open year-round. Patient security: staff secured; no runaway pursuit. Rural setting. Not-for-profit facility affiliated with Delaware County Memorial Hospital/Riddle Memorial Hospital. Licensed by state of Pennsylvania. Accredited by JCAHO.

Participants Accepts: male and female adolescents ages 13–18; male and female adults ages 18–75. Average stay: 27 days. Admission: one parent, court order, depending on program. Treats learning disabilities; substance abuse; compulsive/addictive disorders other than substance abuse and eating disorders. Accepts the mobility impaired; the speech impaired. Special programs for the mobility impaired; those with AIDS. Largest number of participants from Pennsylvania, Delaware, New Jersey.

Program Treatment modalities: Twelve Step Recovery. Family treatment program available.

Staff Total facility staff includes 1 physician, 1 psychologist, 10 registered nurses, 3 practical/vocational nurses, 2 MSW social workers, 1 social worker (non-MSW), 1 teacher, 2 counselors, 1 occupational/recreational therapist, 5 therapists, 1 dietician. Staff is 64% male, 36% female.

Facilities Single building; males and females in coeducational units. Separate residential quarters for adolescents. Separate dining by residential unit available. Basketball courts, playing fields, volleyball.

Education Academic program available at no charge. Serves ages 13–18, grades 7–12. 1 teacher on staff. Cost of educational program covered by local school district.

Costs Average cost: $11,799 per stay. Accepts private insurance, group insurance, Blue Cross/Blue Shield, public funds.

Additional Services Outpatient services for males and females ages 14 and up. Treats behavior disorders; substance abuse; compulsive/addictive disorders other than substance abuse and eating disorders; post-traumatic stress disorder; thought, mood, and personality disorders.

Contact William J. Rachor Jr., Director of Community Relations, main address above. Phone: 215-565-9232. Fax: 215-565-7497.

MOCCASIN BEND RANCH
130 A Street, SW
Miami, Oklahoma 74354
918-542-1836; Fax: 918-542-8730

General Information Residential treatment/subacute facility for adolescents. 22 beds for adolescents. Open year-round. Patient security: unlocked; will pursue and return runaways. Rural setting. For-profit facility affiliated with Sterling Health Care Corporation, Bellevue, WA. Licensed by state of Oklahoma. Accredited by JCAHO.

Participants Accepts: male and female adolescents ages 12–18. Average stay: 90 days. Admission: one parent, court order, depending on program. Treats learning disabilities; behavior disorders; general psychosocial disorders; substance abuse; compulsive/addictive disorders other than substance abuse and eating disorders; post-traumatic stress disorder; thought, mood, and personality disorders. Accepts those receiving psychotropic medication. Largest number of participants from Oklahoma, Kansas, Missouri.

Program Treatment modalities: behavior modification; social learning program; Twelve Step Recovery. Family treatment program available.

Staff 1.1 full-time direct-care staff members per adolescent. Total facility staff includes 1 physician, 1 psychiatrist, 2 registered nurses, 3 practical/vocational nurses, 2 MSW social workers, 1 social worker (non-MSW), 2 teachers, 1 counselor, 3 occupational/recreational therapists, 1 dietician, 9 other direct-care staff members. Staff is 41% male, 59% female.

Facilities Single building; males and females in co-educational units. Central dining. Basketball courts, game room, horseback riding, outdoor tennis courts, playing fields, ropes course, canoeing, camping.

Education Academic program available at no charge. Serves ages 12–18. 2 teachers on staff. Curriculum accredited or approved by Wyandotte School System. Cost of educational program covered by local school district.

Costs Average cost: $350 per day. Accepts private insurance, group insurance, medicaid, Blue Cross/Blue Shield.

Contact Tami Verhoff, Intake Coordinator, main address above. Phone: 918-542-1836 Ext. 500. Fax: 918-542-8730.

MOHONK HOUSE, INC.
66 Weston Road
Westport, Connecticut 06880
203-226-6665; Fax: 203-226-6665

General Information Residential treatment/subacute facility for adolescents. 10 beds for adolescents. Open year-round. Patient security: staff secured; will pursue and return runaways. Suburban setting. Independent not-for-profit facility. Licensed by state of Connecticut.

Participants Accepts: male adolescents ages 12–18. Average stay: 180 days. Admission: one parent, all parties who share custody, court order, voluntary, depending on program. Treats learning disabilities; behavior disorders; general psychosocial disorders; post-traumatic stress disorder. Accepts those receiving psychotropic medication; those with a history of epilepsy; diabetics. Largest number of participants from Connecticut, New York, Massachusetts.

Program Treatment modalities: Gestalt. Family treatment program available.

Staff .8 full-time direct-care staff member per adolescent. Total facility staff includes 1 psychologist, 1 psychiatrist, 1 MSW social worker, 3 counselors, 2 other direct-care staff members. Staff is 75% male, 25% female.

Facilities Multiple buildings. Central dining. Basketball courts, game room, gymnasium, indoor swimming pool, outdoor swimming pool, outdoor tennis courts, playing fields, ropes course, sailboats, motorboats, scuba diving, 125-acre campground.

Education Educational arrangements: children attend local public schools. Educational program held off-site at no charge.

Costs Average cost: $25,000 per year. Accepts private insurance, group insurance, public funds.

Additional Services Outpatient services for males and females ages 12–18. Treats learning disabilities; behavior disorders; general psychosocial disorders; compulsive/addictive disorders other than substance abuse and eating disorders; post-traumatic stress disorder; thought, mood, and personality disorders. Wilderness/survival program for males and females ages 12–18. Treats learning disabilities; behavior disorders; general psychosocial disorders; post-traumatic stress disorder. Camping program for males and females ages 12–18. Treats learning disabilities; behavior disorders; general psychosocial disorders; post-traumatic stress disorder. Gifted education/treatment programs for males ages 12–18. Treats learning disabilities; behavior disorders; general psychosocial disorders.

Contact Dr. David Singer, Director, main address above. Phone: 203-226-6665. Fax: 203-226-6665.

Announcement Mohonk House is a truly unique residential facility especially for gifted and talented adolescents with adjustment and conduct disorders. The ratio of staff to residents (1:2) as well as the large number of resources and imaginative and accelerated programs makes Mohonk unique in the United States.

MONTANA DEACONESS MEDICAL CENTER
1101 26th Street, South
Great Falls, Montana 59405
406-761-1200; Fax: 406-455-4974

General Information General hospital for children, adolescents. Patient security arrangements vary depending on program. Independent not-for-profit facility. Licensed by state of Montana. Accredited by JCAHO.

Participants Accepts: male and female children; male and female adolescents. Average stay: 14 days. Admission: one parent, all parties who share custody, court order, voluntary, physician's referral, depending on program. Treats learning disabilities; behavior disorders; general psychosocial disorders; substance abuse; eating disorders; compulsive/addictive disorders other than substance abuse and eating disorders; post-traumatic stress disorder; thought, mood, and personality disorders.

Contact Chuck Cerny, Director, Psychiatric Program, main address above. Phone: 406-455-5230.

MONTANARI RESIDENTIAL TREATMENT CENTER
291 East Second Street
Hialeah, Florida 33011-1360
305-887-7543; Fax: 305-882-1970

General Information Residential treatment/subacute facility for children, adolescents. Patient security: partially locked. Independent for-profit facility. Licensed by state of Florida. Accredited by JCAHO.

Participants Accepts: male and female children; male and female adolescents. Average stay: 18 months. Admission: one parent, all parties who share custody, court order, voluntary, depending on program. Treats autistic disorders; learning disabilities; behavior disorders; general psychosocial disorders; substance abuse; eating disorders; compulsive/addictive disorders other than substance abuse and eating disorders; thought, mood, and personality disorders.

Staff Staff is 35% male, 65% female.

Costs Average cost: $140 per day.

Contact Paul Hague, Executive Director, main address above. Phone: 305-887-7543.

MOUNTAIN VIEW HOSPITAL
1000 East Highway 6
Payson, Utah 84651
801-465-9201; Fax: 801-465-3370

General Information General hospital for children, adolescents, adults. Open year-round. will pursue and return runaways. Rural setting. For-profit facility affiliated with Health Trust, Inc., Nashville, TN. Licensed by state of Utah. Accredited by JCAHO.

Participants Accepts: male and female children ages up to 12; male and female adolescents ages 13–20; male and female adults ages 21 and up. Average stay: 15 days. Admission: one parent. Treats autistic dis-

orders; learning disabilities; behavior disorders; general psychosocial disorders; substance abuse; eating disorders; compulsive/addictive disorders other than substance abuse and eating disorders; post-traumatic stress disorder; thought, mood, and personality disorders. Accepts the mobility impaired; the vision impaired; the hearing impaired; the speech impaired; those with a history of arson; the sexually compulsive; those with a history of harm to themselves and others; those receiving psychotropic medication; non-English speaking individuals; those with a history of epilepsy. Special programs for the mobility impaired.

Program Treatment modalities: Twelve Step Recovery; inner child; hypnotherapy; co-dependency. Family treatment program available.

Staff Total facility staff includes 106 physicians, 1 psychologist, 2 psychiatrists, 105 registered nurses, 46 practical/vocational nurses, 3 MSW social workers, 3 counselors, 3 physical therapists, 1 occupational/recreational therapist, 2 dieticians. Staff is 25% male, 75% female.

Facilities Single building; males and females in coeducational units. Residential quarters shared with adults. Central dining (shared with adults), in-room dining available. Indoor swimming pool, playing fields, ropes course, weight and exercise room.

Education Academic program available at no charge. Serves ages 10–18, grades 5–12. Curriculum accredited or approved by Utah Teacher Association. Cost of educational program covered by local school district.

Costs Average cost: $353 per day. Accepts private insurance, group insurance, medicare, medicaid, Blue Cross/Blue Shield, public funds.

Additional Services Drug and alcohol rehabilitation services for males and females. Treats learning disabilities; behavior disorders; general psychosocial disorders; substance abuse; eating disorders; compulsive/addictive disorders other than substance abuse and eating disorders; post-traumatic stress disorder; thought, mood, and personality disorders. Outpatient services for males and females. Treats autistic disorders; learning disabilities; behavior disorders; general psychosocial disorders; substance abuse; eating disorders; compulsive/addictive disorders other than substance abuse and eating disorders; post-traumatic stress disorder; thought, mood, and personality disorders. Residential or sub-acute services for males and females. Treats learning disabilities; behavior disorders; general psychosocial disorders; substance abuse; eating disorders; compulsive/addictive disorders other than substance abuse and eating disorders; post-traumatic stress disorder; thought, mood, and personality disorders.

Contact Pam White, Public Relations Director, main address above. Phone: 801-465-9201.

MOUNTAINVIEW PLACE
2135 Southgate Road
Colorado Springs, Colorado 80906
719-633-4114; Fax: 719-578-0857

General Information Residential treatment/subacute facility for children, adolescents. Open year-round. Patient security: staff secured; will pursue and return runaways. Urban setting. For-profit facility affiliated with Healthcare International, Austin, TX. Licensed by state of Colorado. Accredited by JCAHO; Civilian Health and Medical Program of the Uniformed Services, Department of Social Services.

Participants Accepts: male and female children ages 10–12; male and female adolescents ages 13–18. Average stay: 120 days. Admission: all parties who share custody, voluntary, depending on program. Treats learning disabilities; behavior disorders; general psychosocial disorders; substance abuse; eating disorders; compulsive/addictive disorders other than substance abuse and eating disorders; post-traumatic stress disorder; thought, mood, and personality disorders. Accepts the mobility impaired; the vision impaired; those with a history of arson; the sexually compulsive; those with a history of harm to themselves and others; those receiving psychotropic medication; those with a history of epilepsy.

Program Treatment modalities: psychodynamic; behavioral; cognitive-restructuring; family systems. Family treatment program available.

Staff Total facility staff includes 1 physician, 1 psychiatrist, 5 registered nurses, 3 MSW social workers, 2 teachers, 9 counselors, 2 occupational/recreational therapists, 1 therapist, 1 dietician. Staff is 40% male, 60% female.

Facilities Multiple buildings; males and females in coeducational units. Central dining (shared with adults). Basketball courts, game room, gymnasium, horseback riding, playing fields, ropes course.

Education Academic program available at no charge. Serves ages 10–18, grades 4–12. 2 teachers on staff. Curriculum accredited or approved by Harrison Public School District. Cost of educational program sometimes covered by local school district.

Costs Average cost: $450 per stay. Accepts private insurance, group insurance, medicare, Blue Cross/Blue Shield, public funds.

Additional Services Drug and alcohol rehabilitation services for males and females ages 10–18. Treats learning disabilities; behavior disorders; general psychosocial disorders; substance abuse; eating disorders; compulsive/addictive disorders other than substance abuse and eating disorders; post-traumatic stress disorder; thought, mood, and personality disorders.

Contact Janet Miller, Program Manager, main address above. Phone: 719-633-4114. Fax: 719-578-0857.

MOUNTAINVIEW REHABILITATION CENTER, INC.
HCR #1, Box 175
Brodheadsville, Pennsylvania 18322
717-992-5566; Fax: 717-992-8089

General Information Drug and alcohol rehabilitation center for adolescents, adults. Open year-round. Patient security: staff secured; will pursue and return runaways. Rural setting. Independent for-profit facility. Licensed by state of Pennsylvania. Accredited by JCAHO.

Participants Accepts: male and female adolescents ages 12–18; male and female adults ages 19–65. Average stay: 42 days. Admission: one parent, court order, voluntary, depending on program. Treats behavior disorders; general psychosocial disorders; substance abuse; thought, mood, and personality disorders. Accepts those receiving psychotropic medication.

Program Treatment modalities: Twelve Step Recovery. Family treatment program available.

Staff 1.1 full-time direct-care staff members per adolescent. Total facility staff includes 1 physician, 1 psychologist, 1 psychiatrist, 2 registered nurses, 3 practical/vocational nurses, 2 teachers, 4 counselors, 1 occupational/recreational therapist, 1 dietician, 8 other direct-care staff members.

Facilities Multiple buildings; males and females in separate units. Separate residential quarters for adolescents. Separate dining by residential unit available. Basketball courts, ropes course.

Education Academic program available at no charge. Serves ages 12–18, grades 6–12. 2 teachers on staff. Curriculum accredited or approved by Pennsylvania Department of Education. Cost of educational program covered by local school district. Organized sports program offered.

Costs Average cost: $1200 per stay. Accepts private insurance, group insurance.

Contact Pat Ferrara, Admissions Coordinator, main address above. Phone: 717-992-5566. Fax: 717-992-8089.

MOUNTAIN WOOD
500 Old Lynchburg Road
P.O. Box 5546
Charlottesville, Virginia 22905
804-971-8245; Fax: 804-971-1385

General Information Drug and alcohol rehabilitation center for adolescents, adults. 40 beds for adolescents. Open year-round. Patient security: unlocked; will pursue and return runaways. Suburban setting. For-profit facility affiliated with Mediplex Group, Inc., Wellesley, MA. Licensed by state of Virginia. Accredited by JCAHO.

Participants Accepts: male and female adolescents ages 13–18; male and female adults ages 18 and up. Average stay: 30 days. Admission: all parties who share custody. Treats general psychosocial disorders; substance abuse; post-traumatic stress disorder. Accepts the mobility impaired.

Program Treatment modalities: Twelve Step Recovery; individual and group psychodynamic counseling. Family treatment program available.

Staff .3 full-time direct-care staff member per adolescent. Total facility staff includes 1 physician, 1 psychologist, 2 psychiatrists, 2 registered nurses, 5 practical/vocational nurses, 2 MSW social workers, 1 teacher, 1 physical therapist, 1 dietician. Staff is 30% male, 70% female.

Facilities Multiple buildings; males and females in coeducational units. Separate residential quarters for adolescents. Central dining (shared with adults). Basketball courts, game room, gymnasium, playing fields.

Education Academic program available at no charge. Serves ages 13–18, grades 7–12. 1 teacher on staff. Curriculum accredited or approved by State of Virginia.

Costs Accepts private insurance, group insurance, medicaid, Blue Cross/Blue Shield, public funds.

Contact Michael Goodman, Director of Regional Services, 7635 Leesburg Pike, Falls Church, VA 22043. Phone: 703-848-2621. Fax: 703-848-2969.

MOUNT BACHELOR ACADEMY
P.O. Box 7463
Bend, Oregon 97708
800-462-3404; Fax: 503-462-3430

General Information School for adolescents. 82 beds for adolescents. Open year-round. Patient security: staff secured; no runaway pursuit. Rural setting. For-profit facility affiliated with College Health Enterprises, Downey, CA. Licensed by state of Oregon.

Participants Accepts: male and female adolescents ages 13–18. Average stay: 730 days. Admission: all parties who share custody, court order, depending on program. Treats learning disabilities; behavior disorders; general psychosocial disorders; substance abuse; eating disorders; compulsive/addictive disorders other than substance abuse and eating disorders; thought, mood, and personality disorders. Accepts the mobility impaired; the hearing impaired; the speech impaired; those receiving psychotropic medication; non-English speaking individuals; those with a history of epilepsy. Largest number of participants from California, New Jersey, Virginia.

Program Treatment modalities: group counseling; peer counseling. Family treatment program available.

Staff .3 full-time direct-care staff member per adolescent. Total facility staff includes 8 teachers, 8 counselors, 4 other direct-care staff members. Staff is 35% male, 65% female.

Facilities Multiple buildings; males and females in separate units. Basketball courts, game room, gymnasium, outdoor swimming pool, outdoor tennis courts, playing fields.

Education School serves ages 13–18, grades 7–12. 8 teachers on staff. Curriculum is college-preparatory; diploma granted upon completion. Organized sports program offered.

Costs Average cost: $3450 per month. Accepts private insurance, group insurance, medicare, medicaid, Blue Cross/Blue Shield, public funds. Financial aid available.

Additional Services Drug and alcohol rehabilitation services for males and females ages 13–18. Treats learning disabilities; behavior disorders; general psychosocial disorders; substance abuse; eating disorders; compulsive/addictive disorders other than substance abuse and eating disorders; post-traumatic stress disorder; thought, mood, and personality disorders. Wilderness/survival program for males and females ages 13–18. Treats autistic disorders; learning disabilities; behavior disorders; general psychosocial disorders; substance abuse; eating disorders; compulsive/addictive disorders other than substance abuse and eating disorders; post-traumatic stress disorder; thought, mood, and personality disorders.

Contact Jeffry Johnson, Admissions Director, main address above. Phone: 800-462-3404. Fax: 503-462-3430.

MOUNT ST. VINCENT HOME
4159 Lowell Boulevard
Denver, Colorado 80211
303-458-7220

General Information Residential treatment/subacute facility for children. 45 beds for children. Open year-round. Patient security: staff secured. Urban setting. Not-for-profit facility affiliated with Sisters of Charity of Leavenworth, Leavenworth, KS. Licensed by state of Colorado.

Participants Accepts: male and female children ages 5–16. Average stay: 22 months. Admission: all parties who share custody, court order, voluntary, depending on program. Treats learning disabilities; behavior disorders; general psychosocial disorders; compulsive/addictive disorders other than substance abuse and eating disorders; post-traumatic stress disorder; thought, mood, and personality disorders. Accepts the speech impaired; the sexually compulsive; those with a history of harm to themselves and others; those receiving psychotropic medication; those with a history of epilepsy. Special programs for the speech impaired.

Program Treatment modalities: psychodynamic. Family treatment program available.

Staff Total facility staff includes 1 psychologist, 3 psychiatrists, 1 registered nurse, 7 MSW social workers, 8 teachers, 1 speech pathologist, 36 other direct-care staff members.

Facilities Single building; males and females in separate units. Central dining. Basketball courts, gymnasium, outdoor swimming pool, playing fields, mountain lodge.

Education 8 teachers on staff.

Costs Average cost: $1960 per month. Accepts private insurance, group insurance, public funds.

Contact Sandra Sears, Clinical Director, main address above. Phone: 303-458-7220.

MOUNT SINAI HOSPITAL
Fourth and Reed Streets
Philadelphia, Pennsylvania 19147
215-339-3333; Fax: 215-339-3616

General Information Specialty hospital for children, adolescents. 16 beds for adolescents. Open year-round. Patient security: partially locked; will pursue and return runaways. Urban setting. Not-for-profit facility affiliated with Graduate Health System, Philadelphia, PA. Licensed by state of Pennsylvania.

Accredited by JCAHO; Department of Public Welfare.

Participants Accepts: male and female children ages 10–12; male and female adolescents ages 13–17. Average stay: 20 days. Admission: voluntary. Treats learning disabilities; behavior disorders; general psychosocial disorders; substance abuse; thought, mood, and personality disorders. Accepts those with a history of harm to themselves and others; those receiving psychotropic medication; non-English speaking individuals; those with a history of epilepsy. Special programs for the developmentally disabled; those with AIDS.

Program Treatment modalities: psychodynamic; behavior modification. Family treatment program available.

Staff Total facility staff includes 1 physician, 1 psychologist, 2 psychiatrists, 7 registered nurses, 2 MSW social workers, 2 teachers, 1 counselor, 2 occupational/recreational therapists, 1 speech pathologist, 9 therapists. Staff is 50% male, 50% female.

Facilities Multiple buildings; males and females in coeducational units. Central dining (shared with adults). Game room, gymnasium.

Education Academic program available at no charge. Serves ages 10–17. 2 teachers on staff. Curriculum accredited or approved by State of Pennsylvania.

Costs Accepts private insurance, group insurance, medicare, medicaid, Blue Cross/Blue Shield, public funds.

Additional Services Drug and alcohol rehabilitation services for males and females ages 10 and up. Treats behavior disorders; general psychosocial disorders; substance abuse; compulsive/addictive disorders other than substance abuse and eating disorders; post-traumatic stress disorder; thought, mood, and personality disorders.

Contact Jay Cantor, main address above. Phone: 215-339-3835. Fax: 215-339-3616.

THE MOUNT SINAI MEDICAL CENTER
One Gustave Levy Place
New York, New York 10029
212-241-6500; Fax: 212-831-6398

General Information General hospital for children. 15 beds for children. Patient security: entirely locked. Independent not-for-profit facility. Licensed by state of New York. Accredited by JCAHO.

Participants Accepts: male and female children ages 5–12. Average stay: 2 months. Admission: all parties who share custody. Treats autistic disorders; learning disabilities; behavior disorders; general psychosocial disorders; eating disorders; compulsive/addictive disorders other than substance abuse and eating disorders; post-traumatic stress disorder; thought, mood, and personality disorders.

Staff Staff is 25% male, 75% female.

Additional Services Outpatient services for males and females ages up to 18. Treats autistic disorders; learning disabilities; behavior disorders; general psychosocial disorders; eating disorders; compulsive/addictive disorders other than substance abuse and eating disorders; post-traumatic stress disorder; thought, mood, and personality disorders. School for males and females ages 5–12. Treats autistic disorders; learning disabilities; behavior disorders; general psychosocial disorders; eating disorders; compulsive/addictive disorders other than substance abuse and eating disorders; post-traumatic stress disorder; thought, mood, and personality disorders.

Contact Trude Gruber, Social Work Supervisor, main address above. Phone: 212-241-6882.

MULBERRY CENTER, WELBORN HOSPITAL
500 Southeast 4th Street
Evansville, Indiana 47713
812-426-8168; Fax: 812-426-3333

General Information General hospital for children, adolescents, adults. 14 beds for children; 38 beds for adolescents; 114 beds total. Open year-round. Patient security: partially locked; will pursue and return runaways. Urban setting. Independent not-for-profit facility. Licensed by state of Indiana. Accredited by JCAHO.

Participants Accepts: male and female children ages 4–12; male and female adolescents ages 13–18; male and female adults ages 18 and up. Average stay: 14 days. Admission: one parent, court order, depending on program. Treats learning disabilities; behavior disorders; general psychosocial disorders; substance abuse; eating disorders; compulsive/addictive disorders other than substance abuse and eating disorders; post-traumatic stress disorder; thought, mood, and personality disorders. Accepts the vision impaired; the hearing impaired; the speech impaired; those with a history of arson; those with a history of harm to themselves and others; those receiving psychotropic medication; those with a history of epilepsy; sexually traumatized victims. Special programs for the chronically ill; the developmentally disabled; the hearing

impaired. Largest number of participants from Illinois, Kentucky.

Program Treatment modalities: psychodynamic; trauma treatment model/experimental; family systems; Twelve Step Recovery. Family treatment program available.

Facilities Multiple buildings; males and females in coeducational units. Separate residential quarters for children and adolescents. Separate dining by residential unit available. Basketball courts, game room, gymnasium, indoor swimming pool, indoor tennis courts, volleyball.

Education Academic program available at no charge. Serves ages 4–18, grades K–12. Curriculum accredited or approved by local school corporation. Cost of educational program sometimes covered by local school district.

Costs Average cost: $8500 per stay. Accepts private insurance, group insurance, medicare, medicaid, Blue Cross/Blue Shield, public funds.

Additional Services Drug and alcohol rehabilitation services for males and females ages 12 and up. Treats learning disabilities; behavior disorders; general psychosocial disorders; substance abuse; eating disorders; compulsive/addictive disorders other than substance abuse and eating disorders; post-traumatic stress disorder; thought, mood, and personality disorders. Outpatient services for males and females ages 4–90. Treats behavior disorders; general psychosocial disorders; substance abuse; eating disorders; compulsive/addictive disorders other than substance abuse and eating disorders; post-traumatic stress disorder; thought, mood, and personality disorders.

Contact Linda Pruitt, Assistant Director, Mullberry Center, main address above. Phone: 812-426-8467. Fax: 812-426-3333.

MUNSON MEDICAL CENTER— ALCOHOL AND DRUG TREATMENT CENTER
1105 6th Street
Traverse City, Michigan 49684
616-935-6382; Fax: 616-935-6920

General Information Residential treatment/subacute facility for adolescents. Patient security: staff secured. Not-for-profit facility affiliated with Munson Medical Center, Traverse City, MI. Licensed by state of Michigan. Accredited by JCAHO.

Participants Accepts: male and female adolescents. Average stay: 6 weeks. Admission: one parent, all parties who share custody, court order, voluntary, depending on program. Treats substance abuse. Accepts the mobility impaired; the vision impaired; the hearing impaired; the speech impaired; those with a history of arson; those with a history of harm to themselves and others; those receiving psychotropic medication; those with a history of epilepsy.

Staff Staff is 60% male, 40% female.

Costs Average cost: $350 per day.

Additional Services Outpatient services for males and females ages 12–18. Treats substance abuse.

Contact Robert Baker, Adolescent Admissions Coordinator, main address above. Phone: 616-935-6382. Fax: 616-935-6920.

NAMASTE
40 Hob Road
Los Lunas, New Mexico 87031
505-865-6176

General Information Residential treatment/subacute facility for children. 24 beds for children. Open year-round. Patient security: staff secured; no runaway pursuit. Rural setting. Independent not-for-profit facility. Licensed by state of New Mexico. Accredited by JCAHO.

Participants Accepts: male and female children ages 6–12. Average stay: 9 months. Admission: one parent, court order, depending on program. Treats learning disabilities; behavior disorders; general psychosocial disorders; substance abuse; eating disorders; compulsive/addictive disorders other than substance abuse and eating disorders; post-traumatic stress disorder. Accepts those with a history of harm to themselves and others; those receiving psychotropic medication.

Program Treatment modalities: attachment-based treatment model; holistic modalities. Family treatment program available.

Staff 1 full-time direct-care staff member per child. Total facility staff includes 2 physicians, 4 psychologists, 2 psychiatrists, 1 registered nurse, 1 social worker (non-MSW), 3 teachers, 5 counselors, 2 occupational/recreational therapists, 1 speech pathologist, 1 dietician, 22 other direct-care staff members. Staff is 50% male, 50% female.

Facilities Multiple buildings; males and females in coeducational units. Separate dining by residential unit available. Basketball courts, horseback riding, indoor swimming pool, playing fields, ropes course.

Education Academic program available at no charge. Serves ages 6–12, grades 1–6. 3 teachers on staff. Cost of educational program sometimes covered by local school district.

Costs Average cost: $375 per day. Accepts private insurance, group insurance, medicaid, public funds.

Contact Tina Austin, Outreach Director, main address above. Phone: 505-865-6176.

NATIONAL HOSPITAL FOR KIDS IN CRISIS
5300 Kidspeace Drive
Orefield, Pennsylvania 18069
215-799-8000; Fax: 215-799-8001

General Information Psychiatric hospital for children, adolescents. 12 beds for children; 60 beds for adolescents; 72 beds total. Open year-round. Patient security: entirely locked; will pursue and return runaways. Rural setting. Not-for-profit facility affiliated with KidsPeace, Bethlehem, PA. Licensed by state of Pennsylvania. Accredited by JCAHO.

Participants Accepts: male and female children ages 6–12; male and female adolescents ages 13–21. Average stay: 30 days. Admission: one parent, all parties who share custody, court order, voluntary, depending on program. Treats learning disabilities; behavior disorders; general psychosocial disorders; substance abuse; eating disorders; compulsive/addictive disorders other than substance abuse and eating disorders; post-traumatic stress disorder; thought, mood, and personality disorders. Accepts the vision impaired; the hearing impaired; the speech impaired; those with a history of arson; the sexually compulsive; those with a history of harm to themselves and others; those receiving psychotropic medication; those with a history of epilepsy.

Program Treatment modalities: psychosocial; behavioral; psychodynamic; family-oriented. Family treatment program available.

Staff Total facility staff includes 1 physician, 2 psychologists, 2 psychiatrists, 22 registered nurses, 12 MSW social workers, 3 teachers, 64 counselors, 6 occupational/recreational therapists. Staff is 50% male, 50% female.

Facilities Single building; males and females in separate units. Central dining. Basketball courts, game room, gymnasium, indoor swimming pool, playing fields, ropes course.

Education Academic program available at additional cost. Serves ages 6–21, ungraded. 3 teachers on staff. Curriculum accredited or approved by Middle States Association of Schools and Colleges. Cost of educational program covered by local school district.

Costs Accepts private insurance, group insurance, medicaid, public funds.

Additional Services Drug and alcohol rehabilitation services for males and females ages 13–21. Treats learning disabilities; behavior disorders; general psychosocial disorders; substance abuse; compulsive/addictive disorders other than substance abuse and eating disorders; thought, mood, and personality disorders.

Contact Bill Powers, Vice President of Programs, main address above. Phone: 800-854-3123. Fax: 215-799-8001.

Announcement The National Hospital for Kids in Crisis, a division of KidsPeace, opened September 1992. The 72-bed acute inpatient facility offers specialized programs for male and female adolescents and children under 12 experiencing psychiatric disorders. A dual diagnosis unit and intensive residential treatment component are also available. Contact Marcee Stiltner at 1-800-854-3123 for details. Location: 5300 KidsPeace Drive, Orefield, PA 18069.

NAVAJO PINES OUTDOOR RESIDENTIAL TREATMENT CENTER
774 North 800th West
LaVerkin, Utah 84745
801-635-4936; Fax: 801-635-2488

General Information Residential treatment/subacute facility for adolescents. 14 beds for adolescents. Open year-round. Patient security: staff secured; will pursue and return runaways. Rural setting. Independent for-profit facility. Licensed by state of Utah.

Participants Accepts: male and female adolescents ages 13–18. Average stay: 56 days. Admission: one parent, all parties who share custody, depending on program. Treats learning disabilities; behavior disorders; substance abuse; eating disorders; post-traumatic stress disorder; thought, mood, and personality disorders. Accepts the vision impaired; the hearing impaired; the speech impaired; those receiving psychotropic medication.

Program Treatment modalities: Twelve Step Recovery; extensive experiential ropes program. Family treatment program available.

Staff .7 full-time direct-care staff member per adolescent. Total facility staff includes 1 psychologist, 1 psychiatrist, 1 MSW social worker, 2 counselors, 1 occupational/recreational therapist, 1 therapist. Staff is 60% male, 40% female.

Facilities Multiple buildings; males and females in separate units. Central dining. Ropes course.

Education Academic program available at no charge. Serves ages 13–18, grades 8–12. Curriculum accredited or approved by Utah Education Department.

Costs Average cost: $200 per day. Accepts private insurance, group insurance.

Additional Services Drug and alcohol rehabilitation services for males and females ages 13–18. Treats learning disabilities; behavior disorders; substance abuse; eating disorders; compulsive/addictive disorders other than substance abuse and eating disorders; post-traumatic stress disorder; thought, mood, and personality disorders.

Contact David Goodwin, Director, Box 60, LaVerkin, UT 84745. Phone: 801-635-4936. Fax: 801-635-2488.

NEW BEGINNINGS AT NORTHWEST
600 North 130th Street
Seattle, Washington 98133
206-362-6000; Fax: 206-361-0823

General Information Drug and alcohol rehabilitation center for adolescents. 44 beds for adolescents. Open year-round. Patient security: partially locked; will pursue and return runaways. Suburban setting. For-profit facility affiliated with National Medical Enterprisesz, Santa Monica, CA. Licensed by state of Washington. Accredited by JCAHO.

Participants Accepts: male and female adolescents ages 12–19. Average stay: 21 days. Admission: one parent. Treats substance abuse; post-traumatic stress disorder. Accepts the mobility impaired; the hearing impaired; the speech impaired; those with a history of arson; those with a history of harm to themselves and others; those receiving psychotropic medication; non-English speaking individuals; those with a history of epilepsy. Special programs for the mobility impaired; the developmentally disabled; the hearing impaired; the speech impaired; those with AIDS. Largest number of participants from Oregon, Alaska.

Program Treatment modalities: Twelve Step Recovery; reality therapy; Rogerian; Gestalt. Family treatment program available.

Staff .5 full-time direct-care staff member per adolescent. Total facility staff includes 1 physician, 1 psychologist, 1 psychiatrist, 5 registered nurses, 1 MSW social worker, 2 teachers, 5 counselors, 2 occupational/recreational therapists, 1 dietician. Staff is 4% male, 96% female.

Facilities Single building; males and females in separate units. Central dining. Ropes course.

Education   2 teachers on staff.

Costs   Average cost: $14,500 per stay. Accepts private insurance, group insurance, Blue Cross/Blue Shield, public funds.

Contact   Jerry Shultz, Director of Information and Referral, main address above. Phone: 800-362-3446. Fax: 206-361-0823.

NEW BEGINNINGS AT WHITE OAK
Route 16
P.O. Box 56
Woolford, Maryland 21613
410-228-7000; Fax: 410-228-8609

General Information   Drug and alcohol rehabilitation center for adolescents. Patient security: staff secured. For-profit facility affiliated with National Medical Enterprises, Washington, DC. Licensed by state of Maryland. Accredited by JCAHO.

Participants   Accepts: male and female adolescents. Average stay: 35 days. Admission: one parent, all parties who share custody, court order, voluntary, depending on program. Treats substance abuse. Accepts the mobility impaired; the vision impaired; the hearing impaired; the speech impaired.

Staff   Staff is 50% male, 50% female.

Costs   Average cost: $500 per day.

Contact   Maddy Obhrai, Program Director, main address above. Phone: 410-228-7000. Fax: 410-228-8609.

NEW BEGINNINGS OF OPELOUSAS
1692 Linwood Loop
Opelousas, Louisiana 70570
318-942-1171; Fax: 318-948-9101

General Information   Drug and alcohol rehabilitation center for adolescents, adults. Open year-round. Patient security: staff secured; will pursue and return runaways. Small town setting. Independent for-profit facility. Licensed by state of Louisiana. Accredited by JCAHO.

Participants   Accepts: male and female adolescents ages 13–17; male and female adults ages 17 and up. Average stay: 3 months. Admission: one parent, court order, depending on program. Treats behavior disorders; general psychosocial disorders; substance abuse; eating disorders; compulsive/addictive disorders other than substance abuse and eating disorders; post-

traumatic stress disorder; thought, mood, and personality disorders. Accepts the mobility impaired; the vision impaired; the hearing impaired; the speech impaired; the sexually compulsive; those with a history of harm to themselves and others; those receiving psychotropic medication; those with a history of epilepsy; diabetics. Special programs for the developmentally disabled; the vision impaired; the hearing impaired; the speech impaired.

Program   Treatment modalities: Twelve Step Recovery; reality; Gestalt. Family treatment program available.

Staff   Total facility staff includes 3 physicians, 2 psychiatrists, 1 registered nurse, 1 MSW social worker, 1 teacher, 5 counselors, 1 occupational/recreational therapist, 1 speech pathologist, 1 dietician, 5 other direct-care staff members. Staff is 81% male, 19% female.

Facilities   Multiple buildings; males and females in separate units. Residential quarters shared with adults. Separate dining by residential unit available. Basketball courts, game room, gymnasium, outdoor swimming pool, outdoor tennis courts, playing fields, fishing pond, serenity trail, baseball field.

Education   Academic program available at no charge. Serves grades 8–12. 1 teacher on staff. Curriculum accredited or approved by St. Landry Parish School Board. Cost of educational program sometimes covered by local school district. Organized sports program offered.

Costs   Average cost: $100 per day. Accepts private insurance, group insurance, Blue Cross/Blue Shield.

Additional Services   Outpatient services for males and females ages 13 and up. Treats learning disabilities; behavior disorders; general psychosocial disorders; substance abuse; eating disorders; compulsive/addictive disorders other than substance abuse and eating disorders; post-traumatic stress disorder; thought, mood, and personality disorders. Residential or sub-acute services for males and females ages 17 and up. Treats learning disabilities; behavior disorders; general psychosocial disorders; substance abuse; eating disorders; compulsive/addictive disorders other than substance abuse and eating disorders; post-traumatic stress disorder; thought, mood, and personality disorders.

Contact   Kim Signorelli, Clinical Director, main address above. Phone: 318-942-1171. Fax: 318-948-9101.

NEW DIRECTIONS
104 South Lowell
Casper, Wyoming 82601
307-237-6033

General Information Residential treatment/subacute facility for adolescents. Patient security: staff secured. Not-for-profit facility affiliated with Central Wyoming Counseling Center, Casper, WY. Licensed by state of Wyoming.

Participants Accepts: male and female adolescents. Average stay: 45 days. Admission: one parent, all parties who share custody, court order, voluntary, depending on program. Treats substance abuse. Accepts the vision impaired; the hearing impaired; the speech impaired; those with a history of arson; the sexually compulsive; those receiving psychotropic medication.

Staff Staff is 66% male, 34% female.

Costs Average cost: $75 per day.

Contact Don Monson, Supervisor, main address above. Phone: 307-237-6033.

NEW DIRECTIONS, INC.
30800 Chagrin Boulevard
Pepper Pike, Ohio 44124
216-591-0324; Fax: 216-591-1243

General Information Residential treatment/subacute facility for adolescents. 15 beds for adolescents. Open year-round. Patient security: unlocked; will pursue and return runaways. Suburban setting. Independent not-for-profit facility. Licensed by state of Ohio. Accredited by JCAHO; Ohio Department of Alcohol and Drug Addiction Services.

Participants Accepts: male and female adolescents ages 13–19. Average stay: 120 days. Admission: one parent, all parties who share custody, court order, depending on program. Treats learning disabilities; behavior disorders; general psychosocial disorders; substance abuse; eating disorders; post-traumatic stress disorder; thought, mood, and personality disorders. Accepts the mobility impaired; the vision impaired; the hearing impaired; the speech impaired; those with a history of harm to themselves and others; those receiving psychotropic medication. Special programs for those with AIDS; those with sickle cell anemia.

Program Treatment modalities: Twelve Step Recovery. Family treatment program available.

Staff Staff is 35% male, 65% female.

Facilities Single building; males and females in separate units. Central dining. Basketball courts, game room, gymnasium, playing fields, ropes course, volleyball court.

Education Academic program available at additional cost. Serves ages 13–19, grades 7–12. Curriculum accredited or approved by local school district. Cost of educational program covered by local school district.

Costs Average cost: $98 per day. Accepts private insurance, group insurance, medicaid, Blue Cross/Blue Shield, public funds.

Contact Sally Newman, Business Manager, main address above. Phone: 216-591-0324. Fax: 216-591-1243.

NEW DOMINION SCHOOL, INC.
Route 3
Cumberland, Virginia 23040
804-983-2051; Fax: 804-983-2068

General Information School in camp-like setting for adolescents. 64 beds for adolescents. Open year-round. Patient security: staff secured; will pursue and return runaways. Rural setting. Independent for-profit facility. Licensed by state of Virginia.

Participants Accepts: male adolescents ages 11–18. Average stay: 540 days. Admission: all parties who share custody. Treats learning disabilities; behavior disorders; general psychosocial disorders; substance abuse; compulsive/addictive disorders other than substance abuse and eating disorders; thought, mood, and personality disorders. Accepts those with a history of arson; the sexually compulsive; those with a history of harm to themselves and others. Largest number of participants from Virginia, Pennsylvania, West Virginia.

Program Treatment modalities: cognitive/behavioral; social learning; interpersonal. Family treatment program available.

Staff .5 full-time direct-care staff member per adolescent. Total facility staff includes 1 psychologist, 1 registered nurse, 2 MSW social workers, 1 social worker (non-MSW), 6 teachers, 14 counselors, 8 other direct-care staff members. Staff is 85% male, 15% female.

Facilities Multiple buildings. Basketball courts, playing fields, ropes course, pond, stream.

Education School serves ages 11–18, ungraded. 6 teachers on staff. Curriculum is college-preparatory; diploma granted upon completion. Curriculum accredited or approved by Southern Association of Colleges and Schools.

Costs Average cost: $39,000 per stay. Accepts private insurance, group insurance, Blue Cross/Blue Shield, public funds.

Additional Services Aftercare program for males ages 11–18. Treats behavior disorders; general psychosocial disorders; substance abuse; compulsive/addictive disorders other than substance abuse and eating disorders; thought, mood, and personality disorders.

Contact Chris Yates, Director, P.O. Box 540, Dillwyn, VA 23936. Phone: 804-983-2051. Fax: 804-983-2068.

See page 440 for full page description.

NEWGRANGE SCHOOL
52 Lafayette Avenue
Trenton, New Jersey 08610
609-394-2255

General Information School for children, adolescents. Open academic year. Small town setting. Independent not-for-profit facility. Licensed by state of New Jersey.

Participants Accepts: male and female children and adolescents ages 8–18. Treats learning disabilities.

Contact Lois Young, Director, main address above. Phone: 609-394-2255.

NEW HOPE CENTER HOSPITAL
8050 Northview Street
Boise, Idaho 83704
800-843-2207; Fax: 208-327-0594

General Information Freestanding drug and alcohol treatment facility and psychiatric hospital for adolescents. Patient security: staff secured. For-profit facility affiliated with Western Healthcare, Inc., Boise, ID. Licensed by state of Idaho. Accredited by JCAHO.

Participants Accepts: male and female adolescents. Average stay: 4 weeks. Admission: one parent, all parties who share custody, court order, voluntary, depending on program. Treats learning disabilities; behavior disorders; general psychosocial disorders; substance abuse; eating disorders; compulsive/addictive disorders other than substance abuse and eating disorders; post-traumatic stress disorder; thought, mood, and personality disorders.

Costs Average cost: $500 per day.

Contact Nora Wilson, Patient Services Coordinator, main address above. Phone: 800-843-2207. Fax: 208-327-0594.

NEW HOPE FOUNDATION
Route 520
P.O. Box 66
Marlboro, New Jersey 07746
908-946-3030; Fax: 908-946-3507

General Information Drug and alcohol rehabilitation center for adolescents. 50 beds for adolescents. Open year-round. Patient security: staff secured; will pursue and return runaways. Rural setting. Independent not-for-profit facility. Licensed by state of New Jersey. Accredited by JCAHO.

Participants Accepts: male and female adolescents ages 13–18. Average stay: 180 days. Admission: one parent, court order, Department of Youth and Family Services, depending on program. Treats learning disabilities; behavior disorders; general psychosocial disorders; substance abuse; eating disorders; compulsive/addictive disorders other than substance abuse and eating disorders; post-traumatic stress disorder; thought, mood, and personality disorders. Accepts the mobility impaired; the vision impaired; those receiving psychotropic medication; those with a history of epilepsy; pregnant patients. Special programs for those with AIDS. Largest number of participants from New Jersey.

Program Treatment modalities: Twelve Step Recovery; rational emotive therapy; reality therapy; behavior modification (level system). Family treatment program available.

Staff .7 full-time direct-care staff member per adolescent. Total facility staff includes 5 physicians, 1 psychiatrist, 3 registered nurses, 8 practical/vocational nurses, 7 teachers, 15 counselors, 1 occupational/recreational therapist, 1 dietician, 5 other direct-care staff members. Staff is 35% male, 65% female.

Facilities Single building; males and females in co-educational units. Central dining. Basketball courts, gymnasium, playing fields, ropes course.

Education Academic program available at additional cost. Serves ages 13–18, grades 9–12. 7 teachers on staff. Curriculum accredited or approved by Monmouth County Educational Service Commission.

Costs Average cost: $130 per stay. Accepts private insurance, group insurance, Blue Cross/Blue Shield, public funds.

Additional Services Residential or sub-acute services for males and females ages 13–18. Treats learning disabilities; behavior disorders; substance abuse; compulsive/addictive disorders other than substance abuse and eating disorders; post-traumatic stress disorder; thought, mood, and personality disorders.

Contact George Mattie, Chief Executive Officer, main address above. Phone: 908-946-3030. Fax: 908-946-3507.

NEW HOPE TREATMENT CENTER
225 Midland Parkway
Summerville, South Carolina 29485
803-851-5010; Fax: 803-851-5020

General Information Residential treatment/subacute facility for adolescents. 52 beds for adolescents. Open year-round. Patient security: entirely locked; will pursue and return runaways. Suburban setting. Independent for-profit facility. Licensed by state of South Carolina. Accredited by JCAHO.

Participants Accepts: male and female adolescents ages 12–17. Average stay: 217 days. Admission: one parent, all parties who share custody, depending on program. Treats learning disabilities; behavior disorders; general psychosocial disorders; substance abuse; eating disorders; compulsive/addictive disorders other than substance abuse and eating disorders; post-traumatic stress disorder; thought, mood, and personality disorders. Accepts those with a history of arson; the sexually compulsive; those with a history of harm to themselves and others; those receiving psychotropic medication. Special programs for sex offenders. Largest number of participants from South Carolina, Georgia, Michigan.

Program Treatment modalities: Twelve Step Recovery; psychodynamic; behavior modification; cognitive. Family treatment program available.

Staff 1.2 full-time direct-care staff members per adolescent. Total facility staff includes 1 psychologist, 3 psychiatrists, 5 registered nurses, 3 practical/vocational nurses, 4 MSW social workers, 1 social worker (non-MSW), 4 teachers, 13 counselors, 2 occupational/recreational therapists, 21 other direct-care staff members. Staff is 70% male, 30% female.

Facilities Multiple buildings; males and females in coeducational units. Central dining. Basketball courts, gymnasium, playing fields.

Education Academic program available. Serves ages 12–17, ungraded. 4 teachers on staff. Curriculum accredited or approved by South Carolina Department of Education. Organized sports program offered.

Costs Average cost: $275 per day. Accepts private insurance, group insurance, medicare, medicaid, Blue Cross/Blue Shield.

Contact Becky Cuda, Coordinator of Staff Growth and Development, main address above. Phone: 803-851-5010. Fax: 803-851-5020.

NEWMAN CLINIC
1225 Broadway
Quincy, Illinois 62306
217-224-4453; Fax: 217-224-9383

General Information Residential treatment/subacute facility for children, adolescents. Patient security: entirely locked. Independent for-profit facility. Licensed by state of Illinois. Accredited by JCAHO.

Participants Accepts: male and female children; male and female adolescents. Average stay: 12 days. Admission: one parent, all parties who share custody, court order, voluntary, depending on program. Treats learning disabilities; behavior disorders; general psychosocial disorders; substance abuse; eating disorders; compulsive/addictive disorders other than substance abuse and eating disorders; thought, mood, and personality disorders.

Staff Staff is 50% male, 50% female.

Costs Average cost: $400 per day.

Contact John Tripp, P.O. Box 450, Quincy, IL 62301. Phone: 217-224-4453.

NEWPORT HARBOR HOSPITAL
1501 East 16th Street
Newport Beach, California 92663
714-650-9752; Fax: 714-646-6142

General Information Psychiatric hospital for children, adolescents. 14 beds for children; 54 beds for adolescents; 68 beds total. Open year-round. Patient security: partially locked; no runaway pursuit. Urban setting. For-profit facility. Licensed by state of California. Accredited by JCAHO.

Participants Accepts: male and female children ages 6–12; male and female adolescents ages 12–18. Average stay: 44 days. Admission: all parties who share custody, court order, depending on program. Treats learning disabilities; behavior disorders; general psychosocial disorders; substance abuse; eating disorders; compulsive/addictive disorders other than substance abuse and eating disorders; post-traumatic stress disorder; thought, mood, and personality disorders. Accepts the mobility impaired; the speech impaired; those with a history of arson; the sexually compulsive; those with a history of harm to themselves and others; those receiving psychotropic medication. Special programs for the developmentally disabled; the speech impaired. Largest number of participants from California, Pennsylvania, Nevada.

Program Treatment modalities: psychodynamic; behavioral; Twelve Step Recovery. Family treatment program available.

Staff Total facility staff includes 6 physicians, 56 psychologists, 36 psychiatrists, 16 registered nurses, 5 practical/vocational nurses, 3 MSW social workers, 1 social worker (non-MSW), 4 teachers, 50 counselors, 1 occupational/recreational therapist, 4 speech pathologists, 1 dietician, 9 other direct-care staff members. Staff is 35% male, 65% female.

Facilities Multiple buildings. Central dining. Basketball courts, game room, playing fields, volleyball court.

Education Academic program available at no charge. Serves ages 6–18, grades 1–12. 4 teachers on staff. Curriculum accredited or approved by State of California. Cost of educational program sometimes covered by local school district.

Costs Average cost: $11,093 per stay. Accepts private insurance, group insurance, Blue Cross/Blue Shield, public funds.

Contact Michael Deary, Call Center Coordinator, 485 East 17th Street, Suite 351, Costa Mesa, CA 92627. Phone: 714-650-9714. Fax: 714-646-6142.

NEW SPIRIT ADDICTIVE DISORDERS AND MENTAL HEALTH PROGRAM
2411 Fountainview #175
Houston, Texas 77056
713-975-1580

General Information Psychiatric hospital for adolescents, adults. 18 beds for adolescents. Open year-round. Patient security: staff secured; will pursue and return runaways. Urban setting. Independent for-profit facility. Licensed by state of Texas. Accredited by JCAHO.

Participants Accepts: male and female adolescents ages 11–19; male and female adults ages 19 and up. Average stay: 10 days. Admission: one parent. Treats behavior disorders; general psychosocial disorders; substance abuse; eating disorders; compulsive/addictive disorders other than substance abuse and eating disorders. Accepts the speech impaired; those with a

history of harm to themselves and others; those with a history of epilepsy.

Program Treatment modalities: Twelve Step Recovery; trauma resolution therapy. Family treatment program available.

Facilities Multiple buildings; males and females in coeducational units. Separate residential quarters for adolescents. Central dining (shared with adults). Basketball courts, gymnasium, indoor swimming pool, outdoor tennis courts, ropes course.

Education Academic program available at no charge. Curriculum accredited or approved by Houston Independent School District. Cost of educational program covered by local school district. Organized sports program offered.

Costs Average cost: $1000 per day. Accepts private insurance, group insurance, Blue Cross/Blue Shield.

Additional Services Outpatient services for males and females ages 12–18. Treats behavior disorders; general psychosocial disorders; substance abuse; eating disorders; compulsive/addictive disorders other than substance abuse and eating disorders.

Contact Deborah Sopher, Marketing Director, 1755 Saint James Place, Houston, TX 77056. Phone: 713-871-0821. Fax: 713-871-6301.

THE NEW YORK INSTITUTE FOR SPECIAL EDUCATION
999 Pelham Parkway, North
Bronx, New York 10469
718-519-7000; Fax: 718-231-9314

General Information School for children, adolescents. Patient security: staff secured. Independent not-for-profit facility. Licensed by state of New York. Accredited by National Accreditation Council for Agencies Serving the Blind and Visually Impaired.

Participants Accepts: male and female children; male and female adolescents. Average stay: 5 days. Admission: one parent, appointment by Commissioner of Education, depending on program. Treats learning disabilities; behavior disorders.

Education School serves grades K–12. Curriculum accredited or approved by New York State Board of Regents.

Contact Leslie Maeby, Director of Facility, main address above. Phone: 718-519-7000. Fax: 718-231-9314.

Announcement The New York Institute for Special Education was founded as the New York Institute for the Blind in 1831. The Institute has educational programs serving students ranging in age from 6 months to 21 years, including a residential component. Students are blind, visually impaired, learning disabled, emotionally disturbed, and developmentally delayed preschoolers. A full range of support services is available for students and their families.

NIKE HOUSE, INC.
4775 West Pioneer Avenue
Las Vegas, Nevada 89102
702-871-5448

General Information Drug and alcohol rehabilitation center for adolescents. 12 beds for adolescents. Patient security: staff secured. Independent not-for-profit facility. Licensed by state of Nebraska. Accredited by Bureau of Alcohol and Drug Abuse.

Participants Accepts: female adolescents. Average stay: 9 months. Admission: one parent, all parties who share custody, court order, voluntary, depending on program. Treats learning disabilities; behavior disorders; general psychosocial disorders; eating disorders; compulsive/addictive disorders other than substance abuse and eating disorders; thought, mood, and personality disorders.

Staff .6 full-time direct-care staff member per adolescent. Staff is 14% male, 86% female.

Costs Average cost: $1300 per month.

Contact Kevin Broadbent, Director, main address above. Phone: 702-871-5448.

NORTH AMERICAN WILDERNESS ACADEMY
17359 Trinity Mountain Road
French Gulch, California 96033
916-359-2215; Fax: 916-359-2229

General Information Experiential education program for adolescents. Patient security: staff secured. For-profit facility. Licensed by state of California.

Participants Accepts: male and female adolescents ages 12–18. Admission: one parent. Treats learning disabilities.

Staff Staff is 66% male, 34% female.

Education School serves ages 12–18, grades 7–12. Diploma granted upon completion. Curriculum accredited or approved by California State Department of Education.

Costs Average cost: $2000 per month.

Contact David Hull, Executive Director, main address above. Phone: 916-359-2215. Fax: 916-359-2229.

See page 400 for full page description.

NORTH CAROLINA BAPTIST HOSPITALS, INC.
Medical Center Boulevard
Winston-Salem, North Carolina 27157
919-748-2011; Fax: 919-748-2879

General Information General hospital for children, adolescents. Patient security: staff secured. Independent not-for-profit facility. Licensed by state of North Carolina. Accredited by JCAHO.

Participants Accepts: male and female children; male and female adolescents. Average stay: 6 days. Admission: one parent. Treats autistic disorders; learning disabilities; behavior disorders; general psychosocial disorders; substance abuse; eating disorders; compulsive/addictive disorders other than substance abuse and eating disorders; post-traumatic stress disorder; thought, mood, and personality disorders.

Contact Pediatrics Department, main address above. Phone: 919-748-4431.

NORTH COLORADO PSYCHCARE
928 12th Street
Greeley, Colorado 80631
303-352-1056; Fax: 303-352-2258

General Information Psychiatric hospital for adolescents. 22 beds for adolescents. Patient security: partially locked. Independent not-for-profit facility. Licensed by state of Colorado. Accredited by JCAHO.

Participants Accepts: male and female adolescents. Average stay: 6 days. Admission: one parent, all parties who share custody, court order, voluntary, depending on program. Treats behavior disorders; general psychosocial disorders; eating disorders; post-traumatic stress disorder; thought, mood, and personality disorders.

Costs Average cost: $650 per day.

Contact Kim Barbour, Community Relations Representative, main address above. Phone: 303-352-1056. Fax: 303-352-2258.

NORTHRIDGE HOSPITAL
8160 Hamilton Road
Columbus, Georgia 31909
706-576-2500; Fax: 706-576-2525

General Information Psychiatric/chemical dependency rehabilitation facility for children, adolescents. Open year-round. Patient security: entirely locked; no runaway pursuit. Rural setting. Not-for-profit facility affiliated with Columbus Regional Healthcare System, Columbus, GA. Accredited by JCAHO.

Participants Accepts: male and female children ages 4–12; male and female adolescents ages 13–18. Average stay: 17 days. Admission: one parent, court order, depending on program. Treats learning disabilities; behavior disorders; general psychosocial disorders; substance abuse; eating disorders; compulsive/addictive disorders other than substance abuse and eating disorders; post-traumatic stress disorder; thought, mood, and personality disorders.

Program Treatment modalities: Twelve Step Recovery. Family treatment program available.

Facilities Single building; males and females in co-educational units. Central dining (shared with adults). Basketball courts, game room, gymnasium, children's play room.

Costs Accepts private insurance, group insurance, Blue Cross/Blue Shield, public funds.

Contact Donna Nanney, Marketing Director, main address above. Phone: 706-576-2500.

NORTHSHORE PSYCHIATRIC HOSPITAL
104 Medical Center Drive
Slidell, Louisiana 70461
504-646-5500; Fax: 504-649-7573

General Information Psychiatric hospital for adolescents. 18 beds for adolescents. Patient security: partially locked. For-profit facility affiliated with National Medical Enterprises, Washington, DC. Licensed by state of Louisiana. Accredited by JCAHO.

Participants Accepts: male and female adolescents. Average stay: 25 days. Admission: one parent, all parties who share custody, court order, voluntary, depending on program. Treats behavior disorders; general psychosocial disorders; substance abuse; eating disorders; compulsive/addictive disorders other than substance abuse and eating disorders; thought, mood, and personality disorders.

Contact Debbie Ivy, Director, Adolescent Program, main address above. Phone: 504-646-5500.

NORTH STAR HOSPITAL
1650 South Bragaw Street
Anchorage, Alaska 99508
907-277-1522; Fax: 907-277-3031

General Information Psychiatric hospital for children, adolescents. Patient security: partially locked. Not-for-profit facility affiliated with Sterling Health Care Corporation, Bellevue, WA. Licensed by state of Alaska. Accredited by JCAHO.

Participants Accepts: male and female children; male and female adolescents. Average stay: 26 days. Admission: one parent, all parties who share custody, voluntary, depending on program. Treats learning disabilities; behavior disorders; general psychosocial disorders; substance abuse; eating disorders; compulsive/addictive disorders other than substance abuse and eating disorders; post-traumatic stress disorder; thought, mood, and personality disorders.

Costs Average cost: $18,000 per stay.

Contact Candace Mumford, Assessment Coordinator, main address above. Phone: 907-277-1522.

NORTHWEST CHILDREN'S HOME, INC.
419 22nd Avenue
P.O. Box 1288
Lewiston, Idaho 83501-1288
208-743-9404; Fax: 208-746-4955

General Information Residential treatment/subacute facility for children, adolescents. Patient security: staff secured. Independent not-for-profit facility. Licensed by state of Idaho. Accredited by JCAHO.

Participants Accepts: male and female children; male and female adolescents. Average stay: 1 year. Admission: one parent, all parties who share custody, court order, voluntary, depending on program. Treats learning disabilities; behavior disorders; substance abuse; compulsive/addictive disorders other than substance abuse and eating disorders; post-traumatic stress disorder; thought, mood, and personality disorders.

Staff Staff is 50% male, 50% female.

Education Academic program available. Serves ages 6–17. Curriculum accredited or approved by Northwest Association of Schools and Colleges.

Costs Average cost: $150 per day.

Contact Charles Yeaton, Director, Outreach Services, main address above. Phone: 208-743-9404. Fax: 208-746-4955.

NORTHWEST COUNSELING CENTER— THE TURNING POINT PROGRAM
107 East Church Street
P.O. Box 1079
Lexington, Tennessee 38351
901-968-0130; Fax: 901-968-0189

General Information Drug and alcohol rehabilitation center for adolescents. 20 beds for adolescents. Patient security: staff secured. Independent not-for-profit facility. Licensed by state of Tennessee.

Participants Accepts: male and female adolescents. Average stay: 5 months. Admission: all parties who share custody, court order, voluntary, depending on program. Accepts the hearing impaired; the sexually compulsive.

Staff Staff is 40% male, 60% female.

Contact Sandy McBride, Clinical Director, main address above. Phone: 901-968-0130. Fax: 901-968-0189.

NORTHWEST DADE CENTER
4175 West 20th Avenue
Hialeah, Florida 33012
305-825-0300; Fax: 305-826-3039

General Information Psychiatric hospital for adolescents. Patient security: entirely locked. Independent not-for-profit facility. Licensed by state of Florida. Accredited by JCAHO.

Participants Accepts: male and female adolescents. Average stay: 2 months. Admission: one parent, all parties who share custody, voluntary, depending on program. Treats learning disabilities; behavior disorders; general psychosocial disorders; eating disorders; post-traumatic stress disorder; thought, mood, and personality disorders. Accepts the mobility impaired; the vision impaired; the hearing impaired; the speech impaired; those with a history of arson; those with a history of harm to themselves and others; those receiving psychotropic medication; non-English speaking individuals; those with a history of epilepsy.

Staff Staff is 65% male, 35% female.

Costs Average cost: $275 per day.

Contact Dr. Ana Rivas-Vazquez, Clinical Director, main address above. Phone: 305-825-0300.

NOVA THERAPEUTIC COMMUNITY
3473 Larimore Avenue
Omaha, Nebraska 68111
402-455-8303; Fax: 402-455-7050

General Information Drug and alcohol rehabilitation center for adolescents. 30 beds for adolescents. Patient security: staff secured. Independent not-for-profit facility. Licensed by state of Nebraska. Accredited by Therapeutic Community.

Participants Accepts: male and female adolescents. Average stay: 12 months. Admission: one parent, all parties who share custody, court order, voluntary, depending on program. Treats substance abuse. Accepts the mobility impaired; the vision impaired; the hearing impaired; the speech impaired; those with a history of arson; the sexually compulsive; those with a history of harm to themselves and others; those receiving psychotropic medication; those with a history of epilepsy.

Staff Staff is 50% male, 50% female.

Costs Average cost: $53 per day.

Contact Angela Thode, Intake Coordinator, main address above. Phone: 402-455-8303. Fax: 402-455-7050.

OAK CREST CENTER
1601 Gordon Cooper Drive
Shawnee, Oklahoma 74801
800-669-4625; Fax: 405-275-2425

General Information Psychiatric hospital for children, adolescents. Patient security: entirely locked. For-profit facility affiliated with Sterling Health Care Corporation, Bellevue, WA. Licensed by state of Oklahoma. Accredited by JCAHO.

Participants Accepts: male and female children; male and female adolescents. Average stay: 45 days. Admission: one parent, all parties who share custody, court order, voluntary, depending on program. Treats learning disabilities; behavior disorders; general psychosocial disorders; substance abuse; post-traumatic stress disorder; thought, mood, and personality disorders.

Staff Staff is 75% male, 25% female.

Additional Services Outpatient services for males and females ages 5–18. Treats learning disabilities; behavior disorders; general psychosocial disorders; substance abuse; post-traumatic stress disorder; thought, mood, and personality disorders.

Contact Roger Wilkens, Director of Clinical Services, main address above. Phone: 800-669-4625. Fax: 405-275-2425.

OAK GROVE INSTITUTE
24275 Jefferson Avenue
Murrieta, California 92562
714-677-5599; Fax: 714-698-0461

General Information Residential treatment/subacute facility for children, adolescents. Open year-round. Patient security: unlocked; will pursue and return runaways. Suburban setting. Independent for-profit facility. Licensed by state of California. Accredited by JCAHO; Civilian Health and Medical Program of the Uniformed Services.

Participants Accepts: male and female children and adolescents ages 9–18. Average stay: 90 days. Admission: one parent, all parties who share custody, court order, voluntary, depending on program. Treats learning disabilities; behavior disorders; general psychosocial disorders; substance abuse; eating disorders; post-traumatic stress disorder; thought, mood, and personality disorders. Accepts the mobility impaired; those with a history of harm to themselves and others; those receiving psychotropic medication. Special programs for the chronically ill; the developmentally disabled. Largest number of participants from California, Nevada.

Program Treatment modalities: milieu therapy; behavioral therapy; psychodynamic; social learning model. Family treatment program available.

Staff Total facility staff includes 1 physician, 2 psychologists, 2 psychiatrists, 4 registered nurses, 4 practical/vocational nurses, 7 MSW social workers, 9 teachers, 60 counselors, 3 occupational/recreational therapists, 1 speech pathologist, 1 dietician, 10 other direct-care staff members.

Facilities Multiple buildings. Central dining. Basketball courts, outdoor swimming pool, outdoor tennis courts, playing fields.

Education Academic program available at no charge. Serves ages 9–18, grades 4–12. 9 teachers on staff. Curriculum accredited or approved by California Department of Education. Cost of educational program sometimes covered by local school district. Organized sports program offered.

Costs Accepts private insurance, group insurance, public funds.

Additional Services Day treatment and day school for males and females ages 9–18. Treats learning disabilities; behavior disorders; general psychosocial

disorders; eating disorders; post-traumatic stress disorder; thought, mood, and personality disorders.

Contact Cindy Stober, Intake Coordinator, main address above. Phone: 714-677-5599. Fax: 714-698-0461.

OAK GROVE TREATMENT CENTER
6436 Mark Drive
Burleson, Texas 76028
817-483-0989; Fax: 817-561-1309

General Information Residential treatment/subacute facility for children, adolescents. 12 beds for children; 29 beds for adolescents; 41 beds total. Open year-round. Patient security: partially locked; will pursue and return runaways. Rural setting. Independent for-profit facility. Licensed by state of Texas. Accredited by JCAHO; Civilian Health and Medical Program of the Uniformed Services.

Participants Accepts: male and female children ages 6–12; male and female adolescents ages 12–18. Average stay: 150 days. Admission: all parties who share custody, voluntary, depending on program. Treats learning disabilities; behavior disorders; general psychosocial disorders; substance abuse; eating disorders; compulsive/addictive disorders other than substance abuse and eating disorders; post-traumatic stress disorder; thought, mood, and personality disorders. Accepts those with a history of harm to themselves and others; those receiving psychotropic medication; those with a history of epilepsy; the sexually/physically abused. Special programs for dual diagnosis. Largest number of participants from Texas, Oklahoma, New Mexico.

Program Treatment modalities: psychodynamic; behavioral modification; rational emotive. Family treatment program available.

Staff 1.4 full-time direct-care staff members per child or adolescent. Total facility staff includes 1 physician, 1 psychologist, 4 psychiatrists, 4 registered nurses, 5 practical/vocational nurses, 2 MSW social workers, 1 social worker (non-MSW), 3 teachers, 3 counselors, 3 occupational/recreational therapists, 1 dietician, 48 other direct-care staff members. Staff is 25% male, 75% female.

Facilities Multiple buildings; males and females in separate units. Central dining. Basketball courts, game room, outdoor swimming pool, playing fields, volleyball.

Education Academic program available at no charge. Serves ages 6–18, grades 1–12. 3 teachers on staff. Curriculum accredited or approved by Texas

Education Agency. Cost of educational program covered by local school district.

Costs Average cost: $350 per day. Accepts private insurance, group insurance, medicaid, Blue Cross/Blue Shield.

Contact Peggy McGuigan, Director Admissions, main address above. Phone: 817-483-0989. Fax: 817-561-1309.

OAKHILL RESIDENTIAL TREATMENT CENTER
450 Montford Avenue
Asheville, North Carolina 28801
704-254-3201; Fax: 704-258-8095

General Information Residential treatment/subacute facility for adolescents. 18 beds for adolescents. Open year-round. Patient security: staff secured; will pursue and return runaways. Urban setting. For-profit facility affiliated with Highland Hospital, Asheville, NC. Licensed by state of North Carolina. Accredited by JCAHO.

Participants Accepts: male and female adolescents ages 12–18. Average stay: 181 days. Admission: all parties who share custody. Treats autistic disorders; learning disabilities; behavior disorders; general psychosocial disorders; substance abuse; eating disorders; compulsive/addictive disorders other than substance abuse and eating disorders; post-traumatic stress disorder; thought, mood, and personality disorders. Accepts the vision impaired; those with a history of harm to themselves and others; those receiving psychotropic medication; those with a history of epilepsy. Special programs for the developmentally disabled; the vision impaired.

Program Treatment modalities: Twelve Step Recovery; biopsychosocial; psychodynamic; behavioral. Family treatment program available.

Staff Total facility staff includes 1 psychologist, 1 psychiatrist, 5 registered nurses, 1 MSW social worker, 2 teachers, 1 occupational/recreational therapist, 1 therapist, 1 dietician, 15 other direct-care staff members.

Facilities Multiple buildings; males and females in coeducational units. Central dining. Basketball courts, game room, gymnasium, outdoor swimming pool, outdoor tennis courts, playing fields, ropes course.

Education Academic program available at additional cost. Serves ages 12–80, grades K–12. 2 teachers on staff. Curriculum accredited or approved by State

of North Carolina. Cost of educational program sometimes covered by local school district.

Costs Average cost: $14,000 per month. Accepts private insurance, group insurance, Blue Cross/Blue Shield, public funds.

Additional Services Drug and alcohol rehabilitation services for males and females ages 12 and up. Treats autistic disorders; learning disabilities; behavior disorders; general psychosocial disorders; substance abuse; eating disorders; compulsive/addictive disorders other than substance abuse and eating disorders; post-traumatic stress disorder; thought, mood, and personality disorders. Outpatient services for males and females ages 17 and up. Treats autistic disorders; learning disabilities; behavior disorders; general psychosocial disorders; substance abuse; eating disorders; compulsive/addictive disorders other than substance abuse and eating disorders; post-traumatic stress disorder; thought, mood, and personality disorders. Partial hospitalization/acute-care psychiatric hospital for males and females ages 12 and up. Treats autistic disorders; learning disabilities; behavior disorders; general psychosocial disorders; substance abuse; eating disorders; compulsive/addictive disorders other than substance abuse and eating disorders; post-traumatic stress disorder; thought, mood, and personality disorders.

Contact Jane Lawson, Program Coordinator, main address above. Phone: 704-254-3201. Fax: 704-258-8095.

OAKLAND SCHOOL
Boyd Tavern
Keswick, Virginia 22947
804-293-9059

General Information School for children, adolescents. Open September to May. Patient security: unlocked; will pursue and return runaways. Rural setting. Independent not-for-profit facility. Licensed by state of Virginia.

Participants Accepts: male and female children and adolescents ages 8–17. Average stay: 2 years. Admission: one parent. Treats learning disabilities.

Program Treatment modalities: individualized.

Staff Total facility staff includes 14 teachers, 4 counselors, 13 other direct-care staff members. Staff is 29% male, 71% female.

Facilities Multiple buildings; males and females in separate units. Central dining (shared with adults). Basketball courts, game room, gymnasium, horseback riding, outdoor swimming pool, outdoor tennis courts, playing fields.

Education School serves ages 8–17, ungraded. 14 teachers on staff. Curriculum accredited or approved by Virginia Department of Education. Organized sports program offered.

Costs Average cost: $19,330 per stay. Accepts public funds.

Additional Services Camping program for males and females ages 8–14. Treats learning disabilities.

Contact Judith Edwards, Assistant Director, main address above. Phone: 804-293-8965.

Announcement Since 1950 parents have put their trust in Oakland School. Approximately 95% of students who finish the program go into regular education. Oakland specializes in rapid remediation of reading disabilities and in bringing students to grade level. There are exceptional recreation programs and facilities.

OAKLAWN
330 Lakeview Drive
P.O. Box 809
Goshen, Indiana 46526
219-533-1234

General Information Psychiatric hospital for children, adolescents, adults. 12 beds for children; 24 beds for adolescents; 76 beds total. Open year-round. Patient security: partially locked; will pursue and return runaways. Rural setting. Independent not-for-profit facility. Licensed by state of Indiana. Accredited by JCAHO.

Participants Accepts: male and female children ages 6–12; male and female adolescents ages 13–17; male and female adults ages 18 and up. Average stay: 31 days. Admission: one parent, all parties who share custody, court order, depending on program. Treats learning disabilities; behavior disorders; general psychosocial disorders; substance abuse; eating disorders; compulsive/addictive disorders other than substance abuse and eating disorders; post-traumatic stress disorder; thought, mood, and personality disorders. Accepts the mobility impaired; the vision impaired; the sexually compulsive; those with a history of harm to themselves and others; those receiving psychotropic medication; those with a history of epilepsy. Special programs for the chronically ill; the mobility impaired.

Program Treatment modalities: psychodynamic; Twelve Step Recovery; behavioral; experiential. Family treatment program available.

Staff Total facility staff includes 1 physician, 3 psychologists, 4 psychiatrists, 47 registered nurses, 8 MSW social workers, 4 teachers, 7 occupational/recreational therapists, 1 dietician, 76 other direct-care staff members. Staff is 33% male, 67% female.

Facilities Single building; males and females in co-educational units. Separate residential quarters for children and adolescents. Central dining (shared with adults). Basketball courts, gymnasium, playing fields, jogging course, fishing pond.

Education Academic program available at no charge. Serves ages 6–17, ungraded. 4 teachers on staff. Curriculum accredited or approved by State Department of Education.

Costs Average cost: $540 per day. Accepts private insurance, group insurance, medicare, medicaid, Blue Cross/Blue Shield, public funds.

Additional Services Outpatient services for males and females. Treats autistic disorders; learning disabilities; behavior disorders; general psychosocial disorders; substance abuse; eating disorders; compulsive/addictive disorders other than substance abuse and eating disorders; post-traumatic stress disorder; thought, mood, and personality disorders.

Contact Sharon Miller, Admissions Counselor, main address above. Phone: 219-533-1234.

THE OAKS TREATMENT CENTER
1407 West Stassney Lane
Austin, Texas 78745
512-444-9561; Fax: 512-445-5533

General Information Psychiatric hospital for children, adolescents. Patient security: partially locked. For-profit facility affiliated with Healthcare International, Inc., Austin, TX. Licensed by state of Texas. Accredited by JCAHO.

Participants Accepts: male and female children; male and female adolescents. Average stay: 6 months. Admission: one parent, all parties who share custody, court order, voluntary, depending on program. Treats learning disabilities; behavior disorders; general psychosocial disorders; substance abuse; eating disorders; compulsive/addictive disorders other than substance abuse and eating disorders; post-traumatic stress disorder; thought, mood, and personality disorders.

Contact Sandra McDaniel, Admissions Manager, main address above. Phone: 800-843-6257. Fax: 512-445-5533.

OAKVIEW TREATMENT
3100 North Ridge Road
Ellicott City, Maryland 21043
800-223-7770; Fax: 301-465-0923

General Information Drug and alcohol rehabilitation center for adolescents, adults. 17 beds for adolescents. Open year-round. Patient security: partially locked; no runaway pursuit. Urban setting. Not-for-profit facility. Licensed by state of Maryland. Accredited by JCAHO.

Participants Accepts: male and female adolescents ages 13–19; male and female adults ages 19–67. Average stay: 30 days. Admission: one parent, all parties who share custody, court order, voluntary, depending on program. Treats behavior disorders; general psychosocial disorders; substance abuse; thought, mood, and personality disorders.

Program Treatment modalities: Twelve Step Recovery; psychodynamic. Family treatment program available.

Staff Total facility staff includes 1 physician, 12 registered nurses, 1 MSW social worker, 1 social worker (non-MSW), 10 teachers, 2 counselors, 2 occupational/recreational therapists, 1 dietician.

Facilities Single building; males and females in co-educational units. Separate residential quarters for adolescents. Central dining (not shared with adults). Game room, ropes course, volleyball.

Education Academic program available at no charge. Serves ages 13–19. 10 teachers on staff. Cost of educational program covered by local school district. Organized sports program offered.

Costs Average cost: $480 per day. Accepts private insurance, group insurance, medicare, Blue Cross/Blue Shield, public funds.

Contact Shellie Leveton, Director of Adolescent Admissions, main address above. Phone: 800-223-7770. Fax: 301-465-0923.

ODYSSEY ADOLESCENT PROGRAM
625 South, 200 East
Salt Lake City, Utah 84111
801-363-0203; Fax: 801-359-3864

General Information Residential treatment/subacute facility for adolescents. 27 beds for adolescents. Patient security: unlocked. Independent not-for-profit facility. Licensed by state of Utah.

Participants Accepts: male and female adolescents. Average stay: 9 months. Admission: one parent, all parties who share custody, court order, voluntary, depending on program. Treats learning disabilities; behavior disorders; general psychosocial disorders; substance abuse; eating disorders; compulsive/addictive disorders other than substance abuse and eating disorders; post-traumatic stress disorder; thought, mood, and personality disorders.

Staff Staff is 62% male, 38% female.

Costs Average cost: $75 per day.

Contact Mary Siebert, Admissions Counselor, main address above. Phone: 801-363-0203. Fax: 801-359-3864.

O'NEILL VALLEY HOPE
Box 918
O'Neill, Nebraska 68763
402-336-3747

General Information Drug and alcohol rehabilitation center for adolescents, adults. Open year-round. Patient security: staff secured; no runaway pursuit. Small town setting. Not-for-profit facility affiliated with Valley Hope Association, Norton, KS. Licensed by state of Nebraska. Accredited by JCAHO.

Participants Accepts: male and female adolescents ages 13–19; male and female adults ages 19–85. Admission: one parent. Treats behavior disorders; general psychosocial disorders; substance abuse; eating disorders; compulsive/addictive disorders other than substance abuse and eating disorders; post-traumatic stress disorder; thought, mood, and personality disorders. Accepts the mobility impaired; those receiving psychotropic medication; those with a history of epilepsy. Special programs for the mobility impaired.

Program Treatment modalities: Twelve Step Recovery; behavior modification; reality therapy. Family treatment program available.

Staff Total facility staff includes 1 physician, 1 psychologist, 1 psychiatrist, 6 registered nurses, 5 practical/vocational nurses, 6 counselors.

Facilities Multiple buildings; males and females in separate units. Residential quarters shared with adults. Central dining (shared with adults). Basketball courts, game room, playing fields.

Education Educational arrangements: private tutoring. Educational program held on-site at additional cost.

Costs Average cost: $4700 per stay. Accepts private insurance, group insurance, medicaid, Blue Cross/Blue Shield.

Contact Kaye L. Chohon, Director, main address above. Phone: 402-336-3947.

OPERATION PAR
13800 66 Street, North
Largo, Florida 34641
813-538-7250; Fax: 813-536-7512

General Information Drug and alcohol rehabilitation center for adolescents. 30 beds for adolescents. Patient security: staff secured. Independent not-for-profit facility. Licensed by state of Florida.

Participants Accepts: male and female adolescents. Average stay: 7 months. Admission: one parent, all parties who share custody, court order, voluntary, depending on program. Treats substance abuse. Accepts the mobility impaired; the vision impaired; the hearing impaired; the speech impaired; those with a history of epilepsy.

Staff Staff is 40% male, 60% female.

Costs Average cost: $70 per day.

Contact Intake, main address above. Phone: 813-538-7250. Fax: 813-536-7512.

OPERATION SPRINGBOARD
HC 4
P.O. Box 406
Canyon Lake, Texas 78133
512-964-2800; Fax: 512-964-2514

General Information Residential treatment/subacute facility for adolescents. 22 beds for adolescents. Open year-round. Patient security: staff secured; will pursue and return runaways. Rural setting. Independent for-profit facility. Licensed by state of Texas. Accredited by JCAHO; Department of Human Services, Texas Commission on Alcohol and Drug Abuse.

Participants Accepts: male and female adolescents ages 12–18. Average stay: 120 days. Admission: one parent, voluntary, depending on program. Treats learning disabilities; behavior disorders; general psychosocial disorders; substance abuse; eating disorders; compulsive/addictive disorders other than substance abuse and eating disorders; post-traumatic stress disorder; thought, mood, and personality disorders. Accepts the mobility impaired; those with a history of arson; the sexually compulsive; those with a history of harm to themselves and others; those receiving psychotropic medication. Largest number of participants from Texas.

Program Treatment modalities: Twelve Step Recovery; psychodynamic; positive peer culture. Family treatment program available.

Staff .9 full-time direct-care staff member per adolescent. Total facility staff includes 1 physician, 2 psychologists, 1 psychiatrist, 1 registered nurse, 3 practical/vocational nurses, 3 MSW social workers, 2 teachers, 2 counselors, 1 occupational/recreational therapist, 1 speech pathologist, 2 therapists, 1 dietician, 20 other direct-care staff members. Staff is 40% male, 60% female.

Facilities Multiple buildings; males and females in separate units. Central dining. Basketball courts, game room, gymnasium, horseback riding, outdoor swimming pool, playing fields, camping, obstacle course.

Education Academic program available at no charge. Serves ages 12–18, grades 5–12. 2 teachers on staff. Curriculum accredited or approved by Comal County Independent School District. Cost of educational program sometimes covered by local school district.

Costs Average cost: $250 per day. Accepts private insurance, group insurance, public funds.

Contact Clifford Craig, Admissions Director, main address above. Phone: 512-964-2800. Fax: 512-964-2514.

OPPORTUNITIES
808 Pitt Road
Scott, Louisiana 70583
318-896-3451

General Information Drug and alcohol rehabilitation center for adolescents, adults. 15 beds for adolescents. Open year-round. Patient security arrangements vary depending on program; will pursue and return runaways. Rural setting. Independent for-profit facility. Licensed by state of Louisiana.

Participants Accepts: male and female adolescents ages 13–21; male and female adults ages 21 and up. Admission: one parent, all parties who share custody, court order, voluntary, depending on program. Treats behavior disorders; general psychosocial disorders; substance abuse; eating disorders; compulsive/addictive disorders other than substance abuse and eating disorders; post-traumatic stress disorder; thought, mood, and personality disorders. Accepts those receiving psychotropic medication; those with a history of epilepsy.

Program Treatment modalities: psychodynamic; Twelve Step Recovery. Family treatment program available.

Staff 1.2 full-time direct-care staff members per adolescent. Total facility staff includes 2 physicians, 1 psychiatrist, 2 MSW social workers, 6 counselors, 2 therapists, 1 dietician, 1 other direct-care staff member.

Facilities Multiple buildings; males and females in coeducational units. Residential quarters shared with adults. Central dining (shared with adults). Basketball courts, game room, outdoor swimming pool, playing fields.

Education Academic program available at no charge. Serves ages 13–21, grades 7–12. Cost of educational program covered by local school district.

Costs Average cost: $2250 per month. Accepts private insurance, group insurance.

Additional Services Outpatient services for males and females ages 13–21. Treats behavior disorders; general psychosocial disorders; substance abuse; eating disorders; compulsive/addictive disorders other than substance abuse and eating disorders; post-traumatic stress disorder; thought, mood, and personality disorders. Residential or sub-acute services for males and females ages 13–21. Treats general psychosocial disorders; substance abuse; eating disorders; compulsive/addictive disorders other than substance abuse and eating disorders; post-traumatic stress disorder; thought, mood, and personality disorders. Extended care/halfway program ages 13–21. Treats general psychosocial disorders; substance abuse; eating disorders; compulsive/addictive disorders other than substance abuse and eating disorders; post-traumatic stress disorder.

Contact Tony Thibedeau, Admission Coordinator, main address above. Phone: 318-896-3451.

ORCHARD HOME
917 Belmont Street
Watertown, Massachusetts 02172
617-489-1760; Fax: 617-489-6641

General Information Residential treatment facility and school for adolescents. 12 beds for adolescents. Open year-round. Patient security: staff secured; will pursue and return runaways. Suburban setting. Not-for-profit facility affiliated with New England Home for Little Wanderers, Boston, MA. Licensed by state of Massachusetts. Accredited by Council on Accreditation of Services for Families and Children.

Participants Accepts: female adolescents ages 11–17. Average stay: 500 days. Admission: one parent, all parties who share custody, court order, voluntary, depending on program. Treats learning disabilities; behavior disorders; general psychosocial disorders; substance abuse; eating disorders; compulsive/addictive disorders other than substance abuse and eating disorders; post-traumatic stress disorder; thought, mood, and personality disorders. Accepts the sexually compulsive; those with a history of harm to themselves and others; those receiving psychotropic medication. Largest number of participants from Massachusetts.

Program Treatment modalities: psychodynamic. Family treatment program available.

Staff 3.3 full-time direct-care staff members per adolescent. Total facility staff includes 1 psychologist, 1 psychiatrist, 1 registered nurse, 3 MSW social workers, 6 teachers, 18 counselors, 1 speech pathologist, 9 other direct-care staff members. Staff is 25% male, 75% female.

Facilities Multiple buildings. Central dining. Basketball courts, game room, playing fields.

Education Academic program available. Serves ages 11–17, ungraded. 6 teachers on staff. Curriculum accredited or approved by Watertown Public Schools, Massachusetts Department of Education. Cost of educational program covered by local school district.

Costs Average cost: $69,238 per stay. Accepts public funds.

Additional Services Outdoor summer education program for males and females ages 11–17. Treats learning disabilities; behavior disorders; general psychosocial disorders; post-traumatic stress disorder; thought, mood, and personality disorders.

Contact Jessica Buck, Associate Director, main address above. Phone: 617-489-1760. Fax: 617-489-6641.

ORCHARD PLACE
925 Southwest Porter Avenue
Des Moines, Iowa 50315
515-285-6781; Fax: 515-285-8925

General Information Psychiatric medical institute for children, adolescents. 63 beds for children; 15 beds for adolescents; 78 beds total. Open year-round. Patient security: staff secured; will pursue and return runaways. Urban setting. Independent not-for-profit facility. Licensed by state of Iowa. Accredited by JCAHO; Council on Accreditation of Services for Families and Children.

Participants Accepts: male and female children ages 5–16; male and female adolescents ages 13–18. Admission: one parent, all parties who share custody, court order, voluntary, parental rights terminated, depending on program. Treats learning disabilities; behavior disorders; general psychosocial disorders; substance abuse; eating disorders; compulsive/addictive disorders other than substance abuse and eating disorders; post-traumatic stress disorder; thought, mood, and personality disorders. Accepts the mobility impaired; the vision impaired; the speech impaired; those with a history of arson; the sexually compulsive; those with a history of harm to themselves and others; those receiving psychotropic medication; those with a history of epilepsy; sexual abuse survivors.

Program Treatment modalities: psychodynamic. Family treatment program available.

Staff .7 full-time direct-care staff member per child or adolescent. Total facility staff includes 1 physician, 3 psychologists, 4 psychiatrists, 3 registered nurses, 2 practical/vocational nurses, 18 MSW social workers, 3 social workers (non-MSW), 13 teachers, 2 occupational/recreational therapists, 4 therapists, 2 dieticians. Staff is 33% male, 67% female.

Facilities Multiple buildings; males and females in both coeducational and separate units depending on program. Separate dining by residential unit available. Basketball courts, game room, gymnasium, playing fields, playground equipment.

Education Academic program available at no charge. Serves ages 5–18, grades K–12. 13 teachers on staff. Curriculum accredited or approved by Des Moines Public School District. Cost of educational program covered by local school district. Organized sports program offered.

Costs Average cost: $120 per day. Accepts private insurance, group insurance, medicare, medicaid, Blue Cross/Blue Shield, public funds.

Additional Services In-home services program for males and females ages 5–18. Treats behavior disorders; general psychosocial disorders; compulsive/addictive disorders other than substance abuse and eating disorders; post-traumatic stress disorder; thought, mood, and personality disorders.

Contact Leslie Held, Admissions Coordinator, main address above. Phone: 515-285-6781. Fax: 515-285-8925.

OUR HOME, INC.
510 Nebraska Southwest
Huron, South Dakota 57350
605-353-1025; Fax: 605-353-1061

General Information Residential treatment/subacute facility for adolescents. 108 beds for adolescents. Patient security: staff secured. Independent not-for-profit facility. Licensed by state of South Dakota. Accredited by Division of Drug and Alcohol Abuse.

Participants Accepts: male and female adolescents. Average stay: 50 days. Admission: one parent, all parties who share custody, court order, voluntary, depending on program. Treats substance abuse. Accepts the sexually compulsive; those with a history of harm to themselves and others.

Staff Staff is 50% male, 50% female.

Contact Doug Murano, Chemical Dependency Services Coordinator, main address above. Phone: 605-353-1025. Fax: 605-353-1061.

OUR LADY OF PEACE HOSPITAL
2020 Newburg Road
Louisville, Kentucky 40232
502-451-3330; Fax: 502-451-0080

General Information Psychiatric hospital for children, adolescents. Patient security: partially locked. Not-for-profit facility affiliated with Sisters of Charity of Nazareth Health System, Nazareth, KY. Licensed by state of Kentucky. Accredited by JCAHO.

Participants Accepts: male and female children; male and female adolescents. Average stay: 27 days. Admission: one parent, all parties who share custody, court order, voluntary, depending on program. Treats autistic disorders; learning disabilities; behavior disorders; general psychosocial disorders; substance abuse; eating disorders; compulsive/addictive disorders other than substance abuse and eating disorders; post-traumatic stress disorder; thought, mood, and personality disorders.

Staff Staff is 28% male, 72% female.

Contact 24 Hour Help Line. Phone: 502-451-3333.

OUR LADY OF THE LAKE REGIONAL MEDICAL CENTER—TAU CENTER
5000 Hennessey Boulevard
Baton Rouge, Louisiana 70808
504-767-1320

General Information Drug and alcohol rehabilitation center for adolescents. Patient security: staff secured. Not-for-profit facility affiliated with Franciscan Missionary of Our Lady, Baton Rouge, LA. Licensed by state of Louisiana. Accredited by JCAHO.

Participants Accepts: male and female adolescents. Average stay: 18 days. Admission: one parent, all parties who share custody, court order, voluntary, depending on program. Treats substance abuse. Accepts those receiving psychotropic medication; non-English speaking individuals; those with a history of epilepsy.

Staff Staff is 40% male, 60% female.

Costs Average cost: $345 per day.

Contact Barbara Buckel, Director, main address above. Phone: 504-767-1320.

OUTREACH HOUSE/BRENTWOOD
400 Crooked Hill Road
Brentwood, New York 11717
516-231-3132

General Information Drug and alcohol rehabilitation center for adolescents. 40 beds for adolescents. Patient security: staff secured. Not-for-profit facility affiliated with Outreach Project, Woodhaven, NY. Licensed by state of New York.

Participants Accepts: male and female adolescents. Average stay: 15 months. Admission: one parent, court order, voluntary, depending on program. Treats substance abuse. Accepts the mobility impaired; the vision impaired; the hearing impaired; the speech impaired; those with a history of arson; those with a history of harm to themselves and others; those receiving psychotropic medication; those with a history of epilepsy.

Staff Staff is 40% male, 60% female.

Education Academic program available at no charge. Serves ages 12–17. Curriculum accredited or approved by Suffolk County Board of Cooperative Educational Services II School Board. Cost of educational program covered by local school district. Organized sports program offered.

Contact John Sheehan, Director of Adolescent Services, 89-15 Woodhaven Boulevard, Woodhaven, NY 11421. Phone: 718-847-9233. Fax: 718-849-1093.

OUTREACH HOUSE/RIDGEWOOD
1416 Wierfield Street
Ridgewood, New York 11385
718-847-9233; Fax: 718-849-1093

General Information Drug and alcohol rehabilitation center for adolescents. 36 beds for adolescents. Patient security: staff secured. Not-for-profit facility affiliated with Outreach Project, Woodhaven, NY. Licensed by state of New York.

Participants Accepts: male and female adolescents. Average stay: 15 months. Admission: one parent, court order, voluntary, depending on program. Treats substance abuse. Accepts the vision impaired; the hearing impaired; the speech impaired; those with a history of arson; those with a history of harm to themselves and others; those receiving psychotropic medication; those with a history of epilepsy.

Staff Staff is 50% male, 50% female.

Education Academic program available at no charge. Serves ages 12–17. Curriculum accredited or approved by New York City Board of Education. Cost of educational program covered by local school district. Organized sports program offered.

Contact John Sheehan, Director of Adolescent Services, 89-15 Woodhaven Boulevard, Woodhaven, NY 11421. Phone: 718-847-9233. Fax: 718-849-1093.

PACIFIC GATEWAY HOSPITAL
1345 Southeast Harney
Portland, Oregon 97202
503-234-5353; Fax: 503-232-0069

General Information Psychiatric hospital for adolescents, adults. 38 beds for adolescents. Open year-round. Patient security: entirely locked; will pursue and return runaways. Urban setting. For-profit facility affiliated with Sterling Health Care Corporation, Bellevue, WA. Licensed by state of Oregon. Accredited by JCAHO.

Participants Accepts: male and female adolescents ages 11–17; male and female adults ages 18 and up. Average stay: 28 days. Admission: all parties who share custody, court order, depending on program. Treats learning disabilities; behavior disorders; general psychosocial disorders; substance abuse; eating disorders; compulsive/addictive disorders other than substance abuse and eating disorders; post-traumatic stress disorder; thought, mood, and personality disorders. Accepts the mobility impaired; the vision impaired; the hearing impaired; the speech impaired; those with a history of arson; the sexually compulsive;

those with a history of harm to themselves and others; those receiving psychotropic medication; those with a history of epilepsy.

Program Treatment modalities: cognitive-behavioral; Twelve Step Recovery. Family treatment program available.

Staff 2 full-time direct-care staff members per adolescent. Total facility staff includes 2 physicians, 4 psychologists, 6 psychiatrists, 16 registered nurses, 5 practical/vocational nurses, 4 MSW social workers, 3 teachers, 28 counselors, 4 occupational/recreational therapists, 1 dietician, 2 other direct-care staff members. Staff is 50% male, 50% female.

Facilities Single building; males and females in co-educational units. Separate residential quarters for adolescents. Central dining (not shared with adults), in-room dining available. Game room, exercise room, volleyball court.

Education Academic program available at no charge. Serves ages 11–17, grades 6–12. 3 teachers on staff. Curriculum accredited or approved by State of Oregon.

Costs Accepts private insurance, group insurance, medicare, medicaid, Blue Cross/Blue Shield, public funds.

Additional Services Outpatient services for males and females ages 11–17. Treats learning disabilities; behavior disorders; general psychosocial disorders; substance abuse; eating disorders; compulsive/addictive disorders other than substance abuse and eating disorders; post-traumatic stress disorder; thought, mood, and personality disorders.

Contact Mark Lenetsky, Director, Clinical Outreach, main address above. Phone: 503-234-5353. Fax: 503-232-0069.

PACIFIC LODGE BOYS' HOME
4900 Serrania Avenue
Woodland Hills, California 91364
818-347-1577; Fax: 818-883-5452

General Information Residential treatment/subacute facility for adolescents. 76 beds for adolescents. Open year-round. Patient security: unlocked; no runaway pursuit. Suburban setting. Independent not-for-profit facility. Licensed by state of California.

Participants Accepts: male adolescents ages 13–18. Average stay: 270 days. Admission: all parties who share custody, court order, depending on program. Treats learning disabilities; behavior disorders; general psychosocial disorders; substance abuse; compulsive/addictive disorders other than substance abuse

and eating disorders; post-traumatic stress disorder; thought, mood, and personality disorders. Accepts those with a history of arson; the sexually compulsive; those with a history of harm to themselves and others; those receiving psychotropic medication; those with a history of epilepsy.

Program Treatment modalities: psychodynamic; family systems; limited behavioral modification. Family treatment program available.

Staff 1 full-time direct-care staff member per adolescent. Total facility staff includes 2 psychologists, 2 psychiatrists, 1 registered nurse, 4 MSW social workers, 7 social workers (non-MSW), 54 counselors, 1 occupational/recreational therapist, 1 dietician. Staff is 50% male, 50% female.

Facilities Multiple buildings. Central dining. Basketball courts, gymnasium, outdoor swimming pool, playing fields, fitness room, indoor and outdoor volleyball.

Education Academic program available at no charge. Serves ages 13–18, grades 7–12. Curriculum accredited or approved by Los Angeles County Schools. Cost of educational program covered by local school district. Organized sports program offered.

Costs Average cost: $3331 per stay. Accepts private insurance, group insurance, public funds.

Additional Services Drug and alcohol rehabilitation services for males ages 13–18. Treats substance abuse. Sex offender program for males. Treats behavior disorders; general psychosocial disorders; substance abuse.

Contact Cliff Topel, Admissions Coordinator, Box 308, Woodland Hills, CA 91365. Phone: 818-886-6543. Fax: 818-883-5452.

PAHL, INC.—PAHL HOUSE
106-108 9th Street
Troy, New York 12180
518-272-0206; Fax: 518-272-0208

General Information Drug and alcohol rehabilitation center for adolescents. Patient security: staff secured. Not-for-profit facility affiliated with Pahl, Inc., Troy, NY. Accredited by Department of Substance Abuse Services.

Participants Accepts: male and female adolescents. Average stay: 8 months. Admission: one parent, all parties who share custody, court order, voluntary, depending on program. Treats substance abuse. Accepts the mobility impaired; the hearing impaired; the speech impaired; those with a history of arson; those receiving psychotropic medication; those with a history of epilepsy.

Additional Services Transitional apartments for males and females ages 16–25. Treats substance abuse.

Contact Janice Prichett, Clinical Director, main address above. Phone: 518-272-0206. Fax: 518-272-0208.

PALMDALE HOSPITAL MEDICAL CENTER
1212 East Avenue S
Palmdale, California 93550
805-273-2211; Fax: 805-273-0719

General Information General hospital for adolescents. 21 beds for adolescents. Patient security: entirely locked. For-profit facility affiliated with Affiliated Medical Enterprises, Orange, CA. Licensed by state of California. Accredited by JCAHO.

Participants Accepts: male and female adolescents. Average stay: 21 days. Admission: one parent. Treats behavior disorders; general psychosocial disorders; substance abuse; eating disorders; compulsive/addictive disorders other than substance abuse and eating disorders; post-traumatic stress disorder; thought, mood, and personality disorders.

Staff Staff is 50% male, 50% female.

Costs Average cost: $27,000 per stay.

Contact Intake Coordinator, main address above. Phone: 805-265-6417.

PALMVIEW HOSPITAL
2510 North Florida Avenue
Lakeland, Florida 33805
813-682-6105; Fax: 813-688-5597

General Information Psychiatric hospital for adolescents. Patient security: entirely locked. Not-for-profit facility affiliated with Health Management Asssociates, Naples, FL. Licensed by state of Florida. Accredited by JCAHO.

Participants Accepts: male and female adolescents. Average stay: 21 days. Admission: all parties who share custody, court order, voluntary, depending on program. Treats autistic disorders; learning disabilities; behavior disorders; general psychosocial disorders; substance abuse; eating disorders; compulsive/addictive disorders other than substance abuse and

eating disorders; post-traumatic stress disorder; thought, mood, and personality disorders.

Staff Staff is 50% male, 50% female.

Additional Services Drug and alcohol rehabilitation services for males and females ages 12–18. Treats autistic disorders; learning disabilities; behavior disorders; general psychosocial disorders; substance abuse; eating disorders; compulsive/addictive disorders other than substance abuse and eating disorders; post-traumatic stress disorder; thought, mood, and personality disorders.

Contact Admissions Department, main address above. Phone: 813-682-6105. Fax: 813-688-5597.

PALOMARES GROUP HOMES
1525 Hamilton Avenue
San Jose, California 95155
408-265-9092; Fax: 408-265-0299

General Information Residential treatment/subacute facility for adolescents. 36 beds for adolescents. Open year-round. Patient security: staff secured; will pursue and return runaways. Urban setting. Independent not-for-profit facility. Licensed by state of California.

Participants Accepts: male and female adolescents ages 11–19. Average stay: 365 days. Admission: one parent, all parties who share custody, court order, private insurance, Mental Health Department, depending on program. Treats learning disabilities; behavior disorders; general psychosocial disorders; substance abuse; eating disorders; compulsive/addictive disorders other than substance abuse and eating disorders; post-traumatic stress disorder; thought, mood, and personality disorders. Accepts the sexually compulsive; those with a history of harm to themselves and others; those receiving psychotropic medication; those with a history of epilepsy. Largest number of participants from California.

Program Treatment modalities: psychodynamic; behavioral; family systems. Family treatment program available.

Staff 1.4 full-time direct-care staff members per adolescent. Total facility staff includes 1 psychiatrist, 1 teacher, 40 counselors, 1 occupational/recreational therapist, 6 therapists. Staff is 50% male, 50% female.

Facilities Multiple buildings; males and females in both coeducational and separate units depending on program. Separate dining by residential unit available. Basketball courts, game room, horseback riding, indoor swimming pool, outdoor swimming pool, playing fields, ropes course.

Education   Academic program available at additional cost. Serves ages 11–19, grades 4–12. 1 teacher on staff. Curriculum accredited or approved by California State Department of Education. Cost of educational program sometimes covered by local school district.

Costs   Average cost: $60,000 per year. Accepts private insurance, group insurance, Blue Cross/Blue Shield, public funds.

Additional Services   Special education school; short-term treatment and assessment for males and females ages 11–19. Treats learning disabilities; behavior disorders; general psychosocial disorders; substance abuse; eating disorders; compulsive/addictive disorders other than substance abuse and eating disorders; post-traumatic stress disorder; thought, mood, and personality disorders.

Contact   Tracy J. True, Clinical Director, main address above. Phone: 408-265-9092. Fax: 408-265-0299.

PALOS COMMUNITY HOSPITAL
80th Avenue and McCarthy Road
Palos Heights, Illinois 60463
708-361-4500

General Information   General hospital for adolescents. 46 beds for adolescents. Patient security: entirely locked. Not-for-profit facility affiliated with St. George's Corporation, Palos Heights, IL. Licensed by state of Illinois. Accredited by JCAHO.

Participants   Accepts: male and female adolescents. Average stay: 3 weeks. Admission: one parent, voluntary, depending on program. Treats learning disabilities; behavior disorders; general psychosocial disorders; substance abuse; eating disorders; compulsive/addictive disorders other than substance abuse and eating disorders; post-traumatic stress disorder; thought, mood, and personality disorders.

Contact   Intake, main address above. Phone: 708-361-4500 Ext. 5448.

PARC PLACE
5116 East Thomas Road
Phoenix, Arizona 85018
602-952-9111; Fax: 602-840-7567

General Information   Freestanding drug and alcohol rehabilitation and behavioral health facility for adolescents. 45 beds for adolescents. Open year-round. Patient security: unlocked. Suburban setting. Independent for-profit facility. Licensed by state of Arizona. Accredited by JCAHO.

Participants   Accepts: male and female adolescents ages 12–20. Average stay: 45 days. Admission: one parent. Treats learning disabilities; behavior disorders; general psychosocial disorders; substance abuse; eating disorders; post-traumatic stress disorder; thought, mood, and personality disorders.

Program   Treatment modalities: Twelve Step Recovery; psychosocial. Family treatment program available.

Staff   1.3 full-time direct-care staff members per adolescent. Total facility staff includes 1 physician, 2 psychologists, 1 psychiatrist, 6 registered nurses, 4 practical/vocational nurses, 2 MSW social workers, 1 social worker (non-MSW), 2 teachers, 6 counselors, 1 occupational/recreational therapist, 2 therapists, 1 dietician, 18 other direct-care staff members. Staff is 47% male, 53% female.

Facilities   Multiple buildings; males and females in separate units. Central dining. Basketball courts, gymnasium, outdoor swimming pool, playing fields, volleyball court.

Education   Academic program available at no charge. Serves ages 12–20, grades 6–12. 2 teachers on staff. Curriculum accredited or approved by Maricopa County Accommodations School District. Cost of educational program sometimes covered by local school district.

Costs   Average cost: $630 per day. Accepts private insurance, group insurance, Blue Cross/Blue Shield.

Additional Services   Outpatient services for males and females ages 12–20. Treats learning disabilities; behavior disorders; general psychosocial disorders; substance abuse; eating disorders; compulsive/addictive disorders other than substance abuse and eating disorders; post-traumatic stress disorder; thought, mood, and personality disorders.

Contact   Cindy Caiazzo, Director of Admissions, main address above. Phone: 602-952-9111. Fax: 602-840-7567.

PARKER VALLEY HOPE
22422 East Main Street
Parker, Colorado 80134
303-841-7857; Fax: 303-841-6526

General Information Drug and alcohol rehabilitation center for adolescents, adults. 4 beds for adolescents. Open year-round. Patient security: staff secured; will pursue and return runaways. Rural setting. Not-for-profit facility affiliated with Valley Hope Association, Norton, KS. Licensed by state of Colorado. Accredited by JCAHO; Colorado State Health Department, Alcohol and Drug Abuse Council.

Participants Accepts: male and female adolescents ages 17–18; male and female adults ages 19–85. Average stay: 30 days. Admission: one parent. Treats substance abuse. Accepts the mobility impaired; the vision impaired; those receiving psychotropic medication. Largest number of participants from Colorado, Kansas.

Program Treatment modalities: Twelve Step Recovery; MMPI/ASAM criteria; SASSY testing; spiritual (non-denominational) recovery. Family treatment program available.

Staff 4.5 full-time direct-care staff members per adolescent. Total facility staff includes 1 psychologist, 10 registered nurses, 5 counselors, 2 other direct-care staff members. Staff is 40% male, 60% female.

Facilities Multiple buildings; males and females in coeducational units. Residential quarters shared with adults. Central dining (shared with adults). volleyball court.

Costs Average cost: $160 per day. Accepts private insurance, group insurance, Blue Cross/Blue Shield.

Contact Diane Sander, Community Relations, main address above. Phone: 303-841-7857. Fax: 303-841-6526.

PARKLAND HOSPITAL
2414 Bunker Hill
Baton Rouge, Louisiana 70808
504-927-9050; Fax: 504-927-4403

General Information Psychiatric hospital for children, adolescents, adults. 12 beds for children; 24 beds for adolescents. Open year-round. Patient security: partially locked; will pursue and return runaways. Urban setting. For-profit facility affiliated with Health Care Corporation of America, Nashville, TN. Licensed by state of Louisiana. Accredited by JCAHO.

Participants Accepts: male and female children ages 4–12; male and female adolescents ages 12–19; male and female adults ages 20 and up. Average stay: 15 days. Admission: all parties who share custody. Treats learning disabilities; behavior disorders; general psychosocial disorders; substance abuse; eating disorders; compulsive/addictive disorders other than substance abuse and eating disorders; post-traumatic stress disorder; thought, mood, and personality disorders. Accepts the mobility impaired; the vision impaired; the hearing impaired; the speech impaired; those with a history of arson; the sexually compulsive; those with a history of harm to themselves and others; those receiving psychotropic medication; non-English speaking individuals; those with a history of epilepsy. Special programs for the chronically ill; the mobility impaired; the hearing impaired; the speech impaired; those with AIDS. Largest number of participants from Louisiana.

Program Treatment modalities: cognitive-behavioral approach; rational emotive therapy; Twelve Step Recovery; Gestalt Therapy. Family treatment program available.

Staff Total facility staff includes 12 physicians, 2 psychologists, 13 psychiatrists, 30 registered nurses, 6 MSW social workers, 4 social workers (non-MSW), 3 teachers, 3 counselors, 3 occupational/recreational therapists, 1 therapist, 1 dietician, 4 other direct-care staff members. Staff is 40% male, 60% female.

Facilities Single building; males and females in separate units. Central dining (shared with adults), in-room dining available. Game room, gymnasium, outdoor swimming pool, outdoor tennis courts, ropes course, miniature golf course, par course, walking track.

Education Academic program available. Serves ages 5–18, grades K–12. 3 teachers on staff. Curriculum accredited or approved by State of Louisiana Board of Education.

Costs Accepts private insurance, group insurance, medicare, medicaid, Blue Cross/Blue Shield.

Additional Services Drug and alcohol rehabilitation services for males and females ages 12 and up. Treats learning disabilities; general psychosocial disorders; substance abuse; eating disorders; compulsive/addictive disorders other than substance abuse and eating disorders; post-traumatic stress disorder; thought, mood, and personality disorders. Outpatient services for males and females ages 6 and up. Treats learning disabilities; behavior disorders; general psychosocial disorders; substance abuse; eating disorders; compulsive/addictive disorders other than substance abuse and eating disorders; post-traumatic stress disorder; thought, mood, and personality disorders. Camping program for males and females ages 5–12. Treats learning disabilities; behavior disorders; general psychosocial disorders; thought, mood, and personality disorders.

Contact Bev Waldrop, Marketing Director, main address above. Phone: 504-927-9050. Fax: 504-927-4403.

PARK RIDGE CHEMICAL DEPENDENCY
1565 Long Pond Road
Rochester, New York 14626
716-723-7000; Fax: 716-723-6715

General Information Residential treatment/subacute facility for children, adolescents. Patient security: staff secured. Not-for-profit facility affiliated with Park Ridge Hospital, Rochester, NY. Licensed by state of New York. Accredited by JCAHO.

Participants Accepts: male and female children; male and female adolescents. Average stay: 60 days. Admission: one parent, all parties who share custody, court order, voluntary, depending on program. Treats substance abuse.

Staff Staff is 40% male, 60% female.

Costs Average cost: $14,000 per stay.

Additional Services Outpatient services for males and females ages 11–18. Treats substance abuse.

Contact Jim Shipman, Admissions Coordinator, main address above. Phone: 716-723-7723.

PARKSIDE AT BAPTIST HOSPITAL OF SOUTHEAST TEXAS
3450 Stagg Drive
Beaumont, Texas 77701
409-839-5376; Fax: 409-839-5118

General Information Psychiatric hospital for adolescents, adults. 20 beds for adolescents. Open year-round. Patient security: staff secured; will pursue and return runaways. Urban setting. Not-for-profit facility affiliated with Baptist Health Care System, Beaumont, TX. Operated by Parkside Medical Services, Park Ridge, IL. Licensed by state of Texas. Accredited by JCAHO; Texas Commission on Alcohol and Drug Abuse, Texas Association of Alcohol and Drug Counselors.

Participants Accepts: male and female adolescents ages 12–18; male and female adults ages 18 and up. Average stay: 21 days. Admission: one parent, all parties who share custody, court order, voluntary,

depending on program. Treats learning disabilities; behavior disorders; general psychosocial disorders; substance abuse; eating disorders; thought, mood, and personality disorders. Accepts those with a history of arson; the sexually compulsive; those with a history of harm to themselves and others; those receiving psychotropic medication; those with a history of epilepsy. Special programs for the developmentally disabled. Largest number of participants from Texas, Louisiana.

Program Treatment modalities: psychotherapy; psychodynamics; Twelve Step Recovery. Family treatment program available.

Staff 4 full-time direct-care staff members per adolescent. Total facility staff includes 2 psychologists, 13 psychiatrists, 15 registered nurses, 11 practical/vocational nurses, 2 MSW social workers, 1 teacher, 8 counselors, 1 occupational/recreational therapist, 8 other direct-care staff members. Staff is 30% male, 70% female.

Facilities Single building; males and females in co-educational units. Separate residential quarters for adolescents. Central dining (shared with adults), in-room dining available. Basketball courts, game room, gymnasium, indoor swimming pool.

Education Academic program available. Serves ages 12–18, grades 7–12. 1 teacher on staff. Curriculum accredited or approved by Texas Education Agency.

Costs Average cost: $10,000 per stay. Accepts private insurance, group insurance, medicaid, Blue Cross/Blue Shield.

Additional Services Drug and alcohol rehabilitation services for males and females ages 11 and up. Treats substance abuse; thought, mood, and personality disorders. Outpatient services for males and females ages 18 and up. Treats learning disabilities; behavior disorders; general psychosocial disorders; substance abuse; thought, mood, and personality disorders.

Contact Mike Giniger, main address above. Phone: 409-839-5376. Fax: 409-839-5118.

PARKSIDE LODGE OF BIRMINGHAM
1189 Albritton Road
P.O. Box 129
Warrior, Alabama 35180
205-647-1945; Fax: 205-647-3626

General Information Residential treatment/subacute facility for adolescents, adults. Open year-round. Patient security: partially locked; no runaway pursuit. Rural setting. Not-for-profit facility affiliated with

Lutheran General Hospital, Chicago, IL. Licensed by state of Alabama. Accredited by JCAHO.

Participants Accepts: male and female adolescents ages 12–18; male and female adults ages 19–27. Admission: one parent, all parties who share custody, court order, depending on program. Treats general psychosocial disorders; substance abuse; eating disorders; compulsive/addictive disorders other than substance abuse and eating disorders; post-traumatic stress disorder. Accepts the mobility impaired; the hearing impaired; the sexually compulsive; those with a history of harm to themselves and others; those receiving psychotropic medication; those with a history of epilepsy.

Program Treatment modalities: Twelve Step Recovery. Family treatment program available.

Staff Total facility staff includes 1 physician, 1 psychologist, 7 registered nurses, 2 teachers, 2 counselors, 1 occupational/recreational therapist, 2 dieticians, 6 other direct-care staff members. Staff is 60% male, 40% female.

Facilities Multiple buildings; males and females in coeducational units. Separate residential quarters for adolescents. Central dining (shared with adults). Basketball courts, ropes course, Nautilus, volleyball.

Education Academic program available. Serves grades 7–12. 2 teachers on staff. Organized sports program offered.

Costs Average cost: $15,000 per month. Accepts private insurance, group insurance, Blue Cross/Blue Shield.

Additional Services Drug and alcohol rehabilitation services for males and females ages 12–27. Treats general psychosocial disorders; substance abuse; eating disorders; compulsive/addictive disorders other than substance abuse and eating disorders; post-traumatic stress disorder. Outpatient services for males and females ages 12–27. Treats substance abuse; eating disorders; compulsive/addictive disorders other than substance abuse and eating disorders.

Contact Bob Durham, Adolescent Program Director, main address above. Phone: 205-647-1945. Fax: 205-647-3626.

PARKSIDE LODGE OF CONNECTICUT
Route 7
P.O. Box 668
Canaan, Connecticut 06018
203-824-5426; Fax: 203-824-1016

General Information Drug and alcohol rehabilitation center for adolescents, adults. 14 beds for adolescents. Open year-round. Patient security: staff secured. Rural setting. Not-for-profit facility affiliated with Parkside Medical Services Corporation, Park Ridge, IL. Licensed by state of Connecticut. Accredited by JCAHO; Connecticut Health Department, Connecticut Division for Child and Youth Services.

Participants Accepts: male and female adolescents ages 13–19; male and female adults ages 19 and up. Average stay: 30 days. Admission: one parent, court order, voluntary, depending on program. Treats learning disabilities; behavior disorders; general psychosocial disorders; substance abuse; eating disorders; post-traumatic stress disorder; thought, mood, and personality disorders. Largest number of participants from New York, Connecticut, Massachusetts.

Program Treatment modalities: Twelve Step Recovery; psychodynamic; behavioral; reality-based. Family treatment program available.

Staff .7 full-time direct-care staff member per adolescent. Total facility staff includes 1 physician, 1 psychologist, 2 psychiatrists, 14 registered nurses, 3 practical/vocational nurses, 2 MSW social workers, 1 social worker (non-MSW), 1 teacher, 10 counselors, 1 occupational/recreational therapist, 1 dietician, 10 other direct-care staff members. Staff is 60% male, 40% female.

Facilities Multiple buildings; males and females in coeducational units. Separate residential quarters for adolescents. Central dining (shared with adults). Basketball courts, game room, outdoor swimming pool, playing fields, volleyball court, therapeutic challenge course.

Education Academic program available at additional cost. Serves ages 13–19, ungraded. 1 teacher on staff. Curriculum accredited or approved by Connecticut Department of Education. Cost of educational program covered by local school district. Organized sports program offered.

Costs Average cost: $14,250 per stay. Accepts private insurance, group insurance, Blue Cross/Blue Shield.

Additional Services Outpatient services for males and females ages 18 and up. Treats substance abuse.

Contact Andrea S. Wilson, Executive Director, main address above. Phone: 203-824-5426. Fax: 203-824-1016.

PARKSIDE LODGE OF DUBLIN
804 Industrial Boulevard
Dublin, Georgia 31021
912-275-0353; Fax: 912-275-4876

General Information   Drug and alcohol rehabilitation center for adolescents, adults. 10 beds for adolescents. Open year-round. Patient security: staff secured; will pursue and return runaways. Rural setting. Not-for-profit facility affiliated with Parkside Medical Services Corporation, Parkridge, IL. Licensed by state of Georgia. Accredited by JCAHO.

Participants   Accepts: male and female adolescents ages 13–18; male and female adults ages 18 and up. Average stay: 42 days. Admission: one parent. Treats substance abuse. Accepts the mobility impaired; those with a history of harm to themselves and others; those receiving psychotropic medication; those with a history of epilepsy. Largest number of participants from Georgia, South Carolina, Massachusetts.

Program   Treatment modalities: Twelve Step Recovery; rational emotive therapy; Gestalt. Family treatment program available.

Staff   Total facility staff includes 1 physician, 1 psychologist, 6 registered nurses, 1 MSW social worker, 1 teacher, 4 counselors, 1 occupational/recreational therapist, 1 dietician, 10 other direct-care staff members. Staff is 57% male, 43% female.

Facilities   Single building; males and females in coeducational units. Separate residential quarters for adolescents. Central dining (shared with adults). Basketball courts, game room, playing fields, ropes course.

Education   Academic program available at no charge. Serves ages 13–18, grades 7–12. 1 teacher on staff.

Costs   Average cost: $20,712 per stay. Accepts private insurance, group insurance, Blue Cross/Blue Shield, public funds.

Additional Services   Outpatient services for males and females ages 13 and up. Treats substance abuse.

Contact   Samuel Love, Program Director, P.O. Box 1285, Dublin, GA 31040. Phone: 912-275-0353. Fax: 912-275-4876.

PARKSIDE LODGE OF KATY
5638 Medical Center Drive
Katy, Texas 77494
713-392-3456; Fax: 713-392-8670

General Information   Freestanding drug, alcohol, and psychiatric, rehabilitation center for adolescents, adults. 10 beds for adolescents. Open year-round. Patient security: staff secured; will pursue and return runaways. Suburban setting. Not-for-profit facility affiliated with Parkside Medical Services Corporation, Chicago, IL. Licensed by state of Texas. Accredited by JCAHO; Texas Commission on Alcohol and Drug Abuse.

Participants   Accepts: male and female adolescents ages 12–18; male and female adults ages 17 and up. Average stay: 30 days. Admission: one parent, court order, depending on program. Treats behavior disorders; general psychosocial disorders; substance abuse; eating disorders; compulsive/addictive disorders other than substance abuse and eating disorders; post-traumatic stress disorder; thought, mood, and personality disorders. Accepts the mobility impaired; the speech impaired; the sexually compulsive; those with a history of harm to themselves and others; those receiving psychotropic medication; those with a history of epilepsy.

Program   Treatment modalities: Twelve Step Recovery; reality therapy; psychodynamic; trauma resolution. Family treatment program available.

Staff   Total facility staff includes 2 physicians, 1 psychologist, 1 psychiatrist, 7 registered nurses, 5 practical/vocational nurses, 2 MSW social workers, 1 social worker (non-MSW), 1 teacher, 15 counselors, 1 occupational/recreational therapist, 1 dietician, 21 other direct-care staff members. Staff is 50% male, 50% female.

Facilities   Multiple buildings; males and females in coeducational units. Residential quarters shared with adults. Central dining (shared with adults). Basketball courts, playing fields, ropes course, weight room.

Education   Academic program available at no charge. Serves ages 12–18, grades 6–12. 1 teacher on staff. Curriculum accredited or approved by Katy Independent School District.

Costs   Average cost: $17,000 per stay. Accepts private insurance, group insurance, Blue Cross/Blue Shield, public funds.

Additional Services   Outpatient services for males and females ages 17 and up. Treats general psychosocial disorders; substance abuse; eating disorders; compulsive/addictive disorders other than substance abuse and eating disorders; post-traumatic stress disorder. Residential or sub-acute services for males and females ages 17 and up. Treats behavior disorders; general psychosocial disorders; substance abuse; eating disorders; compulsive/addictive disorders other than substance abuse and eating disorders; post-traumatic stress disorder; thought, mood, and personality disorders.

Contact   Deborah P. Burdett, Marketer/Clinician, 11111 Richmond, #200, Houston, TX 77082. Phone: 713-977-3456. Fax: 713-977-7633.

PARKSIDE LODGE OF MUNDELEIN
24647 North Highway 21
Mundelein, Illinois 60060
708-634-2020; Fax: 708-913-2375

General Information   Drug and alcohol rehabilitation center for adolescents. 68 beds for adolescents. Open year-round. Patient security: staff secured; will pursue and return runaways. Suburban setting. Not-for-profit facility affiliated with Parkside Medical Services Corporation, Park Ridge, IL. Licensed by state of Illinois. Accredited by JCAHO; Illinois Department of Alcohol and Substance Abuse.

Participants   Accepts: male and female adolescents ages 13–21. Average stay: 21 days. Admission: one parent. Treats substance abuse; eating disorders. Accepts the mobility impaired; the vision impaired; those with a history of harm to themselves and others; those receiving psychotropic medication; those with a history of epilepsy. Largest number of participants from Illinois.

Program   Treatment modalities: Twelve Step Recovery; eclectic treatment modalities. Family treatment program available.

Staff   Total facility staff includes 2 physicians, 2 psychologists, 2 psychiatrists, 9 registered nurses, 2 MSW social workers, 1 teacher, 4 counselors, 1 occupational/recreational therapist, 1 dietician. Staff is 60% male, 40% female.

Facilities   Single building; males and females in separate units. Central dining. Basketball courts, game room, gymnasium, playing fields, ropes course.

Education   Academic program available at no charge. Serves ages 13–21, ungraded. 1 teacher on staff. Cost of educational program covered by local school district. Organized sports program offered.

Costs   Average cost: $500 per stay. Accepts private insurance, group insurance, Blue Cross/Blue Shield.

Additional Services   Wilderness/survival program ages 13–17. Treats substance abuse; eating disorders.

Contact   Dan Untch, Administrator, main address above. Phone: 708-634-2020. Fax: 708-913-2375.

PARKSIDE LODGE OF WISCONSIN, INC.
313 Stoughton Road
Edgerton, Wisconsin 53534-0111
608-884-3381

General Information   Drug and alcohol rehabilitation center for adolescents, adults. 16 beds for adolescents. Open year-round. Patient security: staff secured; will pursue and return runaways. Small town setting. Not-for-profit facility affiliated with Parkside Medical Services Corporation, Park Ridge, IL. Licensed by state of Wisconsin. Accredited by JCAHO.

Participants   Accepts: male and female adolescents ages 12–18; male and female adults ages 19 and up. Average stay: 15 days. Admission: one parent, voluntary, depending on program. Treats learning disabilities; substance abuse.

Program   Treatment modalities: twelve step recovery; reality therapy; family systems. Family treatment program available.

Staff   .2 full-time direct-care staff member per adolescent. Total facility staff includes 2 physicians, 1 psychologist, 1 psychiatrist, 6 registered nurses, 1 MSW social worker, 1 teacher, 2 counselors, 1 dietician, 6 other direct-care staff members.

Facilities   Single building; males and females in co-educational units. Separate residential quarters for adolescents. Central dining (not shared with adults). Basketball courts.

Education   Academic program available at no charge. Serves ages 12–19, grades 7–12. 1 teacher on staff.

Costs   Accepts private insurance, group insurance, medicaid, Blue Cross/Blue Shield.

Additional Services   Outpatient services for males and females ages 12–19. Treats substance abuse.

Contact   Barbara Snell, Youth Treatment Director, main address above. Phone: 608-884-3381.

PARKSIDE RECOVERY CENTER AT CHARLESTON AREA MEDICAL CENTER
501 Morris Street
P.O. Box 1547
Charleston, West Virginia 25326
304-348-6060; Fax: 304-340-7294

General Information   General hospital for adolescents, adults. 18 beds for adolescents. Open year-round. Patient security: staff secured; will pursue and return runaways. Urban setting. Independent not-for-profit facility. Licensed by state of West Virginia. Accredited by JCAHO.

Participants Accepts: male and female adolescents ages 13–19; male and female adults ages 18 and up. Average stay: 22 days. Admission: one parent, court order, depending on program. Treats behavior disorders; general psychosocial disorders; substance abuse; compulsive/addictive disorders other than substance abuse and eating disorders; post-traumatic stress disorder; thought, mood, and personality disorders. Accepts the mobility impaired; the vision impaired; the hearing impaired; those receiving psychotropic medication; those with a history of epilepsy. Special programs for the chronically ill; the hearing impaired.

Program Treatment modalities: Twelve Step Recovery; behavior modification; medical model. Family treatment program available.

Staff Total facility staff includes 2 physicians, 2 psychologists, 3 psychiatrists, 15 registered nurses, 1 MSW social worker, 1 teacher, 6 counselors, 1 occupational/recreational therapist, 1 dietician. Staff is 15% male, 85% female.

Facilities Single building; males and females in co-educational units. Separate residential quarters for adolescents. Central dining (not shared with adults). Basketball courts, game room, gymnasium.

Education Academic program available at no charge. Serves ages 12–18, ungraded. 1 teacher on staff. Curriculum accredited or approved by Kanawha County Home Bound Program. Cost of educational program covered by local school district.

Costs Average cost: $9000 per stay. Accepts private insurance, group insurance, medicare, medicaid, Blue Cross/Blue Shield, public funds.

Additional Services Drug and alcohol rehabilitation services for males and females ages 12 and up. Treats behavior disorders; general psychosocial disorders; substance abuse; compulsive/addictive disorders other than substance abuse and eating disorders; post-traumatic stress disorder; thought, mood, and personality disorders. Outpatient services for males and females ages 18 and up. Treats substance abuse.

Contact Jerri Buck, Admissions Specialist, main address above. Phone: 304-348-6060. Fax: 304-340-7294.

PARKSIDE RECOVERY CENTER AT FREEMAN HOSPITAL
1102 West 32nd Street
Joplin, Missouri 64801
417-782-8800; Fax: 417-625-6636

General Information General hospital for adolescents, adults. 6 beds for adolescents. Open year-round. Patient security: staff secured; no runaway pursuit. Small town setting. Not-for-profit facility affiliated with Parkside Medical Services Corporation, Park Ridge, IL. Licensed by state of Missouri. Accredited by JCAHO.

Participants Accepts: male and female adolescents ages 12–18; male and female adults ages 18 and up. Average stay: 12 days. Admission: one parent, all parties who share custody, court order, depending on program. Treats behavior disorders; general psychosocial disorders; substance abuse; compulsive/addictive disorders other than substance abuse and eating disorders; post-traumatic stress disorder; thought, mood, and personality disorders. Accepts the mobility impaired; the vision impaired; the hearing impaired; the speech impaired; those receiving psychotropic medication; those with a history of epilepsy. Special programs for the chronically ill; the mobility impaired; the developmentally disabled; the vision impaired; the hearing impaired; the speech impaired; those with AIDS. Largest number of participants from Missouri, Oklahoma, Kansas.

Program Treatment modalities: Twelve Step Recovery; reality therapy; rational emotive therapy; family therapy. Family treatment program available.

Staff 5.3 full-time direct-care staff members per adolescent. Total facility staff includes 1 physician, 3 registered nurses, 9 practical/vocational nurses, 1 teacher, 2 counselors. Staff is 31% male, 69% female.

Facilities Single building; males and females in co-educational units. Residential quarters shared with adults. Central dining (shared with adults), in-room dining available. Game room, playing fields.

Education 1 teacher on staff. Educational arrangements: supervision of homework from schools. Educational program held on-site at no charge.

Costs Average cost: $400 per day. Accepts private insurance, group insurance, medicare, Blue Cross/Blue Shield.

Additional Services Drug and alcohol rehabilitation services for males and females ages 12 and up. Treats behavior disorders; general psychosocial disorders; substance abuse; eating disorders; compulsive/addictive disorders other than substance abuse and eating disorders; post-traumatic stress disorder; thought, mood, and personality disorders. Outpatient services for males and females ages 12 and up. Treats general psychosocial disorders; substance abuse.

Contact James Schnackenberg, Program Director, main address above. Phone: 417-782-8800. Fax: 417-625-6636.

PARKSIDE YOUTH CENTER
2221 64th Street
Woodridge, Illinois 60517
708-719-0980; Fax: 708-719-0012

General Information Drug and alcohol rehabilitation center for adolescents. 40 beds for adolescents. Open year-round. Patient security: staff secured; will pursue and return runaways. Small town setting. Not-for-profit facility affiliated with Parkside Medical Services Corporation, Park Ridge, IL. Licensed by state of Illinois. Accredited by Illinois Department of Alcohol and Substance Abuse.

Participants Accepts: male and female adolescents ages 13–21. Average stay: 90 days. Admission: voluntary. Treats behavior disorders; general psychosocial disorders; substance abuse; eating disorders; post-traumatic stress disorder; thought, mood, and personality disorders. Accepts the mobility impaired; the vision impaired; the hearing impaired; the speech impaired; those receiving psychotropic medication.

Program Treatment modalities: Twelve Step Recovery; disease concept; therapeutic community. Family treatment program available.

Staff .3 full-time direct-care staff member per adolescent. Total facility staff includes 1 physician, 1 MSW social worker, 1 teacher, 1 counselor, 1 occupational/recreational therapist, 7 dieticians.

Facilities Single building; males and females in co-educational units. Basketball courts, game room, gymnasium, playing fields, ropes course.

Education Academic program available at no charge. Serves ages 14–18, grades 8–12. 1 teacher on staff. Curriculum accredited or approved by North Central Association of Colleges and Schools. Cost of educational program sometimes covered by local school district.

Costs Average cost: $130 per day. Accepts private insurance, group insurance, Blue Cross/Blue Shield, public funds.

Contact Mary Jane Bressler, Program Director, main address above. Phone: 708-719-0980. Fax: 708-719-0012.

PARKSIDE YOUTH CHEMICAL DEPENDENCY PROGRAM
807 North Main Street
Bloomington, Illinois 61738
309-829-0755

General Information Residential treatment/subacute facility for adolescents, adults. 10 beds for adolescents. Open year-round. Patient security: staff secured; no runaway pursuit. Small town setting. Not-for-profit facility affiliated with Parkside Medical Services Corporation, Park Ridge, IL. Licensed by state of Illinois. Accredited by JCAHO.

Participants Accepts: male and female adolescents ages 12–18; male and female adults ages 18 and up. Average stay: 24 days. Admission: voluntary. Treats behavior disorders; general psychosocial disorders; substance abuse; thought, mood, and personality disorders. Accepts the mobility impaired; the vision impaired; the hearing impaired; the speech impaired; the sexually compulsive; those receiving psychotropic medication. Special programs for the hearing impaired; the speech impaired; those with AIDS.

Program Treatment modalities: Twelve Step Recovery; psychodynamic; group, individual, and family therapies. Family treatment program available.

Staff .9 full-time direct-care staff member per adolescent. Total facility staff includes 3 physicians, 2 psychologists, 2 psychiatrists, 10 registered nurses, 1 teacher, 7 counselors, 1 speech pathologist, 1 dietician, 10 other direct-care staff members. Staff is 30% male, 70% female.

Facilities Single building; males and females in co-educational units. Separate residential quarters for adolescents. Central dining (shared with adults). Basketball courts, game room, gymnasium, ropes course.

Education Academic program available at no charge. Serves ages 12–18. 1 teacher on staff. Curriculum accredited or approved by State of Illinois Education Department. Cost of educational program covered by local school district.

Costs Accepts private insurance, group insurance, medicare, Blue Cross/Blue Shield.

Additional Services Outpatient services for males and females ages 12 and up. Treats substance abuse.

Contact Nancy Haggund, Admissions Specialist, main address above. Phone: 309-829-0755. Fax: 309-829-0760.

PARKVIEW EPISCOPAL MEDICAL CENTER—CHILD AND ADOLESCENT PSYCHIATRIC SERVICE
400 West 16th Street
Pueblo, Colorado 81003
719-584-4457; Fax: 719-584-4342

General Information   General hospital for children, adolescents. Patient security: staff secured. Independent not-for-profit facility. Licensed by state of Colorado. Accredited by JCAHO.

Participants   Accepts: male and female children; male and female adolescents. Average stay: 12 days. Admission: one parent, all parties who share custody, court order, voluntary, depending on program. Treats learning disabilities; behavior disorders; general psychosocial disorders; substance abuse; compulsive/addictive disorders other than substance abuse and eating disorders; post-traumatic stress disorder; thought, mood, and personality disorders.

Staff   Staff is 40% male, 60% female.

Additional Services   Outpatient services for males and females ages 2–18. Treats learning disabilities; behavior disorders; general psychosocial disorders; substance abuse; compulsive/addictive disorders other than substance abuse and eating disorders; post-traumatic stress disorder; thought, mood, and personality disorders.

Contact   Terry Barnett, Program Director, main address above. Phone: 719-584-4457. Fax: 719-584-4342.

PARKVIEW HOSPITAL OF TOPEKA
3707 Southwest 6th Avenue
Topeka, Kansas 66606
913-235-3000; Fax: 913-295-4012

General Information   Psychiatric hospital for children, adolescents. Patient security: entirely locked. For-profit facility affiliated with National Medical Enterprises, Santa Monica, CA. Licensed by state of Kansas. Accredited by JCAHO.

Participants   Accepts: male and female children; male and female adolescents. Average stay: 23 days. Admission: one parent, all parties who share custody, court order, voluntary, depending on program. Treats autistic disorders; learning disabilities; behavior disorders; general psychosocial disorders; substance abuse; eating disorders; compulsive/addictive disorders other than substance abuse and eating disorders; post-traumatic stress disorder; thought, mood, and personality disorders.

Contact   Information and Referral Services, P.O. Box 1220, Topeka, KS 66606. Phone: 913-235-3000. Fax: 913-295-4012.

PARKWAY HOSPITAL
6001 Research Park Boulevard
Madison, Wisconsin 53719
608-238-5151; Fax: 608-238-2305

General Information   Psychiatric hospital for children, adolescents, adults. 12 beds for children; 20 beds for adolescents; 62 beds total. Open year-round. Patient security: partially locked; will pursue and return runaways. Suburban setting. For-profit facility affiliated with Hospital Corporation of America, Nashville, TN. Licensed by state of Wisconsin. Accredited by JCAHO; State of Wisconsin Department of Health and Human Services.

Participants   Accepts: male and female children ages 4–12; male and female adolescents ages 13–18; male and female adults ages 19 and up. Average stay: 20 days. Admission: voluntary. Treats learning disabilities; behavior disorders; general psychosocial disorders; substance abuse; eating disorders; compulsive/addictive disorders other than substance abuse and eating disorders; post-traumatic stress disorder; thought, mood, and personality disorders. Accepts the mobility impaired; the vision impaired; the hearing impaired; the speech impaired; those with a history of arson; the sexually compulsive; those with a history of harm to themselves and others; those receiving psychotropic medication; non-English speaking individuals; those with a history of epilepsy. Special programs for the chronically ill; the mobility impaired; the developmentally disabled; the vision impaired; the hearing impaired; the speech impaired; those with AIDS. Largest number of participants from Wisconsin, Michigan, Minnesota.

Program   Treatment modalities: multi-family therapy. Family treatment program available.

Staff   .3 full-time direct-care staff member per child or adolescent. Total facility staff includes 17 physicians, 2 psychologists, 15 psychiatrists, 46 registered nurses, 6 MSW social workers, 3 social workers (non-MSW), 2 teachers, 5 counselors, 3 occupational/recreational therapists, 2 dieticians, 30 other direct-care staff members.

Facilities   Single building; males and females in co-educational units. Central dining (shared with adults). Game room, gymnasium, courtyards, outdoor playground.

Education Academic program available at no charge. Serves ages 7–12, grades 1–6. 2 teachers on staff. Cost of educational program sometimes covered by local school district.

Costs Accepts private insurance, group insurance, medicare, medicaid, Blue Cross/Blue Shield, public funds.

Additional Services Dual diagnosis program for adolescents and adults for males and females ages 4 and up. Treats learning disabilities; behavior disorders; general psychosocial disorders; substance abuse; eating disorders; compulsive/addictive disorders other than substance abuse and eating disorders; post-traumatic stress disorder; thought, mood, and personality disorders.

Contact Carol Brooks, Director of Marketing, main address above. Phone: 608-238-5151. Fax: 608-238-2305.

PARMADALE
6753 State Road
Parma, Ohio 44134
216-845-7700; Fax: 216-845-5910

General Information Residential treatment/subacute facility for children, adolescents. 12 beds for children; 148 beds for adolescents; 160 beds total. Open year-round. Patient security: staff secured; will pursue and return runaways. Suburban setting. Not-for-profit facility. Licensed by state of Ohio. Accredited by JCAHO.

Participants Accepts: male and female children ages 10–12; male and female adolescents ages 13–18. Average stay: 9 months. Admission: all parties who share custody, court order, depending on program. Treats autistic disorders; learning disabilities; behavior disorders; general psychosocial disorders; substance abuse; eating disorders; compulsive/addictive disorders other than substance abuse and eating disorders. Accepts the mobility impaired; the vision impaired; the hearing impaired; the speech impaired; those with a history of arson; the sexually compulsive; those with a history of harm to themselves and others; those receiving psychotropic medication. Special programs for the developmentally disabled. Largest number of participants from Ohio, Indiana, West Virginia.

Program Treatment modalities: applied behavior analysis; skillstreaming; Twelve Step Recovery; structural family therapy. Family treatment program available.

Staff 1.9 full-time direct-care staff members per child or adolescent. Total facility staff includes 2 physicians, 4 psychologists, 1 psychiatrist, 2 registered nurses, 2 practical/vocational nurses, 30 MSW social workers, 5 social workers (non-MSW), 19 teachers, 8 counselors, 1 speech pathologist, 1 dietician, 222 other direct-care staff members. Staff is 47% male, 53% female.

Facilities Multiple buildings; males and females in separate units. Separate dining by residential unit available. Basketball courts, game room, gymnasium, outdoor swimming pool, outdoor tennis courts.

Education 19 teachers on staff.

Costs Average cost: $40,000 per stay. Accepts private insurance, group insurance, public funds.

Additional Services Drug and alcohol rehabilitation services for males and females ages 12–18. Treats learning disabilities; behavior disorders; general psychosocial disorders; substance abuse; eating disorders; compulsive/addictive disorders other than substance abuse and eating disorders. Outpatient services for males and females ages 3–18. Treats learning disabilities; behavior disorders; general psychosocial disorders; substance abuse.

Contact Anne Mengerink, Intake Director, main address above. Phone: 216-845-7700. Fax: 216-845-5910.

PARSONS CHILD AND FAMILY CENTER
60 Academy Road
Albany, New York 12208
518-426-2600; Fax: 518-426-2792

General Information Residential treatment/subacute facility for children, adolescents. 25 beds for children; 58 beds for adolescents; 83 beds total. Open year-round. Patient security: staff secured. Suburban setting. Independent not-for-profit facility. Licensed by state of New York. Accredited by JCAHO; Council on Accreditation of Services for Families and Children.

Participants Accepts: male and female children ages 7–12; male and female adolescents ages 13–21. Average stay: 1 year. Admission: one parent, voluntary, depending on program. Treats autistic disorders; learning disabilities; behavior disorders; general psychosocial disorders; eating disorders; post-traumatic stress disorder; thought, mood, and personality disorders. Accepts the vision impaired; the hearing impaired; the speech impaired; those with a history of harm to themselves and others; those receiving psychotropic medication; those with a history of epilepsy.

Special programs for the chronically ill; the developmentally disabled.

Program Family treatment program available.

Staff 3.5 full-time direct-care staff members per child or adolescent. Total facility staff includes 1 physician, 4 psychologists, 7 psychiatrists, 14 registered nurses, 5 practical/vocational nurses, 65 MSW social workers, 5 social workers (non-MSW), 60 teachers, 80 counselors, 2 occupational/recreational therapists, 5 speech pathologists, 3 therapists, 1 dietician. Staff is 30% male, 70% female.

Facilities Multiple buildings. Separate dining by residential unit available. Basketball courts, game room, gymnasium, outdoor swimming pool, playing fields.

Education Academic program available. Serves ages 5–21, ungraded. 60 teachers on staff. Curriculum accredited or approved by New York State Education Department. Organized sports program offered.

Costs Accepts medicaid, public funds.

Additional Services Outpatient services for males and females ages 5–21. Treats autistic disorders; learning disabilities; behavior disorders; general psychosocial disorders; substance abuse; thought, mood, and personality disorders.

Contact Deborah Singer, Director of Assessment and Referral Services, main address above. Phone: 518-426-2624. Fax: 518-426-2792.

PARTHENON PAVILION AT CENTENNIAL MEDICAL CENTER
2401 Murphy Avenue
Nashville, Tennessee 37203
615-342-1400; Fax: 615-342-4450

General Information Psychiatric hospital for adolescents, adults. 20 beds for adolescents. Open year-round. Patient security arrangements vary depending on program; will pursue and return runaways. Urban setting. For-profit facility affiliated with Hospital Corporation of America, Nashville, TN. Licensed by state of Tennessee. Accredited by JCAHO.

Participants Accepts: male and female adolescents ages 12–18; male and female adults ages 19 and up. Average stay: 20 days. Admission: one parent, all parties who share custody, court order, depending on program. Treats learning disabilities; behavior disorders; general psychosocial disorders; substance abuse; eating disorders; compulsive/addictive disorders other than substance abuse and eating disorders; post-traumatic stress disorder; thought, mood, and person-

ality disorders. Accepts the mobility impaired; the vision impaired; the hearing impaired; the speech impaired; those with a history of arson; the sexually compulsive; those with a history of harm to themselves and others; those receiving psychotropic medication; non-English speaking individuals; those with a history of epilepsy. Special programs for the chronically ill; the mobility impaired; the developmentally disabled; the vision impaired; the hearing impaired; the speech impaired; those with AIDS. Largest number of participants from Tennessee, Kentucky.

Program Treatment modalities: Twelve Step Recovery; psychodynamic. Family treatment program available.

Staff .8 full-time direct-care staff member per adolescent. Total facility staff includes 3 physicians, 1 psychologist, 65 psychiatrists, 114 registered nurses, 22 practical/vocational nurses, 16 MSW social workers, 3 teachers, 19 occupational/recreational therapists, 63 other direct-care staff members. Staff is 21% male, 79% female.

Facilities Single building; males and females in co-educational units. Separate residential quarters for adolescents. Central dining (shared with adults). Basketball courts, game room, gymnasium.

Education Academic program available at no charge. Serves ages 12–18, grades 7–12. 3 teachers on staff. Curriculum accredited or approved by State of Tennessee Department of Education. Organized sports program offered.

Costs Accepts private insurance, group insurance, medicare, medicaid, Blue Cross/Blue Shield, public funds.

Additional Services Outpatient services for males and females. Treats learning disabilities; behavior disorders; general psychosocial disorders; eating disorders; compulsive/addictive disorders other than substance abuse and eating disorders; post-traumatic stress disorder; thought, mood, and personality disorders.

Contact Susan French, Director of Community Assistance Program, main address above. Phone: 615-342-1450. Fax: 615-342-4450.

PASSAGES RESIDENTIAL TREATMENT CENTER
1155 Idaho Street
El Paso, Texas 79902
915-544-4000; Fax: 915-532-0733

General Information Residential treatment/subacute facility for adolescents. 24 beds for adolescents.

Open year-round. Patient security: partially locked; will pursue and return runaways. Urban setting. For-profit facility affiliated with Hospital Corporation of America, Nashville, TN. Licensed by state of Texas. Accredited by JCAHO; Texas Department of Human Services.

Participants Accepts: male and female adolescents ages 13–17. Average stay: 9 months. Admission: all parties who share custody, court order, depending on program. Treats behavior disorders; general psychosocial disorders; substance abuse; post-traumatic stress disorder; thought, mood, and personality disorders. Accepts the mobility impaired; the speech impaired; those with a history of arson; those with a history of harm to themselves and others; those receiving psychotropic medication; those with a history of epilepsy. Largest number of participants from Texas, New Mexico.

Program Treatment modalities: cognitive-behavioral; psychodynamic. Family treatment program available.

Staff .6 full-time direct-care staff member per adolescent. Total facility staff includes 1 psychologist, 1 psychiatrist, 3 registered nurses, 2 practical/vocational nurses, 1 MSW social worker, 1 social worker (non-MSW), 1 teacher, 6 counselors, 2 occupational/recreational therapists, 2 therapists, 1 dietician. Staff is 57% male, 43% female.

Facilities Single building. Basketball courts, game room, gymnasium, indoor swimming pool, ropes course.

Education Academic program available at no charge. Serves ages 13–17, grades 7–12. 1 teacher on staff. Curriculum accredited or approved by El Paso Independent School District. Cost of educational program covered by local school district.

Costs Average cost: $425 per day. Accepts private insurance, group insurance, Blue Cross/Blue Shield, public funds.

Additional Services Drug and alcohol rehabilitation services for males and females ages 12–18. Treats behavior disorders; general psychosocial disorders; substance abuse; compulsive/addictive disorders other than substance abuse and eating disorders; post-traumatic stress disorder; thought, mood, and personality disorders. Residential or sub-acute services for males and females ages 13–17. Treats behavior disorders; general psychosocial disorders; substance abuse; post-traumatic stress disorder; thought, mood, and personality disorders.

Contact Joseph A. Trillo, Program Director, main address above. Phone: 800-444-1231. Fax: 915-532-0733.

THE PAVILION/WEST FLORIDA REGIONAL MEDICAL CENTER
2191 Johnson Avenue
Pensacola, Florida 32514
904-494-5000; Fax: 904-494-5107

General Information Psychiatric hospital for adolescents. 16 beds for adolescents. Patient security: entirely locked. For-profit facility affiliated with Hospital Corporation of America, Nashville, TN. Licensed by state of Florida. Accredited by JCAHO.

Participants Accepts: male and female adolescents. Average stay: 12 days. Admission: one parent, all parties who share custody, court order, voluntary, depending on program. Treats learning disabilities; behavior disorders; general psychosocial disorders; substance abuse; eating disorders; post-traumatic stress disorder; thought, mood, and personality disorders.

Staff Staff is 50% male, 50% female.

Costs Average cost: $750 per day.

Contact Cynthia Ayres, Administrator, main address above. Phone: 904-494-5000. Fax: 904-494-5107.

PEACE RIVER CENTER CARE CENTERS
655 North Jackson Street
Bartow, Florida 33830
813-533-8982

General Information Residential treatment/subacute facility for children, adolescents. 10 beds for children; 20 beds for adolescents; 30 beds total. Open year-round. Patient security arrangements vary depending on program. Not-for-profit facility affiliated with Peace River Center. Licensed by state of Florida.

Participants Accepts: male and female children ages 6–17. Admission: voluntary, ward of the state, depending on program. Treats autistic disorders; learning disabilities; behavior disorders; general psychosocial disorders; eating disorders; compulsive/addictive disorders other than substance abuse and eating disorders; post-traumatic stress disorder; thought, mood, and personality disorders. Accepts the sexually compulsive; those with a history of harm to themselves and others; those receiving psychotropic medication; those with a history of epilepsy.

Program Treatment modalities: eclectic. Family treatment program available.

Staff Total facility staff includes 1 physician, 5 psychologists, 1 psychiatrist, 1 registered nurse, 1 MSW social worker, 4 social workers (non-MSW), 6 teachers, 10 counselors, 2 occupational/recreational therapists, 39 other direct-care staff members. Staff is 40% male, 60% female.

Facilities Multiple buildings; males and females in coeducational units. Separate dining by residential unit available. Basketball courts, game room, playing fields.

Education Academic program available at no charge. Serves ages 6–17, grades K–12. 6 teachers on staff. Cost of educational program covered by local school district.

Costs Accepts private insurance, group insurance, Blue Cross/Blue Shield, public funds.

Additional Services Day treatment for males and females ages 6–17. Treats autistic disorders; learning disabilities; behavior disorders; general psychosocial disorders; eating disorders; compulsive/addictive disorders other than substance abuse and eating disorders; post-traumatic stress disorder; thought, mood, and personality disorders.

Contact Judy Godwin, Supervisor, CARE Centers, main address above. Phone: 813-533-8982.

PENINSULA PSYCHIATRIC HOSPITAL
2244 Executive Drive
Hampton, Virginia 23666
804-827-1001; Fax: 804-838-7694

General Information Psychiatric hospital for children, adolescents, adults. 10 beds for children; 20 beds for adolescents; 125 beds total. Open year-round. Patient security: partially locked; will pursue and return runaways. Urban setting. For-profit facility affiliated with Hospital Corporation of America, Nashville, TN. Licensed by state of Virginia. Accredited by JCAHO.

Participants Accepts: male and female children ages 3–12; male and female adolescents ages 13–17; male and female adults ages 18 and up. Average stay: 12 days. Admission: one parent, court order, depending on program. Treats autistic disorders; learning disabilities; behavior disorders; general psychosocial disorders; substance abuse; eating disorders; compulsive/addictive disorders other than substance abuse and eating disorders; post-traumatic stress disorder; thought, mood, and personality disorders. Accepts the mobility impaired; the vision impaired; the hearing impaired; the speech impaired; those with a history of arson; the sexually compulsive; those with a history of harm to themselves and others; those receiving psychotropic medication; non-English speaking individuals; those with a history of epilepsy.

Largest number of participants from Virginia, North Carolina.

Program Treatment modalities: Twelve Step Recovery; psychoeducational; problem-solving therapy: individual, family, group. Family treatment program available.

Facilities Single building; males and females in coeducational units. Separate residential quarters for children and adolescents. Central dining (shared with adults). Basketball courts, game room, gymnasium, horseback riding, indoor swimming pool, outdoor tennis courts, playing fields, ropes course, weight room.

Education Academic program available at no charge. Serves ages 5–18, grades K–12. Curriculum accredited or approved by Virginia Department of Education.

Costs Average cost: $900 per day. Accepts private insurance, group insurance, medicare, Blue Cross/Blue Shield, public funds.

Additional Services Drug and alcohol rehabilitation services for males and females ages 13 and up. Treats substance abuse; compulsive/addictive disorders other than substance abuse and eating disorders. Outpatient services for males and females ages 3 and up. Treats learning disabilities; behavior disorders; general psychosocial disorders; substance abuse; eating disorders; compulsive/addictive disorders other than substance abuse and eating disorders; post-traumatic stress disorder; thought, mood, and personality disorders.

Contact Lois Mueller, Director of Admissions, main address above. Phone: 804-827-1001. Fax: 804-838-7694.

PENINSULA VILLAGE
Jones Bend Road
P.O. Box 100
Louisville, Tennessee 37777
615-970-1814; Fax: 615-970-1875

General Information Residential treatment/subacute facility for adolescents. 120 beds for adolescents. Open year-round. Patient security: partially locked; will pursue and return runaways. Rural setting. Independent for-profit facility. Licensed by state of Tennessee. Accredited by JCAHO.

Participants Accepts: male and female adolescents ages 13–18. Average stay: 265 days. Admission: one parent, court order, depending on program. Treats learning disabilities; behavior disorders; general psychosocial disorders; substance abuse; eating disorders; compulsive/addictive disorders other than substance abuse and eating disorders; post-traumatic stress disorder; thought, mood, and personality disorders. Accepts the speech impaired; the sexually compulsive; those with a history of harm to themselves and others; those receiving psychotropic medication; those with a history of epilepsy. Largest number of participants from Tennessee, North Carolina, Michigan.

Program Treatment modalities: psychodynamic. Family treatment program available.

Staff 1.1 full-time direct-care staff members per adolescent. Total facility staff includes 2 physicians, 3 psychologists, 2 psychiatrists, 10 registered nurses, 2 practical/vocational nurses, 6 MSW social workers, 10 teachers, 3 occupational/recreational therapists, 1 dietician, 68 other direct-care staff members. Staff is 50% male, 50% female.

Facilities Multiple buildings; males and females in separate units. Central dining. Basketball courts, game room, indoor swimming pool, outdoor swimming pool, outdoor tennis courts, playing fields, ropes course, running trails.

Education Academic program available at no charge. Serves ages 13–18. 10 teachers on staff. Curriculum accredited or approved by State of Tennessee. Cost of educational program sometimes covered by local school district.

Costs Average cost: $110,000 per stay. Accepts private insurance, group insurance, Blue Cross/Blue Shield, public funds.

Additional Services Drug and alcohol rehabilitation services for males and females ages 13–18. Treats learning disabilities; behavior disorders; general psychosocial disorders; substance abuse; eating disorders; compulsive/addictive disorders other than substance abuse and eating disorders; post-traumatic stress disorder; thought, mood, and personality disorders.

Contact Kim Taylor, Admissions Director, main address above. Phone: 615-970-3255. Fax: 615-970-1866.

PERCEPTION HOUSE
134 Church Street
Willimantic, Connecticut 06226
203-450-0151; Fax: 203-450-0205

General Information Drug and alcohol rehabilitation center for adolescents. 4 beds for adolescents. Patient security: staff secured. Not-for-profit facility

affiliated with Perception Programs, Willimantic, CT. Licensed by state of Connecticut.

Participants Accepts: male and female adolescents. Average stay: 2 months. Admission: one parent, all parties who share custody, court order, voluntary, depending on program. Treats substance abuse. Accepts the vision impaired; the hearing impaired; those with a history of arson; the sexually compulsive; those with a history of epilepsy.

Contact Ian Bland, Outreach Coordinator, main address above. Phone: 203-450-0151. Fax: 203-450-0205.

PERSONAL ENRICHMENT THROUGH MENTAL HEALTH SERVICES
11254 58th Street, North
Pinellas Park, Florida 34666
813-545-5636; Fax: 813-545-1537

General Information Residential treatment/subacute facility for children, adolescents. Open year-round. Patient security: partially locked; no runaway pursuit. Suburban setting. Independent not-for-profit facility. Licensed by state of Florida. Accredited by JCAHO; Association of Children's Psychiatric Services.

Participants Accepts: male and female children and adolescents ages 6–17. Average stay: 436 days. Admission: one parent, all parties who share custody, court order, voluntary, depending on program. Treats learning disabilities; behavior disorders; general psychosocial disorders; substance abuse; eating disorders; compulsive/addictive disorders other than substance abuse and eating disorders; post-traumatic stress disorder; thought, mood, and personality disorders. Accepts the mobility impaired; the hearing impaired; the speech impaired; those with a history of arson; the sexually compulsive; those with a history of harm to themselves and others; those receiving psychotropic medication; non-English speaking individuals; those with a history of epilepsy. Largest number of participants from Florida.

Program Treatment modalities: psychodynamic; structural (Minuachin); systems (Bowen). Family treatment program available.

Staff Total facility staff includes 1 physician, 3 psychologists, 3 psychiatrists, 1 registered nurse, 1 practical/vocational nurse, 1 MSW social worker, 2 social workers (non-MSW), 4 occupational/recreational therapists, 1 dietician, 30 other direct-care staff members. Staff is 50% male, 50% female.

Facilities Multiple buildings; males and females in both coeducational and separate units depending on program. Separate dining by residential unit available. Basketball courts, playing fields.

Education Academic program available at no charge. Serves ages 6–17, ungraded. Curriculum accredited or approved by Pinellas County School Board. Cost of educational program covered by local school district.

Costs Accepts private insurance, group insurance, medicare, medicaid, Blue Cross/Blue Shield, public funds.

Additional Services Crisis stabilization unit for males and females ages 6–17. Treats behavior disorders; general psychosocial disorders; thought, mood, and personality disorders.

Contact Chris Walker, Director of Child Residential Services, main address above. Phone: 813-545-5636. Fax: 813-545-1537.

PETTERSEN HOUSE
6020 Hohman Avenue
Hammond, Indiana 46320
219-931-0427

General Information Residential treatment/subacute facility for adolescents. Patient security: staff secured. Not-for-profit facility affiliated with Tri-City Community Mental Health Center, East Chicago, IN. Licensed by state of Indiana. Accredited by Bureau of Addiction Services of Indiana.

Participants Accepts: male and female adolescents. Average stay: 3 months. Admission: court order, voluntary, depending on program. Treats substance abuse. Accepts the vision impaired; the hearing impaired; the speech impaired; those with a history of harm to themselves and others; non-English speaking individuals.

Staff Staff is 30% male, 70% female.

Costs Average cost: $120 per day.

Contact Michael Taylor, Program Supervisor, main address above. Phone: 219-931-0427.

PHILADELPHIA CHILD GUIDANCE CENTER
34th Street and Civic Center Boulevard
Philadelphia, Pennsylvania 19104
215-243-2600; Fax: 215-243-2847

General Information Psychiatric hospital for children, adolescents, adults. 19 beds for children; 19 beds for adolescents; 38 beds total. Open year-round. Patient security arrangements vary depending on program; will pursue and return runaways. Urban setting. Independent not-for-profit facility. Licensed by state of Pennsylvania. Accredited by JCAHO.

Participants Accepts: male and female children ages 7–12; male and female adolescents ages 13–17; male and female adults ages 18–20. Average stay: 25 days. Admission: one parent, all parties who share custody, court order, court authorization for child in custody of child welfare system, depending on program. Treats learning disabilities; behavior disorders; general psychosocial disorders; eating disorders; post-traumatic stress disorder; thought, mood, and personality disorders. Accepts the mobility impaired; the vision impaired; the hearing impaired; the speech impaired; those with a history of arson; the sexually compulsive; those with a history of harm to themselves and others; those receiving psychotropic medication; non-English speaking individuals; those with a history of epilepsy. Special programs for the chronically ill; the hearing impaired. Largest number of participants from Pennsylvania, New Jersey, Delaware.

Program Treatment modalities: family therapy; psychoeducational program; individual and group therapy; milieu therapy. Family treatment program available.

Staff 2.5 full-time direct-care staff members per child or adolescent. Total facility staff includes 1 physician, 6 psychologists, 8 psychiatrists, 14 registered nurses, 3 practical/vocational nurses, 3 MSW social workers, 1 social worker (non-MSW), 4 teachers, 2 occupational/recreational therapists, 42 other direct-care staff members. Staff is 40% male, 60% female.

Facilities Single building; males and females in separate units. Separate residential quarters for children and adolescents. Central dining (not shared with adults). Basketball courts, gymnasium, playing fields.

Education Academic program available at no charge. Serves ages 7–18, ungraded. 4 teachers on staff. Curriculum accredited or approved by Pennsylvania Department of Education.

Costs Average cost: $800 per day. Accepts private insurance, group insurance, medicaid, Blue Cross/Blue Shield, public funds.

Additional Services Drug and alcohol rehabilitation services for males and females ages 10–18. Treats substance abuse. Outpatient services for males and females ages up to 18. Treats learning disabilities; behavior disorders; general psychosocial disorders; substance abuse; eating disorders; compulsive/addictive disorders other than substance abuse and eating disorders; post-traumatic stress disorder; thought, mood, and personality disorders. Residential or subacute services for males and females ages 6–14. Treats learning disabilities; behavior disorders; general psychosocial disorders; post-traumatic stress disorder; thought, mood, and personality disorders. Intensive family/home-based program for males and females ages up to 18. Treats learning disabilities; behavior disorders; general psychosocial disorders; compulsive/addictive disorders other than substance abuse and eating disorders; post-traumatic stress disorder; thought, mood, and personality disorders.

Contact Rosalyn Weinstein, Director of Admissions and Referrals, main address above. Phone: 215-243-2800. Fax: 215-243-2847.

Announcement Philadelphia Child Guidance Center is a comprehensive mental health organization serving children/adolescents with emotional problems. Strong focus on family; inpatient, outpatient; two apartments for families with preschool children or who require intensive treatment. Specialization in eating disorders, chronic illnesses. Affiliated with University of Pennsylvania and Children's Hospital of Philadelphia.

PHILHAVEN—A CONTINUUM OF PSYCHIATRIC SERVICES
283 South Butler Road
Mount Gretna, Pennsylvania 17064
717-273-8871; Fax: 717-270-2455

General Information Residential facility with inpatient, outpatient, and acute partial care services for children, adolescents. Patient security: entirely locked. Independent not-for-profit facility. Licensed by state of Pennsylvania. Accredited by JCAHO.

Participants Accepts: male and female children; male and female adolescents. Average stay: 23 days. Admission: one parent, all parties who share custody, court order, voluntary, depending on program. Treats autistic disorders; learning disabilities; behavior disorders; general psychosocial disorders; substance abuse; eating disorders; compulsive/addictive disorders other than substance abuse and eating disorders;

post-traumatic stress disorder; thought, mood, and personality disorders.

Contact Philhaven Services, main address above. Phone: 717-273-8871.

PHOENIX ACADEMY
23981 Sherilton Valley Road
Descanso, California 91916
619-445-0405; Fax: 619-445-9028

General Information Residential treatment/subacute facility for adolescents. Patient security: staff secured. Not-for-profit facility affiliated with Phoenix House, New York, NY. Licensed by state of California.

Participants Accepts: male and female adolescents. Average stay: 15 months. Admission: one parent, all parties who share custody, court order, voluntary, depending on program. Treats substance abuse.

Staff Staff is 60% male, 40% female.

Contact Ronald Plotts, Director, P.O. 370, Descano, CA 91916. Phone: 619-445-0405. Fax: 619-455-9028.

PHOENIX ACADEMY
35 Piermont Road, Building D
Rockleigh, New Jersey 07647
201-768-1171; Fax: 201-768-1882

General Information Drug and alcohol rehabilitation center for adolescents. 36 beds for adolescents. Patient security: staff secured. Not-for-profit facility affiliated with Phoenix House Foundation, New York, NY. Licensed by state of New Jersey.

Participants Accepts: male and female adolescents. Average stay: 1 year. Admission: one parent, all parties who share custody, court order, voluntary, depending on program. Treats substance abuse. Accepts the mobility impaired; the vision impaired; the hearing impaired; the speech impaired; non-English speaking individuals; those with a history of epilepsy.

Staff Staff is 65% male, 35% female.

Education Academic program available at no charge. Serves ages 14–18, grades 8–12. Curriculum accredited or approved by Bergen County Special Education Services. Organized sports program offered.

Contact Glenn Nichols, Director, main address above. Phone: 201-768-1171. Fax: 201-768-1882.

PHOENIX HOUSE
503 Oceanfront Walk
Venice, California 90291
310-392-3070; Fax: 310-392-9068

General Information Long-term drug rehabilitation for adolescents. 50 beds for adolescents. Open year-round. Patient security: unlocked; no runaway pursuit. Urban setting. Independent not-for-profit facility. Licensed by state of California.

Participants Accepts: male and female adolescents ages 12–17. Average stay: 1 year. Admission: one parent, court order, depending on program. Treats substance abuse. Largest number of participants from California.

Program Treatment modalities: behaviorism. Family treatment program available.

Staff Total facility staff includes 1 psychologist, 1 registered nurse, 3 MSW social workers, 3 teachers, 35 counselors, 1 occupational/recreational therapist, 1 dietician.

Facilities Single building; males and females in coeducational units. Central dining.

Education Academic program available. Serves ages 12–17, ungraded. 3 teachers on staff. Organized sports program offered.

Contact Intake Coordinator, main address above. Phone: 310-392-3070. Fax: 310-392-9068.

THE PIKE SCHOOL, INC.
P.O. Box 101
Haverhill, New Hampshire 03765
603-989-5862

General Information School for adolescents. 36 beds for adolescents. Open year-round. Patient security: unlocked; will pursue and return runaways. Rural setting. Independent not-for-profit facility. Licensed by state of New Hampshire. Accredited by State of New Hampshire Department of Health, State of New Hampshire Department of Children and Youth Services.

Participants Accepts: male adolescents ages 11–17. Average stay: 18 months. Admission: all parties who share custody, court order, school district, depending on program. Treats learning disabilities; behavior disorders; post-traumatic stress disorder. Largest number of participants from New Hampshire, Maine, Vermont.

Staff 1 full-time direct-care staff member per adolescent. Total facility staff includes 1 psychologist, 1 registered nurse, 34 MSW social workers, 6 teach-ers, 3 counselors, 1 occupational/recreational therapist, 22 other direct-care staff members. Staff is 60% male, 40% female.

Facilities Multiple buildings. Separate dining by residential unit available. Basketball courts, gymnasium, playing fields, ropes course.

Education School serves ages 11–17, grades 6–10. 6 teachers on staff. Curriculum accredited or approved by New Hampshire State Department of Education, Bureau of Special Education. Organized sports program offered.

Costs Accepts public funds.

Additional Services Residential or sub-acute services for males ages 11–17. Treats learning disabilities; behavior disorders. Wilderness/survival program for males ages 10–17. Treats learning disabilities; behavior disorders.

Contact Thomas Priston, Clinical Director, P.O. Box 299, Pike, NH 03780. Phone: 603-989-5882.

Announcement The Pike School is a nonprofit organization that provides special education and residential treatment for 36 learning disabled and emotionally handicapped boys ages 10-18. Primary goals are to enhance learning abilities, interpersonal relationship skills, and autonomous functioning. Equally important is the resolution of past trauma so that behavior, thought, and effect can be coordinated into a more rewarding daily experience. Learning strategies, cooperative learning, and experiential and vocational training are used in the academic setting. Reality therapy/cognitive restructuring is used to aid youngsters. Adaptive interpersonal behavior management system is employed to facilitate growth and development.

PINE CREST HOSPITAL
2301 North Ironwood Place
Coeur d'Alene, Idaho 83814
800-221-5008; Fax: 208-664-1805

General Information Psychiatric hospital for children, adolescents. Patient security: entirely locked. For-profit facility affiliated with Sterling Health Care Corporation, Bellevue, WA. Licensed by state of Idaho. Accredited by JCAHO.

Participants Accepts: male and female children; male and female adolescents. Admission: one parent, all parties who share custody, court order, voluntary, depending on program. Treats autistic disorders; learning disabilities; behavior disorders; general psychosocial disorders; substance abuse; eating disorders; compulsive/addictive disorders other than substance abuse and eating disorders; post-traumatic stress disorder; thought, mood, and personality disorders.

Costs Average cost: $600 per day.

Contact Jim Serratt, Admissions Director, main address above. Phone: 800-221-5008. Fax: 208-664-1805.

PINE GROVE HOSPITAL
7011 Shoup Avenue
Canoga Park, California 91307
818-348-0500

General Information Psychiatric hospital for adolescents. Patient security: partially locked. For-profit facility affiliated with National Medical Enterprises, Santa Monica, CA. Licensed by state of California. Accredited by JCAHO.

Participants Accepts: male and female adolescents. Average stay: 14 days. Admission: one parent, court order, voluntary, depending on program. Treats behavior disorders; general psychosocial disorders; substance abuse.

Additional Services Partial hospitalization for males and females ages 12 and up. Treats behavior disorders; general psychosocial disorders; substance abuse.

Contact Information and Referrals, main address above. Phone: 818-348-0500.

PINELANDS HOSPITAL
4632 Northeast Stallings Drive
P.O. Bo 1004
Nacogdoches, Texas 75963-1004
409-560-5900; Fax: 409-560-0008

General Information Psychiatric hospital for children, adolescents, adults. 10 beds for children; 12 beds for adolescents; 38 beds total. Open year-round. Patient security: entirely locked; will pursue and return runaways. Small town setting. For-profit facility affiliated with Psych Group, Inc., Wayne, PA. Licensed by state of Texas. Accredited by JCAHO.

Participants Accepts: male and female children ages 4–12; male and female adolescents ages 13–18; male and female adults ages 18 and up. Average stay: 24 days. Admission: one parent, voluntary, depending on program. Treats autistic disorders; learning disabilities; behavior disorders; general psychosocial

disorders; substance abuse; eating disorders; compulsive/addictive disorders other than substance abuse and eating disorders; post-traumatic stress disorder; thought, mood, and personality disorders. Accepts the mobility impaired; the speech impaired; those with a history of harm to themselves and others; those receiving psychotropic medication; those with a history of epilepsy. Special programs for the developmentally disabled.

Program Treatment modalities: cognitive-behavioral; Twelve Step Recovery. Family treatment program available.

Staff Total facility staff includes 6 physicians, 2 psychologists, 4 psychiatrists, 8 registered nurses, 2 MSW social workers, 2 teachers, 4 counselors, 3 occupational/recreational therapists, 1 speech pathologist, 3 therapists, 1 dietician. Staff is 60% male, 40% female.

Facilities Multiple buildings; males and females in coeducational units. Separate residential quarters for children and adolescents. Central dining (shared with adults). Basketball courts, game room, horseback riding, outdoor swimming pool, outdoor tennis courts, playing fields.

Education Academic program available at no charge. Serves ages 4–18, grades K–12. 2 teachers on staff. Curriculum accredited or approved by Texas Education Agency. Cost of educational program covered by local school district.

Costs Average cost: $750 per day. Accepts private insurance, group insurance, medicare, medicaid, Blue Cross/Blue Shield.

Additional Services Drug and alcohol rehabilitation services for males and females ages 4–18. Treats autistic disorders; learning disabilities; behavior disorders; general psychosocial disorders; substance abuse; eating disorders; compulsive/addictive disorders other than substance abuse and eating disorders; post-traumatic stress disorder; thought, mood, and personality disorders. Outpatient services for males and females ages 4–18. Treats autistic disorders; learning disabilities; behavior disorders; general psychosocial disorders; substance abuse; eating disorders; compulsive/addictive disorders other than substance abuse and eating disorders; post-traumatic stress disorder; thought, mood, and personality disorders. Residential or sub-acute services for males and females ages 4–18. Treats autistic disorders; learning disabilities; behavior disorders; general psychosocial disorders; substance abuse; eating disorders; compulsive/addictive disorders other than substance abuse and eating disorders; post-traumatic stress disorder; thought, mood, and personality disorders.

Contact Myrna Armistead, Intake Coordinator, main address above. Phone: 409-560-5900. Fax: 409-560-0008.

PINE MEADOWS SCHOOL
17359 Trinity Mountain Road
French Gulch, California 96033
916-359-2211; Fax: 916-359-2229

General Information School for adolescents. Open year-round. Patient security: staff secured. Independent not-for-profit facility. Licensed by state of California.

Participants Accepts: male and female adolescents ages 12–18. Average stay: 18 months. Admission: all parties who share custody. Treats learning disabilities; behavior disorders.

Facilities Multiple buildings.

Education School serves ages 12–18, grades 7–12. Diploma granted upon completion. Curriculum accredited or approved by California State Department of Education.

Costs Average cost: $4000 per month.

Contact David Hull, main address above. Phone: 916-359-2211. Fax: 916-359-2229.
See page 442 for full page description.

PINE RIDGE SCHOOL
1075 Williston Road
Williston, Vermont 05461
802-434-2161; Fax: 802-434-5512

General Information School for adolescents. 90 beds for adolescents. Open academic year. Small town setting. Independent not-for-profit facility. Licensed by state of Vermont.

Participants Accepts: male and female adolescents ages 13–18. Average stay: 3 years. Admission: voluntary. Treats learning disabilities. Largest number of participants from New Hampshire, Vermont, New Jersey.

Program Treatment modalities: Orton Gillingham; metacognition; reality therapy.

Staff .6 full-time direct-care staff member per adolescent. Total facility staff includes 1 registered nurse, 19 teachers, 3 counselors, 21 therapists, 7 other direct-care staff members. Staff is 27% male, 73% female.

Facilities Multiple buildings. Central dining. Gymnasium, playing fields, ropes course.

Education School serves ages 13–18, ungraded. 19 teachers on staff. Diploma granted upon completion. Tutor is available. Curriculum accredited or approved by New England Association of Schools and Colleges. Organized sports program offered.

Costs Average cost: $30,500 per year. Accepts public funds.

Additional Services Camping program for males and females ages 9–18. Treats learning disabilities. Transition program for recent high school graduates for males and females. Treats learning disabilities.

Contact Dee Goodrich, Director of Admissions, main address above. Phone: 802-434-2161.

THE PINES RESIDENTIAL TREATMENT CENTER AND THE PHOENIX AT PORTSMOUTH PSYCHIATRIC CENTER
825 Crawford Parkway
Portsmouth, Virginia 23704
804-393-0061; Fax: 804-393-1029

General Information Residential treatment/subacute facility for children, adolescents, adults. 36 beds for children; 284 beds for adolescents; 344 beds total. Open year-round. Patient security: staff secured; will pursue and return runaways. Small town setting. For-profit facility affiliated with First Hospital Corporation, Norfolk, VA. Licensed by state of Virginia. Accredited by JCAHO.

Participants Accepts: male and female children ages 5–12; male and female adolescents ages 13–17; male and female adults ages 18–21. Average stay: 548 days. Admission: all parties who share custody, court order, voluntary, depending on program. Treats learning disabilities; behavior disorders; general psychosocial disorders; substance abuse; eating disorders; compulsive/addictive disorders other than substance abuse and eating disorders; post-traumatic stress disorder; thought, mood, and personality disorders. Accepts the speech impaired; those with a history of arson; the sexually compulsive; those with a history of harm to themselves and others; those receiving psychotropic medication; those with a history of epilepsy. Special programs for the developmentally disabled. Largest number of participants from D.C., Maryland, Virginia.

Program Treatment modalities: developmental/interpersonal; cognitive-behavioral; family systems; psychophysiological. Family treatment program available.

Staff   2.2 full-time direct-care staff members per child or adolescent. Total facility staff includes 1 physician, 7 psychologists, 5 psychiatrists, 21 registered nurses, 13 practical/vocational nurses, 15 MSW social workers, 17 social workers (non-MSW), 69 teachers, 1 speech pathologist, 3 therapists, 1 dietician, 368 other direct-care staff members. Staff is 42% male, 58% female.

Facilities   Multiple buildings; males and females in separate units. Separate residential quarters for children and adolescents. Central dining (not shared with adults). Basketball courts, game room, gymnasium, outdoor swimming pool, outdoor tennis courts, playing fields, indoor and outdoor volleyball courts.

Education   Academic program available at additional cost. Serves ages 5–21, grades K–12. 69 teachers on staff. Curriculum accredited or approved by Virginia Association of Independent Special Education Facilities, CORE (multi-agency licensure). Cost of educational program covered by local school district. Organized sports program offered.

Costs   Average cost: $374 per day. Accepts private insurance, medicaid, Blue Cross/Blue Shield, public funds.

Contact   Merrill Friedman, Referral Development Director, main address above. Phone: 804-393-0061. Fax: 804-393-1029.

See page 444 for full page description.

PINEY RIDGE CENTER, INC.
1000 Hospital Road
Waynesville, Missouri 65583
314-774-5353; Fax: 314-774-2907

General Information   Residential treatment/subacute facility for adolescents. 48 beds for adolescents. Open year-round. Patient security: staff secured; will pursue and return runaways. Small town setting. For-profit facility affiliated with Family Care Services, Inc., Waynesville, MO. Accredited by JCAHO.

Participants   Accepts: male and female adolescents ages 11–18. Average stay: 150 days. Admission: one parent, all parties who share custody, court order, depending on program. Treats learning disabilities; behavior disorders; general psychosocial disorders; substance abuse; eating disorders; compulsive/addictive disorders other than substance abuse and eating disorders; post-traumatic stress disorder; thought, mood, and personality disorders. Accepts the mobility impaired; the vision impaired; the hearing impaired; the speech impaired; those with a history of arson; the sexually compulsive; those with a history of harm to themselves and others; those receiving psychotropic medication; those with a history of epilepsy. Largest number of participants from Missouri, Kansas.

Program   Treatment modalities: Twelve Step Recovery; psychodynamic; behavioral. Family treatment program available.

Staff   Total facility staff includes 1 physician, 1 psychologist, 2 psychiatrists, 4 registered nurses, 7 practical/vocational nurses, 5 MSW social workers, 3 teachers, 2 counselors, 3 occupational/recreational therapists, 1 speech pathologist, 1 dietician, 28 other direct-care staff members.

Facilities   Multiple buildings; males and females in separate units. Central dining. Basketball courts, game room, gymnasium, horseback riding, indoor swimming pool, outdoor swimming pool, outdoor tennis courts, playing fields, ropes course.

Education   Academic program available at no charge. Serves ages 11–18. 3 teachers on staff. Curriculum accredited or approved by North Central Association of Colleges and Schools.

Costs   Average cost: $435 per day.

Additional Services   Drug and alcohol rehabilitation services for males and females ages 11–18. Treats autistic disorders; learning disabilities; behavior disorders; general psychosocial disorders; substance abuse; eating disorders; compulsive/addictive disorders other than substance abuse and eating disorders; post-traumatic stress disorder; thought, mood, and personality disorders. Outpatient services for males and females ages 3 and up. Treats autistic disorders; learning disabilities; behavior disorders; general psychosocial disorders; substance abuse; eating disorders; compulsive/addictive disorders other than substance abuse and eating disorders; post-traumatic stress disorder; thought, mood, and personality disorders.

Contact   Deena Stolowski, Admission Director, P.O. Box 935 SRB, Waynesville, MO 65583. Phone: 314-774-5353. Fax: 314-774-2907.

PIONEER RANCH
4000 East Granite Dells Road
Payson, Arizona 85541
602-474-1674; Fax: 602-474-8174

General Information   Drug and alcohol rehabilitation center for adolescents. 25 beds for adolescents. Patient security: staff secured. Not-for-profit facility affiliated with Amity, Inc., Tucson, AZ. Licensed by state of Arizona.

Participants   Accepts: male adolescents. Average stay: 9 months. Admission: one parent, all parties who share custody, court order, voluntary, depending on program. Treats learning disabilities; behavior disorders; general psychosocial disorders; substance abuse; compulsive/addictive disorders other than substance abuse and eating disorders; post-traumatic stress disorder; thought, mood, and personality disorders.

Staff   Staff is 34% male, 66% female.

Costs   Average cost: $122 per day.

Contact   Val Alexander, Program Manager, P.O. Box 32200, Tucson, AZ 85751-2200. Phone: 602-474-1674. Fax: 602-474-8174.

POPLAR SPRINGS HOSPITAL
350 Poplar Drive
Petersburg, Virginia 23805
804-733-6874; Fax: 804-861-5625

General Information   Psychiatric hospital for children, adolescents, adults. 10 beds for children; 52 beds for adolescents; 100 beds total. Open year-round. Patient security: partially locked; will pursue and return runaways. Small town setting. For-profit facility affiliated with Hospital Corporation of America, Nashville, TN. Licensed by state of Virginia. Accredited by JCAHO; Health Care Financing Administration.

Participants   Accepts: male and female children ages 3–12; male and female adolescents ages 12–18; male and female adults ages 18 and up. Average stay: 12 days. Admission: one parent, all parties who share custody, court order, voluntary, depending on program. Treats learning disabilities; behavior disorders; general psychosocial disorders; substance abuse; eating disorders; compulsive/addictive disorders other than substance abuse and eating disorders; post-traumatic stress disorder; thought, mood, and personality disorders. Accepts the mobility impaired; the vision impaired; the hearing impaired; the speech impaired; those with a history of arson; the sexually compulsive; those with a history of harm to themselves and others; those receiving psychotropic medication; non-English speaking individuals; those with a history of epilepsy. Special programs for the chronically ill; the mobility impaired; the developmentally disabled; the vision impaired; the hearing impaired; the speech impaired; those with AIDS. Largest number of participants from Virginia, North Carolina.

Program   Treatment modalities: Twelve Step Recovery. Family treatment program available.

Staff   Total facility staff includes 1 psychologist, 35 registered nurses, 12 practical/vocational nurses, 4

MSW social workers, 6 social workers (non-MSW), 2 teachers, 2 counselors, 3 occupational/recreational therapists, 2 therapists, 1 dietician, 51 other direct-care staff members. Staff is 24% male, 76% female.

Facilities   Single building; males and females in co-educational units. Separate residential quarters for children and adolescents. Central dining (shared with adults). Basketball courts, gymnasium, outdoor swimming pool, outdoor tennis courts.

Education   Academic program available at no charge. Serves ages 4–18, grades K–12. 2 teachers on staff. Curriculum accredited or approved by State Department of Education.

Costs   Accepts private insurance, group insurance, medicare, Blue Cross/Blue Shield, public funds.

Additional Services   Drug and alcohol rehabilitation services for males and females ages 12 and up. Treats learning disabilities; behavior disorders; general psychosocial disorders; eating disorders; compulsive/addictive disorders other than substance abuse and eating disorders; post-traumatic stress disorder; thought, mood, and personality disorders. Residential or sub-acute services for males and females ages 11–21. Treats learning disabilities; behavior disorders; general psychosocial disorders; substance abuse; eating disorders; compulsive/addictive disorders other than substance abuse and eating disorders; post-traumatic stress disorder; thought, mood, and personality disorders.

Contact   David Nissen, Director of Respond, main address above. Phone: 804-733-6874. Fax: 804-861-5625.

PORTER-STARKE SERVICE, INC. AND VALE PARK PSYCHIATRIC HOSPITAL
701 Wall Street
Valparaiso, Indiana 46383
219-464-8541; Fax: 219-462-3975

General Information   Psychiatric hospital for children, adolescents, adults. 13 beds for children; 12 beds for adolescents; 56 beds total. Open year-round. Patient security: partially locked; will pursue and return runaways. Suburban setting. Independent not-for-profit facility. Licensed by state of Indiana. Accredited by JCAHO.

Participants   Accepts: male and female children ages 10–13; male and female adolescents ages 13–18; male and female adults ages 18 and up. Average stay: 21 days. Admission: all parties who share custody, court order, depending on program. Treats learning disabilities; behavior disorders; general psychosocial disorders; substance abuse; eating disorders; compulsive/addictive disorders other than substance abuse and eating disorders; post-traumatic stress disorder; thought, mood, and personality disorders. Accepts the vision impaired; the hearing impaired; the speech impaired; those with a history of harm to themselves and others; those receiving psychotropic medication; non-English speaking individuals; those with a history of epilepsy. Special programs for the chronically ill. Largest number of participants from Illinois.

Program Treatment modalities: psychodynamic; Twelve Step Recovery; reality therapy; rational emotive therapy. Family treatment program available.

Staff Total facility staff includes 5 physicians, 3 psychologists, 3 psychiatrists, 35 registered nurses, 4 practical/vocational nurses, 14 MSW social workers, 3 teachers, 5 occupational/recreational therapists, 1 dietician, 75 other direct-care staff members. Staff is 35% male, 65% female.

Facilities Multiple buildings; males and females in coeducational units. Separate residential quarters for children and adolescents. Separate dining by residential unit available. Game room, gymnasium, ropes course.

Education Academic program available at no charge. Serves ages 10–18, ungraded. 3 teachers on staff.

Costs Average cost: $13,650 per stay. Accepts private insurance, group insurance, medicare, medicaid, Blue Cross/Blue Shield, public funds.

Additional Services Outpatient services for males and females. Treats learning disabilities; behavior disorders; general psychosocial disorders; eating disorders; compulsive/addictive disorders other than substance abuse and eating disorders; post-traumatic stress disorder; thought, mood, and personality disorders. Challenge (Ropes) Program for males and females ages 10 and up. Treats learning disabilities; behavior disorders; general psychosocial disorders; substance abuse; eating disorders; compulsive/addictive disorders other than substance abuse and eating disorders; post-traumatic stress disorder; thought, mood, and personality disorders.

Contact Mary Beth Schultz, Director of Admissions, main address above. Phone: 219-464-8541. Fax: 219-465-1295.

PORTLAND ADVENTIST MEDICAL CENTER ADOLESCENT TREATMENT PROGRAM
10123 Southeast Market Street
Portland, Oregon 97216
503-254-5437; Fax: 503-251-6318

General Information General hospital for adolescents. 12 beds for adolescents. Patient security: staff secured. Not-for-profit facility affiliated with Adventist Health Systems West, Sacramento, CA. Licensed by state of Oregon. Accredited by JCAHO.

Participants Accepts: male and female adolescents. Average stay: 7 days. Admission: one parent, court order, voluntary, depending on program. Treats autistic disorders; learning disabilities; behavior disorders; general psychosocial disorders; substance abuse; eating disorders; post-traumatic stress disorder; thought, mood, and personality disorders.

Staff Staff is 40% male, 60% female.

Costs Average cost: $675 per day.

Contact John Custer, Administrative Director, main address above. Phone: 503-254-5437. Fax: 503-251-6318.

PRAIRIE VIEW, INC.
1901 East 1st Street
Newton, Kansas 67114
316-283-2400; Fax: 316-283-6364

General Information Psychiatric hospital for adolescents, adults. 30 beds for adolescents. Open year-round. Patient security: unlocked; will pursue and return runaways. Small town setting. Independent not-for-profit facility. Licensed by state of Kansas. Accredited by JCAHO.

Participants Accepts: male and female adolescents ages 13–18; male and female adults ages 18 and up. Average stay: 30 days. Admission: one parent, court order, depending on program. Treats autistic disorders; learning disabilities; behavior disorders; general psychosocial disorders; substance abuse; eating disorders; compulsive/addictive disorders other than substance abuse and eating disorders; post-traumatic stress disorder; thought, mood, and personality disorders. Accepts those with a history of arson; the sexually compulsive; those with a history of harm to themselves and others; those with a history of epilepsy. Largest number of participants from Kansas.

Program Treatment modalities: psychodynamic; cognitive-behavioral; Twelve Step Recovery.

Staff .2 full-time direct-care staff member per adolescent. Total facility staff includes 2 psychologists, 3 psychiatrists, 14 registered nurses, 3 MSW social workers, 3 teachers, 2 counselors, 5 occupational/recreational therapists, 37 other direct-care staff members. Staff is 42% male, 58% female.

Facilities Multiple buildings; males and females in coeducational units. Residential quarters shared with adults. Central dining (shared with adults). Basketball courts, game room, gymnasium.

Education Academic program available at no charge. Serves ages 9–19, ungraded. 3 teachers on staff. Curriculum accredited or approved by State of Kansas Special Purpose Schools.

Costs Average cost: $550 per day. Accepts private insurance, group insurance, medicare, medicaid, Blue Cross/Blue Shield, public funds.

Additional Services Drug and alcohol rehabilitation services for males and females ages 12 and up. Treats autistic disorders; learning disabilities; behavior disorders; general psychosocial disorders; substance abuse; eating disorders; compulsive/addictive disorders other than substance abuse and eating disorders; post-traumatic stress disorder; thought, mood, and personality disorders. Outpatient services for males and females ages 3 and up. Treats autistic disorders; learning disabilities; behavior disorders; general psychosocial disorders; substance abuse; eating disorders; compulsive/addictive disorders other than substance abuse and eating disorders; post-traumatic stress disorder; thought, mood, and personality disorders. Residential or sub-acute services for males and females ages 12–18. Treats autistic disorders; learning disabilities; behavior disorders; general psychosocial disorders; substance abuse; eating disorders; compulsive/addictive disorders other than substance abuse and eating disorders; post-traumatic stress disorder; thought, mood, and personality disorders.

Contact Melva Caldwell, Director of Admissions, main address above. Phone: 316-283-2400. Fax: 316-283-6364.

PRESSLEY RIDGE SCHOOL AT OHIOPYLE
Box 25
Ohiopyle, Pennsylvania 15470
412-329-8300 Ext. 01

General Information Residential treatment and outdoor camping for adolescents. 60 beds for adolescents. Open year-round. Patient security: staff secured; will pursue and return runaways. Rural setting. Not-for-profit facility affiliated with Pressley Ridge Schools, Pittsburgh, PA. Licensed by state of Pennsylvania. Accredited by Department of Public Welfare.

Participants Accepts: male adolescents ages 10–16. Average stay: 1 year. Admission: all parties who share custody, court order, depending on program. Treats learning disabilities; behavior disorders; general psychosocial disorders; thought, mood, and personality disorders. Accepts those receiving psychotropic medication.

Program Family treatment program available.

Staff .6 full-time direct-care staff member per adolescent. Total facility staff includes 1 psychologist, 1 psychiatrist, 1 practical/vocational nurse, 6 social workers (non-MSW), 3 teachers, 12 counselors, 9 other direct-care staff members. Staff is 85% male, 15% female.

Facilities Multiple buildings. Central dining. Outdoor swimming pool, playing fields.

Education Academic program available at no charge. Serves ages 10–16, ungraded. 3 teachers on staff. Curriculum accredited or approved by Middle States Association of Colleges and Schools.

Costs Average cost: $110 per stay. Accepts medicaid, public funds.

Contact Scot L. Thomas, Coordinator of Family Services, main address above. Phone: 412-329-8300 Ext. 01.

PRIMARY CHILDREN'S RESIDENTIAL TREATMENT CENTER
497 Colorow Way
Salt Lake City, Utah 84010
801-588-4980; Fax: 801-588-4960

General Information Residential treatment/subacute facility for children. 33 beds for children. Open year-round. Patient security: partially locked; will pursue and return runaways. Suburban setting. Not-for-profit facility affiliated with Intermountain Health Care Corporation, Salt Lake City, UT. Licensed by state of Utah. Accredited by JCAHO; Civilian Health and Medical Program of the Uniformed Services.

Participants Accepts: male and female children ages 6–13. Average stay: 11 months. Treats autistic disorders; learning disabilities; behavior disorders; general psychosocial disorders; post-traumatic stress disorder; thought, mood, and personality disorders. Accepts the speech impaired; the sexually compulsive; those with a history of harm to themselves and others; those receiving psychotropic medication; those with a history of epilepsy. Special programs for the speech impaired. Largest number of participants from Utah, Nevada, Idaho.

Program   Treatment modalities: behavioral; cognitive. Family treatment program available.

Staff   Total facility staff includes 1 physician, 1 psychologist, 2 psychiatrists, 2 registered nurses, 6 MSW social workers, 2 teachers, 36 counselors, 1 occupational/recreational therapist, 1 speech pathologist, 11 other direct-care staff members. Staff is 52% male, 48% female.

Facilities   Single building; males and females in co-educational units. Separate dining by residential unit available. Basketball courts, game room, gymnasium, playing fields, playground.

Education   Academic program available at no charge. Serves ages 6–12, grades K–6. 2 teachers on staff. Cost of educational program covered by local school district.

Costs   Average cost: $190 per day. Accepts private insurance, group insurance, medicaid, Blue Cross/Blue Shield, public funds.

Contact   James L. Anderson, Administrative Director, main address above. Phone: 801-588-4980. Fax: 801-588-4960.

PRIMARY CHILDREN'S RESIDENTIAL TREATMENT PROGRAM
5770 South, 1500 West
Salt Lake City, Utah 84123
801-262-6199; Fax: 801-265-3065

General Information   Residential treatment/subacute facility for children. 12 beds for children. Open year-round. Patient security: staff secured; will pursue and return runaways. Suburban setting. Not-for-profit facility affiliated with Intermountain Health Care Corporation, Salt Lake City, UT. Operated by Primary Children's Medical Center- Department of Psychiatry, Salt Lake City, UT. Licensed by state of Utah. Accredited by JCAHO.

Participants   Accepts: male children ages 5–11. Average stay: 225 days. Admission: one parent, court order, depending on program. Treats learning disabilities; behavior disorders; post-traumatic stress disorder; thought, mood, and personality disorders. Accepts the sexually compulsive; those with a history of harm to themselves and others; those receiving psychotropic medication. Special programs for the developmentally disabled.

Program   Family treatment program available.

Staff   .6 full-time direct-care staff member per child. Total facility staff includes 1 psychologist, 1 psychiatrist, 4 registered nurses, 1 practical/vocational nurse, 2 MSW social workers, 1 teacher, 1 physical therapist, 1 occupational/recreational therapist, 1 dietician, 4 other direct-care staff members. Staff is 50% male, 50% female.

Facilities   Multiple buildings; males and females in separate units. Separate dining by residential unit available. Basketball courts, game room, gymnasium, playing fields.

Education   Academic program available at no charge. Serves ages 5–11, grades K–4. 1 teacher on staff. Curriculum accredited or approved by Salt Lake School District.

Costs   Accepts private insurance, group insurance, medicare, medicaid, Blue Cross/Blue Shield, public funds.

Additional Services   Drug and alcohol rehabilitation services for males and females ages 11–17. Treats behavior disorders; general psychosocial disorders; substance abuse; eating disorders; compulsive/addictive disorders other than substance abuse and eating disorders; post-traumatic stress disorder; thought, mood, and personality disorders. Outpatient services for males and females ages 5 and up. Treats behavior disorders; general psychosocial disorders; substance abuse; eating disorders; compulsive/addictive disorders other than substance abuse and eating disorders; post-traumatic stress disorder; thought, mood, and personality disorders.

Contact   Ron Jackson, Intake Director, main address above. Phone: 801-262-6199. Fax: 801-265-3065.

PROCTOR COMMUNITY HOSPITAL
5409 North Knoxville Avenue
Peoria, Illinois 61614
309-691-1000; Fax: 309-691-4543

General Information   General hospital for adolescents. 10 beds for adolescents. Patient security: partially locked. Independent not-for-profit facility. Licensed by state of Illinois. Accredited by JCAHO.

Participants   Accepts: male and female adolescents. Average stay: 5 weeks. Admission: one parent, all parties who share custody, court order, voluntary, depending on program. Treats substance abuse. Accepts the mobility impaired; the vision impaired; the hearing impaired; the speech impaired; those with a history of arson; the sexually compulsive; those with a history of harm to themselves and others; those receiving psychotropic medication; those with a history of epilepsy.

Staff   Staff is 60% male, 40% female.

Costs   Average cost: $265 per day.

Contact   Eric Zehr, Interim Executive Director, main address above. Phone: 309-691-1000. Fax: 309-691-4543.

PROJECT REBOUND
98 Cumberland Street
Bangor, Maine 04401
207-941-1600

General Information   Residential treatment/subacute facility for adolescents. 12 beds for adolescents. Patient security: staff secured. Not-for-profit facility affiliated with Wellspring, Inc., Bangor, ME. Licensed by state of Maine.

Participants   Accepts: male adolescents. Average stay: 4 months. Admission: one parent, voluntary, depending on program. Treats substance abuse.

Staff   .7 full-time direct-care staff member per adolescent. Staff is 25% male, 75% female.

Contact   Laura Richards, Program Manager, main address above. Phone: 207-941-1600.

PROJECT REHAB—SHILOH FAMILY
750 Cherry Street, SE
Grand Rapids, Michigan 49503
616-774-9536

General Information   Drug and alcohol rehabilitation center for adolescents. Patient security: staff secured. Independent not-for-profit facility. Licensed by state of Michigan. Accredited by JCAHO.

Participants   Accepts: male and female adolescents. Average stay: 6 months. Admission: one parent, all parties who share custody, court order, voluntary, depending on program. Treats substance abuse. Accepts the mobility impaired; the vision impaired; the hearing impaired; the speech impaired; those with a history of arson; the sexually compulsive; those with a history of harm to themselves and others; those receiving psychotropic medication; those with a history of epilepsy.

Contact   Donna Maas, Operations Supervisor, main address above. Phone: 616-774-9536.

PROVIDENCE HOSPITAL FIRST STEP
1233 Main Street
Holyoke, Massachusetts 01040
413-539-2818

General Information   Hospital-based detox short-term intensive treatment program for adolescents. 26 beds for adolescents. Patient security: staff secured. Not-for-profit facility affiliated with Sisters of Providence, Holyoke, MA. Licensed by state of Massachusetts. Accredited by JCAHO.

Participants   Accepts: male and female adolescents. Average stay: 13 days. Admission: one parent, court order, voluntary, depending on program. Treats substance abuse. Accepts the mobility impaired; those with a history of arson; those receiving psychotropic medication; non-English speaking individuals; those with a history of epilepsy.

Costs   Average cost: $350 per day.

Contact   Ralph Samuelsen, Director of Adolescent Programs, main address above. Phone: 413-539-2818.

PROVIDENCE HOSPITAL HONOR HOUSE
1233 Main Street
Holyoke, Massachusetts 01040
413-533-4500

General Information   Residential treatment/subacute facility for adolescents. 20 beds for adolescents. Patient security: staff secured. Not-for-profit facility affiliated with Sisters of Providence, Holyoke, MA. Licensed by state of Massachusetts. Accredited by JCAHO.

Participants   Accepts: male and female adolescents. Average stay: 3 months. Admission: one parent, court order, voluntary, depending on program. Treats substance abuse.

Costs   Average cost: $91 per day.

Contact   Ralph Samuelsen, Director of Adolescent Programs, main address above. Phone: 413-539-2818.

PROVO CANYON SCHOOL
4501 North University Avenue
P.O. Box 1441
Provo, Utah 84603
800-848-9819; Fax: 801-227-2095

General Information Residential treatment/subacute facility for adolescents. 210 beds for adolescents. Open year-round. Patient security: partially locked; will pursue and return runaways. Small town setting. For-profit facility affiliated with Charter Medical Corporation, Macon, GA. Licensed by state of Utah. Accredited by JCAHO.

Participants Accepts: male and female adolescents ages 12–18. Average stay: 330 days. Admission: one parent, all parties who share custody, court order, depending on program. Treats learning disabilities; behavior disorders; general psychosocial disorders; substance abuse; post-traumatic stress disorder; thought, mood, and personality disorders. Accepts those receiving psychotropic medication. Largest number of participants from California, Texas, Washington.

Program Treatment modalities: Twelve Step Recovery; reality therapy; hypnotherapy; Gestalt therapy. Family treatment program available.

Staff .7 full-time direct-care staff member per adolescent. Total facility staff includes 3 physicians, 1 psychologist, 2 psychiatrists, 7 registered nurses, 6 practical/vocational nurses, 2 MSW social workers, 18 social workers (non-MSW), 21 teachers, 64 counselors, 4 occupational/recreational therapists, 1 dietician, 8 other direct-care staff members. Staff is 56% male, 44% female.

Facilities Multiple buildings; males and females in separate units. Basketball courts, game room, gymnasium, indoor swimming pool, outdoor swimming pool, outdoor tennis courts, playing fields, ropes course, bowling alley.

Education Academic program available. Serves ages 12–18, grades 7–12. 21 teachers on staff. Curriculum accredited or approved by Northwest Association of Schools and Colleges. Organized sports program offered.

Costs Accepts private insurance, group insurance, medicaid, Blue Cross/Blue Shield, public funds.

Contact Janett Benson, Admissions Counselor, main address above. Phone: 800-848-9819. Fax: 801-227-2095.
See page 446 for full page description.

QUEST
23000 Mountain View Road
Boonville, California 95415
707-895-2613

General Information Boarding school and camp for children, adolescents. 10 beds for children; 10 beds for adolescents; 20 beds total. Open academic year. Patient security: unlocked; will pursue and return runaways. Rural setting. Independent for-profit facility. Licensed by state of California.

Participants Accepts: male children; male adolescents. Average stay: 2 years. Admission: one parent, all parties who share custody, court order, depending on program. Treats learning disabilities; behavior disorders. Accepts the hearing impaired; the speech impaired; non-English speaking individuals. Largest number of participants from California, Florida.

Staff .4 full-time direct-care staff member per child or adolescent. Total facility staff includes 5 teachers, 1 therapist. Staff is 67% male, 33% female.

Facilities Multiple buildings. Central dining (shared with adults). Basketball courts, game room, outdoor swimming pool, playing fields.

Education School serves ages 6–18, grades 1–8. 5 teachers on staff. Curriculum is college-preparatory; diploma granted upon completion.

Costs Average cost: $21,400 per year. Accepts private insurance.

Contact Robin C. Harris, Director, P.O. Box 400, Boonville, CA 95415. Phone: 707-895-2613.
See page 448 for full page description.

QUINCO BEHAVIORAL HEALTH SYSTEMS
2075 Lincoln Park Drive
Columbus, Indiana 47201
812-379-2341; Fax: 812-376-4875

General Information Psychiatric hospital for adolescents. 12 beds for adolescents. Patient security: entirely locked. Independent not-for-profit facility. Licensed by state of Indiana. Accredited by JCAHO.

Participants Accepts: male and female adolescents. Average stay: 2 weeks. Admission: one parent, all parties who share custody, court order, voluntary, depending on program. Treats autistic disorders; learning disabilities; behavior disorders; general psychosocial disorders; substance abuse; eating disorders; compulsive/addictive disorders other than substance abuse and eating disorders; post-traumatic stress disorder; thought, mood, and personality disorders.

Costs   Average cost: $500 per day.

Contact   Robert Siegmann, Director of Hospital Services, main address above. Phone: 812-379-2341. Fax: 812-376-4875.

RAMAPO ANCHORAGE CAMP
P.O. Box 266
Rhinebeck, New York 12572
914-876-4273

General Information   Camp for children. 160 beds for children. Open summer. Rural setting. Independent not-for-profit facility. Licensed by state of New York. Accredited by American Camping Association.

Participants   Accepts: male and female children. Average stay: 27 days. Treats learning disabilities; behavior disorders. Accepts those with learning disabilities; those with behavior disorders.

Staff   1 full-time direct-care staff member per child. Total facility staff includes 2 registered nurses, 2 MSW social workers, 120 counselors, 30 other direct-care staff members.

Facilities   Multiple buildings; males and females in separate units. Central dining. Basketball courts, game room, gymnasium, playing fields, ropes course, lake for boating/swimming, hiking trails, computer center.

Education   Academic program available at no charge. Academic program is ungraded. Organized sports program offered.

Contact   Michael Kunin, Assistant Director, main address above. Phone: 914-876-4273.

RAPHA ADOLESCENT TREATMENT PROGRAM
2709 Hospital Boulevard
Grand Prairie, Texas 75051
214-641-5300; Fax: 214-641-5372

General Information   General hospital for adolescents. 24 beds for adolescents. Open year-round. Patient security: entirely locked. Suburban setting. For-profit facility affiliated with RAPHA, Inc., Houston, TX. Licensed by state of Texas. Accredited by JCAHO.

Participants   Accepts: male and female adolescents ages 12–18. Average stay: 29 days. Admission: one

parent, all parties who share custody, court order, depending on program. Treats autistic disorders; learning disabilities; behavior disorders; general psychosocial disorders; substance abuse; eating disorders; compulsive/addictive disorders other than substance abuse and eating disorders; post-traumatic stress disorder; thought, mood, and personality disorders. Largest number of participants from Texas.

Program   Treatment modalities: Christ-centered program; psychodynamic; Twelve Step Recovery with Christian perspective; individual/family/group psychotherapy. Family treatment program available.

Staff   .4 full-time direct-care staff member per adolescent. Total facility staff includes 3 psychologists, 2 psychiatrists, 8 registered nurses, 6 practical/vocational nurses, 2 MSW social workers, 2 teachers, 3 counselors, 2 occupational/recreational therapists, 1 dietician, 25 other direct-care staff members. Staff is 50% male, 50% female.

Facilities   Single building; males and females in co-educational units. Separate dining by residential unit available. Basketball courts, game room, gymnasium, indoor swimming pool, playing fields, ropes course.

Education   Academic program available at no charge. Serves ages 12–18, grades 7–12. 2 teachers on staff. Curriculum accredited or approved by Arlington Independent School District. Cost of educational program covered by local school district.

Costs   Average cost: $835 per day. Accepts private insurance, group insurance, Blue Cross/Blue Shield.

Contact   Don Avezedo, Program Director, main address above. Phone: 214-641-5300. Fax: 214-641-5372.

RAPID CITY REGIONAL HOSPITAL— ADDICTION RECOVERY CENTER
915 Mountain View Road
Rapid City, South Dakota 57702
605-399-7200; Fax: 605-399-7018

General Information   Residential treatment/subacute facility for adolescents. Patient security: staff secured. Not-for-profit facility affiliated with Rapid City Regional Hospital, Rapid City, SD. Licensed by state of South Dakota. Accredited by JCAHO.

Participants   Accepts: male and female adolescents. Average stay: 42 days. Admission: one parent, all parties who share custody, court order, voluntary, depending on program. Treats substance abuse. Accepts the mobility impaired; the hearing impaired; those with a history of epilepsy.

Staff   Staff is 50% male, 50% female.

Costs   Average cost: $10,750 per stay.

Contact   Sheri Settle, Clinical Coordinator, main address above. Phone: 605-399-7200. Fax: 605-399-7018.

RECOVERY SERVICES COUNCIL, INC.— RECOVERING ADOLESCENT PROGRAM
1642 West Douglas
Wichita, Kansas 67203
316-265-8562; Fax: 316-265-4304

General Information   Residential treatment/subacute facility for adolescents. Patient security: staff secured. Independent not-for-profit facility. Licensed by state of Kansas.

Participants   Accepts: male and female adolescents. Average stay: 45 days. Admission: one parent, court order, voluntary, depending on program. Treats learning disabilities; behavior disorders; general psychosocial disorders; substance abuse; eating disorders; compulsive/addictive disorders other than substance abuse and eating disorders; post-traumatic stress disorder; thought, mood, and personality disorders.

Staff   Staff is 70% male, 30% female.

Costs   Average cost: $100 per day.

Contact   Jack Hanson, Program Director, main address above. Phone: 316-265-8562. Fax: 316-265-4304.

RED WILLOW ADOLESCENT CHEMICAL DEPENDENCY TREATMENT, INC.
4400 Southwest 110th Avenue
Beaverton, Oregon 97005
503-792-3697; Fax: 503-526-8657

General Information   Drug and alcohol rehabilitation center for adolescents. 35 beds for adolescents. Patient security: staff secured. Independent for-profit facility. Licensed by state of Oregon. Accredited by Commission on Accreditation of Rehabilitation Facilities.

Participants   Accepts: male and female adolescents. Average stay: 45 days. Admission: one parent, all parties who share custody, court order, voluntary, depending on program. Treats substance abuse. Accepts the mobility impaired; the vision impaired; the speech impaired; those with a history of arson; those receiving psychotropic medication.

Staff   Staff is 40% male, 60% female.

Costs   Average cost: $185 per day.

Additional Services   Outpatient services for males and females ages 12 and up. Treats substance abuse.

Contact   Kim Brucks, Program Director, P.O. Box 25751, Portland, OR 97225. Phone: 503-792-3697. Fax: 503-526-8657.

REED ACADEMY
1 Winch Street
Framingham, Massachusetts 01701
508-877-1222; Fax: 508-877-7477

General Information   School for children. 23 beds for children. Open year-round. Patient security: staff secured; will pursue and return runaways. Suburban setting. Independent not-for-profit facility. Licensed by state of Massachusetts. Accredited by Massachusetts Department of Social Services; Office for Children.

Participants   Accepts: male and female children ages 7–14. Average stay: 720 days. Admission: school referral, Department of Social Services, state agencies. Treats learning disabilities; behavior disorders; general psychosocial disorders; post-traumatic stress disorder; thought, mood, and personality disorders. Accepts the vision impaired; the hearing impaired; the speech impaired; those receiving psychotropic medication; those with a history of epilepsy. Special programs for the developmentally disabled. Largest number of participants from Massachusetts.

Program   Treatment modalities: milieu therapy; group therapy; educational family counseling. Family treatment program available.

Staff   .9 full-time direct-care staff member per child. Total facility staff includes 2 psychologists, 1 practical/vocational nurse, 3 social workers (non-MSW), 7 teachers, 5 counselors, 1 speech pathologist. Staff is 10% male, 90% female.

Facilities   Single building; males and females in separate units. Central dining. Basketball courts, gymnasium, playing fields.

Education   School serves ages 7–14, ungraded. 7 teachers on staff. Curriculum accredited or approved by Massachusetts Department of Education.

Costs   Average cost: $43,149 per year. Accepts public funds.

Additional Services   Camping program for males and females ages 5–14. Treats learning disabilities;

behavior disorders; general psychosocial disorders; post-traumatic stress disorder; thought, mood, and personality disorders.

Contact Diane Engel, Executive Secretary, main address above. Phone: 508-877-1222. Fax: 508-877-7477.

THE REGENT HOSPITAL
425 East 61st Street
New York, New York 10021
212-935-3400; Fax: 212-891-8690

General Information Psychiatric hospital for adolescents, adults. 20 beds for adolescents. Open year-round. Patient security: partially locked; no runaway pursuit. Urban setting. Independent for-profit facility. Licensed by state of New York. Accredited by JCAHO.

Participants Accepts: male and female adolescents ages 13–22; male and female adults. Average stay: 30 days. Admission: one parent, legal guardian, depending on program. Treats learning disabilities; behavior disorders; general psychosocial disorders; substance abuse; eating disorders; compulsive/addictive disorders other than substance abuse and eating disorders; post-traumatic stress disorder; thought, mood, and personality disorders. Accepts the vision impaired; the hearing impaired; the speech impaired; those with a history of arson; those with a history of harm to themselves and others; those receiving psychotropic medication; non-English speaking individuals; those with a history of epilepsy.

Program Treatment modalities: psychodynamic; Twelve Step Recovery; cognitive-behavioral; psycho-educational. Family treatment program available.

Staff Total facility staff includes 1 physician, 2 psychologists, 4 psychiatrists, 5 MSW social workers, 12 social workers (non-MSW), 2 teachers, 20 counselors, 8 occupational/recreational therapists, 1 therapist.

Facilities Single building; males and females in co-educational units. Separate residential quarters for adolescents. Central dining (not shared with adults).

Education Academic program available. Serves ages 12–18, ungraded. 2 teachers on staff. Curriculum accredited or approved by New York City Board of Education.

Costs Average cost: $1778 per stay. Accepts private insurance, group insurance.

Additional Services Outpatient services for males and females ages 13 and up. Treats behavior disorders; general psychosocial disorders; substance abuse.

Contact Paula Smith, Community Relations Director/Office Manager, main address above. Phone: 212-891-8622. Fax: 212-891-8690.

REGIONAL MENTAL HEALTH CLINIC
15565 Northland Drive, Suite 903E
Southfield, Michigan 48075
313-557-1401

General Information Drug and alcohol rehabilitation center for children, adolescents, adults. Open year-round. Patient security: unlocked; will pursue and return runaways. Suburban setting. Independent for-profit facility. Licensed by state of Michigan. Accredited by JCAHO.

Participants Accepts: male and female children ages 4–10; male and female adolescents ages 10–16; male and female adults. Admission: all parties who share custody, voluntary, depending on program. Treats learning disabilities; behavior disorders; substance abuse; eating disorders; compulsive/addictive disorders other than substance abuse and eating disorders; post-traumatic stress disorder; thought, mood, and personality disorders. Accepts the mobility impaired; the speech impaired; those with a history of arson; the sexually compulsive; those with a history of harm to themselves and others; those receiving psychotropic medication; those with a history of epilepsy. Special programs for the developmentally disabled.

Program Treatment modalities: rational emotive therapy; Michano Family; Twelve Step Recovery. Family treatment program available.

Staff .1 full-time direct-care staff member per child or adolescent. Total facility staff includes 7 psychologists, 2 psychiatrists, 3 MSW social workers. Staff is 42% male, 58% female.

Facilities Single building.

Costs Accepts private insurance, group insurance, medicare, medicaid, Blue Cross/Blue Shield.

Additional Services Outpatient services for males and females ages 4 and up. Treats learning disabilities; behavior disorders; general psychosocial disorders; substance abuse; eating disorders; compulsive/addictive disorders other than substance abuse and eating disorders; post-traumatic stress disorder; thought, mood, and personality disorders.

Contact Jane Hakes, Clinical Director, main address above. Phone: 313-557-1401.

REHABILITATION INSTITUTE OF CHICAGO
345 East Superior Street
Chicago, Illinois 60611
312-908-6930; Fax: 312-908-4300

General Information Rehabilitation hospital for children, adolescents, adults. Open year-round. Patient security: unlocked; no runaway pursuit. Urban setting. Independent not-for-profit facility. Licensed by state of Illinois. Accredited by JCAHO; Commission on Accreditation of Rehabilitation Facilities.

Participants Accepts: male and female children ages up to 12; male and female adolescents ages 12–21; male and female adults ages 21 and up. Average stay: 29 days. Admission: one parent, all parties who share custody, voluntary, physician, social worker referral, depending on program. Treats learning disabilities; behavior disorders. Accepts the mobility impaired; the speech impaired. Special programs for the mobility impaired; the speech impaired; amputees, those with brain and spinal cord injuries, cerebral palsy, neuromuscular disease, spina bifida.

Program Treatment modalities: neurodevelopmental treatment; sensory integration. Family treatment program available.

Staff Total facility staff includes 19 physicians, 13 psychologists, 92 registered nurses, 11 practical/vocational nurses, 12 MSW social workers, 3 teachers, 8 counselors, 57 physical therapists, 51 occupational/recreational therapists, 19 speech pathologists, 31 therapists, 2 dieticians, 296 other direct-care staff members.

Facilities Single building; males and females in coeducational units. Residential quarters shared with adults. Central dining (shared with adults). Game room, weight lifting.

Education Academic program available at no charge. Serves grades K–12. 3 teachers on staff. Curriculum accredited or approved by Chicago Board of Education. Cost of educational program covered by local school district. Organized sports program offered.

Costs Average cost: $900 per day. Accepts private insurance, group insurance, medicare, medicaid, Blue Cross/Blue Shield, public funds.

Additional Services Outpatient services for males and females. Treats learning disabilities; behavior disorders. Physical rehabilitation programs for males and females. Treats learning disabilities; behavior disorders.

Contact Richard Fitts, Director of Admitting and Referral Relations, main address above. Phone: 312-908-6066. Fax: 312-908-1369.

THE REHABILITATION INSTITUTE OF PITTSBURGH
6301 Northumberland Street
Pittsburgh, Pennsylvania 15217
412-521-9000; Fax: 412-521-0570

General Information Rehabilitation facility for children, adolescents. Patient security: staff secured. Independent not-for-profit facility. Licensed by state of Pennsylvania. Accredited by JCAHO; Commission on Accreditation of Rehabilitation Facilities.

Participants Accepts: male and female children; male and female adolescents. Average stay: 30 days. Admission: one parent, all parties who share custody, voluntary, depending on program. Treats autistic disorders; behavior disorders; general psychosocial disorders; eating disorders.

Costs Average cost: $48,000 per stay.

Contact Bea Maier, PhD, Program Director, main address above. Phone: 412-521-9000 Ext. 228. Fax: 412-521-0570.

RENAISSANCE CENTER FOR ADDICTIONS
600 East Boulevard
Elkhart, Indiana 46514
219-523-3370; Fax: 219-523-3133

General Information General hospital for children, adolescents. Patient security: staff secured. Independent not-for-profit facility. Licensed by state of Indiana. Accredited by JCAHO.

Participants Accepts: male and female children; male and female adolescents. Average stay: 9 days. Admission: one parent, all parties who share custody, court order, voluntary, depending on program. Treats learning disabilities; behavior disorders; general psychosocial disorders; substance abuse; eating disorders; compulsive/addictive disorders other than substance abuse and eating disorders; post-traumatic stress disorder; thought, mood, and personality disorders.

Staff Staff is 28% male, 72% female.

Costs Average cost: $559 per day.

Additional Services Outpatient services for males and females ages 5 and up. Treats learning disabilities; behavior disorders; general psychosocial disorders; substance abuse; eating disorders; compulsive/addictive disorders other than substance abuse and eating disorders; post-traumatic stress disorder; thought, mood, and personality disorders.

Contact Dick Dunn, Assistant Director, P.O. Box 1329, Elkhart, IN 46515-1329. Phone: 219-523-3370. Fax: 219-523-3133.

Contact Theresa Walsh, Executive Director, main address above. Phone: 215-536-9070. Fax: 215-536-4788.

RENEWAL CENTERS
2705 Old Bethlehem Pike
P.O. Box 597
Quakertown, Pennsylvania 19070
215-536-9070; Fax: 215-536-4788

General Information Drug and alcohol rehabilitation center for adolescents. 26 beds for adolescents. Open year-round. Patient security: staff secured; will pursue and return runaways. Rural setting. Not-for-profit facility affiliated with Lifequest, Quakertown, PA. Licensed by state of Pennsylvania. Accredited by JCAHO.

Participants Accepts: male and female adolescents ages 12–18. Average stay: 28 days. Admission: one parent, all parties who share custody, court order, voluntary, depending on program. Treats behavior disorders; general psychosocial disorders; substance abuse; post-traumatic stress disorder; thought, mood, and personality disorders. Accepts the mobility impaired; the hearing impaired; the speech impaired; those receiving psychotropic medication; those with a history of epilepsy. Special programs for the developmentally disabled. Largest number of participants from Pennsylvania, New Jersey.

Program Treatment modalities: Twelve Step Recovery; multi/family/group therapy; assessment; psychoeducational. Family treatment program available.

Staff Total facility staff includes 4 physicians, 1 psychologist, 1 psychiatrist, 6 registered nurses, 2 MSW social workers, 1 social worker (non-MSW), 3 teachers, 4 counselors, 1 occupational/recreational therapist, 1 therapist, 1 dietician, 8 other direct-care staff members. Staff is 45% male, 55% female.

Facilities Single building; males and females in separate units. Basketball courts, game room.

Education Academic program available at no charge. Serves ages 12–18, grades 6–12. 3 teachers on staff. Curriculum accredited or approved by Pennsylvania Board of Education. Cost of educational program covered by local school district. Organized sports program offered.

Costs Average cost: $400 per stay. Accepts private insurance, group insurance, Blue Cross/Blue Shield, public funds.

Additional Services Outpatient services for males and females ages 12–25. Treats general psychosocial disorders; substance abuse.

THE RENFREW CENTER
475 Spring Lane
Philadelphia, Pennsylvania 19128
215-482-5353; Fax: 215-482-7390

General Information Freestanding psychiatric care facility treating eating disorders for adolescents, adults. 10 beds for adolescents. Open year-round. Patient security: staff secured; will pursue and return runaways. Suburban setting. Independent for-profit facility. Licensed by state of Pennsylvania. Accredited by JCAHO.

Participants Accepts: male and female adolescents ages 15–18; male and female adults ages 18 and up. Average stay: 45 days. Admission: voluntary. Treats general psychosocial disorders; substance abuse; eating disorders; post-traumatic stress disorder; thought, mood, and personality disorders. Accepts the speech impaired; those with a history of harm to themselves and others; those receiving psychotropic medication; those with a history of epilepsy.

Program Treatment modalities: psychodynamic; community/relational-orientation; feminist orientation. Family treatment program available.

Staff 6.6 full-time direct-care staff members per adolescent. Total facility staff includes 2 physicians, 4 psychologists, 3 psychiatrists, 20 registered nurses, 1 practical/vocational nurse, 14 MSW social workers, 2 dieticians, 20 other direct-care staff members. Staff is 15% male, 85% female.

Facilities Multiple buildings. Residential quarters shared with adults. Central dining (shared with adults).

Education Academic program available at no charge. Serves ages 15–17, ungraded. Cost of educational program covered by local school district.

Costs Average cost: $800 per day. Accepts private insurance, group insurance, Blue Cross/Blue Shield.

Contact Hap Rogers, Assistant Administrator, main address above. Phone: 215-482-5353. Fax: 215-482-7390.

THE RENFREW CENTER OF FLORIDA
7700 Renfrew Lane
Coconut Creek, Florida 33073
305-698-9222; Fax: 305-698-9007

General Information Residential treatment/subacute facility for adolescents, adults. Open year-round. Patient security: staff secured. Suburban setting. For-profit facility affiliated with The Renfrew Center, Philadelphia, PA. Licensed by state of Florida. Accredited by JCAHO.

Participants Accepts: female adolescents ages 14–18; female adults ages 18 and up. Average stay: 7 weeks. Admission: voluntary. Treats behavior disorders; general psychosocial disorders; substance abuse; eating disorders; compulsive/addictive disorders other than substance abuse and eating disorders; post-traumatic stress disorder; thought, mood, and personality disorders. Accepts the mobility impaired; the vision impaired; the hearing impaired; the speech impaired; the sexually compulsive; those with a history of harm to themselves and others; those receiving psychotropic medication; those with a history of epilepsy; diabetics. Special programs for the mobility impaired; the vision impaired; the hearing impaired; the speech impaired; those with AIDS. Largest number of participants from Florida.

Program Treatment modalities: psychodynamic. Family treatment program available.

Staff Total facility staff includes 2 physicians, 3 psychologists, 3 psychiatrists, 4 registered nurses, 10 MSW social workers, 7 occupational/recreational therapists, 2 dieticians. Staff is 2% male, 98% female.

Facilities Multiple buildings. Separate residential quarters for adolescents. Central dining (shared with adults). Outdoor swimming pool, aerobics room.

Education Educational program held on-site at no charge. Cost of educational program covered by local school district.

Costs Average cost: $850 per day. Accepts private insurance, group insurance, Blue Cross/Blue Shield.

Contact Adrienne Ressler, Director of Professional Relations, main address above. Phone: 305-698-9222. Fax: 305-698-9007.

RESEARCH PSYCHIATRIC CENTER
2323 East 63rd Street
Kansas City, Missouri 64130
816-444-8161; Fax: 816-333-4495

General Information Psychiatric hospital for children, adolescents, adults. 12 beds for children; 24 beds for adolescents; 100 beds total. Open year-round. Patient security: entirely locked; will pursue and return runaways. Urban setting. For-profit facility affiliated with Hospital Corporation of America and Health Midwest. Licensed by state of Missouri. Accredited by JCAHO.

Participants Accepts: male and female children ages 5–13; male and female adolescents ages 13–17; male and female adults ages 18 and up. Average stay: 12 days. Admission: all parties who share custody. Treats autistic disorders; learning disabilities; behavior disorders; general psychosocial disorders; substance abuse; eating disorders; compulsive/addictive disorders other than substance abuse and eating disorders; post-traumatic stress disorder; thought, mood, and personality disorders. Accepts the mobility impaired; the vision impaired; the hearing impaired; the speech impaired; those with a history of harm to themselves and others; those receiving psychotropic medication. Special programs for the developmentally disabled. Largest number of participants from Missouri, Kansas.

Program Treatment modalities: individual/group psychotherapy; transactional analysis; cognitive therapy; rational emotive therapy. Family treatment program available.

Staff Total facility staff includes 9 physicians, 1 psychologist, 1 psychiatrist, 17 registered nurses, 4 practical/vocational nurses, 6 MSW social workers, 1 teacher, 4 occupational/recreational therapists, 2 dieticians, 9 other direct-care staff members. Staff is 14% male, 86% female.

Facilities Single building; males and females in co-educational units. Separate residential quarters for children and adolescents. Central dining (shared with adults). Basketball courts, gymnasium, outdoor swimming pool.

Education Academic program available at no charge. Serves ages 6–18, grades 1–12. 1 teacher on staff.

Costs Accepts private insurance, group insurance, medicare, Blue Cross/Blue Shield.

Contact Kathy Moots, Intake Services Manager, main address above. Phone: 816-444-8161. Fax: 816-333-4495.

THE RESIDENTIAL TREATMENT CENTER
2904 Bedford Road
Bedford, Texas 76021
800-477-9797; Fax: 817-545-8982

General Information Residential treatment/subacute facility for children, adolescents. 20 beds for children; 41 beds for adolescents; 61 beds total. Open year-round. Patient security: entirely locked; will pursue and return runaways. Suburban setting. For-profit facility affiliated with National Medical Enterprises, Santa Monica, CA. Licensed by state of Texas. Accredited by JCAHO.

Participants Accepts: male and female children ages 5–12; male and female adolescents ages 13–18. Admission: all parties who share custody, court order, voluntary, depending on program. Treats learning disabilities; behavior disorders; general psychosocial disorders; substance abuse; eating disorders; compulsive/addictive disorders other than substance abuse and eating disorders; post-traumatic stress disorder; thought, mood, and personality disorders. Accepts the mobility impaired; the vision impaired; the hearing impaired; the speech impaired; those with a history of arson; the sexually compulsive; those with a history of harm to themselves and others; those receiving psychotropic medication; non-English speaking individuals; those with a history of epilepsy; pregnant patients. Special programs for the chronically ill; the mobility impaired; the developmentally disabled. Largest number of participants from Louisiana, California, Indiana.

Program Treatment modalities: social behavioral; Twelve Step Recovery. Family treatment program available.

Staff .9 full-time direct-care staff member per child or adolescent. Total facility staff includes 1 psychologist, 1 psychiatrist, 9 registered nurses, 2 practical/vocational nurses, 2 MSW social workers, 1 social worker (non-MSW), 5 teachers, 2 counselors, 2 occupational/recreational therapists, 3 therapists, 1 dietician, 11 other direct-care staff members. Staff is 25% male, 75% female.

Facilities Single building; males and females in separate units. Central dining. Basketball courts, game room, gymnasium, outdoor swimming pool, ropes course, sand volleyball court.

Education Academic program available at no charge. Serves ages 5–18, grades K–12. 5 teachers on staff. Curriculum accredited or approved by Hurst Euless Bedford Independent School District.

Costs Accepts private insurance, group insurance, medicaid, Blue Cross/Blue Shield, public funds.

Contact Director of Admissions, main address above. Phone: 800-477-9797. Fax: 817-545-6941.

THE RETREAT
555 Southwest 148th Avenue
Sunrise, Florida 33325
305-370-0200; Fax: 305-370-7312

General Information Psychiatric hospital for children, adolescents. Patient security: entirely locked. Independent for-profit facility. Licensed by state of Florida. Accredited by JCAHO.

Participants Accepts: male and female children; male and female adolescents. Average stay: 30 days. Admission: one parent, court order, voluntary, depending on program. Treats learning disabilities; behavior disorders; general psychosocial disorders; substance abuse; eating disorders; compulsive/addictive disorders other than substance abuse and eating disorders; post-traumatic stress disorder; thought, mood, and personality disorders.

Costs Average cost: $900 per day.

Contact Karen Mitchell, main address above. Phone: 318-370-0200.

RIDGEVIEW INSTITUTE
3995 South Cobb Drive
Smyrna, Georgia 30080-6397
404-434-4568; Fax: 404-431-7026

General Information Psychiatric hospital for children, adolescents, adults. 40 beds for adolescents. Open year-round. Patient security: partially locked; will pursue and return runaways. Suburban setting. Independent not-for-profit facility. Licensed by state of Georgia. Accredited by JCAHO.

Participants Accepts: male and female children ages 8–12; male and female adolescents ages 12–18; male and female adults ages 18 and up. Average stay: 25 days. Admission: all parties who share custody. Treats autistic disorders; learning disabilities; behavior disorders; general psychosocial disorders; substance abuse; eating disorders; compulsive/addictive disorders other than substance abuse and eating disorders; post-traumatic stress disorder; thought, mood, and personality disorders. Accepts the mobility impaired; the vision impaired; the hearing impaired; the speech impaired; those with a history of arson; the sexually compulsive; those with a history of harm to themselves and others; those receiving psychotropic medication; non-English speaking individuals; those with a history of epilepsy.

Program Treatment modalities: Twelve Step Recovery; cognitive-behavioral; experiential. Family treatment program available.

Facilities Multiple buildings; males and females in coeducational units. Separate residential quarters for children and adolescents. Central dining (shared with adults), separate dining by residential unit available. Basketball courts, game room, outdoor swimming pool, playing fields.

Education Academic program available at no charge. Serves ages 8–18, grades 5–12. Curriculum accredited or approved by Georgia Accrediting Association, Georgia Department of Education.

Costs Average cost: $800 per day. Accepts private insurance, group insurance, medicare, Blue Cross/Blue Shield, public funds.

Additional Services Drug and alcohol rehabilitation services for males and females ages 8 and up. Treats learning disabilities; behavior disorders; general psychosocial disorders. Private school program for ADHD sufferers for males and females ages 12–18. Treats learning disabilities; behavior disorders; general psychosocial disorders; substance abuse; eating disorders; compulsive/addictive disorders other than substance abuse and eating disorders; post-traumatic stress disorder; thought, mood, and personality disorders.

Contact Valerie Morvan, Director of Marketing, main address above. Phone: 404-434-4568. Fax: 404-431-7026.

RIDGEVIEW PSYCHIATRIC HOSPITAL AND CENTER, INC.
240 West Tyrone Road
Oak Ridge, Tennessee 37830
615-482-1076; Fax: 615-481-6164

General Information Psychiatric hospital for adolescents. 15 beds for adolescents. Patient security: partially locked. Independent not-for-profit facility. Licensed by state of Tennessee. Accredited by JCAHO.

Participants Accepts: male and female adolescents. Average stay: 14 days. Admission: one parent, all parties who share custody, court order, voluntary, depending on program. Treats behavior disorders; general psychosocial disorders; eating disorders; compulsive/addictive disorders other than substance abuse and eating disorders; post-traumatic stress disorder; thought, mood, and personality disorders.

Staff Staff is 40% male, 60% female.

Contact Gary Stoegbauer, Program Director, main address above. Phone: 615-482-1076.

RIMROCK FOUNDATION
1231 North 29th Street
P.O. Box 30374
Billings, Montana 59107
406-248-3175; Fax: 406-248-3821

General Information Freestanding rehabilitation center for adolescents. Open year-round. Patient security: staff secured; will pursue and return runaways. Small town setting. Independent not-for-profit facility. Licensed by state of Montana. Accredited by JCAHO.

Participants Accepts: male and female adolescents ages 14–18. Average stay: 35 days. Admission: one parent. Treats learning disabilities; behavior disorders; general psychosocial disorders; substance abuse; eating disorders; compulsive/addictive disorders other than substance abuse and eating disorders; post-traumatic stress disorder; thought, mood, and personality disorders. Accepts the sexually compulsive; those with a history of harm to themselves and others; those receiving psychotropic medication; those with a history of epilepsy.

Program Treatment modalities: Twelve Step Recovery; psychodynamic; group therapy. Family treatment program available.

Staff Total facility staff includes 3 physicians, 1 psychologist, 2 psychiatrists, 3 registered nurses, 9 practical/vocational nurses, 2 MSW social workers, 1 teacher, 15 counselors, 16 occupational/recreational therapists, 1 dietician. Staff is 66% male, 33% female.

Facilities Single building; males and females in coeducational units. Residential quarters shared with adults. Central dining (shared with adults). Basketball courts, gymnasium, indoor swimming pool, outdoor tennis courts, playing fields.

Education Academic program available at no charge. Serves ages 14–18, grades 7–12. 1 teacher on staff. Curriculum accredited or approved by school districts. Cost of educational program covered by local school district. Organized sports program offered.

Costs Average cost: $7200 per stay. Accepts private insurance, Blue Cross/Blue Shield, public funds.

Additional Services Residential or sub-acute services for males and females ages 14 and up. Treats learning disabilities; behavior disorders; general psychosocial disorders; substance abuse; eating disorders; compulsive/addictive disorders other than substance abuse and eating disorders; post-traumatic stress disorder; thought, mood, and personality disorders.

Contact   Barbara Hansen, Intake Coordinator, main address above. Phone: 406-248-3175. Fax: 406-248-3821.

RIVENDELL OF UTAH
5899 West Rivendell Drive
West Jordan, Utah 84088
801-561-3377; Fax: 801-569-2959

General Information   Residential treatment/subacute facility for adolescents. 60 beds for adolescents. Open year-round. Patient security: staff secured; will pursue and return runaways. Suburban setting. For-profit facility affiliated with Vendell Healthcare, Inc., Nashville, TN. Licensed by state of Utah. Accredited by JCAHO; Civilian Health and Medical Program of the Uniformed Services.

Participants   Accepts: male and female adolescents ages 12–18. Average stay: 170 days. Admission: one parent. Treats learning disabilities; behavior disorders; general psychosocial disorders; substance abuse; eating disorders; compulsive/addictive disorders other than substance abuse and eating disorders; post-traumatic stress disorder; thought, mood, and personality disorders. Accepts those with a history of arson; those with a history of harm to themselves and others; those receiving psychotropic medication; those with a history of epilepsy. Largest number of participants from California, Montana.

Program   Treatment modalities: positive peer culture; Twelve Step Recovery for dual diagnosis. Family treatment program available.

Staff   .8 full-time direct-care staff member per adolescent. Total facility staff includes 1 physician, 4 psychologists, 2 psychiatrists, 6 registered nurses, 8 MSW social workers, 5 teachers, 17 counselors, 4 occupational/recreational therapists, 1 speech pathologist, 1 dietician. Staff is 68% male, 32% female.

Facilities   Single building; males and females in co-educational units. Central dining (shared with adults). Basketball courts, game room, gymnasium, playing fields, ropes course.

Education   Academic program available. Serves ages 12–18, grades 6–12. 5 teachers on staff. Curriculum accredited or approved by Utah and California State Boards of Education, Northwest Association of Schools and Colleges.

Costs   Average cost: $275 per day. Accepts private insurance, group insurance, medicare, medicaid, Blue Cross/Blue Shield, public funds.

Additional Services   Drug and alcohol rehabilitation services for males and females ages 12–18. Treats learning disabilities; behavior disorders; general psychosocial disorders; substance abuse; eating disorders; compulsive/addictive disorders other than substance abuse and eating disorders; post-traumatic stress disorder; thought, mood, and personality disorders.

Contact   Rachel Adams, Assessment and Referral Supervisor, main address above. Phone: 801-561-3377. Fax: 801-569-2959.

RIVENDELL PSYCHIATRIC CENTER
1035 Porter Pike
Bowling Green, Kentucky 42103
502-843-1199; Fax: 502-782-9996

General Information   Psychiatric hospital for children, adolescents. Patient security: entirely locked. For-profit facility affiliated with Vendell Healthcare, Inc., Nashville, TN. Licensed by state of Kentucky. Accredited by JCAHO.

Participants   Accepts: male and female children; male and female adolescents. Average stay: 45 days. Admission: one parent, all parties who share custody, court order, voluntary, depending on program. Treats autistic disorders; learning disabilities; behavior disorders; general psychosocial disorders; substance abuse; eating disorders; compulsive/addictive disorders other than substance abuse and eating disorders; post-traumatic stress disorder; thought, mood, and personality disorders.

Staff   Staff is 40% male, 60% female.

Contact   Admissions Coordinator, main address above. Phone: 502-843-1199. Fax: 502-782-9996.

RIVENDELL PSYCHIATRIC CENTER
55 Basin Creek Road
Butte, Montana 59701
406-494-4183; Fax: 406-494-5869

General Information   Psychiatric hospital for children, adolescents. Patient security: entirely locked. For-profit facility affiliated with Vendell Healthcare, Inc, Nashville, TN. Licensed by state of Montana. Accredited by JCAHO.

Participants Accepts: male and female children; male and female adolescents. Admission: one parent, court order, voluntary, depending on program. Treats autistic disorders; learning disabilities; behavior disorders; general psychosocial disorders; substance abuse; eating disorders; compulsive/addictive disorders other than substance abuse and eating disorders; post-traumatic stress disorder; thought, mood, and personality disorders.

Staff Staff is 50% male, 50% female.

Contact Marla Wilkin, Director of Marketing, main address above. Phone: 406-494-4183. Fax: 406-494-5869.

RIVENDELL PSYCHIATRIC CENTER
3770 Rivendell Drive
Seward, Nebraska 68434
402-643-3770; Fax: 402-643-2109

General Information Psychiatric hospital for children, adolescents. 16 beds for children; 32 beds for adolescents; 48 beds total. Open year-round. Patient security: entirely locked; will pursue and return runaways. Rural setting. For-profit facility affiliated with Vendell Healthcare, Inc., Nashville, TN. Licensed by state of Nebraska. Accredited by JCAHO.

Participants Accepts: male and female children ages 5–12; male and female adolescents ages 12–18. Average stay: 32 days. Admission: one parent, all parties who share custody, court order, depending on program. Treats learning disabilities; behavior disorders; general psychosocial disorders; substance abuse; post-traumatic stress disorder; thought, mood, and personality disorders. Accepts the mobility impaired; the vision impaired; the hearing impaired; the speech impaired; those with a history of arson; the sexually compulsive; those with a history of harm to themselves and others; those receiving psychotropic medication; non-English speaking individuals; those with a history of epilepsy.

Program Treatment modalities: family systems therapy. Family treatment program available.

Staff 1.6 full-time direct-care staff members per child or adolescent. Total facility staff includes 6 physicians, 11 psychologists, 5 psychiatrists, 24 registered nurses, 2 practical/vocational nurses, 6 MSW social workers, 1 social worker (non-MSW), 6 teachers, 4 counselors, 5 occupational/recreational therapists, 1 speech pathologist, 1 therapist, 1 dietician, 46 other direct-care staff members. Staff is 45% male, 55% female.

Facilities Single building. Basketball courts, gymnasium, ropes course, outdoor volleyball court.

Education Academic program available at no charge. Serves ages 5–18, grades K–12. 6 teachers on staff. Curriculum accredited or approved by Nebraska Department of Education. Cost of educational program sometimes covered by local school district.

Costs Average cost: $26,560 per stay. Accepts private insurance, group insurance, medicare, medicaid, Blue Cross/Blue Shield, public funds.

Additional Services Drug and alcohol rehabilitation services for males and females ages 12–18. Treats behavior disorders; general psychosocial disorders; substance abuse; eating disorders; compulsive/addictive disorders other than substance abuse and eating disorders; post-traumatic stress disorder; thought, mood, and personality disorders. Outpatient services for males and females ages 5–18. Treats autistic disorders; learning disabilities; behavior disorders; general psychosocial disorders; substance abuse; eating disorders; compulsive/addictive disorders other than substance abuse and eating disorders; post-traumatic stress disorder; thought, mood, and personality disorders. Day treatment program for males and females. Treats behavior disorders; general psychosocial disorders; substance abuse; eating disorders; compulsive/addictive disorders other than substance abuse and eating disorders; post-traumatic stress disorder; thought, mood, and personality disorders.

Contact Vern Larson, Administrator, main address above. Phone: 402-643-3770. Fax: 402-643-2109.

RIVERNORTH TREATMENT CENTER
5505 Shreveport
Pineville, Louisiana 71360
318-640-0222; Fax: 318-640-0222

General Information Psychiatric and substance abuse treatment facility for adolescents. 15 beds for adolescents. Patient security: entirely locked. For-profit facility affiliated with Hallmark Health Care, Atlanta, GA. Licensed by state of Louisiana. Accredited by JCAHO.

Participants Accepts: male and female adolescents. Average stay: 18 days. Admission: one parent, all parties who share custody, court order, voluntary, depending on program. Treats autistic disorders; learning disabilities; behavior disorders; general psychosocial disorders; substance abuse; eating disorders; compulsive/addictive disorders other than substance abuse and eating disorders; post-traumatic stress disorder; thought, mood, and personality disorders.

Staff   Staff is 34% male, 66% female.

Contact   Cindy Nardini, Program Director, main address above. Phone: 800-256-1999.

RIVER OAK CENTER FOR CHILDREN
5445 Laurel Hills Drive
Sacramento, California 95841
916-344-2295; Fax: 916-344-3303

General Information   Residential treatment/subacute facility for children. 68 beds for children. Open year-round. Patient security: staff secured; will pursue and return runaways. Suburban setting. Independent not-for-profit facility. Licensed by state of California.

Participants   Accepts: male and female children ages 5–13. Average stay: 15 months. Admission: all parties who share custody, court order, voluntary, depending on program. Treats learning disabilities; behavior disorders; general psychosocial disorders; post-traumatic stress disorder; thought, mood, and personality disorders. Accepts the speech impaired; those with a history of arson; the sexually compulsive; those with a history of harm to themselves and others; those receiving psychotropic medication; those with a history of epilepsy. Special programs for the developmentally disabled; the speech impaired.

Program   Family treatment program available.

Staff   1.2 full-time direct-care staff members per child. Total facility staff includes 2 psychologists, 3 psychiatrists, 2 registered nurses, 7 MSW social workers, 10 social workers (non-MSW), 10 teachers, 80 counselors, 2 occupational/recreational therapists, 1 speech pathologist, 2 therapists, 1 dietician. Staff is 40% male, 60% female.

Facilities   Multiple buildings; males and females in coeducational units. Basketball courts, game room, gymnasium, playing fields.

Education   Academic program available at additional cost. Serves ages 5–13, grades K–7. 10 teachers on staff. Curriculum accredited or approved by State of California.

Costs   Average cost: $4366 per month. Accepts private insurance, medicare, Blue Cross/Blue Shield.

Additional Services   Outpatient services for males and females ages 5–13. Treats autistic disorders; learning disabilities; behavior disorders; general psychosocial disorders; substance abuse; eating disorders; compulsive/addictive disorders other than substance abuse and eating disorders; post-traumatic

stress disorder; thought, mood, and personality disorders. Specialized foster care for males and females ages 5–13. Treats learning disabilities; behavior disorders; general psychosocial disorders; substance abuse; eating disorders; compulsive/addictive disorders other than substance abuse and eating disorders; post-traumatic stress disorder; thought, mood, and personality disorders.

Contact   Cheryl Prosser, Intake Social Worker, main address above. Phone: 916-344-2295. Fax: 916-344-3303.

RIVER OAKS HOSPITAL
1525 River Oaks Road West
New Orleans, Louisiana 70123
504-733-2273; Fax: 504-733-7020

General Information   Freestanding psychiatric facility for children, adolescents. Patient security: partially locked. For-profit facility affiliated with Universal Health Services, King of Prussia, PA. Licensed by state of Louisiana. Accredited by JCAHO.

Participants   Accepts: male and female children; male and female adolescents. Average stay: 21 days. Admission: one parent, all parties who share custody, court order, voluntary, depending on program. Treats learning disabilities; behavior disorders; general psychosocial disorders; substance abuse; eating disorders; compulsive/addictive disorders other than substance abuse and eating disorders; post-traumatic stress disorder; thought, mood, and personality disorders.

Contact   Lois Laughlin, Director of Admission and Referrals, main address above. Phone: 504-733-2273.

RIVERSIDE HOSPITAL
1314 West Edgewood Drive
Jefferson City, Missouri 65109
314-659-8000; Fax: 314-659-8090

General Information   Psychiatric hospital for children, adolescents. Patient security: entirely locked. For-profit facility affiliated with Sterling Health Care Corporation, Bellevue, WA. Licensed by state of Missouri. Accredited by JCAHO.

Participants   Accepts: male and female children; male and female adolescents. Average stay: 14 days. Admission: one parent, all parties who share custody, court order, voluntary, depending on program. Treats autistic disorders; learning disabilities; behavior disorders; general psychosocial disorders; substance abuse; eating disorders; compulsive/addictive disorders other than substance abuse and eating disorders; post-traumatic stress disorder; thought, mood, and personality disorders.

Staff Staff is 50% male, 50% female.

Costs Average cost: $750 per day.

Additional Services Outpatient services for males and females ages 3–18. Treats autistic disorders; learning disabilities; behavior disorders; general psychosocial disorders; substance abuse; eating disorders; compulsive/addictive disorders other than substance abuse and eating disorders; post-traumatic stress disorder; thought, mood, and personality disorders.

Contact Phyllis Shockley, Admissions Coordinator, main address above. Phone: 314-659-8000. Fax: 314-659-8090.

RIVERVIEW SCHOOL, INC.
551 Route 6A
East Sandwich, Massachusetts 02537
508-888-0489; Fax: 508-888-1315

General Information School for adolescents. 109 beds for adolescents. Open academic year. Patient security: partially locked; will pursue and return runaways. Rural setting. Independent not-for-profit facility. Licensed by state of Massachusetts.

Participants Accepts: male and female adolescents ages 12–21. Average stay: 3 years. Admission: all parties who share custody. Treats autistic disorders; learning disabilities; eating disorders. Accepts the mobility impaired; the vision impaired; the hearing impaired; the speech impaired; those with a history of epilepsy. Special programs for the mobility impaired; the developmentally disabled; the speech impaired. Largest number of participants from Massachusetts, California, New York.

Program Treatment modalities: Orton Gillingham; total language development approach; criterion-based instruction; social skills development.

Staff Total facility staff includes 2 psychologists, 1 registered nurse, 1 MSW social worker, 2 social workers (non-MSW), 22 teachers, 1 speech pathologist.

Facilities Multiple buildings; males and females in separate units. Residential quarters shared with adults. Central dining (shared with adults). Basketball courts, game room, gymnasium, horseback riding, indoor swimming pool, outdoor tennis courts, playing fields.

Education School serves ages 12–21, grades 7–PG. 22 teachers on staff. Curriculum is college-preparatory; diploma granted upon completion. Curriculum accredited or approved by New England Association of Schools and Colleges. Organized sports program offered.

Costs Average cost: $29,000 per year. Accepts private insurance, group insurance, public funds. Financial aid available.

Additional Services Summer school program for males and females ages 18–23. Treats learning disabilities.

Contact Janet Lavoive, Director of Admissions, main address above. Phone: 508-888-0489. Fax: 508-888-1315.

Announcement The Riverview School offers a unique residential coeducational program for 110 adolescents who are marginally handicapped intellectually and have identifiable learning disabilities. In a structured, supportive environment, students learn the skills that will enable them to pursue postsecondary educational/vocational options or return to their home communities.

THE ROAD BACK
7 Forest Street
Attleboro, Massachusetts 02703
508-222-5811; Fax: 508-222-8687

General Information Residential treatment/subacute facility for adolescents. 22 beds for adolescents. Patient security: staff secured. Not-for-profit facility affiliated with Attleboro Area Youth and Family Services, Attleboro, MA. Licensed by state of Massachusetts.

Participants Accepts: male and female adolescents. Average stay: 3 months. Admission: one parent, all parties who share custody, court order, voluntary, depending on program. Treats learning disabilities; behavior disorders; general psychosocial disorders; substance abuse; eating disorders; compulsive/addictive disorders other than substance abuse and eating disorders; post-traumatic stress disorder; thought, mood, and personality disorders.

Staff Staff is 50% male, 50% female.

Costs Average cost: $225 per day.

Contact Laurice Girouard, Program Director. Phone: 508-222-5811.

THE ROCK CREEK CENTER
40 Timberline Drive
Lemont, Illinois 60439
708-257-3636; Fax: 708-257-8846

General Information Psychiatric hospital for adolescents, adults. 15 beds for adolescents. Open year-round. Patient security: staff secured; will pursue and return runaways. Small town setting. Independent for-profit facility. Licensed by state of Illinois. Accredited by JCAHO.

Participants Accepts: male and female adolescents ages 12–18; male and female adults ages 18 and up. Average stay: 40 days. Admission: one parent, legal guardian, depending on program. Treats learning disabilities; behavior disorders; general psychosocial disorders; substance abuse; eating disorders; compulsive/addictive disorders other than substance abuse and eating disorders; post-traumatic stress disorder; thought, mood, and personality disorders. Accepts those with a history of harm to themselves and others; those receiving psychotropic medication. Special programs for the chronically ill.

Program Treatment modalities: psychodynamic.

Staff Total facility staff includes 1 physician, 8 psychologists, 9 psychiatrists, 54 registered nurses, 9 practical/vocational nurses, 4 MSW social workers, 3 social workers (non-MSW), 4 teachers, 42 counselors, 4 occupational/recreational therapists, 2 therapists, 3 dieticians, 2 other direct-care staff members. Staff is 45% male, 55% female.

Facilities Multiple buildings; males and females in coeducational units. Separate residential quarters for adolescents. Central dining arrangements vary. Game room.

Education Academic program available at no charge. Serves ages 12–18, grades 6–12. 4 teachers on staff. Curriculum accredited or approved by North Central Association of Schools and Colleges, Illinois State Board of Education.

Costs Average cost: $990 per stay. Accepts private insurance, group insurance, medicare, Blue Cross/Blue Shield.

Additional Services Outpatient services for males and females ages 5 and up. Treats learning disabilities; behavior disorders; general psychosocial disorders; substance abuse; eating disorders; compulsive/addictive disorders other than substance abuse and eating disorders; post-traumatic stress disorder; thought, mood, and personality disorders. Partial hospitalization program for adolescent males and females. Treats learning disabilities; behavior disorders; general psychosocial disorders; substance abuse; eating disorders; compulsive/addictive disorders other than substance abuse and eating disorders; post-traumatic stress disorder; thought, mood, and personality disorders.

Contact Karen Lemaster, Director of Marketing, main address above. Phone: 708-257-3636. Fax: 708-257-8846.

See page 450 for full page description.

ROCKY MOUNTAIN ACADEMY
Route One
Bonners Ferry, Idaho 83805
208-267-7522; Fax: 208-267-3232

General Information School for adolescents. 170 beds for adolescents. Open year-round. Patient security: unlocked; will pursue and return runaways. Rural setting. Independent for-profit facility. Licensed by state of Idaho.

Participants Accepts: male and female adolescents ages 13–18. Average stay: 30 months. Admission: all parties who share custody. Treats learning disabilities; behavior disorders; general psychosocial disorders; substance abuse; eating disorders; compulsive/addictive disorders other than substance abuse and eating disorders; thought, mood, and personality disorders. Accepts those receiving psychotropic medication; those with a history of epilepsy. Largest number of participants from California, Washington, Georgia.

Program Treatment modalities: group psychotherapy; individualized therapy. Family treatment program available.

Staff .4 full-time direct-care staff member per adolescent. Total facility staff includes 1 psychologist, 1 psychiatrist, 1 registered nurse, 2 social workers (non-MSW), 15 teachers, 35 counselors, 5 other direct-care staff members. Staff is 70% male, 30% female.

Facilities Multiple buildings; males and females in separate units. Central dining (shared with adults). Basketball courts, playing fields, ropes course, pond.

Education School serves ages 13–18. 15 teachers on staff. Curriculum is college-preparatory; diploma granted upon completion. Curriculum accredited or approved by Northwest Association of Schools and Colleges. Organized sports program offered.

Costs Average cost: $3465 per month. Accepts private insurance, group insurance. Financial aid available.

Contact Ranel Hanson, Admissions Director, main address above. Phone: 208-267-7522. Fax: 208-267-3232.

See page 452 for full page description.

ROGERS MEMORIAL HOSPITAL
34700 Valley Road
Oconomowoc, Wisconsin 53066
414-646-4411; Fax: 414-646-3158

General Information Psychiatric hospital for children, adolescents. Patient security: staff secured. Independent not-for-profit facility. Licensed by state of Wisconsin. Accredited by JCAHO.

Participants Accepts: male and female children; male and female adolescents. Average stay: 20 days. Admission: all parties who share custody, voluntary, depending on program. Treats learning disabilities; behavior disorders; general psychosocial disorders; substance abuse; eating disorders; compulsive/addictive disorders other than substance abuse and eating disorders; post-traumatic stress disorder; thought, mood, and personality disorders.

Costs Average cost: $9455 per stay.

Contact Bernice Shotola, Admissions Coordinator, main address above. Phone: 800-767-4411.

ROLLING HILLS HOSPITAL
1000 Rolling Hills Lane
Ada, Oklahoma 74820
405-436-3600; Fax: 405-436-3958

General Information Psychiatric hospital for children, adolescents, adults. 6 beds for children; 16 beds for adolescents; 40 beds total. Open year-round. Patient security: entirely locked; will pursue and return runaways. Rural setting. For-profit facility. Operated by Mediplex Group, Inc., Wellesley, MA. Licensed by state of Oklahoma. Accredited by JCAHO.

Participants Accepts: male and female children ages 5–12; male and female adolescents ages 13–17; male and female adults ages 18 and up. Average stay: 45 days. Admission: one parent, all parties who share custody, court order, depending on program. Treats learning disabilities; behavior disorders; general psychosocial disorders; substance abuse; compulsive/addictive disorders other than substance abuse and eating disorders; post-traumatic stress disorder; thought, mood, and personality disorders. Accepts the mobility impaired; the vision impaired; the hearing impaired; the speech impaired; those with a history of arson; the sexually compulsive; those with a history of harm to themselves and others; those receiving psychotropic medication; those with a history of epilepsy. Special programs for the hearing impaired. Largest number of participants from Oklahoma.

Program Treatment modalities: cognitive-behavioral therapy; psychodynamic therapy; experiential therapy; Twelve Step Recovery. Family treatment program available.

Staff Total facility staff includes 3 physicians, 1 psychologist, 2 psychiatrists, 5 registered nurses, 7 practical/vocational nurses, 1 MSW social worker, 2 teachers, 2 counselors, 2 occupational/recreational therapists, 1 dietician, 12 other direct-care staff members. Staff is 44% male, 56% female.

Facilities Single building; males and females in co-educational units. Separate residential quarters for children and adolescents. Central dining (shared with adults). Playing fields, ropes course, exercise room with Universal gym.

Education Academic program available at no charge. Serves ages 5–18, grades 1–12. 2 teachers on staff. Curriculum accredited or approved by Byng School District I-16. Cost of educational program covered by local school district.

Costs Average cost: $30,000 per stay. Accepts private insurance, group insurance, medicare, medicaid, Blue Cross/Blue Shield.

Additional Services Drug and alcohol rehabilitation services for males and females ages 13–17. Treats learning disabilities; behavior disorders; general psychosocial disorders; substance abuse; compulsive/addictive disorders other than substance abuse and eating disorders; post-traumatic stress disorder; thought, mood, and personality disorders. Outpatient services for males and females ages 5 and up. Treats behavior disorders; general psychosocial disorders; substance abuse; compulsive/addictive disorders other than substance abuse and eating disorders; post-traumatic stress disorder; thought, mood, and personality disorders.

Contact Sherri Owen, Executive Director, main address above. Phone: 405-436-3600. Fax: 405-436-3958.

ROSECRANCE CENTER
1505 North Alpine Road
Rockford, Illinois 61107
815-399-5351; Fax: 815-398-2641

General Information Drug and alcohol rehabilitation center for adolescents. 28 beds for adolescents. Open year-round. Patient security: staff secured. Suburban setting. Independent not-for-profit facility. Licensed by state of Illinois. Accredited by JCAHO; State of Illinois Department of Alcoholism and Substance Abuse.

Participants Accepts: male and female adolescents ages 12–18. Average stay: 42 days. Admission: one parent, all parties who share custody, court order, voluntary, Department of Children and Family Services referrals, depending on program. Treats substance abuse. Accepts the mobility impaired; the vision impaired; the hearing impaired; the speech impaired; those with a history of epilepsy.

Program Treatment modalities: Twelve Step Recovery. Family treatment program available.

Staff Total facility staff includes 1 psychiatrist, 3 registered nurses, 3 practical/vocational nurses, 4 MSW social workers, 3 teachers, 26 counselors, 1 occupational/recreational therapist, 1 dietician.

Facilities Multiple buildings; males and females in separate units. Central dining. Basketball courts, game room, playing fields, ropes course.

Education Academic program available at no charge. Serves ages 12–18, ungraded. 3 teachers on staff. Curriculum accredited or approved by local school district. Cost of educational program covered by local school district. Organized sports program offered.

Costs Average cost: $395 per day. Accepts private insurance, group insurance, medicaid, Blue Cross/ Blue Shield, public funds.

Additional Services Outpatient services for males and females ages 12–18. Treats substance abuse.

Contact Lynne Vass, Director of Resource Development, main address above. Phone: 815-399-5351. Fax: 815-398-2641.

ROTARY YOUTH CAMP
22310 East Colbern Road
Lee's Summit, Missouri 64063
816-246-6311

General Information Camp for children, adolescents. 35 beds for children; 10 beds for adolescents. Open summer. Patient security: staff secured; will pursue and return runaways. Suburban setting. Not-for-profit facility affiliated with Mattie Rhodes Counseling and Art Center, Kansas City, MO. Accredited by American Camping Association.

Participants Accepts: male and female children ages 6–12; male and female adolescents ages 13–16. Average stay: 6 days. Admission: one parent, all parties who share custody, depending on program. Treats learning disabilities; behavior disorders; general psychosocial disorders; post-traumatic stress disorder; thought, mood, and personality disorders. Accepts the mobility impaired; the vision impaired; the hear-

ing impaired; the speech impaired; those with a history of harm to themselves and others; those receiving psychotropic medication; non-English speaking individuals; those with a history of epilepsy.

Staff Total facility staff includes 1 registered nurse, 5 MSW social workers, 11 counselors. Staff is 40% male, 60% female.

Facilities Multiple buildings; males and females in separate units. Central dining. Basketball courts, game room, outdoor swimming pool, playing fields, archery, canoeing, hiking.

Additional Services Outpatient services for males and females ages 5–70. Treats learning disabilities; behavior disorders; general psychosocial disorders; substance abuse; eating disorders; compulsive/addictive disorders other than substance abuse and eating disorders; post-traumatic stress disorder; thought, mood, and personality disorders.

Contact Bob Walden, Director, main address above. Phone: 816-246-6311.

ROXBURY
601 Roxbury Road
Shippensburg, Pennsylvania 17257
717-532-4217; Fax: 717-532-4003

General Information Drug and alcohol rehabilitation center for adolescents, adults. 6 beds for adolescents. Open year-round. Patient security: staff secured; will pursue and return runaways. Small town setting. For-profit facility affiliated with First Hospital Corporation, Norfolk, VA. Licensed by state of Pennsylvania. Accredited by JCAHO.

Participants Accepts: male and female adolescents ages 14–19; male and female adults ages 20 and up. Average stay: 42 days. Treats behavior disorders; general psychosocial disorders; substance abuse; eating disorders; compulsive/addictive disorders other than substance abuse and eating disorders; post-traumatic stress disorder; thought, mood, and personality disorders. Accepts the mobility impaired; the vision impaired; those with a history of harm to themselves and others; those receiving psychotropic medication.

Program Treatment modalities: Twelve Step Recovery; medical model. Family treatment program available.

Staff 2.5 full-time direct-care staff members per adolescent. Total facility staff includes 1 physician, 6 practical/vocational nurses, 4 counselors, 3 other direct-care staff members. Staff is 47% male, 53% female.

Facilities Single building; males and females in co-educational units. Residential quarters shared with adults. Central dining (shared with adults). Indoor swimming pool, playing fields, ropes course.

Education Educational arrangements: supervised homework is part of treatment plan. Educational program held on-site at no charge. Cost of educational program sometimes covered by local school district. Organized sports program offered.

Costs Average cost: $380 per day. Accepts private insurance, group insurance, Blue Cross/Blue Shield, public funds.

Contact Rebecca N. Washinger, Business Manager, main address above. Phone: 717-532-4217. Fax: 717-532-4003.

SACRED HEART GENERAL HOSPITAL
2222 Coburg Road
Eugene, Oregon 97401
503-686-7399; Fax: 503-686-8398

General Information Psychiatric hospital with dual diagnosis program for children, adolescents. Patient security: entirely locked. Not-for-profit facility affiliated with Health and Hospital Services, Bellevue, WA. Licensed by state of Oregon. Accredited by JCAHO.

Participants Accepts: male and female children; male and female adolescents. Average stay: 22 days. Admission: one parent, all parties who share custody, court order, voluntary, depending on program. Treats autistic disorders; learning disabilities; behavior disorders; general psychosocial disorders; substance abuse; eating disorders; compulsive/addictive disorders other than substance abuse and eating disorders; post-traumatic stress disorder; thought, mood, and personality disorders.

Staff Staff is 50% male, 50% female.

Costs Average cost: $431 per day.

Additional Services Outpatient services for males and females ages 6–18. Treats autistic disorders; learning disabilities; behavior disorders; general psychosocial disorders; substance abuse; eating disorders; compulsive/addictive disorders other than substance abuse and eating disorders; post-traumatic stress disorder; thought, mood, and personality disorders.

Contact Michael Goldrick, Director, main address above. Phone: 503-686-7399. Fax: 503-686-8398.

SACRED HEART MEDICAL CENTER, DEPARTMENT OF PSYCHIATRY
West 101 Eighth Avenue
TAF-C9
Spokane, Washington 99220-4045
509-455-3131

General Information General hospital for children, adolescents. 8 beds for children; 14 beds for adolescents; 24 beds total. Open year-round. Patient security: entirely locked; no runaway pursuit. Urban setting. Licensed by state of Washington. Accredited by JCAHO.

Participants Accepts: male and female children ages 4–12; male and female adolescents ages 12–18. Average stay: 19 days. Admission: one parent. Treats learning disabilities; behavior disorders; general psychosocial disorders; eating disorders; post-traumatic stress disorder; thought, mood, and personality disorders. Accepts the mobility impaired; the vision impaired; the hearing impaired; the speech impaired; those with a history of arson; the sexually compulsive; those with a history of harm to themselves and others; those receiving psychotropic medication; non-English speaking individuals; those with a history of epilepsy. Largest number of participants from Washington, Idaho, Montana.

Staff Total facility staff includes 1 psychologist, 6 psychiatrists, 1 practical/vocational nurse, 1 MSW social worker, 4 teachers, 2 physical therapists, 6 occupational/recreational therapists, 2 speech pathologists, 2 dieticians.

Facilities Single building; males and females in co-educational units. Central dining. Basketball courts, game room, gymnasium, playing fields.

Education Academic program available at additional cost. Serves ages 4–18, grades N–12. 4 teachers on staff. Cost of educational program covered by local school district.

Costs Accepts private insurance, group insurance, medicare, medicaid, Blue Cross/Blue Shield, public funds.

Contact Dr. Michael Manz, Associate Director, Chief, Psychiatric Center for Children and Adolescents, main address above. Phone: 509-455-3016. Fax: 509-455-4890.

ST. AGNES HOSPITAL—ADDICTION SERVICES
430 East Division Street
Fond du Lac, Wisconsin 54935
414-929-1380; Fax: 414-929-1306

General Information   General hospital for adolescents. 8 beds for adolescents. Patient security: staff secured. Independent not-for-profit facility. Licensed by state of Wisconsin. Accredited by JCAHO.

Participants   Accepts: male and female adolescents. Average stay: 25 days. Admission: one parent, all parties who share custody, court order, voluntary, depending on program. Treats substance abuse. Accepts the mobility impaired; the vision impaired; the hearing impaired; the speech impaired; those with a history of arson; the sexually compulsive; those with a history of harm to themselves and others; those receiving psychotropic medication; those with a history of epilepsy.

Staff   Staff is 10% male, 90% female.

Costs   Average cost: $350 per day.

Additional Services   Outpatient services for males and females ages 13–17. Treats substance abuse. Halfway house for males and females ages 13–17. Treats substance abuse.

Contact   Darrell Aldrich, Director, main address above. Phone: 414-929-1390. Fax: 414-929-1306.

SAINT ALBANS PSYCHIATRIC HOSPITAL
P.O. Box 3608
Radford, Virginia 24143
703-639-2481

General Information   Psychiatric hospital for children, adolescents. Patient security: partially locked. Not-for-profit facility. Licensed by state of Virginia. Accredited by JCAHO.

Participants   Accepts: male and female children; male and female adolescents. Admission: one parent, all parties who share custody, court order, voluntary, depending on program. Treats behavior disorders; general psychosocial disorders; substance abuse; eating disorders; compulsive/addictive disorders other than substance abuse and eating disorders; post-traumatic stress disorder; thought, mood, and personality disorders.

Contact   Robert Terrell, Chief Executive Officer, main address above. Phone: 703-639-2481.

ST. ANN'S HOME, INC.
100A Haverhill Street
Methuen, Massachusetts 01844
508-682-5276

General Information   Residential treatment/subacute facility for children, adolescents. 68 beds for children; 22 beds for adolescents; 90 beds total. Open year-round. Patient security: staff secured; will pursue and return runaways. Suburban setting. Independent not-for-profit facility. Licensed by state of Massachusetts. Accredited by Massachusetts Department of Social Services; Office for Children.

Participants   Accepts: male and female children ages 6–12; male and female adolescents ages 13–17. Average stay: 550 days. Admission: one parent, all parties who share custody, court order, depending on program. Treats learning disabilities; behavior disorders; general psychosocial disorders; eating disorders; compulsive/addictive disorders other than substance abuse and eating disorders; post-traumatic stress disorder; thought, mood, and personality disorders. Accepts the speech impaired; those with a history of arson; the sexually compulsive; those with a history of harm to themselves and others; those receiving psychotropic medication; those with a history of epilepsy. Special programs for the speech impaired. Largest number of participants from Massachusetts, New Hampshire, Rhode Island.

Program   Treatment modalities: psychodynamic therapy; behavior modification therapy; psychotropic medication. Family treatment program available.

Staff   1.8 full-time direct-care staff members per child or adolescent. Total facility staff includes 3 psychologists, 3 psychiatrists, 4 registered nurses, 1 practical/vocational nurse, 15 MSW social workers, 5 social workers (non-MSW), 20 teachers, 100 counselors, 2 occupational/recreational therapists, 1 speech pathologist, 1 therapist, 10 other direct-care staff members. Staff is 30% male, 70% female.

Facilities   Multiple buildings; males and females in separate units. Separate dining by residential unit available. Basketball courts, game room, gymnasium, horseback riding, outdoor tennis courts, playing fields.

Education   Academic program available at no charge. Serves ages 6–17, ungraded. 20 teachers on staff. Curriculum accredited or approved by Massachusetts Department of Education approval as special needs school. Cost of educational program sometimes covered by local school district. Organized sports program offered.

Costs   Accepts private insurance, public funds.

Additional Services   Outpatient services for males and females ages 6–17. Treats behavior disorders;

general psychosocial disorders; eating disorders; compulsive/addictive disorders other than substance abuse and eating disorders; post-traumatic stress disorder; thought, mood, and personality disorders. Day treatment and special education program for males and females ages 6–17. Treats learning disabilities; behavior disorders; general psychosocial disorders; eating disorders; compulsive/addictive disorders other than substance abuse and eating disorders; post-traumatic stress disorder; thought, mood, and personality disorders.

Contact Patrick T. Villani, PhD, Executive Director, main address above. Phone: 508-682-5276.

ST. CHRISTOPHER'S JENNIE CLARKSON CHILD CARE SERVICES—DOBBS FERRY CAMPUS
71 South Broadway
Dobbs Ferry, New York 10522
914-693-3030; Fax: 914-693-8325

General Information Residential treatment/subacute facility for adolescents. Open year-round. Patient security: staff secured; will pursue and return runaways. Suburban setting. Independent not-for-profit facility. Licensed by state of New York. Accredited by JCAHO; Council of Family and Child Care Agencies, Community Council of Greater New York, Federation of Protestant Welfare Agencies, Inc.

Participants Accepts: male and female adolescents ages 12–19. Admission: court order. Treats learning disabilities; behavior disorders; general psychosocial disorders; substance abuse; post-traumatic stress disorder; thought, mood, and personality disorders. Accepts those with a history of harm to themselves and others; those receiving psychotropic medication.

Program Treatment modalities: psychodynamics. Family treatment program available.

Staff Total facility staff includes 4 physicians, 6 psychologists, 3 psychiatrists, 3 registered nurses, 7 practical/vocational nurses, 12 MSW social workers, 28 social workers (non-MSW), 10 other direct-care staff members. Staff is 35% male, 65% female.

Facilities Multiple buildings. Separate dining by residential unit available. Basketball courts, game room, gymnasium, playing fields.

Education Academic program available at no charge. Serves ages 12–19, ungraded. Curriculum accredited or approved by New York State Education Department. Cost of educational program covered by local school district.

Costs Average cost: $158 per stay. Accepts medicaid, public funds.

Contact Andrea Naso Nord, Director of Public Relations, main address above. Phone: 914-693-3030. Fax: 914-693-8325.

ST. CHRISTOPHER'S JENNIE CLARKSON CHILD CARE SERVICES—VALHALLA CAMPUS
Route 22
Valhalla, New York 10595
914-949-0665; Fax: 914-949-0130

General Information Residential treatment/subacute facility. Open year-round. Patient security: staff secured; will pursue and return runaways. Suburban setting. Independent not-for-profit facility. Licensed by state of New York. Accredited by JCAHO; Council of Family and Child Care Agencies, Community Council of Greater New York, Federation of Protestant Welfare Agencies, Inc.

Participants Admission: court order. Treats learning disabilities; behavior disorders; general psychosocial disorders; substance abuse; post-traumatic stress disorder; thought, mood, and personality disorders. Accepts those with a history of harm to themselves and others; those receiving psychotropic medication.

Program Treatment modalities: psychodynamics. Family treatment program available.

Staff Total facility staff includes 4 physicians, 6 psychologists, 3 psychiatrists, 3 registered nurses, 7 practical/vocational nurses, 12 MSW social workers, 28 social workers (non-MSW), 10 other direct-care staff members. Staff is 35% male, 65% female.

Facilities Multiple buildings; males and females in separate units. Separate dining by residential unit available. Basketball courts, game room, gymnasium, playing fields.

Costs Average cost: $158 per stay. Accepts medicaid, public funds.

Contact Andrea Naso Nord, Director of Public Relations, main address above. Phone: 914-693-3030. Fax: 914-693-8325.

ST. CLARE'S HOSPITAL CHEMICAL DEPENDENCY TREATMENT CENTER
915 East 5th Street
Alton, Illinois 62002
618-463-5655

General Information Acute care facility with inpatient and outpatient programs for adolescents. 10 beds for adolescents. Patient security: staff secured. Independent not-for-profit facility. Licensed by state of Illinois. Accredited by JCAHO.

Participants Accepts: male and female adolescents. Average stay: 21 days. Admission: one parent, all parties who share custody, court order, voluntary, depending on program. Treats learning disabilities; behavior disorders; general psychosocial disorders; substance abuse; eating disorders; compulsive/addictive disorders other than substance abuse and eating disorders; post-traumatic stress disorder; thought, mood, and personality disorders.

Staff Staff is 20% male, 80% female.

Contact Suzanne Ringhausen, Program Director, main address above. Phone: 618-463-5600.

ST. CLOUD CHILDREN'S HOME
1726 7th Avenue, South
St. Cloud, Minnesota 56301
612-251-8811; Fax: 612-251-3198

General Information Residential treatment/subacute facility for children, adolescents. Patient security: staff secured. Not-for-profit facility affiliated with Catholic Charities of the Diocese, St. Cloud, MN. Licensed by state of Minnesota. Accredited by Council on Accreditation of Services for Families and Children.

Participants Accepts: male and female children; male and female adolescents. Average stay: 9 months. Admission: one parent, all parties who share custody, court order, depending on program. Treats autistic disorders; learning disabilities; behavior disorders; general psychosocial disorders; substance abuse; post-traumatic stress disorder; thought, mood, and personality disorders.

Staff Staff is 50% male, 50% female.

Costs Average cost: $120 per day.

Contact John Doman, Director, main address above. Phone: 612-251-8811. Fax: 612-251-3198.

ST. FRANCIS ACADEMY—CAMELOT
50 Riverside Drive
Lake Placid, New York 12946
518-523-3605; Fax: 518-523-1470

General Information Residential treatment/subacute facility for adolescents. 26 beds for adolescents. Open year-round. Patient security: staff secured; will pursue and return runaways. Rural setting. Not-for-profit facility affiliated with St. Francis Academy, Inc., Salina, KS. Licensed by state of New York. Accredited by JCAHO; New York State Department of Social Services, Civilian Health and Medical Program of the Uniformed Services.

Participants Accepts: male adolescents ages 12–18. Admission: one parent, all parties who share custody, court order, depending on program. Treats learning disabilities; behavior disorders; general psychosocial disorders; substance abuse; post-traumatic stress disorder; thought, mood, and personality disorders. Accepts those with a history of arson; those receiving psychotropic medication; those with conduct disorders. Largest number of participants from New York, D.C., Ohio.

Program Family treatment program available.

Staff 1.4 full-time direct-care staff members per adolescent. Total facility staff includes 1 physician, 1 psychologist, 1 psychiatrist, 4 registered nurses, 5 MSW social workers, 2 social workers (non-MSW), 4 teachers, 4 counselors, 1 occupational/recreational therapist, 2 therapists, 1 dietician, 10 other direct-care staff members. Staff is 81% male, 19% female.

Facilities Single building. Central dining. Basketball courts, game room, gymnasium, outdoor tennis courts, playing fields, ropes course.

Education Academic program available at additional cost. Serves ages 12–18, grades 7–12. 4 teachers on staff. Curriculum accredited or approved by New York State Department of Education. Organized sports program offered.

Costs Average cost: $300 per day. Accepts private insurance, group insurance, Blue Cross/Blue Shield, public funds.

Additional Services Wilderness/survival program for males ages 12–18. Treats behavior disorders; general psychosocial disorders; substance abuse; compulsive/addictive disorders other than substance abuse and eating disorders; post-traumatic stress disorder; thought, mood, and personality disorders. Dual diagnosis for males ages 12–18. Treats behavior disorders; substance abuse; post-traumatic stress disorder; thought, mood, and personality disorders.

Contact Thomas H. Webb, Admissions Officer, main address above. Phone: 518-523-3605. Fax: 518-523-1470.

THE SAINT FRANCIS ACADEMY INCORPORATED
509 East Elm
P.O. Box 1340
Salina, Kansas 67401
800-423-1342; Fax: 913-825-2502

General Information   Open year-round. Patient security: staff secured; will pursue and return runaways. Suburban setting. Independent not-for-profit facility. Accredited by JCAHO.

Participants   Admission: all parties who share custody.

Contact   David Lang, Director of Admission, main address above. Phone: 800-423-1342. Fax: 913-825-2502.

THE SAINT FRANCIS ACADEMY, INC.
509 East Elm
Salina, Kansas 67402
913-825-0541; Fax: 913-825-2502

General Information   Residential treatment/subacute facility for adolescents. 85 beds for adolescents. Open year-round. Patient security: staff secured; will pursue and return runaways. Small town setting. Independent not-for-profit facility. Licensed by state of Kansas. Accredited by JCAHO.

Participants   Accepts: male adolescents ages 12–18. Average stay: 270 days. Admission: one parent, all parties who share custody, court order, depending on program. Treats learning disabilities; behavior disorders; substance abuse; compulsive/addictive disorders other than substance abuse and eating disorders; post-traumatic stress disorder; thought, mood, and personality disorders. Accepts those with a history of arson; the sexually compulsive; those with a history of harm to themselves and others; those receiving psychotropic medication; those with a history of epilepsy. Special programs for the developmentally disabled. Largest number of participants from New York, Kansas, Nebraska.

Program   Treatment modalities: behavior modification; cognitive therapy. Family treatment program available.

Staff   1 full-time direct-care staff member per adolescent. Total facility staff includes 3 physicians, 3 psychologists, 3 psychiatrists, 6 registered nurses, 5 MSW social workers, 4 social workers (non-MSW), 7 teachers, 18 counselors, 3 therapists, 2 dieticians, 29 other direct-care staff members. Staff is 60% male, 40% female.

Facilities   Multiple buildings. Central dining. Basketball courts, game room, gymnasium, horseback riding, playing fields, ropes course.

Education   Academic program available at additional cost. Serves ages 12–18, grades 7–12. 7 teachers on staff. Curriculum accredited or approved by local school district. Cost of educational program sometimes covered by local school district.

Costs   Average cost: $265 per day. Accepts private insurance, medicaid, Blue Cross/Blue Shield, public funds.

Additional Services   Drug and alcohol rehabilitation services for males ages 12–18. Treats learning disabilities; behavior disorders; substance abuse; compulsive/addictive disorders other than substance abuse and eating disorders; post-traumatic stress disorder; thought, mood, and personality disorders. Wilderness/survival program for males and females ages 10–14. Treats learning disabilities; behavior disorders; post-traumatic stress disorder; thought, mood, and personality disorders.

Contact   Richard Burnett, Vice President/Clinical, main address above. Phone: 913-825-0541. Fax: 913-825-2502.

ST. JOHN MEDICAL CENTER
St. John Heights
Steubenville, Ohio 43952
614-264-8000; Fax: 614-264-8620

General Information   General hospital for adolescents, adults. 18 beds for adolescents. Open year-round. Patient security: staff secured; will pursue and return runaways. Urban setting. Not-for-profit facility affiliated with Franciscan Services Corporation, Sylvania, OH. Licensed by state of Ohio. Accredited by JCAHO.

Participants   Accepts: male and female adolescents ages 13–18; male and female adults ages 18 and up. Average stay: 18 days. Admission: one parent, all parties who share custody, court order, voluntary, depending on program. Treats behavior disorders; general psychosocial disorders; substance abuse; post-traumatic stress disorder; thought, mood, and personality disorders.

Program   Treatment modalities: Twelve Step Recovery.

Facilities   Single building; males and females in co-educational units. Separate residential quarters for adolescents. Central dining (not shared with adults). Basketball courts, game room, gymnasium.

Education Academic program available at no charge. Serves ages 13–18, grades 8–12.

Costs Average cost: $525 per day. Accepts private insurance, group insurance, medicare, medicaid, Blue Cross/Blue Shield.

Additional Services Outpatient services for males and females ages 18 and up. Treats substance abuse.

Contact Pamela Rhodes, Marketing Representative, main address above. Phone: 614-264-8020. Fax: 614-264-8620.

ST. JOSEPH HEALTH CENTER
300 First Capitol Drive
St. Charles, Missouri 63301
314-947-5020; Fax: 314-947-5064

General Information General hospital for adolescents. 18 beds for adolescents. Open year-round. Patient security: entirely locked; no runaway pursuit. Suburban setting. Independent not-for-profit facility. Licensed by state of Missouri. Accredited by JCAHO.

Participants Accepts: male and female adolescents ages 12–18. Admission: all parties who share custody. Treats learning disabilities; behavior disorders; general psychosocial disorders; substance abuse; eating disorders; compulsive/addictive disorders other than substance abuse and eating disorders; post-traumatic stress disorder; thought, mood, and personality disorders. Accepts the mobility impaired; those with a history of arson; those with a history of harm to themselves and others; those receiving psychotropic medication; those with a history of epilepsy. Special programs for the mobility impaired; those with AIDS. Largest number of participants from Missouri, Illinois.

Program Treatment modalities: Twelve Step Recovery (dual diagnosis); psychodynamic therapy; cognitive therapy; expressive therapy. Family treatment program available.

Staff 1.9 full-time direct-care staff members per adolescent. Total facility staff includes 1 psychologist, 8 psychiatrists, 10 registered nurses, 3 MSW social workers, 1 teacher, 10 counselors, 2 occupational/recreational therapists. Staff is 50% male, 50% female.

Facilities Single building; males and females in coeducational units. Central dining. Game room, gymnasium, outdoor swimming pool, crafts room.

Education Academic program available at no charge. Serves ages 12–18, grades 6–12. 1 teacher on staff.

Costs Average cost: $435 per day. Accepts private insurance, group insurance, medicaid, Blue Cross/Blue Shield.

Additional Services Drug and alcohol rehabilitation services for males and females ages 12–18. Treats learning disabilities; behavior disorders; general psychosocial disorders; substance abuse; eating disorders; compulsive/addictive disorders other than substance abuse and eating disorders; post-traumatic stress disorder; thought, mood, and personality disorders. Outpatient services for males and females ages 10–18. Treats autistic disorders; learning disabilities; behavior disorders; general psychosocial disorders; substance abuse; eating disorders; compulsive/addictive disorders other than substance abuse and eating disorders; post-traumatic stress disorder; thought, mood, and personality disorders. Acute inpatient/partial hospitalization for males and females ages 12–18. Treats learning disabilities; behavior disorders; general psychosocial disorders; substance abuse; eating disorders; compulsive/addictive disorders other than substance abuse and eating disorders; post-traumatic stress disorder; thought, mood, and personality disorders.

Contact Linda Street, Intake Coordinator, main address above. Phone: 314-947-5020. Fax: 314-947-5064.

ST. JOSEPH'S CARONDELET CHILD CENTER
739 East 35th Street
Chicago, Illinois 60616
312-624-7443; Fax: 312-624-7676

General Information Residential treatment/subacute facility for children, adolescents. Patient security: staff secured. Independent not-for-profit facility. Licensed by state of Illinois.

Participants Accepts: male children; male adolescents. Average stay: 2 years. Admission: one parent, all parties who share custody, court order, voluntary, depending on program. Treats learning disabilities; behavior disorders; general psychosocial disorders; eating disorders; compulsive/addictive disorders other than substance abuse and eating disorders; post-traumatic stress disorder; thought, mood, and personality disorders.

Staff Staff is 50% male, 50% female.

Additional Services Day treatment program for males and females ages 5–18. Treats learning disabilities; behavior disorders; general psychosocial disorders; eating disorders; compulsive/addictive disorders other than substance abuse and eating disorders; post-traumatic stress disorder; thought, mood, and personality disorders.

Contact Thomas G. Eagan, Program Director, main address above. Phone: 312-624-7443. Fax: 312-624-7676.

SAINT JOSEPH'S CHILDREN'S HOME
South Main Street
P.O. Box 1117
Torrington, Wyoming 82240
307-532-4197

General Information Residential treatment/subacute facility for children, adolescents. Patient security: staff secured. Not-for-profit facility affiliated with Cheyenne Diocese, Cheyenne, WY. Licensed by state of Wyoming. Accredited by Wyoming Department of Family Services.

Participants Accepts: male and female children; male and female adolescents. Average stay: 9 months. Admission: one parent, all parties who share custody, court order, depending on program. Treats learning disabilities; behavior disorders; general psychosocial disorders; substance abuse; eating disorders; posttraumatic stress disorder; thought, mood, and personality disorders.

Staff Staff is 35% male, 65% female.

Costs Average cost: $85 per day.

Contact Lori Stromberg, Residential Coordinator, main address above. Phone: 307-532-4197.

ST. JOSEPH'S HOME FOR CHILDREN
1121 East 46th Street
Minneapolis, Minnesota 55407
612-827-6241; Fax: 612-827-7954

General Information Children's emergency shelter and residential treatment center for children, adolescents. 30 beds for children; 76 beds for adolescents; 106 beds total. Open year-round. Patient security: staff secured. Urban setting. Not-for-profit facility affiliated with Catholic Charities of Archdiocese of St. Paul, Minneapolis, MN. Licensed by state of Minnesota. Accredited by JCAHO.

Participants Accepts: male and female children ages up to 12; male and female adolescents ages 13–17. Admission: one parent, all parties who share custody, court order, voluntary, depending on program. Treats

behavior disorders; general psychosocial disorders; thought, mood, and personality disorders. Accepts the hearing impaired; those receiving psychotropic medication. Special programs for the developmentally disabled; the hearing impaired.

Program Treatment modalities: milieu treatment modality; Erickson's stages of development. Family treatment program available.

Staff Total facility staff includes 2 physicians, 1 psychologist, 1 psychiatrist, 14 registered nurses, 1 practical/vocational nurse, 12 MSW social workers, 10 teachers, 145 counselors, 2 occupational/recreational therapists, 1 speech pathologist, 60 other direct-care staff members. Staff is 39% male, 61% female.

Facilities Multiple buildings; males and females in coeducational units. Central dining (shared with adults), separate dining by residential unit, in-room dining available. Basketball courts, game room, gymnasium, playing fields, vita course, weight room.

Education Academic program available. Serves ages 6–17, grades 1–12. 10 teachers on staff. Curriculum accredited or approved by Minneapolis Public Schools Board of Education. Organized sports program offered.

Costs Average cost: $115 per day. Accepts private insurance, group insurance, Blue Cross/Blue Shield, public funds.

Additional Services Outpatient services for males and females ages 7–17. Treats learning disabilities; behavior disorders; general psychosocial disorders; compulsive/addictive disorders other than substance abuse and eating disorders; thought, mood, and personality disorders.

Contact Douglas H. Goke, Administrator, main address above. Phone: 612-827-6241. Fax: 612-827-7954.

ST. JOSEPH'S VILLA
3300 Dewey Avenue
Rochester, New York 14616
716-865-1550; Fax: 716-865-5219

General Information Residential treatment/subacute facility for adolescents. 93 beds for adolescents. Open year-round. Patient security: unlocked; will pursue and return runaways. Suburban setting. Independent not-for-profit facility. Licensed by state of New York. Accredited by JCAHO; American Association of Children's Residential Centers, New York State Division of Alcoholism and Substance Abuse Services, New York State Office of Mental

Health, New York State Department of Social Services.

Participants Accepts: male and female adolescents ages 11–19. Average stay: 1 year. Admission: all parties who share custody, court order, voluntary, depending on program. Treats learning disabilities; behavior disorders; general psychosocial disorders; substance abuse; eating disorders; post-traumatic stress disorder; thought, mood, and personality disorders. Accepts the speech impaired; those with a history of arson; those receiving psychotropic medication.

Program Treatment modalities: psychodynamic; milieu/behavior modification; Twelve Step Recovery. Family treatment program available.

Staff Total facility staff includes 1 physician, 4 psychologists, 3 psychiatrists, 6 registered nurses, 20 MSW social workers, 20 teachers, 75 counselors, 5 occupational/recreational therapists, 1 speech pathologist, 1 dietician, 20 other direct-care staff members. Staff is 50% male, 50% female.

Facilities Multiple buildings; males and females in separate units. Separate dining by residential unit available. Basketball courts, game room, gymnasium, outdoor swimming pool, playing fields, ropes course, project adventure stations, canoeing.

Education Academic program available. Serves ages 11–19, grades 4–12. 20 teachers on staff. Curriculum accredited or approved by New York State Education Department. Cost of educational program sometimes covered by local school district. Organized sports program offered.

Costs Average cost: $107 per day. Accepts medicaid, public funds.

Additional Services Drug and alcohol rehabilitation services for males ages 13–18. Treats learning disabilities; behavior disorders; general psychosocial disorders; substance abuse; post-traumatic stress disorder; thought, mood, and personality disorders. Outpatient services for males and females ages 12–21. Treats behavior disorders; general psychosocial disorders; thought, mood, and personality disorders. Group homes for males and females ages 11–18. Treats learning disabilities; behavior disorders; general psychosocial disorders; eating disorders; post-traumatic stress disorder; thought, mood, and personality disorders.

Contact Cheryl Olney, Director of Intake, main address above. Phone: 716-865-1550. Fax: 716-865-5219.

ST. LUKE'S BEHAVIORAL HEALTH CENTER
1800 East Van Buren
Phoenix, Arizona 85006
602-251-8100; Fax: 602-251-8694

General Information Freestanding psychiatric and chemical dependency facility for children, adolescents. Independent not-for-profit facility. Licensed by state of Arizona. Accredited by JCAHO.

Participants Accepts: male and female children; male and female adolescents. Treats behavior disorders; substance abuse; compulsive/addictive disorders other than substance abuse and eating disorders; post-traumatic stress disorder; thought, mood, and personality disorders.

Contact Main address above. Phone: 602-251-8535.

ST. LUKE'S GORDON RECOVERY CENTER
3200 West 4th Street
Sioux City, Iowa 51102
712-258-4578

General Information Drug and alcohol rehabilitation center for adolescents. 30 beds for adolescents. Patient security: staff secured. Not-for-profit facility affiliated with St. Luke's Health System, Sioux City, IA. Licensed by state of Iowa. Accredited by JCAHO.

Participants Accepts: male and female adolescents. Average stay: 65 days. Admission: one parent, all parties who share custody, court order, voluntary, depending on program. Treats substance abuse. Accepts the mobility impaired; the vision impaired; the hearing impaired; the speech impaired; those with a history of arson; those with a history of harm to themselves and others; those receiving psychotropic medication; those with a history of epilepsy.

Staff Staff is 50% male, 50% female.

Costs Average cost: $200 per day.

Contact Robert Campbell, Manager of Adolescent Inpatient Services, 2700 Pierce Street, Sioux City, IA 51104. Phone: 712-258-4578.

ST. LUKE'S HOSPITAL
1026 A Avenue, NE
Cedar Rapids, Iowa 52402
319-369-7211

General Information General hospital for children, adolescents. Patient security: entirely locked. Independent not-for-profit facility. Licensed by state of Iowa. Accredited by JCAHO.

Participants Accepts: male and female children; male and female adolescents. Average stay: 3 weeks. Admission: one parent, all parties who share custody, court order, voluntary, depending on program. Treats learning disabilities; behavior disorders; general psychosocial disorders; eating disorders; post-traumatic stress disorder; thought, mood, and personality disorders.

Staff Staff is 15% male, 85% female.

Costs Average cost: $600 per day.

Additional Services Outpatient services for males and females ages 1 and up. Treats learning disabilities; behavior disorders; general psychosocial disorders; substance abuse; eating disorders; compulsive/addictive disorders other than substance abuse and eating disorders; post-traumatic stress disorder; thought, mood, and personality disorders.

Contact Kent Jackson, Child/Adolescent Services Manager, P.O. Box 3026, Cedar Rapids, IA 52406-3026. Phone: 319-369-8356. Fax: 319-369-8036.

ST. MARY-CORWIN REGIONAL MEDICAL CENTER
1008 Minnequa Avenue
Pueblo, Colorado 81004
719-560-5610; Fax: 719-560-4646

General Information General hospital for children, adolescents, adults. 4 beds for children; 8 beds for adolescents; 30 beds total. Open year-round. Patient security: partially locked; will pursue and return runaways. Urban setting. Not-for-profit facility affiliated with Sisters of Charity Health Systems, Cincinnati, OH. Licensed by state of Colorado. Accredited by JCAHO.

Participants Accepts: male and female children ages 2–12; male and female adolescents ages 13–18; male and female adults ages 19 and up. Average stay: 10 days. Admission: court order, voluntary, depending on program. Treats autistic disorders; learning disabilities; behavior disorders; general psychosocial disorders; substance abuse; eating disorders; compulsive/addictive disorders other than substance abuse and eating disorders; post-traumatic stress disorder; thought, mood, and personality disorders. Accepts the mobility impaired; the vision impaired; the hearing impaired; the speech impaired; those with a history of arson; the sexually compulsive; those with a history of harm to themselves and others; those receiving psychotropic medication; non-English speaking individuals; those with a history of epilepsy. Special programs for the chronically ill; the mobility impaired; the developmentally disabled; the vision impaired; the hearing impaired; the speech impaired; those with AIDS.

Program Treatment modalities: recovery program; Mom, Pops, and Tots; behavior modification; partial hospitalization. Family treatment program available.

Staff .9 full-time direct-care staff member per child or adolescent. Total facility staff includes 3 registered nurses, 1 teacher, 4 counselors, 1 occupational/recreational therapist, 1 therapist, 1 other direct-care staff member. Staff is 27% male, 73% female.

Facilities Single building; males and females in coeducational units. Separate residential quarters for children and adolescents. Central dining (not shared with adults). Basketball courts, game room, gymnasium, outdoor tennis courts.

Education Academic program available at no charge. Serves ages 6–18, grades K–12. 1 teacher on staff. Organized sports program offered.

Costs Average cost: $400 per day. Accepts private insurance, group insurance, medicare, medicaid, Blue Cross/Blue Shield, public funds.

Additional Services Drug and alcohol rehabilitation services for males and females ages 12–18. Treats behavior disorders; general psychosocial disorders; substance abuse; post-traumatic stress disorder; thought, mood, and personality disorders. Outpatient services for males and females ages 3–18. Treats autistic disorders; learning disabilities; behavior disorders; general psychosocial disorders; substance abuse; eating disorders; compulsive/addictive disorders other than substance abuse and eating disorders; post-traumatic stress disorder; thought, mood, and personality disorders.

Contact Linda Young, main address above. Phone: 719-560-5610. Fax: 719-560-4646.

SAINT MARY OF NAZARETH HOSPITAL CENTER
2233 West Division
Chicago, Illinois 60622
312-770-2000; Fax: 312-770-2392

General Information General hospital for children, adolescents, adults. 15 beds for adolescents. Open year-round. Patient security: partially locked; will pursue and return runaways. Urban setting. Independent not-for-profit facility. Licensed by state of Illinois. Accredited by JCAHO.

Participants Accepts: male and female children ages 1–12; male and female adolescents ages 12–18; male and female adults ages 18 and up. Average stay: 21 days. Admission: one parent. Treats learning disabilities; behavior disorders; general psychosocial disorders; substance abuse; eating disorders; compulsive/addictive disorders other than substance abuse and eating disorders; post-traumatic stress disorder; thought, mood, and personality disorders. Accepts those with a history of harm to themselves and others; those receiving psychotropic medication; non-English speaking individuals; those with a history of epilepsy.

Program Treatment modalities: psychodynamic; psychiatric medical model. Family treatment program available.

Staff Total facility staff includes 4 psychologists, 15 psychiatrists, 39 registered nurses, 13 MSW social workers, 1 teacher, 41 counselors, 6 occupational/recreational therapists, 1 therapist. Staff is 35% male, 65% female.

Facilities Single building; males and females in co-educational units. Central dining (not shared with adults). Basketball courts, game room, gymnasium, playing fields, exercise bike, weights.

Education Academic program available at no charge. Serves ages 12–18. 1 teacher on staff. Cost of educational program sometimes covered by local school district. Organized sports program offered.

Costs Average cost: $15,000 per stay. Accepts private insurance, group insurance, medicaid, Blue Cross/Blue Shield, public funds.

Additional Services Outpatient services for males and females ages up to 18. Treats learning disabilities; behavior disorders; general psychosocial disorders; substance abuse; compulsive/addictive disorders other than substance abuse and eating disorders; post-traumatic stress disorder; thought, mood, and personality disorders.

Contact Michael Pelletier, Director, Mental Health, main address above. Phone: 312-770-2606.

ST. MARY'S ADOLESCENT SUBSTANCE ABUSE CENTER
1111 3rd Street, SW
Dyersville, Iowa 52040
319-875-2951; Fax: 319-875-2957

General Information General hospital for adolescents. 18 beds for adolescents. Patient security: staff secured. Not-for-profit facility affiliated with Mercy Health Care, Dubuque, IA. Accredited by JCAHO.

Participants Accepts: male and female adolescents. Average stay: 26 days. Admission: one parent, all parties who share custody, court order, voluntary, depending on program. Treats substance abuse. Accepts the mobility impaired; the vision impaired; the hearing impaired; the speech impaired; those with a history of arson; the sexually compulsive; those with a history of harm to themselves and others; those receiving psychotropic medication; those with a history of epilepsy.

Staff Staff is 25% male, 75% female.

Contact Dianna Kirkland, Program Coordinator, main address above. Phone: 319-875-2951. Fax: 319-875-2957.

ST. MARY'S HILL HOSPITAL
2350 North Lake Drive
Milwaukee, Wisconsin 53211
414-291-1650; Fax: 414-291-1688

General Information Psychiatric hospital for children, adolescents. Patient security: entirely locked. Not-for-profit facility affiliated with St. Mary's Hospital, Milwaukee, WI. Licensed by state of Wisconsin. Accredited by JCAHO.

Participants Accepts: male and female children; male and female adolescents. Average stay: 14 days. Admission: one parent, all parties who share custody, court order, voluntary, depending on program. Treats autistic disorders; learning disabilities; behavior disorders; general psychosocial disorders; substance abuse; eating disorders; compulsive/addictive disorders other than substance abuse and eating disorders; post-traumatic stress disorder; thought, mood, and personality disorders.

Staff Staff is 50% male, 50% female.

Costs Average cost: $650 per day.

Additional Services Outpatient services for males and females ages 4–19. Treats autistic disorders; learning disabilities; behavior disorders; general psychosocial disorders; substance abuse; eating disorders; compulsive/addictive disorders other than substance abuse and eating disorders; post-traumatic stress disorder; thought, mood, and personality disorders.

Contact Greg Kresse, Program Director of Child and Adolescent Services, main address above. Phone: 414-291-1683. Fax: 414-294-1688.

ST. MARY'S MEDICAL CENTER
900 Oak Hill Avenue
Knoxville, Tennessee 37917
615-971-6011; Fax: 615-971-7823

General Information General hospital for adolescents. 16 beds for adolescents. Patient security: entirely locked. Independent not-for-profit facility. Licensed by state of Tennessee. Accredited by JCAHO.

Participants Accepts: male and female adolescents. Average stay: 3 weeks. Admission: one parent, all parties who share custody, voluntary, depending on program. Treats autistic disorders; learning disabilities; behavior disorders; general psychosocial disorders; substance abuse; eating disorders; compulsive/addictive disorders other than substance abuse and eating disorders; post-traumatic stress disorder; thought, mood, and personality disorders.

Staff Staff is 10% male, 90% female.

Costs Average cost: $550 per day.

Contact Brenda Robinson, Nurse Manager, main address above. Phone: 615-971-7550. Fax: 615-971-7823.

ST. MARY'S REGIONAL MEDICAL CENTER, NEW FOUNDATION CENTER FOR ADDICTIONS AND BEHAVIORAL HEALTH
235 West 6th Street
Reno, Nevada 89520
702-789-3111

General Information General hospital for adolescents. 16 beds for adolescents. Patient security: staff secured. Independent not-for-profit facility. Licensed by state of Nevada. Accredited by JCAHO; Bureau of Alcohol and Drug Abuse.

Participants Accepts: male and female adolescents. Average stay: 26 days. Admission: one parent, all parties who share custody, court order, voluntary, depending on program. Treats learning disabilities;

behavior disorders; general psychosocial disorders; substance abuse; eating disorders; compulsive/addictive disorders other than substance abuse and eating disorders; post-traumatic stress disorder; thought, mood, and personality disorders.

Staff Staff is 40% male, 60% female.

Costs Average cost: $350 per day.

Contact Marilyn Taylor, Program Director, main address above. Phone: 702-789-3111.

ST. PETER CHEMICAL DEPENDENCY CENTER
4800 College Street
Lacey, Washington 98503
800-332-0465; Fax: 206-491-2332

General Information Drug and alcohol rehabilitation center for adolescents. 24 beds for adolescents. Patient security: partially locked. Not-for-profit facility affiliated with Sisters of Providence. Licensed by state of Washington. Accredited by JCAHO.

Participants Accepts: male and female adolescents. Average stay: 30 days. Admission: one parent, all parties who share custody, court order, voluntary, depending on program. Treats substance abuse. Accepts the mobility impaired; the hearing impaired; those with a history of arson; those with a history of harm to themselves and others; those receiving psychotropic medication; those with a history of epilepsy.

Staff Staff is 40% male, 60% female.

Costs Average cost: $330 per day.

Contact Bruce Hendry, Admissions Coordinator, main address above. Phone: 800-332-0465. Fax: 206-491-2332.

ST. ROSE RESIDENCE
3801 North 88th
Milwaukee, Wisconsin 53222
414-466-9450; Fax: 414-466-0730

General Information Residential treatment/subacute facility for children, adolescents. 10 beds for children; 38 beds for adolescents; 48 beds total. Open year-round. Patient security: staff secured; no runaway pursuit. Urban setting. Independent not-for-profit facility. Licensed by state of Wisconsin. Accredited by JCAHO.

Participants Accepts: female children ages 7–12; female adolescents ages 13–17. Average stay: 403

days. Admission: all parties who share custody, court order, depending on program. Treats learning disabilities; behavior disorders; general psychosocial disorders; substance abuse; eating disorders; compulsive/addictive disorders other than substance abuse and eating disorders; post-traumatic stress disorder; thought, mood, and personality disorders. Accepts the speech impaired; those with a history of arson; the sexually compulsive; those with a history of harm to themselves and others; those receiving psychotropic medication; those with a history of epilepsy. Largest number of participants from Wisconsin, Illinois, Indiana.

Program Treatment modalities: pyschodynamic; systems approach. Family treatment program available.

Staff 1.1 full-time direct-care staff members per child or adolescent. Total facility staff includes 1 psychiatrist, 1 registered nurse, 5 MSW social workers, 20 social workers (non-MSW), 10 teachers, 2 occupational/recreational therapists, 1 speech pathologist, 1 dietician, 7 other direct-care staff members. Staff is 15% male, 85% female.

Facilities Single building. Separate dining by residential unit available. Basketball courts, game room, gymnasium, playing fields.

Education Academic program available. Serves ages 7–17, ungraded. 10 teachers on staff. Curriculum accredited or approved by State of Wisconsin. Organized sports program offered.

Costs Average cost: $3980 per month. Accepts private insurance, Blue Cross/Blue Shield, public funds.

Additional Services Outpatient services for females ages 7–18. Treats learning disabilities; behavior disorders; general psychosocial disorders; substance abuse; eating disorders; compulsive/addictive disorders other than substance abuse and eating disorders; post-traumatic stress disorder; thought, mood, and personality disorders.

Contact James Maro, Director, Child Care, main address above. Phone: 414-466-9450. Fax: 414-466-0130.

ST. VINCENT AND SARAH FISHER CENTER RESIDENTIAL TREATMENT PROGRAM
27400 West Twelve Mile Road
Farmington Hills, Michigan 48334-4200
313-626-7527; Fax: 313-626-0865

General Information Residential treatment/subacute facility for children, adolescents. Open year-

round. Patient security: unlocked; will pursue and return runaways. Suburban setting. Licensed by state of Michigan. Accredited by Council on Accreditation of Services for Families and Children.

Participants Accepts: male and female children ages 4–11; male and female adolescents ages 11–16. Average stay: 450 days. Admission: court order, Department of Mental Health with consent of parent, depending on program. Treats learning disabilities; behavior disorders; general psychosocial disorders; eating disorders; thought, mood, and personality disorders. Accepts the speech impaired; those with a history of arson; the sexually compulsive; those with a history of harm to themselves and others; those receiving psychotropic medication; those with a history of epilepsy.

Program Treatment modalities: psychodynamic. Family treatment program available.

Staff .1 full-time direct-care staff member per child or adolescent. Total facility staff includes 1 registered nurse, 1 practical/vocational nurse, 1 occupational/recreational therapist, 1 dietician.

Facilities Multiple buildings; males and females in separate units. Separate dining by residential unit available. Basketball courts, game room, gymnasium, playing fields.

Education Educational arrangements: Farmington Public School. Educational program held off-site at no charge. Cost of educational program covered by local school district. Organized sports program offered.

Costs Average cost: $180 per day. Accepts medicaid, public funds.

Contact Catherine Lamb, Program Director, main address above. Phone: 313-626-7527. Fax: 313-626-0865.

ST. VINCENT MEDICAL CENTER
2213 Cherry Street
Toledo, Ohio 43608-2691
419-321-3232; Fax: 419-321-3810

General Information General hospital for children, adolescents. Patient security: staff secured. Not-for-profit facility affiliated with Covenant Health Systems, Inc., Lexington, MA. Licensed by state of Ohio. Accredited by JCAHO.

Participants Accepts: male and female children; male and female adolescents. Average stay: 19 days. Admission: all parties who share custody, court order, depending on program. Treats learning disabilities; behavior disorders; general psychosocial disorders; substance abuse; eating disorders; compulsive/addictive disorders other than substance abuse and eating disorders; post-traumatic stress disorder; thought, mood, and personality disorders.

Contact Linda Heineman, Administrative Director of Behavioral Health Services, main address above. Phone: 419-321-4785.

ST. VINCENT'S ADOLESCENT PSYCHIATRIC SERVICES
455 St. Michael's Drive
Santa Fe, New Mexico 87501
505-989-5372; Fax: 505-989-5208

General Information General hospital for adolescents. 14 beds for adolescents. Open year-round. Patient security: entirely locked; no runaway pursuit. Small town setting. Independent not-for-profit facility. Licensed by state of New Mexico. Accredited by JCAHO.

Participants Accepts: male and female adolescents ages 12–18. Average stay: 25 days. Admission: one parent, all parties who share custody, court order, depending on program. Treats learning disabilities; behavior disorders; general psychosocial disorders; substance abuse; eating disorders; post-traumatic stress disorder; thought, mood, and personality disorders. Accepts the mobility impaired; the vision impaired; the hearing impaired; the speech impaired; those with a history of arson; the sexually compulsive; those with a history of harm to themselves and others; those receiving psychotropic medication; non-English speaking individuals; those with a history of epilepsy.

Program Treatment modalities: psychodynamic; chemical dependency track utilizing Twelve Step Recovery model. Family treatment program available.

Staff Total facility staff includes 2 physicians, 2 psychologists, 2 psychiatrists, 8 registered nurses, 1 teacher, 10 counselors, 2 physical therapists, 2 occupational/recreational therapists, 1 speech pathologist, 2 therapists, 1 dietician. Staff is 40% male, 60% female.

Facilities Single building; males and females in coeducational units. Separate dining by residential unit available. Basketball courts, gymnasium, outdoor tennis courts, playing fields, ropes course, low elements course.

Education Academic program available. Serves ages 12–18, grades 6–12. 1 teacher on staff. Curriculum accredited or approved by New Mexico State Department of Education. Organized sports program offered.

Costs Average cost: $16,000 per stay. Accepts private insurance, group insurance, medicaid, Blue Cross/Blue Shield, public funds.

Additional Services Drug and alcohol rehabilitation services for males and females ages 12–18. Treats learning disabilities; behavior disorders; general psychosocial disorders; substance abuse; eating disorders; compulsive/addictive disorders other than substance abuse and eating disorders; post-traumatic stress disorder; thought, mood, and personality disorders. Outpatient services for males and females ages 12–18. Treats learning disabilities; behavior disorders; general psychosocial disorders; substance abuse; eating disorders; compulsive/addictive disorders other than substance abuse and eating disorders; post-traumatic stress disorder; thought, mood, and personality disorders. Partial hospital program-family systems for males and females ages 12–18. Treats learning disabilities; behavior disorders; general psychosocial disorders; substance abuse; eating disorders; compulsive/addictive disorders other than substance abuse and eating disorders; post-traumatic stress disorder; thought, mood, and personality disorders.

Contact Olivia Cohen, Clinical Intake Coordinator, main address above. Phone: 505-989-5372. Fax: 505-989-5208.

SALVATION ARMY ADDICTION TREATMENT SERVICES
3624 Waokanaka Street
Honolulu, Hawaii 96817
808-595-6371

General Information Drug and alcohol rehabilitation center for adolescents. 10 beds for adolescents. Patient security: staff secured. Not-for-profit facility affiliated with Salvation Army, Honolulu, HI. Licensed by state of Hawaii. Accredited by Commission on Accreditation of Rehabilitation Facilities.

Participants Accepts: male adolescents. Average stay: 9 months. Admission: one parent, all parties who share custody, court order, voluntary, depending on program. Treats substance abuse. Accepts the mobility impaired; the vision impaired; the hearing impaired; the speech impaired; those with a history of arson; those with a history of epilepsy.

Costs Average cost: $80 per day.

Contact Richard Walsh, Program Director, main address above. Phone: 808-595-6371.

THE SALVATION ARMY TREATMENT PROGRAMS FOR WOMEN AND CHILDREN
2950 Manoa Road
Honolulu, Hawaii 96822
808-988-7423; Fax: 808-988-5285

General Information Residential drug/alcohol treatment and psychiatric day treatment program for children, adolescents, adults. 15 beds for children; 6 beds for adolescents. Open year-round. Patient security: staff secured. Suburban setting. Independent not-for-profit facility. Licensed by state of Hawaii. Accredited by JCAHO; Commission on Accreditation of Rehabilitation Facilities.

Participants Accepts: male and female children ages 1–8; female adolescents ages 15–18; female adults ages 18 and up. Average stay: 18 months. Admission: one parent, court order, voluntary, depending on program. Treats learning disabilities; behavior disorders; general psychosocial disorders; substance abuse; eating disorders; compulsive/addictive disorders other than substance abuse and eating disorders; post-traumatic stress disorder. Accepts the mobility impaired; the vision impaired; the hearing impaired; the speech impaired; those receiving psychotropic medication; those with a history of epilepsy. Largest number of participants from Hawaii.

Program Treatment modalities: Twelve Step Recovery; psychodynamic; eclectic; humanistic. Family treatment program available.

Staff Total facility staff includes 2 psychiatrists, 1 registered nurse, 1 practical/vocational nurse, 3 MSW social workers, 4 teachers, 8 counselors, 9 other direct-care staff members. Staff is 23% male, 77% female.

Facilities Multiple buildings.

Education Academic program available at no charge. Serves ages 3–18, ungraded. 4 teachers on staff. Cost of educational program covered by local school district.

Costs Accepts public funds.

Contact Claire Woods, Director, Women and Children's Services, main address above. Phone: 808-988-7423. Fax: 808-988-5285.

THE SANDSTONE CENTER
4201 Texas Avenue, South
College Station, Texas 77840
409-690-3030; Fax: 409-690-0870

General Information Psychiatric hospital for children, adolescents, adults. 10 beds for children; 25 beds for adolescents; 70 beds total. Open year-round. Patient security: entirely locked; will pursue and return runaways. Small town setting. For-profit facility affiliated with Innovative Healthcare, Birmingham, TX. Licensed by state of Texas. Accredited by JCAHO; Mental Health and Mental Retardation.

Participants Accepts: male and female children ages 5–12; male and female adolescents ages 13–18; male and female adults ages 17 and up. Average stay: 26 days. Admission: one parent, court order, voluntary, depending on program. Treats learning disabilities; behavior disorders; general psychosocial disorders; substance abuse; eating disorders; compulsive/addictive disorders other than substance abuse and eating disorders; post-traumatic stress disorder; thought, mood, and personality disorders. Accepts the mobility impaired; the vision impaired; the speech impaired; those with a history of arson; the sexually compulsive; those with a history of harm to themselves and others; those receiving psychotropic medication; those with a history of epilepsy.

Program Treatment modalities: Twelve Step Recovery; psychodynamic; behavioral modification. Family treatment program available.

Staff Total facility staff includes 6 physicians, 2 psychologists, 3 psychiatrists, 13 registered nurses, 3 practical/vocational nurses, 2 MSW social workers, 1 social worker (non-MSW), 1 teacher, 1 counselor, 2 occupational/recreational therapists, 1 dietician, 6 other direct-care staff members. Staff is 40% male, 60% female.

Facilities Single building; males and females in co-educational units. Separate residential quarters for children and adolescents. Central dining (shared with adults). Gymnasium, outdoor swimming pool.

Education Academic program available at no charge. Serves ages 5–18, grades 1–12. 1 teacher on staff. Curriculum accredited or approved by College Station Independent School District.

Costs Average cost: $23,530 per stay. Accepts private insurance, group insurance, medicare, Blue Cross/Blue Shield, public funds.

Additional Services Drug and alcohol rehabilitation services for males and females ages 17 and up. Treats general psychosocial disorders; substance abuse; compulsive/addictive disorders other than substance abuse and eating disorders; post-traumatic stress disorder; thought, mood, and personality disorders.

Residential or sub-acute services for males and females ages 5 and up. Treats behavior disorders; general psychosocial disorders; substance abuse; eating disorders; compulsive/addictive disorders other than substance abuse and eating disorders; post-traumatic stress disorder; thought, mood, and personality disorders.

Contact Mary Lou Millett, Director of Admissions, main address above. Phone: 409-690-3030. Fax: 409-690-0870.

SANDY PINES HOSPITAL
11301 Southeast Tequesta Terrace
Tequesta, Florida 33469
407-744-0211; Fax: 407-575-1445

General Information Psychiatric hospital for children, adolescents. 15 beds for children; 45 beds for adolescents; 60 beds total. Open year-round. Patient security: entirely locked; no runaway pursuit. Small town setting. For-profit facility affiliated with Health Management Associates, Inc., Naples, FL. Licensed by state of Florida. Accredited by JCAHO; Health and Rehabilitative Services.

Participants Accepts: male and female children ages 3–11; male and female adolescents ages 12–18. Average stay: 22 days. Admission: one parent, all parties who share custody, court order, depending on program. Treats autistic disorders; learning disabilities; behavior disorders; general psychosocial disorders; substance abuse; eating disorders; compulsive/addictive disorders other than substance abuse and eating disorders; post-traumatic stress disorder; thought, mood, and personality disorders. Accepts the mobility impaired; the vision impaired; the hearing impaired; the speech impaired; those with a history of arson; the sexually compulsive; those with a history of harm to themselves and others; those receiving psychotropic medication; those with a history of epilepsy.

Program Treatment modalities: multi modality; multi disciplinary; Twelve Step Recovery. Family treatment program available.

Staff Total facility staff includes 5 psychiatrists, 14 registered nurses, 1 practical/vocational nurse, 7 MSW social workers, 3 teachers, 15 counselors, 4 occupational/recreational therapists, 1 speech pathologist, 1 therapist, 1 dietician. Staff is 40% male, 60% female.

Facilities Single building; males and females in co-educational units. Central dining. Gymnasium, horseback riding, outdoor swimming pool, ropes course.

Education Academic program available at no charge. Serves ages 3–18, grades N–12. 3 teachers on staff. Curriculum accredited or approved by Martin County School District. Cost of educational program sometimes covered by local school district. Organized sports program offered.

Costs Average cost: $20,000 per stay. Accepts private insurance, group insurance, Blue Cross/Blue Shield.

Additional Services Residential or sub-acute services for males and females ages 13–18. Treats learning disabilities; behavior disorders; general psychosocial disorders; substance abuse; eating disorders; compulsive/addictive disorders other than substance abuse and eating disorders; post-traumatic stress disorder; thought, mood, and personality disorders.

Contact Cynthia Shulman, Director of Admissions, main address above. Phone: 407-744-0211. Fax: 407-575-1445.

SAN MARCOS TREATMENT CENTER, A BROWN SCHOOLS NEUROPSYCHIATRIC HOSPITAL
P.O. Box 768
San Marcos, Texas 78667-0768
800-251-0059; Fax: 512-392-2212

General Information Residential treatment/subacute facility for children, adolescents, adults. Open year-round. Patient security: partially locked; will pursue and return runaways. Small town setting. For-profit facility affiliated with Healthcare International, Austin, TX. Licensed by state of Texas. Accredited by JCAHO; Civilian Health and Medical Program of the Uniformed Services.

Participants Accepts: male and female children ages 4–12; male and female adolescents ages 13–17; male and female adults ages 18–23. Admission: one parent, all parties who share custody, court order, depending on program. Treats autistic disorders; learning disabilities; behavior disorders; general psychosocial disorders; substance abuse; eating disorders; compulsive/addictive disorders other than substance abuse and eating disorders; post-traumatic stress disorder; thought, mood, and personality disorders. Accepts the speech impaired; those with a history of arson; the sexually compulsive; those with a history of harm to themselves and others; those receiving psychotropic medication; those with a history of epilepsy. Special programs for the developmentally disabled. Largest number of participants from Illinois.

Program Treatment modalities: biopsychosocial medical model; sexual abuse program for victims and perpetrators; neuropsychiatric program. Family treatment program available.

Staff 1.3 full-time direct-care staff members per child or adolescent. Total facility staff includes 2 physicians, 4 psychologists, 5 psychiatrists, 20 registered nurses, 10 practical/vocational nurses, 6 MSW social workers, 9 social workers (non-MSW), 16 teachers, 3 counselors, 1 physical therapist, 6 occupational/recreational therapists, 3 speech pathologists, 5 therapists, 1 dietician, 13 other direct-care staff members.

Facilities Multiple buildings; males and females in coeducational units. Separate residential quarters for children and adolescents. Central dining arrangements vary. Basketball courts, game room, gymnasium, horseback riding, outdoor swimming pool, outdoor tennis courts, playing fields, ropes course.

Education Academic program available at additional cost. Serves ages 4–23, grades K–12. 16 teachers on staff. Curriculum accredited or approved by Southern Association of Colleges and Schools. Cost of educational program sometimes covered by local school district. Organized sports program offered.

Costs Accepts private insurance, group insurance, medicaid, public funds.

Contact Lonnie Forester, Director of Information and Referrals, main address above. Phone: 800-251-0054. Fax: 512-392-2212.

SAN PABLO TREATMENT CENTER, INC.
2801 North 31st Street
Phoenix, Arizona 85008
602-956-9090; Fax: 602-956-3018

General Information Residential treatment/subacute facility for adolescents. 36 beds for adolescents. Open year-round. Patient security: staff secured; no runaway pursuit. Urban setting. Independent not-for-profit facility. Licensed by state of Arizona. Accredited by JCAHO.

Participants Accepts: male adolescents ages 12–17. Average stay: 8 months. Admission: one parent, all parties who share custody, court order, depending on program. Treats learning disabilities; behavior disorders; compulsive/addictive disorders other than substance abuse and eating disorders; thought, mood, and personality disorders. Accepts those receiving

psychotropic medication; those with affective, conduct, oppositional, or adjustment disorders.

Program Treatment modalities: Adlerian Approach; cognitive therapy; reality therapy; behavior modification. Family treatment program available.

Staff .9 full-time direct-care staff member per adolescent. Total facility staff includes 2 physicians, 1 psychiatrist, 2 registered nurses, 5 social workers (non-MSW), 8 teachers, 4 counselors, 1 speech pathologist, 3 therapists, 1 dietician, 15 other direct-care staff members. Staff is 67% male, 33% female.

Facilities Multiple buildings. Central dining. Basketball courts, game room, outdoor swimming pool, outdoor tennis courts, playing fields.

Education Academic program available at additional cost. Serves ages 12–17. 8 teachers on staff. Curriculum accredited or approved by Arizona and California Departments of Education. Cost of educational program sometimes covered by local school district.

Costs Average cost: $180 per day. Accepts private insurance, group insurance, medicaid, public funds.

Contact Hal Elliott, Program Director, main address above. Phone: 602-956-9090. Fax: 602-956-3018.

See page 454 for full page description.

SCHNEIDER CHILDREN'S HOSPITAL OF LONG ISLAND
270-05 76th Avenue
New Hyde Park, New York 11042
718-470-8000

General Information General hospital for children, adolescents. Patient security: staff secured. Not-for-profit facility affiliated with Long Island Jewish Medical Center, New Hyde Park, NY. Licensed by state of New York. Accredited by JCAHO.

Participants Accepts: male and female children; male and female adolescents. Average stay: 8 days. Admission: one parent. Treats autistic disorders; learning disabilities; behavior disorders; general psychosocial disorders; substance abuse; eating disorders; post-traumatic stress disorder; thought, mood, and personality disorders.

Staff Staff is 50% male, 50% female.

Costs Average cost: $1600 per day.

Contact Dr. Esther Wender, Chief of Developmental and Behavioral Pediatrics, main address above. Phone: 718-470-3540.

SCOTTSDALE CAMELBACK HOSPITAL
7575 East Earl Drive
Scottsdale, Arizona 85251
602-941-7500; Fax: 602-994-5558

General Information Psychiatric hospital for children, adolescents. 8 beds for children; 12 beds for adolescents; 20 beds total. Open year-round. Patient security: entirely locked. Urban setting. Not-for-profit facility affiliated with Samaritan Health Systems, Phoenix, AZ. Licensed by state of Arizona. Accredited by JCAHO.

Participants Accepts: male and female children ages 3–12; male and female adolescents ages 12–18. Average stay: 1 day. Admission: all parties who share custody, court order, depending on program. Treats autistic disorders; learning disabilities; behavior disorders; general psychosocial disorders; substance abuse; eating disorders; compulsive/addictive disorders other than substance abuse and eating disorders; post-traumatic stress disorder; thought, mood, and personality disorders. Accepts the mobility impaired; the vision impaired; the hearing impaired; those with a history of arson; the sexually compulsive; those with a history of harm to themselves and others; those receiving psychotropic medication; non-English speaking individuals; those with a history of epilepsy.

Program Treatment modalities: psychodynamic; Twelve Step Recovery; behavior management; milieu therapy. Family treatment program available.

Staff Total facility staff includes 1 practical/vocational nurse, 2 MSW social workers, 4 teachers, 4 counselors, 1 occupational/recreational therapist, 1 speech pathologist, 1 dietician.

Facilities Multiple buildings; males and females in coeducational units. Central dining (shared with adults), in-room dining available. Basketball courts, game room, gymnasium, outdoor swimming pool, outdoor tennis courts, playing fields.

Education Academic program available. Serves ages 3–18, grades 1–12. 4 teachers on staff. Organized sports program offered.

Costs Average cost: $735 per stay. Accepts private insurance, group insurance, medicare, medicaid, Blue Cross/Blue Shield, public funds.

Contact Judith Verwolf, Director of the Child and Adolescent Program, main address above. Phone: 602-941-7500. Fax: 602-994-5558.

SEAFIELD PINES HOSPITAL
Route 9
Keene, New Hampshire 03431
603-357-2308; Fax: 603-357-7808

General Information Drug and alcohol rehabilitation center for adolescents. Patient security: staff secured. For-profit facility affiliated with Seafield, Inc., Westhampton, NY. Licensed by state of New Hampshire. Accredited by JCAHO.

Participants Accepts: male and female adolescents. Average stay: 42 days. Admission: one parent, all parties who share custody, court order, voluntary, depending on program. Treats substance abuse. Accepts the vision impaired; the hearing impaired; the speech impaired; those with a history of arson; the sexually compulsive; those with a history of harm to themselves and others; those receiving psychotropic medication; those with a history of epilepsy.

Staff Staff is 60% male, 40% female.

Contact Edward Schreiber, Clinical Director, main address above. Phone: 603-357-2308.

SEA PINES REHABILITATION HOSPITAL
101 East Florida Avenue
Melbourne, Florida 32901
407-984-4600; Fax: 407-984-4627

General Information Residential treatment/subacute facility for children, adolescents. Patient security: staff secured. For-profit facility affiliated with National Medical Enterprises Rehabilitation Hospital Division, Santa Monica, CA. Licensed by state of Florida. Accredited by JCAHO.

Participants Accepts: male and female children; male and female adolescents. Average stay: 2 months. Admission: one parent, all parties who share custody, depending on program. Treats learning disabilities; post-traumatic stress disorder; thought, mood, and personality disorders.

Staff Staff is 40% male, 60% female.

Contact Admitting Office, main address above. Phone: 800-356-6816.

SEATTLE INDIAN HEALTH BOARD
611 12th Avenue, South
Seattle, Washington 98114
206-324-9360

General Information Residential treatment/subacute facility for adolescents. 10 beds for adolescents. Patient security: staff secured. Independent not-for-profit facility. Licensed by state of Washington. Accredited by JCAHO.

Participants Accepts: male and female adolescents. Average stay: 2 months. Admission: one parent, all parties who share custody, court order, voluntary, depending on program. Treats behavior disorders; general psychosocial disorders; substance abuse; eating disorders; compulsive/addictive disorders other than substance abuse and eating disorders; post-traumatic stress disorder; thought, mood, and personality disorders.

Costs Average cost: $150 per day.

Contact Rebecca Gonzales, main address above. Phone: 206-324-9360.

SEMI-INDEPENDENT LIVING
524 Madison
Steubenville, Ohio 43952
614-282-5338

General Information Residential treatment/subacute facility for adolescents. 5 beds for adolescents. Patient security: staff secured. Not-for-profit facility affiliated with Jefferson County Mental Health Services Board, Inc., Steubenville, OH. Licensed by state of Ohio.

Participants Accepts: male adolescents. Average stay: 1 year. Admission: one parent, all parties who share custody, court order, voluntary, depending on program. Treats learning disabilities; behavior disorders; general psychosocial disorders; thought, mood, and personality disorders.

Staff .2 full-time direct-care staff member per adolescent.

Costs Average cost: $4500 per month.

Contact Deborah McGee, Administrative Director, main address above. Phone: 614-282-5338.

THE SETTLEMENT HOME FOR CHILDREN
1600 Peyton Gin Road
Austin, Texas 78758
512-836-2150; Fax: 512-836-2159

General Information Residential treatment/subacute facility for adolescents. 32 beds for adolescents. Open year-round. Patient security: unlocked; will pursue and return runaways. Urban setting. Independent not-for-profit facility. Licensed by state of Texas. Accredited by Texas Department of Human Services.

Participants Accepts: female adolescents ages 9–17. Average stay: 12 months. Admission: all parties who share custody. Treats learning disabilities; behavior disorders; general psychosocial disorders; eating disorders; compulsive/addictive disorders other than substance abuse and eating disorders; post-traumatic stress disorder; thought, mood, and personality disorders. Accepts those receiving psychotropic medication.

Program Treatment modalities: individual therapy; group therapy; recreational and creative arts therapies; milieu therapy—structure, feedback, nurturance. Family treatment program available.

Staff .8 full-time direct-care staff member per adolescent. Total facility staff includes 1 psychologist, 1 psychiatrist, 1 registered nurse, 3 MSW social workers, 2 social workers (non-MSW), 8 counselors, 6 therapists, 10 other direct-care staff members. Staff is 15% male, 85% female.

Facilities Multiple buildings. Central dining. Basketball courts, game room, gymnasium, playing fields, ropes course.

Education Educational arrangements: Austin Independent School District. Educational program held off-site at no charge. Cost of educational program covered by local school district.

Costs Average cost: $101 per day. Accepts private insurance, group insurance, medicaid, Blue Cross/Blue Shield, public funds.

Contact Director of Admissions, main address above. Phone: 512-836-2150. Fax: 512-836-2159.

SEVEN HAWKS WILDERNESS PROGRAM
Route 3
Box 87A
Waverly, Tennessee 37185
615-296-1835; Fax: 615-296-1878

General Information Wilderness/survival program for adolescents. 150 beds for adolescents. Patient security: staff secured. For-profit facility affiliated with Residential Management Services, Dickson, TN. Licensed by state of Tennessee.

Participants Accepts: male and female adolescents. Average stay: 12 months. Admission: one parent, all parties who share custody, court order, voluntary, depending on program. Treats learning disabilities; behavior disorders; substance abuse; post-traumatic stress disorder; thought, mood, and personality disorders.

Staff Staff is 60% male, 40% female.

Costs Average cost: $103 per day.

Contact Kim Moore, Admissions Director, 222 Church Street, Dickson, TN 37055. Phone: 800-467-2206. Fax: 615-446-3985.

SHADOW MOUNTAIN INSTITUTE
6262 South Sheridan Road
Tulsa, Oklahoma 74133
918-492-8200; Fax: 918-250-4875

General Information Residential treatment/subacute facility for children, adolescents. 33 beds for children; 75 beds for adolescents; 108 beds total. Open year-round. Patient security: partially locked; no runaway pursuit. Suburban setting. For-profit facility affiliated with Century HealthCare Corporation, Tulsa, OK. Licensed by state of Oklahoma. Accredited by JCAHO.

Participants Accepts: male and female children ages 5–11; male and female adolescents ages 12–18. Average stay: 45 days. Admission: one parent, all parties who share custody, court order, voluntary, depending on program. Treats learning disabilities; behavior disorders; general psychosocial disorders; substance abuse; eating disorders; compulsive/addictive disorders other than substance abuse and eating disorders; post-traumatic stress disorder; thought, mood, and personality disorders. Accepts the mobility impaired; the vision impaired; the hearing impaired; the speech impaired; those with a history of arson; the sexually compulsive; those with a history of harm to themselves and others; those receiving psychotropic medi-

cation; non-English speaking individuals. Special programs for the sexually abused; adopted children and families.

Program Family treatment program available.

Facilities Multiple buildings; males and females in both coeducational and separate units depending on program. Central dining. Basketball courts, game room, gymnasium, playing fields, ropes course.

Education Academic program available at no charge. Serves ages 5–18, grades K–12. Curriculum accredited or approved by Tulsa Public Schools. Cost of educational program sometimes covered by local school district.

Costs Average cost: $10,000 per stay. Accepts private insurance, group insurance, public funds.

Additional Services Drug and alcohol rehabilitation services for males and females ages 5–18. Treats learning disabilities; behavior disorders; general psychosocial disorders; substance abuse; eating disorders; compulsive/addictive disorders other than substance abuse and eating disorders; post-traumatic stress disorder; thought, mood, and personality disorders. Partial hospitalization with in-home family therapy for males and females ages 5–18. Treats learning disabilities; behavior disorders; general psychosocial disorders; substance abuse; eating disorders; compulsive/addictive disorders other than substance abuse and eating disorders; post-traumatic stress disorder; thought, mood, and personality disorders.

Contact Phil Cottrell, Director of Referral Services, main address above. Phone: 918-492-8200. Fax: 918-250-4875.

See page 414 for full page description.

SHEPPARD PRATT HOSPITAL
601 North Charles Street
Baltimore, Maryland 21204
410-938-3000; Fax: 410-938-4532

General Information Psychiatric hospital for children, adolescents, adults. 12 beds for children; 84 beds for adolescents; 303 beds total. Open year-round. Patient security: entirely locked. Suburban setting. Not-for-profit facility affiliated with Sheppard and Enoch Pratt Health System, Baltimore, MD. Licensed by state of Maryland. Accredited by JCAHO.

Participants Accepts: male and female children ages 4–12; male and female adolescents ages 12–19; male and female adults ages 18 and up. Admission: custodial parent or legal guardian. Treats learning disabilities; behavior disorders; general psychosocial disorders; substance abuse; eating disorders; compulsive/addictive disorders other than substance abuse and eating disorders; post-traumatic stress disorder; thought, mood, and personality disorders. Accepts those with a history of harm to themselves and others; those receiving psychotropic medication; those with a history of epilepsy. Special programs for the chronically ill; those with dissociative disorders.

Program Treatment modalities: psychotherapy; cognitive-behavioral therapy; psychopharmacology; Twelve Step programs. Family treatment program available.

Facilities Multiple buildings; males and females in coeducational units. Separate residential quarters for children and adolescents. Central dining (not shared with adults), in-room dining available. Basketball courts, game room, gymnasium, indoor swimming pool, outdoor tennis courts, playing fields.

Education Academic program available. Serves ages 5–12, grades K–12. Curriculum accredited or approved by State of Maryland. Cost of educational program covered by local school district. Organized sports program offered.

Costs Accepts private insurance, group insurance, medicare, medicaid, Blue Cross/Blue Shield.

Additional Services Outpatient services for males and females. Treats behavior disorders; general psychosocial disorders; substance abuse; eating disorders; compulsive/addictive disorders other than substance abuse and eating disorders; post-traumatic stress disorder; thought, mood, and personality disorders.

Contact Mat Merker, Director of Admissions, main address above. Phone: 410-938-3800. Fax: 410-938-3828.

SIERRA TUCSON ADOLESCENT CARE
39580 South Lago del Oro Parkway
Tucson, Arizona 85737
602-792-5858; Fax: 602-825-3639

General Information Psychiatric hospital for adolescents. 60 beds for adolescents. Open year-round. Patient security: staff secured; will pursue and return runaways. Rural setting. Independent for-profit facility. Licensed by state of Arizona. Accredited by JCAHO.

Participants Accepts: male and female adolescents ages 13–17. Average stay: 45 days. Admission: all parties who share custody. Treats learning disabilities; behavior disorders; general psychosocial disorders; substance abuse; eating disorders; compulsive/addictive disorders other than substance abuse and

eating disorders; post-traumatic stress disorder; thought, mood, and personality disorders. Accepts the mobility impaired; the vision impaired; the hearing impaired; the speech impaired; those with a history of arson; the sexually compulsive; those with a history of harm to themselves and others; those receiving psychotropic medication; those with a history of epilepsy.

Program Treatment modalities: Twelve Step Recovery; Sierra model; focused expressive psychotherapy. Family treatment program available.

Staff Total facility staff includes 1 physician, 2 psychiatrists, 6 registered nurses, 3 practical/vocational nurses, 1 MSW social worker, 1 teacher, 11 counselors, 1 occupational/recreational therapist, 1 dietician.

Facilities Multiple buildings; males and females in coeducational units. Central dining. Basketball courts, gymnasium, horseback riding, outdoor tennis courts, playing fields, ropes course, climbing wall.

Education Academic program available at no charge. Serves ages 13–17, ungraded. 1 teacher on staff.

Costs Average cost: $33,750 per stay. Accepts private insurance, group insurance, Blue Cross/Blue Shield, public funds.

Additional Services Drug and alcohol rehabilitation services for males and females ages 13–17. Treats autistic disorders; learning disabilities; behavior disorders; general psychosocial disorders; substance abuse; eating disorders; compulsive/addictive disorders other than substance abuse and eating disorders; post-traumatic stress disorder; thought, mood, and personality disorders.

Contact Pete Anderson, National Outreach Counselor, main address above. Phone: 602-792-5858. Fax: 602-825-3502.

Announcement Sierra Tucson's Adolescent Care program offers a truly original approach to adolescent treatment. The adolescent experiences change, rather than just hearing about the need for it. The treatment environment at Adolescent Care is both safe and nurturing so that each patient receives the respect he or she deserves. The dedicated staff ensures that each young person receives the best opportunity possible for successful recovery.

See page 456 for full page description.

SILVER HILL HOSPITAL
208 Valley Road
New Canaan, Connecticut 06840
203-966-3561; Fax: 203-966-1075

General Information Psychiatric hospital for adolescents, adults. 10 beds for adolescents. Open year-round. Patient security: partially locked; will pursue and return runaways. Small town setting. Independent not-for-profit facility. Licensed by state of Connecticut. Accredited by JCAHO; American Hospital Association.

Participants Accepts: male and female adolescents ages 13–18; male and female adults ages 18 and up. Average stay: 36 days. Admission: one parent, all parties who share custody, court order, voluntary, depending on program. Treats learning disabilities; behavior disorders; general psychosocial disorders; substance abuse; eating disorders; compulsive/addictive disorders other than substance abuse and eating disorders; post-traumatic stress disorder; thought, mood, and personality disorders. Accepts the mobility impaired; the vision impaired; the hearing impaired; the speech impaired; the sexually compulsive; those with a history of harm to themselves and others; those receiving psychotropic medication; non-English speaking individuals; those with a history of epilepsy. Special programs for the chronically ill. Largest number of participants from Connecticut, New York, New Jersey.

Program Treatment modalities: Twelve Step Recovery; psychotherapy; psychopharmacology; life skills training. Family treatment program available.

Staff Total facility staff includes 2 physicians, 2 psychologists, 13 psychiatrists, 46 registered nurses, 8 practical/vocational nurses, 10 MSW social workers, 4 teachers, 2 counselors, 1 physical therapist, 8 occupational/recreational therapists, 39 therapists, 1 dietician, 11 other direct-care staff members.

Facilities Multiple buildings; males and females in coeducational units. Separate residential quarters for adolescents. Basketball courts, game room, gymnasium, indoor swimming pool, outdoor tennis courts, playing fields.

Education Academic program available. Serves ages 13–18, grades 7–12. 4 teachers on staff. Curriculum accredited or approved by State Board of Education. Cost of educational program covered by local school district. Organized sports program offered.

Costs Average cost: $5000 per month. Accepts private insurance, group insurance, Blue Cross/Blue Shield.

Additional Services Outpatient services for males and females ages 13 and up. Treats learning disabilities; behavior disorders; general psychosocial disorders; substance abuse; eating disorders; compulsive/addictive disorders other than substance abuse and eating disorders; post-traumatic stress disorder; thought, mood, and personality disorders.

Contact Anne Cassidy, Director of Admissions, main address above. Phone: 203-966-3561. Fax: 203-966-1075.

SMITH CENTER RESIDENTIAL TREATMENT
5400 Kirkwood Boulevard, SW
Cedar Rapids, Iowa 52404
319-364-0259; Fax: 319-364-1162

General Information Residential treatment/subacute facility for children. 44 beds for children. Open year-round. Patient security: staff secured; will pursue and return runaways. Urban setting. Independent not-for-profit facility. Licensed by state of Iowa. Accredited by JCAHO.

Participants Accepts: male and female children ages 5–13. Average stay: 14 months. Admission: court order, physician pre-certification, depending on program. Treats learning disabilities; behavior disorders; general psychosocial disorders; post-traumatic stress disorder; thought, mood, and personality disorders. Accepts the vision impaired; the hearing impaired; the speech impaired; those with a history of arson; the sexually compulsive; those with a history of harm to themselves and others; those receiving psychotropic medication; those with a history of epilepsy. Largest number of participants from Iowa.

Program Treatment modalities: family-based residential treatment; Psychiatric Medical Institute for Children; positive peer culture; behavior management. Family treatment program available.

Staff 1.4 full-time direct-care staff members per child. Total facility staff includes 1 psychologist, 1 psychiatrist, 1 registered nurse, 26 counselors, 2 occupational/recreational therapists, 10 therapists, 1 dietician, 19 other direct-care staff members. Staff is 45% male, 55% female.

Facilities Single building; males and females in separate units. Central dining. Basketball courts, gymnasium, playing fields, baseball diamond, jungle gym.

Education Academic program available at no charge. Serves ages 5–13, grades K–7. Curriculum accredited or approved by Iowa Department of Public Education. Cost of educational program covered by local school district. Organized sports program offered.

Costs Average cost: $125 per day. Accepts private insurance.

Additional Services Outpatient services for males and females ages 5–18. Treats learning disabilities; behavior disorders; general psychosocial disorders; post-traumatic stress disorder; thought, mood, and personality disorders. Residential or sub-acute services for males and females ages 13–18. Treats behavior disorders; compulsive/addictive disorders other than substance abuse and eating disorders.

Contact Phil Lala, Operations Manager, main address above. Phone: 319-364-0259. Fax: 319-364-1162.

SNOWDEN AT FREDERICKSBURG
1200 Kirkland Boulevard
Fredericksburg, Virginia 22401
703-372-3900; Fax: 703-372-3918

General Information Freestanding drug and alcohol treatment center and psychiatric care facility for adolescents. Patient security: entirely locked. For-profit facility affiliated with Mary Washington Hospital MediCorp, Fredericksburg, VA. Licensed by state of Virginia. Accredited by JCAHO.

Participants Accepts: male and female adolescents. Admission: one parent, all parties who share custody, court order, voluntary, depending on program. Treats autistic disorders; learning disabilities; behavior disorders; general psychosocial disorders; substance abuse; eating disorders; compulsive/addictive disorders other than substance abuse and eating disorders; post-traumatic stress disorder; thought, mood, and personality disorders.

Contact Jim Legge, Director, main address above. Phone: 703-372-3900. Fax: 703-372-3918.

SOLONO PARK HOSPITAL
2101 Courage Drive
Fairfield, California 94533
707-427-8000; Fax: 707-427-2126

General Information Psychiatric hospital for children, adolescents, adults. 8 beds for children; 10 beds for adolescents; 80 beds total. Open year-round. Patient security: partially locked; will pursue and return runaways. Rural setting. For-profit facility affiliated with National Medical Enterprises, Washington, DC. Licensed by state of California. Accredited by JCAHO.

Participants Admission: one parent, all parties who share custody, court order, physician, depending on program. Treats learning disabilities; behavior disorders; general psychosocial disorders; substance abuse; eating disorders; compulsive/addictive disorders other than substance abuse and eating disorders; post-traumatic stress disorder; thought, mood, and personality disorders. Accepts the mobility impaired; the vision impaired; the hearing impaired; the speech impaired; those with a history of harm to themselves and others; those receiving psychotropic medication. Special programs for the developmentally disabled; the hearing impaired; the speech impaired.

Program Treatment modalities: psychodynamic (individual and group psychotherapy); behavior modification; expressive therapies; milieu therapy. Family treatment program available.

Staff Total facility staff includes 39 physicians, 1 psychologist, 6 psychiatrists, 12 MSW social workers, 2 dieticians.

Facilities Single building; males and females in co-educational units. Separate residential quarters for children and adolescents. Central dining (shared with adults), in-room dining available. Basketball courts, game room, gymnasium, outdoor swimming pool, ropes course, enclosed yard areas with lawns.

Education Academic program available. Serves ages 10–17, ungraded. Curriculum accredited or approved by Solono County Unified School District.

Costs Accepts private insurance, group insurance, medicare, medicaid, Blue Cross/Blue Shield, public funds.

Contact Denise L. Steele, Community Relations Director, main address above. Phone: 707-427-6442. Fax: 707-427-6404.

SONIA SHANKMAN ORTHOGENIC SCHOOL
University of Chicago
1365 South 60th Street
Chicago, Illinois 60637
312-702-1203; Fax: 312-702-1304

General Information Residential treatment/subacute facility for children, adolescents. Open year-round. Patient security: staff secured; will pursue and return runaways. Urban setting. Not-for-profit facility affiliated with University of Chicago, Chicago, IL. Licensed by state of Illinois. Accredited by Illinois Office of Education; contracts with Illinois Department of Children and Family Services and Illinois Department of Mental Health.

Participants Accepts: male and female children ages 5–13; male and female adolescents ages 13–21. Average stay: 5 years. Admission: one parent, all parties who share custody, court order, over 14 voluntary, depending on program. Treats learning disabilities; behavior disorders; general psychosocial disorders; eating disorders; post-traumatic stress disorder; thought, mood, and personality disorders. Accepts the mobility impaired; the vision impaired; the hearing impaired; the speech impaired; those with a history of arson; the sexually compulsive; those with a history of harm to themselves and others; those receiving psychotropic medication; non-English speaking individuals. Special programs for the chronically ill; the developmentally disabled. Largest number of participants from Illinois, New York, Michigan.

Program Treatment modalities: psychodynamic; milieu therapy. Family treatment program available.

Staff Total facility staff includes 2 psychologists, 1 psychiatrist, 1 MSW social worker, 5 social workers (non-MSW), 20 teachers, 1 therapist. Staff is 45% male, 55% female.

Facilities Multiple buildings; males and females in separate units. Central dining. Basketball courts, game room, gymnasium, playing fields.

Education Academic program available. Serves ages 6–21, grades K–PG. 20 teachers on staff. Curriculum accredited or approved by Office of Education. Organized sports program offered.

Costs Average cost: $60,000 per year. Accepts private insurance, group insurance, medicare, medicaid, Blue Cross/Blue Shield, public funds.

Contact Elizabeth F. Hulsizer, main address above. Phone: 312-702-1203. Fax: 312-702-1304.

SONORA DESERT HOSPITAL
1920 West Rudasill Road
Tucson, Arizona 85704
602-297-5500; Fax: 602-544-0208

General Information Psychiatric hospital for children, adolescents, adults. 8 beds for children; 18 beds for adolescents; 78 beds total. Open year-round. Patient security: entirely locked; will pursue and return runaways. Suburban setting. Independent for-profit facility. Licensed by state of Arizona. Accredited by JCAHO.

Participants Accepts: male and female children ages 3–12; male and female adolescents ages 13–18; male and female adults ages 18 and up. Average stay: 10 days. Admission: one parent, all parties who share custody, court order, depending on program. Treats autistic disorders; learning disabilities; behavior disorders; general psychosocial disorders; substance abuse; eating disorders; compulsive/addictive disorders other than substance abuse and eating disorders; post-traumatic stress disorder; thought, mood, and personality disorders. Accepts the mobility impaired; the vision impaired; the hearing impaired; the speech impaired; those with a history of arson; the sexually compulsive; those with a history of harm to themselves and others; those receiving psychotropic medication; non-English speaking individuals; those with a history of epilepsy.

Program Treatment modalities: family relations; Twelve Step Recovery; behavioral; cognitive-behavioral. Family treatment program available.

Staff Total facility staff includes 16 registered nurses, 1 practical/vocational nurse, 5 MSW social workers, 5 teachers, 10 therapists, 5 other direct-care staff members.

Facilities Multiple buildings; males and females in coeducational units. Separate residential quarters for children and adolescents. Central dining (shared with adults). Basketball courts, gymnasium, outdoor swimming pool, exercise room with free weights and Nautilus equipment.

Education Academic program available at no charge. Serves ages 3–18, grades N–12. 5 teachers on staff. Curriculum accredited or approved by North Central Association of Colleges and Schools, Arizona State Department of Education. Cost of educational program sometimes covered by local school district.

Costs Accepts private insurance, group insurance, medicare, medicaid, Blue Cross/Blue Shield, public funds.

Additional Services Drug and alcohol rehabilitation services for males and females ages 3–18. Treats learning disabilities; behavior disorders; general psychosocial disorders; eating disorders; compulsive/addictive disorders other than substance abuse and eating disorders; post-traumatic stress disorder; thought, mood, and personality disorders. Outpatient services for males and females ages 3–18. Treats learning disabilities; behavior disorders; general psychosocial disorders; eating disorders; compulsive/addictive disorders other than substance abuse and eating disorders; post-traumatic stress disorder; thought, mood, and personality disorders.

Contact Judith Black, Director of Respond, main address above. Phone: 602-297-5500. Fax: 602-544-0208.

SORENSON'S RANCH SCHOOL
410 North 1st East
P.O. Box 219
Koosharem, Utah 84744
801-638-7318; Fax: 801-638-7582

General Information Residential treatment/subacute facility for adolescents. 51 beds for adolescents. Open year-round. Patient security: staff secured; will pursue and return runaways. Rural setting. Independent for-profit facility. Licensed by state of Utah. Accredited by American Camping Association.

Participants Accepts: male and female adolescents ages 13–18. Average stay: 365 days. Admission: one parent, all parties who share custody, depending on program. Treats learning disabilities; behavior disorders; general psychosocial disorders; substance abuse; eating disorders; compulsive/addictive disorders other than substance abuse and eating disorders; post-traumatic stress disorder; thought, mood, and personality disorders. Accepts those receiving psychotropic medication. Special programs for the developmentally disabled. Largest number of participants from California, Washington, Oregon.

Program Treatment modalities: behavior modification; individual experiential learning; natural consequences.

Staff .3 full-time direct-care staff member per adolescent. Total facility staff includes 1 psychiatrist, 1 registered nurse, 2 MSW social workers, 1 social worker (non-MSW), 7 teachers, 35 other direct-care staff members.

Facilities Multiple buildings; males and females in coeducational units. Central dining (shared with adults). Basketball courts, game room, gymnasium, horseback riding, playing fields.

Education School serves ages 13–18, grades 7–12. 7 teachers on staff. Curriculum is college-preparatory; diploma granted upon completion. Curriculum accredited or approved by Northwest Association of Schools and Colleges.

Costs Average cost: $2500 per month. Accepts private insurance, group insurance, medicare, medicaid, Blue Cross/Blue Shield, public funds.

Additional Services Drug and alcohol rehabilitation services for males and females ages 13–18. Treats learning disabilities; behavior disorders; general psychosocial disorders; substance abuse; eating disorders; compulsive/addictive disorders other than substance abuse and eating disorders; post-traumatic stress disorder; thought, mood, and personality disorders.

Contact Burnell Sorenson, Admissions Director, P.O. Box 440219, Koosharem, UT 84744-0219. Phone: 801-638-7318. Fax: 801-638-7582.

Announcement Sorenson's facility is designed to help troubled teens, school dropouts, or those who are having problems with parents, substance abuse, etc. Structured programs of behavior modification and natural consequences are incorporated with professional therapy. Ranch and mountain experiences serve as rewards: horseback riding, animal care, farming, fishing, outcamping, etc.

See page 458 for full page description.

SOUTHERN OREGON ADOLESCENT STUDY AND TREATMENT CENTER
210 Tacoma Street
Grants Pass, Oregon 97526
503-476-3302

General Information Residential treatment/subacute facility for adolescents. 12 beds for adolescents. Open year-round. Patient security: staff secured; will pursue and return runaways. Rural setting. Independent not-for-profit facility. Licensed by state of Oregon. Accredited by JCAHO; State of Oregon Mental Health and Developmental Disabilities Division, Day and Residential Treatment Standards.

Participants Accepts: male adolescents ages 12–18. Average stay: 24 months. Admission: one parent, all parties who share custody, court order, depending on program. Treats learning disabilities; behavior disorders; general psychosocial disorders; substance abuse; compulsive/addictive disorders other than substance abuse and eating disorders; post-traumatic stress disorder; thought, mood, and personality disorders. Accepts the vision impaired; those with a history of arson; the sexually compulsive; those with a history of harm to themselves and others; those receiving psychotropic medication; those with a history of epilepsy. Largest number of participants from Oregon.

Program Treatment modalities: psychodynamic; family systems; groups systems; cognitive-behavioral. Family treatment program available.

Staff 1.5 full-time direct-care staff members per adolescent. Total facility staff includes 1 physician, 1 psychologist, 1 psychiatrist, 1 registered nurse, 3 MSW social workers, 2 teachers, 5 counselors, 5 other direct-care staff members. Staff is 85% male, 15% female.

Facilities Multiple buildings. Central dining. Basketball courts, game room, playing fields.

Education Academic program available at additional cost. Serves ages 12–18, ungraded. 2 teachers on staff. Curriculum accredited or approved by State of

Oregon Department of Education. Cost of educational program sometimes covered by local school district.

Costs Average cost: $215 per day. Accepts medicaid, public funds.

Contact Frank Kennedy, Clinical Supervisor, main address above. Phone: 503-476-3302.

SOUTHMORE MEDICAL CENTER
906 East Southmore
Pasadena, Texas 77502
713-475-5985; Fax: 713-475-5934

General Information General hospital for children, adolescents. Patient security: entirely locked. Independent for-profit facility. Licensed by state of Texas. Accredited by JCAHO.

Participants Accepts: male and female children; male and female adolescents. Average stay: 10 days. Admission: one parent, all parties who share custody, court order, voluntary, depending on program. Treats learning disabilities; behavior disorders; general psychosocial disorders; substance abuse; eating disorders; compulsive/addictive disorders other than substance abuse and eating disorders; post-traumatic stress disorder; thought, mood, and personality disorders.

Staff Staff is 40% male, 60% female.

Costs Average cost: $400 per day.

Contact Steve Musgraves, Program Director, main address above. Phone: 713-475-5985. Fax: 713-475-5934.

SOUTH OAKS
400 Sunrise Highway
Amityville, New York 11701
516-264-4000; Fax: 516-264-0613

General Information Psychiatric hospital for children, adolescents, adults. 12 beds for children; 83 beds for adolescents; 334 beds total. Open year-round. Patient security: partially locked; no runaway pursuit. Suburban setting. Independent for-profit facility. Licensed by state of New York. Accredited by JCAHO.

Participants Accepts: male and female children ages 10–12; male and female adolescents ages 13–21; male and female adults ages 22 and up. Admission: one parent. Treats behavior disorders; general psychosocial disorders; substance abuse; eating disorders; compulsive/addictive disorders other than substance abuse and eating disorders; post-traumatic stress disorder; thought, mood, and personality disorders.

Program Treatment modalities: team treatment; Twelve Step Recovery. Family treatment program available.

Staff Total facility staff includes 7 psychologists, 20 psychiatrists, 73 registered nurses, 1 practical/vocational nurse, 14 MSW social workers, 47 counselors, 5 occupational/recreational therapists, 4 therapists, 5 dieticians, 108 other direct-care staff members.

Facilities Multiple buildings; males and females in coeducational units. Separate residential quarters for children and adolescents. Central dining (shared with adults). Basketball courts, gymnasium, outdoor tennis courts, playing fields.

Education Academic program available at no charge. Serves grades 5–12. Curriculum accredited or approved by Board of Cooperative Educational Services. Cost of educational program covered by local school district. Organized sports program offered.

Costs Accepts private insurance, group insurance, medicare, medicaid, Blue Cross/Blue Shield.

Additional Services Outpatient services for males and females. Treats substance abuse.

Contact Nita Ireland, Director of Admissions, main address above. Phone: 516-264-4000.

SOUTHWEST WASHINGTON MEDICAL CENTER—TURNAROUND
400 Northeast Mother Joseph Place
Vancouver, Washington 98664
206-256-2170; Fax: 206-256-6466

General Information General hospital for adolescents. 12 beds for adolescents. Patient security: staff secured. Independent not-for-profit facility. Licensed by state of Washington. Accredited by JCAHO.

Participants Accepts: male and female adolescents. Average stay: 35 days. Admission: one parent, all parties who share custody, court order, voluntary, depending on program. Treats substance abuse.

Costs Average cost: $215 per day.

Contact Dennis Malmer, Executive Director, main address above. Phone: 206-256-2170.

SOUTHWOOD COMMUNITY HOSPITAL
111 Dedham Street
Route 1A
Norfolk, Massachusetts 02056
508-668-0385; Fax: 508-668-1481

General Information General hospital for adolescents. 10 beds for adolescents. Patient security: staff secured. Not-for-profit facility affiliated with Neponset Valley Health System, Norfolk, MA. Licensed by state of Massachusetts. Accredited by JCAHO.

Participants Accepts: male and female adolescents. Average stay: 8 days. Admission: one parent, all parties who share custody, court order, voluntary, depending on program. Treats autistic disorders; learning disabilities; behavior disorders; general psychosocial disorders; substance abuse; eating disorders; compulsive/addictive disorders other than substance abuse and eating disorders; post-traumatic stress disorder; thought, mood, and personality disorders.

Contact Rhoda Stevens, Associate Director, Inpatient Services, main address above. Phone: 508-668-0385.

SPARTANBURG REGIONAL MEDICAL CENTER
101 East Wood Street
Spartanburg, South Carolina 29303
803-560-6185; Fax: 803-591-6001

General Information General hospital for children, adolescents. Patient security: entirely locked. Independent not-for-profit facility. Licensed by state of South Carolina. Accredited by JCAHO.

Participants Accepts: male and female children; male and female adolescents. Average stay: 13 days. Admission: one parent, all parties who share custody, voluntary, depending on program. Treats behavior disorders; general psychosocial disorders; substance abuse; eating disorders; thought, mood, and personality disorders.

Staff Staff is 30% male, 70% female.

Costs Average cost: $337 per day.

Contact Helen West, Director of Psychiatric Unit, main address above. Phone: 803-560-6763.

SPAULDING YOUTH CENTER
Memorial Drive
Northfield, New Hampshire 03276
603-286-8901; Fax: 603-286-8650

General Information Residential treatment/subacute facility for children, adolescents. 41 beds for children; 7 beds for adolescents; 48 beds total. Open year-round. Patient security: staff secured. Rural setting. Independent not-for-profit facility. Licensed by state of New Hampshire.

Participants Accepts: male and female children ages 6–16; male and female adolescents ages 16–21. Admission: court order, public school placements, depending on program. Treats autistic disorders; learning disabilities; behavior disorders; general psychosocial disorders; post-traumatic stress disorder. Accepts the speech impaired; those with a history of arson; those with a history of harm to themselves and others; those receiving psychotropic medication; those with a history of epilepsy. Special programs for the developmentally disabled. Largest number of participants from New Hampshire, Massachusetts, Maine.

Program Treatment modalities: behavior modification; group and individual therapy; milieu therapy.

Staff 1.8 full-time direct-care staff members per child or adolescent. Total facility staff includes 2 physicians, 3 psychologists, 1 psychiatrist, 2 registered nurses, 1 practical/vocational nurse, 2 MSW social workers, 2 social workers (non-MSW), 28 teachers, 33 other direct-care staff members. Staff is 40% male, 60% female.

Facilities Multiple buildings; males and females in coeducational units. Central dining. Basketball courts, game room, gymnasium, playing fields, ropes course, cross-country skiing, hiking trails.

Education Academic program available at additional cost. Serves ages 6–21, ungraded. 28 teachers on staff. Curriculum accredited or approved by New Hampshire, Massachusetts, New Jersey Departments of Education. Cost of educational program sometimes covered by local school district.

Costs Accepts public funds.

Contact Gail Tapply, Admissions Coordinator, main address above. Phone: 603-286-8901.

SPRING SHADOWS GLEN HOSPITAL
2801 Gessner
Houston, Texas 77080
713-462-4000; Fax: 713-744-1645

General Information Psychiatric hospital for children, adolescents, adults. Open year-round. Patient security: partially locked. Suburban setting. For-profit facility affiliated with Memorial City Medical Center, Houston, TX. Licensed by state of Texas. Accredited by JCAHO.

Participants Accepts: male and female children; male and female adolescents; male and female adults. Admission: all parties who share custody, voluntary, depending on program. Treats learning disabilities; substance abuse; eating disorders; compulsive/addictive disorders other than substance abuse and eating disorders; post-traumatic stress disorder; thought, mood, and personality disorders. Accepts the mobility impaired; the vision impaired; the hearing impaired; the speech impaired; those with a history of arson; the sexually compulsive; those with a history of harm to themselves and others; those receiving psychotropic medication; non-English speaking individuals; those with a history of epilepsy. Special programs for the chronically ill; the developmentally disabled; the speech impaired.

Program Treatment modalities: Twelve Step Recovery; psychodynamic psychotherapy (group and individual). Family treatment program available.

Staff Total facility staff includes 1 psychologist, 29 registered nurses, 12 practical/vocational nurses, 10 MSW social workers, 4 social workers (non-MSW), 4 teachers, 5 counselors, 1 dietician, 42 other direct-care staff members.

Facilities Multiple buildings; males and females in coeducational units. Separate residential quarters for children and adolescents. Central dining (shared with adults). Game room, gymnasium, outdoor swimming pool, outdoor tennis courts, playing fields.

Education Academic program available at no charge. Serves ages 6–17, grades 1–12. 4 teachers on staff. Curriculum accredited or approved by Spring Branch Independent School District. Cost of educational program covered by local school district.

Costs Accepts private insurance, group insurance, medicare, Blue Cross/Blue Shield.

Contact Marty Mead, Intake Coordinator, main address above. Phone: 713-462-4000. Fax: 713-744-1645.

STARR COMMONWEALTH
Starr Commonwealth Road
Albion, Michigan 49224
517-629-5591; Fax: 517-629-2317

General Information Residential treatment/subacute facility for adolescents. 185 beds for adolescents. Open year-round. Patient security: staff secured; will pursue and return runaways. Rural setting. Independent not-for-profit facility. Licensed by state of Michigan. Accredited by Council on Accreditation of Services for Families and Children.

Participants Accepts: male adolescents ages 12–17. Average stay: 365 days. Admission: court order. Treats learning disabilities; behavior disorders; general psychosocial disorders; substance abuse; compulsive/addictive disorders other than substance abuse and eating disorders; thought, mood, and personality disorders. Accepts the mobility impaired; the vision impaired; the hearing impaired; the speech impaired; those with a history of arson; the sexually compulsive; those with a history of harm to themselves and others; those with a history of epilepsy. Largest number of participants from Michigan.

Program Treatment modalities: psychoeducational model; guided group interaction. Family treatment program available.

Facilities Multiple buildings. Separate dining by residential unit available. Basketball courts, game room, gymnasium, indoor swimming pool, outdoor tennis courts, playing fields, ropes course, racquetball courts.

Education Academic program available. Serves ages 12–17, ungraded. Curriculum accredited or approved by local intermediate school district. Cost of educational program covered by local school district. Organized sports program offered.

Costs Average cost: $126 per day. Accepts public funds.

Additional Services Outpatient services for males and females. Treats autistic disorders; learning disabilities; behavior disorders; general psychosocial disorders; substance abuse; eating disorders; compulsive/addictive disorders other than substance abuse and eating disorders; post-traumatic stress disorder; thought, mood, and personality disorders. Wilderness/survival program for males and females. Treats autistic disorders; learning disabilities; behavior disorders; general psychosocial disorders; substance abuse; eating disorders; compulsive/addictive disorders other than substance abuse and eating disorders; post-traumatic stress disorder; thought, mood, and personality disorders.

Contact Martin L. Mitchell, Vice President for Program, main address above. Phone: 517-629-5591. Fax: 517-629-2317.

THE STARTING PLACE
2057 Coolidge Street
Hollywood, Florida 33020
305-925-2225; Fax: 305-921-1845

General Information Drug and alcohol rehabilitation center for adolescents. Patient security: staff secured. Independent not-for-profit facility. Licensed by state of Florida.

Participants Accepts: male and female adolescents. Average stay: 3 months. Admission: one parent, all parties who share custody, court order, voluntary, depending on program. Treats learning disabilities; behavior disorders; general psychosocial disorders; substance abuse; eating disorders; compulsive/addictive disorders other than substance abuse and eating disorders; post-traumatic stress disorder; thought, mood, and personality disorders.

Contact James Kraut, Director of Admissions, main address above. Phone: 305-925-2225.

STARTING POINT CHEMICAL DEPENDENCY RECOVERY HOSPITAL
8773 Oak Avenue
Orangevale, California 95662
916-988-5700; Fax: 916-988-5699

General Information Drug and alcohol rehabilitation center for adolescents, adults. 30 beds for adolescents. Open year-round. Patient security: staff secured; no runaway pursuit. Suburban setting. For-profit facility affiliated with Comprehensive Care Corporation, Chesterfield, MO. Licensed by state of California. Accredited by JCAHO.

Participants Accepts: male and female adolescents ages 12–18; male and female adults ages 18 and up. Average stay: 28 days. Admission: one parent, all parties who share custody, court order, depending on program. Treats behavior disorders; general psychosocial disorders; substance abuse. Accepts the mobility impaired; the vision impaired; the hearing impaired; the speech impaired; the sexually compulsive; those receiving psychotropic medication; those with a history of epilepsy.

Program Treatment modalities: Twelve Step Recovery. Family treatment program available.

Staff .3 full-time direct-care staff member per adolescent. Total facility staff includes 1 physician, 1 psychologist, 4 registered nurses, 7 practical/vocational nurses, 2 MSW social workers, 2 teachers, 1 occupational/recreational therapist, 3 other direct-care staff members. Staff is 50% male, 50% female.

Facilities Single building; males and females in co-educational units. Separate residential quarters for adolescents. Central dining (shared with adults). Basketball courts, game room, playing fields.

Education Academic program available at no charge. Serves ages 12–18, ungraded. 2 teachers on staff. Cost of educational program covered by local school district.

Costs Average cost: $17,000 per stay. Accepts private insurance, group insurance, Blue Cross/Blue Shield.

Contact Judy Kelso, Marketing Supervisor, main address above. Phone: 916-988-5700. Fax: 916-988-5699.

STONY LODGE HOSPITAL
40 Croton Dam Road
Ossining, New York 10562
914-941-7400; Fax: 914-941-4102

General Information Psychiatric hospital for adolescents. 61 beds for adolescents. Patient security: entirely locked. Independent for-profit facility. Licensed by state of New York. Accredited by JCAHO.

Participants Accepts: male and female adolescents. Average stay: 20 days. Admission: one parent, all parties who share custody, depending on program. Treats learning disabilities; behavior disorders; general psychosocial disorders; substance abuse; eating disorders; compulsive/addictive disorders other than substance abuse and eating disorders; post-traumatic stress disorder; thought, mood, and personality disorders.

Contact Admissions Department, P.O. Box 1250, Briarcliff Manor, NY 10510. Phone: 914-941-7400.

STORMONT VAIL REGIONAL MEDICAL CENTER
1500 Southwest 10th Street
Topeka, Kansas 66604
913-354-6000; Fax: 913-354-5073

General Information General hospital for children, adolescents. Patient security: entirely locked. Independent not-for-profit facility. Licensed by state of Kansas. Accredited by JCAHO.

Participants Accepts: male and female children; male and female adolescents. Average stay: 22 days. Admission: one parent, all parties who share custody, court order, voluntary, depending on program. Treats autistic disorders; learning disabilities; behavior disorders; general psychosocial disorders; substance abuse; eating disorders; post-traumatic stress disorder; thought, mood, and personality disorders.

Staff Staff is 40% male, 60% female.

Costs Average cost: $400 per day.

Contact Linda Opat, Charge Nurse, main address above. Phone: 913-354-6395. Fax: 913-354-5073.

SUMMIT CAMP, INC.
RD 3
Duck Harbor Road
Honesdale, Pennsylvania 18431
717-253-4381; Fax: 717-253-2934

General Information Camp for children, adolescents. 100 beds for children; 100 beds for adolescents; 200 beds total. Open summer. Patient security: staff secured; will pursue and return runaways. Rural setting. Independent for-profit facility. Licensed by state of Pennsylvania. Accredited by American Camping Association.

Participants Accepts: male and female children ages 7–12; male and female adolescents ages 13–17. Average stay: 53 days. Admission: one parent, voluntary, depending on program. Treats learning disabilities; behavior disorders. Accepts the speech impaired; those receiving psychotropic medication; those with a history of epilepsy. Largest number of participants from New York, New Jersey.

Program Treatment modalities: group work approach; individual supportive counseling; adaptive recreation.

Staff .7 full-time direct-care staff member per child or adolescent. Total facility staff includes 1 physician, 4 registered nurses, 2 MSW social workers, 3 teachers, 95 counselors, 3 occupational/recreational therapists, 28 other direct-care staff members.

Facilities Multiple buildings; males and females in separate units. Central dining. Basketball courts, game room, gymnasium, outdoor swimming pool, outdoor tennis courts, playing fields.

Education Academic program available at no charge. Serves ages 7–17. 3 teachers on staff. Organized sports program offered.

Costs Average cost: $4950 per stay.

Contact Regina Skyer, Associate Director, main address above. Phone: 800-323-9908.

Announcement Summit Camp offers a unique full-service program for children and adolescents with average or above intelligence whose primary disability is attention deficit disorder with secondary learning and/or adjustment difficulties. Summit features a structured environment in which the acquisition and refinement of appropriate social skills and positive self-attitude are stressed.

SUMMIT SCHOOL/CHILDREN'S RESIDENCE CENTER
339 North Broadway
Upper Nyack, New York 10960
914-358-7772; Fax: 914-358-1270

General Information Residential treatment/subacute facility for children, adolescents, adults. 15 beds for children; 77 beds for adolescents; 102 beds total. Open year-round. Patient security: unlocked; will pursue and return runaways. Suburban setting. Independent not-for-profit facility. Licensed by state of New York. Accredited by New York State Department of Social Services.

Participants Accepts: male and female children ages 8–12; male and female adolescents ages 13–19; male and female adults ages 20–22. Average stay: 600 days. Admission: all parties who share custody, voluntary, depending on program. Treats learning disabilities; behavior disorders; general psychosocial disorders; substance abuse; eating disorders; compulsive/addictive disorders other than substance abuse and eating disorders; post-traumatic stress disorder; thought, mood, and personality disorders. Accepts those with a history of harm to themselves and others; those receiving psychotropic medication; those with a history of epilepsy. Largest number of participants from New York, New Jersey, Illinois.

Program Treatment modalities: therapeutic community; special education. Family treatment program available.

Staff 1.3 full-time direct-care staff members per child or adolescent. Total facility staff includes 1 physician, 1 psychologist, 2 psychiatrists, 2 registered nurses, 7 MSW social workers, 17 teachers, 53 counselors, 1 speech pathologist, 1 dietician, 50 other direct-care staff members. Staff is 58% male, 42% female.

Facilities Multiple buildings; males and females in separate units. Separate residential quarters for children and adolescents. Central dining (shared with adults). Basketball courts, game room, gymnasium, outdoor swimming pool, outdoor tennis courts, playing fields.

Education Academic program available. Serves ages 8–22, ungraded. 17 teachers on staff. Curriculum accredited or approved by New York State Department of Education. Organized sports program offered.

Costs Accepts private insurance, public funds.

Contact Dr. Bruce Goldsmith, main address above. Phone: 914-358-7772. Fax: 914-358-1270.

SUNCREST HOSPITAL OF SOUTH BAY
4025 West 226th Street
Torrance, California 90505
310-373-7733; Fax: 310-375-6904

General Information Freestanding psychiatric hospital/drug and alcohol treatment center for adolescents. 24 beds for adolescents. Patient security: partially locked. Independent for-profit facility. Licensed by state of California. Accredited by JCAHO.

Participants Accepts: male and female adolescents. Average stay: 21 days. Admission: one parent, all parties who share custody, court order, voluntary, depending on program. Treats behavior disorders; general psychosocial disorders; substance abuse; eating disorders; compulsive/addictive disorders other than substance abuse and eating disorders; post-traumatic stress disorder; thought, mood, and personality disorders.

Staff Staff is 50% male, 50% female.

Contact Tom Inlay, Manager of Needs Assessment and Referral Center, main address above. Phone: 800-221-2672.

SUNDOWN RANCH, INC.
Route 4
P.O. Box 182
Canton, Texas 75103
903-479-3933; Fax: 903-479-3999

General Information Drug and alcohol rehabilitation center for adolescents, adults. 23 beds for adolescents. Open year-round. Patient security: staff secured; will pursue and return runaways. Rural setting. Independent for-profit facility. Licensed by state of Texas. Accredited by JCAHO.

Participants Accepts: male and female adolescents ages 12–17; male and female adults ages 17–24. Average stay: 120 days. Admission: one parent, all parties who share custody, court order, voluntary, depending on program. Treats learning disabilities; behavior disorders; general psychosocial disorders; substance abuse; eating disorders; compulsive/addictive disorders other than substance abuse and eating disorders; post-traumatic stress disorder; thought, mood, and personality disorders. Special programs for the developmentally disabled. Largest number of participants from Texas, Florida, Kansas.

Program Treatment modalities: Twelve Step Recovery; family systems model; rational motive therapy; trauma resolution therapy. Family treatment program available.

Staff .3 full-time direct-care staff member per adolescent. Total facility staff includes 1 physician, 1 psychologist, 3 psychiatrists, 1 registered nurse, 4 practical/vocational nurses, 2 MSW social workers, 1 teacher, 3 counselors, 1 speech pathologist, 1 dietician, 26 other direct-care staff members. Staff is 50% male, 50% female.

Facilities Multiple buildings; males and females in separate units. Residential quarters shared with adults. Central dining (shared with adults). Basketball courts, horseback riding, outdoor swimming pool, outdoor tennis courts, playing fields, ropes course, volleyball courts, horseshoes, arts and crafts room.

Education Academic program available at no charge. Serves ages 12–24. 1 teacher on staff. Curriculum accredited or approved by Martins Mill Independent School District. Cost of educational program covered by local school district. Organized sports program offered.

Costs Average cost: $365 per day. Accepts private insurance, group insurance, Blue Cross/Blue Shield, public funds.

Contact Steve Echols, Business Manager, main address above. Phone: 903-479-3933. Fax: 903-479-3999.

SUNNY HILLS CHILDREN'S SERVICES
300 Sunny Hills Drive
San Anselmo, California 94960
415-457-3200; Fax: 415-456-4679

General Information   Residential treatment/subacute facility for adolescents. 40 beds for adolescents. Open year-round. Patient security: unlocked; will pursue and return runaways. Suburban setting. Independent not-for-profit facility. Licensed by state of California. Accredited by JCAHO.

Participants   Accepts: male and female adolescents ages 13–18. Average stay: 545 days. Admission: one parent, all parties who share custody, court order, voluntary, depending on program. Treats autistic disorders; learning disabilities; behavior disorders; general psychosocial disorders; substance abuse; eating disorders; compulsive/addictive disorders other than substance abuse and eating disorders; post-traumatic stress disorder; thought, mood, and personality disorders. Accepts the hearing impaired; the speech impaired; those with a history of arson; the sexually compulsive; those with a history of harm to themselves and others; those receiving psychotropic medication. Special programs for the developmentally disabled; the hearing impaired; the speech impaired.

Program   Treatment modalities: Sunny Hills Treatment Program; group therapy; family therapy; milieu therapy. Family treatment program available.

Staff   1.6 full-time direct-care staff members per adolescent. Total facility staff includes 2 physicians, 2 psychiatrists, 3 registered nurses, 2 MSW social workers, 4 social workers (non-MSW), 3 teachers, 40 counselors, 1 occupational/recreational therapist, 1 dietician, 7 other direct-care staff members.

Facilities   Multiple buildings; males and females in separate units. Separate dining by residential unit available. Basketball courts, game room, gymnasium, outdoor swimming pool, playing fields.

Education   Academic program available at additional cost. Serves ages 13–18, ungraded. 3 teachers on staff. Curriculum accredited or approved by California State Department of Special Education. Cost of educational program sometimes covered by local school district. Organized sports program offered.

Costs   Average cost: $58,000 per stay. Accepts private insurance, group insurance, medicaid, Blue Cross/Blue Shield, public funds.

Additional Services   Drug and alcohol rehabilitation services for males and females ages 13–18. Treats substance abuse.

Contact   Robert R. McCallie, Executive Director, main address above. Phone: 415-457-3200. Fax: 415-456-4679.

SUNRISE, INC.
523 Main
Larned, Kansas 67550
316-285-3462

General Information   Drug and alcohol rehabilitation center for adolescents. Patient security: staff secured. Independent not-for-profit facility. Licensed by state of Kansas.

Participants   Accepts: male and female adolescents. Average stay: 180 days. Admission: one parent, all parties who share custody, voluntary, social rehabilitation services, depending on program. Treats substance abuse. Accepts the hearing impaired; the speech impaired; those receiving psychotropic medication.

Staff   Staff is 50% male, 50% female.

Costs   Average cost: $13 per day.

Contact   Dennis Augustine, Executive Director, main address above. Phone: 316-285-3462.

SUN TOWERS BEHAVIORAL HEALTH CENTER
300 Waymore Drive
El Paso, Texas 79902
915-544-3223; Fax: 915-541-3927

General Information   Psychiatric hospital for adolescents, adults. 16 beds for adolescents. Open year-round. Patient security: partially locked; will pursue and return runaways. For-profit facility affiliated with Columbia Hospital Corporation, Fort Worth, TX. Licensed by state of Texas. Accredited by JCAHO.

Participants   Accepts: male and female adolescents ages 13–17; male and female adults ages 18 and up. Average stay: 19 days. Admission: court order. Treats learning disabilities; behavior disorders; general psychosocial disorders; substance abuse; eating disorders; post-traumatic stress disorder; thought, mood, and personality disorders. Accepts the mobility impaired; the vision impaired; the speech impaired; the sexually compulsive; those receiving psychotropic medication; those with a history of epilepsy.

Program   Treatment modalities: Twelve Step Recovery; psychodynamic. Family treatment program available.

Staff   1.4 full-time direct-care staff members per adolescent. Total facility staff includes 5 registered nurses, 2 practical/vocational nurses, 1 MSW social worker, 4 social workers (non-MSW), 1 teacher, 3 counselors, 2 occupational/recreational therapists, 1 speech pathologist, 1 dietician, 2 other direct-care staff members. Staff is 50% male, 50% female.

Facilities   Multiple buildings; males and females in coeducational units. Game room, outdoor swimming pool.

Education   Academic program available. Serves ages 13–18, grades 5–12. 1 teacher on staff. Cost of educational program covered by local school district.

Costs   Average cost: $700 per stay. Accepts private insurance, group insurance, medicare, Blue Cross/Blue Shield.

Additional Services   Outpatient services for males and females ages 13 and up. Treats learning disabilities; behavior disorders; general psychosocial disorders; substance abuse; eating disorders; compulsive/addictive disorders other than substance abuse and eating disorders; post-traumatic stress disorder; thought, mood, and personality disorders.

Contact   Arlene Ormsby, Marketing/Public Relations Director, main address above. Phone: 915-544-3223. Fax: 915-541-3927.

SUWS ADOLESCENT PROGRAM
16771 Northeast 80th Street
Suite 201
Redmond, Washington 98052
206-881-7173; Fax: 206-881-2827

General Information   Outdoor therapeutic treatment program for adolescents. Patient security: unlocked. Independent for-profit facility. Licensed by state of Idaho.

Participants   Accepts: male and female adolescents ages 13–18. Average stay: 21 days. Admission: one parent, voluntary, depending on program. Treats learning disabilities; behavior disorders; substance abuse.

Costs   Average cost: $5200 per stay.

Contact   Admissions Office, P.O. Box 171, Redmond, WA 98073. Phone: 206-881-7173. Fax: 206-881-2827.

Announcement   SUWS's effective 21-day impact program in Idaho departs weekly year-round and helps adolescents who may be experiencing rebellion against parental or school authority, anger due to adoption, frustration with parents' divorce, low self-esteem; runaways, who are bright but unmotivated, depressed, manipulative, expelled or suspended. Boys and girls, 13–18. Deals with low self-esteem, immaturity and brings most teenagers out of their fantasy world and back to reality. References provided.

THE SYCAMORES
2933 North El Nido Drive
Altadena, California 91001
818-798-0853; Fax: 818-798-4531

General Information   Residential treatment/subacute facility for children. Open year-round. Patient security: staff secured; will pursue and return runaways. Suburban setting. Independent not-for-profit facility. Licensed by state of California.

Participants   Accepts: male children ages 6–14. Average stay: 14 months. Admission: one parent, all parties who share custody, court order, depending on program. Treats learning disabilities; behavior disorders; general psychosocial disorders; post-traumatic stress disorder; thought, mood, and personality disorders. Accepts those with a history of harm to themselves and others; the abused; the emotionally disturbed. Largest number of participants from California.

Program   Treatment modalities: cognitive behavioral modification; group and individual therapy. Family treatment program available.

Staff   1.3 full-time direct-care staff members per child. Total facility staff includes 3 psychologists, 1 psychiatrist, 2 registered nurses, 1 practical/vocational nurse, 5 MSW social workers, 10 teachers, 10 therapists. Staff is 50% male, 50% female.

Facilities   Multiple buildings. Separate dining by residential unit available. Basketball courts, game room, playing fields.

Education   Academic program available at additional cost. Serves ages 6–14, ungraded. 10 teachers on staff. Curriculum accredited or approved by State of California. Cost of educational program covered by local school district. Organized sports program offered.

Costs   Average cost: $55,650 per year. Accepts private insurance, public funds.

Additional Services   Drug and alcohol rehabilitation services for males ages 6–14. Treats learning disabilities; behavior disorders; general psychosocial disorders; post-traumatic stress disorder; thought, mood, and personality disorders.

Contact   Phillip Krave, Intake Coordinator, main address above. Phone: 818-798-0853. Fax: 818-798-4531.

Announcement   In close cooperation with cognitive behavior therapist Dr. Donald Meichenbaum, The Sycamores is pioneering a treatment model that seeks to alter a child's destructive behavior and emotions by teaching the child new thinking skills, such as problem solving, anger control, and how to initiate and maintain healthy relationships.

TALISMAN SUMMER CAMP
601 Camp Elliott Road
Black Mountain, North Carolina 28711
704-669-8639; Fax: 704-669-4067

General Information Camp for children, adolescents. Open summer. Patient security: staff secured; will pursue and return runaways. Rural setting. Not-for-profit facility affiliated with Talisman School, Inc., Black Mountain, NC. Licensed by state of North Carolina.

Participants Accepts: male and female children ages 9–17; male and female adolescents ages 9–17. Average stay: 4 weeks. Admission: all parties who share custody. Treats learning disabilities; behavior disorders. Largest number of participants from North Carolina.

Program Treatment modalities: positive peer culture; group dynamics. Family treatment program available.

Staff Total facility staff includes 1 registered nurse, 2 MSW social workers, 10 counselors.

Facilities Multiple buildings; males and females in coeducational units. Central dining. Game room, playing fields, lake, canoes.

Costs Average cost: $2500 per stay.

Contact Catherine Buie, Director, main address above. Phone: 704-669-8639. Fax: 704-669-4067.

TAMARACK CENTER
2901 West Fort George Wright Drive
Spokane, Washington 99204-5202
509-326-8100

General Information Residential treatment/subacute facility for adolescents. 11 beds for adolescents. Open year-round. Patient security: staff secured. Suburban setting. Independent not-for-profit facility. Licensed by state of Washington. Accredited by JCAHO.

Participants Accepts: male and female adolescents ages 12–18. Average stay: 547 days. Admission: court order, voluntary, depending on program. Treats learning disabilities; behavior disorders; general psychosocial disorders; substance abuse; eating disorders; compulsive/addictive disorders other than substance abuse and eating disorders; post-traumatic

stress disorder; thought, mood, and personality disorders. Accepts the mobility impaired; the vision impaired; the hearing impaired; the speech impaired; those with a history of arson; the sexually compulsive; those with a history of harm to themselves and others; those receiving psychotropic medication. Special programs for the chronically ill; the mobility impaired; the developmentally disabled; the vision impaired; the hearing impaired; the speech impaired; those with AIDS. Largest number of participants from Washington.

Program Family treatment program available.

Staff 2.9 full-time direct-care staff members per adolescent. Total facility staff includes 1 physician, 1 psychologist, 1 psychiatrist, 3 registered nurses, 1 MSW social worker, 1 social worker (non-MSW), 1 teacher, 12 counselors, 2 physical therapists, 1 occupational/recreational therapist, 1 therapist, 1 dietician, 19 other direct-care staff members. Staff is 40% male, 60% female.

Facilities Multiple buildings; males and females in coeducational units. Central dining. Game room.

Education Academic program available at no charge. Serves ages 12–18. 1 teacher on staff. Curriculum accredited or approved by District 81 of Washington State. Cost of educational program covered by local school district.

Costs Average cost: $276 per day. Accepts private insurance, medicaid, public funds.

Contact Fay Cadwallader, Admission/Discharge/Aftercare Coordinator, main address above. Phone: 509-326-8100.

TAMPA BAY ACADEMY
12012 Boyette Road
Riverview, Florida 33569
813-677-6700; Fax: 813-671-3145

General Information Residential treatment/subacute facility for children, adolescents. 25 beds for children; 55 beds for adolescents; 80 beds total. Open year-round. Patient security: staff secured; will pursue and return runaways. Suburban setting. Independent for-profit facility. Licensed by state of Florida. Accredited by JCAHO; Health and Rehabilitative Services.

Participants Accepts: male and female children and adolescents ages 4–18. Average stay: 150 days. Admission: one parent. Treats learning disabilities; behavior disorders; general psychosocial disorders; substance abuse; eating disorders; post-traumatic stress disorder; thought, mood, and personality disorders. Largest number of participants from Florida.

Program Treatment modalities: psychoeducational; medical. Family treatment program available.

Staff 1.3 full-time direct-care staff members per child or adolescent. Total facility staff includes 2 psychiatrists, 4 registered nurses, 2 practical/vocational nurses, 6 MSW social workers, 8 teachers, 3 counselors, 3 occupational/recreational therapists, 4 therapists, 40 other direct-care staff members. Staff is 40% male, 60% female.

Facilities Multiple buildings; males and females in separate units. Central dining. Basketball courts, game room, gymnasium, horseback riding, outdoor swimming pool, outdoor tennis courts, playing fields.

Education Academic program available at no charge. Serves ages 4–18, grades N–12. 8 teachers on staff. Curriculum accredited or approved by Florida Council of Independent Schools. Organized sports program offered.

Costs Average cost: $415 per day. Accepts private insurance, group insurance, Blue Cross/Blue Shield, public funds.

Additional Services Drug and alcohol rehabilitation services for males and females ages 12–18. Treats learning disabilities; behavior disorders; general psychosocial disorders; substance abuse; eating disorders; compulsive/addictive disorders other than substance abuse and eating disorders; post-traumatic stress disorder; thought, mood, and personality disorders. Outpatient services for males and females ages 4 and up. Treats learning disabilities; behavior disorders; general psychosocial disorders; substance abuse; eating disorders; compulsive/addictive disorders other than substance abuse and eating disorders; post-traumatic stress disorder; thought, mood, and personality disorders. Partial hospitalization program for males and females ages 4–18. Treats learning disabilities; behavior disorders; general psychosocial disorders; substance abuse; eating disorders; compulsive/addictive disorders other than substance abuse and eating disorders; post-traumatic stress disorder; thought, mood, and personality disorders.

Contact Elaine Baron DeRiso, Director of Admissions and Case Management, main address above. Phone: 813-677-6700. Fax: 813-671-3145.

Announcement Tampa Bay Academy highlights include highest JCAHO accreditation: With Commendation; CHAMPUS SELECT approved; full-time child psychiatrists; all licensed therapists; treatment for sexual and substance abuse; separate children's program; 24-acre campus, including pool and equestrian program; weekend and long-distance family therapy; inn rooms on-site for parents.

TANAGER PLACE
2309 C Street, SW
Cedar Rapids, Iowa 52404
319-365-9164; Fax: 319-365-6411

General Information Residential treatment/subacute facility for children, adolescents. 10 beds for children; 50 beds for adolescents; 60 beds total. Open year-round. Patient security: staff secured; no runaway pursuit. Urban setting. Independent not-for-profit facility. Licensed by state of Iowa. Accredited by JCAHO.

Participants Accepts: male and female children ages 7–11; male and female adolescents ages 12–17. Average stay: 280 days. Admission: one parent, all parties who share custody, court order, depending on program. Treats learning disabilities; behavior disorders; general psychosocial disorders; compulsive/addictive disorders other than substance abuse and eating disorders; post-traumatic stress disorder; thought, mood, and personality disorders. Accepts the mobility impaired; those with a history of arson; the sexually compulsive; those with a history of harm to themselves and others; those receiving psychotropic medication; those with a history of epilepsy. Largest number of participants from Iowa.

Program Treatment modalities: psychodynamic; dyadic. Family treatment program available.

Staff .3 full-time direct-care staff member per child or adolescent. Total facility staff includes 1 psychiatrist, 4 registered nurses, 3 practical/vocational nurses, 8 MSW social workers, 6 social workers (non-MSW), 4 teachers, 17 counselors, 6 occupational/recreational therapists, 2 dieticians, 30 other direct-care staff members.

Facilities Multiple buildings; males and females in both coeducational and separate units depending on program. Separate dining by residential unit, in-room dining available. Basketball courts, game room, gymnasium, playing fields, obstacle course.

Education Academic program available at additional cost. Serves ages 10–14, grades 5–10. 4 teachers on staff.

Costs Accepts private insurance, group insurance, medicaid, public funds.

Contact Jerry Anderson, Program Director, main address above. Phone: 319-365-9164. Fax: 319-365-6411.

TAYLOR HOME, INC.
3131 Taylor Avenue
Racine, Wisconsin 53405
414-553-4100

General Information Residential treatment/subacute facility for adolescents. 52 beds for adolescents. Open year-round. Patient security: unlocked; will pursue and return runaways. Urban setting. Independent not-for-profit facility. Licensed by state of Wisconsin.

Participants Accepts: male and female adolescents ages 12–17. Average stay: 180 days. Admission: court order. Treats behavior disorders; substance abuse; compulsive/addictive disorders other than substance abuse and eating disorders. Accepts the sexually compulsive; those with a history of harm to themselves and others.

Program Treatment modalities: errors in thinking. Family treatment program available.

Staff .6 full-time direct-care staff member per adolescent. Total facility staff includes 1 psychiatrist, 1 MSW social worker, 2 social workers (non-MSW), 3 teachers, 22 counselors, 4 occupational/recreational therapists. Staff is 50% male, 50% female.

Facilities Multiple buildings; males and females in separate units. Central dining. Basketball courts, game room, gymnasium, outdoor tennis courts, playing fields, ropes course.

Education Academic program available at no charge. Serves ages 11–17, grades 6–12. 3 teachers on staff. Curriculum accredited or approved by Racine Unified School District. Cost of educational program covered by local school district.

Costs Average cost: $2743 per month. Accepts public funds.

Additional Services Outpatient services for males and females ages 11–17. Treats behavior disorders; substance abuse; compulsive/addictive disorders other than substance abuse and eating disorders.

Contact Alice Portis-Patterson, Program Manager, main address above. Phone: 414-553-4100.

TAYLOR MANOR HOSPITAL
4100 College Avenue
P.O. Box 396
Ellicott City, Maryland 21041-0396
410-465-3322; Fax: 410-461-7075

General Information Psychiatric hospital for adolescents, adults. 40 beds for adolescents. Open year-round. Patient security: entirely locked; will pursue and return runaways. Suburban setting. Independent for-profit facility. Licensed by state of Maryland. Accredited by JCAHO.

Participants Accepts: male and female adolescents ages 10–18; male and female adults ages 18 and up. Average stay: 31 days. Admission: one parent, all parties who share custody, court order, depending on program. Treats autistic disorders; learning disabilities; behavior disorders; general psychosocial disorders; substance abuse; eating disorders; compulsive/addictive disorders other than substance abuse and eating disorders; post-traumatic stress disorder; thought, mood, and personality disorders. Accepts the mobility impaired; the vision impaired; the hearing impaired; the speech impaired; the sexually compulsive; those with a history of harm to themselves and others; those receiving psychotropic medication; those with a history of epilepsy.

Program Treatment modalities: behavior modification; eclectic; family therapy intervention. Family treatment program available.

Staff Total facility staff includes 7 psychologists, 10 psychiatrists, 43 registered nurses, 6 practical/vocational nurses, 4 MSW social workers, 5 social workers (non-MSW), 10 teachers, 64 counselors, 10 occupational/recreational therapists, 1 dietician, 7 other direct-care staff members.

Facilities Multiple buildings; males and females in coeducational units. Separate residential quarters for adolescents. Separate dining by residential unit available. Basketball courts, game room, gymnasium, outdoor swimming pool, playing fields, nature trails.

Education Academic program available at no charge. Serves ages 10–18, grades 7–12. 10 teachers on staff. Curriculum accredited or approved by Howard County Board of Education. Cost of educational program sometimes covered by local school district. Organized sports program offered.

Costs Average cost: $550 per day. Accepts private insurance, group insurance, medicare, medicaid, Blue Cross/Blue Shield.

Additional Services Drug and alcohol rehabilitation services for males and females ages 10 and up. Treats substance abuse. Outpatient services for males and females ages 1 and up. Treats learning disabilities; behavior disorders; general psychosocial disorders; substance abuse; eating disorders; compulsive/addictive disorders other than substance abuse and eating disorders; post-traumatic stress disorder; thought, mood, and personality disorders.

Contact Pamela Causey, Public Relations Director, main address above. Phone: 410-465-3322. Fax: 410-461-7075.

TEEN CHALLENGE CHRISTIAN ACADEMY
P.O. Box 1160
Sundance, Wyoming 82729
307-283-2544; Fax: 307-283-2987

General Information School for adolescents. 45 beds for adolescents. Open year-round. Patient security: staff secured; will pursue and return runaways. Rural setting. Independent not-for-profit facility. Licensed by state of Wyoming.

Participants Accepts: male and female adolescents ages 12–18. Admission: all parties who share custody. Treats behavior disorders; general psychosocial disorders; substance abuse; eating disorders; compulsive/addictive disorders other than substance abuse and eating disorders. Accepts the vision impaired; the hearing impaired; the speech impaired. Largest number of participants from California, Colorado, Idaho.

Staff .3 full-time direct-care staff member per adolescent. Total facility staff includes 1 social worker (non-MSW), 2 teachers, 6 counselors, 1 dietician, 6 other direct-care staff members. Staff is 55% male, 45% female.

Facilities Multiple buildings; males and females in separate units. Central dining. Basketball courts, gymnasium, playing fields.

Education School serves ages 12–18, grades 7–12. 2 teachers on staff. Curriculum is college-preparatory; diploma granted upon completion. Curriculum accredited or approved by Accelerated Christian Education.

Costs Average cost: $960 per stay. Financial aid available.

Contact Kevin Carroll, Program Director, main address above. Phone: 307-283-2544.

TEEN ENRICHMENT CENTER, INC.
542 Valley Way
Milpitas, California 95035
408-942-8761; Fax: 408-942-8764

General Information Residential treatment/subacute facility for adolescents. 24 beds for adolescents. Patient security: staff secured. Independent not-for-profit facility. Licensed by state of California.

Participants Accepts: female adolescents. Average stay: 12 months. Admission: one parent, all parties who share custody, court order, voluntary, depending on program. Treats learning disabilities; behavior disorders; general psychosocial disorders; substance abuse; eating disorders; compulsive/addictive disord-

ers other than substance abuse and eating disorders; post-traumatic stress disorder.

Staff .4 full-time direct-care staff member per adolescent. Staff is 10% male, 90% female.

Costs Average cost: $3000 per month.

Contact Jessie Story, Executive Director, main address above. Phone: 408-942-8761. Fax: 408-942-8764.

TEN BROECK HOSPITAL
8521 LaGrange Road
Louisville, Kentucky 40242
502-426-6380; Fax: 502-429-5787

General Information Mental health hospital and chemical dependency treatment facility for children, adolescents. Patient security: staff secured. For-profit facility affiliated with United Medical Corporation, Tampa, FL. Licensed by state of Kentucky. Accredited by JCAHO.

Participants Accepts: male and female children; male and female adolescents. Average stay: 17 days. Admission: one parent, all parties who share custody, court order, voluntary, depending on program. Treats autistic disorders; learning disabilities; behavior disorders; general psychosocial disorders; substance abuse; eating disorders; compulsive/addictive disorders other than substance abuse and eating disorders; post-traumatic stress disorder; thought, mood, and personality disorders.

Staff Staff is 57% male, 43% female.

Education Academic program available. Serves ages 4–18, grades 1–12.

Additional Services Wilderness/survival program for males and females ages 3 and up. Treats autistic disorders; learning disabilities; behavior disorders; general psychosocial disorders; substance abuse; eating disorders; compulsive/addictive disorders other than substance abuse and eating disorders; post-traumatic stress disorder; thought, mood, and personality disorders.

Contact Intake Department, main address above. Phone: 502-426-6380. Fax: 502-429-5787.

TENNESSEE CHRISTIAN MEDICAL CENTER
500 Hospital Drive
Madison, Tennessee 37115
615-865-2373; Fax: 615-865-0251

General Information General hospital for children, adolescents. Patient security: entirely locked. Not-for-profit facility affiliated with Adventist Health System, Orlando, FL. Licensed by state of Tennessee. Accredited by JCAHO.

Participants Accepts: male and female children; male and female adolescents. Average stay: 20 days. Admission: one parent, all parties who share custody, court order, voluntary, depending on program. Treats autistic disorders; learning disabilities; behavior disorders; general psychosocial disorders; substance abuse; eating disorders; compulsive/addictive disorders other than substance abuse and eating disorders; post-traumatic stress disorder; thought, mood, and personality disorders.

Contact Terry Owen, Vice President of Marketing, main address above. Phone: 615-865-2373.

THE TERRACES
1170 South State Street
Ephrata, Pennsylvania 17522
717-859-4100; Fax: 717-859-2131

General Information Drug and alcohol rehabilitation center for adolescents. Patient security: staff secured. For-profit facility affiliated with Addiction Recovery Corporation, Rockville, MD. Licensed by state of Pennsylvania. Accredited by JCAHO.

Participants Accepts: male adolescents. Average stay: 21 days. Admission: one parent, all parties who share custody, court order, voluntary, depending on program. Treats behavior disorders; general psychosocial disorders; substance abuse; thought, mood, and personality disorders. Accepts the vision impaired; the hearing impaired; the speech impaired; those receiving psychotropic medication; those with a history of epilepsy.

Staff .4 full-time direct-care staff member per adolescent.

Costs Average cost: $450 per day.

Contact Linda Wellington, Director of Administration, main address above. Phone: 717-859-4100.

THOMPSON CHILDREN'S HOMES
6801 Saint Peter's Lane
P.O. Box 25129
Charlotte, North Carolina 28229
704-536-0375; Fax: 704-531-9266

General Information Residential treatment/subacute facility for children, adolescents. 30 beds for children; 8 beds for adolescents. Open year-round. Patient security: unlocked; will pursue and return runaways. Suburban setting. Independent not-for-profit facility. Licensed by state of North Carolina. Accredited by North Carolina Child Care Association.

Participants Accepts: male and female children ages 5–12; male adolescents ages 8–18. Average stay: 700 days. Admission: all parties who share custody. Treats learning disabilities; behavior disorders; general psychosocial disorders. Accepts the hearing impaired; the speech impaired. Special programs for the developmentally disabled. Largest number of participants from North Carolina.

Program Family treatment program available.

Staff 1.1 full-time direct-care staff members per child or adolescent. Total facility staff includes 1 physician, 1 psychiatrist, 1 registered nurse, 6 MSW social workers, 4 teachers, 15 counselors, 3 occupational/recreational therapists, 10 dieticians. Staff is 25% male, 75% female.

Facilities Multiple buildings; males and females in both coeducational and separate units depending on program. Central dining (shared with adults), separate dining by residential unit available. Basketball courts, game room, gymnasium, indoor swimming pool, playing fields.

Education Academic program available at no charge. Serves ages 5–12, grades K–6. 4 teachers on staff. Curriculum accredited or approved by Charlotte-Mecklenburg School System. Organized sports program offered.

Costs Average cost: $48,000 per year. Accepts private insurance, group insurance, medicare, public funds.

Additional Services Outpatient services for males and females ages 5–12. Treats behavior disorders; general psychosocial disorders.

Contact Steven Sally, Program Director, main address above. Phone: 704-536-0375. Fax: 704-531-9266.

THREE SPRINGS OF COURTLAND
101 Madison Street
Courtland, Alabama 35618
205-637-2199; Fax: 205-637-8911

General Information Residential treatment/subacute facility for adolescents. 33 beds for adolescents. Open year-round. Patient security: entirely locked; will pursue and return runaways. Small town setting. Independent for-profit facility. Licensed by state of Alabama. Accredited by JCAHO.

Participants Accepts: male adolescents ages 12–17. Average stay: 365 days. Admission: one parent, all parties who share custody, court order, depending on program. Treats learning disabilities; behavior disorders; general psychosocial disorders; substance abuse; compulsive/addictive disorders other than substance abuse and eating disorders; post-traumatic stress disorder; thought, mood, and personality disorders. Accepts the sexually compulsive; those with a history of harm to themselves and others; those receiving psychotropic medication. Largest number of participants from Tennessee, Alabama, Georgia.

Program Treatment modalities: cognitive-behavioral. Family treatment program available.

Staff .6 full-time direct-care staff member per adolescent. Total facility staff includes 1 psychologist, 2 psychiatrists, 1 registered nurse, 5 practical/vocational nurses, 4 MSW social workers, 2 social workers (non-MSW), 3 teachers, 5 counselors, 1 occupational/recreational therapist, 1 dietician, 5 other direct-care staff members. Staff is 50% male, 50% female.

Facilities Multiple buildings. Central dining. Basketball courts, game room, gymnasium, playing fields.

Education Academic program available at no charge. Serves ages 12–17, grades 4–12. 3 teachers on staff. Curriculum accredited or approved by State of Alabama Department of Education. Cost of educational program sometimes covered by local school district.

Costs Average cost: $250 per day. Accepts private insurance, group insurance, Blue Cross/Blue Shield, public funds.

Contact Scott Carpenter, Admissions, P.O. Box 370, Courtland, AL 35618. Phone: 205-637-2199. Fax: 205-637-8911.
See page 460 for full page description.

THREE SPRINGS OF DUCK RIVER
RR 1
Nunnelly, Tennessee 37137
615-729-5040; Fax: 615-729-9525

General Information Residential treatment/subacute facility for adolescents. 60 beds for adolescents. Open year-round. Patient security: unlocked; will pursue and return runaways. Rural setting. Independent for-profit facility. Licensed by state of Tennessee.

Participants Accepts: male adolescents ages 11–17. Average stay: 365 days. Admission: one parent, all parties who share custody, court order, depending on program. Treats learning disabilities; behavior disorders; general psychosocial disorders; substance abuse; post-traumatic stress disorder; thought, mood, and personality disorders. Largest number of participants from Tennessee, Illinois.

Program Treatment modalities: cognitive-behavioral; reality therapy. Family treatment program available.

Staff .7 full-time direct-care staff member per adolescent. Total facility staff includes 1 physician, 1 psychologist, 1 psychiatrist, 1 practical/vocational nurse, 1 MSW social worker, 2 social workers (non-MSW), 4 teachers, 13 counselors, 1 dietician, 8 other direct-care staff members. Staff is 69% male, 31% female.

Facilities Multiple buildings. Central dining. Basketball courts, game room, gymnasium, playing fields, ropes course.

Education Academic program available at no charge. Serves ages 10–17, grades 3–12. 4 teachers on staff. Curriculum accredited or approved by State of Tennessee Department of Education. Cost of educational program sometimes covered by local school district.

Costs Average cost: $100 per day. Accepts private insurance, group insurance, Blue Cross/Blue Shield, public funds.

Additional Services Wilderness/survival program for males ages 11–17. Treats learning disabilities; behavior disorders; general psychosocial disorders; substance abuse; post-traumatic stress disorder; thought, mood, and personality disorders.

Contact Toni Kline, Director of Family Services, P.O. Box 297, Centerville, TN 37033. Phone: 615-729-5040. Fax: 615-729-9525.
See page 460 for full page description.

THREE SPRINGS OF NORTH CAROLINA
P.O. Box 1320
Pittsboro, North Carolina 27312
919-542-1104; Fax: 919-782-4956

General Information Residential treatment/subacute facility for adolescents. 80 beds for adolescents. Open year-round. Patient security: staff secured; will pursue and return runaways. Rural setting. Independent for-profit facility. Licensed by state of North Carolina. Accredited by JCAHO.

Participants Accepts: male adolescents ages 10–17. Treats behavior disorders; general psychosocial disorders; substance abuse; thought, mood, and personality disorders. Accepts those with a history of harm to themselves and others; those receiving psychotropic medication. Largest number of participants from North Carolina, South Carolina, Georgia.

Program Treatment modalities: outdoor therapeutic programming; Twelve Step Recovery; cognitive-behavioral group therapy; adventure-based counseling. Family treatment program available.

Staff 1.1 full-time direct-care staff members per adolescent. Total facility staff includes 4 psychiatrists, 5 registered nurses, 2 practical/vocational nurses, 3 MSW social workers, 5 social workers (non-MSW), 6 teachers, 10 counselors, 2 dieticians. Staff is 50% male, 50% female.

Facilities Multiple buildings. Central dining. Basketball courts, horseback riding, outdoor swimming pool, playing fields.

Education Academic program available at no charge. Serves ages 11–17, grades 6–12. 6 teachers on staff. Curriculum accredited or approved by North Carolina private school certification.

Costs Accepts private insurance, group insurance, Blue Cross/Blue Shield.

Contact Theresa Rall, Admissions Coordinator, main address above. Phone: 919-542-1104.
See page 460 for full page description.

THREE SPRINGS OF PAINT ROCK VALLEY
P.O. Box 20
Jackson County
Trenton, Alabama 35774
205-776-2303; Fax: 205-776-2561

General Information Residential treatment/subacute facility for adolescents. 108 beds for adolescents. Open year-round. Patient security: unlocked; will pursue and return runaways. Rural setting. Independent for-profit facility. Licensed by state of Alabama.

Participants Accepts: male and female adolescents ages 10–17. Average stay: 365 days. Admission: one parent, all parties who share custody, court order, depending on program. Treats learning disabilities; behavior disorders; general psychosocial disorders; substance abuse; post-traumatic stress disorder; thought, mood, and personality disorders. Largest number of participants from Alabama, Tennessee, Georgia.

Program Treatment modalities: cognitive-behavioral; reality therapy; Twelve Step Recovery. Family treatment program available.

Staff .4 full-time direct-care staff member per adolescent. Total facility staff includes 1 psychologist, 1 psychiatrist, 1 registered nurse, 5 MSW social workers, 2 social workers (non-MSW), 5 teachers, 16 counselors, 1 dietician, 5 other direct-care staff members. Staff is 50% male, 50% female.

Facilities Multiple buildings; males and females in separate units. Central dining. Basketball courts, game room, gymnasium, outdoor swimming pool, outdoor tennis courts, playing fields, ropes course.

Education Academic program available at no charge. Serves ages 10–17, grades 3–12. 5 teachers on staff. Curriculum accredited or approved by State of Alabama Department of Education. Cost of educational program sometimes covered by local school district.

Costs Average cost: $36,500 per stay. Accepts private insurance, group insurance, Blue Cross/Blue Shield, public funds.

Additional Services Wilderness/survival program for males and females ages 10–17. Treats learning disabilities; behavior disorders; general psychosocial disorders; substance abuse; compulsive/addictive disorders other than substance abuse and eating disorders; post-traumatic stress disorder; thought, mood, and personality disorders.

Contact Thelathia Morris, Admissions, main address above. Phone: 205-776-2503. Fax: 205-776-2561.
See page 460 for full page description.

THRESHOLD YOUTH SERVICES
1401 Valley Drive
Sioux Falls, South Dakota 57105
605-334-6686; Fax: 605-335-3121

General Information Residential treatment/subacute facility for children, adolescents. Patient security: staff secured. Independent not-for-profit facility. Licensed by state of South Dakota.

Participants Accepts: male and female children; male and female adolescents. Average stay: 1 year. Admission: one parent, all parties who share custody, court order, voluntary, depending on program. Treats behavior disorders; general psychosocial disorders; substance abuse; eating disorders; compulsive/addictive disorders other than substance abuse and eating disorders; post-traumatic stress disorder; thought, mood, and personality disorders.

Staff Staff is 25% male, 75% female.

Costs Average cost: $64 per day.

Additional Services Outpatient services for males and females ages 10–22. Treats behavior disorders; general psychosocial disorders; substance abuse; eating disorders; compulsive/addictive disorders other than substance abuse and eating disorders; post-traumatic stress disorder; thought, mood, and personality disorders.

Contact Pam Bollinger, Executive Director, main address above. Phone: 605-334-6686. Fax: 605-335-3121.

TODAY, INC.
295 North Woodbourne Road
P.O. Box 908
Newtown, Pennsylvania 18940
215-968-4713; Fax: 215-968-8742

General Information Drug and alcohol rehabilitation center for adolescents, adults. Open year-round. Patient security: staff secured; no runaway pursuit. Suburban setting. Independent not-for-profit facility. Licensed by state of Pennsylvania. Accredited by JCAHO; Office of Drug and Alcohol Programs, Division of Youth and Family Services, Department of Public Welfare.

Participants Accepts: male and female adolescents ages 13–21; male adults ages 22–35. Average stay: 45 days. Admission: one parent, court order, depending on program. Treats behavior disorders; general psychosocial disorders; substance abuse; eating disorders; thought, mood, and personality disorders.

Program Treatment modalities: behavior modification; Twelve Step Recovery; psychodynamic. Family treatment program available.

Staff .7 full-time direct-care staff member per adolescent. Total facility staff includes 1 physician, 1 psychiatrist, 1 registered nurse, 5 teachers, 6 counselors, 2 dieticians, 6 other direct-care staff members. Staff is 55% male, 45% female.

Facilities Multiple buildings; males and females in coeducational units. Separate residential quarters for adolescents. Central dining (shared with adults). Basketball courts, game room, outdoor swimming pool, playing fields, ropes course, volleyball.

Education Academic program available at no charge. Serves ages 13–18, ungraded. 5 teachers on staff. Curriculum accredited or approved by Neshaminy School District. Cost of educational program covered by local school district. Organized sports program offered.

Costs Average cost: $5625 per stay. Accepts private insurance, group insurance, Blue Cross/Blue Shield, public funds.

Additional Services Outpatient services for males and females ages 18 and up. Treats substance abuse.

Contact Sylvia Lefcourt, Community Relations, main address above. Phone: 215-968-4713. Fax: 215-968-8742.

TOUCHSTONE COMMUNITY, INC.
3420 East Shea Boulevard, Suite 150
Phoenix, Arizona 85024
602-953-9024; Fax: 602-953-9217

General Information Residential facility with outpatient and prevention programs for adolescents. 24 beds for adolescents. Patient security: staff secured. Independent not-for-profit facility. Licensed by state of Arizona. Accredited by JCAHO.

Participants Accepts: male adolescents ages 12–16. Average stay: 4 months. Admission: one parent, all parties who share custody, court order, voluntary, depending on program. Treats learning disabilities; behavior disorders; general psychosocial disorders; substance abuse; compulsive/addictive disorders other than substance abuse and eating disorders; post-traumatic stress disorder; thought, mood, and personality disorders.

Staff 3 full-time direct-care staff members per adolescent.

Additional Services Outpatient services for males and females ages 2–18. Treats learning disabilities; behavior disorders; general psychosocial disorders; substance abuse; compulsive/addictive disorders other than substance abuse and eating disorders; post-traumatic stress disorder; thought, mood, and personality disorders. School for males ages 12–16. Treats learning disabilities; behavior disorders; general psychosocial disorders; substance abuse; compulsive/addictive disorders other than substance abuse and eating disorders; post-traumatic stress disorder; thought, mood, and personality disorders.

Contact Tim Dunst, President, main address above. Phone: 602-953-9024.

TRICENTER
707 West Messmer Street
Milwaukee, Wisconsin 53209
414-372-7200; Fax: 414-372-8655

General Information Residential treatment/subacute facility for adolescents. 20 beds for adolescents. Patient security: staff secured. Not-for-profit facility affiliated with Lutheran Social Services of Wisconsin and Upper Michigan, Milwaukee, WI. Licensed by state of Wisconsin. Accredited by Council on Accreditation of Services for Families and Children.

Participants Accepts: male and female adolescents. Average stay: 1 year. Admission: one parent, all parties who share custody, court order, voluntary, depending on program. Treats learning disabilities; behavior disorders; general psychosocial disorders; substance abuse.

Staff Staff is 50% male, 50% female.

Costs Average cost: $112 per day.

Contact Tim Wildrick, Program Director, main address above. Phone: 414-372-7200. Fax: 414-372-8655.

TRINITY LUTHERAN HOSPITAL
3030 Baltimore Avenue
Kansas City, Missouri 64108
816-753-4600; Fax: 816-751-4623

General Information General hospital for children, adolescents. Patient security: entirely locked. Not-for-profit facility affiliated with Health Midwest, Kansas City, MO. Licensed by state of Missouri. Accredited by JCAHO.

Participants Accepts: male and female children; male and female adolescents. Average stay: 21 days. Admission: one parent, all parties who share custody, court order, voluntary, depending on program. Treats autistic disorders; learning disabilities; behavior disorders; general psychosocial disorders; substance abuse; eating disorders; compulsive/addictive disorders other than substance abuse and eating disorders; post-traumatic stress disorder; thought, mood, and personality disorders.

Contact Gail Cyr, Clinical Director of Child and Adolescent Mental Health Services, main address above. Phone: 816-753-4600.

TRUCKEE MEADOWS HOSPITAL
1240 East Ninth Street
Reno, Nevada 89520
702-323-0478; Fax: 702-789-4203

General Information Psychiatric hospital for children, adolescents, adults. 14 beds for children; 35 beds for adolescents; 95 beds total. Open year-round. Patient security: entirely locked; will pursue and return runaways. Urban setting. For-profit facility affiliated with Hospital Corporation of America, Nashville, TN. Licensed by state of Nevada. Accredited by JCAHO.

Participants Accepts: male and female children ages 3–12; male and female adolescents ages 13–17; male and female adults ages 18 and up. Average stay: 14 days. Treats learning disabilities; behavior disorders; general psychosocial disorders; substance abuse; eating disorders; compulsive/addictive disorders other than substance abuse and eating disorders; post-traumatic stress disorder; thought, mood, and personality disorders. Accepts the mobility impaired; the vision impaired; the hearing impaired; the speech impaired; those with a history of arson; those with a history of harm to themselves and others; those receiving psychotropic medication; non-English speaking individuals; those with a history of epilepsy. Largest number of participants from Nevada, California.

Program Treatment modalities: Twelve Step Recovery; group therapy; multifamily. Family treatment program available.

Staff Total facility staff includes 13 physicians, 44 psychologists, 19 psychiatrists, 16 registered nurses, 2 practical/vocational nurses, 7 MSW social workers, 5 social workers (non-MSW), 100 teachers, 4 counselors, 7 occupational/recreational therapists, 12 other direct-care staff members.

Facilities Multiple buildings; males and females in coeducational units. Separate residential quarters for children and adolescents. Separate dining by residential unit, in-room dining available. Basketball courts, game room, gymnasium, outdoor swimming pool, ropes course.

Education Academic program available at no charge. Serves ages 5–18, grades K–12. 100 teachers on staff. Curriculum accredited or approved by Nevada Department of Education.

Costs   Accepts private insurance, group insurance, medicare, medicaid, Blue Cross/Blue Shield, public funds.

Additional Services   Drug and alcohol rehabilitation services for males and females ages 18 and up. Treats general psychosocial disorders; substance abuse; eating disorders; compulsive/addictive disorders other than substance abuse and eating disorders; post-traumatic stress disorder; thought, mood, and personality disorders. Outpatient services for males and females ages 4 and up. Treats behavior disorders; general psychosocial disorders; substance abuse; eating disorders; compulsive/addictive disorders other than substance abuse and eating disorders; post-traumatic stress disorder; thought, mood, and personality disorders.

Contact   Mark Lanier, Front End Systems Director, main address above. Phone: 800-242-0478. Fax: 702-789-4203.

TUCSON PSYCHIATRIC INSTITUTE YOUTH HOSPITAL
7220 East Rosewood Street
Tucson, Arizona 85710
602-296-2828; Fax: 602-290-1465

General Information   Psychiatric hospital for children, adolescents. 10 beds for children; 38 beds for adolescents; 48 beds total. Open year-round. Patient security: entirely locked; will pursue and return runaways. Suburban setting. For-profit facility affiliated with National Medical Enterprises, Santa Monica, CA. Licensed by state of Arizona. Accredited by JCAHO.

Participants   Accepts: male and female children ages 5–12; male and female adolescents ages 13–17. Average stay: 180 days. Admission: all parties who share custody, court order, depending on program. Treats learning disabilities; behavior disorders; general psychosocial disorders; substance abuse; post-traumatic stress disorder; thought, mood, and personality disorders. Accepts those with a history of harm to themselves and others; those receiving psychotropic medication.

Program   Family treatment program available.

Staff   1.3 full-time direct-care staff members per child or adolescent. Total facility staff includes 3 physicians, 3 psychiatrists, 10 registered nurses, 10 practical/vocational nurses, 6 MSW social workers, 6 teachers, 2 occupational/recreational therapists, 1 dietician, 15 other direct-care staff members.

Facilities   Single building; males and females in co-educational units. Central dining. Basketball courts, gymnasium, outdoor swimming pool, outdoor tennis courts, playing fields.

Education   Academic program available at additional cost. Serves ages 6–17, grades 1–12. 6 teachers on staff. Curriculum accredited or approved by Arizona State Board of Education. Cost of educational program covered by local school district.

Costs   Accepts private insurance, group insurance, medicare, medicaid, Blue Cross/Blue Shield, public funds.

Additional Services   Drug and alcohol rehabilitation services for males and females ages 6 and up. Treats behavior disorders; general psychosocial disorders; substance abuse; eating disorders; compulsive/addictive disorders other than substance abuse and eating disorders; post-traumatic stress disorder; thought, mood, and personality disorders. Outpatient services for males and females ages 3 and up. Treats behavior disorders; general psychosocial disorders; eating disorders; compulsive/addictive disorders other than substance abuse and eating disorders; post-traumatic stress disorder; thought, mood, and personality disorders. Residential or sub-acute services for males and females ages 5–17. Treats learning disabilities; behavior disorders; general psychosocial disorders; substance abuse; eating disorders; compulsive/addictive disorders other than substance abuse and eating disorders; post-traumatic stress disorder; thought, mood, and personality disorders.

Contact   J. Chris Hall, Director of Referral and Information, main address above. Phone: 602-296-2828. Fax: 602-290-1465.

TULANE UNIVERSITY MEDICAL CENTER
1415 Tulane Avenue
New Orleans, Louisiana 70112
504-588-5263; Fax: 504-585-4047

General Information   General hospital for children. 8 beds for children. Patient security: staff secured. Independent not-for-profit facility. Licensed by state of Louisiana. Accredited by JCAHO.

Participants   Accepts: male and female children. Average stay: 6 weeks. Admission: one parent, all parties who share custody, voluntary, depending on program. Treats autistic disorders; behavior disorders; eating disorders; post-traumatic stress disorder; thought, mood, and personality disorders.

Contact Dr. Richard Dalton, Director of Children's Neuropsyche Inpatient Unit, main address above. Phone: 504-588-5800.

TURNOFF, INC.
71-175 Aurora Road
Desert Hot Springs, California 92240
619-329-9596

General Information Residential treatment/subacute facility for adolescents. Patient security: staff secured. Independent not-for-profit facility. Licensed by state of California.

Participants Accepts: male and female adolescents. Average stay: 12 months. Admission: one parent, all parties who share custody, court order, voluntary, depending on program. Treats substance abuse. Accepts those with a history of arson; those with a history of harm to themselves and others; those with a history of epilepsy.

Staff Staff is 60% male, 40% female.

Costs Average cost: $2800 per month.

Contact Danny Levitoff, Executive Director, main address above. Phone: 619-329-9596.

TUSTIN HOSPITAL MEDICAL CENTER
14662 Newport Avenue
Tustin, California 92680
714-669-4483; Fax: 714-730-5282

General Information General hospital for adolescents. 10 beds for adolescents. Patient security: staff secured. Independent for-profit facility. Licensed by state of California. Accredited by JCAHO.

Participants Accepts: male and female adolescents. Average stay: 20 days. Admission: one parent, all parties who share custody, court order, voluntary, depending on program. Treats substance abuse. Accepts the mobility impaired; the vision impaired; the hearing impaired; the speech impaired; those with a history of arson; those with a history of harm to themselves and others; those receiving psychotropic medication; those with a history of epilepsy.

Staff Staff is 25% male, 75% female.

Costs Average cost: $470 per day.

Contact Michael Dean, Program Director, main address above. Phone: 714-669-4483. Fax: 714-730-5282.

TWIN LAKES CENTER FOR DRUG AND ALCOHOL REHABILITATION
P.O. Box 909
Somerset, Pennsylvania 15501-0909
814-443-3639

General Information Drug and alcohol rehabilitation center for adolescents, adults. 10 beds for adolescents. Open year-round. Patient security: staff secured; will pursue and return runaways. Rural setting. Not-for-profit facility affiliated with Somerset Health Services, Inc., Somerset, PA. Licensed by state of Pennsylvania. Accredited by JCAHO.

Participants Accepts: male and female adolescents ages 13–18; male and female adults ages 18 and up. Average stay: 42 days. Admission: voluntary, parental and court referrals, depending on program. Treats substance abuse.

Program Treatment modalities: Twelve Step Recovery. Family treatment program available.

Staff 2 full-time direct-care staff members per adolescent. Total facility staff includes 2 physicians, 1 psychologist, 1 psychiatrist, 1 registered nurse, 6 practical/vocational nurses, 1 MSW social worker, 2 counselors, 1 occupational/recreational therapist, 5 other direct-care staff members. Staff is 55% male, 45% female.

Facilities Multiple buildings; males and females in coeducational units. Separate residential quarters for adolescents. Central dining arrangements vary. Playing fields.

Education Academic program available at no charge. Serves ages 13–18, grades 7–12. Curriculum accredited or approved by Pennsylvania Department of Education. Cost of educational program covered by local school district.

Costs Average cost: $5880 per stay. Accepts private insurance, group insurance, Blue Cross/Blue Shield, public funds.

Additional Services Outpatient services for males and females ages 13 and up. Treats substance abuse.

Contact Frank Hershberger, Clinical Director, main address above. Phone: 814-443-3639.

TWO RIVERS PSYCHIATRIC HOSPITAL
5121 Raytown Road
Kansas City, Missouri 64133
816-356-5688; Fax: 816-358-5395

General Information Psychiatric hospital for adolescents, adults. 20 beds for adolescents. Open year-round. Patient security: entirely locked; will pursue and return runaways. Suburban setting. Independent for-profit facility. Licensed by state of Missouri. Accredited by JCAHO.

Participants Accepts: male and female adolescents ages 11–17; male and female adults ages 18 and up. Admission: one parent, all parties who share custody, court order, voluntary, Division of Family Services referrals, depending on program. Treats learning disabilities; behavior disorders; general psychosocial disorders; substance abuse; eating disorders; compulsive/addictive disorders other than substance abuse and eating disorders; post-traumatic stress disorder; thought, mood, and personality disorders. Accepts the mobility impaired; the vision impaired; the hearing impaired; the speech impaired; those with a history of arson; the sexually compulsive; those with a history of harm to themselves and others; those receiving psychotropic medication; those with a history of epilepsy. Special programs for the chronically ill; the developmentally disabled; the vision impaired; the hearing impaired; the speech impaired; those with AIDS.

Program Treatment modalities: Masters and Johnson Sexual Trauma Program; dual diagnosis/addictions; adolescent recovery program; adult psychiatric program. Family treatment program available.

Staff 1.6 full-time direct-care staff members per adolescent. Total facility staff includes 1 physician, 3 psychologists, 3 psychiatrists, 12 registered nurses, 2 practical/vocational nurses, 4 MSW social workers, 1 teacher, 2 counselors, 4 occupational/recreational therapists, 1 speech pathologist, 1 therapist, 1 dietician. Staff is 15% male, 85% female.

Facilities Single building; males and females in co-educational units. Separate residential quarters for adolescents. Separate dining by residential unit available. Basketball courts, game room, gymnasium, playing fields.

Education Academic program available at no charge. Serves ages 11–18, grades 7–12. 1 teacher on staff. Curriculum accredited or approved by State of Missouri.

Costs Average cost: $850 per day. Accepts private insurance, group insurance, medicare, medicaid, Blue Cross/Blue Shield, public funds.

Additional Services Drug and alcohol rehabilitation services for males and females ages 11–18. Treats learning disabilities; behavior disorders; general psychosocial disorders; substance abuse; eating disorders; compulsive/addictive disorders other than substance abuse and eating disorders; post-traumatic stress disorder; thought, mood, and personality disorders.

Contact Linda Berridge, Marketing Director, main address above. Phone: 816-356-5688. Fax: 816-358-5395.

TYLER RANCH, INC.
West 4921 Rosewood Avenue
Spokane, Washington 99208-3740
509-327-6900

General Information Residential treatment/subacute facility for children, adolescents. 16 beds for children. Open year-round. Patient security: staff secured; will pursue and return runaways. Suburban setting. Independent not-for-profit facility. Licensed by state of Washington. Accredited by Department of Social and Health Services.

Participants Accepts: male children ages 5–12; male adolescents ages 12–18. Average stay: 1 year. Admission: all parties who share custody. Treats learning disabilities; behavior disorders; general psychosocial disorders; substance abuse; compulsive/addictive disorders other than substance abuse and eating disorders; thought, mood, and personality disorders. Accepts those with a history of arson; the sexually compulsive; those with a history of harm to themselves and others; those receiving psychotropic medication; those with a history of epilepsy. Special programs for those with Fetal Alcohol Syndrome. Largest number of participants from Washington, California, Oregon.

Program Treatment modalities: Twelve Step Recovery; behavior modification; reality therapy.

Staff Total facility staff includes 1 psychologist, 2 MSW social workers, 2 counselors, 2 other direct-care staff members. Staff is 86% male, 14% female.

Facilities Single building. Separate dining by residential unit available. Basketball courts, game room, gymnasium, ropes course.

Costs Average cost: $2000 per month. Accepts private insurance.

Additional Services Drug and alcohol rehabilitation services for males ages 6–12. Treats learning disabilities; behavior disorders; general psychosocial disorders; substance abuse; compulsive/addictive disorders other than substance abuse and eating disorders; thought, mood, and personality disorders.

Contact Jon W. Tyler, Executive Director, main address above. Phone: 509-327-6900.

Announcement Tyler Ranch considers each individual a special placement with programs customized to specific needs. Tyler blends education, discipline, goal setting, responsibility, structure, and all activities within a family-style home setting that includes appropriate professional support systems. Accomplishment and emotional growth are both encouraged and rewarded.

TYRONE HOSPITAL DETOX UNIT
1 Hospital Drive
Tyrone, Pennsylvania 16686
814-684-1255 Ext. 233; Fax: 814-684-1255
Ext. 300

General Information General hospital for adolescents, adults. 6 beds for adolescents. Open year-round. Patient security: unlocked; no runaway pursuit. Small town setting. Not-for-profit facility affiliated with Tyrone Hospital, Tyrone, PA. Licensed by state of Pennsylvania. Accredited by JCAHO; Office of Drug and Alcohol Programs of Pennsylvania.

Participants Accepts: male and female adolescents ages 14–20; male and female adults ages 21–72. Average stay: 5 days. Admission: voluntary. Treats substance abuse. Accepts the mobility impaired; the vision impaired; the hearing impaired; the speech impaired; those with a history of epilepsy. Special programs for the chronically ill. Largest number of participants from Pennsylvania.

Program Treatment modalities: Twelve Step Recovery. Family treatment program available.

Staff Total facility staff includes 1 physician, 1 psychologist, 4 registered nurses, 2 practical/vocational nurses, 4 counselors, 1 physical therapist, 1 dietician. Staff is 2% male, 98% female.

Facilities Single building; males and females in separate units. Residential quarters shared with adults. Central dining (shared with adults).

Costs Average cost: $700 per day. Accepts private insurance, group insurance, medicare, Blue Cross/Blue Shield.

Additional Services Drug and alcohol rehabilitation services for males and females ages 14–72. Treats substance abuse.

Contact Judy Deer, Director, Detox Unit, main address above. Phone: 814-684-1255 Ext. 233. Fax: 814-684-1255 Ext. 300.

UNIVERSITY HOSPITAL
1116 North Kedzie Avenue
Chicago, Illinois 60651
312-276-5200; Fax: 312-276-1046

General Information Freestanding psychiatric/drug and alcohol center for children, adolescents. Patient security: entirely locked. Independent not-for-profit facility. Licensed by state of Illinois. Accredited by JCAHO.

Participants Accepts: male and female children; male and female adolescents. Average stay: 16 days. Admission: one parent, voluntary, guardianship, depending on program. Treats autistic disorders; learning disabilities; behavior disorders; general psychosocial disorders; substance abuse; eating disorders; compulsive/addictive disorders other than substance abuse and eating disorders; post-traumatic stress disorder; thought, mood, and personality disorders.

Staff Staff is 50% male, 50% female.

Contact Mike Huber, Director of Marketing, main address above. Phone: 312-276-5200.

UNIVERSITY OF SOUTH FLORIDA PSYCHIATRY CENTER
3515 East Fletcher Avenue
Tampa, Florida 33613
813-972-3000; Fax: 813-972-7098

General Information Psychiatric hospital for children, adolescents. Patient security: entirely locked. For-profit facility affiliated with Hospital Corporation of America, Nashville, TN. Licensed by state of Florida. Accredited by JCAHO.

Participants Accepts: male and female children; male and female adolescents. Average stay: 14 days. Admission: one parent, all parties who share custody, court order, voluntary, agency with custody, depending on program. Treats learning disabilities; behavior disorders; general psychosocial disorders; eating disorders; compulsive/addictive disorders other than substance abuse and eating disorders; post-traumatic stress disorder; thought, mood, and personality disorders.

Costs Average cost: $15,000 per stay.

Contact Respond Department, main address above. Phone: 813-972-3000.

UNIVERSITY PAVILION
7425 North University Drive
Taramac, Florida 33321
305-722-9933; Fax: 305-726-1567

General Information Psychiatric hospital for children, adolescents. Patient security: entirely locked. For-profit facility affiliated with Hospital Corporation of America, Nashville, TN. Licensed by state of Florida. Accredited by JCAHO.

Participants Accepts: male and female children; male and female adolescents. Average stay: 17 days. Admission: one parent, all parties who share custody, court order, voluntary, depending on program. Treats behavior disorders; general psychosocial disorders; substance abuse; eating disorders; compulsive/addictive disorders other than substance abuse and eating disorders; post-traumatic stress disorder; thought, mood, and personality disorders.

Contact Lee Mattuizzo, Director of Respond, main address above. Phone: 305-722-9933. Fax: 305-726-1567.

UTA HALEE GIRLS' VILLAGE
10625 Calhoun Road
Omaha, Nebraska 68112
402-453-0803; Fax: 402-453-1247

General Information Residential treatment/subacute facility for adolescents. 55 beds for adolescents. Open year-round. Patient security: partially locked; will pursue and return runaways. Suburban setting. Independent not-for-profit facility. Licensed by state of Nebraska. Accredited by JCAHO; American Association of Psychiatric Services for Children, Department of Social Services, Department of Health.

Participants Accepts: female adolescents ages 12–18. Average stay: 15 months. Admission: one parent, all parties who share custody, court order, depending on program. Treats learning disabilities; behavior disorders; general psychosocial disorders; substance abuse; post-traumatic stress disorder; thought, mood, and personality disorders. Accepts those with a history of harm to themselves and others; those receiving psychotropic medication; those with a history of epilepsy. Largest number of participants from Nebraska, Iowa.

Program Treatment modalities: psychodynamic; structural/strategic family therapy; reality therapy; behavior modification. Family treatment program available.

Staff 1.1 full-time direct-care staff members per adolescent. Total facility staff includes 1 physician, 1 psychologist, 1 psychiatrist, 1 registered nurse, 1 practical/vocational nurse, 11 MSW social workers, 12 teachers, 1 counselor, 4 occupational/recreational therapists, 1 dietician, 56 other direct-care staff members. Staff is 8% male, 92% female.

Facilities Multiple buildings. Central dining, separate dining by residential unit available. Basketball courts, game room, gymnasium, outdoor tennis courts, playing fields.

Education Academic program available at additional cost. Serves ages 12–18, grades 7–12. 12 teachers on staff. Curriculum accredited or approved by Nebraska Board of Education. Organized sports program offered.

Costs Average cost: $90,900 per stay. Accepts private insurance, medicaid.

Contact Lindy Ottoson, Admissions/Community Education, main address above. Phone: 402-453-0803. Fax: 402-453-1247.

UTAH VALLEY REGIONAL MEDICAL CENTER
1034 North 500 West
Provo, Utah 84604
801-373-7850; Fax: 801-371-7186

General Information General hospital for children, adolescents. Patient security: partially locked. Not-for-profit facility affiliated with Intermountain Health Care Corporation, Salt Lake City, UT. Licensed by state of Utah. Accredited by JCAHO.

Participants Accepts: male and female children; male and female adolescents. Average stay: 30 days. Admission: one parent, all parties who share custody, court order, voluntary, depending on program. Treats autistic disorders; learning disabilities; behavior disorders; general psychosocial disorders; substance abuse; eating disorders; compulsive/addictive disorders other than substance abuse and eating disorders; post-traumatic stress disorder; thought, mood, and personality disorders.

Staff Staff is 50% male, 50% female.

Education Academic program available at no charge. Serves ages 3–18, grades K–12. Curriculum accredited or approved by public school district. Cost of educational program covered by local school district. Organized sports program offered.

Costs Average cost: $700 per day.

Contact   Michael Cain, Program Director, main address above. Phone: 801-373-7850. Fax: 801-371-7186.

VALLEY VIEW/REDIRECTION
Swiss Hill Road
P.O. Box 26
Kenoza Lake, New York 12750
800-955-2869; Fax: 914-482-3516

General Information   Drug and alcohol rehabilitation center for adolescents, adults. 50 beds for adolescents. Open year-round. Patient security: staff secured; will pursue and return runaways. Rural setting. Independent for-profit facility. Licensed by state of New York. Accredited by JCAHO; New York State Division of Alcoholism and Alcohol Abuse, New York State Division of Substance Abuse Services.

Participants   Accepts: male and female adolescents ages 12–21; male and female adults ages 22 and up. Average stay: 42 days. Admission: one parent, all parties who share custody, court order, depending on program. Treats substance abuse. Accepts the hearing impaired; those receiving psychotropic medication. Special programs for the hearing impaired.

Program   Treatment modalities: Twelve Step Recovery; multi-family group therapy; psychodynamic; psycho-educational. Family treatment program available.

Staff   Total facility staff includes 2 physicians, 1 psychiatrist, 8 registered nurses, 2 practical/vocational nurses, 4 MSW social workers, 2 teachers, 6 counselors, 3 therapists, 12 other direct-care staff members. Staff is 50% male, 50% female.

Facilities   Multiple buildings; males and females in separate units. Separate residential quarters for adolescents. Central dining (shared with adults). Basketball courts, horseback riding, indoor swimming pool, outdoor swimming pool, playing fields.

Education   Academic program available at no charge. Serves ages 12–21, grades K–12. 2 teachers on staff. Curriculum accredited or approved by New York City Board of Education Off-site Educational Services. Organized sports program offered.

Costs   Average cost: $700 per day. Accepts private insurance, group insurance, medicare, Blue Cross/Blue Shield.

Contact   Richard Santiago, Marketing Director, main address above. Phone: 800-955-2869. Fax: 914-482-3516.

VALLEY VIEW SCHOOL
Oakham Road
P.O. Box 338
North Brookfield, Massachusetts 01535
508-867-6505; Fax: 508-867-3300

General Information   Residential treatment/subacute facility for adolescents. 42 beds for adolescents. Open year-round. Patient security: staff secured; no runaway pursuit. Rural setting. Independent not-for-profit facility. Licensed by state of Massachusetts. Accredited by American Association of Psychiatric Services for Children.

Participants   Accepts: male adolescents ages 12–17. Admission: all parties who share custody. Treats learning disabilities; behavior disorders; general psychosocial disorders; thought, mood, and personality disorders. Largest number of participants from Illinois, New Jersey, California.

Program   Treatment modalities: therapeutic milieu; structured environment; individual and group psychotherapy.

Staff   .8 full-time direct-care staff member per adolescent. Total facility staff includes 3 psychologists, 1 psychiatrist, 1 registered nurse, 2 MSW social workers, 10 teachers, 1 counselor, 11 other direct-care staff members. Staff is 80% male, 20% female.

Facilities   Multiple buildings. Central dining (shared with adults). Basketball courts, game room, gymnasium, outdoor tennis courts, playing fields, skateboarding ramp.

Education   Academic program available at no charge. Serves ages 12–17, ungraded. 10 teachers on staff. Curriculum accredited or approved by North Brookfield School Committee. Cost of educational program sometimes covered by local school district. Organized sports program offered.

Costs   Average cost: $36,000 per year. Accepts private insurance, public funds.

Contact   Philip G. Spiva, PhD, Director, main address above. Phone: 508-867-6505. Fax: 508-867-3300.

Announcement   Valley View accepts boys who are oppositional, ADHD, beyond comfortable management by their family, and unmotivated. A relatively gentle group without drug or court history. Therapeutically, structure, accountability, and self-esteem are stressed. Unique aspects include outdoor activities, athletics, drama, and foreign travel. See Peterson's Guide to Independent Secondary Schools 1992-93.

VANDERBILT CHILD AND ADOLESCENT PSYCHIATRIC HOSPITAL
1601 23rd Avenue, South
Nashville, Tennessee 37212
615-327-7000; Fax: 615-327-7114

General Information Psychiatric hospital for children, adolescents. Open year-round. Patient security: entirely locked. Independent for-profit facility affiliated with Hospital Corporation of America and Vanderbilt University Division of Psychiatry, Nashville, TN. Licensed by state of Tennessee. Accredited by JCAHO; National Association of Private Psychiatric Hospitals.

Participants Accepts: male and female children and adolescents ages 4–21. Average stay: 25 days. Admission: one parent, all parties who share custody, court order, depending on program. Treats learning disabilities; behavior disorders; general psychosocial disorders; substance abuse; eating disorders; post-traumatic stress disorder; thought, mood, and personality disorders.

Staff Staff is 45% male, 55% female.

Facilities Single building. Gymnasium, indoor swimming pool.

Costs Average cost: $930 per stay.

Contact Sharon Pakis, Director of Marketing, main address above. Phone: 615-327-7000. Fax: 615-327-7114.

See page 462 for full page description.

THE VANGUARD SCHOOL
2249 Highway 27, North
Lake Wales, Florida 33853
813-676-6091; Fax: 813-676-8297

General Information School for children, adolescents. Open academic year. Patient security: unlocked; no runaway pursuit. Rural setting. Independent not-for-profit facility. Licensed by state of Florida.

Participants Accepts: male and female children ages 9–13; male and female adolescents ages 13–21. Admission: voluntary. Treats learning disabilities. Accepts the speech impaired; those receiving psychotropic medication; those with a history of epilepsy. Special programs for the speech impaired. Largest number of participants from Florida, Georgia, Louisiana.

Program Treatment modalities: remedial academics eclectic.

Staff .5 full-time direct-care staff member per child or adolescent. Total facility staff includes 2 psychologists, 2 registered nurses, 25 teachers, 2 counselors, 1 speech pathologist, 40 other direct-care staff members. Staff is 38% male, 62% female.

Facilities Multiple buildings; males and females in both coeducational and separate units depending on program. Central dining. Basketball courts, game room, gymnasium, outdoor swimming pool, outdoor tennis courts, playing fields.

Education School serves ages 9–20. 25 teachers on staff. Curriculum is college-preparatory; diploma granted upon completion. Curriculum accredited or approved by Florida Council of Independent Schools. Organized sports program offered.

Costs Average cost: $19,800 per stay. Financial aid available.

Contact Joan Pleines, Admissions Registrar, main address above. Phone: 813-676-6091. Fax: 813-676-8297.

Announcement The Vanguard School, in Lake Wales, was established in 1966 to provide a residential and day coed program to serve the needs of learning-disabled students. The program is highly individualized and remedial. The goal is to offer each student academic, social, and personal growth in a supportive environment.

VENICE HOSPITAL
540 The Rialto
Venice, Florida 34285
813-485-7711; Fax: 813-483-7699

General Information General hospital for children, adolescents. Patient security: partially locked. Independent not-for-profit facility. Licensed by state of Florida. Accredited by JCAHO.

Participants Accepts: male and female children; male and female adolescents. Admission: one parent, all parties who share custody, depending on program. Treats behavior disorders; substance abuse; eating disorders.

Staff Staff is 20% male, 80% female.

Contact Bruce Collison, Marketing Director, main address above. Phone: 813-483-7604.

VICTORY MEMORIAL HOSPITAL (CHEMICAL DEPENDENCY PROGRAMS)
1324 North Sheridan Road
Waukegan, Illinois 60085
708-688-4357; Fax: 708-360-4099

General Information   General hospital for adolescents, adults. 5 beds for adolescents. Open year-round. Patient security: staff secured; will pursue and return runaways. Suburban setting. Not-for-profit facility affiliated with Victory Health Services, Waukegan, IL. Licensed by state of Illinois. Accredited by JCAHO; Illinois Department of Public Health, Illinois Department of Alcohol and Substance Abuse.

Participants   Accepts: male and female adolescents ages 12–18; male and female adults ages 18 and up. Average stay: 33 days. Admission: voluntary. Treats general psychosocial disorders; substance abuse; compulsive/addictive disorders other than substance abuse and eating disorders; post-traumatic stress disorder; thought, mood, and personality disorders. Accepts the mobility impaired; the vision impaired; the hearing impaired; the speech impaired; those with a history of arson; those with a history of harm to themselves and others; those receiving psychotropic medication; those with a history of epilepsy. Special programs for the chronically ill; the mobility impaired; those with medical problems.

Program   Treatment modalities: medical model/social model; Twelve Step Recovery; psychodynamic; behavioral. Family treatment program available.

Staff   7 full-time direct-care staff members per adolescent. Total facility staff includes 1 physician, 1 psychologist, 1 psychiatrist, 7 registered nurses, 2 practical/vocational nurses, 1 MSW social worker, 1 social worker (non-MSW), 7 counselors, 1 occupational/recreational therapist, 1 therapist, 1 dietician, 1 other direct-care staff member. Staff is 38% male, 62% female.

Facilities   Single building; males and females in co-educational units. Residential quarters shared with adults. Central dining (shared with adults), in-room dining available. Basketball courts, game room, gymnasium, outdoor tennis courts, playing fields.

Education   Academic program available at additional cost. Serves ages 12–18, ungraded. Cost of educational program covered by local school district. Organized sports program offered.

Costs   Average cost: $13,000 per stay. Accepts private insurance, group insurance, medicare, Blue Cross/Blue Shield.

Additional Services   Drug and alcohol rehabilitation services for males and females ages 15 and up. Treats general psychosocial disorders; substance abuse; compulsive/addictive disorders other than substance abuse and eating disorders; post-traumatic stress disorder; thought, mood, and personality disorders. Outpatient services for males and females ages 12 and up. Treats general psychosocial disorders; substance abuse; compulsive/addictive disorders other than substance abuse and eating disorders; post-traumatic stress disorder; thought, mood, and personality disorders. Residential or sub-acute services for males and females ages 15 and up. Treats general psychosocial disorders; substance abuse; compulsive/addictive disorders other than substance abuse and eating disorders; post-traumatic stress disorder; thought, mood, and personality disorders.

Contact   Dianne Wilcox, Assessment Counselor/Nurse, main address above. Phone: 708-360-4089. Fax: 708-360-4099.

VILLA DEL SOL TREATMENT CENTER
1951 West 25th Street
Yuma, Arizona 85364
602-344-8413; Fax: 602-344-4966

General Information   Residential treatment/subacute facility for adolescents. 16 beds for adolescents. Open year-round. Patient security: partially locked; no runaway pursuit. Rural setting. Independent for-profit facility. Licensed by state of Arizona. Accredited by JCAHO.

Participants   Accepts: male and female adolescents ages 12–18. Average stay: 152 days. Admission: one parent, all parties who share custody, court order, depending on program. Treats learning disabilities; behavior disorders; general psychosocial disorders; substance abuse; eating disorders; compulsive/addictive disorders other than substance abuse and eating disorders; post-traumatic stress disorder; thought, mood, and personality disorders. Accepts the mobility impaired; the vision impaired; the hearing impaired; those with a history of arson; the sexually compulsive; those with a history of harm to themselves and others; those receiving psychotropic medication; non-English speaking individuals; those with a history of epilepsy. Special programs for the mobility impaired. Largest number of participants from Arizona, Idaho, California.

Program   Treatment modalities: psychodynamic; Twelve Step Recovery; family systems; reality/behavioral. Family treatment program available.

Staff   1.8 full-time direct-care staff members per adolescent. Total facility staff includes 2 psychiatrists, 4 registered nurses, 1 practical/vocational nurse, 2 MSW social workers, 2 teachers, 1 counselor, 1 occupational/recreational therapist, 1 dietician, 14 other direct-care staff members. Staff is 50% male, 50% female.

Facilities Multiple buildings; males and females in coeducational units. Central dining. Game room, outdoor swimming pool, playing fields.

Education 2 teachers on staff.

Costs Average cost: $424 per stay. Accepts private insurance, group insurance, medicaid, Blue Cross/Blue Shield, public funds.

Additional Services Drug and alcohol rehabilitation services for males and females ages 12–17. Treats learning disabilities; behavior disorders; general psychosocial disorders; substance abuse; eating disorders; compulsive/addictive disorders other than substance abuse and eating disorders; post-traumatic stress disorder; thought, mood, and personality disorders. Outpatient services for males and females. Treats learning disabilities; behavior disorders; general psychosocial disorders; substance abuse; eating disorders; compulsive/addictive disorders other than substance abuse and eating disorders; post-traumatic stress disorder; thought, mood, and personality disorders.

Contact Celia Renteria, Director of Admissions, main address above. Phone: 602-344-8413. Fax: 602-344-4966.

VILLA MARIA RESIDENTIAL TREATMENT CENTER
2300 Dulaney Valley Road
Timonium, Maryland 21093
410-252-4700; Fax: 410-252-3040

General Information Residential treatment/subacute facility for children. 86 beds for children. Patient security: staff secured. Not-for-profit facility affiliated with Associated Catholic Charity, Baltimore, MD. Licensed by state of Maryland. Accredited by JCAHO.

Participants Accepts: male and female children ages 5–13. Average stay: 16 months. Admission: one parent, all parties who share custody, court order, voluntary, depending on program. Treats learning disabilities; behavior disorders; general psychosocial disorders; eating disorders; post-traumatic stress disorder; thought, mood, and personality disorders.

Staff Staff is 45% male, 55% female.

Costs Average cost: $238 per day.

Contact Zarina Noronha, Co-Director of Clinical Services, main address above. Phone: 410-252-4700.

VIRGINIA BEACH PSYCHIATRIC CENTER
1100 First Colonial Road
Virginia Beach, Virginia 23454
804-496-6000; Fax: 804-481-0484

General Information Psychiatric hospital for children, adolescents, adults. 10 beds for children; 10 beds for adolescents. Open year-round. Patient security: entirely locked; will pursue and return runaways. Suburban setting. For-profit facility affiliated with First Hospital Corporation, Norfolk, VA. Licensed by state of Virginia. Accredited by JCAHO.

Participants Accepts: male and female children ages 4–12; male and female adolescents ages 12–18; male and female adults ages 18 and up. Average stay: 14 days. Admission: one parent, court order, depending on program. Treats learning disabilities; behavior disorders; general psychosocial disorders; substance abuse; eating disorders; compulsive/addictive disorders other than substance abuse and eating disorders; post-traumatic stress disorder; thought, mood, and personality disorders. Accepts the mobility impaired; the vision impaired; the hearing impaired; the speech impaired; those with a history of arson; the sexually compulsive; those with a history of harm to themselves and others; those receiving psychotropic medication; non-English speaking individuals; those with a history of epilepsy; those with heart disease; diabetics; those with various medical disabilities. Special programs for those with injuries to the brain or central nervous system. Largest number of participants from Virginia.

Program Treatment modalities: dual diagnosis; psychodynamic; cognitive-behavioral; Twelve Step Recovery. Family treatment program available.

Staff .1 full-time direct-care staff member per child or adolescent. Total facility staff includes 4 physicians, 3 psychologists, 14 psychiatrists, 40 registered nurses, 1 practical/vocational nurse, 3 MSW social workers, 3 social workers (non-MSW), 3 teachers, 60 counselors, 3 occupational/recreational therapists, 1 therapist, 1 dietician. Staff is 25% male, 75% female.

Facilities Single building; males and females in coeducational units. Separate residential quarters for children and adolescents. Separate dining by residential unit, in-room dining available. Basketball courts, game room, gymnasium, playground.

Education Academic program available at no charge. Serves ages 5–18, grades K–12. 3 teachers on staff. Curriculum accredited or approved by Commonwealth of Virginia Board of Education.

Costs Average cost: $12,000 per stay. Accepts private insurance, group insurance, medicare, Blue Cross/Blue Shield, public funds.

Additional Services Drug and alcohol rehabilitation services for males and females ages 14 and up. Treats behavior disorders; general psychosocial disorders; substance abuse; eating disorders; compulsive/addictive disorders other than substance abuse and eating disorders; post-traumatic stress disorder; thought, mood, and personality disorders. Neurobehavioral management program for males and females ages 18 and up. Treats behavior disorders; substance abuse.

Contact Joanna Parsick, Regional Marketing Director, main address above. Phone: 804-496-6000. Fax: 804-481-0484.

VISTA DEL MAR CHILD AND FAMILY SERVICES
3200 Motor Avenue
Los Angeles, California 90034
310-836-1223; Fax: 310-839-2820

General Information Residential treatment/subacute facility for children, adolescents. Patient security: staff secured. Independent not-for-profit facility. Licensed by state of California. Accredited by JCAHO.

Participants Accepts: male and female children; male and female adolescents. Average stay: 12 months. Admission: one parent, all parties who share custody, court order, voluntary, depending on program. Treats learning disabilities; behavior disorders; general psychosocial disorders; substance abuse; eating disorders; compulsive/addictive disorders other than substance abuse and eating disorders; post-traumatic stress disorder; thought, mood, and personality disorders.

Costs Average cost: $4000 per month.

Contact Ruth Wildhorn, Director of Admissions, main address above. Phone: 310-836-1223 Ext. 230.

WALDEN/SIERRA, INC.
Saint Andrew's Church Road
California, Maryland 20619
301-863-6661; Fax: 301-862-4880

General Information Residential treatment/subacute facility for adolescents. 14 beds for adolescents. Patient security: staff secured. Independent not-for-profit facility. Licensed by state of Maryland.

Participants Accepts: female adolescents. Average stay: 18 months. Admission: one parent, all parties who share custody, court order, voluntary, depending

on program. Treats behavior disorders; general psychosocial disorders; substance abuse; compulsive/addictive disorders other than substance abuse and eating disorders.

Staff Staff is all female.

Contact Leslie Walker, Residential Supervisor, main address above. Phone: 301-862-4212. Fax: 301-862-4880.

WALKER CENTER
1120 A Montana Street
Gooding, Idaho 83330-1858
208-934-8461; Fax: 208-934-5437

General Information Specialty hospital for children, adolescents. Patient security: partially locked. Independent not-for-profit facility. Licensed by state of Idaho. Accredited by JCAHO.

Participants Accepts: male and female children; male and female adolescents. Average stay: 16 days. Admission: court order, voluntary, depending on program. Treats behavior disorders; general psychosocial disorders; substance abuse; eating disorders; compulsive/addictive disorders other than substance abuse and eating disorders; post-traumatic stress disorder; thought, mood, and personality disorders.

Staff Staff is 35% male, 65% female.

Costs Average cost: $6500 per stay.

Contact Martin Mueller, Administrator, main address above. Phone: 208-934-8461.

WALLA WALLA GENERAL HOSPITAL'S ADDICTION RECOVERY CENTER
1025 South 2nd Avenue
Walla Walla, Washington 99362
509-522-4357; Fax: 509-527-0226

General Information General hospital for children, adolescents. Patient security: staff secured. Independent not-for-profit facility. Licensed by state of Washington. Accredited by JCAHO.

Participants Accepts: male and female children; male and female adolescents. Average stay: 28 days. Admission: one parent, all parties who share custody, court order, voluntary, depending on program. Treats substance abuse; eating disorders. Accepts the mobility impaired; the vision impaired; the hearing impaired; the speech impaired; those with a history of arson; those with a history of harm to themselves and others; those receiving psychotropic medication; those with a history of epilepsy.

Staff Staff is 50% male, 50% female.

Costs Average cost: $207 per day.

Additional Services Day treatment program for males and females ages 14–18. Treats substance abuse; eating disorders.

Contact Jamie Gavin, Director, P.O. Box 1398, Walla Walla, WA 99362. Phone: 509-522-4357. Fax: 509-527-0226.

WALTHAM HOUSE
409 Lexington Street
Waltham, Massachusetts 02154
617-489-1760; Fax: 617-489-6641

General Information Residential treatment/subacute facility for adolescents. 11 beds for adolescents. Open year-round. Patient security: staff secured; will pursue and return runaways. Suburban setting. Not-for-profit facility affiliated with New England Home for Little Wanderers, Boston, MA. Licensed by state of Massachusetts. Accredited by Council on Accreditation of Services for Families and Children.

Participants Accepts: male and female adolescents ages 11–17. Average stay: 500 days. Admission: one parent, all parties who share custody, court order, voluntary, depending on program. Treats learning disabilities; behavior disorders; general psychosocial disorders; substance abuse; eating disorders; compulsive/addictive disorders other than substance abuse and eating disorders; post-traumatic stress disorder; thought, mood, and personality disorders. Accepts the sexually compulsive; those with a history of harm to themselves and others; those receiving psychotropic medication. Largest number of participants from Massachusetts.

Program Treatment modalities: psychodynamic. Family treatment program available.

Staff 2.7 full-time direct-care staff members per adolescent. Total facility staff includes 1 psychologist, 1 psychiatrist, 1 registered nurse, 3 MSW social workers, 6 teachers, 12 counselors, 1 speech pathologist, 7 other direct-care staff members. Staff is 25% male, 75% female.

Facilities Multiple buildings; males and females in coeducational units. Central dining. Basketball courts, game room, playing fields.

Education Academic program available. Serves ages 11–17, ungraded. 6 teachers on staff. Curriculum accredited or approved by Watertown Public Schools,

Massachusetts Department of Education. Cost of educational program covered by local school district.

Costs Average cost: $69,238 per stay. Accepts public funds.

Additional Services Outdoor summer education program for males and females ages 11–17. Treats learning disabilities; behavior disorders; general psychosocial disorders; post-traumatic stress disorder; thought, mood, and personality disorders.

Contact Frank Mammano, Associate Director, main address above. Phone: 617-647-9956. Fax: 617-489-6641.

WARREN SECURE RESIDENTIAL PROGRAM
Carlyle Center for Mental Health
6902 Chicago Road
Warren, Michigan 48092
313-939-4940; Fax: 313-939-1567

General Information Residential treatment/subacute facility for children, adolescents. 10 beds for children; 18 beds for adolescents. Open year-round. Patient security: entirely locked; will pursue and return runaways. Suburban setting. Not-for-profit facility affiliated with Grosse Pointe Woods—Children's Home of Detroit, Grosse Pointe Woods, MI. Licensed by state of Michigan. Accredited by JCAHO.

Participants Accepts: male and female children ages 6–13; male and female adolescents ages 13–18. Average stay: 4 months. Admission: all parties who share custody, voluntary, depending on program. Treats learning disabilities; behavior disorders; general psychosocial disorders; compulsive/addictive disorders other than substance abuse and eating disorders; thought, mood, and personality disorders. Accepts those with a history of harm to themselves and others; those receiving psychotropic medication; those with a history of epilepsy. Largest number of participants from Michigan.

Program Treatment modalities: psychodynamic; behavioral; cognitive. Family treatment program available.

Staff .7 full-time direct-care staff member per child or adolescent. Total facility staff includes 1 physician, 1 psychiatrist, 1 registered nurse, 3 MSW social workers, 1 social worker (non-MSW), 1 occupational/recreational therapist. Staff is 45% male, 55% female.

Facilities Single building; males and females in coeducational units. Central dining. Basketball courts, game room, gymnasium, outdoor swimming pool, outdoor tennis courts, playing fields.

Education Academic program available at no charge. Serves ages 6–18, grades 1–12. Curriculum accredited or approved by North Central Association of Colleges and Schools. Cost of educational program covered by local school district.

Costs Average cost: $198 per day. Accepts private insurance, group insurance, public funds.

Additional Services Camping program for males and females ages 6–18. Treats learning disabilities; behavior disorders; general psychosocial disorders; compulsive/addictive disorders other than substance abuse and eating disorders; thought, mood, and personality disorders.

Contact Kitty Walters, Director of Social Services, main address above. Phone: 313-939-4940.

WATERFORD COUNTRY SCHOOL
78 Hunts Brook Road
P.O. Box 408
Quaker Hill, Connecticut 06375
203-442-9454; Fax: 203-442-2228

General Information Residential treatment/subacute facility for children, adolescents. Open year-round. Patient security: staff secured; will pursue and return runaways. Rural setting. Independent not-for-profit facility. Licensed by state of Connecticut. Accredited by Council on Accreditation of Services for Families and Children.

Participants Accepts: male and female children and adolescents ages 8–18. Average stay: 550 days. Admission: all parties who share custody. Treats learning disabilities; behavior disorders; general psychosocial disorders; thought, mood, and personality disorders. Accepts the mobility impaired; the speech impaired; the sexually compulsive; those with a history of harm to themselves and others; those receiving psychotropic medication; non-English speaking individuals; those with a history of epilepsy. Special programs for the developmentally disabled. Largest number of participants from Connecticut.

Program Treatment modalities: integrate special education/therapeutic plan; reality-based behavior modification; skill building for daily living. Family treatment program available.

Staff Total facility staff includes 1 psychologist, 1 psychiatrist, 2 registered nurses, 3 MSW social workers, 4 social workers (non-MSW), 8 teachers, 1 speech pathologist, 1 dietician, 57 other direct-care staff members. Staff is 35% male, 65% female.

Facilities Multiple buildings; males and females in coeducational units. Central dining, separate dining by residential unit available. Basketball courts, game room, gymnasium, horseback riding, playing fields.

Education Academic program available at additional cost. Serves ages 10–18, ungraded. 8 teachers on staff. Curriculum accredited or approved by Connecticut State Department of Education.

Costs Average cost: $59,600 per stay. Accepts private insurance, group insurance, public funds.

Additional Services Emergency shelter: crisis intervention; short-term treatment (up to 60 days) for males and females ages 8–18. Treats behavior disorders; general psychosocial disorders; post-traumatic stress disorder; thought, mood, and personality disorders.

Contact Patricia Martin, Intake Coordinator, main address above. Phone: 203-442-9454. Fax: 203-442-2228.

WATER OAK SPECIALTY HOSPITAL
2634 G, Capital Circle, NE
Tallahassee, Florida 32308
904-487-0335

General Information Residential treatment/subacute facility for adolescents. 16 beds for adolescents. Open year-round. Patient security: unlocked; will pursue and return runaways. Urban setting. Independent not-for-profit facility. Licensed by state of Florida. Accredited by JCAHO.

Participants Accepts: male and female adolescents ages 10–16. Average stay: 500 days. Admission: all parties who share custody. Treats behavior disorders; general psychosocial disorders; post-traumatic stress disorder; thought, mood, and personality disorders. Accepts those with a history of arson; those with a history of harm to themselves and others; those receiving psychotropic medication; those with a history of epilepsy.

Program Treatment modalities: behavior modification. Family treatment program available.

Staff 1.1 full-time direct-care staff members per adolescent. Total facility staff includes 1 physician, 1 psychiatrist, 1 registered nurse, 2 MSW social workers, 12 other direct-care staff members. Staff is 75% male, 25% female.

Facilities Single building; males and females in coeducational units. Central dining. Basketball courts, game room.

Education Educational program held off-site at no charge. Cost of educational program covered by local school district. Organized sports program offered.

Costs Accepts private insurance, group insurance, medicaid, Blue Cross/Blue Shield, public funds.

Contact Dana Dykes, Social Worker, main address above. Phone: 904-487-0335.

WAVERLY CHILDREN'S HOME
3550 Southeast Woodward Street
Portland, Oregon 97202
503-234-7532; Fax: 503-233-0187

General Information Residential treatment/subacute facility for children, adolescents, adults. 38 beds for children; 5 beds for adolescents; 43 beds total. Open year-round. Patient security: staff secured; will pursue and return runaways. Urban setting. Independent not-for-profit facility. Licensed by state of Oregon. Accredited by Day and Residential Treatment Standards, Mental Health Division; Department of Human Resources.

Participants Accepts: male and female children ages 3–13; male and female adolescents ages 12–18; female adults ages 19–30. Average stay: 14 months. Admission: all parties who share custody. Treats learning disabilities; behavior disorders; general psychosocial disorders; post-traumatic stress disorder; thought, mood, and personality disorders. Accepts the speech impaired; those with a history of arson; those with a history of harm to themselves and others; those receiving psychotropic medication; non-English speaking individuals. Special programs for the speech impaired; child abusers. Largest number of participants from Oregon, California.

Program Treatment modalities: family systems; parent support; Dreikors Parenting Concepts. Family treatment program available.

Staff Total facility staff includes 1 physician, 1 psychologist, 1 psychiatrist, 2 registered nurses, 4 MSW social workers, 3 social workers (non-MSW), 8 teachers, 1 counselor, 1 speech pathologist, 44 other direct-care staff members. Staff is 40% male, 60% female.

Facilities Single building; males and females in separate units. Separate residential quarters for children and adolescents. Separate dining by residential unit available. Basketball courts, game room, gymnasium, playing fields.

Education Academic program available at no charge. Serves ages 3–14, grades K–7. 8 teachers on staff. Curriculum accredited or approved by Department of Education. Cost of educational program

sometimes covered by local school district. Organized sports program offered.

Costs Average cost: $3900 per month. Accepts private insurance, medicaid, public funds.

Additional Services Outpatient services for males and females ages 7–14. Treats learning disabilities; behavior disorders; general psychosocial disorders; post-traumatic stress disorder. Residential or subacute services for males ages 7–14. Treats learning disabilities; behavior disorders; general psychosocial disorders; post-traumatic stress disorder; thought, mood, and personality disorders. Day treatment for males and females ages 6–14. Treats learning disabilities; behavior disorders; general psychosocial disorders; post-traumatic stress disorder; thought, mood, and personality disorders.

Contact Cynthia A. Thompson, Executive Director, main address above. Phone: 503-234-7532. Fax: 503-233-0187.

WAYLAND FAMILY CENTERS
11225 North 28th Drive, Suite A 100
Phoenix, Arizona 85029
602-375-7230; Fax: 602-375-7243

General Information Residential treatment/subacute facility for children, adolescents. Patient security: staff secured. Independent not-for-profit facility. Licensed by state of Arizona. Accredited by JCAHO.

Participants Accepts: male and female children; male and female adolescents. Average stay: 6 months. Admission: one parent, all parties who share custody, court order, voluntary, depending on program. Treats learning disabilities; behavior disorders; general psychosocial disorders; substance abuse; eating disorders; post-traumatic stress disorder; thought, mood, and personality disorders.

Staff Staff is 50% male, 50% female.

Costs Average cost: $151 per day.

Additional Services Outpatient services for males and females ages 6–18. Treats learning disabilities; behavior disorders; general psychosocial disorders; substance abuse; eating disorders; post-traumatic stress disorder; thought, mood, and personality disorders.

Contact Doug Barshter, Assistant Director, 11225 North 28th Drive Suite A 100, Phoenix, AZ 85029. Phone: 602-375-7230. Fax: 602-375-7243.

WELLSPRING
21 Arch Bridge Road
Bethlehem, Connecticut 06751-0370
203-266-7235; Fax: 203-266-5830

General Information Residential treatment/subacute facility for adolescents, adults. 16 beds for adolescents. Open year-round. Patient security: staff secured; will pursue and return runaways. Rural setting. Independent not-for-profit facility. Licensed by state of Connecticut. Accredited by JCAHO.

Participants Accepts: male and female adolescents ages 13–18; male and female adults ages 19 and up. Admission: voluntary. Treats learning disabilities; behavior disorders; general psychosocial disorders; substance abuse; eating disorders; compulsive/addictive disorders other than substance abuse and eating disorders; post-traumatic stress disorder; thought, mood, and personality disorders. Accepts those receiving psychotropic medication; those with a history of epilepsy. Largest number of participants from New York, Connecticut.

Program Treatment modalities: psychodynamic; therapeutic community; family therapy; creative-expressive therapy. Family treatment program available.

Staff Total facility staff includes 2 physicians, 10 psychologists, 2 psychiatrists, 3 registered nurses, 5 practical/vocational nurses, 1 MSW social worker, 1 social worker (non-MSW), 2 teachers, 18 counselors, 1 occupational/recreational therapist, 1 therapist, 1 dietician, 4 other direct-care staff members. Staff is 40% male, 60% female.

Facilities Multiple buildings; males and females in coeducational units. Separate residential quarters for adolescents. Central dining (shared with adults). Game room, playing fields, theater.

Education Academic program available at additional cost. Serves ages 13–18, ungraded. 2 teachers on staff. Cost of educational program sometimes covered by local school district.

Costs Average cost: $385 per day. Accepts private insurance, group insurance, Blue Cross/Blue Shield.

Additional Services Outpatient services for males and females ages 13 and up. Treats behavior disorders; general psychosocial disorders; eating disorders; compulsive/addictive disorders other than substance abuse and eating disorders; post-traumatic stress disorder; thought, mood, and personality disorders. Day treatment for males and females ages 13 and up. Treats behavior disorders; general psychosocial disorders; eating disorders; compulsive/addictive disorders other than substance abuse and eating disorders; post-traumatic stress disorder; thought, mood, and personality disorders.

Contact William Genovese, Administrator, main address above. Phone: 203-266-7235. Fax: 203-266-5830.

WENDY PAINE O'BRIEN TREATMENT CENTER
1300 North 77th Street
Scottsdale, Arizona 85257
602-945-7999; Fax: 602-947-1865

General Information Residential treatment/subacute facility for adolescents. Patient security: staff secured. Not-for-profit facility affiliated with Cambelback Health System. Licensed by state of Arizona. Accredited by JCAHO.

Participants Accepts: male and female adolescents. Average stay: 3 months. Admission: one parent, all parties who share custody, voluntary, depending on program. Treats autistic disorders; learning disabilities; behavior disorders; general psychosocial disorders; substance abuse; eating disorders; compulsive/addictive disorders other than substance abuse and eating disorders; post-traumatic stress disorder; thought, mood, and personality disorders.

Staff Staff is 50% male, 50% female.

Costs Average cost: $395 per day.

Contact Mike Todd, Executive Director, main address above. Phone: 602-945-7999.

WESTBRIDGE ADOLESCENT CENTER
1830 East Roosevelt
Phoenix, Arizona 85006
602-254-0884; Fax: 602-258-4033

General Information Residential treatment/subacute facility for adolescents. 104 beds for adolescents. Open year-round. Patient security: partially locked; no runaway pursuit. Urban setting. For-profit facility affiliated with Century HealthCare Corporation, Tulsa, OK. Licensed by state of Arizona. Accredited by JCAHO; Civilian Health and Medical Program of the Uniformed Services.

Participants Accepts: male and female adolescents ages 12–22. Admission: one parent, court order, depending on program. Treats learning disabilities; behavior disorders; general psychosocial disorders; substance abuse; eating disorders; post-traumatic stress disorder; thought, mood, and personality disorders. Accepts the mobility impaired; the vision impaired; the hearing impaired; the speech impaired;

those with a history of arson; those with a history of harm to themselves and others; those receiving psychotropic medication; non-English speaking individuals; those with a history of epilepsy; sexual perpetrators. Special programs for the speech impaired; diabetics.

Program Treatment modalities: systems theory. Family treatment program available.

Staff .3 full-time direct-care staff member per adolescent. Total facility staff includes 7 physicians, 30 psychologists, 31 psychiatrists, 18 registered nurses, 8 practical/vocational nurses, 7 MSW social workers, 9 social workers (non-MSW), 6 teachers, 5 occupational/recreational therapists, 1 speech pathologist, 4 therapists, 1 dietician, 36 other direct-care staff members. Staff is 28% male, 72% female.

Facilities Multiple buildings; males and females in coeducational units. Central dining. Basketball courts, game room, outdoor swimming pool, outdoor tennis courts, playing fields, ropes course.

Education Academic program available at no charge. Serves ages 12–22, grades 6–12. 6 teachers on staff. Curriculum accredited or approved by Arizona Department of Education. Organized sports program offered.

Costs Accepts private insurance, group insurance, medicaid, Blue Cross/Blue Shield, public funds.

Additional Services Ropes course for males and females ages 12–22. Treats autistic disorders; learning disabilities; behavior disorders; general psychosocial disorders; substance abuse; eating disorders; compulsive/addictive disorders other than substance abuse and eating disorders; post-traumatic stress disorder; thought, mood, and personality disorders.

Contact Elizabeth Yaeger, Admissions Director, main address above. Phone: 602-254-0884. Fax: 602-258-4033.

See page 414 for full page description.

WESTBRIDGE CENTER FOR CHILDREN
720 East Montebello
Phoenix, Arizona 85014
602-277-5437; Fax: 602-277-5558

General Information Psychiatric hospital for children. 55 beds for children. Open year-round. Patient security: partially locked; will pursue and return runaways. Urban setting. For-profit facility affiliated with Century HealthCare Corporation, Tulsa, OK. Licensed by state of Arizona. Accredited by JCAHO.

Participants Accepts: male and female children ages 3–14. Admission: one parent, court order, depending

on program. Treats learning disabilities; behavior disorders; general psychosocial disorders; substance abuse; eating disorders; compulsive/addictive disorders other than substance abuse and eating disorders; post-traumatic stress disorder; thought, mood, and personality disorders. Accepts the hearing impaired; the speech impaired; those with a history of arson; the sexually compulsive; those with a history of harm to themselves and others; those receiving psychotropic medication; non-English speaking individuals; those with a history of epilepsy. Special programs for the hearing impaired; the speech impaired; those with AIDS.

Program Treatment modalities: behavior modification; psychotherapy; brief therapy; family systems therapy. Family treatment program available.

Staff Total facility staff includes 5 registered nurses, 2 practical/vocational nurses, 4 MSW social workers, 4 teachers, 2 occupational/recreational therapists, 1 speech pathologist, 1 therapist, 1 dietician, 33 other direct-care staff members. Staff is 37% male, 63% female.

Facilities Multiple buildings; males and females in coeducational units. Basketball courts, game room, outdoor swimming pool, playing fields, ropes course.

Education Academic program available. Serves ages 3–14, ungraded. 4 teachers on staff. Curriculum accredited or approved by Arizona Department of Education. Cost of educational program sometimes covered by local school district. Organized sports program offered.

Costs Accepts private insurance, group insurance, medicaid, Blue Cross/Blue Shield, public funds.

Additional Services Partial hospitalization for males and females ages 3–14. Treats learning disabilities; behavior disorders; general psychosocial disorders; substance abuse; eating disorders; compulsive/addictive disorders other than substance abuse and eating disorders; post-traumatic stress disorder; thought, mood, and personality disorders.

Contact Vicki A. Bloom, Director of Admissions, main address above. Phone: 602-277-5437. Fax: 602-277-5558.

See page 414 for full page description.

WESTCENTER REHABILITATION FACILITY, INC.
2105 East Allen Road
Tucson, Arizona 85719
602-795-0952; Fax: 602-323-4335

General Information Drug and alcohol rehabilitation center for adolescents, adults. 8 beds for adolescents. Open year-round. Patient security: staff secured; will pursue and return runaways. Suburban setting. For-profit facility affiliated with Summit Health, Ltd., Burbank, CA. Licensed by state of Arizona. Accredited by JCAHO.

Participants Accepts: male and female adolescents ages 13–18; male and female adults ages 17–85. Average stay: 28 days. Admission: one parent, court order, depending on program. Treats behavior disorders; general psychosocial disorders; substance abuse; eating disorders; compulsive/addictive disorders other than substance abuse and eating disorders; post-traumatic stress disorder; thought, mood, and personality disorders. Accepts the mobility impaired; the vision impaired; the hearing impaired; the speech impaired; those receiving psychotropic medication; those with a history of epilepsy.

Program Treatment modalities: Twelve Step Recovery; psychotherapy. Family treatment program available.

Staff Total facility staff includes 1 physician, 2 psychologists, 2 psychiatrists, 12 registered nurses, 4 practical/vocational nurses, 2 MSW social workers, 8 counselors, 2 therapists, 1 dietician, 8 other direct-care staff members. Staff is all female.

Facilities Single building. Residential quarters shared with adults. Central dining (shared with adults). Basketball courts, game room, outdoor swimming pool, outdoor tennis courts, spa, sport court.

Education Academic program available at no charge. Serves ages 13–18, grades K–12. Curriculum accredited or approved by State of Arizona.

Costs Average cost: $650 per day. Accepts private insurance, group insurance, medicare, Blue Cross/Blue Shield, public funds.

Additional Services Outpatient services for males and females ages 13–18. Treats behavior disorders; general psychosocial disorders; substance abuse; eating disorders; compulsive/addictive disorders other than substance abuse and eating disorders; post-traumatic stress disorder; thought, mood, and personality disorders. Partial hospitalization for males and females ages 13–18. Treats behavior disorders; general psychosocial disorders; substance abuse; eating disorders; compulsive/addictive disorders other than substance abuse and eating disorders; post-traumatic

stress disorder; thought, mood, and personality disorders.

Contact Allan 'Chip' Harrington, Chief Executive Officer, main address above. Phone: 602-795-0952.

WESTERN INSTITUTE OF NEUROPSYCHIATRY
501 Chipeta Way
Salt Lake City, Utah 84108
801-583-2500; Fax: 801-582-8471

General Information Psychiatric hospital for children, adolescents. Patient security: entirely locked. For-profit facility affiliated with National Medical Enterprises, Santa Monica, CA. Licensed by state of Utah. Accredited by JCAHO.

Participants Accepts: male and female children; male and female adolescents. Average stay: 14 days. Admission: one parent, all parties who share custody, court order, voluntary, depending on program. Treats learning disabilities; behavior disorders; general psychosocial disorders; substance abuse; eating disorders; compulsive/addictive disorders other than substance abuse and eating disorders; post-traumatic stress disorder; thought, mood, and personality disorders.

Staff Staff is 50% male, 50% female.

Contact Elizabeth Murphy, Program Director, Child and Adolescent Services, main address above. Phone: 801-583-2500.

WESTLAKE ACADEMY
42 Institute Road
North Grafton, Massachusetts 01536
508-839-6282; Fax: 508-839-3084

General Information Residential treatment/subacute facility for adolescents. 13 beds for adolescents. Open year-round. Patient security: entirely locked; will pursue and return runaways. Small town setting. Not-for-profit facility affiliated with Health and Education Services, Salem, MA. Licensed by state of Massachusetts. Accredited by JCAHO.

Participants Accepts: male and female adolescents ages 13–18. Average stay: 547 days. Admission: all parties who share custody. Treats learning disabilities; behavior disorders; general psychosocial disorders; post-traumatic stress disorder; thought, mood, and personality disorders. Accepts those with a history of harm to themselves and others; those receiving psychotropic medication; those with a history of epilepsy. Special programs for the developmentally disabled. Largest number of participants from Massachusetts, Pennsylvania, New Hampshire.

Program Treatment modalities: psycho-social/educational milieu treatment. Family treatment program available.

Staff 2.3 full-time direct-care staff members per adolescent. Total facility staff includes 1 psychologist, 1 psychiatrist, 2 registered nurses, 1 MSW social worker, 4 teachers, 15 counselors, 1 occupational/recreational therapist, 1 dietician, 4 other direct-care staff members. Staff is 50% male, 50% female.

Facilities Single building; males and females in coeducational units. Central dining (shared with adults). Basketball courts, gymnasium, playing fields, ropes course, sailing.

Education Academic program available at additional cost. Serves ages 13–18, grades K–12. 4 teachers on staff. Curriculum accredited or approved by Local Education Authorities.

Costs Accepts medicaid, public funds.

Contact Donald Mosher, Director, main address above. Phone: 508-839-6282. Fax: 508-839-3084.

WEST VALLEY CAMELBACK HOSPITAL
5625 West Thunderbird Road
Glendale, Arizona 85306
602-588-4700; Fax: 602-843-1727

General Information Psychiatric hospital for children, adolescents, adults. 12 beds for children; 28 beds for adolescents; 64 beds total. Open year-round. will pursue and return runaways. Urban setting. Not-for-profit facility affiliated with Camelback Behavioral Health Services and Samaritan Health System, Phoenix, AZ. Licensed by state of Arizona. Accredited by JCAHO.

Participants Accepts: male and female children ages 3–12; male and female adolescents ages 13–18; male and female adults ages 19 and up. Average stay: 24 days. Admission: one parent, all parties who share custody, court order, depending on program. Treats learning disabilities; behavior disorders; general psychosocial disorders; substance abuse; eating disorders; compulsive/addictive disorders other than substance abuse and eating disorders; post-traumatic stress disorder; thought, mood, and personality disorders. Accepts the mobility impaired; the vision impaired; the hearing impaired; the speech impaired; those with a history of arson; the sexually compulsive; those with a history of harm to themselves and others;

those receiving psychotropic medication; non-English speaking individuals; those with a history of epilepsy. Special programs for the chronically ill; the mobility impaired; the developmentally disabled; the vision impaired; the hearing impaired; the speech impaired. Largest number of participants from Arizona.

Program Treatment modalities: Twelve Step Recovery; behavior management; family systems; psychodynamic. Family treatment program available.

Staff 1.2 full-time direct-care staff members per child or adolescent. Total facility staff includes 6 physicians, 14 psychologists, 15 psychiatrists, 16 registered nurses, 4 practical/vocational nurses, 2 MSW social workers, 3 social workers (non-MSW), 2 teachers, 9 counselors, 1 physical therapist, 3 occupational/recreational therapists, 1 speech pathologist, 1 dietician, 14 other direct-care staff members. Staff is 25% male, 75% female.

Facilities Multiple buildings; males and females in coeducational units. Separate residential quarters for children and adolescents. Central dining (shared with adults). Basketball courts, game room, outdoor swimming pool, playing fields.

Education Academic program available at no charge. Serves ages 3–18, grades K–12. 2 teachers on staff. Curriculum accredited or approved by Arizona State Department of Education.

Costs Accepts private insurance, group insurance, medicare, medicaid, Blue Cross/Blue Shield, public funds.

Additional Services Drug and alcohol rehabilitation services for males and females ages 12 and up. Treats learning disabilities; behavior disorders; general psychosocial disorders; substance abuse; eating disorders; compulsive/addictive disorders other than substance abuse and eating disorders; post-traumatic stress disorder; thought, mood, and personality disorders. Outpatient services for males and females. Treats learning disabilities; behavior disorders; general psychosocial disorders; substance abuse; eating disorders; compulsive/addictive disorders other than substance abuse and eating disorders; post-traumatic stress disorder; thought, mood, and personality disorders. Residential or sub-acute services for males and females ages 12–18. Treats learning disabilities; behavior disorders; general psychosocial disorders; substance abuse; eating disorders; compulsive/addictive disorders other than substance abuse and eating disorders; post-traumatic stress disorder; thought, mood, and personality disorders.

Contact Dale Rinard, Chief Executive Officer, main address above. Phone: 602-588-4700.

WETUMKA GENERAL HOSPITAL— SECOND CHANCE
325 South Washita
Wetumka, Oklahoma 74883
800-256-8223; Fax: 405-452-5815

General Information Drug and alcohol rehabilitation center for adolescents. Patient security: staff secured. Independent not-for-profit facility. Operated by Preferred Management Company, Shawnee, OK. Licensed by state of Oklahoma. Accredited by JCAHO.

Participants Accepts: male and female adolescents. Admission: one parent, all parties who share custody, court order, voluntary, depending on program. Treats substance abuse. Accepts the mobility impaired; the vision impaired; the hearing impaired; the speech impaired; those with a history of arson; the sexually compulsive; those with a history of harm to themselves and others; those receiving psychotropic medication; those with a history of epilepsy.

Staff Staff is 50% male, 50% female.

Contact Gary Cowan, Admissions Coordinator, main address above. Phone: 800-256-8223. Fax: 405-452-5815.

WIDE HORIZONS RANCH, INC.
27442 Oak Run and Fern Road
Oak Run, California 96069
916-472-3223

General Information Residential treatment/subacute facility for children. 12 beds for children. Open year-round. Patient security: staff secured; will pursue and return runaways. Rural setting. Independent not-for-profit facility. Licensed by state of California.

Participants Accepts: male children ages 9–17. Average stay: 3 years. Admission: all parties who share custody, court order, depending on program. Treats autistic disorders; learning disabilities; behavior disorders; post-traumatic stress disorder; thought, mood, and personality disorders. Accepts those with a history of harm to themselves and others; those receiving psychotropic medication. Largest number of participants from California.

Staff 1.3 full-time direct-care staff members per child. Total facility staff includes 1 psychiatrist, 3 teachers, 12 counselors. Staff is 50% male, 50% female.

Facilities Multiple buildings. Separate dining by residential unit available. Basketball courts, game room, gymnasium, outdoor swimming pool, playing fields.

Education Academic program available at no charge. Serves ages 9–17. 3 teachers on staff. Curriculum accredited or approved by State of California.

Costs Accepts private insurance, group insurance, medicare, medicaid, Blue Cross/Blue Shield, public funds.

Contact Administrator, main address above. Phone: 916-472-3223.

WILDERNESS TREATMENT CENTER
200 Hubbart Dam Road
Marion, Montana 59925
406-854-2832; Fax: 406-854-2835

General Information Drug and alcohol rehabilitation center for adolescents, adults. Open year-round. Patient security: unlocked; no runaway pursuit. Rural setting. Independent for-profit facility. Licensed by state of Montana.

Participants Accepts: male adolescents ages 13–22; male adults ages 21–25. Average stay: 60 days. Admission: one parent. Treats substance abuse. Accepts the hearing impaired; the speech impaired. Largest number of participants from Montana, Colorado, Texas.

Program Treatment modalities: Twelve Step Recovery. Family treatment program available.

Staff Total facility staff includes 2 physicians, 1 psychologist, 2 registered nurses, 1 teacher, 12 counselors, 1 dietician. Staff is 80% male, 20% female.

Facilities Multiple buildings. Residential quarters shared with adults. Central dining (shared with adults). Basketball courts, ropes course.

Education Academic program available at no charge. Serves ages 13–25, ungraded. 1 teacher on staff. Cost of educational program sometimes covered by local school district.

Costs Average cost: $13,500 per stay. Accepts private insurance, group insurance, Blue Cross/Blue Shield, public funds.

Additional Services Wilderness/survival program for males ages 13–25. Treats substance abuse.

Contact Kay Holmes, Admissions, main address above. Phone: 406-854-2832. Fax: 406-854-2835.
See page 464 for full page description.

WILEY HOUSE TREATMENT CENTERS
1650 Broadway
Bethlehem, Pennsylvania 18015-3998
800-854-3123; Fax: 215-799-8001

General Information   Residential treatment/subacute facility for children, adolescents. 55 beds for children; 381 beds for adolescents; 456 beds total. Open year-round. Patient security: staff secured; will pursue and return runaways. Urban setting. Independent not-for-profit facility affiliated with KidsPeace, Bethlehem, PA. Licensed by state of Pennsylvania. Accredited by JCAHO; American Association of Psychiatric Services for Children.

Participants   Accepts: male and female children ages 6–12; male and female adolescents ages 12–18. Admission: one parent, all parties who share custody, court order, voluntary, depending on program. Treats learning disabilities; behavior disorders; general psychosocial disorders; substance abuse; eating disorders; compulsive/addictive disorders other than substance abuse and eating disorders; post-traumatic stress disorder; thought, mood, and personality disorders. Accepts the vision impaired; the hearing impaired; the speech impaired; those with a history of arson; the sexually compulsive; those with a history of harm to themselves and others; those receiving psychotropic medication; those with a history of epilepsy. Largest number of participants from Maryland, New York, New Jersey.

Program   Treatment modalities: behavior management; psychotherapeutic; Twelve Step Recovery; therapeutic recreation. Family treatment program available.

Staff   Total facility staff includes 4 physicians, 5 psychologists, 12 psychiatrists, 8 registered nurses, 5 practical/vocational nurses, 13 MSW social workers, 11 social workers (non-MSW), 51 teachers, 243 counselors, 1 speech pathologist, 2 therapists, 1 dietician, 50 other direct-care staff members. Staff is 40% male, 60% female.

Facilities   Multiple buildings; males and females in separate units. Central dining. Basketball courts, game room, gymnasium, indoor swimming pool, playing fields.

Education   Academic program available at additional cost. Serves ages 5–18, grades K–12. 51 teachers on staff. Curriculum accredited or approved by Pennsylvania Department of Education, Middle States Association of Schools and Colleges. Organized sports program offered.

Costs   Accepts private insurance, group insurance, medicaid, public funds.

Additional Services   Partial hospitalization for males and females ages 6–18. Treats learning disabilities; behavior disorders; general psychosocial disorders; substance abuse; thought, mood, and personality disorders.

Contact   Ginger Papp, Supervisor of Admissions, main address above. Phone: 800-854-3123. Fax: 215-799-8001.

See page 466 for full page description.

WILEY HOUSE TREATMENT CENTERS OF NEW ENGLAND
Route 180
P.O. Box 787
Ellesworth, Maine 04605

General Information   Residential treatment/subacute facility for children, adolescents. 14 beds for children; 20 beds for adolescents; 34 beds total. Open year-round. Patient security: staff secured; will pursue and return runaways. Rural setting. Independent not-for-profit facility affiliated with KidsPeace, Bethlehem, PA. Licensed by state of Maine. Accredited by JCAHO; American Association of Psychiatric Services for Children.

Participants   Accepts: male children ages 10–12; male and female adolescents ages 13–18. Admission: one parent, all parties who share custody, court order, voluntary, depending on program. Treats learning disabilities; behavior disorders; general psychosocial disorders; substance abuse; compulsive/addictive disorders other than substance abuse and eating disorders; post-traumatic stress disorder; thought, mood, and personality disorders. Accepts the speech impaired; those with a history of arson; those with a history of harm to themselves and others; those receiving psychotropic medication; those with a history of epilepsy. Largest number of participants from Maine, New Hampshire, Connecticut.

Program   Treatment modalities: behavior management; psychotherapeutic; Twelve Step Recovery; therapeutic recreation. Family treatment program available.

Staff   1.1 full-time direct-care staff members per child or adolescent. Total facility staff includes 1 psychologist, 1 psychiatrist, 1 registered nurse, 2 MSW social workers, 4 teachers, 1 occupational/recreational therapist, 1 dietician, 28 other direct-care staff members. Staff is 28% male, 72% female.

Facilities   Multiple buildings; males and females in both coeducational and separate units depending on program. Central dining. Basketball courts, game room, gymnasium, playing fields, lake, canoes.

Education Academic program available at additional cost. Serves ages 10–18, ungraded. 4 teachers on staff. Curriculum accredited or approved by Maine Department of Education, Middle States Association of Colleges and Schools. Cost of educational program covered by local school district.

Costs Accepts private insurance, group insurance, public funds.

Contact Mark Scott, Intake Worker, main address above. Phone: 207-667-0909. Fax: 207-667-6348.

WILLIAM S. HALL PSYCHIATRIC INSTITUTE
1800 Colonial Drive
Columbia, South Carolina 29202
803-734-7170; Fax: 803-734-0791

General Information Psychiatric hospital with inpatient, outpatient, and residential programs for children, adolescents. Patient security: partially locked. Not-for-profit facility. Licensed by state of South Carolina. Accredited by JCAHO.

Participants Accepts: male and female children; male and female adolescents. Average stay: 2 months. Admission: one parent, all parties who share custody, court order, voluntary, depending on program. Treats autistic disorders; learning disabilities; behavior disorders; general psychosocial disorders; eating disorders; post-traumatic stress disorder; thought, mood, and personality disorders.

Staff Staff is 20% male, 80% female.

Contact Dr. Thomas Bariston, Director of Admissions, P.O. Box 202, Columbia, SC 29202. Phone: 803-734-7170.

WILLOW CREEK HOSPITAL
7000 Highway 287, South
Fort Worth, Texas 76017
817-572-3355; Fax: 817-572-8018

General Information Psychiatric hospital for adolescents, adults. 64 beds for adolescents. Open year-round. Patient security: entirely locked; will pursue and return runaways. Rural setting. For-profit facility affiliated with Columbia Hospital Corporation, Fort Worth, TX. Operated by Century Healthcare Corporation, Tulsa, OK. Licensed by state of Texas. Accredited by JCAHO; Texas Commission on Alcohol and Drug Abuse.

Participants Accepts: male and female adolescents ages 11–18; male and female adults ages 18–80. Average stay: 21 days. Admission: all parties who share custody. Treats behavior disorders; general psychosocial disorders; substance abuse; eating disorders; compulsive/addictive disorders other than substance abuse and eating disorders; post-traumatic stress disorder; thought, mood, and personality disorders. Accepts the mobility impaired; the vision impaired; the hearing impaired; the speech impaired; those with a history of arson; the sexually compulsive; those with a history of harm to themselves and others; those receiving psychotropic medication; those with a history of epilepsy. Largest number of participants from Texas.

Program Treatment modalities: Twelve Step Recovery; brief solution-focused therapy; psychodynamic; family therapy. Family treatment program available.

Staff .3 full-time direct-care staff member per adolescent. Total facility staff includes 30 registered nurses, 4 MSW social workers, 4 teachers, 4 counselors, 3 occupational/recreational therapists, 2 therapists, 1 dietician, 24 other direct-care staff members. Staff is 40% male, 60% female.

Facilities Multiple buildings; males and females in coeducational units. Separate residential quarters for adolescents. Central dining (shared with adults). Basketball courts, game room, gymnasium, outdoor swimming pool, outdoor tennis courts, playing fields, ropes course.

Education Academic program available at no charge. Serves ages 11–18, ungraded. 4 teachers on staff. Curriculum accredited or approved by Kennedale Independent School District. Cost of educational program sometimes covered by local school district.

Costs Accepts private insurance, group insurance, medicaid, Blue Cross/Blue Shield.

Additional Services Drug and alcohol rehabilitation services for males and females ages 11–18. Treats behavior disorders; general psychosocial disorders; substance abuse; eating disorders; post-traumatic stress disorder; thought, mood, and personality disorders. Residential or sub-acute services for males and females. Treats behavior disorders; general psychosocial disorders; substance abuse; eating disorders; post-traumatic stress disorder; thought, mood, and personality disorders.

Contact Bob Porter, Associate Administrator, main address above. Phone: 817-572-3355. Fax: 817-572-8018.

See page 414 for full page description.

WINCHESTER MEDICAL CENTER, INC.
1840 Amherst Street
Winchester, Virginia 22601
703-722-8000; Fax: 703-722-8734

General Information   General hospital for adolescents. 16 beds for adolescents. Patient security: entirely locked. Independent not-for-profit facility. Licensed by state of Virginia. Accredited by JCAHO.

Participants   Accepts: male and female adolescents. Average stay: 20 days. Admission: one parent, court order, voluntary, depending on program. Treats behavior disorders; general psychosocial disorders; substance abuse; eating disorders; compulsive/addictive disorders other than substance abuse and eating disorders; thought, mood, and personality disorders.

Costs   Average cost: $522 per day.

Contact   Wes Williams, Marketing Director, main address above. Phone: 703-722-8735.

WINNICOH RESIDENTIAL TREATMENT CENTER FOR CHILDREN
10300 Southwest Eastridge Street
Portland, Oregon 97225
503-297-2252

General Information   Psychiatric hospital for children. 10 beds for children. Open year-round. Patient security: partially locked; no runaway pursuit. Suburban setting. For-profit facility affiliated with Community Psychiatric Centers, Laguna Hills, CA. Licensed by state of Oregon. Accredited by JCAHO.

Participants   Accepts: male and female children ages 8–14. Admission: all parties who share custody. Treats learning disabilities; behavior disorders; general psychosocial disorders; substance abuse; compulsive/addictive disorders other than substance abuse and eating disorders; post-traumatic stress disorder; thought, mood, and personality disorders. Accepts the mobility impaired; the vision impaired; the hearing impaired; the speech impaired; those with a history of arson; the sexually compulsive; those with a history of harm to themselves and others; those receiving psychotropic medication. Largest number of participants from Oregon.

Program   Treatment modalities: positive peer culture; behavioral; cognitive restructuring. Family treatment program available.

Staff   .7 full-time direct-care staff member per child. Total facility staff includes 5 physicians, 1 registered nurse, 1 MSW social worker, 1 teacher, 1 occupational/recreational therapist, 2 other direct-care staff members.

Facilities   Single building; males and females in co-educational units. Central dining (shared with adults). Game room, gymnasium.

Education   Academic program available at no charge. Serves ages 8–14, ungraded. 1 teacher on staff. Curriculum accredited or approved by Northwest Association of Schools and Colleges.

Costs   Average cost: $350 per day. Accepts private insurance, group insurance, Blue Cross/Blue Shield.

Additional Services   Outpatient services for males and females ages 6–12. Treats behavior disorders; general psychosocial disorders. Residential or subacute services for males and females ages 8–14. Treats learning disabilities; behavior disorders; general psychosocial disorders; substance abuse; compulsive/addictive disorders other than substance abuse and eating disorders; post-traumatic stress disorder; thought, mood, and personality disorders.

Contact   Jan Thomson, Clinical Coordinator, main address above. Phone: 503-297-2252. Fax: 503-297-6613.

WOODBOURNE CENTER, INC.
1301 Woodbourne Avenue
Baltimore, Maryland 21239
410-433-1000; Fax: 410-433-1459

General Information   Residential treatment/subacute facility for adolescents. 44 beds for adolescents. Open year-round. Patient security: staff secured; will pursue and return runaways. Urban setting. Independent not-for-profit facility. Licensed by state of Maryland. Accredited by JCAHO.

Participants   Accepts: male and female adolescents ages 11–18. Admission: one parent, all parties who share custody, court order, depending on program. Treats learning disabilities; behavior disorders; general psychosocial disorders; substance abuse; compulsive/addictive disorders other than substance abuse and eating disorders; post-traumatic stress disorder; thought, mood, and personality disorders. Accepts those with a history of arson; those with a history of harm to themselves and others; those receiving psychotropic medication.

Program   Treatment modalities: cognitive-behavioral; psychopharmacological intervention; crisis prevention; environmental modification. Family treatment program available.

Staff   Total facility staff includes 1 physician, 1 psychologist, 2 psychiatrists, 3 registered nurses, 1 practical/vocational nurse, 6 MSW social workers, 9 teachers, 50 counselors, 2 occupational/recreational therapists, 1 speech pathologist, 1 therapist, 1 dietician, 6 other direct-care staff members. Staff is 60% male, 40% female.

Facilities Multiple buildings; males and females in both coeducational and separate units depending on program. Central dining. Basketball courts, gymnasium, outdoor swimming pool, playing fields.

Education Academic program available at no charge. Serves ages 11–18, ungraded. 9 teachers on staff. Curriculum accredited or approved by Maryland State Department of Education. Cost of educational program sometimes covered by local school district. Organized sports program offered.

Costs Average cost: $299 per day. Accepts medicaid, public funds.

Additional Services Outpatient services for males and females ages 6–14. Treats learning disabilities; behavior disorders; general psychosocial disorders; compulsive/addictive disorders other than substance abuse and eating disorders; post-traumatic stress disorder; thought, mood, and personality disorders. Treatment in foster care for males and females ages 4–16. Treats behavior disorders; general psychosocial disorders; substance abuse; eating disorders; compulsive/addictive disorders other than substance abuse and eating disorders; post-traumatic stress disorder; thought, mood, and personality disorders.

Contact Beulah Newby, Admissions Coordinator, main address above. Phone: 410-433-1000. Fax: 410-433-1459.

WOODBURY EXTENDED CARE
1665 Woodbury Drive
Woodbury, Minnesota 55125
612-436-6623; Fax: 612-436-8855

General Information Drug and alcohol rehabilitation center for adolescents. 40 beds for adolescents. Patient security: staff secured. Not-for-profit facility affiliated with Fairview Hospital, Minneapolis, MN. Licensed by state of Minnesota. Accredited by JCAHO.

Participants Accepts: male and female adolescents. Average stay: 60 days. Admission: one parent, all parties who share custody, court order, voluntary, depending on program. Treats substance abuse. Accepts the vision impaired; the hearing impaired; the speech impaired; the sexually compulsive; those with a history of harm to themselves and others; those

receiving psychotropic medication; those with a history of epilepsy.

Staff Staff is 60% male, 40% female.

Costs Average cost: $200 per day.

Contact Randy Forsman, Program Manager, main address above. Phone: 612-436-6623. Fax: 612-436-8855.

WOODLAND HOSPITAL
1650 Moon Lake Boulevard
Hoffman Estates, Illinois 60194
708-882-1600; Fax: 708-843-6557

General Information Psychiatric hospital for children, adolescents, adults. 16 beds for children; 24 beds for adolescents; 100 beds total. Open year-round. Patient security: entirely locked; will pursue and return runaways. Suburban setting. For-profit facility affiliated with Hospital Corporation of America, Nashville, TN. Licensed by state of Illinois. Accredited by JCAHO.

Participants Accepts: male and female children ages 4–12; male and female adolescents ages 13–18; male and female adults ages 18–90. Average stay: 23 days. Admission: all parties who share custody. Treats learning disabilities; behavior disorders; general psychosocial disorders; eating disorders; compulsive/addictive disorders other than substance abuse and eating disorders; post-traumatic stress disorder; thought, mood, and personality disorders. Accepts the mobility impaired; those with a history of arson; the sexually compulsive; those with a history of harm to themselves and others; those receiving psychotropic medication.

Program Treatment modalities: psychodynamic; behavior modification. Family treatment program available.

Staff Total facility staff includes 1 physician, 1 psychologist, 1 psychiatrist, 30 registered nurses, 1 MSW social worker, 3 social workers (non-MSW), 2 teachers, 25 counselors, 4 occupational/recreational therapists, 3 therapists, 2 dieticians, 8 other direct-care staff members. Staff is 36% male, 64% female.

Facilities Single building; males and females in coeducational units. Separate residential quarters for children and adolescents. Central dining (shared with adults). Basketball courts, gymnasium, ropes course, exercise equipment.

Education Academic program available at additional cost. Serves ages 4–18, grades K–12. 2 teachers on staff. Curriculum accredited or approved by North Central Illinois Association on Accreditation of

Schools. Cost of educational program sometimes covered by local school district.

Costs Accepts private insurance, group insurance, medicare, Blue Cross/Blue Shield.

Contact Edie Corneils, Respond Director, main address above. Phone: 708-843-6546. Fax: 708-843-6557.

WOODRIDGE ADOLESCENT UNIT
394 Ridgecrest Circle
Clayton, Georgia 30525
706-782-3100; Fax: 706-782-4873

General Information Psychiatric hospital for adolescents, adults. 13 beds for adolescents. Open year-round. Patient security: staff secured; will pursue and return runaways. Rural setting. Not-for-profit facility affiliated with Woodlands Foundation, Inc., Baton Rouge, LA. Licensed by state of Georgia. Accredited by JCAHO.

Participants Accepts: male and female adolescents ages 12–18; male and female adults ages 19 and up. Average stay: 28 days. Admission: one parent. Treats learning disabilities; behavior disorders; general psychosocial disorders; substance abuse; eating disorders; compulsive/addictive disorders other than substance abuse and eating disorders; post-traumatic stress disorder; thought, mood, and personality disorders. Accepts the mobility impaired; the vision impaired; the hearing impaired; the speech impaired; the sexually compulsive; those with a history of harm to themselves and others; those with a history of epilepsy.

Program Treatment modalities: family systems; Twelve Step Recovery; psychodynamic; relational. Family treatment program available.

Staff 1.5 full-time direct-care staff members per adolescent. Total facility staff includes 3 physicians, 1 psychologist, 1 psychiatrist, 3 registered nurses, 4 practical/vocational nurses, 1 MSW social worker, 1 social worker (non-MSW), 1 teacher, 2 counselors, 1 occupational/recreational therapist, 1 dietician.

Facilities Multiple buildings; males and females in separate units. Separate residential quarters for adolescents. Central dining (not shared with adults). Basketball courts, game room, indoor swimming pool, hiking trails.

Education Academic program available at no charge. Serves ages 12–17, grades 8–12. 1 teacher on staff. Organized sports program offered.

Costs Average cost: $20,000 per stay. Accepts private insurance, group insurance, medicare, Blue Cross/Blue Shield.

Additional Services Drug and alcohol rehabilitation services for males and females ages 12–18. Treats general psychosocial disorders; substance abuse; eating disorders; compulsive/addictive disorders other than substance abuse and eating disorders; post-traumatic stress disorder; thought, mood, and personality disorders. Outpatient services for males and females ages 12–18. Treats general psychosocial disorders; substance abuse; eating disorders; compulsive/addictive disorders other than substance abuse and eating disorders; post-traumatic stress disorder; thought, mood, and personality disorders.

Contact Amy Wuttke, Program Coordinator, main address above. Phone: 706-782-0465. Fax: 706-782-4873.

Announcement The Woodridge Adolescent Unit is located in the beautiful and serene Blue Ridge Mountains. The facility is designed, located, and staffed to provide total healing and growth to clients. Woodridge provides a strong relationship model that fosters trust, positive relationships with others, and movement toward health and personal fulfillment.

WOODRIDGE HOSPITAL
403 State of Franklin Road
Johnson City, Tennessee 37604
615-928-7111; Fax: 615-928-7110

General Information Freestanding drug and alcohol rehabilitation center and psychiatric hospital for children, adolescents. Patient security: partially locked. Not-for-profit facility affiliated with Watauga Mental Health Services, Inc., Johnson City, TN. Licensed by state of Tennessee. Accredited by JCAHO.

Participants Accepts: male and female children; male and female adolescents. Average stay: 21 days. Admission: one parent, court order, voluntary, depending on program. Treats autistic disorders; learning disabilities; behavior disorders; general psychosocial disorders; substance abuse; eating disorders; compulsive/addictive disorders other than substance abuse and eating disorders; post-traumatic stress disorder; thought, mood, and personality disorders.

Staff Staff is 50% male, 50% female.

Costs Average cost: $440 per day.

Additional Services Day treatment program for males and females ages 12–18. Treats substance abuse.

Contact Robert Werstlein, PhD, Program Director, main address above. Phone: 615-928-7111. Fax: 615-928-7110.

WOODS PSYCHIATRIC INSTITUTE OF CENTRAL TEXAS
4800 East Rancier
Killeen, Texas 76543
817-690-3555; Fax: 817-690-8166

General Information Residential treatment/subacute facility for children, adolescents. 16 beds for children; 48 beds for adolescents. Open year-round. Patient security: partially locked; will pursue and return runaways. Small town setting. For-profit facility affiliated with Woods Clinical Management, Abilene, TX. Licensed by state of Texas. Accredited by JCAHO.

Participants Accepts: male and female children ages 6–17; male and female adolescents ages 6–17. Average stay: 150 days. Admission: one parent. Treats learning disabilities; behavior disorders; general psychosocial disorders; substance abuse; eating disorders; post-traumatic stress disorder; thought, mood, and personality disorders. Accepts those with a history of arson; the sexually compulsive; those with a history of harm to themselves and others; those receiving psychotropic medication; those with a history of epilepsy.

Program Treatment modalities: general systems theory; object relations; psychodynamic; positive behavioral reinforcement. Family treatment program available.

Staff 1 full-time direct-care staff member per child or adolescent. Total facility staff includes 1 physician, 2 psychiatrists, 7 registered nurses, 4 practical/vocational nurses, 7 MSW social workers, 3 teachers, 2 occupational/recreational therapists, 1 dietician, 40 other direct-care staff members. Staff is 50% male, 50% female.

Facilities Multiple buildings; males and females in separate units. Central dining. Basketball courts, game room, gymnasium, outdoor swimming pool, playing fields, ropes course.

Education Academic program available at no charge. Serves ages 6–17, grades K–12. 3 teachers on staff. Curriculum accredited or approved by Texas Education Agency, Killeen Independent School District. Cost of educational program covered by local school district.

Costs Average cost: $60,000 per stay. Accepts private insurance, Blue Cross/Blue Shield.

Additional Services Outpatient services for males and females ages 4 and up. Treats behavior disorders; general psychosocial disorders; compulsive/addictive disorders other than substance abuse and eating disorders; post-traumatic stress disorder; thought, mood, and personality disorders.

Contact Brenda Coley, Referral Coordinator, main address above. Phone: 817-690-3555. Fax: 817-690-8166.

WOODVIEW-CALABASAS HOSPITAL
25100 Calabasas Road
Calabasas, California 91302
818-222-1000; Fax: 818-222-3847

General Information Psychiatric hospital for adolescents, adults. 21 beds for adolescents. Open year-round. Patient security: partially locked. Suburban setting. For-profit facility affiliated with Neuro Affiliates, Inc., Calabasas, CA. Licensed by state of California. Accredited by JCAHO.

Participants Accepts: male and female adolescents ages 12–17; male and female adults ages 21 and up. Average stay: 13 days. Admission: one parent, all parties who share custody, court order, voluntary, depending on program. Treats learning disabilities; behavior disorders; general psychosocial disorders; substance abuse; eating disorders; compulsive/addictive disorders other than substance abuse and eating disorders; post-traumatic stress disorder; thought, mood, and personality disorders. Accepts the mobility impaired; the vision impaired; the hearing impaired; the speech impaired; those with a history of harm to themselves and others; those receiving psychotropic medication; those with a history of epilepsy. Largest number of participants from California, Nevada.

Program Treatment modalities: Twelve Step Recovery. Family treatment program available.

Staff .8 full-time direct-care staff member per adolescent. Total facility staff includes 1 psychiatrist, 2 practical/vocational nurses, 1 MSW social worker, 1 teacher, 1 occupational/recreational therapist, 1 therapist, 1 dietician, 1 other direct-care staff member. Staff is 5% male, 95% female.

Facilities Single building; males and females in coeducational units. Separate residential quarters for adolescents. Central dining (shared with adults). Basketball courts, game room, outdoor swimming pool, ropes course.

Education Academic program available at no charge. Serves ages 12–17, ungraded. 1 teacher on staff. Cost of educational program covered by local school district.

Costs Accepts private insurance, group insurance, medicare, Blue Cross/Blue Shield.

Additional Services Drug and alcohol rehabilitation services for males and females ages 18 and up. Treats behavior disorders; general psychosocial disorders; substance abuse; compulsive/addictive disorders other than substance abuse and eating disorders; post-traumatic stress disorder; thought, mood, and personality disorders.

Contact Chris Redman, Director, First Call, main address above. Phone: 818-222-1000. Fax: 818-222-3847.

WORDSWORTH RESIDENTIAL TREATMENT PROGRAM
Pennsylvania Avenue and Camp Hill Road
Fort Washington, Pennsylvania 19034
215-643-5400; Fax: 215-643-0595

General Information Residential treatment/subacute facility for children, adolescents. 20 beds for children; 62 beds for adolescents. Open year-round. Patient security: staff secured; will pursue and return runaways. Suburban setting. Independent not-for-profit facility. Licensed by state of Pennsylvania. Accredited by JCAHO.

Participants Accepts: male and female children ages 5–12; male and female adolescents ages 13–21. Average stay: 18 months. Admission: voluntary. Treats learning disabilities; behavior disorders; general psychosocial disorders; post-traumatic stress disorder; thought, mood, and personality disorders. Accepts the mobility impaired; the speech impaired; those with a history of harm to themselves and others; those receiving psychotropic medication; those with a history of epilepsy. Largest number of participants from Pennsylvania, Maryland.

Program Treatment modalities: behavioral; psychodynamic; humanistic; family systems. Family treatment program available.

Staff .5 full-time direct-care staff member per child or adolescent. Total facility staff includes 3 psychologists, 2 psychiatrists, 3 registered nurses, 2 practical/vocational nurses, 6 MSW social workers, 10 teachers, 6 counselors, 5 occupational/recreational therapists, 1 speech pathologist, 2 therapists, 1 dietician,

4 other direct-care staff members. Staff is 53% male, 47% female.

Facilities Multiple buildings; males and females in coeducational units. Central dining, separate dining by residential unit available. Basketball courts, game room, gymnasium, playing fields.

Education Academic program available at additional cost. Serves ages 5–21, grades K–12. 10 teachers on staff. Curriculum accredited or approved by Pennsylvania, Maryland, Washington, D.C., and New Jersey Departments of Education. Cost of educational program covered by local school district. Organized sports program offered.

Costs Average cost: $51,000 per stay. Accepts private insurance, group insurance, medicaid, Blue Cross/Blue Shield, public funds.

Additional Services Outpatient services for males and females ages 5–21. Treats autistic disorders; learning disabilities; behavior disorders; general psychosocial disorders; substance abuse; eating disorders; compulsive/addictive disorders other than substance abuse and eating disorders; post-traumatic stress disorder; thought, mood, and personality disorders. Psychiatric day partial hospital for males and females ages 5–21. Treats learning disabilities; behavior disorders; general psychosocial disorders; post-traumatic stress disorder; thought, mood, and personality disorders.

Contact Joan Parsons, Admissions Coordinator, main address above. Phone: 215-643-5400 Ext. 412. Fax: 215-643-0595.

YALE PSYCHIATRIC INSTITUTE
Cedar Street
New Haven, Connecticut 06520
800-275-9253; Fax: 203-785-7855

General Information Psychiatric hospital for children, adolescents, adults. 33 beds for adolescents. Open year-round. Patient security: partially locked; will pursue and return runaways. Urban setting. Not-for-profit facility affiliated with Yale School of Medicine, New Haven, CT. Operated by Yale University, New Haven, CT. Licensed by state of Connecticut. Accredited by JCAHO.

Participants Accepts: male and female children ages up to 12; male and female adolescents ages 13–19; male and female adults ages 20 and up. Average stay: 15 days. Admission: one parent, court order, depending on program. Treats autistic disorders; learning disabilities; behavior disorders; general psychosocial disorders; substance abuse; eating disorders; compulsive/addictive disorders other than substance abuse and eating disorders; post-traumatic stress disorder; thought, mood, and personality disorders. Accepts the mobility impaired; the vision impaired; the hearing impaired; those with a history of harm to themselves and others; those receiving psychotropic medication; non-English speaking individuals; those with a history of epilepsy. Special programs for the chronically ill; the mobility impaired; the developmentally disabled; the vision impaired; the hearing impaired.

Program Treatment modalities: pharmacotherapy; psychotherapy; family systems. Family treatment program available.

Staff Total facility staff includes 1 physician, 7 psychologists, 16 psychiatrists, 3 registered nurses, 14 MSW social workers, 1 social worker (non-MSW), 18 teachers, 1 counselor, 15 occupational/recreational therapists, 1 dietician, 29 other direct-care staff members.

Facilities Multiple buildings; males and females in coeducational units. Separate residential quarters for children and adolescents. Central dining arrangements vary. In-room dining available Basketball courts, game room, gymnasium.

Education Academic program available at additional cost. Serves ages 13–19, grades 7–12. 18 teachers on staff. Curriculum accredited or approved by City of Hamden School System. Cost of educational program covered by local school district.

Costs Average cost: $810 per day. Accepts private insurance, group insurance, medicare, Blue Cross/Blue Shield, public funds.

Additional Services Drug and alcohol rehabilitation services for males and females ages 19 and up. Treats autistic disorders; learning disabilities; behavior disorders; general psychosocial disorders; substance abuse; eating disorders; compulsive/addictive disorders other than substance abuse and eating disorders; post-traumatic stress disorder; thought, mood, and personality disorders. Outpatient services for males and females ages 14 and up. Treats autistic disorders; learning disabilities; behavior disorders; general psychosocial disorders; substance abuse; eating disorders; compulsive/addictive disorders other than substance abuse and eating disorders; post-traumatic stress disorder; thought, mood, and personality disorders.

Contact Admissions Office, main address above. Phone: 203-785-7201. Fax: 203-737-2590.

YELLOWSTONE TREATMENT CENTERS
1732 South 72nd Street, West
Billings, Montana 59106
406-656-3001; Fax: 406-656-0021

General Information Residential treatment/subacute facility for children, adolescents. 9 beds for children; 95 beds for adolescents; 104 beds total. Open year-round. Patient security: partially locked. Rural setting. Independent not-for-profit facility. Licensed by state of Montana. Accredited by JCAHO.

Participants Accepts: male children ages 6–12; male and female adolescents ages 12–18. Admission: one parent, all parties who share custody, court order, voluntary, depending on program. Treats learning disabilities; behavior disorders; general psychosocial disorders; substance abuse; eating disorders; compulsive/addictive disorders other than substance abuse and eating disorders; post-traumatic stress disorder; thought, mood, and personality disorders. Accepts the mobility impaired; the vision impaired; those with a history of arson; the sexually compulsive; those with a history of harm to themselves and others; those receiving psychotropic medication; those with a history of epilepsy. Special programs for the developmentally disabled. Largest number of participants from Montana, Wyoming, Illinois.

Program Treatment modalities: reality therapy; cognitive behavioral; psychodynamic; experiential. Family treatment program available.

Staff 1.9 full-time direct-care staff members per child or adolescent. Total facility staff includes 1 physician, 6 psychologists, 2 psychiatrists, 5 registered nurses, 12 practical/vocational nurses, 13 MSW social workers, 3 social workers (non-MSW), 13 teachers, 2 counselors, 3 occupational/recreational therapists, 1 speech pathologist, 2 therapists, 2 dieticians, 130 other direct-care staff members. Staff is 47% male, 53% female.

Facilities Multiple buildings; males and females in separate units. Basketball courts, game room, gymnasium, horseback riding, indoor swimming pool, outdoor tennis courts, playing fields, ropes course.

Education Academic program available. Serves ages 6–18, grades 1–12. 13 teachers on staff. Curriculum accredited or approved by Montana Office of Public Instruction, Northwest Association of Schools and Colleges. Cost of educational program sometimes covered by local school district. Organized sports program offered.

Costs Average cost: $245 per day. Accepts private insurance, group insurance, medicaid, Blue Cross/Blue Shield, public funds.

Contact Trisha Elk, Admissions Director, main address above. Phone: 800-726-6755. Fax: 406-656-0021.

See page 468 for full page description.

YORK PLACE
234 Kings Mountain Street
York, South Carolina 29745
803-684-4011; Fax: 803-684-8002

General Information Residential treatment/subacute facility for children. 36 beds for children. Open year-round. Patient security: staff secured; will pursue and return runaways. Small town setting. Affiliated with Episcopal Dioceses of South Carolina, Columbia, SC. Licensed by state of South Carolina. Accredited by JCAHO; South Carolina Department of Social Services, Department of Health and Environmental Control.

Participants Accepts: male and female children ages 6–12. Average stay: 400 days. Admission: one parent, legal guardian, depending on program. Treats learning disabilities; behavior disorders; general psychosocial disorders; compulsive/addictive disorders other than substance abuse and eating disorders; post-traumatic stress disorder; thought, mood, and personality disorders. Accepts the hearing impaired; those with a history of arson; the sexually compulsive; those with a history of harm to themselves and others; those receiving psychotropic medication. Largest number of participants from South Carolina, Georgia, North Carolina.

Program Treatment modalities: milieu therapy; psychodynamic; family and individual therapy.

Staff 1 full-time direct-care staff member per child. Total facility staff includes 1 registered nurse, 4 teachers, 20 counselors, 2 occupational/recreational therapists, 5 therapists, 4 other direct-care staff members. Staff is 28% male, 72% female.

Facilities Multiple buildings; males and females in coeducational units. Separate dining by residential unit available. Basketball courts, gymnasium, indoor swimming pool, outdoor tennis courts, playing fields.

Education Academic program available at no charge. Serves ages 6–12, grades 1–8. 4 teachers on staff. Curriculum accredited or approved by South Carolina Department of Education. Cost of educational program sometimes covered by local school district.

Costs Average cost: $176 per day. Accepts private insurance, group insurance, medicaid, Blue Cross/Blue Shield, public funds.

Contact Barry Allison, Admissions and Continuing Care Director, main address above. Phone: 803-684-8005. Fax: 803-684-8002.

YOUTH AND SHELTER SERVICES, INC.
232½ Main Street
P.O. Box 1628
Ames, Iowa 50010
515-233-3141

General Information Drug and alcohol rehabilitation center for adolescents. Patient security: staff secured. Independent not-for-profit facility. Licensed by state of Iowa.

Participants Accepts: male and female adolescents. Average stay: 7 months. Admission: one parent, all parties who share custody, court order, voluntary, depending on program. Treats behavior disorders; general psychosocial disorders; substance abuse. Accepts the mobility impaired; the vision impaired; the hearing impaired; the speech impaired; the sexually compulsive.

Staff Staff is 30% male, 70% female.

Costs Average cost: $105 per day.

Contact Dorothy Tschopp, Program Coordinator, main address above. Phone: 515-233-3141.

YOUTH HOME, INC.
5905 Forest Place
Suite 100
Little Rock, Arkansas 72207-5245
501-666-1960; Fax: 501-666-3349

General Information Residential treatment/subacute facility for adolescents. 58 beds for adolescents. Open year-round. Patient security: entirely locked; will pursue and return runaways. Suburban setting. Independent not-for-profit facility. Licensed by state of Arkansas. Accredited by JCAHO.

Participants Accepts: male and female adolescents ages 12–18. Average stay: 150 days. Admission: court order. Treats learning disabilities; behavior disorders; general psychosocial disorders; substance abuse; eating disorders; compulsive/addictive disorders other than substance abuse and eating disorders; post-traumatic stress disorder; thought, mood, and personality disorders. Accepts the speech impaired; those with a history of arson; those with a history of harm to themselves and others; those receiving psychotropic medication; those with a history of epilepsy. Largest number of participants from Arkansas.

Program Treatment modalities: reality therapy; bio-psychosocial; family systems; psychodynamic. Family treatment program available.

Staff 2.2 full-time direct-care staff members per adolescent. Total facility staff includes 3 psychiatrists, 5 registered nurses, 12 practical/vocational nurses, 4 MSW social workers, 5 social workers (non-MSW), 6 teachers, 74 counselors, 1 occupational/recreational therapist, 1 therapist, 1 dietician, 13 other direct-care staff members. Staff is 31% male, 69% female.

Facilities Multiple buildings; males and females in separate units. Separate dining by residential unit available. Basketball courts, game room, playing fields.

Education Academic program available at no charge. Serves ages 12–18, grades 7–12. 6 teachers on staff. Curriculum accredited or approved by Arkansas State Department of Education.

Costs Average cost: $313 per day. Accepts private insurance, group insurance, medicaid, Blue Cross/Blue Shield, public funds.

Contact Main address above.

YOUTH SERVICE BUREAU OF PORTER COUNTY—NIEQUIST CENTER
304 North Morgan
Valparaiso, Indiana 46383
219-464-9585

General Information Residential treatment/subacute facility for adolescents. 15 beds for adolescents. Patient security: staff secured. Not-for-profit facility affiliated with Youth Service Bureau of Porter County, Valparaiso, IN. Licensed by state of Indiana.

Participants Accepts: male and female adolescents. Average stay: 1 year. Admission: one parent, all parties who share custody, court order, voluntary, depending on program. Treats learning disabilities; behavior disorders; general psychosocial disorders; substance abuse; eating disorders; compulsive/addictive disorders other than substance abuse and eating disorders; post-traumatic stress disorder; thought, mood, and personality disorders.

Staff Staff is 20% male, 80% female.

Costs Average cost: $125 per day.

Additional Services Outpatient services for males and females ages 7–17. Treats learning disabilities; behavior disorders; general psychosocial disorders; substance abuse; eating disorders; compulsive/addic-

tive disorders other than substance abuse and eating disorders; post-traumatic stress disorder; thought, mood, and personality disorders.

Contact Jerry Montgomery, Program Director, 253 West Lincolnway, Valparaiso, IN 46383. Phone: 219-464-9585.

YOUTH VILLAGES—DEER VALLEY CAMPUS
P.O. Box 560
Linden, Tennessee 37096
615-589-2500; Fax: 615-589-2005

General Information Residential treatment/subacute facility for adolescents. 50 beds for adolescents. Open year-round. Patient security: staff secured; will pursue and return runaways. Rural setting. Independent not-for-profit facility. Licensed by state of Tennessee. Accredited by JCAHO.

Participants Accepts: female adolescents ages 10–17. Admission: one parent, all parties who share custody, court order, Department of Human Services, Mental Health and Youth Development referrals, depending on program. Treats learning disabilities; behavior disorders; general psychosocial disorders; substance abuse; eating disorders; compulsive/addictive disorders other than substance abuse and eating disorders; post-traumatic stress disorder; thought, mood, and personality disorders. Accepts the hearing impaired; the speech impaired; the sexually compulsive; those with a history of harm to themselves and others; those receiving psychotropic medication.

Program Treatment modalities: behavior modification; Twelve Step Recovery. Family treatment program available.

Staff .5 full-time direct-care staff member per adolescent. Total facility staff includes 1 physician, 1 psychologist, 1 psychiatrist, 1 registered nurse, 1 practical/vocational nurse, 4 teachers, 4 counselors, 20 therapists.

Facilities Multiple buildings; males and females in separate units. Basketball courts, gymnasium, outdoor swimming pool, playing fields.

Education 4 teachers on staff.

Costs Average cost: $345 per day. Accepts private insurance, group insurance.

Contact Susan Walker, Assistant Director of Marketing, P.O. Box 341154, Memphis, TN 38184. Phone: 901-867-8832. Fax: 901-867-8937.

YOUTH VILLAGES—DOGWOOD VILLAGE CAMPUS
2890 Bekemeyer Drive
Arlington, Tennessee 38002
901-867-8832; Fax: 901-867-8937

General Information Residential treatment/subacute facility for adolescents. 80 beds for adolescents. Open year-round. Patient security: staff secured; will pursue and return runaways. Suburban setting. Independent not-for-profit facility. Licensed by state of Tennessee. Accredited by JCAHO.

Participants Accepts: male and female adolescents ages 9–21. Average stay: 12 months. Admission: one parent, all parties who share custody, court order, Department of Human Services, Mental Health and Youth Development referrals, depending on program. Treats learning disabilities; behavior disorders; general psychosocial disorders; substance abuse; eating disorders; compulsive/addictive disorders other than substance abuse and eating disorders; post-traumatic stress disorder; thought, mood, and personality disorders. Accepts the hearing impaired; the speech impaired; the sexually compulsive; those with a history of harm to themselves and others; those receiving psychotropic medication. Largest number of participants from Tennessee, Arkansas, Maryland.

Program Treatment modalities: behavior modification; Twelve Step Recovery. Family treatment program available.

Staff .9 full-time direct-care staff member per adolescent. Total facility staff includes 1 physician, 6 psychologists, 1 psychiatrist, 2 registered nurses, 3 practical/vocational nurses, 8 teachers, 8 counselors, 1 occupational/recreational therapist, 8 therapists, 1 dietician, 32 other direct-care staff members. Staff is 50% male, 50% female.

Facilities Multiple buildings; males and females in separate units. Basketball courts, gymnasium, outdoor swimming pool, playing fields.

Education Academic program available at no charge. Serves ages 10–21, grades K–12. 8 teachers on staff. Curriculum accredited or approved by Shelby County, Perry County. Cost of educational program sometimes covered by local school district. Organized sports program offered.

Costs Average cost: $345 per day. Accepts private insurance, group insurance.

Additional Services Drug and alcohol rehabilitation services for males ages 12–18. Treats behavior disorders; general psychosocial disorders; substance abuse; compulsive/addictive disorders other than substance abuse and eating disorders; post-traumatic stress disorder; thought, mood, and personality disorders.

Contact Susan Walker, Assistant Director of Marketing, P.O. Box 341154, Memphis, TN 38184. Phone: 901-867-8832. Fax: 901-867-8937.

YOUTH VILLAGES—MEMPHIS BOYS TOWN CAMPUS
7410 Memphis-Arlington Road
Memphis, Tennessee 38135
901-386-2040; Fax: 901-386-1691

General Information Residential treatment/subacute facility for adolescents. 58 beds for adolescents. Open year-round. Patient security: staff secured; will pursue and return runaways. Suburban setting. Independent not-for-profit facility. Licensed by state of Tennessee. Accredited by JCAHO.

Participants Accepts: male and female adolescents ages 12–21. Admission: one parent, all parties who share custody, court order, Department of Human Services, Mental Health and Youth Development referrals, depending on program. Treats learning disabilities; behavior disorders; general psychosocial disorders; substance abuse; eating disorders; compulsive/addictive disorders other than substance abuse and eating disorders; post-traumatic stress disorder; thought, mood, and personality disorders. Accepts the hearing impaired; the speech impaired; the sexually compulsive; those with a history of harm to themselves and others; those receiving psychotropic medication.

Program Treatment modalities: behavior modification; Twelve Step Recovery. Family treatment program available.

Staff .7 full-time direct-care staff member per adolescent. Total facility staff includes 1 physician, 3 psychologists, 1 psychiatrist, 1 registered nurse, 2 practical/vocational nurses, 3 teachers, 5 counselors, 3 therapists, 1 dietician, 20 other direct-care staff members.

Facilities Multiple buildings; males and females in separate units. Basketball courts, gymnasium, outdoor swimming pool, playing fields.

Education 3 teachers on staff.

Costs Average cost: $345 per day. Accepts private insurance, group insurance.

Contact Susan Walker, Assistant Director of Marketing, P.O. Box 341154, Memphis, TN 38184. Phone: 901-867-8832. Fax: 901-867-8937.

Expanded Descriptions

THE ACADEMY

French Gulch, California

Type: Experiential education program

Affiliation: Associated with the North American Wilderness Academy; for-profit

Population Served: Grades 7 through 12 with one year postgraduate available

Size: Limited to 17 students per class

Head of Facility: David W. Hull, President

Contact: The Academy, 17351 Trinity Mountain Road, French Gulch, California 96033; 916-359-2215 or 800-358-6292

THE FACILITY
The Academy is completely different from a traditional school. The Academy's campus is the North American continent with all its unique places for learning. Whether spending time at Colonial Williamsburg, in the Smithsonian, outdoors studying Anasazi ruins in the four-corners area of the United States, traveling, or camping, students find themselves in new places, confronted with physical and educational challenges.

ELIGIBILITY
The Academy is ideally suited for students who are having trouble staying on task in school and who learn better by seeing, touching, and doing. Many students have experienced previous school failure combined with occasional conflicts with teachers and authority figures. Some students share low self-esteem, lack of confidence, and impulsive behavior. Others arrive needing to learn, set, and achieve personal goals, develop greater social skills, and increase their confidence, leadership ability, or level of education.

Those who test limits or are insensitive to the needs of others will also benefit from the program. The Academy has enabled students who are doing poorly in school or trapped in a negative peer group to find the motivation and courage to break away from the past and move positively into the future.

The Academy will not accept students who are mentally retarded, developmentally disabled, psychotic, suicidal, physically abusive, felony offenders, or out-of-control and in need of a residential treatment program.

ASSESSMENT
Psychological and educational testing is available to all students by resident staff on an as-needed basis. Depending upon the psychological test performed, there may be an additional charge.

Additionally, most students are educationally tested on an annual basis to determine their progress.

PROGRAMS
Classes are divided into travel groups according to age and year in school and are composed of, at most, seventeen students. Each class travels to the best location in the United States, Canada, and Mexico to experientially learn each subject. As it takes a minimum of 60 hours to complete a course, the Academy teaches two courses every six weeks. The Academy works to integrate what is read with a hands-on approach. Class lectures are kept to a minimum so students can translate what is read into learning through doing and experiencing rather than just hearing and reading.

Each class travels with one of two rotating staff teams, composed of a wilderness instructor, a school counselor, and a teacher. Students and staff camp in a combination of wilderness, public, and private campgrounds. With the guidance of the school counselor, each class meets daily to work out all interpersonal issues. All issues facing the group are resolved at the group meetings.

Education within the Academy is contracted from Pine Meadows School, a nonpublic school licensed by the State Department of Education. Units, grades, and diplomas earned by students transfer to public and private schools as well as colleges. All teachers have a California credential.

Each class learns basic survival and camping skills as well as advanced first aid during the first four to six weeks in the local northern California mountains. During this period students earn their health and physical education credits as they learn the skills that will prepare them for traveling and camping in the months ahead. Students also learn how to cook, take care of their equipment, and work together as a team. Once the basics for surviving and working cooperatively as a group are learned and followed, students are ready to travel.

All high school subjects necessary for entrance into a university or college are taught from September through June, with an optional summer school session available. The survival and rescue skills instruction continues as the students travel and take academic and elective courses. As the year progresses, the wilderness instructor continues to increase the sophistication of the training and creates new challenges for the class. Survival and rescue skills training supplements the experiential education program well. Students find that wilderness training teaches self-reliance, independence, and self-esteem, while developing interpersonal skills. Rescue training teaches problem solving and sequential thinking skills, leadership, teamwork, and the ability to listen and follow instruction.

Each student learns how to organize and conduct a simulated rescue and in the process develops leadership skills. As students learn to handle negative events in a positive and assertive manner, the Academy's adolescents gain the tools they need to avoid being victimized as they progress through life.

STAFF
All of the Pine Meadows School teachers assigned to the Academy are fully credentialed in the state of California. The Academy's staff members hold various human services degrees combined with extensive backgrounds in special education, counseling, and adolescent group work. Additionally, most staff have current certificates for first responder, vertical rescue, swift water rescue, tracking, and many other wilderness and rescue skills.

SPECIAL PROGRAMS

The Academy provides students with a wonderfully wide variety of cultural opportunities. As each class travels through the North American continent, students visit art galleries as well as attend plays and a variety of musical presentations. The music, art, and drama courses are semester classes where students have the opportunity to meet with musicians, actors, and artists to supplement the normal course curriculum.

CONTINUITY OF TREATMENT

Students may continue their education at the Academy until they obtain a high school diploma. Students may also transfer to a traditional boarding school or return home and attend a local school. The decision on what is best for the student usually rests on the amount of maturity the student has gained over the years at the Academy.

BUILDINGS AND GROUNDS

Due to the unique nature of the Academy's program, it is impossible to describe a single "campus." The classroom for the Academy's students is the North American continent, with its myriad opportunities for instruction, wonder, and challenge.

ADMISSION AND FINANCIAL INFORMATION

Many students enter the Academy at the beginning of the fall semester in early September. However, most parents enroll their child at any time, with students able to join their classes usually within seven days. Parents or students who wish to receive an application may contact the corporate office of the North American Wilderness Academy Monday through Friday from 8:30 to 5 p.m. at 916-359-2215 or 800-358-6292. Total cost for September to June is $19,850: $1000 is deposited with the application, and two payments, each $9425, are then due on August 15 and December 15. Upon receipt of the application and deposit, an arrival time will be determined.

ADOLESCENT CENTER FOR CHANGE

La Verkin, Utah

Type: Residential treatment center

Affiliation: A corporately owned, for-profit organization

Population Served: Male and female, ages 11 to 17

Size: 24 students

Contact: Narvin Lichfield, Post Office Box 3109, Saint George, Utah 84770; 800-637-0701

THE FACILITY

The Adolescent Center for Change (ACC), licensed by the state of Utah, is a behavior modification program consisting of professional therapy, accredited academics, and a highly structured daily schedule. In addition, ACC's combined treatment-educational and adventure process helps the student to form positive habit patterns. Outdoor recreation on the weekends provides students with supervised physical exercise, opportunities for cultural exposure, and travel that will enrich their overall experience at ACC.

Through positive, genuine affirmation, students regain or discover the self-esteem and self-confidence that they often lack. Once this process has begun, the students become "internally motivated"; they begin acting responsibly not for others but for themselves, having personally realized and experienced the benefits of thoughtful, responsible action.

Parents are positively involved in a student's experience, initially through telephone calls with a therapist and later through visits to ACC if it is deemed beneficial or necessary.

ACC is open year-round and is located in La Verkin, Utah, 20 miles from the mouth of Zion Canyon.

ELIGIBILITY

ACC treats adolescents with attitude, behavior, emotional, and substance-abuse problems. While treatment-resistive adolescents and involuntary admissions are common, ACC recognizes that the student is as much a participant in the process as the parents and staff. Therefore, students are required to take an active part in establishing specific treatment goals at the beginning of the program. Students function in small-group settings that allow for individualized attention and a high staff-to-adolescent ratio.

There is a three-month minimum and a thirty-six-month maximum program length. The actual length of treatment is determined on an individual basis. Successful program completion is achieved once treatment goals have been realized, at which point the student can return home or to another fostering environment.

ACC's adolescents come from around the country, with a concentration from California and other western states.

ASSESSMENT

ACC performs a complete assessment of the student, including an examination of the student's social history, paying particular attention to the length and severity of the problems being addressed. ACC then decides if the student

is right for the program and if the type of treatment offered by ACC will be effective and beneficial to the student.

While ACC does accept outside references and referrals, most important is an examination of the family and the history of interfamily relationships.

PROGRAMS

ACC's 24-hour, supervised therapeutic milieu provides the proper balance of individual, group, and family therapy, all under the direction of experienced professionals. The proven treatment process, combined with a challenging daily schedule, instills positive behavioral changes.

ACC's focus during the week is on academics, therapy, and fitness. Students attend classes for 6 hours daily as well as adhere to a daily fitness regimen. There are two individual and three group therapy sessions weekly.

On weekends, ACC's focus is on wilderness and recreational excursions. Throughout the week, students earn the right to participate in weekend activities that include hiking and camping getaways to the Grand Canyon and to Great Basin, Zion, Bryce, and other national parks and recreation areas. These supervised trips allow for self-discovery in a wilderness setting and provide unmatched opportunities to experience some of the earth's greatest wonders.

STAFF

Treatment programs at ACC are overseen by experienced, credentialed psychiatrists and therapists, while the educational portion of ACC's program is overseen by credentialed, certified teachers.

CONTINUITY OF TREATMENT

If circumstances require it, additional therapy or other types of follow-up programs can be arranged. ACC is happy to recommend and communicate with other professionals or support groups in a student's home area.

BUILDINGS AND GROUNDS

ACC's main building is located 20 miles from the mouth of majestic Zion Canyon. The building is divided into two units, one male and one female, where students share a semiprivate room with its own bath. ACC is located within an hour's drive of some of the nation's most beautiful landscapes and recreation facilities. Recreational opportunities are varied and seasonal but can include working on a ropes course, hiking, white-water rafting, and others.

ADMISSION AND FINANCIAL INFORMATION

ACC focuses on changes needed and not time frames. As a result, ACC agrees to work with a student for a minimum of three months and a maximum of thirty-six months. When the student achieves his or her treatment goals anytime within those boundaries, he or she is able to return home or to a less restrictive environment. Due to the scope and thoroughness of the initial evaluations and program planning, the first month at ACC is billed at a cost of $5900. Subsequent months are billed at $2400 each or $80 per day. ACC is willing to work with any insurance carrier and has found that reimbursement can often be obtained by working through insurance carriers' individual case managers.

Camp Huntington

High Falls, New York

Type: Therapeutic recreation; independent living and work training programs

Affiliation: Operated by Camp Huntington, Inc.

Population Served: Learning disabled, neurologically impaired, attention deficit disorder, mildly to moderately developmentally disabled males and females; ages 6 to 21 in the children, teen, and young adult program and ages 21 and up in the adult program

Head of Facility: Bruria K. Falik, Ph.D.

Contact: Dr. Bruria K. Falik, Director; Bruceville Road, RR 2, Box 27, High Falls, New York 12440; 914-687-7840 or 914-687-7927; fax: 914-687-7211

THE CAMP

Camp Huntington was established in 1961 as a privately owned residential summer camp for boys and girls with learning and developmental disabilities. Located in the historic town of High Falls, New York, at the foot of the Catskill Mountains, Camp Huntington enjoys a natural rustic environment and a lovely view of the surrounding countryside. The camp's nearly 50 acres stretch almost a mile along the Roundout Creek. Through a variety of educational and recreational activities, the camp's purpose is to cultivate children's personal growth and cater to their special needs. First-time campers, campers who have attended other special or regular camps, and parents have found the experience at Camp Huntington to be rewarding and beneficial.

The camp's director, Dr. Bruria Falik, has a background uniquely suited to effectively handle the camp's special population. Dr. Falik has a Ph.D. in clinical child psychology and is an active New York State–certified school psychologist and behavioral psychotherapist. In her many years of teaching and clinical experience with special populations, she has been extensively involved in parent education, staff training, program development, and workshop instruction. Her children, Daniel and Sandy, are active members of the camp staff and help each child feel the warmth and acceptance that are so essential to a successful camp experience.

ELIGIBILITY

The camp serves children and young adults from the United States, Canada, Europe, and Asia who have mild to moderate learning and developmental disabilities. Camp Huntington's aim is to create a diverse community of campers who learn and grow with each other. Admission is based on the director's evaluation of a child's potential to benefit from the programs offered at Camp Huntington. Included among the programs offered at Camp Huntington is a program for autistic children. An adult vacation program serves adults ages 21 and older. Children with outstanding physical handicaps or severe behavior disorders are not eligible to apply.

Programs are therapeutic in design, with emphasis on recreation and learning. Special attention is devoted to each camper's specific needs. Staff members are selected with care to address the specific needs of all campers. A staff-to-camper ratio of 1 to 3 is maintained and, if necessary, one-on-one care can be specially arranged. All programs aim to maintain and advance campers' progress, enhance self-esteem and interpersonal skills, and encourage personal growth.

ASSESSMENT

Interviews and evaluations are conducted by the director. Assessments from a child's school, psychologist, and family physician are all requested. At camp, no rigid evaluative process is attempted. Rather, daily journals are maintained by staff and summarized for parents. Special evaluations of a camper's progress are provided upon request.

PROGRAM

Huntington's wide variety of activities, both educational and recreational, provide a wide range of cognitive and physical developmental possibilities. In well-equipped activity centers, in nature huts, in a home economics cottage, at the pool, and on athletic fields, children learn valuable skills and enjoy fun-filled summer days with friendly peers. Activity periods are designed to offer campers the special focus they need.

Arts and crafts activities include art therapy with painting, clay, fabric, and woodcrafts. In the arts, programs include music, dance and movement therapy, drama, talent shows, puppet theater, dances, professional entertainment, and selected movies.

Outdoor living activities include gardening, scouting, nature hikes, and campfires. Home economics teaches skills in hygiene, first aid, cooking, and table setting. The academics program includes occupational education, consumer economics, communication skills, reading, perceptual training, speech and language therapy, and behavioral counseling.

A full range of sports activities is offered. Campers are encouraged to participate to the extent of their abilities in baseball, basketball, volleyball, soccer, tennis, handball, Ping-Pong, badminton, miniature golf, and bowling. Horseback riding is available at a local ranch.

An important emphasis of the camp is instructional and recreational swimming at the camp's beautiful pool. Swimming is one of the campers' favorite activities. Constant supervision is provided by Red Cross–certified Water Safety Instructors who are experienced in adaptive aquatics.

Selected adolescent and adult campers may choose the work training program, in which up to 2 hours each day are spent in independent living skills, food services, child care, office skills, and building and grounds maintenance.

Mealtimes are important too, and counselors are on hand to provide assistance. The camp's proximity to supply sources ensures that fresh milk, fruits and vegetables, prime quality meats, poultry, fish, and eggs are always available in abundance. Menus are both varied and well-balanced. Special diets can be arranged on request.

STAFF

Camper programs are staffed with psychologists, special education teachers, nurses, occupation and recreation therapists, and second-year and older college students majoring in psychology, special education, social work, peer counseling, art, music, and dance therapy. In addition, recommendations of mental health and dietary specialists contribute to the ongoing development of the camp's program. All staff contribute to the campers' well-being and an overall atmosphere of acceptance and loving care.

BUILDINGS AND GROUNDS

Separate campuses for boys and girls are located on either side of a small, mountain-fed brook. Campers sleep in cheerful, airy cabins, with between five and eight campers to a cabin. All cabins are equipped with showers, sinks, and toilets. The camp's facilities include spacious dining centers, recreation halls, activity centers, nature huts, an arts-and-

crafts building, a home economics cottage, an academics building, an Olympic-size swimming pool, and extensive playing fields and athletic facilities.

ADMISSION AND FINANCIAL INFORMATION

Registration begins in November. Interested parents can inquire about early payment plans. Tuition may be tax deductible as a medical expense. Camperships are awarded to over 30 percent of all campers. Tuition assistance can be arranged with the director. A nonprofit division of the camp reviews applications to determine tuition assistance.

THE CASCADE SCHOOL

Whitmore, California

Type: Coeducational boarding school
Affiliation: Corporate ownership; for-profit
Population Served: Male and female, ages 13 to 18
Size: 150 students
Head of Facility: Michael Allgood, President
Contact: Admissions, Post Office Box 9, Whitmore,
California 96096; 916-472-3031; fax: 916-472-3414

THE SCHOOL

The Cascade School was founded in 1984 and is designed to provide an educational program for high school students who have the capability to succeed academically but who have been failing to achieve their potential. As a result, they have fallen behind in their educational and social development, further impeding their progress. The Cascade School is characterized by its unique ability to redirect and motivate these underachieving adolescents. Its educational program is based on the belief that in order for students to progress successfully, they must be committed to learning, be willing to assume responsibility for themselves and their actions, and be aware of the rich possibilities their futures have to offer.

The Cascade School is situated on 250 acres of forest and meadowland in the foothills of the Cascade Mountains of northern California. Surrounded by wilderness forest preserves and a national park, the Cascade School is 45 minutes from the city of Redding. The rural location provides an ideal setting for a variety of outdoor activities, sports, and wilderness challenges.

The Cascade School is owned and operated by its founding faculty and is organized by a five-member Board of Directors. The plant is valued at approximately $6 million.

ELIGIBILITY

Students who enroll in the Cascade School are usually distinguished by the fact that education has ceased to be an attainable goal. Typically, they are discouraged and unhappy; they are unwilling to accept their parents' direction and support. Students' low self-esteem is sometimes masked by bravado or marked by lonely withdrawal, truancy, adherence to popular fad, and turning to the "wrong crowd." They have begun the downward spiral that often leads to dropping out of school or even drug and alcohol abuse. At the Cascade School young people are able to reverse this undesirable trend and grow toward healthy adulthood.

Students with a history of arson, violent or criminal behavior, or uncontrolled sexual "acting-out" are not appropriate candidates for admission.

ASSESSMENT

In most cases, students are referred by educational consultants who submit complete assessments prior to the interview. If the applicant has not been professionally tested and evaluated, the school will recommend that an evaluation be performed by its consulting psychologist. The Cascade School continues to assess students as they progress through the program.

PROGRAMS

The essence of the Cascade School's curriculum is the Personal Growth and Development Program, in which students participate in a year-round intensive curriculum designed to accelerate personal growth and development while rebuilding academic skills. The program provides integrated educational and counseling components that challenge students intellectually, physically, and emotionally. The Personal Growth and Development Program averages two years in length and is determined by individual needs and circumstances.

Assemblies are scheduled throughout the year to present lectures, concerts, and theatrical productions. Three times each year, trips are taken to the Oregon Shakespeare Festival to study classical and contemporary drama, and study tours are taken to San Francisco. Summers provide the opportunity for a variety of field experiences and academic enrichment.

All students are expected to perform roles of service within the school community and to participate in service activities in Whitmore or Redding. The student government offers a variety of committees: Big Brothers, Big Sisters, Tutor Guild, Disciplinary Council, Activities and Entertainment, HOPE (community service) Committee, Environmental Awareness Club, Poets' Society, language clubs, and the Drama Club. Festivals at the Cascade School center on traditional holidays and events that are special to the school: Halloween, Thanksgiving, Hanukkah, Christmas, Easter, Passover, Founders Day, and Summer Games, a four-day Olympic-style athletics competition.

The schedule of daily activities is full and varied. Academic classes are scheduled from 8 a.m. to 2:45 p.m. each weekday, with breaks for tea-time and lunch. Afternoons until 4:30 p.m. are devoted to art electives, physical education, and Forums. Committee and group meetings occupy the time until supper at 6. Evenings provide the time for study and discussion, music or play rehearsal, or conferences with counselors. Each student is expected to do his or her assigned chores at some time during the day.

A variety of weekend activities are planned from which students may choose. The Student Council meets on Saturday afternoon, and a movie is shown in the evening. On Sunday, a large brunch is served, followed by group activities in which participation is optional. For students who have earned the privilege, transportation is provided to Redding for shopping and recreation. Personal Growth and Development Workshops are held two to three times per month, usually on weekends.

The summer curriculum offers a variety of classes, from science field study to ceramics, as well as remedial work in academic subjects. Most courses center on physically active and creative subjects that include field study or studio work. Each summer, several three-week treks are conducted in wilderness areas of northern California.

STAFF

Nineteen teachers (twelve men and seven women) and twenty-one counselors (eleven men and ten women) constitute the forty-member faculty. Each student is assigned a counselor who firmly but lovingly guides the student through the difficult process of self-exploration and growth. Counselors conduct triweekly group discussions, called Forums, and a series of workshops that provide the opportunity for in-depth exploration of values, goals, and personal experiences. Individual guidance counseling encourages the student to participate in self-assessment and goal setting. Counselors report regularly to parents regarding their child's progress and conduct family workshops several times each year.

The campus currently houses twelve faculty members and their families; additional residences are under construction. The teaching faculty holds four doctoral, six master's, and fourteen bachelor's degrees. The Cascade School provides in-service training in counseling techniques for all of its faculty. In addition to its counseling and teaching staff, the Cascade School employs a full-time registered nurse and has a physician on campus twice a week.

Michael Allgood, President, with twenty-three years' experience as an educator, counselor, and administrator (fourteen of which were spent as a headmaster), inspired and led the group that founded the Cascade School. He continues to serve as the head of the school.

CONTINUITY OF TREATMENT
Workshops are offered to assist parents in creating a post-Cascade plan with their children as well as in setting goals and boundaries before the child leaves the school. There is also an alumni follow-up program conducted by the counseling staff, and students are welcome to come back to visit the campus. Over 95 percent of Cascade graduates go on to college or university. The alumni, many still of college age, retain a keen interest in the school and visit the campus frequently.

BUILDINGS AND GROUNDS
The Cascade School has three dormitory buildings for boys and three for girls, each housing between six and twenty-nine students. Two to four students share each unit. Dormitories and large living spaces are comfortably furnished to provide a homelike setting.

The library, computer center, and common areas are found in the Lodge. The Pavilion houses a performing arts studio/theater, practice rooms, and two classrooms. Thirteen additional classrooms and laboratories are included in the humanities, science, and fine arts buildings. Two ponds, playing fields, three classrooms at the fitness center, and a swimming pool provide space for physical education activities. A counseling center complex and dining hall are new additions to the campus.

ADMISSION AND FINANCIAL INFORMATION
The Cascade School enrolls students from various parts of the United States and some other countries. Applications are accepted for grades 7–12. Students are selected on the basis of the likelihood of their benefiting from Cascade's overall program. On-campus interviews of the student and parents are required. Interview impressions, along with school records, results of testing, and recommendations of counselors and teachers, are taken into consideration by the admissions committee.

Inquiries are welcome at any time of the year, and parents are encouraged to make an appointment for a campus tour and interview. Depending upon available openings, students may be admitted as soon as all application information is presented.

There is no fee for application. Tuition is $3400 per month with fees at admission totaling $1500. In addition, parents are asked to deposit $1000 in an account to be drawn upon for allowances and personal expenses. Tuition is billed monthly, and all deposits are refundable.

Cedar Crest
Residential Treatment Center

Belton, Texas

Type: Psychiatric residential treatment center

Affiliation: An affiliate of Hospital Corporation of America

Population Served: Male and female, ages 4 to 17

Size: Licensed capacity, 70 beds

Head of Facility: Richard N. Rickey, M.A., M.P.H., Administrator/CEO; Pankaj Naik, M.D., Medical Director, Child and Adolescent Psychiatrist

Contact: Admissions Department, Cedar Crest RTC, 3500 South I-H 35, Belton, Texas 76513; 817-939-2100 or 800-888-4071

THE FACILITY

Cedar Crest is a Residential Treatment Center (RTC) for children and adolescents. The center is designed for young people who do not require a locked, acute-care facility but who are emotionally or behaviorally incapacitated to the degree that they require the help of a special environment to acquire age-appropriate functioning in school, family, peer, and community life spheres. The center is also designed for those who require continuing care after psychiatric hospitalization or who need a 24-hour therapeutic program that is less restrictive than a hospital environment yet more structured than an outpatient setting.

Cedar Crest is accredited with commendation by the Joint Commission on Accreditation of Healthcare Organizations. It is also licensed as a child and adolescent residential treatment center by the Texas Department of Human Services.

ELIGIBILITY

Cedar Crest RTC best serves children and adolescents, ages 4 to 17, who are unable to manage a completely open environment yet have progressed beyond the point of requiring a locked, acute-care facility. Referrals from physicians, mental health professionals, and child service agencies are accepted.

While Cedar Crest RTC is able to successfully treat a number of problems, there are some that are best treated elsewhere. Cedar Crest RTC cannot accept those young people who have IQs below 70, are at a significant suicidal risk, who require acute psychiatric or medical care, or are acutely psychotic.

ASSESSMENT

Once admitted, each individual receives a complete evaluation and assessment of his or her psychiatric, psychological, psychosocial, educational, and physiological needs.

This assessment serves as the basis for the development of a comprehensive, individualized treatment plan that guides the staff through the child's care at Cedar Crest. Treatment plans are reviewed at least monthly by the multidisciplinary treatment team and are then modified to reflect changes and progress in the resident's treatment.

PROGRAMS

Cedar Crest RTC offers three distinct programs designed to meet the unique needs of latency children, adolescents, and dually diagnosed residents. Each resident is assigned to a program based upon age, sex, and therapeutic need.

Recognizing that adolescent boys and girls have distinct needs and recognizing that coed living areas may raise issues that can be detrimental to treatment, Cedar Crest operates separate programs for adolescent males and females. Various modalities are used with these groups, including relationship building with staff and peers and milieu therapy, which focuses strongly on the group as a community. Special programming is also offered for various special needs such as adoption, sexual issues, and stepchildren.

All residents participate in milieu therapy daily, individual therapy at least once per week, group therapy 3 to 4 times per week, and ongoing family therapy. Family commitment and involvement are required throughout each step of treatment so that the family's support becomes the cornerstone of the child's recovery.

Cedar Crest provides a full range of educational services throughout the year. From August to May, services are provided through Belton Independent School District, which is accredited by the Texas Education Association. During the summer, Cedar Crest provides an enrichment program with a variety of learning opportunities.

The activity therapy staff provides a variety of activities, recreational events, therapeutic outings, and special events as well as helping residents to develop leisure skills and social skills, learn ways to relieve stress, and discover new talents and interests.

The Cedar Crest treatment philosophy is based on a firm belief that only loving, dignified, considerate treatment allows a patient to grow.

STAFF

Cedar Crest is staffed by an interdisciplinary team of fully credentialed psychiatrists, clinical psychologists, clinical social workers, nursing staff, and mental health associates. The clinical team also includes activity therapists, nutritionists, and special education professionals.

SPECIAL PROGRAMS

Programming for latency children ages 4 to 12 is separate from that provided for adolescents. Program components such as level systems, point sheets, privileges, and consequences are designed to meet the needs of latency children. A highly structured milieu combined with their therapies provides many opportunities for this special population to resolve their emotional issues and learn age-appropriate coping skills.

Special programming for dual diagnoses residents is designed to ensure that both psychiatric and substance abuse issues are fully addressed. These residents are incorporated with the adolescent male or female milieus while receiving special Twelve-Step and process groups as well as attending NA and AA on campus.

CONTINUITY OF TREATMENT

Beginning at admission, discharge planning is a crucial component of the treatment process. Initial plans are developed and documented after the psychosocial assessment has been performed and include discharge criteria, estimated length of stay, and postdischarge plans. Discharge plans are reevaluated regularly to meet any changing needs of the patient. Every effort is made to refer the resident back to the referring professional in order to facilitate continuity of care. In the event the referring professional was not seeing the resident in therapy prior to admission, the referring professional will be contacted for discharge recommendations and/or notification. Residents and parents are encouraged to actively participate in discharge planning, making contacts with aftercare resources, in order to promote responsibility and commitment.

BUILDINGS AND GROUNDS

Cedar Crest's 30-acre campus is located on a beautiful wooded hill overlooking the central Texas Lampasas Valley. The environment is a campus setting rather than a hospital, with acres of trees, hiking trails, and streams. Cedar Crest's campus is open with four separate cottages for residents,

each room containing two beds and a private bath. Residents also benefit from a central dining room, a fully equipped gymnasium with state-of-the-art weight equipment, an outdoor swimming pool, and on-campus schooling.

ADMISSION AND FINANCIAL INFORMATION

By reviewing past and present clinical information, the admissions process ensures that each resident is suitable for Cedar Crest's program prior to admission. Approval or denial is normally determined by the medical director within 48 hours.

Services are covered by CHAMPUS and most major insurers. Admissions and business office staff are available to provide a thorough financial analysis prior to placement.

Those families needing assistance or information on travel arrangements may contact the admissions department at 800-888-4071.

CEDU MIDDLE SCHOOL

Running Springs, California

Type: Coeducational boarding school for preadolescents and adolescents with special emotional or educational needs

Affiliation: An independent, for-profit organization

Population Served: Boys and girls, ages 9½ to 13½

Size: 50 preadolescents and adolescents

Head of Facility: Dr. Barry D. Boatman, Middle School Director

Contact: Saul G. Rudman, Director of Admissions, P.O. Box 1176, Running Springs, California 92382; 714-867-2725; fax: 714-867-9483

THE SCHOOL
The CEDU Middle School's program combines the successful philosophy of CEDU Education, founded in 1966, with contemporary and effective behavioral, developmental, emotional, and academic programs. The Middle School is a year-round coeducational boarding school for children and adolescents 9½ to 13½, grades 5 through 8, with special needs. The Middle School is located on a serene, 76-acre forested campus midway between Lake Arrowhead and Lake Big Bear in the community of Running Springs, California. The Middle School provides an environment conducive to personal and academic growth and uses a working animal farm at the center of the program.

The school is 60 miles from Palm Springs and 90 miles east of Los Angeles. CEDU's ideal setting allows for a wide variety of active sports, wilderness programs, and academic learning opportunities. The program is directed by Barry D. Boatman, Doctor of Psychology and Licensed Marriage, Family, and Child Therapist. James Powell, Ph.D., and Ronald Cook are the Director and the President of CEDU Schools, respectively. Steven Morgan, Ph.D., is the Licensed Clinical Consulting Psychologist.

ELIGIBILITY
CEDU Middle School students, despite their high potential, have often experienced frustration in a traditional educational setting and are in need of additional structure and support to aid their overall development. Many have experienced poor interpersonal relationships, failure in school, behavioral difficulties, hyperactivity, attention disorders, or problems with their families. The CEDU Middle School views these problems as the outward expression of underdeveloped or misdirected inner forces that can also manifest themselves as a lack of motivation and self-discipline, low self-esteem, and poor judgment. The Middle School accepts children on medication; a consulting psychiatrist addresses students' medication needs, and a full-time registered nurse administers prescribed medications.

ASSESSMENT
Referrals come from professional-academic personnel, educational consultants, psychiatrists, psychologists, social workers, MFC Counselors, and alumni and parents.

Acceptance is based largely on the admission interview itself, yet a completed application, transcripts, former records, and all written and verbal evaluations from the referring source are requested. Application and admission may take place at any time during the year, with every effort made to accommodate families with an immediate need. Initial acceptance of the CEDU Middle School by the prospective student is not expected, nor does any lack of initial acceptance act as a deterrent to enrollment.

PROGRAMS
CEDU'S Middle School program is designed to ensure mastery of the skills basic to all learning and integrates four main components: personal growth, academics, fine arts, and life/animal sciences. A student's placement is developed and monitored via CEDU Middle School's personalized Comprehensive Education Plan (CEP). The individualized instruction, in conjunction with a maximum class size of twelve, helps the student experience immediate success and develop a positive self-image. Each student's CEP is developed to address their unique academic, physical, social, and emotional needs. Upon completion of a yearlong comprehensive evaluation, the student's continuing education is determined.

The Personal Growth Module focuses on daily Communication Groups designed to teach, or reteach, ways to identify dysfunctional patterns and habits in order to replace them with new, functional ones. These groups, combined with a positive-reinforcement focus, structured peer-group interaction, and daily individual support counseling, provide an effective environment conducive to personal and academic growth.

The Core Academic Module centers on composition, communication skills, active listening skills, creative writing, language arts, social studies, science, computer science, mathematics, and algebra.

The Fine Arts Module is designed to evoke self-expression and creativity from the student. Various art mediums, including sculpture, ceramics and three-dimensional art, woodworking, painting, and drawing, are also explored. Music, drama, and dance are also important parts of the Fine Arts Module.

The Life/Animal Science Module, which includes farm science, animal science, physical science, geology, biology, agriculture, ropes courses, and wilderness experiences, enables the student to build positive self-esteem, a strong work ethic, and overall successful behavioral patterns.

As a major element of the students' personal growth program, physical conditioning is integrated into almost all aspects of the school. Students participate in team and individual sports, a special weeklong Olympic competition, weight-training, dance, aerobics, wilderness experiences, nature hikes, ropes courses, horseback riding, swimming, and racquet sports. The mountain resort location of the school provides for many snow sports as well as fishing, boating, and hiking. Students enjoy a variety of other activities, including movies, plays, sporting events, and field trips to museums, parks, and cultural centers. Trips are made in groups under strict faculty supervision.

STAFF

CEDU Middle School is staffed with full-time teachers and counselors, live-in dorm parents, a farm manager, consulting psychiatrists and psychologists, social workers, a licensed nursing staff, speech pathologists, dieticians, and educational resource specialists.

SPECIAL PROGRAMS

Parent Support Groups are formed according to general geographical areas and meet frequently to share growth as a family unit. In addition, parents are invited to participate in three extended weekend Parent Seminars each year. These seminars address parents' concerns and provide families with a thorough understanding of their child's experiences at CEDU Middle School. The Middle School also offers intensive individualized and specialized programs for the extremely challenging child with special needs.

CONTINUITY OF TREATMENT

Most CEDU students continue their education in some of the finest high schools in the nation. Students who successfully graduate from the Middle School program have the option of continuing in the CEDU High School Program if appropriate. Graduates routinely demonstrate self-confidence, emotional stability, and a healthy life-style upon graduation.

BUILDINGS AND GROUNDS

The Middle School campus is focused around a working animal farm complete with horses, sheep, lambs, chickens, goats, ducks, geese, rabbits, cows, and various other farm animals. The western theme, combined with the curative element of the students' hands-on interaction with the animals, has proved to be a very valuable component in the program.

Students are housed in dormitory buildings, with two to four students sharing a furnished room and bath. Laundry facilities are available in each building. Other facilities include a computer lab, study library, kitchen facilities, dining rooms, offices, living rooms, and family rooms. The campus also offers a dance studio, gym, and swimming pool. Current expansion projects include a "Total Concept Facility" around the working animal farm, utilizing the western theme to expand the horse programs.

ADMISSION AND FINANCIAL INFORMATION

In addition to the comprehensive student history obtained from parents, a thorough review of written and verbal assessments provided by the referral source and any previous placements or counselors forms the basis for acceptance. Parents are encouraged to call the admissions office to schedule a tour of the campus. While on campus, parents become familiar with the school and its programs and have an opportunity to meet with CEDU students, faculty, and administrators.

A completed application and $35 application fee are required prior to enrollment.

The current CEDU Middle School tuition is $3550 per month. This fee includes academic education, room and board, support counseling, and program costs. A registration fee of $800 and an enrollment and orientation fee of $900, covering the first eighteen days, are due upon enrollment. The student expense account requires a refundable deposit of $250. Parents are provided with a list of required clothing and personal items needed upon enrollment. A one-time linen fee of $125 is also assessed. The admissions office should be contacted for information on individual insurance or financial assistance applications.

CEDU SCHOOL

Running Springs, California

Type: Coeducational boarding school for adolescents with special emotional or educational needs

Affiliation: An independent, for-profit organization

Population Served: Male and female, ages 13½ to 17½

Size: 100 adolescents

Head of Facility: Ronald W. Cook, President

Contact: Saul G. Rudman, Director of Admissions, Post Office Box 1176, Running Springs, California 92382; 714-867-2722; fax: 714-867-9483

THE SCHOOL

Founded in 1966, CEDU School provides a place where adolescents can develop intellectually, emotionally, socially, and physically. The 76-acre campus is open year-round and is located in Running Springs, California. At an altitude of 6,030 feet, midway between Lake Arrowhead and Big Bear Lake, CEDU is surrounded by the San Bernardino National Forest. The school is 60 miles from Palm Springs and 90 miles east of Los Angeles.

The ideal setting accommodates active sports and wilderness programs, a farm, and vocational training. CEDU School is a privately owned, independent entity, accredited by the Western Association of Schools and Colleges (WASC), and enjoys considerable alumni participation and support.

ELIGIBILITY

CEDU students are generally young people who have experienced frustration in a traditional educational setting and are in need of additional structure and support for their overall development. The school seeks applicants who possess the ability to achieve academically, although this ability may have been hampered by learning difficulties or life circumstances.

Despite CEDU students' high potential, they may have experienced a combination of problems prior to enrollment including poor interpersonal relationships, failure in school, or problems with their families. Some students have a history of attention deficit disorder and/or depression and may have experimented with drugs and/or alcohol. The school does enroll students receiving certain psychotropic medications. Many students have demonstrated a lack of discipline and conflict with their families. Approximately one third of CEDU's students explore adoption-related issues during their stay.

ASSESSMENT

Referrals come from professionals including academic personnel, educational consultants, psychiatrists, psychologists, social workers, counselors, and current and alumni parents of CEDU students. Acceptance is based largely on the admissions interview itself, yet a completed application, transcripts, and former records as well as written and verbal evaluations from the referring source are requested. Application and admission may take place at any time during the year. If it is determined that an immediate need

exists, the admissions staff will make every effort to accommodate the family. It is not expected that the prospective student will initially embrace his or her placement in, and the structured nature of, the CEDU School. This partial resistance is anticipated and does not serve as a deterrent to enrollment.

PROGRAMS

The CEDU School curriculum focuses on emotional growth and academic achievement. The academic curriculum is designed to ensure mastery of the skills basic to all learning. Each student's class schedule is determined according to his or her achievement level in each subject area. The maximum class size is twelve, and the overall student-to-faculty ratio is 3:1. Individualized programs range from one-to-one remedial tutoring to college-preparatory studies.

Among the subjects offered are American and world history, U.S. government, geography, introductory mathematics, algebra, geometry, biology, geology, literature, creative writing, language arts, Shakespeare, theater, composition, issues in science, botany, computer sciences, health, physical education, a cappella singing, instrumental music, painting, drawing, ceramics, sculpture, and wilderness skills. SAT preparation as well as college and career counseling are also offered.

To graduate, a student must complete 240 units of credit. These must include the following: 40 units of English, 40 units of social science, 20 units of mathematics, 20 units of science, 20 units of physical education, 10 units of fine arts or foreign language, 10 units of health, and 80 units of electives. Graduates receive a diploma accredited by WASC.

The academic program operates year-round; during the two-week period between each academic quarter, academic studies and activities alternate. Report cards are sent to parents after each quarter along with an evaluation of the student's overall progress.

Each day begins at 7 a.m. and is filled with a balanced mixture of classes, emotional growth groups, work, sports and recreation, and free time, until the Last Light meeting of the entire student body at 9 p.m.

Regular and recurring group sessions and extended thematic workshops help students develop self-awareness, establish healthy relationships, and assume responsibility for their actions and resulting consequences. Speech and language therapy, as well as testing and remediation for special learning difficulties, is available.

Physical conditioning, as a major element of personal growth, is integrated into almost all aspects of the school, from sports and vocational experiences to dance and wilderness experiences. All students participate in a wilderness program designed to promote fitness, self-discipline, group problem-solving skills, and self-confidence. The challenges of the wilderness program range from hikes and jogging to cross-country skiing and rock and mountain climbing. In addition, students participate in off-campus wilderness excursions of various lengths.

Students are actively involved in the direction of the school through participation in Student Government, committees, and general meetings. Students attend movies, plays, and sporting events and take field trips to museums, parks, and cultural centers throughout California. Students enrolled in theater class present a major theatrical production each quarter. As students progress through the school program, they take on increased responsibility for setting their own goals as well as designing and implementing plans to achieve them.

STAFF

CEDU is staffed with forty-five full-time teachers and counselors, one consulting psychiatrist, four psychologists, two licensed social workers, one registered nurse, one speech pathologist, one dietician, and one educational resource specialist.

SPECIAL PROGRAMS

The Alumni Program, through which alumni visit the school on weekends, provides students with positive and supportive role models. Parent Support Groups are formed according to general geographical areas and meet frequently to share growth as a family unit. Parents are invited to participate in three extended weekend Parent Seminars each year. The seminars address parent concerns and provide families with a thorough understanding of their child's experiences at CEDU School.

CONTINUITY OF TREATMENT

Most CEDU students continue their education at some of the finest colleges and universities in the nation. Students leaving CEDU without a diploma receive a Certificate of Completion and are assisted in finding the most appropriate high school placement. Graduates routinely demonstrate increased self-confidence, emotional stability, and a healthy life-style.

BUILDINGS AND GROUNDS

The main lodge houses an expansive log living room, several large family rooms, offices, the computer lab, a study library, kitchens, and a dining room. Students are housed in five dormitory buildings with two to four students sharing each furnished dormitory room and bath. Laundry facilities are available in each building. The campus includes a working farm facility for vocational training, a comprehensive ropes course, a dance studio, a gymnasium, and a swimming pool.

ADMISSION AND FINANCIAL INFORMATION

In addition to a comprehensive student history obtained from parents, admission to CEDU is largely based on a thorough review of written and verbal assessments from the referral source and any previous placements or counselors. Parents are encouraged to telephone the admissions office to schedule a tour of the campus. While on campus, parents are familiarized with the school and its programs and have an opportunity to meet with CEDU students, faculty, and administrators.

A completed application along with a $35 application fee is required prior to enrollment. The current CEDU School tuition is $3550 per month and is billed monthly. This fee includes academic education, room and board, support counseling, and program costs. A registration fee of $850 and an enrollment and orientation fee of $900, which covers the first eighteen days, are all due upon enrollment. The student expense account requires a refundable deposit of $250. A one-time linen fee of $125 is also billed. The admissions office should be telephoned in order to discuss individual insurance or application for financial assistance.

CENTURY HEALTHCARE CORPORATION

Tulsa, Oklahoma

Type: Psychiatric treatment centers offering inpatient and outpatient programs for children and adolescents

Population Served: Male and female, ages 3 to 11 in children's units, 12 to 18 in adolescent units

Size: Seven facilities with total of 384 inpatient beds

Contact: Bob Reid, Director of Marketing and Strategic Planning, Century HealthCare Corporation, Suite 200, 7615 East 63rd Place, Tulsa, Oklahoma 74133; 918-250-9651 or 800-BRIDGES

THE FACILITIES

Century HealthCare Corporation began in 1971 with the nation's only freestanding acute-care psychiatric hospital exclusively for children and adolescents. The company now consists of seven separate facilities that treat children and adolescents throughout the Southwest.

Each facility operates under the philosophy of providing the most appropriate, least restrictive, and most cost-effective treatment programs for troubled youth through a comprehensive continuum of treatment options. A variety of inpatient and outpatient programs provide evaluation; individual, group, and family therapies; special topic-oriented therapies; and after-care services, all of which offer troubled youth a chance to succeed.

Century has continually pioneered successful treatment philosophies and methods. The company introduced the first partial hospitalization program, the first in-home therapy program, and, most recently, the country's first medical/psychiatric program to address chronic medical conditions along with emotional or behavioral disorders.

In 1990, the company commissioned one of the psychiatric industry's first standardized, quantitative research studies to examine the effectiveness of its treatment programs. The outcome of the study is dramatic. Of the sample of 434 patients who were treated at various Century facilities, only 18 percent required readmission to another facility; industry averages for recidivism range from 35 to 90 percent.

This study also assisted managed health-care providers in evaluating the cost effectiveness of Century's treatment programs.

All Century facilities are accredited by the Joint Commission on Accreditation of Health Care Organizations. Additionally, most facilities are approved by the Civilian Health and Medical Program of Uniformed Services (CHAMPUS).

ELIGIBILITY

Century accommodates children and adolescents who are clinically diagnosed with a variety of specific needs. Patients with adoption/attachment issues, attention deficit hyperactivity disorder, dual diagnosis, chronic medical conditions, and severe behavioral difficulties, such as sexual abuse and perpetration or fire-setting, are accommodated, in addition to those with many other special needs. Some facilities will accommodate involuntary admissions.

ASSESSMENT

At each facility, an admissions director works with an evaluation team to determine the most appropriate level of treatment for each child or adolescent. A comprehensive, personalized treatment plan is developed, based on the patient's individual needs, to utilize the most appropriate level of care in Century's continuum. A treatment team works with the patient and family throughout the program to evaluate the youth's progress and modify the treatment to meet the patient's changing needs. Youth may enter the continuum at any level and move through the continuum as their treatment progresses.

Century facilities accept referrals from parents, teachers, mental health professionals, and other concerned persons, as well as hospitals, mental health centers, and other referral agencies.

PROGRAMS

The levels of care offered include psychiatric diagnosis, crisis intervention, acute-care hospitalization, residential treatment, partial hospitalization, transitional living, in-home therapy, and a wide range of after-care services for children, adolescents, and their families.

All Century facilities offer residential treatment and partial hospitalization programs. These programs are for youth who are experiencing emotional and/or behavioral problems at home and school but are not a significant threat to the health of the home environment. Residential treatment provides intensive, structured, 24-hour care in a medically supervised environment. Partial hospitalization provides the same therapeutic components as residential treatment; however, the setting is less restrictive, and the patient is permitted to return home in the evenings and on weekends.

Most Century facilities also offer inpatient acute care to provide a safe and secure environment for youth experiencing devastating and life-threatening problems. Once the patient is stabilized, he or she is transferred to a less intensive setting.

All inpatient programs include specialized Treatment Tracks to address special issues. These topic-oriented programs are conducted by nationally known professionals with recognized expertise in areas such as fire-setting, attention deficit hyperactivity disorders, the occult/Satanism issues, substance abuse, sexual abuse, sexual perpetration, divorce, adoption/attachment issues, and others.

Traditional individual outpatient therapy and child and adolescent support groups are available through many Century facilities.

STAFF

Each patient's treatment team consists of a psychologist, a psychiatrist, therapists, a teacher, and nurses.

SPECIAL PROGRAMS

All inpatient treatment includes accredited education programs that allow the patients to continue to progress in their local school system.

Patients benefit from recreational physical activities that serve as an integral part of the therapeutic process, including a state-of-the-art ropes course at most facilities. These activities challenge patients to address important aspects of team building, leadership, trust, and self-esteem.

Century also offers preventive services and parenting skills programs that help equip families with the proper foundation for dealing with a child or adolescent's development or rehabilitation.

CONTINUITY OF TREATMENT
Outpatient therapy is often used as an after-care component following treatment in a more restrictive inpatient setting.

BUILDINGS AND GROUNDS
All Century facilities are located on spacious campuses among natural surroundings. Each facility provides a comfortable, therapeutic environment specifically designed and decorated to appeal to the age of its patients. A relaxed, nonthreatening environment is an important element in providing less restrictive, more effective treatment.

ADMISSION AND FINANCIAL INFORMATION
Final admission decisions are made by each facility's medical and professional staff with the patient's family and the referring professional.

Costs for services at Century facilities are covered by most major medical insurance programs. Century maintains contracts with several national, regional, and local managed care companies; HMOs; self-insured health providers; and other health providers as a result of its specialized continuum of programs. Century facilities also maintain payor contracts with state and local entities and with CHAMPUS.

Experienced financial counselors assist families in determining the extent of insurance benefits available under their specific policies. Other payment plans are available based upon financial circumstances.

To inquire about Century's continuum of care or a specific level of care, call Century HealthCare at the number above.

Century HealthCare
Products and Services Matrix

		PROGRAM		BRIDGES CONTINUUM OF CARE											
		Children	Adolescents	Preventive/Educational Services	Crisis Intervention	Psychiatric Diagnosis/Evaluation	Traditional Outpatient Therapy	In-Home Psychiatric Therapy	Partial Hospitalization	Transitional Living	Therapeutic Foster Homes	Inpatient Sub-Acute Residential Treatment	Inpatient Long-Term Care	Inpatient Acute Care	After-Care Programs
CHAMPIONS	Houston, Texas	•	•	•		•		•	•			•	•		•
CHEYENNE MESA	Colorado Springs, Colorado		•	•	•	•			•			•	•		
HIGH POINTE	Oklahoma City, Oklahoma	•	•	•	•	•			•			•	•	•	
SHADOW MOUNTAIN INSTITUTE	Tulsa, Oklahoma	•	•	•	•	•	•	•	•		•	•	•	•	•
WESTBRIDGE CHILDREN	Phoenix, Arizona	•		•	•	•			•			•	•	•	•
WESTBRIDGE ADOLESCENT	Phoenix, Arizona		•	•	•	•	•	•	•	•		•	•	•	•
WILLOW CREEK	Arlington, Texas		•	•	•	•			•			•	•	•	•

CROTCHED MOUNTAIN
FOUNDATION

Greenfield, New Hampshire

Type: Preparatory school and rehabilitation center for children and adolescents with multiple handicaps

Affiliation: Subsidary of Crotched Mountain Foundation

Population Served: Male and female, grades K–12, ages 6 to 22

Size: Licensed capacity: 131; 115 students

Head of Facility: David A. Jordan, President

Contact: Debra Flanders, Admissions Manager, Crotched Mountain Preparatory School and Rehabilitation Center, 1 Verney Drive, Greenfield, New Hampshire 03047; 603-547-3311; Fax: 603-547-3232

THE SCHOOL
The Crotched Mountain Preparatory School and Rehabilitation Center was founded in 1936 by Harry A. Gregg and spans over 50 years of active service to children with special needs. Since the early 1950s, Crotched Mountain has existed as an expression of private commitment to the education, therapy, and rehabilitation of children whose needs require an extra measure of dedication and expertise. Crotched Mountain welcomes children who are challenged with a wide range of physical handicaps, learning disabilities, behavioral disorders, and special medical needs. Treatment for all children is individualized, integrated, and team-mediated.

The Crotched Mountain Foundation Quality Assurance Office coordinates and monitors program activities for the purpose of assuring the governing body and administration that Crotched Mountain Preparatory School and Rehabilitation Center functions at a level of quality described as optimal. Through a variety of surveys, audits, and site visits, the Quality Assurance Coordinator provides a continuous system of tracking that ensures that the School is providing the best possible service to its students.

Located less than 2 hours from Boston on a breathtaking 1,400-acre rural campus in Greenfield, New Hampshire, the School operates on both a 180-day school calendar and a 220-day school schedule, which includes a summer educational program. A subsidiary of Crotched Mountain Foundation, Crotched Mountain Preparatory School is a member of the National Association of Independent Schools and is accredited by the Independent School Association of Northern New England (ISANNE), National Association of Private Schools for Exceptional Children (NAPSEC), and New England Association of Schools and Colleges (NEASC).

ELIGIBILITY
Crotched Mountain Preparatory School administers to a wide range of students, including children and adolescents with multiple handicaps, cerebral palsy, spina bifida, visual and hearing impairments and other neurological disabilities, autism, developmental disorders, mental retardation, behavioral and emotional disorders, medical syndromes, seizure disorders, and traumatic brain injury.

Crotched Mountain does not accept sex offenders, children with drug and alcohol problems, or involuntary admissions.

The students are from New England, the Middle Atlantic states, Arizona, Florida, Virgin Islands, and the Pacific Rim.

ASSESSMENT
To determine the suitability of a student's admission to the School at Crotched Mountain, the following information must be provided and be current within one year of the application: complete medical history, primary care, medication, and seizure records (if applicable); recent history, physical (within the last twelve months), and diagnoses; an updated immunization record and report on visual screening; reports of the most recent psychological, neurological, orthopedic, psychiatric, and audiological consultations; current evaluations and progress reports from therapy programs, such as physical, occupational, and speech therapy; a current signed Individual Education Plan (IEP), educational evaluations, and progress notes; behavioral information (database, graph, program); activities of daily living assessment; and a complete social history summary.

A student being considered for admission at Crotched Mountain must undergo a thirty- to sixty-day evaluation period. A case manager is assigned and is responsible for the overall coordination during this period. There are assessments in the areas of education; physical, occupational, and speech therapies; and audiological, medical, and psychological services. The student's emotional and behavioral development is also assessed.

PROGRAMS
Academic and vocational classes contain no more than eight students with classroom settings and resources designed for maximum flexibility. Central to the structure of the learning process is the IEP, custom designed for each student and devised by the student's parents, the local educational agencies, and the student's Crotched Mountain team. Each student's IEP revolves around major, student-centered interdisciplinary goals to create an individualized curriculum designed to help students achieve their highest potential. Crotched Mountain's educational services include a K–12 academic curriculum, functionally based curricula, and a full range of prevocational and vocational programs, such as electricity, horticulture, a full workshop area, computer-aided drafting and machining (CAD/CAM), office occupations, and computer literacy. Computer technology is used extensively throughout the school. A typical school day runs from 8:30 a.m. to 3 p.m. with 1 hour for lunch.

In addition, the school offers independent living skills training through its home economics program, community access and awareness programs, specialized programs for head-injured adolescents, driver education services, and a fully equipped Instructional Media Center, which is integrated into all educational programs.

Twenty-four-hour medical supervision at Crotched Mountain is provided by a team of four pediatricians and a variety of consulting medical specialists. The medical director, a board-certified pediatrician, manages the development and administration of all physician services. Other medically related services available at Crotched Mountain include a dental clinic and orthopedic, neurological, podiatric, electroencephalogram (EEG), videofluoroscopy, dietary and nutritional, pharmaceutical, laboratory, and X-ray diagnostic services. Monadnock Community Hospital, a fully equipped community facility, is located 8 miles away. Crotched Mountain also maintains relationships with major teaching hospitals in Boston, Massachusetts, and Hanover, New Hampshire.

Clinical rehabilitation services at Crotched Mountain include physical therapy, occupational therapy, speech and language intervention, augmentative communication, audiology, psychology, a dysphagia/feeding team, rehabilitation engineering, and recreational programming. The efforts of clinical services are linked closely with the goals of the School through each student's IEP.

Crotched Mountain's physical education program provides a well-rounded learning experience through movement, sports, and games. Students are given the opportunity to participate according to their physical abilities. Physical education activities include Special Olympics, archery, bowling, creative dance, golf, skiing, hiking, weight lifting (isokinetics), and a summer swimming program on a private beach.

STAFF
There are 217 faculty and staff members involved in direct care who hold bachelor and graduate degrees in special education, psychology, therapeutic recreation, and other related fields. They are assisted by teachers' assistants and teachers' aides. The faculty-student ratio ranges from 1:1 to 1:4. The School seeks to hire faculty who are creative, sensitive, and dedicated to enabling each child reach his or her highest potential. The School prides itself on its tailored rehabilitation and therapeutic programs, ministered with dignity and love.

SPECIAL PROGRAMS
After-school activities consist of sports, recreational events, homework, and relaxation. The Therapeutic Recreation Department and Residential Services provide ample opportunities for participation in cultural and recreational activities in the community, including plays, concerts, movies, museums, and hikes. In addition, care is taken to provide the students with opportunities to visit local shopping centers, libraries, and any other local attractions. Bowling, bingo, dances, boy scouts and girl scouts, and other activities are available on campus.

Arrangements are made for Catholic, Protestant, and Jewish services and religious instruction throughout the year.

CONTINUITY OF TREATMENT
Case Management seeks to ensure that each student maximizes his/her potential by advocating for adequate and appropriate services and follow-through of the IEP. Case Managers serve as liaisons to parents or guardians, the local school district, and any other agencies. Case Managers seek to empower parents and guardians to become effective advocates for their children.

BUILDINGS AND GROUNDS
The campus includes a twenty-six-classroom school, a pool and therapy complex, a specialty hospital, group homes, a health center, lakefront property, athletic fields, staff housing, and a day-care center.

Students live on-campus in a residential complex of nine group homes and in Foxmeadow Apartments, a complex for independent living, also on campus. This group-home neighborhood of four-bedroom ranch-style houses includes a park area and playground. The homes are fully equipped with wheelchair accessible appliances, kitchen facilities, new and modern furnishings, and a guest room for visitors.

Crotched Mountain maintains a fully licensed specialty hospital nursing facility for medically involved children who require ongoing nursing services. The nursing facility is adjacent to the School and makes it possible for students with significant medical challenges to attend Crotched Mountain Preparatory School and participate fully in educational and therapeutic programs.

The beautiful, new James E. Chandler Pool Complex is available for use by all students attending Crotched Mountain. Within the complex is a 25-yard recreation pool as well as a 25-foot by 25-foot therapy pool, which has a hydraulic floor that adjusts the depth to the level most beneficial to the student. Students participate in several aquatic programs, including Special Olympics, scuba diving, swimming lessons, and recreational swims. Physical and occupational therapy sessions take place in the therapy pool.

ADMISSIONS AND FINANCIAL INFORMATION
Crotched Mountain accepts most major medical plans, Medicare, and Medicaid. Local school districts and private payment arrangements may also be arranged. The admissions office makes every effort to assist students and families with the process of admission and is extremely flexible in maintaining an orderly flow of information among the student, family, referent, and Admissions Committee.

New Orleans, Louisiana

Type: Psychiatric hospital and residential treatment center

Affiliation: Hospital Corporation of America

Population: Male and female; children, adolescents, and adults

Size: Child Acute Program–24; Adolescent Acute Program–56; Residential Treatment Center–56; total child and adolescent services–136

Heads of Facility: Greg Steele, Chief Executive Officer; Robert Lancaster, Medical Director

Contact: Nancy Cranton, Director of Respond, DePaul Hospital, 1040 Calhoun Street, New Orleans, Louisiana 70118; 504-899-8282 or 800-548-4183; fax: 504-897-5775

THE HOSPITAL

In the midst of the chaos that marked the year 1861, a small group of nuns began treating the mentally ill in New Orleans.

Since then, the Daughters of Charity of St. Vincent de Paul, and now the Hospital Corporation of America, have brought a new age of enlightenment to the treatment of mental health issues. The evolution of psychiatry and chemical dependency can be seen throughout DePaul's 130 years of growth and progress.

DePaul is located on a 13-acre campus in the heart of uptown New Orleans. Carefully spaced buildings, oak trees, spacious lawns, and flower gardens all contribute to a feeling of security and tranquility.

Owned by the Hospital Corporation of America, DePaul Hospital is accredited by the Joint Commission on Accreditation of Healthcare Organizations, is licensed by the state of Louisiana, and approved to care for CHAMPUS and Medicare patients.

DePaul provides care for all age groups: children, adolescents, and adults.

ELIGIBILITY

DePaul's rich heritage and diversity of care stand alone in the New Orleans area. Presenting problems (for children and adolescents) include depression, substance abuse, conduct disorders, eating disorders, sexual trauma issues, family problems, issues of suicide, chronic problems at school, and attention deficit hyperactivity disorder.

Most admissions to DePaul are voluntary, but the hospital does accept involuntary admissions.

The majority of acute-care patients come from the communities surrounding New Orleans. DePaul Hospital Residential Treatment Center is the only CHAMPUS-approved residential facility in Louisiana and Mississippi. Residential patients come from all over the southeastern United States.

ASSESSMENT

Admission to DePaul Hospital is reviewed by the admission and assessment center. The assessments, which are available 24 hours a day, seven days a week, help determine which treatment options would be most beneficial to the patient. If a child or adolescent does not have a personal physician or psychiatrist, DePaul's trained staff helps decide what is needed and then refers the patient to a child or adolescent psychiatrist or mental health professional.

All admission decisions are made by board-eligible or board-certified psychiatrists or addictionists. Referrals can be made by family physicians, psychologists, social workers, school counselors, ministers, agencies, or caring individuals.

Residential Treatment Center admissions are based on clinical criteria. During the initial telephone conversation, clinical information is necessary to determine if the patient needs residential care. Before a decision is made, a complete packet of information, including, but not limited to, an educational assessment, a social history, and psychiatric and psychological evaluations, must be reviewed by DePaul's clinical staff.

PROGRAM

DePaul offers a full continuum of treatment, including acute inpatient, residential, outpatient, partial hospitalization, and aftercare.

The Child and Adolescent Service, which uses behavior modification and insight therapy to treat young people under the age of 18, is one of the largest and most comprehensive in the United States. DePaul believes that children and adolescents should be treated separately from adults in an environment that is created especially for children.

The five child and adolescent programs are the Children's Program, the Adolescent Acute Program, the Pre-Adolescent Residential Behavior Modification Treatment Program, the Adolescent Residential Behavioral Modification Treatment Program, and the Adolescent Residential Program.

Three adult programs are also offered for both chemical dependency and psychiatric issues.

STAFF

DePaul feels that it is the quality of their staff that distinguishes their care. While the campus and facilities are comprehensive and provide patients with an environment that is conducive to their progressing in their treatment, the quality of care enjoyed by the patients is a direct result of the effort of DePaul's caring, dedicated staff.

DePaul's well-trained staff includes physicians, psychologists, psychiatric technicians, nurses, teachers, pastoral counselors, social workers, a speech therapist, creative arts therapists, and a host of other support people.

DePaul takes a multidisciplinary approach to treatment, with contributions to each patient's case made from each represented specialty. From the day of admission, each patient has an individualized treatment plan and a treatment team that plan for the patient's discharge. This ensures that the patients are working toward achievable goals and will be reunited with their families as soon as possible.

SPECIAL PROGRAMS

For children and adolescents, the educational experience at DePaul includes the Lancaster Academy, which is an accredited school for K through 12. The classrooms are equipped with state-of-the-art teaching aids, such as computers, to aid educational growth. A low student-to-teacher ratio is further enhanced by having master's-level teachers on staff.

CONTINUITY OF TREATMENT

DePaul considers the continuity of treatment important. Once inpatient treatment draws to a close, DePaul believes in caring for the patient on an outpatient basis, through partial hospitalization, or in aftercare. Upon discharge, the patient is returned to the referring professional for outpatient treatment. Arrangements can also be made through the Respond Office to match community resources with the patient's needs.

The staff at DePaul works closely with families and the child's support systems to maximize gains while in treatment.

BUILDINGS AND GROUNDS

DePaul Hospital has seven main buildings. The five floors of the Lancaster Building are strictly for children and adolescents; residential living areas occupy the first four floors with the school housed on the fifth floor. Each floor is secure and

separate, specific to age and level of care needed. The adult patients at DePaul are housed in two other buildings on campus.

Much of the Lancaster Building was recently renovated, and, as a result, DePaul is able to offer both private and semiprivate rooms, depending on the child's needs. Each floor has a creative arts therapy area, a day room with a TV and video games, a kitchen area, and a group room. A free-standing cafeteria, located across campus, is available for children and adolescents depending on the specific patient's progress.

Patients enjoy the use of a full-court indoor gym, Olympic-size swimming pool, outdoor volleyball courts, and gardens. Art therapy, ceramics, movement and dance, and recreational, leisure, and vocational therapies are some of the special activities utilized during treatment.

One very special aspect of DePaul Hospital is that the hospital is located next to Audubon Park. The jogging path, oak trees, lagoons with ducks, and pavilions are perfect counterparts to DePaul's own grounds.

ADMISSION AND FINANCIAL INFORMATION

The admission and assessment center can help make all the necessary medical and financial arrangements for admission. The cost of treatment for both acute inpatient care and residential treatment is covered by most health-care insurers. The extent of coverage and other financial considerations can be discussed prior to admission.

For a free assessment or admission information, call the Respond Office at 800-548-4183.

DESISTO SCHOOL

Stockbridge, Massachusetts

Type: Coeducational, college-preparatory boarding school for students with special emotional and educational needs

Affiliation: The DeSisto School

Population Served: Adolescents and young adults, 13 to 20 years of age

Size: Licensed for 175 beds

Head of Facility: A. Michael DeSisto, Executive Director

Contact: Constance Real, Director of Admissions, The DeSisto School, Route 183, Stockbridge, Massachusetts 01262; 413-298-3776; fax: 413-298-5175

THE SCHOOL

Michael DeSisto founded the DeSisto School in 1978. The campus is located in Stockbridge, Massachusetts, 150 miles west of Boston, 65 miles south of Albany, 160 miles north of New York, and 2 miles from Tanglewood, the summer home of the Boston Symphony Orchestra.

DeSisto was founded on the belief that an individual's intellectual and emotional lives are interdependent. The school's program is designed to create a nurturing environment in which a student's problems can be confronted openly, promoting responsibility and academic and emotional growth. DeSisto's environment requires each student to take control of his or her life's direction and progress. The intellect is stimulated through an active, participatory, and creative academic program. Emotional growth is facilitated by a highly refined, comprehensive, and extensive set of support structures and interactions. Problems with relationships and intimacy are frequently core issues for DeSisto's students. Confronting and working toward the resolution of issues allows the responsible and creative person within to emerge.

Family involvement is required. Monthly parent support groups are facilitated by school staff throughout the United States. Weekend parent workshops, parent/child workshops, and family therapy sessions are essential components of the program. Faculty, students, parents, and therapists interact constantly, creating the consistency and continuity the program requires for success.

DeSisto School's curriculum is approved by the Berkshire Hills Regional School District in accordance with Massachusetts General Laws, Chapter 76, Section 1. DeSisto School works closely with Special Educational Departments in order to serve those students on Individual Educational Plans (IEP).

DeSisto School is a nonprofit corporation under the direction of a seven-member Board of Trustees.

ELIGIBILITY

A typical adolescent coming to DeSisto has been unsuccessful at home and/or in other settings and is in need of structure and therapy. He or she is an adolescent unable to live at home due to persistent emotional, psychiatric, and/or drug-related problems and is not able to benefit from outpatient therapy. Presenting diagnoses and conditions often include adjustment disorders, substance abuse, conduct and anxiety disorders, depression, borderline and narcissistic personality disorders, addictions, suicidal and self-mutilating behaviors, and eating disorders. Admission referrals come from all areas of the United States. While most admissions are voluntary, accommodations can be made for involuntary admissions when appropriate. DeSisto is very proud of its ability to individualize treatment modalities to better serve its students.

ASSESSMENT

Admission referrals are made by professionals, parents, educational consultants, and other schools. Admission is based on an intensive intake interview focusing on individual and family psychodynamics; psychological and psychiatric evaluations; psycho-educational, cognitive testing; and school records.

PROGRAMS

DeSisto School is therapeutic in its entirety. Both staff and students form the support community that is crucial to the success of DeSisto's highly refined behavior modification program. Students participate in individual psychotherapy, one to two times weekly and in groups daily. Additional focus groups (adoption, return-from-hospital, inner child, sexuality) are essential; twelve-step groups, including AA, OA, SLAA, and NA, are utilized both on and off campus. Psychodrama, art, recreation, and therapy are incorporated when appropriate. Family work includes intensive multifamily weekend workshops and individual family therapy sessions.

It is the comprehensive nature of the entire therapy program that helps students begin to reduce the self-defeating acting-out behaviors, build self-awareness, and develop a sense of responsibility for themselves and others. Students develop appropriate methods of recognizing and meeting needs and interacting with the world.

Admissions are made year-round. Completion and graduation varies with each student, but the average length of stay is two to three years.

STAFF

DeSisto School is staffed with highly motivated and committed people who are expected to model life's growth processes.

The DeSisto staff includes credentialed secondary-level teachers, a certified special educational instructor, an academic counselor, advisers, dance instructors, and voice and drama specialists. The clinical staff includes a fully credentialed psychiatrist, general and specialty therapists, a nursing staff, activities therapists, and specialists in the areas of eating disorders and chemical dependency.

SPECIAL PROGRAMS

Taking its founding premise seriously requires the school to be both emotionally therapeutic and academically motivating. To accomplish this takes an interdisciplinary staff and a consistency and continuity of both structure and timing. The school's special activities component is clearly an example of such design quality. Options include drama, dance, athletics, cooking, music studies, arts, country cultural study, marine biology in the Florida Keys, and student-designed projects.

Academics and tutorials continue throughout the year. Auxiliary programs include European and domestic trips, dinner-theater programs, cross-country biking, hiking, and camping. Junior College classes are also available. Religious preferences and services are supported. Nutritional needs and medication requirements are addressed by the appropriate staff.

Parents are required to participate in the monthly group sessions that are held in the parents' geographic area and facilitated by the school staff. Special focus groups are designed for parents, as are parent and child workshops. On-campus and off-campus twelve-step programs are suggested and encouraged when appropriate for students and parents.

CONTINUITY OF TREATMENT

Throughout the program, the focus is on preparing the student for a successful transition to his or her home community. Students completing DeSisto's program should be able to participate in either a college or employment setting. Students are experienced in their ability to determine what they need and how to find it in their community.

The postgraduate program is a unique component of DeSisto School. The program begins with graduation and continues for a minimum of one year. During this period the student and/or parents may need to reconnect with the school and its support system as part of the transition process. Alumni support groups are encouraged, and summer work experience is available. Individual therapy and twelve-step

programs available in the student's own community are familiar supports and may be continued. Parental and family groups are effective tools and should also continue for at least one year.

BUILDINGS AND GROUNDS

A beautiful nineteenth-century mansion is the center of DeSisto's 300-acre Massachusetts campus. Students live in dormitories supervised by resident Dorm Parents. The number of students per room usually varies from two to four, and the dorms function as close family units with 24-hour supervision. The school buildings, gymnasium, dining hall, and dormitories are within sight of the Administrative Mansion. Faculty housing is conveniently located throughout the central campus.

ADMISSION AND FINANCIAL INFORMATION

The admissions office works with parents and professionals in processing enrollments, which are accepted year-round. When necessary, a family interview can be arranged quickly and the prospective student can be enrolled immediately. The student need not be compliant, though this is not the norm. The 1992–93 cost for 365 days is approximately $34,000 plus individual weekly therapy sessions, which are billed at an estimated $4000. The total cost of the program has been accepted by the Internal Revenue Service as an allowable medical expense.

The school works with parents on payment plans and has provided financial aid up to 5 percent of the annual gross budget.

In the past, the school has received full payment from participating insurance programs. Public school funding may also be approved for students with appropriate IEPs.

Devon, Pennsylvania

Type: A nationwide network of residential, day, and community-based treatment programs

Affiliation: Nonprofit, private

Population Served: Male and female, ages 3 to geriatric, who have a wide range of emotional and developmental disorders

Size: Licensed capacity, nationwide: 2,000; Devereux programs are located in 13 states

Head of Facility: Ronald P. Burd, President and CEO

Contact: National Referral Services, 19 South Waterloo Road, Devon, PA 19333; 800-345-1292, ext. 3045, or 215-964-3045

THE ORGANIZATION

Devereux was founded in 1912 by a remarkable Philadelphia educator, Helena Trafford Devereux, who recognized the need of special people to feel useful, successful, and worthwhile. She provided opportunities for individuals whose needs were frequently unmet by traditional school systems or other organizations.

Pioneering the multidisciplinary approach to treatment, Helena Devereux brought together professionals in psychiatry, psychology, education, social work, and other disciplines to design, develop, and implement treatment plans tailored to the needs of each individual in care.

While Devereux programs vary in the types of educational and treatment programs provided, they are steadfast in ensuring that every experience in the daily life of each client is therapeutic. Activities encourage success and achievement while discouraging frustration and failure.

This emphasis on extracting full therapeutic benefit from all activities complements Devereux's broad spectrum of settings, ranging from the most protective to the least restrictive. These elements have made Devereux one of the largest and most comprehensive organizations of its kind.

Devereux programs provide services around-the-clock, year-round.

Established in 1991, Devereux's regional structure allows individuals in care to be treated as close to their homes and communities as possible. The organization is structured in four parts. In the Northeast Region, programs are offered in Massachusetts, Connecticut, and New York, while the Mid-Atlantic Region is served by programs in New Jersey, Pennsylvania, Delaware, and Maryland. Programs in Georgia, Tennessee, and Florida serve the Southeast Region, and Texas-, Arizona-, and California-based programs serve the Western Region.

Devereux is licensed and approved by appropriate education and health-care agencies, including the Joint Commission on Accreditation of Healthcare Organizations (JCAHO), the Commission on Accreditation of Rehabilitation Facilities (CARF), and other accreditors.

Devereux is governed by a national Board of Trustees; many centers have volunteer auxiliary and/or advisory boards. In addition, many boards have family representation.

ELIGIBILITY

Individuals admitted to Devereux programs may exhibit the following presenting problems: psychiatric disorders, behavioral disturbances, emotional disturbances, neurological impairments, developmental and learning disabilities, mental retardation, autism, and post-traumatic head injuries.

Other problems most frequently encountered include dual diagnoses (by definition: a primary diagnosis of mental retardation and a secondary of emotional disorder).

Homicidal or fire-setting histories are carefully considered by specific centers.

Admissions are based on facility treatment resources and Devereux's ability to effectively manage the presenting problems of particular clients. Exclusions are determined by treatment teams on a case-by-case basis.

PROGRAMS

All Devereux treatment centers follow multidisciplinary treatment modalities, with each modality—clinical, educational, residential, and recreational—given equal emphasis in the program plan for each individual.

Devereux's continuum of care ranges from the most protective setting to the least restrictive environment, providing a client with the ability to move from secure through intermediate to open residential settings.

An important element of Devereux's programming is that initially individuals, depending on their presenting problems, may be placed in any of the above settings.

Basic requirements for treatment at Devereux are individually determined.

Devereux clients have their own daily schedules as indicated in their individual treatment program plan. As their progress changes or as needs dictate, the treatment plan is modified.

The Devereux treatment network includes five specialized psychiatric hospitals for children and adolescents and a center for young adults with head trauma.

Special features within the Devereux network include the following: vocational and prevocational programs as well as actual job experiences; a program for hearing-impaired, emotionally disturbed adolescent males; programs in several states for youngsters with autism; a program for individuals who have Prader-Willi syndrome or Tourette syndrome; programs for survivor groups—including the sexually abused and the abuser; step-down programs for eating disorders and substance abuse (both following acute care); and other individually tailored programs.

For young people approaching graduation, criteria are individually addressed, based on intellectual ability and academic growth of the client. In some programs, graduates may receive a diploma from Devereux or from their own school district.

Scheduled to open in the fall of 1992 is the Devereux Hospital and Neurobehavioral Institute of Texas. Located on 49 acres in the Houston suburb of League City, the facility will serve individuals from 6 to 36 who have severe emotional disturbances, severe conduct disorders, pervasive developmental disorders, or brain injury.

Families are encouraged to participate in the client's treatment program—either through home visits or family visits to the program.

STAFF

Across the country, Devereux employs more than 2,800 full-time and 850 part-time direct-care, administrative, and support staff.

Staffing includes fully credentialed professionals in the following categories: psychiatry (child, adolescent, and adult), psychology, education, (elementary, secondary, and special education), medicine, pediatrics, nutrition and dietetics, art, music and dance therapy, physical education, therapies, such as occupational, physical, and speech; animal-assisted therapy, dietetics and nutrition, social services, and vocational rehabilitation.

A typical Devereux treatment team includes the following: a psychiatrist, medical doctor, psychologist, social worker, educator, and other professionals as indicated.

SPECIAL PROGRAMS

Devereux clients are exposed to a wealth of cultural, educational, and recreational activities in the communities where centers are located. In addition, some centers have teams of volunteers who provide new and enriching learning experiences for clients.

Across the country, hundreds of Devereux clients participate in Special Olympics competitions; others belong to Boy and Girl Scout Troops, and many belong to such support groups as Al-Anon and Al-Ateen.

Devereux offers focused seminars to families of individuals with special needs. These workshops are offered not only to Devereux families but also to the community in general.

CONTINUITY OF TREATMENT

From the day of admission, Devereux staff—working with referral sources, families, and the individual, when appropriate—are preparing for a smooth transition to the next level of care. As indicated in the program section of this description, Devereux's continuum of care ranges from the most protective to the least restrictive setting.

In most Devereux centers, clients can progress to transitional and independent living—in a wide range of environments, including group homes or apartments.

Devereux, in some locations, offers the following programs: respite care, partial hospitalization, and foster care. The majority of Devereux centers also offer day care.

BUILDINGS AND GROUNDS

Devereux clients reside in warm, homelike settings in suburban and/or rural campuses. Residences are conducive to therapy as well as comfort.

ADMISSION AND FINANCIAL INFORMATION

Devereux accepts a wide range of payment options and is a preferred provider for several managed health-care companies. Admissions procedures vary among Devereux centers.

Admissions staff members are vigilant in assisting clients and their families with the admission process; each is committed to maintaining an orderly flow of information among family, referral source, clinical treatment team, and client when appropriate.

ÉLAN SCHOOL

Poland Spring, Maine

Type: Boarding school
Affiliation: Corporate ownership—Élan One Corp.; for-profit
Population Served: Male and female, ages 13 to 20
Size: Unrestricted
Head of Facility: Joseph Ricci, Executive Director
Contact: Deanna L. Atkinson, Admissions Director, Élan School, RR1, Box 370, Poland Spring, Maine 04274-9711; 207-998-4666; fax: 207-998-4660

THE SCHOOL
Founded in 1970, Élan School is a carefully conceptualized, caringly administered residential community for adolescents with behavioral, emotional, or adjustment problems. Students are often estranged from their families, have fallen prey to negative peer pressure, or have failed in school. Élan's unique program helps adolescents see the causes and consequences of their conduct and teaches them the skills of responsible living.

Élan's mission is to change the direction of adolescents whose lives seem out of control. Élan accomplishes this in a therapeutic community, under strong staff direction and supervision, using positive peer pressure and relatively high levels of confrontation.

Élan encourages substantial family involvement, with emphasis on repairing and rebuilding strained parent/child relationships.

Élan is open year-round and corporately controlled.

The 32-acre campus is located in a small, rural resort community in central Maine, 40 minutes from Portland and 20 minutes from Lewiston/Auburn. The property is bordered on two sides by woods and on one side by a lake; vehicle access is limited to one unpaved road. The remote site is conducive to privacy and its proximity to Upper Range Pond affords recreational pursuits in season.

Élan is accredited by the Maine Department of Education as a private special purpose school, grades 7–12. Staff memberships include Maine Association of Directors of Services for Exceptional Children, Guidance Counselors Association, Independent Educational Consultants Association, Maine Association for Counseling and Development, and American Orthopsychiatric Association.

While moral support and networking are provided informally by parents and alumni, there is no financial support provided directly by the school.

ELIGIBILITY
Students who exhibit defiance of authorities, underachievement, and poor peer and/or family relationships are eligible for admission to Élan.

Main diagnoses among Élan students are conduct disorder, attention deficit disorder, and oppositional defiant disorder.

Students not considered for admission are those who have a major mental illness, have cognitive deficits, are actively violent, need psychotropic medications, have a physical condition requiring major dietetic restriction or constant medical attention, or are non-English-speaking.

At the time of admission, minor students need not express a willingness to cooperate; however, students 18 and over (not court-committed) must be interviewed to ascertain their personal commitment to the full eighteen- to twenty-four-month program.

Involuntary admissions are common and referral to private security transport providers is available upon request.

Students are admitted at any time year-round (scheduled and emergencies) and have come from all parts of the U.S. and abroad. Numbers of males and females fluctuate as a result of "rolling admissions" and the current population is seventy-four males and fifty-seven females.

ASSESSMENT
Professional and personal referrals are accepted, and the data needed for admission assessment is as follows: Psychological Evaluation including social history, presenting problem, IQ and Personality Test results, diagnosis (where not available, equivalent documentation is acceptable), and Education Summary listing present grade, learning disabilities and IEP (special education students).

All services provided at Élan are based on external referrals and assessments.

Psychological Evaluations can be arranged; IEPs, Kaufman's Achievement Tests, and other tests are administered as needed.

PROGRAMS
The basic goal at Élan is the development and internalization of a positive value system. For some students, this amounts to a characterological change.

Élan expects students to continue to practice the life skills learned at Élan after graduation from the program. The Re-Entry Phase is designed to provide a transition to the reduced structure of post-Élan (everyday) living. Outpatient therapy may be considered essential, ancillary, or unnecessary depending upon the individual.

The principal modalities of education used at Élan are group therapy, life skills learning, and milieu therapy within a total therapeutic community.

Graduation criteria are 20 credits: (education) 4 English, 1 U.S. history, 1 other history, 2 science (1 lab), 2 math, 1 art (humanities, theater, music), 1 physical education, 1/2 health (program), 1 applied psychology, 2 life skills, successful completion of the Re-Entry Phase, and electives.

A full week includes 25 hours of educational programming, 6 hours of individual counseling, and 10 hours of group counseling.

There is a complex hierarchy of job positions with multiple opportunities for success, failure, and resilience in the face of failure, with emphasis on achievement and an "everything must be earned" philosophy. Small class size, a student-to-teacher ratio of 10:1, and an adjustable curriculum help to meet students' special needs. Additionally, students are actively involved in creating a positive educational environment; school during evening hours allows students to work through behaviors that interfere with concentration and learning. Teachers are certified in their subject areas and in one or more areas of special education. Students receive immediate feedback on both positive and negative behaviors, are held accountable for their own behavior, and are motivated to take an active role in planning for their futures. Quarterly progress reports reflect both educational and therapeutic progress.

Élan is a testing site for the PSAT, SAT, and ACT.

A typical weekday schedule includes jobs, counseling, recreation, and physical education between 8 a.m. and 6:30 p.m., followed by school until 10:30 p.m. On weekends there are religious services (as requested) as well as free time, trips, and movies.

Parents visit Élan at the four- to six-month point for a scheduled, structured counseling session with the student and therapeutic staff. Following that Parent Group, parents take their child (and usually another Élan student) off-grounds (not home) for the weekend. Two or three months after the initial Parent Group, students begin taking progressively longer home visits contingent upon their progress in rebuilding the relationship as well as overall progress. Additional meetings at the school are scheduled if needed.

STAFF

Élan's staff is made up of a clinical director/Ph.D., an M.S.W., an L.S.W., two nurses, a physician (1 day per week on-site, 24-hour on call), twenty-two therapeutic staff (degreed/experienced), sixteen special education teachers (dual certified: special education/subject area), a guidance director, a special education director, and a certified physical education instructor.

A typical treatment team consists of a therapeutic educational coordinator, a therapist, a caseworker, a director of education, and a guidance director. Weekly meetings between the teaching and therapeutic teams are held to assess progress and problem areas and plan strategies. Informal consultations among clinicians are conducted on an as-needed basis.

SPECIAL PROGRAMS

Élan offers trips (winter skiing, white-water rafting, deep-sea fishing, sailing, windsurfing, water skiing, camping, bicycling, colleges, theater, restaurants), tours (e.g., Washington, D.C., Boston), seminars, and "ethnic meals" (prepared by students).

Élan School is nonsectarian. Students' participation in religious services and activities is voluntary but encouraged.

CONTINUITY OF TREATMENT

Élan prepares students for college or a return to high school and plans cooperatively with school districts. If it is deemed necessary, a recommendation and/or referral for additional therapy is made.

The last three months of Élan's program, entitled the Re-Entry Phase, are individually constructed to facilitate a confident and productive transition into the community.

BUILDINGS AND GROUNDS

Among Élan's thirteen buildings, three large frame houses serve as dormitories and house forty-five students each. There is coed dining, working and studying, counseling, separate male/female bathrooms, and dorm-style bedrooms that have four to six people per room. Staff live off-grounds, but a rotating 43-hour work week provides round-the-clock supervision and familiarity with all students.

A physician visits Élan one day a week and is on call at all other times. Two full-time nurses attend to minor medical problems, monitor overall health, and refer to area physicians and dentists when necessary. An area hospital and ambulance service handle emergencies.

Meals are prepared in a central kitchen and served family-style in house dining rooms to staff and students.

The wooded, lakeside campus affords a full waterfront program. Special trips utilize Maine's many outdoor recreational opportunities.

ADMISSION AND FINANCIAL INFORMATION

The 1992 total annual cost is $38,755 and is billed monthly at $3229.58 (components: education, $11,327; counseling and related services, $15,622; room and board, $11,806). The daily rate is $106.18. A student's personal account for sundries averages $100 per month and is billed separately.

Students may be eligible for coverage under psychological/psychiatric benefits by private carriers as "case management," "exception," or "alternative to normal plan benefits," etc.

All fees are billed monthly. Fees due the day of admission are the balance of the present month (if before the 15th; after the 16th, the following month's fees also) plus three-month prepayment (applied to final three months of program) and student personal account deposit of $200. No financial aid is provided by Élan School directly; however, students not funded privately (this designation includes full or partial private health insurance contributions) may be eligible for assistance through local school districts if coded special education, or public welfare, or any combination of the above. At present, 80 percent of students receive full or partial assistance.

A current Psychological Evaluation and Educational Summary are reviewed by the Admissions Committee. Questions of appropriateness are resolved by telephone; in some cases, a personal interview is required. If criteria are met, the referral source is notified, funding is verified, and admission arrangements are made. Students are admitted Monday through Thursday. By the date of admission, school transcripts, birth certificate, immunizations, admissions application, medical authorizations, and any applicable legal documents must be submitted. Visits are encouraged, prior to enrollment if possible; but in emergency situations, parents are given a tour on admission day. A student's legal guardian must accompany him or her on the day of admission.

Katonah, New York

Type: Psychiatric hospital with four adolescent units
Affiliation: Operated by Four Winds, Inc.
Population Served: Male and female, ages 13 to adult, 13 to 17 in adolescent units
Size: Licensed capacity, 175; 55 adolescents
Head of Facility: Samuel C. Klagsbrun, M.D.
Contact: Diane Biumi, Director of Admissions, 800 Cross River Road, Katonah, New York 10536; 914-763-8151 or 800-KATONAH

THE HOSPITAL

The "new" Four Winds was established in 1978, when psychiatrist Samuel C. Klagsbrun, M.D., purchased Four Winds Hospital, a psychiatric hospital located on a beautiful and serene 55-acre campus 50 miles north of New York City. Today, under the clinical direction of Dr. Klagsbrun, Four Winds provides a broad range of psychiatric treatment services for adolescents, young adults, and adults.

The hospital is accredited by the Joint Commission on Accreditation of Healthcare Organizations (JCAHO) and is licensed by the New York State Office of Mental Health.

ELIGIBILITY

Patients must be in need of acute psychiatric care. Most admissions are voluntary, but under appropriate clinical circumstances Four Winds is able to accommodate involuntary admissions.

Four Winds places a high priority on integrating the care of patients with multiple problems. Clinical specialists with particular expertise in each problem area are available to each patient's treatment team. Among treatment modalities available are focused groups for patients sharing a common problem and educational services that address the special academic and treatment needs of the patients.

In addition to general psychiatric treatment services, Four Winds offers special clinical services to patients with dual diagnosis/chemical dependency, eating disorders, and to those burdened by severe and persistent emotional illness. Treatment for all patients is individualized, integrated, and team-mediated.

ASSESSMENT

Following an intensive period of evaluation, each patient's program is designed to meet his or her unique needs and issues. The protocol for individual evaluation includes a comprehensive psychodiagnostic assessment, a psychoeducational evaluation, a family dynamics assessment, a school assessment, a detailed assessment of cognitive functioning, a neuropsychological evaluation (when indicated), forensic psychological testing (when indicated), and numerous screening assessments to determine further testing.

PROGRAM

Patients participate in a variety of intensive, structured therapeutic activities daily. These include individual and group therapy, focused groups on special topics (such as issues related to medication), psychodrama, art therapy,

recreation therapy, and discharge-preparation group. Families are an important part of treatment and participate weekly in family therapy and multiple family-group therapy. Activities of clear therapeutic benefit, such as schooling, AA and NA meetings, supervised study (1 evening hour per day), and structured recreation, are an integral part of the program, when clinically appropriate.

Adolescent patients are subject to a system that lowers the level of supervision and raises the level of responsibility for those who are progressing well. Both staff members and peers participate in setting the levels. Higher-level patients have significant freedom and may be allowed to leave the grounds briefly with their families; lower-level patients are restricted to direct staff observation.

The length of stay at Four Winds varies. A patient may be hospitalized for a week or less for a diagnostic evaluation; intensive treatment will take longer. The goals for treatment include proper and comprehensive diagnosis, stabilization of symptoms, preparation for less intensive care in other settings, networking community resources to support the patient after discharge, connecting families with appropriate support services and preparing them to support the patient's care, and adjusting educational planning to meet education needs. Patients are ready for discharge to a less intensive setting when those goals are attained.

STAFF

The adolescent service is staffed with an interdisciplinary team of fully credentialed psychiatrists, clinical psychologists, clinical social workers, nursing staff, and mental health workers. The clinical team also includes activities therapists, nutritionists, and educators. In addition, specialists in the areas of eating disorders, severe and persistent mental illness, dual diagnoses (psychiatric/chemical dependency), and learning disabilities participate in the treatment on a fully integrated basis, following initial evaluation and elaboration of the individual treatment plan.

ANCILLARY SERVICES

Four Winds Hospital provides educational services through an on-campus secondary school. The curriculum includes college-preparatory work as well as basic skills. Special emphasis is on finding creative ways to meet the needs of learning-disabled and emotionally disturbed children. The school also emphasizes life skills and coping mechanisms for patients with emotional and cognitive handicaps, as well as assessment, discharge planning, and advocacy to ensure that educational needs are met after discharge.

Physical development and recreation are addressed through a well-structured program of recreation therapy, physical education, and other supervised recreational endeavors. This is supported with highly qualified professional staff and the best of recreation equipment.

Most medical issues not requiring medical hospitalization can be addressed at Four Winds–Westchester. Northern Westchester Hospital, a fully equipped community facility, is located minutes away. Nutritional needs are addressed by dietary evaluation and counseling in conjunction with the patient's overall treatment plan.

Four Winds supports spiritual development on a fully individual basis; the hospital offers an elective ecumenical religious service weekly.

CONTINUITY OF TREATMENT

Four Winds views the treatment it provides as one important aspect within a clinical care continuum, offering the opportunity to focus intensively on evaluation, relief of symptoms, and careful discharge planning. Most patients begin their therapeutic work before admission, and, to help maintain continuity, the hospital relies on clinical data supplied by the patient's referring therapist and maintains contact with that clinician during hospitalization. Upon discharge, the patient continues outpatient treatment with the referring professional to the extent clinically appropriate. Arrangements may also be made with community resources to ensure continuing support.

Both discharge planners in the education program and the social work staff of the hospital plan from the day of admission for a smooth transition to the next level of care. Patients who are able to return home at night but still require intensive therapeutic support may live at home and attend a full day of activities on their old unit under the Transitional Aftercare Day Program.

An intensive outpatient program called CHOICES is available after school for adolescents with drug and/or alcohol problems as part of the full-service clinic for adolescents and adults.

Through its office in New York City, Four Winds offers complete outpatient psychiatric evaluations and an educational consulting service for all ages.

BUILDINGS AND GROUNDS

Patients reside in homelike, fifteen-bed cottages, or units, with their own treatment program and full-time interdisciplinary clinical team. This intimate setting and consistent staffing allow patients to feel comfortable and secure.

Within each of the four adolescent units, boys are on separate corridors from girls. Rooms normally contain two beds, but singles and triples are available to accommodate varying clinical conditions and issues. Private bath facilities are located within a few doors of each room.

Four Winds' patients share the use of a central dining facility; food is comparable to that available in better restaurants. They also share a fully equipped gymnasium, an exercise room, an outdoor swimming pool, and a challenge course. The grounds are spacious, lending an open and noninstitutional quality.

ADMISSION AND FINANCIAL INFORMATION

Four Winds Hospital accepts most major medical plans, Medicare, and Medicaid (for patients younger than 21 or older than 65). Private payment arrangements may also be negotiated. Four Winds is on the preferred provider list of several managed care companies. The admissions office is extremely flexible in assisting patients and families with the potentially burdensome process of admission into a hospital setting and is committed to maintaining an orderly flow of information among patient, family, referrent, and clinical treatment team. Four Winds is available to admit patients 24 hours a day, 7 days a week.

THE GREENWOOD SCHOOL

Putney, Vermont

Type: Boarding school

Affiliation: Nonprofit

Population Served: Dyslexic males ages 8 to 15

Size: 40 students

Head of Facility: Thomas D. Scheidler, M.S.

Contact: John Alexander, Admissions Coordinator, RR 2, Box 270, Putney, Vermont 05346; 802-387-4545; fax: 802-387-5396

THE SCHOOL

The Greenwood School was established in 1978 by Tom and Andrea Scheidler, the Greenwood School's directors, and a board of trustees comprised of parents of current and graduated students. The school's mission is to remediate the language deficits of bright, dyslexic boys while at the same time encouraging them to develop their strengths in the areas of art, drama, music, sports, and leadership capabilities. The verdant hills of Putney, Vermont (2½ hours from Boston and 4 hours from New York City) are home to the 100-acre campus.

Greenwood is accredited by both the state of Vermont and the New England Association of Schools and Colleges.

ELIGIBILITY

The typical Greenwood student presents something of an educational enigma. Intelligence tests demonstrate that Greenwood's students possess average or superior ability yet show a marked deficit in specific language and mathematical skills. Because of this inequity between ability and performance, students may be misunderstood and judged as lacking in intelligence or motivation.

Those students who have undergone emotional stress as a result of their learning problems customarily improve after experiencing academic and social success at Greenwood.

The program does not accept applicants with primary or emotional behavior disorders.

ASSESSMENT

Independent educational consultants or psychologists refer most candidates. These professionals administer a wide range of diagnostic tests to determine whether the candidate's learning profile is compatible with Greenwood's program. In some cases, a neuropsychological report is also necessary. For students not referred by a consultant, Greenwood requires appropriate test results as part of the admission process. Prospective Greenwood students and at least one parent or guardian are also required to come to the campus for an interview and some short, informal testing.

PROGRAM

The goal of Greenwood is to help students bridge the gap between their potential and present level of achievement. Greenwood believes that in order to raise a student's academic performance to a level appropriate for his intelligence, he must feel that he is part of the learning community. Visitors to Greenwood remark on the scholarly atmosphere and mutual support among the students.

A language-intensive program specially designed for Greenwood students distinguishes Greenwood from other junior boarding schools. Greenwood's remedial language program offers individualized training in basic and advanced skills and is based on the Orton-Gillingham approach, which stresses the integration of the visual, auditory, and kinesthetic senses. Students spend an hour a day in language class studying and practicing reading, spelling, comprehension, handwriting, and writing from dictation.

Because written work is such a difficult process for most dyslexic students, Greenwood devotes an additional period to writing instruction. In writing classes, students learn grammar, punctuation, sentence and paragraph construction, and creative expository writing. Before graduating, students receive practical instruction in writing both research and term papers. Word processors aid students in the writing process as students learn to type, edit, and structure their work.

Many learning disabled students also have difficulty with math. Greenwood's math classes are small and grouped according to individual ability. Concepts, computational skills, and beginning algebra are taught. Students who have particular difficulty with fundamentals receive special attention and help. The math program uses manipulatives, calculators, and other methods developed by the faculty to aid students in acquiring skills. The game of Village, a creative math program, is popular with the students and unique to Greenwood.

Because science and social studies classes usually require extensive reading, many Greenwood students have fallen behind in these subjects. Through lectures, discussions, videotapes, and group projects, students learn and review important concepts. The language-trained teachers encourage students to employ appropriate language skills to content-area work.

Although Greenwood students have specific learning disabilities that affect their performance in academic classes, Greenwood's students are creative and excel in art, music, and drama. To develop these talents, Greenwood has a strong fine arts program. All fine arts teachers are masters in their profession and are eager to share their experience and insights with the students.

Greenwood feels that it is important to balance the academic efforts of the day with a variety of seasonal sports and outdoor activities, including soccer, hiking, biking, swimming, cross-country and downhill skiing, ice skating, sledding, and softball. To further improve concentration and coordination, students participate in a judo class each Saturday afternoon. The sports and activities programs are important aspects of Greenwood as they address the physical needs of the students while fostering a sense of cooperation and respect among the participants.

STAFF

While the Greenwood program is structured and maintains definite behavioral expectations, the atmosphere remains relaxed and friendly. Faculty involvement in the dormitory and extracurricular life helps develop a good understanding of all the dimensions of a student's life.

There are thirteen resident teachers who, in addition to teaching responsibilities, share after-school, evening, and

428

weekend coverage. Of the thirteen, three are dorm parents, with one being the director of student life. There are three nonresident, part-time teachers who teach during the academic day. All sixteen teachers have bachelor's degrees and seven have master's degrees.

To ensure a unified approach throughout the curriculum, all Greenwood faculty members receive an intensive internship in the Orton-Gillingham approach to remedial language teaching. A resident master and several regularly scheduled consultants provide ongoing supervision.

To service the other needs of the school, there is an eight-person support staff, including a business manager and two secretaries, three cooks, and two maintenance personnel.

SPECIAL PROGRAMS
Although all Greenwood students receive assistance in developing their ability to use language as a communication tool, students with a greater need for this skill receive additional oral language training from a speech-language pathologist. This special training includes spoken syntax, following directions, word finding, listening, and vocabulary development.

Counseling services with local psychologists are also available for those students in need of specialized therapy.

Both special language training and additional counseling services are billed separately.

CONTINUITY OF TREATMENT
The Greenwood School program, through its positive emphasis on individual strengths combined with an intensive

remedial program, prepares its students for mainstream education. As a result, 95 percent of Greenwood students advance to private and public high schools where they succeed in meeting academic and social demands. The remaining 5 percent continue their secondary studies in specialized remedial schools. Greenwood graduates have enrolled at Tilton, Brewster, Proctor, Trinity-Pawling, Tabor, Forman, Eaglebrook, and Gould.

BUILDINGS AND GROUNDS
Students live in Founders Hall, which has eighteen student rooms, three faculty apartments, and two common rooms. The Leland Best Academic Center holds nine classrooms, an auditorium, a computer center, an AV center, a science lab, an art studio, and a library. A connected wing houses the kitchen, the dining room, and a music studio. Himmel House and the Director and Assistant Director's homes house the remainder of the resident teachers. A multipurpose facility for physical education and large gatherings was completed in 1992. A woodshop and small administrative building complete the list of buildings on campus.

A network of trails, winding through the 100+ acres, provides enjoyment for hikers, mountain bikers, and cross-country skiers. A 2-acre pond refreshes students during the warm, humid days of May and June.

ADMISSION AND FINANCIAL INFORMATION
The Greenwood School has an enrollment of forty boys and an average of twelve to fourteen openings per year. Students come from all over the United States and Canada and from several foreign countries. Students between the ages of 8 and 13 are eligible for admission. Tuition, room, and board for the 1992–93 school year are $25,710. Limited financial aid is available (distributed to approximately 15 percent of the enrollment).

HCA Grant Center Hospital

Miami, Florida

Type: Psychiatric hospital with residential treatment program, children's and adolescent programs

Affiliation: Hospital Corporation of America

Population Served: Male and female, 3-years-old to adult; children's program 3 to 13; adolescent 14 to 16; young adult 16 to 20

Size: Licensed capacity–140 beds; 110 children and adolescents

Head of Facility: Larry Melby, Administrator

Contact: John Guglietta, RN, Director of Admissions/Respond, 20601 Southwest 157th Avenue, Miami, Florida 33187; 305-251-0710; in Florida: 800-237-2823; fax: 305-253-1005

THE HOSPITAL

HCA Grant Center Hospital is a private 140-bed, psychiatric hospital dedicated to caring for the emotional problems of families.

Founded initially as a school for children with special problems, the facility opened its doors as a hospital in 1974. In 1985, the hospital was purchased by the Hospital Corporation of America.

Grant Center is one of five psychiatric facilities in Florida affiliated with HCA. In addition to owning forty-eight psychiatric hospitals in the U.S., HCA is also the parent of seventy-four medical and surgical facilities. HCA's corporate headquarters are in Nashville, Tennessee.

Serving south Florida families for generations, this year-round facility emphasizes family therapy as a part of the healing process. The 20-acre campus in rural southwest Dade County (just south of Miami) accommodates a fully accredited school, K through 12, as well as classes for GED.

The wide variety of therapeutic modalities, including individual and group therapy, supplement the family therapy. All patients enjoy, and benefit from, the activity therapy. Activities such as team sports, swimming in the pool, dance, horticulture, art, ceramics, and music are incorporated into each therapeutic regime.

The hospital is accredited by the Joint Commission on the Accreditation of Healthcare Organizations and is licensed by the state of Florida. The school, Redlands Academy, is fully accredited by the Southern Association of Colleges and Schools and the Florida Council of Independent Schools.

ELIGIBILITY

Admission criteria vary depending upon a variety of factors. Children or adolescents may be exhibiting a variety of behaviors, including suicidal or aggressive behaviors and unmanageable behavior that does not respond to normal limit-setting, possibly harming oneself and others. In addition, candidates' histories may include abuse of drugs or alcohol, excessive suspiciousness, hallucinations, and psychosomatic symptoms and failure of outpatient or other less intensive treatment.

HCA Grant requires that all patients be medically stabilized prior to admission.

Involuntary admissions are accepted and follow all State of Florida Baker Act regulations.

ASSESSMENT

A free initial screening is offered to all callers. The Respond® Department, under a physician's supervision, makes recommendations and referrals to appropriate programs and outside community agencies based on each patient's needs.

PROGRAMS

HCA Grant Center realizes that emotional problems are complicated. It is very difficult to determine causes and select the best treatment. Because of this, the hospital's expert staff offers various programs so each child can be placed in the treatment setting that is best suited to him or her.

HCA Grant's Children's Treatment is designed for children ages 3 to 13 and focuses on personal responsibility. At the same time, it allows these young people the freedom they need for individual growth. Children are grouped according to age and similar clinical needs and problems, and staff members are available 24 hours a day. The program helps each child learn to use personal skills to cope more effectively with internal and external conflicts. There is emphasis on group interaction, communication, and the sharing of ideas in a structured and supervised environment.

The Adolescent Treatment Program is divided into two tracks. One is for 14- to 16-year-olds; the other is for young adults 16 to 21 years of age. A major emphasis is placed on helping adolescents learn to make better decisions for themselves. This is achieved through goal setting and developing increased awareness of the consequences of decisions and actions. Young adults work on independence and self-reliance.

An addictive disease may result from substance abuse, sexual abuse, or eating disorders. At HCA Grant Center, patients with a dual diagnosis are placed on teams with individuals with similar case histories. Participants also attend AA and NA meetings at the hospital. A major key to therapy is an emphasis on self-responsibility and a positive self-image.

The Partial Hospitalization for Children and Adolescents Program provides daily care, five days per week, without hospitalization. This includes school, group and activity therapy, family support, and management of acute patient conditions.

Partial hospitalization can be effective as well as transitional for inpatients returning to their families or for children who need intensive therapy without hospitalization. The program is open Monday through Friday from 7:30 a.m. to 5 p.m. Additional days and hours can be provided for individual cases. The hospital will coordinate patient transportation to and from the hospital.

The Residential Treatment Program for Adolescents and Children offers children and adolescents longer-term care at a lower daily rate. This less intensive, structured environment concentrates on instruction in daily living and job skills. The program also works to improve social skills, such as controlling anger and negotiating. Residents learn how to look for and obtain a job, including specifics on interviewing and résumé preparation. Another focus of the unit is on daily living skills such as nutrition, finance management, and consumer awareness. A plan is designed for each resident and each patient is monitored by a well-rounded team of professionals.

An alternative to hospitalization or daily supervision is the outpatient counseling centers—HCA Family Services. The counseling centers have expert staff who are trained to deal with addictive and emotional problems.

Located off campus, HCA Family Services provides programs for children and adults. As with HCA Grant Center Hospital inpatients, a full range of services is available. The flexible programs offer a wide variety of therapies and treatment options. The initial consultation is free. Most insurance plans cover service, and a flexible fee scale is also available.

Because being the parent of an ADD child can be almost as difficult as being the child suffering from the disorder, HCA Grant has a family-oriented approach to treatment. The hospital's specially trained team of physicians, psychologists, nurses, and counselors design each treatment program, which, in conjunction with new research and information, has resulted in many success stories in the treatment of ADHD/ADD. The program includes a parenting skills group, psychological testing, a social skills group for children, tutoring, and medication if necessary. The program is offered on both an outpatient and inpatient basis.

STAFF

An interdisciplinary team of professionals includes psychiatrists, psychologists, clinical social workers, nurse specialists, therapists, pharmacists, dieticians, and educators. Medical specialists cover a broad spectrum of subspecialties including eating disorders, victims of sexual abuse, addiction disorders, learning disabilities, attention deficit disorders, and post-traumatic stress disorders.

SPECIAL PROGRAMS

Many outreach programs are sponsored each year by the hospital. In addition to educational programs for the medical and education communities, there are numerous community programs. The hospital offers a speakers' bureau service to professional or civic organizations in the community. Lectures, workshops, and screenings are offered in locations throughout the county in both English and Spanish. Many of the programs are free of charge. For a schedule of upcoming programs, to be placed on the hospital mailing list, or to request a speaker, contact the hospital's marketing department.

CONTINUITY OF TREATMENT

Hospitalization is only one part of the ongoing treatment needed for emotional problems in children and adolescents. Therefore, when a patient is discharged, his or her treatment must continue. The treatment team at HCA Grant Center and the attending physician will recommend the follow-up and ongoing care necessary. The Partial Hospitalization Program offers an option for patients to attend school and therapy during the day and return home to their families at night. The Residential Treatment Program offers less intensive medical supervision within the framework of a highly structured therapeutic environment. HCA Family Services outpatient centers also offer counseling, workshops, and support groups in a community setting.

BUILDINGS AND GROUNDS

Tropical grass-covered huts, barbecue areas, and orchards give HCA Grant Center's country-like grounds a welcoming atmosphere. An abundance of activities are available for residents and students. Two tennis courts, a basketball court, and a playground are used for practice and friendly competition. Soccer and softball are played on full-sized fields. For those who prefer water sports, an Olympic-size swimming pool is provided. Programs and facilities address both the mind and body; by incorporating this total approach each individual is allowed to reach his or her highest potential.

The colorful gardens, landscaping, and horticultural areas are inviting and fulfilling for those who enjoy more tranquil activities. Separate facilities for art therapy, dance, music, and drama complement the campus. The environmental surroundings of HCA Grant Center Hospital are truly unique as well as being soothing and conducive to the overall treatment of patients.

Completely separate living quarters for children and adults ensure the privacy and integrity of each program.

ADMISSION AND FINANCIAL INFORMATION

Those in need of HCA Grant Center's services may call the facility and inquire regarding the programs. Information and preliminary details are gathered and a free face-to-face psychosocial screening is offered; based on the results, recommendations are made.

Payment plans may be arranged with the Patient Accounts Department with the approval of the administration.

Most insurance program and managed-care plans are accepted. There is a sliding fee scale for outpatient services only.

HCA Willow Springs Center

Reno, Nevada

Type: Psychiatric residential treatment center

Affiliation: Hospital Corporation of America; for-profit

Population Served: Male and female children, ages 5 to 12; male and female adolescents, ages 13 to 17

Size: Licensed capacity–10-bed children's unit; 64-bed adolescent unit

Head of Facility: Robert E. Marshall, M.Ed., Executive Director

Contact: Wayne Hoff, M.S., L.A.S.W., Admissions Coordinator, 690 Edison Way, Reno, Nevada 89502; 702-858-3303 or 800-448-9454

THE HOSPITAL

Willow Springs Center opened in 1988 in Reno, Nevada, offering a full continuum of care and services for troubled children and adolescents. Willow Springs is located on 5 acres and offers the scenic beauty of the Sierra Nevada Mountains as well as easy access to international airport services. The facility and grounds are designed to provide a supportive environment for patients and families, utilizing a multilevel system of treatment programs.

Willow Springs Center was created to help children, adolescents, and families overcome psychiatric difficulties and return to healthier lives. The center, its caring staff, and its comprehensive programs are all dedicated to a common goal: to help children, adolescents, and families identify their problems and work toward solutions.

The center is accredited by the Joint Commission on the Accreditation of Healthcare Organizations, is licensed by the state of Nevada, and is a CHAMPUS-approved facility.

ELIGIBILITY

Patients must be in need of 24-hour care in a setting less restrictive than acute hospitalization or unable to effect progress in an outpatient setting. Potential patients must be sufficiently whole intellectually, cognitively, and emotionally to benefit from residential treatment. Additionally, patients should not be a danger to themselves or others, not actively assaultive, suicidal, self-destructive, or an extreme elopement risk; nor can patients manifest grossly psychotic or manic behavior requiring containment or exhibit significant mental, emotional, or behavioral problems that cannot be adequately treated in the existing home or school environment.

Diagnoses most likely to be admitted are attention deficit disorder, anxiety disorder, affective disorder, substance abuse, dual diagnoses, and other psychiatric or behavioral disorders that can be treated effectively in a residential treatment center model.

Patients who are not likely to be accepted are those who are severely or moderately retarded, require intensive medical or skilled nursing care, or are severely handicapped and require daily help in hygiene, self-care, and/or locomotion.

ASSESSMENT

The screening process includes reviews of a recent case history and physical, psychological, and psychiatric assessments. A psychological assessment includes an evaluation of intellectual, emotional, and academic levels. Patients referred without prior assessments may be admitted to an acute-care psychiatric inpatient unit for a brief evaluation that is usually completed within ten to fourteen working days. Another option is to be evaluated as an outpatient, either by arrangement of the referral source or through the Willow Springs Center on-call system (fees and billing arrangements for assessments are the responsibility of the private practitioners). On occasion an assessment can be conducted at Willow Springs Center by the on-site admissions coordinator available at the center.

PROGRAMS

Every Willow Springs Center program utilizes a wide variety of therapy treatments. Each patient may participate in individual, family, and group therapy as determined by the treatment plan.

Individual therapy sessions create helpful relationships with counselors and assist patients in identifying their problems and developing appropriate coping skills.

Group therapy focuses on sharing problems common among children and adolescents. All patients are encouraged to look at their feelings through the eyes of their peers. This gives patients support and guidance and helps develop new coping skills.

Family therapy sessions let family members share feelings, improve communication, and learn more about each other. Parent support groups and parent training sessions are also an important part of family therapy.

The Children's Program provides residential treatment for children between the ages of 5 and 12 and is designed to treat behaviors and/or disorders that can occur during childhood years. The program is designed to help the child begin to learn healthy ways to express feelings while working on self-control and building self-esteem.

In Willow Springs' Children's Program, the family plays a vital role in treatment. Parents and family members are strongly encouraged to participate in support groups, educational courses, special activities, and family therapy that teaches family members how to communicate with their children and with each other.

The treatment team coordinates each child's treatment plan. Under the direction of a psychiatrist, each child receives a comprehensive evaluation, and, based on the findings, an individualized plan is designed. The plan is reviewed and revised frequently to reflect the child's progress.

A comprehensive offering of services is incorporated into each treatment plan. These services can include individual, group, and family therapy; education and support; occupational and recreational therapies; education and educational therapy; and discharge planning and aftercare support.

The goal of the Children's Program is to help the children learn acceptable behavior patterns, develop confidence, and function successfully in family and school.

The Adolescent Program provides residential treatment

for teens, ages 13 to 17, who may be experiencing chemical dependency, depression, anxiety, problems at school or home, or other emotional and behavioral problems.

The special needs of teens troubled by the transition from adolescence to adulthood are addressed in individualized treatment plans, with specific goals to guide treatment. Professional and sensitive treatment teams work closely with each adolescent to achieve these goals as quickly as possible.

Therapy is essential to the treatment process. Each teen may participate in individual, family, group, and recreational therapy as determined by the treatment plan.

Family involvement is also vital to each teen's treatment. Family therapists, counselors, and case managers involve family members in the treatment process and inform them of progress.

The goal of the Adolescent Program is to help teens develop the self-confidence, trust, and the responsibility necessary to move successfully into young adulthood as well as to return to their family, school, and community.

STAFF

The treatment-team approach is used to coordinate every aspect of patient care. Upon admission, each patient is assigned a case manager who works with the attending physician to coordinate assessment, treatment, and aftercare.

An experienced, multidisciplinary team of mental health professionals is also assigned to each patient, and an individualized treatment plan is carefully developed. All professionals involved in a patient's care work together as a team.

Professional treatment teams include psychiatrists, clinical psychologists, marriage and family therapists, licensed clinical social workers, case managers, staff nurses, mental health technicians, activity therapists, and teachers.

SPECIAL PROGRAMS

At Willow Springs Center, education is a vital part of the treatment process and is fully integrated into the treatment plan. Truckee Meadows School, a fully accredited private school, provides elementary and secondary education to all Willow Springs' residents. Students attend school daily, where they earn credits that are transferable after treatment.

Recreational and allied therapies encourage the vital physical, emotional, and mental releases of the treatment process. Leisure management skills are developed through exercise, sports, games, and community outings. Other recreational therapy involves team building, trust games, and problem-solving experiences.

Willow Springs Center offers the Challenge by Choice (ROPES) course, which encourages emotional, physical, and intellectual growth. The activities are not competitions. They are opportunities to develop communication, leadership, and problem-solving skills. Individuals are challenged to go beyond their perceived boundaries—to take risks as the group supports them. Challenge by Choice builds the relationships that develop team spirit and cooperation.

The course is a three-phase program of outdoor group activities, utilizing a series of elements including ropes, cables, and logs that create various obstacles or "Challenges." The individual's right to not participate is always

respected, thereby creating a "Choice."

Challenge by Choice helps people realize that many obstacles they face in life come from within and can be overcome.

CONTINUITY OF TREATMENT

Discharge plans for each patient are developed in order to help continue the progress achieved at Willow Springs Center. Discharge planning is coordinated with the patient, the patient's family, and the treatment team. The discharge plan addresses the patient's individual treatment plans, specifying additional therapy, if needed, and assisting with necessary arrangements.

BUILDINGS AND GROUNDS

Willow Springs residents live in a dormitory setting, thus providing 24-hour interaction with peers as well as a full-time interdisciplinary clinical staff. This setting and consistent staffing allows patients to feel secure and comfortable.

Within the adolescent unit, boys are on separate corridors from girls. Rooms contain two beds and bath facilities. The children's unit contains the boys' area at opposite ends of the corridor from the girls' area. Rooms contain two beds, and private bath facilities are located within a few doors of each room.

Willow Springs patients share the use of a central dining facility, where food is prepared by a master chef and is comparable to the food served in better restaurants. Patients also share a fully equipped gymnasium, an exercise room, a spacious courtyard for recreational activities, and the Challenge by Choice course.

ADMISSION AND FINANCIAL INFORMATION

Willow Springs Center accepts CHAMPUS and most major medical plans, as well as Nevada Medicaid. Private payment arrangements may also be negotiated. Costs vary between programs and services. The cost to the patient depends upon the exact nature of treatment as well as the type of health insurance and extent of coverage. Willow Springs Center can assist in exploring funding options. The insurance liaisons are experienced at accessing the coverage for longer-term treatment and can sometimes uncover alternatives that aren't readily discernible.

Admissions to Willow Springs Center may be generated by referrals from physicians, psychologists, school counselors, youth agencies, social workers, marriage and family counselors, police, families, or other concerned individuals.

Referrals and admissions may be arranged by contacting the Willow Springs Admissions Coordinator. A free evaluation is available to facilitate the referral and admission process. The admissions office is extremely flexible in assisting patients and families with the potentially burdensome process of admission into a residential setting and is committed to maintaining an orderly flow of information between the patient, family, referral source, and clinical treatment team.

HILLTOP

Running Springs, California

Type: Coeducational residential program for young adults at risk

Affiliation: An independent, for-profit organization

Population Served: Males and females, ages 17½–27, with emotional, educational, and emancipation needs

Size: 38 students

Head of Facility: Jayne Selby-Longnecker

Contact: Deborah A. Scott, Director of Enrollment, P.O. Box 595, Running Springs, California 92382; 714-867-7054 or 714-582-8761

THE FACILITY

The Hilltop community was established in 1984 as an adjunct to CEDU School. CEDU education founder Mel Wasserman identified the need for a program designed specifically to address the emotional, educational, and emancipation needs of young adults at risk. Today, the year-round program continues its commitment to help participants develop the necessary skills to live responsibly and independently in today's challenging world.

Located outside the southern California mountain resort community of Running Springs, Hilltop's ideal setting accommodates active sports, wilderness programs, and access to a variety of excellent educational, vocational, and extracurricular activities in neighboring communities.

ELIGIBILITY

Hilltop participants are young adults whose ability to assume personal responsibility and sustained emancipation may have been hampered by life circumstances, learning difficulties, and/or counterproductive personal choices. Prospective applicants have generally experienced frustration in traditional settings and are in need of additional structure and support for their successful overall development.

Despite individual potential, Hilltop students have generally experienced a combination of problems prior to enrollment, often including academic failure, attention deficit disorder, depression, family difficulties, drug and alcohol usage, poor motivation, lack of discipline, and problem issues related to adoption.

Young adults with physical disabilities and/or requiring psychotropic or other medications are considered on an individual basis. While enrollment is voluntary, it is not expected that the prospective student will initially embrace the structured nature of the Hilltop program. This partial resistance is to be expected and does not serve as a deterrent to enrollment.

ASSESSMENT

Appropriate admission and program participation is based upon a combination of assessments prior to, during, and following enrollment. Both written and verbal evaluations and information are requested from the referring source. The majority of referrals come from professionals (psychiatrists, psychologists, hospital program directors, discharge planners, counselors, social workers, educational consultants) and parents (both current and alumni).

Information and evaluations received during the enrollment process are used in conjunction with the on-site evaluation and orientation that takes place during the initial thirty- to sixty-day enrollment period within the Hilltop community.

PROGRAM

Hilltop focuses on the emotional growth, education, and emancipation goals and objectives of each of its students. The foundation of the program is the emotional growth curriculum designed to meet individual needs and issues.

The curriculum is designed for each student individually and contains specific goals and objectives. The components are initially very structured, move toward increased responsibility, and culminate in the achievement of individual emancipation. The length of the program varies, depending on the goals, objectives, and motivation of the student.

In addition, regular and recurring group sessions and thematic workshops serve to further support the individual student. While the twice-weekly sessions and quarterly workshops are led by experienced and credentialed faculty, the emotional growth work is done by students both as individuals and as a group.

The academic portion of the curriculum is designed to ensure mastery of the skills basic to learning. Each student's academic component is determined according to his or her individual achievement level. Academics are fully integrated into the Hilltop program. After initial assessment of transcripts, an individual educational and/or vocational plan is established. Students may earn a high school diploma in addition to attending and participating in one of the many fine college programs in the surrounding area. An ongoing assessment of progress is made by the faculty adviser, who is responsible for making sure that the students' academic needs are being met and challenged.

Emancipation skills and goals are learned and attained through a variety of daily life activities and off-site work experiences.

STAFF

Faculty and staff bring a rich variety of educational and counseling disciplines to the Hilltop program. Staff and faculty are selected for their ability to understand the problems facing young adults as well as their personal level of academic achievement. Credentials range from counseling, special education, teaching, and social work to Ph.D. designations. In addition, specialists in eating disorders, chemical dependency, and learning disabilities participate on an individual and integrated basis.

CONTINUITY OF TREATMENT

Hilltop's primary goal is to help young adults at risk develop the necessary skills to live both emotionally healthy and independently responsible lives following graduation from the program. A student's initial Hilltop Individual Plan provides the avenue to move through to achievement and actualization of this goal.

Independent Living is an additional and auxiliary component to the initial Hilltop program and exists as an option to graduates. Participants live in individual houses physically separate from the clustered community setting. By offering participation in the Hilltop program on a part-time and as-needed basis, Independent Living offers the graduate an adjustment period in a "real world" environment where choices and responsibility for choices can be experienced. Independent Living participants are expected to attend school and/or work a full-time job. Many choose a combination of education and employment. Length of time spent in Independent Living varies from student to student but averages between three and six months.

BUILDINGS AND GROUNDS

The essence of student life at Hilltop is the formation of a positive peer group. To help accomplish this, students live in a clustered community of cabin-type homes, with males and females living separately. Each house represents an individual peer unit and is overseen by a senior student and staff counselor. It is the intimate setting and consistent peer interaction that enables Hilltop students to feel secure, safe, and able to begin their emotional growth journey.

Students are involved in life skills immediately. All cooking, cleaning, laundry, and managing of living space is done individually. Hilltop subscribes to a conservative dress and hygiene code. Although a staff member is on grounds at all times, students are expected to live and act responsibly.

ADMISSION AND FINANCIAL INFORMATION

Application and admission take place year-round. If an immediate need exists, the admissions staff will make every effort to accommodate the family.

Tuition is $3550 per month and is billed on a monthly basis. This fee includes room, board, support counseling, and basic academic, education, and program costs. Additional registration, orientation, linen, and student expense account fees are due upon enrollment. Costs for high school, college, vocational education, field trips, and individual psychological counseling are billed as incurred and applicable. Please call directly for specific fee information.

THE JOHN DEWEY ACADEMY

Great Barrington, Massachusetts

Type: Residential, college-preparatory, therapeutic high school

Population Served: Coeducational, ages 15 to 21

Size: 50 students

Head of Facility: Thomas Edward Bratter, Ed.D., President

Contact: Thomas Edward Bratter or Henry T. Radda, Ph.D., Dean of Students, Searles Castle, 389 Main Street, Great Barrington, Massachusetts 01230; 413-528-9800; fax: 413-528-5662.

THE SCHOOL

Founded in 1985 by Drs. Bratter and Radda, The John Dewey Academy wants to be judged by the performances of its graduates and the reputations of the institutions of higher education they attend. Graduation from a prestigious college is crucial to maximize the probability of future educational, professional, and social success and to seal permanently painful, past performances. The Academy's mission is to prove to mental health professionals and educators that when adolescents whose self-destructive behavior has made them at risk are placed in an uncompromising environment with stressfully high expectations, they can transcend nihilistic pasts and achieve the greatness of which they are capable.

The Academy is open year-round. It is located on 90 acres, with just a 3-hour drive to Boston and New York City.

The Academy is accredited by the National Independent Private Schools Association and approved by the Massachusetts Department of Education.

The academics, college placement, and teaching philosophy of the Academy are discussed in the following publications: Bratter, et al., "The Effective Education Professional: Politician, Psychologist, Philosopher, Professor & Parent," *Journal of Humanistic Education and Development*, 1991; Glasser, "A Residential College Preparatory Therapeutic High School: A Dialogue with Tom Bratter," *Journal of Counseling and Development*, 1990; and Bratter, et al., "The John Dewey Academy: A Pragmatic, Moral, Thinking Curriculum in a Drug-Free Environment," *Journal of Reality Therapy*, 1989.

ELIGIBILITY

The Academy seeks students who possess superior intuitive and intellectual ability, although, frequently, standardized testing fails to confirm this potential. It is not unusual for students to have significant educational deficits. Some have abused psychoactive substances, failed in school, and engaged in sexual promiscuity. A few have stolen but are not hard-core sociopaths who are dangerous to society. Although labeled "unmotivated" by their families, friends, and teachers, they are, in fact, unconvinced they can succeed, and this becomes the crucial educational challenge: to inspire them to learn and to try.

During their formative years, some students suffered from parental acts of accidental deprivation or deliberate cruelty. Several have been bruised, battered, and bloodied by their families. They may ward off painful feelings with a voracious sense of entitlement; no one can realistically satisfy their escalating demands. Family members and friends sometimes become dehumanized objects to gratify their needs.

Others project an aura of hostility to protect themselves from being hurt. This alienates and antagonizes adults.

All are sensitive to their feelings but ignore the needs and rights of others. Internally they are hemorrhaging, but they project a facade of grandiosity to hide feelings of shame, fear, guilt, self-contempt, and self-doubt. Not infrequently they are misdiagnosed as demoralized and depressed because they conceal their anger and rage, which is often directed at themselves. By testing limits (ubiquitous in adolescence) and creating constant crises by their behavior, these students have imprisoned themselves in a "no win– no exit" labyrinth where the expectation of failure becomes a painful, negative self-fulfilling prophesy.

They are described to be characterologically difficult, showing prominent features of the DSM-III-R Axis II diagnoses of borderline and narcissism. Many are viewed as oppositional character disordered whose problems are exacerbated by hyperactivity and/or an attention deficit disorder with an accompanying bipolar condition. Prior to attending The John Dewey Academy, 50 percent are medicated with Prozac, Lithium, or Ritalin. None of the students currently attending the Academy are medicated, which reflects the school's premise that psychotropic medicine does not modify irresponsible and self-destructive attitudes. A safe, supportive, and structured environment helps these adolescents to stabilize, which generally eliminates the need for medication.

The Academy cannot help those who suffer from profound and prolonged psychiatric dysfunctions. Anyone who lacks the internal control to regulate behavior requires a more intensive residential setting. Actively anorexic and suicidal individuals are excluded, as are those who suffer from clinical endogenous depression, organic disorders, schizophrenia, or psychosis. They require a secure setting not provided by this Academy. There is no provision for involuntary placement. Students retain the freedom to leave and are not detained against their wishes.

PROGRAM

Special attention is given to the student's psychosocial-spiritual-moral growth. The goal is to help the student regain self-respect. All adolescents need to establish a stable personal identity. Concurrently, they need to learn how to form positive peer relationships. At the Academy, groups are conducted by credentialed mental health professionals at least three times a week to achieve these goals. A confrontational, teaching, interpretive, reasoning approach is utilized to encourage group members to recognize that constructive and creative change is possible by accepting responsibility for behavior. The group discourages passivity or feeling victimized by conditions beyond personal control. In a group setting, the adolescent can relate to peers who offer insight and suggestions that are often the catalysts for self exploration and change. As the member accepts responsibility for past self-destructive behavior, the group helps the student resolve painful intrapsychic and interpersonal problems. Members learn how to depend on others and be dependable, to trust and be trusted, to help and be helped, to respect and be respected, to give and to receive.

There are time-limited and theme-related groups that focus on such areas as adoption, divorce, fourth step, substance abuse, and eating disorders. Five times a week, there are leaderless groups where adolescents provide support for each other and in so doing learn how to praise, communicate responsible concern, and show affection.

Individual and family psychotherapy are provided. Students spend 25 percent of their time specifically with therapeutics discussed in the following publications: Bratter, et al., "The Residential Therapeutic Caring Community: A Safe, Secure, Structured and Supportive Treatment Milieu for Self-Destructive, Psychologically Intact Adolescents Who Have Superior Intellectual and Creative Abilities," *Psychotherapy: Theory, Research and Practice,* 1993; Bratter, "Group Psychotherapy with Alcohol and Drug Addicted Adolescents: Special Clinical Concerns and Challenges," in *Adolescent Group Psychotherapy,* editors F. J. C. Azima and L. H. Richmond, Madison, Connecticut: International Universities Press, 1989; and Bratter, et al., "Mentoring: Extending the Psychotherapeutic and Pedagogical Relationships with Adolescents," *Journal of Reality Therapy,* 1989.

Students are expected to take control of their lives. Empowerment is important. Students maintain the premises, answer phones, and order and prepare the food. After proving to the satisfaction of the staff that they are responsible, some students are permitted to have cars so they can attend college, do internships with congressmen or local state representatives, serve as teacher's assistants, or do volunteer work in local agencies.

The Academy stimulates intellectual and cognitive growth by equipping the student with the academic skills needed to succeed at a competitive college. The Academy seeks to create a learning environment where it is safe to experiment with new ideas and discover the connections between facts and wisdom, using imagination and intuition to find constructive solutions. The student is encouraged to gain the ability to make decisions in a realistic, ethical, and moral context. The educational objectives are to help the student think critically and communicate effectively both orally and in writing. The curriculum instills critical thinking abilities in a questioning-questing environment. The three R's have been expanded to include responsibility, reality, relevance, reverence, respect, renewal, and relatedness. Students are educated not only to perform academic tasks but also to develop strategies to cope with change in a technological society. The learning environment encourages intellectual, affective, and moral development and helps define, not dictate, the synergetic and dynamic relationship between the individual and society.

The curriculum is comprehensive and academically demanding. There is unavoidable pressure. The student is expected to work a minimum of 3 hours a day, 6 days a week. French, Greek, Italian, Latin, Spanish, and Russian are taught. Physics and precalculus are offered. Those who are more advanced can take courses at Williams College and Smith College.

STAFF
The clinical staff comprises two psychologists, a social worker, and a guidance counselor. The average age of the ten-person teaching staff is 45. All have their master's degrees. Four have their doctorates.

There is constant communication. Twice a week there are faculty meetings so the staff can design an individualized educational plan, taking into account the student's academic and psychological strengths and weaknesses.

CONTINUITY OF TREATMENT
Virtually all John Dewey graduates go on to college. Academy students attend Antioch, Bucknell, Clark, Connecticut, Hobart, NYU, Pitzer, St. John's College (Maryland), Sarah Lawrence, Scripps, Syracuse University's College of Visual and Performing Arts, Trinity (Connecticut), Union, University of Chicago, Wellesley, Wheaton (Massachusetts), and Williams. Of the students who have graduated since the Academy's founding in 1985, 50 percent have made the dean's list at their respective colleges.

BUILDING AND GROUNDS
Listed on the National Register of Historic Places, Searles Castle was built at a cost of $2.3-million in 1888. No more than four students share large rooms, some of which have private baths.

ADMISSION AND FINANCIAL INFORMATION
The admissions process is complex. There is no objective criterion. Consideration of standardized test scores and previous academic performance is minimal because they do not reflect potential or probability of success. An interview, conducted by the clinical staff and students, is the most significant criterion because it reveals the prospective student's attitude, which is considered the most realistic predictor for success. The applicant needs to acknowledge that past problems were created by poor choices, not by conditions beyond personal control; to make a commitment to change; to convince the staff of a willingness to work diligently academically; and to agree to stay for at least two years. During the interview, the applicant will be asked, "Why should The John Dewey Academy admit you?" No one is admitted without an interview. The candidate can request friends, family members, and professionals to write letters of recommendation.

Each student spends a probationary period of at least ten days becoming better acquainted with the Academy before deciding whether or not to remain. The Academy reserves the right to deny admission during this probationary period. No admission is automatic. There is a risk of rejection, although rarely is anyone rejected who sincerely wants to change. Only those who can cope with a painful rejection should apply. The ultimate decision to admit is determined by a majority vote of the students.

Tuition for fifty-two weeks is $38,000. The Academy is not eligible to receive third-party payments because its primary identity is a school; however, a few insurance companies and school districts have agreed to pay when convinced the patient needed prolonged residential treatment. There are provisions for some students to reduce tuition through a work-study program, and about 30 percent of the students receive scholarship stipends granted by the Academy. In exceptional cases of outstanding personal merit and documented financial need, full scholarships are given.

JULIA DYCKMAN ANDRUS MEMORIAL

Yonkers, New York

Type: Treatment Center

Affiliation: Privately owned, nonprofit

Population Served: Male and female, ages 7 to 15

Size: Residential Treatment Center–57; Diagnostic Center–10; Day Treatment Program–10

Head of Facility: Gary O. Carman, Ph.D.

Contact: Sheri Bloom, CSW, Director of Admissions, Julia Dyckman Andrus Memorial, 1156 North Broadway, Yonkers, New York 10701; 914-965-3700; fax: 914-965-3883

THE FACILITY

Founded in 1928 as a children's home by philanthropist John E. Andrus, in memory of his wife Julia Dyckman Andrus, the Julia Dyckman Andrus Memorial (JDAM) offers a long-term residential treatment program, a short-term diagnostic center, and a day treatment program for children.

Located on an open 107-acre campus setting, JDAM is dedicated to providing a comprehensive treatment and educational program for emotionally troubled boys and girls.

Until the early 1960s, Andrus operated as a home for needy and orphaned children. Gradually, the focus of the Andrus program shifted to meet the changing needs of the children and their families. Today, Andrus is a multifaceted treatment center designed to care for children while working with their families toward the eventual goal of returning the youngsters to their home, whenever feasible.

Andrus's unique New York State–approved on-grounds school, the Orchard School, provides a wide range of special education services for its student population. While the primary focus is on teaching children the basic skills of reading, mathematics, and writing, the school also offers an interactive computer program that makes the learning process fun, while enhancing and reinforcing basic learning skills. Art, woodshop, and music are also offered as part of the school's varied curriculum.

After sixty years of service, the Julia Dyckman Andrus Memorial's mission remains the same: "To Give Opportunity to Youth".

ELIGIBILITY

Children and their families must recognize the need for residential or day treatment in order to take full advantage of the multimodal treatment approach, which includes individual, group, family, and milieu therapies. Although Andrus successfully addresses a wide range of behavioral and emotional problems, it cannot effectively address all of them. Among those children who cannot be effectively served by Andrus are those who are actively psychotic, retarded, autistic, have an extensive history of antisocial, severely aggressive, or delinquent behavior, have a history of primary substance or alcohol abuse, or exhibit chronic runaway behavior.

ASSESSMENT

To determine a youngster's appropriateness for residential or day treatment, information required for consideration should include a social history, psychological and psychiatric evaluations, educational records, and pertinent medical information. This initial assessment along with a preplacement interview helps to determine the initial goals for treatment.

PROGRAMS

The Orchard School, a New York State–approved school, was established in 1972 to educate children with emotional and learning problems. Within an overall student-to-faculty ratio of 3:1, students are introduced to comprehensive, computer-managed education programs that evaluate academic performance. Through this method of computer-managed instruction, youngsters often improve their rate of learning dramatically and significantly increase their repertoire of reading and mathematical skills.

The Orchard School encourages students, whenever possible, to return to community school. A few youngsters in ninth grade or below do not require special education and attend mainstream programs at neighborhood schools. Andrus maintains an excellent relationship with local school districts, and its children are well-received, closely monitored, and carefully supervised. The school is recognized by the U.S. Department of Education as a "National Exemplary School."

The Residential Treatment Program is designed to provide comprehensive therapeutic services for fifty-seven children between the ages of 7 and 15. Children live in four cottages on campus: three for boys and one for girls.

The belief in a child's capacity to grow and change is central to the Residential Treatment Program. Each cottage is staffed by trained Child Behavior Specialists who work with youngsters in daily living skills, peer relationships, and self-development. Activity groups, special trips, and campuswide events enrich the daily life at Andrus. Further opportunities for fun and skill development are offered through the Recreation Department. Intramural sports, swimming instruction, and music lessons are among the many activities available. The child's education program is provided by the Orchard School or, in some cases, by an appropriate community school setting coordinated by the Orchard School staff.

STAFF

Central to the treatment program at Andrus is its clinical staff that includes psychiatric social workers, a clinical psychologist, and a staff psychiatrist. The clinical staff works in close conjunction with a child behavior specialist in order to determine the most effective treatment for the youngster.

Andrus also provides an infirmary staff including a consulting medical director, full-time nurses, and aides. When required, the facilities of nearby St. John's Riverside Hospital are available.

While the Julia Dyckman Andrus Memorial's ultimate goal is to reunite children and families, JDAM prides itself on its staff's ability to provide youngsters with a joyous experience.

SPECIAL PROGRAMS

Included within JDAM is the Andrus Diagnostic Center, a short-term residential program for emotionally troubled children, ages 5 to 10, for whom there are long-term planning questions. A multidisciplinary clinical team conducts a comprehensive assessment of the needs and strengths of the child and uses this information to develop appropriate discharge plans.

A child admitted to the Diagnostic Center can expect to stay between thirty and ninety days. The initial phase of treatment emphasizes specialized evaluations by a social worker, psychiatrist, psychologist, physician, educators, recreation therapist, and residential staff. At the conclusion of the four-week diagnostic phase, the staff presents the findings and recommendations to the family and responsible agency. The following sixty days are used to implement the recommendations for long-term planning. During this period, treatment continues. The Program Director coordinates the individual, group, and family services while a recreation therapist conducts play and development activities. Educational services, including a preschool readiness program as well as a Special Education Diagnostic classroom, are provided in the Orchard School.

The Diagnostic Center expects maximum participation from the family and responsible agency in the evaluation and planning process. Visiting in the spacious facility is coordinated by the center's staff.

The Day Treatment Program offers comprehensive services at Andrus to students who can remain home during the treatment process. Those in day treatment attend the Orchard School while a multidisciplinary team from Andrus coordinates an individualized treatment plan on an outpatient basis. Only children referred from the School District Committees of Special Education (CSE) can be accepted for either ten- or twelve-month placement.

CONTINUITY OF TREATMENT

Each child and family is served by a multidisciplinary team representing Clinical Services, Education, Recreation, and Residential Life. The child and family's social worker coordinates the individualized treatment plan that addresses both the problems and strengths identified in the first months of placement. Treatment plans include weekly individual counseling and biweekly family counseling that is designed to explore new and more effective ways of coping with the youngsters' problems. The child and family meet with the treatment team every three months both to review goals and expectations and to assess progress toward discharge.

The group incentive system, correlating behavioral expectation and privileges, provides clear indications to each

child of progress being made in each specific area of the program. Children are encouraged to identify changes leading to eventual discharge and return to community life.

BUILDINGS AND GROUNDS

Children participating in the residential program live in one of five Tudor-style cottages that can accommodate up to fourteen youngsters. Each cottage is staffed by a team of child behavior specialists.

Athletic, social, and cultural programs on campus and throughout Metropolitan New York are utilized to meet both the individual and social needs of the children. The activities program is centralized at the McGee Field House, which houses the gymnasium, an indoor swimming pool, and a multipurpose game room. Outdoor facilities, such as softball and hardball fields, playground facilities, and tennis, basketball, and volleyball courts, offer a wide range of activities.

ADMISSION AND FINANCIAL INFORMATION

Children are referred by parents, educators, mental health professionals, or social service agency staff. When appropriate, the Director of Admissions will schedule a preplacement interview. This visit provides an opportunity for the family, child, and/or referral source to meet the staff and tour the campus. If a child is accepted, admission can take place at any time during the year. Boys and girls ages 5 through 13 are accepted for admission without regard to race, color, creed, religion, or national origin. Departments of Social Services and school district placements are charged a per-diem rate set by New York State. As a nationally accredited treatment center, Andrus accepts third-party payments and is on the provider list of several managed-care companies. Private payments may also be negotiated.

NEW DOMINION SCHOOL, INC.

Dillwyn, Virginia

Type: Wilderness school and treatment program

Affiliation: For-profit corporation

Population Served: Males, ages 11–18

Size: 64 students

Head of Facility: Melvin Klement, Executive Director; James M. O'Connor, M.A., M.S.W., Administrator; William Hyson, Ph.D, Educational Director

Contact: Chris Yates, Director, New Dominion School, Post Office Box 540, Dillwyn, Virginia 23936; 804-983-2051; fax: 804-983-2058

THE SCHOOL

New Dominion School, founded in 1976, serves youths who are experiencing emotional, behavioral, and learning problems. The major objectives at New Dominion School are to help a youth take positive control of his life, realize his self-worth, and return to his family and community as a responsible, contributing member of society.

The school is located on 500 acres in the rolling countryside of rural Virginia, 45 miles south of Charlottesville. This natural environment provides healthy outlets for energy and emotions and is conducive to activities that foster the development of self-discipline, self-confidence, and self-esteem. New Dominion operates a second wilderness program in western Maryland.

New Dominion School's year-round curriculum is accredited by the Southern Association of Colleges and Schools, and New Dominion is a member of the Virginia Association of Independent Special Education Facilities.

ELIGIBILITY

New Dominion's students possess at least average intellectual abilities, but factors such as poor self-esteem, emotional disturbance, negative peer relationships, involvement in drugs and alcohol, and delinquent behavior necessitate longer-term therapeutic intervention for the student.

Youths who are most appropriate for enrollment are those whose treatment needs can be met in New Dominion School's highly structured, disciplined, optimistic, and nurturing atmosphere.

New Dominion School does not accept youths who are below average in intellectual functioning, organically impaired, medication dependent, physically limited, actively suicidal, or clearly sociopathic.

Upon enrollment, the concerned parties and the student decide upon three relevant treatment goals and resolve to be committed to working toward the ultimate goal of healing broken trust and successfully reentering the community.

Most of New Dominion's students come from the mid-Atlantic states, with concentrations from Virginia, Maryland, Pennsylvania, and West Virginia.

ASSESSMENT

As a part of the application process for enrollment, New Dominion School's treatment team requires that a psychological assessment, along with educational materials and a family history, be submitted for review. If feasible, an on-site interview is scheduled with the youth and his parents or guardian to further assess the applicant's compatibility with New Dominion School's program. Interviews in the student's home community can be arranged if needed. After enrollment, an Individualized Education Plan and Treatment Plan are developed with the participation of the parents and the youth's treatment and educational staff. If subsequent psychological assessment is needed for postprogram placement or evaluation, it will be arranged with the consulting psychologist.

PROGRAM

Goals for students at New Dominion School include developing an increasing awareness of one's own needs, emotions, behavior, thoughts, and intentions; awareness of and sensitivity to the needs of others; taking personal responsibility for decisions and actions; developing interpersonal skills in expressing feelings and resolving conflicts; acquiring a desire to learn and explore creative talent; achieving academic success; developing good health habits and physical fitness; working cooperatively with others; and developing a positive self-image.

In order to achieve these goals, the students are challenged to meet their basic needs and experience both the positive and negative consequences of their actions. New Dominion utilizes a group-process problem-solving model in which youths and staff live together in structured therapeutic units consisting of ten boys and two full-time live-in adult counselors, with supervisory support available as needed. With the guidance and modeling of the trained staff, students participate in helping each other make positive changes and achieve goals. A positive group experience is formed to replace a negative peer group in the community. Trust relationships are formed by youths and staff working cooperatively in resolving problems and working toward mutual goals and positive outcomes.

Individual and group treatment is available 24 hours a day, seven days a week. When problems arise, a group member calls for a group meeting to resolve the issues. In this way, a youth's difficulties in relating to others are not treated in isolation from his daily actions. Instead, they are dealt with immediately, when they occur. If necessary, a student may be temporarily removed from the group, to work on the problem on an individual basis, until he is ready to return to the group and resolve the problem constructively.

Because most of the students have experienced problems in school, New Dominion utilizes an accredited experiential education curriculum until the student is ready to benefit from more formal classes. In fact, students earn their way into the formal academic program as they progress in achieving treatment goals. In this way, students are able to take charge of their education as they work through problems that have hindered success in the past.

New Dominion School offers a full range of accredited courses, from college-prep (leading to a New Dominion high school diploma) to GED preparation to remedial or secondary-level courses, to help students succeed in traditional school settings upon returning home.

Typically, completion of the program and readiness to return home take between fourteen and eighteen months.

Treatment-team meetings are held quarterly, and reports are sent to parents regarding both treatment and academic progress. In addition, the family work staff is always available to give an update, hold a family conference, or provide assistance.

STAFF

New Dominion School employs forty-five faculty and staff for sixty-four students. The twelve trained live-in group leaders, all holding a bachelor's degree or higher, participate in ongoing staff training and development. Supervisory personnel are advanced counselors and are highly trained and experienced. Teachers hold certification in specialties providing K–12–accredited curriculum and individualized instruction. Family support staff are given direction by the social worker/administrator. Routine nursing, clinic care, and referral to local physicians is provided. The licensed psychologist provides training and consultation, and New Dominion employs the services of an additional clinical psychologist who is certified in treating sexual abuse issues.

SPECIAL PROGRAMS

New Dominion provides weekly AA/NA meetings as well as a group led by a clinical psychologist, certified by the American Association of Sex Educators, Counselors, and Therapists, for students needing specialized assistance in dealing with sexual abuse issues. Family and aftercare support groups meet in

several areas, including Virginia, Pennsylvania, and Maryland.

Backpacking, canoeing, and bicycling wilderness trips are available to the groups who are at an appropriate level to derive maximum therapeutic benefit from this type of intensive programming.

CONTINUITY OF TREATMENT

Readiness for graduation from New Dominion is based upon demonstrable changes and progress in the group, at home, in academic achievement, and in the community.

As students progress in achieving treatment goals, there is a gradual transition toward home, and emphasis is placed on developing a viable postprogram plan.

Upon completion of the program, parents and students may attend one of the family support groups or may seek follow-up assistance from the family support staff. Postprogram plans include returning to public or private school, high school graduation, or completion of the GED program, followed by employment, entry into military service, or college enrollment.

BUILDINGS AND GROUNDS

The central campus comprises five cedar buildings that house a dining hall, administrative offices, a school, a library, a clinic, a movie theater, a vocational arts facility, and a shower house and laundry. Each group has its own village that is designed, built, and maintained by the group and located in an outlying wooded area of the property. Each village consists of residential, dining, cooking, and recreational structures. Wood stoves are used for heat in the winter. The 500-acre campus includes woods, fields and streams, ponds for fishing and swimming, playing fields, a basketball court, an archery course, and low ropes course.

ADMISSION AND FINANCIAL INFORMATION

Tuition is $73.31 per day and is billed on a monthly basis. Parents are responsible for clothing costs and also for prescription medication if needed. Depending upon distance from school, some transportation costs may be assumed by parents.

New Dominion operates on a year-round basis and accepts applicants for enrollment at any time. The family support staff and treatment team work closely with the family to help with information and support. Some insurance plans have assumed payment costs; for privately paid placements, individualized payment schedules can be arranged.

PINE MEADOWS SCHOOL

French Gulch, California

Type: Residential school

Affiliation: Private, for-profit

Population Served: Male and female, ages 12 to 18

Size: 41 students

Head of Facility: David W. Hull, President

Contact: Director of Admissions, 17351 Trinity Mountain Road, French Gulch, California 96033; 916-359-2211

THE SCHOOL

Pine Meadows is an established, private residential school located in the foothills of the beautiful Trinity Alps of northern California. Pine Meadows operates year-round for youths needing a structured, therapeutic treatment and educational program. The school is located on a former 556-acre cattle ranch that was originally the site of a large Wintu Indian village. Pine Meadows is just 20 minutes from Whiskeytown Lake and 45 minutes from the city of Redding. Students live in comfortable cottages and attend classes in a wonderfully situated, comprehensive facility.

The school is licensed by both the State Department of Social Services and the State Department of Education. It accepts boys and girls between the ages of 12 and 18 who are having behavioral, emotional, and educational problems. Students come to the school from throughout the United States. Pine Meadows is also licensed by the U.S. Department of Justice to accept students from other countries. There is no minimum time limit to completing the program at Pine Meadows.

ELIGIBILITY

Pine Meadows is a positive alternative for teenagers who cannot be educated within the normal public school offerings of programs.

Prior to entering Pine Meadows, students are often described by their parents as being impulsive, defiant, untruthful, self-destructive, manipulative, angry, and lazy. It is not unusual to hear of problems that include some involvement with drugs, alcohol, sex, stealing, physical and verbal abuse, defiance of authority, and negative peer relationships.

The individual counseling and attention provided at Pine Meadows slowly nourish the development of internal controls. At the same time, the imposed external controls of the program's rules and structure limit the acting-out behavior and emphasize that the student's normal negative behaviors will be unsuccessful in manipulating either the staff or the students.

As incentive for positive behavior, Pine Meadows uses a daily performance point system. Rewards and privileges are entirely based upon the point level attained by the student.

As the students progress, the internal controls of self-discipline and responsibility begin to emerge. The positive attention and rewards students receive for their positive behaviors build self-confidence and give them the feeling that success is always within their grasp. They eventually develop a positive pattern of behavior and the internal controls to successfully meet the challenges that will face them in life.

Pine Meadows cannot accept all referrals. Students not appropriate for placement are those who are mentally retarded, developmentally disabled, psychotic, on probation for serious felonies, actively suicidal, or who have been involved in setting fires.

ASSESSMENT

Psychological and educational testing is available to all students by resident staff on an as-needed basis. Depending upon the psychological tests performed, there may be an additional charge.

Additionally, most students are educationally tested on an annual basis to determine their progress.

PROGRAMS

All students are assigned a therapist upon entering the program and are required to meet formally each week for a minimum of one hour of individual therapy with the assigned clinician. Students are also required to attend weekly group and family therapy sessions. Weekly family therapy, usually done over a conference telephone, is an important ingredient in reducing the amount of time it takes to complete the program.

In addition to the traditional individual, group, and family telephone therapies, Pine Meadows offers art therapy for students who are "closed" emotionally. Crisis intervention is used on a situational basis by a large number of qualified staff to augment all formal treatment.

All Pine Meadows students have an individual education and treatment plan developed within the first six weeks of placement. Each plan is tailored to the individual academic and emotional needs of the student. Goals and specific objectives are listed and agreed upon between the principal, assigned counselor, parent, and student.

The educational program is divided between academic classes and vocational training in which all students participate. Students attend classes from 8:30 a.m. until 3 p.m. each day, 210 school days each year. Included in this schedule is a summer school session of six weeks. Emphasis in the academic classes is placed upon the basics of successful communication (written and oral) and learning. Classes are small, seldom exceeding more than ten students, and are taught by credentialed special education teachers. An individual curriculum is prepared for each student. Every effort is made to help the students experience an expanding number of successes in their daily work. This slowly increases their self-confidence in handling academic work and decreases negative behavior in the classroom.

At 5 p.m. dinner is served to all students. Following clean-up, students are allowed time for personal phone calls. Evening activities include classes in survival training, music, study hall, leather crafts, stress reduction, table games, sports, and discussion groups. Students are required to attend three or four of these special activities every day to widen their education and strengthen their ability to relate appropriately to peers and adults.

Students are required to be in their cottages at 9:30 p.m. on school nights, with lights off prior to 10 p.m. On weekends, students must be in their cottages before 10:30 p.m. with lights off before 11 p.m. and have the option of sleeping in until brunch on Saturday and Sunday.

Permanent change is a slow process that is characterized at Pine Meadows by six stages. Movement from one stage to the next is determined by monthly meetings that allow staff to evaluate long-term patterns of behavior change. The time that it takes to move from one stage to the next is totally dependent upon the student. In order for a student to have the greatest chance of success following graduation from Pine Meadows, all six stages must be completed.

Students who are on stages three through six may visit their homes during vacation periods if they have earned the privilege. An exception to this policy is the Christmas break when students may visit home for between several days and two weeks, depending upon their behavior.

STAFF
All of Pine Meadows' teachers are fully credentialed in the state of California and all of Pine Meadows' therapists have at least an M.A. or higher in their field. A detailed description of faculty members' qualifications is available upon request.

SPECIAL PROGRAMS
Ranching and agriculture classes are offered to all students. Taught by a credentialed teacher with years of ranching experience, the program takes advantage of a large amount of acreage by raising a variety of farm animals and vegetable crops. Students learn how to care for and ride the horses and work with various livestock and crops.

Pine Meadows occasionally conducts exciting educational travel experiences, depending upon the number of students eligible to attend. The most popular is a nine-day trip to Washington, D.C., and Virginia, where students visit and learn about various historic sites.

CONTINUITY OF TREATMENT
Students who complete Pine Meadows' six stages are ready to return to a normal educational setting. Most students who graduate with a diploma proceed to college or university. Students who complete the program and need to finish high school usually return home and attend either a public school, or preferably, a boarding school. Pine Meadows' graduates typically function at their highest level of performance within the more structured environment of a boarding school.

BUILDINGS AND GROUNDS
Pine Meadows School is situated in a beautiful valley surrounded by mountains that are forested with oaks and pines. A river running through campus provides excellent fishing for the students. West of the river is the barn, agriculture science area, boys' cottages, and all classrooms. The east side of the river has the offices, cafeteria, and girls' cottages. Most cottages sleep six students, with two students in each room. All cottages are heated and have their own bathrooms and showers.

ADMISSION AND FINANCIAL INFORMATION
Pine Meadows operates on a July through June fiscal year and publishes its rates for that period. There are three basic payment plans:

Plan A - Monthly rate for payment *after* service is provided: $4454. This is the average monthly cost charged to organizations, companies, insurance carriers, and public agencies that require a month of service to be performed prior to Pine Meadows billing for reimbursement.

Plan B - Monthly rate for payment *before* service is provided: $4000. This is the rate charged to parents, and payment must arrive prior to the monthly anniversary admission date. First and last months' payments must be received no later than the first day of placement.

Plan C - Monthly rate with partial scholarship. This rate depends upon the amount of the scholarship given.

Pine Meadows is willing to work with any insurance carriers, and students may apply for, and be awarded, partial scholarships.

THE PINES
TREATMENT CENTER

A Residential Treatment Center For Children and Adolescents

Portsmouth, Virginia

Type: Multicampus adolescent residential treatment facility

Affiliation: Operated by First Hospital Corporation, Norfolk, Virginia

Population Served: Male and female, ages 5 to 21

Size: 326 residents

Head of Facility: Edward C. Irby Jr., Executive Director

Contact: Merrill A. Friedman, Referral Development Director, 825 Crawford Parkway, Portsmouth, Virginia 23704; 804-393-0061; fax: 804-393-1029

THE FACILITY

The Pines Residential Treatment Center is a multicampus operation that evolved from FHC of Portsmouth. The Pines consists of four distinct programs, located on two sites within the city of Portsmouth, Virginia. The facilities are centrally located and provide excellent opportunities for community activities and involvement. The facility is accredited by the Joint Commission on Accreditation of Healthcare Organizations (JCAHO) and is licensed by the state of Virginia.

ELIGIBILITY

Those likely to benefit from the programs offered within The Pines are those individuals who have a DSM-III diagnosis of psychiatric illness for residential care; those with a significant impairment of social, interpersonal, educational, or vocational functioning that requires the provision of multidisciplinary treatment interventions; or those for whom appropriate community or family resources do not exist. In addition, potential candidates must be able to functionally participate in the treatment program and must display the potential to both benefit from the program and transfer to a lower level of care within a predictable period of time. It is also common for potential candidates to have failed in less restrictive settings and experienced multiple psychiatric hospitalizations. Those individuals not appropriate for programs offered by The Pines are those who are in need of detoxification, those who are acutely or severely disorganized, or those whose unstable medical conditions require intensive medical management.

ASSESSMENT

The Pines Residential Treatment Center welcomes referrals from social services agencies, court service units, local education agencies, mental health practitioners, private physicians, the candidate, family, and others. Multidisciplinary teams that include the resident, parents, and referral sources devise individual treatment plans that are specific to each resident's needs.

PROGRAMS

The Phoenix Program is one of four programs providing intensive, highly structured treatment for adolescents and young adults with severe emotional and behavioral disturbances. Such disturbances are typically characterized by self-destructive behavior; highly impulsive, aggressive, and sometimes violent behavior; chronic failure in school; an inability to develop relationships with peers and adults; and other problems often complicated by emotional deprivation. The Phoenix Program serves a much-needed role, positioned between acute psychiatric hospitalization and open residential treatment.

The Behavioral Studies Program provides multiple treatment units in a highly structured residential treatment environment for adjudicated and nonadjudicated male and female sexual offenders from youth to young adult ages. Separated according to age, level of emotional maturity, and cognitive capabilities, each resident receives a comprehensive psychological assessment. This profile is based on results from physiological laboratory tests as well as other, more traditional, methods and indicates specific therapeutic intervention techniques that guide the formulation of an individualized treatment plan.

The Open Adolescent Program, for adolescents and young adults ages 14 to 22, is based in two townhouses (one for males and one for females) where each unit targets the developmental and clinical needs of its specific population. Older adolescents learn independent living skills through vocational training, on- and off-campus employment programs, GED preparation, and driver education. For younger adolescents and those who need a greater degree of structure and treatment intensity, there are two other single-sex units.

The Children and Youth Program provides intermediate- to long-term residential treatment for emotionally disturbed youngsters ages 5 to 14. The program offers a secure and structured environment in which residents can utilize the therapeutic resources to remedy problems that affect social, interpersonal, and educational functioning.

Each resident's program follows an Individualized Service Plan that is directed by a multidisciplinary team under the leadership of a child psychiatrist. The therapeutic milieu incorporates individual, group, family, and behavioral interventions as well as pharmacotherapy when indicated. A year-round education program, directed by teachers, counselors, and recreation staff, in conjunction with ample outdoor and recreational activities, addresses each child's special learning needs while promoting a balanced life.

STAFF

The Pines Residential Treatment Center is staffed by a team of psychiatrists, psychologists, social workers, direct-care staff, educators, and activities/recreation counselors. This cohesive multidisciplinary team is an integral part of the resident's course of treatment from the time of referral to the time of discharge.

CONTINUITY OF TREATMENT

Believing that continuity of the caregiver is one of the central variables ensuring success for the transition of residential patients back into the community, the treatment teams offer alternative residential settings. Forty specialized community-based-program beds, which are in five different houses across the street from the main campus, meet this need. Each program is uniquely designed to meet the transitional and independent living needs of the residents.

Those residents who do not require group placement work, throughout the course of treatment, toward their eventual return to the community. A follow-up program to track each resident's success functions as a treatment tool in discharge planning.

BUILDINGS AND GROUNDS
The facilities are exceptional, offering many recreational resources, including gymnasiums, tennis courts, ball fields, swimming pools, and a vocational education and training center.

ADMISSION AND FINANCIAL INFORMATION
State funds, Blue Cross/Blue Shield, CHAMPUS, and other major insurance carriers are accepted. The Pines Residential Treatment Center does not discriminate on the basis of race, color, religion, or national origin.

CHARTER
PROVO CANYON SCHOOL

Provo, Utah

Type: Residential treatment
Affiliation: Charter Medical Corporation; for-profit
Population Served: Male and female, ages 12 to 18
Size: 210 students
Head of Facility: Robert R. Harrison, Administrator
Contact: Ms. Gina Van Valkenburg, Provo Canyon School, 4501 North University Avenue, Post Office Box 1441, Provo, Utah 84103; 801-227-2000

THE SCHOOL
Provo Canyon School, founded in 1971, is located in Provo, Utah, a university town of 70,000, at the foot of majestic Mount Timpanogos in the Wasatch range of the Rocky Mountains.

Provo Canyon School's overall goal is to help each patient resolve the therapeutic issues necessary to facilitate a successful reintegration into home and society. By experiencing growth opportunities, patients are encouraged to care for themselves and for others. Through these growth experiences, patients have the opportunity to increase self-esteem and achieve personal goals. Although Provo Canyon School has created a highly structured environment, it believes that patients must do their own therapeutic work to succeed. Provo Canyon School supports the students in that work and encourages them to develop their individual potential. Staff members encourage patients to practice behavior that motivates growth and development in academics, behavior, and personal values.

Provo Canyon School is fully accredited by the Joint Commission on Accreditation of Healthcare Organizations (JCAHO).

ELIGIBILITY
Adolescents ages 12 to 18 are accepted with a variety of adjustment problems related to family, communication difficulties, lack of respect for the rights of others, running away, persistent lying, stealing within the home, argumentativeness, noncompliant behaviors, physical aggressiveness, lack of emotional bonding, or violations of family rules. There may be problems related to personal and emotional functioning, substance abuse, poor self-image, impulsivity, inadequate judgment-making skills, low frustration tolerance, depression, and temper outbursts. Provo Canyon School also works with teens who have academic difficulties related to disruptive or delinquent behaviors, poor performance, or mild to moderate learning disabilities. Provo Canyon School's program is not appropriate for youngsters with severe psychotic disorders or other psychiatric illnesses that require acute hospitalization or those who have significant physical handicaps that would limit their ability to participate fully in treatment. Provo Canyon School is also not appropriate for students with severe learning disabilities. Other exclusionary criteria include brain injury or impairment, organic brain syndrome, chronic violent behavior, severe sexual disorders, pregnancy, or significant medical illness.

Average enrollment is 190 students, generally with 60 percent boys and 40 percent girls. Students come from all across the United States, including Alaska, and reflect all socioeconomic levels.

ASSESSMENT
The admissions process requires submission of records of prior treatment or placements, with particular emphasis on psychological testing, psychiatric evaluation, and social and behavioral history. Upon admission, each student completes an internal assessment process that includes a medical history and physical examination, a psychiatric evaluation, a psychological evaluation, substance-abuse testing, a social history, and an academic assessment.

The referring therapist, physician, or counselor is involved in treatment planning as much as possible. Based on the initial assessment, all treatment plans are individualized and developed by the student's treatment team and regularly modified as appropriate.

PROGRAM
The treatment program provides weekly individual and group therapy, including specialized groups for such issues as sexual abuse and anger management. Provo Canyon also offers a full therapeutic recreation program and a state-licensed, long-term drug and alcohol treatment program based on the Twelve-Step model. Thus, most youngsters in the program receive up to five therapeutic interventions per week in addition to daily unit processing meetings.

One of the aspects that makes Provo Canyon School unique from other mental health treatment programs is its very strong academic component. A fully accredited and licensed junior high and high school program is offered that provides a multitrack approach to meeting the needs of a full academic spectrum, from patients working at the honors level to learning disabled patients requiring resource classes.

Provo Canyon School is licensed by the Northwest Association of Schools and Colleges as well as by the states of Utah and California. The Individual Education Plan is used to track academic progress. Patients generally attend seven academic periods a day in Provo Canyon's year-round school, allowing patients to receive nearly one and one-half years of academic credit in one year. Since many of the patients are behind academically when they arrive, Provo Canyon School's ability to accelerate their patients' education so that they can catch up with their peers is a significant benefit.

Since many of the youngsters who are admitted to the program have a history of running away, have acting-out tendencies, and can occasionally become aggressive, Provo Canyon School maintains a secure area in the facility. The secure area consists of an orientation unit for new patients, as well as an "investment" unit for those who have had major behavioral infractions. Within the investment area are seclusion rooms for youngsters who choose to act dangerously to themselves or others. The use of these rooms must be approved by the psychiatrist, and the youngsters are regularly monitored while they regain control of their behavior. As soon as they are in control, their therapist works with them to move them toward their appropriate level.

As the adolescents progress through the program, they move from the "orientation" status to open units on campus where they have more freedom and responsibilities. While these units are not locked, they are supervised at all times.

During a typical day, students wake up at 7 a.m. and have approximately ½ hour to dress, make their beds, and take care of their personal hygiene. Breakfast is served from 7:30 to 8 a.m., followed by time for students' unit responsibilities. Students are involved in school from 8:20 a.m. until 2:40 p.m., attending eight periods, including a lunch break and a study hall. From 2:45 until 5 p.m., students are involved in individual, group, or recreation therapy, or unit activities. Dinner is served from 5 to 6:30 p.m., followed by a variety of activities including on- or off-campus work experience, intramurals, swimming, gym time, homework time, and on- or off-campus recreational activities. In the evenings students have a ½ hour snack time with access to the school store, where they may spend a portion of their allowance on a variety of snack items. Following showers, students must be in bed by 10 p.m., and have their lights out by 10:20 p.m.

The program provides 24-hour nursing services, and contracted family medicine physicians are on campus daily as needed for illnesses or injuries of a minor nature. More serious needs are handled via contracts with local hospitals. Patients who need psychotropic medication are seen weekly by the psychiatrist. Initial nursing assessments and physical exams are performed on campus by the nursing staff and contracted physician.

STAFF

Provo Canyon School's commitment to helping adolescents is reflected in the tenure of the staff. The average length of service for the senior staff is more than eleven years. The 220 full- and part-time staff includes twenty-two therapists, twenty-four teachers, sixteen nurses, and over eighty group-living staff as well as a complement of support services personnel.

The therapy staff reflects a range of disciplines including psychiatry, psychology, family therapy, social work, and therapeutic recreation. The teaching staff reflects Provo Canyon School's belief that expertise in the subject matter is as important as special education credentials. The teachers, most of whom are prepared at the master's level, are able to provide challenge and support appropriate to the intellectual abilities of all students.

SPECIAL PROGRAMS

Northern Utah offers unparalleled outdoor recreational opportunities. During winter, snow skiing (downhill and cross-country) is a popular activity. During the summer months, hiking, caving, and trips to Lake Powell for waterskiing and camping keep the calendar full. Provo Canyon School's Therapy Without Walls offers a highly structured six-day wilderness experience for selected adolescents. Participation in all of these activities is dependent on behavioral stability.

As an organization, Provo Canyon School has no religious affiliation but does seek to meet the needs of its students by providing a basic offering of religious services. The school provides a nondenominational chaplain who conducts regular religious services each Sunday and has ties with representative clergy from established religious faiths

who provide individual and small-group services upon request. It is Provo Canyon School's policy to provide students with the opportunity to pursue spiritual growth consistent with family choices and the dictates of their own consciences.

BUILDINGS AND GROUNDS

Provo Canyon School enjoys the advantage of two separate campuses, totaling 12 acres. Therapeutic and diversional recreation is emphasized in the program.

Facilities include the traditional complement of gymnasium, swimming pool, and outdoor competitive athletic fields as well as a complete bowling alley, skateboard ramps, and a climbing wall. Provo Canyon School offers areas dedicated to the creative arts, including pottery ovens and a complete photography laboratory. The 500-seat auditorium has a full range of audiovisual support and provides a setting for music, drama, and special presentations.

ADMISSION AND FINANCIAL INFORMATION

There are two basic rates of payment available at Provo Canyon School. The first is $239 per day. This rate includes room and board, routine academic services, all psychiatric and psychological services, all therapeutic and behavioral modification services, first-aid supplies and nursing services, laundry services, supervised use of recreational equipment and facilities, and supervised work projects.

Pharmacy charges, laboratory charges, and charges for outside medical and dental visits (i.e., office calls, drug screening, H.C.G. tests, etc.), are billed on a per-usage basis.

The second rate is billed at a flat rate of $252 per day, which includes the pharmacy and laboratory charges associated with psychiatric care. Under either option, the family is responsible for personal amenities and additional expenses, which generally average $75 per month.

Limited scholarship funds are available. Awarding of scholarships is based entirely on family financial need.

Admission is on a continuous basis, and initial inquiry is welcome at any time. There is no separate fee for the admission process. Provo Canyon School strongly encourages parents to be at the school during the admission process. While a formal interview is not required, a complete package of information must be provided before a decision can be made. Families may request information and admission packages by calling 800-848-9819.

QUEST
Residential School

Boonville, California

Type: Boarding school
Affiliation: Corporate ownership; nonprofit
Population Served: Male, ages 6 to 18
Size: Approximately 20 students
Heads of Facility: Robin C. Harris, Donna L. Harris, Directors
Contact: Mr. or Mrs. Harris, Post Office Box 400, Boonville, California 95415; 707-895-2613

THE SCHOOL
Quest was founded in 1984 to meet the intellectual, emotional, and social needs of children and adolescents who have mild learning or behavior difficulties and who need a highly individualized, caring, and familylike setting. Quest is not a clinical treatment facility but an early-intervention boarding school that operates on an academic calendar with typical vacation periods.

Quest is situated on a majestic 40-acre mountainside in California's redwood country. While the location is clearly rural, Quest is only 4 miles from Boonville, a town of 1,500 people, 2 hours north of San Francisco. The school enjoys a distinct four-season, moderate climate and is only 20 miles from the Pacific Ocean at an elevation of 1,500 feet. The terrain and clear mountain nights are perfect for stargazing and contribute to the serenity of the setting.

Quest is a nonprofit corporation governed by a five-person board of directors.

ELIGIBILITY
Typical students are those with attention deficit disorders, dyslexia, or other learning difficulties who are not thriving in a traditional school setting. Motivation and attendance problems may be present despite adequate academic ability. Low self-esteem, poor peer relationships, rebellion, and anger and frustration are typical. In addition, the student may deny that he has any control over his behavior or that a problem even exists. Frequently, he is not functioning satisfactorily as a member of his family and is not meeting his responsibilities. Sometimes the family itself is dysfunctional. Whatever the specific circumstances, consistency and structure are needed to prevent the escalation of these behaviors.

Students who are out of control, have severe emotional or social difficulties, or whose behavior is related to substance abuse are not eligible for Quest's program. Parents need to know that their son will not be exposed to appreciably greater negative influences while enrolled at Quest. Indeed, some children are at Quest simply because they need a positive experience.

Enrollment is voluntary, with the greatest emphasis placed upon the student's commitment to participate in a program of growth and change, although he may not be able to verbalize that commitment at the time of enrollment. Specific intelligence scores are not a factor in enrollment and entrance testing is not required. Each student is accepted at his present level of achievement.

Very young students do well at Quest. Much care is taken with children who need extra care and nurturing—hugs during the day and tucking-in at night—and whose daily hygiene requirements may need supervision.

ASSESSMENT
Because Quest accepts students at face value, the school prefers to move slowly through an informal diagnostic regimen rather than administer an initial battery of tests, which may be threatening and perhaps inconclusive. Because classes are very small and a great deal of the instruction is tutorial, the faculty determines students' needs relatively easily. Previous evaluations and psychological histories are studied carefully and objectively.

PROGRAMS
Quest's primary goal is that each boy become a truly happy and fully functioning individual with an increased sense of self-worth and the capacity for introspection.

Students learn to deal effectively with anger and frustration, improve the quality of their peer relationships, handle authority, earn trust, accept responsibility, and develop a positive work ethic. By learning to be contributing, thoughtful members of a group, they develop attitudes and behaviors consistent with harmonious family relationships.

Structure and consistency are essential. Students' enthusiasms are encouraged and their freedoms valued within a framework of clearly set guidelines and limits. Quest utilizes a four-level system, of which the fourth level is one of reasonable responsibilities and privileges. All students enter on this level. The goal is to remain there. Lower levels carry diminished freedom and privileges, and the climb back to Level Four is a challenge. A weekly point-earning system provides a continuum of positive reinforcement.

Students and staff share responsibilities of daily living. Students clean their living quarters each day and must choose from a list of daily chores. In addition, each has a permanent assignment such as care of the chickens or rabbits or maintenance of the school van. Students also help in the preparation of meals.

Extensive group and individual counseling, staff and peer counseling, and conflict resolution programs are utilized. A required Mastership class teaches stress management and relaxation techniques, and hypnotherapy services are available.

The academic program is individualized, ranging from remedial to college-preparatory courses. Students may be mainstreamed or remain through grade 12. Most students advance academically at a rate greater than 1:1 years because they progress, unimpeded, at their own pace in each subject area. Comprehensive reports are issued throughout the year, and a high level of communication is maintained with parents.

The elective program is impressively varied for a school of Quest's size. Not only are elective classes a career exploration vehicle, but success in an elective area is often the springboard to enhanced self-esteem. Students may take three or four electives. Most choose woodcraft/construction, auto mechanics, art and design, and culinary arts.

Physical education and recreation are noncompetitive. Archery, weight-lifting, hiking, and jogging are popular throughout the year. Swimming, water skiing, camping, backpacking, and fishing are carried on in fall and spring. A three-day snow-skiing trip is taken each winter.

Periodic weekend visitations by parents may commence following a satisfactory adjustment period.

STAFF

A full-time residential faculty is maintained to provide a faculty-to-student ratio of 1:3. Academic and counseling programs are coordinated by the Directors, credentialed teachers with a combined fifty years' experience in special education, public school administration, and counseling. The faculty shares living group supervision.

SPECIAL PROGRAMS

Quest's Student Industry Program offers children and adolescents an opportunity to participate in a business. Typical industries include book publishing, prefabricated storage buildings, and a culinary product.

A special summer program is provided for boys, ages 6 to 12, who have learning or behavior difficulties similar to those of Quest's regular student body.

CONTINUITY OF TREATMENT

Much time is spent in career education, determining interests and assessing options. Plans are developed between the student, faculty, and parents for continued education. Most students enter a community college or technical school. Many have gone on to four-year colleges and universities. For students reentering mainstream elementary or secondary education, the faculty assists with educational planning for the ensuing year.

BUILDINGS AND GROUNDS

Quest's facility is a former resort. A huge lodge with 24-foot ceilings and a massive fireplace overlooks the swimming pool. The former restaurant is now the dining room. Students live in two-bedroom cottages, carpeted and heated, each with a full bath. Between four and six students live in each cottage. Cottages are adjacent to staff homes for optimum supervision. Living areas are widely separated, so younger students live at some distance from older ones, with separate and inviolate play areas.

The comfortable and inviting library has 3,000 volumes and an extensive periodicals room. Classroom buildings, conference rooms, and shops complete the home away from home. Groves of redwood, fir, and madrone serve as outdoor classrooms, conference areas, and wonderful sites for clubhouses and tree forts.

ADMISSION AND FINANCIAL INFORMATION

Tuition is $21,400 for the academic year, payable in two installments or monthly by arrangement. Students may enroll during the year with tuition prorated. Tuition is inclusive. There are no special fees for books and materials, recreation, or other "extras." A reasonable weekly student allowance must be provided.

A visit and interview are an important part of the enrollment procedure. However, because some students come from considerable distances, a visit may not be possible. In this event, other options can be explored.

ᴄɦᴇ ᴘᴏᴄᴋ ᴄʀᴇᴇᴋ ᴄᴇɴᴛᴇʀ

Lemont, Illinois

Type: Private psychiatric hospital that includes adolescent inpatient, partial hospitalization, and NCA–accredited high school programs

Affiliation: Rush Presbyterian St. Luke's Hospital; for-profit

Population Served: Male and female, age 11 through adulthood

Size: 45 inpatient beds and 50 partial hospitalization beds

Directors of Facility: Ian Aitken and Jesse Viner, M.D.

Contact: Ms. Edie Comeils, RN, 40 Timberline Drive, Lemont, Illinois 60439; 708-257-3636 or 800-669-2426; fax: 708-257-8846

THE FACILITY

In June 1989, the Rock Creek Center opened its doors to treat severely disturbed adults and adolescents in need of inpatient hospitalization. The Rock Creek Center was the first psychiatric facility of its kind in its geographical area. Since opening, the hospital has maintained its original commitment to provide longer-term individualized psychiatric treatment to men and women in need. In addition, Rock Creek Center has expanded its inpatient program to include shorter lengths of stay.

The treatment approach is eclectic and encompasses psychodynamic models as well as behavioral, biological, familial, social, and vocational interventions. Family treatment is an integrated component of the therapeutic model.

The Rock Creek Center is located on 42 acres of land approximately 30 miles southwest of downtown Chicago. Patients reside in single-story lodges designed to maximize patient/staff collaboration within the treatment milieu. Treatment evolves within the context of a therapeutic community where patients are encouraged to actively engage in their treatment.

The Rock Creek Center is accredited by both the Joint Commission on Accreditation of Healthcare Organizations and the North Central Accreditation for Junior High and High Schools.

ELIGIBILITY

The Rock Creek Center treats patients who suffer from depression, psychosis, schizophrenia, suicidality, anorexia, bulimia, multiple personality disorder, narcissistic personality disorder, manic depressive and bipolar disorder, and substance abuse.

Although many patients have severe learning problems, the Rock Creek Center does not admit patients with severe mental retardation or severe organic impairment.

Patients may be admitted on a voluntary, involuntary, or informal basis.

ASSESSMENT

Following an initial, intensive period of evaluation, each patient's program is designed to meet the individual patient's and family's needs. The evaluation can include a comprehensive nursing assessment, a psychiatric evaluation, a family evaluation, a psychoeducational evaluation, an educational assessment, a biological evaluation, neuropsychological testing (when indicated), and other screening assessments. Additional assessments may include a substance abuse evaluation, an eating disorders assessment, or a language evaluation.

Professional referrals are not necessary. Individuals can call the Rock Creek Center directly to schedule an evaluation or to receive admission information on any of the Rock Creek Center's programs.

PROGRAMS

The Rock Creek Center is able to offer a comprehensive diagnostic assessment and treatment plan. This process includes engaging the patient and family in a psychotherapeutic relationship in order to begin the work required to resolve long-standing problems. Patients participate in vocation evaluation and training, psychodrama, group and individual art therapy, and individual, group, music, family, multiple family, and recreation therapy. Adolescents attend a fully accredited junior high school program that serves students twelve months a year. Class size does not exceed five students, and students' abilities range from remedial to honors level. The unique hospital school includes a fully equipped laboratory for science and offers learning disabled students prescriptive instruction to meet their learning needs.

The Rock Creek Center Adolescent Inpatient Program offers intensive psychiatric treatment to adolescents. The program incorporates individual and group therapy, intensive milieu therapy, family therapy, academic education, and a variety of therapeutic and recreational activities.

Patients are admitted 24 hours a day, seven days a week. Calls regarding admission are directed to the Consultation, Referral and Admissions Department.

As with all of the 24-hour programs at the Rock Creek Center, the Adolescent Inpatient Program distinguishes itself by offering a full-time medical staff to conduct and review treatment and lead the intensive, community-milieu program. Moreover, the noninstitutional setting is an important factor in reducing stress often generated by hospitalization.

The unique eating disorders and substance abuse services at the Rock Creek Center provide patients with comprehensive assessments and individually designed treatment programs. Assessment, consultation, and treatment are available to adolescent and adult patients hospitalized for long or brief periods.

The Rock Creek Center Community Clinic offers a full range of outpatient services for individuals, couples, and families as well as specific, clinically focused groups. The Clinic serves children, adolescents, and adults.

STAFF

The adolescent service interdisciplinary staff includes credentialed psychiatrists, clinical psychologists, clinical social workers, nurses, mental health counselors, recreational therapists (including an artist-in-residence), an occupational therapist, and a nutritionist. Areas of clinical specialties include dual diagnosis, eating disorders, and psychopharma-cological treatment.

SPECIAL PROGRAMS

The school day is a core component of adolescent treatment at the Rock Creek Center. Both inpatient adolescents and those attending the partial hospitalization program are enrolled in school at the Learning Center of the Rock Creek Center. Each student's instructional program provides academic challenge, enrichment, and success.

The educational program is designed to foster the student's cognitive strengths, address limitations, and provide remediation. The Learning Center's staff strives to build a sense of competence, responsibility, and self-worth into prescriptive and group teaching in order to help form an appropriate educational program.

The school within the Learning Center has earned North Central Accreditation for Junior High and High School Programs as well as approval by the Illinois State Board of Education for administering a therapeutic school. The school operates as a departmentalized high school, meeting Monday through Friday, twelve months a year. The curriculum is taught by Illinois-certified high school teachers and special-ists in learning disabilities and behavioral disorders. Thoughtful classroom placement and heterogeneous groups afford cooperative learning and modeling from peers as well as teachers.

The partnership among the Learning Center's staff, the student, the student's parents, and the home-school contact person provides the linkage necessary to ensure post-hospitalization success.

CONTINUITY OF TREATMENT

A patient may be hospitalized at the Rock Creek Center for a week or less for a diagnostic evaluation; intensive treatment may require a longer inpatient or partial hospitalization stay.

The goals for treatment include a comprehensive diagnosis, stabilization of symptoms, preparation for less intensive or restrictive care, networking to community resources for post-discharge support available to patients and families, and educational planning at an elementary, secondary, or college level. Patients, staff, and families work toward achieving these goals prior to discharge.

BUILDINGS AND GROUNDS

The Rock Creek Center is located on 42 acres of wooded property. Patients live in single-story lodges that each house sixteen patients. Each lodge has one triple, three single, and five double rooms, each with a private bath. Although each lodge has a fully equipped kitchen, the main dining room is where main meals are eaten by staff and adolescent and adult patients.

ADMISSION AND FINANCIAL INFORMATION

The admissions office at the Rock Creek Center is open to receive calls 24 hours a day, seven days a week and can be reached by calling 708-257-3636 or 800-669-2426. Evening, night, and weekend calls are received by the campus supervisor.

The Rock Creek Center's all-inclusive fee covers room and board, therapist's fees, medication, nursing care, school, family therapy, music, recreation and occupational therapy, diagnostic testing, and all other assessment and treatment modalities that occur on campus. Medicare and private insurance are appropriate funding resources. Rock Creek Center's business office provides assistance in identifying benefits.

ROCKY MOUNTAIN ACADEMY

Bonners Ferry, Idaho

Type: Boarding school

Affiliation: CEDU Schools

Population served: Male and female, ages 13 to 18

Size: Approximately 160 students

Heads of School: Doug Kim-Brown, Headmaster, and Robert W. Spear Jr., President

Contact: Ranel Hanson, Admissions Director, Rocky Mountain Academy, Route One, Bonners Ferry, Idaho 83805; telephone: 208-267-7522

THE SCHOOL

Rocky Mountain Academy (RMA) was founded in 1982. A CEDU school, Rocky Mountain provides students with a safe place to develop emotionally, intellectually, socially, and physically. CEDU Education, developed in 1967, addresses the emotional and intellectual needs of the whole child.

RMA's year-round curriculum includes extensive family involvement, as family issues are explored and resolved during parent and family seminars and workshops. Held throughout the year, these workshops offer parents an in-depth understanding of their child's experience as well as an opportunity to address the dynamics of the student-family relationship. In addition to the workshops, parent and family visits take place on and off campus and provide opportunities for families to reestablish relationships.

The school occupies a 120-acre site in the scenic mountains of northern Idaho. Located 6 miles outside of the small farming town of Bonners Ferry, the campus is within a short drive of the Canadian border. RMA's setting and facilities perfectly accommodate a curriculum that includes a challenging academic program, athletics, wilderness expeditions, a working farm, and vocational training. All activities at the school focus on the emotional development of the students.

RMA is a private institution governed by a four-member Board of Directors. It is a fully accredited special-purpose high school as recognized by the Northwest Association of Schools and Colleges.

ELIGIBILITY

RMA students, despite their high potential, have experienced poor interpersonal relationships, failure in school, or problems within the family. They have had difficulties at home or in traditional academic settings. Many have low self-esteem, poor peer relationships, and difficulty accepting responsibility for their behavior. The highly structured and nurturing environment at the Academy assists students in untangling the failures, frustrations, and angers of their past.

The school seeks applicants who possess the ability to achieve emotionally and academically, although this ability may have been hampered by learning difficulties, life circumstances, or counterproductive personal choices. The Academy's active program is not meant to be easy; however, it is not beyond the ability of any young person who is of average intelligence.

The school enrolls young people from all geographic regions of the United States as well as several foreign countries. Students on certain psychotropic medications may be eligible for enrollment upon the review of medical records and history. Home enrollment and escort services are available upon request.

ASSESSMENT

To ensure proper placement at Rocky Mountain Academy, a complete developmental and psychological history is obtained on all candidates for admission. Previous educational and clinical assessments and diagnostic workups are reviewed by the Academy's professional staff to facilitate enrollment and program planning. Additional assessment, if needed, is completed by the staff.

PROGRAMS

Rocky Mountain Academy's goals for students include personal accountability, improved family relations, and sharpened decision-making and problem-solving skills. Graduates are better equipped to steer themselves in a positive direction as they meet the challenges of young adulthood.

RMA's extensive emotional-growth curriculum utilizes experientially based education to assist students in redirecting their energies. Group and individual counseling coupled with nine emotional-growth workshops are the fundamental cornerstones of the program.

Rocky Mountain Academy offers individualized academic programs ranging from college-preparatory to remedial studies. The four-quarter school year, a maximum class size of twelve students, and an overall student-faculty ratio of 3:1 allow students to catch up on missed academic studies and to advance at a faster rate. Report cards, along with an evaluation of the student's overall progress, are sent to parents each quarter. In addition, parents are updated regularly by their Family Resource Coordinator.

All students participate in a Wilderness Program designed to promote fitness, self-discipline, group problem-solving skills, and self-confidence. Students are challenged by canoeing, hiking, jogging, cross-country skiing, and rock- and mountain-climbing. Off-campus wilderness excursions, varying in length from four to fourteen days, assist students in breaking through their self-imposed limitations.

Standards of conduct at RMA are based on acceptable social values of group living. They support a system by which students can strive to achieve self-worth, responsibility, and maturity. To sustain an environment in which students are encouraged to maintain good health and make positive choices, negative influences such as violence and drug and alcohol use are not permitted.

STAFF

Rocky Mountain Academy's faculty members are highly trained to work with adolescents and young adults. In addition to completing the emotional-growth curriculum, each faculty member actively participates in ongoing training and development.

RMA's clinical staff includes a nurse, a licensed psychiatrist, and a neuropsychologist, offering medical supervision, diagnostic services, and individual therapy as needed.

CONTINUITY OF TREATMENT

Each faculty adviser assists students, parents, and any appropriate consulting professionals in creating a postgraduate plan for continued success. Students and their families develop a plan of action and set goals for the student's future and for their relationships. More than 85 percent of RMA graduates go on to such colleges and universities as Boston University, Emory, Syracuse, UCLA, and Willamette.

BUILDINGS AND GROUNDS

RMA's campus includes twenty-two buildings plus numerous athletic fields and outdoor experiential learning sites. Students are housed in dormitory buildings with rooms large enough to maximize the development of a variety of friendships and small enough to encourage closeness. Four to six students share each furnished room and the accompanying large bathroom area. Laundry facilities are available in each dorm. Faculty houses are part of or near each dorm, providing 24-hour access to faculty members.

Rocky Mountain Academy's dining room is a focal point of the campus. Open to the kitchen, with its wood-burning cooking stoves and frequent smells of fresh-baked breads, the dining room allows students and faculty to relax and spend time together.

The campus houses a weavery, a tepee, a pond, a sauna, sand volleyball courts, athletic fields, a ropes course and climbing wall, a vegetable garden, and extensive hiking trails.

ADMISSION AND FINANCIAL INFORMATION

Tuition is $3465 per month and is billed monthly. This fee includes counseling, room and board, academic and vocational education, and program costs. A nonrefundable registration and orientation fee of $1250 is charged. The student expense account requires a $250 refundable deposit. A one-time linen fee of $210 is also billed. These fees are due upon enrollment. Some financial aid is available.

Application and admission may take place at any time during the year. If an immediate need exists, the admissions staff will make every effort to accommodate the family. Acceptance to the Academy is based largely on an admissions interview with the student and parents. Visits should be scheduled in advance by writing or telephoning the admissions office. A completed application, transcripts, and former records and evaluations are required by the date of enrollment. The application fee is $35.

Phoenix, Arizona

Type: Residential psychiatric and day treatment center for adolescent males

Affiliation: Private; nonprofit

Population Served: Males ages 12 to 18

Size: Licensed capacity of 36 beds for residential treatment; 60 beds for day treatment

Head of Facility: Lowell E. Andrews, M.S., President

Contact: Hal Elliott, M.Ed., Vice President and Program Director, Post Office Box 32650, 2801 North 31st Street, Phoenix, Arizona 85064-2650; 602-956-9090; fax: 602-956-3018

THE FACILITY

San Pablo Treatment Center is a private, not-for-profit residential psychiatric treatment center dedicated to the treatment and education of young men. The center provides a full continuum of care, including academic remediation and residential psychiatric and day treatment.

San Pablo's governing Board of Directors represents civic and business leaders as well as professional and concerned citizens who are interested in the welfare of young people.

San Pablo has been accredited by the Joint Commission on Accreditation of Healthcare Organizations (JCAHO) since 1974 and is licensed by the Arizona Department of Health. St. Paul's Academy is approved by the Arizona and California Departments of Education and has been accepted as a candidate for accreditation by the North Central Association of Colleges and Schools.

ELIGIBILITY

San Pablo admits those young men who can best benefit from the structured, supervised therapeutic environment offered in the residential and day treatment programs. Youths considered for placement include those who are emotionally disturbed, have conduct/behavior problems, have learning disabilities or development problems in need of specialized education, and those whose school, family, and social adjustment problems require special attention. Chemically dependent youths are considered for admission following detoxification. Those not considered appropriate for San Pablo placement include youths who are severely delinquent, autistic, drug dependent, or below average intelligence.

Admission is based upon psychological, psychiatric, social, and educational information and a preadmission interview. Referrals should be directed to the Program Director.

PROGRAM

San Pablo provides a highly structured environment of therapy and positive incentives designed to restore self-worth. The center recognizes the dignity and value of the youths it serves.

Three basic treatment modalities comprise the San Pablo program. These are the Clinical, Milieu, and Education Programs. The following three levels of treatment are provided, depending on a young man's needs: intensive care, regular care, and open care.

Changes in the level of treatment administered are made by the treatment team, based on acknowledged therapeutic progress. Failure to meet goals or misuse of privileges results in the loss of privileges and an opportunity to refocus on treatment needs. A minimum of a one-year commitment is requested.

The Clinical Program provides the medical, dental, and nursing staff necessary to cope with the physical and psychiatric needs of the young men within the program. Services are provided by the staff psychiatrist (Medical Director), house physician, registered nurses, and other medical consultants as required. Nursing and medical care are available on a 24-hour basis.

Each individual is assigned a therapist responsible for all phases of treatment under the direct supervision of the Medical Director. Upon admission, a complete treatment plan outlining medical, psychological, social, educational, vocational, recreational, and family needs is prepared. Specific criteria for discharge are established. Each treatment plan is thoroughly reviewed quarterly or more frequently if necessary.

Psychiatric and psychological services are provided under the direction of the Medical Director, who has overall responsibility for each young man's treatment. Upon admission, a thorough psychiatric evaluation is prepared. All cases are reviewed weekly in the clinical staff meeting. Psychiatric examinations are completed quarterly and a medication review is completed monthly. Psychological evaluation is provided by consulting psychologists when required. Psychoneurological, speech, and hearing evaluations as well as specific therapeutic services are obtained as dictated by treatment needs.

San Pablo refers individual cases to more appropriate programs when necessary. Former placements are followed up on a regularly scheduled basis for two years following discharge.

San Pablo's Milieu Program is built around highly structured activities that include a daily schedule of dormitory chores, meals, education, study time, group activities, and recreation. On-campus recreation activities include swimming, basketball, volleyball, and weight training. Track, tennis, golf, and bowling are available nearby. Weekend off-campus activities such as hiking, camping, and fishing are also provided. Those who are doing well in the program are encouraged to participate.

A three-phase program for providing personal development and practical work experience for residents includes on- and off-campus jobs in addition to summer and weekend employment. Residents are encouraged to earn their own spending money through the work-skills program.

Residents may be involved in religious training if they choose. An ecumenical approach provides exposure to a variety of religious beliefs and while participation is not required, it is encouraged.

Each young man is required to establish daily goals and to critique his success. Peers and staff offer feedback as well. Target goals reflect the basic elements of the Individual Treatment Plan.

San Pablo's Educational Program is designed to meet the specialized needs of each student. Upon admission, academic strengths and weaknesses are assessed through testing, observation, and records. Specific educational goals and methods of instruction are established. Parents are encouraged to participate in this process. Report cards are prepared and sent to parents quarterly.

Certified special education and secondary teachers address the intellectual, behavioral, emotional, and social needs of each individual. Courses are provided in language arts, mathematics, history, science, health, computer literacy, and vocational and physical education. Special education services are provided to remediate skill deficiencies and address learning disabilities. Coordination with each student's local school district ensures that individual needs are addressed and academic advancement is achieved. High school and eighth grade diplomas are awarded.

Instruction is delivered in a variety of ways. Field trips, community theater groups, movies, and guest speakers are used to supplement classroom instruction. The computer lab plays an integral role in teaching computer literacy and reinforcing content area skills.

Each student's vocational aptitude as well as his preferences and interests are assessed yearly. Vocational education, as part of the school curriculum, provides practical experience in the safe use of tools, woodworking, electrical and maintenance skills, project design and planning, and small-engine repair.

STAFF

A multidisciplinary team including a therapist, director of education, personal counselor, registered nurse, and clinical director develops an individualized treatment plan for each young man. Changes in treatment are made by the team, based upon therapeutic progress.

The academic program is supervised by a director of education and staffed by seven full-time certified teachers who are experienced in their disciplines.

Paraprofessional staff includes a resident supervisor and day, evening, and overnight youth-care workers. A consulting staff of clinical psychologists, physicians, dentists, a speech pathologist/audiologist, and a dietician provide additional, ongoing services.

Staff-to-child ratios are 1:8 for clinical staff, 1:6 for child-care staff, and 1:10 for educational staff.

CONTINUITY OF TREATMENT

Return to the home and community is the goal for each resident.

San Pablo also offers a Day Treatment Program for those who do not require the intensive, 24-hour supervision of an inpatient residential program. Day treatment delivers a multidisciplinary program for psychological, psychiatric, academic, and behavioral problems in the same therapeutic environment provided to San Pablo residents.

Those admitted to day treatment participate fully in clinical, academic, and preparatory life programs.

Appropriate candidates for day treatment include those who require a transition from inpatient to outpatient treatment and those requiring a more comprehensive, highly structured program than outpatient treatment can provide.

BUILDINGS AND GROUNDS

Located on an 8-acre urban campus in a quiet residential area of central Phoenix, San Pablo has five homelike cottages that accommodate four to ten young men. A pool, a recreation facility, an occupational therapy workshop, and individual and group counseling rooms are located on the spacious, tree-lined campus. St. Paul's Academy is located on a separate campus one mile away. St. Paul's campus provides classroom facilities, a dining hall, and academic and counseling offices. St. Paul's serves San Pablo residents as well as providing academic remediation and treatment for day students.

ADMISSION AND FINANCIAL INFORMATION

San Pablo Treatment Center accepts reimbursement from qualified health insurance plans and is on the preferred provider list of a number of managed-care companies. Private payment arrangements may also be negotiated. All or a portion of treatment may be tax deductible.

For referral or admission information, contact the Program Director at 602-956-9090.

San Pablo is an equal opportunity employer and does not discriminate on the basis of age, sex, color, or national origin. San Pablo does not discriminate in the provision of services or employment on the basis of handicap.

SIERRA TUCSON ADOLESCENT CARE

Tucson, Arizona

Type: Psychiatric hospital

Affiliation: Sierra Tucson Companies, Inc., a publicly held, for-profit company

Population Served: Adolescent males and females, ages 13 to 17 (ages 18 to 21 may be considered for admission after clinical review)

Size: Licensed 60-bed facility

Head of Facility: Wyatt Webb, Executive Director

Contact: Steve Leonard and Kathy Shingler, Intake Counselors, 39580 South Lago del Oro Parkway, Tucson, Arizona 85737; 602-624-4000 or 800-624-2233; fax: 602-825-3502

THE HOSPITAL

Sierra Tucson Adolescent Care opened in September 1991. It was developed and established by its parent organization, Sierra Tucson Companies, in response to the public's request for a high-quality model of adolescent care. Dr. James Graham is the Medical Director of Sierra Tucson Adolescent Care as well as Corporate Medical Director for Sierra Tucson Companies. Sierra Tucson developed a medically supervised, fully integrated, psychological, biological, whole person approach to the treatment of addictions and mental health disorders known as The Sierra Model. This treatment model integrates and combines philosophies and practices from the medical, psychological, family systems, and self-help communities. The Twelve Step/Family Systems principles that are the foundation of the Sierra Tucson chemical-dependency program have been broadened to include more intensive psychiatric care. The Sierra Model emphasizes the involvement and treatment of family members during the patient's stay.

The facility is located on 160 acres among the foothills of the Santa Catalina Mountains and is open year-round. The campus is located approximately 12 miles north of Tucson in high desert surroundings, conducive to healing and natural serenity. The hospital is under the supervision of Sierra Tucson Companies' corporate office and board of directors. Sierra Tucson Adolescent Care is an acute-care facility licensed by the state of Arizona as a psychiatric hospital. It is accredited by the Joint Commission on Accreditation of Healthcare Organizations.

ELIGIBILITY

Patients must be in need of acute psychiatric care. Sierra Tucson places a high priority on the individual care of patients with multiple problems. Because of the multifaceted origins and manifestations of physical, sexual, and emotional abuse; depression; anxiety; relationship dependencies; and other stress-related disorders, Sierra Tucson believes that chemical dependency and behavioral disorders are most effectively treated utilizing an interdisciplinary staff of physicians, psychiatrists, registered nurses, and highly qualified, certified therapists with specific background and training in adolescent treatment. An integrated, individualized treatment plan is created for each of the patients and is team mediated. Sierra Tucson serves adolescent boys and girls and

their families from a national audience as well as from Europe and Mexico. While Sierra Tucson is a staff-secured facility, involuntary admissions are not accepted at this time. A patient must have a degree of willingness to participate in the clinical program. A preadmission assessment can be arranged by contacting an admission counselor. There is no fee for this service.

ASSESSMENT

Each patient is initially admitted to the Detoxification, Orientation, and Evaluation (DOE) unit. Sierra Tucson's philosophy is based upon the belief that each adolescent is a unique individual with inherent rights and dignity and that each patient requires specific treatment to meet individual needs. The DOE process, generally three to five days, is a support function; its mission is to prepare the adolescent for treatment. Each patient is carefully screened and assessed to ensure appropriateness for treatment and to ensure that the individual's specific needs are addressed. Each patient is seen by the medical director, and all medical, psychological, and educational assessments begin at this time.

PROGRAMS

All treatment programs, while tailored to the individual, contain several common elements. These include the guiding philosophy and Twelve Steps of Alcoholics Anonymous (with an emphasis on spirituality), intense feelings work, the disease concepts of addictions, and the integration of family system issues into the treatment process. Patients are presented with an integrated program of group therapy, family therapy, lectures, video presentations, and counseling for fitness, nutritional, and spiritual needs. Specialty groups address such issues as grief resolution, living skills, dysfunctional families, and sexual awareness. The staff utilizes a variety of treatment modalities specific to the individual's disorder. Among the most effective therapies are anger and shame reduction, reality, inner child, insight oriented, family systems, guided imagery, gestalt, and psychodrama. Sierra Tucson maintains close contact with the patient's referral source through weekly phone calls and works toward developing a plan for continuing care after the patient's discharge from the facility. This offers a continuum of care effective in the prevention of relapse. Sierra Tucson Adolescent Care provides a psycho-educational program staffed with certified teachers to promote a success-oriented educational atmosphere and utilizes the nationally recognized NovaNET computer system developed by the University of Illinois. Each classroom has an educational assistant assigned, under the direction of the teacher, to assist the students. Academic instruction is individualized and promotes positive educational achievement, coping skills, appropriate peer relationships, and positive self-image. Homeschool officials are informed of recommendations for academic credit and instructional strategies, placement, and approaches geared to further develop the patient's social and study skills.

Experiential treatment components are a strength of Sierra Tucson's programs. The Integrated Riding Resource Program is designed to elevate the troubled adolescent's self-esteem using the therapeutic qualities of riding and caring for horses. Skills for communication, relationship building, choice making, and intimacy are practiced and learned. Riding activities develop self-awareness, build confidence, and cultivate concentration and self-discipline. The STIR-RUP Program is facilitated by staff and supervised by a master's-level therapist. Another very successful experiential component is the Wilderness Recovery Program. The use of safe, therapeutic outdoor and wilderness activities provides the patient and other group members with the opportunity to learn trust, cooperation, and personal empowerment. Patients are assisted in experiencing personal growth through participation in the Outdoor Wilderness Course, the indoor Climbing Wall, and other therapeutic, structured outdoor activities. Each participant learns he or she has unique contributions or strengths to add to the group.

Family involvement is an important component of the Sierra Tucson philosophy of care. The exploration of the family system is emphasized during the seven-day Family Week. Also, children as young as 6 years of age participate in the specially designed Children's Program, which is geared to each child's emotional and developmental level. It incorporates a group dynamics format, utilizing art, music, and other expressive therapies.

Continuing care assessment begins during the initial admission to DOE. The continuing care coordinator works with the family and referent on developing a continuing care plan that utilizes a network of community resources nationwide. This plan seeks to support the patient and family after discharge, to connect them with the appropriate support services, and to prepare the family and patient for the patient's reentry into the home community. Prior to leaving Adolescent Care, patients are prepared for this most important phase of recovery through Going Home groups.

STAFF
Sierra Tucson Adolescent Care is staffed with an interdisciplinary team of physicians, psychiatrists, psychologists, nurses, teachers, and therapists. The clinical team also includes a Wilderness Program Director, Recreational Therapist, Nutritionist, and certified teacher. A treatment team for an individual patient includes the primary therapist, family therapist, sexual concerns therapist, psychiatrist, the medical director, the recreation therapist, a certified teacher, and a nutritionist as well as support staff, nursing staff, and a continuing care counselor. The multidisciplinary team meets daily to assess individual patient progress and to implement and update the individual's treatment plan through a case review process.

CONTINUITY OF TREATMENT
Continuing care and discharge planning are an integral part of the complete treatment approach at Sierra Tucson. The treatment team, patient, and family members, as well as the referent, begin to develop a continuing care plan during the first week of care. The continuing care counselor meets with each adolescent and family to discuss what the patient's needs will be upon returning home. In individual sessions, specific plans for appropriate continuing care referrals are established.

Sierra Tucson has developed a nationwide referral network of care providers, extended care facilities, therapists, and alumni sponsors. This network is an integral part of the complete treatment program and is necessary in preparing and assisting each patient for return to the home community. Appropriate levels of support services are also sought and recommended for the patient's family members.

BUILDINGS AND GROUNDS
Patients reside in semiprivate rooms (maximum of three per room) with individual closets, study areas, and private bath. All Sierra Tucson buildings are accessible to the handicapped. There are two dormitories built in traditional Santa Fe southwestern style. There are separate corridors for boys and girls within each of these dormitories. Sierra Tucson provides a central dining facility and a nutritionally balanced meal plan for patients. The use of refined sugars and caffeine is restricted, yet the food is comparable to that available in good-quality restaurants. Patients also share the use of a full-size lap pool, sand volleyball court, and basketball and tennis courts. The grounds are spacious, open, safe, and of exceptional quality. The facility has an outdoor kiva community area for meetings and commencements. Medical services for patients are provided on-site with the exception of surgical needs. Northwestern Hospital, a fully equipped community facility, is located minutes away.

ADMISSION AND FINANCIAL INFORMATION
Sierra Tucson Adolescent Care accepts most major medical plans and CHAMPUS insurance. Private payment arrangements may also be made. The admissions office will assist patients and families with the process of assessment, admission, and confirming financial arrangements for the facility. The toll-free number for admission is 800-624-2233. Sierra Tucson Adolescent Care is committed to the confidential, respectful, and professional care of the patient, family, and referent professional.

SORENSON'S RANCH SCHOOL, INC.

Koosharem, Utah

Type: Treatment center and school for troubled teens
Affiliation: Corporate ownership; for-profit
Population Served: Male and female, ages 13 to 18
Size: Licensed capacity, 71
Head of Facility: Shane B. Sorenson, Director
Contact: Burnell Sorenson, Admissions Director, 410 North 100 East, Koosharem, Utah 84744-0219; 801-638-7318 or 800-748-4549; fax: 801-638-7582

FACILITY

Sorenson's Ranch School, Inc., was founded by Burnell and Carrol Sorenson as a summer camp in 1959 and became a year-round school in 1982. As long-time educators, they recognized the need for a school to address the unique needs of young people. The business is family-owned and -operated and the administration is available round-the-clock.

Sorenson's goal is to help teens realize that they must be prepared to be held accountable for their own actions and be able to function successfully as positively contributing members of society. Parental involvement is desirable but not mandatory.

The 200-acre ranch is on the border of Koosharem, a small town of ninety families, nestled in an isolated high-mountain valley. The next-largest town is 35 miles away.

Sorenson's Ranch School is licensed as a mental health and substance-abuse treatment center with the Utah State Human Services Department. The school is also accredited by the Northwest Association of Schools and Colleges and the American Camping Association. Sorenson's utilizes a multitreatment approach in order to provide treatment that addresses each student's specific needs.

ELIGIBILITY

Students' histories often include problems with parents, substance abuse, low or nonexistent self-esteem, learning disabilities, running away, dropping out of or being expelled from school, and extreme mental stress. The student profile of thirty-one girls and forty boys shows that Sorenson's students possess above-average scholastic ability and do not have any severe mental or physical problems.

Students are not denied entrance on the basis of race, religion, creed, sex, or national origin. Although Sorenson's is not a lock-up facility, it is able to accept involuntary admissions and can provide arrangements for placement.

ASSESSMENT

Diagnostic data and background materials are helpful in determining eligibility for placement. Professional referrals are not required. The school reserves the right to expel a teenager within the first thirty days if it is found that the student is detrimental to the overall health of the school community.

Placement may be made by parents, insurance companies, social services, concerned individuals, members of the clergy, or others. Referrals are also occasionally made to

wilderness programs when behavior may be enhanced by a high-intensity survival experience.

PROGRAM

Therapy and education are provided for troubled teens. Individualized treatment plans are created and include reality therapy, natural consequences, a Twelve-Step approach, behavior modification through experiential learning, and living activities in a safe, natural, outdoor-type environment.

Young people set weekly goals for themselves and must accept responsibility for their own actions. Excuses or previous circumstances are not acceptable explanations for negative behaviors. Students learn to accept the consequences of their good and bad behavior and adjust their subsequent behavior accordingly. Sorenson's understands that everyone makes mistakes sometimes. At the same time, they stress that students must understand that with choices and freedom comes personal responsibility.

A point system is used and points are awarded or taken away in direct relation to good or bad behavior. Students learn that as a result of positive behavior, they can participate in various outings, gain more freedom within the school, and increase their allowance. Conversely, as a result of consistent negative behavior, students engage in activities such as digging ditches, hauling manure, and weeding.

The working ranch activities include animal care and horse training and riding. The program of experiential learning activities also includes outcamping and recreational activities.

Sorenson's educational program is designed so that students are given the proper guidance and counseling in order to learn at their own rate. For those students who are behind in school, Sorenson's open-entry and open-exit policy facilitates catching-up in school.

The competency-based curriculum provides all the courses needed for students to earn a high school diploma. School is held year-round, and credits may be earned for survival experience when students participate in licensed programs. Formal and informal group and individual therapy sessions are held.

STAFF

Specialists include professionals (psychiatrist, LCSWs, MSWs, SSW, RN), trained care-workers, and certified educational staff. A typical treatment team is headed by a personal counselor who integrates treatment plans with other professionals and acts as the contact person with parents or placement agencies. The counselor acts as a personal advocate as well as a mentor for the student.

SPECIAL PROGRAMS

Placement into community homes is an option open to advanced students. This program provides the students with a stepping-stone for eventual reintegration with the student's own family as well as an experiential model within a functioning family.

CONTINUITY OF TREATMENT

The average length of stay at Sorenson's Ranch School is one year, and, depending on the individual, transition may be to a home, another school, or college of some type. Most students leave with the ability to function as a positive member of society and are able to demonstrate renewed self-esteem and an orientation toward goal achievement.

BUILDINGS AND GROUNDS

Facilities at the ranch include student housing in ten cabins and dorms, all with connected restrooms. Students sleep in a ranch setting with an average of four students in each room. There are counseling offices, a kitchen, an infirmary, and the lodge, which houses a multipurpose room for dining and activities. A classroom complex, an industrial arts center with two shops, a full gymnasium, a library, and animal/tack facilities are in outlying buildings.

ADMISSION AND FINANCIAL INFORMATION

Fees, as of November 1992, are $2600 per month; first and final months' payments, plus a $400 deposit for personal expenses, are required up front. Insurance, social service, educational, or other placements without prepayments are billed an additional $100 per month. Scholarships and financial aid are not available.

THREE SPRINGS

Huntsville, Alabama

Type: Six residential treatment programs for adolescents

Affiliation: Operated by Three Springs, Inc.

Population Served: Male and female, ages 11–17

Size: Licensed capacity for programs varies from 33 to 60; total 270

Head of Facilities: Christopher Burns, M.A.

Contact: Amy Sobieszczyk, 247 Chateau Drive, Huntsville, Alabama 35801; 205-880-3339

THE FACILITIES
Established in 1985, Three Springs is dedicated to providing comprehensive and cost-effective residential mental health treatment services for adolescents with emotional and behavioral difficulties. Six programs operate year-round at four locations. Set in rural areas, each program is within 60 miles of a metropolitan community (Huntsville, Nashville, or Raleigh). The cognitive-behavioral model is employed to treat a broad range of mental health issues.

Each program maintains state licensure, with the programs in Pittsboro, North Carolina, and Courtland, Alabama, accredited by the Joint Commission on Accreditation of Healthcare Organizations.

ELIGIBILITY
Residents must be in need of short-term (3–5 months) or long-term (9–12 months) residential treatment. A full-scale IQ of 85 or greater is desired. Candidates for the outdoor programs must have no physical conditions that would preclude participation in outdoor activity. Admission may be voluntary or involuntary, with appropriate considerations given to meet either circumstance.

Treatment services are designed to meet the needs of youths with a wide variety of emotional and behavioral diagnoses. In addition, secondary substance abuse issues are clinically addressed for youths who have completed a rehabilitation program or are at risk of developing substance abuse problems.

ASSESSMENT
Although many referrals are made by private professionals, Three Springs accepts direct parental referrals with appropriate professional recommendation. A comprehensive examination of a psychological/psychiatric evaluation, social assessment, family history, medical history, educational assessment, and previous interventions is made. If required, a complete psychiatric assessment can be completed at the residential center in Courtland, Alabama.

PROGRAM
The fundamental goal of the program is to help the resident gain the skills needed to accept full responsibility for his or her behavior. In doing so, the resident learns to assert his or her rights and apply skills in dealing with presenting problems as well as to communicate and fulfill needs in appropriate ways. In order to provide an environment that promotes trust and confidence, Three Springs offers its residents a highly structured daily schedule.

Following a master treatment plan, formulated by an interdisciplinary team, each resident participates daily in therapeutic, educational, and recreational activities. Nightly group meetings are utilized to address personal and group issues and to evaluate personal and group goals. The residents receive individual counseling as well as group counseling to address shared questions dealing with sexual/physical abuse, substance abuse, sexual issues, and self-esteem. Experiential outings, vocational activities, and adventure programming are also offered.

A stage and level system adds structure to the program. A resident's stage is related to his or her demonstrated responsibility and determines the level of privileges. Movement through the stages is completely individualized and dependent upon the motivation of the resident. As a child progresses through the stages, tasks of greater responsibility are assigned and mutual trust is gained. Ceremonies are held to celebrate advancement through the stages. These ceremonies give tangible evidence of progress. Graduation is based upon maximum growth of the resident, not completion of a preset standard.

Since family involvement is important in addressing the resident's current problems, families are requested to participate in therapy sessions, parent support groups, and parent training workshops. In-person family conferences are held before home visits or by phone conference if distance is a constraint.

STAFF
Three Springs believes that treatment involves all aspects of development and that no one individual or service can effectively meet every need. For this reason, the clinical team is derived from many disciplines participating together to assist the resident. The treatment team consists of psychiatrists, psychologists, social workers, nurses, and direct care staff. Other members of the team include teachers, activity therapists, nutritionists, and pharmacists. Each contributes expertise in the formulation of the resident's individual treatment plan. Through professional cooperation and consideration, each member is able to make an effective contribution to ensure a well-rounded approach to address the resident's needs.

SPECIAL PROGRAMS
Three Springs provides educational services through private schools located within the treatment programs. Academic work is tailored to an individual's needs. A low student-teacher ratio provides residents with individualized attention. The educational programs are integrated with overall treatment planning, and specialized attention is given to learning disabilities and emotional conflicts. Classroom academics are supplemented by experiential learning opportunities.

A summer program is also available for troubled youths who require an intensive, highly structured, short-term intervention program. Three Springs' Summer Program enables the individual to develop basic problem-solving skills, to accept personal responsibility, and to learn to live cohesively with others.

Parents are required to participate in two parent weekends that consist of educational workshops, support groups, family therapy, and recreation. Aftercare services are offered for three months.

CONTINUITY OF TREATMENT

Three Springs' education and social service staff provides assistance in reacclimating youths to the home and school environments. Aftercare services include continual family conferences, supportive services, and monthly group meetings with other aftercare residents. These groups offer an avenue for discussion and support in developing appropriate solutions to common problems. A support group for parents of aftercare residents is also provided.

The referring professional is regularly informed of the child's progress during treatment. Whenever possible, the referring professional is invited to participate in discharge planning, and his or her services are recommended in conjunction with the aftercare services provided.

BUILDINGS AND GROUNDS

Three Springs' facilities are modern brick buildings, built or remodeled to facilitate the treatment of adolescents. The outdoor treatment programs are each located on over 350 acres of rural woodlands. Residents live in groups of eight to twelve on campsites with four to six platform tents, a cooking area, group meeting sites, and privy. A large central area of brick buildings houses classrooms, a dining hall,

showers, laundry facilities, and administrative offices. Recreational facilities are located within the buildings or in the gymnasium next door.

The intermediate and secure residential centers consist of one central building. Great attention is paid to design and furnishings in order to avoid an environment that suggests institutionalization. Rooms consist of two beds, and bathrooms are located close to each room. Private rooms are available when therapeutically appropriate. By meeting personal goals, residents earn the privilege of purchasing and displaying personal objects in their rooms.

Arrangements have been made with local medical and dental clinics to provide services to the residents. Local hospitals are utilized for more intensive medical needs.

ADMISSION AND FINANCIAL INFORMATION

Three Springs accepts most major medical insurance plans. Private payments can also be arranged. All services within Three Springs' programs are included in the daily rate. These services include individual counseling, group and family counseling, educational and social services, nursing services, and room and board. A referral package consists of an admission application, a health history, a psychological or mental status report, and any available social history. The most updated materials should be included to provide an accurate picture of the youth's current needs. After a review of the application, the admission staff will contact the referral source to discuss suitability of placement. A preadmission clinical interview is conducted before or on the scheduled admission date to assess suitability and motivation for treatment.

VANDERBILT CHILD & ADOLESCENT PSYCHIATRIC HOSPITAL

Nashville, Tennessee

Type: Full-service psychiatric hospital

Size: Licensed for 88 beds, acute-care facility

Affiliation: Joint venture with Vanderbilt University Division of Psychiatry and Hospital Corporation of America (HCA)

Population Served: Male and female, ages 4 to 21

Head of Facility: Gail Oberta, Administrator; William Bernet, M.D., Medical Director

Contact: Mark Watson, LCSW, Director LCSW, Director of RESPOND, 1601 Twenty-third Avenue South, Nashville, Tennessee 37212

THE FACILITY

Vanderbilt Child and Adolescent Psychiatric Hospital (VCAPH) opened its doors in 1985. VCAPH has pioneered the development of specialized treatment for children's affective disorders, emotional trauma recovery, dual diagnoses, forensics, and partial hospitalization programs.

VCAPH is located on the Vanderbilt campus in Nashville, Tennessee, and is intersected by three major in-state highway systems. Managed by a joint board of HCA and Vanderbilt staff members, VCAPH is directed by the Hospital Administrator and Medical Director.

VCAPH is accredited through Joint Commission, Tennessee State Licensure of Mental Health and Mental Retardation. The hospital is also a member of the National Association of Private Psychiatric Hospitals.

ELIGIBILITY

VCAPH accepts males and females ages 4 to 21. Specific eligibility requirements are described under the heading PROGRAMS.

Parental or guardian consent for participation in a program must be obtained through the time a patient is 15.

While VCAPH is a secured facility and can accept court-referred admissions, Vanderbilt is not equipped to serve those children who are severely mentally retarded.

PROGRAMS

VCAPH's programs are centered on the need to provide a place for assessment and treatment of children and adolescents with psychiatric problems. Each program is supported by a multidisciplinary team of professionals, including psychiatrists, nurses, educators, social workers, and nutritionists. The treatment approach emphasizes family involvement, practical living skills, and aftercare. Each clinical program is under the direction of a board-certified child and adolescent psychiatrist.

The **Affective Disorders Program** has experienced the most success in treating patients ages 12 to 19 who have been diagnosed with major depressive disorder, dysthymia, concurrent mood disorder, bipolar affective disorder, and anxiety disorders, including panic, schizophrenia, and other psychoses.

In addition, episodes of suicide, aggression, family problems, school problems, sexual as well as physical abuse, and other disruptive behaviors are often present in the histories of patients appropriate for the Affective Disorders Program.

The Affective Disorders Program is not able to accept those patients who are moderately or severely mentally retarded, sexual perpetrators, or exhibiting dangerously violent behavior.

Vanderbilt provides its patients with a safe, secure, structured environment. This environment serves to create a supportive milieu for the implementation of multimodal treatment of the patient and family/support system as well as to alleviate severe depressive/anxious symptomatology and permit safe return to an outpatient environment.

Within the Affective Disorders Program, milieu, interpersonal and educational group, pharmacological, family, and individual therapies are used. Each week, patients participate in at least three individual therapy sessions and a minimum of 10 hours of group therapy. During the various types of therapy, Vanderbilt emphasizes appropriate verbal expression of feelings, rather than acting out, and the exploration of the impact of life circumstances on the evaluation of psychiatric illness.

In order to maintain gains acquired during inpatient treatment, patients may need multimodality outpatient care. Vanderbilt works with patients and families to ensure appropriate step-down care.

The **Emotional Trauma Recovery Program** (ETRP) treats males and females ages 12 to 18. ETRP's patients are usually the victims of trauma due to physical or sexual abuse, often compounded by divorce or dysfunctional relationships with stepparents. As a result, clients' histories typically include indications of low self-esteem, poor school performance, legal problems, poor communication skills, and poor anger control.

ETRP creates a structured, predictable program in order to provide a calming, safe milieu for the patients. Within this environment, group and peer interaction is primary. Patients are taught an association of normalcy when confronted with peers' problems in comparison to their own problems.

Each week, patients are required to attend 1 and 4 hours of individual and group therapy, respectively. In addition, patients attend 4 hours of school each week.

Visiting hours are every Saturday and Sunday from 2 to 4 p.m., and additional visits can be arranged with an M.D.'s order.

The length of stay at ETRP is usually brief and must be related to continued care afterward.

The **Chemical Dependency Program** at VCAPH specializes in the treatment of dual disorders. Dual disorders commonly refer to substance abuse or chemical dependency compounded by emotional, behavioral, or psychiatric problems. Additional coexisting problems may include, but are not limited to, affective, posttraumatic stress, attention deficit, and eating disorders. Patients appropriate for the Chemical Dependency Program are assessed for admission to inpatient treatment. Typically, patients and oftentimes their families are experiencing symptoms of the patient's problems that necessitate consideration of inpatient treatment.

The Chemical Dependency Program serves males and females ages 11 to 18. Many have experienced problems in relation to legal matters as well as to their education, families, and social activities.

Program goals include comprehensive evaluations and assessments and individualized treatment planning based on the results of the evaluation process. The program also has a number of quality assurance indicators to monitor family involvement in treatment, aftercare planning, effectiveness of treatment, patient progress measures, and accuracy of assessment.

The Chemical Dependency Program offers a free aftercare program for the patients and their family members. This service is available for as long as is necessary. A plan for continued care is developed in conjunction with each patient and family prior to discharge; these plans are based on patient need and vary accordingly. Typically, they may include involvement in Twelve-Step groups and other therapies as indicated.

A variety of therapeutic interventions are utilized. These include, but are not limited to, group psychotherapy, individual, milieu, family, and recreational therapy as well as structure, level system, educational services, and Twelve-Step education and affiliation. The program is highly structured; patients typically spend 4 hours per day in school, 3 to 4 hours in group therapy, 2 hours in recreational therapy, and 1 to 2 hours in individual therapy. Visitation is arranged by the patient's therapist and typically occurs on weekends for 2 hours.

Vanderbilt's **Children's Program** treats ten children ages 5 to 11. These children may have been diagnosed with PTSD or ADHD and may typically exhibit one or a combination of the following behaviors: hyperactivity, violence toward others, behavior problems related to sexual acting out, firesetting, anxiety, depression, bedwetting, noncompliance with rules and authority figures, destruction of property, cruelty to animals, truancy, obesity, anorexia, self-abuse, and suicidal ideation.

The program uses a combination of milieu, education, and recreational therapy, in addition to psychotherapy, and is designed to emphasize praise and reward for children who take responsibility for their actions. A typical day includes school; individual, activity, group, and milieu therapy; rest and play time; and group meetings.

Visits are usually limited to weekends but may be individualized according to the child's needs.

STAFF

VCAPH's staff is made up of child and adolescent psychiatrists, child and adolescent fellows and residents, master's-level licensed social workers, nurse specialists, nurses, activity therapists, speech therapists, certified teachers, child and adolescent psychologist interns, and registered dieticians.

An individualized treatment team consists of a child and adolescent psychologist, a primary nurse, a primary educator, an activity therapist, and a social worker. The team meets regularly to discuss the ongoing progress and goal setting for each individual patient.

BUILDINGS AND GROUNDS

VCAPH is a free-standing building, associated with the Vanderbilt Medical Center and University. The patients' rooms are semiprivate with bathrooms and are organized by program. Each program has group rooms, two activity rooms, a kitchen, and laundry facilities. The facility also includes an indoor swimming pool and a junior high gymnasium. Patients eat in the dining room, with the exception of the patients in the children's program; they eat in a separate dining room.

ADMISSION AND FINANCIAL INFORMATION

VCAPH accepts most major insurance carriers, CHAMPUS, and Tennessee Medicaid.

All admissions are handled through the RESPOND Program, 615-327-7000.

WILDERNESS TREATMENT CENTER

Marion, Montana

Type: Chemical dependency inpatient treatment for adolescents and young adults

Affiliation: Operated by Wilderness Alternative Schools; incorporated as a for-profit organization

Population Served: Male, ages 14 to 24 in adolescent treatment

Size: Two 25-bed facilities

Head of Facility: John Brekke, President

Contact: Kay Holmes, Admissions Coordinator, 200 Hubbart Dam Road, Marion, Montana 59925; 406-854-2832

THE FACILITY

Wilderness Treatment Center (WTC) was founded in 1983 by John Brekke, when he purchased a large working dude ranch, The M Lazy V Ranch in Marion, Montana, and converted it into an inpatient treatment center. WTC was founded on the philosophy of the Twelve-Step Program combined with an Outward Bound type modality. In 1987 Wilderness Treatment Center purchased a 3,300-acre working cattle ranch called the "I Am Third Ranch" in Wilsall, Montana. It has since become an identical 25-bed program with JCAHO-accreditation as well as state licensure.

ELIGIBILITY

Appropriate patients must be in need of inpatient treatment with a primary diagnosis of chemical dependency. Most admissions are voluntary but under appropriate clinical circumstances Wilderness Treatment Center is capable of accommodating involuntary admissions.

The clinical staff is capable of dealing with all problems that the chemically dependent adolescent displays. The staff places a heavy emphasis on dealing with self-esteem issues. There are also issue-specific groups on dual diagnosis, sexuality, and other behavioral problems. Treatment for all patients is individualized, integrated, and team managed.

ASSESSMENT

Prior to admission, all patients must have participated in an independent assessment that specifically focused on chemical dependency. The assessment must be completed by a qualified independent clinician.

Upon admittance, Wilderness Treatment Center will complete its own assessment (approximately three to five days) to verify the assessment provided by the patient. Wilderness Treatment Center's assessment includes a psych-social history, prediagnostic interview, psychological testing, and a complete physical.

PROGRAM

Wilderness Treatment Center is a sixty-day program for chemically dependent adolescents and young adults. For the first thirty days, the patient is in therapy Monday through Thursday from 9 a.m. to 8:30 p.m. This therapy includes group, lecture, and individual therapy. Since both of the programs are located on working cattle ranches, students engage in work therapy on Fridays and Saturdays. Work therapy is overseen by a therapist and deals effectively with high-energy patients. The patients complete the first three steps of AA and NA in this phase.

WILDERNESS COMPONENT

This phase lasts sixteen days in the winter and twenty-one days in the summer. Wilderness trips are not survival trips, as WTC's kids are already survivors when they arrive. The wilderness phase is success oriented and designed to deal with patients who display a low self-worth. All trips have four to six patients, who are accompanied by a therapist and a trained wilderness instructor. The patients are well-clothed, well-fed, and provided with good equipment.

In the first week, patients are taught the skills necessary to function as Group Leaders. Each patient gets the opportunity to be "leader of the day," in which he is responsible for the group and their travel. After the first week, the instructors are primarily helpers and ensure safety on the trip, while the patients make the decisions. The goals of the wilderness expedition are increased self-esteem, cooking for the group, and minimum-impact camping.

Before a patient completes his wilderness phase he must make a complete list of his assets and liabilities (Step 4) so that when he returns to the center he will know the direction his aftercare will take.

WTC has been featured in a number of publications as well as on TV. WTC was featured in the documentary "Over the Influence" and NBC Nightly News with Tom Brokaw in addition to appearing in, among others, the magazines *National Geographic, Montana,* and *Freedom.*

STAFF

Wilderness Treatment Center facilities are each supervised by a medical director. The medical director oversees an interdisciplinary team of fully accredited chemical dependency counselors, psychologists, nurses, dieticians, pharmacists, a nutritionist, and certified wilderness instructors. Wilderness Treatment Centers' philosophy has the certified chemical dependency therapist as the primary person responsible for the patient's treatment, utilizing the above staff. Wilderness Treatment Center maintains a 5:1 patient-to-staff ratio.

SPECIAL PROGRAMS

For long-term recovery it is essential that families participate in the patient treatment process. Ninety percent of the family members attend a one-week, on-campus family program that includes group therapy, lectures, individual treatment plans, and one day on the ropes course with the patient. Sunday recreation is therapeutically designed to enhance self-esteem and is overseen by a therapist. Sunday's activities can include rock climbing, rappelling, cross-country skiing, and fly fishing.

BUILDINGS AND GROUNDS

Both treatment centers are located on large working cattle ranches in the mountains of Montana. Even though they are in rural settings, both centers remain extremely accessible to major airports. The centers are licensed health-care facilities that provide their patients with wide-open spaces and a sense of freedom. Patients at both centers live in semiprivate rooms with individual bathrooms. Food is cooked in a high-quality kitchen and served in a dining room setting.

ADMISSION AND FINANCIAL INFORMATION

Wilderness Treatment Center's cost ranges from $225 to $265 per day. This charge is all-inclusive. Wilderness Treatment Center accepts most major medical plans and private payment arrangements may also be negotiated. The admission office is happy to assist the families with the admission process in whatever way possible.

WileyHouse Treatment Centers℠
THE NATIONAL CENTER FOR KIDS IN CRISIS

Bethlehem, Pennsylvania

Type: Twenty-eight sites in Pennsylvania, Maine, and Indiana, offering varying levels of residential treatment programs, partial hospitalization, psychoeducational programs, outpatient services, and in-home counseling

Affiliation: A nonprofit organization owned by KidsPeace

Population Served: Varies according to location and treatment facility

Size: Varies according to location and treatment facility

Head of Facility: John P. Peter, President and CEO; Corporate Headquarters, 1650 Broadway, Bethlehem, Pennsylvania 18015-3998

Contact: Ms. Ginger Papp, 5300 KidsPeace Drive, Orefield, Pennsylvania 18069; 800-8KID-123; fax: 215-799-8424

THE FACILITY

For over a century, Wiley House Treatment Centers has designed its services to meet the specific needs of troubled children and their families. William Thurston, in 1882, became aware of the needs of youths in the Lehigh Valley. He acted by opening a home for their care and bearing the expense of maintaining the home until it was incorporated in 1886. In 1895, Captain James Wiley purchased 6 acres of land and built a residence that was to serve children and youths for the next three quarters of a century.

Throughout the decades since then, Wiley House Treatment Centers has received gifts, contributions, and bequests from Lehigh Valley citizens that enabled it to continue providing quality services for the children in its care. Since the early 1970s, Wiley House Treatment Centers has responded to the need for continuity of care by expanding existing programs and developing an integrated continuum of treatment programs that is currently offered to thousands of children and families in the Lehigh Valley and throughout the nation.

Additionally, Wiley House Treatment Centers has continued to provide services at its various sites throughout Pennsylvania, Indiana, and Maine.

Wiley House Treatment Centers is open year-round and is accredited by JCAHO (Joint Commission on Accreditation of Healthcare Organizations), the Middle States Association of Colleges and Schools, and the American Association of Psychiatric Services for Children.

The specific Wiley House Treatment Centers site used by the individual is determined by the type of treatment undertaken and location of the individual. Residential programs take place in clusters of cottages where the child interacts with peers and staff throughout his or her stay.

ELIGIBILITY

Wiley House Treatment Centers' multidisciplinary treatment teams have experienced positive outcomes treating mood disorders, adjustment disorders, sexual disorders, and personality disorders. Specialized treatment tracks focus on the treatment of sexual victimization, sexual offenders, depression/suicidal gestures, abandonment issues, fire-setting, family problems, and other specialized issues as the need arises. Wiley House Treatment Centers' treatment teams typically consist of board-certified child and adolescent psychiatrists, licensed clinical psychologists, social workers, members of educational and nursing staffs, mental health workers, and members of recreational and crisis prevention intervention staffs.

Wiley House Treatment Centers is not prepared to deal with individuals who require 24-hour medical attention, who are actively suicidal or homicidal, or who are severely mentally or physically challenged.

Wiley House Treatment Centers accepts court-ordered placements as well as voluntary placements, and the population at Wiley House Treatment Centers is made up of children from around the country and around the globe.

ASSESSMENT

There are no specific tests that Wiley House Treatment Centers requires for admission, but a social history, a psychological and/or psychiatric evaluation no older than six months, education history, and medical history are extremely helpful in assessing a child's needs. Within a week of a child's admission into a Wiley House Treatment Center, a battery of tests are done in order to help the treatment team formulate a treatment plan that will best suit the needs of the child. This battery of tests can include a psychiatric evaluation, a nursing assessment, and an assessment of the child's academic abilities. If it is deemed the best solution, diagnostic units in eastern Pennsylvania can provide a ten- or forty-five-day program for children ages 6 to 17 for whom no clear service plan exists or for those children whose placements have not been successful in the past.

PROGRAMS

Depending upon the specific circumstances of the child being treated, Wiley House Treatment Centers tries to assist the child in returning to a less restrictive home environment and emancipate him or her into a community where he or she can function safely and responsibly.

Among the modalities used by Wiley House Treatment Centers are individual, group, family, recreation, speech, play, and reality therapy as well as behavior modification, life space counseling, and life skills training. The modality or combination of modalities used is decided upon by the treatment team, taking into consideration effectiveness, needs, and response by the child. In using these types of treatment, Wiley House Treatment Centers hopes to successfully discharge a child once his or her treatment goals and objectives have been realized. These goals, established early on by the treatment team and others concerned about the child's well-being, determine when a child is ready to "graduate." Parental and family visitation varies and permission is based upon whether visitation will hinder overall treatment progress.

STAFF

Specific certification and composition of any Wiley House Treatment Centers' staff varies according to the size, location, and focus of a given center. A treatment team can include but is not limited to licensed clinical psychologists, educational staff, nursing staff, board-certified child and adolescent psychiatrists, mental health workers, recreational staff, crisis prevention intervention staff, and social workers.

SPECIAL PROGRAMS

There is a variety of associated family care that is available to family members of children in treatment. The Family Support Program offers partial hospitalization for parents of children in day programs while the Family Training and After-Care Programs provide ongoing and post-treatment therapies to the families of children who have been in the residential program.

The In-Home Youth/Parent Counseling Program's purpose is to avoid the need for out-of-home placement. A counselor works with the adolescent and the parents in the home in an effort to establish or reestablish communication so that residential or partial hospitalization treatment is unnecessary.

CONTINUITY OF TREATMENT

Wiley House Treatment Centers is equipped to provide varying degrees of outpatient and step-down care. Step-down care and full treatment are available through Wiley House Treatment Centers' Day Treatment, Partial Hospitalization, and Family Support Programs as well as their In-Home Counseling, Outpatient, and Psycho-Educational Services. Additional arrangements for continued care are made on an as-needed basis.

BUILDINGS

In the majority of the residential programs offered by Wiley House Treatment Centers, residential areas are clusters of cottages where children live, work, and interact with peers and staff. The dormitories house ten to twenty children who are grouped according to age and condition being treated. Staff and children eat meals together in central dining halls. Wiley House Treatment Centers also offers a variety of activities for the children, including swimming, gymnastics, baseball, softball, a ropes course, and other recreational facilities.

In addition to those sites that currently exist, Wiley House Treatment Centers is scheduled to open its National Hospital for Kids in Crisis in autumn 1992.

ADMISSION AND FINANCIAL INFORMATION

Wiley House Treatment Centers maintains contracts with several county and state agencies as well as with various managed-care organizations. Private insurance will frequently cover much of the cost of treatment.

More specific financial information can be accessed by calling 1-800-8KID-123.

	POPULATION SERVED				SERVICES PROVIDED													SPECIALIZED TREATMENT TRACKS			
Wiley House Treatment Centers / National Hospital for Kids in Crisis / KidsPeace	Children - Boys	Children - Girls	Adolescents - Boys	Adolescents - Girls	Acute Inpatient Program/Dual Diagnosis	Acute Residential Treatment	Diagnosis/Assessment	Family Therapy	In Home Counseling Program	Psycho-Educational Services	Recreational Programs	Residential Treatment/Extended	24 Hour Emergency Shelter Care	Substance Abuse Treatment	Training/Aftercare for Families	Training Program (CEU)	Preventative/Education Services	Mood/Adjustment/Agression	Personality Disorders	Sexual Abuse Victims	Sexual Abuse Offenders
Residential Center, Bethlehem, Pa	■	■	■	■		■	■	■		■	■	■		■	■			■	■	■	■
Residential Center, Orefield, Pa.	■	■	■	■		■	■	■		■	■	■		■	■			■	■	■	■
Diagnostic Unit, Saylorsburg, Pa.			■	■		■	■	■		■	■		■	■	■			■	■	■	■
Diagnostic Unit, Schnecksville, Pa	■	■				■	■	■		■	■		■	■	■			■	■	■	■
ITF (15 Locations in Pa.)	■	■	■	■				■	■	■			■	■	■			■	■	■	■
Residential Community-Based - 11th Ave., Beth., Pa.	■					■	■	■		■	■	■		■	■			■	■	■	■
Residential Community-Based - Linden St., Beth., Pa.			■			■	■	■		■	■	■		■	■			■	■	■	■
ITF, South Bend and Indianapolis, Indiana	■	■	■	■				■	■	■			■	■		■		■	■	■	■
National Hospital for Kids in Crisis, Orchard Hills, Pa.(Jan. 93)	■	■	■	■	■	■	■	■		■	■	■	■	■	■	■	■	■	■	■	■
W.H.T.C. of New England, Ellsworth, Maine			■			■	■	■		■	■	■		■	■			■		■	

YELLOWSTONE
Treatment Centers

Billings, Montana

Type: Residential psychiatric treatment center for children and adolescents

Affiliation: Nonprofit

Population Served: Male and female, ages 8 to 17

Size: Licensed capacity of 104 beds in 10 separate treatment units

Head of Facility: Loren Soft, Executive Director

Contact: Trisha Eik, Director of Admissions, 1732 South 72nd Street, West Billings, Montana 59106; 406-656-3001 or 800-726-6755

THE TREATMENT CENTERS

Yellowstone Treatment Centers was founded in 1957 as Yellowstone Boys' Ranch to serve the needs of abused and neglected boys in Montana and Wyoming. In response to regional and national requests for services, Yellowstone has grown over the past thirty-five years to serve seriously emotionally disturbed children and adolescents on its 400-acre rural campus. Ten minutes west of Billings, Yellowstone offers a range of specialized residential treatment services, including learning disabled, ADHD/ADD, developmentally delayed, juvenile sexual offender, and psychiatric intensive care.

Yellowstone is accredited by the Joint Commission on Accreditation of Healthcare Organizations (JCAHO) and licensed by the Montana Department of Health and the Montana Department of Family Services.

ELIGIBILITY

Children and adolescents may be referred to Yellowstone by psychiatrists, psychologists, private therapists, social workers, school counselors, hospital discharge planners, employee assistance coordinators, managed-care firms, families, members of the clergy, and juvenile court workers. Treatment programs are designed to serve a variety of patients who are experiencing traditional psychiatric disorders. The range of psychopathology includes the DSM III-R categories of conduct, oppositional, anxiety, identity, attention deficit, affective, and personality disorders.

Behavioral manifestations of the disorders successfully treated at Yellowstone include impulsivity, substance experimentation, sexual acting out, truancy, suicide attempts, self-destructive incidents, underdeveloped social skills, language and motor developmental lags, poor academic performance, verbal aggression, and property destruction.

Treatment for all residents is individualized and incorporates a team approach that is supervised by a staff psychiatrist.

ASSESSMENT

Prior to admission, a referral screening committee reviews the most recent psychiatric, psychological, and social assessments available on the patient. On the day of admission, the patient and family are interviewed by a psychiatrist who performs a psychiatric assessment. A nurse completes a health screen and within 24 hours the pediatrician performs a physical exam. From this information, the initial 72-hour

treatment plan is developed. Within eight days after admission, the psychiatric, psychological, social, educational, health, dietary, recreation, and speech assessments are completed and placed in the individual's record. On day thirteen, the treatment team meets to develop the master treatment plan.

PROGRAM

Yellowstone is committed to a medical model emphasizing the role of diagnosis and treatment. Individualized treatment programs are based on the interactive nature of symptoms and individual psychological, environmental, and biological functioning. The therapeutic environment builds positive relationships between staff and youths. A major goal of treatment is to teach youths to form trusting relationships with others. In addition to individual, group, and family therapies, clients receive feedback twice daily from staff and peers on how well goals and objectives specified in the individual treatment plan are being met. As prescribed by the treatment team, clients may also participate in pharmacological, experiential, art, music, expressive, or substance abuse therapies.

All treatment is focused on returning the youth to the family or the least restrictive community-based services appropriate for continuing his or her growth and development. Aftercare planning begins at the time of admission and is reviewed every twenty-eight days during the master treatment plan update. Because all treatment is individualized, length of stay varies between sixty and ninety days in the Intensive Care Unit to twenty-four months in the specialized treatment units.

Families are strongly encouraged to participate in therapy and regular visitation. Lodging and meals are provided on-campus at no charge when families attend therapy and planned visitation.

Individual treatment is based on the belief that emotional growth occurs as a result of personal insight, inner emotional healing, adjustment in maladaptive family and behavioral patterns, and spiritual experience. The treatment team, consisting of a psychiatrist, nurse, primary therapist, education specialist, mental health worker, recreation therapist, and pastoral-care staff, meets every twenty-eight days to review progress and update goals and objectives in the master treatment plan.

STAFF

Yellowstone provides an interdisciplinary team of credentialed psychiatrists, clinical psychologists, master's- and doctoral-level therapists, nursing staff, regular and special education instructors, dieticians, recreational therapists, and mental health workers. Trained and certified specialists in the areas of learning disabilities, substance abuse, occupational therapy, pastoral-care, and the ropes course also assist the treatment team.

SPECIAL PROGRAMS

The education center at Yellowstone is unique in many respects. The center is a public school accredited by the Montana Department of Public Instruction and Northwest Accreditation of Schools but serves only students who are residents of Yellowstone. The formulation of each student's individualized education plan is based on assessment, learning style, past achievement, social skills, future goals, and the master treatment plan. The education plan includes annual goals, behavioral objectives, course work, teaching strategies, and evaluation procedures.

Yellowstone provides pastoral-care services to meet students' social, intellectual, emotional, and spiritual development needs. In addition to weekly nondenominational services, the campus chaplain trains and supervises counselors in each unit who are available to assist youths at any time.

Recreation and physical development needs are met through structured recreational therapy, physical education, team sports and activities, such as skiing, horseback riding, hiking, swimming, and bicycling. All activities are supervised by trained and certified activities therapists.

Most medical services are provided on-campus by the pediatrician and nursing staff. Billings has two excellent regional medical centers that are able to meet any needs requiring hospitalization.

CONTINUITY OF TREATMENT

Yellowstone understands that residential treatment is a separate and distinct level of care requiring 24-hour supervision that is impossible to maintain in the normal home environment. This supervision is directed toward the attainment of specific goals and objectives. The residential program brings together many professional disciplines to provide effective treatment. This cooperative effort provides a highly structured, comprehensive yet flexible approach to promoting change.

Discharge planning for each youth begins at admission. During each twenty-eight-day treatment, aftercare plans are reviewed by the treatment team and updated in the master treatment plan. While the primary therapist is responsible for ensuring that all aftercare services are arranged, each member of the treatment team is available to discuss treatment needs with community-based caregivers. Prior to discharge, the family, aftercare providers, and home school are invited to meet with the treatment team. Therapeutic follow-up is done by the primary therapist at fourteen, thirty, and sixty days following discharge.

A guiding principle of Yellowstone Treatment Centers is that a youth's family is irreplaceable. Belief in this principle results in a strong emphasis on family participation in therapy. When families are not able to participate in regular weekly family therapy due to travel constraints, arrangements are made prior to admission for the family to participate in conjoint long distance therapy. This provides a better opportunity for success and reintegration into the home and community following treatment at Yellowstone.

BUILDINGS AND GROUNDS

A 400-acre rural setting is home to Yellowstone's 60-acre residential campus. While at Yellowstone, residents live in ten-bed lodges staffed by a full-time treatment team consisting of the primary therapist, mental health workers, and a unit manager. Meals are provided in a central dining hall where residents sit together as a family unit.

The campus also includes a fully staffed 24-hour-a-day medical clinic, a recreational complex that includes a full-sized gymnasium, an indoor swimming pool, and indoor and outdoor ropes courses. Educational services are provided in a twelve-classroom complex that includes a library, a computer lab, and vocational training opportunities. Nondenominational worship services are available in the on-campus chapel.

ADMISSION AND FINANCIAL INFORMATION

Services at Yellowstone Treatment Centers are covered by most insurance companies or by Medicaid. Private payment arrangements can also be negotiated. Yellowstone is a preferred provider with several managed-care companies and will negotiate contracts with any third party payor. The staff of the admissions office works closely with families, reference sources, and third-party payors to smoothly negotiate the paperwork requirements and ensure that all arrangements are handled prior to admission.

Glossary

Mental Illnesses Affecting Children and Adolescents

Children and adolescents are as likely to suffer from mental illnesses as adults. However, some mental illnesses are more likely to affect children and adolescents, and some manifest themselves differently in children than they do in adults. . . . The definitions below offer only the most basic facts about an illness.

Alcohol and Drug Abuse: Teens abuse drugs and alcohol because they are addicted to them, because they are "self-medicating" or numbing the emotional pain of another mental illness (e.g., depression), because of peer pressure, or for many other reasons. One of the easiest ways to define alcohol or drug dependency is a need to take the drug to feel "normal." Withdrawal symptoms may occur if the alcohol or drug is taken away. Typical warning signs include:

- a drop in school performance
- deterioration of family relationships
- isolation
- a marked change in dress or appearance
- a change in group of friends
- physical changes, such as red eyes, persistent cough, or difficulty sleeping
- delinquent behavior

Depression: A disturbance in mood lasting at least two weeks and characterized by sadness, hopelessness, and irritability may be much more serious than just "the blues." Depression usually also includes at least four of these symptoms:

- change in appetite
- change in sleeping patterns
- loss of interest in activities formerly enjoyed
- loss of energy; fatigue
- feelings of worthlessness or inappropriate guilt
- inability to concentrate or think; indecisiveness
- recurring thoughts of death; threatened or attempted suicide

Reprinted with permission from *When Your Child Needs Psychiatric Hospitalization,* © 1990 The National Association of Private Psychiatric Hospitals. To order the complete pamphlet (at a cost of $1), contact the NAPPH at 1319 F Street, NW, Suite 1000, Washington, DC 20004; 202-393-6700.

Conduct Disorder: A repetitive and persistent destructive or hostile behavior pattern that violates the rights of others or deviates significantly from age-appropriate norms and rules may be diagnosed as conduct disorder. The conduct is far more serious than ordinary mischief and is often dangerous to the child or to others. Teenagers with a conduct disorder usually have trouble at home and/or school, are often sexually active at a young age, and may run away from home, set fires, or commit crimes. Conduct disorder may be a manifestation of an underlying depression.

Anorexia Nervosa: A refusal to eat a balanced diet resulting in a loss of at least 25 percent of body weight is indicative of a mental illness, especially if there is no known physical illness accounting for the inability to maintain a normal weight for height and age. The disorder most often strikes teenage girls who have low self-esteem and an irrational belief that they are fat, regardless of how thin they become. Without treatment, the self-induced starvation can lead to death.

Bulimia: Another eating disorder primarily affecting girls, bulimia is characterized by a compulsion to binge (eat a large amount of food rapidly, usually in less than two hours) and then to purge (rid oneself of the food) by self-induced vomiting or the use of laxatives. Weight can fluctuate by as much as ten pounds during binge-and-purge cycles. Girls who suffer from bulimia are aware that their eating patterns are abnormal and they fear being unable to stop eating voluntarily. Binges are usually followed by a depressed mood and self-disgust. Bulimia leads to dehydration, hormonal imbalance, and the depletion of important minerals, and it can have serious consequences for the adolescent's later physical development.

Anxiety: Young people suffer from three major types of anxiety disorder:

- **Separation Anxiety:** Excessive anxiety about those to whom the youth is attached, most often parents. Symptoms include a reluctance or refusal to go to school in order to stay home with the attachment figure and an unrealistic fear or worry that something will happen to the parent. Although it usually begins between the ages of 6 and 12, it can develop suddenly during teenage years.

- **Avoidant Disorder:** An excessive shrinking from strangers for at least six months—to the extent that it interferes with social functioning, peer relationships, and satisfying relationships with family members and friends—may indicate the need for a professional evaluation of your child's mental health.

- **Overanxious Disorder:** Excessive worrying or fearful behavior that does not focus on a specific situation or object and that persists for at least six months. Signs include an unrealistic worry about future events, an excessive need for reassurance, an inability to relax, and frequent physical complaints, such as headaches or stomachaches.

Attention Deficit Hyperactivity Disorder (ADHD): Youngsters suffering from ADHD are excessively impulsive, have serious trouble paying attention, and find it difficult to focus on a task. They are easily distracted and often cannot organize work or cooperate in sports. This illness is ten times more common in boys than in girls, and it typically develops by the age of three.

Manic Depression: Wide mood swings from extreme elation to severe depression that occur in cycles may signal a manic-depressive disorder. During the manic phase teens are hyperactive and become overly involved in activities that often have painful consequences. They talk loudly, change topics abruptly, and may go days without sleep or getting hungry. Most manic depression begins before the age of 30. Current treatments are highly effective in treating this disease.

Schizophrenia: A psychotic disorder lasting more than six months, schizophrenia is accompanied by disturbances in thought, feelings, behavior, and the use of words. Symptoms may include inappropriate emotions or delusions, such as "they are plotting against me." Three-quarters of schizophrenics develop the disease between the ages of 16 and 25.

Psychosis: A psychotic disorder is a severe mental disorder characterized by an extreme impairment in the person's ability to think, respond emotionally, remember, communicate, or understand reality. Someone who is psychotic often has hallucinations (seeing or hearing things that don't exist) or may regress into behavior appropriate for a much younger child. A psychosis greatly interferes with meeting the ordinary demands of life and usually requires close medical supervision.

Mental Health Professionals

Nearly all psychiatric hospitals use a team approach to treating children and adolescents. Members of [a] child's team will include a variety of mental health professionals who offer different, specialized skills to help [the] child get better. Find out what role each team member will play in [the] treatment and each member's responsibilities. Mental health professionals likely to be involved include:

- **Psychiatrist:** A fully trained and licensed physician (MD or DO) who has completed three to four years of training in general psychiatry after medical school. [The] child may also be treated by a child/adolescent psychiatrist who has completed two years of specialized training in child and adolescent psychiatry. Psychiatrists may be certified by the American Board of Psychiatry and Neurology.

- **Clinical Psychologist:** A licensed mental health professional with a doctoral (PhD) degree in clinical psychology from an accredited institution and an additional one to two years of supervised training in an inpatient setting.

- **Clinical Nurse Specialist:** A registered nurse (RN) who is licensed by the state and may be certified by the American Nurses Association for child and adolescent psychiatric nursing or adult psychiatric nursing after two years of supervised psychiatric practice and a certification examination.

- **Clinical Social Worker:** A mental health professional with a master's degree in social work (MSW) and a minimum of two years of supervised clinical experience in an inpatient setting. Some states require licensure for clinical social workers and others do not. A clinical social worker may be a member of the American Academy of Certified Social Workers (ACSW) or be listed in the National Association of Social Workers' *Register of Clinical Social Workers.*

Other mental health professionals who may play an important part in [the] child's treatment include drug/alcohol counselors, occupational therapists, teachers, and dieticians.

Resources for More Information

American Academy of Child and Adolescent Psychiatry

3615 Wisconsin Avenue, N.W.
Washington, DC 20016
202/966-7300

The AACAP has a membership of over 5,000 child and adolescent psychiatrists and provides information on mental illnesses affecting children, adolescents, and their families as well as on issues such as child development, sexual abuse, and divorce.

American Psychiatric Association

1400 K Street, N.W.
Washington, DC 20005
202/682-6000

Representing 37,500 psychiatric physicians, APA offers information on diagnosis and treatment of mental illnesses, including alcohol and substance abuse.

American Psychological Association

750 First Street, N.E.
Washington, DC 20002
202/336-5500

APA is the leading scientific and professional society of doctorally trained psychologists in the United States and is the world's largest association of psychologists. With 114,000 members and affiliates, APA works to advance psychology as a profession, as a science, and as a means of promoting human welfare.

National Alliance for the Mentally Ill

2101 Wilson Boulevard #302
Arlington, VA 22201
703/524-7600

NAMI is a self-help organization, with nearly 1,000 local affiliate chapters, that emphasizes mutual support, public education, research, and advocacy for people with serious mental illnesses and their families.

National Association of Private Psychiatric Hospitals

1319 F Street, N.W., Suite 1000
Washington, DC 20004
202/393-6700

NAPPH represents the nation's more than 300 nongovernmental, specialty psychiatric hospitals and will provide information about all aspects of hospitalization for mentally ill or chemically dependent children and adults.

National Council of Community Mental Health Centers

12300 Twinbrook Parkway, Suite 320
Rockville, MD 20852
301/984-6200

Representing more than 500 members in 48 states, the NCCMHC works to enhance member effectiveness in public policy, business development, and managerial effectiveness. Fundamental to the National Council strategy is the development of a grassroots advocacy organization built on state provider associations and provider agency members.

National Institute of Mental Health

5600 Fishers Lane
15-105 Parklawn Building
Rockville, MD 20857
301/443-3600

NIMH is the federal government research agency responsible for developing better understanding of, and treatments for, mental illnesses. Other helpful government agencies are the National Institute of Drug Abuse (NIDA) and the National Institute of Alcohol Abuse and Alcoholism (NIAAA).

National Mental Health Association

1021 Prince Street
Alexandria, VA 22314
703/684-7722

NMHA is the nation's only citizens' volunteer advocacy organization concerned with all aspects of mental health and mental illnesses. With 600 affiliates in 43 states and the District of Columbia, NMHA has been working for America's mental health since 1909.

Many of these national organizations have state and/or local chapters listed in the telephone directory. Your state or local departments of public health and mental health will also be helpful sources of information.

Reprinted with permission from *When Your Child Needs Psychiatric Hospitalization,* © 1990 The National Association of Private Psychiatric Hospitals. To order the complete pamphlet (at a cost of $1), contact the NAPPH at 1319 F Street, NW, Suite 1000, Washington, DC 20004; 202-393-6700.

Index

A **bold page number** indicates an Expanded Description.
An *italic page number* indicates an Announcement.